OSKAR SCHINDLER

OSKAR SCHINDLER

THE UNTOLD ACCOUNT OF

His Life, Wartime Activities,

AND THE TRUE STORY BEHIND

the List

DAVID M. CROWE

Westview Press
A MEMBER OF THE PERSEUS BOOKS GROUP

Published in the United States of America by Westview Press, A Member of the Perseus Books Group.

Find us on the world wide web at www.westviewpress.com

Westview Press books are available at special discounts for bulk purchases in the United States by corporations, institutions, and other organizations. For more information, please contact the Special Markets Department at the Perseus Books Group, 11 Cambridge Center, Cambridge, MA 02142, or call (617) 252-5298 or (800) 255-1514, or email special.markets@perseusbooks.com.

Text design by Brent Wilcox
Set in 10.5 point Sabon

Library of Congress Cataloging-in-Publication Data
Crowe, David
    Oskar Schindler : the untold account of his life, wartime activities, and the true story behind the list / David M. Crowe.
        p. cm.
    Includes bibliographical references and index.
    ISBN 0-8133-3375-X (alk. paper)
    1. Schindler, Oskar, 1908–1974.   2. Righteous Gentiles—Biography.
3. Righteous Gentiles in the Holocaust.   4. Holocaust, Jewish (1939–1945).   I. Title.
D804.66.S38C76   2004
940.53'1835'092—dc22

                                                                                    2004013879

The paper used in this publication meets the requirements of the American National Standard for Permanence of Paper for Printed Library Materials Z39.48-1984.

10   9   8   7   6   5   4   3   2   1

TO
Sol Urbach
AND
Chris and Tina Staehr

CONTENTS

PREFACE AND ACKNOWLEDGMENTS

The initial idea for this book came about during a conversation I had in the fall of 1996 with my editor at Westview Press, Peter Kracht, who is now the Editorial Director of Praeger Publishers. Peter and I had worked together on several books, and he wanted to know whether I had any ideas for a new one. I told him that I would love to do a biography of Oskar Schindler because, despite his fame and new place in the Holocaust field, there was no scholarly work on him. Peter was intrigued by the idea and told me to send him a book precis and outline. The rest, as they say, is history.

I began working on this book in 1997 and never imagined that it would take seven years to complete. The discovery of the vast collection of Oskar Schindler's private papers in 1997 and its public release two years later forced me to expand my research because these papers raised new questions about Schindler and opened up new avenues of research. I worked with several editors at Westview Press during this period. The most important was Steve Catalano, who carefully nurtured the book through its final stages. He is an author's editor.

During my research, I had to rely on the expertise and kindness of quite a few people who are far too numerous to mention individually. Needless to say, the pace and depth of my research would have been far less successful if it had not been for these individuals. Little appeared in the historical literature on Oskar Schindler, so I had to rely on Thomas Keneally's novel, *Schindler's List,* and Steven Spielberg's film of the same title as my initial guideposts to research. My research plan was quite simple— to go back to the beginning of Schindler's life in Bohemia and Moravia and then gradually move forward chronologically with research in the Czech Republic, Poland, Germany, Israel, Argentina, and the United States. My plan was to blend archival research with interviews of anyone who knew Oskar or Emilie Schindler.

I also decided that to explore successfully the archives of the Czech Republic, Poland, Germany, and Argentina, I would need research assistants to help me with my work and interviews in each country. I should like to thank Dr. Ilona Klímová, Konstancja Szymura, David Fuhr, and Dr. Adriana Brodsky for their invaluable assistance during the numerous trips I made to these countries during the course of my research. I also had to rely on linguists to help me translate the mountain of documents, much of it handwritten, in eight languages. I should like to thank Jenny Raabe, Yudit Natkin, and Tomasz Jaskiewisz's tireless translating of very difficult, hard-to-read and aging documents.

Equally important were individual archivists, historians, and others in the Czech Republic, Poland, Israel, Germany, Argentina, and the United States who did everything possible to insure the success of my work. In the Czech Republic, I should like to thank Dr. Jitka Gruntová and Radoslav Fikejz; in Great Britain, Robin O'Neil; in Poland, Leszek Świątek; in Israel, Dr. Sara Bardosh, Dr. Mordechai Paldiel, and Dr. Moshe Bejski; in Germany, Mietek Pemper, Dr. Wolf Buchmann, Dr. Uwe Vorkötter, Claudia Keller, Stefan Braun, Susan and Michael Fuhr, and Dr. Dieter and Ursula Trautwein; in Argentina, Francisco Wichter, Ilse Chwat, Monika Caro, Ilse Wartenslebens, Elias Zviklich, Werner Krowl, and Roberto Alemann; and in the United States, Elinor Brecher, Sherry Hyman, Ned Comstock, and Daisy Miller. I am eternally grateful to each of the Schindler Jews who shared their memories of Oskar Schindler with me.

It is difficult to find the adequate words to thank my wife, Kathryn, for all of the hard work and support she put into helping make this book possible. In addition to carefully reading each chapter and offering advice on every aspect of the book, she cheerfully put up with my long absences during the research and writing phases of the manuscript. This book would not have been possible without her undivided love, support, and encouragement.

I should like to dedicate this book to three individuals who played an important and inspiring role in all aspects of my research and writing—Sol Urbach and Chris and Tina Staehr. Sol was that rare Schindler Jew who worked for Oskar Schindler in Emalia and Brünnlitz. More important, he was able throughout the course of my research and writing to give me realistic, unromantic insights into the heart and mind of Oskar Schindler during the war years. Chris and Tina Staehr have been equally gracious and helpful. I was particularly moved by their generosity and sensitivity when it came to the question of the vast Oskar Schindler *Koffer* (suitcase) collection. Instinctively, they insisted that it be sent to Yad Vashem in Israel as a gift to the Jewish people. I am absolutely convinced that this is exactly what Oskar, who deeply loved Israel and is buried in Jerusalem, would have wanted.

This book is also written in memory of several people who passed away as I was working on it: my beloved brother-in-law, Richard H. Moore; Leopold Pfefferberg-Page; and Dr. Dieter Trautwein.

David M. Crowe
April 10, 2004

1.

SCHINDLER'S EARLY LIFE (1908–1938)

It WAS THE WINTER OF 1947-1948 IN MUNICH. TED FEDER, A former American GI, was now deputy director of the Munich office of the American Jewish Joint Distribution Committee (the Joint; AJJDC). His boss, Samuel L. Haber, called Ted into his office and told him: "Ted, there's a German out there who wants to see me. See him, see what he wants, and get rid of him." When Ted Feder walked into the outer office, he saw a German sitting there in traditional Bavarian clothing: winter *Lederhosen* (leather breeches with knee socks) and a felt cap with a feather in it. As Feder uncomfortably approached the German, a side door opened and one of the office's other workers, a Holocaust survivor, saw the German and cried out in Yiddish, "Uns grettet, uns grettet [He saved us, he saved us]." The survivor then fell to his knees and began to kiss the German's hands. The German was Oskar Schindler.[1]

At that time, Oskar Schindler was an impoverished former Sudeten German factory owner desperately searching for ways to survive financially during the postwar hardships in Germany. With the exception of the 1,098 *Schindlerjuden* (Schindler Jews) who survived the war in large part because of Schindler's efforts, few people knew of his exploits. Yet to many *Schindlerjuden,* he was already a god-like figure. This adoration was the basis for Schindler's extremely close relationship with many of his survivors until his death in 1974. "My Jews or my children," as he often

1

called them, overlooked Schindler's human failings and continually searched for ways to help their flawed hero maintain some semblance of a normal life, first in Germany, later in Argentina, and again in Germany. They helped him financially and looked for ways to honor him and tell the world about his unique efforts to save them during the Holocaust. The *Schindlerjuden* were driven, for the most part, by the deep love and admiration they had for him. When faced with Schindler's shortcomings, particularly after the war, many would explain that it was these very character flaws that made him so effective during the Holocaust. In reality, their love for Oskar Schindler was so deep and reverential that some would simply shrug off talk about his drinking and womanizing and say, "Oh, that's just Oskar."

Yet who was this Oskar Schindler? Was he truly the revered savior portrayed in Steven Spielberg's film *Schindler's List*? Or was he a womanizing alcoholic with questionable business skills? The only way to answer these questions is to look at the complete life of this controversial figure.

Early Life, 1908–1935

Oskar Schindler was born on April 28, 1908, in Svitavy (German, Zwittau), a Moravian town in the Austrian-Hungarian empire. Schindler's family, like many of their neighbors in the region, were Sudeten (southern) Germans. Their first language and culture was German, as opposed to the thriving Czech culture in other parts of the Czech lands of Bohemia and Moravia. The Schindler family originally came to the region from Vienna in the early sixteenth century. Oskar's father, Johann (Jan) Hans, came from the village of Moravsky Lacnov (German, Mährisch Lotschnau). Oskar's mother, Franziska (Frantiska) "Fanny" Luser, was from the same village; she married Johann "Hans" Schindler in 1907. Oskar was the eldest of two children. His sister, Elfriede, was born in 1915.[2]

Svitavy seems to have changed little from the time that Oskar Schindler lived there as a child. Even now, Svitavy seems remote, although it is only an hour's drive from the Czech Republic's second largest city, Brno, and three hours from the capital, "Golden" Prague. Vienna is only a few hours south of Brno. Though the Czechoslovak government drove the Sudeten Germans en masse from Czechoslovakia after World War II, their presence still lingers in the architecture and in the surnames of some residents in this part of the Czech Republic. When you mention this, most Czechs living in Svitavy, Brněnec (Brünnlitz), and the surrounding villages remind you that they are Czechs, not Germans.

The trip from Brno to Svitavy is like a step back in time. The fields are lush and green during the summer, and the rolling landscape is dotted with forests and clusters of orange-tiled village roofs. There is a sense of relaxed comfort and prosperity here, though Czech income statistics suggest otherwise. The locals complain that low property values are attractive to Germans looking for cheap summer homes. Svitavy is a quiet city. The city center is small, attractive but unimpressive. Fanny Schindler bought a home in one of Svitavy's more prominent neighborhoods, No. 24 Iglauerstrasse. The Schindler home overlooked a private park that was given to the city in 1933. The park is now known as the Jana Palacha Park, named after a Czech student who immolated himself in 1969 to protest the Soviet invasion that ended the 1968 "Czech Spring" flirtation with democracy. In 1993, Germany's Sudeten German community erected a monument to Oskar Schindler on the edge of Jana Palacha Park, just across the street from his boyhood home. Yet, although most Czechs would agree that Jan Palach is a legitimate hero and martyr, they are less certain about Oskar Schindler, who, some feel, played a role in the destruction of the Czechoslovak Republic before World War II.[3]

Before the Depression, Hans Schindler made a comfortable living making and selling farm machinery. He made certain that his family remained close to their Austrian German roots even after Svitavy became part of the Czechoslovak Republic in 1918. After World War II, Oskar frequently referred to himself as an Austrian to distinguish himself from the "Prussians," whom he blamed for the war and its atrocities. He was also proud of his Sudeten German roots. Oskar was baptized in the Catholic faith when he was one month old. Though he nominally remained a Roman Catholic throughout his life, he seemed to have little affection for Catholicism, at least until the later years of his life.[4]

We know very little about Oskar's early life, though his father's heavy drinking and womanizing might indicate that life in the Schindler home was less than perfect. In 1915, Oskar began *Volksschule* (elementary school) in Svitavy and later attended *Realschule* (secondary school). He went on to the *Höheres Realgymnasium* (technical school), where he was expelled in 1924 for forging his grade report. After he returned to school, his classmates nicknamed him "Schindler the crook." Though he later graduated, Oskar was not an outstanding student and never took the *Abitur* exam for admission to college or university. He would remind acquaintances after the war that he was a businessman, not a scholar. After graduation from the *Realgymnasium,* Oskar attended several trade schools in Brno, where he took courses on machinery, heaters, and chauffeuring. He passed exams to qualify in each of these fields.[5]

During this period, the first hint of trouble with his father began to surface. According to Oskar's wife, Emilie, soon after Oskar turned seventeen, Hans accused his son of stealing some insurance premiums. Emilie claimed that Hans sold insurance on the side and stole some of the premiums after he ran into financial difficulties. Some of Hans's clients reported the thefts to the police, who questioned Hans. Emilie said in her memoirs, *Where Light and Shadow Meet* (1997), that Hans told the police that Oskar had stolen the money. Emilie, who married Oskar in 1928, had little respect for her father-in-law. She blamed Oskar's worst traits, particularly his drinking and his womanizing, on his father. She said that Hans was a "hopeless alcoholic" who got so drunk on one occasion that he raped his sister-in-law. A daughter who was born of this crime died at the age of fourteen.[6]

Emilie "Milli" Pelzl met Oskar in the fall of 1927. Emilie, who was seven months older than Oskar, lived in the small Moravian village of Staré Maletín (German, Alt Moletein). Svitavy, which was about twenty-five miles to the southwest, was by comparison a booming metropolis. Emilie claimed that her family's roots in the region dated back to the Middle Ages. Emilie, whose father, Josef, was a prosperous farmer, had a happy childhood. She had fond memories of her parents and her paternal grandparents, who lived with them, and of her older brother Franz. Emilie described her mother, Marie, as a patient and lovely woman who was her "mirror and model." Emilie shared her love for horses with her hardworking father, who returned from World War I stricken with malaria and heart trouble. For the rest of his life, this broken man dwelled on his suffering and, as time went on, became more and more of a stranger to his family. As Emilie's relationship with her father became more distant, she drew closer to her brother, Franz.[7] Compared to her later life with and without Oskar, Emilie's life in Staré Maletín was idyllic. She loved the natural world and animals, particularly horses. Nature, she said, always had "a magical attraction" for her. She also developed a stubborn streak that later enabled her to survive many heartaches and difficulties.[8]

One of Emilie's other childhood interests was Gypsies. She said in her memoirs that Gypsies had fascinated her since her childhood. Officials in Staré Maletín would permit the nomadic Gypsies to camp only for a few days at a time at a predesignated site, usually at the edge of the village. These limitations were common throughout Central and Eastern Europe. Emilie would frequently visit the Gypsies and listen to their music and stories. Their tales of the world beyond Staré Maletín fascinated her. What most intrigued Emilie about the Gypsies was their nomadic lifestyle and independent spirit. Emilie said that it was an old Gypsy fortuneteller, whom she came across in an abandoned granary, who first warned her about the difficult life that awaited her.[9] After holding the girl's small hands in her own, the Gypsy told Emilie:

> I see, child, that your lifeline is long. You will have a long life, longer than you think. But you will also experience much pain and suffering. You will meet a man who will take you away from here. You will love him above all, although you will not be happy at his side. I also see other people around you, but I do not know who they are or what they are doing. There are other things, my child, that I do not dare tell you.[10]

The Gypsy frightened Emilie, who ran out of the granary and into her mother's arms. When her mother asked her what was wrong, Emilie refused to tell her. Emilie said that she kept the incident a secret until 1949. She told Oskar of the Gypsy's predictions as they sailed to Argentina in 1949. Oskar hugged her and said, "You can no longer believe in these things and go on torturing yourself. If you have not been happy up to now, I will see to it that you are in the future. You can be sure that I love you."[11] Sad to say, Oskar failed to keep his promise.

Oskar met Emilie during a business trip to Josef Pelzl's farm in the fall of 1927. Oskar, who had been working for his father for three years, accompanied him to try to sell Emilie's father a new electric generator for their house. While Hans talked endlessly about the advantages of electricity in the Pelzl home, Oskar, whom Emilie described as slender with "broad shoulders, blond hair, and deep blue eyes," seemed bored. On the other hand, according to Emilie, Oskar could not take his eyes off of her. She thought his flirtations were a bit ridiculous, though Oskar's "particularly dignified stance" impressed her. After several trips to the Pelzl farm, Oskar finally charmed his way into Emilie's heart. His mother and sister visited Emilie's family as the relationship became more serious. Finally, Oskar asked to see Josef, Marie, and Emilie together to ask for Emilie's hand in marriage. He told them that he wanted to unite his life to Emilie's, so that "we can build a future together." Emilie's life at home was becoming difficult because of family illness, and she found Oskar's charm and looks irresistible. Yet she told a German reporter in 1994 that her father had warned her about Oskar's false charm. Regardless, she accepted his marriage proposal.[12]

The wedding took place in Svitavy on March 6, 1928. Afterwards, Oskar and Emilie moved in with Oskar's parents on Iglauerstrasse 24. The newlyweds occupied the upstairs of the house; Oskar's family lived downstairs. Emilie had few happy memories of life in the Schindler home. Hans was a crude, uneducated, abusive drunk. Fanny, whom Oskar adored, was "elegant and pleasant," though almost totally bedridden. Oskar's young teenage sister, Elfriede, who was unattractive and homely, was starved for attention; she grew close to Emilie, who tried to give Elfriede what little attention she could, though Emilie felt overburdened by the responsibilities of taking care of the Schindler household as well as her own family in Staré Moletín. Oskar was little help because he traveled frequently on business.[13]

Yet it was not business or a new wife that most interested Oskar in 1928; it was motorcycle racing. Oskar always had an interest in fast automobiles and motorcycles. By 1926, he had already gained quite a reputation as a reckless speedster on his red Italian Galloni 500 cc motorcycle with sidecar. According to one of his old friends, Erwin Tragatsch, it was the only motorcycle of this type in the Czechoslovak Republic. As Oskar became more interested in motorcycle racing, he began to look for a faster machine. In 1928, he bought a 250 cm Königsswellen Moto-Guzzi, a racing motorcycle reputed to be one of the fastest in Europe. Presumably, Hans bought both motorcycles for Oskar.[14]

Oskar entered his first race in May 1928. The course began in Brno and finished in the town of Soběšice just north of Brno. Though Tragatsch referred to the event as a "mountain race," the course was more hilly than mountainous. Oskar, riding his red Moto-Guzzi, finished third in his first race. His third-place victory so thrilled Oskar that he soon entered another race at the Alvater course, on the German border. Oskar competed with nine other racers in his motorcycle class. This time, though, two other racers also drove Moto-Guzzis. During most of the race, Oskar remained in fifth place. He moved into fourth place when one of his competitors on a Moto-Guzzi dropped out. He took third place when Kurt Henkelmann, a seasoned racer on a Werks-DKW, ran out of gas. As Henkelmann pushed his motorcycle towards the finish line, Oskar passed him, thinking he was in third place. For some unknown reason, Oskar stopped just before the finish line, much to the dismay of the crowd, which shouted for him to cross over it. While he was mistaking their shouts for applause, Henkelmann pushed his motorcycle over the finish line to take third place. According to Tragatsch, this was Schindler's last race. Supposedly, he gave up motorcycle racing because he could no longer afford it.[15]

Soon after Oskar met Emilie, he quit working for his father to take a job with the Moravian Electric Company (MEAS; *Moravská elektrotechnická akciová společnost*) in Brno. He left MEAS after his marriage and ran a driving school in Šumperk, which is about fifty-five miles northeast of Svitavy. His career with the driving school was cut short by an eighteen-month stint in the Czechoslovak army. He served in the Tenth Infantry Regiment of the Thirty-first Army and by 1938 was a lance-corporal in the reserves. Oskar later said of his active duty in the Czech army that he "played more at sports than at soldiering."[16]

Oskar rejoined MEAS when he returned from active duty. In 1931, MEAS went bankrupt and Oskar was unemployed for a year. Hans was unable to help Oskar and Emilie because the Depression had forced him to close his farm machinery business. This situation frustrated Emilie. Her father had given Oskar a dowry of 100,000 Czech crowns ($2,964) and he had squandered it on a fancy car and other unimportant things. When she questioned Oskar about these excesses, he replied, "Emilie, you are too austere, a real ascetic. While, on the other hand, I am by nature a sybarite [a resident of the ancient Greek-Italian city of Sybaris who loved luxury and pleasure]."[17]

Like his father, Oskar had grown fond of drinking. In a 1951 letter to the Viennese-born German-American film maker, Fritz Lang, Oskar said that among his greatest pleasures at that time in his life were the "Heuriger" (new wines) taverns of Vienna. He would occasionally visit his prosperous uncle, Adolf Luser, who published the monthly *Der Getreue Eckehart (The Faithful Eckehart)* in the Austrian capital. Heuriger cafés dotted the suburban areas around Vienna and were favorite drinking spots for the Viennese and tourists alike. Oskar described his uncle's publication as "fast völkischer Verlag" (an almost nationalistic or populist publication). The Germans forced Adolf to shut down *Der Getreue Eckehart* after they occupied Austria in the spring of 1938. Adolf died soon afterwards, even though the DAF (*Deutsche Arbeitsfront*; German Labor Front) paid Oskar's uncle more than RM 4 million ($1.6 million) in compensation. According to Oskar, his uncle died of grief over "den Verlust seines Lebenswerkes" (loss of his life's work).[18]

Oskar's "sybaritic" nature got the best of him during his year of unemployment. The police arrested him twice in 1931 and 1932 for misdemeanors "against physical security of body and health," meaning public drunkenness, disorderly conduct, and assault. The police jailed him for twenty-four hours and fined him 50 Czech crowns ($1.48) for his first misdeeds. They jailed him twice again in 1932 for similar misdeeds. He got four days in jail and a 200-crown ($5.93) fine for his new brush with the law and eight hours in jail and a fine of 100 crowns ($2.96) for his third conviction. This would not be his last run-in with the police in the 1930s. Oskar had two more brushes with the law between 1932 and 1935. On January 21, 1938, a court in Svitavy sentenced him to two months in jail. The judge also ordered that Schindler was to be deprived of food every fourteenth day of his sentence. He was released after a month in jail.[19]

What we do not know is the nature of his crime because the specific records on his case were either lost or destroyed. There is even some question about the accuracy of the dates. According to Dr. Jitka Gruntová, the foremost Czech expert on Schindler, at least one Czech historian, Milan Štyrch, claims that Schindler was given this sentence on November 5, 1938, not January 21, for his espionage crimes. However, the criminal register of the regional Criminal Court in Brno lists January 21 as the date of the sentence. It is unlikely that the Czechs would have sentenced him to prison on the eve of his parole as part of the Munich Agreement. Given his past history of public disorderliness and drunkenness, Oskar could have been imprisoned for crimes involving such misbehavior. It is also possible that he was arrested and jailed as a warning from officials concerned about his Abwehr activities. We will never know.[20]

Frustrated by his unemployment and legal problems, Oskar went to Berlin in 1931 to find work. Later, he admitted that he became interested in communism while in the German capital, though this statement might have been an attempt to neutralize the pro-Nazi claims against him during his arrest and interrogation for spying in 1938. After his return from Germany, Oskar bought a chicken farm. He quickly lost interest in this venture and became a representative of the Jaroslav Simek Bank of Prague. He worked for the Simek Bank for six years selling government property. In January 1938, he left this firm and began to sell government property on installments for a businessman in Brno.[21]

Oskar's conduct and lack of direction frustrated Emilie. She felt he constantly "lied and deceived" her, but she was always taken in by his boyish pleas for forgiveness. She admired his kindness and willingness to help others. When she complained to Oskar's mother about his behavior, Fanny said, "Oskar is now married, and it is his wife's obligation to educate him, my dear Emilie." Emilie hoped things would improve after the couple moved from the Schindler home to one of their own on 16 Baderova Street, a house that had belonged to a well-to-do Svitavy family. Emilie described the new home as a mansion complete with elegant furnishings and crystal chandeliers.[22]

The new home had little impact on their marriage, which had not been strong. Once Oskar got back on his feet financially, he became involved in an affair with an old school friend, Aurelie Schlegel, who worked as a secretary for his father. Aurelie bore Oskar two children out of wedlock. Edith was born in 1933, and Oskar Jr. two years later. It is difficult to determine what type of relationship Oskar had with Aurelie after the children were born, though if his relationship with them after the war is any indication, he probably neglected both of them. After the war, Oskar told Ruth Kalder Göth, Amon Göth's wartime mistress, that he had determined that the boy, Oskar Jr., was not his son. It is therefore not surprising that Aurelie raised both children alone.[23]

At the end of World War II, Oskar Jr. disappeared when the Russians occupied Svitavy. According to Oskar Jr.'s sister, Edith Schlegl, her brother was serving in a German military unit when the Soviets captured him. More than likely, he was serving with a Hitler Youth (HJ; *Hitlerjugend*) unit. During the last year of the war, such units had sprung up all over the Greater Reich as part of the *Volkssturm* (People's Militia), which tried to enlist all able-bodied men in the desperate attempt to defend Hitler's collapsing empire. Though most of the young men in these groups were in the fifteen-to-seventeen-year-old range, there were also boys as young as eight serving in some of them. According to one Allied report in the summer of 1945, rumors abounded about the ongoing sabotage activities of feared HJ "Werewolf" commando units in the former Sudetenland.[24]

Aurelie Schlegel, who changed her name to Schlegl after World War II, tried to locate Oskar Jr. through the Red Cross, but could never find him. According to Edith Schlegl, her mother, who died in Germany in 1997, never got over the loss of her son. They both attended Oskar's funeral in Frankfurt in 1974, though Edith said she had had little contact with her father after the war. In fact, few people knew of Oskar's children. Consequently, everyone at his funeral in Frankfurt in 1974 was shocked to see a large flower arrangement with the following words on it: "Alles Liebe von deinem Sohn und deiner Tochter" (Love from your son and daughter). Needless to say, Oskar's affair with Aurelie Schlegel damaged his marriage to Emilie, who knew of the illegitimate children.[25] Emilie knew about the affair and heard rumors about the two illegitimate children. She wrote in her memoirs that she discovered in the 1990s that Oskar's illegitimate son was living in Argentina. She said that his mother had "mistreated him terribly" and that he had wandered "aimlessly through the streets of the town, left to his own devices and eccentric behavior."[26]

In the midst of his affair with Aurelie Schlegel, Oskar's beloved mother died after a two-year illness. His sister, Elfriede, had cared for her during this period. Afterwards, she married Herr Tutsch, an official with the state railway system, and they lived in a "very big apartment furnished to him by the railway." Hans Schindler, who had abandoned his wife just months before her death, then sold the family home and moved into an apartment of his own. Oskar never forgave his father, who died in 1945, for leaving his mother. Thomas Keneally says that Oskar openly criticized his father among family and friends for his treatment of Fanny. Yet he also seemed "blind to the resemblance between his own faltering marriage and his parents' broken one."[27] In many ways, Oskar had already become much like his father.[28]

In 1941, several friends arranged for a reconciliation between Oskar and his father; knowing that Hans would be at a certain public coffee house in Svitavy, they took Oskar there. Oskar approached his father and offered his hand, which Hans accepted. From then on, whenever Oskar was in Svitavy, he visited his father; and until Hans died in 1945, Oskar sent his father a bank draft of RM 1,000 every month. According to Oskar, this sum allowed his father "to live a pleasant existence, to buy the medicines which he needed, to have the help he needed in the apartment, and not to have to worry about the economic structure of his own life." Oskar's grandmother, aunt, and other relatives still lived in Svitavy, and he tried to visit them every four to five months.[29]

Oskar never talked much about his sister, though he did reveal in a 1964 interview that she died in 1945 "as a result of her treatment at the hands of the Russians when they occupied the country." Elfriede Tutsch bore three children, who survived the war. One of his nieces, presumably Traude Ferrari, who became close to Emilie, worked in the sales department of an automobile firm, first in Düsseldorf and later in Italy. Another niece held a similar position in Düsseldorf, and Oskar's nephew was a supervisor for a textile wholesale company in Ingoldstadt.[30]

Oskar never discussed the impact his mother's death had on him, though it seemed to have stirred his restless spirit. The same year, he joined Konrad Henlein's Sudeten German Party and made his first contacts with the German military's counterintelligence branch, Abwehr.[31] These first moves into the world of politics and pro-German activity would forever change Oskar Schindler's life. Throughout his life, Schindler remained close to his Sudeten German roots. His work for Abwehr in the immediate years before World War II was in the Sudeten portions of Czechoslovakia, and most of his operatives were Sudeten Germans like himself. He also made frequent visits to Germany. The contacts and skills he learned as an Abwehr agent were key to understanding his later successes in Kraków and Brünnlitz. It was no accident that in 1944 he chose to move his Kraków factory to Brünnlitz, which is just south of Svitavy. His ties to the Sudeten portion of the former Czechoslovakia were strong, and he had hoped to rebuild his life there after the war. When that hope faded, he was bitter and expressed strong resentment towards Czechoslovakia's last prewar president, Edvard Beneš, whom he called a "Scharlatan." He told Fritz Lang that Beneš had weakened Sudeten German rights before the region was annexed by Germany in 1938. After Oskar returned to Germany from Argentina in the late 1950s, he became involved with the Sudeten German community in Frankfurt. Some of his more liberal German friends were taken aback by Oskar's ties to the exiled Sudeten German community in West Germany, which they regarded as extremely conservative. Yet to understand Oskar Schindler and his ties to Abwehr and Germany, one must look briefly at the Sudeten Germans and their troubles in Czechoslovakia between 1918 and 1938. This was a special world to Oskar Schindler and events there during the interwar years deeply affected him throughout his life.[32]

The Sudeten Germans in Czechoslovakia, 1918–1938

The Czechoslovak Republic came into existence at the end of World War I in the midst of the breakup of the Austro-Hungarian empire.[33] The country's new leaders, President Tomáš G. Masaryk, Foreign Minister Edvard Beneš, and Minister of War General Milan Štefánik, insisted that those portions of Bohemia, Moravia, and Silesia with large German populations would remain part of the new state. Historically, the Germans had been the "pre-eminent national group" in the Czech lands, a status that would change with the creation of the Czechoslovak state. By 1921, the population of 13.6 million included 3.1 million Germans. As World War I came to an end in the fall of 1918, Sudeten German leaders in Vienna created the provinces of German Bohemia and Sudetenland with the idea that these ethnically autonomous regions would become part of a new German Austria. The Czech military occupation of the two provinces in November 1918 ended these dreams.[34]

Instead, the Czech Germans became part of the new Czechoslovak republic. Initially, most Czech Germans, who lived primarily in Bohemia, refused to accept their fate and longed for union with Austria or Germany.[35] One of the first demands of the Sudeten Germans in the new Czechoslovak Republic was national autonomy; but Masaryk denied this right because the republic's leaders wanted their new state to display a purely Czechoslovak face. On the other hand, Czechoslovak leaders were amenable to greater cultural autonomy for the Sudeten Germans and other minorities. German culture and education thrived in the predominantly German portion of Czechoslovakia, though it suffered in other parts of the country. Gradually, many Sudeten German politicians decided that it was in their best interest to work with other Czechoslovaks for the greater good of the nation.[36]

Despite this greater spirit of cooperation, most Czech Germans were never satisfied with the rights afforded them by Czech and Slovak politicians in Prague. Their frustrations intensified after the Sudetenland, with its outdated factories and businesses, which concentrated on luxury goods for export, was hit hard by the Depression.[37] Many frustrated Sudeten Germans unfairly charged that the Czech government was doing little to alleviate their growing unemployment and other problems.[38] In this environment, it is not surprising that the historic distrust between the Czechs and the Germans should now resurface and affect Sudeten German politics.

The most dramatic political change among the Sudeten Germans was a shift in voter support from the mainstream German parties to two extreme right wing groups: the German Nationalists (DNP; *Deutsche Nationalpartei*) and the German Nazis (DNSAP; *Deutsche Nationalsozialistische Arbeiterpartei*). Before the Depression, these parties had not done well in national elections. Once the Depression struck, the ultra-right Sudeten parties gained a greater following among German voters. By 1935, the vast majority of Sudeten Germans were casting their votes for the country's only remaining extreme right pro-Nazi party, Konrad Henlein's SdP *(Sudetendeutsche Partei).*[39]

This upsurge in Sudeten German support for the extreme right came partially in response to Adolf Hitler's strong nationalistic message and Nazi successes in reviving Germany's battered economy after he took power as chancellor on January 30, 1933. The prospect of a dynamic Sudeten German Nazi movement in their own midst now worried many Czechoslovak politicians, including some Germans. They were particularly concerned about the impact of such movements on the viability of the Czechoslovak democracy.[40]

In 1929, the Sudeten Nazis created a Peoples' Sports Association *(Volkssportverband)*, modeled on the German Nazis' SA *(Sturmabteilung;* storm detachment or troops). Between 1930 and 1932, Sudeten German Nazi Party membership grew from 30,000 to more than 61,000. This upsurge in Nazi Party membership and activity greatly troubled Czechoslovakia's leaders, including some German politicians. What particularly concerned them was that Germany's support for the DNSAP had radicalized the Sudeten Nazi movement. In early 1932, the Prague government began a crackdown against the Sudeten Nazi Party and, on October 25, the National Assembly passed a law that allowed the government to outlaw subversive organizations such as the DNSAP and the DNP.[41] Several weeks earlier, both parties' leaders voted to dissolve their movements, which the government officially suspended in early October. A few days earlier, Konrad Henlein, a gym teacher and activist in two nationalistic Sudeten German movements, the Comrades' Union (KB; *Kameradschaftsbund)* and the Gymnastics Union or Association *(Turnverband),* announced the creation of the Sudeten German Home Front (SHF; *Sudetendeutsche Heimatfront).* Henlein hoped that the SHF would bring together all Sudeten German political parties under one banner. Henlein, as head of the new party, did everything possible to keep the Czechoslovak government from outlawing the SHF. He constantly reassured Czechoslovak leaders of his loyalty to Czechoslovakia and its democratic traditions, a policy advocated by Germany at this time.[42]

In fact, after the dissolution of the Nazi Party in Czechoslovakia, Hans Steinacher, the head of the Volk League for Germandom Abroad (VDA; *Volksbund für das Deutschtum im Ausland)* and co-chair of the *Volksdeutsch* Council, an organization created by Rudolf Hess, who oversaw Reich policies towards ethnic Germans abroad, contacted Henlein and informed him that Germany intended to pursue a policy of accommodation with the Czech government to protect the rights and well being of the Sudeten Germans.[43]

On the other hand, at Hitler's insistence, aid was given to individual Sudeten Nazis whom the Czechs had prosecuted for their activities. Berlin also maintained contact with Henlein, though it was not ready to support him actively. This all changed in the spring of 1935 as Henlein's party gained more Sudeten German support in its campaign for the May 19 elections. The Reich now wanted to use Henlein's organization to build a stronger Nazi power base in Czechoslovakia, though Berlin preferred Henlein's more extreme propaganda chief, Karl Hermann Frank.[44]

As the campaign for the 1935 elections shifted into high gear, Czechoslovak and mainstream German politicians grew increasingly concerned about Henlein's movement; but, despite Henlein's reassurances of his loyalty to Czechoslovakia and its democracy, his rallies, with their Nazi-like atmosphere, did much to neutralize his declarations that he was not Adolf Hitler's puppet. Moreover, many of Henlein's followers were former Sudeten Nazis who admired Hitler and Germany.[45] Yet it was not just the growing pro-Nazi sentiments among the Sudeten Germans that troubled Czechoslovak leaders; they also worried about the disciplined, aggressive campaign waged by Henlein's party before the May 19 elections. It reminded some Czechoslovaks of similar tactics in Germany three years earlier that helped bring Hitler to power. Some Czechoslovak politicians feared that an SHF victory could have severe implications for the country's democratic traditions. Widely distributed pamphlets attacked Jews and communists and called for Sudeten Germans to rally behind World War I veterans like Henlein. The SHF propagandists were careful to attack German-speaking Jews and communists, not those of Czechoslovak origins.[46]

Growing political demands ultimately led President Masaryk's government to consider outlawing the SHF before the election, though Masaryk ultimately decided that allowing Henlein's party to function within the confines of the Czechoslovak democratic system was better than forcing it to operate illegally. But he would only do so if Henlein agreed to change the party's name.[47] The SHF now became the Sudeten German Party (SdP; *Sudetendeutsche Partei*) and appeared on the ballot of the May 19, 1935, elections.[48] The SdP received the largest percentage (15.2 percent) of the 8.2 million votes cast in the election. Over 63 percent of the Sudeten Germans in Bohemia voted for the SdP and 56 percent in Moravia-Silesia. The SdP gained 44 seats in the three-hundred-member House of Deputies and 23 out of 150 seats in the Senate. Collectively, Czechoslovakia's right- and left-wing extremist parties gained 40 percent of the vote, which gave them 119 seats in the Chamber of Deputies and 59 seats in the Senate.[49] To counter the new strength of Henlein's party and build a viable governing coalition, Prime Minister Jan Malypetr invited all mainstream German parties except the SdP to join the government.[50]

Oskar Schindler and Abwehr: Early Contacts and the Sudeten Crisis

Despite the results of the 1935 election, Czechoslovakia entered the last four years of its prewar history with a viable political system.[51] Internationally, Germany was the greatest threat to Czech security, particularly after Hitler's illegal occupation of the Rhineland in 1936. Because the Nazi list for "elections" to the Reichstag after the takeover of the Rhineland included Sudeten Germans, Germany's ties to Henlein's party and its long-range goals for Czechoslovakia were underscored. As Gerhard Weinberg notes, German military planners were already contemplating moves towards Czechoslovakia, and Hitler's diplomats were laying the groundwork for such action.[52]

One of the important elements in such planning was Abwehr (German, *abwehren*—to ward or fend off) the counterintelligence and counterespionage branch of the Wehrmacht, the term for the German armed forces in Nazi Germany from 1935 until 1945. Created in 1920, Abwehr was designed to aid military defense work for the Weimar Republic's armed forces *(Reichswehr)*. Once Hitler came to power, Abwehr became a much more aggressive tool of German military policy, particularly under *Konteradmiral* (Rear Admiral, later *Admiral*), Wilhelm Canaris, who ran Abwehr from 1935 until 1944. Evidence suggests that Abwehr made its initial contact with Sudeten Germans in Czechoslovakia as early as 1928. By the time that Henlein scored his tremendous electoral victory in 1935, Abwehr had a well-established network of agents in Czechoslovakia.[53]

Yet Abwehr was involved in more than counterintelligence and counterespionage, important elements in the ongoing power struggles between the Nazi Party and the military in Germany and elsewhere. In Czechoslovakia, Abwehr was involved in Sudeten German affairs, particularly the power struggle within the SdP between Henlein and the "traditionalists," whom Abwehr supported, and the "radicals," who had the backing of Germany's SD *(Sicherheitsdienst;* Security Service) and the Gestapo *(Geheime Staatpolizei,* or secret state police, founded in 1933). The SD was the SS's *(Schutzstaffeln;* defense and protection squads of the Nazi

Party) counterespionage and intelligence service under Reinhard Hey-drich.[54] SD and Gestapo involvement in Sudeten German affairs began after the dissolution of the DNSAP in Czechoslovakia in 1933. Worried over the flood of Sudeten German Nazis into Germany, Rudolf Hess created a joint SD-Gestapo Sudeten German Control Center *(Sude-tendeutsche-Kontrollstelle)* to interview the recently arrived Sudeten Germans, weed out spies, and gather information on developments in Czechoslovakia. As the self-proclaimed guardians of Nazism, it is not surprising that the SD and the Gestapo soon became involved in a power struggle between radicals and traditionalists in the SdP. Early in its involvement with Sudeten German questions, the SD and the Gestapo sided with the more radical wing of the SdP and maintained close ties with former members of the outlawed NDSAP. Abwehr became the ally of Henlein and the traditionalist faction of the SdP, which initially sought to work within the confines of the Czechoslovak republic.[55]

In some ways, Oskar Schindler's work for Abwehr either reflected or helped mold his own opinions towards different factions of the Nazi movement in Czechoslovakia and Germany. There was no love lost between Abwehr and Heydrich's SD and the Gestapo. Early in his career as an Abwehr agent, Oskar developed a distrust of the SD, the Gestapo, and other Nazi Party organizations that would affect his actions during World War II. Yet, like most Abwehr agents, he also learned to work with these organizations because they played such a major role in the intelligence-gathering world of Nazi Germany. Finally, as an Abwehr agent, Oskar Schindler developed the skills and contacts that helped him save almost 1,100 Jews during the Holocaust.

An ethnic map of Czechoslovakia in 1935 indicates that the Svitavy district of northwest Moravia was a Sudeten German island surrounded by Czechs. According to Radoslav Fikejz, it was also an important SdP center. Given the political climate and the groundswell of support for the SdP at this time, it should come as no surprise that Oskar Schindler joined Henlein's party in 1935. Though Oskar later claimed that he did not join the SdP until 1938, substantial evidence supports his earlier membership, including his application for Nazi Party membership in the fall of 1938.[56]

Emilie Schindler and Radoslav Fikejz agreed that Oskar made his initial contacts with Abwehr in Kraków, where, in 1935, Oskar had a liaison with a woman who was an Abwehr agent.[57] In his written interrogation report for the Czech secret police in 1938, Oskar said that his initial interest in working for Abwehr came in the winter of 1936–1937, when he was in

Berlin. During this visit, he was staying with Ilse Pelikanová, a Sudeten German from Šumperk (Mährisch Schönberg), where Oskar had once run a driving school. Ilse told Oskar that she knew some Wehrmacht officers and suggested that the two of them might be interested in working "für Deutschland." Oskar said that he presumed she was talking about working for the *Deutscher Nachrichtendienst* (German intelligence service). He added that Ilse talked about "Steuerflüchtlingen und von Ueberwachen von Emigranten [tax evaders and inspecting emigrants]." Oskar was not interested in such activities at the time and did not take Ilse seriously because he thought she was an "unwollwärtige und histärische Person" [*unwollwertige und hysterische Person;* invalid and hysterical person]. Hysterical or not, Czechoslovak authorities regarded Ilse as a German agent.[58]

Oskar downplayed his work with Abwehr in the years immediately after World War II because of the stigma associated with such service. He also knew that the Czechs were looking for him as a war criminal. However, after he returned to Germany from Argentina, he became a little more open about his work with Canaris's organization. In 1966, Oskar wrote two documents, a *Lebenslauf* (c.v., curriculum vitae) and a list of important dates in his life. In these documents, he admitted that he had joined Abwehr in 1936 and served with Abwehrstelle II's Commando VIII unit, whose headquarters were in Breslau (today, Wrocław, Poland). He was probably part of Abwehr III (counterespionage) initially, since in 1936 Abwehr II dealt principally with cipher and radio monitoring. When Canaris reorganized Abwehr in 1938, the new Abwehr II absorbed some of the old Abwehr III's responsibilities, particularly those dealing with foreign minorities. The new Abwehr II was responsible for, among other things, agitating abroad and developing fifth columns.[59]

In his 1951 letter to Fritz Lang, who had fled Germany soon after Hitler took power to avoid becoming head of the Nazi film industry, Oskar downplayed his work with Abwehr. He told the film maker that his next contacts with Abwehr came innocently in the summer of 1938. Several years earlier, he had met "a very nice, humorous girl" while on business in the Riesen Gebirge (Riesengebirge) mountains that ran along the German, Polish, and Czechoslovak borders. In the summer of 1938, Oskar's "humorous girl" asked him to help her cross the Czechoslovak-German border illegally. Oskar explained that she was afraid of dealing with Czechoslovak border officials because her brother had fled to Germany the year before for political reasons. Oskar drove her to the border, where one of her relatives showed them where to avoid border officials.

The relative advised Oskar to cross on foot. Schindler, though, demurred because he was "not a fan of morning walks through the dew-fresh grass, especially with suitcases." Instead, he drove into Germany along the footpath. Once in Germany, a "well-dressed civilian" escorted Oskar and his friend to a hotel in Ziegenhals, where the girl's brother lived. Oskar claimed that he met an officer in Ziegenhals who liked his "impudent deed" and advised him to stay in Germany. Oskar reminded the officer that he had a wife and a job in Svitavy and that he had to return soon. Later that evening, several Germans caused a commotion near the border crossing to provide a cover while Oskar raced across in his car. Schindler told Lang that he made this illegal crossing once more on foot to see this young woman in Ziegenhals. After the second trip, the Czechoslovak police arrested him.[60]

Who was this mysterious woman and what connection did she have to Abwehr? Schindler provided the answers in his 1938 statement to the Czech secret police after his arrest. Her name was Gritt Schwarzer, whom Oskar met on a weekend holiday in Rumburg (Czech, Rumberk) in 1936. Later, Gritt became the manager of the Juppebad Hotel in Ziegenhals (today, the Polish town of Głuchołazy) just across the Czechoslovak border in Germany. Their chance meeting marked the beginning of their three-year romantic relationship and of Oskar's more direct involvement in Abwehr activities. Over the years, Oskar and Gritt corresponded and met occasionally in Germany when Oskar traveled there on business. One of their liaisons took place in Freiwalden, just south of Berlin. According to Thomas Keneally, Gritt introduced Oskar to Eberhard Gebauer, an Abwehr agent who asked Oskar to supply Canaris's organization with military information from southern Poland, where Oskar frequently traveled.[61]

Yet details about Oskar's Abwehr activities in the testimony of other Sudeten Germans recruited by Oskar and by the Czech secret police before and after World War II show a much more seasoned spy than the one painted by Schindler. A highly confidential Czech secret police report dated July 28, 1938, concluded that Oskar was "a spy of big caliber and an especially dangerous type." This conclusion was reached partly because the Czechoslovak police considered Schindler's contact person in Germany, Kreuziger, "one of the leading figures of the German Empire espionage service." In a November 1945 Czech secret police report about SD and Abwehr activities in Czechoslovakia before World War II, Oskar appears first in an unalphabetized list of nine Czechoslovaks engaged in serious activities against Poland. His name also appears frequently in other postwar Czech secret police investigations of spying in pre-1939 Czechoslovakia.[62]

According to Dr. Sobotka, the head of the police directorate in Brno who oversaw Schindler's confession and signed it, what made Oskar so good at his work were his manipulative skills, his natural eloquence, his intelligence, and his good observation techniques. Yet, unlike many of the Sudeten Germans who chose to work for Abwehr or other German groups at this time, Oskar Schindler was not motivated by Sudeten German patriotism. According to Dr. Sobotka, Oskar was "a very frivolous man of shady character whose only aspiration [was] to obtain easily and without work a lot of money." Oskar openly admitted to his Czech interrogators that he had joined Abwehr because of money. Before he became a German spy, he had a monthly income of between 8,000 and 10,000 Czech crowns ($277–$346), though his weakness for alcohol and women kept him constantly in debt. Dr. Sobotka said that Oskar was so desperate for money that he would even risk treasonous activities against his own country to obtain it.[63]

What specifically, then, did Oskar Schindler do as a German spy and what was it that led to his arrest in the summer of 1938? Second, what was his relationship to Abwehr after his pardon by German authorities in the Sudetenland after the Munich Accord in the fall of 1938? The detailed Czech secret police reports that were written during Oskar's three-month incarceration in 1938 and after World War II provide some clues to his activities, as do Emilie's memoirs and statements by Oskar himself. Abwehr was careful about the foreigners it chose to work in military counterintelligence. The Central Office in Berlin kept tabs on the political sentiments of Sudeten Germans and considered many of them unreliable because of religious, political, and nationalistic reasons. Oskar's SdP membership gave him some credibility as a potential spy, though his greed and intelligence were probably also important elements in the decision of Abwehr's field agents to use Schindler to help compromise Czechoslovak military security. His being in the military reserves was also useful to them. Their trust in him made him an important agent in a highly sensitive area that was important to German plans for the takeover of the Sudetenland and the rest of Czechoslovakia. After Schindler was pardoned in the fall of 1938, Abwehr promoted him and sent him as second in command of a group of twenty-five agents operating out of Ostrava (Mährisch-Ostrau) on the Czechoslovak-Polish border. Oskar now worked with Abwehr to help plan the invasion of Poland.[64]

Oskar Schindler operated in a strategically important area for the German military as it planned the takeover of Czechoslovakia and later

Poland. Abwehr made its first forays into the Czechoslovak Republic in the late 1920s. Admiral Canaris intensified these contacts in January 1935 through Henlein's liaison in Berlin, Friedrich Bürger. Canaris would later brag that Abwehr had "discovered" Henlein. This is an exaggeration, but it is true that Abwehr was one of the first German organizations to realize the value of Henlein and the SdP to the Third Reich. The SD and the Gestapo remained suspicious of the SdP leader; in 1936, one SD report called Henlein "a slave of Rome" who was seriously damaging Germany's efforts to draw closer to the Sudeten Germans.[65]

Canaris's liaison with Henlein was *Major* (Major) Helmut "Muffel" Groscurth, the head of Untergruppe IS (a subgroup of Abwehr I). At this time, Abwehr was divided into three major sections, Abwehr I (secret intelligence service); Abwehr II (cipher and radio monitoring); and Abwehr III (counterintelligence), which was responsible for war sabotage and minorities abroad.[66] Abwehr underwent several changes while Oskar Schindler was connected with the organization. In 1935, Hitler's decision to reinstate universal military service meant, at least from Canaris's perspective, new dangers to Germany's military security from abroad. To deal with this threat, Canaris greatly expanded Abwehr III. One of its new subsections was Abwehr IIIF, under Lt. Commander Richard Protze. One of the responsibilities of Protze's group was to recruit foreigners from across the German border to work for Abwehr. Soon after Canaris took over Abwehr, he decided to become more aggressive outside Germany. Each Abwehr office *(Abwehrstelle)* in Germany's nine (later thirteen) military districts was to set up its own intelligence operations team. Each unit of three to six agents was known as a Private Orchestra *(Hauskapelle)* overseen by a conductor *(Kapellmeister)*. One of the prime tasks of the *Hauskapellen* was to recruit agents who could infiltrate foreign spy agencies. They were aided by a special group of informants who were part of a *Hotelorganisation*. These informants worked in hotels and resorts and watched foreign spies. They also helped identify foreigners who might be willing to work for Canaris's organization. Abwehr IIIF agents at regional border stations worked with the green-uniformed border police *(Grenzpolizei)* to try to convince foreigners to work for military counterintelligence.[67]

Oskar Schindler probably worked for Abwehr IIIF in Opava first under *Major* Plathe. Gestapo reports in 1940 about a break-in at Schindler's apartment in Märisch Ostrau in 1939 show that *Major* Plathe remained Oskar's command officer through 1940.[68] Nothing in the German or Czech secret police files verifies this save for a statement Oskar made to the Czech secret police on July 23, 1938. The inclusion of this in Dr. Sobotka's official report five days later suggests that he accepted Schindler's statement as fact. In discussing his initial contacts with a Sudeten German Abwehr agent, whom Oskar referred to as "Kreuziger," he said that "Kreuziger" told him "to refuse cooperation with the department [Abwehr] II A, which deals only with political issues, such as propaganda, pamphlets, etc." This reference was not to the old Abwehr II, which had been responsible for cipher (code) and radio monitoring, but to a brand-new Abwehr II. Earlier that year, Canaris had reorganized Abwehr in response to new changes in OKW (*Oberkommando der Wehrmacht*; Wehrmacht High Command) under *General* Wilhelm Keitel. Abwehr now became the Bureau Abwehr (*Amtsgruppe* A), complete with a Foreign Office, an administrative Central Division, and three branches. Abwehr I remained the secret intelligence service, and Abwehr II, now under Groscurth, was responsible for psychological warfare, international agitation, and the cultivation of fifth columns abroad. Abwehr IIA referred to the Central Office in Berlin under Groscurth.[69]

There are four major accounts and collections about Oskar Schindler's work for Abwehr. The first was his own testimony to the Czechoslovak secret police after his arrest in Svitavy on July 18, 1938. The second is the interrogation statement of Leo Pruscha, a Sudeten German whom Oskar had recruited to work for Abwehr. The Czechs arrested Pruscha on July 19. The third document on Oskar's Abwehr activities is the report signed by Dr. Sobotka for the Police Directorate in Brno, where criminal charges were prepared against Schindler and Pruscha. Emilie also gives some important details about Oskar's Abwehr work in her memoirs, particularly his activities against Poland in 1939. Some minor interrogation reports by the Czech secret police in the summer of 1938 also allude to Schindler's activities.

I also discovered in Brno a fifty-five-page collection of Gestapo reports on the break-in at Oskar and Emilie's apartment in 1939. The investigation, which took over a year, provides some interesting insights into Oskar's Abwehr activities in 1939 and 1940. Finally, a collection of testimony gathered by the Czechoslovak Ministry of the Interior and the Czechoslovak Governmental Commission for Persecution of Nazi War Criminals after World War II presents important testimonies and information on Schindler. One can piece together a fairly clear picture of Oskar's work for Abwehr in 1938 and 1939 from these accounts. However, some of the statements, particularly Oskar's, have to be taken less seriously because he was charged with espionage and faced the death penalty. Certainly he did everything possible to downplay his role as an Abwehr agent. He always minimized his Abwehr activities, particularly after World War II, because he was still under investigation for espionage and war crimes in Czechoslovakia and Poland. The most accurate account is probably that of Leo Pruscha. His testimony about his relationship with Oskar is amazingly honest. He readily admitted to working for Oskar because of his deep sense of Sudeten German nationalism. Pruscha said he worked for the Germans because he was a patriot, though he certainly did not shy away from taking money for his efforts.

Dr. Sobotka's final report indicates that the Czechoslovak secret police had been watching Oskar for some time and had a dossier on him. It is doubtful that they could have come up with detailed information about many personal aspects of Oskar's life in just ten days after his arrest. What is remarkable about Dr. Sobotka's report is how accurately it characterizes Oskar's motives, needs, and personal characteristics. Czechoslovak police officials were aware of his human weaknesses and strengths well before he arrived in Kraków in the early days of World War II. The act that led to Oskar's arrest in the summer of 1938 was his effort to get Pruscha, a ticket clerk for the Czechoslovak national railways in Brno, to obtain military and rail information vital to the Wehrmacht's preparations for an invasion of Czechoslovakia in the fall of 1938.

A year earlier, Czechoslovakia had become the prime topic of discussion among Germany's military planners. From 1935 to 1937, Czechoslovakia was a favorite target of Hitler's propaganda machine, which depicted the country as a "tool" of Soviet foreign policy. The Führer now began to explore several options for Czechoslovakia, the boldest being its conquest; Hitler thought conquest would shorten Germany's borders and provide the Third Reich with a larger German population, particularly after the hated Czechoslovaks had been driven out. Hitler hoped to isolate Czechoslovakia from its European allies, particularly from France and Great Britain, by severing diplomatic relations and emphasizing the "grievances" of the Sudeten Germans.[70]

The issue was pushed along by the growing radicalization of the Sudeten German population in Czechoslovakia, particularly after Hitler occupied Austria (the *Anschluss,* or union) on March 13, 1938. Many Sudeten Germans were certain that Hitler would make them a part of the Third Reich on his birthday, April 20. Henlein's greatest rival in the SdP, Karl Hermann Frank, who had excellent ties to Himmler and the SS, was certain that Hitler would soon annex the Sudetenland and make it a part of the Third Reich. Many around Frank in the SdP supported this dream.[71]

By the fall of 1937, with a severely weakened political base, Henlein wrote to Hitler and proposed the German annexation of Bohemia and Moravia.[72] Hitler later told the Sudeten Nazi leader that his tactic in Czechoslovakia should be to make demands that "are unacceptable to the Czech government." He added that he "intended to settle the Sudeten German problem in the not-too-distant future." Hitler also told Henlein, "From tomorrow you'll be my Viceroy [Staathalter]. I will not tolerate difficulties being made for you by any department whatsoever within the Reich." These words meant a lot to Henlein because also present at the three-hour meeting were Karl Hermann Frank, Rudolf Hess, Hitler's deputy Führer, Joachim von Ribbentrop, Germany's foreign minister, and Werner Lorenz, head of the VoMi.[73]

Henlein returned to Czechoslovakia and began to pursue a two-fold policy that outwardly promised continued loyalty to the Czechoslovak state while privately supporting German annexation of the Sudetenland. In his famous April 24 speech before the SdP congress in Karlovy Vary (Karls-bad), Henlein laid out eight demands for autonomy within the Czechoslovak Republic. If the Prague government had accepted them all, it would have "been tantamount to union with Germany." Three days earlier, Hitler met with the new head of the OKW, Generalleutnant Wilhelm Keitel, and discussed his thinking on the Czechoslovak question. He told Keitel that he did not intend to destroy Czechoslovakia unless an extreme crisis occurred. Hitler wanted to avoid a major international confrontation over Czechoslovakia. His plan was to justify Germany's slow military buildup by intensifying international tensions over the plight of the Sudeten Germans. The crisis would end with a surprise attack by Germany or one triggered by an incident "arranged" within Czechoslovakia.[74]

Henlein played his new role well. Hitler told him to avoid a settlement of the Sudeten question with the Czechoslovak government and to keep Great Britain neutral during the crisis. On May 20, the OKW gave Hitler an interim directive for Operation Grün (Green), which was based on the idea that political developments within Czechoslovakia might prompt German action. In a meeting with prominent German military leaders on May 28, Hitler said the attack on Czechoslovakia, which he thought would begin on October 1, was a prelude to a later move against Germany's western neighbors.[75] Two days later, OKW presented the Führer with a refined directive for Operation Grün, which began with Hitler's statement that it was his "unalterable decision to smash Czechoslovakia by military action in the near future. It is the business of the political leadership to await or bring about the suitable moment from a political and military point of view."[76]

General Keitel told *Admiral* Canaris that Abwehr was to help prepare for the invasion of Czechoslovakia "by means of propaganda, subversion, and reconnaissance." Some thought was also given in OKW to an Abwehr assassination of the German ambassador to Czechoslovakia, Ernst Eisenlohr, to justify an attack against Czechoslovakia. Abwehr propaganda was meant to "intimidate Czechoslovakia" and weaken "her resistance with threats." Abwehr was also to use its propaganda outlets to send "instructions to the national minorities to support the armed struggle." The operational plan for the invasion of Czechoslovakia also said that after German units had moved into Czechoslovakia, "co-operation with the Sudeten German frontier population, deserters from the Czechoslovak army and elements of the sabotage service" could greatly enhance German successes.[77]

Oskar Schindler's work during the summer of 1938 was linked to Abwehr's need to provide its combat (K) and sabotage (S) teams *(K and S-Verbände)* with reliable maps and information on Czechoslovak troop movements, military fortifications, and other strategically important data. Abwehr stationed its K and S teams just across the Czechoslovak-German border; they were thus prepared to move once the invasion began. The K and S teams were to reconnoiter landings sites for the Seventh Air[borne] Division in the Freudenthal (Bruntál) region, which was about fifty miles northeast of Svitavy. This was also to be a staging area for the Eighth Army Corps. Oskar Schindler's intense efforts to recruit Sudeten Germans with knowledge of vital military information was important to Abwehr's invasion plans.[78]

Schindler's Activities as an Abwehr Agent: Summer 1938

At the time of his arrest on July 19, 1938, Leo Pruscha (Czech, Průša) was a forty-six-year-old station "manipulantem," or railway worker, who sold tickets in Brno. His arrest photograph shows a well-dressed middle-aged man in a striped suit and bow tie. His features are very striking with a strong chin and nose. Pruscha was born in Okříšky, a small village about thirty-five miles west of Brno. His family moved to Brno after his father, a railway worker, was killed in an accident in 1897. He was not a strong student, and in 1910 his mother convinced him to drop out because of poor grades. He found a job as a typist at the railway traffic office in Brno. In early 1914, he joined the Austrian army and served in Olomouc and Kraków for three and a half months. After his return from the military, he became a telegraph operator at a small station in Miroslav, southeast of Brno. He met his future wife in Miroslav, and she bore him a daughter in 1915. Pruscha was recalled to active duty after World War I broke out in August 1914 and was wounded twice. He remained in the army until the end of the war in 1918 and married on his return. He returned to his railway job in Miroslav, now part of the new Czechoslovak Republic. Railway officials later transferred him to Hrušovany nad Jevišovkou. They moved him again to Nezamyslice for poor job performance. Pruscha improved enough to earn a transfer to Brno in 1934 or 1935, where he worked in Department V/5, which prepared train schedules. By 1938, he was selling train tickets.[79]

Pruscha had a base monthly railway salary of 640 crowns ($22.16) and a special clerical bonus of 750 crowns ($25.96). He supported his wife and daughter, who was a law student, on this income. Though Pruscha told his interrogators that he decided to help Abwehr because he was "under the influence of a national fever due to the current political climate," the Czech secret police thought otherwise. There is no question that Pruscha was a passionate Sudeten German, but he also desperately needed money. The Czech police reported that he had accumulated debts and had a drinking problem. Four months before his arrest, one of his coworkers, Ladislav Novak, said that authorities had found money missing from Pruscha's cash register. He also had a record of antigovernment activity dating back to 1935, when the police investigated him for violating the antitreason Law for the Protection of the Republic. Pruscha admitted that he once had been a member of the outlawed DNSAP and had only recently joined Henlein's SdP. His wife and daughter had joined the SdP much earlier. His statements and those of others lead one to conclude that Leo Pruscha was a staunch Sudeten German nationalist with strong Nazi leanings.[80]

Oskar first met Pruscha in 1931, though Pruscha claimed that he did not meet Oskar until July 1938. At the time of their first meeting, Oskar was again working for MEAS in Brno and admittedly spent a lot of time in coffee shops and taverns. Oskar said that he remembered Pruscha as a drunk and a Sudeten German patriot who had serious financial problems. Oskar got to know Pruscha through a brother-in-law, Ondrej Schulz, whom Oskar had known for some time. Schindler did not meet Pruscha again until the summer of 1938, when Oskar recruited him to obtain vital Czechoslovak railway and troop movement information for Abwehr.[81]

Oskar told the Czechoslovak secret police in 1938 that his efforts began innocently. On July 1, he decided to visit Gritt Schwarzer in Ziegenhals, Germany, where she had recently begun to manage the Hotel Juppebad. Oskar said that when he arrived at the Czechoslovak border town of Zlaté Hory (Zuckmantel), he decided he would have to cross the frontier illegally because he did not have a passport. He persuaded a local Sudeten German innkeeper, Fölkel, to "show" him a path across the border, then crossed at 10:00 P.M. When he reached Germany, Oskar called Gritt; she arranged for a private car so that he could drive to Ziegenhals. When he arrived at the Juppebad Hotel, Gritt was attending a "joyous" dinner party. While Oskar waited for her, he was drawn into a conversation with a stranger, who later introduced himself as Peter. When Peter learned that Oskar was from the Czechoslovak Republic, he said that lot of Sudeten Germans in the Reich made good money working for the Fatherland.[82]

A "tipsy" German, Kreuziger, soon joined Oskar and Peter and congratulated Schindler for his interest in working for Abwehr. Oskar and Kreuziger met the next day and talked further about Abwehr. Kreuziger was interested in Oskar's business connections and his areas of travel. He also wanted to know whether he was in the Czechoslovak military and his rank. Kreuziger was obviously trying to determine Oskar's full value to Abwehr because Gritt had probably already told Kreuziger about his talents and political reliability. The German agent was particularly interested in contacts that Oskar had with people who might have important economic or military information. Abwehr was being flooded by requests for such information from throughout the Wehrmacht, and its agents were desperate for anything that would enhance military preparations for Operation Green. Kreuziger also warned Oskar not to have anything to do with Abwehr IIA, which was responsible for "political things and propaganda." If he did, his relationship with Kreuziger's "orchestra" would be affected.[83]

Kreuziger was disappointed that Oskar did not have business ties in Slovakia. Though Slovakia had a sizeable ethnic German population, it was not as dependable as the Sudeten German community in Bohemia and Moravia. Moreover, Slovakia shared most of its frontier with Poland and Hungary, not the Greater Reich. Members of the radical wing of the Slovak People's Party, the Ludaks, developed close, if unfruitful, ties with German intelligence agents and the SdP. Most Ludak contacts came through the German consulate in Bratislava or through the SS's Ethnic German Central Office (VoMi; Volksdeutsche Mittelstelle). Unfortunately for Abwehr, the VoMi was now completely under Himmler's control after the appointment of SS-Obergruppenführer Werner Lorenz as head the agency in 1937.[84]

Kreuziger also wanted to know whether Oskar had relationships with military officers or government workers who might be interested in working for Germany. He said that Oskar should develop closer ties with such people, but should approach them carefully and subtly about the nature of the work. Kreuziger said it was important to gather detailed information about each person's job. The Reich agent said he would pay all of Oskar's Abwehr-related expenses. Once Oskar proved himself, Kreuziger said he could provide an advance to cover future expenses. Oskar mentioned that he already had a job and might have to take time off to do his Abwehr work. Kreuziger promised that he would reimburse Oskar for financial shortfalls. The German agent added that he might be able to give Schindler as much as RM 1,000 to RM 2,000 ($400 to $800) for future reimbursement expenses and that Oskar should personally deliver all information to him. Kreuziger promised Oskar that in the future one or two motorcycles would be made available to him for his work and intelligence deliveries. Kreuziger also wanted Oskar to meet his "conductor," or boss, an Abwehr major, on July 7 in Ziegenhals. The major needed to get to know Oskar, assess his capabilities, and give him further details about his work. In the meantime, Oskar was to see whether his acquaintances might be useful to what Kreuziger called the Reich German Intelligence Service (Reichsdeutscher Nachrichtendienst).[85]

In an emergency, both men agreed that Oskar could call Gritt at the Juppebad Hotel, who would get in touch with Kreuziger. Peter could then meet him at the border and take him to Ziegenhals. Kreuziger told Oskar that Peter would meet him that evening and help him cross back into Czechoslovakia. Oskar spent the rest of the day at the Hotel Juppebad engaged in "private matters." Peter met him at 6:00 P.M. and drove him to the frontier. The German agent told Oskar that he would wait for him at the city market in Zlaté Hory on July 7 and take him across the frontier.[86]

On July 7, a friend, Julius Heger, drove Oskar the sixty miles from Svitavy to Zlaté Hory in a rented car. Heger dropped him off at a local inn and Schindler walked to a prearranged place to meet Peter. The German spy pretended not to recognize Oskar and walked towards a church. He then went along the same path that the innkeeper Fölkel had shown

Oskar on July 1. Oskar followed Peter and met him outside Zlaté Hory. They both crossed the frontier illegally and walked to the German Customs House manned by the border police. Peter dialed 514, Kreuziger's number, and told him that Oskar was in Germany. Kreuziger said that he and his boss, the mysterious Abwehr *major*, were too busy to collect Oskar by car. Instead, Kreuziger said he would meet them at the Customs House on a motorcycle. Kreuziger soon arrived, Gritt accompanying him in a sidecar. Oskar climbed inside with Gritt, and Kreuziger drove them to a local tavern in Ziegenhals. Oskar, Gritt, and Kreuziger spent the evening drinking and discussing insignificant topics. Peter was also in the tavern, though he did not join Oskar and the others. At 2:00 A.M., Oskar learned that the *major* was not coming; Peter took Oskar back to the border and helped him walk into Czechoslovakia. Oskar spent the rest of the night in the Hotel Tietze in Zlaté Hory. The next morning, Heger drove him back to Svitavy. Along the way, Oskar stopped to visit with some of his customers.[87]

On July 9, the day after Oskar returned to Svitavy from Germany, he drove to Brno. He normally went to Brno once a week on business and knew the city well. He spent most of the day conducting business and then went to Pruscha's apartment at Jilova 3. According to Pruscha, a stranger appeared at his door at 4:00 P.M. on July 9 and introduced himself as Oskar Müller. Pruscha referred to Schindler as Oskar Müller throughout his July 23, 1938, interrogation report for the Czech secret police. Pruscha said that the stranger knew of him through his brother-in-law, Ondrej Schulz. Pruscha told his interrogators that he knew nothing about Schulz's whereabouts. Because Pruscha's wife and daughter were in the front room, "Müller" said he would like to talk privately with Leo in another room. Oskar asked Pruscha whether anyone could hear them in the adjoining room, and Pruscha assured him that no one could.[88]

At this point, their testimonies diverge considerably. Oskar said that he told Pruscha: "I am ordered to ask you whether you are willing to deliver material and reports to the German Reich, as far as you can obtain it at the Bahn [railway; *Eisenbahn*]." Oskar put 100 Czech crowns ($3.46) on the table and asked Pruscha to meet him in Svitavy the next day. Pruscha said that "Müller" told him that he was from the "Říše" (empire or Reich) and had worked for Germany for two years. He stated that because Pruscha was a good German, he could not refuse any request from Oskar. Pruscha then asked "Müller" what he wanted him to do. Oskar answered that he wanted Leo to give him information on railway facilities and transports.

He said that Pruscha would learn more about his duties after the two of them went to Germany. Leo told "Müller" that he had no passport. Oskar replied that it was not important and that his connections could take them safely across the border. Oskar was still worried that someone would hear them and asked Leo to go outside with him. Pruscha refused and said that he wanted to think about "Müller's" offer before making a decision. He was on vacation and had time to think the matter over. Before he left, Oskar reminded Leo that he expected to meet him at the Restaurace u Ungar in Svitavy the next day. "Müller" advised Leo to take the noon "fast train" from Brno and, once in Svitavy, to board the bus marked "Hotel Unger." Leo said that he was not sure whether he would come. "Müller" then gave him 100 crowns for expenses. Schindler reminded him not to discuss their conversation, particularly with Leo's wife and daughter.[89]

On Sunday, July 10, Pruscha boarded the noon train for Svitavy and arrived at 12:22 P.M. Oskar, who had driven back to Svitavy the night before, went to the train station to see whether Leo had come. However, he did not approach Pruscha because he wanted to make sure that no one else was with him. After a while, Oskar walked up to him and, according to Pruscha, they took a bus to the Hotel Unger (today, Hotel Slavia). Schindler said that they walked to the hotel. "Müller" told Leo that he wanted to take him to Germany that afternoon and Pruscha agreed. Oskar took Pruscha to the hotel restaurant and told him to order breakfast. Schindler left Leo at the table and returned some time later. He told Leo that he had arranged transportation to Germany. Oskar again used Julius Heger's rented car and a driver. As they drove to Zlaté Hory from Svitavy, Leo told "Müller" about his job at the state railway system. Oskar said he found most of the conversation confusing and uninteresting. He told Leo that once in Germany, they would meet with an Abwehr *major* who would tell Pruscha more about what they wanted from him. They had a late lunch at the train station in Zábřeh, where Oskar waited for a new driver. When he did not show up, Oskar arranged for the Svitavy driver to take them to Zlaté Hory. As they got closer to the frontier, Oskar said he hoped that he could locate the Abwehr *major*.[90]

At this point, Leo seems to have gotten cold feet. He told "Müller" that he was not sure whether he had any valuable information for the Germans because he worked for the railway system's commercial service. Oskar, however, disagreed. He had already decided that Pruscha would be of great help to Abwehr. Perhaps Schindler knew that Pruscha was a reserve sergeant in Telegraph Battalion No. 3 in the Czechoslovak army. He

told Leo that the *major* wanted all information he had on military transports and related matters. "Müller" also wanted to know whether Pruscha
had friends in the Czechoslovak military. Leo answered that he knew several officers. One, Igl, was retired; the other, Vaclav Ryba, was a warrant
officer and a construction supervisor. Pruscha said he doubted that Ryba
would be interested in working for the Germans. Oskar replied that he
did not think Igl would be of value as he was retired, but he was interested
in Ryba and would negotiate with him separately.[91]

"Müller" told Leo that it was important for him always to carry money
to pay for the expenses he would incur if he met people who might have
valuable information. Oskar said that Leo should treat them to food and
drink while they talked. He added that he could give Pruscha 100 to 200
crowns ($3.50 to $7.00) now but that Leo would have to request larger
sums beforehand from Oskar. "Müller" would have to get approval for
larger amounts from Abwehr. While they were talking, the car broke
down, which delayed their trip. On the outskirts of Zlaté Hory, Oskar
and Leo got out of the rented car. Oskar said he ordered the driver to take
it about six miles to Jeseník (Freiwaldau) and wait for his call to return.
Pruscha said the driver took them to Zlaté Hory's town square, not the
outskirts. Leo added that "Müller" told him to wait in the car while he
visited a customer. After about fifteen minutes, Oskar returned and both
men waited in a cafe for Peter. Schindler returned to the car and ordered
the driver to leave after giving him written instructions about a later
pickup time and location. Oskar went off again and left Leo on a park
bench. Bored and hungry, Pruscha bought a pastry in a bakery and Oskar
joined him there. They walked around the square for almost an hour before Oskar decided that Peter was not coming. He told Pruscha that he
would take him across the border himself.[92]

They followed the familiar path behind the church and across some
fields to a pub just 150 steps from the border. "Müller" told Leo to relax.
They would soon be in Germany. Both men crossed the border near
Skřivánkov (Lerchenfeld) between 4:00 P.M. and 5:00 P.M. on July 10
without detection. They walked a bit farther and entered a German pub
through the kitchen, from where Oskar called Kreuziger's 514 number.
Thirty minutes later, a rental car and driver arrived to take them to
Ziegenhals. Oskar said that it was Kreuziger who picked them up, though
Pruscha said he did not meet the German agent until they arrived in
Ziegenhals. The driver took them to a local hotel, the *Deutsches Haus*
(German House). They went to the hotel restaurant and Oskar introduced

Leo to Kreuziger, whom Pruscha referred to as "Kreuz" or "Kreuz ing his interrogation.[93]

At this point, the testimonies of Schindler and Pruscha vary considerably. Oskar said that after Kreuziger picked the two men up at the border, he took them to the *Deutsches Haus*. Afterwards, they went pub hopping until 3:00 or 4:00 A.M. and never discussed business. According to Schindler, Kreuziger picked them up the next morning at 9:00 A.M. at the *Deutsches Haus* and took them to his apartment. They stayed there for about an hour discussing Abwehr business. Pruscha claims that the bulk of their conversation took place in a private room at the *Deutsches Haus* the evening before. He told the Czechoslovak secret police that after he and "Müller" met Kreuziger in the restaurant at the *Deutsches Haus* on the evening of July 10, the three men had drinks and exchanged pleasantries. After a while, they went to a private room in the restaurant where Kreuziger interviewed Pruscha. The Brno railway clerk told Kreuziger that he was in bad financial shape and was not being promoted because he was a German. He emphasized that he and his family had a "strong national conscience." Kreuziger said that he was glad that Leo was willing to work for Abwehr and regretted that his boss, the *major*, could not meet him. Leo reminded him that he was a mere railway clerk who worked in the commercial affairs division. Kreuziger said that was fine, though he was only interested in military information. Oskar added that Leo would be able to see military transports and facilities in Brno and could share this information with Abwehr. Kreuziger was desperate for details about the Czechoslovak state railways system because the Wehrmacht intended to use it to transfer "the bulk of the field army" into Czechoslovakia.[94]

Pruscha now began to address Kreuziger as "Herr *Major*" and said that he would try to get him some "traffic graphicons." Kreuziger said that he knew nothing about graphicons and asked Leo to explain them. Pruscha said that a graphicon was "a graphical visualization of the train schedules and longitudinal intersection of the tracks where one can see the fluctuation (ascent and descent) along a [train's] route." Kreuziger said he would be interested in seeing the graphicons. Leo also promised to provide him with information on military railway facilities and transports. "Herr *Major*" was particularly interested in details about military transports. He told Pruscha that he wanted anything on troop movements not only during mobilization but also when there was peace. The partial Czechoslovak mobilization on May 20–21 had caught the Germans by surprise and Abwehr wanted to be certain that this did not happen again.[95]

Kreuziger also wanted to know about the military storage facilities in Brno. Pruscha said he knew nothing about them. The *major* then opened up a railway map of Czechoslovakia with names of stations in Czechoslovak and German. He was particularly interested in the border crossings from Austria via Břeclav (Lundenburg) and Hrušovany n. Jevišovkou. Kreuziger also wanted to know about the condition and construction of the rail lines between these two cities and Brno. Břeclav was about thirty miles southeast of Brno and Hrušovany twenty-seven miles to the southwest. Vienna was about fifty miles below each town. German forces operating out of Austria would want to gain quick control of these important rail heads in their move northward to Brno and beyond. Pruscha, who had once been stationed in Hrušovany, told Kreuziger that there was a double track between Brno and Břeclav and a single line between Hrušovany and Brno. Kreuziger wanted to know the distance between the two cities and Brno. He also asked whether the Czechoslovak military had occupied these particular rail lines during their mobilization in May. Pruscha said that he had been sick during the partial call up, but was certain that the army had seized the bridges and carefully watched all rail lines. He added that there was a separate rail line out of Hrušovany westward to Znojmo (Znoim), which lay just north of the Austrian border. Kreuziger was interested in this information because there was a Czechoslovak military garrison in Znojmo. He asked Leo whether he knew how many troops were stationed in Znojmo. Pruscha said that he did not know how many soldiers were there.[96]

Kreuziger then asked Leo what he knew about the railway connections into Slovakia. Though it is uncertain whether Kreuziger knew the details of Operation Green, it entailed a very well-coordinated, rapid movement of troops into Czechoslovakia during the last half of the four-day campaign. The focal point of the German invasion was Prague, but it was also important that German forces quickly reach the important railhead at Brno and from there, Slovakia. One of the important challenges for the Wehrmacht in Operation Green was the prevention of "a withdrawal by the Czech Army into Slovakia." Hitler, the driving force behind Operation Green, also hoped a quick victory would forestall Allied intervention in support of the Czechoslovaks.[97]

The wide informational net that Kreuziger had cast reflected Abwehr's desperate effort to gather as much information as possible for the various Wehrmacht units requesting it. This worrisome search for data on the Czechoslovak military was justified. The Czechoslovaks could field four armies with 800,000 to 1 million men under arms. Thousands of fortified positions, ranging from machine gun posts to heavy fortresses, dotted the country's frontiers. The most formidable of Czechoslovakia's defenses was the Czech Maginot Line, which ran from Nachod to Ostrava. In 1934, Prague sent military specialists to France to study that nation's Maginot Line. With the help of French advisers, the Czechoslovaks began to construct a series of heavy fortifications, which the Germans referred to as the Beneš Line, to defend their northwestern frontier with Germany. Though it was not intended for completion until 1946, parts of the Czechoslovak Maginot Line were almost complete on the eve of the Sudeten crisis. In 1938, the Czechoslovaks also began to build lighter defense works along its frontier with recently annexed Austria. These fortifications were manned by special elite border units under eight Border Sector Commands. Abwehr reports on the strength of these defenses were so contradictory that Canaris feared that he had fallen out of favor with Hitler because of their inaccuracy.[98]

Czechoslovakia's defensive strategy was to move out of Bohemia and create a military barrier in Moravia in expectation of attacks from Austria and Silesia. The Czechoslovak First Army was to defend Bohemia and the Second and Fourth Armies were to protect Moravia. The Third Army was positioned along the Hungarian border. And although the British and the French differed over the ability of the Czechoslovaks successively to slow down a German assault while awaiting Allied help, the size and strength of Czechoslovakia's armed forces worried German military planners. Moreover, there was every indication that the Czechoslovaks would put up fierce resistance if attacked. Radomír Luža reports that when the army's commanders learned of the Allied decision to give away part of their country at Munich in late September, they urged Beneš to reject the accord and "go to war regardless of the consequences." The same commanders, though, told Beneš that they could not hold out more than three weeks without the support of their western allies. The fact that the Germans worked frantically in the summer of 1938 to strengthen their own defensive and offensive posture against Czechoslovakia underscores a deep respect for the Czechoslovak military.[99]

In light of this, it is not surprising that Kreuziger was under pressure to find out anything he could about rail lines into Slovakia and their planned use by the military. Pruscha was not able to tell him much, which frustrated Kreuziger. Pruscha told the German agent that the rail connection out of Brno to Slovakia was along the Vlarska route, but added that he was familiar only with the rail lines to Veselí nad Moravou, which is about fifteen miles from the Slovak border. He told Kreuziger that there was nothing special about this particular rail line. Leo said it was about ninety miles from Brno to Veselí. Kreuziger also wanted to know about the rail line between Brno and Jihlava in the northwest. Leo answered that he knew nothing about this route. Kreuziger was also interested in rail connections through Bohumin and its crossing into Germany. Pruscha said that he knew only about the line between Brno and Nezamyslice, which had a single track and no special features. Kreuziger also inquired about the rail link between Brno and Nemecky Brod (today, Havičkův Brod; [Deutsch Brod]), which was equidistant between Prague and Brno. Was it, he wondered, a double-tracked line? Leo said it had only a single track and that only a local rail shuttle used it. Kreuziger then asked about the railway lines between Brno and Prague. Pruscha thought there were double tracks on this particular route, though he knew little about it. At this point, Schindler entered the discussion and said that he was quite familiar with the Brno-Prague line. It had double tracks and nine tunnels. Finally, Kreuziger asked Pruscha whether the Czechoslovak military was building new bases or making other preparations near the rail lines under discussion. He also wanted to know whether anything had been done to increase military security along each route. Pruscha said he knew nothing about new installations, preparations, or enhanced security.[100]

At this point, Kreuziger reemphasized that he remained very interested in military matters. Schindler, perhaps sensing Kreuziger's frustration with Pruscha's lack of such knowledge, answered that they both knew one soldier, Ryba, who worked in military construction. Leo said he doubted they could convince Ryba to work for Abwehr. Oskar assured Kreuziger that he would begin to work on Ryba and was sure he could win him over. If Schindler was successful in convincing Ryba to work with him, Kreuziger responded, he would need information on "defense works, the direction of their embrasures [parapet of a fortification for firing cannon], thickness of walls, location of fortifications and, if possible, the plan of the fortifications." One of the key concerns in German military planning was the quick breaching of Czechoslovakia's considerable border fortifications. The Wehrmacht also worried about the buildup of new fortifications along the Czechoslovak-Austrian border, particularly after the May Crisis. Operation Green laid out as one of the principal tasks of the army and the *Luftwaffe* (airforce) the rapid destruction of Czechoslovak border defenses and fortifications. One of the key elements in these efforts was "cooperation with the Sudeten German frontier population" and "deserters from the Czechoslovak Army."[101]

Kreuziger now turned to Pruscha and said that he should give any information he gathered to Schindler. The German agent thought it would be a good idea for Leo to bring a bit of information as a gesture of his willingness to work with military counterintelligence. Pruscha answered that because he was on vacation, he would not be able to get hold of anything until after July 14. He promised he would have something for Schindler in Brno by July 16. Kreuziger told Leo that he would generously pay for all his expenses and reward him accordingly for valuable information. Pruscha said that "as a nationalist German" he did not want to make any "profits" out of this. He felt "it was the moral obligation of a German to do these kinds of duties." He reemphasized his "Germanness" to Kreuziger and said that his daughter also belonged to Henlein's SdP. This did not seem to interest Kreuziger. The Abwehr agent promised Leo that if something ever happened to him, he could get him a job in Germany. If Pruscha ever needed anything, he should ask Oskar "Müller."[102]

Leo Pruscha told the Czech police that their conversation ended late in the evening. They walked to another restaurant where many people were dancing. Along the way, people greeted Kreuziger as they walked along the street. About midnight, they went back to the *Deutsches Haus* and drank coffee and wine in a "special room." Kreuziger left after an hour and the two Sudeten Germans went to their separate rooms on the first floor of the *Deutsches Haus*. The next morning, Kreuziger met the two at the *Deutsches Haus* restaurant at 9:00 A.M. Pruscha said that another German met them there, though he was never formally introduced to him. It was the mysterious Peter. He described Peter in some detail to his Czechoslovak interrogators. He was about forty years old and about 165 cm (5'3"). He thought he might have had one gold tooth. Peter had dark hair and dressed in a well-worn dark grey coat. He wore a hat of similar color and a shirt with a "sawed-on collar" without a tie. Leo said that they stayed in the restaurant until about 1:00 P.M., when Oskar left.[103]

Schindler claimed that only Kreuziger met them in the restaurant at 9:00 A.M. and took them to his apartment where the German agent lived with his family. Oskar told his Czechoslovak interrogators that they talked for about an hour. He noted that he had spotted Peter in the kitchen, though he never came out to talk with Schindler and the others. Kreuziger asked Oskar and Leo to stay for lunch, but Oskar declined because he had to meet Gritt Schwarzer. Before he left, he arranged for

Kreuziger to have Peter meet him at 3:00 P.M. with a car. He promised Kreuziger that he would return to Zlaté Hory on July 18 or 19 with the materials from Pruscha. Because "Müller" was uncertain about which day he would come to the frontier, Kreuziger said he would have Peter wait there each day between 6:00 P.M. and 8:00 P.M.[104]

At this point, the testimonies of Schindler and Pruscha diverge again. Oskar said that after his meeting with Gritt, he met Peter and Leo at the prearranged spot in Ziegenhals, where a car was waiting for them. Leo evidently felt he did not have enough time to get the information that Kreuziger wanted and told Oskar he needed an extra day or so. "Müller" told Peter that he would not come to Zlaté Hory on July 17 or 18 but on July 18 or 19. Pruscha's account is different. He said that Kreuziger met the two Sudeten Germans in the *Deutsches Haus* on the morning of July 11. Oskar excused himself at 1:00 P.M. while Leo and Peter went to a street corner near the restaurant. At 1:45 P.M., Schindler returned with a car which drove them to the German border village of Arnoldsdorf (Pruscha said Altmansdorf). "Müller" then called for a car to meet them on the Czechoslovak side of the frontier. Oskar and Peter left Pruscha hidden in a room at a local restaurant. Schindler finally returned and they walked together to a red church in Arnoldsdorf. Suddenly, Peter walked past them and signaled them to walk quickly towards the Czechoslovak border. He gave hand signals when it was safe to cross the border. They crossed at the same spot that Oskar had first learned on July 1 and walked safely to Skřivánkov. About halfway to Zlaté Hory, Peter passed them on a bicycle. They met him in a pub in Zlaté Hory. Pruscha went to the bar and bought a beer and some sausages while Oskar and Peter stood in the hallway talking. After Leo had finished, "Müller" paid his tab and they walked towards the train station along a special route laid out by Peter. They arrived at the station at 5:15 P.M. and caught a train ten minutes later for Mikulovice.[105]

In Mikulovice, they changed trains for Jeseník (Fryvaldov in both testimonies). On their arrival, Schindler got off the train and told him to meet him in Zábřeh (Hohenstadt), where he would give Pruscha the coat that he had left in the car in Germany. He said he was getting off in Jeseník because he had customers to visit there. When Leo got into Zábřeh at 10:00 P.M., Oskar was waiting for him. Unknown to Pruscha, Schindler's private car and driver were waiting for him in Zábřeh. Oskar said that as he was being driven to Zábřeh, he remembered that there were no more late evening connections from there to Brno. Consequently, he met Leo at the train station and offered to take him to Svitavy by private car because otherwise he would have to wait four hours for another train. Before they left, Oskar took Leo to the *Zur Eiche* (by the Oak Tree) tavern while he "settled a private matter." Pruscha explained that "Müller" told him to have dinner and wait for him. After fifteen minutes, Oskar returned with the driver and the three of them had dinner together. He paid the bill with a 100 crown ($3.46) note and gave the change of 60 crowns ($2.14) to Leo. As they were driving to Svitavy, Leo and Oskar agreed to meet in Brno at 9:30 P.M. on July 16 at the Europa Café. If for some reason one of them was not there, they would meet the next evening at 10:00 P.M. in the Grimm restaurant on the Vaclavska in Brno. Pruscha promised that he would try to have the graphicons. When they reached Svitavy, Oskar took Leo to the Unger Hotel to wait for his train to Brno. Oskar left Pruscha at the hotel and went home.[106]

Schindler stopped at this point in his interrogation statement and explained that he wanted to add another remark by Pruscha to his testimony. Oskar said that Pruscha told him that he had a good German friend in Brno, Vaclav Ryba, who was a "military master builder." Leo added that he regularly played cards with Ryba. According to Schindler, Pruscha would try to "attract him to our thing," but that they would have to deal with Ryba very carefully because he was "known to be very correct and dutiful." Ryba constructed barracks in Slovakia but returned home on weekends. His financial situation was "stable." Pruscha felt it best that he talk to Ryba alone. If he seemed interested, Oskar could meet with him. Regardless of Ryba's interest, Leo promised to introduce him to "Müller."[107]

Pruscha spent the last two days of his vacation at home and returned to work on Thursday, July 14. The following day, July 15, he went to the pub *U Hradecký* on Rasinova street, where he met Ryba, who was having a drink in the beer garden with an architect, Nemecek. Pruscha was surprised to see Ryba, who usually came to Brno only on weekends. The Czechoslovak army officer explained that he came home early because "he had to arrange things in Brno." After Nemecek left, Leo spoke to Ryba in German and asked him how he would react should he be asked to do something for his "German culture and way of life." Ryba immediately understood the intent of Pruscha's question. He asked "my dear Leo" whether he had forgotten that Ryba was a soldier. If a civilian was caught doing such things, Ryba sharply added, he might get a year. A soldier would get "a bullet." Pruscha said that after these comments he decided not to try to "win Ryba over for espionage anymore because [he] was discouraged by his words." Ryba left the pub to go to lunch and Leo stayed behind and ate his packed lunch. Afterwards, he returned to work.[108]

The next day, Pruscha went to Department V of the directorate of the Czechoslovak National Railways to find Ladislav Novak. He also approached another employee, Pokorny, who worked in the lithographic department. Pokorny told Leo that he did not have any spare graphicons to give him. At noon, he went to the outer office where Novak worked and asked that he meet him in the corridor. Pruscha explained that he had scratched some graphicons he had been preparing for his boss. When he tried to repair them with glue, he irreparably damaged them. His boss was quite angry, and Leo hoped he could get some new ones to give his supervisor when he returned from vacation "to put the whole thing right." Novak told Pruscha that he would give him new ones only if Leo gave him the damaged graphicons. Novak was in charge of the drawing and production of graphicons in his department. Since 1936, railway authorities had treated them as confidential and kept them under lock and key because of their strategic military value. Graphicons with military margins had to be put in a special case. Anyone who wanted a graphicon, such as a station master, had to sign a written release form to obtain it. At the end of each year, all graphicons had to be returned to Novak's department, where the old ones were burned. Pruscha knew this but begged Novak to give him some new ones immediately so that he could finish working on them over the weekend. Novak gave him the only two he had for the routes from Brno to Hrušovany nad Jevišovkou and Břeclav-Brno-Česká Třebová. They were missing the military margins, or "tear off slips." Novak reiterated that he would give Leo replacements if he would bring in the damaged graphicons. He added that he doubted that Pruscha had ruined them all. Instead, Ladislav suspected, Leo had lost them. Pruscha thanked Novak for the graphicons and promised to buy him a beer in return, though Novak declined. Pruscha took the graphicons back to his railway office. Leo also got a copy of a 1930 graphicon, which he later gave to "Müller."[109]

As Pruscha was meeting with Novak in the offices of the railway directorate, Oskar Schindler boarded a noon train for Brno. He conducted "several private and business matters" most of the afternoon and went to the Europa Café at 9:00 P.M. Leo spent the evening at the Hradecky pub and left about 9:15 P.M. for his meeting with "Müller" at the Europa. Oskar was frustrated when Leo did not arrive by 9:30 P.M. and left. As he was walking down the street he met Pruscha and asked where they could go to talk. He suggested the Hradecky pub. According to Schindler, Leo said that he had just paid gas and electric bills and had no money. He lamented that he had not even been able to pay his earlier bar tab at the Hradecky. His wife was out, so he could not even get money from her. Oskar gave Leo 100 crowns ($3.46) as they walked down the street. In the tavern, they ordered beers and began to talk about the graphicons that Leo had brought with him. Pruscha had them in his coat pocket and advised "Müller" to hide them in the same place in his coat. Schindler said that Pruscha gave him a package with the graphicons inside and put it in his briefcase. Leo apologized because the military information was missing from the graphicons but thought he knew where "he could get them." He promised to get more for Kreuziger.[110]

Oskar then asked Leo about Ryba. The ticket agent told "Müller" about the conversation he had with him. He repeated his question to Ryba in German as well as his response. Leo felt that "we cannot do anything with him." Schindler disagreed and said he was not turned off by Ryba's answer. He would like Leo to introduce the two of them. "Müller" would try to convince Ryba to work for him. Pruscha said that he played cards every Sunday with Ryba and others between 10:00 A.M. and noon at the Grimm pub. Oskar said he would meet him there the next day and try to talk to Ryba. He spent the night in Brno and went to the Grimm tavern about 11:00 A.M. Leo and Ryba, whom the other players called Vaclav, were already at the Grimm pub with the usual Sunday group. When Schindler arrived, Leo introduced him to everyone. One of the members of the card-playing group was the retired military officer Igl whom Pruscha had earlier mentioned to "Müller." Ryba asked Schindler whether he was a colleague of Leo's and Oskar replied that they were old acquaintances. Schindler watched the group play cards and kept his eye on Ryba, whom Pruscha had described as the "master builder."[111]

At noon, Ryba got up to leave. Leo stopped him and asked whether he would come back that evening, but Ryba said he did not know. Schindler told Leo that if that was the case, he would return as well. "Müller" took a tram to town where he had lunch and Leo went home. He returned to the Grimm tavern at 9:00 P.M. and Oskar came in half an hour later. They waited for Ryba for two and a half hours and finally decided that he was not going to show up. "Müller" asked Pruscha whether he thought Ryba knew what was going on. Leo answered that he thought he did. Schindler shrugged this off and said he would try to talk to him next Sunday. He still felt that he could convince Ryba to work with them. Oskar said in his testimony that he never intended to make Ryba an offer at their first meeting because he thought that getting him to work for Abwehr "would be much more difficult than in Pruša's case." It was almost midnight and both men agreed to meet the following Wednesday or Thursday at the Hradecky pub or the following Sunday at Grimm's. The next day, Oskar Schindler was arrested by the Czech police for his espionage activities. They arrested Leo Pruscha the following day.[112]

The incident that led to their arrests was Oskar Schindler's effort to recruit Rudolf Huschka, a sergeant major in the state police. Schindler had known Huschka for quite a while. According to a 1966 report of the Czechoslovak Ministry of the Interior (secret police), Schindler met Huschka while Oskar, dressed in his reserve corporal's military uniform, was inspecting fortifications near Opava and Králíky. Oskar had a meeting planned with Huschka on July 13 or 14 after his weekend with Pruscha, Kreuziger, Gritt, and Peter in Ziegenhals. He met the state police sergeant in the Ungar Hotel bar in Svitavy. Oskar began his conversation with Huschka carefully. He wanted to find out what Huschka knew and whether it would be worth the effort to recruit him. Schindler was probably frustrated with Pruscha's limited knowledge of military affairs and wanted to be certain that if he invested the same amount of time in recruiting Huschka that it would be fruitful. He also wanted to impress Kreuziger with a better "catch." Schindler asked the state policeman whether his agency "had institutions or other things of military-political significance." Oskar met with Huschka over the next few days and told him that he would do what he could "to work out a connection with competent authorities in Germany." Schindler said that the policeman was delighted over his willingness "to create access to the *reichsdeutschen Nachrichtendienst.*" Huschka was particularly concerned about his pay and promised regular deliveries of important information to Oskar. They agreed to meet at the Hotel Ungar at 10:00 P.M. on Monday July 18.[113]

Oskar arrived on time and both men began to talk about Abwehr matters. According to Oskar, Huschka tried to give him an envelope containing important information, which Oskar refused to accept. It is possible that Schindler knew the police had him under surveillance in the hotel lobby. While they were talking, several policemen, Dr. Janda and Inspector Hrbek, as well as the head of Svitavy's police unit, Tomek, arrested Schindler and Huschka. They were taken to local police headquarters for an initial interrogation. Schindler quickly confessed to espionage and was sent to the National Police Office in Šumperk. The police promised "certain considerations" if he confessed and threatened to arrest Emilie and Oskar's father, Hans, if he did not. After further "interrogations and confrontations," authorities sent him to the headquarters of the Police Directorate in Brno, where authorities prepared criminal charges against him.[114]

There is no criminal case file on Huschka. According to several reports prepared on Schindler after World War II by the Czechoslovak Ministry of the Interior and the Commission for the Persecution of Nazi War Criminals, the Germans arrested Huschka after Hitler took over the Sudetenland in the fall of 1938. They imprisoned Huschka in Opava and later executed him. The War Crimes Commission's report accused Schindler of causing Huschka's death. There is nothing other than this one report to substantiate the charge.[115]

Oskar Schindler was in prison from July 18 until October 7, 1938, when he was released and transferred from Brno to Svitavy, which had just become part of the Third Reich because of the Munich Agreement.[116] Schindler seldom spoke about his imprisonment and there is disagreement over his sentence. After the war, Oskar told his close friend, Dr. Dieter Trautwein, that the Czechs tortured him during his interrogation by putting a rubber hose down his throat. This, Oskar explained, was the reason for his raspy voice, not his chain smoking. The police also broke into his home just after they arrested him and ransacked it for evidence. The police claimed they found the graphicons under Schindler's bed, though Emilie said in her memoirs that they were "hidden behind a bedroom mirror." In her 1981 interview with the British film maker Jon Blair, Emilie claimed that the graphicons were hidden in a bathroom panel. She said the police searched their home several times before they found them. On their last visit, they went right to them.[117]

No available record exists of a trial or sentencing for Oskar in Brno. The same is true for Leo Pruscha. Emilie says that Oskar received the death penalty, but Robin O'Neil, a retired British police inspector who spent more than a decade investigating Schindler's life, stated that he got two years imprisonment. Some Czech historians argue that the sentence was fourteen years. After Oskar's arrest, Emilie contacted Kreuziger to see what he could do for Oskar. He seemed disinterested in Oskar's fate. In reality, there was little he could do given the developing crisis between Czechoslovakia and Germany over the Sudetenland.[118]

Hitler's determination to invade Czechoslovakia created a dangerous international crisis in the late summer and early fall of 1938. It also caused an uproar in the Wehrmacht, where army leaders raised serious questions about Germany's ability to fight a war in Europe, particularly if Czechoslovakia's allies decided to fight to stop Hitler's aggression. Two days before Oskar Schindler's arrest, *General* Ludwig Beck, the army Chief of Staff, sent *General* Walther von Brauchitsch, the army's commander in chief, a memorandum arguing that an attack on Czechoslovakia would bring England and France into a war that would "be a general catastrophe for Germany, not only a military defeat." Unfortunately, although some top generals, including Canaris, agreed with Beck, they were not willing to openly challenge Hitler because of the impact such a move would have on their careers and their sense of soldierly duty to the state. When Hitler finally learned of the generals' concerns, he flew into a rage. On August 15, he told them that he was determined to crush Czechoslovakia in early fall. Three days later, von Brauchitsch accepted Beck's resignation as Chief of Staff. He was replaced by Franz Halder, who would become the central figure in coup discussions that included several prominent Abwehr officers.[119]

The Führer's hunch that Britain and France were unwilling to go to war over Czechoslovakia strengthened his determination to attack Czechoslovakia in the early fall of 1938. For months, London and Paris pursued a policy that tried to pressure the Beneš government to make concessions to Henlein while trying to keep the SdP leader from becoming too aggressive in summer-long talks with Prague. But when Beneš finally did, it shocked the SdP leadership, who now looked for an excuse to derail further discussions.[120]

In the midst of the crisis, the Beneš government was determined to defend Czechoslovak independence at all costs. Schindler's arrest was part of a Czechoslovak effort to do everything possible to thwart Germany's efforts to compromise the country's defenses. Czech authorities took Schindler's espionage seriously. The Czechs continued to arrest suspected spies and arms smugglers throughout September and declared martial law in parts of Bohemia after spontaneous antigovernment demonstrations broke out on September 12 and 13. Prague extended martial law throughout Bohemia and Moravia several days later and outlawed the SdP.[121]

At the same time, Neville Chamberlain informed Hitler that he was willing to fly to Germany immediately "to find a peaceful solution" to the Sudeten crisis. The Führer agreed to meet with the British prime minister in Obersalzberg in two days. In the interim, Henlein advised Hitler to demand the immediate "cession of regions with more than 50 percent German population," which the Wehrmacht would occupy within twenty-four hours." Hitler liked this idea and used it as his core demand when he met Chamberlain on September 15. Two days later, Britain and France acceded to Hitler's wishes and so informed President Beneš.[122]

The fate of Czechoslovakia and the Sudetenland now rested in the hands of Adolf Hitler. Yet Hitler was not appeased; he wanted all of Czechoslovakia and seemed willing to risk full-scale war to get it. His willingness to risk German defeat to achieve his goals had caused deep consternation in Wehrmacht circles for some time and triggered talk of a coup in the highest echelons of the Wehrmacht. At its center were several Abwehr officers who planned to kidnap and assassinate Adolf Hitler after he gave the order to invade Czechoslovakia in late September. Hitler's decision to accept a brokered settlement in Munich on September 29 ended this spate of coup discussions.[123]

At the center of the plot to assassinate Hitler was Canaris's deputy, *Oberst* (later *Generalleutnant*) Hans Oster. Though Canaris remained dutiful to Hitler, he "permitted individual officers to conspire against the regime." According to Klemens von Klemperer, "under Canaris the Abwehr became 'not only a nest of spies but also a nest of conspirators.'" In many ways, Oster was like Schindler, "dapper, elegant, agile, outgoing and unafraid and, if anything, singularly lacking caution." Over time, one of the people drawn into this broader circle of Abwehr contacts was Oskar Schindler. These ties would be important to him during the war. Without them, he would never have been able to save the large number of Jews that he did. His continual interaction with anti-Hitler Abwehr officers also served to fortify his own misgivings about Hitler and the Nazi regime, though they would not blossom until later in the war.[124]

Before Hitler decided to settle the Sudeten crisis at the end of September, Henlein formed, with Hitler's approval, the Sudeten German Free Corps (FK; *Sudetendeutscher Freikorps*), which began raids along the German-Czechoslovak border. The Führer wanted to orchestrate a series of incidents that would give him an excuse to invade Czechoslovakia. Canaris supplied Henlein's units with some of the intelligence information that Schindler and other Abwehr agents had gathered during the summer. Abwehr also supplied the FK with arms and money.[125]

On September 28, representatives from Germany, Britain, France, and Italy met in Munich to resolve the Sudeten crisis. Over the next thirty-six hours, Chamberlain, Mussolini, and France's prime minister, Edouard Daladier, dismembered Czechoslovakia without consulting the Prague government. The result was the Munich Agreement of September 29, 1938. According to its terms, the Wehrmacht would begin to occupy Czech territories where over 50 percent of the population was German between October 1 and 10. Population transfers would take six months. Britain and France agreed to guarantee Czechoslovakia's new frontiers. Italy and Germany would not do so until Prague had worked out the problems of the country's Polish and Hungarian minorities. Section 8 stipulated that within four weeks the Czechoslovak government would release Sudeten Germans who no longer wanted to serve in the armed forces or the police. During this same time frame, Prague was to release "Sudeten German prisoners who [were] serving terms of imprisonment for political offenses." Within a week, Oskar Schindler was out of prison and back in Svitavy.[126]

His imprisonment ended a frightening time for him; yet it also gave him opportunities as Abwehr began to prepare for Hitler's takeover of the rest of Czechoslovakia and, later, Poland. His imprisonment also brought him rewards, a promotion, and important credibility as a German's German. He had made the next to ultimate sacrifice for the Führer. For the most part, though, this had more to do with Schindler's greed than a fanatical sense of German nationalism. Oskar was too selfish for that. He was too egocentric to care deeply for anything or anyone other than himself and his own pleasures. Yet he was smart enough to realize that he could parlay his recent heroism into something more exciting than espionage and, when war came, military service. Consequently, he learned to play whatever role was necessary at a given moment to further his own selfish interests. In time, these skills would enhance Schindler's efforts to save his Jewish workers. But first he had to find his own moral center, and that would be difficult in the Nazi German world that he was about to enter.

2.

SCHINDLER THE SPY

OSKAR SCHINDLER RETURNED TO SVITAVY IN EARLY OCTOBER 1938 as a hero. After the war, several of his acquaintances told Czechoslovak investigators that Hitler had rewarded him with an automobile and other valuables. In the opening of his historical novel *Schindler's List*, Thomas Keneally wrote that Oskar wore "a large ornamental gold-on-black enamel *Hakenkreuz* (swastika)." Steven Spielberg made great visual use of this Nazi badge in his film *Schindler's List*. By using this important Nazi symbol, both artists were trying to imply that Oskar Schindler was a highly decorated Nazi Party member who later used this honor to help save "his Jews." Yet which badge, if any, did he wear? Was it the standard party badge with the black swastika on a white background circled in red with *National-sozialistische-D.A.P. (Deutsche Arbeiterpartei;* German Workers' Party) in gold lettering, or was it one of the two forms of the distinctive Golden Party Badge *(Goldenes Parteiabzeichen)* and the Golden Honor Award of the NSDAP *(Goldenes Ehrenzeichen der NSDAP)?* Though none of the scores of survivors interviewed for this book remembers a Nazi badge on Oskar's coat lapels, one Jewish survivor who knew Schindler during the war and later accused him of mistreatment claimed that Oskar always wore the Blood Order *(Blutorden)* medal, Nazism's highest award. It is doubtful that Oskar received the Blood Order; this honor was reserved for the 2,000 Nazi "Old Fighters" who took part in Adolf Hitler's abortive Beer Hall *Putsch* on November 9, 1923. Over the years, the Blood Order was also given to other Nazi heroes, particularly if they had served long prison terms or had been injured for the cause. The Golden Party Badge was Nazism's next highest honor, though it had two forms. The standard, individually numbered Golden Party Badge was initially reserved for the party's first 100,000 members, though later it was also given to party favorites or heroes. The Golden Party Badge bore a distinctive gold cluster surrounding the traditional party badge. According to John Weitz, who used Spielberg's image of Oskar as an example of the power of this award, the wearer of the Golden Party Badge could expect special treatment at theaters and restaurants.[1]

The much more prestigious Golden Honor Award of the NSDAP was awarded specifically by Adolf Hitler to individuals who had offered distinguished service to the Party and state. The Nazis' semi-official newspaper, the *Völkischer Beobachter (People's Observer)*, called it "the supreme badge of honor of the Party." Though both gold party badges were quite similar in appearance, the Golden Honor Award had Adolf Hitler's initials stamped on the back as well as the date of the award. Hitler awarded only 650 of the Golden Honor Awards during his time as Germany's dictator.[2]

If Oskar was a highly decorated hero, he said little about it. We do not know much about his life after his release from prison in the fall of 1938. He did consider himself a martyr and blamed his arrest and confinement on his own carelessness (Leitsinn, *Leichtsinn*). He claimed he was now unemployed because his old firm was in Brno, which was in what remained of Czechoslovakia after the Munich accord. On November 1, 1938, Oskar applied for Nazi Party (NSDAP; *National-sozialistische Deutsche Arbeiterpartei;* National Socialist German Workers Party) membership. Sudeten Germans who had belonged to Konrad Henlein's SdP were eligible for membership if they had been SdP continuous members since 1935. Though the Nazi Party accepted Oskar for provisional membership on February 2, 1939, the party's district court raised questions about his numerous arrests in the 1930s, which Oskar had listed on his membership application. Using guidelines drawn up by Rudolf Hess in 1937, local party officials were to investigate each applicant to insure that their political attitudes were in line with those of the party. They also applied the 1935 Nuremberg Laws to each application, the Law to Protect German Blood and German Honor and the Reich Citizenship Law; this was to insure that the potential member had neither Jewish blood nor a Jewish spouse. Party functionaries also examined an applicant's moral character. If an applicant's qualifications for membership were in doubt, the matter was turned over to the local or district party courts *(Parteigerichte),* which would rule on the matter.[3]

Eight months after Oskar applied to Nazi Party membership, Dr. Gerlich, a Nazi Party official in the Reichsgau Sudetenland headquarters in Reichenberg, forwarded Oskar's application to the party's district court *(Kreisgericht)* in Zwittau (formerly Svitavy) for further investigation. Dr. Gerlich said that the court should examine two matters: Oskar's claim that he had been a continuous member of the SdP since 1935, and his police record. Dr. Gerlich said that the party district court should obtain a copy of Oskar's criminal files from the district attorney's office in Zwittau. He added that if they found only the convictions that Schindler had listed on his party application, these would not be enough to keep him from becoming a party member in good standing "if he is otherwise of good character and politically acceptable."[4]

Several days before the Czechoslovakians released Oskar from prison, German forces began to move into the Sudetenland. Initially, Svitavy was not included in the territory ceded to Nazi Germany, but that would change. The Munich Agreement stated that an international commission made up of Germany, Czechoslovakia, Great Britain, Italy, and France would decide on border disputes between Prague and Germany, Poland, and Hungary. One area of particular interest to Hitler was the Svitavy region, Schindler's home district. An ethnic German island on the Bohemian-Moravian border, Svitavy rested at the center of the main rail links between eastern and western Czechoslovakia. Three days after the signing of the Munich accord, Hitler personally told the German negotiators to insist on this piece of territory in their border talks with Czechoslovak officials. By the time Oskar Schindler returned to Svitavy, it was about to become part of Germany.[5]

Hitler Moves to Dismember Rump Czechoslovakia (October 1938–March 1939)

As Oskar recovered physically and psychologically from his jail term, Germany began its integration of the Sudetenland into the Third Reich. Konrad Henlein became *Reichskommissar* for the newly created Sudeten German territory *(Reichskommissar für die sudetendeutschen Gebiete)* and Karl Hermann Frank his deputy *Kommissar*. Reich officials began an immediate campaign of *Gleichschaltung* (reordering) to Nazify the Sudetenland. Almost 99 percent of the Sudeten German population approved this move during Reichstag elections on December 4, when they voted to support the Führer and the *grossdeutsche Reich*. An active policy to force non-Germans to leave the Sudetenland was connected with the campaign of Nazification. The SdP, which was integrated into the NSDAP on December 11, 1938, began a policy of intimidation against Czech and Jewish businesses. SdP members put signs reading *Tschechisches Geschäft* (Czech business or shop) and *Jüdisches Geschäft* on all Czech and Jewish stores and businesses in the Sudetenland. During the November 9–10, 1938, anti-Jewish *Kristallnacht* riots, the SdP led anti-Jewish demonstrations. The intimidation campaign worked. About 140,000 Czechs, including 12,000 Germans, fled the Sudetenland for Czechoslovakia in the months after the German takeover of this region.[6]

If the Sudeten Germans thought that Hitler would bring them a better life, they were sorely misled. Though Germany was able to deal firmly with the region's unemployment, it did so with a heavy hand. Nazi Germany was a dictatorship; Czechoslovakia a democracy. These differences became readily apparent to most Sudeten Germans over time. Many Sudeten Germans came to resent the arrival of the Reich German carpetbaggers, who dominated government and business. At the instigation of Karl Hermann Frank, the Germans purged many of Konrad Henlein's old SdP associates, including his closest ally, Walter Brand, who spent some time in the Sachsenhausen concentration camp outside Berlin. After Germany occupied the rest of Czechoslovakia in March 1939, the Sudeten Germans began to resent what they felt was Reich German favoritism towards Czechs in the new Protectorate of Bohemia and Moravia, whom they wanted expelled from the region. Certainly Oskar Schindler was affected by Sudeten German resentment towards Reich officialdom during and after World War II.[7]

In the midst of the Reich German effort to Nazify the Sudetenland, Abwehr officials debriefed Oskar Schindler and gave him some leave to recover from his imprisonment. They soon promoted Oskar and made him second in command of a team of Abwehr agents in Mährisch Ostrau (formerly Moravská Ostrava, Moravian Ostrava; today Ostrava) on the Sudeten-Polish border. One Czech investigation of Oskar's activities in Märisch Ostrau suggests, though, that his position was so high in the local Abwehr organization that some of its agents considered him the practical head of its operations in the former Czech city.[8]

During this interim, Hitler began to plan for the takeover of the rest of Czechoslovakia. According to Gerhard Weinberg, Wehrmacht officers in the Sudetenland heard of these plans as early as October 3, 1938. Within a week, military planning for the invasion of the remainder of Czechoslo-

SCHINDLER THE SPY 49

vakia was well under way in Berlin. On October 21, Hitler issued his directive to the Wehrmacht for the takeover of the rest of Czechoslovakia. It is now apparent that Schindler was involved in these efforts and was sent by Abwehr to Moravská Ostrava in early 1939 to help plan Germany's takeover of the rest of Bohemia and Moravia. Schindler's efforts, though, would be less significant than his later work in helping plan the invasion of Poland; Hitler was still suspicious of Admiral Canaris and Abwehr because they had not supplied the Wehrmacht with accurate information about Czechoslovakia in 1938. Instead, Hitler decided to force a political separation of Slovakia from the rest of Czechoslovakia by using SD terrorists in preparation for his takeover of the Czech lands.[9]

Yet even before German forces moved into the Czech lands (Bohemia and Moravia) on March 14, 1939, Germany's allies, Hungary and Poland, further humiliated Czechoslovakia by using Prague's fragile international situation to cash in on those parts of the Munich Accord that stipulated discussions about disputed territory. In little more than a month after the completion of the Munich Agreement, Poland was able to acquire Těšín and several small areas along the Polish-Slovak border, and Hungary gained more than 4,500 square miles of territory in eastern Slovakia in the German-Italian-sponsored First Vienna Award of November 2, 1938. By the end of the first week of November 1938, Czechoslovakia had been forced to cede almost 19,000 square miles of territory and more than 5 million people to Germany, Hungary, and Poland. The loss of a third of its population and territory devastated the Czechoslovak economy and denuded its defense system.[10]

Under a new president, Dr. Emil Hácha, the Czechoslovak government sought to repair its relations with Germany and seek Anglo-French guarantees of its remaining frontiers as provided in the Munich Agreement. The British and the French did not approach Germany and Italy about this until February 8, 1939, only weeks before Hitler planned to move against the remainder of Czechoslovakia. Once again, the major powers allowed Hitler to determine the course of international affairs in Europe. Five days later, Hitler told *General* Keitel, the head of OKW, and *General* Brauchitsch, the army's commander-in-chief, that he planned to move against Czechoslovakia in mid-March.[11]

Hitler needed only excuses to justify his move, and German plans were already underway to fabricate one in league with Slovak politicians. The unstable political climate in Slovakia after Munich had forced the recently appointed head of the Slovak government, General Jan Syrový, to give in to the demands of Father Jozef Tiso, the head of the fascist Hlinka's Slovak People's Party (HSL'S; *Hlinkova slovenská l'udová strana*) to make Czechoslovakia a federal republic. On November 23, 1938, Czech and Slovak leaders agreed to create a federal Czecho-Slovak state. Six weeks earlier, Father Tiso had become Slovakia's premier.[12] The federal union with the Czech lands did not satisfy radicals within the HSL'S, who demanded full independence for Slovakia. They looked to Germany for support and promoted their cause through anti-Semitic and anti-Czech movements such as the Hlinka Guards (HG; *Hlinkova garda*), an SA-like movement that blended Nazi and fascist ideals. Gradually, HSL'S extremists transformed Slovakia into a single party state and society.[13]

Talk of Slovak independence became widespread. Hitler thought the HSL'S leaders would be ready partners in the final eradication of Czecho-Slovakia. Slovakia's drift into the German camp and rumors of Germany's imminent takeover of Czecho-Slovakia prompted President Hácha to ask Slovak leaders on March 1, 1939, to reaffirm their loyalty to the Czecho-Slovak Republic and abandon talk of independence. When the Tiso government failed to make such pledges, Hácha fired Tiso and some of his cabinet. He appointed a Slovak interim government and moved some military units into Slovakia. Ferdinand Durčanský, one of Tiso's dismissed ministers, fled to Vienna and asked Hitler to intervene.[14]

On March 13, Hitler called Tiso and Durčanský to Berlin, where the Führer gave them until the following day to declare Slovakia's independence. If they refused or hesitated, Slovakia would be divided between Germany, Hungary, and Poland. Tiso acceded; on March 14, 1939, the Slovak parliament declared Slovak independence. In the meantime, German agents fabricated incidents in Bohemia and Moravia that the Reich press claimed were aimed at Sudeten Germans. Hitler now had the two excuses he needed to justify his move into Bohemia and Moravia: political instability and continued Czech mistreatment of Sudeten Germans in Bohemia and Moravia.[15]

While Tiso and Durčanský met with Hitler in Berlin, the Czech cabinet urged President Hácha to rush to Berlin to meet with Hitler. As their train sped north towards Berlin, German units marched into the strategically important Czech town of Moravská Ostrava. Though Hácha and his foreign minister, František Chvalkovský, arrived in Berlin at 10:40 P.M., Hitler kept them waiting until the early hours of the morning to tell them that they had no choice but to agree to the forced takeover of Czecho-Slovakia. When Hácha hesitated, Hermann Göring, the powerful head of the *Luftwaffe,* threatened to destroy Prague if the president refused to agree to the passive acceptance of the German takeover of Czecho-Slovakia. Hácha, who conferred with his cabinet in Prague during the three-hour meeting, was also forced to sign a joint German-Czech statement that placed full control of Czecho-Slovakia in the "hands of the Führer of the German Reich." Hácha, overwhelmed by the severity of the moment and the knowledge that his cabinet opposed his signature, fainted. At 4:00 A.M. on Wednesday, March 15, 1939, Czecho-Slovakia ceased to exist. Europe would never be the same again.[16]

As German forces marched into the Czech lands, Father Tiso, under pressure from Hitler, declared Slovak independence. The Wehrmacht quickly occupied Slovakia, which became a German protected state *(Schutzstaat).* Though Slovakia appeared to function as an independent country throughout the war, in reality it was a German puppet state run by staunch pro-Nazis around Father Tiso. Slovakia became the Third Reich's propaganda showpiece in that part of Europe and Slovak troops fought alongside Germans during World War II. The Tiso government adopted German-style anti-Semitic laws and 75 percent of Slovak Jews (c. 135,000 in 1930) died during the Holocaust.[17]

According to the postwar testimony of Alois Polansky, who worked as a chauffeur for Abwehr and the SD in Mährisch Ostrau in 1939, Oskar Schindler was already working as an Abwehr agent in Moravská Ostrava when German forces moved into Bohemia and Moravia on March 14 and 15. Renamed Mährisch Ostrau after the German takeover, Moravská Ostrava was considered a strategically vital city because of its proximity to the Polish border. The SdP had staged incidents there in early September 1938 to derail its talks with Prague, and Hitler refused to let the Poles occupy it as part of their takeover of Těšín and other bits of Czechoslovak territory a month later because of its economic value to the Reich. It was fear of a Polish move into Moravská Ostrava in March 1939 that prompted Hitler to take the city over before the formal move of German troops into Bohemia and Moravia.[18]

Oskar Schindler in Moravská Ostrava/Mährisch Ostrau, 1939

In January 1939, Oskar and Emilie Schindler moved to Moravská Ostrava (Mährisch Ostrau), their home for most of 1939. Even after he moved to Kraków in September 1939 to explore new business opportunities, Oskar continued to list Mährisch Ostrau as his home. In the spring of 1940, Oskar applied for a driver's license at the Police Directorate in Mährisch Ostrau and listed as his address 25 Parkstraße (Sadova Street), though later Gestapo reports on Schindler and the break-in at his apartment said that Oskar and Emilie lived at 27 Parkstraße. Perhaps they occupied two apartments, one an Abwehr office and their living quarters next door. Before the war, Germans and Jews lived side by side on Sadova Street. Once fighting began, its Jewish residents disappeared, though its German families kept their homes. Mährisch Ostrau's mayor lived next door to Emilie and Oskar, and not far away was the city hall and the headquarters of the SD and the Gestapo. According to Emilie, Wehrmacht barracks stood across the street. Oskar kept the apartment at 25 Sadova throughout the war. Emilie lived there from 1939 to 1941, when she finally joined Oskar in Kraków. For the next four years, Oskar evidently maintained it for his girlfriend, Irena Dvorzakova, who worked at the Vitkovice steel works. Irena stayed in the apartment in Mährisch Ostrau apartment until late 1945 or early 1946, when she moved to Vratislav. Oskar visited the apartment for the last time in April 1945, when he collected some of his belongings.[19]

Oskar and Emilie would hardly recognize Ostrava today. It is a major industrial center and the Czech Republic's third largest city after Prague and Brno. By Czech standards, Ostrava is a relatively modern town that sprung up after the Austrian emperor, Joseph II, united what remained of Silesia with Moravia after Frederick the Great of Prussia conquered most of it four decades earlier. In the nineteenth century, Austrian Mährisch Ostrau became an important Austrian industrial center because of its coal mines and iron furnaces. Though there was a strong German presence in Ostrava, it was predominantly a Czech town. By the 1930s, less than 20 percent of Ostrava's population was German.[20] Modern Ostrava does not look or feel like a gloomy industrial town and it retains much of its prewar charm. Trolleys still meander along tracks in the middle of the streets and the pace is slow and relaxed. In many ways, modern Ostrava is still the traditional entranceway to the beautiful rolling hills and rich farmland of Moravia.

It is about three hours by car from Kraków to Ostrava on surprisingly modern roads. The several important roads and railways that converge through the city make it an important terminus for train, truck, and car traffic. Oskar said little about his assignment in Mährisch Ostrau after the war. He told Fritz Lang that he took the assignment to protect himself from charges that he continued to maintain relations with Jewish friends and acquaintances after the Germans moved into the Sudetenland. Though there is no evidence to discount Oskar's claim, he probably took the Abwehr assignment in Moravská Ostrava because it meant a promotion and better pay. After the war, he told Fritz Lang that he joined Abwehr because it was "the most realistic option amidst the bustle of the grouping formations" and because of the influence of his father, who was loyal to the "traditions of the KK [*kaiserliche und königliche,* imperial and royal] army."[21]

Whatever his motivation, Oskar Schindler was actively engaged in espionage for Abwehr well before the German takeover of the remnant of Czechoslovakia in March 1939. Alois Polanski says that he drove his boss, *Leutnant* Görgey, an Abwehr officer, three times to meet with Schindler in Moravská Ostrava before the German move into Czechoslovakia. Their last meeting was probably on March 12, 1939, three days before Hitler absorbed Bohemia and Moravia. Though Moravská Ostrava was still part of Czechoslovakia, Abwehr used it as a prime listening post for developments within the country. As Hitler planned his second move against Czecho-Slovakia, though, Canaris was determined not to be excluded from planning for Hitler's next moves. Abwehr looked constantly for collaborators within Czechoslovakia and carefully watched the activities of Czechoslovak intelligent agents. To strengthen his intelligence-gathering operations in Czechoslovakia, Canaris even approached General František Moravec, head of Czech military intelligence, about collaboration between the two agencies. General Moravec never responded to Canaris's offer.[22]

The move to Moravská Ostrava upset Emilie because she had to leave their large, comfortable home in Zwittau. The serenity of Zwittau was replaced by the hustle and bustle of their new apartment on 25 Sadova, in the center of Moravská Ostrava. Emilie said that the apartment was just across the street from a Wehrmacht base, though this would not have been possible until the spring of 1939. According to Emilie, the Schindler home became an Abwehr office with four workers, including Irena Dvorzakowa, Oskar's newest lover. Dr. Mečislav Borak, a Czech expert on Schindler's activities in Ostrava, doubts that Oskar had a full-fledged office in his home. This was the same conclusion reached by Gestapo investigators in 1940. Certainly Oskar kept some Abwehr materials in the apartment, but he later told Gestapo officials who were investigating the Polish break-in that he had never kept important Abwehr materials at 25–27 Parkstraße.[23]

Emilie served as Oskar's office manager and handled his routine Abwehr office work in addition to her housekeeping chores. Emilie had some sort of security clearance to do this work because she was also responsible for receiving, processing, and hiding the numerous secret files they received. Her only protection was a German Luger that they hid in a closet. The work she did for Oskar was the extent of her operational duties.[24]

Although their work was deadly serious, there were a few moments of comic relief. Soon after they moved to Moravská Ostrava, Oskar bought forty carrier pigeons so that he could send messages to other Abwehr operatives. In addition to her office duties, Emilie had to feed the pigeons and clean their cages. According to Emilie, Oskar soon lost interest in the pigeons and never used them to carry messages. After a few months of pigeon duty, Emilie decided to set them free without telling Oskar. She chose a beautiful day, but, at first, they hesitated to leave their cages. Once free, they circled the Schindler home once, then flew away. Later, they returned to Ostrava to the frustration of Oskar's superiors, who complained that the Schindlers had not taken good care of these valuable servants of the Third Reich.[25]

Abwehr, Oskar Schindler, and German Plans for the Invasion of Poland

Though Hitler had allowed Admiral Canaris and Abwehr to play a secondary role in helping plan the takeover of rump Czechoslovakia, they were considered too vital to German military planning to be kept in the background for long. Moreover, Canaris was determined not to let Abwehr commit the same mistakes that had so hurt the organization in the fall of 1938. He approached planning for the attack against Poland with renewed vigor and ingenuity. Oskar Schindler would be important to Abwehr's plans.[26]

According to one Abwehr report, in the months before the invasion of Poland Oskar and his twenty-five agents were actively engaged smuggling arms and men into the Těšín area where they trained for secret combat operations. Schindler was involved in similar Abwehr activities in the Sillein (Žilinia) region. Two Abwehr agents with whom Oskar worked closely during this period were Herbert Hipfinger, who used the cover name Forster, and a second agent known only by a letter designation.[27]

In the days after the German dismemberment of what remained of Czechoslovakia, European leaders searched for clues to Hitler's next moves. Romania and Poland seemed to be next in line for a German takeover. Romania was dropped from the potential victim's list when, on March 23, it signed an economic agreement with Germany giving Hitler control over most of its oil and farm products. Fearful of an imminent German move against Poland after Warsaw rejected Hitler's demand for Danzig and transit rights across the Polish Corridor in return for Germany's guarantees of Poland's western borders, Prime Minister Neville Chamberlain told the British Parliament on March 31 that his government would come to the aid of Poland if its independence was threatened. Hitler, who wanted Poland in the German camp before the Reich dealt with Britain and France, decided that war was the only way to resolve the Polish question. On April 3, 1939, the Wehrmacht was ordered to begin initial planning for an invasion of Poland.[28]

Moravská Ostrava had been an important Abwehr listening post into Poland before Hitler dismembered Czecho-Slovakia in the spring of 1939. Now known as Mährisch Ostrau in the new German Protectorate of Bohemia and Moravia (Böhren und Mähren), it became an important staging and information gathering point for Abwehr, the SS, the SD, and the Gestapo as they prepared for the invasion of Poland. Canaris was one of a handful of Wehrmacht officers who received a copy of the Hitler-OKW initial April 3 directive for *Fall Weiss* (Case White) for the future destruction of Poland. Updated on April 11 and then periodically during the spring and summer, it was predicated on the political isolation of Poland before German units destroyed Polish military forces in the field. It anticipated an action date on or after September 1, 1939.[29]

Canaris briefed the commanders of Abwehr I, which was responsible for gathering information about the military strength and armaments of foreign nations and Abwehr II, Schindler's group, which dealt with sabotage, countersabotage, and commando operations. Abwehr II was now under the command of *Oberst* Erwin Lahousen, a former officer in the Austrian intelligence service. Initially, Abwehr I, under *Oberst* Hans Piekenbrock, was to carry the burden of Abwehr plans against Poland. This involved intelligence flights over Polish military positions and the use of intelligence agents within Poland to gather information on military installations and arms. When OKW complained about the failure of Abwehr I's efforts to supply them with adequate information about the Polish military, Canaris turned to Lahousen and Abwehr II to supply him with the information so vitally needed by the Wehrmacht for planning the invasion of Poland.[30]

As plans evolved throughout the late spring and early summer of 1939, it became evident that the commando squads of Abwehr II were to play a first-strike role in the German attack on Poland that fall. Abwehr II units were to sneak into Poland in civilian clothing and be ready to move just before the German military assault. From the German perspective, Polish military planners had committed a serious error when they decided to move two thirds of their forces along the border with Germany instead of keeping them east of the Vistula and San Rivers, where they might have been able to mount a more successful rearguard action. Polish military authorities made this decision to protect the country's major industrial areas. Unfortunately, this action aided the Germany military because it allowed the Wehrmacht to destroy the Polish armed forces early in its assault. Abwehr II's responsibility in all of this was to sneak into Poland and try to disarm the explosives set by the Poles to destroy industrial and communication sites as the Wehrmacht moved in Poland.[31]

Of particular concern to Abwehr II in the Mährisch Ostrau area were the railroad tunnel and twin tracks in the Jablunkov Pass forty miles to the southeast. This important rail line was the principal rail connection between Vienna, Warsaw, and the Balkans. If not captured, it could seriously affect Wehrmacht moves into southern Poland. Abwehr II commando squads operating out of nearby Mosty u Jablunkova just north of Jablunkov Pass and Žilinia (Sillein) in Slovakia were to attack Polish defenders guarding the tunnel and seize it in the early hours of the invasion before the Poles could blow it up. *Leutnant* Hans-Albrecht Herzner was to recruit, train, and lead the Abwehr II-Breslau team of twenty-four men drawn from the SA and the *Grenzpolizei* to seize the Jablunkov tunnel. Oskar's unit, Abwehr II-Breslau, Aktion Kommando Unit VIII under the command of *Major* Plathe, was to monitor Herzner's operation and provide Abwehr headquarters information about its success or failure.[32]

Other Abwehr II-Breslau commando squads were to prepare to seize and destroy bridges and railroad tracks inside Poland once the attack began. Some teams wore Polish uniforms as disguises. As plans for Operation *Weiss* intensified during the summer of 1939, the head of the SD's foreign intelligence service, *SS-Standartenführer* Heinz Jost, approached Canaris about a special operation approved by Hitler that would require 150 Polish uniforms as well as Polish military documents and arms for the Germans who would wear them. Jost also wanted Canaris to supply him with 364 men to work with the SD on this top secret operation. Because of the nature of the operation, Jost told Canaris that he could not divulge its function. Canaris concluded that Jost wanted the Polish uniforms for a provocative action against Poland.[33]

The idea of disguising German forces as Polish soldiers to create an incident that would enable Hitler to justify his invasion of Poland came from *Generalleutnant* Erich von Manstein, the Chief of Staff of Army Group South, who was responsible for attacking the heavily industrialized area of Upper Silesia just to the northwest of Mährisch Ostrau. Manstein wanted to dress three battalions of German shock troops in Polish uniforms to seize Upper Silesia in the early hours of the invasion. Although Hitler rejected the plan, Reinhard Heydrich, the head of the Security Police and the SD, took Manstein's ideas and revised the plan.[34]

Heydrich's plan, given the code name "Tannenberg," called for dressing SD operatives in Polish uniforms; they would attack other SD men dressed as German *Grenzpolizei* on the Polish-German border. The phony Polish troops would then seize the German radio station at Gleiwitz (now Polish Gliwice), about forty miles north of Mährisch Ostrau. The phony Polish soldiers would also attack a nearby German forestry station and a border post. When the Germans in Polish uniforms had finished their attacks, they would bring in dead bodies from concentration camps to ensure that everything looked authentic. The SS gave the dead inmates the code name *Konserven* (canned goods).[35]

What did all this have to do with Oskar Schindler? According to Emilie Schindler, it was Oskar who obtained and stored the Polish uniforms in their Mährisch Ostrau apartment before they were sent to Heydrich's operatives for the attack on the radio station at Gleiwitz. Emilie adds that they bought their first Polish uniform from a Polish soldier and then sent it to Berlin, where it was reproduced in large quantities.[36] It is possible that a random Polish uniform was obtained this way, but most were obtained from Polish ethnic Germans who had deserted the Polish army and fled to Germany. They gladly turned over their uniforms to the Wehrmacht. This was Oskar's only involvement in this aspect of the attack on Poland. According to historian Dr. Jaroslav Valenta, a member of the Czech Academy of Sciences, even if Schindler had stored large quantities of Polish uniforms, weapons, and cigarettes in his apartment, it was doubtful he had much to do with the Gleiwitz attack because his operational area was around Polish Těšín near the Slovak border. Because of this, most of his time was spent planning for the German attack on the railway tunnel at Jablunkov Pass.[37]

Emilie made their work in Mährisch Ostrau seem ordinary, though it really was not. The several break-ins to their apartment were initially thought to be the work of Polish intelligence agents. The first took place on July 12, 1939, when Eugen Sliwa, a petty criminal recently released from a Czech forced labor camp, broke into Schindler's Parkstraße apartment. The Czech police arrested Sliwa five days later for several break-ins in the area. Though Sliwa seemed to have stolen nothing of importance, Oskar was concerned about involving the Gestapo in the investigation. Instead, at least according to the detailed Gestapo reports, Schindler dealt directly with the Czech police on the robbery. Schindler, like the Gestapo, thought that Sliwa was working for Polish intelligence. Oskar was so upset by the robbery that he questioned Sliwa in jail about his contacts with Polish agents; he also took Sliwa to the Polish border to identify the Polish agent who, Sliwa claimed, had paid him to break into Schindler's apartment. Sliwa was also taken to Mährisch Ostrau to look for the Polish spy.[38]

The Gestapo did not hear of the robbery until some time later. The investigating agents were furious because neither Schindler nor the commander of the local Czech uniformed police, Niemetz, had informed them of the burglary. From the perspective of the Gestapo, the "affair Sliwa" had been bungled. A May 8, 1940, Gestapo report from its Mährisch Ostrau office noted that Otto "Zeiler" (Oskar Schindler) was quite well known to them. The Gestapo did not consider him to be a true Abwehr agent. Instead, the report called Schindler a confidant of *Major* Plathe who commanded Abwehr operations in Gleiwitz. The Gestapo knew Schindler "because of his arbitrary actions and sometimes senseless doings." The Gestapo did not consider him a German official, merely a confidant. This distinction was going to be important in the Gestapo's determination about whether to pursue its investigation of Sliwa and Schindler.[39]

Once local police officials completed their investigation, they sent a report of their findings to the Gestapo in Brno. The Gestapo then summoned "Otto Zeiler" (Oskar Schindler) to discuss the case. Schindler, however, failed to appear and, with the invasion of Poland, "went to Poland with the advancing troops and has not been seen in Mährisch Ostrau again." Schindler, the May 8, 1940, Gestapo report concluded, was still working for Abwehr in Poland or the Balkans. Sliwa remained in Czech police custody until the spring of 1940, when he was handed over to the German police. According to local Gestapo officials, it was now time for the "affair to be brought to a close." Schindler's unwillingness to help the Gestapo in its investigation hindered its ability to determine whether Sliwa's break-in was an act of counterespionage or a common robbery. The Gestapo had no idea at this time what had been stolen from Schindler's apartment because Oskar refused to talk with them.[40]

This report, though, did not end the matter. A second report two days later from Gestapo headquarters in Brno suggested that "Zeiler" be located and that Sliwa, whom a later Gestapo report called an "utterly degenerate, work-shy, irresolute person" (a crime in Nazi Germany), be re-interrogated by the Gestapo.[41] After the Gestapo again questioned Sliwa, it sent the matter to the German District Court *(deutsches Amtsgericht)* for final deliberation. The court ruled that it was difficult to determine whether Schindler's office was an official Abwehr office or simply a message center office because "Zeiler [Schindler] was only an Abwehr 'confidant.'" The only way to find out whether "Zeiler's" office was an office of the Reich would be to contact *Major* Plathe in Gleiwitz. Until this could be done, Sliwa would remain in German custody. The court noted that the Kripo *(Kriminalpolizei;* criminal police) had located Schindler, who now resided in Kraków at Lipova No. 4, and suggested that "further action regarding Schindler be initiated from there."[42]

This matter passed through judicial channels until it reached the Supreme Judge of the Reich at the People's Court *(Volksgerichtshof)* in Berlin. On July 23, 1940, the Supreme Judge's office requested "what is known about the personality and official duties of engineer Zeiler" from Gestapo officials in Mährisch Ostrau.[43] Local court officials responded on August 10 that Sliwa's break-in was "not of a political nature" and that his claim that he had been recruited by a Polish agent was "merely an excuse." Sliwa had broken into five homes between June 21 and July 14, 1939, and was now being questioned about each of them. The house on Parkstraße 25–27 "was not occupied by the Gestapo or any other military or civilian service office" but by an Abwehr confidant. As far as the court could tell, "Zeiler" or Schindler, who now lived in Kraków, still worked for Abwehr under *Oberstleutnant* Plathe. Further investigation indicated that "Schindler alias Zeiler had not stored any important papers in his apartment." All Sliwa stole were a "few love letters," five handkerchiefs, a purse containing 170 Czech crowns ($5.80), a lady's gold wrist watch worth 400 crowns ($13.68), and a piggy bank.[44]

The Gestapo, though, disagreed with the People's Court. The Gestapo office in Brno wrote to its suboffice in Mährisch Ostrau on August 23, 1940, that the "facts of the case unquestionably seem to indicate high treason to the detriment of the Reich." The documents Sliwa stole from

"Engineer Zeiler's" Abwehr office were of "extraordinary importance to the Polish authorities." The Gestapo in Brno requested that agents in Mährisch Ostrau question Sliwa again and "present him to the investigative attorney for high treason." However, it was suggested that the agents not question Schindler because he was "outside the country." They also urged a "speedy settlement" of the Sliwa matter.[45]

The attorney general of the People's Court in Mährisch Ostrau disagreed with the Gestapo's conclusion and noted in his final report that Sliwa, a "completely depraved and unprincipled person," was telling a lie when he claimed that he had been hired by a Polish agent to break into "Zeiler's" office. When he was dealing with Czech officials, Sliwa admitted to the thefts because "the punishment will not be very severe due to the Czech mentality." But when he confesses to a German, he hides behind "the assertion that he was induced to do this" because he knew that "German courts proceed harshly, without ceremony, in such matters." In other words, Sliwa wanted "to shift the guilt for this whole affair into someone else's shoes." The attorney general concluded that there was no high treason here and that only "a case of breaking and entering theft" was involved. It ordered that Sliwa be turned over to local Protectorate authorities.[46] On October 22, 1940, the District Court in Mährisch Ostrau sentenced Sliwa to eleven months of hard labor. The Gestapo, though, seemed unwilling to accept this decision, and on November 13 requested the transfer of all of the files on Sliwa and the Polish consulate in Mährisch Ostrau to its headquarters in Brno.[47] This might explain why Schindler had so much trouble with the Gestapo during his years in Kraków. Certainly the Gestapo in Kraków knew of his unwillingness to cooperate with Gestapo officials in Mährisch Ostrau. This, in turn, probably led to the increased surveillance of a man some in Gestapo headquarters in Brno thought was associated with a robbery involving high treason. Oskar would be arrested by the Gestapo three times in Kraków and Brünnlitz. A few of the arrests were undoubtedly meant to teach a lesson to the man who had earlier proved so uncooperative.

This was not the only attempt by Polish agents to break into the Schindler apartment. On another occasion, a prowler woke Emilie up when he shined his flashlight into the apartment. She was sleeping in the apartment's office, a converted bedroom, because she and Oskar had just had a fight about his love affair with Irena Dvorzakowa. While Oskar slept blissfully in their bedroom, Emilie took the Luger to the office window and fired two shots into the air inside the office. She saw a shadow disappear outside, and the shots startled the guard, who was sleeping on duty. Again, the suspicion was that a Polish agent had tried to break into the apartment.[48]

Our information about Oskar's activities as an Abwehr agent in Mährisch Ostrau in 1939 comes from various sources: Emilie's memoirs; the Gestapo reports on the Sliwa robbery; the post-World War II Czechoslovak investigations of Oskar's activities, which included the testimony of fellow agents; and an Abwehr report on the activities of combat and other Abwehr units in the Těšín area in the months before the invasion of Poland. Oskar also briefly discussed his Abwehr activities with Martin Gosch in an interview in Paris in 1964. As will be seen in more detail in a later chapter, immediately after World War II the Czechoslovakian government began intensive investigations of Sudeten Germans and others who had collaborated with the Third Reich to determine who should be punished for their crimes. Oskar Schindler's name came up frequently in these investigations. The principal testimony against Oskar came from two Sudeten Germans, Alois Polansky, who worked for Abwehr in Oppa (Czech Opava) and the SD in Mährisch Ostrau, and Joseph "Sepp" Aue, who later worked for Oskar in Kraków. The Abwehr report does not mention Schindler specifically, though that was not all that uncommon because some agents were only mentioned by letters or numbers to disguise their identity.

According to these interrogation reports, Polansky was born in Těšín in 1894. He saw action on the Russian and Italian fronts in the Austrian-Hungarian army during World War I. After the war, he managed a garage until 1938 and joined Abwehr in early 1939. He continued to work for Abwehr throughout the war and held positions in Bratislava (German Pressburg) and Mährisch Ostrau. After the war, the Czechoslovaks sentenced Polansky to fifteen years in prison for his collaboration with the Germans. Polansky's testimony gives us the most complete picture we have of Oskar's Abwehr work in the months before the outbreak of World War II. As mentioned earlier, Polansky drove *Leutnant* György to meet with Oskar on three occasions before Hitler took over Bohemia and Moravia in March 1939. Oskar, who now used the code name OSI, or Zeiler, would meet with György at the Hotel Palace in Moravská Ostrava. On one occasion, which Polansky identifies as possibly March 12, 1939, he drove the two agents to Visolaje in Slovakia, where Oskar and György met with two Abwehr operatives who spoke Czech and Slovak. Schindler translated for *Leutnant* György. After half an hour, *Leutnant* György asked Polansky whether he felt it was safe to drive to Bily Kriz (White

Cross) in the nearby Beskydy (Beskid) mountains. Polansky thought it was too dangerous because of the snow. The four Abwehr agents told Polansky to stay behind while they took a sleigh to Bily Kriz. Three hours later, György and Oskar returned alone. Polansky later learned that one of the two strangers was from Žilinia, the Slovak staging area for one of the two teams responsible for taking the Jablunkov Pass.[49]

After they left Visolaje, Polansky drove Oskar and György to Raškovice, which was equidistant between Moravská Ostrava and the Jablunkov Pass. Once there, they met with a farmer, Julius Fischer, who took them to meet with another agent, Vilém Moschkorsch (Moschkorz), who was from nearby Staříč. Oskar and Moschkorsch went off by themselves to talk for half an hour. After they returned to the car, Polansky drove Moschkorsch to Staříč and then took Oskar back to Moravská Ostrava.[50]

When they were back in Moravská Ostrava, Polansky drove Oskar to the Podrum wine cellar. Sitting at another table were two Abwehr agents who had been waiting for Oskar. One of the two strangers was Kobierský, an Abwehr agent who worked closely with Schindler and György. Oskar left Polansky and György alone while he went to talk with Kobierský and the other agent. When Oskar returned, he told *Leutnant* György of their conversation and then left the wine bar. Afterwards, Polansky drove György to the Café Palace, where he met Oskar again. The two agents talked for two hours and then were driven back to the Podrum, where they had dinner. Afterwards, Kobierský and another agent sat at a nearby table, where Oskar soon joined them. After a lengthy conversation with the two Abwehr agents, Oskar returned to give *Leutnant* György a letter and some documents that Polansky thought were plans of some sort. Polansky later identified the strangers that Oskar met on March 12, 1939, during his two visits to the Podrum as František Unger, an Abwehr operative who also worked with the SD, and Bedřich Schestag, also an Abwehr agent.[51]

Other agents who worked with Schindler during this period were Waltraud Vorster, Ervin (Evžen) and Ladislav Kobiela, Dr. Walter Titzel, Hildegard Hoheitova, and Josef Urbánek. Kobiela's real name was Oskar Schmidt. All these local Czechoslovak operatives were on the Czech most-wanted list after World War II. Charges were filed against all these agents and collaborators after the war; Vorster, the only one who could be found, was sentenced to fifteen years in prison. The Abwehr and postwar Czech reports also mention two other agents who worked with Oskar, a Herr Zimmermann from Česky Těšín who also worked closely with Lts. Lang and György, and František Cienciala (Činčala/Czincala) from Svibiče.[52]

Yet the most interesting of all the operatives and collaborators that Oskar worked with during his time in Moravská Ostrava/Mährisch Ostrau was Josef "Sepp" Aue. During the war, Aue worked for Oskar in Kraków, where Schindler helped him to obtain a factory. Aue turned on his friend after the war and gave damaging testimony about Oskar's Abwehr activities to the Czech secret police. On the other hand, Aue had no compunction about trying to reestablish contact with prominent *Schindlerjuden* after his meetings with Czech authorities.[53]

Sepp Aue was an illegitimate Jew whose mother, Emilie Goldberg, raised her son as a Roman Catholic in Bruntál, about fifty miles northwest of Moravská Ostrava. Aue was his mother's maiden name. According to a letter that Aue wrote to Itzhak Stern in 1948, his father was killed in Auschwitz in 1942. Aue's mother married Karl Lederer, who died in 1937. After World War II, she emigrated to Israel. Aue was able to hide his Jewish background by becoming a staunch Sudeten German nationalist. In late 1938, Aue applied for membership in the Nazi Party. Aue first met Oskar through his contacts as a money trader. After the German takeover of the Sudetenland, Aue made a living exchanging currency from Czech Jews fleeing the Greater Reich. He met Schindler through his principal moneylending contact, Helena Bohdanova, a fur trader in Cieszyn. According to Aue, Oskar, who initially introduced himself only as "Zeiler," forced Aue to work for him by threatening to charge him with violating German currency laws. Oskar "Zeiler" did show Aue identification that indicated he was a member of Kripo, the German criminal police. "Zeiler" warned Aue that he could be sent to prison for his illegal activities. There was, according to "Zeiler," an alternative. Sepp Aue could work for him gathering military intelligence along and inside the Polish border. He added that it was Aue's duty as a good German to work for the Reich.[54]

Oskar "Zeiler" Schindler was initially interested in military activities and movements at the Polish railway station at Bohumín. This was an important rail center that Hitler, against the advice of German military leaders and diplomats, had permitted Poland to seize as German troops marched into Bohemia and Moravia in March 1939. Aue was not a very good agent. Oskar told Aue to go to the Bohumín area in the spring of 1939 and gather as much information as he could on Polish military installations and important troop movements. Aue became so confused with the maps that he decided to lie to Oskar. According to Aue, he gave Oskar false information when he met with him at the Hotel Palace after he returned to Mährisch Ostrau. Oskar quickly saw through Aue's lies and concluded that he was not fit for intelligence work. He promised Aue that he would try to find other work for him. For some reason, Oskar liked Sepp Aue and took him to Kraków after the outset of World War II. After the war, Aue returned Oskar's friendship by testifying against him in Czechoslovakia. Czech authorities considered Aue's testimony against Oskar so significant that they thought Aue should be turned over to Polish authorities for further investigation. There is no evidence, though, that the Czechs did this. Moreover, Aue was never charged with anti-German activity and continued to live in Ostrava after the war. He later told Itzhak Stern that his experiences after the war were "indescribable."[55]

Two other important Sudeten German Abwehr operatives were Karel Gassner and František Turek. According to Robin O'Neil, Gassner was Schindler's boss in Ostrava. Czech postwar investigative reports indicate that Gassner operated under the pseudonym "Princ." He was listed first on the Czech "most wanted" list for local Abwehr operatives in the Moravská Ostrava area after the war, followed by Oskar Schindler. Gassner, who was born in 1885 in Plzeň (Pilsen), was much older than Oskar and probably lacked his energy and charm, which might explain why some Abwehr operatives considered Schindler the effective head of the unit in Mährisch Ostrau. The Czech secret police report describes Gassner as elderly, grey, and slim with a slight hunchback. This was in striking contrast to his tall, blond second in command, Oskar Schindler.[56]

According to Josef Aue, Fransisek Turek was Oskar's right-hand man in Mährisch Ostrau. Turek was a Czech theater painter who had worked for Abwehr in Opava during the First Czech Republic (1918–1938). The Germans valued Turek because he spoke fluent Czech, Polish, and Russian. As an Abwehr agent, Turek was actively engaged in smuggling German arms into Slovakia and Poland. According to Aue, Turek, who also worked with Oskar Schindler in Kraków, bragged one night in Kraków, after a few too many drinks, that he had discovered a Czechoslovak arms depot in Slovakia after the German takeover of the Sudetenland. He reported this to his Abwehr superiors, who rewarded him with 10,000 Czech crowns ($294). He also told Aue that he killed a Polish border guard in the early hours of the German move into Těšín on September 1, 1939. Like Oskar, Fransisek Turek moved to Kraków after the war began, where he became *Treuhänder* (trustee) for the Laudon Company, which manufactured crockery.[57]

Yet more important to Oskar than his Sudeten German contacts were the German Abwehr officers whom he worked with in Mährisch Ostrau and Kraków. According to Czech investigative records after the war, six

German officers oversaw Abwehr activities in the Opava-Moravská Os-trava/Mährisch Ostrau area of the former Czechoslovak Republic before World War II: *Major* (later *Oberstleutnant*) Plathe, *Hauptmann* Kristiany, *Leutnant* Görgey, *Leutnant* Decker, and *Leutnant* Rudolf (or Karel) Lang. After the war, Oskar praised some of these officers, particularly Plathe and *Major* (later *Oberstleutnant*) Franz von Korab, for their efforts in se-curing Oskar's release from Gestapo detention and helping Oskar protect his Jewish workers. We have to rely on these sources for our information about their efforts because most Abwehr records were destroyed during World War II.[58]

Major Franz von Korab commanded Abwehr operations in Těšín and later, Kraków. Over time, Schindler and von Korab became close friends. In his 1951 letter to Fritz Lang, Oskar described von Korab as his "best friend in the Krakower years." According to Emilie, *Major* von Korab's mother was Jewish. For a long time, he was able to keep this a secret until one of his nephews inadvertently slipped and let the authorities know about his uncle's secret. *Major* Korab was stripped of his rank and mili-tary honors and kicked out of the military. He spent the last year of the war in Prague, where he was killed by Czech partisans because he was a German-speaking civilian. Von Korab's wife then moved to Vienna, where she lived after the war. Emilie said that *Major* Korab looked like the clas-sic Aryan Nazi with his blond looks and "Appolonian" stature. She felt that despite his Jewish background, *Major* Korab "represented better than most, including the Führer himself, the paragons of race and beauty that Nazism was championing." According to Robin O'Neil, Korab made the initial contacts that enabled Oskar to lease a former Jewish factory in Kraków after the war began. Two months after the war ended, Oskar thanked von Korab and a handful of other German officers for their courageous efforts to help Jews.[59]

Leutnant Lang worked closely with Oskar in Mährisch Ostrau and with *Leutnant* György, who often went by the civilian name of Dr. Greiner. Sepp Aue reported that before the German takeover of what re-mained of Bohemia and Moravia in March 1939, he frequently saw Schindler give Lang and György "various papers, packages" and other "luggage" or "baggage" *(zavazadla)*, an indication that Oskar supplied the two German agents with a great deal of information about the Czech military. Lang originally worked for Abwehr in Opava; after the conquest of Poland he was transferred to Prague. During the war, he was released from military service because of a serious motorcycle accident injury.[60]

Indications are that Oskar's German superiors thought highly of him. According to Alois Polansky, he received numerous awards, including a Horch, an extremely expensive road car designed by August Horch, the founder of Audi, for his work in 1938 and 1939. But according to Eva Marta Kisza, one of Schindler's mistresses, the two of them were walking down a Berlin street when Oskar spotted a light blue Horch in a showroom window. Emilie said that the luxurious two-seater Horch had been made for the Shah of Iran, but because of the war, it was never delivered. Eva added that the impulsive Oskar fell in love with the car and convinced his Abwehr superiors to give him the money to buy it. During the war he had the Horch painted gray. The car became Oskar's most prized possession and he used it to escape capture by Soviet troops at the end of World War II.[61]

Since this all took place during the war, Oskar probably never returned to the business world. More than likely, Schindler never fully left Abwehr. Those who work in intelligence are forever sworn to secrecy. As will be seen later, the fact that Abwehr sent him on a special mission to Turkey in 1940 indicates the great trust that Canaris's organization put in his skills.[62]

Yet what were the principal fruits of Oskar Schindler's espionage efforts in the spring and summer of 1939? According to Dr. Mečislav Borak, Schindler was involved in German plans for the invasion of Poland, particularly the seizure of the Gliwice radio station and the takeover of the Jablunkov Pass railway tunnel and tracks during the early hours of the German attack. However, Professor Jaroslav Valenta of the Historical Institute of the Czech Academy of Sciences doubts that Schindler played much of a role in the seizure of the radio station at Gliwice because this was not in his area of operation; moreover, the seizure was controlled by the SS and the SD, though supported by Abwehr. According to Professor Valenta, most historic evidence tends to support this conclusion. Still, direct and indirect evidence does suggest that Oskar played an active role in German efforts to seize the Jablunkov Pass.[63]

Abwehr, Schindler, and the Invasion of Poland

As Britain, France, and the Soviet Union searched for ways diplomatically and militarily to thwart a German invasion of Poland in the spring and early summer of 1939, the Wehrmacht and Abwehr moved ahead with plans for the invasion of Poland.[64] If there was an uncertain factor in this planning, it was the response of the Soviet Union to an invasion of Poland. German military planners had assumed that the Poles would try to hold back German forces long enough for Stalin to respond. This never happened. As Anglo-French-Soviet talks faltered over Stalin's insistence that he be given the right to act defensively against any country on his western frontier that seemed to be moving into the German camp, low-level nonaggression talks began between Moscow and Berlin. Though they did not bear fruit until August 23 and 24, 1939, the talks between Germany and the Soviet Union removed the immediate prospect of war between these two countries and made Stalin an active participant in the takeover of Poland.[65]

Once Hitler was certain that an agreement with Stalin was possible, he established the final timetable for the attack on Poland. On August 12, 1939, Canaris put all his espionage units on full alert. Two days later, Hitler met with his Wehrmacht chiefs in his Berghof mountain retreat outside Munich. The following day, Canaris ordered his commando and sabotage units to move into position in Poland. On August 19, two trucks from Abwehr II delivered uniforms to the SD for the 364 Abwehr and SS operatives who were to take part in the phony assaults just inside Poland. Three days later, Hitler met again with a larger body of Wehrmacht commanders, including Canaris. Also in attendance was Hermann Göring, who was about to be named head of the Ministerial Council for the Defense of the Reich *(Ministerrat für die Reichsverteidigung)* and Hitler's official successor, and Foreign Minister Joachim von Ribbentrop. On Hitler's instructions, all his top officers wore civilian clothing. At the end of the meeting, which, as usual, the Führer dominated, he told his military leaders that he expected the attack on Poland to begin in four days. His parting words: "I have done my duty. Now do yours."[66]

At 4:05 P.M. on August 25, the Wehrmacht High Command under *General* Wilhelm Keitel issued the order to invade Poland. Canaris immediately sent his combat and sabotage teams into action. Two and a half hours later, though, Keitel ordered his units to stand down at 8:30 P.M. because of new political developments. Great Britain, which Hitler had hoped to isolate through an alliance offer, instead signed a mutual assistance treaty with Poland that day. Benito Mussolini, Hitler's Pact of Steel ally, now informed the Führer that Italy was militarily unprepared to join in a war that would probably include Britain and France. *Oberst* Edwin Lahousen frantically informed *Admiral* Canaris that his agents overseeing the attack on the Jablunkov Pass railway tunnel had lost contact with the sabotage team under *Leutnant* Hans-Albrecht Herzner. The fear now was that Herzner's squad would provoke the very war that the Führer had just called off. Desperate Abwehr II radio operators in Germany and northern Slovakia did everything possible to contact the missing unit. Oskar Schindler's Commando VIII unit was the main physical link to Herzner's squad. On the morning of August 26, Oskar's team informed Abwehr headquarters that it had heard reports of heavy rifle fire near the Jablunkov Pass and concluded that it was probably *Leutnant* Herzner's unit.[67]

Hours later, Canaris received more information about *Leutnant* Herzner's activities. At 3:55 A.M. on August 26, Herzner's unit was sent to the Eighth Army, which was part of Army Group South; this was the first official dispatch of World War II. It reported that it had taken nearby Mosty u Jablunkova station but had failed to take the Jablunkov tunnel. Herzner's squad then captured a locomotive and tried to enter the tunnel, but the Poles repelled this effort as well. The Abwehr team, which was now trapped behind Polish lines, was ordered to fight its way to the Slovak border. It met stiff resistance from Polish police forces, who now tried to block the German team's way out of Poland. By early afternoon, Herzner's unit remained under heavy Polish fire as it tried to move across the Slovak border in the Raková-Čadca region. Just before it entered Slovak territory, *General* Keitel ordered Herzner to remain in Poland.[68]

Hitler had never intended to halt his invasion of Poland; instead, he delayed his assault for a few days to convince the British to abandon their guarantees to Poland and pressure Mussolini to reconsider his position about joining Hitler in war. By August 28, Hitler had decided to invade Poland on September 1.[69]

On the afternoon of August 31, 1939, the special Abwehr, SS, and SD units that were to initiate the mock attacks were given the code words *Grossmutter gestorben* (Grandmother is dead). This was the signal for their final moves into Poland. A stunned Admiral Canaris, who received his orders for the initial assaults at 5:30 P.M, broke down and cried. For Canaris, war meant the end of Germany.[70] Two and a half hours later, Germans dressed in Polish uniforms fired shots across the Polish border and left the dead prisoners as "evidence" of Polish aggression. Another group under *SS-Sturmbannführer* Alfred Naujocks attacked and captured the radio station at Gleiwitz. The phony "Polish" occupiers then announced, in Polish, an attack on Germany. Hitler now had his justification for war.[71]

The following day, the *Völkischer Beobachter* informed the German people that Polish rebels had moved into German territory and Adolf Hitler told the Reichstag that the Reich would now respond to fourteen "border incidents" of the previous night. The reality was quite different. Hitler had signed the final directive for the attack on Poland at noon on August 31. Seventeen hours later, five German armies moved into Poland, preceded by several Abwehr commando squads. Over the next few days, Hitler rejected the demands of Britain and France to withdraw as a prelude to negotiations. On September 3, London and Paris declared war on the Third Reich. By the time Soviet forces, after considerable German prodding, began to occupy their portion of eastern Poland, the Wehrmacht had almost completed its conquest of Poland and the destruction of Poland's once proud military forces. Though some Polish units were able to escape into neutral territory, the Germans were able to defeat those that remained in Poland by October 6.[72]

Kraków and the Early Months of the German Occupation

Kraków, Poland, would be Oskar Schindler's home from 1939 to 1944. According to Emilie, he "fell in love with the bustling life and beauty of the city and did not want to leave; he was more faithful to it than to many of his women, certainly more than to me." Kraków was also one of the first major Polish cities taken by the Wehrmacht in September 1939. Two German armies, Army Group North under *General* Fedor von Bock and Army Group South under Gerd von Runstedt invaded Poland in the early morning hours of September 1, 1939. Runstedt's Fourteenth Army, operating out of Slovakia, was responsible for taking southern Poland, particularly the fortified city of Lvov. The Fourteenth Army was also to stop Polish units from moving into the safety of Hungary and Romania. In the first hours of combat, units of the Fourteenth Army took the difficult Jablunkov Pass from its Polish defenders. That evening, the force of the German attack saw the disorganized Polish Kraków Army flee in the face of the German assault. By September 5, the Fourteenth Army was on the outskirts of Kraków, which surrendered the next day. It would be another month before German forces completed the conquest of Poland.[73]

Five weeks after Kraków surrendered to the Germans, Oskar Schindler made the three-hour trip from Mährish Ostrau to Kraków to explore the possibility of resuming his business career. When he arrived in Kraków,

Abwehr officers had their hands full dealing with the fallout from defunct German plans to initiate a revolt in those parts of Poland and the Soviet Union with large Ukrainian populations. On September 19, Canaris had personally asked *Oberst* Erwin Lahousen, the head of Abwehr II, to set up operations in Kraków to deal with the large influx of Ukrainians fleeing Soviet troops, who had just moved into their occupation zone in Poland. Three and a half weeks earlier, Moscow and Berlin had signed the Nazi-Soviet nonaggression pact and a secret accord that divided Poland almost equally between both countries.[74]

For several years, Canaris and other Abwehr leaders had played with the idea of stirring up nationalist sentiment among the large Ukrainian minority in Poland and, at the opportune moment, uniting Ukrainians in Poland and the Soviet Union into a pro-Nazi Greater Ukrainian state. The Nazi-Soviet accord dashed hopes that such a state would come into existence.[75] At German prodding, the Soviet Union, which had just concluded an armistice with Japan, ending a four-month war on the Mongolian-Manchurian border, sent the Red Army to occupy its treaty zone in Poland. Vladimir Potemkin, the vice commissar of foreign affairs, told the Polish ambassador to Moscow, Waclaw Grzybowski, that Stalin did so to protect the Ukrainians and Belorussians in Poland.[76]

Most of Poland's 4.4 million Ukrainians (1931 census) were now trapped in Stalin's new Polish territory, and more than 0.5 million lived in German-occupied Poland. During the next year, about 20,000 to 30,000 Ukrainians left Soviet Poland for the German zone. Soon after the war began, Abwehr set up a relief organization in Kraków to help the Ukrainian refugees. For the rest of World War II, Kraków would be a center of Ukrainian nationalist activity that was officially encouraged by the Germans. Many of the guards who oversaw Oskar Schindler's workers in Kraków and Brünnlitz were drawn from this large Ukrainian emigré community.[77]

The German invasion and conquest of Poland was brutal. According to Ian Kreshaw, occupied Poland was to become an "experimental playground" for the SS and the Nazi Party, both of which would play a key role in ruling Poland after it was conquered. Hitler regarded ethnic Poles as that "dreadful [racial] material" who stood in the way of his dreams of a greater Aryan-pure Germany. On August 22, Hitler told his top generals to "act brutally" towards all Poles. The Führer viewed Poland's Jews "as the most horrible thing imaginable." Hitler added that the aim of war was physically to annihilate the enemy, in this case the Poles. His special

Einsatz squads had "orders mercilessly and pitilessly to send men, women, and children of Polish extraction and language to their death."[78]

Consequently, during the six years the Germans occupied Poland, they waged two wars against the Polish population: one against Polish Jews and one against non-Jewish Poles. Once in Poland, the Germans were determined to destroy the heart of the intellectual leadership or core of the Polish people and isolate the Jews from occupied Polish society. Specially trained *Einsatzgruppen* (special action groups) made up of 2,700 men from the SD, Sipo, and the SS were sent into Poland to combat so-called hostile elements. Initially used in the takeover of Austria in 1938 (the *Anschluß*) to establish police security, over time the *Einsatzgruppen* expanded their mission to include the neutralization or eradication of all societal elements deemed racially or physically dangerous to the German control of Bohemia, Moravia, Poland, and later, the Soviet Union. In 1941, the *Einsatzgruppen* became the principal killing squads the Germans used in their effort to mass murder all Jews in the Soviet Union.[79]

Five *Einsatzgruppen* swept into Poland behind the Wehrmacht in early September 1939. What Ian Kreshaw calls an "orgy of atrocities" followed; it put earlier Nazi brutalities in the Greater Reich "completely in the shade." The Germans were determined to wipe out Poland's religious, political, and intellectual leaders as well as the nobility. Ultimately, this campaign against Poland's elite resulted in 60,000 deaths.[80]

Jews also suffered terribly during this period. In Kraków, which was occupied by the Fourteenth Army and *Einsatzgruppe* I under *SS-Brigadeführer* Bruno Streckenbach, many of the city's 60,000 Jews fled the Nazi terror campaign. Yet the Jews in Kraków and elsewhere in Poland suffered not only from abuses at the hands of the *Einsatzgruppen* but also from atrocities committed by the Wehrmacht.[81] One of the first Wehrmacht officers to voice concerns about this was Admiral Canaris, who ordered his Abwehr officers to watch the activities of the *Einsatzgruppen* and to report the atrocities they committed. Though Canaris was too cautious to lodge a formal complaint with Hitler, he did share his concerns with *General* Keitel on September 12 at the special armored "Führer Train" headquarters in Upper Silesia. Canaris told Keitel that he had heard of the shootings of Poles and Jews and of plans that the clergy and the nobility were to be "exterminated (*ausgerottet*)." Canaris seemed worried that the Wehrmacht would be blamed for these killings. Keitel said that Hitler had already decided on the matter and had told *General* Franz Halder, the army Chief of Staff, that if the military wanted no part in such actions, they should stand aside and let the *Einsatzgruppen* do their work. A month after this conversation, Oskar Schindler arrived in Kraków, where some of the worst atrocities had already taken place. As an active Abwehr officer, he was probably soon privy to the atrocities and to Canaris's order that Abwehr keep an eye on the *Einsatzgruppen*.[82]

The Creation of the General Government

If Poland was the racial laboratory for the SS, then the General Government was its killing field. With the exception of the Russian front from 1941 onwards, the General Government was the most brutal place in the Third Reich. In a meeting with important Nazi and Wehrmacht leaders in mid-October 1939, Hitler laid out the practical and ideological framework for the General Government. It was not to be treated like a German province nor was it to have a strong economy. Hitler intended the quality of life for the Poles there to be low and viewed the General Government as a primary source for forced labor. He viewed German efforts there as a *Volkstumskampf* (hard ethnic struggle) that should have no legal restrictions. Nazi control of this part of Poland would "allow us to purify the Reich area too of Jews and Polacks." German activity in the General Government, Hitler told the gathering, was "the devil's work."[83] It was in this environment that Oskar Schindler would work so hard to save his Jewish workers in Kraków.

German plans for the administration and division of Poland after its conquest were put into place unevenly and reflected Hitler's uncertainty over the future fate of the Polish nation. The Führer gave some thought to creating a rump Polish state, though he remained unsure about the exact nature of this entity until October 1939. His uncertainty centered around Stalin's hesitancy to occupy his portion of Poland and the West's response to German peace feelers in September and early October.[84] In the meantime, the Wehrmacht wanted to restore to normalcy all the areas it had conquered as quickly as possible. Before the invasion of Poland, it set up special "CdZs enemy country" (*Chef der Zivilverwaltung*, chief of civil administration) offices attached to each of the invading armies to oversee this process.[85]

Almost immediately, conflicts began between Nazi Party officials and the military over the appointments and powers of the new CdZs. Sometimes, Hitler countered military appointments. The result was a growing conflict between the Wehrmacht and party officials that was to continue in various ways in occupied Poland throughout the war. Part of Oskar Schindler's genius in saving his Jews was his ability to work within the shadows of this conflict and use it to his advantage.

By the end of September, Hitler had approved the army's "Organization of the Military Administration in the Occupied, formerly Polish, Territories." Southern East Prussia and eastern Upper Silesia were given special provisions; the rest of German-occupied Poland was divided into four military districts (Danzig-West Prussia, Posen, Łódź, and Kraków) overseen by the military aided by a civilian administration. The four districts were overseen by Commander in Chief East Gerd von Runstedt, who also commanded the Łódź military district. The senior civilian administrator under Runstedt was Hans Frank, a Nazi "Old Fighter" and its most powerful legal expert. Other prominent Nazis such as *SS-Obergruppenführer* Albert Forster (Danzig) and future *SS-Obergruppenführer* Arthur Greiser (Posen) held the chief administrative positions in the other military districts. The Kraków military district's civilian administrator was to be *SS-Obergruppenführer* Arthur Seyß-Inquart, a former Austrian chancellor who would later hold important administrative positions as deputy governor of the General Government and Reich Commissioner of the Netherlands. Each of these men were tried and convicted as war criminals after World War II.[86]

Hitler's appointment of top Nazis to these administrative positions in Poland meant that the traditional party infighting that had so plagued German administration elsewhere now would become rampant throughout Poland. Petty jealousy and backbiting now became the hallmarks of a Nazi Party-dominated administrative system that was about to undergo another major change as Hitler agreed to a new administrative structure for Poland that transferred governing power to the Nazi Party. Wehrmacht leaders had never been comfortable about administering a civilian area once a conflict had ended and order was restored. Administration was something best left to civilians, not soldiers. Germany's military leaders were particularly glad to be rid of the political responsibilities of such administration.[87]

Friction between the army and Nazi administrators intensified as army commanders became more and more critical of the brutality of the *Einsatzgruppen* against the Polish population. Hitler sided with the SS and told Joseph Goebbels on October 13 that the army was "too soft and yielding." Four days later, he took the SS and the police out from under the military's jurisdiction in Poland. The SS and other Nazi Party organs and functionaries would now be given a free hand to expand their experiments in what remained of the Polish "racial laboratory."[88]

The transformation of Poland into a civilian-administered area did not end army protests. Over several months, *Generalleutnant* Johannes Blaskowitz, Commander in Chief East, sent his superior, army commander Walther von Brauchitsch, two memos severely criticizing the reign of terror unleashed by the SS in Poland against civilians. Blaskowitz was fearful that if these activities were not halted, they could severely damage the German nation. Blaskowitz felt that the "brutalization and moral depravity" practiced by the SS could easily "spread like a plague among valuable German men." The person principally responsible for spreading news among the officer corps about Blaskowitz's memorandums was *Major* Helmut "Muffel" Groscurth, former head of Abwehr *Untergruppe* IS and a close associate of Hans Oster, Admiral Canaris's Chief of Staff.[89]

Hitler, who saw Blaskowitz's first memo, called his ideas childish. According to the Führer, you could not fight a war using Salvation Army methods. The army leadership responded weakly to Blaskowitz's complaints and worked out a compromise with Himmler and *General* Fedor von Bock sent a memorandum to all army commanders that decried the "unfortunate misinterpretations" of the security forces in Poland but said that their "'otherwise uncommonly harsh measures towards the Polish population of the occupied areas' were justified by the need to 'secure German *Lebensraum* and the solutions to ethnic political problems ordered by the Führer.'" In the spring of 1940, Himmler spoke to senior army leaders in Koblenz and said that though he never saw such harsh actions himself, the policies were necessary to deal with the subversive actions of Polish nationalists and Bolsheviks. Though Blaskowitz remained in the army, he held secondary posts and was never promoted to *Generalfeldmarschall.*[90]

Within days after the Wehrmacht had defeated the last pockets of Polish resistance in early October, plans began in earnest for the final territorial realignment of German-occupied Poland. Wilhelm Stuckhart, a state secretary in the Reich Interior Ministry, prepared several decrees for Hitler dealing with Polish regions that were to be integrated into the Greater Reich and the creation of a General Government for central and southern Poland. With Hitler's approval, the new General Government for the Occupied Areas of Poland *(Generalgouvernement für die besetzten polnischen Gebiete)* was to come into existence on October 26, with Hans Frank as governor general *(Generalgouverneur)*. Part of northwestern Poland was integrated into the Danzig-West Prussia *Reichsgau* under *Reichsstatthalter* and *Gauleiter* Albert Forster, and East Prussia was governed by *Gauleiter* Erich Koch. The area around the Polish city of Łódź was integrated into the Warthegau under *Reichstatthalter* and *Gauleiter* Arthur Greiser, and eastern Upper Silesia became East Upper Silesia. Two years later, East Upper Silesia was divided into two *Gaue:* Lower Silesia, its capital in Breslau (today Wrocław); and Upper Silesia, its capital in Kattowice (Katowice).[91]

Within weeks after Oskar Schindler arrived in Kraków, the creation of the General Government, with Kraków as its capital, was almost completed. Hitler had personally chosen Hans Frank to rule the new General Government. For the next five years, Schindler worked with officials close to Frank and lived literally in the shadows of Frank's headquarters and official residence, Wawel Castle. Born in Karlsruhe in 1900, Frank was a legitimate "Old Fighter" who joined the Nazi Party in the fall of 1923. A law student in Munich, he took part in the legendary Beer Hall Putsch on November 8 and 9, 1923, when Hitler tried unsuccessfully to seize control of the Bavarian state government. He became Hitler's personal lawyer and founded what later became the National Socialist League of Law Guardians (NSRB; *Nationalsozialistischer Rechtwahrerbund*). As the Nazi's top lawyer, Frank was involved in several thousand cases involving the Nazi Party before Hitler's accession to power in 1933.[92]

Frank won a Reichstag seat in the 1930 elections and served as Bavarian Minister of Justice from 1933 to 1934. He created the Academy for German Law *(Akademie für deutsches Recht)* in 1933 and served as its president until 1941. In 1934, Frank became a Reich Minister without Portfolio. Yet despite his numerous positions and awards, Frank never entered Hitler's inner circle. Generally, Hitler disliked lawyers. More important, throughout his Nazi career, Frank made moves and statements that alienated the Führer. For example, in 1934, Frank argued that the SA leaders murdered in the Röhm Purge (Night of the Long Knives) should have received trials.[93]

At a distance, none of this seemed seriously to affect Frank's career. When the war began, he had joined the reserve battalion of the Potsdam Ninth Infantry Regiment. When he became the chief administrative head *(Oberverwaltungschef)* of the Wehrmacht's occupied Polish territories, he lobbied hard for the governor general's position and hoped it would increase his power. Even before he became governor general, he began to transform the administrative structure he had inherited from the military.

Chaos abounded, which later worked to Oskar Schindler's advantage. Technically, only Frank and Hermann Göring, the chair of the Ministerial Council for the Defense of the Reich *(Ministerrat für die Reichsverteidigung)*, could issue decrees in the General Government. Yet it was not Göring, who was also head of the Four Year Plan *(Vierjahresplan)*, which oversaw economic war planning, who became a threat to Frank. Early on, Göring made Frank his defense commissioner in the General Government to oversee his interests there. Instead, the threats came from elements in the Party, government, and military who longed for access to the General Government's resources and manpower.[94]

Frank and the SS in the General Government

Frank brought considerable power and prestige to his position as governor general. From his perspective, he was answerable only to Hitler and tried to adopt the *Führerprinzip* of absolute authority under one leader throughout the General Government. To underscore his imperial pretensions and to reduce the significance of the Poles' modern capital, Warsaw, Frank chose Kraków, the political and intellectual seat of Polish kings, as the capital of the General Government. He chose as his official residence Wawel Castle, the medieval home of Poland's Catholic prelates and monarchs. But Frank preferred to spend as much time as possible in the neo-Gothic castle once owned by the Polish architect Adolf Szyszko-Bohuzs on the outskirts of the city in Przegorzały overlooking the Vistula River. Nazi Party officials in Berlin jokingly referred to the Government General as the "Frank-reich" (Hans Frank's kingdom), a play on the German word for France and a reference to the early medieval German-French kingdom. Frank's imperiousness affected his family. His wife, Brigitte, saw herself as the "Queen of Poland" and acted out the part in a most corrupt way; in fact, charges of corruption against Frank and his family seriously undermined his authority. In the spring of 1942, Frank met with Hitler, Dr. Hans Lammers, the head of Hitler's Reich Chancellery, and Martin Bormann, the Führer's alter ego and private secretary, over charges of corruption. When Frank promised to reform, particularly with regard to his wife's family, Hitler seemed satisfied. Frank got away with his crimes because other Nazi officials, who were as corrupt as Frank, feared that pressing their charges too firmly against him could backfire. We shall see that this was not the last of Frank's troubles with his enemies or with the Führer.[95]

Frank's cronies in crime and genocide were the officials he appointed to help him run the General Government. His first deputy governor was Arthur Seyß Inquart, an Austrian-trained lawyer who had earlier served as the Reich governor *(Reichsstatthalter)* of Austria and Reich Minister without Portfolio. After the conquest of The Netherlands in the spring of 1940, Seyß Inquart became the Reich Commissioner for the Netherlands, a position he held until the end of the war. In the fall of 1945, Seyß Inquart and Frank were tried and convicted of several of the four counts of the 1945–1946 Nuremberg trial of twenty-two major Nazi war criminals: conspiracy, crimes against peace, war crimes, and crimes against humanity. Both were hanged on October 16, 1946, in Nuremberg.[96]

After Seyß Inquart's departure, Dr. Josef Bühler, who testified at Frank's trial and was himself later tried and executed in Poland for war crimes, ran the day-to-day affairs of the General Government as its state secretary *(Staatssekretär).* Bühler oversaw the twelve (later fourteen) major administrative divisions of the "Frank-reich." The central administration of the General Government was divided into major divisions *(Hauptabteilungen)* that dealt with education, railways, postal service, the economy, and so forth. Because these divisions were similar to those in the Reich, German officials in Berlin and elsewhere often went directly to the General Government's divisions to do business, thus bypassing the power-hungry governor. Bühler made matters worse by occasionally setting up offices that conflicted directly with the work of the General Government's major divisions.[97]

The General Government was divided into four, and then later, five districts: Kraków, Lublin, Radom, Warsaw, and Galicia. Each district was ruled by a *Gouverneur,* who was usually a Party member, and a civilian *Amtschef.* Each district's governor enjoyed an absolute local authority that occasionally conflicted with the interests of the General Government. During his five years in Kraków, Oskar Schindler had to deal frequently not only with General Government officials headquartered in Kraków but also with the Kraków district's governor, *SS-Brigadeführer* Otto Gustav Freiherr Wächter and his successors, *SS-Brigadeführer* Dr. Richard Wendler and Dr. Curt Ludwig von Burgsdorff.[98]

Frank's efforts to wield absolute control over the General Government were complicated not only by the bloated administrative system he tried to govern but also by his limited authority over key elements in the Nazi dictatorship—the SS and the military. Though Frank was able to hold his own with the Wehrmacht, he was, according to Hans Umbreit, "on a losing ticket from the start" when it came to Himmler and the SS. Himmler was the Reich Führer-SS and Chief of the German Police *(Reichsführer-SS und Chef der Deutschen Polizei)*. He had under him the newly created Reich Main Security Office (RSHA; *Reichssicherheitshauptamt*), Germany's new super police organization, and was also Reich Commissioner for the Fortification of the German Volk-Nation *(Reichskommissar für die Festigung des deutschen Volkstums)*. This latter position gave Himmler considerable authority to press his claim as the guardian of police and political authority in the Nazis' new "racial laboratory." Because Himmler was much closer to Hitler than Frank when it came to dealing with the "Jewish question," the Reich Führer's position in the General Government was further strengthened.[99]

Himmler's principal representative in the General Government was the Higher SS and Police Leader (HSSPF; *Höherer SS-und Polizeiführer*). The HSSPF oversaw the various branches of the Order-Keeping Police (Orpo; *Ordnungspolizei*) and Sipo (Security Police; *Sicherheitspolizei*), which included the Gestapo, Kripo *(Kriminalpolizei*; criminal police) and the Border Police *(Grenzpolizei)*. The HSSPF had under him subordinates who oversaw SS and police matters in the five districts of the General Government. During his five years in Kraków, Oskar Schindler not only had to deal with two General Government HSSPFs (Friedrich Wilhelm Krüger, 1939–1943; Wilhelm Koppe, 1943–1945) but also with the Kraków district's HSSPFs (Karl Zech; Schedler; Julian Scherner, 1942–1943; and Teobald Thier).[100]

Originally, Himmler saw the HSSPF as the overseer of the various police forces and SS units in areas under German control. During the war, he tried to expand powers of the HSSPF to include authority over all political and racial matters in the Third Reich. Consequently, Himmler and his subordinates became Frank's principal competitors in the General Government during Frank's long years of rule there.[101]

The Wehrmacht and the Armaments Inspectorate in the General Government

Because Frank had no authority in military matters, the Wehrmacht was less problematic to Frank than Himmler and the SS. Frank had the greatest difficulties with *General* Blaskowitz and played an important role in his dismissal. Blaskowitz was succeeded by *Generalleutnant* Curt Ludwig Baron von Gienanth, who held the title of Military Commander in the

General Government *(Militärbefehlshaber im Generalgouvernement)* and, in 1942, Military Commander of the General Government District *(Wehrkreisbefehlshaber im Generalgouvernement)*. In 1943, *General der Infantrie* Siegfried Haenicke replaced Gienanth as commander of the General Government military district.[102]

The relationship between Frank, the HSSPF, and the military was always tense, particularly after the outbreak of war with the Soviet Union in 1941 and the transformation of the General Government into the prime killing center of the Final Solution, the German plan to mass murder of all the Jews of Europe. Though we now know that the Wehrmacht played more of a collaborationist role in this mass murder campaign against Jews, the deadliest military complicity took place in occupied parts of the Soviet Union. Regardless, the Wehrmacht regarded the General Government as an important staging area for its war with the Soviet Union and resented the conflicting goals of the SS and its various police operatives, who came to see the General Government less as a war zone than as a killing field.[103]

Oskar Schindler's success in protecting and saving his Jewish workers in Kraków and Brünnlitz centered around his close ties with Wehrmacht officers in Kraków, Berlin, and elsewhere. As previously mentioned, his ties within Admiral Canaris's Abwehr were essential to his work. Equally important, however, were his links to the Wehrmacht's Armaments Inspectorate *(Rüstungsinspektion)* and Himmler's Security Police, Sipo. On three occasions after the war, Schindler specifically thanked his friends in Abwehr, the Armaments Inspectorate, and Sipo for their help not only in aiding his Jews but also for arranging to have him released after his three arrests during the war. In his letter to Fritz Lang in 1951, Oskar explained their motives. He said that the supportive officers in Abwehr and the Armaments Inspectorate were "partly anti-Nazi, or at least opponents of the SS and its methods." He added that they were "on the side of Canaris during the ever-widening gap between the Abwehr and the SD."[104]

The person he always mentioned first in his postwar statements about helpful Wehrmacht officers was *Generalleutnant* Maximillian Schindler, the head of the Armaments Inspectorate in the General Government. As the war with the Soviet Union lengthened, the military viewed the General Government, with its large human labor resources, as an important element in war production. And key to Wehrmacht war planning in the General Government was Oskar Schindler's namesake, *General* Schindler. Though not related to Oskar Schindler, the Sudeten German businessman let everyone he dealt with in the General Government think that he and

General Schindler were relatives; indeed, some thought that Oskar was *General* Schindler's son. The fictitious tie between the two men worked to Oskar's advantage, though Maximillian Schindler and his Sudeten German namesake had very little in common. Born in 1881 in Bavaria, Maximillian Schindler had served as an infantry officer in World War I. According to Oskar, *General* Schindler later was a German delegate to the League of Nations and also served as Military Attaché to the German embassy in Warsaw. In September 1939, *General* Schindler became the OKW's representative for industrial matters in Poland *(Industriebeauftragter des OKW in Poland)* and then head of the Armaments Inspectorate of the General Government *(Inspektor der Rüstungsinspektion im Generalgouvernement)*, with the rank of *General*. In 1944, he became the head of the Armaments Inspectorate West *(Rüstungsbeautragter West)*. He settled in Munich after the war and died in 1963.[105]

General Schindler was also one of only a handful of officers whom Oskar thanked at the end of the war for helping him save his Jews. What we know about *General* Schindler's activities in the General Government comes from a study of German defense and armaments production, *Geschichte der deutschen Wehr-und Rüstungwirtschaft (1919–1943/45)*, by the head of the Armaments Inspectorate, *General* Georg Thomas, and Albert Speer's *Der Sklavenstaat (The Slave State)*. Though neither work provides clues as to *General* Schindler's political sentiments, he must have been well respected throughout the German armaments industry because he remained in his post after Thomas's dismissal in 1943. Oskar Schindler's choosing to put *General* Schindler at the top of his small list of officers who helped him during the war also says a lot about Maximillian Schindler. One possible assumption is that *General* Thomas, himself a vocal critic of Hitler's inadequate wartime military plans, provided *General* Schindler with the same type of protection that Admiral Canaris did for his own rebellious officers and administrators. The relationship between Thomas and Canaris is particularly intriguing, as we shall see. Though they were never close, their erstwhile antipathy to Hitler's ongoing war efforts periodically brought them together.

Given Oskar's friendship with *General* Schindler, it should come as no surprise that he also had close ties with two other prominent Armaments Inspectorate officers, *Oberstleutnant* Ott, the head of the Wehrmacht's Armaments Inspectorate in Kraków, and *Oberstleutnant* Süßmuth, who headed the Armaments Inspectorate office in Troppau (Opava) in what had become the Protectorate of Bohemia and Moravia. Later, *Oberstleut-*

nant Süßmuth, at least according to Oskar, was instrumental not only in helping Oskar get permission to move his factory from Kraków to Brünnlitz in the fall of 1944, but he also had about 3,000 Polish Jewish women transferred from Auschwitz to smaller forced labor camps, where they all survived the war. Ott died at the end of the war or soon thereafter; Süßmuth settled in Vienna.[106]

Oskar was also close to another armaments specialist, Erich Lange of the Army High Command's (OKH; *Oberkommando des Heeres*) Ordnance Department *(Heereswaffenamt)*. Lange, an engineer, would play a key role in getting Schindler's Jewish workers released from their brief incarceration in the Auschwitz and Groß Rosen (Polish, Rogożnica) concentration camps in the fall of 1944 while en route from Kraków to Brünnlitz. Emilie described Lange as a gentleman who always wore civilian clothing whenever he visited the Schindlers in Brünnlitz to show "his disapproval of the Nazi regime." Lange frequently mentioned that he worked for Germany and not the Nazi regime. Emilie found Erich Lange to be "most cordial and friendly" with a strong "sense of justice" and moral integrity.[107]

The most interesting thing about the support that Oskar received from important figures in the Armaments Inspectorate is the similarity between these ties and those with Abwehr. Some Abwehr officers, particularly those who helped and befriended Oskar, were operating under the umbrella protection of Admiral Canaris, who shared some of their sympathies. Could the same be said of Armaments Inspectorate officers? Yes. *General* Thomas also had serious misgivings about Hitler and the Nazis, though they had less to do with Nazi political and racial policies than with Hitler's ill-thought-out military plans. Regardless, Thomas would be increasingly seen by Nazi leaders as a defeatist and critic of the Nazi regime. And like Canaris, he would be arrested after the July 20, 1944 assassination plot against Hitler for his activities.

Thomas and Canaris

Yet who was Georg Richard Thomas? He was the son of a factory owner from Forst in eastern Germany. He joined a Junker unit in 1908 and was commissioned a lieutenant in 1910. He served on the Western Front in World War I. A decorated officer, he remained in the army after the war and he became a protégé of Ludwig Beck, later Hitler's Chief of the General Staff of the Army *(Chef des Generalstabes Wehrmacht)* and later an anti-Nazi resistance leader. Named Chief of Staff of the Army's Weapons Office (*Chef des Stabes des Heereswaffenamts*) in 1930, Thomas would be the center of military planning for the German armed forces when Adolf Hitler came to power three years later. The rearming of Germany had long been one of Adolf Hitler's priorities. Well before his public announcement of German rearmament in 1935, Hitler had greatly increased state expenditures for Germany's armed forces. Some in the military, Thomas and Canaris among them, would argue on the eve of World War II that Germany was not ready to fight a lengthy war. And they were right. Hitler's efforts to rearm and build a modern economy had created tremendous tensions between the military and civilians charged with revitalizing various sectors of Germany and preparing it for war.[108]

How did Thomas fit into all this? According to the Reich Defense Law of 1935, which was amended in 1938, the Minister for Economic Affairs, who also served as the General Plenipotentiary for the Economy *(GBW; Generalbevollmächtigter für die Wirtschaft),* would oversee general supervision of businesses important to the war economy. During wartime, the Wehrmacht, particularly Thomas's office, would supervise businesses involved in armaments production. Hitler tried to resolve the conflicting demands and needs of both groups by putting Hermann Göring in charge of a new overall economic rebuilding program in 1936—the Four Year Plan *(Vierjahresplan)*—which envisioned a nation and military ready for war once the plan was completed. Göring quickly became Germany's economic dictator, though the military, which retained control over armaments production, did everything possible to reassert its control by hammering out a special relationship with the GBW.[109]

Though Germany made tremendous strides in the early years of the Four Year Plan, its efforts to rearm for Hitler's goal of a lengthy conflict backed by a full war economy fell far short of the military's needs in even a limited war. In the summer of 1939, *General* Thomas told Wehrmacht leaders that Germany's economic preparation for war had weakened over the past year and that supplies of essential raw materials would last only a few months. Thomas hoped his report would help Wehrmacht leaders talk Hitler out of war; but if war came, it should be "total war" against Poland and the countries of southeastern Europe to acquire vital raw materials.[110]

After he read Thomas's negative report, *Admiral* Canaris asked the general to talk to *General* Keitel, the head of OKW, about the inadvisability of war over Poland. This was the beginning of a special relation-

ship between Thomas and Canaris that lasted at least until Thomas resigned as head of Defense Economy and Chief Armanents Office (*Wi-Rü
Amt Werkwirtschafts-und Rüstungshauptamt*) in 1943. Thomas, long a
voice in the wilderness about Germany's military readiness to fight aggressive war, was frustrated when Albert Speer (whom Hitler appointed in
1942 as his new Reich Minister for Armaments and Munitions [Rmf-
BuM; *Reichsminister für Bewaffnung und Munition*]), decided to place
Thomas's regional officers and armaments inspectors directly under Rmf-
BuM. Though Thomas still commanded Wi-Rü, his power and influence
were reduced considerably by Speer's move.[111]

Canaris had become acquainted with Thomas when the latter commanded the army's Weapons Office *(Heereswaffenamt)*. By the time Canaris approached Thomas about the Wehrmacht's war preparedness,
Thomas was recognized as the military's foremost armaments expert. Yet
Thomas was more than that and Canaris knew it. The forty-nine-year old
Thomas was also a well-placed and influential officer with strong misgivings about the Nazi system. He was particularly shaken by the twin crises
in 1938 surrounding the resignation of Minister of War Werner von
Blomberg, on charges that he had married a prostitute, and the dismissal
of Supreme Military Commander Werner von Fritsch, who was charged
with being a homosexual. The failure of the army's leadership to protest
Fritsch's treatment troubled many officers, including Thomas and Canaris, who saw in the Fritsch crisis an assault on their treasured military
values. Hitler now used both situations to his advantage by assuming full
personal control of the Wehrmacht through the newly created OKW
under Keitel. The Fritsch crisis was also an important watershed for
Thomas, Canaris, and other officers later involved in various aspects of
the anti-Hitler resistance.[112]

It was no accident that in August 1939 Canaris tried to enlist Thomas's
help in convincing *General* Keitel of the foolishness of war at that time. In
early 1940, both men were drawn together around the issuance of the "X-
Report," but this time they were on different sides of the resistance fence.
In the fall of 1939, a new conspiracy plot against Hitler developed initially with Canaris's approval that involved Thomas and Abwehr officers
such as *Oberst* Hans Oster, now head of Abwehr's Central Division and
Canaris's Chief of Staff, and *Sonderführer* K (*Hauptmann*) Dr. Johannes
von Dohnányi, the brother-in-law of Dietrich Bonhoeffer. The recently appointed Dohnányi officially served as adviser to Canaris and Oster on military and foreign policy, though he also worked to expand Abwehr's anti-

Hitler contacts. Also working with Oster and Dohnányi was *Oberstleutnant* Helmut Groscurth, Canaris's Abwehr liaison with the OKH, and retired *Generalleutnant* Ludwig Beck, now one of the principal figures in the military opposition to Hitler.[113]

Soon after the German invasion of Poland, Oster convinced Canaris to appoint a new army second lieutenant, Dr. Josef Müller, to Abwehr's main office in Munich. Oster intended to use *Leutnant* Müller, a staunch Catholic, to establish ties with the British government by way of the Vatican. Oster and other conspirators wanted to determine the interest of the British in peace terms in the aftermath of a coup that would topple Hitler and form a new government. Müller's contact with the Vatican was a Jesuit priest, Father Robert Leiber. From the end of September 1939 until early 1940, Müller, who was known in intelligence documents as "Mr X," met several times with Leiber, who transmitted information to Müller about the Vatican's contacts with the British government. The Abwehr officers hoped to take the British terms to General Franz Halder, the army's Chief of Staff, and his boss, army commander *Oberst* General Walther von Brauchitsch, in hopes they would support the coup and halt plans for the German invasion of Western Europe. The result of these talks was the controversial "X Report," which was prepared by Dohnányi in January 1940 and delivered by *General* Thomas to *General* Halder in early April 1940. The mysteriously rewrittèn "X Report" had little effect on Halder and Brauchitsch because they did not see it until just before the invasion of Denmark and Norway.[114]

Despite Hitler's successes in the spring and early summer of 1940, Thomas and Canaris remained concerned about Hitler's aggressive war plans. Yet both men played both ends against the middle as they sought to promote and protect their own careers. After Canaris learned of the details of *Aufbau Ost* (buildup in the east) in August 1940, the initial planning stage for Hitler's planned assault against the Soviet Union, he asked Thomas to prepare a detailed report about the ability of the Wehrmacht to wage such an extensive war. Thomas, now enamored with the expansion of his own vast power, particularly after his appointment as head of *Werkwirtschafts-und Rüstungshauptamt* on August 1, 1940, saw the invasion of the Soviet Union as a means of resolving some of Germany's raw material and labor problems. Consequently, he had no problem supporting Göring's plan to let I. G. Farben build factories at Auschwitz to make synthetic rubber and gasoline.[115] After Thomas was made head of the Economic Organization East *(Ostorgan-*

isation; Wirtschaftsorganisation Ost) in 1941, he became less sanguine; in reports to OKH and Keitel, he spoke of huge military shortages. There is some sense that Thomas might have been trying to convince Hitler to reconsider his attack against the Soviet Union. Thomas continued his negative reports when the war with Russia began. Over time, Keitel came to view Thomas's reports as "defeatist," and Hitler refused to read them.[116]

Yet something else was also lurking in Thomas's mind, particularly once the invasion of the Soviet Union began. Thomas visited the Russian front in the fall of 1941 and learned first hand the policy of mass murder adopted by Hitler and the SS. According to Ulrich Hoffmann, a prominent civilian leader in the resistance, Thomas visited selected commanders on the Russian front in an unsuccessful effort to drum up new support for a coup in August or September 1941. By this time, talk was widespread in upper Wehrmacht circles about the atrocities being committed in Russia. On September 15, Canaris signed a memorandum prepared by Count Helmuth James von Moltke, a military and international affairs expert at OKW and head of the Kreisau resistance circle. The memo, which was given to Keitel, voiced strong objections to the recent OKW decisions regarding Soviet POWs. Thomas, who had close ties with Moltke and Canaris, was probably consulted about its contents.[117]

As the atrocities continued, the Wehrmacht was drawn deeper and deeper into the genocidal circle through its support of the various SS killing squads. In October, *General* Thomas visited *General* Brauchitsch, to discuss the rising tide of atrocities in the Soviet Union. The army commander already knew of the "beastliness" that was rampant in the east, and realized that he had to share responsibility for it.[118] Yet these discussions were never acted upon, probably because of the air of victory surrounding Germany's dramatic successes in the Soviet Union. Moreover, the resistance was not well organized, and resistance leaders were now being watched by various branches of Germany's super police organization, the RSHA. More serious discussions of a coup would come after the failed offensive before Moscow in 1941–1942 and the terrible losses at Stalingrad a year later. By that time, Thomas and Canaris's reputations and careers were damaged beyond repair.[119]

Hitler briefly removed Canaris as head of Abwehr in early 1942 after Himmler accused him of using Jewish agents. Though Canaris was able to convince the Führer to return him to his command, his influence waned considerably after this incident. At about the same time, Thomas lost out in a power struggle with Albert Speer, who became the new Minister of Armaments and Munitions after Todt's accidental death. By the end of the year, Thomas had lost all authority over armaments issues and in early 1943 asked to be relieved of his military duties. A few months later, the military, with the aid of the Gestapo, arrested Dohnányi for corruption; Oster was placed under house arrest and transferred to the *Führer-Reserve,* where he could still wear his military uniform. Ultimately, Oster was dismissed from the service. Though the military cleared Dohnányi in 1944, he was now turned over to the RSHA. In early 1944, Hitler fired Canaris. Abwehr was taken over by the RSHA. Thomas, Canaris, Oster, and others involved in various resistance activities during the war were arrested and tortured after the July 20, 1944, assassination attempt on Hitler's life. Canaris, Oster, and Dohnányi were executed at Flossenbürg concentration camp on April 9, 1945. Thomas managed to survive the war. He died in American custody at the end of 1945.[120]

What do all of these developments and intrigues have to do with Oskar Schindler? Quite a bit. Schindler relied heavily on his ties with Abwehr and the Armaments Inspectorate, particularly General Schindler, to help him acquire the vital armaments contracts necessary to open or keep his factories running in Kraków and Brünnlitz (Brnenec).[121] Emilie also used Oskar's contacts with Abwehr and the Armaments Inspectorate to get him out of jail on numerous occasions during their years in Kraków. Moreover, Schindler's work as a courier for the Jewish Agency in Budapest was partly facilitated through his Abwehr ties. What is difficult to determine is the impact of these connections on Schindler's personal feelings towards Hitler and the Nazi system. Was his effort to use and later save the Jews who worked for him in Kraków and Brünnlitz affected by his ties with Abwehr and Armaments Inspectorate officers who held anti-Hitler and anti-Nazi sentiments?

3.

SCHINDLER AND
THE EMALIA CONTROVERSY

THERE SEEMS TO BE SOME QUESTION ABOUT WHEN OSKAR Schindler first came to Kraków after the outbreak of World War II. Emilie Schindler says in her memoirs that Oskar went to Kraków in mid-October, but Thomas Keneally places him there at the end of the same month. Robin O'Neil says that Oskar received orders from Abwehr on October 17, 1939, to report immediately to *Major* Franz von Korab in Kraków for further duties. Yet other sources indicate that Oskar was in Kraków well before the third week of October because of his importance to Abwher regionally. O'Neil says in his unpublished manuscript on Oskar Schindler, *The Man from Svitavy,* that "Oskar had followed on the heels of the invading German army" into Kraków, which surrendered to the Wehrmacht on September 6. This is almost the identical phrase used in a Gestapo investigation in 1940 centering around the July 1939 break-in of Oskar's apartment in Mährisch Ostrau. It stated that Schindler "had gone to Poland with the advancing German troops."[1]

This explanation is more probable than the idea that Oskar did not arrive in Kraków until the third week of October. He already had an apartment in Poland's ancient capital by this time, a sign that he was already familiar with the intricacies of the new German administrative system there. Then what did happen to bring Oskar to Kraków on October 17?

More than likely, it was the date of his permanent formal transfer to Abwehr headquarters in the new capital of the General Government. Traveling with him was another Abwehr agent, Josef "Sepp" Aue. Indications are that Schindler and Aue were sent to Kraków to open businesses that would serve as Abwehr fronts. We do not know whether the two men were close friends or not, but they shared accommodations in Poland for the next few months.[2]

Keneally and O'Neil both claim that Oskar already had possession of the luxurious apartment at Straszewskiego 7/2 made famous in the film *Schindler's List*. Today, the original top-floor apartment, with its wonderful balcony view of Wawel Castle and the small Planty Park across the street, is still as elegant as it was when Oskar lived there. But this was probably not his first apartment in Kraków. Though there is no question that Oskar ultimately lived at Straszewskiego 7/2, Polish court records in Kraków dealing with the lease of his first factory there in early 1940 and his signed sworn statement for the Gestapo in Kraków on August 22, 1940, about the robbery in Mährisch Ostrau the previous summer, listed two addresses. The first was on busy Krasińskiego Zygmunta, 24; the second was Fenna Serena Gasse 14/8. This seems logical because it is doubtful that Oskar had the means to live in the grand style that later became his hallmark. When he moved to Kraków in the fall of 1939, he was still an Abwehr officer searching for a front and a new career. And remember, he still maintained a home at Parkstraße 25 in Mährisch Ostrau for Emilie. His move from Krasińskiego Zygmunta to the quieter Fenna Serena Gasse, on the edge of Stare Miasto, and finally to the exquisite apartment on Straszewskiego, reflects his own success as a businessman in Kraków.[3]

Nonetheless, Oskar did not live a spartan life in his new apartment on Fenna Serena Gasse 14/8. Leopold "Poldek" Pfefferberg-Page, a *Schindlerjude* perhaps more important than anyone else in ultimately bringing Schindler's story to the world, first met Oskar at the apartment of Poldek's mother, Mila Pfefferberg-Page, in the fall of 1939. Page, who died in the spring of 2001, was born in Kraków on March 20, 1913. He attended the prestigious Jagiellonian University, no small feat, given the growing spirit of anti-Semitism in Poland's universities and the calls for restrictions on Jewish enrollment. A year after Poldek earned his master's degree in 1936, some Polish universities adopted a "seating ghetto" policy that required Jewish students to sit in segregated parts of classrooms. Yet for anyone who knew the feisty Poldek Pfefferberg-Page, the restrictions and taunts that he met as a university student only stiffened his resolve to complete his education.[4]

After graduation, Poldek taught physical education in a Jewish gymnasium (college preparatory high school) until the war broke out in 1939. Whenever I mentioned certain Schindler Jews during the few conversations we had, he would remind me that this or that person had once been one of his students. He served as a lieutenant in the Polish army, probably with the Eleventh Infantry Division, which retreated to Przemyśl, a medieval fortress town on the Polish-Soviet Ukrainian border, after its defeat at the hands of the German Fourteenth Army near the San River on September 10–12. Three days later, after a fierce defense by the city's Polish troops, Przemyśl fell to the Germans. Poldek, who was wounded in the San River battle, recovered in the military hospital in Przemyśl until he was captured by the Germans. While there, he worked for the Poles and then the Germans as a hospital orderly. German hospital authorities gave him a pass that allowed him to travel with ambulance crews working in the city.[5]

He took advantage of the pass while in transit from Przemyśl to the Greater Reich. One night, he was on a POW train for captured Polish officers that stopped in Kraków. The Polish officers were taken off of one train, Poldek among them, to wait for a new one. An hour or two before dawn, the bold Poldek approached the sleepy, lone German soldier guarding the several hundred officers in the first class waiting room in one of Kraków's railway stations and showed him the military ambulance pass that had allowed him to move freely throughout Przemyśl. Poldek fluttered the impressive-looking multi-stamped document in front of the soldier's face and explained in German the rights of movement afforded him in the document. The flabbergasted guard nodded his head in approval as Poldek walked out the door of the waiting room and into the dark streets of his beloved Kraków.[6]

Schindler, whom Pfefferberg-Page would later call his closest friend, first met Poldek in less than auspicious conditions. In fact, Page intended to kill the unknown German during their first encounter. After his escape, Poldek blended in with the hundreds of other Polish officers still moving freely throughout Kraków because the Germans had not had time to process them. As an escaped POW, Poldek hid out with friends, visiting his parents only under the most secretive conditions. According to Thomas Keneally, who worked closely with Page when he wrote *Schindler's List,* said that Page felt so comfortable in Kraków in the early months of the German occupation that he was able to return to his teaching job.[7]

If he did, the window of opportunity was narrow. The war broke out on the same day that many Jewish schools throughout Poland were about to open. Some state-run Jewish schools tried to reopen at the end of September, though official permission was not granted until October 8, when military authorities agreed that all schools in operation before the war could begin the fall term. When the General Government came into existence, Nazi officials ordered all Jewish schools closed. The doors of the last Jewish school in Poland were shut on December 4, 1939. Jewish students and teachers were also forbidden to attend or teach in the limited number of non-Jewish schools now allowed to operate in the General Government. Though German policy towards Polish education would change over the next few years, Frank and Himmler both thought the schools that provided Poles with the necessary skills to serve the economic needs of the Greater Reich should remain open. Elementary and vocational schools were allowed limited classes, but universities and gymnasia, traditionally centers of intellectual enlightenment and bastions of Polish culture, were closed.[8]

Poldek Page had been working with his mother's interior decorating business and first met Oskar Schindler at his mother's apartment on ul. (*ulica;* street) Grodzka 48. Grodzka is one of the main streets running just to the north of Wawel Castle to the center of Stare Miasto, the elegant Rynek Krakowski (Kraków Market Square). The Pfefferberg apartment was on what remains one of the most historic and beautiful streets in Kraków. Though many of Kraków's Jews lived in the nearby old Jewish quarter, Kazimierz, there were others, particularly more secular Jewish families who were later saved by Oskar Schindler such as the Pfefferbergs and the Müllers, who lived in other parts of Kraków.

From Poldek's initial perspective, Oskar Schindler symbolized all that was evil about Poland's German occupiers. But when Schindler knocked on Mina Pfefferberg's apartment door in November 1939, Poldek's initial fear was arrest by the Gestapo as an escaped POW. The ever cautious Poldek went to the kitchen door, one of two hallway entrance ways into the Pfefferberg apartment, and peered out. He immediately thought it was the Gestapo because the tall, blondish, well-dressed German was wearing a Nazi Party badge on his lapel. The Gestapo was responsible for threats to internal state security. Now that the military had relinquished control over Kraków, the Gestapo was responsible for arresting so-called enemies of the state. As a Jew and an escaped POW, Poldek qualified. For the former high school teacher and Polish officer, this meant life, and possibly death, in a concentration camp if arrested. For his parents, it could also mean the loss of their home and personal possessions.[9]

Consequently, Leopold Page had a lot to fear when he saw Oskar Schindler at the front door of his mother's apartment. Mina was terrified, and Poldek hid in the kitchen when she went to the door. Ideally, he would try to escape; but, if necessary, he was prepared to shoot Schindler with the .22 pistol he kept hidden in his parent's apartment. When Mina opened the door, Oskar saw the terror on her face and quickly reassured her: "Don't worry," he said, "I'm not here to arrest anybody, I am here to make business with you because I took an apartment, a Jewish apartment, and I pay money to this Jewish fellow, and he said that you were in interior decorating, and he was decorating his apartment." Poldek, who by this time was standing behind the double doors separating the dining room from the living room, was relieved. As Schindler struggled to speak with Mrs. Pfefferberg in broken Polish, Poldek came through the door and interpreted for them. Though Oskar would later become fluent in Polish, it is doubtful that he knew very much in 1939. But Czechs and Poles can understand each other if they converse in their separate languages. My Polish research assistant, Konstancja Szymura, and I had this experience in the summer of 2000 when we were looking for Emilie Schindler's remote Bohemian village. As we stopped frequently to ask directions, we spoke in Polish and received directions in Czech.[10]

Leopold Page would later say that he felt an immediate closeness to Oskar Schindler, and by the end of their first meeting they had become friends. Oskar was so reassuring that Mina Pfefferberg agreed to decorate his new apartment. Oskar then asked Poldek whether he would find him some black market items for his new apartment as well as other black market goods. Little did Schindler know how well connected Leopold Page was to the thriving black market in Kraków. Almost from the moment he escaped German military detention, Poldek was active in the black market jewel trade. Poles, Jews and non-Jews alike, but particularly Jews, were desperate for food, which the Germans carefully restricted.[11]

When World War II broke out, the Germans initiated a Reich-wide rationing system based on race. Hitler was determined that the German people would not suffer the same economic hardships they had endured during World War I, so the real burden of rationing fell on the shoulders of the occupied peoples, particularly the Jews. Ration books were distributed to Kraków's Jews through the Temporary Jewish Religious Community and later the *Judenrat* (Jewish Council). In fact, food and the illnesses that came from lack of it became the largest initial problem faced by the *Judenräte* throughout German-occupied Poland.[12]

The food shortages faced by Kraków's Jewish community were similar to those suffered by Jews in other parts of Poland during World War II. In 1939, the *Stadtkommissar* (city commissioner) in Łódź, for example, decreed that Jews were supposed to receive 25 percent of the city's food allocations. In reality, Jews got much less because of problems with food distribution and deliberate German efforts to starve them. By the end of 1940, Warsaw's Jews were allotted only 3,250 grams of bread apiece; the city's Aryans received 6,100 grams. Warsaw's Jews also got no sugar, flour, meat, eggs, or potatoes, which were reserved for non-Jews. The Polish historian Eugeniusz Duraczyński estimated that the average daily food allotment for residents in Warsaw in 1941 was 2,613 calories for Germans, 669 calories for Poles, and 184 calories for Jews. Because of the underground economy, some Poles were able to buy food to increase their daily caloric intake by 1,000 to 1,500 calories.[13]

Underground activity was much more difficult for the General Government's impoverished Jewish population, particularly after the creation of the ghetto system, which severely restricted their ability to buy food on the black market. The *Judenräte* throughout the General Government were able to set up food acquisition, production, and distribution systems, but they were barely able to raise Jewish caloric intake slightly above the 1,000 calories deemed necessary to sustain life over a long period. The situation worsened after Hans Frank decided in the fall of 1942 to stop supplying food to the 1.2 million Jews in the General Government not involved in jobs considered vital to the German economy. Starvation had now become an active German tool of mass death for Jews.[14]

When Oskar Schindler first talked to Page about helping him learn the Kraków black market system, he was thinking less about basic foodstuffs than the elegant life he hoped to live as a prosperous businessman and sometime Abwehr agent. One of the things that interested Schindler during his first meeting with Poldek was the fine blue silk shirt that the former Polish officer was wearing. Oskar asked him whether he could purchase more and how much they would cost. Though Poldek could buy them for Zł 5 ($1.56) apiece, he told Schindler that one shirt would cost him Zł 25 ($7.81). He added that he would need Oskar's shirt size and an advance payment. Oskar gave

Poldek RM 200 ($8.00). It was enough for Page to buy eighty shirts for Schindler, and the overly generous Oskar knew this. The following week, Oskar received a dozen shirts from Poldek. Thus began a close friendship that was to last until Oskar's death in 1974. And though it was black marketeering that drew the two men together, there was also something else. Poldek Page and Oskar Schindler were similar in many ways. Both men were independent, self-assured, strong-minded, and intrepid individuals. These characteristics served them both well during and after the Holocaust.[15]

Page, though, had little to do with Oskar's next step in becoming a prosperous German businessman in Kraków. Though Oskar had enough ambition and guile for several men, he needed other contacts to help him open his first business in the General Government's new capital. From a distance, it would seem that not much effort was needed because Jewish properties were available to most Germans for the taking. But not in November 1939. By the time Oskar made his first visit to the Pfefferberg-Page apartment, German authorities were well on their way to depriving the city's 60,000 Jews of their rights, dignity, and property. On September 8, *SS-Brigadeführer* Bruno Streckenbach, the head of the First Operational Group of the SD and SS, ordered that all Jewish businesses were to display a Star of David on their windows by the next evening. On the same day, *SS-Oberscharführer* Paul Siebert, the head of Sipo's Jewish affairs office, appointed Dr. Marek Bieberstein, a prominent prewar Jewish community leader, as head of the Temporary Jewish Religious Community in Kraków. Ten weeks later, this organization, still under Bieberstein, was transformed into a *Judenrat*. The *Judenräte*, which were used throughout German-occupied Europe, were to act as liaisons between the Germans and a city's Jewish community and carry out the Nazi administration's orders.[16]

The first official decree of Dr. Bieberstein's administrative board came on September 21, when Bieberstein asked the city's Jews to begin working to fill in the various antiaircraft ditches throughout Kraków. This was the beginning of the German forced-labor practices that transformed the General Government's Jews into slaves of the Third Reich. Once Hans Frank was in power, he decreed that all Jews between twelve and sixty were obligated to work for a two-year term in a forced labor camp. Frank's subordinate, *SS-Gruppenführer* Otto Wächter, the governor of the Kraków district, decreed on November 18, 1939, that all Jews in his district older than twelve were required to wear a white band with a blue Star of David sewn on it. Wächter added that the white band had to be 10 cm wide and the star had to be 8 cm in diameter. The Kraków governor defined a Jew as someone "who is or was a believer in the Jewish faith" and whose mother or father "is or was a believer in the Jewish faith." This order included temporary as well as permanent Jewish residents of Kraków.[17]

The final blow to Jewish dignity and pride soon followed when a series of decrees and regulations stripped Jews of their homes, businesses, and personal property. Oskar Schindler, like many other German carpetbaggers, would benefit greatly from these developments. But Jews had already lost many of their possessions during the random military and civilian plundering during the invasion and occupation of Poland in September 1939. In November, the Germans froze all Jewish and foreign assets in banks and other financial institutions and permitted them to keep only Zł 2,000 ($625) in cash. On December 5–6, 1939, the Germans blockaded all Jewish homes in Kazimierz and other parts of Kraków and brutally confiscated everything collectively valued more than Zł 2,000 ($625) from individual Jewish residences. Several days earlier, Kraków's Jews had to report and then turn in their motor vehicles. On January 24, 1940, the city's Jews were given five weeks to register their remaining property with the German authorities. They were also forbidden to change their addresses. According to Dr. Roland Goryczko, the lawyer appointed by the Polish trade court to handle the business affairs of the bankrupt Jewish factory just leased by Oskar Schindler, the registration order marked the beginning of official German confiscation of Jewish property in the General Government.[18]

In the midst of all of this, Oskar Schindler began his inquiries about Jewish property. The logical path for him was through the office of the Main Trusteeship Office East (HTO; *Haupttreuhandstelle Ost*), created by Hermann Göring on November 1, 1939, and headed by Max Winkler, a close associate of Joseph Goebbels and Reich Commissioner of the German Film Industry. Though headquartered in Berlin, the HTO had branch offices *(Treuhandstellen)* throughout German-occupied Poland, including Kraków. Those in each of the General Government's four districts were overseen by the General Government Trustee Office (*Treuhandstelle für das General Gouvernement*). Göring's directive, later clarified in early 1940, recognized two methods of property seizure based on taking over *(Beschlagnahme)* property rights and confiscation *(Einziehung)*. According to a new directive issued by Göring on January 24, 1940, the HTO could take over or confiscate all property deemed important to the public interest. Local HTO offices would then be responsible for overseeing the stolen property and putting it in the hands of carefully selected *Treuhänder* (trustee). Polish property that was not officially registered with the Germans was considered ownerless and was subject to seizure by the HTO. Jewish property seized by the HTO, the military, or other organs of state for the benefit of the Reich was not bound by Göring's property seizure directives. For Jews, the only things exempt from seizure were personal items.[19]

When Oskar Schindler began to look for confiscated Polish property to build his new business career in the fall of 1939, the seizure of Polish property, whether it be public, private, or Jewish, was just getting under way. Jewish property was certainly being stolen in the immediate months after the German conquest by the military, the police, and a few civilians. On September 29, for example, the military issued a decree allowing for the immediate seizure of property that was improperly managed or that belonged to absentee owners, an action that became a pretext for the confiscation of much Jewish property. Oskar, though, despite his Abwehr ties, had to follow a more formal, legalistic route to acquire property in Kraków at this time.[20]

Jewish property was still hard to acquire in such situations because Jews in the General Government were not required to register their property with the HTO until late January 1940. And it was not until September 17, 1940, that Göring issued a new directive ordering immediate confiscation of all Jewish property in Poland with the exception of personal belongings and RM 1,000 ($400) in cash. These regulations were enforced unevenly throughout German-occupied Poland. In Kraków, for example, the new rule was applied only to homes that brought in rent of more than Zł 500 ($156.25) a month. Yet most of the private property seized in Poland by the Reich was Jewish-owned. The only exception was state-owned Polish property, which Frank declared in the fall of 1940 was now the property of the General Government. At the end of 1941, Germans only owned 157 private businesses out of 2,973 in Kraków. Non-Jewish Poles owned the rest.[21]

Initially, some effort was made to compensate Jews for their extensive property losses. Early in the occupation, the Germans seemed interested only in larger Jewish businesses and homes, though, over time, the Jews in the General Government lost everything. In Kraków, for example, the HTO agreed to pay former apartment house owners 75 percent of the property's value; by the summer of 1940, the HTO reduced these payments to 50 percent. Jews who had money in the state-owned Polish Post State Savings Bank *(Pocztowa Kasa Oszczędności)* were allowed to take out only 10 percent of their savings, and their total withdrawals from their individual accounts could be no more that Zł 1,000 ($312.50). Those who had money in the Jewish credit unions after November 18, 1940, lost everything because they were liquidated on this date.[22]

On February 18, 1941, the General Government's Trustee Office laid out specific guidelines for compensating former Jewish property owners. The first criteria for payment was that the former Jewish owner could not support himself from other sources of income. Second, if compensation was given, it could be no greater than a quarter of the former property owner's net income. Moreover, German compensation could not exceed Zł 250 ($78) a month. Given that it required about Zł 1,300 ($406.25) a month in 1941 to meet the basic cost of living expenses in the General Government, these limits were another indication of German efforts to rid themselves of the Jewish population well before the implementation of the Final Solution. A third HTO criteria stipulated that compensation given could not affect the value of the seized property. Finally, and this was the most damaging to Jewish hopes of compensation, the HTO directive stated that Jewish property seized for the benefit of the Reich was not subject to compensation. Once the property was taken over, the new German owner was not obligated to pay any of the confiscated property's prewar debts to Polish creditors. At the same time, the new owners had the right to demand payments from Poles for debts owed the former owners. Oskar Schindler would benefit from these German debt regulations.[23]

Some of the worst initial losses suffered by Polish Jews came in the midst of random property seizures by the Wehrmacht and the police forces in the early months of the war. Göring and Himmler both claimed extensive authority to seize property for the good of the Reich, which was then not subject to compensation consideration. Winkler, who technically answered to Göring, claimed the same rights for the HTO. The military and the police, and occasionally bold civilians, had no qualms about raiding a Jewish business, factory, or home and stealing everything inside. Stella Müller-Madej, a *Schindlerjude*, tells one such story in her memoirs. Early one November morning in 1939, three SS men entered her family's spacious apartment on fashionable ul. Szymanowskego Karola. Like the Pfefferbergs, the Müllers were secular Jews who chose to live in a predominantly Polish neighborhood. At first, the Germans thought they had the wrong apartment because of its elegance and Stella's mother, Bertha, a

Jew of German descent with blond hair and green eyes who spoke impeccable German. Bertha politely informed the SS officer that she was Jewish. After a moment of hesitation, the SS officer informed Bertha that her family had half an hour to vacate the apartment. They would not be allowed to take anything with them. The officer assured the Müllers that they would receive a detailed inventory of everything in the apartment. The family quickly dressed and added extra layers of clothes. Bertha was also able to sneak a few items from her jewelry box, though she was sure the Germans would keep their word about a receipt for the confiscated items. But when they walked out the door, they lost everything. Such tragic stories were repeated time and again throughout German-occupied Poland during the first years of the war.[24]

These developments had a direct impact on Oskar Schindler's ability to acquire property in the early months after the outbreak of World War II. The extensive Trustee offices *(Treuhandstellen)* were just being set up as he was looking for a cheap piece of property in Kraków. Moreover, Oskar was in a hurry to begin his new business, whether it be for profit or as an Abwehr front. Even if he was receiving some of his startup money from Abwehr, he still did not have unlimited funds. And he now had two homes, a wife, and several mistresses to take care of. Most important, he needed good business advice. If his wartime and postwar experiences are any indication, Oskar Schindler was not much of a businessman. He was extremely impatient, particularly when it came to details, and did not handle money well. He would need someone to help him find an appropriate business to invest in and someone to run it. Perhaps Steven Spielberg best captured the essence of all of this in the fictitious scene in *Schindler's List* that had Liam Neeson (Schindler) and Ben Kingsley (Itzhak Stern) together in an office. Neeson was trying to find out whether Kingsley knew of any Jewish businessmen willing to put up funds to help him open a factory. In return for their investment, Neeson explained, they would receive manufactured goods to trade on the black market. When Kingsley asked what Neeson would bring to the bargain, he responded, "I would see that it had a certain panache. That's what I'm good at, not the work, not the work. Presentation."[25]

Schindler, Stern, and Bankier

Josef "Sepp" Aue told the Czech secret police after World War II that Oskar Schindler was the principal figure involved in helping him acquire a business in Kraków during the early months of the war. According to Aue, all this was linked to the activities of two Abwehr operatives in Kraków at the time, Walter Muschka and Oskar Schmidt, who went by the cover name of Ervin Kobiela. Aue claimed that Muschka was head of an office in Kraków that oversaw the confiscation of Jewish property. Robin O'Neil claims that Muschka was head of the General Government's Trustee Office in Kraków, though this office did not exist at the time. More than likely, Muschka oversaw a Wehrmacht *Wirtschaftsstelle* that handled Jewish property confiscations. According to Aue, Abwehr's office in Kraków was headed by *SS-Sturmbannführer* Otto Kipka. *SS-Hauptsturmführer* Rolf Czurda served as his deputy. This link between Abwehr and the SS was not as strange as it seemed. Ties between both organizations had grown closer in the days leading up to the war and would become even closer. They had both worked together on the invasion of Poland, and some Abwehr officers in Poland were drawn from SS units. Abwehr officers had trained members of the SS Standby Troops (VT; *Verfügungstruppen*), the forerunner of the Waffen SS (Armed SS), in security and counterespionage matters, and members of Himmler's newly created super police organization, the RSHA, taught Abwehr officers police tactics. At a distance, ties between Abwehr and the Gestapo, an arm of RSHA, were so close that some anti-Nazis thought that Abwehr was an extension of the Gestapo. The special relationship between Abwehr and various branches of RSHA, which would wane during the war, would often work in Oskar Schindler's favor.[26]

Certainly Schindler and Aue's ties to Abwehr helped them acquire property in Poland. When they arrived together in Poland in late September 1939, Oskar immediately took Sepp to meet with Muschka and Kobiela. Kobiela took Aue aside and asked him what type of business he wanted. Sepp replied that it did not really matter to him. Kobiela suggested that he might be interested in a Jewish firm, J. L. Buchheister & Co., at 15 Stradom Street. When Aue agreed, both men went to the shop, where Kobiela introduced himself as a clerk for the Wehrmacht's *Wirtschaftsstelle* (Economic Planning Office). Kobiela demanded that the owner give him the contents of his cash register as well as a detailed inventory of all of his shop's goods and other possessions. The Abwehr agent then told Mr. Buchheister that when he had completed the inventory, he should leave the shop and never return. The shop was now controlled by Josef "Sepp" Aue. He said that when he took it over it had on hand about Zł 650,000 ($203,125) in textiles and Zł 500 ($156.25) in cash. Like Schindler, Aue formally took control of this company in early 1940 after official confiscation regulations were put in place.[27] Though Aue told the Czech secret police that he stopped working for Abwehr when he came to Kraków, his asking known Abwehr operatives to help him find a factory negates this claim. Though he might not have formally been working for Abwehr, he could never escape obligations to Canaris's organization, at least while he remained in Kraków. In fact, he was part of a larger Sudeten-German Abwehr network that was actively involved in property acquisitions in the General Government's capital in the early months of the war. Muschka and Korbiel, for example, not only helped Schindler and Aue acquire property but also helped Oskar's right-hand man in Ostrava, František Turek, acquire a business there.[28]

Thomas Keneally tells a different story about Aue and Schindler's relationship, which he based on interviews with Jewish survivors. The Czech secret police files and Schindler's own comments about this were not available to the Australian novelist when he did his research for *Schindler's List* in the early 1980s. According to Keneally, Aue and Schindler first met at a party in late October 1939 at the apartment of one of Schindler's girlfriends, a Sudeten German *Treuhander* named Ingrid. Sepp Aue invited Oskar to drop by his office the next day. It was during this meeting that Schindler was supposed to have first met Itzhak Stern. Stern, at home with the flu, had been called to the office by Aue to check into a payment discrepancy involving two German soldiers and one of the company's Jewish bookkeepers. While Stern was trying to resolve this matter, Aue introduced him to Schindler, a meeting that would begin a lifelong friendship. According to Keneally, though Stern spent only a few minutes with Oskar, he was able to review the business records of the Polish Jewish firm, Rekord, Ltd., that Schindler proposed to take over. Stern told Oskar that he was familiar with this company and that his brother, Natan, had worked for one of Rekord's Swiss creditors. He explained that Rekord, which had made enamelware, had been badly managed and had gone bankrupt. After glancing at Rekord's books for three minutes, Stern told Oskar that it was a good business, particularly with military contracts looming on the horizon. He added that Rekord had been grossing more than Zł 0.5 million ($94,340) a year and that new equipment could easily be acquired to expand its production. Stern went on to tell Schindler that the best way to acquire Rekord was through the Polish Trade Court instead of the *Treuhandstelle*. What Schindler could do, suggested Stern, was lease Rekord with the option later to buy it outright.

"As a *Treuhänder*," Stern noted, "only a supervisor, you were completely under the control of the Economics Ministry." According to Keneally, the first meeting between Schindler and Stern ended with a modest philosophical discussion on religion. Stern's last comment was a quote from the Talmud: "He who saves the life of one man saves the world." Keneally implied that Oskar seemed to agree with this thought, and has Stern saying that "it was at this moment that he . . . dropped the right seed in the furrow." This is the beginning of the story that it was Stern who gave Oskar Schindler the timely business advice he needed to acquire Rekord, Ltd., and planted the seed that later led to Schindler's decision to hire and save Jewish workers.[29]

Stern tells a somewhat different story. In fact, what we know about the early phase of Stern's relationship with Oskar comes from the detailed testimony Stern gave to Dr. Kurt Jakob Ball-Kaduri, who worked for Yad Vashem in Jerusalem, in late 1956, and the testimony he provided Martin Gosch and Howard Koch in 1964. Both men were preparing a film script for a movie on Oskar Schindler. Over the next year, Stern supplied Dr. Ball-Kaduri with supplemental details and documents. The Yad Vashem archivist was simultaneously corresponding with Oskar Schindler in Buenos Aires. With the exception of Schindler's own postwar accounts, Stern's lengthy testimony in German and his remarks to Gosch and Koch are some of the most important accounts we have of Oskar's wartime activities. Even before Dr. Ball-Kaduri got to know Stern and Schindler, he had already gained a reputation for accuracy. Prosecutors in the 1961–1962 trial of Adolf Eichmann used testimony collected by Dr. Ball-Kaduri. During the trial, State Attorney Ya'acov Bar-Or noted that Dr. Ball-Kaduri, a specialist in the history of Central European Jews, began to record their testimonies after the end of the Holocaust. When Yad Vashem (Yad Vashem Holocaust Martyrs' and Heroes' Remembrance Authority) came into existence in 1953, Dr. Ball-Kaduri volunteered to continue his work for the new Israeli Holocaust memorial institution. Bar-Or told the Eichmann court that Dr. Ball-Kaduri's recorded testimonies "constitute today the only record and the only proof about some most important events."[30]

According to Stern, his first meeting with Oskar Schindler took place on November 18 or 19, 1939, not late October. At the time, Stern was at home, ill and suffering a high fever. Aue, who had just taken over Buchheister, called Stern into the office to resolve a situation involving one of the Jewish clerks accused of theft. The day before, two German soldiers had walked into Aue's new shop and bought several bolts of cloth worth Zł 60 ($18.75) with an outdated 1858 German bill and a 1914 German occupation note. The morning after the sale, Buchheister's German bookkeeper saw the bills in the cash register and accused the Jewish clerk of stealing Zł 60 and replacing the money with outdated German bills. Stern listened to the story and realized that if he did not resolve it quickly, the Jewish clerk could be shot. Stern told Aue: "Well, this is a piece of false money—we don't need this—and I forgot about it anyway, that we had charged this up to a matter of profit and loss." Stern then took the two bills and threw them into a nearby stove. Aue really liked the way that Stern handled the matter and told him that he wanted to share something confidential. Stern assured Aue that anything he told him in confidence would remain their mutual secret. Aue then introduced Stern to Oskar Schindler.[31]

Schindler was interested in acquiring a business and wanted his advice, according to Stern. At this point, Oskar took a financial balance statement out of his pocket about a company called Rekord, Ltd. and wanted to know Stern's opinion about its financial health. Stern's brother, an attorney, had represented a Swiss company that was suing Rekord, Ltd. and knew a great deal about its economic history. Stern recommended that Oskar rent or purchase a business and not take one over as a trustee. From Stern's perspective, the owner of a factory "was relatively free in the employment of Jews" and would be more personally connected to the factory than a trustee, who would operate the factory for the Reich. Stern said that at one point in their conversation, he forgot he was talking to a German; he told Schindler that the Talmud said that if one man could save another, it was like saving the whole world. Schindler was amazed that Stern knew what he did about Rekord, Ltd. and asked him how a Jew was privy to such information. The day before, Aue had asked Stern to analyze and explain to him a recent set of regulations from Berlin on labor and related costs in Poland. This was how Stern had learned so much about the advantages of renting or buying property as opposed to taking it over as a trustee. Stern knew this was highly sensitive information but told Oskar that it had been readily available in many German newspapers. Oskar looked at Stern and said, "Don't tell me this. I know better than that." He then affectionately patted Stern on the back as they walked into Aue's office to discuss politics and philosophy.[32]

This is all that Stern had to say about his first meeting with Oskar. The second meeting took place on December 4; this is when Oskar obliquely warned him of the forthcoming German raid on Jewish homes: "Tomorrow you'll see a big thing, and you'll find out what the Germans can do." Oskar was trying to tell Stern of a deadly German *Aktion*, though Stern and his friends, who were suspicious of Schindler, refused to heed his warning. Afterwards, Stern regretted his understandable hesitancy to believe anything a German told him and became more trusting of Schindler.[33]

The difference between Stern's and Keneally's accounts of how Schindler met Stern are nothing compared to Steven Spielberg's decision to cast Itzhak Stern as Schindler's Jewish alter ego in *Schindler's List*. Spielberg, or more appropriately his final scriptwriter, Steven Zaillian, intended Stern to be Schindler's subconscious, a composite figure encompassing three people: Abraham Bankier, Mietek Pemper, and Stern. Mietek Pemper, though, told me that Steven Spielberg told him during the filming of *Schindler's List* in Kraków in 1993 that Itzhak Stern was a composite of Stern and Pemper. Spielberg said nothing to him about Abraham Bankier. This decision made for good cinema, but it was bad history. Bankier was the financial genius who ran Schindler's factory in Kraków. Stern himself readily admitted to Dr. Ball-Kaduri that "he never worked for Schindler in Kraków, and he also at no time was living in the Jewish camp near the Schindler factory." Instead, Stern continued to work for J. L. Buchheister & Co., and later for the Progress metalworking factory, first in Kraków and later in the Płaszów concentration camp. Both were run by a trustee, Herr Unkelbach, whose Progress factory was shut down by Amon Göth, the commandant at Płaszów, because Unkelbach had been too lenient towards his Jewish workers. Stern then went to work for Göth in the camp's administrative offices.[34]

So if Stern did not work closely with Schindler from 1939 to 1944, what was the reason for his relationship with the Sudeten German businessman? Moreover, why was he given so much more prominence in Keneally's novel and Spielberg's film than equally important figures such as Pemper and Bankier? Certainly Schindler thought highly of Stern and maintained contacts with him throughout the war. In a letter to Dr. Ball-Kaduri on September 9, 1956, Oskar wrote: "Seldom in my life have I encountered people of his standard. His high ethical values, his fearless willingness to help, his sacrificial efforts for his brothers combined with modesty in his own life have repeatedly caused my great admiration and respect. Mr. Isaak Stern has been a substantial part of the reason why my rescue efforts were successful." But what was the nature of their relationship? It had little to do with the running of Schindler's Emalia factory because Bankier did that brilliantly. More than likely, it had to do with Stern's contacts in Göth's office and his invaluable ties to the Kraków Jewish community's leadership.[35]

As we shall see later, in 1943 Oskar Schindler became a courier and go-between for the Jewish Agency for Palestine, which was trying to filter money into Poland to help Jews and determine the depth of Germany's deadly policies towards Jews there. Soon after the war broke out, Stern went to work for the Society for the Protection of Health (TOZ; *Towarzystwo Ochrony Zdrowia)*, which was created and funded by the American Jewish Joint Distribution Committee (the Joint; AJJDC). Stern headed TOZ operations in Kraków and was responsible for the health of Jews in the city. TOZ operated different types of medical facilities and, as long as the Germans permitted it, gave training courses for nursing personnel. When necessary, TOZ opened soup kitchens for orphaned children. Once sent to Płaszów, Stern became an important contact for Schindler and the Jewish Agency. Stern supplied Schindler with information about conditions in the camp, and Schindler supplied him with funds from the Jewish Agency to help the Jewish prisoners there.[36]

Though Keneally said that Stern had the manners of a Talmudic scholar and an East European intellectual, his relationship with Schindler had more to do with business and survival than with intellectual matters. In some ways, Schindler and Stern were quite different, though they also had things in common. What drew the two men together was opportunity. Schindler was an impatient and impulsive personality; Stern was thoughtful and calm. Both men exuded a certain strength. And in their own ways, Schindler and Stern were brave men. Jews who worked for Amon Göth lived in constant fear for their lives. Stern was no exception. Yet he prided himself on his calm nature, particularly when he dealt with Germans. Both men also came from business families. Stern's father, Menachem, was a successful bookkeeper. To prepare himself to follow his father, Stern studied trade science in Vienna and Kraków before he joined J. L. Buchmeister. Though he was only nine years older than Oskar, Stern was more of a father figure to Schindler than an elder brother. But it would be wrong to depict him as Oskar's friend, at least during the war. Friendship requires a level of personal contact that was not permitted between Germans and Jews during the Holocaust. Moreover, Oskar Schindler was still a German and Jews who wished to survive had to maintain a distance from all Germans.

Numerous *Schindlerjuden* have told me that despite what Oskar Schindler did for them, during the war they were distrustful of him because he was a German. Not until the war ended did they feel comfortable with a more trusting relationship with their "savior."[37]

Yet one other Jew was equally or more important to Oskar Schindler during the war: Abraham Bankier. After Oskar leased Emalia, his friends kidded him about his acquisition. They said that "all his fortune consisted of was a Jew by the name of Bankier and ten enamel pot covers." Janka Olszewska, one of Oskar's closest Polish friends and who still lives in Kraków, said that Emalia was run by Schindler and Bankier. She added that together they looked like the "comic heroes of some silent movie." To Janka, they looked like Mutt and Jeff, "Bankier, short and fat, and Schindler tall and slim." Janka's statement about Bankier's importance to Schindler and Emalia is supported by numerous statements by Schindler and other Jews such as Sol Urbach, who worked for Oskar in Kraków and Brünnlitz and had access to his office complexes. According to Urbach, Bankier had an office behind Schindler's at Emalia. Schindler's office was decorated with the usual Nazi art and photos for his German clients, but Bankier received Polish businessmen in his plain rear office.[38]

Victor Dortheimer, one of the few Schindler Jews who worked for Oskar at Emalia and Brünnlitz, confirmed the importance of Bankier to Schindler's operations in Kraków. Dortheimer was never consulted by Keneally or Spielberg even though he considered himself Schindler's personal master painter: "I had a personal relationship with the Director [Schindler]. All the time I was in the Emalia factory, Stern was never seen. Bankier was the boss, he had his own office and never wore the 'star.'"[39] Dortheimer later told two German reporters that it was Bankier who was responsible for bringing the first Jewish workers to Emalia. Bankier had a special pass that let him come and go from the ghetto to the factory. At first, he took a group of twenty Jewish workers from the ghetto to the factory and back each day; in fact, he was the one principally responsible for bringing many of the Jews to Emalia, thus saving their lives.[40]

Bankier's genius centered around his black market skills, which provided Schindler with substantial profits and the money he used to help his Jewish workers. Bankier obtained quantities of metal beyond the factory's quota to make extra pots and pans, which he then used to purchase goods on the black market. Bankier was always the one blamed for black market deals that went bad. He risked his life, Dortheimer explained, time and again, but Schindler remained unmolested. Because of this, Bankier became indispensable to Oskar Schindler. When Dortheimer attended the London premiere of *Schindler's List*, he spotted Steven Spielberg. As Spielberg's body guards pushed him away, Dortheimer shouted to Spielberg, "It's all wrong." Later, he told two German reporters: "Schindler was our savior. But in the Emalia factory Bankier was the key figure. Without Bankier there would have been no Schindler."[41]

Bankier traveled frequently with Oskar around Kraków. Oskar thought so highly of Bankier that he told Jewish Agency representatives in Budapest in November 1943 that because Bankier had "a clear overview of the whole business," he could, "without worrying, go away for four weeks, and know that he [would] faithfully substitute" for him.[42] Bankier enjoyed such a position of privilege that Schindler got into trouble for it. One day after the opening of the ghetto in the early spring of 1941, *SS-Hauptscharführer* Wilhelm Kunde and *SS-Oberscharführer* Hermann Hubert Heinrich, whom Schindler described as two of the most feared SS men in the ghetto, met with Oskar at Emalia. They said they had just learned from the Gestapo about Bankier's privileged position in the factory. What followed was a detailed SS investigation of the operation at Emalia, which was assisted by a representative from the Trustee Office. Evidently they were looking for a legal violation so they could close the factory and turn it over to the Trustee Office. They found nothing and left Oskar and Bankier alone, at least for a while. Schindler later found out that a former disgruntled employee, Natan Wurzel, had told another ghetto resident, Mr. Spitz, about Bankier's special position at Emalia. Spitz in turn told Kunde and Heinrich.[43]

It is no accident, then, that Oskar first thanked Bankier and then Stern in his July 1945 financial report about his wartime activities. Over the years, Oskar developed a deep affection for Bankier. In a letter to Stern in the fall of 1956, Oskar included some pictures from the "Old Time." One of them was of Oskar and Bankier, whom Oskar affectionately called "Boguslav." The photo, he wrote, "awakens many memories in me."[44] Unknown to Oskar, his beloved loyal Bankier had recently died in Vienna. For daily activities, then, Bankier was much more important to Oskar than Stern. Almost 80 percent of Oskar's business dealings were on the black market and it was Bankier who did most of the trading. Bankier's skills as a businessman and a black marketeer provided Oskar Schindler with the vast resources he needed to hire, house, feed, transfer, and save hundreds of Jewish workers.

Schindler, Emalia, and the Wurzel-Wiener Controversy

The reason that Bankier became so close to Oskar was through his earlier ties with Rekord, Ltd. Given the nature of the German occupation,
one would presume that Oskar's takeover of a former Jewish business
would have been easy. In many ways, it was, though after the war it
would lead to a series of charges so serious that some questions were
raised in Israel in 1962 about whether Oskar Schindler should be named
a Righteous Gentile. Even if these charges had not been made, broader
ones arose in the 1980s and 1990s after the appearance of Keneally's
novel and Spielberg's film. They centered around the idea that, despite his
motivations, Schindler was no better than a thief when he acquired Jewish property in German-occupied Poland. At a distance, this was a general charge that could be made against any German who took over Jewish property in German-occupied Poland. But for Oskar Schindler, the
charge was more personal because one of the two Jews who waged a
campaign against Schindler in the courts and media of Argentina and Israel was a *Schindlerjude.*

The reason so little has been written about these charges is that until recently not much information was available and most of them were in Hebrew at Yad Vashem. Thomas Keneally alluded to the controversy in his
novel but did not deal with it in detail. Schindler's defense of his actions
can be found in the recently discovered Schindler *Koffer* (suitcase) files
now at Yad Vashem. But to get the full story behind Schindler's acquisition
of the former Polish Jewish factory, *Pierwsza Małopolska Fabryka Naczyń
Emaliowanych i Wyrobów Blaszanych "Rekord," Spółka, z ograniczoną
odpowiedzialnością w Krakowie* (First Little Polish Limited Liability Factory of Enamel Vessels and Tinware, Record, Limited Liability Company
in Kraków), one must look also at the extensive Polish Okręgowy (Trade)
court records in Kraków on this subject.[45] Also revealing is the extensive
collection of documents supplied by Schindler to West German officials in
the 1950s and 1960s in his efforts to qualify for *Lastenausgleich* (equalization of burdens) compensation for his lost factories in Kraków and
Brünnlitz. Collectively, these files detail the steps that Oskar Schindler took
first to lease and then to buy the bankrupt Jewish factory. His decision to
allow Abraham Bankier full control of his factory's daily affairs is linked
to all this. The Polish court records also carefully document efforts by the
principal figure involved in the postwar controversy, Natan Wurzel, to be
awarded compensation for what he felt was stolen property.

Rekord, Ltd. was the joint endeavor of three Jewish businessmen in Kraków, Michał Gutman, Wolf Luzer Glajtman, and Izrael Kohn, who bought a small enamelware factory built in 1935. These men were not on the famous "Schindler's List" in the fall of 1944. They filed papers for the incorporation of their enamel and tinware factory on March 17, 1937, in Kraków. Rekord, Ltd. was set up with Zł 100,000 ($18,939) in capital. Each of the new owners received shares in Rekord Ltd., each share being worth Zł 500. Wolf Glajtman contributed Zł 50,000 ($9,470) for a hundred shares, and Luzer and Kohn Zł 25,000 ($4,735) for fifty shares apiece.[46]

In the fall of 1937, a new partner, Herman Hirsch, bought into the firm for Zł 12,000 ($2,273) and twenty-four shares, which reduced the capital investments of Glajtman (now Zł 48,000, Kohn (Zł 20,000), and Gutman (Zł 20,000). This ownership arrangement was also expanded to include Wolf Luzer Glajtman's four brothers, Uszer, Szyj, Leibisch, and Zalka, as well as his brothers-in-law, Abraham Bankier and Abram Szydłowski. They would collectively be given sixty-six shares of Rekord, Ltd., with the stipulation that Wolf Luzer Glajtman would always keep thirty shares for himself. Herman Hirsch was also given the right to transfer his shares to his wife, Adela, or to his brother-in-law, Natan Wurzel, or his wife, Gustawa Wurzel. Hirsch also gave the Wurzels proxy rights to act in his stead on business matters.

The board of directors consisted of the owners, though only one, Bankier, who was the factory manager, could be dismissed. This arrangement would not go into effect until the end of 1938. Wolf Luzer Glajtman and Bankier had the right to sign checks and enter into business deals for the company, but Michał Gutman had to approve checks for more than Zł 2,000 ($379). A year later, a new partner was brought into the business, Hersz Szpigelman, who invested Zł 3,000 ($566) in the firm. Rekord, Ltd.'s base capitalization remained at Zł 100,000. This reduced Michał Gutman's investment in the firm to Zł 17,000 ($3,208).[47]

It would seem to be an optimum time to open a factory in Kraków—unless you were Jewish. Poland, like many of its Central and East European neighbors, had suffered terribly in the immediate years after World War I. The country's economic ills had been one of the issues that led to Marshal Józef Piłsudski's military coup in 1926. A modest economic recovery followed, but ended with the Depression in the early 1930s. A year after Piłsudski's death in 1935, government officials launched an economic recovery plan that saw industrial production increase rapidly.

It now seemed that the time was ripe for the opening of new business ventures in Poland. Unfortunately, part of the government's economic plan was the reduction of the role of Jews in the Polish economy. Prime Minister General Felicjan Sławoj Składkowski of Poland perhaps best summed up official attitudes towards the Jews' role in the Polish economy when he said in 1936 that there should be an "economic struggle [against the Jews] by all means—but without force." In reality, Poland's Jews had suffered from almost two decades of economic anti-Semitism. According to Ezra Mendelsohn, what was new was the government's support of such policies. The ongoing economic pauperization of Poland's large Jewish population now intensified with a new round of boycotts and other anti-Semitic actions.[48]

The question is what effect, if any, economic anti-Semitism had on Rekord, Ltd., which filed for bankruptcy in the summer of 1939. Polish court records reveal little about the reasons for the company's failure except to say that it was in bad financial shape. The factory was making goods for the Polish military and was operating under military mobilization orders by this time. The owners somehow thought that if they could find a way to come up with extra cash to pay their creditors, they could keep the factory running. This is what led to the controversy with Natan Wurzel.[49]

The controversy between Rekord, Ltd.'s primary owners and Natan Wurzel initially had nothing to do with Oskar Schindler. He was drawn into it after he leased the factory in the fall of 1939. Though the factory had trouble paying its bills, it had tremendous assets in its machines, buildings, and other factory property. A detailed financial report prepared on March 17, 1939, in preparation for the sale of Rekord, Ltd.'s property before its official declaration of bankruptcy showed fixed and liquid assets valued at Zł 681,559 ($128,596). The company owed almost as much to its creditors and was only able to break even because of the original Zł 100,000 investment of its owners. The value of its machinery and dies was Zł 223,309 ($42,293). It was the machinery and its ownership that was the center of the controversy between Natan Wurzel, Michał Gutman, and Wolf Luzer Glajtman. The sources on this disagreement are the letters of both sides in Polish trade court records. Each party tells his side differently, which means the truth is somewhere in between these accounts.[50]

The problem began with the sale of Rekord, Ltd.'s machines to Natan Wurzel during the company's auction of the factory's possessions. According to Gutman and Glajtman, the auction was just a formality designed to keep the factory running by selling the machines to Wurzel, who would take the machines in pawn to satisfy the money loaned to Rekord, Ltd. by his brother-in-law, Herman Hirsch. Gutman and Glajtman thought Wurzel would keep the machines in trust until the factory was back on its feet. The controversy arose when Wurzel tried to take possession of the machines and sell them to someone else. Wurzel bought the machines and dies at the auction for Zł 46,000 ($8,679), though they were worth more. As part of this deal, Gutman and Glajtman also gave Wurzel an additional Zł 10,000 ($1,887) to buy the machines for Rekord, Ltd's use. When Wurzel tried to take possession of the machines, Gutman and Glajtman stopped him. By early August, it seemed as though both sides had come to an agreement. Gutman and Glajtman found a buyer for the factory, who agreed to pay Wurzel Zł 60,000 ($11,321) for the machines and dies. When this deal fell through, the controversy reignited.[51]

By this time, both sides were using lawyers and the courts. It does not appear that Gutman and Glajtman denied Wurzel's technical ownership of the equipment, but they disagreed with him about his intent. According to them, Wurzel, who handled the negotiations for himself and his brother-in-law, Herman Hirsch, reneged on an under-the-table arrangement that would have kept the factory under Gutman, Glajtman, and Bankier's control.[52] When the war began, Wurzel's charges shifted to Oskar Schindler and centered around not only ownership of the machines and the factory but also claims that Schindler had physically abused one of Wurzel's partners, Julius Weiner.

But what about Natan Wurzel's initial dispute with Gutman and Glajtman? It remained in the Polish courts, which continued to operate after Germany conquered Poland. Only in 1942, as Oskar prepared to buy the former Rekord, Ltd. factory, was the controversy revisited by the Polish regional trade court's legal representative *(syndyk)*, attorney *(Adwokat)* Dr. Bolesław Zawisza, who oversaw affairs for the former Rekord, Ltd. In the spring of 1942, Dr. Zawisza contacted Natan Wurzel in an effort to clarify the ownership before the so-called auction of June 26, 1942, where Oskar Schindler bought the former Rekord, Ltd. At the time, Wurzel was living in the ghetto of a Polish town, Brzesko, about forty miles east of Kraków. Wurzel sent Dr. Zawisza a letter on April 20, 1942, giving his side of the controversy. Among other things, Wurzel renounced his claims to the controversial machines. Dr. Zawisza went to Brzesko on May 27,

1942, to confirm Wurzel's statement. During this meeting, Wurzel stated that he did receive money from the two factory owners not only to buy the machines in the fictitious auction but also to buy Rekord, Ltd.'s considerable holdings of enamel pots and pans. He added that Gutman and Glajtman gave him Zł 10,000 ($1,887) to do this. He borrowed the additional Zł 36,000 ($6,792) from Israel Kohn. On July 24 and August 3, 1942, Wurzel sent Dr. Zawisza two more letters in which he changed his story again and claimed that he had sold the machines on the eve of the war to an engineer named Bruliński. Wurzel added in his final letter that he had made a statement in August 1939 renouncing his claim to the machines, which he had bought for Rekord, Ltd. He explained that he decided to make this final statement because he had heard the factory was about to be sold.[53]

One can only speculate about why Wurzel decided to change his stories. By this time, Wurzel said, he had already had some pretty nasty encounters with Oskar Schindler; more important, Jews were trying to avoid drawing attention to themselves. The Final Solution was in its early stages and Brzesko's Jews were particularly vulnerable. About 4,000 Jews lived in the Brzesko ghetto, which the Germans had opened in 1940. Over the next two years, the Germans would send another 1,000–1,500 Jews there. In September 1942, 2,000 Brzesko Jews were sent to the Bełżec death camp 150 miles to the northeast. A year later, the Germans ordered the Brzesko ghetto closed and sent its remaining 3,000 Jews to their deaths in Auschwitz. In the midst of these horrors, the Germans also massacred another 500 Brzesko Jews. Today, a monument in the Jewish cemetery marks the site of their mass grave.[54]

Consequently, fear influenced Wurzel's statements in 1942. It is possible to clarify what really happened by comparing the statements of Glajtman, Gutman, Wurzel, and Schindler in the Polish court records before and during the war with their comments after the war. The information must be then linked to the next part of Natan Wurzel's claims, which centered around charges of brutality and theft against Oskar Schindler. These events, if they took place, occurred in the early months of the war when Oskar Schindler took over Rekord, Ltd.

Oskar Schindler Acquires Rekord, Ltd.

Itzhak Stern said in his Yad Vashem testimony that he did not meet Oskar Schindler until November 19 or 20, 1939. According to Polish court records, by that time Oskar had already taken possession of the factory. On November 13, the HTO's Trustees for Trade and Industry (*Treuhänder für Handel und Gewerbe*) in Kraków approved Oskar's lease of Rekord, Ltd. The next day, Schindler signed a hastily prepared handwritten document acknowledging his lease; he took the keys, but did not sign a formal lease until January 15, 1940. Dr. Roland Goryczko, who acted as the Polish trade court's legal representative, handled the legalities for the lease agreement. Oskar bought Rekord, Ltd.'s equipment for Zł 28,000 ($8,750) and paid the court a quarterly rent of Zł 2,400 ($750). This hasty arrangement was made to prevent Rekord, Ltd. from being seized by the German Trustee Office as a formerly owned Jewish factory.[55]

According to the lease agreement, Oskar Schindler was "obliged to run the factory in an efficient way according to its social and technical requirements. Also, he is supposed to use all means possible to produce enamelware vessels and hire as many workers as possible." The lease also stipulated that Oskar was to compensate his employees in a just and appropriate way. He could not change the type of goods that he produced without the permission of the trade court judge responsible for the leased factory. Oskar could also use the name of the former factory, though he decided to rename it the *Deutsche Emalwarenfabrik Oskar Schindler* (German Enamelware Factory Oskar Schindler). For convenience, Schindler and his workers referred to the renamed German factory simply as Emalia. The address of Emalia remained the same as Rekord, Ltd., ul. Lipowa 4. Because Oskar was only leasing the former company, a different address would be used in all Polish court matters dealing with the former Jewish factory; that address was ul. Romanowicza Tadeusza 9, a street running adjacent to the factory.[56]

Dr. Goryczko was appointed the trade court's legal representative several weeks earlier to look into its financial state, particularly charges of property theft. On his first visit on October 20, he found several former workers living in the company's offices. One of them, Jozef Janda, was a guard and was paid four times the normal salary for a guard. Dr. Goryczko found no evidence of theft. While there he took the keys to the company's storeroom and also got the keys for the machines from Natan Wurzel, who, Goryczko noted, owned the machines. He also took the company's records. Goryczko prepared a list of the company's creditors in anticipation of a sale of the company's finished enamelware. The sale was announced for November 6, though it never took place because Oskar

Schindler began negotiations with Goryczko for the lease of Rekord, Ltd. Six days after Oskar took control of the factory, Dr. Goryczko completed a detailed, twenty-seven-page inventory of the factory's machinery and stores. Presumably Oskar saw a rough draft of the inventory before he signed the preliminary lease agreement.[57]

Schindler's factory was located in Podgórze, a suburb of Kraków. The factory was equidistant from Kazimierz, the historic Jewish quarter of Kraków just across the Vistula (Wisla) River, and two Jewish cemeteries two miles to the south on Jerozolimska Street. Though Oskar could not know it, his factory would sit at the edge of the Kraków Jewish ghetto after it was opened in the spring of 1941. The following year, the SS would open the infamous Płaszów Forced Labor Camp *(Zwangsarbeitslager Plaszow des SS- und Polizeiführers im Distrikt Krakau)* on the site of the Jewish cemeteries on Jerozolimska Street. All Schindler's Jewish workers would initially live here when the camp opened.

Kraków's industrial quarter, Podgórze, was substantially working class and still retains that flavor. Unlike the neighborhoods just across the Vistula surrounding Stare Mesto, Podgórze is a bit run down. Schindler's factory at 4 Lipowa is several blocks away from the *Plac Zgody* (Peace Square) in a subdistrict of Podgórze, Kraków Zabłocie. Oskar would occasionally tell people that Emalia was located in Zabłocie. A major rail line runs through Podgórze and trains stop at the station there, Kraków Zabłocie. The railroad tracks through Podgórze also separate the industrial part of the district from its residential area. Today, Schindler's factory rests in the middle of a complex of factories just as it did during the war.

From a distance, little seems to have changed at Emalia. The old gated entranceway is still there as is the striking glass stairway leading to the former Schindler offices. The sign over the entrance now reads Krakowskie Zakłady Elektroniczne "Telpod" (Kraków Electronic Works "Telpod"). Several firms now have offices in the buildings that once housed Schindler's factory. New buildings have been built on the site and the old brick smokestack was torn down in the late 1990s. Security is modestly tight there, particularly if one tries to go upstairs to find Schindler and Bankier's offices. I was once able to sneak upstairs, only to discover that no one in the various firms on the top floor of Emalia's former business quarters had any idea where Oskar had his elegant offices. Sol Urbach, that rare *Schindlerjude* who worked for Oskar in Kraków and Brünnlitz, often worked in Schindler's office at Emalia as a carpenter.

He said that Schindler's office was just at the top of the stairs. Abraham Bankier's office was behind Schindler's office. Because so much had changed at 4 Lipowa, Steven Spielberg used only the gated entrance and the glass stairway in his film. The factory interior shots were done at an enamelware factory in Olkusz about thirty miles northwest of Kraków.[58] Though Spielberg was probably not aware of it, Olkusz was the hometown of Wolf Luzer Glajtman, the principal founder of Rekord, Ltd.

The Wurzel-Wiener Affair Continues

The controversy between Oskar Schindler and Natan Wurzel became quite ugly in the 1950s and deeply troubled Oskar. Here was the acknowledged German "savior" of almost 1,100 Jews being accused by a Jew of theft and physical abuse. Wurzel, who after the war moved to Israel and changed his name to Antoni Korzeniowski, found an ally in *Schindlerjude* Julius Wiener. In 1955, both men mounted publicity and legal campaigns against Oskar Schindler that centered around charges of physical abuse and theft. Wiener's charges of physical abuse were the most serious. Yet Julius Wiener was also the more timid of the two. In a letter to Wiener on May 21, 1955, Wurzel told him that he "must not be like the young woman who, after her first disappointment in love, decides to enter a monastery."[59]

It is not clear what prompted Natan Wurzel/Antoni Korzeniowski to bring his charges against Schindler. On October 30, 1951, he wrote the Tel Aviv office of the Joint requesting information on the whereabouts of Oskar Schindler. He explained, in Polish, that Schindler knew the fate of his family and that he wanted to contact him "in order to obtain full information about my lost relatives." Ten days later, Helen Fink, an administrative assistant at the Joint, responded that she believed Schindler had moved to Argentina. She suggested he write their office in Buenos Aires for further information.[60]

Whatever his intentions, he did not follow through on them for another four years, when he wrote letters to various Jewish organizations in Israel charging Schindler with theft and brutality. Wurzel told Wiener that "it is our duty to find a good and conscientious lawyer, maybe in Tel Aviv, who will take it on himself to conduct the trial. We must offer this lawyer a share in the proceeds of the trial as payment for his work." Wurzel was partly motivated by the desire to be compensated for what he claimed was his stolen factory, Rekord, Ltd. And perhaps this is the key to Wurzel and

Wiener's charges against Oskar Schindler. Like many Holocaust survivors struggling to rebuild a life in Israel, a young and poor country, they were driven by a desire for some type of compensation for their losses; indeed, Wurzel and Wiener had not only lost family members in the Holocaust but also their worldly possessions. In his May 21, 1955, letter to Wiener, Wurzel told him that Schindler "lives well, with wealth, without worries." But little did they know that at the time that Oskar Schindler was also in poor financial shape.[61]

Schindler, of course, denied that Wurzel had ever owned the factory. The charges prompted Oskar to send a detailed letter in response to several Schindler Jews in Israel in April 1955. This was followed by a detailed, well-thought-out *Bericht* (report) on October 30, 1955, that discussed his efforts to save Jews in Kraków and Brünnlitz from 1939 to 1945.[62] Particularly important about these letters is their view into the "office politics" of the Jews who first began to work for Schindler after he leased Rekord, Ltd. Because Wurzel's statements lack the detail of Oskar's letters and statements, much of the following story is drawn from Schindler's perspective. Schindler's account of how he acquired Rekord, Ltd. follows pretty closely that found in the Polish trade court records. The biggest flaw in his story is the claim that he acquired his factory "legally." Certainly he followed a proper "legal" course with the Polish trade court, but nonetheless Oskar Schindler was able to lease a former Jewish factory for a pittance of what it was worth. Moreover, even though Rekord, Ltd. had gone bankrupt just before the war began, it remained the confiscated property of Poland's new German rulers after the outbreak of World War II. So buried in Wurzel's charges, and to a lesser degree Wiener's, was the pain of these humiliating losses.[63]

According to Oskar, he decided to lease Rekord, Ltd. only after lengthy discussions with various wholesale suppliers, among them Samuel Wiener (Julius's father), Samuel Kempler, and the Landaus. They all assured Oskar that they would have no trouble moving the goods he produced in his newly acquired factory. Oskar said that he had been offered several factories but that the promises of the Jewish wholesalers had prompted him to lease Rekord, Ltd.[64] This Jewish connection is important because Schindler would come to rely on Rekord, Ltd.'s former Jewish owners to help run Emalia. When he reopened the factory, he hired seven Jewish workers, among them Wolf Luzer Glajtman, Uszer Glajtman, Natan Wurzel, and Abraham Bankier, and 250 non-Jewish Polish employees.[65]

Natan Wurzel worked for Schindler for about eighteen months. According to Oskar, Wurzel became an active player in an "egotistical power struggle among the top group of my employees" that centered around efforts "to gain my favor and to win influence over me."[66] Wurzel, like all Polish workers, Jewish and non-Jewish alike, had to register with the Labor Exchange *(Arbeitsamt)* for a work assignment. Schindler, who initially trusted Wurzel, used his influence with the corrupt Labor Exchange to secure him a job at Emalia. And then the trouble began. According to Oskar, Wurzel was responsible for Wolf Luser Glajtman's dismissal after he told Schindler that Glajtman had embezzled Zł 4,000 ($1,250) when he brought sheet metal from the Synger Sosnowitz factory. Oskar investigated the matter and discovered that Glajtman had sent the money to his wife in Olkusz to help his family. Oskar fired Glajtman and informed the Labor Exchange of his dismissal. But this was not the end of the Glajtman affair. Soon after Wolf Glajtman's dismissal, Wurzel told Schindler that Wolf's brother, Uszer Glajtman, an ammunition maker at Emalia, was making mistakes. Wurzel added that Uszer was also taking advice from Wolf. Oskar did not fire Uszer but transferred him to the warehouse.[67]

It began to dawn on Schindler that Natan Wurzel was a bit of a manipulator. Oskar now began to rely on Abraham Bankier more and more because he thought Bankier was "more decent." By this time, Wurzel had succeeded in having his rivals for Schindler's favor neutralized or fired. Only Bankier remained in the "top group." If Oskar is to be believed, Wurzel now set out to destroy Bankier. On one occasion, he personally attacked Bankier in front of the chief purchasing agent for the Higher SS and Police Leader (HSSPF, *Der Höhere SS-und Polizeiführer*), Friedrich Wilhelm Krüger. For one Jew to attack another Jew in front of an SS officer was dangerous and potentially deadly. The buyer, whom Oskar never identified, persecuted Bankier for months after Wurzel's attack. On one occasion, the drunken buyer came to Emalia to find and shoot Bankier. Fortunately, he could not find him.[68]

After this incident, Oskar took Natan Wurzel aside and told him, in front of witnesses, not to incite Emalia's customers against Bankier. This did little to stop Wurzel, who told several of the German trustees whom Oskar did business with that Bankier was "in cahoots" with another Jewish worker, Samuel Kempler, who worked for František Turek. Turek had been Oskar's right-hand man in the Abwehr office in Moravská Ostrava before the war and was now the trustee of a factory in Kraków. Turek was furious with Bankier and fired Kempler. When Turek visited

Emalia, he insulted and humiliated Bankier. Oskar periodically stepped in to "slow Turek down." But Wurzel's criticism of Bankier continued. If there was anything wrong at the factory, whether it be not enough vodka or too few promotions, Wurzel would always say "[w]*vinna Bankiera (guilty Bankier)*."[69]

Though Wurzel was tough on the other Jews who worked for Schindler, he got along well with Emalia's German customers, Wehrmacht officers, and members of the SS. He even had a good relationship with *SS-Hauptsturmführer* Rolf Czurda, the head of the SD's foreign defense division in Kraków; because of this, Oskar said, Wurzel developed a sense of false security that led to his dismissal. But it was Wurzel's allies at Emalia who told Oskar that Wurzel had taken money from a German client in Tarnów named Baytscher. These funds were meant to pay for furniture and transportation. Instead, Wurzel took the money he received from Baytscher and spent it. Schindler informed the Labor Office of Wurzel's dismissal but did not inform the Gestapo or the police of his crime. But this was not the end of Natan Wurzel. For several months after his dismissal, he would drop by Emalia and ask for handouts so he would not go hungry. Often the naive Bankier would intercede for him.[70]

This was a mistake. Whatever positive relationship Wurzel had with Schindler and Czurda now changed. Czurda was the SD's liaison with the Armaments Inspectorate and would visit Emalia three or more times a week to collect the "significant" gifts that Oskar would give him. Though Czurda had nothing to do with Jewish labor issues, Schindler saw him as a potential "business confidant" because of his ties to the Armaments Inspectorate. Czurda was always driven to Emalia in a private car and usually arrived drunk. During one visit after Wurzel's dismissal, Czurda ran into Wurzel at Emalia. During their conversation, the drunk Czurda took offense at something Wurzel said to him. He then slapped him twice in the face in front of Oskar and his secretary, Elisabeth Kühne. Oskar and Ms. Kühne stepped between the two to prevent further harm to Wurzel. Wurzel later claimed that Schindler had ordered Czurda to hit him. Esther Schwartz, a Jewish clerk who knew Wurzel and worked for Oskar in one of his subsidiary business in Kraków until 1943, testified in Israel in 1963 that news of Wurzel's beating caused quite an uproar in the Kraków ghetto. After she heard the story, she recalled that she had heard Oskar tell Marta, who ran the subsidiary business for him, "After I gave him [Wurzel] the 'hairdo,' he finally agreed to sign." Esther concluded that Oskar was talking about Natan Wurzel.[71]

Julius Wiener testified after the war that he learned of Wurzel's beating after he heard people talking about it near the entrance to the ghetto. After the beating, which took place in the summer of 1941, Wurzel was taken to an apartment on Limanowskiego Bolesława Street, one of the main thoroughfares running through the ghetto. When Julius entered the room, he saw Wurzel lying unconscious on the bed. Wiener, who also claimed to have been beaten on Schindler's orders, was shocked by what he saw. Wurzel, he testified, "looked like one blue mass of flesh with blood trickling down." Natan's brother told Julius that Schindler had ordered Wurzel to come to the factory. Once inside, Schindler told him to sign a document stating that he had earlier sold the factory to a Christian. When Natan refused, Schindler told him to wait. After a few minutes, several SS men took Wurzel into a separate room, where they brutally beat him. Frantic with pain, Wurzel begged for mercy. The SS men then asked whether he was prepared to sign Schindler's document. He agreed. Wurzel then stumbled into Schindler's office and signed the required document without reading it. Before he left, he was told not to say anything about the "incident." If he did, he was reminded, there was nearby Auschwitz. Natan could barely walk when he left the factory. His brother hired a carriage to take him back to the ghetto.[72]

In his charges against Schindler after the war, Wurzel agreed that he was forced to sign false statements on the day of the beating about Rekord, Ltd.'s former owners and about the factory's bankruptcy proceedings. Later, he claimed that the Gestapo, working with Dr. Zawisza, forced him to sign other documents about Rekord, Ltd. in Brzesko. What is interesting about this claim is that Oskar's version of the story, told from memory ten years after the war, is more in line with the events recorded in the Polish trade court records than Wurzel's account. According to Oskar, it was Dr. Zawisza and another attorney, J. Hrycan, who visited Wurzel in Brzesko on May 27, 1942. Wurzel said he was forced to sign the "false documents in terror," a claim that Oskar disputed. He said that Hrycan was an elderly white-haired man and Dr. Zawisza was a passive invalid who had lost an arm in World War I. Both men worked for Emalia to earn a living and had always been extremely polite in their dealings with Wurzel.[73]

Oskar said that Natan Wurzel was able to turn the slapping incident with Czurda into "a quite profitable collaboration" between himself, Czurda, and the SD. This new relationship also enhanced Wurzel's "chance for escape." Oskar learned from a business acquaintance, a

Baltic German trustee from Riga, Herr Sommer, that Wurzel occasionally visited Czurda in his Kraków apartment. Czurda in turn met with Wurzel in Brzesko. Sommer periodically worked as a translator in Czurda's office. Moreover, Czurda's secretary, Frau Schürz, confirmed all this when Oskar asked her about these stories. She added that Czurda even got Wurzel a job working for a German Jew, Alexander Förster, a known SD agent. Oskar stated that Förster used Wurzel as a driver in an escape scheme for wealthy Jews. After they paid the appropriate bribes, these Jews would be driven to the border, where they would be picked up by the SS, robbed, and murdered. According to Oskar, at this point, "the famous buddies Förster and Wurzel cashed in on their fees and *Lapuvka* (bribe) in any case."[74]

Förster and Wurzel's efforts seriously affected the Jewish Agency's smuggling routes in and out of Poland from Hungary. Dr. Chaim Hilfstein, who worked for the JSS (*Jüdische Soziale Selbsthilfe;* Jewish Self-Help Association), the only Jewish aid society allowed to work in the General Government, prepared a report on the phony smuggling ring. Oskar took this report to Budapest on one of his first missions for the Jewish Agency and handed it over to Dr. Reszőe (Rudolf or Israel) Kasztner, the vice chairman of the Relief and Rescue Committee of Budapest (Va'ada; *Va'adat ha-Ezra ve-ha-Hatsala be-Budapest*), which, among other things, helped smuggle Jews into Hungary from Poland, Germany, and Slovakia. Va'ada considered the report serious enough to change its smuggling routes into Hungary.[75]

Dr. Rudi Sedlacek, an Austrian dentist from Vienna who worked with the Jewish Agency, gave further information about Förster's activities to an old friend, *Major* Franz von Korab. He in turned shared Sedlacek's report with an SS officer, Kraus, who responded, "Hands off Förster." According to Oskar, the SD left Förster alone as long as they needed him. When the German Jew was no longer useful to them, he was *überstellt* (handed over). Oskar claimed that he had been told that Förster had been murdered by some of his victims just after the war ended.[76]

Förster is discussed in some depth in the memoirs of Malvina Graf, a survivor of the Kraków ghetto and Płaszów, and Tadeusz Pankiewicz, a Righteous Gentile who ran a pharmacy in the Kraków ghetto. The son of a piano maker from Leipzig, Förster spied for the Germans throughout the war. The forty-year-old-Förster was a dancer appearing in a Kraków café, the Feniks, when the war broke out. Though Jewish, he never wore the required white arm band with the blue Star of David, even if he went outside of the ghetto. Because of his privileged position, Förster was able to leave the ghetto whenever he wanted. Pankiewicz and Graf said Förster had a three-bedroom apartment near the entrance to the ghetto and ran a restaurant-dance bar in the same building. He kept a second apartment at the Hotel Royale in Kraków, which Malvina Graf's relatives had once owned.[77]

Pankiewicz said that Förster was on personal terms with several Gestapo agents. He would greet some of them with the personal *Du* (thou or you); they would then shake his hand after he had raised it in salute. One of Förster's duties was to arrange private all-night parties at his nightclub for high-ranking Gestapo officers. As the drunken Gestapo officers left Förster's parties, they would fire their revolvers in the air. Some Jews believed that Förster had a private office in Gestapo headquarters on Pomorska Street and "would sit there in a German uniform." Other rumors had him writing the Gestapo's *Stimmungs-Berichte* (opinion polls), publications that analyzed the mood of the ghetto's population.[78]

In May 1942, the Germans began to transport Jews from the Kraków ghetto to death camps. During the roundups, Förster would always stand beside the Gestapo and supervise the *Aktionen*. He would occasionally intervene to prevent certain Jews from being put on the transports. It was known that Förster took bribes and gifts to help Jews, though sometimes he helped them for humanitarian reasons. Graf stated in her memoirs that he helped many, many Jews get the appropriate work stamps on their identity cards *(Kennkarten)* and in so doing saved them from the transports.[79]

Förster's ties to the SS and the Gestapo did not protect him from mistreatment and jail. On one occasion, he was arrested and sent to the Jewish Security Police (OD; *Jüdischer Ordnungsdienst*) jail. The OD was a Jewish police force in the Kraków ghetto headed by Symcha Spira. Tadeusz Pankiewicz said that *Leutnant* Oswald Bousko, the vice commandant of the *Schutzpolizei* (municipal police, or gendarmes) that guarded the ghetto and often helped Jews, explained to him the reason for Förster's arrest. The day before his arrest, Förster had sent Hermann Heinrich a bouquet of roses to celebrate Heinrich's promotion. Heinrich opened Förster's gift at a celebration party at Gestapo headquarters. As a joke, Heinrich called the OD and told them to arrest Förster. Some felt that Heinrich also wanted to let Förster know that he was still a member of an "inferior race," regardless of his ties to the Gestapo. The morning after Förster's arrest, Heinrich went to the OD jail and ordered Förster released. Both men left the jail laughing and joking.[80]

After the Germans closed the ghetto in the spring of 1943, Förster stayed in Kraków. Rumor had it that he was sent on a three-week "secret mission" to Hungary and later charged with working for the British. Förster left Kraków again and was arrested and imprisoned in Montelupich prison. Pankiewicz said that Förster was probably liquidated by the Gestapo. Afterwards, the Gestapo spread rumors that the charges against Förster had no merit and that he had been released. Some stories had him parachuting into Great Britain on a secret mission. Two Schindler Jews, the musicians Hermann and Henry Rosner, wrote to Pankiewicz after the war from the United States and told him that they knew someone who had been jailed with Förster. According to this witness, the Gestapo had clubbed Förster to death.[81] Though it is difficult to verify the stories about Förster's activities after the Kraków ghetto closed, it is interesting that he went to Hungary on several "missions" at about the same time as Oskar Schindler. Was there a connection? We will never know.

Oskar Schindler's charge that Wurzel was involved with Förster in an illegal escape scam is extremely serious. In his 1955 letter to several *Schindlerjuden* in Israel, Oskar told them of a story that he had heard from Janina ("Janka") Pithard-Olszewska, a secretary for the enamelware wholesale company, Shlomo Wiener Ltd., that sold Emalia's products. Janka said that one evening she paid a visit to a Polish friend who had an apartment near Gestapo headquarters. Wurzel and Förster were at the apartment and Janka heard them work out plans for the escape of seven young rabbis to Hungary. At some point in the planning, Janka told Oskar, *SS-Hauptsturmführer* Heinrich Hamann and another SS officer joined in the discussions. Janka was shocked by the cold-bloodied cynicism of the discussions, particularly Wurzel and Förster's concern about the amount of money they would make. She was also disturbed by Wurzel's criticism of Oskar and his efforts to aid his Jewish workers.[82]

Janka Olszewska was from the Vilnius (Wilno) region of Poland. A month after the German-Soviet invasion of Poland, Stalin transferred Vilnius, which many Lithuanians claimed as their historic capital, to Lithuania. Janka's husband was drafted into the Polish army soon after the war began and disappeared. With her husband gone and their estate destroyed, Janka decided to go to Kraków and live with her father. She did not know that her father had died while a prisoner of the Germans. After several months in a German transit camp, Janka reached Kraków. Germans now lived in her father's apartment, so she stayed with her in-laws. This was where she met Oskar Schindler. Schindler was interested in renting an apartment in one of the homes owned by Janka's in-laws. She was struck by the fact that Oskar offered to pay for the apartment, whereas most Germans in Kraków simply "requisitioned" the apartments they wanted.[83]

Janka met Oskar several times when he came by her in-laws' apartment to pay the rent. On one visit, Schindler brought his girlfriend, Marta G. (Eva Kisch Scheuer), a Czech from Silesia (Śląsk) who now lives near New York. Marta G. was born in Zaolzie, Czechoslovakia, which was taken over by Poland in 1938. She lost her job as a teacher and began to smuggle goods across the Polish-Czech border to make a living. Though engaged, she also developed a relationship with Oskar Schindler. The Polish police became suspicious of her trips across the frontier, and particularly of her relationship with Oskar. To avoid arrest, she decided to escape to Czechoslovakia with her fiancé. Evidently, the Polish border police spotted them trying to cross the frontier and shot her fiancé to death. They arrested Marta and imprisoned her in Lvov. When Oskar arrived in Kraków, he began to look for Marta. During his search he went to Montelupich prison, where he would later be incarcerated. When she was released from prison, Marta went to Kraków and lived with Oskar; later, she moved into her own apartment on ul. Ujejskiego Kornela.[84]

Schindler set Marta up in business. She ran a small shop at ul. 51 Krakówska, near Kazimierz, that sold Oskar's enamelware. The former Jewish business has once been owned by Shlomo Wiener. When she learned that Janka was unemployed, Marta offered her a job as a bookkeeper. In the office with Marta and Janka were four Jews and an ethnic German (*Volksdeutscher*). Janka had no background in business and learned everything she needed to know from a bookkeeping textbook. Janka handled all Marta's business negotiations with Bankier and Schindler. She negotiated her deals with Bankier and settled all financial matters with Oskar. She got to know the factory and its Jewish and Polish workers quite well. On one occasion, the Polish underground (*Armia Krajowa*) approached Janka about acquiring specially made kettles and bowls for its field kitchens. When she went to pay Oskar, he refused to take her money because, he said, it was "all for the Polish 'bandits' in the woods—the partisans." On another occasion, Oskar asked Janka to help him conduct the roll call of his Jewish workers for Amon Göth, the dreaded commandant of the Płaszów forced labor camp. After Göth left, Schindler told

Janka that, because of her, Göth had decided not to kill any of his Jewish workers that day.[85]

This was not all that Oskar had to say about Wurzel in his 1955 letter to his *Schindlerjuden* friends in Israel. He was particularly offended by Wurzel's accusation that Oskar ordered an official from the Foreign Exchange *(Devisen)*, Werner, to take a 14-carat diamond from Wurzel. Oskar, of course, denied this charge and said that he doubted Wurzel ever had such an expensive diamond. The problem with this charge, Oskar said, was that Werner and Wurzel worked together, often in league with František Turek. Oskar constantly warned his workers to be wary of Turek, who would often try to swindle anyone selling him their valuables. On one occasion, a young Jewish worker named Weil came to the factory to buy scrap metal. Weil used the money from the sale of the scrap dishes to care for his mother in the ghetto. When he got to Emalia, Weil called Wurzel from the guard's office at the front entrance. Later, Abraham Bankier told Oskar that on this particular day Weil had 150 grams of *Bruchgold* (broken gold) to sell. Wurzel advised Weil to sell it to Turek. When Bankier learned of this, he tried to reach Weil by phone at Turek's factory, but was too late; Weil had already lost his gold. When Weil arrived at Turek's factory, he was made to wait until Werner showed up. He identified himself as an agent of the Foreign Exchange Office and took the gold from Weil. Oskar did not know whether Wurzel received a commission for the "transaction."[86]

Julius Weiner and Charges of Brutality Against Oskar Schindler

Oskar's charges against Natan Wurzel were in direct response to Wurzel and Weiner's claims of theft, brutality, and other crimes against him. One of their claims, which Oskar never denied but always kept under wraps, was his work for Abwehr. He told his friends in Israel in 1955 that all his acquaintances knew of his ties to Abwehr. In fact, Oskar explained, it "was precisely these friendly connections [with Abwehr] which in situations of no escape created help and often enabled my work of rescue."[87]

But the charges that Oskar never adequately dealt with were those made by Julius Weiner, Natan Wurzel's hesitant partner in the campaign against Oskar Schindler. Details about Julius Wiener's charges against Oskar Schindler did not surface in any detail until 1962, when Schindler was nominated to be included in the first group of the Righteous Among the Nations (Righteous Gentiles) honored at Yad Vashem in Israel. Because of the controversy, the Designation of the Righteous Commission, chaired by Supreme Court Justice Moshe Landau, investigated Wurzel and Wiener's charges.

According to the testimony that Julius Wiener gave the Designation of the Righteous Commission on August 6, 1963, his father, Shlomo Wiener, owned the largest kitchenware, ironware, and cutlery business in Poland before the war. This claim was backed up by Esther Schwartz (Erna Lutinger), who had worked at the Wiener firm as a clerk since 1926. She said that Shlomo Wiener owned the business, located on ul. 51 Krakówska, and his son served as its sales representative. On October 15, 1939, Oskar Schindler came to the Weiner offices with his lover, Marta G. (Eva Kisch Scheuer). When Weiner entered the salesroom, Schindler locked the outer door, went to the cash register, and took out all the money. Mrs. Schwartz testified that Oskar then told everyone in the office that the "good times were over and that he would introduce new arrangements." Schindler, waving a gun, continued to shout and threaten, particularly the elderly Shlomo Wiener, whom he called a crook and a thief. When Julius Wiener's wife protested that it was not the way to treat an elderly man, Schindler shouted, "Pig, Talmudist! Now you will know me and Hitler!" Initially, Mrs. Schwartz thought that they were being "attacked by robbers." Instead, Oskar Schindler was taking over their business.[88]

Schindler then ordered all the Wiener employees to leave the premises. He locked the offices and took Julius and Shlomo to the Trustee Office in Kraków. Julius Wiener said that Oskar continued to insult his father. At the Trustee Office, Schindler made Shlomo kiss a portrait of Hitler. As he humiliated the old man, he sneeringly said, "This is your friend [Hitler], kiss him and give him thanks." Both Wieners then had to sign an unfamiliar document, which, Julius later found out, transferred their property to Schindler. The following day, Oskar returned to announce that he was now the trustee of the Wiener business and that Marta would serve as his representative. Though Oskar paid both Wieners a monthly salary of Zł 700 ($218.75), Shlomo was not allowed on the premises. Before the war, Shlomo Wiener had paid his son Zł 1,000 ($312.50) a month. Esther Schwartz said that Oskar came to the warehouse every day with Marta and constantly discussed business matters with Julius Wiener, who continued to run the office. Initially, Oskar treated Julius with courtesy and, because Marta had few business skills, apparently depended heavily on his advice. Julius called Marta "a soulless puppet necessary only for official purposes." This all changed when Oskar acquired Emalia.[89]

On November 15, 1939, Schindler told Julius Wiener to fetch some enamelware from Natan Wurzel at Schindler's new factory. Normally, Lola Halperin did this sort of thing. When Julius replied that he had a lot of paperwork to do and commented that Lola normally did this type of work, Schindler became angry. He told Julius that he should not forget who was the boss and who was the employee. Oskar added that he expected his orders "to be fulfilled immediately." If not, Julius might be sent "to a place from which no one had yet returned."[90]

When he arrived at Schindler's new factory, Julius went to the scales, where someone else weighed the products he was to carry back to the wholesale store. In his 1956 testimony, Julius Wiener said that "other workers" weighed the goods. In 1963, he testified that Natan Wurzel weighed the enamelware. As the items were weighed, Julius carefully wrote these figures down. In a 1956 statement supporting Wiener's account, Natan Wurzel said that Schindler ordered a workman to put extra goods into the shipment to be picked up by Julius Wiener.[91]

After Wiener returned, Schindler called him into his office and berated him in front of other office workers. Oskar claimed that Wiener had taken too much merchandise and was trying to pilfer extra enamelware for himself. Julius, who was "pale as death," tried to explain that the mistake had been caused by Natan Wurzel, who had not properly weighed the enamelware. He added that he had not weighed the items personally and had only written down the numbers dictated to him by Wurzel. Julius asked Oskar to explain why he thought he would do such a thing. What good would it do to steal things from one of Schindler's businesses only to profit another of them? In his 1956 testimony, Julius stated that Schindler shouted in reply, "You are a swindler and a thief who does it from habit. Get out of here. If you dare to cross the threshold of this establishment again, it will cost you your head." In his 1963 testimony, Julius said that Schindler replied that he thought Julius was a cheat, a thief, and a *Scheißjude* (shitty Jew). When Wiener tried to respond, Schindler physically threw him out of the office door and told him never to return.[92]

Julius spent a sleepless night worrying about the incident with Oskar. The following day was *Shabbat,* the Jewish sabbath, and Julius decided to talk with Schindler about the "infinite nonsense of his accusation." At this point, Julius Wiener's two statements on the affair differ. In his 1963 testimony, he says that he went first to Schindler's new factory to talk to Natan Wurzel about the mis-weighed enamelware. In his 1956 statement, he says he spoke only to Schindler's secretary, who told him to wait for Oskar. After a lengthy wait, Schindler came out of his office but refused to talk to Julius. Wiener was determined to talk with Oskar and continued to sit outside his office. Natan Wurzel said that Wiener spent part of his time with him walking around the factory galleries. He claimed that when Oskar saw Wiener with him, he told Wurzel: "I will kill Wiener." After this threat, Schindler, at least according to Wurzel, called the SS. Some time later, six SS men (in 1963 Julius Wiener said they were from the Gestapo), showed up. Oskar told their leader to give Wiener "the haircut." The policemen took Julius to a side room and locked the door. They punched him so badly that he lost consciousness. Outside, Natan Wurzel could hear the cries and groans of Julius Wiener. The policemen poured buckets of water on him to wake him up and called him "a cursed Jew." One of his tormentors gave him a warning: "If you dare to come again to worry the manager of the factory or if you dare to approach the *Treuhandstelle,* you will go to a place from where there is no return." Julius replied that he would never go to either place. When Wiener staggered from the side room, Natan Wurzel testified, he was "bruised, soiled with blood, full of wounds from burns." He was afraid to help Julius at that moment "because of my dread of the terrible force of the Nazi beast." The bloody, bruised, and humiliated Julius Wiener was too ashamed to show himself in public and was afraid to go home until after dark.[93]

Schindler then returned to Marta's store on Krakówska Street and said in a loud voice: "Now he will not dare to come to the business any more." Esther Schwartz overheard Schindler's comments to Marta. That evening, she went to see Julius Wiener at his home in the courtyard just across from his old company. Esther found Julius in bed, his blood all over the sheets. His wife was applying cold compresses to his face, which was black and blue from the beating. Julius Wiener was bedridden for three days. Afterwards, he was afraid to leave his home because he lived so close to Schindler and Marta's business. Oskar continued to pay both Wieners a salary for three months and then cut them off financially. Julius Wiener's wife went to Schindler several times to ask for help, but he always refused her request.[94]

Several days after the beating, Julius Wiener ran into Natan Wurzel and Uszer Glajtman, who told him that on the day of the weighing incident Schindler told the warehouse worker who was to weigh the enamelware for Julius secretly to add some extra goods to the shipment. Natan Wurzel confirmed this account in 1956. Wiener thought that Oskar had created the entire incident as a pretext to dismiss him and his father from the firm. He also felt that the only reason Schindler had been initially kind to him was to "gain my trust and persuade me to introduce him to our company." When Oskar had achieved his goal, Julius testified, "he kicked me out into the street like a useless piece of furniture, leaving my father and I without any means to live."[95]

Esther Schwartz continued to work for Schindler until 1943 at the former Wiener firm. After Oskar took over the Wieners' business, he raised everyone's salary to insure their continued loyalty. Many of the goods sold by Schindler's subsidiary were under the auspices of a *Bezugsschein* (raw materials license), though some of the enamelware was sold on the black market. Schindler always conducted his illegal business in cash. Though Marta continued to run the former Wiener business, it was apparent to Esther Schwartz and the other workers that Oskar Schindler was their real boss.[96]

Julius Wiener had no more contact with Oskar Schindler until the fall of 1944, when he discovered that Schindler was transferring his factory from Kraków to Brünnlitz in the Protectorate of Bohemia and Moravia (Böhren und Mähren). Julius learned that he was on the famous "Schindler's List," though he was not certain why because he had nothing to bribe the principal author of the list, Marcel Goldberg. He did not want to be on the list because he was afraid of Oskar Schindler. When he arrived in Brünnlitz, Julius tried to avoid Schindler. But one evening, while working on the night shift, he met Oskar, who asked him about his father, Shlomo. Julius testified that "he did not want to say that his father had been murdered," so he said he had died. Oskar replied, "Yes, yes, your poor father." Oskar then wanted to know where Julius worked in the factory. Julius replied that he worked "in *Bonderei* [the worst work in the factory]." Schindler also asked whether Julius had enough food; Julius replied that he had enough to eat. This was the last contact Julius Wiener had with Oskar Schindler. Yet he remained bitter about how Schindler had treated him and his father. Unlike most *Schindlerjuden* who put Oskar Schindler on a pedestal after the war, the well-educated Wiener, who migrated to Israel in 1950, thought that Schindler had helped Jews only "to create an alibi for himself."[97]

Who was telling the truth? The evidence is inconclusive. After looking into the matter, the Designation of the Righteous Commission in Israel told Schindler in 1963 that it could not reach a conclusion about the matter without "an initial, detailed investigation of all the facts," which it did not "feel legitimized to undertake." The testimony it did hear about the charges was insufficient to draw any conclusions. Though Natan Wurzel, Julius Wiener, and Esther Schwartz's testimony supported the allegations, that of another witness, Simah Hartmann (Gelcer), added little to their accounts. She testified in the summer of 1963 that, although it was Schindler who drove Shlomo Wiener out of business, she knew nothing about Oskar's mistreatment of him. Moreover, she said that Oskar was quite kind to her during the two years she had worked for him.[98]

Oskar Schindler had denied the charges for years. Because he was never asked by the Designation of the Righteous Commission to testify, all we have is his own response to the charges in 1955 and 1956 and a detailed letter of support from a select group of Schindlerjuden in Israel to the Designation of the Righteous Commission on December 10, 1961. In his 1955 letter, Schindler listed twenty witnesses in Israel, Poland, the United States, West Germany, and Austria who could support his claims and provide further evidence. On the list were some of the most important people in the Schindler story: Itzhak Stern, Abraham Bankier, Marta Eva Scheuer, Dr. Roland Goriczko, and Leopold "Podek" Pfefferberg-Page. Unfortunately, only one person on Schindler's 1955 list of witnesses, Itzhak Stern, signed the December 10, 1961, letter, and this is why it did so little to address Wiener and Wurzel's specific charges. It leveled modest criticism at Wurzel and Wiener but then fell back on the larger good that Oskar Schindler did during the Holocaust when he saved almost 1,100 Jews from death. The authors asked how could a man who was "trusted by the Jews" for five and a half years, a man who saved Jews, who "acted on their behalf" and who "interfered in their favor in every way" be accused of hurting Jews? Moreover, they argued, though the German nationalization of Jewish property in the General Government was no more than theft, Schindler was only operating under German law when he took over the property claimed by Wurzel and Wiener. The letter goes on to say that even if Natan Wurzel was correct and he did own the machines that he later signed over to Schindler, there was a greater good, and that was

Oskar Schindler's continued ownership of the former Rekord, Ltd. If this had not happened, Oskar Schindler could not have saved his Jews, either in Kraków or Brünnlitz.[99]

Yet why did they not say more? Because they did not know anything else. Most of the Jews saved by Oskar Schindler in 1944 and 1945 did not work for him during the early part of the war. His use of Jewish labor began slowly and by the end of 1941 he only had 190 Jews working for him. And even those who worked for him seldom saw him or knew him very well. Oskar was often away on business for long periods. He would appear only briefly on the factory floor.[100]

Perhaps Simon Jeret, one of Schindler's closest friends in Israel, though not a signatory of the 1961 letter, best captured all this when he told Oskar in a letter of December 17, 1956, in response to the Wurzel and Wiener charges, that

> I can hardly remember the Wurzel in question, and of course I have no notion of any diamond. It is difficult to go back to the years 1940–1942, the time when all Jewish enterprises, in particular factories, things, and equipment were confiscated, which is why, necessarily, all Jewish proprietors lost their property and assets and went under. I therefore do not understand what sorts of demands Wurzel poses today, on what grounds, and how far he is justified in them.[101]

In other words, Jeret, like most of the Jews saved by Oskar Schindler during the Holocaust, simply did not know anything about the charges leveled against Schindler by Natan Wurzel and Julius Wiener.

Could they be true? Of course. The Oskar Schindler of 1939 was a very different person from the Oskar Schindler of 1941 or 1942. He had suffered greatly for the Reich in 1938 and 1939 and was probably caught up in the excitement of Germany's incredible victory over Poland in the fall of 1939. Ever the opportunist, Schindler came to Kraków as a carpetbagger to make his fortune and nothing was going to get in his way. He was steeled by months in a Czech prison and a modestly dangerous life as a German spy. But could Oskar Schindler have ordered or taken part in the mistreatment of a Jew? Perhaps the best person to answer this is one of the *Schindlerjuden* who worked longest for him in Kraków and Brünnlitz, Sol Urbach.

Each one of those who have done significant work on the Schindler story has developed a special relationship with one or two Schindler

Jews who helped bring the past to life. For me, it was Sol Urbach. Sol, who now lives in Delray Beach, Florida, called me in 1999 after he learned that I would be speaking at Ramapo College. Over the next few years, I spent a great deal of time with Sol and his wonderful wife, Ada, also a Holocaust survivor, at their homes in New Jersey and Florida. Sol was born in 1927 in the Polish village of Kalwaria-Zebrzydowska, about thirty-five miles southwest of Kraków. A year after he was born, his father, David, moved the family to Romania. In 1933, as political and economic unrest swept Romania, authorities kicked the Urbachs out of Romania.[102]

Once in Poland, authorities jailed Sol and his family for several days. Jews in the border village where they were being held heard of their plight and helped free them. After their brief incarceration, the Urbachs were sent to Lvov and then settled in the village of Borek Fałęcki, about twenty-eight miles north of Kraków. Sol attended school in Kraków though his family continued to live in Borek Fałęcki even after the Germans conquered Poland. His parents decided to go into hiding in Borek after the Germans ordered them to move to the Kraków ghetto in May 1941. They thought the war would soon be over and that they would be safer in Borek. In 1942, some of their Polish Christian friends who knew they were in hiding warned the Urbachs that they would not be able to keep their secret for long. Soon after this warning, the Urbachs smuggled themselves into the Kraków ghetto, but Sol remained in Borek Fałęcki.[103]

At the time, Sol was working with a Christian furniture maker, Mr. Kaminski, who told him that he would hide him if Sol continued to work for him. He refused, though, to hide Sol in his home in Borek. Instead, he said that Sol could hide in his workshop. Sol said he was terrified of being discovered, particularly at night when it was dark and he was alone. About a week after his family had gone to Kraków, he heard a noise outside the workshop. He said it was probably a cat, but it frightened him so much that he decided he could no longer live this way; he walked from Borek to Kraków and joined his family in the ghetto.[104]

After he sneaked into the ghetto, Sol found his father, mother, and five siblings living in one room in the basement of a large building. The family had entered the ghetto too late to find anything better. It was now the early fall of 1942. Soon after his arrival, Sol was walking through the ghetto's central square, Plac Zgody (Peace Plaza; today, *Plac Bohaterów Getta;* Plaza of Ghetto's Heroes). On a nearby corner was Tadeusz Pankiewicz's pharmacy, *Pod Orłem* ("under the Eagle"). Several blocks away was one of Oskar Schindler's factories, Emalia. An action was about to take place that would save Sol Urbach's life.[105]

As Sol was walking through the plaza, two German trucks pulled up beside him. Several SS men jumped out and began a random roundup of ninety to a hundred Jewish males. Such roundups had been going on in the ghetto since it was founded, and they often meant death for those caught in the German dragnet. After the SS loaded the Jews on the two trucks, they drove to the backyard of a nearby factory. When the Jews got out of the trucks, the SS ordered them into formation. Nearby, Sol noticed a civilian in short Tyrolean pants bent over a woodworking machine. When the Jews had lined up, the civilian came over and said, "You've brought me kids." The SS leader tartly responded, "You keep what we deliver." The civilian was Oskar Schindler and Sol Urbach was now a slave laborer at Emalia.[106]

According to Sol, with the exception of a handful of Jews already working for Oskar, such as Bankier, he was in the first group of male Jews to work for Schindler. And though they were forced to work for this unknown German, they soon came to value their jobs. Sol Urbach became part of that rare fraternity of *Schindlerjuden* who worked for Oskar in Kraków and Brünnlitz. He worked as a carpenter in both camps and often worked in Schindler's offices.[107] He saw Schindler as much as any of the *Schindlerjuden* who worked for the Sudeten German businessman but has always been careful not to overstate his relationship to Schindler either during or after the war. Moreover, he has always approached the Schindler story with a certain scholarly detachment that I came to value greatly as I sought better to understand Schindler and his motivations.

During one of my visits with Sol, I asked him his opinion about the charges of Wurzel and Wiener. I wanted to know whether he thought the charges could be true. His response was, "Of course."

He then went on to explain that his first impression of Oskar Schindler was not very positive. To Sol, Schindler was a typically harsh, uncaring Nazi. There was nothing in Schindler's words or bearing on the day Sol was brought to Emalia to indicate otherwise. But over time, Sol added, Schindler began to change.[108] The Oskar Schindler of 1942 was not the same man in 1944 or 1945.

Yet Sol Urbach's comments still do not tell us definitively whether Oskar Schindler could have mistreated Natan Wurzel, Shlomo Wiener, and Julius Wiener. Two other clues might help. The first was Natan Wurzel's decision to withdraw his charges in 1963. He told Julius Wiener that he had made a "business agreement" with Schindler and suggested that Wiener "forget the matter."[109] Did Schindler pay Wurzel off because he felt guilty about the way that he had treated him or did he simply want to silence him because he was finally receiving the recognition he felt he had long deserved for helping Jews during the war? Knowing Schindler's financial problems at that time, it was probably Schindler's Jewish friends in Israel who paid Wurzel off.

Perhaps the real clues lie in statements made by Schindler himself. In a letter to Dr. Ball-Kaduri in 1956, Oskar wrote: "I am far from being a saint. I am an immoderate human being and have many more flaws than the great majority of those who walk through life so very mannered and polished." This was possibly a reference to Wurzel, who, Oskar once claimed in a letter to Simon Jeret, had "Oxford manners." In his 1956 letter to Ball-Kaduri, Oskar went on to talk about the dozen Jewish women he had "sacrificed . . . to the orgies of the SS Uebermenschen [superior human beings]."[110] In other words, Oskar Schindler was willing to admit that he had made decisions during the war that had harmed Jews.

Perhaps the most revealing of his comments came during an impromptu speech he made at a banquet given in his honor on May 2, 1962, in Tel Aviv by the *Schindlerjuden* then living in Israel. Oskar had come to Israel to receive his Righteous Among the Nations award from Yad Vashem. Unwittingly, he walked back into the middle of the Wurzel-Wiener controversy. But the hundreds of adoring *Schindlerjuden* who met him at the airport and attended the banquet tried to do everything they could to ease his pain. Many of them gave testimonials about Oskar, and towards the end of the evening, Oskar rose to thank them and say a few words. He alluded to the Wurzel-Wiener controversy and said simply, "The truth has already been told by yourselves," meaning that the good things that Oskar did for the *Schindlerjuden* during the war were the proper response to Wurzel and Wiener. Yet at the end of his brief comments, Oskar mentioned the "hard problems" he constantly faced when dealing with the Jews and the Germans during his Holocaust years in Kraków. There were occasions, he admitted, when it was "not at all simple to bring about a situation in which no beatings should occur." But he also added that though he had not "kissed" them, he had "tried to help as best [he] could, in those cases where [they] could not help [them]selves."[111]

Oskar would never have admitted at this time to any of the charges made against him by Natan Wurzel or Julius Wiener, particularly in light of the support that he had received from his Israeli *Schindlerjuden* on the controversy. But he was willing to admit that he had committed abuses of Jews, whether they be physical or otherwise. Oskar Schindler lived in a schizophrenic world that required him to balance his need to succeed in Nazi Germany's "racial laboratory" with his concern for his Jewish workers. During his early years in Kraków Schindler was more interested in making money than anything else; to achieve his goal, he made the necessary moral and economic compromises. But as the war and the Holocaust changed, so did Oskar Schindler.

4.

SCHINDLER IN KRAKÓW

THE NAZI-DOMINATED WORLD THAT OSKAR SCHINDLER ENTERED in the fall of 1939 was one plagued by moral and economic corruption. Beyond being Hitler's new "racial laboratory," the General Government, that part of Poland not integrated directly into the Greater Reich or occupied by the Soviet Union, quickly became a kingdom ripe for German exploitation. Greed and the desire for instant wealth often replaced racial ideals as the driving forces behind the German occupation of what remained of Poland. Though these principles often clashed, sometimes the Germans used them to rationalize the exploitation of stolen Polish and Jewish resources.

The General Government really consisted of three worlds: one German, one Polish, and one Jewish. At a distance, the German world of the General Government was the most normal, though this was a façade. Karl Baedeker published one of his famous travel guides in 1943 for Hitler's so-called racial laboratory, *Das Generalgouvernement: Reisehandbuch von Karl Baedeker*. It could be purchased at Alfred Fritzsche's German book store on Adolf Hitler-Platz in Kraków for Zł 14 ($4.37).[1] Though it seems bizarre to publish a travel guide for the most infamous killing field of the Holocaust, this was the twisted world of Nazi Germany and the General Government. Soldiers on leave from the Eastern Front as well as businessmen probably found the detailed guide quite useful. Governor General Hans Frank wrote a welcoming note for Badeker's guidebook:

For those traveling to the Reich from the East, the General Government provides some glimpse of the charm of home; for those traveling from the Reich to the East, the General Government provides the first greeting of an Eastern world.[2]

Baedeker published his 1943 guide at the height of the Final Solution *(Endlösung)*, but he made no mention of the five death camps then in operation in the General Government. Auschwitz and Bełżec are identified only as train stations. In his section on Warsaw, Baedeker said that one could take the train from the former Polish capital to Białystok via Malkinia. Few knew that Malkinia was the nearest station to the Treblinka death camp.[3]

Baedeker opened the section of his guidebook on "Krakau und Umgebung" (Kraków and Environs) with the usual travel guide discussion of transportation, information, hotels, restaurants, and theaters. It included a detailed map, in color, of the city. Kasimir (Kasimierz), the former Jewish quarter, is listed on the lower right portion of the map. The name Podgorze is listed at the very bottom of the map, though there is nothing to indicate that it was once the site of a Jewish ghetto. The new forced labor camp at nearby Płaszów is also not mentioned, but the travel guide does indicate that you would take the Krakau-Płaszów line eastward to Tarnów and Przemyśl.[4]

The Baedeker guide could also help you find more than just theaters, hotels, and restaurants. It listed all of the important Nazi Party and General Government offices, and its maps listed the newly renamed streets, plazas, and other sites of Kraków. You could also consult Dr. Max Freiherr du Prel's more extensive guide to the complex inner workings of the General Government, *Das General Gouvernement* (1942). Schindler certainly kept a copy in his office at Emalia. It had articles on every facet of regulated life in the General Government. The most valuable part of du Prel's edited work, though, was the detailed list of state, Party, and police officials at every level of the General Government. And Hans Frank wrote the introductory statement, as he did for Badeker's guide.[5]

For daily news on events in the General Government and Kraków, Schindler and other Germans read the *Krakauer Zeitung,* which began daily publication on November 9, 1939. With a circulation of 100,000, it became what du Prel called the "newspaper of the East."[6]

The *Krakauer Zeitung* reported the usual war news, which was given extensive coverage on its front and back pages. But it also carried historical articles and the usual ads that one would find in a normal newspaper. The ads could lead you to a good optician or a place to buy a Pelikan pen. You would also find announcements for the performances of the Kraków Philharmonic, the General Government's State Theater, and the SS- und Polizei-Theater. And if Oskar needed a German office worker, he had to look no farther than the Krakauer Zeitung's want ad and personal section. Two pages in each sixteen-page edition were devoted to sports news and restaurant ads. One can easily see Oskar looking through the Krakauer Zeitung each morning over coffee at his office on ul. Lipowa 4. In the fall of 1943, he probably read the anti-Semitic series on prominent eighteenth-and nineteenth-century Jews and the article on Jewish art, "Jüdisches parasitentum ohne Maske (Jewish Parasites Without a Mask)." He was also no doubt intrigued by Hanns Stock's article on the fifth anniversary of the German takeover of the Sudetenland.[7]

This façade of normalcy did not exist for the General Government's 15 million Poles. Hitler regarded Hans Frank's racial laboratory as a source of cheap manpower for the Third Reich's industrial and agricultural needs. The General Government's non-Jewish population was to be allowed minimal educational and cultural opportunities. They were a subjugated people who existed for one purpose: to serve the unskilled labor needs of the Third Reich. Soon after Frank became the head of the General Government, he decreed that all Poles between eighteen and sixty were obligated to work for the Reich. On December 14, 1939, he expanded this obligation to include young people between fourteen and eighteen years old.[8]

A little more than 10 percent (1.7 million) of the General Government's Poles, including Ukrainians, had been sent to the Third Reich as forced laborers by 1944. About one sixth of these Polish forced laborers were POWs. This does not include the 400,000–480,000 Poles put into concentration camps by the Germans and used as forced laborers there. These Poles became the nucleus of the Third Reich's forced labor population that totaled almost 6 million by the fall of 1944. Yet Poles, and later Soviet forced laborers, were viewed differently from other non-Germans forced to work in the Third Reich. In the spring of 1940, Himmler wrote that the Poles were to be regarded as "a leaderless worker people (Arbeitsvolk)" who were to provide Nazi Germany an annual pool of laborers for farm work, road building, construction, and quarry work. Hitler agreed with Himmler's thoughts on this matter. To insure that the Poles knew their place in the Reich, severe restrictions

were placed on their movements. They were also made to wear a special
badge and were put under orders to avoid sexual intercourse with Germans. To insure the latter restriction, Himmler ordered that special
brothels be set up just for Poles.[9]

Though some Poles had gone voluntarily to the Reich as laborers in the
early months of the war, tales of harsh treatment and low wages eventually made it difficult for the Germans to recruit the large numbers of Poles
they needed to work in Germany, particularly on farms. The forced
roundups of Polish workers that followed prompted a run on falsified certificates of employment in the General Government. The *Arbeitsämter*
could give these certificates only to workers in local government or the armament industry. In time, the Germans distrusted the certificates because
so many were forged.[10]

By 1940, Schindler ran three businesses in Kraków: Emalia, the Shlomo
Wiener enamelware firm, and the Prokosziner Glashütte, a glassware factory just across the street from the main Emalia complex. Collectively,
Schindler's three firms employed hundreds of non-Jewish Poles. Oskar
never said much about the Poles who worked for him and it is hard to determine exactly how many he employed during the war. In the several reports about his wartime activities that Oskar prepared after the war, he
noted that at its peak of operations in 1944, Emalia employed from 1,700
to 1,750 workers, 1,000 of them Jews. He took a small number of Polish
workers with him when he moved to his new factory in Brünnlitz in the
Protectorate of Bohemia and Moravia in the fall of 1944, though the nucleus of the labor force at his new factory consisted of the 1,000 Jews on
the famous "Schindler's List." Oskar left behind 650 Polish workers to
continue operations at Emalia until Soviet forces occupied Kraków in January 1945. Oskar also employed from 350 to 380 workers at his
Prokosziner glass factory in Kraków. According to Oskar, he became the
leaseholder of the glass factory through a direct contract with Fi-
nanzpräsident Hermann Senkowsky, who also oversaw the former Polish
State Monopolies for Tobacco, Spirits, Salt, Matches, and Lottery (*Polnische Staatsmonopole für Tabak, Spiritus, Salz, Zündholz und Lotterie*)
in the General Government. By the time Schindler was forced to close the
glass factory in 1943 because of railroad construction, it was producing
about 1 million vodka bottles a month. Because Oskar did not include the
costs of running the glass factory in his postwar reports detailing his expenses for saving Jews, we can conclude that most of the Prokosziner
workers were probably non-Jewish Poles.[11]

In many ways, the non-Jewish Poles working for Schindler were the backbone of his operations. Schindler had a small staff of Germans who helped oversee all aspects of plant operations, though he relied on Poles to supervise his workforce. His Polish workers, unlike his Jewish slave laborers, were free to come and go and were treated more or less as normal employees by other Germans, particularly the SS. In a report he prepared in Argentina in 1955 on his wartime activities, Schindler said that "the hundreds of Polish workers [he employed] offered a valuable bridge to the Aryan side and kept the contact to the city [of Kraków] intact for them [his Jewish workers]." This bridge was usually to the black market.[12]

Sol Urbach gave one instance of how this bridge to the outside worked. Sol initially worked as a metal presser at Emalia, but soon got a job with a woodworker named Wojcik and his sons. Sol was responsible for maintaining the blackout shades in Schindler's offices and also did other small woodworking chores in Emalia's offices. Wojcik's sons used their positions at Emalia to steal goods from Schindler and sell them on the black market. They forced Sol to help them. He felt that he had no choice but to work with Wojcik's sons if he wanted to keep his job in the woodworking shop. Sol was the key to their operations because he lived in the factory's barracks, which Schindler constructed for his Jews after the Kraków ghetto was closed in 1943. Because Sol's duties gave him easy access to Schindler's offices, Wojcik's sons would occasionally force Sol to enter an office at night and lower the pots and pans they had stolen earlier in the day out of the window. Sol wrapped the pots and pans in paper and lowered them to Wojcik's sons in the street below with ropes supplied by the brothers. If caught, Sol would have paid with his life.[13]

According to Schindler, he had seven Jews and 250 Poles working for him within three months after he took over Emalia. Edith Wertheim was in that first group of Schindler Jews. She said that Oskar wanted six girls to work in his factory and that Abraham Bankier was responsible for choosing them. She testified that she had no idea why she was chosen because she was "not a beauty." On the other hand, she was a "very nice, clean girl with extremely long hair in two braids." When Edith and the other young girls were brought to the factory to meet Schindler, they were all frightened of him. Oskar immediately sensed their fear and said, "Children, don't be scared. You don't need to worry because as long as you are working for me, you are going to live through the war." Later, some of the other girls expressed doubt about Schindler because he was a Nazi. But

Edith said, "Girls, I believe him. He's a nice guy." They responded, "Are you stupid?"[14]

During the course of the war, the number of Jews and Poles working for Schindler increased substantially. He declared that he had employed 150 Jewish workers by the end of 1940; the numbers increased to 550 in 1942; 900 in 1943; and 1,000 in 1944.[15] These figures tend to contradict those given by some of the first Jews who worked for Schindler at Emalia. Edith Wertheim, for example, said that she was among the first small group of Jewish women hired by Schindler in the spring of 1941; Sol Urbach said he was one of the first group of a hundred males the SS rounded up in early fall 1942. By the time Oskar built his Emalia sub-camp in 1943, Wertheim said he had only thirty Jewish women working for him. It is possible that Oskar exaggerated these figures, particularly for the early years of the war.[16]

What prompted this dramatic increase in Jewish workers? Part of it was cost, part of it was efficiency, and part of it was Schindler's efforts to save Jews. He initially hired Jewish workers because they were much cheaper than Polish workers. Dr. Menachim Stern, Itzhak Stern's nephew, said that his uncle convinced Schindler to hire more Jewish women. One day Stern said, "You know how men are, they need their women to produce well." So Oskar decided to increase the size of his female work force to keep his men happy.[17] Though the Germans tried to freeze salaries and prices in occupied Poland at prewar levels, the system did not work very well because of the growing dependency on the black market. In time, more than 80 percent of the General Government's population needs were provided by the black market. This applied to every aspect of the General Government's economy. Schindler maintained two separate bookkeeping systems for his businesses, one for legitimate business and one for the black market. Schindler also had to maintain two wage scales for his Polish workers. The official wage scales were frozen at prewar levels of Zł 200 to Zł 300 ($62.50–$93.75) a month, but the unofficial wage scales could range from Zł 8 to Zł 35 ($2.50–$10.94) an hour. Even so, by 1944 an average Polish worker's salary was worth only about 8 percent of its prewar level. On the other hand, it cost Schindler only Zł 5 ($1.56) a day for a Jewish worker. This salary was paid directly to the SS, which had control over all Jewish workers.[18]

Yet Schindler was motivated by more than cost. Over time, Jewish workers proved to be more reliable and efficient than Polish workers. To keep their war economy going, the Germans forced more and more foreign laborers, particularly Poles, to work in factories throughout the Third Reich; this caused a severe labor shortage in Polish factories. Factory owners raised salaries and even provided free meals to keep Polish workers on the job. Despite such incentives, absenteeism was rampant among Polish workers. One Polish scholar, Czesław Madajczyk, has estimated that by 1943 about a third of all Polish workers were regularly absent from work. It was normal, in fact, for a Polish worker to work four days a week at his regular job and spend the rest of his time working in the black market. One of the most popular jokes at the time centered around two Polish friends who had not seen each other for some time. After meeting on the street, one friend asks the other:

"What are you doing?"
"I am working in the city hall."
"And your wife, how is she?"
"She is working in a paper store."
"And your daughter?"
"She is working in a plant."
"How the hell do you live?"
"Thank God, my son is unemployed."[19]

Oskar Schindler was in Kraków for one reason only, and that was to make money. A lot of money. And it was the black market that gave him this opportunity. The most lucrative business was with the Wehrmacht, which brought huge amounts of goods through its contacts with the Polish black market. According to Jan Gross, the potential for great profits on such deals was enormous, and it was easy to make a fortune in a short time. Schindler quickly grasped the importance of contacts with the black market, which is why he gave Abraham Bankier such a prominent position at Emalia. And it was probably profit that motivated Schindler, no doubt prodded by the trusted Bankier, to hire more and more Jewish workers.[20]

Over time, though, Oskar Schindler did more than employ Jewish workers. He convinced the monstrous Amon Göth, the commandant of the Płaszów forced labor camp, to allow him to build a sub-camp with barracks and other facilities for his Jewish workers. Schindler even provided housing for 450 Jewish workers from nearby German factories. He became the protector of his Jewish workers and kept them healthy and well fed. And when other factory owners began to shut down their factories and return to the Reich with their profits in the face of the westward march of Stalin's Red Army, Schindler arranged to open a new sub-camp and factory, Brünnlitz, near his home town of Svitavy, where he employed over 1,000 Jewish workers, most of whom survived the war. What brought about this transformation? How did a man of questionable morals who came to Kraków in the early months of World War II simply to make a great deal of money become one of the Holocaust's most heralded Righteous Gentiles? This question begs no easy answer, though it probably lies in the evolution of Germany's horrible mistreatment and eventual mass murder of the Jews, first in the General Government, and then in the rest of German-dominated Europe. Living as he did in the heart of the Nazis' principal killing ground during the Holocaust, Oskar Schindler was surprisingly knowledgeable about German plans to murder all the Jews of Europe. His transformation ran parallel to the development of the Third Reich's deadly Jewish policies between 1939 and 1942.

German Policy Toward the Jews in Kraków and the General Government, 1940–1942

By the fall of 1940, the German administrators in Kraków had stripped the 60,000 Jews living there of most of their legal and property rights. Yet Kraków's Jews lost more than their property. They were also stripped of their jobs in non-Jewish businesses and institutions and robbed of most of their bank accounts and other investments. Though the local branch of the Main Trusteeship Office East (HTO; *Haupttreuhandstelle Ost*) in Kraków agreed to compensate former apartment house owners 75 percent of their former property's value, this was reduced to 50 percent in the summer of 1940. Over the next six months, German compensation to Jewish property owners dwindled to almost nothing. And even if Jewish property owners did receive compensation, they were severely limited in their access to these funds in the Polish Post State Savings Bank or in Jewish credit unions.[21]

The gradual impoverishment of Kraków's Jews was part of the greater German effort to rip Jews from the fabric of General Government society. On April 11, 1940, Hans Frank met with several Wehrmacht generals who complained that they had to live in apartment buildings where the only other tenants were Jews. The following day, at a meeting with his department chiefs in the Mining Academy in Kraków, Frank said that the situation was intolerable: If the Nazis wanted to maintain their authority in the General Government, German officials should not have to meet Jews when they entered or left their homes because they might "be subjected to the risk of falling victims to epidemics." Consequently, the Governor General informed his administrators that he intended to rid Kraków of as many Jews as possible by November 1, 1940. Frank admitted that his scheme would result in a massive deportation of Jews. Yet such an action had to take place because "it was absolutely intolerable that thousands and thousands of Jews should slink about and have dwellings in a town which the Führer had done the greatest honour of making the seat of a high Reich authority." Frank added that he intended to make Kraków "the town freest of Jews in the General Government."22

The Nazis had struggled with the so-called Jewish question since Hitler had become chancellor of Germany in early 1933. Over a six-year period, they had stripped Jews in the Greater Reich of all of their economic, professional, and political rights in an effort to force them to leave Hitler's Nazi kingdom. In Poland, they faced new problems because of the size of the Jewish population. Reinhard Heydrich, the Chief of the Security Police and the SD *(Chef der Sicherheitspolizei und des SD)* and soon to be head of the Nazis' new super police organization, the Reich Security Main Office *(RSHA; Reichssicherheitshauptamt)*, laid out the Germans' general blueprint for dealing with the Jews of Poland in a memo, "The Problem of the Jews in the Occupied Areas," that followed a September 21, 1939, meeting with *Einsatzgruppen* leaders in Berlin. Besides providing the guidelines for the creation of the *Judenräte* and other issues, Heydrich also spoke of the "final goal" towards the Jews, which, he said, would take some time. The first stage of this long-range "game plan" was the "concentration of the Jews from the countryside to larger cities." Jews from those parts of Poland who were to be integrated into the Greater Reich were dumped into an area in the interior of Poland that later became the General Government. Towns and cities chosen as concentration areas were to be near a railway line or junction; Jewish communities with fewer than five hundred people were to be dissolved and the inhabitants moved to the nearest concentration point.23

Essentially, Heydrich was thinking of the creation of a ghetto system throughout what remained of German-occupied Poland. On September 20, 1939, *General* Franz Halder, commander of the Army General Staff, noted in his diary that the "ghetto idea exists in broad outline"; two days later, Heydrich told *General* Walther von Brauchitsch, the Army commander in chief, that he planned to create a Jewish state near Kraków under German administration. Brauchitsch protested, and *Reichsführer-SS* Heinrich Himmler, Heydrich's boss, intervened to assure the army chief that this was a long-range objective that would be realized in the future. The time frame for meeting this goal, a year, was laid out into another memo Heydrich sent to his department chiefs in the RSHA on September 27, 1939. The plan, which Hitler had approved, was to send all Greater Reich Jews to urban ghettos in the soon-to-be created General Government. These transfers would give Reich officials a "better chance of controlling them [the Jews] and later removing them." Reich Gypsies, or Roma, were also included in this directive.[24]

The idea of ghettos for Jews was nothing new. The first ghetto for Jews was created in Venice in 1516. The idea of forcing Jews to live in separate parts of cities spread to other European countries over the next four centuries. The purpose of the ghetto was to limit Jewish contact with Christians and to control Jewish economic activities. With the coming of the Enlightenment and the emancipation of the Jews, ghettos fell into disfavor in Christian Europe. The last ghetto in Europe, in Rome, was closed in 1870. The Nazis revived ghettos for Jews seven decades later.[25]

What complicated all of this was the uncontrolled movement of Jews and Poles into the General Government from the recently conquered western Polish territories and Jews and Gypsies from the Greater Reich. There were about 600,000 Jews in the conquered Polish western provinces. Frank also expected that another 400,000 Jews would be sent into his "kingdom" from the Greater Reich. Himmler also intended to move about 400,000 Poles from this region into the General Government. Once this transfer program was completed by the spring of 1940, the General Government would have a Jewish population of 2 million.[26]

Initially, the idea was to create a special Jewish reservation in the Lublin district. However, once the massive transfer began on December 1, 1939, Frank became concerned over the implications of such large population movements within his so-called kingdom. With the backing of Hermann Göring, Frank insisted that he be given full control over all shipments of Jews and others into the General Government. On March 23, 1940, Göring halted all further transports into the General Government. It was in the aftermath of this controversy that Frank decided to force Kraków's Jews out of the city. The expulsions were to take place in two phases. On May 18, 1940, German authorities announced that Kraków's Jews had three months to leave the city for another town in the General Government. Those who left by August 15, 1940, could choose their new place of settlement and take all their personal possessions with them. Those who did not leave voluntarily would be expelled after August 15 and would be limited to 25 kilograms (55 lbs.) of baggage per person; all other property would be transferred to the Kraków district Trustee Office.[27]

In his April 12, 1940, meeting with his department heads, Frank had said that from 5,000 to 10,000 Jews would have to remain in Kraków because the Germans needed their handicraft, trade, and business skills. Frank expanded this number to 15,000 in his May 18 decree. The *Judenrat* under Dr. Bieberstein was to insure that all Kraków Jews complied with the May 18 regulations. Initially, the *Judenrat* asked Jews who had come to Kraków from other parts of Poland to consider voluntary resettlement. When this appeal did not work, the *Judenrat* reminded the city's Jews of the August 15 deadline. On July 23, German authorities informed the *Judenrat* that it would not change the August 15 date for voluntary departures. Two days later, a notice signed by Dr. Bieberstein appeared in the new Jewish newspaper, the *Gazeta Żydowska*, reminding Kraków's Jews of the German regulations regarding voluntary resettlement. It also included information about other cities in the General Government where Jews could settle.[28] The notice ended with

> therefore we ask all Jews of Cracow to change the place of residence voluntarily and immediately irrespective of the fact if the order to move has been delivered or not. The permits to travel by train, identity documents and all sort of information concerning the possible reductions can be obtained from the Migration Committee of the Jewish Community in Cracow, in Brzozowa 5.[29]

Though many Jews did leave Kraków during this period, far too many Jews were still in the city on August 15. The Germans responded by forming a joint German-Jewish eviction committee that issued special residency permits, the *Ausweis*, for Jews who could stay in Kraków. The committee, however, issued far more permits than the number allowed legally to stay in the city. An official investigation concluded that the reason for the excess permits was bribery or an honest desire to help fellow Jews. It also indicated that some former Kraków Jews had returned illegally to the city because they could not find homes in other parts of the General Government.[30]

The failure of the voluntary resettlement program frustrated the Germans; on November 25, 1940, the Kraków district's governor, *SS-Brigadeführer*

Otto Wächter, issued a new decree in Polish and German about illegal Jewish residents in the city. He stated that "in order to cleanse Cracow of its Jews and leave in it only those Jews whose professions are still needed," it was now forbidden for Jews to enter Kraków. Only Jews with the *Ausweis (dokument odroczenia)* could remain in the city. The *Ausweis* had to be carried at all times; those caught without it would be expelled from Kraków. Jews without the *Ausweis* had to present themselves at the Regional District Office for Refugees on ul. 3 Pawia between December 2 and December 11, 1940. This was to be done alphabetically over a five-day period. Wächter warned that the Germans intended to enforce the new decree and warned that anyone who failed to abide by it would be severely punished.[31]

By this time, Wächter had already gained a reputation for brutality. A year earlier, he reported to Frank that posters had appeared all over the city on November 11 commemorating Polish independence day. The governor general ordered Wächter to arrest and shoot one man from every building on which the posters appeared. Wächter dutifully rounded up 120 Poles for execution. Consequently, no one should have been surprised when Wächter began his brutal round up of Jews throughout Kraków, regardless of whether they had the *Ausweis* or not. Jews caught in the Nazi dragnet were sent to the former Austrian fort on ul. Mogilska and then, after they were opened, to ghettos in Warsaw, Lublin, Hrubieszów, and Biała Podlaska. A year earlier, Biała Podlaska had been the terminus point of the first SS death march, which involved eight hundred Jewish prisoners of war from the Polish army. The Germans continued to inter Jewish POWs in a camp in Biała Podlaska until 1941, when the camp was closed.[32]

The Germans harassed the Jews who stayed in Kraków. In January and February 1941, they forced all Jews over age sixteen to spend a set number of days clearing the streets of snow. At the same time, Wächter decreed that all Jews living in the city would have to replace their *Ausweis* with a new identity document, the *Kennkarte*. But before they could receive the new document, Jews had to submit the old *Ausweis* with confirmation of the actual number of days they had worked in January 1941. On February 27, 1941, Wächter declared the *Ausweis* an invalid document. The only Jews allowed to remain in Kraków after this date were those with the *Kennkarte* or those promised one.[33]

Four days later, Wächter published a 13-point ordinance in the *Krakauer Zeitung* that announced the creation of the Kraków Jewish Living Quarter *(Jüdischer Wohnbezirk)*, or ghetto. Wächter explained that the ghetto, which would be in the suburb of Podgórze, was being established for security and health reasons. Though the Germans opened the first Jewish ghetto in Piotrków Trybunalski near Łódź in the fall of 1939, they did not begin to open ghettos in earnest for six more months. The opening of ghettos in the General Government took place randomly between 1940 and 1942. The first was opened in Łódź, which was now part of the Greater Reich, on May 1, 1940. Six months later, the Germans opened another in Warsaw. Tadeusz Pankiewicz, the beloved Christian pharmacist in the Kraków ghetto, said that by early 1941, rumors were widespread that more ghettos would soon be opened in other parts of the General Government. Kraków's Jews hoped the new ghetto would include Kazimierz, the historic Jewish quarter in Kraków. Jews had lived in Kazimierz since 1495. Though long regarded as one of the poorer sections of Kraków, the "Jewish town" was the vibrant religious, cultural, and intellectual center for the city's Jews. Consequently, Wächter's decision to force Kraków's remaining Jews across the Vistula river to the run-down industrial district of Podgórze shocked many of the city's Jews.[34]

The second point of Wächter's ordinance specifically established the boundaries of the new ghetto. Its northernmost border was the Vistula River. From there it would run along the rail line linking central Kraków with the suburb of Płaszów. It would include the central market square of Podgórze and end just below the Krzemionki Hills. The highest point here is Lasota Hill, where Oskar Schindler and his mistress, Amelia (Ingrid), an Abwehr agent, supposedly watched the violent closing of the Kraków ghetto in March 1943. Schindler's Emalia factory on ul. 4 Lipowa was only a few blocks away from the ghetto's western wall.[35]

Wächter's decree ordered all Polish residents living in those parts of Podgórze to move to Kazimierz by March 20, 1941. Jews were given the same amount of time to move to the ghetto. About 3,500 Poles lived in three hundred homes in Podgórze. Many of them were stunned by the German orders. They organized meetings and explored ways to prevent the transfers. Parishioners of Podgórze's striking neo-Gothic St. Joseph's Church asked their vicar, the Reverend Jozef Niemezynski, to discuss their concerns with the Germans. Father Niemezynski told Wächter that to create a ghetto in Podgórze just beyond the church's grounds would work a severe hardship on his parishioners. For one thing, the Catholic priest argued, many of the faithful now forced to move to Kazimierz would have not only to cross the Vistula to attend church, they would also have to walk completely around the walled-off ghetto to get there. Father Niemezynski was told that there were already too many churches in Kraków. In fact, Wächter said, the vicar was lucky that St. Joseph's was not in the ghetto itself. If it were, then "all the faithful from the parish would be lost." Other representatives told the Germans that it would be impossible to move some of their businesses and workshops to Kazimierz because of inadequate facilities there. Their appeals fell on deaf ears. The March 3 ordinance stood.[36]

The *Judenrat* was responsible for insuring that the transfers and the opening of the ghetto went smoothly. Excluded from the transfers from Podgórze to Kazimierz were major factories and businesses producing goods for the Wehrmacht. The Germans also permitted one other Aryan business to remain open in Podgórze, Tadeusz Pankiewicz's pharmacy, *Pod Orłem* (Under the Eagle; today, Museum of National Remembrance). Pankiewicz and his Polish staff, Irena Droździkowska, Helena Krywaniuk, and Aurelia Daner-Czortkowa, had to live outside the ghetto. According to Pankiewicz, the pharmacy, situated as it was on one of the ghetto's main squares, *Plac Zgody* (Peace Square; today, *Plac Bohaterów Getta,* Plaza of Ghettos Heroes), "became witness to the inhuman deportations, monstrous crimes and the constant degradation of human dignity and self-respect of the occupants." More important, Pankiewicz's pharmacy provided the ghetto's Jews with important contacts with the outside world. *Schindlerjude* Stella Müller-Madej described Pankiewicz as "a wonderful human being" and remained close to him after the war. On one occasion, he hid Stella under his desk during a German *Aktion* or roundup in the ghetto. In 1983, Pankiewicz was declared a Righteous Gentile (Righteous Among the Nations) by Yad Vashem in Israel.[37]

Within days of Wächter's March 3 decree, 15,000 Jews began to abandon their homes in Kasimierz and slowly make their way across the Vistula to the three hundred or so homes in Podgórze abandoned by the 3,500 Poles who once lived in them. The Poles, in turn, took up residence in the former Jewish homes in Kasimierz. What was once a normal, though rundown, suburb of Kraków now became a crowded Jewish ghetto where disease and hunger were constant threats to human life. Stella Müller-Madej described the traumatic forced march into the ghetto:

A lot of people were heading for the Ghetto, big groups and small. Some were carrying only bundles, and others had all their possessions loaded on horse carts. Daddy was pushing a nondescript wagon that he had borrowed from the janitor.

It was a beautiful sunny day, but no one was smiling about the splendid weather. The whole crowd around us was grey, gloomy and sad. I felt bad because we must have looked the same in such company. To cheer things up, I said to Daddy, who was pushing the cart with a vacant expression on his face, "Let's pretend it's our car, and we'll step on the gas and run from the bridge here down to Zgoda Square, OK?"[38]

An excited Stella jumped up on the cart, only to see the family's bundles tumble to the ground. After helping Stella put them back on the cart, her father began cheerfully to push it along the street. Stella and Adam, her brother, followed along

skipping and letting out Indian whoops. Mummy and my brother picked up the parcels that fell along the way. Some people looked at us indignantly, while others laughed at the sight. I heard somebody say, "Quite right. We shouldn't let it get us down. It's not as though we were going to our death."[39]

It is not a long walk from Kazimierz to Podgórze, though it probably seemed an eternity to those Jews carrying their lifelong possessions with them on unwieldy carts, wagons, or their backs. Stella and her family probably crossed over the Piłsudski Bridge, Kraków's oldest, though they could have crossed another one just upriver. Because Germans destroyed all of Kraków's bridges on the Vistula at the end of the war, the second bridge into the ghetto no longer exists, though one can still see its markings from across the river.[40]

Stella and her family were given a room with a kitchen in a building on ul. Czarnieckiego; the common toilet was in the courtyard. The place was dirty and filled with roaches. Stella's mother, Tusia, declared that she would "rather not live at all than vegetate for even a week in such conditions." Tusia returned to her grandmother's apartment outside of the ghetto for a few days while Stella's father, Zygmunt, did what he could to make the room livable. In one of the Holocaust's illogical twists, Stella's grandmother was not required to move into the ghetto.[41]

There is a vivid photographic collection in the Archiwum Państwowe in Kraków that paints a graphic picture of the forced Jewish exodus into the ghetto. To facilitate the rapid movement of Jews from Kazimierz and other points in the city to Podgórze, the Germans forced Jews either to walk or take trains or boats across the Vistula to the ghetto. Whatever household goods were permitted in the ghetto were loaded on decrepit horse-drawn wagons; men, women, and children carried whatever personal goods they could. Often, Jews had to push their furniture and other personal items on aging carts. Germans guards were everywhere and they constantly checked and rechecked identity cards. The stress of the transfer showed darkly on the face of every victim.[42]

The forced move into the ghetto came just before one of Judaism's most important religious holidays, Passover (Pesach), which in 1941 was between April 12 and 19. The Germans often chose a period around a special Jewish religious holiday such as Passover or Rosh Hashana to implement a major transfer or roundup. The idea was to use the period of strict Jewish religious observance to catch their victims when they were most off guard. Whether this was the intent in March 1941 is uncertain. Regardless, because of Passover, the ghetto remained quiet until after the week-long holiday. Afterwards, bricklayers began to construct the three-meter (9.8 feet) wall around the ghetto. They placed over the Podgórze Market Square entranceway a large blue Star of David. Below it was a phrase in Yiddish: *Jüdischer wojnbecirk* (Jewish Housing Estate). Two large blue lamps stood above this entranceway; the Germans had workers finish the walls near it with what appeared to be the tops of Jewish gravestones. The Germans also decreed that all signs and other public inscriptions in Polish had to be redone in Hebrew throughout the ghetto. The only exception was the Polish sign over the entranceway to Tadeusz Pankiewicz's pharmacy, *Pod Orłem*.[43]

The three entrances into the ghetto were guarded by Polish police in navy blue uniforms. Though circumstances varied from ghetto to ghetto, particularly in the General Government, the Polish police had authority over the Jewish Security Police (OD; *Jüdischer Ordnungsdienst*) in the ghetto. The main entrance into the Kraków ghetto was at Podgórze Square, where the Germans opened the offices of the *Judenrat* and the German police. A second gate was built at the southeast rear of the ghetto at ul. Limanowskiego. The Germans constructed a third gate at the northeast entrance to *Plac Zgody* just before you crossed the Vistula on what is today Most (Bridge) Powstańców Ślaskich. If you were a Jewish worker fortunate enough to have a *Blauschein* issued by the Labor Office *(Arbeitsamt)*, you could work outside the ghetto. You would leave for your job as a slave laborer through the Podgórze Square gate and return that evening through the one at *Plac Zgody*.[44]

The population in the ghetto changed frequently. Soon after the ghetto opened in the spring of 1941, the Germans shipped Jews there from surrounding villages. That fall, authorities deported 2,000 Jews without proper identification from the ghetto.The roundups and deportations were planned by the Germans and undertaken with the help of the OD. In anticipation of the Kraków ghetto, the *Judenrat* created the Jewish OD force in Kraków at German instigation on May 5, 1940; the agency was headed by a former glazier, Symcha Spira, who was recruited by the *Judenrat*. Tadeusz Pankiewicz said that before the war Spira was an Orthodox Jew who wore a full beard and a long black capote. By the time he became head of the OD, he was clean shaven and wore a tailored uniform bearing many official looking insignias. *Schindlerjude* Malvina Graf described Spira as an immoral person who had many lovers. He also had serious health problems. The Germans liked him because he carried out their orders quickly and efficiently.[45]

Though requirements varied from ghetto to ghetto, OD candidates had to have completed some military service, fit certain weight and height requirements, have an unblemished past, and be nominated by several individuals. The successful nominee would then have to be approved by the *Judenrat*. In Kraków and several other ghettos, the Germans had their favorite nominees, such as Spira, whose nominations could not be challenged.[46] The Kraków Jewish OD was divided into two sections, the Civil Division *(Zivilabteilung)* and the "uniformed" regular OD. Jewish members of the Civil Division wore neckties and blue coats and the regular OD wore coats buttoned to the neck. Members of both OD units wore armbands on their right sleeves with *Ordnungsdienst* in Hebrew. The Gestapo had direct contact with members of the Civil Division; members of the regular OD received their orders from the *Judenrat*. The responsibilities of the OD combined those of a normal civilian police force with those of prison guards. They also had the right to impose sentences traditionally handed out by courts. But what people most remember about the OD was their help during roundups and deportations. In time, the OD became the most despised symbol of the Nazi system throughout the ghetto. Many OD policemen fell prey to the rampant corruption that plagued German rule in the General Government, which only added to Jewish hatred of these units.[47]

The Jewish OD were only part of a complex network of *Judenrat* organizations and facilities created to deal with the complexities of life and society in the Kraków ghetto. Among the most important was the Jewish Self-Help Society (JSS, *Jüdische Soziale Selbsthilfe*; *Żydowska Samopo-*

moc Społeczna) at ul. Józefińka 18. The JSS, headed by Dr. Michał Weichert, was created in the spring of 1940 at the instigation of the Joint,
which was searching for a Jewish-run organization in German-occupied
Poland to distribute welfare aid to Polish Jews. The Germans insisted,
though, that the JSS become part of a Nazi-run Main Welfare Council
(NRO; *Naczelna Rada Opiekuncza)* that also had Polish and Ukrainian
delegates. The NRO first came under the jurisdiction of the Nazi
Party's National Socialist People's Welfare agency (NSV; *Nationalsozialistische Volkswohlfahrt)* and later Hans Frank's Population and Welfare
agency (BuF; *Bevölkerungswesen und Fürsorge)*, created in April 1940.
The Germans insisted that the German Red Cross, which was part of the
NSV, act as the JSS liaison with the Joint. The JSS was a General Gov-
ernment-wide organization. Both the JSS and the Joint had offices in
Warsaw and Kraków.[48]

Weichert, who longed for independence from JSS headquarters in Warsaw and the Kraków *Judenrat,* partially got his wish after Germany declared war on the United States on December 11, 1941, and closed the
Joint office in Warsaw. Though Joint Warsaw continued to operate illegally, it lost control of its JSS offices elsewhere in the General Government. Undeterred, the ambitious Weichert continued to run the Kraków
JSS office, now in the ghetto and later in Płaszów. Initially, Weichert tried
to help Jews throughout the General Government, though when the SS
took over all Jewish matters in the General Government on June 3, 1942,
his efforts were increasingly limited to Kraków's Jews. By this time, with
an eye towards the closing of the ghettos in the General Government, the
SS ordered the dissolution of the NRO. Weichert was permitted to take
over a new organization, the Jewish Aid Center (JUS; *Jüdische Unterstützungsstelle)*, which was responsible for providing Jews in slave labor
camps with whatever aid arrived for them from abroad. JUS continued to
operate even after the the Kraków ghetto was closed in the spring of
1943, aided by at least one future *Schindlerjude,* Dr. Chaim Hilfstein. The
SS finally shut down JUS in August 1943, though Weichert continued to
work for the Polish relief organization, the Chief Aid Committee *(Rada
Głowna Opiekuncza).* Weichert somehow managed to continue to send
goods into the German slave labor camps. In early 1944, the Germans allowed him to reopen JUS; when the Germans closed it again in the summer of 1944, Weichert went into hiding. He survived the Holocaust, but
many Jews, as well as the Polish courts, viewed him with suspicion. He
was tried several times in Poland because of suspected collaboration with

the Germans. He was found innocent on each occasion and ultimately migrated to Israel.[49]

One of the most fascinating aspects of Weichert's efforts to help Jews in the General Government was his contact with Oskar Schindler. There is no direct evidence concerning their relationship; but as both men were deeply involved in efforts to help Jews in the ghetto and in Płaszów, Weichert and Schindler probably had some sort of working relationship, particularly after Schindler made his first trip to Budapest in 1943 to bring Jewish Agency funds back to Kraków. According to Dr. Aleksander Bieberstein, a Schindler Jew who wrote one of the most important books on the Jews of Kraków during the war, two of Weichert's contacts in Kraków were Itzhak Stern and Mietek Pemper, two of Oskar Schindler's closest Jewish associates during and after the war. Stern and Pemper, who worked in the office of Płaszów camp commandant Amon Göth, supplied Dr. Weichert with "secret documents and decrees," which he turned over to the Polish underground. Dr. Bieberstein also says that Weichert supplied Schindler with his first shipment of medicines after he had moved part of his factory from Kraków to Brünnlitiz in the fall of 1944. Dr. Bieberstein was a prominent physician who headed the Hospital for Infectious Diseases in Kraków before the war and continued to serve in this position when the Germans moved it to the ghetto. Tadeusz Pankiewicz described Dr. Bieberstein as "an exceptional human being" who continued his hospital administrative work in Kraków after the war until his migration to Israel.[50]

There were three hospitals, an orphanage, and a post office in the Kraków ghetto, as well as a public bath complete with facilities for delousing and disinfecting. It is unclear, though, whether this also served as a *mikvah* (Jewish ritual bath). Sol Urbach said that he remembered the *mikvah* before the war because it was near the home of his relatives, who used it. However, he had no memory of the public bath in the Kraków ghetto; he said that while they lived in the ghetto, people found ways to maintain their own personal hygiene. He never was deloused or disinfected while in the ghetto and never had to carry an *Entlausungsschein* (delousing certificate), a document required elsewhere that certified the carrier had been deloused and disinfected.[51]

Religion and Jewish education flourished in the ghetto, though the latter was officially outlawed.[52] There were three synagogues in the Kraków ghetto and Tadeusz Pankiewicz said that people continued to observe *Shabbat* and the Jewish holidays while living there. He said that their suffering was always evident on their faces during these times of worship. He often observed Orthodox men and women standing outside the makeshift synagogue near the rear of his pharmacy separately reciting their prayers on *Shabbat*. He added that the *Kaddish,* the prayers for the dead, were frequently recited in almost every Jewish ghetto home.[53]

Yet hints of normalcy in the Kraków ghetto were a façade. The threat of violence and death was constant. Stella Müller-Madej's family lived in constant fear for their personal safety, particularly that of their children. Stella was eleven years old when the ghetto opened and her brother, Adam, was fifteen. Adam and his parents had to leave Stella alone every day to go to work. Stella's parents instructed her to avoid the ghetto wall areas, strangers, and "quarrels with children." The day-time hours were very lonely for the young girl; she recalled she "kick[ed] around the Ghetto streets as if [she] were in a bewitched world." As the child of secular Jewish parents, she found the "little rabbis," the Orthodox Jewish children with their hair locks and conservative dress, "especially irritating." But what really frightened her was the random violence. On one occasion before the completion of the ghetto wall, a gang of Polish children began to pick on her. When a Polish worker helping to build the wall intervened, his colleague admonished him to "let the kids have fun with the little Jew." He then said, "Hey, Sarah [the Germans by this time required all Jews to have a Jewish name, often Sarah for females, and to carry an *Amtsbestätigung* documenting such a change], here's an apple for you." Then he threw the apple in Stella's face, bloodying her nose. Angry with his coworker, the kind Polish worker shouted, "You son of a bitch, I'll show you! Aren't they putting them through enough hell without us?" He then came over, wiped Stella's face clean of blood, and warned her that it would be best if she did not return to the wall construction site "because something really bad might happen." He then asked Stella's name. Ashamed of the behavior of his coworker, he told Stella that his name was Antoni. In fact, he added, it would be okay if she came back to the construction site. If she did, he would bring her a toy.[54]

Though Stella's parents forbade her to return to the wall construction site or to speak to Antoni, she did so surreptitiously. On one occasion, Antoni gave her a black puppy, whom Stella named Blackie. The puppy became Stella's constant companion in the ghetto. In fact, though her parents had originally opposed her keeping him, they later agreed that Blackie was a good companion for Stella in these dangerous times. When the Germans had completed the ghetto walls, the atmosphere grew more deadly. Random acts of violence became more widespread and people no longer walked normally from place to place. In fear, they scurried about quickly to avoid being shot or beaten by Germans or Poles. The rumors of such mistreatment and death were often as frightening as the actual deeds. Stella constantly heard stories of German soldiers driving around in cars killing Jews "like birds on a roof," or of children being tossed off a hill overlooking the ghetto by the "Blacks," or the Baudinists *(Baudienst)*, Poles drafted initially by the Germans for construction work and occasionally used to help the Germans with some of their Jewish roundups. But what most frightened Stella were the stories of Auschwitz she heard her father, who was now an OD man, whisper secretly to her mother.[55]

Yet it was not education, religion, or even the fear of indiscriminate violence that concerned most ghetto residents; it was work. A job and the precious *Blauschein* that came with it was the bridge to life for Kraków's Jews. Her father, Zygmunt, had worked long hours in a quarry before he became an OD man. Adam was employed in a nail factory in the nearby Grzegózki district, and her mother, Tusia, ran the office of an Austrian German button factory on ul. Agnieszki near Kazimierz. The wife of the factory owner, Frau Holzinger, became friends with Tusia. She gave Stella's mother extra food, which she smuggled back into the ghetto. According to Stella, none of the Germans who met Tusia in the Holzinger office believed she was a Jew. On one occasion, Mrs. Holzinger invited Tusia to a reception in her home. Tusia hesitated, but Mrs. Holzinger insisted and promised to drive her back to the ghetto when the party was over. Everything went well until Tusia's Jewish armband fell out of her purse in front of some of the German guests. A few were members of the SS. Mrs. Holzinger tried to explain away the incident as a joke, but Tusia feared it would cost her her job. It did not.[56]

Some Jews worked outside the ghetto; others found employment in factories and other concerns within the ghetto's walls. In an effort to bring some normalcy to life in the ghetto, several bakeries, dairies, and restaurants opened in the spring of 1941. One restaurant had a night club that featured the orchestra and two musicians who were made famous in *Schindler's List:* violinist Henry Rosner and his brother, accordionist Leopold Rosner. The restaurant and bar were owned by Alexander Förster, who often entertained guests from the Gestapo there. Jews could provide the entertainment at such functions, but they could never be a part of them. With the exception of a few well-placed Jews such as Förster and Spira Symcha, few Jews could afford such luxuries or had the energy for them. Jews fortunate enough to have a job worked long, hard hours and usually came home exhausted, not only from the work but from the stress of living as forced laborers and prisoners of the Germans and their Polish collaborators.[57]

German labor policies for Jews varied throughout the General Government and changed as the Germans developed new confinement and death policies for them. In the summer of 1940, Dr. Max Frauendorfer, head of Hans Frank's Labor Division *(Hauptabteilung Arbeit)*, issued regulations that laid out general guidelines for the use and payment of Jewish workers in the General Government. The police were to deal with questions regarding Jewish labor, though in reality it was overseen by Frauendorfer's labor offices throughout the General Government. Frauendorfer argued that it was necessary to use Jewish labor because so many Poles were being sent to Germany to work. He added that many Polish Jews were skilled laborers and were to be used as part of the normal labor pool throughout the General Government. Because the Jewish Councils had limited resources, Frauendorfer decreed that Jews used in the normal labor market were to be paid salaries equal to 80 percent of that paid Polish workers. These guidelines did not apply to Jews used as forced labor.[58]

Frauendorfer's policies were totally ineffective. Polish and German businessmen were unwilling to pay Jews wages anywhere near Frauendorfer's rates; if they were paid anything at all, it was usually in foodstuffs bought on the Aryan side. In all likelihood, the food given to Tusia Müller by Mrs. Holzinger was probably her salary. This situation worsened with the opening of the ghettos, which limited the ability of many Jews to continue to work openly in the free Polish or German side of the economy outside of the ghetto. This was particularly true after the Germans had begun to think seriously about the so-called Final Solution of the Jewish Question in the fall of 1941. Their plan would involve closing most ghettos, though questions remained about the use of Jews in slave labor situations, particularly after the experiment with Soviet POW slave labor had failed.[59]

Various factories and businesses in the ghetto were owned by Poles and Germans, who used Polish and Jewish workers. One of the more famous was opened on the site of the former Optima Chocolate Factory on ul. Węgierska opposite the Jewish Orphanage, which was run by JSS. The factory, which was operated by the *Zentrale für Handwerklieferungen,* employed Jewish craftsmen who made shoes, furs, and clothing for the Germans.[60]

Julius Madritsch, Raimund Titsch, and Oskar Schindler

Another well-known factory in the ghetto was owned by a Viennese businessman, Julius Madritsch. He came to Kraków in the spring of 1940 to keep from being drafted into the Wehrmacht. Though he initially became a trustee for two Jewish confectionary stores, Hogo and Strassberg, at the end of 1940, Madritsch soon was able to open a sewing factory that employed Jewish and Polish workers. Early on, Madritsch gained a reputation similar to Schindler's when it came to the treatment of his Jewish employees. Most of the *Schindlerjuden* I interviewed knew of Madritsch and said he had a reputation as a good man who treated his Jewish workers well. Mila Levinson-Page worked for Madritsch and said he was "wonderful to his Jews." Helen Sternlicht Rosenweig, one of two Jewish maids who worked for Amon Göth in Płaszów, remembered Madritsch well. Unlike Oskar, she recalled, Julius Madritsch never ran around with women. And on one occasion, Julius brought Helen medicine for her ailing mother.[61]

The two men became friends. And when it came time for Marcel Goldberg to make up the famous "Schindler's List" in the fall of 1944, Schindler told Goldberg to be sure to include Madritsch's people. Several years after Oskar Schindler was nominated to be a Righteous Gentile, Julius Madritsch and his factory manager, Raimund Titsch, were declared Righteous Gentiles by Yad Vashem. If you stand at the site of Schindler's carob tree at Yad Vashem, you can see Madritsch and Titsch's trees on the Avenue of the Righteous. Yet after the war, the friendship between Schindler and Madritsch soured because of a dispute over the transfer of some of Madritsch's Jews to Brünnlitz and related matters. Oskar, though, always remained fond of Titsch.[62]

But Titsch was more than just a good human being; he was also an excellent photographer who secretly took photographs of Amon Göth and the Płaszów forced labor camp after Madritsch moved his sewing factory there in 1943. It is Titsch who has provided us with pictures of the overweight, half-naked Göth; some show him armed for target practice, live Jews his targets; other show him standing with his vicious dogs, Rolf and Ralf. Titsch, who knew the photographs were deadly evidence, always kept them hidden, even after the war. According to Thomas Keneally, Titsch did not have them developed but instead hid them in a park in Vienna. Titsch learned after the war that he was listed as a traitor in the files of ODESSA (*Organisation der ehemaligen SS-Angehörigen;* Organization of Former SS-Members), a secret SS network, and feared for his life. In 1963, Leopold Page bought the secret photographs from Titsch for $500, who was seriously ill with heart disease. Later, Page would donate the entire Titsch collection to the United States Holocaust Memorial Museum in Washington, D.C.[63]

Madritsch's story, which is drawn from his brief memoirs, *Menschen in Not! (People in Distress),* is important for the details he gives us about the inner workings of the German administrative system in Kraków, particularly as it relates to helping Jews. What Schindler and Madritsch achieved was far too complex to have been done without the help of others. Madritsch's story provides a deeper look into the complexities of life and business for factory owners like himself and Oskar Schindler. Yet Madritsch's account of his years in Kraków also provides us with a deeper look into the world of Oskar Schindler. Until the last year of the war, Schindler and Madritsch seemed quite close. Schindler even asked Madritsch to move his sewing factory to Brünnlitz. Madritsch's account of his failed efforts to gain permission for the move, his attempts to put some of his Jews on Goldberg's "Schindler's List," and his donation of fabric to Schindler adds depth to the Schindler story.[64]

Madritsch wrote in his memoirs that he sought to avoid the draft not because he was a shirker, but to avoid serving as an involuntary mercenary for the "'new apostles' [the Nazis], who had already forced on [his] homeland the blessings of the Thousand Year Reich." There is no doubt that Schindler and Madritsch were drawn together by their common Austrian heritage. The key to success for a German businessman in the General Government was well-placed contacts and Madritsch, like Schindler, had many. He got his start in business through a friend, Fritsch, who managed the Stafa department store in Kraków. Fritsch in turn introduced Madritsch to Dr. Adolf Lenhardt, a Viennese economic specialist with the General Government. Lenhardt helped Madritsch find a position as a textile specialist with the Textile Trade Association in Kraków *(Textilfachmann zur Textilhandelsges m. b. H., Krakau)* and later managed Madritsch's second sewing factory in Tarnow. At the same time, Madritsch became trustee for the two confectionery businesses.[65]

Madritsch was even-handed in his dealings with his Polish and Jewish workers, who gave him insight "into the methods that the German civil administration and the SS and police chiefs were using." Soon after he got into the confectionery business, Madritsch learned that he could make a great deal more money manufacturing textiles. When word spread among the Jewish community that Madritsch was considering opening a textile factory, representatives of the Judenrat approached him about the prospect of hiring Jewish specialists. Madritsch's greatest difficulties with German authorities came after the opening of the Kraków ghetto. He had to intervene constantly with the SS, the police, and the Labor Office to obtain work permits for his Jewish workers. An Austrian countryman, *Major* Ragger, frequently intervened for Madritsch with the SS and the police. But he had more trouble with the Labor Office, which insisted that he hire Poles instead of Jews. General Government labor officials charged that Madritsch was "a saboteur of the Jewish transfer [into the ghetto] and could encounter difficulties with the Gestapo." Evidently, this did not deter Madritsch, who was able to hire an increasing number of Jewish workers because they were "important to the war effort."[66]

In the midst of the opening of the Kraków ghetto in the spring of 1941, Madritsch was finally drafted into the Wehrmacht. From April 1941 until November 1942, he had to turn over the trusteeship of his factory to Heinz Bayer. He had been quite concerned about who would take over his half completed sewing factory because the previous trustee, Lukas, an SA (*Sturmabteilung,* Storm Division; Storm Troopers) *Führer,* had initiated a reign of terror over the workers. Raimund Titsch, Madritsch's "collaborator," continued to run the factory and kept Madritsch, who was stationed in Vienna, informed about developments there and in Kraków. Titsch kept a detailed account of all the firm's business affairs in a personal diary. Before Bayer assumed management, he met with Madritsch in Vienna, where they decided to set up a new business; they would use Madritsch's special business certificate, which gave him the right to operate a factory that produced goods for the military and allowed him to use Jewish workers. But like Schindler, Madritsch also relied on several Jewish workers, such as Naftali Hudes and Mr. Karp, for advice on setting up his new factory.[67]

All of this took place in the spring and summer of 1942 when the SS was opening its death camps for Jews throughout occupied Poland and struggling with the Wehrmacht over control of Jewish workers. Heinz Bayer began to suffer from eye problems and stress caused by "the relentless persecution of the Jews." Over time, Bayer became unfit for work; in August 1942, he resigned his position with Madritsch's firm and returned to Vienna. Fortunately, the Wehrmacht gave Madritsch several long leaves to return to Kraków and in August 1942 allowed him to return to Kraków permanently. Madritsch was finally released from military service later that year. He said that if his superiors in Vienna had not allowed this, "everything [in Kraków] would have collapsed." Madritsch added that Wehrmacht did not think much of his soldiery skills because his superiors "took only little delight in [his] 'professional' performance."[68] But would this completely explain their decision to grant him such extensive leaves to return to his businesses in Kraków? Probably not. Given the struggle that was taking place between the Armaments Inspectorate and the SS over Jewish labor in 1942, it is quite possible the Wehrmacht concluded that Julius Madritsch was more valuable to them running a military-related factory in the General Government than manning a desk in Vienna.[69]

The Controversy over Jewish Labor and the Final Solution

Madritsch returned to Kraków just as German policies towards Poland's Jews were undergoing a dramatic, deadly change. When the Nazi leadership had set in motion plans for the mass murder of Europe's Jews, they struggled for months with the role of Jewish labor vis-à-vis the goals of the Final Solution. As the death camps began to open throughout occupied Poland, the idea was to send able-bodied Jews to concentration camps as slave laborers and Jews incapable of work to the death camps. Yet even here there was controversy because of conflicting Nazi racial and economic goals. Though Nazi racial goals initially took precedence over economic ones when it came to the Final Solution, Germany's desperate manpower needs forced Reich leaders to rethink this issue, particularly after the failed experiment using Soviet POWs as slave laborers. By early 1942, the SS began to shift to a policy of destruction through labor. According to Christopher Browning, this meant that "Jews capable of labor were to work productively and die in the process."[70]

In the General Government, though, where Jews had come to play an important role in the industrial labor force, such a policy was counterproductive. This conflict came up during the Wannsee Conference in Berlin on January 20, 1942. Delayed because of the outbreak of war between Germany and the United States, Reinhard Heydrich called the meeting in hopes of obtaining "clarity on questions of principle" regarding the Final Solution from the prominent representatives of various ministries in the government and the Nazi Party who attended the conference. Dr. Josef Bühler, Hans Frank's state secretary *(Der Staatssekretär in der Regierung des Generalgouvernements)* stated that he wanted to put it on

record that the Government-General would welcome it if the final solution *[Endlösung]* of this problem [Jewish labor not essential to the war ef-
fort] was begun in the Government-General, as, on the one hand, the
question of transport there played no major role and considerations of
labor supply would not hinder the course of this Aktion. Jews must be removed as fast as possible from the Government-General, because it was
there in particular that the Jew as carrier of epidemics spelled a greater
danger, and, at the same time, he caused constant disorder in the economic structure of the country by his continuous black market dealings.
Furthermore, of the approximately 2.5 million Jews under consideration,
the majority were in any case unfit for work.[71]

Bühler ended his remarks with a request that "the Jewish question in
this area be solved as quickly as possible."[72] But the idea of concentrating
those Jews essential to the German war effort in slave labor camps also
concerned Bühler, who feared the camps would "destroy the existing organizational forms within which Jews were working and damage their
'multifaceted use.'"[73]

The Wehrmacht, particularly the Armaments Inspectorate (Wi Rü Amt)
under *General* Georg Thomas, was also fearful of such disruptions. Initially, the Armaments Inspectorate had opposed the use of Jewish labor
for security reasons; but by the spring of 1942, the Armaments Inspectorate, working with the SS, used Jewish labor in an aircraft factory in
Mielec. The idea was that Jewish workers would replace Poles and
Ukrainians sent to the Reich as forced laborers. The Wehrmacht then
began to experiment with the use of Jewish labor elsewhere in the General
Government. *General* Maximillian Schindler, the head of the Armaments
Inspectorate in the General Government, was so pleased with this experiment that in May 1942 he proposed the employment of 100,000 Jewish
workers, which would release a similar number of Poles and Ukrainians
for work in the Reich. The following month, *General* Schindler proposed
moving all shoe and clothing factories from the Greater Reich to the General Government, where he would run them using Jewish laborers. In
early July, *General* Schindler and Friedrich Wilhelm Krüger, the HSSPF in
the General Government, worked out an agreement whereby Jews working in the armaments industry would be housed in factory barracks or in
SS-run slave labor camps.[74]

Hans Frank initially supported the idea of keeping some Jews to use as
slave laborers in the General Government. He also seemed to support the

pleas of some German officials that more food was needed to keep the "work Jews" fit for hard labor. But by the summer of 1942, with the war against the Soviet Union entering its second year, concerns over the use of Jewish labor in war production gave way to worries about a serious food shortage in the Third Reich. This fear played into the hands of Heinrich Himmler, who on July 19, 1942, announced that the General Government must be cleared of all Jews by the end of the year. The only exceptions were Jews in forced labor camps in Warsaw, Kraków, Częstochowa, Radom, and Lublin. All firms employing Jews were to be closed or transferred into these forced labor camps. Exceptions had to be approved personally by Himmler. The *Reichsführer-SS* added that these moves "were necessary for the new order in Europe as well as for the 'security and cleanliness' of the German Reich and its spheres of interest." Himmler added that violations of his decree "would endanger peace and order and would create in Europe 'the germ of a resistance movement and a moral and physical center of pestilence.'"[75]

Two days before the issuance of Himmler's deportation decree, Krüger informed *General* Schindler of the termination of all deals between the SS and the Armaments Inspectorate dealing with Jewish labor. Krüger also told *General* Schindler of the new plan to house all Jewish workers essential to the war effort in newly constructed concentration camps. Because Himmler's overall plan involved the closing of ghettos throughout the General Government, Krüger promised Schindler that this would be done "in agreement with the Armaments Inspectorate."[76]

What *General* Schindler quickly discovered, though, was that Himmler's massive Jewish deportation scheme was seriously affecting military production. Efforts were made to persuade the SS to take actions against Jews only after it discussed the matter with the Armaments Inspectorate. The Armaments Inspectorate also reminded the SS that with the shipment of so many Poles to the Reich, "Jews [were] the sole available labor manpower." The problem was that the only factories covered by this agreement were linked to the defense contract plants *(Rüstungsbetriebe),* armaments factories that had direct contracts with the Armaments Inspectorate. The accord did not cover businesses involved in the production of armaments for firms in the Greater Reich or for the office of the military commander in the General Government.[77]

The Wehrmacht briefly tried to take a stand against Himmler. On August 15, 1942, a meeting was held in Kraków between representatives of the Armaments Inspectorate in the General Government and Krüger's office. Members of the Armaments Inspectorate were told that the plan to use Jewish labor to replace Polish labor was null and void. They were also reminded of Hermann Göring's recent statement:

> We must get away from the notion that the Jew is indispensable. Neither Armaments Inspection nor the other agencies in the Generalgouvernement are willing [would retain] the Jews until the end of the war. The orders that have been issued are clear and hard. They are valid not only for the Generalgouvernement, but for all occupied territories. The reasons for them must be extraordinary.[78]

One of *General* Schindler's representatives, *Hauptmann* Gartzke, countered that the Armaments Inspectorate needed Jewish workers because military "work orders are mounting." He added that "it would be impossible to replace overnight the Jews employed as trained workers in the factories of the Armaments Inspectorate."[79]

At the end of the meeting, the SS and the Armaments Inspectorate seemed to have worked out a compromise. It was agreed that the Jews working for the Armament Inspectorate in the Warsaw ghetto, the largest Jewish slave labor population in the General Government, would be put into a "special armament ghetto" in the Warsaw ghetto and separated from other Jews. However, two days later, Krüger told *General* Schindler that this agreement was now invalid and that the Warsaw ghetto was to be closed. The SS would now take over control of all Jewish laborers in the General Government. The Armaments Inspectorate would have to deal with the SS on all Jewish labor matters. In situations where Jewish labor was permitted, the Armaments Inspectorate not only would need the permission of the SS to obtain Jewish labor but also would have to build the barracks to house them. Given the serious shortage of barracks in the military, this was an impractical demand.[80]

The Wehrmacht's modest attempt to thwart Himmler's efforts ended on September 5, 1942, when *Generalfeldmarschall* Wilhelm Keitel, the head of the OKW, ordered *Generalleutnant* Kurt Ludwig Baron von Gienanth, the military commander in the General Government, instantly to replace with Poles all Jews working for the Armaments Inspectorate and the Wehrmacht. Himmler, who now planned to push for the removal of Gienanth because of earlier reports of SS difficulties with the general, found his task easier after *General* Gienanth sent a letter to OKW on September 18 underscoring the ridiculousness of Himmler's scheme:

So far, the Generalgouvernement has been directed to release Polish and Ukrainian workers for the Reich and replace them with Jewish workers. For the utilization of Jewish manpower for the war effort, purely Jewish factories or partial factories have been formed [and] Jewish camps set up for employment in the factories. According to government documents— Main Division for Labor—the sum total of commercial workers [in the Generalgouvernement] is somewhat more than one million, including 300,000 Jews. Of these, some 100,000 are skilled workers. In the individual factories working for the Wehrmacht, the number of Jews among the skilled workers keeps shifting between 25 and 100 percent; it is 100 percent in the textile plants making winter clothing. In other plants, for instance in the Fuhrmann and Pleskau vehicle factories, the key workers, the cartwrights, are chiefly Jews. The saddlers, with a few exceptions, are Jews. For uniform repairs, private firms employ a total of 22,700 workers now, of whom 22,000, i.e., 97 percent, are Jews, including some 16,000 skilled workers in textiles and leather plants. A purely Jewish factory with 168 employees manufactures harness fittings. The entire production of harnesses in the Generalgouvernement, the Ukraine, and partly in the Reich is dependent on this firm.[81]

Gienanth added that the deportation of the Jews by the SS had seriously slowed war production in the General Government, which meant that top priority winter production orders could not be completed. He was referring, of course, to the dreadful needs of the Wehrmacht as it went into its second harsh winter against the Soviet Union. He warned the OKW that the removal of Jews from the Wehrmacht's factories "would bring about a considerable reduction in the war potential of the Reich and hold up supplies for the front lines as well as for troops in the General Gouvernement." He estimated production gaps of 25 percent to 100 percent if Himmler followed through on his deportation orders.[82]

Himmler responded to Gienanth's letter on October 9 and pointed out that there was a difference between so-called armament enterprises, such as tailor, shoe, and carpentry shops, and real armament factories that produced weapons. Himmler let Gienanth know that he was prepared to take over shops that produced goods such as uniforms for the war effort. He added:

The Wehrmacht should give its orders to us, and we shall guarantee the continuation of deliveries of the desired uniforms. However, if anyone thinks he can confront us here with alleged armament interests, whereas in reality he only wants to protect the Jews and their business, *he will be dealt with mercilessly.*[83]

Himmler added that in real armaments workplaces, Jews were to be segregated into work halls. Over time, the work halls would be integrated into factory camps, and eventually these would be consolidated into several large concentration camp businesses that employed Jews. Himmler thought these special complexes would be located in the eastern part of the General Government. None of this was to be permanent; Himmler pointed out that even these remaining Jews, "in accordance with the Führer's wish, [would] disappear some day." Himmler was proposing that the SS now be directly involved in military-related industries, both through the control of Jewish labor and the making of items such as uniforms.[84]

To insure military compliance, Gienanth was replaced as military commander of the General Government by *General der Infantrie* Siegfried Hanicke. Several days later, *Oberst* Forster, *General* Hanicke's *Oberquartiermeister,* met with Krüger to work out specific details about Himmler's new armaments production proposal. This involved all companies doing business with the Armaments Inspectorate or the military commander of the General Government. Forster and Krüger both agreed there would be a reduction in the use of Jewish labor in the armaments industry though this had to be done by mutual agreement. The Armaments Inspectorate would pay the SS Zł 5 ($1.56) a day for male Jewish workers and Zł 4 a day ($1.25) for female Jewish workers. The businesses involved were allowed to deduct up to Zł 1.60 ($0.50) a day for "maintenance." These funds were to be transferred to the Reich treasury, which had been financing the concentration camp system since 1936. Presuming that a business using Jewish workers took the maximum maintenance allowance, this meant that the SS was paid Zł 3.40 ($1.06) daily for male Jewish workers and Zł 2.40 ($0.75) a day for female Jewish laborers. This was the arrangement that Julius Madritsch and Oskar Schindler began to use in their factories. After the war, Schindler stated that he paid the SS Zł 5 for each of his workers in Emalia.[85]

The new SS-Wehrmacht armaments production agreement did not include the numerous civilian businesses and agencies that used Jewish labor linked to the war effort. Many of these concerns were devastated by the loss of Jewish labor as the SS continued its massive roundup of Jews for the death camps at Auschwitz II—Birkenau, Sobibór, Treblinka, Bełżec, Kuhlmhof (Chełmno), and Majdanek. Frank alluded to these losses in a meeting on December 9, 1942.

> Not unimportant labor reserves have been taken from us when we lost our old trustworthy Jews [altbewährten Judenschaften]. It is clear that the labor situation is made more difficult when, in the middle of the war effort, the order is given to prepare all Jews for annihilation. The responsibility for this order does not lie with the offices of the General-gouvernement. The directive for the annihilation of the Jews comes from higher sources. We can only deal with the consequences of this situation, and we can tell the agencies of the Reich that the taking away of the Jews has led to tremendous difficulties in the labor field. Just the other day I could prove to Staatssekretär [for the Reichsbahn or state-owned railroad] Ganzemüller [Albert], who complained that a large construction project in the Generalgouvernement had come to a standstill, that would not have happened if the many thousands of Jews who were employed there had not been taken away. Now the order provides that the armaments Jews are also to be taken away. I hope that this order, if not already voided, will be revoked, because then the situation will be even worse.[86]

By the time that the SS and the Wehrmacht concluded their agreement in the fall of 1942, the Final Solution was entering its deadliest phase. Before the invasion of the Soviet Union on June 22, 1941, the Germans put together specially trained Einsatzgruppen to initiate a mass murder program aimed principally at Jews but also the communist leadership in the conquered parts of the Soviet Union. There were about 3,000 men in the four major Einsatzgruppen units (A, B, C, and D), many of them members of the SS. They were drawn from all RSHA branches, such as the Gestapo, Sipo, and Kripo, as well as Order Police units and the Waffen-SS. From June 1941 to January 1942, the Einsatzgruppen murdered about 500,000 Soviet Jews.[87] In the midst of what appeared to be another brilliant military victory for Adolf Hitler, the Nazi leadership, led by Heinrich Himmler, Reinhard Heydrich, and Herman Göring, began to make plans for the "Final Solution of the Jewish Question." Heydrich laid out the general outline for the plan in a letter to Göring in the spring of 1941. On July 31, 1941, Göring signed an order prepared by Heydrich that gave him the right to move ahead with planning the Final Solution:

Complementing the task already assigned to you in the decree of January 24, 1939, to undertake, by emigration or evacuation, a solution of the Jewish question as advantageous as possible under the conditions at the time, I hereby charge you with making *all the necessary organizational, functional, and material preparations for a complete solution (Gesamtlö-sung) of the Jewish question in the German area of influence in Europe.* In so far as the jurisdiction of other central agencies may be touched thereby, they are to be involved. I charge you furthermore with submitting to me in the near future an overall plan of the organizational, functional and material measures to be taken in preparing for the implementation of the aspired *final solution of the Jewish question.*[88]

While the German leadership began to plan the Final Solution, the *Einsatzgruppen* and others continued their violent killing campaign against Jews, Gypsies, the handicapped, and the communist elite in the Soviet Union.

But the Final Solution was to involve more than just the mass murder of Jews by the *Einsatzgruppen*. An integral part of the Final Solution centered around the opening of killing centers throughout German-occupied Poland. The Germans already had considerable experience with such techniques in Germany, where from 1939 to 1941, they operated six T-4 killing centers for the German handicapped. The program was sponsored by Hitler's private Chancellery *(Kanzlei des Führers)* and the Reich Ministry of Interior *(Reichsministerium des Innern)* and took its name from the address of the front organization created to maintain the program's secrecy, No. 4 Tiergarten Straße, Berlin. Operation T-4 murdered about 70,000 handicapped Germans principally using carbon monoxide as a gassing agent. The victims' bodies were then cremated. The Germans officially shut down Operation T-4 in the summer of 1941 because its purpose had become public knowledge, though the murder of the handicapped continued not only in Germany but in other parts of Nazi-occupied Europe. Some of the T-4 specialists were brought to the east, where they formed the nucleus of the Final Solution, particularly in the Aktion Reinhard death camps. Working with other specialists from the SS and German businesses, they helped design a variety of killing chambers, vehicles, and crematories to murder and cremate their victims quickly and efficiently.[89]

Though only about half of the 6 million Jews murdered in the Holocaust died in death camps, the six major death camps in occupied Poland came to symbolize the worst of the Holocaust.

The first camp to began gassing Jews as part of the Final Solution was Chełmno (Kulmhof), about forty-five minutes west of Łódź, where the SS used mobile gas vans to asphyxiate their victims. The SS murdered their first group of Jews at Chełmno on December 8, 1941. Estimates are that as many as from 150,000 to 320,00 Jews were murdered at Chełmno from 1941 to early 1945.[90]

The SS opened its most deadly killing center, Auschwitz (Oświęcim), located forty miles west of Kraków, in the summer of 1940 as a concentration camp for Poles. Himmler ordered the opening of a second complex, Auschwitz II-Birkenau, the following spring. In the fall of 1941, Rudolf Höss, Auschwitz's commandant, and his deputy, Karl Fritzsch, killed Soviet POWs in two experiments in Auschwitz I using a cyanide-based fumigant, Zyklon B. Höss ordered the murder of the first Jews at Auschwitz II-Birkenau in mid-February 1942 using this deadly gassing agent. The next year, Höss greatly expanded the killing and body-disposal facilities at Auschwitz II-Birkenau. From 1942 until early 1945, the Germans murdered about 1 million Jews and another 100,000 Gypsies, Soviet POWs, Poles, and others in Auschwitz.[91]

While Höss and Fritsch experimented with Zyklon B, Himmler appointed the Higher SS and Police Leader (HSSPF) in the Lublin district, Odilo Globočnik, to head a program designed to murder all the Jews in the General Government. After the murder of Reinhard Heydrich by Czech partisans on May 27, 1942, those in charge of this campaign named their operation Aktion Reinhard. From November 1941 until July 1942, the SS opened three more death camps as part of Aktion Reinhard at Bełżec, Sobibór, and Treblinka. The Aktion Reinhard death camps were never meant to be permanent; after the murder of what remained of most of the Jews in the General Government, Himmler decided in the spring of 1943 to close the three camps, all traces of their existence to be destroyed.[92]

In late February 1942, the SS began the experimental murder of Jews in the gas chambers at Bełżec, about a hundred miles northeast of Kraków. The SS used carbon monoxide gas in canisters and pumped it into the death chambers. Over the course of ten months, the SS murdered 550,000 to 600,000 Jews at Bełżec.[93] A second Aktion Reinhard camp, Sobibór, was opened north of Lublin in the spring of 1942. During the fourteen months it served as a death camp, the SS murdered as many as 200,000 Jews there. The Germans used a heavy captured Russian diesel engine to pump carbon monoxide into Sobibór's gas chambers and then cremated or buried the bodies in mass graves. Sobibór was transformed into a concentration camp in the summer of 1943, though Himmler closed it after an embarrassing uprising there on October 14, 1943, that saw about half of Sobibór's remaining six hundred prisoners attempt an escape. Only about fifty managed to elude their German captors.[94]

The SS opened the third Aktion Reinhard death camp, Treblinka, to the northeast of Warsaw, in the summer of 1942. Initially a German forced labor camp, Treblinka became, after Auschwitz, the deadliest of the German killing centers in the General Government. Estimates are that about 763,000 Jews and 100,000 non-Jews were murdered in Treblinka. As at Sobibór, carbon monoxide was pumped into gas chambers from a diesel engine. The victims' bodies were then buried in mass graves. As the Germans made plans to close Treblinka, a rebellion broke out on August 2, 1943. About 750 of the 850 Jewish inmates left in Treblinka took part in the uprising. Most were killed or caught within twenty-four hours, but about 90 successfully escaped the initial German dragnet and fled to the interior of Poland.[95]

There was one more death camp in occupied Poland, Majdanek, located in the suburbs of Lublin. Today, one can eerily look at what remains of the concentration and death camp from a nearby apartment window. In the summer of 1941, Himmler ordered Globocnik to open a concentration camp in Lublin for 25,000 to 50,000 prisoners with the idea of "employing them in the workshops and on building sites of the SS and police."[96] The Majdanek inmates were to be used in various SS ventures and to help build an "SS settlement" in Lublin, which Himmler hoped would become the center of SS activities and supply for operations in the Soviet Union. As HSSPF in Lublin, Globocnik saw Majdanek as his personal camp. He had seven gas chambers built there that used Zyklon B, though the Germans also used the gallows and the guillotine to murder their prisoners. About 60 percent of the 360,000 Jews, Poles, Soviet POWs, and others who were murdered in Majdanek died from harsh labor conditions, malnutrition, or disease. The SS began to dismantle Majdanek in the spring of 1944; it was liberated by the Red Army that summer.[97]

Madritsch's Operations in the Kraków Ghetto

Once Madritsch returned permanently to Kraków, he found it difficult to do business with the SS and, in turn, the Wehrmacht's Armaments Inspectorate, without considerable help from others in the General Government's administration. Because of his extensive contacts in the Textile Trade Association in Kraków, Madritsch was able to get an order for uniforms from the Wehrmacht that "qualified [his] firm as an armaments factory." He got a bank loan of Zł 1,370,000 ($428,125) greatly to expand the size of his operations and opened a second factory in Tarnow. He employed eight hundred workers in each factory, many of them Jews. Like Schindler, Julius Madritsch relied upon his German and Polish contacts to keep the factory running. He mentions his most important supporters and collaborators throughout his memoirs. At the end of the introduction to his brief memoirs, he names five upright coworkers who were particularly important in helping Jews and Poles. With the exception of Mrs. Anneliese Pipgorra, who worked in his office, the other four upright coworkers he mentions were from Austria. This list included Raimund Titsch, Dr. Adolf Lenhardt, Mrs. Maria Herling, another office worker, and a police lieutenant, Oswald Bousko, vice commander of Schupo (*Schutzpolizei;* municipal police, or constables) in Podgórze. Madritsch is equally complimentary of his Polish collaborators, whom he considered no less helpful than his German and Austrian friends. He said he "had blind trust in their loyalty, bravery, and intelligence" and felt linked to them in "sincere friendship." Madritsch was also very proud of the relationship between his Jewish and Polish workers and bragged that despite the opposition of the SD, he periodically held adherence nights *(Gefolgsabende)* before the creation of the ghetto that he said were "comparable to family reunions" for his Jewish and Polish workers.[98]

Yet there were also others who were instrumental to his success in helping Jews and Poles during the war. He was particularly dependent on Herr Mißbach, the head of the Textile Trade Association in Kraków. It was Mißbach who gave Madritsch the numerous "certificates documenting the importance of [his] firms for the war effort." According to Madritsch, Mißbach knew exactly the type of information needed on the various reports he supplied the Armaments Inspectorate teams that periodically evaluated Madritsch's operations to insure that he met Wehrmacht production standards. According to Madritsch, Mißbach was so good at preparing these phony reports that he was able to convince the Armaments Inspectorate that he ran the "largest 'armaments' factory in the G.G., even though in reality [Madritsch] produced at least 95 percent for the civil sector."[99]

Madritsch goes on to mention four more mid-level German bureaucrats (Graßnickel, Stoffregen, Reddig, and Schneewind) from the trade association in Kraków who "helped . . . turn out production numbers according to the full number of laborers, even though [Madritsch] had at most 40 percent specialized workers." Madritsch never says whether these officials helped out from the goodness of their hearts or because he bribed them. But regardless of their motives, these officials were able to rewrite reports that made it seem that 40 percent of Madritsch's Jewish workforce was doing the work of "100 percent Jewish expert workers." But his trade association friends did more than pad numbers: They made sure that Madritsch received orders that were easy to produce and used a minimal amount of cloth to insure greater profits.[100]

Like Schindler, Madritsch had to reward German officials and others with extensive bribes and gifts to insure their support. Over time, Madritsch found that doing business in the General Government became more and more expensive. He attributed part of this to the dramatic rise in the cost of living for civil servants in the General Government. Though many Reich officials initially left their families behind in the Reich, they often brought their families to Poland later to cut expenses. Consequently, Madritsch found these officials seemed "less reluctant" to accept bribes from businessmen such as Madritsch and Schindler. Yet an increase in the cost of living was not the only reason that some Germans accepted bribes. Some were simply greedy and corrupt. Regardless of the motivation, how did Madritsch acquire the extra funds for the bribes? He did it by efficiently cutting the cloth he had for uniform production and then having "his people" sell it on the black market. He used the extra funds to bribe German and Polish officials for extra pay or food for his workers.[101]

Though Madritsch never talked about the amount of money he made in Kraków and Tarnow, he did mention the amount of money he had to pay the SS for "subsistence" and for food subsidies. At the peak of his operations in 1943–1944, he was paying the SS Zł 350,000 ($109,375) a month for subsistence and spent Zł 250,000 ($78,125) a month for extra food for his workers. This seems like an incredible amount, but it was not out of line with the amounts paid by Oskar Schindler to the SS or spent for extra food during the same period, though Schindler's figures seem lower than Madritsch's estimates. It is possible that both men exaggerated the amounts they spent during the war to help Jews, but for different reasons. Moreover, Schindler, unlike Madritsch, does not discuss total monthly subsistence payments to the SS. Oskar wrote his principal financial report just after the war ended with the idea of getting compensation first from Jewish organizations and later from the West German government. Madritsch wrote *Menschen in Not!* in 1962 after his name came up as a possible Righteous Gentile candidate in Israel.[102]

The introduction to *Menschen in Not!* was written by Dr. Dawid Schlang, a professor at the University of Vienna and the general secretary of the Zionist Association in Austria. Dr. Schlang wrote, "We can consider him [Madritsch] with pure conscience as a member of the tiny and hidden Zadilkei *[Tzaddik]* Umoth Haolam [thirty-six righteous of the different peoples on whom the world rests]," a reference to the Talmudic legend of the Thirty-Six *Tzaddikim,* or righteous persons. The term *Tzaddik* is used in the Jewish scriptures to describe, among others, Noah, and refers to a person of great moral character who by his lifestyle inspired others to follow a similar path of faith and piety. The Talmudic legend says that no one except G-d knows the identity of the *Tzaddikim,* though the existence of the world depends on their unselfish lives and work.[103]

The evolving labor policies in the General Government, particularly as they related to Jews, created problems as well as opportunities for Oskar Schindler and Julius Madritsch. With the onset of the Final Solution, it became more and more difficult to hire and keep skilled Jewish laborers. On the other hand, the Third Reich's growing labor shortages also created opportunities for German factory owners who were already accustomed to dealing with the General Government's complex and corrupt black market. They discovered that well-placed bribes could get them almost anything, even Jewish workers. The skill of Germans such as Schindler and Madritsch was inherent in their balancing of personal concern for the well-being of their Jewish slave laborers with the broader Nazi demand for the elimination, through mass murder or forced labor, of all Jews from the face of Europe. During the latter years of the war, both German factory owners found a way to weave their way through the complex racial and economic worlds of the General Government, though, in the end, it was Oskar Schindler who did the most to save his Jewish workers.

5.

ORIGINS OF THE SCHINDLER MYTH

DURING HIS TIME IN KRAKÓW, OSKAR SCHINDLER BECAME AN incredibly successful businessman, in part because of the genius of Abraham Bankier. But Oskar's success was shadowed by the growing horror of the German occupation of Kraków and the desperate lives of the Jewish workers with whom he came in contact every day. From 1941 to 1943, they suffered from the threat of deportation to the growing collection of death camps such as nearby Auschwitz, which was the principal killing center of the Final Solution. Oskar's principal Kraków factory, Emalia, was only a few blocks from the ghetto, and he was able to observe first-hand the horrors and degradation of ghetto life. He responded by treating his Jewish workers with kindness and dignity, which in turn attracted the glare of the Gestapo.

Yet how successful was Oskar Schindler as a businessman in Kraków from 1939 to 1944? According to the detailed financial statement that he prepared immediately after the war in Konstanz, Germany, at the insistence of one of his *Schindlerjude,* Rabbi Menachem Levertov, Oskar estimated that the revenue from his kitchenware products at Emalia was about RM 15 million ($6 million) and another RM 0.5 million ($200,000) from Emalia's modest armaments production facility. In a document filed with German authorities from Buenos Aires in 1954, Oskar broke down his annual revenues for enamelware sales from 1940 through 1944. He said that he sold Zł 2.2 million ($687,500) in enamelware in 1940, Zł 2.6 million ($812,500) in 1941, Zł 3 million ($937,600) in 1942, Zł 3.5 million ($1,093,750) in 1943, and Zł 2.6 million ($812,500) in 1944, his last year of production in Emalia. These figures, which Oskar submitted in 1954, are considerably smaller than the figures that he put into his 1945 financial report, which he admitted he had created "out of my memory, without documents or files."[1]

One document in Oskar's *Lastenausgleich* file provides a more in-depth look at Emalia's financial affairs. The firm's 1943 year-end report, completed on May 15, 1944, and signed by Schindler himself, showed that Emalia had a year-end balance of Zł 7,601,054.98 ($2,375,329.60) and net proceeds of Zł 6,744,532.25 ($2,107,666.30). Oskar had undertaken an ambitious expansion program when he took over Emalia in 1939 and it showed up on his ledgers. By the end of 1943, Schindler was heavily in debt. He owed various banks, creditors, and other lenders Zł 3,849,411.11 ($1,202,940.90). He also had other debts totaling almost Zł 1.5 million ($468,750). A good portion of this was simply listed as part of his *"Privatkonto"* (private account). He also had other obligations, including debts to the *"SS u. Polizeiführer"* (Zł 118,360; $36,987.50) and the SS-run *"Judenfonds"* (Zł 35,832.61; $11,558.93). These were payments owed the SS for Jewish labor and support for 1943.[2]

It is difficult to get a clear picture of Emalia's revenues, debts and other expenses because most records for its operations no longer exist. Moreover, Emalia, like all other businesses in the General Government, operated under two sets of books. Those used for Emalia's 1943 report were the "legal" books; another set existed for the black market economy, the principal source of revenue for Schindler. These "legal" books do tell that Schindler bore tremendous costs and obligations. Some of these are listed in his 1943 report, but because this file is incomplete, there is nothing to indicate the salaries he paid his Polish workers. He used Polish laborers almost exclusively to produce his enamelware and Jewish workers in Emalia's armaments shop. This meant that Polish workers were far more valuable to Oskar than his Jewish workers. He used his profits from the production of enamelware to pay the RM 2.64 million ($1,056,000) and "the Jews of [his] factory, in order to secure their survival and to ease their painful fate."[3]

It is also hard to determine how much Schindler spent on his Polish workers. Remember that he continued to operate his Emalia factory exclusively with 650 Polish workers until the Soviets occupied Kraków in January 1945. At his peak of operations in 1944, Oskar employed from 700 to 750 Polish workers at Emalia. He used another 350 Polish workers at his Proksziner vodka bottle plant across the street from Emalia until it closed in 1943. We have no record of what Schindler paid his Polish workers because there were two wage scales for Polish workers in the General Government. Official wage scales were frozen at prewar levels of Zł 200 to Zł 300 ($62.50 to $93.75) a month, though unofficial wages, which were the ones probably paid by Schindler, ranged from Zł 8 to Zł 35 ($2.50 to $10.94) an hour. It took Schindler three months to get Emalia up and running after he acquired it in November 1939. He initially employed seven Jews and 250 Poles, though he increased the size of both work forces substantially over the next few years.[4]

Given the importance of his Polish workers to his initial financial success, it should come as no surprise that some of his harshest conflicts with General Government officialdom at first concerned his Polish workers. He told Fritz Lang, for example, that he constantly complained about the lack of adequate food and consumer goods for his Polish workers. He wrote detailed letters of complaint to *SS-Obergruppenführer* Wilhelm Koppe, who replaced Friedrich Wilhelm Krüger as the HSSPF (*Höhreren SS- und Polizeiführer;* Higher SS and Police Leader) for the General Government in 1943. According to Oskar, he complained about the growing "superman" syndrome among the General Government's bureaucrats; they "would soon ruin the economy" with regulations that would "murder the cow they intend to milk." Koppe later told Oskar that he would not tolerate continued "crass criticism of his agents and their actions," and the only thing that kept him from putting Oskar in a concentration camp were his "well-known positive contributions to the economy."[5]

Evidently such a warning did little to deter Schindler, who continued to protest labor conditions for his Polish workers and the deportation of Polish workers to the Reich. He also helped some of his "Aryan" Polish workers or their friends obtain their freedom from detention or POW camps, helped stop their deportation to Germany as forced laborers, and was even able to persuade German authorities to return some of their apartments. Oskar thought he was protected not only by his own fearlessness and impudence but also by his expertise, which had helped get him elected head of the sheet metal processing industries organization (*Fachgruppe Blechverarbeitenden Industrien*).[6]

In many ways, it would seem foolish openly to criticize the SS, particularly as the Gestapo arrested him three times during the war for bribery and "fraternization" with Poles and Jews. His last arrest in 1944 was the most serious because it involved substantiated charges that Oskar had bribed "the SS leader with a sum that exceeded two hundred thousand

słoty [sic]." In his 1945 financial statement, Oskar said that he spent about
Zł 550,000 ($171,875) bribing SS officials such as Göth, *SS-Oberführer*
Julian Scherner, the HSSPF in the Kraków District, *SS-Obersturmführer*
Rolf Czurda of the SD, and *SS-Untersturmführer* Leonhard John, the
deputy commandant of the Płaszów camp. Göth received about half the
Zł 550,000 ($171,875), so it is quite possible that Scherner, as Kraków's
HSSPF, was the unnamed "SS leader" who took in excess of Zł 200,000
($62,500) in bribes from Oskar.[7]

Yet Oskar seemed fearless when it came to confronting Koppe or
Krüger about matters that affected the financial well-being of his factories. This is probably why he got away with it. He evidently knew his
boundaries when he wrote his letters of protest, and he likely wrote them
in the context of worrying about policies that hurt the economy and thus
the war effort. And there is probably a good chance that Koppe and
Krüger both received bribes from Schindler. Though he never mentions
Koppe or Krüger by name, Oskar does say that in addition to the Zł
550,000 he spent to bribe Göth and others, he also spent "several hundred thousand Zł [złotys]" for "'smaller' presents and countless compensations, which were demanded by SS-officials in exchange for small favors." For these small favors he gave out watches, cameras, saddles,
boots, and shoes, though in three instances he gave SS officials a BMW
sports car, an Adler limousine, and a Mercedes Benz convertible. It is
doubtful that the cars went to lower-level SS officials.[8]

Emalia

Oskar Schindler operated Emalia *(Deutsche Emalwarenfabrik Oskar
Schindler)* from November 1939 until January 1945. Oskar made few references to the running and production of the factory after the war except
in the context of his various claims for compensation. But one can piece together something about the nature of the factory and its complex from
these claims as well as in documents and factory plans found in the *Lastenausgleich* archives in Bayreuth, the famed Schindler *Koffer* (suitcase files)
at the Bundesarchiv in Koblenz, and Yad Vashem in Jerusalem. There is
also documentation on Emalia in Polish court records in the Archiwum
Państwowe in Kraków and the Schindler files in the archives of the Joint in
New York. Though there are still parts of Emalia on its old site on ul.
Lipowa 4 in Kraków, not much of the old factory remains except for the
storied front gate and upstairs office complex. The original factory smoke-

stack was taken down in the late 1990s and many of Emalia's buildings were torn down and replaced by newer structures after World War II.

When Oskar acquired the lease on the bankrupt Jewish factory, Rekord, Ltd., on November 14, 1939, two buildings stood on the site: the factory itself, which included a separate 45-meter-high brick smokestack, and a warehouse. The original complex, all built in 1935, fronted ul. Lipowa. During the next four years, Schindler enlarged his factory. In 1940, he built a pay office and a medical-dental outpatient clinic, a canteen and workers' eating room, and a joint garage-stable. In 1941 and 1942, he erected a large building for stamping and pressing and for storing sheet metal and tools. In 1942, Oskar added the office complex with its gated factory entranceway and glass-enclosed staircase. This complex is about all that remains of the original Schindler factory. The new administration building included Emalia's central office, a small guard and porter room just inside the gate, the central telephone office, the factory co-op, a chemical storage room, a showroom, a new pay office, the employees' kitchen and dining room, the director's office, a conference room, and an apartment for Oskar.[9]

In 1942 and 1943, Schindler added a building for two new low-pressure boilers. During this time he also signed a contract with Siemens Bauunion G.m.b.H. to begin constructing a large hangar-style stamping facility. Siemens began work on the facility in the fall of 1943 and completed it the following summer at a cost of Zł 248,071 ($77,522).[10] As the tide of war changed, Schindler became more concerned about protecting his considerable investment. In 1949, he prepared a report as part of his ongoing efforts to obtain compensation for his lost factories and personal wealth. He based the estimates in this report on another document he completed on May 6, 1945, just two days before he fled Brünnlitz to avoid capture by the Red Army. He estimated the value of Emalia at DM 1,910,000 ($573,573.57).[11]

On July 10, 1943, he took out two insurance policies with Die Versicherungs-Gesellschaft "Silesia" A.G. for Zł 4,110,000 ($1,284,375) to protect his factory from *"Brand, Blitzschlag und Explosion"* (fire, lightning, and explosion). One policy ran from June 7, 1943, to the same date in 1950; the second provided coverage from 1943 to 1953. His annual premium for both policies was Zł 16,113.60 ($5,035.50). On February 11, 1944, Schindler increased his coverage on both policies to Zł 5,137,500 ($1,605,469). However, reflecting the uncertainty of the times, the premiums, Zł 2,167.49 ($677.31), covered only from January 15, 1944 to June 7, 1944.[12]

Oskar's building program intensified after he formally bought Emalia in 1942. And this was no easy task, given the nature of the German bureaucracy. Emalia was the property of the Polish regional trade court in Kraków. Schindler, who initially leased the factory in November 1939, worked with the court's legal representatives, first Dr. Roland Goryczko and later Dr. Bolesław Zawisza. As part of his original lease deal, Oskar bought the former Rekord, Ltd.'s original equipment in early 1940 for Zł 28,000 ($8,750) and paid the court a quarterly rent of Zł 2,400 ($750).[13]

At first, Oskar seemed satisfied with his lease agreement, though when he began to enjoy considerable profits from his investment he became interested in owning Emalia outright. Oskar had cleverly leased Emalia from the Polish trade court just two months before a law requiring the compulsory seizure of Jewish property went into effect. Consequently, Oskar, but more precisely, the court's legal representative, then Dr. Goryczko, could argue that because Rekord, Ltd., once a Jewish business, had gone bankrupt in the summer of 1939 and was now being leased by a German, it could never legally fall under the requirements of the January 15, 1940, compulsory Jewish property seizure law.[14]

Oskar signed a new lease with the Polish trade court on January 31, 1942, but within a few months moved to buy Emalia outright. This was to be done at a public auction, which was announced first for April 21, 1942, but was delayed until June 26, 1942. The reason for the change in date was to insure that all appropriate documents were in place indicating that the factory was not eligible for seizure as a Jewish factory by the Trustee Office. Fortunately, Dr. Zawisza, now the Polish trade court's Emalia representative, had already recommended to the court that Oskar be allowed to buy the property. This meant securing statements from Nathan Wurzel that he was not the former owner of the factory and had no claims against it. Once Zawisza secured these statements, the auction could go forward. Everything was prearranged, obviously with the help of some well-placed bribes, and Oskar Schindler bought Emalia from the Polish trade court for Zł 254,674.66 ($79,585.83) in cash on September 16, 1942. Given that he insured Emalia for over Zł 4 million ($1.25 million) the following year, the purchase would seem like quite a bargain. But remember that by the time that Oskar bought the factory outright in 1942, he had already invested heavily in new equipment and buildings. The funds from the sale of the former Rekord, Ltd. to Oskar Schindler were deposited into a bank in Kraków. Rekord, Ltd.'s creditors could then apply to the court for payment of the company's debts.[15]

Origins of the Schindler Legend

But Oskar Schindler did more than build a factory to make enamelware. After the closing of the Kraków ghetto in 1943, he arranged with Amon Göth, the commandant of Płaszów, the new forced labor camp just two miles from Emalia in the outskirts of Kraków, to build a Płaszów sub-camp at Emalia. But why and how? Embedded in the answers to these questions is a relationship between two men that came to represent opposite moral touchstones in the Holocaust-Oskar Schindler, the "angel" of Emalia and Brünnlitz, and Amon Göth, one of the true monsters in Nazi Germany's devastating war against the Jews. The question of why Oskar Schindler went to the great trouble of building, at his own expense, a large sub-camp with barracks and other facilities not only for his own Jewish workers but also for Jews who worked in neighboring factories lies at the center of the Schindler story. The seed for the Schindler legend took root at Emalia. By the time Oskar Schindler began to plan the transfer of part of his factory and its Jewish workers to Brünnlitz in the summer and fall of 1944, he was fully committed not only to saving his Jewish workers but those from other factories.

But when did Schindler make the decision to undertake the salvation of his Jewish workers? After the war, Oskar remained very close to his former *Schindlerjuden*; in some ways it seemed, particularly in the immediate years after the war, that he could not function without their support and protection. The most important immediate postwar document about this is Schindler's July 1945 financial statement, in which he talks extensively about his efforts to save his Jewish workers. Written at the prodding of Rabbi Levertov, one of his most prominent *Schindlerjuden*, Oskar was no doubt trying to depict himself as someone deeply committed to an ongoing campaign to help Jews from 1939 onward. And though there is no question that Emalia's success was linked to the genius of Abraham Bankier and others, it is difficult to pinpoint a moment when Oskar Schindler decided to work solely to save his Jewish workers. More than likely, it was a gradual decision. Nonetheless, Oskar was motivated for business as well as moral reasons. At the end of the war, he told Mietek Pemper, one of his closest Jewish associates during and after the war, that when the war ended, he hoped the Allies would create a Czechoslovakian state as they had done after World War I. Oskar's dream was that his factory at Brünnlitz could supply a war-devastated Europe with pots and pans, his Jewish workers at the core of his labor force.[16] So in the end,

Oskar Schindler combined his ethical concern over the fate of Jews in the Holocaust with some impractical business dreams.

It should be remembered that the use of Jewish labor in Kraków was good business. A factory owner had to pay Jewish workers much less than their Polish counterparts. Moreover, Jewish workers were more dependable and willing to work longer hours. But when did Oskar really begin to use large numbers of Jewish workers? He would have us believe that the large-scale use of Jews at Emalia began in 1940 and that by late 1942 almost half of his work force were Jews. But Sol Urbach said that when he was rounded up by the SS and transported to Schindler's nearby factory in the fall of 1942, only a handful of Jews worked at Emalia, not the 550 claimed by Oskar. Edith Wertheim said that when Schindler opened his sub-camp at Emalia in 1943, only about thirty women were working for him. However, Oskar probably included 450 Jews from neighboring factories in the figures he cited for the number of Jews he housed in his sub-camp. Consequently, it is possible that he mistakenly thought of these numbers as his own workers because he housed and fed them, though their expenses were paid by other factory owners. This could possibly explain the discrepancy between Sol Urbach's estimate and Oskar's estimate of the number of Jews working at Emalia in 1942–1943.[17]

But more important than this question is the motivation behind Schindler's efforts to help Jewish workers. By the time Sol Urbach came to work for Oskar in 1942, there were already signs of Oskar's sympathy for his Jewish workers. According to Sol, with the exception of being forced to walk to and from Emalia under SS guard, everything was relatively normal there. Sol and the other Jews rounded up at *Plac Zgody* continued to live in the ghetto, which was only a few blocks from Emalia's entrance, until it was closed on March 13–14, 1943. Each morning, Sol's team of *Schindlerjuden*, armed with their *Kennkarten* (identity cards) and their precious work permits, the *Blauscheine*, would meet at the Podgórze Square gate at about seven to await the two-man SS team that would escort them to Emalia. In December 1942, the SS replaced the *Kennkarten* with a *Judenkarte*. Each Jewish worker leaving the ghetto also had to wear a large, prominently displayed "W," "R," or "Z" patch on their outer clothing. The large patches, which were triangular, had SS and police stamps on them. The "W" patch stood for *Wehrmacht*, indicating that the wearer worked in a factory that produced goods for the military. The "R" stood for *Rüstung*, meaning labor for an armaments-producing firm, and the "Z" for *Zivil*, which indicated that the wearer worked in a civilian industry or in agriculture.[18]

Sol and his fellow Jewish laborers worked long twelve-hour shifts. They were given periodic breaks and their meals, which they ate at their work site alongside Polish workers. The meals consisted of soup and bread. Emalia's Jews were integrated into the larger Polish work force but, with the exception of Bankier and a few others, worked as common laborers supervised by Poles. There were no SS guards at Emalia when the ghetto was open. Sol, working as a carpenter's assistant, moved freely about the Emalia complex, which, he said, did not initially have a "camp-like atmosphere." Emalia's main item of production was a ten-inch round pot. The pots began as long sheets of steel that were then cut into large round circles and pressed into pots. Handles were added to the pots, which were then dipped into enamel and baked in an oven.[19]

This healthy atmosphere in Oskar's factory is the first sign we have of Schindler's attitudes towards his Jewish workers. They were treated with dignity. But it could also be argued that, from a business point of view, a well-treated worker will produce more. Were there other factors that might have affected Schindler's drift into a more protective attitude toward his Jewish workers, particularly in 1942? As we shall see, several developments had a direct and indirect impact on Oskar's thinking about the fate of his *Schindlerjuden*.

Oskar and the Gestapo

The first was Oskar's arrest by the Gestapo in late 1941 or early 1942. Oskar had already run afoul of the Gestapo a year earlier because of the break-in to his apartment in Mährisch Ostrau by a Polish thief in 1939. As we have seen, the Gestapo questioned Schindler extensively about this in 1940 and arrested him three times from 1941 to 1944. Oskar never said much about his arrests, which he referred to as "unpleasantries," but he considered the last one the worst. His third incarceration is also the only one mentioned by Emilie in her memoirs. According to Janina Olszewska, the office manager at Oskar's enamelware showroom, Schindler was first arrested by the Gestapo at the end of 1941 and taken to Gestapo headquarters on ul. Pomorska 2, which is in Nowa Wies, several miles from Schindler's factory. The building that housed the hated Gestapo was reopened as the Museum of the Fight and Martyrdom of the Poles in 1939–1945 (*Walka i Męczeństwo Polakow w latach 1939–1945*) in 1982. On the outside of the building, which must be entered from the rear, is a simple but graphic flower-bedecked memorial to the Poles tortured and murdered there during the war. In the basement are the three cells for those who were about to be interrogated by Gestapo agents. Their walls are covered with the names, prayers, and pleadings of the Gestapo's victims.[20]

Oskar said he was arrested because he was "fraternizing with Jews and Poles"; Janina added that he got into trouble because of his "strange contacts with the attaché of the German embassy in Turkey," and other matters. Oskar had warned Janina that something might happen to him and told her that that if he ever was arrested, she should go immediately to his apartment and hide the contents in the upper right-hand drawer of his desk. Immediately after the Gestapo agents took him away, Janina went to his elegant apartment on Straszewskiego 7/2 and hid the drawer's contents in his sofa. Oskar was released a few days later and laughed when he learned where Janina had hidden his secret documents.[21]

Oskar's second arrest was in the spring of 1942 or 1943. A birthday celebration was held on the factory floor for Oskar, and several of his female workers, Christians and Jews, kissed him in front of everyone. Someone present at the April 28 birthday party reported the incident to the SS and the Gestapo. Several days later, two plainclothes Gestapo agents drove up to the factory and encountered Schindler as he crossed Emalia's courtyard. "Are you Herr Schindler?" they asked. Oskar responded, "Who are you?" The two agents said nothing. Instead, one of them then showed Oskar his badge and said, "We would like to have you come with us for a little ride." Oskar then asked the two men whether they had an arrest order. They said, "You can see about that later. Just come with us now." Oskar warned the agents that if they took him without an arrest warrant, "it could turn out to be pretty unpleasant." They replied, "We'll take our chances on that." To which Oskar countered, "Well, in that case, it's a very nice day, and I feel like a ride, so I'll go with you." As the Gestapo car drove out of Emalia's front gate, Oskar heard one of the German engineers who was a loyal Nazi sing a phrase from a German song that went "Well, all good things come to an end."[22]

Schindler was taken to the Gestapo's Montelupich prison, one of the most feared in Poland. After a body search, Oskar was briefly interrogated and then thrown into a jail cell. Schindler concluded, based on the innocuous question the SS officer asked him during the brief interrogation, that they were simply holding him, "apparently for some higher-ups." Oskar asked for an attorney and was told that they "would see about that later." He shared a cell with a high-ranking SS officer and initially suspected that the officer was placed there as a spy, particularly when the officer explained that he was there because he had gone AWOL and had spent two days with a Polish girl. Oskar was suspicious and therefore very careful about what he said to his cell mate. Oskar later found out that the SS officer had been a legitimate prisoner and not a spy.[23]

That evening, Oskar devised a plan to alert his friends about his plight and gain his release. Schindler, who had some money on him, asked the guard to buy him five bottles of vodka. He wrote the telephone numbers of several important Nazi officials on the money he gave the guard and told him that he could have three of the bottles if he telephoned each person on the bills. The guard was to bring back two bottles for Oskar and his cell mate to help them "pass the time" in their dirty cell. The guard evidently did what he was told and called the three names on Oskar's list: Abwehr *Major* Plathe, *General* Maximillian Schindler of the Armaments Inspectorate, and Oskar's secretary, Viktoria Klonowska, whom Schindler called Columbus. She was given the nickname because she had found a place in Kraków where Oskar and his friends "could go and drink and raise hell."[24]

The next day, HSSPF Julian Scherner called Schindler into his office and said, "You must be a very important man, Oskar, to have seventeen people call me in the course of the night to vouch for you, and to let you go free. I've been doing particularly nothing else but answering calls. What do you do that's so useful, that you have all these friends?" Oskar responded, "Well, you know, none of us can really answer that." Scherner told Schindler that he was free to go and that he could call for his car to pick him up. Oskar, however, "wanted a little revenge for this detention." He said, "Oh, I couldn't use the camp car, the gasoline for this purpose [his own car]—that wouldn't be the right use of it, under the law. You brought me here, you'll have to take me back. I want to go back the same way I came." Scherner then ordered the same Gestapo agents who had brought Oskar to Montelupich to drive him back to Emalia in their Mercedes.[25]

Though it would be hard to prove that his problems with the Gestapo had a major impact on his decision later to help his Jewish workers, there is no question that, particularly when combined with other developments in 1942 and 1943, it helped move him along this path. The Gestapo represented everything that Oskar disliked about the Nazi police state system. Presuming that his growing disaffection with Nazi Germany, particularly in relationship with his ties to Abwehr, affected his decision to work more aggressively to aid his Jewish workers, then his mistreatment by the Gestapo probably only strengthened his resolve to do this. Moreover, his arrests and brief incarcerations only intensified his own sensitivity towards the plight of his *Schindlerjuden,* who suffered from brutal SS abuse and imprisonment. Because the Gestapo and the SS were simply part of the same police state network, it is possible that Schindler cast his aid to Jews partly as a form of resistance to this system.

The May–June 1942 Aktion in the Kraków Ghetto

Other developments that probably affected Oskar's attitudes towards the plight of Kraków's Jews centered around the brutal SS roundups and transport of Kraków's Jews to recently opened death camps in 1942. The first operation, which took place in March 1942, involved the roundup of about fifty Jewish intellectuals, who were deported to Auschwitz and death. But a much more thorough and brutally insidious *Aktion* took place between May 28 and June 8, 1942. In late May, the Germans sealed off the ghetto and, working with the members of the JSS (Jewish Self-Help Society; *Jüdische Soziale Selbsthilfe),* the only Jewish aid organization allowed to operate in the ghetto, began randomly to put a new labor stamp on the *Kennkarten.* The Gestapo then set up tables inside a former savings bank *(Kasa Oszczednosci)* and, working side-by-side with JSS representatives, decided who would have their *Kennkarten* stamped. People with specific trades theoretically got the stamp, though many of these decisions were made arbitrarily. Bribery and favoritism also played a role in who got a stamp and who did not. For the most part, people over fifty-five did not get a stamp. Those who did not receive the new stamp were to be deported to the recently opened Bełżec death camp, though the Germans were secretive about this aspect of their plan. Rumors quickly spread among Kraków's Jews about open labor camps in the Ukraine where the deported would work on farms or "newly erected barrack towns where there were restaurants, libraries, and cinemas, accessible to all." Moreover, so the rumor went, Jews were even paid in the new barrack towns.[26]

By this time, there were a little more than 17,000 Jews in the ghetto, and another 2,000 lived there illegally without the *Kennkarte.* Part of the upcoming German *Aktion* was designed to reduce the size of the ghetto population and address the overcrowding situation. On June 1, the Gestapo ordered the Jewish OD under Symche Spira to go to each apartment in the ghetto and bring those without the new labor stamps to *Plac Zgody* in the early morning hours of June 2. Those who heeded the OD's orders brought all their personal belongs with them in suitcases, bundles, and packages. They sweltered in the summer heat and many were overcome with fear about their fate.[27]

As those selected for deportation arrived in the square, an SS film crew climbed to a balcony overlooking the square and began to film the scene. The Gestapo, aided by the *Schutzpolizei* and members of a Waffen SS unit, marched the group to the Kraków Płaszów rail station two miles away, where they were shipped to the Bełżec death camp seventy-five miles northeast of Kraków.[28]

The Germans, however, were dissatisfied with the numbers deported on June 2, and began a much more brutal roundup on June 4. Armed German troops and police lined *Plac Zgody*, which looked more like a war zone than a gathering spot for deportees. For the first time, the Germans were joined by members of the Polish police *(Polnische Polizei)*, or Blue police *(Granatowa policija)*, who wore dark blue uniforms, and members of the *Baudienst*, a labor unit made up of Poles forced into labor by the Germans.[29] Pankiewicz described the roundup:

> The ghetto echoed with shots; the dead and wounded fell; blood marked the German crimes in the streets. There were more and more people in the square. The heat, as on previous days, was unbearable—fire seemed to fall from the sky. Water was unavailable, but even if it were, it was forbidden to the sufferers. People, weakened by heat and thirst, fainted and fell. In front of the pharmacy there was a small army car to which every few minutes the SS men brought valises filled with valuables taken during the searches of the deportees. They took everything from them: rings, wedding bands, gold and steel watches, cigarette cases and even lighters. Some of the unfortunates looked at those waiting their turns, resignation and apathy etched on their faces. These people were already beyond feeling.[30]

To insure greater compliance from the ghetto's Jewish leadership during the June 4 roundup, the Germans dismissed and publicly humiliated the new head of the Judenrat, Dr. Artur Rosenzweig. He and his family were then forced to join the group of Jews about to be deported. Dr. Rosenzweig was replaced by David Gutter, a former magazine salesman. This put him in constant conflict with the most powerful figure in the ghetto, Symche Spira, a favorite of the Gestapo.[31]

What followed for those Jews gathered at *Plac Zgody* was a slow, brutal march to the Kraków-Płaszów rail station. The Germans kicked and beat them along the way and shot those who were too slow or feeble to make the two-mile march in the summer heat. According to Tadeusz Pankiewicz, their route was covered with dead bodies and blood. Because the march took place in broad daylight and followed ul. Wielicka, the only road to Płaszów, it was difficult to hide the tragedy that was unfolding along this long boulevard. When the new group of Jewish deportees reached the rail station, they were sent to Bełżec, where the Germans murdered them.[32]

Two days later, the Germans ordered all Jews remaining in the ghetto to report to the offices of the JSS on Józefińska 18 to receive a new identity card, the *Blauschein*. The Gestapo oversaw the process and decided who would receive the new work card. Their decisions were arbitrary and had nothing to do with the recipients' skills. The only thing that seemed to affect the Gestapo's decisions were bribes funneled through Jewish cohorts such as Aleksander Förster and Symche Spira, or efforts by German factory owners to protect their skilled Jewish workers.[33]

Jews who did not receive the *Blauschein* were then taken to the grounds of the Optima factory two blocks away. The Germans followed this up with a new decree that stated that anyone caught without a *Blauschein* would be shot on the spot. On the morning of June 8, the Germans began to march all the Jews at the Optima factory grounds to the Prokocim rail station two miles north of the Płaszów depot. Like Płaszów, the Prokocim station was then in a remote suburb of Kraków, which helped the Germans keep the deportation out of full public scrutiny. When the Kraków Jews got to the trains, they found other Jews from nearby towns already on board. The Gestapo took about thirty younger Jews off of the train cars before it left for Bełżec. These Jews were sent to the just-opened *Julag* I slave labor camp in nearby Płaszów.[34]

All total, the Germans shipped 7,000 Jews to Bełżec from June 2 to 8, 1942. Though operational only since March 17, 1942, about 80,000 Jews had already been murdered at Bełżec by the time Kraków's Jews arrived there in June. Ultimately, about 600,000 Jews, over a quarter of them from the Kraków region, would die at Bełżec before it closed at the end of 1942.[35]

What impact did these deportations have on Oskar Schindler? For one thing, he was able to save Abraham Bankier and thirteen of his other Jewish workers from certain death on June 8. This event is depicted in one of the most poignant scenes in *Schindler's List,* though Spielberg chose to have Liam Neeson save Itzhak Stern, the composite film character played by Ben Kingsley, instead of Bankier. Thomas Keneally more accurately portrayed this scene as well as the full horror of the June 1942 deportations. Basing his portrayal on Schindler's account of these events, Keneally seems to have expanded greatly Schindler's comments about what actually took place. According to Keneally, Bankier told Schindler that he and the other *Schindlerjuden* had forgotten to pick up their new *Blauscheine* from the Gestapo.[36] One did not "pick up" the *Blauschein* from the Gestapo. You stood in line and hoped you would get one. The only thing that helped one receive a *Blauschein* was bribery, close ties with the Jewish OD's leadership, or intervention by a German factory owner. And it is hard to imagine that Oskar did not intervene to insure that Bankier got the *Blauschein* from the Gestapo.

So what really happened? Here is Oskar's account:

> In Cracow a Mrs. E. [Edith] Kerner [one of Oskar's secretaries] called me one morning with the news that some of my Jewish workers had been arbitrarily added to an extermination transport, which went from the Cracow ghetto to the Prococym train depot, in order to be shipped east. Four hours later I regained my fourteen men from the already closed-up cattle wagons at the Prococym depot (among them A. Bankier, Reich, Leser) despite weak protests by the accompanying SS guards that the number was not right.[37]

This was all Oskar ever said about the incident. The key to what probably happened centers around one word in Oskar's statement: arbitrary. There was no science to the last roundup in the Kraków ghetto in the summer of 1942. It is quite possible that Bankier and the other *Schindlerjuden* were picked up by the Germans even though they had the *Blauschein*. Given Oskar's earlier problems with the Gestapo, it is possible that the Gestapo picked up Bankier and the other Schindler Jews as a warning to Schindler. It is also possible that Oskar was out of town at the time because he traveled frequently. However, given the severity of the Germans moves into the ghetto, his staff would have gotten in touch with him and warned him of the problems some of his Jewish workers were facing. Whatever prompted the attempted deportation of Schindler's fourteen Jewish workers, his dramatic intervention at the Prokocim train station on June 8 saved them from certain death.

But Oskar also tried to save the son and brother of two of his Jewish workers when he arrived at the Prokocim railway station on that hot June day in 1942. According to Leon Leyson (Leib Lejzon), a retired educator who lives in Fullerton, California, Oskar spotted one of Leon's older brothers, Tsalig (Betsalil), in one of the train cars. Leon's father, Moshe, and another of Leon's brothers, David, worked at Emalia. Though Tsalig did not work for Oskar, the German factory owner knew who he was and had seen him at Emalia with Moshe. Oskar offered to take Tsalig off of the train with Bankier and his other Jewish workers. Tsalig, though, refused because he wanted to stay with his girlfriend. This loving gesture cost Tsalig Leyson his life.[38]

Almost losing the irreplaceable Abraham Bankier to the Gestapo must have had a tremendous impact on Oskar. But even if Oskar was involved in saving some of his Jews, what impact did the June 1942 deportations have on his decision to commit his resources totally to this effort? It is hard to say. Oskar had seen war and death in 1938, and he probably saw some anti-Jewish and anti-Polish atrocities in the fall of 1939. But by 1942, such horrors touched him in a more personal way. Initially, though, he probably thought like most Jews that the deportees were being sent to the rumored barrack camps. He had already been involved in trying to help some of his Polish workers from being sent to Germany as forced laborers, so it is quite possible that he believed the rumors about the Jewish barrack towns. In time, though, new stories crept back into Kraków that told not of barrack towns, but of death camps. They were told by a Kraków dentist, Dr. Brachner, who had escaped when one of the transports arrived in Bełżec and hid in a latrine filled with human excrement for several days. One night, he slowly made his way back to the Kraków ghetto. Dr. Brachner told anyone who would listen of the horrors of Bełżec and its three (later six) carbon monoxide-fed gas chambers.[39]

Several months later, Pankiewicz received a letter from a woman who had fled the ghetto on the eve of the October 1942 *Aktion*. Her escape route took her to Bełżec, where she saw first-hand the horrors taking place there. When the trains arrived, she noted, the Germans occasionally kept cars on sidings until they were ready to murder the Jews on them. The cars were carefully guarded by Germans, and the Jews were given no water or food. When it was time for them to be gassed, German guards took the Jews still alive off the train cars and forced them to undress. They were then sent to the gas chambers. Afterwards, their bodies were cremated. The letter ended with an appeal to anyone reading it to spread the word about what was really happening to the Jews at Bełżec and not to believe German lies about the fate of Jews on any future transport to this particular death camp.[40]

Months before Pankiewicz read this letter, the Germans had unsealed the ghetto, but had also reduced its size. The northeastern part of the ghetto running from Podgórski Square between ul. Limanowskiego and ul. Rękawaka was now returned to Polish-German control. The Germans ordered that the walls in this portion of the old ghetto be torn down and barbed wire erected along the new boundaries. The ghetto was no longer as well-hidden from the Aryan side as it had once been. But the reduction in the size of the ghetto made it much more difficult to see into the ghetto from Lasota Hill, the highest point above Podgórze. In Spielberg's *Schindler's List,* this was the point where Oskar Schindler and his mistress, Eva Schauer ("Ingrid"), supposedly saw Amon Göth's brutal closing of the Kraków ghetto on March 13 and 14, 1943. The eastern boundary of the ghetto, which was just on the other side of Rekawa Street, had been deliberately kept away from the foot of Lasota Hill when it first opened because it would have been easy to see into the streets of the ghetto. With the constriction of the ghetto in June 1942, it was even more difficult to see into the ghetto. Though one could probably have seen some things from Lasota Hill with binoculars, the view would have been severely restricted by the buildings outside and within the ghetto. More than likely, the story about Oskar and Eva ("Ingrid") is apocryphal. But, even more important, Oskar had already seen enough brutality before the closing of the ghetto to convince him to commit himself and his resources to helping save Jewish lives.[41]

The October 28, 1942, Aktion in the Kraków Ghetto

Two other things happened in 1942 that helped push Oskar along this path: more deportations from the ghetto in October 1942 and a visit from Abwehr friends interested in recruiting him in their efforts to help and save Jews. The gradual reduction in the size of the Kraków ghetto came in the midst of the greatest killing period of the Final Solution from 1942 through 1943. Making the Germans' task easy was their control of more than half of Europe's Jews in occupied parts of Poland and Russia. And because all six of the death camps, where about one half of the 6 million Jews murdered in the Holocaust died, were located in occupied Poland, the pace of mass murder was made easier. The Germans were so successful in their murderous campaign against the Jews that by the time Amon Göth was sent to close the Kraków ghetto, Heinrich Himmler had decided to shut down the remaining death camps opened as part of "Operation Reinhard" a year earlier. In little more than a year, the Germans had murdered 1,650,000 Jews in Bełżec, Sobibór, and Treblinka. Auschwitz, Kulmhof (Chełmno), and Majdanek remained open.[42]

The demands of the Final Solution drove the periodic German actions and deportations in the Kraków ghetto and elsewhere. The next *Aktion* came on October 28, 1942. The day before, Spira, Gutter, and other Jewish leaders were informed of the coming German moves in the ghetto. Though Gutter and Spira were pledged to secrecy, word spread quickly that a new wave of deportations would start on October 28. Some ghetto residents prepared hiding places while others sought refuge with friends outside of Kraków. By 9:00 P.M., October 27, armed *Sonderdienst* (Special Service) police under Orpo, the German Order Police, had surrounded the ghetto. The *Sonderdienst* units were made up of Latvians, Lithuanians, and Ukrainians who had volunteered for German service. At the same time, the *Judenrat* ordered all ghetto workers to gather at the ghetto's main entrance at Węgierska and Limanowskiego streets early on October 28.[43]

At 6:00 A.M. the next morning, *SS-Sturmbannführer* Willi Haase arrived to take personal charge of the deportation. As in the past, high-ranking SS and SD officers came to watch the roundup. But what was different about this *Aktion* was that German factory and business owners did everything possible to protect their most valuable Jewish specialists from deportation. Only weeks before, the SS and the Armaments Inspectorate had worked out their agreement whereby the SS supplied Jewish slave labor to companies doing business with the Armaments Inspectorate for a set daily rate. Ultimately, these factories were to move their operations to SS-run concentration and labor camps. In one sense, if a German factory owner could now prove that his factory produced goods important to the war effort, it strengthened his ability to protect his more valuable Jewish workers. From Himmler's perspective, of course, even these protected Jews "[would] disappear some day."[44]

Oskar never eluded to this particular *Aktion* in his postwar writings, though he does claim to have known about the "opening of the extermination camps in the Polish territory" in 1942. Given his contacts, he was also probably well versed on the recent agreement between the Armaments Inspectorate and the SS. Consequently, it is hard to imagine that he was not at the entrance to the ghetto at 6:00 A.M. on October 28.[45] Similarly, Julius Madritsch never referred specifically to the October 28 *Aktion* in his wartime memoirs, *Menschen im Not!*, though he does state that

> one transfer action was followed by the next and we were always faced by ever new cries for help [from Jews]. At least I generally got notice of impending plans through informants at the various departments and therefore I could make preparations to deal with the dangers that my people were facing. We lived in a state of constant high pressure during such crises and were always on stand-by, since we knew that something was always planned, we just waited for the "when?" and were afraid of "how?"[46]

As Madritsch's factory was just a half block from the ghetto's entrance, it is probable that Madritsch or his factory manager, Raimund Titsch, were also at the October 28 roundup.

The first phase of the selection centered around the random choice of workers to be deported and those to remain in the ghetto. The Germans ordered all other Jews remaining in the ghetto to gather by 10:00 A.M. along ul. Józefińska near OD headquarters. The Germans added that everyone should leave their apartments unlocked before they left for the gathering point on Józefińska. Once again, the Germans' decision about who would remain and who would be deported was made capriciously. Even physicians, who wore special armbands to protect them from deportation, were ordered to line up for transport. When it became apparent that some Jews were hiding, Haase shouted so all could hear, "Alle Männer und Frauen gehen ruhig nach Hause" (All men and women can now return to their homes). Relieved, the Jews left their hiding places. But Haase was not finished. To draw more Jews into his net, he later announced that the "Ghetto ist Judenrein!" (The ghetto is free of Jews). Though many hidden Jews were not taken in by Haase's latest ruse, others were, and they were bloodily driven to the deportation point by the German, Latvian, and Lithuanian guards who had spread throughout the ghetto.[47]

Soon after 10:00 A.M. on the 28th, the SS and the *Sonderdienst* began to search for Jews hidden throughout the ghetto. Some began desperately to prepare hiding places in their apartments, attics, and basements. Tadeusz Pankiewicz recalled how a friend hid her parents in a pantry in the foyer of their apartment. She took out the shelves and built a hidden space in the back of the pantry to conceal her parents. She then put hooks at the front of the pantry and hung coats on it. The Germans thoroughly searched the apartment, but never discovered the two elderly people hidden behind the coats.[48]

Those found hiding were shot on the spot or beaten as they were being driven to the collection point. By this point, most of the ghetto's Jews were huddled in terror in *Plac Zgody*. As the day progressed, the roundup became more violent and deadly. At noon, the Germans went into the Jewish Hospital at 14 Józefińska and shot all the bedridden patients. One woman who was in labor was thrown into a deportation truck; other patients were shot as they tried to flee. Haase was ever present, surrounded by his assistants. Gutter, Förster, Spira, and other Jewish collaborators, who did everything they could to please their SS masters. When one frantic woman begged Gutter for help, he kicked her and turned away. She then turned to Spira, who walked away while one of his Jewish OD men beat her with his riding crop.[49]

Children and the elderly were singled out during this action and murdered in large numbers. At the Hospital for the Chronically Ill *(Szpitala dla przewlekle Chorych)* at ul. 15 Limanowska, the Germans beat the patients as they forced them down the stairs and into the street. Those on crutches were tripped and forced to crawl on their knees. Once outside, the Germans ordered the elderly patients to climb onto a courtyard wall and jump off. As they fell, the Germans shot them. By 5:00 P.M. on the 28th, the Germans had completed the roundup and were moving the new deportees to the Płaszów train station. They had murdered 600 Jews during the *Aktion* and sent 6,000 to 7,000 to Bełzec. But not all the Jewish victims were murdered by the Germans and their allies; some committed suicide to escape the horror of the ghetto *Aktion* and deportation.[50]

Several weeks after the October 28 deportations, the Germans slightly reduced the size of the ghetto. The eliminated sections, which were to the west of *Plac Zgody*, were those closest to Schindler's factory at 4 Lipowa. According to a decree issued by Frank on November 14, 1942, there were now to be five closed ghettos in the General Government in Kraków, Warsaw, Lwow, Radom, and Częstochowa. The rest of the General Government was now declared *"Judenrein."* Jews living outside one of these ghettos were ordered to return to one of them.[51]

Five thousand Jews remained in the Kraków ghetto. On December 6, 1942, the SS divided it into two sections. Ghetto A was to be for Jews with jobs; Ghetto B was for those without work. The SS also used Ghetto B as a dumping place for another 2,000 Jews from surrounding areas. Ghetto A was subdivided into three specific labor sections corresponding to the "R,"

"W," or "Z" now worn by Jewish laborers. After a few days, each section of the ghetto was sealed off. All that remained of the former Kraków ghetto was a four-square-block area less than half of the original ghetto's size.[52]

The brutal roundup triggered a reaction from the recently formed ŻOB (*Żydowska Organizacja Bojowa;* Jewish Fighting Organization), which in Kraków drew its membership from two Jewish resistance movements in the Kraków ghetto, Akiba, and Hashomir Hatzair. Both were associated with prewar Zionist youth movements in Kraków. Before the 1942 roundups, Akiba and Hashomir had been involved in various underground activities to help Kraków's Jews. However, in 1942, they began to shift their efforts to armed resistance, often in league with the PPR (*Polska Partia Robotnicza;* Polish Workers Party), and its armed wing, the *Gwardia Ludowa* (GL; People's Guard). Working in and outside the ghetto, the Jewish rebels initially committed small acts of sabotage and assassinations of Germans in Kraków and Jewish informers in the ghetto. They also stole German uniforms from Madritsch's Optima factory in the ghetto. However, their most daring raids took place on December 22, 1942, in response to the October 28 *Aktion* in the ghetto.[53]

The goals of the forty young rebels involved in the attacks were to create confusion among the Germans and raise the spirits of the Jews in the ghetto. They also hoped "to shock the apathetic elements in the Polish society."[54] They wanted to kill as many Germans as possible as they attacked cafes, theatres, German military vehicles, and naval vessels on the Vistula. They also planned to raise Polish flags on the city's bridges and lay a wreath at the site of a statue to Adam Mickiewicz, Poland's national poet, which the Germans had torn down.[55]

Operating in squads of three, ŻOB teams struck simultaneously at three cafés in Kraków favored by the SS and other Germans, the Cyganeria, the Esplanada, and the Zakopianka officers club, as well as the officers' casino housed at the National Museum, and the Scala, one of Kraków's most prominent movie theatres on Reichsstraße 4. The most successful raid was on the Cyganeria, which was full at the time of the 7:00 P.M. attack. About eleven Germans died from the hand grenade attack, and many others were injured. Symbolically, ŻOB could have chosen no better site because the Cyganeria was just across the street from the famed City Theatre (today the Słowacki Theatre) and the nearby Church of the Holy Cross *(Kościółśw. Krzyża).* Moreover, it was just before Christmas, and the streets were filled with Germans preparing to celebrate the holidays. The choice of a Christian religious holiday was particularly ironic because the Germans were quite fond of initiating *Aktionen* against Jews during some of their holiest religious days.[56]

The other attacks were less successful or simply did not take place. The German response to the attacks was swift and brutal. They quickly surrounded ŻOB's hiding place in the old Jewish quarter at ul. 24 Skawinska and arrested many of the operation's leaders. At a bar on ul. 3 Żuławeskiego, Adolf Liebeskind, one of the raid's leaders, had a shootout with the Gestapo as they tried to arrest him. He killed two Germans before committing suicide. Hitler was informed of the attack on Christmas Day; but nothing was made public until the end of March 1943, when HSSPF Krüger announced in a meeting in Kraków that the raid on the Cyganeria had been carried out by an underground Zionist youth organization. According to Krüger, it operated out of the Kraków ghetto using false documents and identity cards.[57]

Today, a plaque commemorates the attack at the site of the former Cyganeria Café. It reads:

> On the night between the 24th and 25th of December 1942, a group of soldiers of the People's Army *(Grupa Ludowe)* and the Jewish Fighting Organization [ŻOB] carried out an operation on the Cyganeria hall, which was full of Germans and inflicted heavy losses upon the conqueror.[58]

Jewish sources claim the raids took place on December 22; Polish sources insist it took place on December 24.[59]

But what impact did the raids have on Oskar Schindler? By late December 1942, Schindler had already seen the horror of the German roundups and probably knew something about the mass murders at the death camps in Poland. Remember that everything suffered by his workers, from the attempted deportation of Bankier and the other thirteen *Schindlerjuden* to beatings and murder, was only the tip of the iceberg for Oskar when it came to what he saw and heard about the suffering of the Jews in the Kraków ghetto. As an employer of Jews, he had to keep abreast of the delays and losses suffered when his workers were detained or deported. His factory was only an earshot away from the violence that took place in the ghetto. And each morning as he left his apartment at 7/2 Straszewskiego and drove along the Vistula before crossing it on the bridge at the end of Alle Weichselstraße (today Most Powstańcowzjeżdzie Śląskich), he could see, and probably smell, the decay and horror of the ghetto. And as his driver made his quick left turn on ul. Zabłocie that would take him to T. Romaninowicza and then right to 4 Lipowa, Oskar could glance briefly into the ghetto. His constant complaining to the SS about the problems suffered by his Jewish workers underscored the difficulties that the roundups caused Schindler. And these were issues that Oskar shared and discussed with other factory owners such as Madritsch and those who owned factories next to Emalia. These businessmen included Kurt Hodemann, who ran N.K.F. *(Neue Kühler u. Flugzeugteile-Fabrik)*, an aircraft radiator factory; Kucharski, who owned the *Krakauer Drahtgitter Fabrik*, a wire netting factory; Ernst Kühnpast, who operated a box factory; and Chmielewski, who ran a *Barackenwerk*, or barracks factory. What drew them together, beyond the desire to make a lot of money, was their Jewish workers. The first known "Schindler's List" still in existence was dated May 25, 1943, and it deals with the joint transfer of 191 Jewish workers to Emalia, NKF, Kühnpast's box factory, and Chmielewski's barracks factory from, presumably, Płaszów.[60]

The Closing of the Kraków Ghetto

The SS decision to close the Kraków ghetto in March 1943 was part of a broader effort to eliminate all ghettos in the General Government and send their inmates to death or slave labor camps. Though Heinrich Himmler's decree of July 19, 1942, ordered this process completed by December 31, 1942, it took much longer. At the time, Himmler also ordered that, after this date, the General Government was to be free of Jews with the exception of those living in camps in Częstochowa, Kraków, Lublin, Radom, or Warsaw. As the SS gradually emptied each ghetto of its Jews and sent them to one of five death camps in the General Government, it also opened or expanded slave labor camps for Jews chosen to live a few more months. This is what the SS did in Kraków, where a slave labor camp was opened at Płaszów while the Germans slowly destroyed the ghetto and its population.[61]

The closing of the Kraków ghetto in Podgórze by Amon Göth on March 13–14, 1943, was, at least as depicted by Steven Spielberg in *Schindler's List*, a dramatic, transforming moment for Oskar Schindler. While watching Oskar and his mistress, Eva ("Ingrid"), look down upon the ghetto as it is being cleared by the SS, one senses his shock and surprise. From that moment on, Oskar Schindler was never the same man. The seed for this scene was a similar one in Thomas Keneally's novel; both portrayals were probably drawn from the notes that Martin Gosch and Howard Koch put together after their lengthy interviews with Schindler in 1964 in preparation for writing a script for a proposed MGM movie about Schindler, *To the Last Hour*. According to them, Schindler was on horseback on a hill overlooking the Jewish ghetto when it was closed in 1941, two years earlier than it really happened. According to Gosch and Koch, Schindler, who was alone, was "affected . . . profoundly" by what he saw.[62] Itzhak Stern's comments about the impact of the closing of the ghetto on Oskar was probably another source for this mythical story. According to Stern, the murder of the children in the ghetto's *Kinderheim* (children's home) during the brutal closing of the Kraków ghetto on March 13–14, 1943, prompted Oskar's firm commitment to do everything he could to save as many Jews as possible. Stern said that this was the "crucial incident that unsettled Schindler's mind. Schindler had changed overnight and was never the same man again."[63] Though Oskar would undoubtedly be shocked by the murder of the *Kinderheim* children, other evidence suggests that he had already chosen his path sometime before this tragedy. The *Kinderheim* horror simply made him more determined to help as many Jews as he could.

But the vivid scene described by Keneally that centered around not only the violent *Aktion* in the ghetto and the little girl in the red coat dealt with the violent roundup of Jews on June 8–10, 1942, not the closing of the ghetto on March 13–14, 1943. Spielberg took Keneally's description of this roundup, which centered around the little girl in red, and put her in the context of Amon Göth's closing of the ghetto in 1943. Unfortunately, lost in all this were Itzhak Stern's comments about what most affected Schindler during the closing of the ghetto—the murder of the children in the *Kinderheim* orphanage—not shock at the sight of Göth's brutal *Aktion* from atop Lasota Hill. Perhaps Keneally, who barely touched on the closing of the ghetto in his historical novel, best captures this moment, particularly as it relates to Oskar Schindler, when he admits that "we do not know in what condition of soul Oskar Schindler spent March 13, the ghetto's last and worst day."[64]

There is nothing to indicate that Oskar and his mistress were ever on Lasota Hill on March 13th or 14th. He was well aware of the coming *Aktion* and was more concerned about the fate of his Jewish workers; in fact, Oskar was so well informed about the forthcoming ghetto liquidation that he told Sol Urbach and his other Jewish workers on March 12 to remain at Emalia until the *Aktion* was over. Julius Madritsch confirmed this and said that the "total evacuation of the ghetto did not come as a surprise. For a long time it had been discussed." Before an *Aktion*, the Germans surrounded the ghetto and outlying areas with various paramilitary units. Given the seriousness of the closing of the ghetto, Oskar probably stayed in his apartment at the factory; it would have been difficult for him to go to the factory once the *Aktion* began because the back streets to it ran beside the ghetto. The idea that Oskar somehow took all this so casually that he took two horses from his stable and then somehow made his way with Eva around the ghetto to Lasota Hill as it was being besieged by the SS is simply not realistic.[65]

This decision, to keep his Jewish workers at Emalia for several days until the March 1943 *Aktion* was over, was one of the first instances we have of Oskar Schindler aggressively working to save Jewish lives. And although it could be argued that this was simply good business, it was a daring, potentially dangerous move. The SS was careful about keeping tabs on its slave laborers, and for someone to order his workers not to go back to camp with their SS escorts was dangerous. It is possible, of course, that Schindler had arranged this earlier with Göth, but this is difficult to prove because Göth had just taken over command of Płaszów in February 1943 and had his hands full not only completing the construction of a large slave labor camp but also eliminating the Kraków ghetto. It would take time for Oskar to develop the special relationship he had with Göth and it is doubtful that he had enough time before the ghetto's liquidation to do this.

Yet given all this, the closing of the Kraków ghetto is still a defining moment in the Schindler story. Oskar had never been around viciousness and bloodshed on such a large scale, particularly so close to his prosperous world. And now, all his Jewish workers and friends were being forced to live in a much more rigid and deadly environment than the ghetto. And each day, their lives were at the mercy of a madman: Amon Göth. All I interviewed who had worked for Göth in Płaszów said that they lived in constant fear for their lives. They were absolutely convinced that someday Göth would kill them on a whim. Oskar Schindler, directly or indirectly, was their island of hope and life.

If anything came to symbolize the evil that Schindler and his Jews had to contend with over the next eighteen months, it was the massacre of the ghetto *Kinderheim* children during the March 13–14, 1943 *Aktion*. The last few months in the ghetto were a time of terror and uncertainty. The approximately 7,000 Jews who remained were often beaten, harassed, and threatened with deportation by the SS and their subordinates. If there was a safe haven, it seemed to be in the *Kinderheim* (children's home) or one of the ghetto's remaining hospitals. The Germans had ordered the *Judenrat* to open a *Kinderheim* in early 1943. David Gutter and Symche Spira took part in the ceremonies celebrating its opening. By this time, the SS was sending a growing number of Jewish workers to work at Płaszów, which was still under construction, or to factories outside the ghetto. The *Kinderheim* was designed as a daycare facility where parents could leave their children while they worked for the SS or factory owners. For many children and their parents, the Jewish-run *Kinderheim*, with its staff of caring professionals, was an island in a sea of terror. But it, too, would be overwhelmed by the same horror that was engulfing most Jews in Poland.[66]

The *Kinderheim* was placed in Ghetto B, a subtle hint of its future. Ghetto B was the SS dumping ground for Jews deemed unfit for labor and earmarked for deportation to death camps once the Germans closed the ghetto. And though the Jews in the ghetto did not learn of plans to close the ghetto until 11:00 A.M. on March 13, 1943, all signs had pointed to its ultimate liquidation weeks before. The Germans had been rounding up workers for months to help build one of three *Julags* (*Jüdischelager*; Jewish camps) in Płaszów (Julag I), Prokocim (Julag II), and Bieżanów (Julag III) in the suburbs of Kraków. Most of those taken to build the Julags or to work in factories outside the ghetto were housed in Julag I at Płaszów. As the population in the ghetto dwindled, stores began to shut and basic foodstuffs disappeared. On March 13, David Gutter issued a decree from Julian Scherner, the HSSPF in the Kraków district, that all residents in Ghetto A had four hours to prepare for a move to Płaszów. Scherner's decree added that on March 14 everyone in Ghetto B should be prepared to board trains for deportation.[67]

Scherner's simple orders were a cover for the terror about to be unleashed by the Gestapo and the SS. It would be overseen by *SS-Sturmführer* Amon Leopold Göth, a thirty-five-year-old Austrian who had joined the Nazi Party in 1930 and the SS two years later; as commandant of the new Płaszów forced labor camp, he was in charge of closing both ghettos. Tadeusz Pankiewicz described Göth as a tall, handsome, overweight, blue-eyed German who had already gained a reputation for brutality during the brief period he had served as Płaszów's commandant. Göth entered the ghetto on the morning of March 13 wearing a long black leather coat. He carried a riding crop in one hand and a small automatic rifle in the other. His large vicious dogs, Rolf and Ralf, walked beside him.[68]

As they prepared for transfer or deportation, the Jews were most concerned about the fate of their children. Most realized that the Germans would not permit parents to take their children to Płaszów even though the Germans said they were building a children's barracks there. When it was completed, they promised, the children would be moved from the *Kinderheim* to Płaszów. Some parents refused to believe another German lie and prepared hiding places. Others fled the ghetto to save their children and even crossed over from Ghetto A to Ghetto B to buy their children a little more time. But some parents in Ghetto A tried to sneak their children into Płaszów by hiding them in bundles or squeezing them in the transfer line at the ghetto's entrance on the afternoon of March 13. Pankiewicz provided many parents with drugs to help their children sleep while in hiding. Göth, however, was determined to keep all children out of Płaszów; he carefully searched the bags and clothing of the departing Jews in search of hidden children. When he found one, he wrenched the unfortunate child from his or her hiding place and beat the parents if they resisted him. The children usually fled in terror and were then forced into the *Kinderheim*. By late afternoon, Ghetto A was empty but for the children and a few members of the *Judenrat*.[69]

Though there was considerable violence in the clearing of Ghetto A, it was nothing compared to what was about to take place in Ghetto B. To the Germans, the residents of Ghetto B were expendable. As the sun rose on March 14, the terrified Jews of Ghetto B began to fill *Plac Zgody*. They carried all their worldly possessions. As they gathered in the square, heavily armed SS, Gestapo, and *Sonderdienst* surrounded them. As they had done the day before, top German officials watched the deportation. What followed was an orgy of blood and death. The first to die were the patients in the main Jewish Hospital on Józefińska Street. As they had done the day before in Ghetto A's hospital, the Germans, led by *SS-Oberscharführer* Albert Hujar, began to murder the patients in their beds. When one visitor, Dr. Katia Blau, refused to leave the bedside of one of her friends, Hujar told her to stand up and turn around. She told Hujar that she was not afraid to die; Hujar then shot her in the back of the head. The Germans also murdered several of the hospitals physicians. Lola Feldman Orzech, a Schindler Jew, said that the Germans also threw her grandmother out of the hospital's third floor window to her death.[70]

The favorite killing place for the German executioners was an alley near *Plac Zgody*. Tadeusz Pankiewicz watched the shootings from the back window of his pharmacy. The principal victims were the elderly and children. They were taken from the crowd on *Plac Zgody* or from hiding places in Ghetto B. The Germans, Latvians, Lithuanians, and Ukrainians involved in the *Aktion* went from apartment to apartment looking for Jews in hiding. Those not shot on the spot were often murdered when they arrived at *Plac Zgody*. When the Germans entered the *Kinderheim*, they put the smallest children into baskets and loaded them on wagons. Older children were taken to *Plac Zgody* and shot.[71]

Those not murdered by the Germans and their collaborators were lined up in *Plac Zgody* and separated according to gender and fitness for work. Elderly males were forced to race to prove their fitness for labor. What transpired was a humiliating scene of elderly males running as fast as they could for their lives. As they ran, they were taunted by jeers from the crowd of Germans and others in the square. And though these elderly males were told they would live if they won, more often than not their "reward" was a shot in the back of the head. Göth personally selected 150 men for a work detail at Płaszów, though Willi Haase, Göth's boss, said that was too many and ordered seventy-five members of Göth's Jewish detail executed on the spot. The other seventy-five Jews were forced to strip the bodies of the recently murdered ghetto Jews and put them on wagons for transport to Płaszów for burial. *Schindlerjuden* Victor Dortheimer and Murray Pantirer were put on one of the burial details. Dortheimer was ordered to "dig mass graves." As the wagons filled with dead bodies covered with branches arrived from Ghetto B, Pantirer and Dortheimer had to bury or burn them in the newly dug graves. According to Pantirer: "In one case we asked a German to give a 'kindness' shot to a young kid who was still alive. The German told us it was a shame to waste a bullet on a Jew."[72]

Sol Urbach and Murray Pantirer both lost close family members in the March 1943 *Aktion*. Sol's brother, Samuel, was shot in the deportation line; Murray's father, Lezur, was murdered when he refused to leave his wife, who was holding the hand of a child. Jews who had managed to survive the brutal roundup in Ghetto B were placed onto large trucks brought to the ghetto's entrance. They were forced to leave their bundles in the square; children discovered hidden in bundles or among the adults were taken from their parents and shot behind Pankiewicz's pharmacy. The SS and the *Sonderdienst* beat the Jews as they left the square and tried to board the trucks. When the trucks were loaded, all that remained in *Plac Zgody* were children and abandoned bundles. Some were in prams; others stood alone and bewildered among the scattered bundles and luggage. The SS took the children by the hands and calmly led them to the execution spot behind

Pankiewicz's phamarcy. To save ammunition, the SS would occasionally line up several children and murder them with one shot; sometimes they put several children in a baby carriage and killed them with one bullet.[73]

The only shadow of humanity in all this were the efforts of Oswald Bousko (an Austrian policeman), Julius Madritsch and Raimund Titsch to save as many lives as they could before and during the March 13–14 *Aktion* in the ghetto. In his memoir, Tadeusz Pankiewicz talks at length about Bousko's efforts to help Jews. Julius Madritsch also brings up Bousko's efforts in *Menschen in Not!*; and *Schindlerjude* Aleksander Bieberstein discusses Bousko's efforts to save Jews in his memoir-history, *Zagłada Żydów w Krakowie*. Thomas Keneally mentions him periodically in his historical novel.

Pankiewicz, who is the principal source of our information on Bousko, first met the Viennese policeman during the June 1942 *Aktion* as he walked out of the Kraków ghetto. Bousko, tall and blond, looked at Pankiewicz's papers and then screamed at him, wanting to know why the Polish pharmacist was leaving the ghetto without a police escort. Bousko told Pankiewicz that he could be shot on the spot without such protection. In future, Bousko suggested, the pharmacist should call him at the *Schupo* station, and he would personally provide Pankiewicz with an escort home. Over time, Pankiewicz learned that Bousko was the son of an unimportant Austrian government official who had once studied to be a Catholic monk. Bousko left the monastery and joined the Nazi Party in Austria. When Engelbert Dollfuß, Austria's chancellor, outlawed the Nazi Party in the summer of 1933, Bousko joined an illegal SS unit set up by Himmler to act as a fifth column against the Austrian government. After the German conquest of Austria in 1938, Bousko became an opponent of the Nazis.[74]

Once in Kraków in the summer of 1942, Bousko did everything possible to help the ghetto's Jews. He used his loud scream to hide his deeper intentions. He not only helped Jews escape from the ghetto but supplied them with food. Occasionally, he would accept bribes for some of his efforts and, when he fled Kraków in the summer of 1944, he carried a suitcase full of his ill-gotten contraband with him. These actions did nothing, though, to lessen the legend of his deeds. It also did not prevent Yad Vashem from naming him, along with Madritsch and Titsch, a Righteous Among the Nations (Righteous Gentile) in 1964. Bousko's file is kept with the files of Julius Madritsch and Raimund Titsch in the Department of the Righteous at Yad Vashem, which reviews nominations for Righteous

Among the Nations recognition. In addition to a few documents citing Bousko's efforts, Yad Vashem also has a copy of Madritch's memoir. There is nothing, though, to indicate that the Department of the Righteous was aware of Pankiewicz's *Apteka w Getcie Krakowskim,* which was first published in Poland in 1947 and in Israel in 1985. If so, Yad Vashem might have had second thoughts about naming Bousko a Righteous Gentile; one of its criteria for consideration of this great honor is that the "rescuer did not exact any material reward or compensation at the time of the rescue, and did not require any promise of compensation, either oral or in writing, as a condition for the aid he was giving." Regardless, Pankiewicz, Bieberstein, Madritsch, and Keneally all agree that many Jews and Poles owed their lives to Oswald Bousko.[75]

Just before the closing of the ghetto in March 1943, Bousko worked with Julius Madritsch to help save more Jews from death. He led many families, particularly those with children, out of the front gate and into Madritsch's nearby factory. The youngest children were given something to make them sleep and were carried into Madritsch's factory in backpacks. In the meantime, Madritsch arranged to have the children placed in the homes of Poles in the city. Madritsch also convinced some Wehrmacht soldiers driving to Tarnow to take some of the Jewish escapees to a factory he owned there. Several weeks later, Madritsch got permission from the SS to transfer three hundred Jews from his Kraków factory to a similar one in Tarnow, sixty miles east of Kraków. Madritsch's factory in Tarnow was very similar to the one in Kraków. Each employed about eight hundred workers and had three hundred sewing machines. After the war, Madritsch turned the sewing machines over to the Joint, asking the American Jewish relief organization to return them to his former workers. On March 25–26, 1943, 232 Jewish men, women, and children left Kraków by rail for Madritsch's factory in Tarnow. Each one was protected by an SS "acceleration of an urgent armaments order."[76]

Oswald Bousko remained in Kraków until the summer of 1944, when he injected himself with a drug that made him severely ill to avoid being sent to the Eastern Front. After several weeks in a German hospital, Bousko disappeared with two Jewish children and a Polish mistress. His Schupo boss suspected he had been kidnapped by Polish partisans and began a search for his subordinate. Bousko wrote to his commander and claimed that indeed he had been captured by partisans. After a further investigation, Schupo concluded that Bousko was lying. The police intensified their search and captured him as he tried to make his way back to Germany. He was put in Montelupich prison in Kraków and then transferred to Danzig, where Bousko tried to feign insanity. He was courtmartialed and executed on October 18, 1944. Afterwards, German officials in Kraków blamed many of their earlier problems with Jews, whether it be escape, black marketering, bribery, or other things, on Bousko and his non-Jewish accomplices.[77]

When the Ghetto B *Aktion* was over, the Germans had murdered 1,000 Jews in the roundup and deported another 4,000. About half this numbered were shipped immediately to Auschwitz via Płaszów. The Germans murdered 1,492 in Crematorium II in Auschwitz II-Birkenau; 484 men and 24 women were integrated into the Auschwitz slave labor force. On March 16, the SS shipped another thousand Ghetto B Jews to Auschwitz. Fifteen men and 26 women became slave laborers; the rest were gassed in Birkenau. Approximately 150 Jews were shot by Ukrainian guards in Płaszów because there was no room for them on the Auschwitz transports. Among those murdered by the Germans and their collaborators in the Kraków ghetto on March 13–14, 1943, were the beloved relatives of many *Schindlerjuden*.[78]

Oskar did not mention the March 13 and 14 actions in his postwar writings. He knew enough, though, about Göth's plans to tell his Jewish workers from Płaszów on the evening of March 12 to stay at Emalia until the closing of the ghetto was complete. He was also stunned by the murders of the *Kinderheim* children. Though Oskar was never much of a father to his two illegitimate children, after the war he drew very close to the children of his Schindler Jews. The testimony of those who knew him after the war suggests that he had a soft spot for children. It is not surprising, then, that he should have been particularly shocked by the mass murder of so many of Kraków's Jewish children during the brutal closing of the ghetto on March 13 and 14, 1943.

The Little Girl in Red

Oskar's love of children provided the basis for the story of the famous little girl in red in Keneally's novel and Spielberg's film. The little girl in the red coat, the only color in the black-and-white portions of the film save for a candle at the beginning, stood out in *Schindler's List* not only during her naive search for safety during the closing of the ghetto but also in a later scene where her dead body was found among others about to be burned. Because the little girl in red was based on a real person, if she was buried in one of the mass graves at Płaszów, her body would have been exhumed and burned in the fall of 1944 by a secret *Aktion* 1005 *Kommando* unit.

The first of these highly secret squads, known as *Sonderkommando* 1005, was created on orders from Heinrich Müller, the head of the Gestapo, in the summer of 1942 and placed under the command of *SS-Standartenführer* Paul Blobel, a seasoned SD officer and *Einsatzgruppe* commander who had already gained quite a reputation for thoroughness and brutality at Babi Yar and elsewhere. Blobel's task was to oversee an *Enterdungsaktion* (Exhumation Action) throughout German-occupied Russia, and later Poland, to eliminate the traces of mass murder victims. The units were made up of members of the SD and Sipo who oversaw a small squad of *Ordnungspolizei* (Orpo; Order police). They supervised the Jewish and other slave laborers who exhumed the bodies, put them on large pyres for burning, and then collected the ashes for disposal. During the final phase of these operations, the slave laborers crushed all remaining bones and looked through the ashes for valuables not discovered in earlier searches. When an *Aktion* 1005 unit had completed a particular operation, it cleared the site and murdered all the slave laborers involved in the exhumation and cremation work. In the summer of 1944, Wilhelm Koppe, the HSSPF in the General Government, held a meeting in Kraków with the commanders of SD, Sipo, and the Order Police from the General Government's five districts. Each district was to create its own *Aktion* 1005 unit and begin operations as soon as possible. The Kraków district's *Aktion* 1005 unit cleared the mass graves of Płaszów, which contained about 8,000 bodies, in the fall of 1944. Though the *Aktion* 1005 units had been created initially because of concern for health problems related to the mass grave sites, fear of discovery by the nearby Red Army later drove the German efforts. One of the bodies possibly exhumed and cremated in the fall 1944 *Enterdungsaktion* in Płaszów was that of the little girl in red.[79]

According to Douglas Brode, Steven Spielberg and his scriptwriter, Steven Zaillian, used the little girl in red as their "Rosebud," a reference to the symbolic last word in *Citizen Kane*. The little girl in the red dress would serve as the "Rosebud" symbol in *Schindler's List* and be the emotional prism through which Oskar Schindler would truly awaken to the horrors of the Holocaust all around him. Three writers, Keneally, then Kurt Luedtke, and finally Zaillian, tried their hands at transforming Keneally's novel into a script for television or a movie. Luedtke had difficulty unlocking the mystery behind Schindler's reasons for helping Jews during the Holocaust. Spielberg felt that Zaillian could resolve this dilemma. The key was the little girl in the red dress. In some ways, the innocent child was like Oskar Schindler. As she walks through the ghetto she seems oblivious to the violence and death around her. Later, she becomes a victim of its horror. From Spielberg's perspective, the closing of the ghetto was a transforming moment for Oskar Schindler: He is no longer able to deny the mass murder taking place before his very eyes.[80]

As I have already discussed, Oskar Schindler was probably never on Lasota Hill with Eva, his mistress, whom Keneally and Spielberg incorrectly called Ingrid, either on June 9, 1942, the date that Keneally used to describe this scene, or on March 13 or 14, 1943, the dates most similar time frame-wise to Spielberg's depiction of Ingrid and Oskar watching Genia, the little girl in red, from atop Lasota Hill. Franciszek Palowski, a prominent Polish journalist who served as Spielberg's technical consultant and adviser during the filming of *Schindler's List* in Kraków in 1993, said that "it is not certain that it [the scene on Lasota Hill] really happened." Moreover, there seems to be some question about the identity of Schindler's mistress at the time. This is not an unimportant issue because it seems as though his Kraków girlfriends had ties to Abwehr and the Gestapo that were useful to Oskar. Keneally's novel and Spielberg's film both center on one Schindler girlfriend, Ingrid. Emilie said in her memoirs, *Where Light and Shadow Meet*, that Keneally got this wrong in his book. Emilie said that, in reality, Ingrid was really Amelia, an Abwehr agent. But later, in her second set of memoirs, *Ich, Emilie Schindler*, Emilie said that Ingrid was really "Marta Eva." Keneally said that "Ingrid" was a Sudeten German *Treuhänder* with ties to Abwehr; Viktoria Klonowska was "a Polish secretary" and "the beauty of Oskar's front office." Oskar "immediately began a long affair" with Viktoria. Both sets of Emilie's memoirs agree that Viktoria Klonowska, who had ties to the Gestapo, was Oskar's Polish girlfriend. And according to Keneally, Viktoria was responsible for arranging Oskar's release from Gestapo custody in 1942, 1943, and 1944. So in addition to Emilie, Oskar had a German mistress in Kraków, "Ingrid" or Eva, and a Polish lover, Viktoria. But in the end it was Eva who was closest to Oskar, and she was the model for "Ingrid" in Keneally's novel and Spielberg's film. She went with Oskar and Emilie to Brünnlitz in 1944 and in time became close friends with Emilie. So who was Eva, or

"Ingrid"? Her real name today is Eva Kisch Scheuer and she ran a small showroom in Kraków for Emalia's enamelware.[81]

If Oskar had been on Lasota Hill in 1942 or 1943 as the SS terrorized the ghetto below, probably Eva would have been with him. Moreover, the scene, at least as it was written by Keneally, would not have been as forceful or as meaningful without the presence of someone intimately close to Oskar. This poignant scene was taken directly from Thomas Keneally's novel and is simply historical symbolism.[82] But what inspired Keneally and Spielberg to create this scene? Spielberg and his scriptwriter, Steven Zaillian, got the idea from one of the chapters in Keneally's novel. They compressed two historical events, the June 8–10, 1942, and March 13–14, 1943, *Aktions* in the Kraków ghetto into one scene and added details from Keneally's chapter on Genia, the real little girl in red. Keneally wrote his short chapter on Genia after he interviewed members of the Dresner family, who had a niece, Genia, whom they nicknamed "red cap" because of her fondness for a red cap, coat, and boots, which she insisted on wearing everywhere. All the Dresners—Juda, Chaja, Jonas, and Danuta—would ultimately be saved by Oskar Schindler.[83]

Spielberg's use of the Keneally story about Genia in his film convinced one Polish woman, Roma Ligocka, a cousin of the Polish film maker, Roman Polanski, that she was the young girl in red. After she saw the film during its Kraków premiere, she decided to write her memoirs about her Holocaust experiences, *The Girl in the Red Coat*. If we accept Keneally's research on this matter, it is doubtful if Roma Ligocka was the real girl in the red coat. On the other hand, her memoir, which partially deals with her life as a Jew in occupied Poland during the war, adds to our knowledge about the experiences of a child during the Holocaust.[84]

According to Keneally, Genia's parents had been in line for the June 8, 1942, deportation to Bełżec but somehow managed to escape into the Polish countryside. Her parents hid Genia with a Polish family who, though very kind, later became afraid of being caught with a Jewish child in their home and somehow managed to send three-year-old Genia back into the ghetto to the Dresners. Genia's parents planned to return to the ghetto to be with their daughter. Genia also had other relatives in the ghetto. One of the young child's favorites was her young uncle, Dr. Judas "Idek" Schindel, an internist who survived the war and later settled in Tel Aviv, where he opened a laryngology clinic. Genia lived with Dr. Schindel in the ghetto. On the day of the June 8 roundup, Dr. Schindel asked some neighbors to watch Genia while he was working at the Jewish Hospital on

Węgierska Street. When Genia managed to slip out of their apartment to look for Dr. Schindel, she was picked up by the SS and put in the deportation line. A family friend saw Genia in line and ran to the hospital to tell Dr. Schindel. Though Keneally says that Dr. Schindel found Genia at the deportation gathering site on *Plac Zgody*, the spot was really at the Optima factory site between Krakuska and Węgierska. This changes the scene described by Keneally, which centers around Oskar and Eva ("Ingrid") watching Genia wander aimlessly in the crowd on *Plac Zgody* until an SS officer gently puts her in the deportation line. Yet if for some reason Oskar and Eva had been on Lasota Hill on June 9, it would have been impossible for them to have seen anything at *Plac Zgody* or the Optima factory grounds. The gathering site at the factory was in an enclosed courtyard and it is doubtful that Dr. Schindel could have had any contact with Genia. But Keneally is correct, at least according to Ludmilla Page, the wife of Poldek Page, when he says that Genia was able to sneak out of the deportation line and back to her uncle's apartment. Ludmilla adds that though Genia survived "this deportation [June 8, 1942]" she probably "perished in the next one," which was on October 28, 1942.[85]

The scene created by Keneally, which Spielberg partially copied, took place the day after he saved Bankier, June 9, 1942. In this scene, Oskar and "Ingrid" rode to the top of Lasota Hill, where they saw the brutal roundup below. They were particularly moved by the figure of a small "toddler, boy or girl, dressed in a small scarlet coat and cap." Oskar asked Ingrid about the gender of the child, and she confirmed that it was a girl. Keneally goes on to describe a violent roundup that conflicts with historical facts. The June 8–10, 1942, roundup had been extremely brutal, but the violent scenes described by Keneally do not fit the events of June 9. Moreover, given the summer foliage and the height of the buildings, it would have been difficult, even with binoculars, to have seen the figure of a little three-year-old-girl among the adults in any part of the ghetto.[86]

What was the purpose of putting this scene in the book? Supposedly, Steven Spielberg and his writers did not think Keneally adequately explained the motives behind Schindler's actions during the war. In many ways, though, Keneally did a better job of this than Spielberg and he did it in this long scene. As Oskar and Ingrid watched Genia search for a hiding place, oblivious to all of the pain and suffering around her, Ingrid pleaded with Oskar to do something. But Oskar could do nothing. He was so upset and sickened by what he saw he that he "slipped from his horse, tripped, and found himself on his knees hugging the trunk of a pine tree." What troubled him most was the "lack of [German] shame." He now understood that "no one could find refuge anymore behind the idea of German culture, nor behind those pronouncements uttered by leaders to exempt anonymous men from stepping behind their gardens, from looking out their office windows at the realities on the sidewalk."[87]

Though the scene with Genia is probably fictitious, Thomas Keneally used it to try to explain why Oskar Schindler ultimately went to such efforts to save Jewish lives during the Holocaust. Oskar Schindler was not a complex man. Moreover, the simple explanation given by Keneally fits with Oskar's explanations after the war about why he did what he did. His answers were plain and simple. He helped Jews because what the Germans were doing to them was wrong. In an impromptu speech in Tel Aviv to a large gathering on May 2, 1962, Oskar said that he "tried to do what I had to do."[88] But beyond this, there were other issues that helped transform Oskar into the person that became a "savior" to almost 1,100 Jews. Several years earlier, Oskar gave a more detailed explanation to Kurt Grossmann, who published Oskar's account of his efforts to save Jews during the war in *Die unbesungenen Helden: Menschen in Deutschlands dunklen Tagen (The Unsung Heroes: People in Germany's Dark Days)*. Oskar told Grossmann that the

driving motives for my actions and my inner change were the daily witnessing of the unbearable suffering of Jewish people and the brutal operations of the Prussian *Übermenschen* (superior human beings) in the occupied territories—a bunch of lying hypocrites, sadistic murderers, who with good propaganda had promised to liberate my homeland, the Sudetenland, and in reality degraded it into a colony and plundered it. My trips into foreign countries helped me to form the true and complete picture of *"Großdeutschland,"* thanks to the open criticism and the recognition of facts, all of which was kept secret in the Reich. Additionally there was the hatred which existed between the SS and the SD on the one hand and the Canaris officers, among whom I had honest friends. An essential driving force for my actions was the feeling of a moral duty toward my numerous Jewish classmates and friends, with whom I had experienced a wonderful youth, free of racial problems.[89]

For Schindler, then, there was not only disgust with the brutality and moral dishonesty of the Germans but also something deeper that went back to his Sudeten German roots. And after the war, Emilie and Oskar both told stories about their childhood friendships with Jews. When Emilie was fifteen, her parents sent her to an agricultural school after an unsuccessful year at a Catholic boarding school for girls. During her three years at the agricultural school, Emilie's best friend was a Jew, Rita Gross.[90] Thomas Keneally tells a similar story about Oskar, whose next door neighbor in Svitavy was "a liberal rabbi named Felix Kantor," a Reform or liberal rabbi who believed that "it was no crime, in fact praiseworthy, to be a German as well as a Jew."[91] In 1936, Rabbi Kantor, who is listed in a 1935 German language information book on Zwittau (Svitavy) as Rabbi Felix Kantner, moved his family, which included two sons, to Belgium because of the growing anti-Semitism in Czechoslovakia. In addition, Oskar was also supposed to have had "a few middle-class Jewish friends."[92]

Keneally's stories about Oskar's early friendships with Jews might seem a little self-serving, and even a bit fabricated, but they were confirmed after the war by Herbert Steinhouse, a Canadian journalist who met Oskar in Munich in 1949 and later interviewed him in Paris about his wartime efforts to help Jews. But before Steinhouse was willing to move ahead with his account of the Schindler story, he gathered a large body of testimony from *Schindlerjuden* and others to corroborate what Oskar had told him. One of the people who wrote to Steinhouse said that in addition to being a Schindler Jew who worked for Oskar at Emalia, he was also one of the sons of Rabbi Kantner. Before the war, he told Steinhouse, Oskar was a "true believer," a loyal Sudeten Nazi who accepted everything except the party's ideas on race. He said that Oskar had "been friendly with several of the Sudetenland Jews" in Svitavy and occasionally talked with Rabbi Kantner about Yiddish literature, folktales, and Jewish traditions in eastern Poland. Rabbi Kantner's "Rabbinat," which was located on Brunoplatz 11, oversaw a small Jewish Temple and cemetery. Census figures from 1930 indicate that there were only 168 Jews in Svitavy out of a total population of 10,466.[93]

There is no reason not to accept these stories as being true, though it is hard to verify whether anyone named Kantner worked at Emalia. There is no Kantner on the first "Schindler-type" list from late 1943 nor on the Mauthausen transport lists of August 10, 1944, which included hundreds of male *Schindlerjuden*. The same is true for the original "Schindler's List" of males for October 21, 1944, and the two final "Schindler's Lists" of April 18, 1945 and May 8, 1945. But this proves nothing because the lists kept by the SS for Emalia's Jewish workers have disappeared, probably destroyed in the war or hidden away in some obscure Polish archive.

But one other point should be made about the various factors that ultimately convinced Oskar Schindler to become more aggressive in his efforts to save Jews, and that is the tide of war.

According to Ian Kershaw, the defeat at Stalingrad barely six weeks before the closing of the Kraków ghetto in 1943 had now convinced those "with any sense of realism" who previously held onto "dwindling hopes of victory" that "ultimate defeat" was now a certainty. Though Hitler's power remained strong, loyalty to the Nazi state and Hitler himself began to decline considerably.[94] And although evidence suggests that Schindler had already gained quite a reputation as someone who was kind towards his Jewish workers, it was probably not coincidental that he became more aggressive in his efforts to help Jews after the Stalingrad debacle; in fact, general German disillusionment with Hitler's regime probably helped Schindler. Moreover, as Oskar and others began to think of a postwar Europe without Hitler, some thought had to be given to questions about criminality and responsibility for the crimes of the Third Reich. And beyond this was the practical question of a return to normal life. We do know that at the end of the war, Oskar naively thought he could transform his factory in Brünnlitz into an Emalia-type plant that would produce enamelware for a war-torn Europe in desperate need of bare necessities such as pots and pans. And during his escape westward, this former German spy and armaments manufacturer carried with him a document prepared by his *Schindlerjuden* attesting to his kindness and good treatment of them. His decision to settle in Regensburg, Germany after the war, which was only an hour or two away from the Czech border, indicates that he probably had dreams of returning to his homeland. The forced expulsion of the Sudeten Germans by Czech authorities in the immediate years after the end of World War II insured, though, that Oskar and Emilie Schindler would never be able to return to Czechoslovakia. What Oskar Schindler never counted on was that, after the war, he, like his *Schindlerjuden,* would become a Displaced Person without a homeland.

6.

AMON GÖTH, OSKAR SCHINDLER, AND PŁASZÓW

ONE OF THE GREAT MYSTERIES OF THE OSKAR SCHINDLER STORY was his relationship with Amon Göth, who was played brilliantly by Ralph Fiennes in *Schindler's List.* In 1983, Monika Christiane Knauss, Göth's daughter, wrote a letter to the German magazine, *Der Spiegel,* in response to the publication in Germany of Thomas Keneally's *Schindlers Liste.* She was particularly critical of Keneally's portrayal of her father as "einen Idioten." She claimed that Schindler and her father were the best of friends, though she admitted that Schindler later denied this. She said that after the war Oskar visited her mother, Ruth, and said nothing negative about her father during the visit. Because Monika was only ten months old when her father was executed for war crimes in 1946, she obviously received this information secondhand. She also told *Der Spiegel* that without her father it would have been impossible for Schindler to have saved some of Płaszów's Jews. She ended her 1983 letter by saying that her father's silence also saved Oskar Schindler's life.[1]

Monika's tone was very different in a rambling, forty-eight-hour interview with Matthias Kessler in the spring of 2001, published the following year as *Ich muß doch meinen Vater lieben, oder?* (I Have to Love My Father, or Do I?) And though the *Frankfurter Allgemeine Zeitung* titled its review of the book a *"Biographische Freakshow,"* in reality, the book-length interview was part of an ongoing and painful attempt by a middle-aged woman to come to grips with the monstrous legacy of her father.[2]

Monika, who used the surname Göth for the book, only slowly discovered the truth surrounding her father's brutal past. Her mother, Ruth Irene Kalder, an actress from Breslau (today Wrocław, Poland), had begun to work for Oskar Schindler as a secretary at Emalia in 1942. One evening, Oskar took her to one of the lavish parties put on by Amon Göth at his villa at Płaszów, where the Viennese camp commandant fell head over heels for Ruth, who, some thought, resembled Elizabeth Taylor. Ruth soon moved in with Göth, who had a wife, Anni, and two children, Werner and Inge, in Vienna. Göth told Ruth that she could live with him but that he could never divorce his wife because of his children.[3]

Ruth loved her luxurious life with Amon Göth in Płaszów. Every morning before breakfast, and again in the afternoon, she would go horseback riding. During warm weather, Ruth could be seen sun bathing on the infamous balcony of Göth's villa overlooking the camp. When she was not sunbathing or horseback riding, she could be found on a nearby tennis court. And then, of course, there were the incredible parties given by Göth in the evenings. Ruth Irene Kalder lived a life of luxury and comfort during her two-year relationship with Amon Göth, though she claims she never visited the concentration camp below the villa.[4]

Ruth remained faithful to Göth after his execution; in 1948, with the backing of his father, Franz Amon Göth, she changed her name to Göth after Franz legally affirmed that his son had been engaged to Ruth at the end of the war. The reason there was no wedding, Franz claimed, was the "chaos at the end of the war."[5] Ruth spoke adoringly of Amon Göth, whom she called by his childhood nickname, "Mony." In fact, she named Monika for him. Ruth told Monika very little about her father when she was a child, but when she did it was always in glowing terms. Ruth told her daughter that Amon Göth was a handsome ladies' man who had a beautiful singing voice and threw lavish parties. Ruth once told Monika: "He was my king and I was his queen." She said that Monika should love her father as deeply as her mother. And for a while she did.[6]

But as she grew older, something continued to nag Monika about her father. Even before she became aware of the mysterious dark shadow that surrounded her father's name, someone attacked her when she was in her pram, possibly because she was Amon Göth's child. Then, when Monika was eight years old, an aunt criticized her for crying and told her that if her father could see her, he would "jump out of the Weichsel."[7] What

Monika did not know was that the aunt was alluding to the disposal of Amon Göth's ashes in the Weichsel River in Poland after his execution in 1946. Three years later, when Monika failed to clean a bathroom, she had a terrible fight with her mother. Ruth, who was fanatical about a clean bathroom, said, "You are like your father and will end up like him."[8] The next day, Monika asked her grandmother, who for all practical purposes raised her, what had really happened to her father during the war. Her grandmother told her that her father had been executed because he had killed some Jews in Poland. She added that he had also run a labor camp and killed the Jews for "sanitation" reasons.[9]

When Monika was twelve, she wanted to get to know a Jewish classmate, Ernestine Silber, who was new to her school. One day, Monika followed Ernestine home and was impressed when Ernestine's father hugged her warmly. She remembered wondering what was so bad about Jews because she liked the way Jews treated their children, and remembered wondering what was so bad about Jewish people. That evening, Monika told her mother about Ernestine and her interest in becoming her friend. Ruth replied, "Oh God, I hope Ernestine does not mention your name at home." Monika responded, "Do you think every Jew knows about Amon Göth and the work camp at Płaszów?" Ruth said that the Jews knew the name of Amon Göth. Monika quickly lost interest in becoming Ernestine's friend. "What could I say? I'm the daughter of someone who killed your relatives?"[10]

Monika's struggle with the memory of her father continued into adulthood. After her marriage to a man that abused her, she wondered why she had married "such a brute." Was she, she later asked herself, trying to replicate her father in her marriage or was she punishing herself?[11] She now felt that she had a drawer in her mind called "Amon Göth" and "could keep it closed" if she wanted to.[12]

When she was twenty-five, she met a Jewish survivor from Płaszów, Manfred, in a Munich bar. When Monika noticed the tattoo on his arm, she asked if he was a Jew. She then wanted to know whether he had been in a concentration camp and, if so, where. "In Poland," Manfred responded. But where in Poland, Monika wanted to know. Manfred, who was becoming uncomfortable with the thrust of the conversation, told her it was probably a camp she had never heard of. But she persisted and he told her he had been a prisoner at Płaszów. Monika said she was glad to hear he was in a labor camp instead of a concentration camp. She then asked whether Manfred knew her father. "Who was he?" Manfred

replied. "Göth," said Monika. Manfred, who was Polish, evidently did
not understand Monika's pronunciation of her father's name and said he
knew no one by that name. Shocked, Monika said that Manfred must
have known him because her father had been the commandant at
Płaszów. She pronounced her father's name again, first as "Gätt," then as
"Gööth," and finally as "Amon Gätt." At that point, Manfred turned
white and screamed, "That murderer! That swine!" Stunned, Monika
tried to argue that Płaszów was a labor camp, not a concentration camp.
That was the end of the conversation. Several days later, Manfred and
Monika met again. Manfred refused to talk about the matter any further,
saying that Monika was too young to discuss such things.[13]

It was also during this period that Monika met Oskar Schindler. She
was, of course, too young to have remembered Oskar's first visit with her
mother soon after the war. Monika was now a teenager and Oskar had returned from Argentina several years earlier. They met in a rundown neighborhood near the Central Train Station in Frankfurt. Oskar was too embarrassed by his shabby living conditions to invite Monika and Ruth to
his apartment. Instead, they met at a restaurant. Monika recalled that he
appeared to be unemployed and broke and that her mother had to pay for
the drinks at the restaurant. This is striking because it was not the custom
then for women to pay the bill in a restaurant. Moreover, Oskar consumed quite a few schnapps and cups of coffee. As Monika later told an
Israeli newspaper reporter: "I've never seen anyone drink like Oskar, although he had no money."[14]

Oskar, who also borrowed cigarettes from Monika, told her that she
looked just like her father. Monika came away from the meeting thinking
that he liked her father. She remembered that her mother told her that her
father had once gotten Schindler out of prison, so she felt no compunction
asking Oskar why he did not go to Kraków to help her father when he
learned that Göth had been captured by the Allies. "Monika," Oskar
replied, "it was impossible; they would have hanged me as well even if I
had saved 10,000 Jews."[15] This was the last time that Monika would see
Oskar Schindler.

The publication of Thomas Keneally's *Schindlers Liste* in Germany in
1983 reopened new wounds for Monika and her mother. In the decade or
so since she had met the Płaszów survivor, Manfred, and the appearance
of Keneally's novel, Monika had married and given birth to a daughter,
Yvette. After Keneally's novel came out, Ruth was contacted by the Lon-
don-based, South African-born film maker Jon Blair, who told Ruth that

he was preparing a documentary on the life of Oskar Schindler. In 1982, he visited Steven Spielberg at Universal Studios to see whether he could get permission for the rights to the Schindler story, which Universal owned. According to Blair, Universal was hesitant to give him permission to make the documentary and only did so under pressure from Spielberg, who was not yet ready to make a film about Oskar Schindler. Blair said that Spielberg later told him that "letting [him] make the documentary . . . would be a cheap way for Universal to have their research done for them, and he [Spielberg] of course would have access to [the] film once he came to make his." Blair feels that he wound up "doing a lot of the leg work for him [Spielberg]."[16] Though it is difficult to determine the impact of Blair's eighty-two-minute documentary, *Schindler: His Story as Told by the Actual People He Saved* (Thames Television) on Spielberg, Blair's research is first rate. Moreover, he captured on film interviews of some of the most important people involved in the Schindler story.

Ruth agreed to do the interview with Jon Blair because she thought it would be about Oskar. Instead, at least from her perspective, all Blair wanted to talk about was Amon Göth. This troubled her. Ruth, who spoke excellent English, was, according to Blair, dying from emphysema. It is obvious from watching the interview that Ruth was ill. Yet she chose her words carefully, particularly when she was asked about Amon Göth. She told Blair that Amon Göth was not a brute, at least no more than others in the SS. He did not, she asserted, "kill for the fun of it." Göth's views towards Jews, Ruth said, were similar to those of others in the SS: "They were there to work." But she admitted that Göth "did kill some Jews," though he did not hate them. She also claimed that she told the two Jewish maids who worked for her, whom Göth called "Lena," (Helen Sternlicht; today Helen Sternlicht Rosenzweig) and "Susanna," (Helen Hirsch), that if she could, she "would have saved them [the Jews] all." Helen Rosenzweig, or "Lena," says that Ruth once did make such a statement to both maids.[17]

Blair did ask Ruth about Oskar Schindler, though most of her interview time on the documentary was spent discussing Amon Göth. In response to Blair's question about whether Oskar loved Jews, Ruth said that he was a "lovable opportunist" who needed the Jews and worked with them. Blair then asked Ruth whether she thought Schindler was a good Nazi. "We were all good Nazis," she told him, "we couldn't be anything else." She added that they "had to believe in all of these things." When asked about the plight of the Jews, she answered with a question: "What could we have done? We couldn't have done anything against it."[18]

But according to Monika, there was more to Ruth Kalder's interview with Jon Blair than appeared in the documentary. Ruth had expected to meet just with Jon Blair and was shocked when he showed up with "einem ganzen Fernsehteam (a whole television crew)." And though the interview with Ruth takes up only about five minutes in the documentary, Blair spent many hours with her on the day of the interview. Monika claimed that the interview seemed to "go on and on and on." While Blair and the BBC crew filmed the interview in Ruth's living room, Monika listened from the kitchen. Monika vividly remembered her mother's stunning response when Blair asked how she could live with such a brute: "He was no worse than the rest of them." Monika, who had never discussed her father with her mother, said she could no longer listen to what was going on in the other room. The next day, Ruth Kalder Göth committed suicide, though in fairness to Jon Blair, it must be mentioned that she had talked about doing this in the weeks before the interview. Ruth left Monika a letter that said she no longer wanted to live. She also hoped that her daughter would have good memories of her. And although Monika felt her ties to her mother were more biological than emotional, Ruth's death traumatized her because an important connection to her past was now gone.[19]

In the two decades since her mother's death, Monika continued to struggle with the memory of her father. She saw *Schindlers Liste* in 1994 and was surprised by how much Ralph Fiennes resembled the images of her father she had seen in photographs. The film devastated her; for three days afterwards she was bedridden. For the first time she had caught a true glimpse of the murderous actions of Amon Göth, and she remembered wishing that the killing would stop and that her father, in the end, would become a bit more humane. He never did. As she left the theater, she heard several Germans discussing her father. One called him schizophrenic; another said that without Göth, no Schindler Jews would have survived the war. This comment mirrored her own thoughts in the 1983 letter to *Der Spiegel*. Perhaps to assuage her own sense of guilt at having such a monstrous father, Monika has visited Israel and has studied classical Hebrew at the university where she works in Munich.[20]

She is interested in the Holocaust and admires Simon Wiesenthal, who overcame his own pain and losses during the Holocaust to seek justice against former Nazi war criminals. Monika has also visited Kraków and the remains of Płaszów. Kessler also gave her a translated copy of the large transcript of Amon Göth's war crimes trial in Kraków, which was published in 1947 as *Proces Ludobójcy Amona Leopolda Goetha* by the Central Jewish Historical Commission in Poland. Kessler used some of the points in the transcript as the basis for some of the questions he asked Monika. Needless to say, she was shocked by what she read. At the end of the interview, she told Kessler that though she had once hoped to see her father as a victim of Hitler, Himmler, and National Socialism, she now saw her father as a murderer.[21]

Despite all this, one is drawn back to Monika Göth's letter to *Der Spiegel* in 1983 and her comment that without her father, Oskar Schindler could not have saved his Jews. Evidently these were views held by others, at least according to the the German theater-goer whose comment Monika Göth overheard. Sadly, there are some seeds of truth in what both claimed in 1983 and 1994. From Amon Göth's perspective, Oskar was his friend. In reality, it was a relationship, at least from Oskar's perspective, based purely on necessity. All Oskar's postwar statements about Göth center around two topics: the bribes he paid him and his brutality. Emilie Schindler described Göth as "the most despicable man" she had ever met. She said that Göth had a "double personality." At one moment, he could be a refined Viennese gentleman commenting on the nuances of a piece of classical music, which he listened to constantly. Minutes later, he could show the "most barbaric instincts."[22] Oskar's ability to appeal to the more refined side of Göth's personality was probably the key to his ties to Göth. Oskar understood that though many people were involved in various aspects of his efforts to save his Jews, in the end Amon Göth was the most important one because he was the commandant of Płaszów, where Schindler's Jewish workers initially lived. And even after Oskar convinced Göth to let him build a sub-camp at Emalia, he had to keep Göth happy to insure the sub-camp's future.

But Oskar had to do more to win Göth's confidence; he had to establish a more personal relationship with him. At a distance, this would seem an impossible task, given Göth's SS fanaticism and racial ideals. Yet it must be remembered that there was another side to Amon Göth that few people knew about. Göth, who was the same age as Schindler, came from a well-to-do Viennese family that owned a publishing house specializing in military publications. Though never a serious student, Amon Göth might well have become a prosperous publisher and intellectual if he had not become involved with the Nazi movement in Austria in the 1920s as a student. Instead, he became a war criminal.[23]

Oddly enough, a blend of sophistication with brutality was not uncommon among the SS officer class. Oskar had probably become accustomed to dealings with SS and General Government officials with similar
contradictory traits. Soon after Hitler took power in Germany in early
1933, Heinrich Himmler sought to enhance the reputation of the SS by recruiting new members from the aristocracy and the well-to-do of Germany. By the late 1930s, some of the most prominent noble families in
Germany had members in the SS, principally the SD. In fact, Heinz Höhne
has estimated that almost 19 percent of the *SS-Obergruppenführer* (lieutenant generals), 9.8 percent of its *SS-Gruppenführer* (major generals),
14.3 percent of its *SS-Brigadeführer* (brigadier generals), 8.8 percent of its
SS-Oberführer (senior colonels), and 8.4 percent of its *SS-Standartenführer* (colonels) were from the nobility. The SS also attracted well-educated,
intellectual members of the upper middle class, many of them attorneys or
economists. They seemed drawn to the SS less by ideals than by careerism
and power. These men gave the SS a veneer of sophistication and "legal-
ity." In many ways, Amon Göth became a bit of an anachronism in the SS
because many of the old guard had been driven out by the time war began
in 1939. On the other hand, he also brought with him a certain air of sophistication that fit into the new SS that after 1933 tried to transform itself into Germany's new aristocracy.[24]

Amon Leopold Göth

But who was this Amon Göth and why did he choose the career that ultimately led to his execution as a mass murderer in 1946? It is important
to know something about Göth if we are to understand the challenges
that Oskar Schindler had to face and overcome as he dealt with this figure so central to his efforts to save his Jews. Fortunately, we have a
fairly good body of documentation dealing with Göth's life before and
during the Holocaust. His SS files in the Bundesarchiv Berlin Documentation Center provide a broad outline of his life, including statements by
Göth. A microfilm copy of Göth's SS file is housed in the Foreign
Records Seized (RG 242) collection in the National Archives of the
United States depository in College Park, Maryland; though not as complete as Göth's Bundesarchiv dossier, it does contain a few documents
not found in the Berlin SS files.

The published transcript of Göth's Polish war crimes trial, *Proces Ludobójcy Amona Leopolda Goetha* (Genocide Trial of Amon Göth),

centers around Göth's criminal actions but also gives information about his Nazi and SS career. In addition, the interviews of Ruth Kalder Göth and Monika Göth by Jon Blair, Matthias Kessler, and Israeli journalist Tom Segev provided more information about Amon Göth's life and career. Göth's name comes up quite frequently in Elinor J. Brecher's fine collection of *Schindlerjuden* testimony, *Schindler's Legacy: True Stories of the List Survivors* (1994). I also interviewed Schindler Jews who have unique perspectives on Amon Göth. Among the most important were Mietek Pemper, who worked in Göth's office in Płaszów, and Helen Sternlicht Rosenszweig, who spent almost two years working as a maid for Göth and Ruth at their villa in Płaszów. Together, these sources provide us with good insight into the character, personality, and life of a man his own daughter considered a murderer and most survivors saw as a brutal monster.

The files of most SS men consisted of a set list of eighteen to twenty documents that covered every aspect of their lives and service to the Fatherland. One of the most important documents was the Vitae *(Lebenslauf)*, the third document in Amon Göth's SS file after his personnel sheet with photograph *(Personalbogen mit Lichtbild)* and his Supplemental Sheet and Change in Status Report *(Ergänzungsbogen und Veränderungsmeldungen)*. The first two documents provide a basic secretarial look at the ebbs and flows of Göth's career in the SS. But the most detailed record of his SS career can be found in another document, the Personal data *(Personalangaben)* file, a four-page document in *Fraktur* (Gothic-style print favored by the Nazis) German that details every aspect of Göth's career, including his awards, SS service, education, civilian occupation, family background, marital status and children, Nazi and other party membership information, and foreign travels.

The Vitae is the most revealing document in Amon Göth's SS file, which, when combined with the interview that Ruth Kalder Göth gave to Tom Segev in 1975, gives us a pretty good look at the more human side of one of Nazi Germany's more infamous war criminals. Amon Göth was born on December 11, 1908, in Vienna, Austria, though at least one SS document later in his file lists his birth date as December 14, 1905. His parents were Franz Amon Göth, the owner of *Verlagsanstalt Amon Franz Göth* (Amon Franz Göth Publishing House) for military books in Vienna, and Berta Schwendt Göth. Roman Ferber, a prominent *Schindlerjude* who went on to hold important urban and economic planning positions in New York city government, told Elinor Brecher that Göth sent much of the booty he stole from Jews or acquired on the black market to his family in Vienna, who are "prosperous publishers to this day."[25]

Franz Amon Göth did quite well as a publisher and his son, Amon, was raised in a proper upper-middle-class Viennese Catholic home. He attended public school in Vienna and went to college in Waidhofen an der Thaya, a beautiful but nondescript medieval town in northwestern Austria near the Czech border. Oskar Schindler and Amon Göth were born eight months apart in the Austro-Hungarian Empire and raised within two hundred miles of each other, facts probably not lost on both men. But Göth felt that his life as a child was less than secure. He told Ruth that his parents neglected him, which was the reason he "turned his back on the bourgeois social values" they tried to instil in him.[26] His father spent a lot of time away from home in the United States and Europe; his mother devoted her time to running the publishing house. His parents left the responsibility of raising their son to his father's sister, Kathy. Göth told Ruth that his parents' main concern was that he prepare and educate himself to take over the family publishing house.[27]

Yet knowing that he had a secure future seemed to have the opposite effect on Amon Göth. He was intelligent but uninterested in his schoolwork. The six-foot-four-inch Göth was more interested in athletics than academics. To the great disappointment of his parents, he decided to study agriculture in college but never completed more than a few semesters of work. He returned to Vienna to work in his family's publishing house. From this time on he considered himself a publisher, the occupation he listed in his Nazi Party and SS membership files.[28]

While in college he did acquire an interest in fascism and Nazism, at that time competitive political movements in Austria. In 1925, Göth joined the local youth chapter of the Austrian branch of the Nazi Party (NSDAP; *Nationalsozialistische Deutsche Arbeiterpartei*), which at the time was in the midst of a power struggle between older trade unionists and younger members who admired Adolf Hitler's forceful leadership in Germany. Hitler's Nazi movement had strong roots in pre- and postwar Austria, where two of its precursors, the DAP (*Deutsche Arbeiterpartei*; German Workers Party) and the DNSAP (*Deutsche Nationalsozialistische Arbeiterpartei*; German National Socialist Workers Party), were formed. The DNSAP group split into Austrian and Czech factions after World War I and was the center of Czech Nazism until 1933.[29]

By the time Amon Göth had begun college, there was a strong surge of interest in Austrian Nazism among high school and university students who came from families hurt by postwar Austria's serious economic problems. Their teachers often encouraged their students to join Nazi-sponsored organizations such as the German Athletes Association *(Deutscher Turnerbund)*. Estimates are that 22 percent of the members of the Austrian Nazi Party's paramilitary organization during this period, the Fatherland Alliance *(Vaterländerischer Schutzbund)*, which later was integrated into the German Nazi Party's SA, were students.[30]

Ruth Göth said that Amon told her his interest in Nazism came from a fellow student who had joined the Hitler Youth *(Hitlerjugend)* earlier. Nazism "captured his heart. It knew how to appreciate his physical strength and athletic ability, and fostered friendship and youthful rebellion."[31] Göth's interest in fascism and Nazism continued to grow after he returned to Vienna to begin his short-lived career as a publisher. In 1927, he joined the Styrian Home Protection Organization in Vienna *(Steirischer Heimatschutzverband Wien)*, the strongest and most virulently anti-Semitic wing of the Austrian fascist Home Guard *(Heimwehr)*, the principal fascist competitor of the Nazis in Austria. He was probably attracted to the Home Guard's political strength vis-à-vis the Austrian Nazis' lack of unity.[32]

Göth evidently left the Styrian Home Guard in 1930 after a failed coalition attempt between the Austrian Nazis and the Home Guard on the eve of the Austrian parliamentary elections in the fall of 1930. Both parties did poorly in the election, particularly the Austrian Nazis; afterwards, Alfred Proksch, one of the Austrian Nazis' top leaders, decreed that the country's Nazis could no longer belong to the Nazi Party and the Home Guard. They had to choose between one or the other party. Göth, who had already applied for Nazi Party membership by this time, decided to side with the Nazis. He was awarded full Nazi Party membership on May 31, 1931, when he became member no. 510 764. This meant that he now belonged to what would become a prestigious group within the Nazi Party, the Old Fighters, or Combatants *(Alte Kämpfer)*, who either had been Nazi Party members a year before Hitler took power as German chancellor on January 30, 1933, or had a party membership number below 300 000. Those who had joined the SS, the SA, or the Nazi Party before Hitler's first major Reichstag victory in Germany on September 14, 1930, were particularly revered as "Party comrades."[33]

After he joined Hitler's party, Göth became involved in its Margareten district local group *(Ortsgruppe)* in Vienna but soon joined another *Ortsgruppe* in the Mariahilf district of the city as "pol. Leiter und als SA Mann [political leader and SA man]."[34] And it was probably through his SA membership that he became interested in the SS, which until late 1930 was part of the SA. Ruth Göth said that Amon joined the SS (membership no. 43 673) in 1930 because he was attracted to the "comradeship it promised."[35]

The SS, which was established in 1925 as a special bodyguard for Hitler, grew tremendously under Heinrich Himmler, who became the SS's third leader in 1929. It had 280 members in 1929 and 2,717 members by the end of 1930. Within six months, its membership had grown fivefold and by the fall of 1932 the SS had almost 50,000 members. Given these figures, it is obvious that Göth did not acquire full membership in the SS until 1932. The reason for the contradiction between Göth's SS and Party files, which stated that he joined the SS in 1930, and SS membership statistics that indicate that he could not have joined until 1932, centered around Himmler's decision to model certain SS membership requirements on the Roman Catholic Jesuit religious order, which required a lengthy candidate period before one enjoyed full membership. In other words, Amon Göth was only a candidate member of the SS from 1930 until 1932, when he was awarded full SS membership. And though technically "Old Fighter" status in the SS was reserved for members with SS membership numbers below 10 000, Amon Göth still enjoyed a certain prestige in the SS because he was able to survive Himmler's purge of the older membership from 1933 to 1935 that rid the SS of "patent opportunists, alcoholics, homosexuals, and men of uncertain Aryan background."[36]

In Vienna, Göth served initially with SS *Truppe* (a unit of from twenty to sixty men under a *Truppenführer,* or sergeant) "Deimel" and *Sturm* "Libardi." The SS *Sturm,* the most important of the SS units, was made up of three *Truppen* and was commanded by an *SS-Hauptsturmführer.*[37] In January 1933, he was transferred to the staff of the Fifty-second SS *Standarte,* a regimental-sized unit, where he served as adjutant and *Zügführer* (platoon leader). In the spring of 1933, he was promoted to the rank of *SS-Scharführer* and ordered "to organize the necessary [illegal] measures within the scope of the Fifty-second SS *Standarte,*" which forced him ultimately to flee the "Eastern authorities" [the Austrians], who were hunting him on explosive charges. Göth's 1941 service report said that he "earned great merits for himself" during his service with this unit.[38]

Ruth Göth told Tom Segev in 1975 that in the first half of 1933 Amon was involved in terrorist activity and was being hunted by Austrian officials. He soon fled to Germany, where he became actively involved in smuggling "arms, money, and information" from the Reich into Austria.[39] Amon Göth's illegal SS activities in Austria were part of the Nazi leadership's effort to destabilize the political situation in Austria and wage what the Austrian Nazi *Party Manual* called a "cold war" in that country.[40] It centered around a growing campaign of violence and terror against opponents that began in 1932 and continued until the summer of 1934.[41]

The Nazis' cold war resulted in the outlawing of the Austrian Nazi Party on June 19, 1933. The Austrian Nazi leadership fled to Munich where they established an exile base of operations to continue their reign of terror in Austria. Amon Göth fled with them and was assigned to work in SS Sector VIII, where he took responsibility for smuggling communications equipment into Austria. This was tied to efforts by the Nazis to use a new medium, the radio, to spread their propaganda into Austria, particularly from the middle of 1933 until early 1934. Göth also served as a courier for the SS until he was arrested and detained by the Austrian police in October 1933. Göth's arrest and detention coincided with efforts by the government of Chancellor Engelbert Dollfuß, who was about to declare martial law "to purge [the government] and Austrian society of Nazi party members and sympathizers."[42] According to Göth, he was released for lack of evidence during Christmas 1933. He was lucky. From November 1933 until April 1934, Austrian authorities had convicted 50,000 Nazis of various crimes against the state and society.[43]

Ruth Göth claimed that Amon continued his illegal activities for the SS in Austria by "smuggling weapons, money, and information." She also told Tom Segev that Göth seemed to have "played a role in the murder of Chancellor Engelbert Dollfuß in July 1934."[44] The assassination of the Austrian leader on July 25 was part of an Austrian SS-led attempt to begin a revolt that would lead to a Nazi seizure of power. More than likely, Hitler knew of the coup, though he thought it was linked to an Austrian military move against the Dollfuß regime. The Nazi rebellion was badly organized and doomed to failure, though it did trigger a minor civil war in certain parts of Austria that resulted in the death of hundreds. The Austrians arrested more than 6,000 Nazis involved in different aspects of the coup. Amon Göth was one of those detained by Austrian authorities, though he somehow managed to escape and return to Munich, where Himmler had opened an *SS-Übungslager* (SS Training Camp and Garrison) at the Dachau SS complex just to the northwest of Munich. Next to it was the smaller, infamous Dachau *Konzentrationslager* (KZ; concentration camp). It is not known whether Göth spent any time at the SS facilities at Dachau because he was soon forced out of the SS by his commander, SS Sector VIII's *Oberführer*, Alfred Bigler. All Göth said about his dismissal was that he had encountered "difficulties" with Bigler, who, he claimed, was also soon kicked out of the SS. Göth launched counterclaims against Bigler, though he said these went unanswered because of Bigler's dismissal from the SS.[45] It is difficult to gauge the seriousness of the factors that led to Amon Göth's problems with the SS at this time, though given the infighting within the Austrian Nazi Party, quite possibly they centered around nothing more than personal conflicts between Bigler and Göth. There is no record of Göth's dismissal in his SS file or in the numerous personnel reports written in 1941 on Göth by his superiors in Vienna. The only indication we have that he was not active in SS affairs from 1934 until 1937 is the simple lack of service details in his SS records. Consequently, it is possible that Göth was allowed to rejoin the SS sometime between 1934 and 1937. This was a difficult time for the Austrian SS and the SA, which were supposed to be dissolved after the July coup. Yet both groups were quickly rebuilt, though by 1938 the ranks of the Austrian SS was still 20 percent smaller than it had been in 1934. It maintained a low profile during this period and worked principally at gathering information for the Third Reich as part of the extensive spy network set up by the Germans in the years before the 1938 *Anschluß*. But it is difficult to say whether Göth was involved in SS affairs in Austria or Germany between 1934 and 1937.[46]

The first document we have that indicates Göth's return to Nazi Party activity is a letter he wrote on July 16, 1937, to the headquarters of the Austrian Refugee Society (ARS; *Flüchtlingshilfswerk*) in Berlin. He asked ARS officials for a note permitting the transfer of his party membership to Munich and the confirmation of his Nazi Party number. He gave Pognerstraße 28/III in Munich as his new, permanent address. He explained that his original Party papers had been taken from him after his arrest in Austria in 1933. It is possible that they were destroyed when he was dismissed from the SS, though more than likely they were part of the Nazi Party and SS records seized by Austrian officials after the 1934 coup.[47]

The ARS had been set up before the 1934 coup and afterwards sent money from Nazi party coffers in Germany to help the families of Nazis killed and executed after the failed coup against Dolfuß. German party leaders hoped this would stop the flood of Austrian Nazi refugees into the Reich and create a greater sense of loyalty towards the Reich among Nazi Party members in Austria. The ARS, which was headed by the head of the Austrian SS, Alfred Rodenbücher, also gave money to unemployed Nazis and even loaned funds to Austrian Nazi businessmen who were having problems because of their political beliefs. Göth's request to ARS headquarters in Berlin for copies of his party documents and permission to transfer his party membership to Munich suggests that he was working for the ARS in Austria. It is also possible that Göth received funds from the ARS during this period, though his father kept a tight rein over the family business. Moreover, it is questionable whether Franz Göth would have accepted funds from the Nazis.[48]

What did Amon Göth do from 1934 until 1937? Ruth Göth said that he lived in Munich and tried to "develop his publishing business." Göth's parents, Franz and Berta, urged him "to make a normal life for himself" and get married. Ruth said her grandfather was something of a liberal and was disillusioned with his son's involvement in Nazi politics. Franz Göth later told Ruth that he considered Amon's Nazi activities nothing more than "teenage adventurism." To push their son along the path of normalcy, Franz and Berta even found him a wife, though the marriage ended in divorce after a few months.[49]

Göth returned to Vienna and the SS after the *Anschluß* in the spring of 1938; he soon found himself under pressure to remarry because Himmler required all SS men between twenty-five and thirty to marry and "found a family." He became engaged to Anny Geiger, who had been born in Innsbruck in 1913. But before they could be wed, they had to pass a rigid series of SS tests, including photos of the prospective couple in bathing suits, to insure they possessed the proper physical characteristics. The SS forbade church marriages and required that all SS men be married by their local commander. To move up the ranks, an SS man was expected to turn his back on the Christian faith.[50]

On October 23, 1938, Amon Göth and Anny were married in an SS ceremony; the couple remained married throughout the war. Anny bore three children but there is some confusion about this. Göth's 1941 *SS Personalangaben* lists only two sons, though his 1943 Recommendation for Promotion *(Ernennungsvorschlag)* lists three children: two sons and a daughter who was deceased. Göth's first son was born in the summer of 1939, his second in February 1940. But the respected life of a publisher did not interest Amon Göth as much as Nazism and the SS, and by the time Adolf Hitler conquered Austria in the spring of 1938, he had rejoined his beloved SS. When war broke out, he began full-time service in the SS, though he still considered himself a publisher by trade. Anny and the children lived permanently in Vienna throughout World War II.[51]

In early 1939, Göth was assigned to *SS-Standarte* 89 in Vienna; when war broke out, he was reassigned to SS *Sturmbann* 1/11. On March 9,

1940, Göth proudly noted in his 1941 *Lebenslauf* that he became a member of one of *Reichsführer-SS* Heinrich Himmler's *Sonderkommando* units, where he served as a *Verwaltungsführer* (administrative leader) on the SS operational staff in East Upper Silesia. Eight months later, he was promoted to the rank of *SS-Oberscharführer* (technical sergeant). At the time, he lived in Kattowitz (Kattowice), though he gave as his permanent address Zollerg 25/16, 7 Wien (Vienna).[52]

Upper Silesia, or, as the Germans called it after it was integrated into the Third Reich in 1939, East Upper Silesia *(Ostoberschlesien),* was highly prized during the war for its coal production output, second only to that of the Ruhr Valley in Germany. Equally important was Upper Silesia's industrial capacity. By 1943, it produced 5 percent of Germany's raw iron and 9 pecent of its steel. Robert Ley, the head of the German Labor Front (DAF; *Deutsche Arbeitsfront*), underscored the importance of East Upper Silesia to the war effort in the *Kattowitzer Zeitung* in early 1942: "As one of our mightiest arms producers, the *Gau* of Upper Silesia has the task of contributing to the strengthening of the German armament industry and thus to the achievement of the final victories of our arms."[53]

From the summer of 1941 until late May 1942, Göth served as an *Einsatzführer* (action leader) and a financial administrator with the 1/11th *SS-Standarte Planetta,* where he worked with an *Umsiedlungskommando* (resettlement commando) under *SS-Obersturmbannführer* Franz Weilgung in the Kattowitz office of the Ethnic German Central Office (VoMi; *Volksdeutsche Mittelstelle*), which was part of Himmler's Reich Office for the Integration of the German Volk-Nation *(Reichsamt für den Zusammenschluß des deutschen Volkstums).* Göth's superiors praised his work with the resettlement command and said that he exhibited "superior character and very good SS-comradeship."[54] When the Germans occupied Upper Silesia in the fall of 1939, they created a special "police line" that ran through the Kattowitz district and divided the new district into two distinct parts. The western area of East Upper Silesia, which had a large German population and was the heart of industrialized Silesia, would not only be an area ripe for major industrial development and exploitation but also Germanization. The area east of the police line, which included Auschwitz and the surrounding area, had large Polish and Jewish populations, which the Germans wanted to isolate from the western portion of East Upper Silesia as part of their "ethnic reordering" scheme.[55]

The idea was that the western portion of East Upper Silesia, along with other segments of recently conquered Poland, would become something of a racial laboratory centered around the move of ethnic Germans into the region after the expulsion of Poles and Jews. Different SS-controlled offices under Himmler's newly created Reich Commission for the Strengthening of Germandom (RKFDV; *Reichskommissariat für die Festigung deutsches Volkstums*) would then oversee the transfers and expulsions. The RKFDV's headquarters office in Berlin under *SS-Gruppenführer* Ulrich Greifelt would plan for the resettlement of ethnic Germans and oversee the expulsion of Poles and Jews; the VoMi, under *SS-Obergruppenführer* Werner Lorenz, would be responsible for the physical transfer of the German immigrants; this would include the creation of temporary settlement camps and the selection of leaders within these diverse groups. The *Reichsstatthalter* (governors) of each *Gau* (district or province) in the newly conquered territories were responsible for the care of the new settlers. Himmler's new super police organization, the Reich Security Main Office (RSHA; *Reichssicherheitshauptamt*), headed by Reinhard Heydrich, was in charge of "requisitioning" the property of "anti-state" Jews and Poles and deporting them to the General Government. These organizations, in turn, had to work with other Party and government agencies to insure the success of the German settlement program.[56]

What is important about Göth's role in all of this is that he worked in a part of the Greater Reich where economics took precedent over racial policy when it came to the fate of Jews. Because the SS came to view him not only as a seasoned administrator but also as an expert on Jewish resettlement and transfers, we can surmise that Göth was probably involved in similar policies and programs in East Upper Silesia. Jewish policy in East Upper Silesia was overseen by *SS-Oberführer* Albrecht Schmelt. By the fall of 1940, Schmelt had developed a highly efficient and extremely profitable Jewish slave labor system that housed Jews in a network of two hundred camps scattered throughout East Upper Silesia. If Albrecht Schmelt was Amon Göth's SS role model, then he learned from a master of brutal efficiency and corruption. Schmelt's Jewish slave labor force grew from 17,000 in the fall of 1940 to more than 50,000 by late 1943. The vast sums made by Schmelt and the SS from hiring out his Jewish laborers to factories and other businesses were such that the SS was able to help fund a resettlement program for ethnic Germans in the district and even provide aid to SS men killed in battle. And there was enough wealth left over to help buy an estate, Parzymiechy, where ethnic Germans were trained to become farmers. Schmelt was also able to skim enough money from this program to pay for a private home for himself and put RM 100,000 ($40,000) in his private bank account.[57]

By the time Amon Göth was transferred to Lublin in the summer of 1942, he had become a seasoned administrator. Ten months earlier, he had been promoted to the rank of *Untersturmführer*. His transfer papers stated that he was to work on the staff of *SS-Brigadeführer* Odilo Globočnik, the SSPF (*SS- und Polizeiführer Ost*; SS and Police Leader) in the Lublin district. His transfer documents stated that he was to become part of *"Sonderdienst* [Special Aktion] *Reinhard,"* specializing in *"Judenumsiedlung"* (Jewish resettlement) efforts.[58]

If anyone came to symbolize the brutality of German policy towards Polish Jews during this period, it was Globočnik. But Globočnik was more than just a brute. He was also a crook of the highest order, and he, like Albrecht Schmelt, became a role model for Amon Göth. Like Göth, he was an Austrian Old Fighter who had been arrested and imprisoned several times for illegal Nazi activity before the *Anschluß*. In fact, it is possible that both men knew each other in Austria and Munich. Göth and Globočnik both smuggled explosions into Austria from Germany for the Austrian Nazi Party and spent a lot of time in Munich working for the outlawed party. But here their careers diverged. While Göth's career in the Nazi Party and the SS languished because of his dismissal in 1934, Globočnik, who joined the Nazi Party (Party no. 442 939) and the SS (SS no. 292 776) later than Göth, quickly caught the eye of Himmler when he became an SS member in 1934 (SS No. 292 776). Like Göth, he spent a great deal of time in Munich from 1934 to 1938, where he helped operate a ring smuggling funds into Austria. Globočnik also served as *Gauleiter* of the Kaernten district in Austria.[59]

In early 1939, Globočnik, who at the time was *Gauleiter* of Vienna, was stripped of his rank and honors for corruption. However, Himmler, who thought highly of Globočnik, resurrected his career in the fall of 1939 when he made him the SSPF for Lublin. Globočnik transformed the Lublin district into an economic center for SS firms using Jewish slave labor and also planned to make it the heart of SS and German colonization in Poland. In late 1941, Globočnik was put in charge of what later became known as *Aktion* Reinhard, so-named to honor the memory of Reinhard Heydrich, who was assassinated by Czech partisans on June 4, 1942, in Prague. *Aktion* Reinhard was the SS plan to murder the 2.3 million Jews in the General Government as part of the Final Solution. It centered around the creation of three special "extermination camps"—Bełżec, Sobibór, and Treblinka.[60]

There are documents in Göth's SS files in the Bundesarchiv and in the National Archives as well as a brief reference in his war crimes trial transcript linking Göth to *Aktion* Reinhard. In addition, Mietek Pemper, Göth's Jewish stenographer, shed some light on Göth's activities as an *Aktion* Reinhard staff officer in his testimony during Göth's war crimes trial in 1946. Göth's SS records provide no details about his activities because of the secrecy that surrounded *Aktion* Reinhard. Each of the 450 SS men, police officers, and "euthanasia" specialists chosen to serve with Globočnik were sworn to secrecy and asked to sign a statement pledging that they would say or write nothing about their activities to anyone except members of the *Aktion* Reinhard staff. They also agreed not to take photographs of any of the *Aktionen* of the operation, and to maintain this secrecy even after they completed their service with *Aktion* Reinhard. Göth, along with many of the other Austrians selected to serve with the Globočnik team, worked in one of the three *Aktion* Reinhard death camps. According to Göth's war crimes transcript, he worked directly under *SS-Hauptsturmführer* Hermann Höfle, an Austrian who headed the Main Department *(Hauptabteilung)* and was responsible for planning the roundups from the ghettos and the deportations to the *Aktion* Reinhard death camps. This is where Göth gained the skills that made him an expert in brutally rounding up Jews in ghettos and preparing them for deportation to death camps. Three of the five charges brought against him during his war crimes trial in 1946 dealt with the closing of the Kraków and Tarnów ghettos and the forced labor camp at Szebnie.[61]

Göth spent only six months working for Höfle and Globočnik before he was appointed commandant of the Płaszów forced labor camp in Kraków on February 11, 1943. According to Pemper, he was sent to Płaszów because he had trouble with Höfle.[62] But the lessons he learned during that six-month period in Lublin honed his brutish, murderous skills. Raimund Titsch, the manager of one of the factories in Płaszów, said that even before his arrival, the factory managers and Jews in the camp already knew Göth as the "Bloody Dog of Lublin."[63] It is difficult to say what job Göth had during this period, though his SS file indicates that on October 1 he was assigned to the *"Stab,"* meaning possibly the *Aussiedlungsstab* (Evaluation or Deportation Staff) under Höfle. Göth probably worked on Höfle's headquarters staff because the actual deportations were overseen by local SS leaders and the movement of rail transports were handled by German railroad officials in Kraków. During the brief period he was in Lublin, this group oversaw the building of new, more efficient gas chambers in the three death camps as well as personnel and labor changes designed to make the camps run more efficiently. Yet Göth must have had some experience with ghetto deportations and camp administration because the SS later had high regard for him as a camp commandant and expert on closing ghettos; in fact, the fall of 1942 was one of the most active periods for such "actions" in the General Government.[64]

Mietek Pemper had occasion to see some of Göth's private documents. He explained in a 1996 interview that every so often one of Göth's adjutants, SS-Hauptsturmführer Raimund Gaube, would ask Pemper to help him draft a letter that necessitated looking at Göth's secret documents. Pemper would explain that because of Göth's insistence on perfection, he would have to see all documents relating to the proposed letter. If Göth was away, Gaube would allow Pemper access to these files, but only behind locked doors. Sometimes Gaube would carelessly forget to close the safe, which also contained secret documents. Pemper, who had a photographic memory, would use these opportunities to read everything he could get his hands on. This is how Pemper came across letters relating to Göth's service with Aktion Reinhard. One of the letters that Pemper read but later destroyed during a routine barracks check was from Globočnik to the commandants of Bełżec, Sobibór, and Treblinka. According to Pemper, this letter gave Göth the right to move freely about all three of these camps as an inspector involved in construction matters.[65]

For an ambitious SS man, an appointment to Globočnik's staff was an important career move. And by this time, Amon Leopold Göth was a highly thought-of member of the SS. A July 14, 1941, Certificate of Service (Dienstleistungszeugnis) made out by his commanding officer, SS-Sturmbannführer Otto Winter, praised Göth's loyalty, service, character, proper Weltanschauung (world view), and racial characteristics. Winter added that Göth was also "free from any confessional [religious] ties." Three months later, Winter and his superior, SS-Gruppenführer und Generalleutnant der Polizei Ernst Kaltenbrunner, the head of SS-Oberabschnittes Donau (SS sub-district for Austria), soon to become head of RSHA to replace the murdered Reinhard Heydrich, signed off on a special SS Personal Report (Personal-Bericht) about Göth that went into greater detail about his physical traits as well as his family and financial situation, his personal character, his military and SS background, his training and athletic abilities, his world view, and his knowledge of the SS bureaucracy. At the end of the report, Winter discussed Göth's advancement prospects.[66]

Not surprisingly, Winter gave Amon Göth high marks in every category. Racially, he was deemed to be of Phalian-Eastern extraction with a very good demeanor. Winter wrote that his appearance and behavior were "flawless." Göth's finances were sound and his family situation was considered to be good. Winter considered him bright and well-educated. Göth's "interpretation of life and power of judgement" were considered "affirmative and clear." He was deemed to have no "flaws" and his special strength was his "courageous, determined attitude." He earned affirmative or good marks on all questions about his special police training, his field service, and his knowledge and practice of sports. The only negative was his failure so far to earn his *Sports Badge (Sportabzeichen)*, a reference to the German National Badge for Physical Training *(Deutsches Reichsabzeichen für Leibesübungen)*. Overall, Winter concluded, Amon Göth was an upright National Socialist able to make all the necessary sacrifices required of an SS-man. He added that Göth was well suited to be an SS commander.[67]

Göth, Tarnów, and Szebnie

Anyone familiar with the Oskar Schindler story has read or seen depictions of Amon Göth's brutal closing of the Kraków ghetto in March 1943. But most people are not aware of his efforts to close the Tarnów ghetto on September 3, 1943, and his shutting down of the Szebnie forced labor camp in southeastern Poland from September 21, 1943, through February 3, 1944. Göth did this extra duty for the SS while serving as commandant at the Płaszów forced labor (later concentration) camp. Two of the Polish government's five charges against Göth after World War II dealt with his crimes in Tarnów and Szebnie.[68]

Tarnów, about forty-five miles east of Kraków, is a provincial capital with a rich Jewish history. Though originally a Polish city, Tarnów became part of the Austrian empire after the Russian-led Partitions of Poland in the last quarter of the eighteenth century. Tarnów returned to Polish control at the end of World War I. Under the Austrians, Tarnów became an important regional trading center that attracted a large Jewish population. On the eve of World War II, about 45 percent of Tarnów's population of 56,000 was Jewish. And although many members of Tarnów's Jewish community played an important role in the city's cultural and intellectual leadership, many Tarnów Jews were quite poor. Over the centuries, Tarnów's Jewish community developed a diverse complex of religious, educational, cultural, and self-help institutions to sustain a rich community life. When World War II broke out, thousands of Jews fled to Tarnów from western Poland to escape the German onslaught. By the summer of 1940, there were 40,000 Jews in Tarnów. They suffered from the same harsh anti-Jewish policies as other Jews throughout occupied Poland.[69]

On June 11, 1942, the SS initiated an action against Tarnów's Jews as part of *Aktion* Reinhard in preparation for the creation of a ghetto there. In a brutal Operation where hundreds of Jews were murdered in the streets, the SS rounded up 3,500 Jews and sent them to Bełżec. Four days later, the Germans initiated a second, three-day roundup that saw 10,000 more Jews sent to Bełżec. The SS and their collaborators murdered another 3,000 Jews in the Jewish cemetery and killed 7,000 beside pits dug on Tarnów's Zbylitowska Gora (hill). On June 19, the Germans sealed off an area for the ghetto and forced Tarnów's remaining Jews into it. Over time, the Germans had a high wooden fence built around the ghetto. On September 10, the Germans, working with the *Judenrat,* ordered all Jews to report to Targowica Square near one of the ghetto's two entrances. The 8,000 Jews without a *Blauschein* were rounded up and sent to Bełżec. Over the next month, Jews from the surrounding area were sent to the Tarnów ghetto, which now had a population of about 15,000. On November 15, 1942, the Germans rounded up another 2,500 Jews for deportation to Bełżec and then divided the ghetto into two sections just as they had done in Kraków. Jews deemed fit for work were forced to live in Ghetto A; those who were unable to work were forced into Ghetto B.[70]

Julius Madritsch was one of the Germans who opened a factory in the Tarnów ghetto soon after it opened. This would be the third factory that he ran using Jewish slave laborers. Madritsch had opened his second sewing factory in a ghetto in Bochnia, which was midway between Tarnów and Kraków, earlier in 1942. Madritsch claimed in his memoirs that he had opened the factories in Bochnia and Tarnów because of the "constant begging of the Jewish council [in Kraków]."[71] Madritsch estimated after World War II that he was able to save "another 1,000 to 2,000 human beings" because of his efforts in Tarnów and Bochnia. He had about three hundred sewing machines in the Tarnów ghetto, where he employed eight hundred Jewish workers.[72]

Madrich never said much about the conditions in his sewing factories, although testimony from survivors indicated that he and Raimund Titsch took good care of their workers. Dr. Dawid Schlang, a Schindler Jew who wrote the introduction to Madritsch's memoirs about the war, wrote Yad Vashem about Mr. Madritsch's exemplary conduct towards the Jewish workers: "Many survivors testify to his friendly and humane approach and his continuous care of the Jews."[73] He added that there were many times when Madritsch and his manager, Raimund Titsch, risked their lives to help Jews.[74]

There are several photographs of Jewish women at work on Pfaff sewing machines in the Bochnia ghetto in the archives at the United States Holocaust Memorial Museum in Washington, D.C., and they are probably Madritsch's workers. These are obviously propaganda photos because the male workers in the photographs are wearing coats and ties. The women sit at old-fashioned foot-pedaled sewing machines under spare light near shaded windows. One photo has a male tailor fitting a suit coat on another man, stacks of three-quarter-length, light-colored coats in a pile behind them.[75]

After Amon Göth closed the Kraków ghetto in March 1943, Madritsch's Jewish workers who now worked in his sewing factory in Płaszów begged him to transfer them to his factory in the Tarnów ghetto. Madritsch was somehow able to get permission from the SS to transfer several hundred of his Jewish workers to Tarnów; on the night of March 25–26, 1943, he succeeded in transporting 232 Jewish women, men, and children to the Tarnów ghetto, where they began work in his sewing factory. It probably took considerable bribes to persuade Göth and his SS superiors to agree to this, though Madritsch was probably also able to argue that such a request was reasonable because he would need experienced workers to operate his new factory in the Tarnów ghetto.[76]

Madritsch was proud of his factory in Tarnów, particularly after he was forced to move his operations in the Kraków ghetto to Płaszów, where his new factory was only several hundred yards from Amon Göth's villa. Life in the Kraków ghetto had been harsh, but it was nothing compared to the terror-ridden atmosphere in Płaszów, where Göth took great pleasure in random, daily acts of murder. According to Madritsch, "At this point [after the closing of the Kraków ghetto] the Jews of Tarnów [about 95 kilometers away] led a life that could be looked upon with envy, since they still had a ghetto where everyone had their own apartment and their own bed."[77] Although this is an overstatement by Madritsch, it does show that he was well aware, at least comparatively, of the vast difference between life in the Tarnów ghetto and that in Płaszów under the monstrous Amon Göth.

But life for the Jews in the Tarnów ghetto, which Madritsch described as a comparative "oasis," would soon change. In early September 1943, Amon Göth arrived to close the Tarnów ghetto and ship its Jews to Auschwitz and Płaszów. On September 1, the Tarnów ghetto's Jews were ordered to appear the next morning at the *Appellplatz* at Magdeburg Square. The square was surrounded by heavily armed police, the Gestapo, the SS, Jewish OD men, and others, who began to separate children from their mothers. Over the next two days, different groups were placed in wagons and taken to the train station, where they were shipped to Płaszów and Auschwitz, though no one seemed aware that the transports to Auschwitz meant death. According to the 1946 Polish indictment against Göth, which was based on the testimony of three witnesses, Berek Figa, Leon Leser, and Mendel Balsam, Amon Göth personally shot between thirty and ninety women and children during the ghetto's closing. Martin Balsam testified that the most shocking aspect of the roundup was the forced separation of the children from their mothers. The children were then placed in wagons and sent to their deaths. Göth played an active role in all this; as the roundup ended at mid-day on September 2, Balsam testified, Göth took out his pistol and helped shoot the two hundred children and women left in the ghetto who were not designated to be part of the clean-up crew.[78]

The indictment added that Göth arranged to have 8,000 of Tarnów's Jews deported directly to Auschwitz. Another 3,000 Jews from the Bochnia ghetto and forced labor camp, which were in the process of being liquidated, were added to the Tarnów-Auschwitz transport. This group would soon be sent to Auschwitz. The Polish court records stated that only 400 Jews out of 11,000 made it to Auschwitz, meaning that Göth had the rest murdered along the way; furthermore, there is no mention of a transport arriving in Auschwitz from Tarnów in September 1943. On the other hand, the Auschwitz records do show that two transports of 3,000 Jews each arrived in Auschwitz from Bochnia on August 31 and September 2, 1943. Only 3,000 to 3,500 Jews were in Bochnia at the time, so it is probable that the second transport was made up of Jews from Tarnów. The SS selected 1,075 Jews from the first transport for slave labor and murdered the rest. Only 830 Jews on the second transport were chosen as slave laborers and the rest were murdered in the gas chambers. A few more Jews from Tarnów were sent to the Szebnie forced labor camp near Jasło. Three hundred Jews remained in the Tarnów ghetto to go through the belongings of its former Jewish residents and then clean it up. When their work was done, they were then sent to Płaszów. Mendel Balsam testified that it took two weeks to clean up the Tarnów ghetto after the roundup was completed on September 2, 1943.[79]

We know very little about the history and closing of the Tarnów ghetto, particularly the role played by Amon Göth. Because this was part of the secretive *Aktion* Reinhard operation, no mention was made of Göth's efforts there in his SS service jacket. On the other hand, his SS file shows that he was praised and promoted in the summer of 1943 for his actions in closing the Kraków ghetto and early administration of the Płaszów forced labor camp. This was an extraordinary promotion; Göth jumped two ranks from *SS-Untersturmführer* to *SS-Hauptsturmführer*. According to Mietek Pemper, Göth's Jewish stenographer, the promotion came after HSSPF *Ost SS-Obergruppenführer* Friedrich Wilhelm Krüger inspected Płaszów. Krüger was quite impressed by the large variety of machines in use at Płaszów, though Pemper said that this was a ruse. Gradually, Amon Göth was becoming a master of deception.[80]

In his letter of July 23, 1943, supporting Göth's promotion to *SS-Hauptsturmführer*, *SS-Sturmbannführer* Klein, a member of the HSSPF Ost staff, praised Göth's outstanding and authoritative work, particularly as commandant of the Płaszów forced labor camp. According to Klein, Göth had created "something out of nothing" at Płaszów. Moreover, Klein noted that Göth's "exemplary" efforts to open Płaszów were undertaken with little consideration for his own person."[81] Sacrifices like these, of course, were the things that made a great SS officer. Five days later, the newly promoted Göth was appointed to Section F, the SS and Police *Fachgruppe* (Section of Experts). His expertise: closing ghettos and shipping its inmates to slave labor or death camps.[82]

One of the reasons for the haste in closing the Tarnów ghetto was Göth's growing responsibilities elsewhere. As more and more ghettos were closed during this period throughout the General Government as part of the Final Solution and *Aktion* Reinhard, Płaszów's population was growing considerably, which added to his responsibilities there. But Göth's haste in closing the Tarnów ghetto was driven more by the pace of German mass murder plans in the summer and early fall of 1942. With all six death camps now open and operating to full capacity, the Germans were determined to close the multitude of large and small ghettos throughout occupied Europe. Jews not selected as slave laborers were sent to their deaths. The pace of the German mass murder program of Jews up to this point in the Holocaust was astounding. According to Raul Hilberg, the Germans killed 1.1 million European Jews in 1941 and 2.7 million in 1942. Polish Jews were particularly vulnerable because Himmler had ordered that the General Government be clear of all Jews by the end of 1942 except those designated as slave laborers. The heavy concentration of Jews in close proximity to the six death camps in occupied Poland and the Soviet Union made the Germans' job much easier. But it should be remembered that only about half the Jews murdered in the Holocaust died in these camps. The others died in mass murder campaigns initiated by the *Einsatzgruppen*, in ghetto actions or random actions of violence, during transport, from malnutrition, and other horrible ways.[83]

Once Göth had closed and cleaned up the Tarnów ghetto, he was ordered to close the Szebnie forced labor camp near Jasło, which was fifty miles southeast of Tarnów. If there is a dearth of information on the Tarnów ghetto, this is doubly so for Szebnie; yet, given the large number of concentration camps and sub-camps throughout German-occupied Europe, this is not surprising. During the years of Nazi power in Europe, the Germans set up thousands of large and small detention camps to imprison racial, political, criminal, and military prisoners and "enemies of the state." In addition to the *Konzentrationslager* (KL; concentration camp) there were also *Arbeitslager* (forced labor camps), *Zwangslager* (forcible detention camps), *Zwangsarbeitslager* (penal servitude camps), *Zivilgefangenenlager* (detention camps for civilians), *Straflager* (punitive camps), *Zuchthaus* (penitentary), and *PW Dulags* or *Durchgangslager* (transit camps). The Wehrmacht ran *Soldatenkonzentrationslager* (soldiers' concentration camps) and military prisons as well as a network of *Stalags* (*Stammlager*, or main camps) for enlisted men and officers. Some camps existed only briefly and handled only a small number of prisoners. A classified SHAEF (Supreme Headquarters Allied Expeditionary Force) report listed 615 concentration and detention camps in Nazi-occupied Europe in 1944 but admitted that its statistics were not "entirely reliable." It said that there were 109 camps in Poland in the fall of 1943, including twenty-four concentration camps.[84]

One of the camps mentioned in the SHAEF report was a "Szebunia" (Szebnie) in Jasło County, which it termed a "KL permanent camp."[85] Scattered references to Szebnie can be found in all the principal encyclopedic works on the Holocaust, though there is little detailed information about it. In the fall of 1943, Szebnie also served as a brief transit stop for Jews recently shipped out of the Przemyśl and Rzeszów ghettos. Iwo

Cyprian Pogonowski's *Jews in Poland* provides some details about the liquidation of Szebnie in the fall of 1943. He states that on September 22, 1943, the SS took seven hundred young and elderly Jews from Szebnie to the nearby village of Dobrucowa and murdered them. They then burned the bodies. Pogonowski adds that on November 3, *SS-Sturmbannführer* Willi Haase, who had been a central figure in the deportations and closing of the Kraków ghetto, arrived in Szebnie with an SS contingent, including a number of Ukrainians, to close the camp. Haase ordered the remaining 2,800 Jewish prisoners to strip naked, then began to load them on trains for transport to Auschwitz. When the Jewish prisoners arrived at Auschwitz, a few were selected for hard labor, but most were sent to the gas chambers. Pogonowski adds that on November 5, 1943, the SS executed another five hundred Jewish prisoners still at Szebnie.[86]

The Holocaust Chronicle states that on September 20, 1943, the SS guards at Szebnie put 1,000 Jewish prisoners on trucks and took them to a nearby field "where they shot all of them."[87] They then burned the bodies and dumped the remains in the Jasiolka River. It adds that on November 4, 1943, a rebellion broke out among the Szebnie prisoners, which the SS quickly put down. It then closed the camp and shipped the remaining 3,000 prisoners to Auschwitz. The five-volume official history of the Auschwitz camp, *Auschwitz 1940–1945*, corrects some of these figures. It states, as does Danuta Czech's *Auschwitz Chronicle,* that on November 5, 1932, 4,237 Jews arrived at Birkenau from Szebnie. The SS selected 952 men and 396 women for slave labor and executed the rest.[88]

With the exception of Willi Haase, though, no other SS officer is mentioned in these accounts. Yet one of the five charges brought against Amon Göth in his war crimes trial was that, in the process of closing the Szebnie forced labor camp from September 1943 until early February 1944, he was responsible for "causing the death of several thousand persons."[89] The Polish court's evidence was based on the testimony of various witnesses, including Mietek Pemper, Regina Weiss, and Henryk Faber. Weiss, who was taken to Szebnie from Tarnów, never mentioned Göth in her testimony, though she does support Pogonowski's claim that 2,800 Szebnie Jews were shipped to Auschwitz and murdered in early November 1943. She also partially confirms official Auschwitz statistics about another 1,200 Szebnie Jews sent to Auschwitz at the same time. But, she says, they were Poles, not Jews. Faber said nothing about Göth in his brief testimony.[90]

One of the reasons for this was that Göth had little to do with the closing of the Szebnie camp. Mietek Pemper said that even though Göth was briefly "nominal commandant" there, he soon lost control of Szebnie to Kellermann, who oversaw the its closing, though Göth continued to play an oversight role there. This fits with the testimony of Dr. Aleksander Biberstein, a Schindler Jew and one of the principal witnesses in Göth's trial. In mid-February 1943, Biberstein and another physician, Dr. Zygfryd Schwarz, were ordered by Dr. Weichert's Jewish Aid Society to meet with Göth to talk about "building the [Płaszów] hospital and about the sanitary facilities in the camp."[91] Göth was unusually friendly to both Jewish physicians and offered them cigarettes; he did almost all the talking and told them that at the time he was building two camps, the one in Płaszów and another in Szebnie.[92]

Other evidence presented in Göth's trial gives a more expansive view of the role he played in the clearing and liquidation of the Szebnie forced labor camp. Like many small German forced labor camps, Szebnie had Jewish and Polish workers. There were 4,000 Jewish slave laborers at Szebnie and 1,500 Polish forced laborers. The Göth trial records make no mention of Haase, and given his rank, it is hard to imagine that he was involved directly in the Szebnie roundup, though it is possible he was there briefly as an observer. It was not uncommon for higher-ranking SS officials to show up on the first day of a roundup or the closing of a ghetto or forced labor camp to watch the *Aktion*. In reality, Göth sent one of his lower-ranking subordinates from Płaszów, *SS-Hauptscharführer* Josef Grzimek, to work with Szebnie's commandant, Kellermann, to close the camp, which took place between September 21, 1943 and February 3, 1944. As the camp was being shut down, Göth ordered a detailed inventory of the camp's goods, which were then shipped to Płaszów. Most of the Poles in Szebnie were sent to Płaszów and Bochnia, though it is not certain how many survived the war.[93]

Płaszów

But it is not in Szebnie, Tarnów, or even Kraków where Amon Göth committed his greatest war crimes. It was in Płaszów, the forced labor and later concentration camp he commanded from February 11, 1943 until the SS arrested him for corruption on September 13, 1944. According to the Polish indictment against him, Amon Göth was responsible for the deaths of 8,000 inmates during the time that he ran the camp, though it is difficult to determine the exact number. A recent study undertaken by the Polish Foundation for the Protection of Monuments of National

Memory-Iwona Ruebenbauer-Skwara (Fundacja Opieka nad Pomnkiem Pamieci Narodowej-Iwona Ruebenbauer-Skwara) estimated that the number of Jews and others murdered at Płaszów was between 8,000 and 12,000. Mietek Pemper testified in Göth's trial that "natural mortality" in the camp was very low. About five hundred prisoners were executed for trying to escape, and most of these were killed "by Goeth himself or his subordinates." Pemper estimated that another 5,000 to 6,000 were either executed or were on the May 14, 1944, transport to Auschwitz. Pemper added that the SS murdered about 2,000 Jews during the closing of the Kraków ghetto in the spring of 1943. But these figures must also be put into the context of the actual number of Jews, and, to a much lesser degree, Christian Poles who were sent briefly to Płaszów and then on to concentration or death camps. When Płaszów first opened, it only had about 2,000 prisoners, about half the number it could initially handle. During the next year, its population grew tremendously; at its peak in 1944, it had a permanent population of approximately 30,000. But because it also served as a temporary transit camp, about 150,000 inmates passed through Płaszów. In mid-1943, Płaszów was a sub-camp of Majdanek, but became its own separate concentration camp in early 1944. Until this point, Płaszów housed only Jewish prisoners. A small camp for Polish prisoners guilty of misdemeanors was added in the summer of 1943. When they had served their prison terms, they were released or sent to forced labor camps in Poland. About 3,000 Poles were imprisoned at Płaszów during the war.[94]

Today, it is hard to imagine that this was the site of Amon Göth's brutal camp. Years ago, the Poles turned it into a nature preserve and it has retained its quiet, bucolic nature. Poles who live in the private homes (some in Göth's private villa and the "Gray House," the camp's former prison) and apartments that run along the northern border of the camp on Jerozoliminka, W. Heltmana and Wielicka Streets, can be seen walking their dogs along the paths that traverse the former camp site. Unfortunately, despite a few monuments at the southeastern end of the camp site, little has been done to preserve the largely hidden but important remnants of the camp. On one occasion when I was looking for the remains of the old Jewish mortuary there, I fell into an open grave that had been desecrated by the Germans. It took me three trips to Płaszów over several years before I truly grasped the significance of these ruins. My most important visits took place in the summer of 2000, when I was accompanied first by Jaroslav Zotciak, a landscape architect who had studied and mapped the Płaszów site, and Stella Müller-Madej, a Schindler Jew who lives in Kraków. Both were able to bring Płaszów back to life for me, but in different ways.

The trip with Stella was the most moving. The day before, I had spent a great deal of time with her talking about Schindler and her experiences during the Holocaust, which she has documented in the first volume of her two-part memoir, *Dziewczynka z listy Schindlera* (A Girl from Schindler's List). Stella had lived in Kraków all her life and spent hours telling me and my research assistant, Konstancja Szymura, about her life there before the war. She also shared with us stories about her life in the Kraków ghetto, in Płaszów, and with Oskar Schindler in Brünnlitz. In her fluid, literary way of speaking, she shared with us the range of emotions that she experienced in those long, horrible years during the Holocaust. At the end of the evening, she asked whether we would like her to take us to Płaszów. She also mentioned that she had never been to the site of Schindler's factory on ul. Lipowa and wondered whether I would mind taking her there on the way to Płaszów. I hesitated at first because over the years I had learned to respect the tender emotions of Holocaust survivors, who are often forced to bring back painful memories when they speak about or visit former Holocaust sites. But Stella insisted and Konstancja and I agreed to spend the following afternoon with her at Płaszów and Emalia.

The trip to Emalia had little meaning to Stella because she had never worked there. But her return to Płaszów was as emotional as I expected it to be. The site is large and Stella, who had been there many times before, decided it would be too much for her to walk the complete site. Instead, she drove off the main road onto one of the dirt roads that runs through the camp. Small mounds of trash left there by inconsiderate visitors were mixed in with the open graves and ruins of the barracks. During other trips to Poland, I have visited Auschwitz, Treblinka, and Majdanek with Holocaust survivors. But this visit was different because I had gotten to know Stella very well and was deeply touched by the pain that she experienced as we slowly moved through Płaszów. She would periodically stop the car to point out the location of a barracks or the *Appellplatz*. But when we stopped before Hujowa Górka, the principal mass murder and burial site of the camp, she got out of the car and walked quietly away from us. Konstancja asked whether we should do something to help. I said that what she was feeling and experiencing was very, very personal and that we should leave her alone. Neither of us could imagine the horrible thoughts and memories that came flooding back to her as she stood in the quiet of Płaszów on that pleasant summer day. When she returned to the car, she had regained her composure and suggested that we go into the hills above Kraków for ice cream.

Today, it is hard to realize that at its peak the Płaszów camp covered between 173 and 197 acres. The only significant remains are Amon Göth's villa, the "Grey House," which housed the camp's small prison, and some broken tombstones and open graves of the two Jewish cemeteries desecrated by the Germans as they constructed the forced labor camp on this site. There are also building foundations and raised mounds as well as portions of one of the camp roads built with broken Jewish cemetery headstones, though they are hard to find, particularly in the summer's tall grass. There were three mass murder sites in Płaszów: one in the northern part of the old Jewish cemetery; another, Lipowy Dolek, in the southeastern part of the camp, which also contained a mass grave; and Hujowa Górka, which contains two monuments, one Polish and one Jewish, to honor those who were murdered here. The Polish Martyrs' Monument to all Płaszów victims at Hujowa Górka sits atop the site of a former Austrian fort complete with its old moat. It is one of those striking, stark Soviet-style monuments found throughout Moscow's former empire. The smaller, more tasteful Jewish memorial is down the hill and just across the moat from the Polish memorial. And hidden away in the hills at the eastern edge of the former camp overlooking Płaszów is a stark cross circled in barbed wire to commemorate the Christian Poles who died in Płaszów.[95]

According to Jaroslav Zotciak, the name for the camp, Płaszów, was a bit of a misnomer because it was located in Kraków's Podgórze and Wola Duchacka districts, not in the Płaszów district. It probably got the name Płaszów because its first Jewish prisoners came from *Julag* I, which was in the Płaszów region. In some ways, the site of the future Płaszów forced labor and concentration camp was always a natural island in a sea of Polish development. Today, high rise apartments block the view of the camp from Wielicka street, the large boulevard that runs closest to the former camp site. The buildings now sit where Göth housed his SS troops, and a McDonald's and other commercial buildings stand on or near the site where he stored the goods taken from the camp's inmates. The area has not suffered from further development only because Płaszów was built partly in Krzemionki, where Kraków's prewar Jewish community had two of its most important cemeteries. And just beyond this is the large Christian Podgórski cemetery. So well before World War II, this part of Podgórze had become a sacred place for Jews and Christians.

In 1887, the Jews in Kraków's Old City built their first cemetery in Krzemionki because space was running out in the small cemeteries in Kazimierz. In 1932, the Jews of Podgórze built a much larger cemetery next to the smaller one. The new cemetery contained a beautiful three-domed mortuary that sat at the entrance of the cemeteries and then ran beside Jerozolinska and Abrahama Streets. At one point, Göth used the mortuary as a stable but later had part of it destroyed to build a rail line into the camp. The SS used what remained of the mortuary for a power station. Göth also built Płaszów's main entrance near the site of the entrance to the Jewish cemeteries. SS camp tradition dictated a certain style and architecture for entrances to forced labor and concentration camps that reminds one somewhat of the storied entrance to Auschwitz II-Birkenau. But unlike Birkenau, where train tracks ran through the two-storied entranceway, the train tracks into Płaszów ran beside the entranceway. Two black-and-white-striped guard posts stood beside the two-storied entranceway, which had elongated buildings attached to it on both sides. This style of SS architecture with its "central tower and side wings" had been perfected at Dachau, Buchenwald, and other SS-run camps. According to Wolfgang Sofsky, the camp gate was a "sign of final and irreversible inclusion."[96]

Płaszów's origins centered around the creation of three *Julag*s, or small Jewish labor camps in the Płaszów, Prokocim, and Bielżanów districts of Kraków. Each of the camps was located within a kilometer or two of the future Płaszów forced labor/concentration camp. Henry Weiner, Jack Mintz, and Richard Krumholz, all three future *Schindlerjuden,* worked at one of the *Julag*s. Henry Weiner worked for Siemens-Bauwerke at Julag I in Płaszów, where he built roads; Jack Mintz (Jehuda Minc-Anschell Freimann) and his two brothers, David and Benjamin, worked at *Julag* II in Prokocim, where they built railroad bridges. *Julag* I, which would become the nucleus of the main Płaszów camp, was commanded first by *SS-Unterscharführer* Horst Pilarzik and later Franz Müller.[97]

By the time that Amon Göth became commandant of the new *Zwangsarbeitslager Plaszow des SS- und Polizeiführers im Distrikt Krakau* (Płaszów Forced Labor Camp of the SS and Police Leader in the Kraków District) in February 1943, the SS had gained full control over Jewish labor in the General Government. It had involved a considerable struggle with the Wehrmacht, which now had to go to the SS to get Jewish laborers for its armaments factories in that part of occupied Poland. The considerable administrative changes the SS forced labor and concentration camp system was undergoing made things even more complicated. These had begun in early 1942, when *SS-Obergruppenführer und General der Waffen SS und Polizei* Oswald Pohl, the head of the SS-*Wirtschaftsunternehmen,* brought together the various SS offices that dealt with economic and construction matters into one office, the Economic and Administrative Main Office (WVHA; *Wirtschafts-und Verwaltungshauptamt*) in Oranienburg, a suburb of Berlin. WVHA was divided into four *Amtsgruppen* (Office Groups), with *Amtsgruppe* D (formerly the IKL, or *Inspektion der Konzentrationslager;* Inspector of Concentration Camps) under *SS-Gruppenführer und General der Waffen-SS* Richard Glücks, who oversaw all aspects of the SS camp network. But in reality, the real head of *Amtsgruppe* D was not the incompetent Glücks but the head of *Amtsgruppe* D2, the office of Labor Action of the Prisoners, *SS-Obersturmbannführer* (later, *SS-Standartenführer*) Gerhard Maurer. When Oskar Schindler sought permission to move his factory from Kraków to Brünnlitz in the fall of 1944, he first approached a close friend in the Army High Command's Ordnance Department, Erich Lange, who in turn negotiated with Maurer over the move.[98]

Göth took command of Płaszów ten days after Germany's stunning military defeat at Stalingrad. As the tide of war began gradually to shift in the Allies' favor, Germany's military and industrial manpower needs became more severe and created a conflict between those in the Nazi leadership who wanted to continue their mass murder program of the Jews and those who wanted to balance this with the greater economic interests of the Third Reich. The SS did not give up its goal of ridding Europe of its "racial enemies" and, under Maurer, *Amtsgruppe* D2 sought to balance these goals with the needs of the burgeoning armaments industry. He tried to give SS physicians more control over life and death in the camps to insure a steady supply of slave laborers. Those deemed unfit for the SS labor needs would be murdered. But Maurer was unable to control ongoing, sadistic reigns of terror unleashed by Göth and other commandants. In fact, the SS would not address the issue of indiscriminate murder in the camps until much later.[99]

Today it is impossible to visit the former site of Płaszów and get any sense of the vast complex that was begun there in late 1942. But photographs in the archives of Beit Lohamei Haghetaot in Israel and the United States Holocaust Memorial Museum in Washington, D.C., help bring it to life. In addition, Jaroslav Zotciak shared with me a large map of the concentration camp that he had reconstructed based on materials he discovered in the archives of the *Glowa Komisja Badana Zbrodni Przeciwko Narodowi Polskiemu Instytut Pamieci Narodowej Okregowa*

Komisja w Krakowie (the Main Commission for the Investigation of Crimes Against the Polish Nation). The only difference between this map and the one in Joseph Bau's *Dear God, Have You Ever Gone Hungry?* is that Bau's map shows the camp's crematorium. I have been able to form a much clearer picture of the vast complex that Amon Göth and the SS built between 1942 and 1944 from information that Jaroslav shared with me, as well as from our careful trek across the camp's remains, the accounts I have read or gathered from survivors (particularly Dr. Aleksander Biberstein's *Zagłada Żydów w Krakowie* [Extermination of the Jews in Kraków]), and the photographs I have collected.[100]

It is important to remember that Płaszów evolved slowly over twenty-six months first as a *Julag,* then as a forced labor camp, and was finally a permanent concentration camp complete witha crematory and plans for gas chambers. Most of the evidence we have about Płaszów centers around its existence as one of Nazi Germany's permanent German concentration camps from January 1944 to January 1945. And even here, documents and testimony must be blended with photographs to understand the size and complexity of the concentration camp's operation. There is little information about the Płaszów *Zwangsarbeitslager.* Mietek Pemper testified at Göth's 1946 trial that it was run without rules or orders and that everything was decided by the camp commandant. This was when Göth committed his most brutal and indiscriminate murders. When Płaszów became a concentration camp in 1944, the paperwork required by the SS for such actions tended to hamper, but not end, Göth's ability to kill at will.[101]

At its peak of operations, Płaszów had an SS staff of 636 guards who oversaw 25,000 prisoners. The *Totenkopfwachsturmbanne* (Death Head Guard Formations) at *Konzentrationslager* Kraków-Płaszów were commanded by forty-five officers and noncommissioned officers.[102] According to survivor testimony, other than Amon Göth, *SS-Unterscharführer* Horst Pilarzik and *SS-Oberscharführer* Albert Hujar, the most hated and feared SS men in the camp, were the black-uniformed Ukrainians. According to Mietek Pemper, Pilarzik, who was initially the Jewish specialist for the HSSPF in Kraków, was a "horrific figure during the liquidation of the [Kraków] ghetto" in 1943. Pemper thought Pilarzik was either an alcoholic or a drug addict because "he rampaged like a hungry wolf or tiger," murdering many Jews, during the ghetto's closing. Later, Pilarzik served briefly as Göth's adjutant but was dismissed because he had bragged at a local restaurant that he was the recipient of the Knight's Cross. Hujar was the SS officer in

Schindler's List who, without Göth's prodding, murdered Diana Reiter, the Jewish engineer who questioned SS construction methods.[103]

Schindler Jew Jack Mintz described the black-uniformed Ukrainians as "the best killers."[104] One "Black Uniform," he said, would occasionally stand by the garbage pile outside the camp's inmate kitchen and shoot any desperately hungry Jew who dug through the scraps of food looking for something to eat.[105] The Ukrainian guards at Płaszów wore the black uniforms of the *Allgemeine* (general) or "Black" SS; others on the camp staff wore the grey uniforms of the *Waffen* SS (Armed SS), or "White" SS. The camps were under the control of the Waffen SS, the "Imperial Guard" of Nazi Germany. The use of foreign volunteers or recruits in the SS Death's Head units, which guarded the camp, increased substantially as the war dragged on. The Ukrainian guards at Płaszów and elsewhere were drawn either from the large Ukrainian community in Poland or from Ukrainian prisoners-of-war volunteers who had once served with the Red Army. The Death's Head units also had other foreign volunteers, such as ethnic Germans or Hungarians, who served as guards at Płaszów. Only about 15 percent of a forced labor or concentration camp's personnel were career SS men. The handful of Germans who ran these camps relied heavily on foreign volunteers, recruits for guard service, and a cadre of inmate leaders. The members of the *Wachbattalions,* sentries armed with machine guns and spot lights who guarded the the watch towers and outer perimeters of the camp, were restricted to these zones of authority as well as their contacts with the prisoners. The foreign guards were also an important black market conduit for the inmates who relied on them for illegal foodstuffs, medicines, and other items to make life in these hell holes a little more tolerable.[106]

Initially, *Zwangsarbeitslager* Płaszów was administratively under the auspices of HSSPF *Ost* Friedrich Wilhelm Krüger, though ultimately it was taken over by WVHA and transformed into a permanent concentration camp. The SS gave considerable thought to the structure and boundary networks in its camps. SS guards patrolled the inner boundaries that separated SS personnel facilities and work areas from the prisoners' living complex. This was touched off by an outer perimeter of double barbed wire fences that created a no-man's-land lined with gravel. Eleven watchtowers manned by two members of the *Feldwache* (outpost) SS guard teams were placed along this outer no-man's-land. In addition, there was also an antiaircraft battery placed on a high tower on one of the promontories overlooking the rest of the camp.[107]

Once Płaszów was transformed into a concentration camp, a series of internal boundaries were created by barbed wire fences that essentially divided Płaszów into a series of small camps within a larger camp. This inner network of barbed wire boundaries was designed to create areas of limited access for prisoners and camp staff. Prisoners could enter the SS areas only during working hours, and normally the camp staff and guards did not enter the prisoner compound. To maintain this separation and distance, the SS relied upon a cadre of inmate leaders to serve as liaison between the SS administration and the prisoners. Within this group was what Wolfgang Sofsky has called a gradation of power based on the importance of power. Depending on one's position in this camp hierarchy, an inmate could wield incredible power over his or her peers. The SS camp administration understood the value of this group and permitted them considerable leeway in how they conducted affairs and relations with other prisoners. Some inmate camp leaders used their positions to help others, though some abused their positions.[108]

According to Wolfgang Sofsky, the Nazi concentration camp "was a complete settlement with a network of streets and a railroad siding—a town for personnel and prisoners housing thousands, at times tens of thousands, of people."[109] It was, for all practical purposes, a self-sustaining SS community with all of the attributes and facilities of a small town.

WVHA had specific guidelines for the structure of the camp and the placement and borders for each of its sections. The ideal camp structure and substructure was a rectangle with most camp buildings running along an east-west or north-south axis. Theoretically, on a flat plane, one could stand at one end of a smaller camp and easily see the other end of the camp if one's view was not blocked by buildings or trees. Given the hilly nature of Płaszów, this was a little more difficult, though even here it is possible to observe rudiments of the rectangular design. The center of the camp was the administrative area, which contained the commandant's office as well as branches of all the different WVHA offices that served as liaisons between the camp administration and WVHA offices in Oranienburg. In Płaszów, the administration building sat just to the right of the main entrance as you entered the camp. Consequently, when Oskar Schindler came to Płaszów he did not have far to go to meet with camp officials or to chat with Mietek Pemper and Itzhak Stern. And if he was invited to a party or gathering at Göth's villa, he only had to travel about a quarter of a mile or so down SS Straße to the commandant's very comfortable quarters. This meant that

Schindler probably did not ordinarily see some of the more awful aspects of the camp, which were fairly well-hidden in the distance. But he certainly knew a great deal about them. The administrative offices of the camp were surrounded by barbed wire, as was the communications center just across the street.[110]

SS master planning also dictated comfortable quarters for SS officers and barracks for the guards. In Płaszów, the SS barracks were just across SS Straße from the administrative offices and partially built over the sites of the former Jewish cemeteries. The guards' barracks centered around a self-contained community area with its own kitchens, infirmary, laundry, and other basics. Farther along SS Straße was the housing of the SS officers, including the Göth villa. There was also a small collection of SS houses just beyond the camp's industrial quarter. The industrial part of the camp, which lay just to the left of Göth's villa, housed the workshops of the various factories permitted to operate in the camp. The largest of these was Julius Madritsch's sewing factory, who housed his workshops in six barracks. Furriers and upholsterers also operated in the industrial complex. Resting between this part of the camp and the SS administrative and housing complex was the camp quarry. The balcony of Amon Göth's house looked over a portion of the quarry and it is from here that he occasionally shot workers. It is hard to imagine this today because trees on the back edge of the Göth property block this view. One of the camp's common grave sites, Lipowy Dolek, was wedged between the industrial complex and the quarry.[111]

To the south of the quarry were the camp's printing press and a smaller number of workshops for shoes, watches, electrical goods, and paper. Just beyond this on the southeastern edge of the camp was Hujowa Gorka, or, as the inmates called it, "Prick Hill," the camp's principal execution and burial site. Bergens Straße ran through the middle of the camp and separated the quarry and industrial-manufacturing portion of the camp from the inmates' enclosure. The center of this part of Płaszów was the hated *Appellplatz* (roll call, or parade ground or place), where inmates not only had to endure twice-daily roll calls but also humiliating and at times deadly punishments. The *Appellplatz* was surrounded on two sides by numerous men's barracks. The camp latrines and barracks were located just to the south of this area; the female inmates were housed in barracks just beyond the male complex. The camp's kitchen and food storehouses lay just beyond the inmate's living quarters and were surrounded by barbed wire. Just beyond this small area was the camp's hospital. The barracks of

the *jüdischer Ordnungsdienst* (Jewish "order service," or Jewish camp police) sat between the male and female camps. Far in the distance in the
south were the barracks of the *Feldwache*, who manned the guard towers
and guarded the outer perimeter of the camp.[112]

In the fall of 1943, Amon Göth, prodded by the creatively manipulative
efforts of Mietek Pemper, received permission to transform Płaszów into a
permanent concentration camp, and this assured the survival of many of
the camp's Jewish and Polish workers. In late October 1943, the WVHA
informed Göth that it would be sending *SS-Hauptsturmführer* Wilhelm
Schitli to oversee the camp's transformation from a forced labor camp
into a concentration camp. Schitli had served as *Schutzhaftlagerführer*
(head of the protective custody camp) at the Neuengamme concentration
camp near Hamburg and had begun his SS camp service career at the
Sachenhausen concentration camp in Oranienburg. He served briefly as
the commandant at Arbeitsdorf, a sub-camp of Neuengamme where the
SS hoped to build a light-metals foundry. Schitli was removed from this
post by Oswald Pohl for incompetency and was forced out of the concentration camp administrative service, only to resurface as part of WVHA's
Office Group C, which oversaw camp construction. Once at Płaszów,
Schitli oversaw the division of the camp into separate zones, which were
surrounded by barbed wire. A new guard force under the Waffen SS now
took over the supervision of the camp, particularly the movement of camp
inmates from the living area to the industrial complex.[113]

Mietek Pemper, Itzhak Stern, and the Transformation of Płaszów

Mietek Pemper is one of the most remarkable *Schindlerjuden* in the
Schindler story, not only because of his intimate knowledge about the
inner workings of Płaszów but also his very close friendship with Oskar
Schindler, particularly after the war. Beyond this connection, Mietek
Pemper is just a warm, gentle human being with a phenomenal memory.
Dr. Moshe Bejski, a retired Israeli Supreme Court justice who later became chairman of the Designation of the Righteous Commission at Yad
Vashem, told me when I interviewed him that when it came to facts
about Oskar Schindler, the only other person he trusted more than himself was Mietek Pemper. Because of his keen memory, Pemper became the
principal witness against not only Amon Göth but also Gerhard Maurer,
both of whom were convicted and executed for war crimes. Pemper, who

speaks perfect German, also served as a translator in some of the Auschwitz trials in Kraków in late 1947.[114]

Yet who was this remarkable man? It took a while for me to find out. When I began my initial research for this book, one of the names that kept coming up in interviews with other Schindler Jews was Mietek Pemper's. Because he served as Amon Göth's stenographer and worked with him daily for sixteen months, other survivors explained that Pemper was the only one who could really answer questions about Amon Göth and his relationship with Oskar Schindler. I was also told that Mr. Pemper did not grant interviews and was unapproachable. I later learned during my two lengthy interviews with this very gracious, kind man that his distance came more from a certain humility and shyness, as well as a healthy suspicion of interviewers, than disinterest in telling what he knew about Oskar Schindler and Amon Göth. I encountered this suspicion time and again among other *Schindlerjuden* who were tired of being misquoted. In time, I gained the trust of scores of Schindler Jews because of my sincerity, patience, and scholarly approach to the subject. Over time, I learned to state in my introductory letters to them that I was a scholar, not a journalist. The trust and friendships that I developed with many of the Schinder Jews in the course of my research are some of the richest experiences of my life.

After he attended the Kraków opening of *Schindler's List,* a *New York Times* reporter asked Mr. Pemper why he had "applied" for the job with Amon Göth. Mietek Pemper did not apply for this job; he was chosen by Göth, who asked Jewish congregation leaders in the ghetto to recommend someone who could do clerical work for him. Because Pemper spoke and read perfect German and knew German stenography, he was selected for the job. As a prisoner first in the ghetto and later in Płaszów, there was no way he could have applied for a "position" with Göth. Mietek Pemper was a slave laborer who was forced to work for Amon Göth. For the next sixteen months, his every waking moment was a living hell. He lived in constant fear of being murdered by Göth for the slightest infraction. One does not "apply" for death.[115]

Mietek Pemper, who was born in Kraków, was nineteen years old when World War II broke out. He came from a family with strong ties to the Habsburg world of the Austro-Hungarian empire. His father and uncle had fought proudly in the Austrian army in World War I, and his grandmother, who had great regard for German culture, refused to speak Polish. Soon after the German occupation of Kraków, Pemper got a job as a stenographer with the Temporary Jewish Religious Community (TJRC) in

Kraków, which the Germans intended to act as liaison between their administrators and the city's Jews. He continued to work for the TJRC after
the opening of the ghetto, and it was because of his work with this group
that he was recommended to Amon Göth.[116]

The key to Pemper's survival in the mercurial, deadly world of Amon
Göth was his discretion, luck, and thoroughness when it came to his steno-
graphic work. But behind his quiet demeanor was a determined young
man with a photographic memory who was intent upon gathering every
scrap of information possible about Göth and general SS policies and operations, whether they be in Płaszów or elsewhere. After the war, he was
asked by Jan Sehn, one of the principal architects of Poland's massive war
crimes investigations, whether he knew anything about Gerhard Maurer.
He explained that he could find no one who knew anything about Maurer,
whom Sehn wanted to extradite to Poland for trial. Pemper told Sehn,
whom he had met while preparing for his testimony in Göth's trial, that he
had seen two or three letters a week from Maurer in Göth's office and remembered everything. According to Pemper, Sehn was delighted and "appeared happy like a child" at this news.[117] As a result, Pemper became the
principal prosecution witness against Maurer, just as he had been in Göth's
trial. Pemper's testimony in Maurer's trial shocked the defendant, who
could not believe that a mere stenographer knew so much. According to
Maurer, he had never heard of a Jewish inmate in such a sensitive position
in a Nazi concentration camp.[118]

The principal reason Pemper had such access was the utter chaos and
fear in Göth's office, not only among the Jewish office workers but also the
German and Polish staff. Amon Göth hated office work and was only there
a few hours a day. He was also a night person, which meant that Pemper
was at his beck and call twenty-four hours a day. He was required to spend
each day working full time in Göth's office in the administrative complex
near the front gate, but he also had to go to Göth's villa to take dictation.
He spent a lot of time in Göth's kitchen waiting for the commandant. That
was where he got to know Göth's two Jewish maids, particularly Helen
Hirsch. Göth had a terrible temper and would lose it over the slightest
thing, whether it be a misspelled word or a flower arrangement in his
house that he thought was out of place. Göth's office staff was terrified of
him. Consequently, his officers and civilian staff members would often ask
Pemper to draft letters for them because they were afraid of making mistakes. If the letters were about sensitive issues, Pemper would ask to see the
secret files that were kept in a safe.[119]

Pemper was also helpful to Göth's part-time German secretary, Frau Kochmann, the wife of a Kraków judge. Initially, Pemper was alone in the office until Göth hired Frau Kochmann, who wanted to work in the mornings. Like everyone on Göth's office staff, she soon felt the commandant's wrath. On one occasion, she made the mistake of putting the carbon paper in backwards when she typed a letter for Göth. He flew into a rage and began screaming at her. Frau Kochmann started to cry and later Pemper came up to her and suggested that he prepare the carbon paper in future. Frau Kochmann gladly accepted Pemper's offer. Pemper made certain to supply fresh carbon paper for each letter to insure that he could read it later in a mirror. Once he had gotten to know and trust Oskar Schindler, Pemper shared everything he could with his future savior and friend.

But Mietek Pemper also did something else with the information he was gathering in Göth's office. He decided to do what he could to help convince first Göth and then WVHA of the wisdom of transforming Płaszów into a permanent concentration camp, which he thought would save many lives. The seed for this idea came from two unrelated events in 1942: the transports from the Kraków ghetto to Bełżec and detailed armaments orders that he was asked to read from several hundred German and Polish companies to Kraków's HSSPF offices. David Gutter, the head of the ghetto's *Judenrat,* had been given these letters by Horst Pilarzik, who wanted him to organize them into a more efficient, easily accessible system. Gutter did not have time to do this and asked Pemper to help him. Gutter emphasized the secret nature of these documents and told Pemper to lock himself in a room while he read them and reorganized them. As he was reading these secret files, Pemper learned of SS plans to close the ghettos throughout the General Government and to intern those Jews necessary for armaments production in a few enclosed slave labor camps.[120]

Soon after Pemper became Göth's stenographer at Płaszów, he came face to face with Pilarzik, who remembered that he had helped organize the files he had given Gutter. Pilarzik was now Göth's adjutant. When they met, Pilarzik said to Pemper, "Wash your chest. Do you know what follows now?" Pemper replied, "Yes, you will be shot." Pilarzik was surprised and asked Pemper how he knew this. Pemper said, "That's what 'wash your chest' means. So I must have done something wrong or incomplete." Pilarzik said no, that he did not mean it that way. But he did need the papers Gutter had given Pemper to organize back as quickly as possible.[121]

But something else besides the information in these reports also drove Mietek Pemper. Reports had been passed on to him from ghetto Jews who had been involved in prewar Poland's socialist movement. They had learned from Polish socialist rail workers about the true fate of the transports from the Kraków ghetto to Bełżec. The Polish rail workers had driven the transports close to Bełżec, where the trains had been taken over by Germans and Ukrainians. When the trains were returned to the Polish crews, the cars had blood in them. Pemper also learned that farmers in the fields near Bełżec reported that the train cars smelled like burnt meat. Though it took Pemper and others a long time to accept what was really happening to Poland's Jews, this realization further motivated him to do everything he could to save as many Jewish lives as possible.[122]

Consequently, in August or September 1943, Mietek Pemper told the managers of Płaszów's metalworking shops, including Oskar Schindler, that he needed full production capacity lists for their factories. He had noticed that Göth had become increasingly interested in the daily production reports of the camp's metalworking shops that Pemper gave him. Göth, who was not a detail person, would occasionally make suggestions about what this factory or that workshop could do with its machines to produce more militarily acceptable goods. Göth had written to his father after Stalingrad that he was worried about the outcome of the war. And Göth also knew that if Płaszów closed he would probably be sent to the Russian front because the Waffen SS was constantly transferring its officers and men from the camps to the front and replacing them with older or wounded veterans.[123]

Pemper also shared this information with Oskar Schindler, who was also in the process of setting up a separate armaments wing at Emalia. Schindler's efforts would be strongly supported by Göth since Emalia was a sub camp of Płaszów. As he began planning his statistical game plan, Pemper also told Itzhak and Natan Stern about it one night in their barracks. Both men looked at him and one of them said, "Are you serious or are you aware that it is crazy that we should try to be transformed into a concentration camp?" From their perspective, the concentration camp symbolized the worst that could happen to Poland's Jews. From that moment on, Pemper decided to be more discreet because it was apparent to him that they thought he was insane.[124]

What is interesting about these developments is that Itzhak Stern took most of the credit for preparing the false reports that helped Göth convince WVHA to transform Płaszów into a concentration camp in his interview with Dr. Ball-Kaduri in 1956. According to Dr. Ball-Kaduri's report, "Stern was able to take advantage of the common interest [of coming under

DAW's jurisdiction] and constructed inflated reports about the capability of the camp to the central office." And though he does mention Pemper occasionally, it is clear that he thought of himself as the principal architect of the transformation scheme. It is quite possible that Mietek Pemper never knew about Stern's claim. In 1969, he wrote Oskar Schindler a long letter in which he described his feelings for Stern, who had just passed away. It is apparent from what Pemper said to Oskar that he had almost the same adoring affection for Stern as he had for Oskar, who also cared greatly for Stern, and that he felt his loss deeply: "I have lost a human being who I admired most of all, who had been together [with me] in war and in the camp, who embodied the ideals of the best, which one saw so seldom amidst the unusual circumstances of the KZ period: a willingness to help, selflessness, unpretentiousness to the point of self-denial—always thinking of others, never of the self, never pushing himself into the foreground—truly there was hardly anyone who can and may be named with him in the same breath."[125]

So what really happened? As is usual where perspectives differ, the realities lie somewhere in between. I do know that I was able to confirm almost everything Mietek Pemper told me in the two interviews I did with him. He, too, is a man of incredible integrity. My suspicion is that Mietek Pemper and Itzhak Stern both played a role in preparing the reports that helped convince Göth and WVHA to make Płaszów one of only twenty permanent concentration camps. And although Stern claimed he was the principal figure in promoting the transformation scheme, even he admits in his testimony that it was Pemper who suggested to Göth that they wanted to "make an interesting report about [the] production in the workshops." Moreover, with the exception of the opening statement in which Stern claims sole credit for coming up with the scheme, in the rest of his testimony he constantly uses the term "we."

Regardless of what exactly took place, the testimony of Pemper and Stern gives us some excellent insight into the politics of camp transformation and provides clues into how Oskar Schindler was able to work his miracles within the context of the SS camp administrative system. According to Stern, as the liquidation of camps got under way in the fall of 1943, there was great interest among the SS and many of the business owners in Płaszów to become part of the German Equipment Works (DAW; *Deutsche Ausrüstungswerke GmbH*), the SS-owned economic enterprises in the forced labor and concentration camps. DAW was begun in 1941 to consolidate "the scattered workshops for graft maintained ad hoc by the

[camp] commandaten since the earliest days of Eicke's Dachau."[126] Over time, DAW enterprises in the concentration camps became "workshops and supply industries for the new order that the SS planned for an imaginary peace."[127] In 1941, DAW sales amounted to RM 5.3 million ($2.1 million). Within two years, its annual sales had quadrupled. In 1942, DAW became part of Office Group W under Oswald Pohl. DAW was now W4/1, a subsidiary of the SS Wood Working Industries.[128]

Stern, like Pemper, also had information about the growing German campaign to murder the Jews throughout the General Government who were not involved in essential war work. He recalls reading one newspaper brought in by foreign workers that contained an essay by Joseph Goebbels, Hitler's Minister of Propaganda, stating that "anybody who encountered a Jew in the General Government after December 31, 1943, could slap Goebbels in the face." Stern also testified that in the fall of 1943 the Ukrainian police brought thousands of coats from Lemberg (today, Ukrainian L'viv). One of the Ukrainian guards then told Stern to escape. When Stern asked him why, the guard told him that if he did not, he would suffer the same fate as those in the Janówska camp. Stern then looked at the coats and realized they were covered with blood. The SS, he concluded, had shot the inmates while they were working. There were thousands of coats and other clothing in the Janówska shipment, so they had probably been taken from the bodies of the murdered inmates after a mid-May 1943 action, where the SS had killed 6,000 Janówska inmates. Consequently, by June 1943, Stern had become aware of certain aspects of the Final Solution.[129]

Stern said the incident that triggered the decision to create a report based on phony statistics came after two telegrams were sent to Göth's office from WVHA headquarters in Oranienburg one Sunday. The first telegram demanded an immediate list of all machines in Płaszów; the second, which arrived on the heels of the first, wanted to know how many inmates were in the camp. Because there were no important officers on duty at the time, the office secretary came to see Stern. Stern made a point of noting that Göth did not come into the office that night, and the secretary also chose not to call Pemper. Stern said that "we" decided to advise Göth not simply to supply a report on the number of inmates but to draft a detailed report that also included the number of machines and departments in the camp, including total figures on the number of people working there. Stern said he thought this might impress officials in Oranienburg and possibly convince them to transform Płaszów into a concentration camp.[130]

Yet, according to Stern, it was Mietek Pemper who told Göth about their idea to create "an interesting report about all [their] productions in the workshops." Stern said the report was based on many "false numbers" that included past and future production statistics. The result was a nicely bound book with many drawings and graphs. Göth, who read the final report, knew that it was based on phony statistics and, after checking the numbers, angrily called Stern to his desk and asked him to explain the inconsistencies. Stern told him that "*Wüst* [confusion] promised up this order." Göth then "realized [their] intention, laughed, and continued to read."[131]

Pemper's account is much more precise. Moreover, it seems more realistic because you can sense the fear behind Pemper's every step as he oversaw the creation of the report. He realized after he had gotten the capacity production reports from the factory managers that they were not sufficient to convince WVHA of Płaszów's potential as a concentration camp. Consequently, he went to Schindler and other factory managers and asked them to give him alternative production capacity statistics based on production potentials if they got orders for metal and iron goods. He then insisted that they provide him with details on every possible type of metal good they could produce with the machines they had as well as exacting detail on every item they might possibly produce if the machines were reconfigured to produce something else. Pemper did not tell them why he wanted this data. He also included Schindler's statistics from Emalia in this data.[132]

In the meantime, Pemper learned that Göth had just arranged to trade suits and boots made in the camp for wide Breitwagen typewriters that the commandant had signed over to himself and then leased to the camp. Pemper used one of these wide typewriters to type the capacity lists. In the upper left-hand corner of each page he typed the number of pieces involved in that workshop and added details about the goods, production, and other explanations. He put so much information on each page that he had to use abbreviations to make each section fit on the paper. When he ran out of space, he typed "*od.,*" the German abbreviation for "*oder* (or)." On the next line he would report how many of the above described items the camp could produce. And at the end of this line he would type "*od.*" When he had finished, he showed it to Göth, who was surprised by the numbers and said, "That can't be true, that's impossible that we can produce all of that." And then Göth asked, "How did you do this?" Pemper explained that he had used signed documents from each of the workshop and factory directors. Göth then wanted to know why the figures were not added up. Pemper explained that the figures could not be added up because they were based on alternatives. Göth then asked about the constant use of the "*od.*" at the end of each line. Pemper said he was becoming more and more nervous about Göth's questions and that it was "very hard . . . to keep [his] countenance."[133]

Göth then returned to his office where Pemper could hear him in deep conversation with others. Pemper thought that Göth either considered him a complete idiot who did not know what he was doing or someone who was capable of reading his mind. Pemper realized that Göth would never have told him outright to fabricate such figures because this would have been "extortionable." On the other hand, he knew that Göth had excellent ties to important officials in the General Government. Pemper was convinced that Göth's two-rank promotion several months earlier was linked to the Płaszów inspection visit of HSSPF Krüger, who seemed fond of Göth. Afterwards, one of Krüger's adjutants, Graf Korf, began to make frequent trips to Płaszów to get custom-made suits and boots. Krüger's teenage sons, Eckehart and Jochen, also came occasionally to camp with another of their father's adjutants, *SS-Obersturmführer* Petrus, whom the teenagers treated with great disdain.[134]

Stern describes the next series of events leading up to the decision to declare Płaszów a permanent concentration camp. Soon after Pemper and Stern's report arrived at WVHA headquarters in Oranienburg, *Obersturmführer* Mohvinkel showed up in Płaszów personally to determine the report's accuracy. Though Stern had a low opinion of many of the SS officers sent from Oranienburg on camp inspections, he quickly realized that Mohvinkel knew what he was doing. It would not take the WVHA officer long to realize that the Płaszów report was based on phony statistics. Mohvinkel was accompanied by another official from WVHA, Leclerc, who seemed to speak mostly French. Stern thought he was a spy and a provocateur. While Mohvinkel was looking over the books, Leclerc whispered to Pemper: "It all depends on Mohvinkel, he only has half an hour, then he needs to leave. You have to be careful not to be caught." Consequently, Stern answered Mohvinkel's questions about the report with partial evidence and partial excuses. Leclerc was there "to do the balances." At one point, he told Stern and Pemper that "everything would be fine." Mohvinkel soon left "without noticing our falsifications."[135]

But by the end of 1943, Göth had still heard nothing about the transformation of the camp. Everything, it seemed, now rested on the visit of one of the most powerful men in the Third Reich, *SS-Obergruppenführer* Oswald Pohl, the head of WVHA, in late 1943. Pohl's decision evidently would be based on how many armaments orders that Płaszów would receive from the Wehrmacht. Until this point, the camp's factories had produced few significant metal goods of interest to WVHA and the Wehrmacht. This was where Oskar Schindler and his contacts with the military's Armaments Inspectorate became useful. Stern told Göth that they needed Schindler's arms production orders to document Płaszów's potential as an arms producer. Stern said that Göth told him to talk with Schindler about this and said the arms production orders were the final key to approval. From what Stern says, though, Göth also talked to Schindler personally about this problem. Oskar immediately called *Generalleutnant* Maximillian Schindler, the head of the Wehrmacht's Armaments Inspectorate in the General Government, and *General* Schindler came to Płaszów the following Sunday evening. Schindler's visit was to determine whether Płaszów was "suitable for such production." Pohl was also to be on hand to give instant approval if *General* Schindler thought Płaszów had the potential to produce arms.[136]

Everyone knew, including Oskar Schindler, that Płaszów's production facilities were "too primitive" for this. So Oskar Schindler suggested to Stern that they have a power failure just before the inspection began. *General* Schindler and his officers could then make the inspection with flashlights. When the power went off, Göth was furious. But in the dark, "the workshops looked quite magnificent." *General* Schindler was evidently impressed by what he saw in the dark and now everyone waited for the production orders from him. Time was of the essence because Pohl had to leave Płaszów by 8:00 P.M. to return to Oranienburg. At 7:00 P.M. Stern called Schindler at Emalia and asked about the production orders. Not long afterwards, a soldier brought three large envelopes with the armaments orders from the Armaments Inspectorate to the camp offices. Stern signed for the envelopes, which he was not supposed to do, and gave them to Pemper, who asked one of the SS men in the office to give them to Göth, who was with Pohl in his office. The SS officer was furious with Pemper because he thought it was improper for him to take the envelopes from someone unauthorized to receive them, particularly a Jew. But the officer was also afraid of disturbing Göth. After hesitating a few moments, the SS man entered the commandant's office. Göth patted him on the back and smiled when he gave him the envelopes. Soon afterwards, Pohl approved Płaszów's new status as a concentration camp just before he left. *SS-Hauptsturmführer* Schitli arrived soon afterwards to oversee the transformation of Płaszów, which was completed in early 1944.[137]

Mietek Pemper was extremely proud of the role he played in this process. During one of our visits together, he even gave me a German stamp commemorating the liberation of the concentration camps. From his perspective, inmates of the camps that were being liquidated were often sent immediately to their deaths; those in the permanent camps were given a chance to live longer. This transformation enabled Oskar Schindler to maintain his sub-camp at Emalia and then transfer it to the Protectorate of Bohemia and Moravia (Böhren und Mähren) as a sub-camp of another permanent concentration camp, Groß Rosen. Płaszów's new status, of course, did not alter the murderous environment in Płaszów, whether it be slow death by slave labor, mass execution, or the indiscriminate raging of Göth and other SS men in the camp. Now that the SS was in full control of Płaszów it became a bit more difficult to murder inmates indiscriminately. This change slowed down the death rate in the camp but did not end it.

The Crimes of Amon Göth in Płaszów

In an interview for the *Süddeutsche Zeitung* in early 1997, the reporter asked Mietek Pemper whether Steven Spielberg depicted Amon Göth accurately in the film's "truly horrific scenes." Pemper said that just the opposite was true, meaning there was no way you could capture the evil that was Amon Göth on film. He remembered, for example, a murder that Göth committed while he was dictating a letter to Pemper in his office. Göth kept a mirror there so he could see what was going on outside. While he was talking, he spotted a worker with a wheelbarrow. Pemper was uncertain whether the worker had stopped to rest or maybe did not have a full load of stones in the wheelbarrow. Regardless, Göth walked to the window, shot the man to death, returned to his desk, and asked Pemper, "Where were we in the text?" On another occasion, Pemper saw Göth shoot a female worker for the same reason.[138]

Yet Pemper had seen much worse. He told Spielberg that he watched Göth let his two great Danes, Rolf and Ralf, tear an inmate to death. Pemper also saw the dogs tear "whole pieces of meat" from two inmates who were about to be transferred to another camp. Evidently, the inmates were killed because they had bribed two Ukrainian guards to help transfer them. Spielberg said these stories were too gruesome to put into the film. In his 1946 war crimes trial, Göth told the court that he kept the dogs for breeding purposes. Helen Sternlicht Rosenzweig, one of two Jewish maids who worked for Göth in Płaszów, said that he used a padded glove that covered his arm up to his elbow to train Ralf to attack people. Another Schindler Jew, Henry Silver (Hersch Silberschlag), had volunteered to be a dog handler when he arrived at Płaszów, though he knew nothing about dogs. He fed Göth's "killer canines," as he called them, until he was transferred to other duty. Roman Ferber, one of the children hidden in Płaszów, said that Göth would occasionally mount "hunting missions" for Jews in the camp and used his dogs to ferret anyone hiding illegally there. Fortunately for Ferber and others, the dogs, who bounded ahead of Göth on these "missions," acted as a warning signal and allowed them to hide. But Ferber, also a *Schindlerjude*, remembered that if Göth "didn't like your looks, he would set the dog on you." According to Stella Müller-Madej, Göth murdered another of his dog handlers, Adam Sztab, because the commandant thought the dogs liked Sztab more than their owner.[139]

Viennese-born Raimund Titsch, who managed Julius Madritsch's large sewing factory in Płaszów, remembered being invited to Göth's villa for lunch. Göth thought the soup was too hot and called the Jewish chef from the kitchen to explain why. The chef evidently did not hear Göth calling for him. Göth jumped out of his chair, yelled for the chef to come out of the kitchen, and took him behind the villa. A few moments later, Titsch heard a single pistol shot. Göth had murdered the Jewish chef because of the hot soup.[140]

Mietek Pemper told me that Amon Göth was "an enigma. He could be both brutal, friendly, and playful with officers' children." And though his staff seemed terrified of him, there were some high-ranking SS officers who felt comfortable enough to play jokes on him. *Schindlerjude* Henry Slamovich (Chaim Wolf Szlamowicz) said that one evening in Płaszów a high-ranking camp SS officer came to his barracks and selected twenty Jews who were then marched to Göth's villa. Slamovich was certain that they were all about to get "wiped out." The officer then marched them into the villa, where they heard dancing and loud music. The inmates were taken to the second floor and ordered "to dismantle the beds and take everything out to the basement, so when Goeth comes back with his girlfriend, it would be empty. It was a joke."[141] Slamovich was one of those who testified against Göth in 1946.[142]

There were different levels of violence and death at Płaszów: indiscriminate shootings, single and mass executions, beatings by Göth, and formal punishments such as lashing. From the perspective of the SS, the commandant of a camp was the role model for his subordinates. So just as Göth modeled the behavior of his former superiors, Albrecht Schmelt and Odilo Globočnik, he served as a role model for those in the camp who served under him.[143] Murray Pantirer, a Schindler Jew who came to the United States and committed his life to insuring that the world never forgot Oskar Schindler, said that Göth "couldn't have breakfast or lunch without seeing Jewish blood. Every day he would shoot somebody else at random." And if the commandant was wearing his Tyrolean hat, Płaszów's inmates knew they "were in terrible danger." Whenever Pantirer saw Göth, he would run to the latrine because he knew that Göth would never go in there. If he came into the barracks, Göth would not leave until he had shot a few workers.[144]

Göth deliberately used cruel punishment and the threat of death to maintain the pace and efficiency of work in Płaszów. He also believed in group responsibility, meaning that if one person in a group tried to escape or committed some other infraction, the entire barracks or work team would be punished. And Göth was most dangerous when he was drunk. Mietek Pemper testified that on one particular morning after all night partying, Göth came to the *Appellplatz,* where the inmates were lined up for roll call. He shot one inmate, Sonnenschein, because his coat was too long and another because he simply did not like his looks. On another occasion, Göth walked into the camp's brush factory and shot the foreman out of boredom. He ordered all the workers outside and lined them up. He then began to divide them into two groups. Göth and his small entourage walked back and forth among the both groups and finally left. The terrified workers continued to stand at attention for another thirty minutes until they were ordered back into the workshop. Once inside, everyone became hysterical because they "had come close to being killed."[145]

But Göth did more than threaten work groups. Once, he was standing just inside the camp gate as several work teams were returning from cleaning the streets in Kraków. *Schindlerjude* Julius Eisenstein, who was in one of the work parties, said Göth noticed that "some of the inmates [in one of the labor groups] had bulging pockets. One had bread, one had a salami, and one had canned food."[146] When Göth discovered the contraband, he told the "blacks [Ukrainian guards] ... '*Alle töten!*' Shoot them all!" The Ukrainian guards then took the entire party of fifty to sixty workers to Hujowa Gorka and shot them.[147]

Murray Pantirer remembered another incident in which Göth ordered every other worker in his fifty-man work team shot because one of them had escaped. Göth had the crew lined up and then asked, "Where is the fiftieth?" When nobody responded, he ordered his guards to shoot every other inmate in the group. Henry Slamovich said that something similar happened after a boy escaped from Slamovich's crew, which was repairing railroad tracks. When they returned to camp, Göth, with whip in hand, touched every fifth boy on the nose with his whip and then shot each one. There was no end to this deadly viciousness. Betty (Bronia) Groß Gunz recalled standing next to Schnadl Müller, a close friend, during morning roll call. As Göth rode by on his horse with Rolf and Ralf, he noticed that Schnadl was smiling. Göth shot her to death for this. As Schnadl fell to the ground, Betty instinctively moved towards her. An SS guard struck her with his whip; another hit her in the back and caused so much damage to her kidney that it had to be removed after the war. The next morning Betty managed to make it to work because she was afraid that if she did not show up they would shoot her.[148]

Given the random, indiscriminate nature of death at Płaszów, it should come as no surprise that those working closest to Amon Göth—Mietek Pemper, Itzhak Stern, and Helen Sternlicht Rosenzweig—feared him most because they were in constant contact with him. Pemper felt that working for Göth was a death sentence and he did not think he would survive the war. This was one of the reasons he was so bold in gathering information about Göth. Pemper said that when the war was over, his nerves were shattered because of the pressure of working under Göth. Itzhak Stern said that his family was certain that Göth would kill him and lived in constant fear for his life. One day, Göth did beat Stern after he was ordered to prepare one of the commandant's horses for a ride. Stern, who knew nothing about horses, could not find the stable master and came back to the office to find him. Göth saw him and asked Stern why he had returned. Stern said he had come back to get his hat. According to Stern, Göth then "beat me terribly."[149]

Göth also mistreated both of his Jewish housemaids, Helen Hirsch Horowitz and Helen (Helena) Sternlicht Rosenzweig. To differentiate between the two Helens, Göth renamed them Lena (Helen Hirsch) and Susanna (Helen Sternlicht). Like most people who saw Schindler's List, I thought there was only one Jewish maid working for Göth, Helen Hirsch, though both appeared briefly together in one scene in the film. Both worked for Göth for almost two years and suffered equally from his brutality. Helen Hirsch is the best known of the two maids because she was featured in Keneally's novel and Spielberg's film. She settled in Israel after the war, remarried and, at this writing, still lives there. She is better known than Helen Rosenzweig, who settled in the United States after the war, because she was part of the close-knit circle of Schindler Jews in Israel who provided the testimony that became the basis of the Schindler story later told by Keneally and Spielberg. Helen Hirsch was the older of the two Jewish maids who worked for Göth. She had originally worked in the camp's Jewish kitchen and was chosen by her superior, Leon Myer, to work for Göth. Myer took several weeks to acquaint her with the commandant's personal likes and dislikes. Initially, Helen lived in a special barracks for Jewish workers, but eventually moved into quarters in the cold, damp cellar of Göth's villa. Living with Göth, she said after the war, "was almost like living under the gallows twenty-four hours a day."[150]

Göth set the tone for his treatment of Helen Hirsch the first night she moved into his villa. He seemed to like the dinner she cooked for him as well as the way she served it. During the meal, Göth asked her name and how she had become such a good cook. She told him that she came from a good family and knew how to do such things. Though she was not a "professional" cook, she promised the commandant that she "would do everything she could to please him." Later that evening, Göth came downstairs and asked Helen for the bones from dinner for his dogs. Helen said that she had thrown them out. Göth flew into a rage and began to beat her. In the midst of the beating, Helen got up the courage to ask him why she was hitting her. He responded, "The reason I am beating you now is because you had the temerity to ask me why I was beating you in the first place."[151]

After this, Helen said, "I was convinced that my life was going to be short-lived." She told herself that she would do whatever necessary to live as long as possible. Helen Hirsch and Helen Sternlicht were supposed to do general house chores and cook for the commandant. Helen Hirsch said after the war that Göth would call the maids by either pressing a buzzer that could be heard throughout the villa or by screaming for them. They were at his beck and call twenty-four hours a day and knew that if they took more than a few seconds to respond, he would hit both of them.[152] Göth broke Helen Hirsch's left eardrum during one of these beatings, which left her deaf in that ear. He was angry with her because he did not like the way she had set the dinner table. On another occasion he threw a knife at her and damaged a nerve in her left leg, an injury that left it partially paralyzed. In a rare display of courage, Helen painfully cried out, "Why are you beating me this way? Why don't you shoot me, finish my life? Why do you continue to torture me this way?" Göth looked at her and said, "You still have plenty of time—I need you." On other occasions, Göth would punish Helen Hirsch by making her run up three flights of stairs until she collapsed from exhaustion.[153]

In 1964, Helen Hirsch Horowitz told Martin Gosch and Howard Koch that "insofar as she was concerned, he [Göth] had made some attempts physically and sexually upon her." Gosch and Koch decided not to put this in the film script because "she might be accused even today of having acceded to his physical demands in order to preserve her life, and this does not happen to be true." She told the Hollywood film makers that she re-membered an incident when Göth called her into his room. When Helen entered, she saw that he was drunk and had a whip in his hand. Göth then began to beat her, "tearing off her clothes, attempting to rape her." She began screaming and Göth's mistress, Ruth, came into the room and saved her. Later, during a party, one of Göth's officers, who liked Helen, told her that she would be the last Jew to die in Płaszów because Göth "derived a kind of sadistic satisfaction out of brutalizing her that gave him greater satisfaction than anything else in the world."[154]

It was during one of these parties that Helen Hirsch met Oskar Schindler. Emalia's owner "took her aside, put his arm around her so that Göth would not see them, and gave her a piece of candy as he kissed her. Oskar told Helen, 'I'm not kissing you as a woman, but I am kissing you because I know about you, and I feel so terrible about your circumstances, and I will try in every way that I can to help you.'" From this moment on, Helen told Gosch and Koch, whenever Schindler visited Göth in the villa, he would make a point of taking Helen aside and telling her things to boost her morale. When Płaszów was being closed in the fall of 1944, Oskar told Bankier to put Helen and her sister, Anna, on the female "Schindler's List."[155]

Itzhak Stern later said that he considered Helen Hirsch the "most un-fortunate of all the inmates of the Plaszhow camp." Everyone in the camp, he said, including the Germans, felt sorry for her. Göth always required her to be dressed elegantly in a fresh, starched uniform because he "did not want to be reminded constantly of the Jewishness around him." Helen Hirsch was also not permitted to wear the Star of David. From Stern's per-spective, "he [Göth] tried to manufacture into his own mind that perhaps she was a human being, that she was not just a nothing, a piece of dirt, a Jew, and that he was being served by dirt." Stern felt that what Helen Hirsch suffered under Amon Göth "was "more than ten lifetimes" worth of pain. This was why Stern thought that "no one is more entitled to greater, stronger, more ardent admiration than Helen Horowitz."[156] But the same could be said for Göth's other Jewish maid, Helen Sternlicht Rosenzweig, who served Göth almost as long as Helen Hirsch and suffered the same horrible mistreatment.

Few people know about Helen Sternlicht Rosenzweig, and she is barely mentioned in Spielberg's film. Sol Urbach knew her and arranged to have me meet her one morning at her home in South Florida. He indicated to me that she was uncomfortable talking about her experiences and that I should not expect much. I had learned from interviewing many Schindler Jews that one could never determine how much they would be willing to talk about or how long an interview would last. People who seemed to know a lot often said nothing; others shared a great deal of information. Usually a hesitation to reveal much had more to do with reviving painful memories than disinterest in talking about their wartime experiences.

When I sat down with Helen Rosenzweig, it was obvious that talking about Göth was going to be very, very difficult for her. She said that she dreamed about him every night and that the two years she worked for him were the most fearful time of her life. I told her that if she did not care to talk about him, I understood. But gradually, she began to open up and tell me stories about him. This beautiful, sensitive woman touched me deeply. After we finished, I walked to my car and shuddered. It took me a long time to recover from what she told me that morning.[157]

Helen's family history under German occupation in Kraków was similar to that of other Jews. When the Germans began the construction of Płaszów in late 1942, her mother, Lola, and one of her older sisters, Sydel (Sydonia), were sent to work there. As the ghetto was being liquidated, Helen decided to try to sneak into Płaszów because she did not have the blue *Kennkarte*. She had already learned about the death trains to Bełżec and was desperate to join her sister and mother there. She hid in a milk wagon going to the new camp but was discovered by the driver just before he got there. She managed to escape his grasp and made it into the camp, where she was given a job cleaning barracks. One day while she was cleaning windows, Amon Göth walked in and said, "I want this girl in my house. If she is smart enough to clean windows in the sunshine, I want her."[158]

Helen Rosenzweig worked for Amon Göth for almost two years and lived in the basement of his villa, the last of the three homes that Göth and Ruth lived in during their time at Płaszów. Helen Hirsch, who had begun to work for Göth a little earlier, lived with Helen. They stayed in a small room behind the basement that had two beds and a small bathroom. Helen never mentioned sexual advances from Göth. Mietek Pemper told me that Göth, who had liver and kidney problems, was not attracted to women. In fact, he found the idea that Göth was somehow sexually attracted to Helen Hirsch Horowitz pure "baloney." She was not, he added, "Miss Kraków or Miss Poland."[159] Helen Rozenzweig added that Göth was also a diabetic who drank heavily. He believed firmly in Nazi racial laws and would not have had relations with a Jew. This does not contradict Helen Hirsch's claim that Göth tried to sexually abuse her when he was drunk. However, the idea, as depicted in Steven Spielberg's film, that Göth was somehow infatuated with Helen Hirsch and even toyed with the idea of kissing her is totally fictitious.[160]

Göth, of course, had no qualms about regularly beating and abusing his maids. He first mistreated Helen Rosenzweig one day while she was ironing his shirts. At the time, she styled her hair in braids. Göth was evidently displeased with her work and grabbed her by the braids. He told her: "You stupid Jew, don't you know how to iron a shirt? In Austria, a girl your age knows how to cook and iron." Göth, a big man with large hands, slapped her hard and told "Susanna" that he did not want any sadness in his house, a warning that she was not supposed to cry when he abused her. At the time, Göth had a young valet named Lisiek working for him. One evening after a party, one of the guests said he needed a ride back to town. Lisiek went to the stable to get the carriage. When he returned, Göth asked him why he done this without his permission. Lisiek, frightened, did not answer. Göth then took out his pistol and shot him to death. From this moment on, Helen Rosenzweig lived in constant fear for her life.[161]

One of Helen's greatest conflicts was her desire to be with her mother and two sisters. She told Elinor Brecher that being alone was even worse for her than Göth's abuse. She would look out the window of her room "watching people marching to work. I envied them. I knew they were going to daily hell, with hanging and killing and mutilations in camp, but they were together for whatever happened, and I was alone."[162] Helen Hirsch was very good to Helen Rosenzweig and tried to take care of her, but this simply was not enough. Helen's loneliness was particularly bad when she was on night duty in the villa. Her yearning to be with her family occasionally overwhelmed her and when Göth was away from the villa, she would sneak out and to try to see her mother, who later died during deportation. And when she could, Helen would sneak sandwiches to her sister, Betty (Bronia) Sternlicht Schagrin, as she was marched by the villa on her way to work at Madrisch's nearby factory.[163]

A few months before Helen Rosenzweig was shipped to Auschwitz and then to Schindler's new factory at Brünnlitz, she saw her sisters in a group of women in white kerchiefs headed for a deportation train. Helen ran outside to her sisters and looked back at Göth, who was standing nearby. She said, pleading, "Herr commandant, Herr commandant." Göth, who had a truncheon in his hand, told Helen, "If you don't move away, I'll kill you." An SS guard then told Helen to move away from her sisters and not to look at him. The guard then said that "there weren't enough cattle cars," meaning they had run out of space for this particular transport. The SS man then told Betty and Sydel (Sydonia), who were by now calling out to Helen, to step back from the transport line. In the meantime, Helen Hirsch, who had seen everything, woke Ruth up and told her that "Susanna had run outside." She pleaded with Ruth to help "Susanna." Ruth, who had once told the two maids that she would help them if she could, said there was nothing she could do without Göth's approval. But then she made a phone call. Later, Ruth told Helen Hirsch that she would have to tell Amon what she had done "because of her conscience." Later that day, Göth came downstairs with a pistol in his hand looking for "Susanna." When he could not find her, he beat Helen Hirsch instead. In fact, it was common for Göth to beat one or both maids for something the other did. Later, "Lena" told "Susanna" to keep quiet and say only "*Jawohl, Jawohl*" when she next met the commandant. The next day, Göth saw "Susanna" and said, "You were very lucky." He never mentioned the incident with her sisters again.[164]

One of the favored methods of punishment at Płaszów was lashing, particularly of women. Mietek Pemper testified at Göth's trial that he remembered one SS circular in the camp that dealt with the lashing of women. It ordered that Czech women were to be lashed by Slovak women and Polish females were to be lashed by Russian women. Pemper said he interpreted this to mean that this was "to cause hatred between people of the same race [Slavs]."[165] And though Amon Göth claimed in his trial that lashing prisoners happened only "once in a while," Pemper testified that it was a common form of punishment. And Göth always insisted that the prisoner receive the maximum number of "hits"—fifty—though Pemper remembered that prisoners were often struck more than a hundred times by the lash. This was particularly true when Płaszów was a forced labor camp and not a more strictly regulated concentration camp.[166]

According to Leon Leyson (Leib Lejzon), the guards used whips with small ball bearings at the end. The first lash was "equal to having somebody cut you with a knife."[167] Betty Sternlicht Schragin believes that her sister Sydel was the first woman at Płaszów to receive twenty-five lashes "on the bare buttocks."[168] The SS punished Sydel for letting five girls in her road crew go into the bathroom to warm up because it was so cold outside. And this was not the last time that Sydel was lashed. A year after the first punishment, the SS entered her barracks and said that everyone would be punished for not attending roll call. The women in Sydel's barracks had been told that because it was a holiday they would not have to work. It was also a Sunday and everyone was asleep when the SS entered the barracks. Sydel volunteered to be the first to be lashed. Before she went outside, Betty told her not to yell out in pain. Sydel was taken out and forced to bend over a chair, where a Jewish policeman named Zimmerman, who was later executed by the Poles, did the lashings. Ultimately, all the women in the barracks, including Betty, were beaten. Afterwards, they "couldn't sit for weeks."[169]

If anything came to symbolize the absolute horror of Płaszów, it was the camp's principal execution, burial, and desecration site, Hujowa Gorka. The inmates' nicknamed it "Prick Hill" because it could be seen from almost any part of the camp. There were also two other camp execution and burial sites at Lipowy Dolek and the northern section of the old Jewish cemetery. We also know that Göth had plans to build a crematorium and gas chambers at Płaszów. Mietek Pemper testified at Göth's trial that the crematorium was to serve the camp as well as "Gestapo around the Kraków [area] and others."[170] The site of the crematorium was shown on the camp plans used during Göth's trial though it is difficult to determine from trial testimony whether it was ever built. The gas chambers were never built because the representative of the Erfurt company (probably Topf and Sons, which built the crematoria at Auschwitz) sent to build them, Koller, "was a decent man" who tried to stall construction, saying "it was too cold" to build them.[171]

Most of those who were murdered by Göth or his SS subordinates were buried in Hujowa Gorka. In addition, the 2,000 Jews murdered in the closing of the ghetto in 1943 were also buried in one of the camp's three common grave sites. The Gestapo and the SS in Kraków also sent some of its prisoners to Płaszów for execution. In one instance, an entire Polish wedding party, including the priest and guests, were sent to the camp for execution. Beginning in the fall of 1943, prisoners were brought three or four times a week from Montelupich prison in Kraków to Płaszów for execution, usually in the morning. The prisoners were ordered from the trucks and told to undress. They were then marched to a ditch surrounding Hujowa Gorka and told to lie down. An SS man, a *Genickschußspezialist* (specialist in shooting in the neck), would then administer a *Nackenschuß*, a shot in the nape of the neck. A dental technician, usually a Jew, would then pull the gold teeth out of each victim's mouth. The dead bodies were then covered with a layer of dirt, though once Płaszow became a concentration camp the bodies were burned. The victims' clothes were sent to the camp's storehouses and most of the valuables were taken by the executioners.[172]

The most chilling accounts about the horrible scenes at Hujowa Gorka came from *Schindlerjuden* forced to work on the burial details or for the special *Sonderkommando* 1005 unit sent to the camp in the fall of 1944 to exhume and burn the bodies buried in mass graves there. Henry Wiener was assigned to one of the camp's burial details in the fall of 1943. He remembered they would bring the bodies of young Jewish girls who had been executed for having false papers for burial and the bodies of those executed for the escape of someone else. Before burial, gold teeth were removed from the bodies. Occasionally, those on the burial detail would pocket some of the gold teeth. "You felt like vomiting," Weiner said. "It was just awful. But the SS guy was right behind you with a gun. I never saw anybody having a nervous breakdown in all those years. In my case, I said 'I don't give a damn what they gonna do. We have to keep going and see their defeat, in spite of what they do to us.'"[173]

The *Sonderkommando* 1005 units were created in the summer of 1942 "to prevent the possible reconstruction of the number of victims."[174] They were commanded by *SS-Standartenführer* Paul Blobel, an architect and engineer who had gained a reputation as commander of *Sonderkommando* 4a in Ukraine for "crudity and bloodthirstiness."[175] These units were made up of about twenty men drawn from the SD, Sipo, and the Order Police. They, in turn, used prisoners, particularly Jews, to dig up the bodies and carry them to the pyres specially constructed for this purpose. Blobel and his men began their work in the late summer of 1942 where they experimented with various burning methods at Auschwitz and Chełmno. The one that Blobel and his men devised centered around large pyres that intermixed layers of timber with several thousand bodies. Gasoline or another flammable liquid was poured on the four corners of the pyre and then lit. Body fat from the victims helped stoke the flames.[176] When they had completed their experimental work at Chełmno and Auschwitz, where they emptied mass graves containing over 100,000 bodies, Blobel's units then did the same thing at Bełżec, Sobibór, and Treblinka. Himmler then sent them to occupied Russia and Poland. By the time a *Sonderkommando* 1005 unit arrived in Płaszów in the fall of 1944, their work was coming to an end. Several months earlier, Blobel took command of *Einsatzgruppe Iltis* to fight partisans on the Yugoslav-Austrian border. Many of the men who had served under him in the *Sonderkommando* 1005 units joined his new antipartisan unit.[177]

In the summer of 1944, Blobel and *SS-Obergruppenführer* Wilhelm Koppe, the HSSPF in Kraków, met with SD, Sipo, and police officials to discuss the creation of regional *Sonderkommando* 1005 units to operate throughout the General Government. It was one of these new units that arrived later in Płaszów to begin its grisly work. Spielberg poignantly captured the horror of these efforts in *Schindler's List,* though the scene with the body of "Red Coat" Genia was fictional. Francisco Wichter, the only Schindler Jew remaining in Buenos Aires and a close friend of Emilie Schindler's before her death in 2001, was forced to work for the *Sonderkommando* 1005 unit in Płaszów. A calm, kind, gentle man, it is hard to imagine what he went through during the time that he worked exhuming and burning bodies. Normally, the Germans shot the workers after they had completed their work. Somehow, Francisco survived. The work crews were ordered to dig up the bodies and carry them to the large pyre for burning. Francisco's job was to carry the bodies exhumed the night before to the wooden pyre. One morning as he walked to the stack of bodies, he saw the body of an eighteen-year-old girl sitting up and staring at him. He said he could not eat for two days afterwards and could still see her face.[178]

Maurice Markheim's experiences were even more gruesome. He was forced to work on one of the exhumation details during the winter when the ground was frozen solid. The inmates used axes to open the ground and, according to Markheim, if they struck someone's head, the brains would splash out. "When you discovered the face, you had to holler. A man came down with a pair of pliers, opened the mouth and pulled the gold teeth. You could recognize one thing: a child. [You could tell] a woman from a man by the hair only. The inmates on the exhumation details were forced to eat among the dead bodies and sit close to the pyres that were aflame twenty-four hours a day. After a while, the inmates working among the dead began to smell of death. Markheim said that even after two or three months in Brünnlitz, his body was "still smelling like the dead bodies, because the smell got under your skin."[179]

Jack Mintz (Jehuda Minc; Anschell Freimann) said that they carried the bodies on stretchers from the mass graves and then manually put them on the pyres. He added that the scene in *Schindler's List* where the inmates were loading bodies on a conveyor belt was wrong. Everything was done by hand. They then stacked wood on the bodies and lit the fire with tar paper. Jack worked with his older brother Iser on the exhumation detail. He particularly remembered one of the *Kapo*s (Italian for boss or chief), Ivan, who supervised his work crew. Ivan took gold teeth from the bodies to buy vodka, which he drank constantly. He would hit his workers over the head with a shovel to keep them in line though he seemed to favor Iser, who could take "a whole body on the shovel and put it on the stretcher." As a reward for his toughness, Ivan let Iser go to the kitchen for his crew's food ration. This allowed Iser to have the first bowl of soup, which meant he could scoop "from the bottom, where anything of nutritional value might have sunk."[180]

All these experiences helped those Jews who worked for or were saved by Oskar Schindler during the war appreciate the time they spent in Emalia or Brünnlitz. Oskar Schindler was no angel and certainly had his flaws. Moreover, his motives were not solely humanitarian. He was a business-man who made a great deal of money during the war and hoped to do so afterwards, hopefully with the Jews who were part of his workforce in Kraków and Brünnlitz. But life as an SS slave laborer in one of Oskar Schindler's factories was heaven compared to the constant threat of death in Płaszów under Amon Göth. And even though Oskar Schindler seemed close to Göth, this relationship had more to do with the role he had to play to have a free hand with his Jewish and Polish workers than it did with sympathy for Göth's murderous behavior in Płaszów. Yet many of Schindler's Jews remained suspicious of him because of this relationship and his relationship with the SS until after the war. In conversations among themselves and with other survivors, they came to realize the remarkable efforts of Oskar Schindler to save their lives, regardless of the motivation. Simply stated, they were alive because of him.

7.

SCHINDLER'S EMALIA SUB-CAMP

THE CLOSING OF THE KRAKÓW GHETTO IN THE SPRING OF 1943 created problems as well as potential opportunities for Oskar Schindler. If he wanted to maintain his enamelware operations in Kraków, he would have to consider doing what Julius Madritsch would do—move it to the new Płaszów forced labor camp run by Amon Göth. But there was another option, and that was maintaining his operations in Podgórze as a sub-camp of Płaszów. But to do this, he would have to win the support of Amon Göth, whose goodwill, support, and important ties to SS leaders in the General Government were essential for such an operation.

According to Mietek Pemper, Schindler established contact with Göth soon after the Viennese SS officer took command of Płaszów. Both men evidently hit it off quickly, in part because they were the same age and "were big, athletic, strong, with the feeling that the world belonged to them."[1] Pemper said that this created "a certain sense of connection" between Schindler and Göth despite the considerable differences between them. Schindler, Pemper admitted, was a "contact-artist" who quickly "took advantage" of his new relationship with Amon Göth.[2] Pemper said that Schindler "came from the region that produced the upright soldier Schweijk. And these Schweijk-like features, he played these out wherever it was necessary."[3]

His allusion to Jaroslav Hašek's brilliant Czech satire, *The Good Soldier Švejk* (*Osydy Dobrého Vojáka Švejka za Svetové*; 1921–1922), is interesting and is quite revealing. The central figure in Hašek's novel is Josef

Švejk (Schwejk or Schweik), at first glance a bumbling fool, who served in the Austrian army in World War I. What Švejk does best is confound and trick those around him. Švejk became, for better or worse, a symbol of the Czech national character after World War I. Švejk, Ivan Olbrecht said, was a "smart idiot, perhaps an *idiot savant,* who through his stupid but cunning good nature [had to] win everywhere because it [was] impossible for him not to win." He added: "This is Švejk."[4] But Czechs saw him differently. In pubs throughout Prague during the 1920s and 1930s there were pictures of Švejk which bore the simple statement: "Take it easy!" often followed by "And keep your feet warm!"[5] For many Czechs, Josef Švejk was an extremely adaptable person who made the best of bad circumstances. And this is certainly what Oskar Schindler did. So perhaps Mietek Pemper's characterization of him as a Švejk-like figure is more on the mark than one realizes.[6] Peter Steiner concludes in his analysis of *The Good Soldier Švejk* that

> in a world dominated by power, Švejk is an underdog, the object of manipulation and coercion by inimical social forces that constantly threaten his very existence. Yet, despite the tremendous odds against him, he passes through all the dangers unharmed. Švejk's mythical invincibility makes him a modern "epic hero" with whom his compatriots identify and of whose exploits they talk because they see in him "a modern Saint George, the hero of a saga of a single mind's triumph over the hydra of Authority, Regime, and System—of the mind disguised as feebleminded-ness in the war of absurdity in the guise of Wisdom and Dignity—the sense of Nonsense against the nonsense of Sense."[7]

The horrible world of Oskar Schindler was nothing like that of the mythical figure, Josef Švejk. And Schindler could never be considered feebleminded. Yet both men, both real and fictional, dealt with insurmountable odds to defy the established authoritarian order of the day. Švejk managed to preserve his own dignity, but Oskar Schindler managed to save the dignity and lives of hundreds.

It could certainly be argued that Oskar's adaptability to the worst of circumstances (and individuals) was what made him so successful, particularly when it came to his relationship with Amon Göth; in fact, one wonders whether there was more to Schindler's relationship with Göth than mere business. There is no evidence, for example, to indicate that Julius Madritsch, one of the principal factory owners in Płaszów and a person

who aided and cared as deeply for his Jewish workers as Schindler, ever
became close friends with Göth. Madritsch's relationship with Göth was
strictly business. However, through no fault of his own, Madritsch was
never able to arrange the large-scale transfer of his factory and Jewish
workers to safety in the last year of the war. So perhaps Oskar's close ties
with Göth helped pave the way for his remarkable deed.

Helen Sternlicht Rosenzweig ("Susanna"), told me that Madritsch was
never close to Göth and that she never saw him in the villa with women.
On the other hand, Schindler seemed to have developed a relationship
with Płaszów's commandant based on something more than just business.
We know he was comfortable around Göth and frequented the parties the
commandant hosted regularly at his villa. Certainly Schindler's behavior
around Göth confused "Susanna," though she thought he was essentially
a good man. She often saw Oskar at the villa and came to distrust him because of his friendly attitude toward Göth, whom Oskar called "Mony."
She was also disgusted when she saw Oskar with women other than his
wife. One evening, for example, a drunken Schindler showed up at Göth's
villa accompanied by several women. Occasionally, he would bring Emilie. Helen knew she was Oskar's wife and said she always looked "very
distinguished and refined."[8]

Oskar described the parties he attended at Göth's villa as increasingly
bacchanalian. Schindler often supplied the liquor and the women for such
occasions, which "were apparently very wild." There were usually from
ten to twenty SS and Gestapo officers at Göth's parties, some of them of
high rank. One party took place in the midst of a heavy snow storm. As
snow drifts built up outside Göth's villa, someone suggested that they
throw all the naked women at the party outside in the snow.[9]

"Susanna" remembered an embarrassing incident that involved Oskar
and one of his girlfriends. One day "Susanna" was in the kitchen when
the upstairs bell rang. There were two rooms on the upper floor of Göth's
villa. One had exercise equipment in it and the other contained two beds.
When "Susanna" entered the bedroom, Schindler was lying there naked.
As she walked over to the bed, he grabbed her with his right hand and exclaimed, "Susanna, Susanna!" Oskar then tried to pull her towards him.
"Susanna" was able to resist him by holding on to a nearby armoire. A
naked girl was lying beside Schindler.[10]

Yet in fairness to Schindler, it is important to add that "Susanna" also
talked a lot about Schindler's kindness and his promise to save her. And at
a distance it would seem as though Oskar's special relationship with Göth

was the price he had to pay to maintain some autonomy from the SS and protect his ever-expanding Jewish labor force. But was it really necessary for Schindler to go to such an extent to befriend Göth? Was Amon Göth a key figure in Oskar's ability first to hire and protect his growing Jewish labor force in Emalia and later to transfer his factory, with his Jewish workers, to Brünnlitz? This must all be looked at in the broader context of the complexities of operating factories that used Jewish slave labor in the General Government after 1942.

By the time Göth had closed the Kraków ghetto and fully opened the Płaszów forced labor camp of the SS and Police Leader in the Kraków District *(Zwangsarbeitslager Plaszow des SS- und Polizeiführers im Distrikt Krakau)* in the spring of 1943, the SS was now in full control of the various factories in these camps, which were overseen by the SS's German Equipment Works (DAW; *Deutsche Ausrüstungswerke GmbH*) as part of Oswald Pohl's Office Group W.[11] The SS had always used forced labor in its growing network of camps throughout the Third Reich. However, the nature of this labor changed with the fortunes of war. This was particularly true after Albert Speer became Nazi Germany's economic tsar in early 1942 as Reich Minister for Armaments and Munitions *(Reichsminister für Bewaffnung und Munitionen)*. Walther Schieber, one of Speer's closest advisers and an honorary *SS-Brigadeführer,* approached Himmler soon after Speer's appointment about expanding armaments production in the concentration camps. In response, Himmler, driven by a desire to create more economic autonomy for the SS as well as a desire to help the war effort, decided to revamp the organizational structure of concentration camp administration by appointing Oswald Pohl the new head of WVHA.[12]

On March 16, 1942, after meeting with Himmler, Speer's armament specialists met with Richard Glücks to work out the new arrangement between the Armaments Ministry and the SS. Himmler had earlier insisted that all armaments factories that used concentration camp inmates had to be located within the confines of the camps. Speer's armaments specialists would be responsible for the design of these factories and their administration. The accord concluded "relocated armaments industries in the concentration camps will continue under the guidance of their individual firms, not only for production but under all economic considerations as well."[13]

This was the core arrangement between the SS and the Armaments Ministry that governed the operation of armaments factories in the concentration camps for the rest of the war. According to Michael Thad Allen, "the ministry relied upon the SS to manage the prisoners' bodies—getting rid of those who had been worked to death and supplying fresh replacements. Meanwhile, the Office Group D left technical management to industry."[14] This latter office was part of the SS's Economic and Administrative Main Office (WVHA; *Wirtschafts-und Verwaltungshauptamt*) in Berlin. Though technically under the incompetent *SS-Gruppenführer und Generalleutnant der Waffen-SS* Richard Glücks, *Amtsgruppe* D was really run by the head of *Amtsgruppe* D2, *SS-Obersturmbannführer* (later *SS-Standartenführer*) Gerhard Maurer, who oversaw all aspects of prison labor.[15]

After Maurer assumed his post in 1942, he began to implement policies designed to give a better idea about the number of prisoners in each of *Amtsgruppe* D's camps. From Maurer's perspective, the only way he could properly manage a camp's prison population and get a better sense of its potential labor output was to have more detailed statistics on the health, good and bad, of its inmates. He also gave SS camp physicians a great deal of power periodically to "cull" inmate populations, even at factory sites, to weed out prisoners too sick, injured, or aged to work. The results of these inhumane reforms did see a decrease in slave laborer mortality rates of 10 percent to 2 percent to 3 percent from the end of 1942 until early 1944, though these figures should be put in the context of the rising slave labor population that continued to grow in the camps during the same period.[16]

But the use of slave labor proved problematic and, when combined with other issues, particularly the lack of SS managerial skills in the camps in question, it created serious production problems in the scattered SS armaments factories. Himmler blamed the Armaments Ministry for these failures and, by the spring of 1943, began to suggest more direct SS managerial control over these factories. Yet, months earlier, Speer had already begun to suggest an expanded role for the SS in armaments productions. In a meeting with Hitler, Speer suggested that the SS be given 3 percent to 5 percent of all arms production. He also told Oswald Pohl that the SS should consider dropping its insistence that all SS armaments work be done within the confines of established concentration camps. Himmler, Speer suggested, should consider expanding beyond these camps into "the open fields."[17] Pohl added: "We may put up an electric fence around it; then we can provide the necessary number of prisoners; and then the factory can be run as an SS armaments works."[18]

But *Amtsgruppe* D was not the only WVHA office that Schindler, Madritsch, and Göth would have to deal with in planning the construction of any armament-related factory workshops at Płaszów. They would also have to work with *Amtsgruppe* C, which oversaw all SS construction projects. Office Group C was overseen by *SS-Oberführer* Dr. Hans Kammler, who brought the same ruthless professional skills to his job that Maurer had to Office Group D. Kammler put together a staff of civilian trained engineers who insisted on exacting standards when it came to the construction of SS facilities, whether they be in concentration camps or elsewhere. Over time, Kammler's office gained a solid reputation for excellence not only in the SS but throughout the Third Reich's armaments construction industry. In 1944, Hermann Göring appointed Kammler, with Hitler's approval, as head of *Sonderstab Kammler* (Special Staff Kammler), which oversaw special construction projects for the SS. Kammler reported directly to Himmler, thus bypassing Pohl.[19] Sadly, the admired standards of Kammler's office cost Diana Reiter, a Jewish engineer, her life when she was shot by Albert Hujar in Płaszów for questioning construction standards on a particular building. She was killed by an SS man for trying to enforce SS building regulations.[20]

The other element that Schindler, Madritsch, and other factory owners had to contend with was the Wehrmacht High Command's (OKW; *Oberkommando der Wehrmacht*) Armaments Inspector in the General Government (*Inspektor der Rüstungsinspektion im Generalgouvernement*), *General* Maximillian Schindler, who was responsible for all aspects of armaments production. *General* Schindler's biggest problems centered around labor shortages, which intensified with the transfer of large numbers of Poles to forced labor situations in the Third Reich and the mass murder of Jews. The labor shortage, in turn, affected production goals in factories throughout the region. *General* Schindler had been caught in the middle of the controversy that erupted between the Wehrmacht and Himmler over this issue in 1942. As a result, the SS had gained control over the supply of slave labor used in most armament works in the General Government.[21]

Gerhard Maurer of *Amtsgruppe* D2 now worked to stabilize the labor shortage crisis by reducing concentration camp mortality rates even though the shortages remained one of *General* Schindler's principal concerns. *General* Schindler was also responsible for military production quotas and was the one who initially suggested that factories in the Reich producing uniforms and shoes be transferred to the General Government where they could be made by Jewish slave labor. And any owner, or, for that matter, forced or concentration camp commandant in the General

Government who wanted to have his workshops or factory declared war essential, had to have the approval of *General* Schindler. Amon Göth, for example, could not have Płaszów declared a permanent concentration camp in early 1944 until he had received *General* Schindler's stamp of approval.[22]

What transpired was a complex application process for the opening, expansion, or building of armaments-related facilities that intended to use Jewish slave labor. It began with simultaneous applications to the Armaments Ministry, which would turn the matter over to *General* Schindler's office in Kraków. His office would have to approve of the armaments-related goods produced in the proposed factory. The Armaments Inspectorate was not only concerned about labor resources but also the supply of raw materials for production use and the military value and production quotas of the goods proposed for production. If the workshop or factory was tied to a forced labor or concentration camp, the owner, after receiving the approval of the SS, would inform Maurer's Office Group D2 of his labor needs. It would inspect all housing facilities to see whether they met SS standards and make certain that proper security measures were in place in the factory to prevent prisoners from escaping. Office Group D2 would then issue a permit that allowed the use of slave laborers. Representatives of the newly approved firm could then choose the workers they wanted in their factory or workshop. Depending on the situation, this meant the chosen workers would live in the concentration camp and be marched to and from the camp factory site or would be housed in an SS approved factory sub-camp. By the spring of 1944, Speer's Armaments Ministry took over the entire application process and required all businesses to deal directly with it before final approval.[23]

What further complicated all of this, particularly for Oskar Schindler and Amon Göth, was the fact that they never truly produced military essential items in the factories in Płaszów or Emalia. How did they get away with producing uniforms, enamelware, and other items of questionable military value to a German war machine struggling with a severe arms shortage? A large part of the explanation centers around the power of corruption and favoritism in the General Government, particularly in SS circles.

Yet it should be remembered that the SS was not just interested in the manufacture of weapons, which never became a big part of its burgeoning industrial empire. The SS got into the manufacturing business primarily to give it an economic base from which to supply its outposts in the newly occupied territories in the east, although Speer and the

Wehrmacht suspected that Himmler wanted either to take over the war economy or to use its expanded role in war production to better arm the elite Waffen SS units. Occupied Poland and Russia were the new colonial areas of the Thousand Year Reich, the proposed breeding ground for a superior Aryan race that was slowly to eliminate the inferior races from the face of Europe. The SS needed every kind of manufactured good to maintain itself as Germany's elite racial and spiritual organization. Consequently, though the SS did undertake modest though not overly successful arms production activities at some of its concentration camps, the WVHA often subcontracted its armaments production to maintain the façade that it was contributing to the total war effort while continuing to operate factories of lesser military value through its network of camps and sub-camps and thus insure its economic survival when peace came. And even after the adoption of the new *Siegentscheidend* (Decisive for Victory) theme after Stalingrad, factories under DAW continued to produce goods of questionable value to the desperate war effort. Consequently, when Oskar Schindler sought to add a small wing to his Emalia operations for arms production, it was something of a cover for the pots and pans that Emalia continued to produce throughout most of the war. [24]

The illogic of such policies worked to Oskar Schindler's advantage and enabled him to produce far more valuable black market trade goods than essential military items at Emalia. We know that Schindler considered his armaments work at Emalia an important, though not essential, part of his operations, yet we know little else about it. He stated in his 1945 financial report that he produced about RM 15,000,000 ($6 million) worth of enamelware in Emalia and only about RM 500,000 ($2 million) worth of armaments products.[25] Schindler's interest in developing a small armaments operation at Emalia seemed to develop some time in 1943. Mietek Pemper said that whenever Schindler came to Płaszów during this period to order tools for his factory, he would stop by the camp office to talk to him and Stern. Pemper said that he urged Oskar to create a "sole armaments production, because you can't win a war with kitchenware products." On one occasion Oskar told Pemper that "he was already thinking about shifting production to armaments." Pemper added that "Oskar still had close contacts with his former Abwehr colleagues and very good connections to the Armaments Inspectorate, whose highest boss was *General* Schindler." Most people assumed that General Schindler was a relative of Oskar's, who "never denied clearly" that he and the general were related.[26]

The large, hangar-style factory building constructed by Siemens-Bauunion G.m.b.H. was not completed until the summer of 1944, and this could be one of the reasons Oskar produced little in the way of armament-related items at Emalia. But what was important here was not Oskar's armaments production output but his intention to produce armaments once the large Siemens building was completed. The construction of the armaments factory building, and his use of Jewish labor to help build it, was the key to his success in increasing the size of his slave labor force during this period. Intention, in other words, was more important than reality.

Yet once Oskar received permission from the Armaments Inspectorate and the SS to operate his factory, he could use SS regulations about maintaining low mortality rates among Jewish workers to help create better working conditions for them. Oskar kept them healthy, which in turn kept them out of the hands of the death squads at Płaszów and the transports to death camps. And the key to good health, beyond avoiding beatings and overwork, was food. To an extent, this can be seen as simply good business. The SS was always ready to take away workers deemed unfit for labor. But if a factory owner mistreated his workers to the extent that he had a high mortality rate, which the SS theoretically discouraged, he would have to replace them with unskilled workers who would have to be trained in various production skills. The operation of factories under DAW's watchful eyes, at least from the perspective of the civilian owners, was all about making a profit; it followed that treating one's workers, whether they be Jewish or Polish, was just good business.

Emerging from all this in the fall of 1942 were new opportunities and problems concerning Jewish forced and concentration camp labor. The agreement worked out between the Armaments Inspectorate and the SS about Jewish labor in the General Government left grey areas that Himmler and Pohl sought to take advantage of. Uniform production now became an area of exclusive SS control in the General Government, which explains why Julius Madritsch was forced to move his workers and sewing machines to Płaszów. Schindler, on the other hand, was helped by Himmler's decision to open factories beyond the confines of the SS camps in "the open fields," as Albert Speer put it. But Schindler knew he would need other things to insure the transformation of Emalia into an SS-approved sub-camp away from Płaszów, and that would be the support of Amon Göth, who had important SS connections, and Schindler's ongoing friendship with important figures in the Armaments Inspectorate in the General Government.

The same thing could be said of Julius Madritsch, though his situation was more complex than Schindler's because he needed SS approval not only to move his Kraków operations and workers to the new forced labor camp but also to do the same eventually for his factory in Tarnów. Evidently, *SS-Hauptsturmführer* Julius Scherner, the HSSPF in the Kraków district, opposed the movement of Madritsch's factory in the former ghetto to Płaszów. It is possible that Scherner was aware of Madritsch's considerable efforts to hide, save, and help Jews escape from his factories in Kraków and Tarnów. This could be the explanation for an incident that took place just before the SS began to close the Tarnów ghetto on September 2, 1943. The day before, Madritsch and his Kraków manager, Raimund Titsch, were invited to an 8:00 P.M. dinner at Göth's villa. Both men accepted Göth's invitation with mixed feelings. When they arrived, Göth told them "in a friendly way that tonight the evacuation of all Jews of the Kraków district [which included Tranów and Bochnia] would take place, and that [they] had to be his guests" until the next morning. Göth then left Madritsch and Titsch in the company of two SS officers who "just tormented" them because they could not show how they felt, "much less talk about how afraid [they] were."[27]

At 5:00 A.M. the next morning, Madritsch and Titsch were released and drove immediately to Tarnów, where they met Göth, who was overseeing the brutal closing of the ghetto there. Göth promised Madritsch that none of his "people" would be harmed. Madritsch said that as far as he could tell, none of his Jewish workers were killed in the closing of the Tarnów ghetto. He credited his factory manager, Dr. Adolf Lenhardt, for this. Evidently, Dr. Lenhardt had managed to smuggle some of Madritsch's workers into columns of workers destined for the Kunzendorf forced labor camp at Trzebinia, about twelve miles northeast of Auschwitz. Later, Madritsch and Lehardt drove to Kunzendorf with a plan to help free some of their former workers and help them escape into Slovakia. Their plan was thwarted, Madritsch claimed, "because of the incomprehensible attitude of the Jewish police at Kunzendorf."[28]

Eleven days later, Madritsch received permission from Scherner to open his new factory in Płaszów, though he did not go into details in his wartime memoirs, *Menschen in Not! (People in Distress),* about the "fight" within the SS that broke out over his application to move his sewing factory. Madritsch's new contract with the SS "was valid until the end of the war."[29] Madritsch said that the principal reason for his success was the backing of Amon Göth, who supported the move "solely because [Madritsch and Titsch] were his fellow countrymen."[30]

There is no doubt that Madritsch had to bribe Scherner, Göth, and other SS men for their support. Unlike Oskar, who broke down the amount of money he spent (Zł 750,000; $234,375) for bribes to the SS and others, Madritsch cited only the money he paid the SS each month for subsistence (Zł 350,000; $109,375) and "food subsidies" (Zł 250,000; $78,125). The latter payments to the SS had "to be balanced through sales on the black market."[31] And though Göth and other SS officers undoubtedly skimmed as much of this as they could from the top, Madritsch said that other costs centered around "the constant little gifts for the 'attention of the other side' [which] amounted to considerable sums, since not only prominent persons but also a high number of little people needed to be satisfied." He included in this list of "little people" a small group of Jews who had "friendly relations with the camp commanders."[32] Given the size of his operation, which was a little larger than Schindler's, one would assume that Madritsch was forced to pay bribes that exceeded the estimated Zł 750,000 Oskar Schindler spent on bribes during his years in Kraków.[33]

However, Raimund Titsch said after the war that Madritsch paid Göth far less money in bribes than Schindler. The reason, he explained, had less to do with Madritsch's friendship with Göth, which was far less intimate than the one the commandant had with Schindler. Madritsch's relationship with Göth was "enforced by the war" and influenced by the fact that Göth and Madritsch (and Titsch) were from Vienna. As Titsch later explained, Madritsch and Göth enjoyed a "Viennese rapport" that Schindler "was not able to take advantage of."[34]

Julius Madritsch had to wait six months for approval from the SS and the Armaments Inspectorate to move his sewing factory from the former ghetto to Płaszów. Schindler seemed to have gotten approval sooner, though his comments about this are confusing. In one of his most important postwar accounts about this matter, which he repeated elsewhere, he explained that in "1942 the systematic persecution of Jews began in the entire Polish territory [elimination of Jews from business life, liquidation of the ghettos, opening of death camps]." He went on: "I had to make a decision: Either I would do without the employment of Jews and therefore leave them to their fate, which is what 99 percent of the Kraków firms that had employed Jews did, or I would construct privately a factory camp and have the Jews live and work there." He added that "within a few days a factory camp had been erected, and hundreds of Jews had been saved from deportation." Several important details, though, are missing from this explanation. What is unclear from all of this is the time frame for the construction and opening of the *Schindler Nebenlager* (Schindler sub-camp).[35]

We know from the testimony of *Schindlerjuden* such as Sol Urbach and Mietek Pemper that after the liquidation of the Kraków ghetto in mid-March 1943, Schindler's Jewish workers were housed in barracks at Płaszów and then driven in trucks each day to Emalia for their twelve-hour shifts. Soon, though, the SS decreed that the trucks were needed for the war effort and the prisoners were marched to and from the factory by SS guards. Itzhak Stern said that this changed on September 1, 1943, when Göth decreed that Jewish inmates could no longer work outside of Płaszów or its sub-camps and were to remain in the camps twenty-four hours a day. Poles, on the other hand, could still work outside the camps. But well before Göth issued this decree, Mietek Pemper said that Schindler went to the commandant and argued that the two-mile hike from Płaszów was tiring for his workers and made them less productive. He also told Göth that it would be too expensive to pay to transport them in civilian vehicles. And thus, concluded Pemper, "a few practical arguments—and hundreds of people were protected from the arbitrary actions of the SS people."[36]

This version of how Oskar got to know Amon Göth is quite different from the one that Schindler told Reszőe Kasztner and Shmuel Spring-mann, two Jewish Agency representatives in Budapest in November 1943. Schindler explained that he decided to befriend Płaszów's commandant after Göth informed him that he would no longer supply Emalia with Jewish workers because they had "gone to work [at Emalia] without an SS guard."[37] It is hard to imagine that Jewish workers were ever permit-ted to leave Płaszów without an SS guard contingent, though anything is possible. In my many discussions with Sol Urbach about his experiences at Emalia and Płaszów, he always emphasized the tight control the SS maintained over the Jewish workers, particularly as they were marched first from the ghetto to Emalia and from Płaszów to Emalia and back. The idea that a large unescorted group of Jews from the forced labor camp was permitted to walk the two miles to Schindler's factory along one of Kraków's busiest streets borders on fiction.

Yet when did this all take place? There are several clues and they do not really give us the precise date for the construction of Schindler's sub-camp. The first is the *"Lageskizze"* (camp sketch) dated May 6, 1944. It provides a detailed description, size-wise, of all of the buildings in Emalia including dates of construction. It does not provide such details for the sub-camp, but does note that the *Arbeiter-Wohnlager* (Workers Residential Camp) was constructed in 1942–1943, indicating that Schindler began construction of his sub-camp before the closing of the ghetto. But if that was so, why did he order his workers to remain in the factory when the ghetto was being closed in mid-March 1943 and not return to Płaszów, unless the sub-camp was simply under construction and not ready for occupation? The only clue we have comes from a document from the Żydowski Institut Historyczny (Jewish Historical Institute) in Warsaw dated May 25, 1943. It is a four-page *Verzeichnis* (list) of 191 male Jewish workers who were being transferred to four of the factories that would comprise the *Schindler Nebenlager* (sub-camp): Emalia, N.K.F. *(Neue Kühler-u. Flugzeugteile-Fabrik;* New Radiator and Aircraft Parts Factory), *Kistenfabrik* (Box Factory), and Chmielewski's *Barackenwerk,* which produced barracks for the Military Garrison Management *(Heerestandort-Verw.).* Oskar said that he ultimately housed 450 Jews from these factories in his sub-camp, so this is only a partial list of the Jews who lived in the *Schindler Nebenlager.* There were only seven *Schindlerjuden* on this list, so we can presume that most of the Jews on it worked for the other factories that surrounded Emalia. It is reasonable to assume that, by the late spring of 1943, Schindler's sub-camp was under construction.[38]

But what motivated Amon Göth to agree to Schindler's plan to open a sub-camp at Emalia? It is hard to imagine that he was swayed by Oskar's concerns about his workers being tired out by the daily march to and from Płaszów. Sol Urbach, for example, told me that as the inmates left their barracks each day to be marched to Emalia, their SS guards made them pick up a heavy rock in front of their barracks and carry it to the camp's gate. Each night when they returned to the camp, they had to pick up an equally heavy rock and take it back to the front of their barracks. On the other hand, there is no doubt that Göth was aware of Himmler's recent move away from insistence that all factories using Jewish slave labor be housed in SS-run camps. More than likely, it was this shift in SS policy combined with hefty bribes from Oskar Schindler that convinced Göth to go along with Oskar's plan. Göth knew that such a scheme would be well received by his SS superiors, many of whom were also being bribed by Schindler.[39]

The Schindler Nebenlager in Kraków

Today, there is nothing left of the former Schindler sub-camp site and one doubts whether anyone in the complex of workshops and studios now housed in Emalia's former buildings even knows an SS camp was located there during the war. To build his sub-camp, Oskar bought a former garden shop from a Polish couple, the Brilskis, just behind the Emalia complex. SS standards were strict when it came to the construction of a camp site, and Emalia was no exception. Moreover, the SS expected the owner who proposed to build a sub-camp on his factory grounds to pay the full cost of construction. Oskar estimated that it cost him Zł 600,000 ($187,500) to build the facilities for his Jewish workers and those from surrounding factories. He stated after the war that this involved building "fences, watch towers, numerous barracks, canalization, wash rooms and toilets, emergency rooms for doctors and dentists, 'hospital rooms' for sick men and women, camp kitchen, laundry rooms, barber, food-storage place, office rooms, and watch quarters for guard troops." Schindler also had to pay for the "necessary interior furnishing of the living/sleeping rooms, kitchen and dentistry."[40]

There are several architectural diagrams of the Schindler *Nebenlager*, or *Judenlager*, as it is described in the sub-camp's plans, in the Schindler collection in the Bundesarchiv in Koblenz that gives a better sense of what the sub-camp looked like. To visualize Schindler's factory complex and sub-camp, think of a collection of buildings that narrowly fronted on ul. Lipowa and ran in a perpendicular line from the factory complex in front with its fabled gate and glass stairway and ended with the fenced-in *Judenlager*. The principal factory buildings were just behind the front gate. As you entered the factory grounds, the first thing you saw was a large brick smokestack (this was torn down in the late 1990s). Just behind it and to the left was the *Emailwerk* (enamel works) and to the smokestack's right was the *Stanzwerk* (metal press works). The enamelware that was made in Emalia was first pressed out in the *Stanzwerk* and then carried across to the *Emailwerk,* where the raw pots and pans were dipped in enamel and then dried. In the fall of 1943, Siemens-Bauunion G.m.b.H. began work on a large hangar-like *Neue Halle,* which was intended to house a new stamping plant. After the war, Siemens estimated the cost of construction of the new building at RM 1 million ($400,000). Siemens completed the new and largest building in the Emalia complex in the summer of 1944. The Siemens factory building sits at the back of the former Emalia complex today.[41]

It was no accident that Siemens built Schindler's largest factory building. Siemens, like other prominent German companies during the Nazi era, contributed heavily to the Nazi Party and the SS, which insured that they would receive lucrative SS contracts. Siemens-Bauunion G.m.b.H., headquartered in Munich, was one of the subsidiaries of Siemens & Halske. In 1971, Siemens & Halske's postwar successor, Siemens AG, today one of the world's largest electronics and engineering companies, sold Siemens-Bauunion to Dyckerhoff & Widman. Though Siemens-Bauunion was certainly not in the same league as Krupp and I. G. Farben when it came to the use of Jewish slave labor, it was active in the Kraków area, where it used Jewish workers from the ghetto, the Kraków *Judenlager,* and Płaszów to build a railroad network around the city that involved constructing seventeen bridges across the Vistula River. Siemens-Bauunion stopped using Kraków's Jewish workers in the spring of 1943 after a typhus epidemic broke out in the Płaszów *Judenlager.* Siemens also built the transformer for Płaszów's electric fences.[42]

Immediately after World War II, 6,000 former slave laborers made claims against Siemens and the company ultimately paid DM 7,184,000 ($1,710,460) in compensation. All total, the payment to each Jewish claimant was worth about DM 3,300 ($785). Between 1958 and 1966, Siemens AG, along with I. G. Farben and Daimler-Benz, paid the Claims Conference (Conference on Jewish Material Claims Against Germany) DM 75 million ($17.9 million) for slave labor claims. But in the late 1990s, spurred by the Swiss bank scandal, which underscored not only Switzerland's significant industrial and financial support of the Third Reich and the failure of Swiss banks to do no more than token searches for Holocaust era assets, German companies, fearing new lawsuits, began to consider doing more to settle decades-long slave letter claims. In 1998, Siemens AG set up a $25 million fund to pay further slave labor claims; a year later, in response to several law suits, twelve of Germany's largest companies, including Siemens, now the second largest electronics company in the world, agreed to set up a Holocaust fund worth $3.3 billion to compensate the 230,000–250,000 former slave and forced laborers eligible for such payments, particularly in Central and Eastern Europe.[43] Some *Schindlerjuden* were eligible for payments from one of these compensation funds for their slave labor with Siemens-Bauunion at one of

Kraków's *Judenlager,* at Płaszów, or at Emalia. However, the amounts were usually so small that they were either not worth mentioning to me or were refused because, as some *Schindlerjuden* told me, no amount of money could compensate them for their suffering and losses.

Schindler's *Judenlager* at Emalia was built just behind and to the right of the Siemens factory building. Schindler's factory was wedged in between a number of other factories, so there was limited space for the Jewish camp. It was surrounded by double rows of barbed wire fencing with two watch towers just beyond the fence at either end of the small camp. Two guardhouses were located at either end of the camp just opposite the watch towers. There were three main barracks in the *Nebenlager,* two for men and one across the small courtyard for women. Several smaller *Neue Baracke* (new barracks) stood just behind these to house the other camp facilities. Sol Urbach told me that the barracks, which were prefabricated and probably built next door at Chmielewski's *Barackenwerk,* were put up pretty quickly. Schindler bragged to Kasztner and Springmann that he could build a barracks in seven to eight days. Schindler's detailed financial claims after the war do not provide many details about the *Judenlager,* probably because most of his efforts to secure reparations centered around the lost factory buildings in Kraków and Brünnlitz.[44]

Some confusion remains about the number of inmates housed in Schindler's *Judenlager.* Oskar claimed in his 1945 financial report, which became the basis of much of what he said later about his Jewish workers in Emalia, that 150 Jews were working for him in 1940; 190 in 1942; 550 in 1943; 1,000 in 1944; and 1,100 in 1945. Oskar used the final number of Jews transferred from Płaszów to Brünnlitz as the basis for his 1944 and 1945 financial reports. In the latter case, this included those Jews transferred to Brünnlitz from other camps during the last eight months of the war. From these estimates we can conclude that he used annual year-end figures for the number of Jews he employed at Emalia. But Oskar also said in the same report that he "saved another 450 Jews from deportation" who worked in neighboring factories and were housed in Schindler's *Judenlager.*[45] This means that before he was forced to move his Jewish workers out of Emalia in the late summer of 1944, Oskar Schindler had 1,450 Jews living in his sub-camp. Because about a third of his Jewish workers were female, we can conclude that he housed about 450 women and 900 men, each gender in separate barracks. It is difficult to determine the size of the barracks and how crowded it was in each *Judenlager* housing unit.

Hans Kammler's WVHA D3 construction office set the standards for the construction of concentration and forced labor camps and oversaw the building of Schindler's *Judenlager*. Comparatively, there were eighty-eight barracks at Płaszów; they ultimately housed 25,000 inmates, most of them Jews. Most of the prisoner barracks in Płaszów were built by the Chmielewski firm just next to Emalia. Each barrack held about 300 inmates though the statistics provided by Aleksander Bieberstein in his detailed study of Płaszów indicate that they varied in size according to SS housing needs. If we used Oskar's estimates for the number of Jewish workers he housed in 1943, it seems as though his barracks were built to house 300 workers apiece. But if we add the 450 other Jewish inmates from surrounding factories, it seems as though Oskar had ultimately to cram 450 workers into each of these barracks. Actually, this was not all that uncommon in SS-run camps. Karl Bischoff, the director of central construction at Auschwitz, initially planned to house 550 inmates in the barracks he built in Auschwitz II-Birkenau, but later changed the number to 744 inmates.[46] When Gerhard Maurer asked Amon Göth in the spring of 1944 whether he could house 10,000 Hungarian Jews temporarily until Auschwitz was ready for them, Göth said he could only do this if Maurer permitted him to do two things, "clean the camp out of the elements who were . . . unproductive, people who were old, sick, weak, unable to work, as well as children" and permit him to double the bunk capacity in each barracks by having the Jewish inmates share the bunks in twelve hour shifts.[47] So it was not unheard of to crowd inmates into the standard SS three or four tiered bunks with three to four inmates squeezed into a tiny 4-by-5-foot section. According to Sol Urbach, the barracks in Emalia were identical to those in Płaszów and just as crowded.[48]

But what distinguished Emalia from other sub-camps was the food and safety from SS abuse and murder. Jewish inmates in Płaszów even used a code word, "Paradise," when they wanted to refer to Emalia. Both Oskar Schindler and Julius Madritsch spoke of the money they spent to purchase extra black market food rations, particularly bread, for their workers. Madritsch estimated, for example, that he "brought into the camp about 6,000 loafs of bread, jam, and even cigarettes each week" for his workers as well as "other things that made it possible to fulfill small wishes to simply make life a little easier."[49] Oskar was even more precise. He said after the war that he had to buy all the food for his Emalia workers from 1942 until 1944 on the black market. Oskar wrote that the SS rations from Płaszów amounted to only 40 percent of what his workers needed to remain healthy. There were also occasions when Schindler and Madritsch got some food from Dr. Michał Weichert's Jewish Self-Help Society, which continued to operate in Płaszów until the summer of 1944. Oskar estimated that he spent about Zł 50,000 ($15,625) a month on black market food between 1942 and 1944, though he admitted that this estimate was probably too low. His total cost for extra food for his Jewish workers in Emalia during this period was more than Zł 1.8 million ($562,500).[50]

Dr. Aleksander Bieberstein had a lot to say about food rations when he testified in Amon Göth's trial. Since SS-rationed food for the Schindler *Judenlager* came from Płaszów, his observations tell us a lot about food conditions in both camps. During the construction of Płaszów, Dr. Bieberstein, who worked as a physician in the camp's hospital, treated the SS noncommissioned officer who was in charge of food for the prisoners. He showed Bieberstein the list of food, in grams, that each prisoner was to receive daily and weekly. The list included "meat, fat, marmalade, sugar, cheese, potatoes, gruel, salt, and bread." Soon after he read the list, Dr. Bieberstein got together with another Jewish physician, Dr. Otto Schwarz, and they transformed the food details on the list into calories. According to their calculations, each prisoner was to receive from 2,200 to 2,500 calories per day from the SS. This might sound like an adequate number of daily calories, but Dr. Bieberstein added in his testimony that it was barely enough for someone to survive doing hard manual labor. Inmates in Płaszów, he testified, needed from 4,500 to 5,000 calories a day to survive.[51]

In reality, the inmates in Płaszów received only about 700 to 800 calories from the camp's food rations, which consisted of black coffee without sugar at breakfast, a light, watery soup at lunch, and "vegetable water" in the evening. They also received a daily bread ration of 390 grams (13.6 ounces). Other than bread, the principal food item for the inmates was "sago," a dish made from barley. So if the SS allotted each worker a daily ration of 2,200 to 2,500 calories, and they got only 700 to 800 calories, where did the food go? It was kept for the SS in several large food storehouses in Płaszów. One of the storehouses was located in the Jewish prisoners' complex. But the best foods, which included the finest cuts of meats and fancy liqueurs and vodka, were kept elsewhere for the SS. Göth used some of the extra food that he kept from his prisoners for his parties and to sell on the black market. It is quite probable that some of the food that Schindler and Madritsch bought on the black market in Kraków originally came from the SS storehouses in Płaszów. Dr. Bieberstein stated in Göth's trial that the "money coming from these exchanges [black marketeering] of sugar and other products like fat, was used for maintaining a beautiful horse and cattle breeding, and generally for the accused's [Göth's] private use."[52]

But Emalia's Jewish workers did not rely solely on the black marketeering skills of Oskar Schindler, or, more particularly, of Abraham Bankier, for sustenance. There was also active illegal trading with Emalia's Polish workers, who were able to bring in food and items for barter with the factory's Jews. Schindler Jew Herman Feldman (Hermann Natan Feldmann) always made sure that his sister, Lola Feldman Orzech, had a little extra money each day to buy extra food from the Poles. But after September 1, 1943, when Göth ordered that all Jews remain in Płaszów or its sub-camps twenty-four hours a day, the cost of black market goods, particularly bread, skyrocketed in cost. A loaf of bread that once cost Zł 10 ($3.12) jumped to Zł 90 ($28.12) a loaf. And even if you did have money, the Poles now demanded a pair of shoes for a loaf of bread.[53] Sam and Edith Wertheim remembered trading "bread for cigarettes or the other way around, or socks, or a shirt."[54] But not all of Schindler's Jewish workers had money or goods to trade, so it is difficult to gauge how many of Emalia's workers were able to supplement the rations they got from the SS and Schindler with their own black marketeering. On the other hand, work in Emalia was less rigorous than that in Płaszów and the daily caloric needs were lower than those estimated by Dr. Bieberstein in the main camp.

But the *Schindlerjuden* in Emalia could never forget that they were ultimately under the control of the SS. Each of them was tattooed with the letters "KL" (*Konzentrationslager*; concentration camp) on the left wrist. Dr. Stanley Robbin (Samek Rubenstein), a Jewish physician at Emalia, would often perform the tattoo work. But some of the workers, such as Rena Fagen, defiantly began to suck the ink out of the tattoo soon after it was put on. She once told Elinor Brecher, the author of the invaluable collection of Schindler survivor testimony, *Schindler's Legacy,* that she "wouldn't even find a spot where it was now."[55] Such acts greatly annoyed the SS, who resented the special treatment that Jewish workers got at Emalia.[56]

In fact, keeping the SS at bay was one of Oskar's greatest challenges. Edith Wertheim said that Oskar installed a bell to warn the workers when a Wehrmacht or SS inspection team came into the factory. Henry Slamovich added that when the SS visited Emalia, Oskar "wined them and dined them" when they arrived and then took them on an inspection of the facilities. He added that the SS "never bothered to hit anybody."[57] Dr. Stanley Robbin described what happened when a group of SS visitors from Płaszów visited the small room with three bunks that served as the inmates' hospital. The SS men saw sixteen-year-old Sam Soldinger lying on one of the bunks complaining of a headache. They immediately wanted to know why he was in the hospital and wanted to kill him on the spot because he did not look ill. Oskar was able to talk them out of murdering Sam, who later settled in Phoenix, Arizona.[58]

And though Oskar usually did not have a lot to say after the war about his humanitarian efforts, he did go into some detail about a few of his deeds in a 1955 report he wrote in Buenos Aires about his experiences. The most famous story, which Thomas Keneally discussed in some detail in his novel, centered around a *Schindlerjude* named Lamus. One day Göth and a group of SS officers from Płaszów were inspecting the facilities at Emalia. Göth spotted Lamus pushing a wheelbarrow across the factory yard and thought he was moving too slowly. He ordered his bodyguard, *SS-Rottenführer* Franz Grün, to shoot Lamus on the spot. Grün began to position Lamus against an outside factory wall for execution while Göth and his entourage continued their inspection of the sub-camp. In the meantime, someone from one of the factory buildings who had seen everything rushed up to Oskar's office to tell him of the coming execution. Oskar said that he rushed down stairs and "bought his [Lamus's] life for a liter of vodka, literally one minute before the intended shooting."[59]

On another occasion, two Gestapo officers showed up to arrest Ignacy and Chaja Wohlfeiler and their three children for purchasing illegal Aryan papers. Oskar met the two agents and showed them upstairs to his office, where he wined and dined them. Oskar said that "three hours later two tipsy Gestapo men left the factory without the Wohlfeilers and without incriminating documents."[60] Chaja Wohlfeiler lived to play a modestly important role at the end of the Schindler saga. On May 8, 1945, it was she who embraced the first Russian soldier who helped liberate Brünnlitz.[61]

One Friday, Eduard Danziger and his brother, two Orthodox Jews, accidentally damaged one of the presses at Emalia. Oskar was away at the time and one of the sub-camp's spies reported the accident to Göth. He decided to hang the two brothers at Płaszów that evening to serve as an example to the other inmates. News of the planned execution spread quickly through the camp. In the meantime, Oskar had returned to Emalia and learned of the incident and the planned hangings. He immediately drove the two miles to Płaszów and somehow persuaded Göth to grant both men clemency, who were immediately returned to Emalia and safety.[62]

But there were also other stories from *Schindlerjuden* that were not as frightening and underscored the uniqueness of life in Schindler's sub-camp. Julius Eisenstein remembered, for example, the time he was playing soccer at Emalia and Oskar came up and asked, "How come you didn't give the ball to this guy?"[63] Julius added that by the time Emalia was finally closed in the fall of 1944, we were "spoiled and felt . . . liberated."[64] He thought that life in Emalia was heaven compared to the hell of Płaszów: "We ate a little better and we didn't get a beating every day."[65] And though he was not on the final list for Brünnlitz, he felt that it was the physical strength that he had been able to preserve at Emalia that helped him survive his forced march to the Flossenbürg concentration camp at the end of the war. These sentiments were shared by other Schindler Jews who did not make it to Brünnlitz.[66]

The inmates even found time for romance. When Irene Hirschfeld (Irena/Irka Scheck) arrived at Emalia, she was given a job carrying heavy metal pots on boards for drying after they had been dipped in enamel. She soon lost this job because she kept dropping the pots and was assigned to a nighttime floor sweeping detail. But she never forgot her femininity. Irene had a sheet and pillow case, from which she made a uniform and dyed it blue. She also had a pair of shoes and asked an inmate to make sandals for her from an old pocketbook. She said she "felt so dressed up, you have no idea!"[67] The reason for her attention to her looks was her new husband, Milton Hirschfeld. The couple had been secretly married in the ghetto and were able to walk and hold hands together in an enclosed yard at Emalia. Milton, who worked in the machine shop, made a comb and a signet ring for Irene. She later lost the ring at Auschwitz. Irene always thanked Oskar Schindler for the special times she had alone with Milton in Emalia. "The towers were full of Germans with machine guns, but they never used them." After the war, the Hirschfelds settled briefly in Paris, where they became reacquainted with Oskar Schindler; they ultimately settled in Oceanside, New York, on Long Island.[68]

Lola Feldman Orzech had a boyfriend at Emalia who worked at the N.K.F. factory next door. She said she was able to spend about half an hour each day with him. She added that though she was usually not hungry at Emalia, she was always "dead tired" and only had the energy to "smooch" with her boyfriend. Afterwards, she "went to bed," or, as she put it, "to hay."[69] But Lola also remembered the flirtations of a friend at

Emalia, Herta Nussbaum. Herta's husband worked at *Kabelwerk* and when Oskar Schindler began to flirt with her, she flirted back, hoping to get her husband transferred to Emalia. According to Lola, Herta spoke fluent German, "was blond, *zaftig* [Yiddish; well rounded], busty, but she had good legs." And her harmless flirtations with Oskar worked, because he soon found a job for Herta's husband at Emalia.[70] This is not the only time Oskar flirted with his female Jewish workers. One *Schindlerjude* made a point of telling me that Oskar made serious advances towards her, though out of respect for her I will not reveal her name.

Schindler Jew Barry Tiger (Berl Teiger) offers a different twist to Schindler's life at Emalia, where he had an apartment. Barry had various jobs at Emalia, including cleaning up after Oskar's parties. "They left a mess, but those were some good parties." As Barry told Elinor Brecher: "There were bottles all over the place—they did a lot of boozing—and SS uniforms. And you could find some leftovers there, too: cake and sandwiches. I saw [Schindler] with women. He was a lady-killer."[71]

But when Oskar invited Amon Göth to a party, it was usually at his apartment on Straszewskiego 7/2. It was more luxurious and away from the factory. Oskar was well aware of Göth's murderous ways when he was drunk and he did everything possible to keep him away from his Jewish workers. Emilie Schindler, who despised Göth, remembered one evening of heavy drinking with Göth and other SS officers. As the evening wore on and the SS guests got drunk, there was a knock on the door. It was an army major whom Oskar had invited to the party. Göth, drunk as usual, staggered over to the officer, who was much shorter than he was, and asked scornfully, "Who are you, you ridiculous midget?" The atmosphere changed quickly from one of friendly banter to tension and many guests began to leave, fearing Göth's rage. "You army types," Göth screamed at the major, "You think your hands are clean. You are such aristocrats, you fight with gallantry . . . you don't stick your noses into the carrion. . . . You cowards, you claim to keep your souls clean while we have to act as your guardian angels and watch your backs."[72]

But Oskar had to put up with Göth's tirades and other murderous flaws because he desperately needed his support to maintain his protective cocoon at Emalia. To a point, though, one could argue that the positive, moderate atmosphere that Oskar Schindler created at Emalia for his Jewish workers was simply a good investment in better production. And there is no doubt that this was true. Well fed, modestly secure workers performed much better than those who lived in constant fear for their lives.

And if they produced well, Schindler would make more money. But something happened in 1943 that put Schindler's efforts into a different light: his decision to begin to work first as a courier for the Relief and Rescue Committee of Budapest (Va'ada; *Va'adat ha-Ezra ve-ha-Hatsala be-Budapest*), which had been created two years earlier to help smuggle Jews out of Poland and Slovakia, and later for the Joint Rescue Committee (JRC) of the Jewish Agency of Palestine, an organ of the *Yishuv*, or Jewish community of Palestine that had absorbed Va'ada in early 1943. This involved not only dangerous trips to Budapest to meet with JRC representatives but also work with its representatives, who came to Kraków to try to gain more information about the fate of Jews in the General Government. Oskar also helped smuggle money, goods, and letters for Jews in Płaszów.

Abwehr, the Jewish Agency, and Schindler's Missions to Turkey and Hungary

The link between Oskar Schindler's growing sense of humanity towards his Jewish workers and his ties to Abwehr, particularly as they related to his later work with the Jewish Agency, is intriguing. It is difficult to determine the impact, if any, of his trip there for Abwehr in the fall of 1940 on the Jewish Agency's decision to approach him about a similar trip later. But his trip to Turkey for Abwehr did seem to secure his reputation as someone who was decisive and willing to take some chances for Admiral Canaris's organization. It also got him into trouble with German authorities in Kraków. Janina Olszewska, who ran Oskar's Emalia sales room in Kraków, said that the Gestapo arrested him in late 1941 in part because of "his strange contacts with the attaché in Turkey . . . and his dealings with the Polish and Jewish people."[73]

Oskar provided some details about his Abwehr mission to Turkey in 1940 in his 1951 letter to Fritz Lang. In addition, Josef "Sepp" Aue, Oskar's Czech Abwehr colleague, also mentioned his 1940 mission in his interrogation statements to the Czech secret police after World War II. Schindler told Lang that he was approached by Colonel Reiche, the head of Abwehr operations in Breslau, about a problem the Abwehr chief was having in Turkey. He asked Oskar to go to Ankara to see whether he could do something to resolve the conflict between the Reich diplomatic corps, the Wehrmacht, the SD *(Sicherheitsdienst der Reichführer-SS)*, the Nazi Party's counterespionage and intelligence service, and the Reich Propaganda Ministry (ProMi, *Propagandaministerium*, shortened title of

Joseph Goebbels's Reich Ministry for Volk Enlightenment and Propaganda, *Reichsministerium für Volksaufklärung und Propaganda*). Reiche was concerned that the conflict between these organizations was affecting the gathering and flow of intelligence information from Turkey, a vital field of Abwehr operations, to Canaris's headquarters in Berlin. Abwehr's difficulties, though, were much more complex than this.[74]

According to Oskar, the real problem centered around reserve Abwehr officers attached to the embassy in Ankara who were interested only in protecting their comfortable life style. They were affected by the "diplomats disease" and ran Abwehr operations in Ankara like "vegetable traders." Protected by their diplomatic immunity, these Abwehr officers paid for news in their favorite cafés regardless of its value to Admiral Canaris's organization. They were driven by a desire to "keep up the good life of diets of *Edelvaluta* (hard currency) and a career far from all fronts." But Abwehr's agents in Turkey were also hurt by conflicts with other German intelligence gathering organizations. Oskar told Lang that by the time he arrived in Ankara, Abwehr's operatives in Turkey were either dead, back in the Reich, or working for the SD, the SS intelligence service. There were almost no Abwehr transmissions coming from Ankara via Hamburg to Berlin. Previous efforts to straighten out Abwehr's problems in the Turkish capital had fallen prey to local Nazi Party infighting. So Abwehr sent Oskar Schindler to Ankara to straighten out the mess.[75]

Yet there was more to Abwehr's failures in Turkey than lazy agents. Abwehr intelligence operations abroad often overlapped, and Turkey was no exception.[76] In addition, there were conflicts with various Nazi Party organizations that not only affected Oskar Schindler's attitudes towards the SS, the Gestapo, and other Nazi groups, but also helped explain their own suspicions about him. In 1943, a Luftwaffe intelligence officer noted that spies in Ankara working for the Nazi Party's *Auslandsorganisation* (AO; Foreign Organization), which oversaw and coordinated Nazi Party organizations abroad, were "dilettantes lacking completely in know-how and experience."[77] In the field, the difficulties between Abwehr, the SD, and the AO centered around efforts by these agencies to win over each other's agents to their foreign intelligence gathering operations, which caused security lapses.[78]

These developments, however, only mirrored another issue that affected German intelligence gathering world-wide, the struggle between the SD and Abwehr for control over Germany's intelligence gathering apparatus. Reinhard Heydrich, backed by Heinrich Himmler, had fought for years to gain control of the Reich's foreign intelligence gathering network. After the creation of the RSHA in the fall of 1939, the SD's old Branch III, Ausland, now became RSHA Branch VI, Foreign Intelligence. By the time Oskar Schindler was sent to Ankara, the struggle was in full bloom. The situation in Turkey was particularly sensitive because of efforts by Germany and the Allies to draw Turkey into their respective camps militarily. Moreover, Turkey's geographic and strategic location made it a vital source of information gathering for the Balkans, the Soviet Union, and the Middle East.[79]

Walter Schellenberg, an SD officer who later came to head RSHA VI, said in his memoirs that by 1940 Heydrich had grown deeply suspicious of Canaris and Abwehr. From Heydrich's perspective, Canaris and Abwehr were unreliable for counterintelligence work. Heydrich thought that Canaris had revealed the date for the German invasion of Western Europe to the Allies and thought that the admiral would ultimately pay a price for this. Oskar Schindler's mission to Turkey in the fall of 1940 should be seen in this competitive light. And based on his statements to Fritz Lang in 1951, Schellenberg's assessment of Canaris was correct. Heydrich and Schellenberg had nothing to worry about, at least from Abwehr.[80]

The intense conflicts in Turkey between the SD, Abwehr, and other German intelligence-gathering organizations not only reflected the struggle between Himmler, Heydrich, and Canaris but also underscored the importance of Turkey to Hitler and Germany. Its strategic position and chrome resources kept it at the forefront of German efforts to keep neutral Turkey from aligning itself with Great Britain. Hitler had sent the veteran diplomat Franz von Papen to Ankara because he thought he possessed the necessary "finesse and intrigue" to keep Turkey from drifting into the Allied camp.[81] Von Papen complained that AO and Abwehr agents, though, were constantly "getting in each other's way" and on occasion "denounced each other's agents to the Turkish police."[82] Ultimately, Abwehr learned it could best protect its foreign operatives if they resigned their Nazi Party membership and stopped contacts with AO's agents abroad.[83]

This was the complex world that Oskar Schindler unwittingly entered in the fall of 1940. Oskar's trip took a few weeks. He took the journey in his beloved blue Horch, traveling "8,000 kilometers through the area." Oskar was not much of a typist and he certainly meant 800 kilometers (671 miles). He told Lang that he "saw much . . . not designated [on maps]" and noted three points that were not even mentioned in the Baedeker travel guide he carried with him. This was an interesting comment on the nature of intelligence gathering at that time but also on Oskar's earlier Abwehr training and activities before World War II. Schindler probably used Baedeker's *Konstantinopl und Kleinasien, Balkanstaaten, Archipel, Cypern* as his guide, which he could buy in any German book store in Kraków. More than likely, his route took him from Kraków southward to Budapest and from there through Belgrade in Yugoslavia and then to Sofia, the capital of Bulgaria. Oskar probably entered Turkey at Edirne, which was only a two- to three-hour drive from Istanbul.[84]

Oskar traveled on a diplomatic passport, which required him to present his credentials to Ambassador von Papen upon his arrival and departure. Before the war, Canaris and Ribbentrop had agreed to use the German diplomatic service as a cover for Abwehr agents abroad. The soldiers in the KO units were attached to embassies and consulates and always wore civilian clothing. This afforded Abwehr agents diplomatic immunity and other diplomatic privileges, though it also meant that as "diplomats," they could be expelled from the host country. This proved to hurt Abwehr's efforts later in the war.[85]

Schindler's meeting with von Papen must have been a special occasion for Schindler, given von Papen's past. The former German chancellor, politician, and soldier had served in Hitler's first cabinet as vice chancellor and brought considerable expertise in Turkish affairs when he assumed the ambassadorship in 1939. Yet Oskar was unimpressed with him. He evidently discussed the nature of his mission with the German ambassador, but found that "he only knew of a fraction of the intrigues and incidents among his collaborators." Oskar added that von Papen was "one of the primary objects of the SD." Yet, according to Schindler, the SD seemed more interested in von Papen's "church visits and tennis matches" than facts about "a new Russian-armour piercing shell."[86]

Oskar evidently caused a bit of a ruckus at the German embassy and told Fritz Lang that Reiche had received protests about Schindler's "methods and arguments." He also claimed that his methods, whatever they were, were only momentarily successful. Schindler noted that within months of his departure, Heydrich had effectively neutralized Abwehr operations in Ankara by having some of Colonel Reiche's agents transferred to active fighting units or having their diplomatic passports lifted while they were back in Germany for the Christmas holiday. In fact, these Abwehr officers were even denied temporary visas to return to Ankara to clear out their offices and tie up loose ends. Oskar concluded that "in the long view, the SD was already stronger than the OKH in 1940."[87]

Technically, Oskar's 1940 mission to Turkey was his last official assignment for Abwehr. However, three years later he would undertake another mission that was partially set up by *Major* Franz von Korab, Schindler's old Abwehr friend who commanded Canaris's operations in Těšín and Kraków and had, at least according to Emilie, helped Oskar find his first factory in Kraków. This time, Oskar did not travel on a diplomatic passport but on a visa arranged for him by Abwehr. While there, Oskar met with other Abwehr operatives in the Hungarian capital. There was also some talk of Oskar returning to Turkey to meet with the American ambassador and Jewish Agency representatives there, but this never took place.[88]

By late 1942, Oskar Schindler had already gained a reputation as someone who treated his Jewish workers well. This prompted Va'ada and the Jewish Agency to recruit him as a courier who would smuggle letters and money into the Kraków ghetto and later Płaszów to help buy needed food, medicine, and other goods on the black market for Jews. Oskar told two versions of his initial contact with Va'ada. In his 1945 report, he said his first meeting with a Va'ada representative took place in 1942 when a Viennese dentist and Abwehr agent, Dr. Rudi Sedlacek, walked into his office at Emalia and told Oskar that he was working with the Joint in Budapest. Dr. Sedlacek wanted to know whether Oskar could help him get letters that he had just brought from Palestine to inmates in Płaszów. Oskar told Sedlacek to see his close friend, *Major* Franz von Korab, "who had the same attitude towards Jews" as he did.[89]

But in another report to Yad Vashem a decade later, Oskar stated that he first met Dr. Sedlacek when *Major* Franz von Korab, a half-Jew who headed Abwehr operations in Kraków, brought Dr. Sedlacek with him to Oskar's office. Given his friendship with von Korab, the second version of this story seems more probable, since Schindler would probably have been more receptive to a proposal to help Va'ada if it had been initiated by his close friend, von Korab. According to Joel Brand, the head of *Tiyyul*, Va'ada's program to smuggle Jews out of Poland and Slovakia, Sedlacek "was an intellectual and was ashamed of the colleagues [in Abwehr] with whom he worked. He wished to appear better than they, and in conversation . . . he always stressed the contempt he felt for the other Abwehr agents."[90]

In his 1955 report, Oskar said that he did not know that Dr. Sedlacek was working with Va'ada. It was only during his second visit that Dr. Sedlacek revealed his true intentions to Oskar. By the time Schindler became seriously involved with these efforts, Va'ada had already been taken over by the Jewish Agency's JRC and became its Aid and Rescue Committee *(Va'adah; Va-adat Ezra Vehatzala)* in Budapest. Va'adah was headed by three men: Otto Komoly, a decorated war hero, engineer, and prominent Zionist, who served as its chairman; Reszőe (Israel) Kasztner, his gifted but controversial vice chair; and Shmuel Springmann, a jeweler and diamond merchant with strong ties to Budapest's diplomatic and intelligence community. Springmann served as Va'adah's treasurer. During his trips for the JRC to Budapest, Oskar met with Kasztner and Springmann, though Sedlacek was his principal JRC contact in Kraków.[91]

The decision to approach sympathetic Abwehr agents about helping rescue Jews in Eastern Europe came after the founding of Va'ada in late 1941. Joel Brand, one of the new organization's leaders, was its most flamboyant member and perhaps the most daring. In 1941, he paid Josef Krem, a Hungarian intelligence officer, to help rescue Brand's sister and husband from Kamenets Podolskiy, a Ukrainian city designated by the SS as a mass murder site. This triggered Brand's interest in rescue efforts, particularly from Poland into Hungary. Hungary, a German ally during World War II, adopted strong anti-Semitic policies towards its 825,000 Jews that limited their civil and economic rights. Yet until Germany invaded Hungary in the spring of 1944 to prevent it from shifting sides in the war, it remained a fairly open country where Jewish groups such as the Jewish Agency could operate with some degree of openness. Hungary also became a haven for thousands of Jewish refugees from Poland, Slovakia, and other Central European states.[92]

By the fall of 1942, Va'ada was having to deal with a flood of Jews from Poland and it desperately needed funds to help them. Springmann got in contact with an old school friend and jack-of-all trades, Andor (Bandi) Grosz, who went by the name André György, and asked him to help Va'ada establish contact with Zionist organizations in Istanbul. Springmann's efforts dovetailed with the request of the Istanbul office of the Jewish Agency to organize an "aid and rescue committee" and create a "courier service."[93]

Grosz would be one of the principal figures in the courier service though he did not work for the JRC for free. He always took 10 percent of any money he carried for Brand and Springmann from Istanbul. But

Grosz was more than just a courier. He also helped Va'ada and the Joint Rescue Committee establish important contacts in Budapest with Abwehr, the Wehrmacht's military counterintelligence service. According to Brand, "these people [Abwehr] not only restored ... contacts with the neutral countries, but also established channels of communication with the Jewish communities in Poland, in Czechoslovakia, in Germany proper, and in the other German-occupied territories."[94]

Such contacts were an integral part of the Jewish Agency's efforts in Turkey to do whatever it could to help the Jews in Nazi-occupied Europe. According to Stanford J. Shaw, neutral Turkey became the "Bridge to Palestine" for Europe's desperate Jewish population.[95] Opened in late 1942, the Istanbul branch of the Jewish Agency was headed by Chaim Barlas, who had previously run its Geneva office. By the time Oskar Schindler became involved with the Va'adah and the Jewish Agency, Jewish organizations from Palestine, the United States, and other countries had moved to Istanbul to help Europe's Jews, though the Jewish Agency was the dominant aid organization. Its JRC had delegates from several of these groups, including the influential Joint. During the Holocaust, about half the funding for JRC activities in Europe came from Jewish groups in Palestine and the other half came from the United States and other countries.[96]

One of the JRC's principal goals was to try to maintain contact with the Jewish communities of Central and Eastern Europe. Moshe Shertock, who would become a foreign minister and a prime minister of Israel, spent time during the war looking at JRC operations and called its operations in Istanbul "a peep hole to the other side."[97] Soon after the Jewish Rescue Committee opened its office in Istanbul, its office staff began to write hundreds of letters to Jews in occupied Eastern Europe asking them about conditions there and what it could do to help them. Initially, these letters went through the regular Turkish postal system, though soon the JRC used couriers to carry the letters into Nazi-held territory. Often the couriers were Turkish truck drivers and businessmen, though some diplomats and even representatives of the Papal Legate to Ankara (the Turkish capital), Angela Roncalli, the future Pope John XXIII, worked with the JRC. When the JRC learned of the increasing murders in the Nazi concentration and death camps, the JRC's staff sent letters of condolence to those who survived in hopes that they would continue to supply the Jewish Rescue Committee with information about conditions there. They supplied this information to the British government and hoped that London would lower its restrictions on the number of Jews permitted to enter

Palestine. But couriers such as Schindler did more than carry letters in and out of Nazi territory; they also brought food, clothing, and money with them, which the JRC hoped would be used to help purchase more food and clothing or to bribe German officials to help Jews.[98]

The JRC was particularly interested in recruiting German and Hungarian spies as couriers in hopes that these double agents could provide aid to Jews in Germany. And one of the spies they tried to recruit was Oskar Schindler.[99] It did not take Dr. Sedlacek long to size up Oskar and determine that he would be a willing courier for the Va'ada and later the JRC. As a test, Oskar was given RM 50,000 ($11,905) as well as some letters and other messages to distribute to JRC representatives in Kraków. Schindler did exactly as he was told, and the JRC now knew they could trust him.[100]

During the next year, he made six or seven trips to Kraków to meet with Oskar. According to Schindler, on three occasions Sedlacek brought money to help Jews in Płaszów as well as personal letters for them from Palestine. On one visit, Dr. Sedlacek gave Oskar RM 50,000 ($11,905); on another trip RM 75,000 ($17,857), and a smaller amount on a third trip. These figures differ somewhat from those cited by Dr. Reszőe Kasztner in his 1946 *Der Bericht des Jüdischen Rettungskomitees aus Budapest, 1942–1945 (A Report on the Jewish Rescue Committee in Budapest, 1942–1945)*. He said that Sedlacek brought Schindler "several hundred thousand Reichsmarks" during his three trips to Kraków.[101] Oskar, in turn, gave the money to Dr. Chaim Hilfstein, a Jewish physician at the sub-camp in Emalia, Abraham Bankier, Itzhak Stern, and Leon Salpeter, a prominent prewar Jewish leader and member of the former Kraków ghetto's *Judenrat,* for medicine and food in Emalia and Płaszów. Each of these prominent Jews went with Oskar to Brünnlitz and became some of his staunchest supporters after the war. Dr. Hilfstein told Joel Brand "that this money was always punctually delivered" by Schindler to Jewish representatives in the concentration camp.[102]

Once the JRC determined that Oskar was honest and trustworthy, they invited him to Budapest to give them information on the plight of the Jews in occupied Poland. The Jewish Rescue Committee's leadership saw Schindler as a leading German industrialist in Kraków and an important contact person in the capital of the General Government. Thomas Keneally said that Schindler's trip to Budapest took three days in a "freight van filled with bundles of the party newspaper, *Völkischer Beobachter,*" where Oskar was "closeted with the redolence of printer's ink and among the heavy Gothic print of Germany's official newspaper."[103] The implication that Oskar was somehow smuggled into Hungary in a newspaper truck is far from the truth, though sometimes the JRC did smuggle couriers into Nazi territory this way. According to Oskar, Dr. Sedlacek got him a visa to travel to Budapest.[104]

Oskar met with the JRC delegation in November 1943 in the Hotel Hungaria in Budapest. There is a detailed transcript of this meeting prepared by "Schmuel" (Springmann) and "Israel" (Reszőe Kasztner) in the Schindler *"Koffer"* files in the Bundesarchiv in Koblenz. It is titled *Bekenntnisse des Herrn X (The Confessions of Mr. X)*. Oskar also provided details of his visit with Springmann and Kasztner in his 1945 and 1955 reports. The report written by Kasztner and Springmann provides an insightful, and at times surprising look into the mind of Oskar Schindler. The authors stated that they had met with Oskar Schindler to try "to discover the truth." They said they tried to write down the conversation exactly as it had taken place and added no editorial comments. They also tried to capture the tone of the lengthy conversation with Schindler. They described "Mr. X" as a "tall, blond man with broad shoulders" who was from forty to fifty years old. What they wanted from Schindler, who, they explained, came "from the other side," was details on what was really happening to Jews in the General Government. "What does this terrible world look like behind the walls, viewed by one who at best could only be called an 'objective' spectator?" The two Jewish leaders were "excited and self-conscious" about meeting with Oskar, who "jovially invited" them to take a seat. There was a third person in the room, a *Schaliach* (Hebrew, emissary or courier), who gave Oskar a large package that contained "clothing, special brands of cigarettes and toiletry items." According to Kasztner and Springmann, these items were to be handed over to the SS leader on "whose good will the lives of 20,000 Jews currently depend[ed]."[105]

Oskar began the meeting by handing Springmann and Kasztner several letters from Abraham Bankier, Itzhak Stern and Dr. Chaim Hilfstein for people in Palestine. After a brief discussion about the difficulty of getting goods to Jewish prisoners in Poland, Springmann and Kasztner began to question Oskar about conditions there. Oskar was quite open about "the magnitude of the tragedy," which he described as a chapter of the political mistakes the Germans committed in Europe." He added that "crushing the skulls of infants with a boot [was] not proper military behavior." He thought that Germany's current problems centered around these mistakes and felt that the Wehrmacht had "accomplished great things and could have won the war." He added that German policies "regarding the defeated nations was a wrong one" and made the point of telling the two JRC representatives that he considered himself an Austrian, and was "not responsible for these 'mistakes.' The Prussians [were] to blame instead."[106] Perhaps Schindler forgot that Adolf Hitler was also an Austrian.

At this point, Kasztner and Springmann interrupted Oskar and wanted to know why the Germans were murdering the Jews. Oskar said that the Prussians had been "breeding militarism for two hundred years." During this period, they had no time to "develop their intellect." Now they were playing catch up with other countries that were ahead of them in intellectual development. They had already destroyed the intellectuals in many of the countries they had occupied and added: "You have to admit that the Jews are the most dangerous competitors in the realm of the intellect."[107] Needless to say, Schindler's comments about Jews upset Springmann and Kasztner, but they restrained from responding because they were not there "for the sake of polemics." They noted in the report that they were only interested in the psychological and political reasons for the catastrophe engulfing Europe's Jews. And they seemed to sense that Oskar knew a lot, though he seemed a bit hesitant to tell everything he knew.[108]

The JRC representatives then asked Oskar how many Jews were still in Poland. He replied that there were about seventeen camps in Poland that contained between 220,000 and 250,000 Jews. In addition, he said that there were just as many Jews in hiding, living on Aryan papers, or working for the partisans. Springmann and Kasztner then wanted to know whether there was a universal order to annihilate Jews. If that was true, then why were so many still alive? On the other hand, if there was no such order, why had the Germans already killed so many Jews? Oskar replied that he did not think such an order existed: "I rather assume that each SS leader wanted to outperform the others with annihilation numbers. None of these wanted to risk his career."[109] But, Schindler added, these SS men did not act on their own. "A higher authority most likely gave them the order to destroy dangerous or useless Jews. They executed this order with the brutality they had already used at home."[110] Schindler then described these SS leaders as "primitive people with bestial instincts" who had served previously in internment camps such as Dachau, where they had become "dull, bestialized."[111]

But Oskar, who tended to ramble, had still not answered their question about a "universal decree." Springmann and Kasztner had difficulty

believing that mid-level SS leaders could initiate such crimes without orders from above. Oskar said that there was no doubt that someone from
above "ordered the annihilation," though he doubted that their goal was
"total annihilation."[112] The two JRC representatives then wondered
whether the Jews still alive in Poland had a chance to survive the war.
Oskar told them that he was sure that those still alive would survive the
war and mentioned Himmler's decision several weeks earlier to halt the
murderous assault against Jewish workers in forced labor situations
throughout occupied Poland. Oskar interpreted this to mean that the ten-
dency was obvious: "One wants to preserve the Jewish work force." He
noted that over the past few months, the "smaller camps were liquidated
and able Jewish workers from the province were concentrated around industrial centers."[113]

Christopher Browning, in his comments on this shift in policy, wrote
that the camps designated for preservation "continued in operation until
the approach of the Red Army forced closure, and even then the inmates
were not killed on the spot but rather evacuated westward. Moreover,
within at least some camps, the murderous regimen was significantly
moderated over time. The massive selections and gratuitous killings were
curtailed, and death from exhaustion, malnutrition, and disease dropped
significantly." Browning called this a new period of "precarious stabil-
ity."[114] Oskar Schindler had better insight into this matter than anyone
imagined at the time.

Oskar went on to explain that Himmler's decision to stop the liquidation of the slave labor camps was brought about by the intervention of
the Military Economics and Armaments Office (Wirtschaftsstellen;
Wehrwirtschafts-und Rüstungsamt). He told Springmann and Kasztner
that he had informed the Military Economics and Armaments Office in
Kraków that his Jewish workforce produced "40 percent more than
Poles."[115] He added that Germany's military needs had placed a heavy
burden on the entire Reich and millions had been drawn from the labor
force to fight. Himmler's recent decree halting the destruction of Jewish
workers in the forced labor camps had, according to Schindler, addressed
this issue. Kasztner and Springmann were skeptical, and wanted to know
whether Himmler's new order would be respected. Oskar replied, "Somewhat." He went on to explain that some SS leaders had some problems
breaking the habit of shooting from ten to one hundred Jews a day, an
obvious allusion to Amon Göth. He said that the situation regarding the
Jews that worked in military factories was somewhat different than those

in the ghettos because they, to a certain degree, were protected by the military inspectors of each factory. He added that the military had not "identified themselves with the methods of the SS." Oskar added that he knew of many instances where German soldiers had saved Jews. The Wehrmacht, he stated, had not wanted to submit to the order [Commissar order of June 6, 1941] to shoot Jewish POWs. The SS then insisted that these prisoners be turned over to them, and then shot them. But before the SS did this, they "tested them: if they were circumcised, they were executed."[116]

Oskar, unfortunately, had already bought into the myth that became so prevalent among the German public after World War II: that the Wehrmacht had played no role in the mass murders of Jews and other war crimes. This has been substantively disproved by any number of scholars, though some diehards still cling to the myth that the Wehrmacht was an ageless German institution that had been above the horrors committed by the SS. To them, "after the war, the *Wehrmacht* became every [German] man's bill to a clean conscience."[117] But for anyone who has spent time investigating the implementation of the Final Solution, particularly in occupied parts of the Soviet Union, the role of the Wehrmacht in the mass killings of Jews and others should come as no surprise. The SS and its *Einsatzgruppen* could not have murdered the hundreds of thousands it did without the help of the military.

Springmann and Kasztner then asked Oskar whether he knew how many Jews had been killed since the outbreak of the war. Schindler said that this was difficult to answer and the only figure he could give them was one that he got from the SS: from 4 to 4.5 million. Oskar stated that he thought these figures were exaggerated because the SS seemed to take pride in these numbers. He told them that he had heard one SS officer brag about the murder of 18,000 Jews in one afternoon. Another officer quickly tried to "top this with a different or similar story."[118] But the most deadly phase of the Holocaust was already past; it is therefore quite possible that the Germans could have murdered as many as 4 to 4.5 million Jews by the time Schindler met with the JRC representatives in Budapest.

Oskar did not want to let these gruesome details interfere with social matters, so he tried to ease the tension of the moment by ordering liqueurs for everyone in his hotel room. This led Kasztner and Springmann to admit their "inward anxiety" about the meeting. They asked Schindler's forgiveness as they explained their feelings to him. "Mr. X, forgive us. We sit here and listen to you with apparent calmness. But would you believe that we are not all so calm inwardly." Oskar was taken back by their comment and took it to mean that they did not trust him. He tried to reassure Springmann and Kasztner that they could trust him and took out his passport and his identity card, which had his photograph on it. He told them that it was "issued by the highest military office in Poland," which declared him to be the "manager of a military factory." According to Oskar, his identity card gave him "full freedom to travel across the entire occupied territory."[119] But Oskar failed to grasp the fear both men had of being in German allied territory. Their fears were compounded because they were Jews dealing with a German spy whom they knew little about; Schindler's impressive credentials probably only increased their anxiety.

But then Oskar took out a letter with "Jewish Forced Labor Camp at Z [Płaszów]. Leader of the S.S. and the Police" printed on the top. The letter, which was signed by "Mr. Y," [Göth], stated that SS regulations required that all Jewish workers must be accompanied by guards with guns ready to fire whenever they go from Camp Z to their workplace. "Mr. Y" went on to say in the letter that he had personally discovered that Mr. X's workers had gone to work [at Emalia] without an SS guard and, as a result, Mr. Y would no longer provide him with Jewish workers. Schindler told Kasztner and Springmann that the day he received this letter, he began his "friendship with this S.S. leader [Göth]."[120] Schindler somehow thought the letter and his explanation about the nature of his "difficult and costly" relationship with Amon Göth would reassure Springmann and Kasztner. Yet, as we have already discussed, it is hard to believe that Schindler's workers had somehow managed to walk the two miles from Płaszów to Emalia and back without SS escorts. The SS maintained rigid control over their inmates, particularly those who worked outside the camp.[121]

Oskar then told them that whenever he went to see Mr. Y after this, he would always bring him five or six bottles of French cognac, Göth's favorite, which cost Schindler Zł 2,000 to Zł 3,000 ($625–$937.50) apiece on the black market. Schindler, who never mentioned Göth or Płaszów by name, added that Mr. Y had "at least 300,000 Jews on his conscience." Oskar told them that he hunted with Göth and got drunk with him in an effort to try to make it clear to him that "the murder of the Jew [was] actually senseless and superfluous." Oskar said that he thought his entreaties had made an impact on Mr. Y because since he had gotten to know him "not even 10 percent of the prior number

[were] being shot in the camps overseen by him." Oskar considered it a "great achievement" that he had convinced Mr. Y to let him use Jews in his factory again because SS leader Y was "famous for the fact that no Jews [left] his hands alive."[122]

Schindler then lapsed into another criticism of the SS before Springmann and Kasztner steered him back to a question about what could be done to help the Jews in German-occupied territory. Oskar said that there were three possibilities: "to make money available, [to] send packages with food and medicine, and [to] try to influence the S.S. leaders."[123] To illustrate his first point, Schindler told Springmann and Kasztner that one of their *Schaliachs* (couriers) came to Kraków and wandered around for two days before discovering that Schindler was at Emalia. If he had not found Oskar there, he could not have delivered the *Mantana* (Hebrew, gift). Oskar sent the courier to Abraham Bankier, whom Oskar said had "a clear overview of the whole business." Oskar added: "I can, without worrying, go away for four weeks, and know that he will faithfully substitute for me."[124]

According to Schindler, Bankier then took care of the matter and turned it over to Dr. Hilfstein, who got it into Płaszów. Oskar went on to explain "how utterly complicated and dangerous it is to carry out such an operation." It began with the courier's demand for a receipt, something the Jewish Agency and its couriers always insisted on to insure that the funds were properly delivered. In this particular instance, Schindler and Bankier asked one of their office workers, Ms. Chawera, to witness the signing of the receipt, which she did not want to do because she was afraid it might be a trap. But there were other complications. For example, Schindler wanted to know what would happen if the courier was stopped by a guard, searched, and the receipt was found on him? The police or the SS would then want to know who gave the courier the money. Oskar said that everyone involved in the transfer of the Jewish Agency funds were "gambling with their lives."[125]

He added that Bankier ("meine Jude") was the only one at Emalia who knew about the funds from abroad. This is a bit contradictory; after all, Schindler had already mentioned that Dr. Hilfstein and Ms. Chawera knew some details about the illicit funds. It was, Oskar added, essential that only one or two "absolutely dependable people be let in on the secret, but only with the greatest of care, because among five Jews at least two [were] *Konfidenten* [Polish, *konfident*; agent or informer]."[126] He was particularly suspicious of anyone involved with the *"Hilfstelle,"* evidently a reference to Dr. Michał Weichert's controversial Jewish Aid Center (*jüdische Unterstützungsstelle*), the only Jewish aid agency permitted by the Germans to function in Kraków until the summer of 1943 and again during part of 1944.[127] Oskar reported that on one occasion a "certain Dr." from the *"Hilfstelle"* was given special permission by the SS to look into hygienic conditions of Jewish prisoners in surrounding camps and asked permission to visit Schindler's sub-camp. Schindler called the Gestapo to see whether he should let the physician into the sub-camp. The Gestapo officer said of course he should because the physician in question was "a better Gestapo man" than himself![128]

Finally, Oskar noted, very little of the money sent by Istanbul through Budapest ever reached Kraków, the implication being that much of the money somehow disappeared along the way. Consequently, Bankier, Hilfstein, and others involved in its receipt wanted to be certain that it was distributed by "competent people." Schindler assured Springmann and Kasztner that he did not mean to imply that people in Kraków were unappreciative of the Jewish Agency's funds. It was, in fact, "a great blessing for the people." They had bought flour with the money and on several occasions 3,000 to 4,000 loaves of extra bread. This not only meant extra food rations for the inmates but also forced the black market price of bread to drop from Zł 130 ($40.65) to Zł 40 to 50 ($12.50–$15.62) a loaf. Schindler, Bankier, and others were also able to buy eighty pairs of shoes for barefoot workers who were forced to get coal from the black market in winter.[129]

The conversation then shifted to a much more sensitive subject: the fate of Jewish children in the General Government. Springmann and Kasztner simply wanted to know whether any children were still alive there. Oskar replied: "Only a very few. They have indeed been exterminated."[130] Oskar estimated that about 90 percent of the children up through fourteen years had been "shot or gassed." Some children, though, were still alive "by accident" because, until six weeks ago, there were still two children's camps open. There were also children who remained alive because they had "special protection" or were "the children of the police or the Jewish OD men *[jüdischer Ordungsdienst]*."[131] He knew, for example, of one Jew, "the protegé of an inspector" in Płaszów's business office, who was able to save his two children because he was an OD man. "Thus only the children who belong to the Jewish police are in the Jewish camps."[132]

Oskar said that the fate of the elderly was the same as that for children, particularly those older than fifty. Older inmates did everything they could to look younger, including dying their hair and wearing makeup. But most of those still alive in the camps were between ages fourteen and fifty.[133] Schindler was quite sensitive to the question of age and survival. He noted in his 1945 report that he gave in to the requests of his workers to save their parents "even though many of them were not able to work."[134] In 1942 and 1943, he employed from two to three hundred "new workers," even though he had no work for them. He paid the SS Zł 5 ($1.56) a day for these workers because he had to "maintain the reputation that [his] firm did not have enough laborers." He estimated that it cost him Zł 720,000 ($225,000) to maintain this group of unemployable workers throughout the war.[135]

Kasztner and Springmann then wanted to know the location of those Jews still alive in Poland. Oskar said mainly in Auschwitz. He estimated that there were about 80,000 Jews in Auschwitz but did not know how many of the hundreds of thousands who had been deported there were still alive. His figures were remarkably accurate. Auschwitz records show that on December 31, 1943, there were 85,298 (55,785 men and 29,513 women) prisoners in Auschwitz I, II (Birkenau), and III (Buna-Monowitz). Springmann and Kasztner told Schindler they had heard that Auschwitz was an "extermination camp." Oskar said that was possible, particularly for the "elderly and children." He added that he had also heard that Jews were "gassed and burned there." The Germans, he thought, had "perfected a scientific system there in order to avoid more Katyns," a reference to the Soviet murder and burial of 4,143 Polish officers in Katyń forest in the spring of 1940.[136]

Another issue raised by the Jewish Agency's representatives was the question of *Tiyyul* or escape. Oskar said this would be very difficult because the camps are "very strictly guarded." He explained that the Jewish OD did not want "to endanger their own positions" and, to prevent escapes, called roll two or three times a day to make sure that every inmate was accounted for. A more serious problem was the Jewish *Konfidenten*, or informers, who were the "most dangerous." Oskar noted that one had to deal with five levels of police authority in the General Government: the Gestapo, the German police, the Polish police, the Ukrainian militia, and the Jewish OD men, and you could not bribe them all. But what if you did manage to escape and tried to reach Slovakia or Hungary? "But what if," Oskar asked, "along the way you are stopped by a Polish police officer who was suspicious of you." He earned Zł 150 ($46.87) a month and a third of his income came from money he found on Jews trying to escape.

Consequently, the Polish police were constantly looking for Jews trying to escape or hide as Aryans to fill their own pockets.[137]

Oskar explained that the only Jews able to escape from Poland were those living outside of the camps. He knew, for example, of one instance in which eighteen extremely wealthy Jews bribed the driver of a German Labor Front *(Deutsche Arbeitsfront)* truck, who took them to the Slovak border. The driver hid them in a double floor in the truck. It was stopped at the border, searched, and each of the Jews detained. Sixteen were executed on the spot and two others were returned to Poland. Oskar said that the two Jews who survived were informers. And he knew of hundreds of similar cases of escape attempts.[138]

Schindler was particularly critical of the Jewish OD men in the camps. "You know," he told Springmann and Kasztner, "I lived in the old Austria and had more respect for Jews then than now." He explained that the Jewish OD men in the camps "walk around elegantly dressed, almost like the people from the SS." He added: "They beat their brethren with such devotion that I could not have imagined it." He recounted a story he had heard about a women's camp in Lemberg (today: Ukrainian, Lviv; Polish, Lwów), in which a female Jewish camp leader bashed in "fifty to sixty skulls" a week with a piece of wood. He went on: "As a German, I do not know if I would have been capable of conducting myself [like this] in a camp of Germans."[139] The camp Oskar was referring to was the Janówksa forced labor camp in the suburbs of Lviv, where 30,000 to 40,000 Jews were murdered during the Holocaust.[140]

It is difficult to know how Kasztner and Springmann reacted to Oskar's criticism of other Jews because they tried to keep their own emotions out of their report. But his remarks did prompt them to ask again whether he thought a *"Tiul"* *(Tiyyul)*, or rescue, was possible. Oskar said that you could rescue some people, but only individuals or groups of two or three, and then only after a great deal of preparation. If this was so, the two JRC representatives asked, did the Jews in the General Government have any money they could use to help themselves or could they "help themselves in other ways"? Oskar explained that some Jews had hidden a lot of money. He noted, for example, that during a recent body search at Emalia, which was made under threat of death, the SS discovered "six large laundry baskets with gold, dollars, diamonds, gold watches, złoty, etc."[141] These goods were seized without receipts and taken to Göth's house, where a third of it "turned to dust," meaning it disappeared into Göth's pockets. The rest was turned over to the genera⸍ SS camp fund. But

Schindler admitted that there were only a few Jews with "hidden wealth" and it was often hidden in places now inaccessible to them. So it was important for the Jewish Agency to supply financial resources to help Jews in Płaszów and Emalia.[142]

Springmann and Kasztner then wanted to know whether it was possible to influence SS leaders in Poland to help Jews. Oskar never really answered this question. Instead, he lapsed into an overview of his own career. He mentioned that it disappointed him when the Nazis took over Czechoslovakia, which was one of the reasons he went to Poland. He was proud of the life he had built there, where he earned more than Zł 100,000 ($30,769) a month. He added that he "hoped to carry on" his business in "peace time as well." This is the first hint Oskar gave of his postwar plans.[143]

At some point in this part of the conversation, at least according to Oskar, Dr. Kasztner told Oskar that his efforts to help Jews were well known in "Israel." Oskar said in his 1955 report to Yad Vashem that Dr. Kasztner suggested that he should try to "take even more Jews into [his] protection without shying away from material sacrifices." When Oskar returned to Kraków, Dr. Kasztner sent him lists of names of prominent Jews, "who, upon the wish of Israeli organizations, should be looked for in the camps and brought to [his] factory and be placed under [his] protection." Oskar was proud of his success in fulfilling Dr. Kasztner's wish, and had managed to find sixteen to eighteen people on these lists, whom he brought to Emalia.[144]

Kasztner and Springmann ended their lengthy meeting with Schindler by asking questions about the Jewish Warsaw ghetto uprising that took place from April 19 to May 16, 1943. Oskar said he had heard that a Jewish self-defense organization had been created that "had let wagons with cement derail, built themselves bunkers, bought guns from Italian and German soldiers, and executed suspicious Jews that might betray them."[145] He estimated that 120,000 to 150,000 Jews were still living in the ghetto when the uprising took place. The uprising, Oskar said, lasted two to three weeks. He described it as a "heroic chapter in [the history] of Polish Jewry." He added: "In their desperation they wanted to salvage the honor of the Polish Jews, when everything else already seemed hopeless."[146] He told Springmann and Kasztner that 50,000 Jews escaped from the ghetto along the canals of the Vistula river during the fighting. He did not know what happened to those who escaped. Oskar had heard, though, that Jewish girls had fired at tanks using 0.8 caliber revolvers.

Tens of thousand of Jews died in the uprising and the ghetto was burned to the ground, along with "an immense amount of valuables." He noted that an international commission [Polish Red Cross] on its way to Katyń to investigate the Soviet massacre reported that it could hear the shootings in the distance and see the fires from the ghetto.[147]

Needless to say, Oskar's account of the uprising is not completely accurate, though it does show that he continued to have good contacts with the SS and the Wehrmacht. It is possible that he got his information on the Warsaw uprising from a security conference held in Kraków on May 31, 1943, where the Jewish revolt was discussed. Evidently, there were those in the General Government who were concerned about the loss of the Warsaw ghetto's sizable work force. The Warsaw ghetto was the largest in the General Government and at its peak in the spring of 1941 contained 450,000 Jews crammed into an area of about 760 acres. In the summer of 1942, the Germans began clearing the Warsaw ghetto of Jews and between July and September shipped 300,000 of its residents to nearby Treblinka and death. By the time the uprising took place the following spring, there were only about 60,000 Jews left in the Warsaw ghetto. The uprising was led by the Jewish Fighting Organization (ŻOB; *Żydowska Organizacja Bojowa)*, which drew its membership from twenty-two other Jewish groups. Seven hundred to 750 Jewish young people, armed with pistols, ten rifles, a few machines guns, 2,000 Molotov cocktails, and unbridled courage, took part in the rebellion. They faced the best military power the SS could throw at them, and they kept Himmler's best troops at bay for almost a month. The commander of the SS operation, *SS-Gruppenführer* Jürgen Stroop, a specialist in antipartisan warfare, said in his final report on May 24, 1943, to the General Government's HSSPF Friedrich Wilhelm Krüger, that his units had apprehended 56,065 Jews, which included 7,000 who had been killed in the uprising and a similar number sent to Treblinka. More than likely, these estimates are exaggerated, as were Stroop's estimates of the number of Germans killed and wounded in the ghetto's rebellion. Stroop added that his units had destroyed 631 bunkers, and captured eight rifles, fifty-nine pistols, a few hundred hand grenades and Molotov cocktails, some homemade weapons, and a large amount of ammunition.[148]

At some point in the lengthy discussion about ways to help the Jews in Poland, Springmann and Kasztner asked Oskar about the prospect of going to Turkey to work with the Jewish Agency there and "informing prominent people about the situation of the Jews in Poland and the terrible consequences of the SS policies (liquidation of ghettos, opening of death camps) [on them]."[149] In particular, they mentioned a possible meeting with the American ambassador to Turkey, Lawrence Steinhardt, himself Jewish. Though Steinhardt, American's wartime ambassador to Ankara, "had been rather hesitant on Jewish matters before 1944, once President Roosevelt ordered the creation of the War Refugee Board (WRB) in early 1944," Steinhardt became a "staunch supporter of any serious rescue plan put forward" by Jewish organizations interested in rescuing Jews.[150]

Oskar said the trip to Turkey never took place, though he fretted because Dr. Sedlacek had taken his passport to get him a visa but had never returned it. Given the time frame of the invitation in relation to the creation of the War Refugee Board and increased American efforts to do more to aid Europe's Jews, Oskar's trip probably became less valuable than originally thought, particularly considering the risks involved to the entire Jewish Agency network across Central and Eastern Europe. And it was not as though there was not already ample evidence about the atrocities being committed by the Germans and their collaborators against the Jews. In his *Official Secrets: What the Nazis Planned, What the British and the American Knew,* Richard Breitman has provided documentation showing that a steady flow of such information to the American and British governments took place well before Schindler met Springmann and Kasztner in Budapest in late 1943. The failure of the United States and Great Britain to give these reports serious consideration is a matter unrelated to Oskar Schindler.[151]

Yet one always wonders a little bit about the veracity of some aspects of Schindler's accounts of his wartime activities. There is no doubt that Oskar, often at the instigation of those *Schindlerjuden* closest to him, tried to put the best light possible on his actions during the war. For the most part, though, his accounts hold up pretty well to what historical documents we have that relate to his activities. Itzhak Stern talks about Oskar's relationship with Dr. Sedlacek, and even remembered the latter's visits to Kraków. Joseph Brand and Reszőe Kasztner also mentioned Schindler's visit to Budapest in their postwar accounts. And there is no reason to doubt the accuracy of their report, "The Confessions of Mr. X," particularly in light of some of the blunt statements made by Oskar during their meeting. "The Confessions of Mr. X" does not try to sugarcoat the ideas and feelings of Oskar Schindler, no matter how insensitive they might have been. But the report also showed how well connected Oskar was to the SS, particularly when it came to policies towards Jews in the General Government.[152]

The meeting with Kasztner and Springmann was not the only one that Oskar had during his brief stay in Budapest in late 1943. One evening, Dr. Sedlacek took Oskar to meet one of Abwehr's more infamous agents in the Hungarian capital, Dr. Schmidt, the head of Admiral Canaris's operations there. Joel Brand had first met Dr. Schmidt in a private room in the Moulin Rouge, a well-known night club in Budapest. Joseph Winniger, another Abwehr agent in Budapest, introduced Brand to Schmidt. "So you are Herr Brand, are you?" Schmidt said when he met Brand. "You want to help the 'children,' and I am ready to work with you in this. But we'll always refer to them as 'children' and nothing else. You understand?"[153] "Children" was often the word Oskar Schindler used to describe his Jews.

But Schmidt and his agents did not work for nothing; in fact, according to Brand, money was all they were interested in. They "paid scant heed to humane considerations."[154] But Va'ada, and later the JRC, would pay the Abwehr agents only for results, which often created problems. When Oskar met Dr. Schmidt on one of his visits to Budapest, he came away with the same negative impression of him as Joel Brand. In fact, Joel Brand's memoirs and the "Confessions of Mr. X" suggest that Oskar was not considered part of Dr. Schmidt's greedy Abwehr entourage. This was because Dr. Sedlacek, Oskar's contact with JRC representatives in Budapest, was ashamed of Dr. Schmidt and men like him. He appealed simply to Oskar Schindler's humanity, and this became the key to Oskar's willingness to work with the JRC.[155]

Oskar said that Dr. Sedlacek told him that Schmidt, a journalist, was an Austrian emigrant who had settled in Hungary. Schindler, Sedlacek, and Schmidt had dinner one evening in the Gellert Hotel in Budapest. All Schmidt wanted to talk about was "construction parts purchases, housing projects, and horse races."[156] To Oskar, Schmidt "seemed like an imposter." He said that Dr. Sedlacek told him that Dr. Schmidt had already made a lot of money exchanging money from Jewish aid agencies in Turkey and Palestine. The Gestapo finally caught up with Schmidt and arrested him. The Gestapo found "various quarter-kilo blocks of platinum and jewelry," all derived from the "embezzlement of Jewish money," in the apartment of Schmidt's girlfriend.[157]

Oskar Schindler's first visit to Budapest during the war had not gone well and he returned to Kraków in a bad mood. According to Itzhak

Stern, he was "furious because the Jews he had negotiated with did not yet believe what was happening in the camp."[158] But this did not keep him from continuing to work with Dr. Sedlacek and the Jewish Agency. Oskar made several trips to Budapest to visit Dr. Sedlacek and others working with the Jewish aid organization. Dr. Sedlacek, in turn, visited Oskar six or seven times in Kraków. According to Thomas Keneally, on one of these visits, Oskar managed to bring Sedlacek and a companion, Babar, who openly carried a small camera with him, into Płaszów. They were escorted by Amon Göth. Oskar did not mention this visit in any of his postwar accounts. Keneally got his information from Itzhak Stern's 1956 report to Yad Vashem. It makes fascinating reading.[159]

According to Stern, in July 1943, an OD man told Stern that Oskar Schindler wanted him to see him at his office in Emalia. Stern said that he had an SS contact who periodically let him visit Schindler at his factory, so this request was not unique. But on this occasion, Stern had a high fever and told the OD man that he could not make it. Soon, though, word came back that Oskar desperately wanted to see him. When he arrived at Oskar's upstairs office in Emalia, Stern was introduced to two men. Keneally said it was Sedlacek and the mysterious "Babar," though Stern never identified them by name in his report. The two agents asked Stern about conditions in Płaszów, which made him suspicious of both of them. He took Oskar aside and asked who they were. Oskar told Stern that they were spies from Hungary and Turkey "working for both sides."[160] Stern said that he then gave them details about conditions in Płaszów.[161]

Oskar then called Amon Göth and told him that he was hosting guests for a few days and wanted to invite him to a party for them. During the party, which included, according to Stern, drunken women, Göth invited Oskar and his two mysterious guests to Płaszów to show them his workshops. Göth told Stern and others that it was important that everything worked well during the visit. The implication here is that somehow Göth thought Oskar's guests were important dignitaries. Göth met the Schindler party at his office and escorted them as they walked through the camp. But before they left the administration building, Schindler told Göth that he needed to talk with Stern about one of his orders. Schindler and Stern decided that as soon as the visiting party walked out of the administration building, Stern would follow. At the point where Jewish gravestones had been used to pave one of the camp's roads, Stern was to stop and tie his shoes. One of the visitors, who had a small camera, would then take pictures of the broken tombstones. In fact, "Babar" took pictures throughout the camp. Stern reported that both men were caught at the border as they tried to return to Hungary and the film was seized and destroyed, though he added that "some of the pictures did get through."[162]

There is no reason to doubt Stern's account of the visit of these mysterious guests to Emalia and Płaszów, though his dates do not coincide with Schindler's initial contacts with Abwehr and the Jewish Agency. Possibly Stern was off a year and the visit took place in 1944 instead of 1943. Then there is the question of the identity of both men. If they were stopped at the border and discovered to have sensitive film or photographs on them, one would assume they were arrested for carrying such contraband. If this took place in the summer of 1944 instead of 1943, we cannot be certain that one of the visitors was Dr. Sedlacek because we can trace his activities in Budapest only through the spring of 1944. According to Joseph Brand, after the German occupation of Hungary, Sedlacek and other Abwehr agents tried to inject themselves into Brand's negotiations with Adolf Eichmann in the spring of 1944 over the exchange of Jewish lives for 10,000 trucks, food, and selected war matériel. Brand said that Sedlacek and his cronies did this because they were "afraid they would be completely eliminated and unable to earn any more money if [their] group were to bargain directly with the security service of the SS and with Istanbul."[163] Brand, who had become frustrated with Abwehr, now considered them worse than the SS. His negotiations with Eichmann never bore fruit in part because of German insincerity and Allied opposition to any scheme that might strengthen the German war effort. In the meantime, Dr. Rudi Sedlacek disappeared.[164]

Oskar's Schindler's decision to become more directly involved in efforts to save his Jewish workers coincided with the decline of Germany's military fortunes after the Battle of Stalingrad. By the time he made his first trip to Budapest for talks with Jewish Agency representatives, the Red Army had captured Kiev, the capital of the former Ukrainian Soviet Socialist Republic. The Big Three, Franklin Roosevelt, Winston Churchill, and Joseph Stalin, were about to meet in Teheran to approve plans for the invasion of France the following summer. By early 1944, Soviet forces had breached the old frontier with Poland. And though it would be another seventeen months before the war in Europe ended, Germans such as Oskar Schindler had to confront the likelihood of the collapse and defeat of the Third Reich. Most factory owners ultimately abandoned their operations in Kraków and made plans to return home with the money they had made in Poland. Oskar Schindler, though, followed a path that ultimately cost him his wartime fortune. As he slowly began to make plans in 1944 for the war's end, he chose to flee, though not with Emilie, or one of his mistresses. Instead, he decided to return to his homeland with as many Jewish workers as he could. If his efforts to help and protect his Jewish workers until this period were remarkable, what was about to happen in 1944 bordered on the miraculous; indeed, the idea that one person could save almost 1,100 Jews in the heart of the Holocaust's principal killing fields can be seen in no other light. Yet the events leading up to the transfer of almost 1,100 Jews from various camps to Oskar Schindler's factory camp in Brünnlitz near his hometown of Svitavy were neither simple nor purely moralistic. In fact, events, and the people who pushed Schindler's Jews along the path to salvation, were often driven by less than ideal motives. The reality of the story of the famous "Schindler's List" is very different from the one that has entered the popular history of the Holocaust.

8.

BEGINNING OF THE
END IN KRAKÓW

In ONE OF THE MORE MEMORABLE SCENES IN STEVEN SPIELBERG'S film *Schindler's List,* Oskar Schindler slowly dictates the names he wants Itzhak Stern to type on to the famous "Schindler's List." Schindler seems to struggle to come up with the names of the thousand Jews he wants sent from Płaszów to his new sub-camp at Brünnlitz (Brněnec), near his hometown of Svitavy, in what was then the Protectorate of Bohemia and Moravia (Böhren und Mähren). As Stern nears the completion of the list, he asks Schindler whether he was buying the names on the list from Amon Göth. Schindler replies that the list was costing him a fortune.[1] When Stern completes the list, Schindler takes it to Amon Göth, who says after looking it over that it contains one clerical error: the name Helen Hirsch. Göth tells Schindler that he cannot let Helen Hirsch go because he wants to take her back to Vienna with him. Schindler reminds Göth that he cannot take a Jew home with him after the war and Göth replies that perhaps he should take Helen to the woods and shoot her. Instead, Oskar offers to play a game of cards with Göth to win her freedom. Schindler suggests they play double or nothing. If Göth wins, Oskar will give him Zł 7,400 ($2,312.50); if Göth's winning hand is a "natural," Oskar will pay him Zł 14,800 ($4,625). But if Schindler wins, he can put Helen Hirsch on his list.[2]

This scene, which was taken from Thomas Keneally's historical novel *Schindler's List,* is pure fiction.[3] For one thing, Oskar Schindler had no role in preparing the famous list other than giving *SS-Hauptscharführer* Franz Josef Müller, some general guidelines for the type of workers he wanted on the list. Moreover, Amon Göth was in prison in Breslau when the list was being prepared and played no role in its creation. In reality, the creation of the famous "Schindler's List," like so much of the Schindler story, is much more complex. Its author was not Oskar Schindler, Itzhak Stern, Mietek Pemper, Abraham Bankier, or even Amon Göth. Instead, the person responsible for the preparation of "Schindler's List" was a corrupt Jewish OD man, Marcel Goldberg; he was the assistant of *SS-Hauptscharführer* Franz Müller, who was responsible for the transport lists. Spielberg's version of the creation of the famed "Schindler's List" certainly fits more comfortably with his efforts to underscore Oskar Schindler's decency and concern for his Jewish workers, but the reality is that Schindler had very little to do with it and he admitted as much after the war. In fact, only about a third of the Jews on the list had worked for Oskar Schindler in Kraków before he was given permission to transfer part of his factory operations to Brünnlitz. And more often than not, many of those who were put on Goldberg's list were prominent prewar Cracovian Jews or important Jewish officials in Płaszów. Some Jews were able to bribe their way onto the list, though this was more the exception than the rule. Others were on the list because they had worked for Julius Madritsch or had worked previously for Josef Leipold, Brünnlitz's new SS commandant. And some were on the list just because they were lucky.

The complexities surrounding the creation of the famous "Schindler's List" list underscore the tragic series of events that led to its creation. The list was, Itzhak Stern told Schindler as he completed typing it in the film, "an absolute good, the list is life, all around its margins lies the gulf."[4] The gulf, of course, was the death and horror of the Shoah. And all the Jews who did not make it onto the list faced the possibility of death during the final months of World War II. Germany may have been losing the war, but this had little impact on their fate. The Nazi commitment to rid Europe of all Jews continued until the very end of the conflict.

For the Jews of Płaszów, a contradictory series of events took place in the first half of 1944. Conditions for the camp's general inmate population seemed to improve at about the same time that the number of prisoners there increased as the Germans used Płaszów as a transit camp for large numbers of Hungarian Jews on their way to Auschwitz. Some of the most poignant scenes in Thomas Keneally's novel and Steven Spielberg's film are drawn from this tragic period in the camp's history.

After the SS officially declared Płaszów one of its official concentration camps in early 1944, conditions seemed to improve. Mietek Pemper testified in Göth's 1946 trial that Płaszów's commandant was limited in his deadly behavior by SS regulations on the mistreatment of prisoners in concentration camps, something he had not had to contend with when Płaszów was a forced labor camp. Pemper admitted that during the first months of its existence as a concentration camp, Płaszów "became a place of rest" when compared to earlier conditions.[5] Another *Schindlerjude*, Dr. Aleksandr Bieberstein, a camp physician, testified at the same trial that conditions also improved in other aspects of camp life. Selections were now made by German camp physicians, which meant there were fewer arbitrary deaths based on medical evaluations.[6]

The idea of the SS having regulations about the mistreatment of Jews and other prisoners seems contradictory, but there was a peculiar logic to it. As Heinz Höhne explains it, "the really horrifying feature of the annihilation of the Jews was that thousands of respectable fathers of families made murder their official business and yet, when off duty, still regarded themselves as ordinary law-abiding citizens who were incapable even of thinking of straying from the strict path of virtue."[7] From Heinrich Himmler's perspective, the SS mass murder program was to be "carried out coolly and cleanly." Even as the SS man committed his crimes, he had to remain "decent."[8] Himmler explained to *SS-Sturmbannführer* Alfred Franke-Gricksch, a self-styled protégé of Reinhard Heydrich, that if he found an SS man who had become excessively dutiful or showed a lack of restraint, he had to intervene. "Anyone," Himmler told Franke-Gricksch, "who finds it necessary to dull his senses, or forgets himself in the face of the enemy who is handed over to him, shows that he is no true SS Commander."[9]

And Himmler backed up his ideas about the unreasonable treatment of prisoners with regulations that forbade "independent, individual actions against the Jews" and even required camp guards to sign a statement every three months "acknowledging their duty to refrain from maltreating prisoners."[10] In reality, of course, the camp administration and staff had a great deal of flexibility in how they interpreted these rules and regulations, which Wolfgang Sofsky has called "terror incorporated." The modest limits on concentration staff behavior were counterbalanced by the excessive rules governing inmate behavior. According to Sofsky, "because everything was forbidden to the prisoners, all was permitted for the personnel."[11] From the SS's perspective, the defining point regarding the mistreatment or murder of Jewish prisoners seemed to center around whether the act was personal or political. If a Jew was murdered because of "political" reasons, this was acceptable behavior. If, however, a death was caused by "selfish, sadistic, or sexual" motivations, then the accused SS man could be tried for murder or manslaughter.[12] Such regulations would later be used against Amon Göth in the SS investigation of his multiple crimes, particularly the murder of Wilhelm Chilowicz, the camp's chief Jewish administrator.

The May 14, 1944, Aktion

But whatever new sense of order and moderation that seemed to settle over Płaszów in the first three or four months of 1944 dissipated after Amon Göth got a secret telegram from *SS-Standartenführer* Gerhard Maurer, the head of *Amtsgruppe* D2, a branch of the SS WVHA (*Wirtschafts-und Verwaltungshauptamt*; Economic and Administrative Main office), which oversaw all aspects of concentration camp prison labor.[13] According to Mietek Pemper, who saw the secret message from Maurer to Göth, the head of *Amtsgruppe* D2 wanted to know whether Göth could temporarily handle some additional prisoners from Hungary who were ultimately to be sent to different armament sub-camps from Auschwitz. He went on to explain that SS regulations stipulated that such armaments workers had to be housed in a neighboring camp. Göth replied that he could take up to 10,000 prisoners if Maurer let him "clean out of the camp" the sick, the weak, the elderly, and children. He also wanted permission to "double use the plank beds." Göth went on to explain that he could assign some of his workers to barracks where they would share the same assigned spots in one of the standard plank beds. One worker would be assigned to his or her spot in the collective bunk while the other worker was at his twelve-hour day or night shift. When the shift changed, so did the person who occupied the bunk space. This was Göth's solution to the space problem.[14]

Maurer rejected the idea of assigning two people to the same bunk space because of sanitary concerns, but did give Göth permission to initiate a *Sonderbehandlung* (special treatment), an SS euphemism for a selection or roundup of prisoners that would lead to their murder. Maurer then informed *SS-Obersturmbannführer* Arthur Liebehenschel, Auschwitz's commandant, to expect a transport from Płaszów.[15] Maurer and Liebehenschel were desperate. Six weeks earlier, German forces had occupied Hungary, once a staunch German ally, to prevent it from switching sides in the war. Until this point, Hungarian Jews had suffered from a series of anti-Semitic laws that had restricted their civil and economic rights and forced them into harsh labor service duties but allowed them some semblance of autonomy. This all changed with the German occupation of Hungary in March 1944. A *Sonderkommando* unit headed by Adolf Eichmann accompanied German forces as they entered Hungary and began to implement a Final Solution for Hungary's 825,000 Jews. What followed over the next few months was a highly concentrated ghettoization and deportation program that saw 437,402 Jews rounded up and transported, mainly to Auschwitz, where they were murdered as part of *Aktion Höss*. The SS estimated that it would have to handle from 12,000 to 14,000 Hungarian Jews a day in Auschwitz II-Birkenau and dramatically increased its manpower and killing capacity to handle the new arrivals. The first Jewish transports left Hungary for Auschwitz on May 15 and continued steadily until July 9, 1944. In a few months, the SS was able to murder more than half of Hungary's prewar Jewish population. The transports were halted by Hungary's ruler, Admiral Miklós Horthy, in response to international outcries and the proximity of Soviet forces.[16]

About 10 percent of the Hungarian Jews sent to Auschwitz were deemed fit for slave labor and were transferred to other camps. About 6,000 to 8,000 Hungarian Jews were sent from Auschwitz to Płaszów.[17] Ana Harsanyi Novac was one of those Hungarian Jews who spent a few weeks in Auschwitz before being transferred to Göth's camp. She remembered seeing the sign as she was marched through the front gate that read *Arbeit macht Frei* (Work Will Make You Free).[18] Ana spent six weeks in Płaszów before she was sent back to Auschwitz. Her initial perspectives on the camp were quite different from those of the hardened Polish inmates who had somehow survived Göth's depredations. She described Płaszów, where she and the other new Hungarian inmates were placed in quarantine, "like a real town" where the "barracks look like new houses." She said the new arrivals looked "like real women and real men who might have gathered for a real reason in the square of a real town" as they stood together for evening roll call.[19]

But she soon became disgusted by Göth's fascination with public hangings and his warped fascination with "pageantry." Once the quarantine was lifted, Ana was assigned to work in the quarry, the hardest work in Płaszów, where she lifted and helped pass stones from one end of the quarry to the other. It was there that she saw Göth at his worst. One day, everyone in the quarry, including the *Kapos* (foremen), suddenly stopped working. As one of the *Kapos* yelled out, *"Los, Schweine, bewegt euch"* (Come on, you pigs, move it!), Ana fell to the ground just as Göth jumped over her on his white horse. She described him as "a panting whale, with an enormous belly and fat, pendulous breasts" and medals that "trembled on his breast." As he looked over the work crew, Göth spotted a victim, a young girl, and began to chase her down, hitting her with his riding crop. When the girl accidentally dropped the stone she was carrying on the hoof of the commandant's horse, Göth unleashed one of his dogs on her, who chased the girl through the quarry until she stumbled and fell. Göth's dogs then ripped her apart.[20]

On Sunday, May 7, 1944, about a month before Ana's arrival in Płaszów, Göth ordered the camp's chief German physician, *SS-Hauptsturmführer* Dr. Max Blancke, to initiate a "medical inspection" *(Gesundheitsappell)*. The final selection process was completed a week later. What transpired has been vividly depicted in Keneally's novel and Spielberg's film. Keneally claimed that Göth had organized the medical inspection like a "country fair." The *Appellplatz* in the prisoner's compound was festooned with banners that read "FOR EVERY PRISONER, APPROPRIATE WORK!" and loudspeakers "played ballads and Strauss and love songs."[21]

Dr. Aleksander Bieberstein and Mietek Pemper tell a far less colorful story. The initial medical inspection took place on May 7. After the normal morning roll call ended, Płaszów's head Jewish administrator, Wilek (Wilhelm) Chilowicz, ordered the inmates to remain in place while the SS and Jewish OD men surrounded their barracks. The Jews standing at attention on the *Appellplatz* were particularly unnerved when the children's barrack, the *Kinderheim*, was also surrounded. Murray Pantirer told me that he saw Josef Mengele, Auschwitz's infamous "Angel of Death" nearby, writing down the "names of all the children."[22] After a two-hour wait, Dr. Blancke, accompanied by *SS-Obersturmführer* Philipp Grimm and *SS-Hauptscharführer* Willi Eckert, arrived and ordered the women to return to their barracks. Göth explained that they were attempting to assign work based on an inmate's physical abilities. Inmates determined to be too weak for certain types of jobs would be assigned easier tasks. In the meantime, *SS-Hauptscharführer* Lorentz Landstorfer and OD man Marcel Goldberg manned two tables with red files on them. The other Jewish OD men in the camp stood nearby to insure that each prisoner moved quickly through the inspection line. The prisoners, who were put in alphabetical groups, were ordered to undress and walk briskly in front of Dr. Blancke. Those considered too weak to work were directed to the tables with the red files, where Landstorfer recorded the physical grade given to him by Dr. Blancke. Though it was early May, the weather was cold enough to force the Germans and the OD men to wear extra clothing. The prisoners remained naked. The health inspection ended at about noon. Dr. Blancke and his staff then moved the tables and red folders to the women's barracks, where, aided by *SS-Aufseherin* Alice Orlowski, they went through the same procedure.[23]

Seven days later, the inmates were again ordered to remain on the *Appellplatz* after morning roll call. SS guards stood in front of the entrance to each barracks and guards with light weapons and machine guns stood along the Bergstraße, the main camp road that ran in front of the *Appellplatz*. Göth and his staff soon arrived and put the red folders on a table. They then began to call the names of prisoners with names in the folders to step forward and line up in groups of five abreast, facing the front gate. As SS guards marched the prisoners out of the *Appellplatz* gate, the 294 children in the *Kinderheim* were loaded onto trucks and driven off. Wilhelm Chilowicz tried to convince Göth to save the children of the Jewish OD men and their friends, but Göth allowed only a few to remain behind. Those who survived the *Kindertransport* (children's transport) were all children of important Jewish OD men, Jewish *Kapos*, or children of other prominent Jews in the camp. A few other children were hidden by their parents in the camp's toilets. Dr. Bieberstein, for example, hid a young girl in the hospital's toilet. He added that as the children left the camp, the Germans played a song on the loudspeakers, *"Mutti, kauf mir ein Pferdchen"* (Mummy, buy me a pony). Bieberstein went on to say that it was impossible to describe the scenes that took place as the children were driven out of the camp.[24]

Stella Müller-Madej was on the *Appellplatz* that day and the scene she described was as wrenching as the one portrayed in Spielberg's film. As the women lined up on the *Appellplatz*, everyone sensed that something was different. Stella noted a sight she had never seen before: hundreds of SS men surrounding the prisoners' square, their guns aimed towards the inmates. Stella wondered whether they were going to shoot everyone there. Everyone of importance was at the *Appellplatz*: Göth and his officers; Chilowicz, his assistant, Mietek Finkelstein, Marcel Goldberg, and all the Jewish OD men and *Kapos*. "The atmosphere," she recalled, was "so tense that no one dared look around."[25] In the distance, she noticed two open trucks outside the prisoner compound. And then, as she heard the sound of marching children, she knew why the trucks were there. Led by *Tatele* (Papa) Koch, they marched in rows of five abreast into the *Appellplatz*, where Koch gave Göth the list of children. Göth "waves his whip dismissively, as if he wants to show that it isn't important any more." When he summoned the trucks "with a wave of his whip," they moved to the gate of the *Appellplatz*.[26]

Göth had prepared for what happened next. As the frightened children were forced onto the trucks, "sobs burst from the breasts of mothers and fathers." The children, who until this moment had "been standing there terrified, as quiet as mannequins," began to scream in unison. As German guards pushed them onto the trucks, one child screamed, "Mother, Mummy, Daddy, Tatele, save me! I don't want to go, I'm afraid, get me out of here!" Another small child tried to crawl away on his hands and knees, only to be stopped and thrown back onto the truck by one of the female SS guards. Stella remembered thinking, "No! This is unbearable! The whole *apelplatz* [sic] is howling, the whips are flying, the dogs barking."[27]

As the trucks drove off, their mothers and grandmothers began to rip their clothes and tear their hair. Some even crawled on their hands and knees towards Göth, somehow thinking their appeals might force him to change his mind. All the while, the *Kapos* and SS female guards *(Aufseherinnen)* beat children with their whips and forced them back into line. There was no way, of course, that any of the inmates could have charged the trucks as they did in Spielberg's film. The trucks were outside the prisoners' compound and Göth had scores of his own men and women on hand to insure order. Stella said in her memoirs that as the children left, the SS played "*Mama, komm zurück*" (Mama, come back), a song quite different from the one remembered by Dr. Bieberstein. Another *Schindlerjude*, Joseph Bau, said in his memoirs that the Germans played another German song, "Good night, Mother" *(Gute Nacht Mutter)*.[28] This is the song that Spielberg has the Germans play in the film as the children are being driven off in the trucks. More than likely, the Germans played a va-

riety of songs as they loaded the children onto the trucks, perhaps thinking this would soothe them. When the trucks left the camp, the multitude
of SS guards, OD men, and *Kapos* closed in to restore order. As Göth and
his entourage left, some mothers begged to be shot. The female guards
kicked them and dragged them by the hair back to their place in line on
the *Appellplatz.*[29]

Later that day, word spread in the women's camp that two children,
Jerzy Spira and Juluś Cinz, had been found hiding in the latrine. But another child was also hiding there, Roman Ferber. He chose the latrine because the guards would never go there because of the smell. "The pit was
twelve feet deep. You couldn't have jumped in it or you would have
drowned. People would sit on boards with holes, and the stuff would fall
inside. There were crossboards [under the boards], and this is where we
used to hide, between the crossbars. I cannot describe the smell."[30] The
women wondered how to hide, clothe, and feed the hidden children. They
decided it was best to leave them in the latrine for another day until it was
safe to bring them out. In the meantime, several women volunteered to
take care of them until they could be taken out of the latrine. Later, the
children were hidden in the inmates' *Krankenstube* (sick room) because,
explained Stella Müller-Madej, "the Germans have a frantic fear of sick-
ness [and] seldom go there." Roman Ferber and Jerzy Spira survived and
were later put on "Schindler's List."[31]

Göth sent almost 1,400 Jewish prisoners to Auschwitz that day, including the children. They were sent to the gas chambers soon after their
arrival. Some of them were wearing newly issued striped prisoners' uniforms; others wore clothes with yellow and red stripes painted on them.
The new concentration camp's first escape had taken place on May 5 and
Göth now required all *Außenkommandos* (inmates who worked outside
the concentration camp) to wear the new uniforms to make it harder to
escape. There were not enough uniforms to go around, so those without
them had yellow and red stripes painted on their clothing during roll call.
But because the striped uniforms were in short supply, Płaszów's commandant asked Liebehenschel to return them after he had gassed
Płaszów's former inmates. Göth testified at his trial that the reason he
sent the request to Auschwitz was because that was the designated storage site for camp uniforms in the Kraków region. Pemper added that the
uniforms of the former Hungarian Jewish inmates were never returned to
Płaszów.[32]

The Beginning of the End: Emalia and Płaszów

In many ways, the tragic action at Płaszów on May 14 underscored the contrast between life under Amon Göth and Oskar Schindler. For those forced to continue to live in Płaszów, life remained tenuous. For those two miles away at Emalia, life was more secure. The Jews working at Emalia and living in Schindler's sub-camp were not forced to participate in the May 7 medical inspection in Płaszów, nor were they put onto the May 14 transport to Auschwitz. But as Soviet forces moved closer and closer, the security that many of Schindler's Jews enjoyed at Emalia would soon disappear. There were certain things that even Oskar Schindler could not control. Many who had enjoyed the security of "Schindler's Ark" would soon find themselves in transport to other concentration camps or back at Płaszów. Others who had enjoyed the security of political or financial prominence at Płaszów would take advantage of their situation to have their names and those of their families placed on the famous "Schindler's List." But before that happened, a series of dramatic changes took place at Płaszów in the late summer and early fall of 1944 that affected not only all the Jewish workers employed by Oskar Schindler but also those who lived at Płaszów. And in Berlin, Oskar Schindler pulled whatever strings he could to get permission to move part of his Kraków operations back to a site near his hometown in what was then the Sudeten region of Germany.

According to Itzhak Stern, by early July 1944, rumors spread through the camp about its liquidation. Later that month, Oskar received an order from the Armaments Inspectorate in Kraków to begin to plan the evacuation of the armaments portion of Emalia to Germany. Though it would be another six months before the Red Army would take Kraków, Soviet forces had already crossed the Bug River and moved into Poland on July 17, 1944. Seven months earlier, Amon Göth told Julius Madritsch that the WVHA in Berlin had ordered him to close his factory immediately to make room for German Armament Works (DAW; *Deutsche Ausrüstungswerke*) authorized factories. Madritsch immediately drove to Berlin, where he successfully petitioned the WVHA to keep his factory operating in Płaszów. He based his appeal on the treaty he had signed with HSSPF *Ost* Wilhelm Koppe in the fall of 1943 that guaranteed the operation of his factory "until the end of the war." This contract was now invalid because Płaszów was under WVHA jurisdiction. Madritsch quickly enlisted the help of a fellow Viennese, *Postrat* Grohe, the director of the German postal service in the East, who substantially increased the size of his office's order with Madritsch. Grohe also contacted the directors of the Compulsory Labor Service *(Baudienst)* and the Textile Economic Group *(Wirtschaftsgruppe Textil)*, who wrote Oswald Pohl, the head of WVHA, that "the existence of my [Madritsch's] factories were absolutely necessary [to the war effort]." Consequently, WVHA signed a new agreement with Madritsch on February 24, 1944, to keep his factory open for six more months.[33]

The Reich was desperate to maintain the dramatic rise in armaments output orchestrated by Albert Speer. These concerns even spilled over into the manufacture of uniforms, particularly after the *Erntefest* (Harvest Festival) massacre of 42,000 Jews in the Lublin district on November 3, 1943. *General* Maxmillian Schindler's Armaments Inspectorate in the General Government received numerous complaints about the dramatic impact that Himmler's last major "cleansing" operation in the General Government had on armaments-related production, particularly textiles.[34]

One of the most serious problems facing German industry in the last two years of war was manpower. As more and more German males were drafted into the military, the German economy, particularly armaments-related industries, came to depend more and more on forced and slave foreign labor to sustain the high levels of armaments production. Until the defeat at Stalingrad, the Reich had depended heavily on the conquered parts of the Soviet Union for its largest pool of foreign workers. With the growing loss of Soviet territory after Stalingrad, Germany had to look elsewhere to fill these needs. Poland had supplied the second largest group of forced laborers in the Reich, though by 1944 the Polish labor market was no longer a viable outlet for the Reich's foreign labor needs. This desperation helps explain the dramatic shift in SS attitudes in late 1943 and early 1944 towards the use of Jewish slave labor first in the General Government and later in the Reich as factories began to be moved westward to escape capture by Soviet forces.[35]

Płaszów, for example, had become an important center for the export of Jewish labor to other armament sites in the General Government. On November 16, 1943, for example, 2,500 Jews had been shipped from Göth's camp to Skarżysko-Kamienna to do munitions work for one of Germany's largest arms manufacturers, the Hugo Schneider Aktiengesellschaft Metallwarenfabrik (HASAG) of Leipzig. Two days later, 1,500 Jewish workers were sent from Płaszów to armaments plants in Kielce, Częstochowa, Pionki, Ostrowice, and Starachowice. This was about 15 percent of the Jews working in armaments-related work in the General Government. Hans Frank estimated in early 1944 that only 100,000 Jews were still alive in the General Government. Desperate for manpower, the Armaments Inspectorate in the General Government increased its appeals for Jewish laborers throughout the first half of 1944, but concluded that summer that the "reservoir of Jews will soon be exhausted."[36] Such desperate needs would ultimately play into Oskar Schindler's hands as he planned to move his armaments factory into the Reich later that fall.

Once Oskar got his orders to break up his Jewish sub-camp (he continued to operate the enamelware part of his factory with 650 Polish workers until early 1945), the pace of the evacuation moved quickly. He got permission to keep three hundred workers at Emalia to help take apart and load that part of the factory that would be shipped to the Reich. The other seven hundred or so would be sent immediately to Płaszów. On the day of the selection, which took place at the end of the first week in August 1944, the SS lined Emalia's Jews up as Oskar walked among them, selecting the three hundred Jews who would remain behind. According to Sol Urbach, Schindler first selected the most important Jews at Emalia, such as Abraham Bankier, to remain with him for a few more weeks. Then he began to select other Jews to be a part of Emalia's remaining Jewish work force. As Oskar walked by, Sol decided to speak up, knowing full well that this could bring the wrath of the SS guards on him. He said, *"Herr Schindler, kein Tischer ist geblieben"* (Herr Schindler, you have no carpenter remaining with you). Oskar took Sol by the arm and put him in the group that would remain at Emalia.[37]

For the next two or three weeks, the three hundred Jewish males worked to prepare for Oskar's move to the Reich. Though Schindler was still involved in negotiations about the location of his new factory, he would ultimately ship "two hundred and fifty wagons of machines, production goods, and construction material" to his new camp in the Sudetenland.[38] One incident that seemed to hasten the pace of the work was the crash of an Australian B-24 Liberator bomber on the women's barracks on August 17. Sol said that only the three crew members were killed. Soon afterwards, the three hundred Jewish workers were sent back to Płaszów and integrated into the general camp slave labor pool. Today, there is a small plaque at Telepod, the business complex on the former Emalia site, to honor the three crew members: Flight Leader John P. Liversidge (RAAF), Flight Lt. Pilot William D. Wright (RAF), and Flight Sergeant John D. Clarke (RAF).[39]

But what happened to the other seven hundred Schindler Jews who were sent back to Płaszów? According to Sol Urbach, there were four hundred men in this group and three hundred women. The men were shipped to Mauthausen almost immediately after they got to Płaszów. According to Schindler, "one hot summer day" he was invited to a security conference of the SS leadership at Płaszów. As he entered the camp's main gate, he noticed on the railroad tracks that ran beside the main road leading into Płaszów a long train with scores of "cattle wagons" filled with thousands of inmates. Oskar soon learned that the transport was bound for Mauthausen, a large German concentration camp about a hundred miles west of Vienna, near Linz. Though Oskar did not mention the date, the detailed inmate list in the Mauthausen archives for this particularly transport is dated August 10, 1944. Because Oskar mentioned that the train had been on the siding since early morning, and Jews on the transport mentioned they sat on the siding in the cattle cars for three days, it was probably August 8, 1944. There were 4,589 Jewish males on the Mauthausen transport that day; about 400 were *Schindlerjuden* who had recently worked at Emalia. They were about to be sent to one of the harshest work camps in the Third Reich where almost 60 percent of the 198,000 prisoners sent there during the war died from disease and starvation. More than a third of those who died at Mauthausen were Jews, mostly during the last year of the war. But the Schindler Jews had a much better chance of survival than the others sent there that year.[40] Several Schindler Jews on that transport confirmed Richard Krumholz's statement that when they got to Mauthausen, they were "still physically strong from Schindler, not undernourished." Their time at Emalia gave many of them the stamina they needed to survive the horrors of Mauthausen or other camps.[41]

Oskar knew that some of his former workers were on the transport. He bribed Göth to allow him to supply the cattle cars with drinking water and also got permission to bring hoses from the camp to spray the train cars. As they sprayed the metal tops of the cattle cars with water, Schindler had to suffer from Göth's mockery of his "humanitarian stupidities as well as the jeers of his SS retinue." Oskar had two horse-drawn wagons filled with large containers and buckets brought to Płaszów; when they arrived, he had the buckets filled with water and placed in each train car. He then gave the train guards a basket filled with Schnaps (a German liqueur) and cigarettes "with the plea to open the sliding doors of the wagons" each time the train stopped. Oskar added in his 1955 report to Yad Vashem that though this "action may seem minor, it took courage to help the thirsty ones before a group of powerful SS men" gathered at Płaszów for an important security conference. Several Schindler Jews testified after the war that once the train was underway, the SS did supply the inmates with water during the few times it stopped during its slow three-day journey to Mauthausen.[42]

Spielberg captured this powerful moment in his film, as did Keneally in his novel. But did it really happen? Yes. Abraham Zuckerman, one of Oskar's closest American friends after the war, had worked at Emalia since early 1943. He was on the Mauthausen transport in Płaszów that hot August day in 1944. He told me when I interviewed him and his business partner and fellow *Schindlerjude,* Murray Pantirer (Mejzesz Puntirer), in their Union, New Jersey office, that he and the other Schindler Jews had been put on the cattle cars immediately after they got to Płaszów. Once the cars were filled, they were moved to a rail siding. The rail cars were so tightly packed that the inmates had to stand up. They stood there in the sweltering heat for three days without food or water. Some of the men on the train went crazy; others died from dehydration and starvation. Some of the inmates even drank their own urine. Zuckerman said that "the stench was unbearable. It was impossible to move the corpses."[43]

This probably explains why Marek Finder, the husband of *Schindlerjude* Rena Ferber Finder, passed out when he was put on the Mauthausen transport. Marek did not wake up until he reached Austria. He told me that he felt guilty about not remembering anything about the transport or the Schindler incident and wondered why he could not recall anything during the horrible six or so days on the train. When I told him that his mind and body had probably shut down to protect his sanity, he seemed relieved.[44] Murray Pantirer was one of the Jews who hosed down the train cars. Schindler, who was wearing a white suit, yelled *"Macht schnell!"* (Hurry up) to make the workers with the hoses on top of the train cars move as quickly as they could. Their efforts were hindered because, instead of fire hoses, they used garden hoses to pour water on top of the metal roofs of the cars. Unfortunately, it was so hot in the cars that when the water hit the metal roofs it turned into steam, "simmering those who'd been baking inside." Al Bukiet later testified that the steam "almost killed" them.[45]

It is doubtful whether Oskar could have done more to help his Emalia Jews even if he knew where he was going to be permitted to open his new factory. But at the time he was not even certain of this. Once the Armaments Inspectorate in Kraków informed him that he had to move his factory westward, Oskar was told he could move to any factory site in the Rhineland in the western part of Germany or to a village in the Semmering Pass area in Lower Austria. In his 1956 report to Yad Vashem, Itzhak Stern quoted a letter he had just received from Schindler in which Oskar told him that he had refused this offer because he "would have to leave [his Jewish] workers behind." Stern said Schindler's decision not to abandon his Jewish workers was "characteristic of this man and the determining action of his life."[46]

Yet there was more to Oskar's decision than just wanting to save his Jewish workers. Schindler had already revealed his postwar plans to the Jewish Agency representatives he had met in Budapest a year earlier. He wanted to return to the Sudetenland and start a factory in his former homeland. Mietek Pemper told me that Schindler told him during the latter days of the war that he had moved his factory back to the Svitavy area to restore his family's honor, which had been lost when his father's factory had closed during the Depression. Oskar also did not think that the Soviets would occupy Bohemia and Moravia at the end of the war and that Czechoslovakia would be restored as a nation. His new operations at Brünnlitz could then be transformed into a major source of enamelware for postwar Europe. Oskar hoped that his Jewish workers would stay with him to fulfill his dream.[47]

But what Jews did Oskar have in mind? According to Emilie Schindler, Oskar told her after he got the evacuation order that he did not know many of his workers and knew only "the names of a few who [came] to our office" when something was needed. "But I have no idea about the others."[48] This is probably true, though it contradicts the image of a man struggling in Spielberg's film trying to come up with the names of 1,000 Jewish workers to put on the famous "Schindler's List." Oskar was a busy man during the war and was seldom on the factory floor. Moreover, he did not begin to use Jews in large numbers until 1943 and he left daily supervision and contact with them to others such as Bankier. This did not mean that he did not care about his Jewish workers, or for that matter, the large number of Poles who worked for him. He was simply too busy to get to know many of them.

As Płaszów was being broken up, Oskar seemed initially powerless to do anything to help save his former Emalia workers. To a great extent this was caused by uncertainty about the fate of his small-arms production facility at his Kraków factory. This part of his operations at Emalia is quite mysterious and none of the survivors I talked to knew anything about it. They did, though, remember working in some aspect of enamelware production or general work around Emalia. Oskar said in his 1945 report that the armaments wing of Emalia produced only RM 500,000 ($2 million) as opposed to RM 15,000,000 ($6 million) in enamelware production during the war. He said his Polish workers made the enamelware while his Jewish workers made the arms.[49] It was the production of these arms, and not enamelware, which was still, up to a point, considered vital to the war effort, that convinced the Armaments Inspectorate to support Oskar's efforts to move his armament operations, along with his Jewish workers, to Brünnlitz. Siemens-Bauunion G.m.b.H. had just completed a large building for this, which probably helped Schindler's case because most of the machinery could be moved to wherever Schindler relocated his armaments production facility.

But what types of armaments did Oskar produce at Emalia? Thomas Keneally mentioned in his novel that at Brünnlitz, Schindler made "not one 45 mm shell, not one rocket casing."[50] It is logical to assume that the Armaments Inspectorate approved Schindler's move to the Sudetenland based on the production of the same type of weapons he had made at Emalia. On my first visit to the Brünnlitz factory site, I met a young boy whose family lived in a small house that had once been part of the Schindler factory. He showed me a collection of small shells he had collected from the site. One set of shells were elongated and about ten to twelve inches; the others were shorter but much thicker. These shells were similar in size to three different types of shells produced for the German 3.7 cm *Panzerabwehrkanone* 36, the standard German World War II antitank gun. Francisco Wichter, a Schindler Jew who now lives in Buenos Aires and who was a close friend of Emilie Schindler's, told me that they produced shell casings for antitank guns at Brünnlitz. Francisco had worked for Brünnlitz's commandant, Josef Leipold, at several Heinkel aircraft factories in Poland and knew something about German weaponry. Midway through World War II, the effectiveness of the 1930s era 3.7 *Panzerabwehrkanone* 36 had been reduced because of better Allied armor. The Wehrmacht responded with a "spigot bomb" shell, the 3.7 cm *Stielgranate* 41 (3.7 cm *Aufsteckegeschoß*), which extended the life of the 3.7

Panzerabwehrkanone. This was probably the shell that Oskar produced in Emalia and Brünnlitz.[51]

And though Oskar knew that the continued production of armaments at Brünnlitz would help save the lives of some of his Jewish workers, he was also aware that they would be under the jurisdiction of one of the remaining concentration camps in the Kraków region, Auschwitz or Groß Rosen. But this move was complicated by officials in the Sudetenland, who opposed moving more Jewish workers into the region. But first, at least according to Emilie, Oskar had to contend with Amon Göth's opposition to the move. Oskar said after the war that Göth was supposed to move with Schindler to Brünnlitz. Emilie added that Oskar told her that Göth wanted to ship all of Płaszów's Jewish inmates, including those at Emalia, to Auschwitz. She said in her memoirs that Oskar offered Göth "diamonds, jewelry, money, vodka, cigarettes, caviar," but Göth would not budge. Oskar thought that maybe he should offer Göth "a couple of beautiful women to cheer him up."[52] If Göth was opposed to the move, then his opposition meant nothing after his arrest by the SS on September 13, 1944, for corruption and brutality. Oskar, who was also arrested as part of the Göth investigation, did move a lot of the former Płaszów commandant's war booty to Brünnlitz. Göth, who still seemed to consider Schindler his friend, visited Brünnlitz several times during the latter months of the war while on parole.[53]

Schindler stated after the war that his initial effort to move part of his Emalia operations to the Sudetenland was hampered by opposition from the *"Reichsstatthalter* [Reich Governor] *Reichenberg"* who forbade the employment of Jewish workers "in industry in the Sudetenland." Schindler, was, of course, speaking in prewar terminology. On April 14, 1939, Hitler appointed Konrad Henlein as *Reichsstatthalter* of the *Sudetengau* with Reichenberg (Czech, Liberec) as its capital. By 1944, Henlein was still head of this region, but now was the *Gauleiter* (regional head) of the *Gauleitung Sudetenland* (Sudetenland Region), which was an integral part of the Greater German Reich.[54]

Schindler's claim that Henlein did not permit the use of Jewish slave laborers in the Sudetenland is not true. Though Henlein had implemented the Nazi Party's harsh anti-Semitic policies towards the region's small Jewish population (2,341 in 1939) during the war, there was little he could do to stop the employment of Jews in German factories there. Himmler, for example, had ordered the *Organisation Schmelt,* named after the police chief of Breslau, *SS-Oberführer* Albrecht Schmelt, to set up scores of armaments workshops and small factories in Silesia, and later, in the Sudetenland. Ultimately, Schmelt's factories would employ over 50,000 Jews. Between 1940 and 1944, Schmelt built more than one hundred forced labor camps in Silesia and seventeen in the Sudetenland; they all used Jewish slave laborers. Himmler ordered these closed in 1943 though a number of them remained open as part of Groß Rosen's satellite camp system. Schindler's new camp at Brünnlitz simply became part of the Groß Rosen network. This did not mean, of course, that Oskar did not have to deal with opposition from Nazi leaders in the Sudetenland; he did, though it seemed to come more from local leaders in the Svitavy region than from officials in Reichenberg.[55]

It is quite possible, of course, that Oskar got some resistance from Sudetenland leaders about the prospect of opening a new armaments sub camp in the region. With the war nearing its end, they probably wanted to do everything possible to distance themselves from some of the Third Reich's more damning racial policies. But most of the resistance to Oskar's move came from Wilhelm Hoffman, one of two brothers who owned the large textile factory complex where Schindler wanted to move his small armaments factory. Schindler wanted to lease only a portion of the vast, sprawling complex. After the German occupation of the Sudetenland, the Hoffmans, former cheese and butter makers in Vienna, became *Treuhänder* for the century-old textile factory owned by a Jewish family, the Löw-Beers. The Hoffman brothers purchased the former Löw-Beer factory outright during the war and renamed it *Elisenthaler Tuch- und Hutfabriken Brüder Hoffmann.*[56]

Given that the Hoffmanns had taken over a previously owned Jewish factory, it is not surprising that they would want to stop any Jews from working there in late 1944. Oskar said that Wilhelm, who had strong ties with local Nazi Party officials, did everything he could to stop Oskar from moving into his complex with his Schindler Jews. Hoffmann tried to convince district officials, the Gestapo, and local Nazi Party officials from letting Schindler "judaize" the region with his new factory. Hoffman argued that if they let Schindler open his factory using Jewish workers, they would bring typhus and other diseases with them. Hoffmann also warned local officials that if they let Schindler open his armaments factory, it could subject the entire factory complex to Allied bombing raids.[57]

It took many bribes and the help of two of Oskar's friends in Berlin, Erich Lange of the Army High Command's (OKH; *Oberkommando des*

Heeres) Ordnance Department *(Heereswaffenamt)* and *Oberstleutnant* Süßmuth, who headed the Armaments Inspectorate office in Troppau (Opava), for Oskar finally to receive permission to move his armaments factory to Brünnlitz. Emilie Schindler said that Lange oversaw arms production in the region for the OKH. She liked the well-mannered Lange, who, she said, always wore civilian clothing when he inspected the Schindler factory in Brünnlitz to show his distaste for the "Nazi regime." Lange explained that he was working for "his country and not for a specific government or system," a standard line among Wehrmacht officers, particularly after the war. Emilie added that Lange "was known for his rectitude and sense of justice." But he also had a reputation as a strict adherent of armaments production guidelines, which created some fear during his first inspection of the Schindler factory.[58]

Oskar credited Süßmuth, who worked closely with Lange, with convincing district officials of the value of Schindler's operations. Lange, of course, was Oskar's liaison with Maurer's D2 office, which would make the final decision on Schindler's Armaments Inspectorate proposal to open a factory using Jewish labor. Maurer's office would review Schindler's plans on the housing and care of his Jewish workers and make certain that there was adequate security to prevent escapes. If the plans met D2 guidelines, then they would be approved. And it was Lange who intervened when Oskar's Jews found themselves trapped in Groß Rosen or Auschwitz en route to Brünnlitz and helped to have them released and on their way to the Sudetenland.[59]

Yet Süßmuth was involved in more than just helping Oskar get permission to open his Brünnlitz factory. According to Oskar, he also helped transfer about 3,000 Jewish women from Auschwitz to small textile plants in villages in the *Sudetengau* and southern Poland in the fall of 1944. Süßmuth moved the women out of Auschwitz in small groups of three hundred to five hundred to help them escape "extermination by the SS murderers." Oskar added that this helped these women survive "the last year of the war." Oskar mentioned five villages in his report to Yad Vashem in 1955. Four of them, Freudenthal (Bruntl), Jägerdorf (Krnov), Grulich (Králíky), and Trautenau (Trutnov) were in the Sudetenland; the fifth, Liebau (Legnica), was just over the border in Poland.[60]

Presumably Süßmuth was involved in these transfers at the same time that Oskar was preparing for the transfer of 1,000 Jews from Płaszów to Brünnlitz. Interestingly enough, Auschwitz records do indicate that between October 14 and November 4, 1944, there were four separate transports from Auschwitz II-Birkenau to "other concentration camps" for 322, 348, 497, and 320 women. In addition, there were two larger transports (2,219 and 2,362 women) to "other concentration camps" on October 10 and November 4. Since Auschwitz records usually listed just the main camps in their transit records and not the sub-camps, it is quite possible that these were the women transferred by Süßmuth to other parts of Poland or the Sudetenland.[61]

But it took more than just the intervention of Süßmuth and Lange for Oscar to win final approval for the transfer of his workers from Płaszów to Brünnlitz. It would also take a lot of money and gifts. After the war, Oskar estimated that he spent RM 100,000 ($40,000) on bribes to complete the relocation of his armaments factory. He said that authorities knew that he was pressed for time and that his "generosity would be further increased by delays and displays of disinterest." In other words, authorities in the Sudetenland, the *Ostbahn* (Eastern Railroad), the Armaments Inspectorate, the OKH, the WVHA, Kraków, Płaszów, Auschwitz, and elsewhere involved in the transfer decision took advantage of the situation and used Oskar's desperation to get whatever they could out of him. Schindler was also hurt by the fact that his reputation had been damaged by his arrest by the SS in the early fall of 1944 for corruption. He had to supply these officials with "donation packets" filled with "foreign cigarettes, cigars, Schnaps, coffee, ham, textiles, etc., for astronomical prices on the black market" to keep things running smoothly throughout the late summer and early fall of 1944. And this was just the beginning of the new round of bribery. When Oskar finally got his workers to Brünnlitz, he had to spend even greater sums on "donation packets" for officials in the Sudetenland and Groß Rosen.[62]

The Chilowicz Murders

Oskar described this period as a nerve-racking time of desperation and uncertainty. It involved numerous trips to the Sudetenland and Berlin to sort out the difficulties he was having in getting permission to transfer part of his Emalia operations. These difficulties were complicated by his own arrest by the Gestapo for a few days in September 1944 and his interrogation by SS officials as part of the investigation into Amon Göth's crimes. This investigation and some of the events that led up to it would have a very direct impact on Schindler's efforts to save as many of his Jews as possible. In just a matter of a few weeks in August and September

1944, these developments would bring about several dramatic administrative changes in Płaszów that would play a decisive role in which Jews would be put on "Schindler's List."

One of the most controversial issues in the Holocaust was the role played by those in what Primo Levi described in *The Drowned and the Damned* as a "gray zone" of "*protekcja* [privilege] and collaboration" that existed between the Germans and others who ran the camps and its Jewish prisoners.[63] Levi, an Italian Jew who spent the latter part of the war in Auschwitz and became one of the foremost essayists on the Holocaust, went on to say in his autobiographical *Survival in Auschwitz* that "if one offers a position of privilege to a few individuals in a state of slavery, exacting in exchange the betrayal of a natural solidarity with their comrades, there will certainly be someone who will accept. . . . The more power that he is given, the more he will be consequently hateful and hated."[64] This was certainly true in Płaszów. Some of the most prominent people in the Schindler story, during and after the war, were part of this administrative "grey zone." Yet, with a few exceptions, these were honorable human beings who used their positions to help their fellow Jews. Yet, as Wolfgang Sofsky has pointed out, there was also a camp aristocracy, what Levi called the "Prominents," who wielded vast power and lived lives of comparable luxury unknown to the average prisoner.[65]

The Jewish OD (*jüdischer Ordnungsdienst*; Jewish Order Service) men lived in their own barracks with their families; office functionaries lived together in a barracks set aside for some of the more privileged prisoners. Mietek Pemper admitted in his testimony during Amon Göth's trial in 1946 that there was a time when he received extra food rations because of his special status as a Płaszów stenographer.[66] A member of the "grey zone" also had easier access to the black market and medical facilities. And though Mietek Pemper and Helen Sternlicht Rosenzweig and others like them lived in constant fear for their lives, they had a better chance of surviving the Holocaust than many of the transit prisoners who stayed briefly in Płaszów on their way to Auschwitz or another death camp. Primo Levi, in fact, noted that it was the "Prominents" who represented "a potent majority among survivors."[67] But as Isaiah Trunk has pointed out in his study of the *Judenrat* (Jewish Councils) during the Holocaust, even those Jews forced to work for the Germans would themselves be the Shoah's "final victims."[68] The key here is how one used one's influence and power in the camps. Most of the prominent *Schindlerjuden* in Płaszów used what modest power or influence they had to help others, though there were exceptions. Very often, of course, those they helped were relatives or acquaintances. Those who abused their power came to be, as Primo stated, the "hateful and hated."[69]

In her memoirs, Malvina Graf, a Cracovian Jew who survived the Kraków ghetto and Płaszów but was not on one of "Schindler's Lists," expressed some of her own frustration towards those she thought were among the privileged in Płaszów. She wrote that Göth showed some favoritism towards some of his Jewish prisoners, particularly Mietek Pemper and the two Rosner brothers, Henry and Leopold. Henry and Leopold were both musicians who played frequently for Amon Göth and were featured in the film, *Schindler's List*. She remembered two occasions when Göth intervened to save a friend of Pemper's or Pemper himself. She evidently got her information from her sister, Balbina, who worked for Kerner in the Jewish OD office. On one occasion, a friend of Pemper's, Luisa Lis, was taken to Chuwoja Gorka, Płaszów's principal killing site, for execution. When Göth learned of this, he personally went to "Prick Hill," stopped the executions, took Luisa out of the execution line, and brought her back to the women's camp. Graf's point in all this had less to do with Pemper than with her concern over the feelings of those on Chuwoja Gorka after Göth left with Luisa. "They were given a last bit of hope when their executions were 'stayed' only to see that their deaths had been postponed only momentarily."[70] Graf added that in August 1944, Göth needed someone to type a highly secret letter for him. She claimed that to maintain such secrecy, "any secretary who typed a letter containing information was shot immediately after completing the task." To protect Pemper, Graf claimed, Göth instead asked for a volunteer to come to his villa and prepare the letter. A Mr. Goldstein volunteered, typed the letter, and was then executed.[71]

Anything is possible, of course, though this story does not fit with what we know about the operations of Göth's office. He only allowed his part-time German secretary, Frau Kochmann, to type his most sensitive letters, though he often called Pemper to his villa late at night for dictation. This was a chaotic period in Płaszów and Göth was nervous about Dr. Konrad Morgen's criminal investigations into SS camp corruption elsewhere. This was also when Göth sought permission to murder Chilowicz and several other prominent OD men in the camp on false charges, so it is quite possible that the letter in question was the one to HSSPF Wilhelm Koppe asking permission to kill Chilowicz and other prominent OD men. Pemper, whom Göth seemed to trust, was not expendable because he was too valuable to the commandant. Given the sensitive nature of the letter to Koppe, it would also have been unwise for Göth to have Frau Kochmann type it, because she probably would have shared its contents with her husband, a judge in the city. So it is quite possible that he chose a volunteer to type it, and then had him killed on Chuwoja Gorka. This, of course, is all speculative and had nothing to do with Mietek Pemper. But Graf's comments about Pemper reflect some of the unspoken frustration I have sensed from Jewish survivors of Emala and Płaszów who did not make it to "Schindler's Ark" in Brünnlitz. For every Jew saved by Oskar Schindler, there were many, many more who did not, some of them former *Schindlerjuden* at Emalia. Some survived and others did not because they did not have the connections, means, or luck to make it onto his famous "list of life."

Sadly, the most hated Jews at Płaszów were also the most powerful at one time or another. This list included Wilek (Wilhelm) Chilowicz and his wife, Maria Chilowicz, and his top assistants, Mietek Finkelstein and Maier Kerner.[72] Other prominent OD men were Wilhelm (Wilek) Schnitzer, Chilowicz's secretary, Romek Faeber, and Schoenfeld.[73] Each of them, or at least their fates, would play an important role in determining which Jews would be sent to Oskar Schindler's new camp in Brünnlitz, which meant life, and who would not. Chilowicz was the head of the Jewish OD unit at Płaszów. It was his responsibility to maintain order in the closed Jewish portions of the camp and to help oversee all movements of Jews in and out of the camp. For better or worse, these responsibilities gave Chilowicz and those closest to him vast power over the Jewish inmates in Płaszów.

To visualize this, go back and watch how Steven Spielberg traces the story of Marcel Goldberg, the real author of "Schindler's List," in his film. He begins in the early part of the film with Goldberg sitting near Leopold "Poldek" Page and other Jewish black marketeers in Kraków's Marjacki Bazylika (St. Mary's Basilica) as Oskar Schindler tries to interest them in doing business with a German. What follows throughout the rest of the film is the subtle tale of Goldberg's gradual moral degeneration. Schindler, for example, gives Itzhak Stern first a lighter, then a cigarette case, and finally a watch to bribe Goldberg to send more Jews to his factory from Płaszów. And though Spielberg erroneously made Oskar Schindler and Itzhak Stern the authors of the famous "Schindler's List," it is apparent in his depiction of Goldberg throughout the film that he was aware that this OD man had a lot more to do with this matter than either Schindler or Stern.[74]

What corrupted Chilowicz and men like him was power mixed with greed. Wolfgang Sofsky said that the camp "aristocracy" had "everything the other prisoners lacked: enough to eat, warm clothing, sturdy shoes." They slept in their own beds, were clean-shaven, and did not have to shave their heads. If they were ill, they were given special medical care. They had access to the camp's brothel and to numerous other forms of entertainment. But "during the day, they spread terror in the camp, supported and admired by their servants and lackeys." At night, while playing cards, "they consumed the day's loot—a bottle of liquor, some cigarettes. In the midst of hunger and misery, the aristocracy lived in its own special world."[75] This was the world of Wilek Chilowicz and those closest to him.

In fairness to Chilowicz, a few Schindler Jews, Roman Ferber among them, spoke kindly of him. Chilowicz, who had no children, hid Roman in the camp. But Ferber also admits that Chilowicz was Göth's "flunky" and helped the commandant "amass a fortune on Kraków's black market." He also admitted that Chilowicz "collected quite a nest egg for himself."[76] Dr. Stanley Robbin said that it was Chilowicz who sent him to Emalia, ultimately a life-saving gesture.[77] Abraham Zuckerman remembered one occasion when he and several hundred other Jews were taken by Chilowicz to Chuwoja Gorka after several women had escaped. Zuckerman was fully prepared to die. Instead, Chilowicz just lectured them harshly about the escapes and told everyone to go back to work. Zuckerman thought that Chilowicz "had some compassion . . . and he only put on a display of anger for his Nazi superiors."[78] While she was in Płaszów, Stella Müller-Madej remembered hearing that Chilowicz was "trying to do some good things" for them, although she never saw any of his good deeds. She added that he was "not a kind person" and "shouts at us all the time, calling us sons of bitches, an expression that is always on his lips."[79]

But Chilowicz and his wife, Maria, and many of those who worked as OD men for them, also had very violent, vulgar reputations. Maria Chilowicz, who was in charge of the women's camp, was nicknamed "the duck" because she was bow-legged and walked "like a duck."[80] She, like her husband, always carried a whip and constantly referred to the camp women as "whores." Aleksander Bieberstein considered Wilek and Maria

Chilowicz sadists.[81] Igor Kling remembered how they treated him when he arrived at Płaszów in the spring of 1944 from the Borysław ghetto. Both Chilowiczes met the transport at the camp's front gate. "Chilowicz and his wife, they started cursing us right away. Using such profanity! The women were shocked. I remember he was wearing riding breeches and boots—all shined up—and a white silk shirt. He had a whip in his hand, a full head of hair."[82] Sally Huppert (Sara Peller) remembered trying to sneak a seven-year-old cousin into Płaszów after the closing of the ghetto. She was met at the gate by Göth and Chilowicz, who refused to let her bring the young girl into the camp. Sally tried to hide the young child under her coat but Chilowicz took the girl away. She was presumably murdered soon afterwards.[83]

But more feared than Chilowicz or his wife were two of his assistants, Mietek Finkelstein and Maier Kerner. Stella Müller-Madej said that the inmates in Płaszów feared Finkelstein, who was quite vulgar and "usually a little drunk," more than Amon Göth.[84] Aleksander Bieberstein said that Finkelstein would beat inmates into unconsciousness.[85] But the prisoners were even more afraid of Kerner. Stella said he was "a completely evil man" who inspired "hysterical fear. He waves a cane around and beats people needlessly."[86] But he did more than wave his cane. Bieberstein wrote in his memoirs that, though a religious man, Kerner had no compunction about mistreating prisoners and beating them over and over, particularly in the face.[87] Stella Müller-Madej added that the children in Płaszów, whom Kerner constantly chased with his cane but never hit, made up a Yiddish song about him:

Majer Kerner the bandit, ta-ra-ra-ra-boom,
he knows not what he does, ta-ra-ra-ra-boom,
if we survive, we'll tear out his eyes.[88]

Kerner, Finkelstein, and other top OD men were involved in Chilowicz's effort to amass wealth while they were in Płaszów. Mietek Pemper said that the basis of Chilowicz's wealth came from the goods that Göth had collected from Kraków's Jews after the closing of the ghetto. Though Göth was supposed to send these valuables to the Reichsbank, he told Chilowicz to keep most of it for his [Göth's] own "expenses." These goods became the basis of Göth's black market empire at Płaszów. Chilowicz, who handled Göth's black market deals, always managed to skim something off the top for himself.[89]

But Julius Madritsch said that Chilowicz did more than steal from Göth. Madritsch expressed great disdain for Chilowicz and the other "small number of Jews who, being friendly with the camp commanders, had the nerves not only to betray their fellow Jews and fellow sufferers for invalid, insignificant advantages" but also extorted "special bonuses" from Madritsch and other factory owners "without a sense of shame." Madritsch remembered one occasion when Chilowicz suggested to Göth that they needed to "get rid of 20 percent of our people, since they are too old and the camp was too full." Fortunately, Madritsch and Titsch were able to talk Göth out of this and convinced him that the elderly in the camp were their "most valuable expert workers."[90]

In the end, Chilowicz's power and greed led to his undoing. He became arrogant and bragged that "if no Jews survive the war, Chilowicz will certainly survive it."[91] As the camp was being evacuated, Göth became concerned that Chilowicz would be shipped out of Płaszów to another camp in the Reich. If that happened, he might reveal some of the secrets of Göth's illicit activities. Göth, of course, was well aware of Dr. Konrad Morgen's year-long investigation into corruption in the concentration camp system, and he had plenty to worry about. Yet SS regulations prevented Göth from murdering the Chilowiczes and their top aides outright.

When Płaszów became a concentration camp, the SS imposed stricter rules for the execution and punishment of prisoners. Mietek Pemper testified at Göth's trial that the SS staff now had to sign a declaration that they would not kill any prisoners. If a commandant wanted to execute someone, he would have to send a telegram to SS headquarters in Berlin, where Heinrich Himmler and *SS-Obergruppenführer und Generalleutnant der Polizei* Ernst Kaltenbrunner, the head of RSHA, would review the request and approve or disapprove it.[92] In the Chilowicz case, Göth would argue that Chilowicz was planning a camp revolt. But new regulations stipulated that Göth had to have the approval of local police authorities, not SS headquarters, to murder the Chilowiczes; this meant the approval would come from HSSPF Wilhelm Koppe.[93]

To get Koppe's permission for the Chilowicz executions, Göth had one of his noncommissioned officers, *SS-Oberwachmann* Josef Sowinski, prepare a detailed, false report about a potential camp rebellion led by Chilowicz and other OD men. Over the past eighteen months, there had been major concentration camp or ghetto uprisings in Sobibór, Treblinka, and Warsaw, as well as the July 20, 1944, attempt on Adolf Hitler's life. In this unstable atmosphere, Göth could expect a positive response from Koppe. In his letter to the HSSPF, Göth asked Koppe for permission to stop the revolt and execute its leaders. Several days later, Koppe sent Göth a secret letter giving him the authority to carry out the executions.[94]

Thomas Keneally spent several pages talking about the Chilowicz murders, though his account is different from those of others who were there. In Keneally's account, Amon Göth arranged to have Sowinski try to sneak the Chilowizces, Finkelstein, and Wilek Chilowicz's sister and brother-in-law, Malia and Romek [Moniek] Ferber, out of the camp in a truck. Göth provided Sowinski with a gun to give Chilowicz, and as the truck moved through the front gate of the camp, Göth, Hujar, and several other SS men (Ivan Scharujew and Amthor) stopped them. They found that "Chilowicz' pockets were laden with diamonds, bribes paid him by the desperate inmates of the camp." Göth then, according to Keneally, shot all of them. During his trial in 1946, Göth testified that he shot Chilowicz and the others "because he tried to escape, owned a weapon, and some valuables."[95]

The real story is quite different, though Roman Ferber, Moniek's brother, simply quotes from Keneally's account in his interview with Elinor Brecher. But he adds that the story about the diamonds is fiction: "Those guys weren't that dumb. They buried all that stuff, and some of it was found after the war."[96] But other *Schindlerjuden* tell a different story. On August 12, 1944, the day before the Chilowicz murders, Wilek Chilowicz went to the shipping department at Julius Madritsch's sewing factory complex just up SS Straße from the commandant's villa. Chaskel Schlesinger was working in the shipping department and accompanied Chilowicz, who he thought was "a monster," to the Madritsch warehouse to pick up some fabric. Chilowicz told Schlesinger: "We're not going to let them get away with this. We're going to fight!"[97] At the time, Chaskel had no idea what he was talking about. The next day, Wilek Chilowicz's sister, Malia Ferber, told Margot Schlesinger that Göth had just searched Chilowicz's barracks and found a gun. Chilowicz claimed that Göth had given him the gun.[98]

The same day, August 13, *Schindlerjude* Celina Karp Biniaz remembered seeing Wilek and Maria Chilowicz again working at Madritsch's warehouse. Madritsch was not there at the time. Celina heard that Göth was coming and hid behind some bales of fabric. Göth walked into the warehouse, found Wilek Chilowicz, and shot him to death. When Maria Chilowek ran into the room to see what was happening, Göth shot her as well. Thirty minutes later, Moniek Ferber, Chilowicz's secretary, was walking into his barracks and found Göth and several other SS officers waiting for him. Göth asked Moniek, "Where is your wife?" Ferber called Malia to come out of their room. Göth then shot both of them. During the next few hours, Göth also murdered Mietek Finkelstein, Wilek Schnitzer, and Schoenfeld.[99]

After the shootings, Stella Müller-Madej remembered being forced to go to an area between the men and women's barracks to see the bodies. As the inmates marched to the spot where they lay, she saw Göth on horseback. Near him were two inmates holding a banner that read: "Everybody who puts up resistance will die this way."[100] Mietek Pemper said that a sign next to the bodies explained that Chilowicz had been killed because "he tried to escape, owned a weapon, and some valuables."[101] Chaskel Schlesinger remembered that the sign said they were killed "because they want[ed] to run away, and they had jewels and guns."[102] As the inmates slowly walked past the bodies, Göth told the inmates that this would be their fate if they tried to mount a rebellion. But all Stella could remember was the awful sight of "flies crawling into the nostrils and open mouths of the corpses."[103]

But this was not the end of the ordeal. The inmates were then marched to the *Appellplatz,* where Göth forced them to watch the hanging of two young men. One was so badly beaten that *Kapos* had to carry him to the gallows.[104] The other victim, Adam Sztab, was the leader of ZOB (*Żydowska Organizacja Bojowa;* Jewish Fighting Organization) in Płaszów. ZOB was one of the principal armed Jewish resistance groups in Poland and had led the Warsaw ghetto uprising the year before.[105] Adam had also taken care of Göth's dogs, Rolf and Ralf, which Stella told me was the reason Göth killed him. Stella said in her memoirs that Göth had wanted to kill Adam once before because he had "crossed" the commandant, but Ruth, Göth's mistress, stopped him. But the real reason Göth disliked Adam, Stella told me when I interviewed her in Kraków, was that he was jealous because Rolf and Ralf seemed to like Adam more than they liked Göth. Anything is possible, though it would seem more logical that Göth would have murdered Sztab for his underground activities, not out of jealousy over his dogs. This reasoning was Alexander Bieberstein's explanation behind the hangings.[106]

But Stella knew Adam not as a ZOB leader but as a childhood acquaintance. He had been a close friend of Stella's brother, Adam, and fondly remembered playing with Adam Sztab before the war. She, her brother, and Adam Sztab would play ball in one of Kraków's parks. Once, when Adam Sztab tossed her the ball, he yelled to her, "You're a butterfingers if you don't catch it, Stella."[107] Now Stella had to stand at attention during his execution. Stella was unable to watch the hangings but remembered seeing Adam's body quivering from the hangman's rope. She also remembered Göth telling the inmates that there had been a conspiracy and that the "other rebels will meet a similarly harsh fate."[108] According to Alexander Bieberstein, a sign was put near Sztab's body that read: *"Tak zginą wszyscy, który ukrją broń"* (Anyone who hides weapons will be killed).[109]

It is hard to determine from survivor testimony who exactly was killed in Płaszów on August 13, 1944. Aleksander Bieberstein mentioned Chilowicz and his wife, Finkelstein, Ferber, Schnitzer, and Schoenfeld.[110] Mietek Pemper, the principal witness against Amon Göth in his 1946 trial, spent a lot of time answering questions about the killings during the war crimes proceedings against Göth. He mentioned the "assassination of Chilowicz and his family," which meant the Ferbers and the Chilowiczes.[111] Schindler Jew Chaskel Schlesinger added that in addition to the Chilowiczes and the Ferbers, Göth also murdered two of Chilowicz's nephews that day. Roman Ferber added that Göth also killed another of Chilowicz's sisters, Feiga S. In fact, Ferber noted, Göth killed just about anyone related to Chilowicz. Finally, Stella Müller-Madej mentioned the executions of Adam Sztab and another man.[112] What we do know was that it was a blood bath that sent a chill through the camp. Sometime later, as the Kommando 1005 units were clearing out the mass graves in Płaszów, Iser Mintz found Wilek Chilowicz's body and his gold watch, a birthday gift from Płaszów's Jewish inmates. On the back there was an inscription in German, "Für seinen guten Dienst" (For his good service). After Iser discovered the watch, one of the *Kapos* took it from him, only to discover that it was not real gold. He tossed it back to Iser, who sold it for two or three loaves of bread.[113]

The SS, Crime, and Corruption

The murder of Płaszów's principal Jewish leaders seemed to be the final straw for the SS, which arrested Göth a month later on a variety of charges, including the Chilowicz murders.

Their deaths, when combined with the arrest of Göth and the general disorder surrounding the closing of the camp, created leadership voids that would have a significant impact not only on the authorship of "Schindler's List," but also on the names placed on it.

By 1944, the SS had become an economic force in its own right through its control of a growing complex of factories and other enterprises. SS wealth grew substantially after the seizure of Jewish businesses in Poland and the use of Jewish concentration camp labor in factories controlled by the SS. The SS was able to develop almost total monopolies in furniture, ceramics, and mineral water production, though once the fortunes of war turned against Germany, Himmler's organization began to shift to more armaments production to maintain its economic vitality.[114]

This lust for wealth and profit bred a culture of greed and corruption in the SS, particularly in the General Government. Himmler addressed this issue in a speech to SS officers in the fall of 1944:

> We have become a very corrupt people. But we must not and need not take this very profoundly or with Weltschmerz [pessimistic outlook] tragedy. We shall not gain control of this plague known as corruption in our circles [of the SS] if we do not act against any outbreak of corruption in our circles, unconditionally and unrestrictedly with no ifs, ands, or buts, if we do not barbarically pursue it, degrade the corrupt man, remove him from office, and expose him before his subalterns. However, what actually deserves to be called corruption is not serious in our circles. Still, there are little things to which one does not give a second thought and for which one uses the expression "to liberate something."[115]

Embedded in Himmler's speech was the uncertainty surrounding SS enforcement of its own codes dealing with corruption and criminality.

Himmler saw the SS not only as the guardian of the Nazi state and its values, but also as Nazi Germany's role model, its racial educator. Himmler, working with Richard Walther Darré, an Argentinian German who became head of the SS Race and Resettlement Main Office (RuSHA; *Rasse-und Siedlungshauptamt*) in 1931, saw the SS as "a new racial-German aristocracy." Along with these racial ideals were medieval ideas of honor and chivalry that were to elevate SS members to a special status in Nazi Germany.[116]

Yet this vanguard and protector of the Nazi racial revolution was made up of human beings, and as such they were prey to the failings of a state within a dictatorial state. Corruption became a serious problem within the SS during the war, particularly in the vast complex of concentration, forced labor, and death camps that it ran. Theoretically, the regular SS was subject to normal German criminal and civil law, though in 1939 a separate legal system was developed for the Waffen SS. In reality, though, as *SS-Oberführer* Günther Reinecke, the Chief Judge of the Supreme SS and Police Court explained in his Nuremberg testimony in 1946, the SS "internal disciplinary law consisted of the right of exclusion," meaning that anyone with a criminal record could not be a member of the SS and those who committed crimes as SS members "had to leave the SS." The reality, of course, was quite different. For all practical purposes, the SS remained a law unto itself.[117]

The SS had its own Legal Department *(Hauptamt SS-Greicht)*, which oversaw a network of Supreme SS and Police Courts, SS and Police Courts, and SS and Police Courts Martial. Needless to say, their effectiveness in controlling corruption among an SS membership that declined in quality during the war years was less than sterling, particularly in the General Government. Occasionally, when corruption was blatant, the SS would step in and punish the victim, as it did in the case of *SS-Untergruppenführer* Lorenz Löv, the deputy head of the General Government's Central Administrative Office. Charged with running a large black market ring, Löv was brought to trial in SS and Police Court VI in Kraków and convicted by Chief Judge *SS-Oberführer* Dr. Günther Reinecke, who sentenced him to life imprisonment. Reinecke explained in his secret judgement statement that he chose not to pass a death sentence on Löv because the same charges could have been brought against Hans Frank's family and close associates. After the war, Reinecke explained that such SS criminality could be traced to the infiltration of the SS "by personas and organizations completely alien to the character of the SS." This, of course, was ridiculous, because men such as Amon Göth, Oskar Dirlewanger, and Karl Otto Koch were veteran Nazis who had joined the SS early in their careers.[118]

Oddly enough, there were also SS regulations dealing with the mistreatment of prisoners in the SS camps, even Jews. When acts of sadism were combined with corruption, which often went hand-in-hand, Himmler would periodically unleash investigations. According to Heinz Höhne, "sadism undermined its [the SS] discipline and corruption destroyed its ideology."[119] Occasionally, SS members were even punished for such crimes, though more often than not they got away with it. The contradiction here was that the SS would send legal experts into a camp to investigate an act or two of sadism while thousands were being butchered nearby in the same camp.[120]

A case in point: the investigations initiated by Dr. Georg Konrad Morgen, an assistant judge in the SS and Police Court *(SS- und Polizeigerichte)* in Kraków, against the brutal activities of *SS-Obersturmführer* Dr. Oskar Dirlewanger, a suspected sexual deviant. Dirlewanger ran an SS Death Head Sonderkommando unit *(SS Totenkopfverbände)*, the *SS-Sonderbataillon Dirlewanger*, which waged vicious campaigns against partisans in Poland and the Soviet Union and Jews in the Kraków and Lublin ghettos. In his Nuremberg testimony after the war, Morgen explained that while operating in the Lublin ghetto, Dirlewanger had entertained some SS officers by torturing young Jewish girls to death. Dirlewanger then had soap made from the fat of some of the victims, who died horribly from strychnine poisoning. According to Raul Hilberg, this is one of the first instances that reference was made to the "soap-making rumor."[121]

Morgen's efforts to have Dirlewanger arrested in early 1942 for his crimes were unsuccessful, though this might have prompted the transfer of Dirlewanger's unit to Belorussia several months later. Morgen did quarrel with HSSPF *Ost SS-Obergruppenführer* Friedrich Wilhelm Krüger over his investigations, which resulted in a punishment for Morgen: his transfer to the Russian front with the Waffen SS Viking Division. Though the SS continued to investigate Dirlewanger's crimes, Himmler regarded him as something of an SS hero because of his actions against partisans, particularly in the Warsaw and Slovak uprisings in 1944. Dirlewanger ended the war as an *SS-Oberführer*. He received the War Order of the German Cross *(Kriegsorden des Deutschen Kreuzes)* in gold in 1943 and was one of only 7,200 Germans to receive the Knight's Cross of the Iron Cross *(Ritterkreuz des Eisernen Kreuzes)*. Dirlewanger disappeared after the war and rumors had him in Cairo and France. Actually, he died mysteriously in a French prison, where his body was exhumed in November 1960.[122]

In 1943, Morgen joined the Economic Crimes Office of Kripo, the Reich Criminal Police. The SS and Police Court in District XII, which included the infamous Buchenwald concentration camp, asked Kripo for help in investigating a corruption ring in the camp centered around Buchenwald's former commandant (1937–1941), Karl Otto Koch. The SS and Police Court insisted, though, that Kripo's investigative officer had to be an SS officer. Morgen, who by this time was an *SS-Sturmbannführer* in the Waffen SS, fit the bill. In his investigation, Morgen found a "network of corruption" with "ramifications extending into the other concentration camps."[123] Morgen also discovered evidence of Koch's brutality and decided to link these crimes with Koch's corruption in his final report to Arthur Nebe, the head of Kripo. Nebe refused to act on Morgen's report so Morgen then took the case to Heinrich Müller, the head of the Gestapo. Müller suggested that Morgen see the head of the SS Legal office, *SS-Obergruppenführer* Franz Breithaupt, who concluded that this was a matter for Heinrich Himmler. Ultimately, Morgen sent his report to Himmler, who gave Morgen the go-ahead to initiate criminal proceedings against Koch, his wife and co-conspirator, Ilse, and their cronies.[124]

By this time, Koch, who had been arrested on corruption charges in the winter of 1941 and then quickly released on Himmler's orders, was transferred to Lublin to become commandant of Majdanek, a new Soviet prisoner-of-war camp there. Koch lost his job in the summer of 1942 when the SS brought new charges of criminal negligence against him after several prisoner escapes in Majdanek earlier that spring. The SS later dropped the charges after Koch explained the circumstances of the escapes and gave him a job in Berlin working as a liaison between the SS and the postal service.[125]

Morgen had Koch arrested and brought to Buchenwald, where he personally interrogated Koch. Ultimately, Koch confessed to his crimes and was executed by the SS in the spring of 1945. Once Morgen got Koch's confession, he then initiated similar investigations in other concentration camps where he finally discovered the depth of SS crimes against Jews and other victims. Morgen was not interested in officially approved racial or euthanasia killings, just those of an "arbitrary" nature. Morgen sent SS investigative teams into Buchenwald, where he lived for eight months as part of his efforts against Koch, and also into camps and ghettos in Kraków, Płaszow, Majdanek, Auschwitz, Sachsenhausen, Oranienburg, Dachau, Warsaw, and Vught in the Netherlands. Amon Göth was investigated in the summer of 1944 by one of Morgen's teams. Morgen was able to win two hundred convictions out of the eight hundred cases he investigated in 1943 and 1944. He personally arrested five concentration commandants, two of whom were shot after their convictions. One of those executed was Koch, who was shot by the SS in Buchenwald in April 1945. His wife, Ilse, who was tried as her husband's accomplice, was acquitted.[126]

However, just as Morgen was intensifying his investigations, Himmler ordered Morgen to limit himself to the Koch case. In reality, the SS had become afraid of Morgen and his investigative teams. Stefan Heymann, one of the prisoner clerks at Buchenwald, told American investigators immediately after the war that he [Morgen] was extraordinarily feared and hated by all SS officers in Buchenwald. They breathed easier when Morgen moved back to Berlin because they feared the investigation could also bring to light incriminating material about themselves. And, indeed, they had all been as corrupt and brutal as Koch.[127]

In the summer of 1946, Morgen testified as a defense witness in the International Military Tribunal's Nuremberg case against the SS, one of six Nazi organizations indicted as criminal organizations. The former SS officer and prosecutor then "disappeared into obscurity."[128]

Amon Göth was not the only person under investigation by the SS and the Gestapo with ties to Oskar Schindler. In his July 1945 financial statement, Oskar listed Julian Scherner, the HSSPF in the Kraków district, for example, as one of the principal recipients of bribes he paid to the SS during his five years in Kraków. Another important Kraków-based SS officer jailed for fraud and theft was *SS-Sturmbannführer* Willi Haase, who personally oversaw the brutal *Aktion* in the Kraków ghetto on October 28, 1942. The SS charged Haase with various crimes. The most serious was the theft of paintings from Jewish victims in the ghetto. One of those stolen was by Wojciech Kossak, one of Poland's most famous artists, who coincidentally died in Kraków in the summer of 1942. Kossak's paintings were popular among Germans in Kraków, which added to the severity of Hasse's theft.[129]

When he was interrogated about his crimes, Haase said he got the paintings from Wilhelm Kunde, an SS *Hauptscharführer* and *Kriminalsekretär* who specialized in Jewish affairs. Kunde, of course, denied everything. He claimed that Haase acquired the paintings from two Jewish informers for the Gestapo, Steinfeld and Brodman. Later, Steinfeld said that Haase had ordered the two Jewish informants to give the paintings to Kunde. After the ghetto closed, Kunde would drop by Pankiewicz's pharmacy in the empty ghetto almost every day before the SS shut it down. Kunde seemed to like the Polish pharmacist, who occasionally gave him "gifts." Kunde liked to talk about the war and other matters, and on one occasion, Kunde told Pankiewicz that he had to be very careful about taking bribes because of jealousy among the Germans in Kraków. Kunde said he knew of one SS officer who had drawn attention to himself by depositing vast sums of money in his bank account. When he could not explain where the money came from, the SS arrested him. Kunde said that to avoid any hint of corruption, the only jewelry he wore was a cheap steel watch. He also shunned bars and theaters to avoid calling attention to himself. If he wanted to entertain friends or colleagues, he did it at home.[130]

Oskar Schindler knew all this, and his genius was his ability to use German greed to his advantage when dealing with people like Göth and Scherner. He also understood the importance of discretion and was probably quite careful about flaunting his own well-being. What got Oskar into trouble with the SS and the Gestapo was not only the size and nature of the bribes that he gave SS and other officials, but their indiscreet display of them. It did not help Oskar's case, of course, that he also showed some sympathy towards his Jewish workers. Yet in another sense, Oskar's bribes to prominent SS and General Government officials, combined with his important connections to the military, probably gave him a modicum of protection. There is no doubt, particularly by 1943, that if Schindler had been arrested and thoroughly investigated for corruption, his testimony could probably have ruined the careers of quite a few SS members. But Oskar was also protected because his factories produced goods of value to officials in the General Government and the SS, either directly or as bribes. Yet pots and pans would not seem to be of value to anyone except a housewife. But with the heavy rationing of metal, everyday pots and pans became a scarce item in the Nazi world. Oskar said, for example, that the "need of the office directors [for kitchenware] was unbelievable; the distribution of kitchenware [as bribes] was up to 30,000 kg (66,138 lbs) per year. I even delivered [kitchenware] to their aunts and grandmothers who had been bombed out in the Reich."[131] In addition, Oskar traded Emalia kitchenware for food.[132] But in time, his black market dealings and the bribes he paid to Amon Göth would catch up with him and almost destroy his efforts to use such dealings to help save his Jewish workers.

The Arrest and Investigation of Amon Göth

The arrest of Amon Göth on September 13, 1944, on charges of corruption, abuse, and murder initiated a six-month SS investigation into all aspects of Göth's tenure as Płaszów's commandant from February 1943 until September 1944. This was the last major investigation of Dr. Morgen's SS team of lawyers and judges. Göth's SS file says little about the investigation. On April 14, 1944, the WVHA recommended that Göth be officially accepted as an *SS-Hauptsturmführer* in the Waffen SS reserves and be transferred from the headquarters company of the HSSPF General Government to the WVHA's *Amtsgruppe* D. The reason for the transfer was that Płaszów was now an official concentration camp and no longer under the authority of the HSSPF in the General Government.[133] The request was rejected ten days later by *SS-Brigadeführer und Generalmajor der Waffen-SS* Dr. Adolf Katz because Göth had not completed his basic Waffen SS reserves Leadership Training Course. Until he had done this, Katz said, there was no way to determine whether Płaszów's commandant had proven "his aptitude for being a Waffen-SS Reserves officer."[134]

One reason Göth might have failed to complete his reserve training was his desire to avoid serving in the Waffen SS on the Eastern front. There had been a steady flow of officers and men from the Waffen SS Death's Head Division *(Totenkopfdivision)* battlefield units to and from the concentration camps throughout the war. On the one hand, such a move could have been a career move for Göth; on the other, it terminated his life of luxury and corruption in Płaszów and hindered his plans to use his booty as a nest egg for a comfortable postwar life.[135] Dr. Katz's resistance to Göth's transfer was finally overcome and in early June he officially became part of the Waffen-SS reserves, assigned to 11th *SS-Standarte* (Regiment) *Planetta*, which was headquartered in Vienna. Göth had served with this unit with distinction earlier in the war in Kattowitz.[136]

These are no other documents in Göth's SS file until August 31, 1944, when a note card, with information supplied by Göth, was placed in it that gives his work and home address. He listed "KL. Plaszow, Cracow, P.O. Box 1024, (7a)" as his work address and "Vienna VI/56. Mariahilferstrasse-105" as his home address.[137] Several days later, HSSPF Koppe received a note that included an August 16, 1944, letter from Hans Stauber, the chief treasurer of Army Post Administration Kraków *(Heeresstandortverwaltung Krakau)*, to Heinrich Himmler, about the closing of Płaszów. Stauber was a close friend of Himmler's and at one point in the letter referred to him as Heini. What concerned Stauber about the evacuation of Płaszów was the loss of Jewish labor. He took this as an SS slight against the Wehrmacht in the aftermath of the July 20, 1944, assassination attempt on Adolf Hitler. Stauber pleaded with Heini to do something to resolve this dilemma. He added that "today everyone needs to give of his best and each task must be accomplished in view of the great goal, the imminent final victory." The most interesting part of the letter are his criticisms of the way Płaszów was run. He thought the "fact that one takes, for example, cigarettes, from the prisoners to portion them out among the guards or that a loaf of bread is being offered to the prisoners at Zł 600–1,000 ($187.50–312.50) for sale (supposedly from nearby placed Jews!!) surely casts a bad light on the supervision [of the camp]."[138]

Though it is possible that Stauber's letter to Himmler might have provided some new information for the SS investigation into the numerous charges against Göth, they were not the basis of Dr. Morgen's legal efforts against Płaszów's commandant. According to Mietek Pemper, who testified against Göth in his 1946 trial, the charges came from disgruntled SS men who had served under Göth. They were angry for the cruel way Göth treated them and for "bringing charges against them to the military court [SS and Police Court]." Pemper testified that Göth had reported one SS man for stealing a small sum of money. The SS man told the SS court that he did not understand why he had to be punished so hard when the "commandant owned a great fortune in valuables [and] foreign currencies."[139] However, in 1964, Oskar Schindler told Martin Gosch and Howard Koch, who interviewed him for a film script they were preparing on his life, that the SS was angry because Göth had executed two Jewish prisoners who were spies for Himmler. The SS, Oskar explained, was "determined to get something on him [Göth]," which led to an investigation that revealed Göth's corruption.[140]

The final note in Göth's file was dated September 6, 1944. It is a wire from Koppe to *SS-Standartenführer* Brandt of the Gestapo's office in Koblenz informing him that Göth was still in Kraków-Płaszów. Koppe told Brandt that the camp was about to be completely shut down and that most of its inmates had already been sent elsewhere. He added: "A process of judicial inquiry is going on against *Hauptsturmführer* Goeth because of usurpation of official authority. During the course of the process other suspicious facts that arise will be investigated simultaneously." Exactly a week later, Amon Göth was arrested by the Gestapo and taken to Breslau, where he would remain in jail until October 22, 1944.[141]

There is some confusion about where Göth was actually arrested. Mietek Pemper, who is our principal source on the SS investigation into Göth's crimes, testified at Göth's 1946 trial that he was arrested in Kraków. But he told me during our first interview in 1999 that the SS arrested him in Vienna, where he was visiting his father.[142] Helen ("Susanna") Sternlicht Rosenzweig also remembered Göth's arrest in Płaszów. On the day in question, "Susanna" heard the door bell ring. When she opened the front door, she saw two civilians who asked for

Göth. She told Göth, who was upstairs, about the two men and he came downstairs to meet them. In the meantime, "Susanna" had stopped at the top of the stairs leading down to the kitchen and watched everything. Göth got his hat and "his belt with the gun," and then walked out the front door between the two men. "Susanna" then told Helen Hirsch what she had just seen. "I think they take him away." Helen replied, "You're such a child; who would take him away? He's the chief commander. No one can touch him."[143]

"Susanna" said that she and Helen were alone in the villa for several days. The implication is that Ruth Kalder was also absent. Then they received a telephone call from Göth. "His voice was completely different." He told his maids to pack him some underwear and socks and that someone would pick them up for him. "Then we knew he was arrested and would never come back." "Susanna" said his arrest saved her life; she was certain he would have killed both maids because they "knew too much."[144]

It is possible, of course, that Göth was taken by the two men, who were probably Kripo (Kriminalpolizei; criminal police) agents, to Vienna to get his affairs in order before his formal arrest. Kripo and the SS and Police Courts worked hand-in-hand on the concentration camp investigations. Dr. Morgen had been made head of the investigations because he was a Kripo specialist on economic crimes and was also a Waffen-SS officer.[145] Göth's arrest sent shock waves through Płaszów. Mietek Pemper told me it was like "the Pope['s] being arrested for stealing silver spoons."[146]

What followed was a well-coordinated investigation that involved the detention of Oskar Schindler and various Schindlerjuden. With the exception of Mietek Pemper, the Schindlerjuden interviewed at Płaszów were luckier. On the same day that Göth was taken away by the Kripo agents, an SS and Police Court team arrived in the camp to begin its investigation. SS-Untersturmführer Judge Tauers headed the investigation. He interviewed three Schindlerjuden, Zygmunt Grünberg, an engineer and construction supervisor at Płaszów; Dr. Leon Gross, the chief Jewish physician; and Mietek Pemper.[147] Construction was constantly going on during Göth's reign at Płaszów and Göth seemed always to set unrealistic building deadlines for Grünberg, whom he beat when they were not met. Schindlerjude Joseph Bau said that Grünberg "absorbed in silence blows that would have felled a boxing champion."[148] On one occasion, Göth even held Grünberg's wife and daughter hostage to force him to complete a project in forty-eight hours. Appeals by Grünberg's SS supervisor, SS-

Obersturmführer Huth, could not dissuade Göth from doing any more than extending the deadline by twenty-four hours.[149]

Grünberg, Gross, and Pemper were taken to Göth's villa for interrogation, though the SS investigators released Grünberg and Gross after a few hours. After the initial interrogation of Pemper, the SS officers left him in the villa and went to talk to *SS-Hauptscharführer* Lorentz Landstorfer and *SS-Hauptscharführer* Franz Josef Müller, noncommissioned officers who worked with the Jewish prisoners. Müller, one of the senior noncommissioned officers at Płaszów, had once been in charge of *Julag* I. He also oversaw a lot of the camp construction. Müller had gained a reputation for brutality not only at Płaszów but also at *Julag* I and the Bochnia ghetto. Landstorfer told the investigators that he had seen Pemper type defense plans for a possible partisan attack against the camp. Landstorfer was providing evidence for one of the principal SS charges against Göth: that he had shared some of the camp's secrets with prisoners. Pemper was able to convince Judge Tauer that he did not have access to such secret plans, though the SS investigator said Pemper knew of other camp defense secrets.[150]

For the next two weeks, the SS placed Pemper in solitary confinement in the camp's small jail in the "Grey House," one of the few original buildings still standing at Płaszów. This was a frightening place and even today, standing alone as it does on the edge of the former camp site, has an ominous look about it. Joseph Bau, a draftsman at Płaszów, has provided us with the only detailed look at the principal buildings at Płaszów in his memoirs, *Dear God, Have You Ever Gone Hungry?* The camp's jail was in the basement of the "Grey House," which he described as a "chamber of horrors." There were only a few cells in the basement. One was just large enough for a man to stand in; another was just long enough "for shoving a prone person in headfirst, as in a grave." There were several other isolation cells, which had small slots for water. Nearby was a bench for whipping prisoners with thick leather whips "made from dried-up bulls' genitalia." Few prisoners came out of the "Grey House" alive.[151]

Two weeks after his detention, an elderly SS judge questioned Pemper. During the two-hour interrogation, Pemper gave all the details he knew about Göth's illegal black market deals. He also told him where he could find the correspondence relating to Göth's illicit activities. Pemper went into details about Göth's theft of food from the camp and about the goods he had taken from Jews after the closing of the ghetto that were supposed to be sent to the Reichsbank. When he had completed his testimony, Pemper was released back into the prisoner population. Two weeks later, he was among the seven hundred men selected for transport to Brünnlitz. But this was not the end of his dealings with the SS over Amon Göth's crimes. In late February or early March 1945, he was taken to Groß Rosen and again interrogated by an SS judge from Munich. For the most part, the judge asked Pemper the same questions that he had been asked by the SS court investigators in Płaszów.[152]

In his testimony in Göth's trial in Kraków in 1946, Pemper told the judges that based on the questions asked him by the SS judges in Płaszów and Groß Rosen, he surmised that they were investigating a number of charges against the former Płaszów commandant. This included his theft of valuables from prisoners, which he failed to turn over to the SS, his luxurious lifestyle, and his failure to supply prisoners with adequate nourishment. Pemper told the Kraków court that he also thought the SS was investigating charges against Göth that he had violated concentration camp regulations, particularly when it came to abuses in the penalty company.[153] Dr. Aleksander Bieberstein, who also testified against Göth in 1946, went into some detail about one of Göth's favorite ways to abuse prisoners. It was called the *Mannschaftszug* (crew train) and was devised by Göth and *SS-Untersturmführer* Anton Scheidt. The *Mannschaftszug* was used in the quarry, which operated twenty-four hours a day. Only women were permitted to work there. Polish women worked in the quarry in twelve-hour shifts during the day; Jewish women worked at night. Thirty-five women were attached to each side of a train of small cars on which were loaded 9,000 kilograms (19,800 lbs) of stone for road work at the upper end of the camp. The women involved, who hauled from twelve to fifteen loads per shift, had to move each load up a very steep incline. Göth was proud of the *Mannschaftszug* and, on Christmas Eve 1943, he decided to display his unique form of torture to a group of prominent SS officers gathered at his villa for a party. Needless to say, most of the Germans at the party were disgusted by Göth's display. To counter the negative response, Ruth was able to convince Göth to let the female workers return to their barracks for the night.[154]

Pemper said that one SS judge told him that such work was a "synonym for death" because it meant "very hard work along with beating and often with death." The SS drew a fine line between what it justified as politically approved killings and "selfish, sadistic, or sexual punishment." In fact, in the fall of 1942, the SS legal department *(Hauptamt SS-Gericht)* asked Heinrich Himmler about these very issues. The Reichsführer SS responded that "if the motive is purely political there should be no punishment unless such is necessary for the maintenance of discipline. If the motive is selfish, sadistic, or sexual, judicial punishment should be imposed for murder or manslaughter as the case may be."[155] Pemper said that the SS also charged Göth for the Chilowicz murders and that one SS judge told him that Göth had killed Chilowicz and the other OD men because they knew too much.[156] In the end, Göth's brutal mistreatment of his prisoners came to haunt him, though the SS never charged him with the mass murder of thousands more because Himmler's organization approved of such crimes as politically motivated.

Finally, Pemper testified, the SS charged Göth with allowing his prisoners to see "the secret acts, correspondence, which is unavailable for prisoners." What the SS considered most important in these documents was the personal information, particularly the personnel evaluations of the SS men in the camp. These reports included negative comments that were only supposed to be seen by officers. Even noncommissioned officers could not see these reports. The fact that prisoners who worked in the camp's offices had seen these reports was considered a serious crime by the SS.[157]

In his 1964 statement to Gosch and Koch, Schindler said that after Göth's arrest on September 13, 1944, he "blamed everything on Oskar." Göth, for example, claimed that Schindler had given him the RM 80,000 ($32,000) found on his person when they arrested him. He also told the SS Court investigators that all of the contraband that they had found at Płaszów had come from Schindler. As a final part of their investigation, Dr. Morgen's SS team of lawyers and judges decided to detain Schindler, who at this time was at Brünnlitz preparing for the move of part of his factory from Emalia. On October 14 or 15, the twenty-four Jews unloading the huge wagon loads of goods from Emalia saw SS men snooping around the camp. They quickly hid some of Göth's personal possessions, thinking they belonged to Oskar. They poured the illegal alcohol into the small river that ran beside the factory's grounds, and hid the priceless cigarettes under a large transformer. This would later become the hiding place for Schindler's storehouse of illegal arms. Oskar, who had not seen the SS men, was driving into the factory to eat lunch with his Jewish workers. As he approached the factory gate, two men in civilian clothes approached him and ordered him to get out of his car. They said, "We want to question you." Oskar responded, "This is my factory—if you want to talk to me you can come to my car or else come over to my office." The plainclothesmen then followed Oskar into his office.[158]

When they got to Oskar's office, the SS men asked questions about "Göth's loot." Oskar told them that he knew nothing about the matter. He did admit that he had several of Göth's suitcases, which Göth had asked him to take down, and that they could open them. The suitcases contained only dirty laundry. Oskar quickly surmised that several of his interrogators were SS judges and he knew that he was in a lot of trouble. His first thought was to contact the Abwehr and Wehrmacht friends who had helped him in the past. At this point, Emilie walked into the office and wanted to know why her husband was under arrest. When the SS men refused to give her an answer, Oskar told her to stay out of it, that it was "not her affair." He did get word to Emilie to contact "Columbus," Schindler's secretary, Viktoria Klonowska, in Kraków; she, in turn, would contact someone who could arrange his release.[159]

At this point, the SS judges had Oskar handcuffed and taken by train to Kraków. As he got off the train, Oskar saw an old friend, Herr Hut, who walked up to him and shook his hand. One of the SS escorts chastised Hut for this: "You still dare to shake hands with this man, who is a prisoner?" Hut replied, "Well, under our law he's innocent until proven guilty. As far as I'm concerned, he is a fine man, a man that I always knew, Oskar Schindler—a fine gentleman, and Herr Direktor, not a prisoner." Schindler was then taken to Gestapo headquarters on Pomorska Street and put into one of the small, dark cells in the basement.[160]

That night, Hut came to see Oskar and brought him a good meal with wine. He also told Schindler that Emilie had contacted "Columbus" and that his secretary had begun contacting members of the "rescue network." Ths next day, Oskar was taken into a interrogation room where he was questioned by twelve SS officers and judges. Oskar's defense was fairly simple: "I don't know anything about this. I didn't give any bribes to Goeth—why should I? I didn't need anything from him—I'm on my way to Brünnlitz. I don't need any more Jews, I have all the workers I need. If I gave him this money, which he said I did, I gave it to him as a loan and there was no other reason." He also testified, "I'm not a fag," indicating that there was not a homosexual relationship between them.[161]

Oskar told Koch and Gosch that he was scared during the eight days he was in SS custody. He was no longer certain that his contacts could get him out of jail because the charge of corruption was so serious. He had been brought to Gestapo headquarters instead of Montelupich prison (where he had been incarcerated earlier), which also frightened him because "only the [word of a] top Nazi, Himmler, could save you." So even though

Schindler was treated well by the SS, he feared for his life. One of the Nazi officers who entered his cell spit on him and called him "a Jew-lover, king of the Jews." Later, after his release, Oskar met this SS officer in public and got into a fight with him. Schindler knocked the SS man unconscious.[162]

On the fourth or fifth day of his imprisonment, Hut, "pale, unshaven, drunk," visited Oskar and told him that Płaszów's new commandant, *SS-Obersturmführer* Arnold Büscher, refused to send the three hundred women initially selected to go to Brünnlitz via Auschwitz. According to Schindler, Büscher thought that Oskar was shipping these women to his new camp "for his own special reasons, and that he wasn't sufficiently anti-Jewish." Büscher wanted to take the Schindler women off the list and replace them with a different group of women. Oskar, who was becoming increasingly worried about the length of his detention, now had even more reason to try to find a way to get out of the Gestapo jail.[163]

He asked Hut to contact *General* Schoen, who was evidently in charge of concentration camps in the region, and to tell him that Oskar wanted to see him. More than likely, Koch and Gosch got the name wrong. If this part of the story is true, and there is no reason to doubt Schindler on this point because other sources verify his imprisonment at this time, he probably asked Hut to contact *General* Schindler, who oversaw concentration camp labor for the Wehrmacht's Armaments Inspectorate in the General Government. Regardless, the general did visit Schindler and told him, "Now don't worry, we're going to get you out of here, and we're going to see that the whole blame is placed on Goeth." The next morning, October 21 or 22, Oskar was released. But instead of returning to Emalia, he drove immediately to Płaszów to find out what had happened to the women.[164]

As luck would have it, Oskar arrived as 2,000 women were being loaded onto train cars for the transport to Auschwitz. When Schindler drove through the camp's gate, his women saw him and began to cry out, "There's Schindler . . . Schindler." Oskar told Koch and Gosch that Büscher had a separation order for the Schindler women, though it is unclear what he meant by this. When Oskar got out of his car, Büscher asked, "What are you doing here? You have no business here, you are under arrest." Oskar replied, "You'd be surprised, I have lots of things to do here. I spoke to your boss and do you know what you are doing? You are sabotaging production. Eight days of production for these 300 women. I want you to refer to your list and then separate these 300 women, then take them out of the 9,000 [2,000]—it's an order, and this must be complied with, as I have this word from the head of the War Production in Berlin." Büscher, who doubted what Schindler had just told him, decided to separate the three hundred Schindler women from the rest of the group, though they were all going to Auschwitz.[165]

But this did not end the matter because Büscher "was still determined to get his revenge on Schindler." Büscher wrote Auschwitz's commandant, Richard Baer, to send three hundred other women to Brünnlitz instead of the three hundred original Schindler women from Płaszów. Oskar stated that Büscher did this "just to harass Schindler and out of his hatred for him, because he felt that he was befriending Jews." Then, according to the notes from Martin Gosch and Howard Koch's meeting with Schindler in Paris in November 1964, Oskar went to Baer and said, "Look, if you give me 300 other women, I have to begin training them again, and this is pretty late to do this—the war effort needs the things that we are going to make, and you take away from me the women who are already skilled, the women I've already trained, and this is going to hurt our production down there, so it doesn't make any sense." Baer finally agreed to release the 300 original Schindler women to Oskar in return for a payment of six RM ($2.40) a day for each woman for the time they were in Auschwitz. Baer then pocketed this money.[166]

Unfortunately, as will be seen in the next chapter, the story about how Oskar got his three hundred women out of Auschwitz is fictitious. Schindler did not go to Auschwitz to save them. So how did Gosch and Koch come up with this tale? In 1955 and 1963, Schindler gave Yad Vashem and the West German criminal police a full account of how he had saved these women. This account is also backed up by testimony from Itzhak Stern, Emilie Schindler, and Mietek Pemper, though each account has slight variations. So Schindler either lied to Koch and Gosch in 1964 or fell prey to their continual editorializing during the lengthy interviews. But the story became part of many of the Hollywood myths that arose during this time about Schindler, and some of them ultimately made their way into Steven Spielberg's 1993 film, *Schindler's List*.[167]

The only other time Oskar mentioned this particular detention was in his 1955 report to Yad Vashem. He said that a "recent arrest for several days by the Gestapo and my being turned over to the SS-Court Krakau because of Jewish interests (bribery of officials) cost much local [Sudeten] prestige."[168] Oskar, of course, had been a major contributor to Göth's illegal financial empire and had a lot to worry about. And though Emilie Schindler did not mention his third arrest in her memoirs, Itzhak Stern

said it was Emilie who got Oskar released after eight days "due to connections and [a] great bribe."[169]

The arrest, detention, and questioning of Mietek Pemper and Oskar
Schindler did not seem to help the SS in their investigation of Göth,
who was ultimately released on his own recognizance from prison in
late October 1944. The SS, though, continued to investigate the charges
against him through the early months of 1945. One reason that Göth
was never brought to trial by the SS was Himmler's decision in the
spring of 1944 to limit Morgen's investigations to the Koch case. Morgen, who had set up investigative commissions in most of the concentration camps, evidently pursued the case against Göth against Himmler's wishes. The Morgen investigations had caused quite a stir in the
SS, which oversaw the mass murder of millions of Jews and others during the war. Moreover, given the widespread corruption in the SS, an
aggressive investigator such as Morgen could create all sorts of problems for any number of officers in the large SS network of camps. In the
end, the SS dropped the charges against Göth, though there was enough
evidence to convict him of various crimes. Unfortunately, politics and
the end of the war kept Morgen from adding Amon Leopold Göth's
name to his list of legal victories.[170]

Mietek Pemper told me that when Schindler got permission to open his
new armaments factory in Brünnlitz, Göth, who at one point had thought
of joining Oskar there, contacted Schindler and asked whether he could
send his clothes and other personal belongs to Brünnlitz for storage.
Oskar agreed, though it is uncertain whether he realized how much Göth
planned to send him. Göth sent two large truckloads of goods to
Brünnlitz that he ultimately wanted sent to his home in Vienna.[171] Oskar
explained in 1964 that once he got approval for the move, Göth made an
arrangement with him to move his personal goods to Brünnlitz in return
for some trucks that Oskar needed to help move machinery and other
items to his new factory. Included in Göth's shipment were 200,000 Polish cigarettes, jewelry, and other valuables.[172] Dr. Aleksander Bieberstein
remembered seeing these goods in storage in Brünnlitz. One day, he approached Schindler about the need for a bed or couch for the factory's
small sick room. Oskar told Dr. Bieberstein to go to the storage area and
tell Adolf Elsner, the inmate in charge, to give him a bed. The storage area
was filled with all types of furniture. As Bieberstein looked around, he noticed that many of the items were carefully wrapped. These, Elsner said,
were owned by Amon Göth.[173]

The arrest of Amon Göth and his removal as commandant of Płaszów, particularly when combined with the murder of Wilhelm Chilowicz and his top OD aides, set the stage for one of the most dramatic moments in the Schindler story, the creation of the famous "Schindler's List." Göth's replacement, *SS-Obersturmführer* Arnold Büscher, had his hands full evacuating the large number of Jews and Poles at Płaszów, helping the *Kommando* 1005 unit disinter and burn bodies, and breaking up the camp. Consequently, Büscher had little time to worry about names on transport lists. This task was left to Franz Müller, the overseer of the Jewish labor details. Müller was not particularly interested in what names went on a particular list, and the most important figure in all this, Oskar Schindler, was struggling to overcome resistance to his move to the Sudetenland from local Party figures and business interests. Schindler, too, had more on his mind than the names that went on his famous "list of life" and he had no contact with Müller about it. The only person privy to Oskar Schindler's general wishes about the list was an undistinguished, greedy OD man who would become the author of a list of 1,000 names made famous by Thomas Keneally and Steven Spielberg. This was Marcel Goldberg, Franz Müller's Jewish assistant.

9.

THE CREATION OF "SCHINDLER'S LIST"

Marcel Goldberg is certainly one of the most mysterious yet important figures in the Schindler story. When I began my research for this book, I had a sense of his importance but could find few people who knew anything about him. Thomas Keneally seemed aware of Goldberg's significance to the creation of the "list," but could only conclude that he "had the power to tinker with its edges."[1] From Keneally's perspective, Oskar Schindler was the principal author of his famous "list." He claimed that Schindler brought a "preparatory list" with more than a thousand names on it to Płaszów and that Goldberg and Raimund Titsch, the manager of Julius Madritsch's sewing factory, made slight changes before it was submitted to the SS for final approval. But Keneally also said that there was a "haziness suitable to a legend about the precise chronology of Oskar's list." He added that this haziness didn't "attach to the existence of the list" because there was a copy of it in Yad Vashem's archives.[2]

In reality, Oskar Schindler had absolutely nothing to do with the creation of his famous transport list. He admitted as much to Dr. Stanley Robbin after the war. Dr. Robbin, a Jewish physician at Emalia, was one of those *Schindlerjuden* taken directly from Emalia during the first week of August 1944 and put on the transport for Mauthausen. Dr. Robbin met Oskar in Germany several years later and asked him why so many long-time Emalia workers did not make it onto the list: "He told me he was not responsible for it. He never arranged this, and he apologized."[3]

Moreover, the supposed original list at Yad Vashem, the United States Holocaust Memorial Museum, and in the Schindler *"Koffer"* collection in the Bundesarchiv in Koblenz is dated April 18, 1945. This is the list that Marcel Goldberg is carrying in one scene in *Schindler's List*. The original lists (one for men and one for women), which I discovered during my research, are dated October 21, 1944 (seven hundred men) and November 12, 1944 (three hundred women). The reason it is important to differentiate between the lists created in the spring of 1945 (there were several) is that the names were changing constantly from the time Goldberg created the list in the fall of 1944 to the date of the liberation of Brünnlitz on May 8, 1945, the date of the final "Schindler's List." To speak of one "Schindler's List" is inaccurate and misleading because it clouds the issues surrounding the constantly changing nature of the list. The final lists that were written on May 8, 1945, were different from those created by Goldberg in Płaszów. Some names that had appeared on the list in the fall were unceremoniously removed and replaced by others during the transit to Brünnlitz via Groß Rosen and Auschwitz. At Brünnlitz, new names were added to the male and female lists as small transports from other camps made their way to Schindler's sub-camp in the Sudetenland. As we have each of these transit lists, we can also consider them part of the collection of "Schindler's Lists."

Finally, though Marcel Goldberg was certainly the most important figure in the creation of the male and female lists in Płaszów and played a decisive role in the removal and replacement of certain Schindler men during the transit to Brünnlitz, he lost his authority when he arrived at Schindler's new factory in the Sudetenland. The difference here is that when Goldberg was in charge of the lists in Płaszów, and had at least some influence over the male list in Groß Rosen, greed and personal contacts played a role in who was put on and who was taken off. When the seven hundred men and three hundred women arrived at Brünnlitz, Mietek Pemper and Itzhak Stern were put in charge and things changed. Moreover, Oskar and Emilie Schindler would now play a more direct role in the lives of their Jewish workers. And because Marcel Goldberg had lost his influence and credibility, Jews added to Oskar Schindler's list were on there purely for humanitarian reasons.

But who was Marcel Goldberg and why was he so important to the creation of the original "Schindler's List?" Keneally and Spielberg both seemed to have some sense of his importance to the creation of the famous list. Keneally described him as a "personnel clerk" who took advantage of the fact that Płaszów's new commandant, Büscher, "could not have cared, within certain numerical limits, who went on the list."[4] But Keneally still saw Schindler, and to a lesser degree, Raimund Titsch, as the principal authors of the list. Spielberg picked up on this and dropped Titsch and Madritsch from the story. Why? Madritsch and Titsch were both considered good Germans (or, more accurately, good Austrians), so it is possible that he thought it would be simpler to identify with one hero instead of several. This is the reason he chose to make Itzhak Stern a composite of Stern, Pemper, and Bankier. It is also possible that no one had investigated Madritsch and Titsch's stories. The Schindler story was promoted by Leopold Page and a small group of extremely dedicated *Schindlerjuden.* Though many of them knew extensively about Madritsch and Titsch, they did not consider either of them in Schindler's league.

Unfortunately, the result of all of this is two mythical stories about the creation of "Schindler's List." Keneally did the best he could with the resources at hand; he also did not make the list's creation the centerpiece of his historical novel. When his original book on Schindler came out in Great Britain in 1982, it was titled *Schindler's Ark.* Keneally correctly understood that the significance of what Oskar Schindler did during the Holocaust took place over several years and involved some very special relationships with Jews. *Schindler's Ark,* and its American literary twin, *Schindler's List,* is about the special relationship that Oskar Schindler developed with some of his Jewish workers and acquaintances over a six-year period. Oskar Schindler's story is carefully intertwined with the testimonies of the Jews he came to befriend and help, not just in the fall of 1944 but throughout the war. Spielberg chose to take a much more simplistic approach to the Schindler story.

On the other hand, Spielberg, while admitting Goldberg's corruption, chose to give the audience a more wholesome story that fits with his theme of Oskar Schindler's moral evolution through the film. And how better to do this than link him in authorship of the list with the film's moral touchstone, Itzhak Stern. Telling the truth would have paired Schindler, a heavy drinker and womanizer, with a corrupt Jew, Marcel Goldberg. And if Spielberg had taken Schindler completely out of this phase of the film, he would have robbed it of its heart. If he had linked Schindler with Goldberg, he would simply have strengthened the sense that what really drove Oskar Schindler in all of this was money. But Spielberg did not leave Marcel Goldberg completely out of the story; he created a mini-story within a story through which he traced Goldberg's moral degeneration through the film. So though Spielberg dared not link Goldberg directly to Schindler when it came to the authorship of the list, he at least had enough sense of history to discuss Goldberg's moral failings elsewhere.

The List

Thomas Keneally was carefully guided in his research and interviews by Leopold Page, who was probably uncomfortable with the Goldberg story because it did not fit with his idealistic image of Oskar. This had more to do, at least from Page's viewpoint, with protecting the image of someone he deeply cared for than with anything else. And despite his balanced approach to the Schindler story, there is no question that Thomas Keneally, a kind person in his own right, was affected by Page's adoring attitude. But it is also possible that the Schindler Jews that Keneally interviewed simply did not know much about Goldberg and his role in the creation of the list. Itzhak Stern, who knew everything, was dead, and Keneally had spent only a few hours with Mietek Pemper, these in the Munich airport. Keneally had more time with Dr. Moshe Bejski, by then the acknowledged "dean" of Schindler Jews in Israel. But if I had not spent a lot of time with Bejski and Pemper, and asked specific questions about Goldberg, they probably would not have brought him up.

In the early stages of my research, I asked Dr. Bejski, a retired justice of the Israeli Supreme Court, and Mietek Pemper about Marcel Goldberg. Dr. Bejski simply told me that "Marcel Goldberg prepared the list." He added that if there were vacancies on the list, then people could bribe Goldberg to get on one of them.[5] Mietek Pemper and I talked extensively about Goldberg during my interviews with him in 1999 and 2000. He told me that Goldberg "had a free hand in choosing what people to put on the list." Goldberg's superior, Franz Müller, "did not care what he did."[6] The only other direct witness to all this, Itzhak Stern, did not even mention Goldberg in his 1956 report to Yad Vashem. But in his memoirs, Dr. Aleksander Bieberstein attributed the authorship of "Schindler's List" to Marcel Goldberg.[7]

In fact, most of the *Schindlerjuden* I interviewed knew or had heard that Marcel Goldberg was the author of "Schindler's List," though many of them were fuzzy about details.

But feelings and attitudes towards Goldberg varied. Like Wilek Chilowicz, Marcel Goldberg had supporters, though most Schindler Jews were extremely critical of him. Some were outraged about his efforts to sell places on the lists; others were bitter because he either did not put them on the lists or at some point took them off. Rena Ferber Finder was one of the Schindler Jews who saw firsthand some of Goldberg's treachery. Rena's father, Moniek (Moses) Ferber, had been an OD man in the ghetto and helped Goldberg get a job on the Jewish police force. Rena's family even shared space with the Goldberg family in a ghetto apartment. On December 31, 1942, Moses Ferber and Marcel Goldberg were arrested together. Later, Marcel Goldberg was released, but Moses Ferber was sent to Auschwitz, where he was killed. Rena did not learn of his death until after the war.[8]

Rena told me that she thought that Goldberg was jealous of her father and she was, needless to say, suspicious about why one of the two Jewish OD men arrested on New Year's Eve, 1942, was sent to Auschwitz and death and not the other. Here, she said, we begin to see the real Goldberg. Several months after her father's arrest and disappearance, Rena went to see Goldberg, who by this time was working in Płaszów for Amon Göth, and asked Goldberg to put her and her mother on a list to Schindler's factory. Rena said that as early as 1943 she knew of people who were bribing Goldberg to send them to Emalia. Rena ultimately got a job at Emalia working on a lathe.[9]

Moshe Bejski said that Goldberg was principally interested in diamonds, which he brought with him to Brünnlitz. Sol Urbach said, though, that it was hard for him to imagine anyone having any sort of wealth at this point in the Holocaust. He talked about the strict body searches conducted by the SS before entering Płaszów and explained that the only people he knew who were able to bring valuables into the camp were those who had placed condoms filled with valuables deep inside their rectums.[10] But some people had managed to hide valuables when they entered Płaszów. Roman Ferber's mother, Malia, had two diamonds "drilled into her teeth," as well as other valuables that enabled the family to survive the Holocaust.[11]

Chaskel Schlesinger managed to take several gold rings with him to Płaszów and Brünnlitz, and Pola Gerner Yogev's family spent a fortune in hidden money to keep their elderly grandmother alive. "Everybody tried to save themselves and their families. Some did it by 'ethical' means, some by 'unethical' means."[12] Lola Feldman Orzech kept a 500 złoty ($156.25) note hidden in her hair bun; Roman Ferber carried a $100 bill with him throughout the Holocaust. Moses Goldberg managed to sneak a 1,000-złoty ($312.50) bill into Płaszów, which he used to bribe a *Kapo* to keep him off the *Kommando* 1005 exhumation and burning detail.[13] Sam Wertheim turned some valuables into cash just before he was sent to Płaszów, and then Mauthausen, in August 1944. He asked Leopold Page to give the money to his wife, Edith, who in turn was to give it to Sam's father; Page gave Edith "every single penny," which she hid in a loaf of bread under straw in Płaszów.[14]

By the time that *Schindlerjude* Sam Birenzweig (Zimich Birnzweig) became a prisoner in Płaszów in the early fall of 1944, it was almost empty. The camp, he said, had a vibrant black market fueled by a "Płaszów-area store that still stocked luxury items like vodka and salami." Sam said the store was for "show" because the Germans still wanted "to maintain the illusion that they were winning the war." These luxury items "were like diamonds. I didn't eat good food like this for three or four years! I brought [sic] it inside Płaszów. People there had money. This was terrific!"[15] It is also important to remember Hans Stauber's comments to Heinrich Himmler at about the same time. Stauber, the chief treasurer of the Army Post Administration in Kraków, had complained to the *Reichsführer SS* in early September 1944 about the active black market trading between guards and Jewish prisoners in Płaszów.[16] So there were valuables in Płaszów to buy almost anything, even a human life. It is doubtful, though, that more than a handful of the remaining inmates had anything significant to trade. If they did, it was usually used to buy bread or other foodstuffs to supplement their meager diet.

And though some people bribed Marcel Goldberg to get onto "Schindler's List," most were on it for other reasons. Many of the places, for example, were already predetermined. Mietek Pemper told me, for example, that although Oskar Schindler had little to do with the actual creation of the list, he gave Franz Müller several general guidelines for who he wanted on the list. He first wanted "my people," meaning the remaining Emalia Jews, Madritsch's list of workers, and specially trained metal workers.[17] Beyond this, Goldberg had to add to the list the workers who had accompanied Brünnlitz's new commandant, Josef Leipold, from the aviation factory in Wieliczka. The Jews chosen by Madritsch, or, more precisely, his manager, Raimund Titsch, were the most prominent Jews from his factory. The same was true with the Jews chosen by Leipold.

After the war, Oskar was bitter about what he saw as Julius Madritsch's failure to do more to put a substantial number of his Jewish workers on the list. Oskar first alluded to this in his 1945 financial report. He mentioned as part of his discussion about the transfer of his armaments operations from Emalia to Brünnlitz that Raimund Titsch had been able to rescue "at least part of his Jews to my relocated factory in Bruennlitz. This was a task that in my opinion should have been Mr. Madritsch's obligation." He added that Titsch visited Brünnlitz several times to make sure that his Jews were "not living in danger and also to give them the support and mail of foreign friends."[18]

Oskar was more pointed in his criticism of Madritsch in several letters he wrote to Dr. K. J. Ball-Kaduri, who was investigating the Schindler story in the summer and fall of 1956. On August 24, 1956, Dr. Ball-Kaduri had written Itzhak Stern in Israel and asked him to talk about his experiences in Poland during the Holocaust. Stern let Oskar read the letter and suggested that he also share his experiences with Dr. Ball-Kaduri. Over the next few months, Oskar and Dr. Ball-Kaduri corresponded about Oskar's wartime experiences. In one of his letters, Dr. Ball-Kaduri asked Oskar whether he had a copy of Madritsch's wartime memoirs, *Menschen in Not!* (People in Distress). Oskar had already told Dr. Ball-Kaduri of his frustration with Madritsch, though he did not initially mention him by name. In his letter to the Yad Vashem researcher on September 9, 1956, Oskar talked of being urged during his last months in Emalia "to emigrate to Switzerland in order to save myself and my financial possessions." This would have meant, Oskar explained, "to leave everything to its predestined fate (extermination)." Oskar also admitted that "it took quite a bit of moral strength to say 'no.'" Yet, he wondered, "who would have dared condemn me, if I had left for Switzerland after being imprisoned by the dangerous Gestapo?"[19]

Five and a half weeks later, Oskar sent Dr. Ball-Kaduri a copy of Madritsch's wartime memoirs and told him that he felt "somewhat biased regarding the case of Madritsch, since the greed of this man prevented me from the certain rescue of 300 people, mainly women, from the Madritsch factory." Schindler added that all Madritsch seemed interested in was five wagons of "rickety and rusty sewing machines and questionable textiles," which had already been transferred to Bregenz, Austria, on Lake Constance (or Bodensee, which rests on the Swiss, German, and Austrian borders). Oskar said that Madritsch's machinery and textiles seemed more important to him than "the fate of the people entrusted to him." Titsch was more pointed in his criticism of Madritsch, who, he said, "was content in his safe, secure position, and had no intention of endangering himself, the amount of money that he had made, his position, and his security in general by taking this dangerous step."[20]

For Oskar, the real hero in this story was Titsch who, he thought, deserved "an Iron Cross for humaneness." He said that "Titsch alone was the motor and it was because of his selfless, undaunted actions when Jewish people were helped at the Madritsch factory."[21] Titsch felt the same way about Schindler. After the war, he said, "I look upon Schindler as the greatest adventurer I have ever known; the bravest man I have ever known."[22] Oskar told Dr. Ball-Kaduri that he had discussed the three hundred or so Jewish workers with Madritsch one evening at a party at Büscher's villa. According to Schindler, when he asked Madritsch about putting some of his Jews on the list, Madritsch seemed uninterested. Oskar continued to press him on the matter until Madritsch said, "Dear Oskar, spare yourself your words; it is a lost cause. I am not investing another dime in it." Titsch, who was also at the party, spoke with Oskar later that evening and hastily put together a list with sixty-two names on it. Titsch later admitted that it was difficult to come up with so many names at a loud, drunken party. Oskar said that he was then able to persuade Büscher, who was in a good mood, to sign it. He explained that the Jews on the list would be "factory tailors."[23]

But the hand-written note that Titsch gave to Oskar that night was not the final Madritsch list. I found it in Schindler's "*Koffer*" files, which Chris Staehr discovered in the attic of his father's home in Hildesheim in 1997 and later gave to Yad Vashem. At Chris's insistence, the Bundesarchiv was permitted to make a copy of this large collection before it was sent to Israel. The carefully typed Madritsch list had the names of forty men and twenty women with their camp identification numbers and is dated October 1944. Titsch wrote by hand the following: "*Verzeichnis der von den to Schindler über unser besuchen über nommenen Leute unserer Betriebes.*" This is really poor German which indicates it was written in haste. Essentially it says that "this is the list for Schindler based on our discussion about the people from our closed factories." The typed list was on an outdated letterhead that read *Julius Madritsch, Krakauer Konfektion, Krakau-Podgorze, Ringplatz 3*. Marcel Goldberg signed his name at the bottom of the Madritsch list. According to Martin Gosch and Howard Koch, who interviewed Titsch for a film project they were working on in 1964, "Julius Madritsch, who now lives in Vienna, carries the original copy of this list in his pocket always."[24]

Several interesting things can be learned from this list, particularly when it is tied to Oskar's discussions with Madritsch and Titsch in October 1944. Schindler's list was prepared just after he got permission from the Armaments Inspectorate and the SS to move his armaments operations to Brünnlitz. We know from Oskar's comments that this matter was uncertain until the last minute. And from the time Oskar received his orders to shut down his armaments production at Emalia, Göth and his successor, Büscher, were emptying Płaszów of its Jewish prisoners. With the transport of 4,000 prisoners to the Stutthof concentration camp in Germany in late July 1944, there were still about 20,000 prisoners in Płaszów. On August 6, Göth shipped 7,500 Jewish women to Auschwitz and four days later 4,589 Jewish men to Mauthausen, which reduced the camp's population by almost half. On August 10, another 1,446 Jewish women were sent from Płaszów to Auschwitz; and in September, the SS closed the Polish section of the camp. Only about 7,000 Jews now remained in Płaszów.[25]

They would be shipped out of Płaszów in October in two major transports; when they were gone, all that remained of the former camp population were six or seven hundred prisoners and a skeleton staff of forty to complete the final liquidation of the camp. On October 15, 4,500 men were sent to Groß Rosen; a week later, Büscher sent 2,000 women to Auschwitz. The transports of October 15 and October 22 included the seven hundred men and three hundred women, who were to be sent ultimately to Brünnlitz.[26] Schindler's seemingly last-minute request to Madritsch for three hundred names, principally women, is revealing because he appeared desperate to find names to fill the women's list. One would have presumed that when Oskar told Franz Müller that his first priority was "my people," he meant the men and women who had worked for him at Emalia. We have no idea how many women worked for Oskar at Emalia, but given the 700:300 ration of his 1944 list, one would presume that this was about how many women worked for him in his Kraków factory. But if Oskar was asking Madritsch to fill his female quota almost completely, then little must have been done to protect his former female workers. This probably had less to do with Oskar's concern over the fate of his Emalia workers than his inability to win approval for his move to Brünnlitz until the eve of the next to last liquidation stage for Płaszów. If that was so, there was probably little he could do to keep his individual workers off the ongoing transports out of Płaszów. A case in point, of course, was the Mauthausen transport of August 10. All that Oskar could do in that situation was help make the trip to Austria a little more comfortable for his former Jewish workers. Because Madritsch and Titsch were able to come up with only sixty names at the last minute, Marcel Goldberg had to fill the remaining places for women bound for Brünnlitz. Complicating the matter further, Mietek Pemper told me that the three hundred women on the female Płaszów-Auschwitz-Brünnlitz list "were mainly women who had worked for Oskar Schindler in Emalia." Goldberg, of course, was on the October 15 transport to Groß Rosen, so there is no way to tell whether changes were made on the female list during the next week.[27]

After the war, Madritsch explained what seemed to be his hesitancy to join Schindler in Brünnlitz. He had planned for some time to move his operations to Lower Austria and reopen his factory in Drosendorf. These plans fell through, he explained, because the fields where he wanted to build his barracks for his Jewish workers had not been harvested. Local officials then rejected his application for the move. One wonders whether the real reason for local Austrian disapproval was similar to the one Schindler encountered when he tried to move his armaments factory to the Sudetenland. At this juncture, Madritsch wrote, he accepted Oskar Schindler's offer to move his sewing factory to Brünnlitz. He was given the permission of economic officials in the General Government and the HSSPF *Ost* for the move but failed to get approval from Maurer's D2 Office. Madritsch made several trips to Berlin to argue his case but was finally told that "uniforms are not an essential production item for the war effort. Fighting is possible in civilian clothes, too. Jewish work forces are to be used in the production of ammunition only!"[28]

Actually, Madritsch should not have been surprised by D2's rejection of his application for the move. He had difficulty getting approval to keep his factory open earlier in the year and only received a six-month contract from Maurer's office in February 1944 to keep his sewing factory open in Płaszów. Consequently, D2's rejection of his application to move with Schindler to Brünnlitz was in line with its earlier decisions.[29] But Madritsch did not know that a good part of the vast factory complex where Schindler would open his small armaments factory in Brünnlitz already housed a large SS uniform factory. Mietek Pemper shared this information with me when I interviewed him for a second time in early

2000. I had excitedly brought with me a factory plan that the archives of the United States Holocaust Museum in Washington, D.C., identified as Brünnlitz. Mr. Pemper explained that this was a plan for the SS uniform factory in the larger factory complex where Schindler had his factory. But it was not a plan for Oskar's factory.[30] Maurer's D2 office knew this, which was probably one of the reasons it rejected Madritsch's application. Moreover, given the difficulties Oskar encountered in persuading local officials in the Sudetenland to support his move there, Madritsch's efforts to join Schindler with his large Jewish workforce there could easily have torpedoed Schindler's planned move.

Madritsch said that by August 6, 1944, he had given up hope of ever moving his factory. Gradually, many of Madritsch's 2,000 workers were sent to Auschwitz and Mauthausen. He was initially allowed to keep about three hundred men and two hundred women for cleanup work. They would be placed on the final October transports to Groß Rosen and Auschwitz in October. He said he provided Oskar with a hundred names for his list and also gave him "several hundred meters of textiles from his Krakow stock piles."[31]

But Madritsch's story did not end there. In early September, he visited his family in Vienna, where he and his wife "were buried alive in my mother's house after an air raid on Vienna." But his troubles were only beginning. On November 3, 1944, the SD arrested him in Kraków and put him in the city's infamous Montelupich prison. Three days later, he was transferred to a prison in Berlin. The SD explained that his name had been found on a list of the resistance movement in Poland: "I was supposed to have spread gruesome stories about Plaszow. That's all?" The SD released him after twelve days.[32]

Given all this, why did Oskar feel so betrayed by Madritsch? There is no reason to doubt Madritsch's version of the story. The Jews who worked for him considered him Schindler's equal when it came to the treatment of his Jewish workers. Just after the war, Irvin (Izak) and Phyllis (Feiga Wittenberg) Karp, both Schindler Jews, went to Vienna to testify in support of Madritsch and Titsch's efforts during the Holocaust. Madritsch had taken over their business, Hogo, and Irvin helped run the business for Madritsch. Celina Karp Biniaz, Irvin and Phyllis's daughter, described Madritsch as "more elegant and classy than Schindler." He was, she added, "a good human being with a heart." She was equally complimentary of Titsch, whom she considered "a wonderful man who got caught in the wrong place at the wrong time." During the war, Jakub

Feigenbaum gave Titsch some diamonds to keep for him. When the war ended, he went to Vienna to find Titsch, who returned the diamonds.[33]

Julius Madritsch and Oskar Schindler were very different people. Madritsch had a good working relationship with Amon Göth, yet he never felt the need to cross the line when it came to sharing Göth's passion for wild parties and drinking. Helen Sternlicht-Rosenzweig, one of Amon Göth's two Jewish maids, said that, unlike Oskar, Madritsch was not a womanizer.[34] Madritsch's virtuous ways and kind treatment of his Jewish workers made him, along with Titsch, a prime candidate for nomination as a Righteous Among the Nations in Israel after the war. It is quite possible that Oskar was jealous of Madritsch, who prospered after the war, though this would not explain why he criticized Madritsch just after the war ended. After their escape to Germany, Oskar and Emilie became very close to some of the Jews they had cared for and protected during the Shoah. In this unguarded environment, questions must have been asked about why certain people made the list and others did not. Given Madritsch's reputation as someone friendly and helpful to Jews, some Schindlerjuden must have wondered why some of their friends and relatives who worked for Madritsch were not on the list. Given the inconsistencies, favoritism, luck, bribery, and other factors that went into the creation of the list by Goldberg, it would have been easier to blame questions about the "missing" on Madritsch rather than Oskar Schindler, who was gradually emerging as a saint to many of his former Jewish workers.

But there is no doubt that jealousy was a factor once the issue of Madritsch and Schindler came to the attention of Yad Vashem in the mid-1950s. By this time, Oskar had failed in his business ventures in Argentina, and his efforts to save Jews during the war became an important part of his identity. To suddenly have to share it with Julius Madritsch, a successful man of seeming impeccable character, was probably a little more than Oskar could handle. From Schindler's perspective, Madritsch owed his postwar success to the money he made during the war, and this only added to Schindler's dislike of him. Raimund Titsch, on the other hand, was a different matter. He was not a factory owner and therefore not as threatening to Schindler as Madritsch. Oskar had read Madritsch's memoirs, *Menschen in Not!* but said little about it. He never questioned the accuracy of Madritsch's account, which was filled with countless, daring tales of efforts to help Jews throughout the war. Perhaps Oskar, whose own account of his wartime efforts to save Jews was published in Germany in 1957, was uncomfortable about

Oskar Schindler (sitting at steering wheel) with family. Svitavy, Czechoslovakia, 1920s. (USHMM)

Schindler home in Svitavy, Czech Republic, and Sudeten German monument to Oskar Schindler. (David M. Crowe)

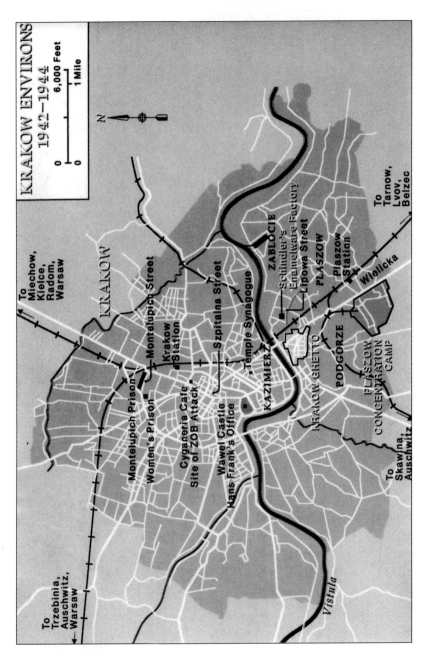

Kraków Environs, 1942–1944. (USHMM *Historical Atlas of the Holocaust*)

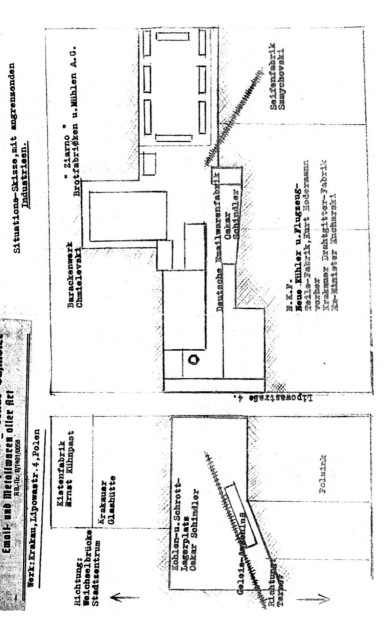

Official factory plan for Emalia, Kraków. (Ami Staehr Collection, Stuttgart)

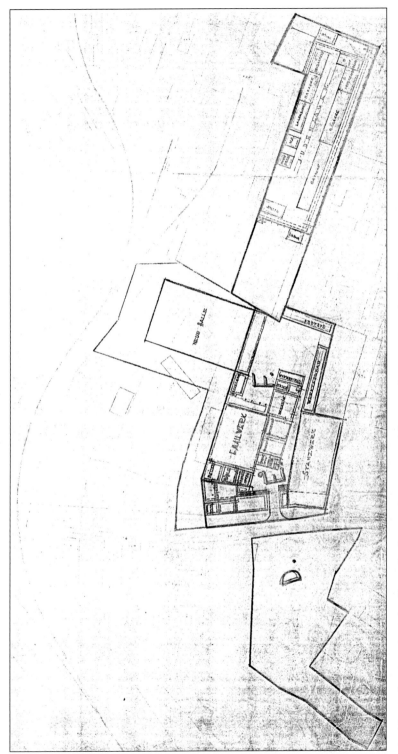

Architect's drawings for *Schindler Nebenlager* (subcamp) at Emalia in Kraków. (Ami Staehr Collection, Stuttgart)

Front Entrance of Emalia today, Kraków. (David M. Crowe)

Glass Staircase at Emalia today, Kraków. (David M. Crowe)

Oskar Schindler (second from left) with his German office staff and Abraham Bankier (third from right). (USHMM)

Oskar Schindler with his Jewish workers at Emalia. (USHMM)

Oskar Schindler parties with German officers in Kraków. (USHMM)

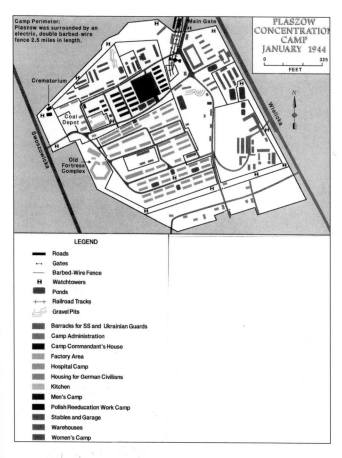

Płaszów Concentration
Camp, January 1944.
(USHMM, *Historical Atlas
of the Holocaust*)

Mietek Pemper,
Augsburg, Germany.
(David M. Crowe)

Płaszów concentration camp, Kraków, 1944. (USHMM)

Płaszów today, Kraków. (David M. Crowe)

Monument to Jewish Dead—Płaszów, Kraków. (David M. Crowe)

Amon Göth on the balcony of his Płaszów villa. (USHMM)

Amon Göth on trial in Kraków, 1946. (USHMM)

Lfd. Nr.	Art	H.Nr.	Name und Vorname	Geb.-Datum	Beruf
1.	Ju.Po.	68821	Kriecher Hirsch	15. 8.1897	Autoschlosser
2.	"	2	Vogel Gedale	5. 7.1901	Fleischermeister
3.	"	3	Biedermann Hirsch	7. 9.1925	Ofensetzergeselle
4.	"	4	Weinberger Nachum	16. 5.1921	Zimmerer
5.	"	5	Wein Wolf	9. 6.1900	Schneidermeister
6.	"	6	Blemmer Jakob	4. 5.1915	Bilanzbuchhalter
7.	"	7	Horn Josef	4. 2.1914	Schreibkraft
8.	"	8	Klinghofer Simon	25. 3.1897	ang.Metallverarb.
9.	"	9	Mahler Abraham	7. 4.1902	ang.Metallverarb.
10.	"	68830	Leichter Josek	25.11.1917	ang.Metallverarb.
11.	"	2	Weinschelbaum Dawid	14. 2.1924	Monteurgeselle
12.	"	3	Rottenberg Beer	9. 8.1920	Elektrikergeselle
13.	"	4	Jakubowicz Jakob	13.11.1927	Maurergehilfe
14.	"	5	Weinschelbaum Pinkus	24. 9.1919	ang.Metallverarb.
15.	"	6	Scheck Jerzy	25.12.1917	Maschinenbautechnik
16.	"	7	Weil Naftali	10. 9.1914	ang.Metallverarb.
17.	"	8	Gottselig Dawid	6. 5.1920	Maurer
18.	"	9	Hornung Josef	6. 9.1911	Bauingenieur
19.	"	68840	Hornung Dawid	25. 2.1919	Maschinenbautechn.
20.	"	1	Birnhack Ignacy	17. 2.1917	Glaser
21.	"	2	Wohlfeiler Ignacy	1.11.1899	Glasermeister
22.	"	3	Taube Maksymilian	17. 6.1927	ang.Metallverarb.
23.	"	4	Hirschfeld Samuel	27. 2.1919	Eisendreher/Fräser
24.	"	5	Taube Emanuel	16. 1.1902	ang.Metallverarb.
25.	"	6	Krug Samuel	15.12.1911	ang.Metallverarb.
26.	"	7	Schlesinger Moses	5. 7.1896	Schlossergeselle
27.	"	8	Tennenbaum Izydor	1.10.1920	Maurer
28.	"	9	Sperber Chaim	7. 7.1903	Schlossergehilfe
29.	"	68850	Scheidlinger Markus	19. 8.1918	Schlossergehilfe
30.	"	1	Horn Eliasz	29. 9.1907	Werkzeugmasch.-Fachm
31.	"	3	Urbach Dawid	18. 2.1896	ang.Metallverarb.
32.	"	5	Lamensdorf Leib	14.12.1890	ang.Metallverarb.
33.	"	6	Kopyto Moses	14. 3.1898	Eisendreher
34.	"	7	Grüss Abraham	6. 9.1906	ang.Metallverarb.
35.	"	8	Hirschberg Herz	16. 5.1927	Schlossergehilfe
36.	"	9	Segal Chaim	30. 3.1907	ang.Mechaniker
37.	"	68860	Schlesinger Abraham	2. 9.1910	Schlosser
38.	"	1	Kinstlinger Joachim	11.11.1915	ang.Metallverarb.
39.	"	2	Oberfeld Adolf	24. 9.1911	ang.Metallverarb.
40.	"	3	Schlang Dawid	8. 7.1903	Klempnergeselle
41.	"	5	Baral Samuel	26.10.1904	Stanzer
42.	"	6	Herz Ludwig	19. 9.1925	Maler
43.	"	7	Hudes Isak	26. 1.1916	Lackierer
44.	"	8	Bleiweiss Efroim	23.12.1906	ang.Metallverarb.
45.	"	9	Heylmann Michal Leib	8. 5.1922	Zimmerer
46.	"	68870	Manskleid Anatol	15. 5.1925	Schlossergehilfe
47.	"	1	Klinghofer Ignacy	30. 1.1925	Autoschlosser
48.	"	2	Lewertow Jakob	10.11.1908	Stanzer
49.	"	3	Herschlag Abraham	2. 3.1920	Schlossergehilfe
50.	"	4	Herschlag Salomon	15. 8.1922	Schlossergehilfe
51.	"	5	Haar Dawid	20.12.1912	Klempner
52.	"	6	Zimmet Dawid	1. 6.1914	ang.Metallverarb.
53.	"	7	Goldschmied Aron	2. 2.1923	Schlossergeselle
54.	"	8	Klingenholz Aron	18. 6.1922	Schlossergeselle
55.	"	9	Morgenbesser Rafal	9.10.1900	Buchhalter
56.	"	68880	Morgenbesser Adam	5. 9.1927	ang.Mechaniker
57.	"	1	Lamensdorf Majer	1.12.1914	Klempnergeselle
58.	"	2	Sternberg Jakob	16.12.1899	Schreibkraft
59.	"	3	Sternberg Jerzy	9. 6.1926	ang.Metallverarb.
60.	"	5	Kinstlinger Moses	21. 7.1906	Tischler

- Blatt 2 -

Male "Schindler's List," *AL Groß-Rosen – AL Brünnlitz*. October 21, 1944.
(Muzeum Auschwitz-Birkenau)

Namensliste des Häftlingszuganges von KL Golleschau (KL Auschwitz)
am 29. Januar 1945

Lfd. Nr.	Häftl. Nummer	KL Au.-Nr.	Jude R.-Nr. Kat.	Name und Vorname	Geburts- datum	Beruf
1.	765	15857	U.	Marisa Ladislaus	26. 9.23	Schneider
2.	2	B11108	Dt.	Baruch Siegfried	3. 5.01	Arbeiter (HA.)
3.	3	B 5713	Ung.	Berger Adolf	29. 3.09	Schneider
4.	4	72294	Poln.	Blackerman Jack	22. 3.22	Schneider
5.	5	A10859	Ung.	Bolassy Tibor	25. 7.18	Tischler
6.	6	B11125	Poln.	Borenstein Josef-Milei	1. 9.98	Taschner
7.	7	B11111	Dt.	Borger Michael	29.12.97	Schneider
8.	8	B 5721	Ung.	Brauer Natan	6. 6.01	Hilfsarb.
9.	9	B11112	Tsch.	Brok Robert	4. 9.16	Hilfsarb.
10.	10	B11121	Dt.	Buchhalter Fritz	9. 1.28	Hilfsarb.
11.	1	B11139	Holl.	Davidsohn Jakob	1. 9.17	Fleischer
12.	2	B 5722	Ung.	Decsi Peter	13. 2.23	Musiker (HA.)
13.	3	B 5726	Ung.	Eckstein Ignac	13. 3.00	Holzsortierer
14.	4	A15276	Ung.	Eisenstein Aron	20. 4.14	Nutmacher
15.	5	B11147	Holl.	van Emden Louis	8. 7.15	Zuschneider
16.	6	B 5729	Ung.	Emerich Karol	23. 7.11	Automechaniker
17.	7	A10999	Ung.	Feldess Sandor	14. 9.98	Telefonarb.
18.	8	B 5734	Ung.	Feuermann Bernard	10.11.93	Sattler
19.	9	B 5735	Ung.	Feuermann Sandor	4. 6.27	Sattler
20.	20	B 5764	Ung.	Forkas Hermann	28.11.99	Hilfsarb.
21.	1	A15897	Ung.	Fränkel Adolf	22.12.13	Bäcker
22.	2	A11051	Ung.	Fried Joseph	24. 4.98	Holzsortierer
23.	3	A15686	Ung.	Edelmann Josi	5.12.99	Chemiker
24.	4	B 5739	Ung.	Friedmann Rudolf	1.12.28	Schlosserlehrl.
25.	5	B 5746	Ung.	Goldberger Arnold	29. 3.29	Hilfsarb.
26.	6	B11178	Holl.	Goudstikker Henry	16. 9.27	Hilfsarb.
27.	7	B11179	Dt.	Grabowski Markus	22. 3.93	Sanitäter
28.	8	B11155	Ung.	Grünfeld Alexander	16.12.03	Schuster
29.	9	B 5757	Slow.	Grünfeld Salomon	10. 9.12	Hilfsarb.
30.	30	B11105	Tsch.	Gellner Artur	1. 5.98	Hilfsarb.
31.	1	B11193	Tsch.	Haas Josef	9. 7.04	Schreibkraft
32.	2	B11201	Dt.	Hansel Otto	4. 8.05	Hilfsarb.
33.	3	B11209	Dt.	Hartog Fritz	23. 5.13	Kraftfahrer
34.	4	A11202	Ung.	Heller Paul	23. 7.10	Hilfsarb.
35.	5	B11202	Tsch.	Hermann Alfred	19. 5.93	Buchhalter
36.	6	A15922	Ung.	Herschkowitz Ignacy	4. 2.96	Hilfsarb.
37.	7	B 5765	Ung.	Hirschel Julius	27.12.00	Bäcker
38.	8	A15920	Ung.	Holasz Gabor	28. 4.01	Hilfsarb.
39.	9	B 5771	Ung.	Howles Joses	22. 4.22	Weber
40.	40	86615	Dt.	Joupe Heins	18.10.15	Bäcker-Heizer
41.	1	B 5777	Ung.	Keiner Armin	30. 1.89	Hilfsarb.
42.	2	B11226	Tsch.	Kellner Eugen	19. 5.17	Schreibkraft
43.	3	B 5779	Ung.	Kellner Joseph	29. 1.20	Hilfsarb.
44.	4	B 5778	Ung.	Kellner Zoltan	13. 5.03	Landwirt
45.	5	A15945	Ung.	Klein Eugen	12. 8.98	Tischler
46.	6	B 5789	Slow.	Kohlmann Natan	6. 5.00	Hilfsarb.
47.	7	B 5795	Ung.	Kohn Markus	7.11. 2	Hilfsarb.
48.	8	B 5774	Ung.	Kowatsch Istvar	19. 5.90	Sattler, Tapez.
49.	9	A11249	Ung.	Kraus Josef	5. 9.25	Buchbinder
50.	76950	B11246	Tsch.	Lampl Heinrich	9. 2.38	Hilfsarb.

Golleschau Transport List, January 29, 1945. (Muzeum Auschwitz-Birkenau)

Oskar Schindler's Brünnlitz factory today. Brněnec, Czech Republic. (David M. Crowe)

Oskar and Emilie after war.
(Yad Vashem)

Oskar Schindler and Itzhak
Stern, Paris 1949. (USHMM
and Tobe Steinhouse)

Leopold Page and Oskar Schindler.
(USHMM)

Oskar Schindler plants his tree at Yad Vashem, Jerusalem, 1962. (USHMM)

Oskar and Ami Staehr,
Israel, 1973. (Ami Staehr
Collection, Stuttgart)

Oskar Schindler's funeral, Jerusalem 1974. Dr. Moshe Bejski is standing at the far left. (Ami Staehr Collection, Stuttgart)

Ami Staehr (on left), Dr. Moshe Bejski, and Erika Bejski at Oskar's grave in the Latin Cemetery, Jerusalem, 1975. (Ami Staehr Collection, Stuttgart)

Ami Staehr in front of Oskar's tree along the Avenue of the Righteous at Yad Vashem, Jerusalem, 1975. (Ami Staehr Collection, Stuttgart)

Chris and Tina Staehr, Tübingen, Germany, 2000. (David M. Crowe)

Sol Urbach and Emilie Schindler, New York, 1993. (Sol Urbach)

Oskar and Emilie's home, 102-108 Viamonte, San Vicente, Argentina. (David M. Crowe)

House built for Emilie by B'nai B'rith, 353 San Martin, San Vicente, Argentina— with author. (David M. Crowe)

Emilie with (from left) Ilse Chwat, Francisco Wichter, author, and Ilse Wartenleben, Hogar los Pinos, May, 2001. (David M. Crowe)

Emilie Schindler, Hogar los Pinos, May, 2001. (David M. Crowe)

Emilie Schindler's grave, Waldkreiburg, Germany, October, 2003. (David M. Crowe)

sharing the limelight with someone whom some *Schindlerjuden* considered Oskar Schindler's equal.[35]

Finally, there is the matter of how many Jews were on the Madritsch-Titsch list. Madritsch said in *Menschen in Not!* that he gave Oskar 100 names while the list that Titsch sent to Goldberg only had sixty names on it. Moreover, only fifty-three of the Madritsch Jews on the Titsch-Goldberg list made it to Brünnlitz. The shifting numbers can only be explained by the whims of Marcel Goldberg. People were desperate to get on the list at the last minute. One of the remarkable things about the two "Schindler's Lists" is the many family groupings. If you had no connections, money, or significant family ties, it was possible you could be replaced by someone who had the money to bribe Goldberg. As Schindler, Madritsch, and Titsch had little say over the actual creation of the two lists, there was no guarantee you would get on it just because one of them suggested your name. Goldberg was smart enough to know that he had to put the important Schindler and Madritsch people on his lists. Margot Schlesinger said that Goldberg was afraid of Titsch, though this was probably not enough to insure that one would finally be put on Goldberg's lists for Płaszów-Groß Rosen-Brünnlitz and Płaszów-Auschwitz-Brünnlitz.[36]

This was probably because Titsch, like Schindler and Madritsch, had developed a special relationship with Göth. Płaszów's commandant was an avid chess player, as was Titsch. One day, Göth asked Titsch to play a game with him, which Titsch won handily. Göth flew into a rage, turned the chess table over, and "stormed out of his office, with his guns on him, and was ready," according to Titsch, "to kill any Jew in sight." After this outburst, Titsch decided to lose to Göth to prevent similar incidents. But he decided to do it very carefully and slowly. Over time, he was able to convince Göth, after losing to him many times, that the commandant was the superior chess player. Titsch made certain that each losing game lasted from three to four hours so that "the camp, and the Jewish people in the camp could breathe easily" during the hours they were playing. And though Titsch and Göth did not play every day, Titsch tried "to engage Goeth in a game of chess whenever possible, because it was in a way his kind of Christian duty [Titsch was a Roman Catholic] to contribute to the welfare of his brother fellow men."[37] Goldberg knew of Titsch's "chess" relationship with Göth as well as their Viennese ties, which is probably the reason he feared Titsch.

Regardless, Goldberg had his own favorites when it came to whom he wanted on his lists and he could be quite bold when he made his choices.

He removed Noah Stockman, the top Jewish leader among the "Budzyner" Jews favored by Brünnlitz's new commandant, *SS-Obersturmführer* Josef Leipold, while the men were in Groß Rosen. Leipold, who had been commandant of the Heinkel aircraft factory camps at Budzyń and Wieliczka (Wilhelmsburg), trusted Stockman and wanted him to play the same role in Brünnlitz that he had at Budzyń and Wieliczka. The group of about fifty to sixty "Budzyners" saw themselves as something special, though they were not powerful enough to prevent Goldberg from removing Stockman from the list in Groß Rosen. This insured continued friction between the Kraków Jewish leadership and the "Budzyners" throughout the rest of the war.[38]

The Budzyń concentration camp was built on the site of a former Polish military industrial complex that included an aircraft factory. The Budzyń military factories were located just north of Kraśnik, which was thirty-five miles southwest of Lublin. After the Germans conquered Poland, the military factories at Budzyń became part of the Hermann Göring Works *(Reichswerke Hermann Göring)* and the Ernst Heinkel Aircraft Company *(Ernst Heinkel Flugzeugwerke A.G.)* took over the Polish aircraft factory. Heinkel had begun to use slave laborers at its new aircraft factory in Oranienburg in 1941. During the next four years, Heinkel-Oranienburg became one of the principal employers of concentration camp labor and a "model for slave labor," complete with a satellite camp of its own in Oranienburg. It also used slave labor in aircraft factories elsewhere. In early 1944, Heinkel reported that it was employing 2,065 prisoners in its factory in Mauthausen-Schwechat and 5,939 in Sachsenhausen. The Germans set up a forced labor camp at Budzyń in 1942 and initially used 500 Jews as slave laborers there. Within a year, 3,000 Jews were working at the various factories at Budzyń. About 10 percent of them were women and children. On October 22, 1942, the SS declared Budzyń a concentration camp and made it a part of the Majdanek network of camps.[39]

In early May 1944, the Heinkel operations at Budzyń were moved to Mielec, about a hundred miles northeast of Kraków. Schindler Jew Francisco Wichter said that about 950 Jews worked at Heinkel's "United East" *Flugzeugwerk* in Mielec. He was not certain about the components he helped manufacture, but speculated they might have been for V-1 and V-2 rockets. On the other hand, *Schindlerjude* Sam Birenzweig remembered helping install windshields on aircraft at Mielec.[40] But Wichter and the other Heinkel Jewish workers would soon move again as part of Hermann Göring's "Fighter Staff" plan to shift vital aircraft production to bomb-proof underground factories. Though run by Karl Otto Saur, the head of the Technical Office in Albert Speer's Ministry for Armaments and Munitions, WVHA's Hans Kammler oversaw the construction of the new aircraft factories. Kammler worked closely with Gerhard Maurer, who supplied the new Fighter Staff factories with concentration camp labor.[41]

Soon after the move to Mielec, the Fighter Staff coordinators began to make plans to transfer Heinkel's Aircraft Company/Works *(Flugzeugwerk)* operations to the Fighter Staff's new underground factory in the Wieliczka salt mines, about ten miles miles east of Kraków. Jewish workers would be drawn from the *Flugzeugwerk* and Płaszów to build the camp, which was named Wilhelmsburg, and then the factory below it. By early June 1944, workers in Wieliczka had constructed the first parts of the Heinkel He 219 Uhu (Owl), one of the most versatile but underproduced aircraft in the Luftwaffe. But by August, with the increased threat of bomb attacks from the U.S. Fifteenth Air Force and the advance of the Red Army, the factory was closed. But even if Wieliczka had not been threatened by the Americans and the Russians, there were serious questions about the wisdom of putting an aircraft factory in a former salt mine. Francisco Wichter and Sam Birenzweig commented on the damage that the salt did to aircraft and machine metal. Some of Wieliczka's Jewish workers were sent to Płaszów, Groß Rosen, Mauthausen, and other camps. The factory itself was moved to Austria, along with some of the other skilled workers.[42]

Josef Leipold was in charge of the Jewish labor camps at the Heinkel operations in Budzyń and Wielizcka. When the Fighter Staff shut down its operations at the salt mines, Leipold joined Göth's staff in Płaszów as an adjutant, though he was still involved with tearing down the barracks and packing up the machinery at Wieliczka. Noah Stockmann remained with Leipold to oversee Jewish workers at the salt mines. Before he came to Płaszów, Stockmann had gained quite a reputation for kindness. Originally from Brest Litovsk, Stockmann was a former Polish army officer who, along with sixty other captured POWs, were permitted to wear their uniforms at Budzyń. Leipold thought this would enable him to distinguish the former POWs from other prisoners.[43] Stockmann did everything he could to make living conditions tolerable in Budzyń. He was, for example, able to arrange for the prisoners to get unleavened bread for a Seder ceremony during Pesach (Passover) in the spring of 1944.[44]

Sam Birenzweig, who worked briefly for Stockmann at Wieliczka, remembered him as "a marvelous guy." Stockmann was uncomfortable selecting workers for life and death, so he told them the truth. The work at Wieliczka would really be hard. If someone was too sick or old to work, he said, they would be put on one of the frequent transports that left the camp. In this way, Birenzweig explained, Stockmann put the burden of life and death on the shoulders of each prisoner. But Stockmann's popularity was probably the cause of his downfall. Once the group of Schindler males arrived at Groß Rosen, Marcel Goldberg found a way to have Stockmann taken off of the list.[45]

Questions of Favoritism and Schindler's Lists

But before any of this happened, Goldberg had to prepare for the final departures of the 1,000 Jews originally on "Schindler's Lists." By the second week of October 1944, only about 7,000 Jews remained in Płaszów. And though Oskar Schindler had only just received final permission to open his factory in Brünnlitz and to move seven hundred men and three hundred women from Płaszów, the two lists indicate that Goldberg had given quite a lot of thought to who would be on them. For one thing, the lists are unusual in that there are so many similar surname groupings on it. Though Oskar did not get permission for the move until late September or early October, Goldberg must have known about his general plans well before this. This is the only way to explain his success in putting certain individuals, their families, and their friends on the list. In little more than two months, Płaszów's inmate population had been reduced by almost 13,000 people. To protect the people he wanted on the list, Goldberg had to take great care to keep them off the large transports that were leaving Płaszów. It was one thing to protect the random OD man, *Kapo*, or *Blockälteste*; it was quite another matter to protect his or her family or friends.

In some ways, the list that Raimund Tisch gave Marcel Goldberg typifies the lumping together of families that appeared on the larger Schindler transport lists. At one point, Madritsch had 3,000 Jews working for him at Płaszów, and when Schindler asked Madritsch and Titsch for a last-minute list of names, they named the people they were most familiar with: their supervisors and other Jews they had relied upon to help administer the large Madritsch sewing concern in the camp. Moreover, in comparing the Madritsch list with the two "Schindler's Lists," it is apparent that there was a concerted effort to put the names of the families of the sixty Madritsch workers on these larger lists. Leib and Estera Hudes, for example, were on Madritsch's list; two other family members, Izak and Naftali Hudes, joined them on "Schindler's Lists." Natan and Leontyna Stern were on Madritsch's list; Aszer, Henryk, and Sala Stern joined them on the larger lists. This meant that the original Madritsch list of sixty was expanded to sixty-eight once extra family members were added. And if you subtract the seven people on the original Madritsch list who did not make it to Brünnlitz, then over 20 percent of those on the Madritsch list were put together with other family members on "Schindler's List."[46]

These family ties were extremely important for survival in Płaszów. Time and again, *Schindlerjuden* told me how they were given better jobs or other special considerations because of their family or personal connections, though they often did not word it quite this way. Personal connections of even the most modest sort could ultimately translate into survival and life for many Schindler Jews. This does not mean that everyone who ultimately got on "Schindler's Lists" had such ties or influence. Many were just lucky. Dr. Moshe Bejski, for example, told me that he had no idea how he got on the list. He learned at the last minute that he was on it but not his two brothers, Izrael and Urysz. He told Goldberg to take him off the list if they were not on it. Later that evening, Goldberg told him to bring his two brothers with him to the train.[47] On the other hand, Ryszard Horowitz admitted that his family were put on the list because "they were well connected."[48]

Ties to Marcel Goldberg were also important. Dr. Aleksander Bieberstein said in his memoirs that though he, his wife, and his daughter were on the lists, Goldberg took them off, despite efforts by Mietek Pemper to change Goldberg's mind. Instead, Dr. Bieberstein said, they were replaced by people who had bribed Goldberg. Dr. Bieberstein was put back on the male list in Groß Rosen after the intervention of Pemper and Itzhak Stern. His wife and daughter were not so lucky. He was also unable to save his nephew, Dr. Artur Bieberstein, from being deported to Flossenbürg.[49] With the exception of one young relative, Emalia's Abraham Bankier was also alone on the list.

The same was true of Josef Bau. But he was alone on it because his wife, Rebecca, who had done manicures for Amon Göth, went to Mietek Pemper and arranged to have herself taken off the female "list" so that her husband, Josef, could be put on the male list. Some time earlier, Rebecca had intervened to save Pemper's mother from being shot by *SS-Rottenführer* Franz Grün. Rebecca was walking through the camp and saw Grün about to shoot Pemper's mother. Rebecca told Grün that if Göth found out he had killed Pemper's mother, the commandant would probably have Grün executed. Rebecca Bau later explained that she had made this sacrifice because "my husband was more important to me than I was, and I wasn't afraid."[50] Josef did not learn of Rebecca's sacrifice until he reached Groß Rosen. In 1971, Josef Bau testified against Grün at a trial in Vienna. The Austrian court sentenced the brutal Płaszów guard to nine years imprisonment for the murder of Bau's father, Abraham, and other Jews. Fourteen years earlier, a Polish court in Kraków had sentenced Grün to life imprisonment.[51]

Aleksander Bieberstein stated bitterly in his memoirs that many of Emalia and Płaszów's most prominent physicians were put on the list because they were friends of Goldberg. This included Dr. Chaim Hilfstein, a Jewish physician at Emalia; Dr. Leon Groß, Dr. Szaja Händler, Dr. Ferdinand Lewkowicz, and Dr. Matylda Löw. On a practical basis, it would seem wise to have as many experienced physicians as you could on any list for a labor camp, particularly in light of SS concern with hygiene. But favoritism did have an impact here. There were eleven members of the Groß family on the list, six Lewkowicz family members, and three Hilfsteins. On the other hand, Dr. Händler was alone on the list and there were only two members of the Löw family on it. Power and influence could not totally protect a family from the killings and murders that had occurred constantly in Kraków and Płaszów since the war began. In other words, even if one was in some sort of leadership or supervisory position at Płaszów, this did not guarantee your survival or that of your family. The vast majority of the Jews on the two "Schindler's Lists" were either there alone or paired with someone else with the same surname. Most of their relatives had already been murdered in the Holocaust.[52]

But this perception of favoritism and corruption surrounding the creation of "Schindler's List" angered a lot of Jews. Aleksander Bieberstein said that "through Goldberg rich OD men and prominent prisoners got on the list."[53] Richard and Lola Krumholz, who had been with Oskar Schindler "since the beginning," presumed they would be on the "list." But Goldberg gave their places to others. Maurice Markheim thought he got on the list at the last minute because his cousin, Herman Feldman, "knew some bigshots." Henry Salmovich never understood how he got on the list. "Usually, the people from Kraków got on it because they had a lot of pull. All those bigshots from the camp—the Jewish police—were from Kraków. I didn't have money or connections."[54]

Jack Mintz was particularly critical of Goldberg, and even Oskar Schindler, about this. He said that many people thought that "Schindler was almighty God, but he wasn't." Though he thought Oskar was "a nice guy," once he got to Brünnlitz, Mintz realized that some of those selected for the list were less than desirable people. "I would say if you selected from the eleven hundred, maybe three hundred should go in a concentration camp after the war. There were a lot of crooks and *Kapos* [on the list]." He blamed Goldberg for this, who had "more power [over the list] than Schindler. Schindler asked for the people he knew, but the rest he didn't know."[55] Such judgements are harsh, but they reflect the frustrations of some of the *Schindlerjuden* who felt so powerless in this critical life-and-death situation.

Yet how truthful are these accusations? In other words, is it possible to determine how many people were on the list because of influence or bribery? It is possible to have some idea of the most important Jews in Płaszów from the more detailed published testimonies such as Aleksander Bieberstein's *Zagłda Żydów w Krakowie* (Extermination of the Jews of Kraków), Stella Müller-Madej's *A Girl on Schindler's List,* and Elinor Brecher's excellent collection of *Schindlerjuden* testimony, *Schindler's Legacy.* There is also an interesting index of postwar testimony collected by the Polish Ministry of the Interior's Main Commission for the Investigation of Hitlerite Crimes in Poland (*Głownej Komisji Badania Zbroni Hitlerowakich w Polsce*) by Magdalena Kunicka-Wyrzykowska, *Indek Imienny Więżniów obpzu w Płaszowie* (Name Index of the Prison Camp in Płaszów). It contains the names of a number of Schindler Jews and a brief history of their experiences during the Holocaust, including the role they played in Płaszów or elsewhere. If you combine these sources with the individual interviews I did with Schindler survivors, it is possible to come up with a pretty good list of the most important Jewish figures in Płaszów. But here the situation gets tricky. For one thing, it would be incorrect to assume that there was something wrong with being on the list because one was in a position of some influence at Płaszów. For every unsavory character like Marcel Goldberg, there were many, many caring Jewish "Prominents" in Płaszów who used their positions to help others. On the other hand, it is also easy to understand the anger and frustration of those who did not make it on to one of Oskar Schindler's lists because, at least from their perspective, they did not have the power or valuables to get themselves or their loved ones on them.[56]

Yet it is possible to identify certain groupings of people on the list and at least determine whether some of them were people of influence. But the multiple, changing "Schindler's Lists" are what make such an analysis difficult beyond even the vaguest implication that to be part of such a surname grouping implied family connections or something immoral. Marcel Goldberg drew up two separate lists for the seven hundred men and the three hundred women who were to be sent to Brünnlitz in the fall of 1944. During my research I discovered several "Schindler's Lists" from the fall of 1944 through the spring of 1945 in the Auschwitz State Museum. These include the original transport list for the men, dated October 21, 1944, from Groß Rosen to Brünnlitz, and two separate female lists for three hundred women dated October 22 (the date the women arrived at Auschwitz from Płaszów) and a separate female Auschwitz to Brünnlitz list dated November 12, 1944. The problem with each of these lists is some of the Schindler men on the Płaszów-Groß Rosen list were taken off by Goldberg and replaced when the seven hundred men arrived at Groß Rosen. The same is true for the list of three hundred women on the Płaszów-Auschwitz transport. In other words, though the number of people removed from the male and female "Schindler's Lists" while in transit to Brünnlitz via Groß Rosen and Auschwitz probably numbered no more than twenty to thirty, the fact remains that the lists drawn up by Marcel Goldberg in Płaszów were different from the lists of men and women who finally reached Schindler's camp in the Sudetenland in October and November 1944.

Further complicating matters, the only two alphabetized lists we have are based on two April 18, 1945, lists that contain the names of 801 men and 297 women. Between the fall of 1944 and the spring of 1945, ninety-eight new people were added to Schindler's lists. The archives and individuals who claim to have the original "Schindler's List" in reality just have the April 18, 1945, list. This is the "list" that Marcel Goldberg has on a clipboard in one scene from Spielberg's *Schindler's List*. But why the difference in numbers between the fall 1944 lists and the April 18, 1945, lists? Between January 29, 1945, and April 11, 1945, three transports arrived at Brünnlitz from German camps at Golleschau (eighty-one Jews), Landskron (six Jews), and Geppersdorf (thirty Jews). Some of the Jews on these transports were either dead when they arrived at Brünnlitz or died a few days later. In addition, several Schindler Jews died while in Brünnlitz or were sent to other camps. Beyond this, there were several Jews, such as Wrozlavsky (Benjamin) Breslauer and Alfred Schonfeld, who simply "trickled" into Brünnlitz during the latter months of the war. But the April 18, 1945, list is not the final "Schindler's List." There was a final list made up on May 8, 1945, the last day before Oskar and Emilie Schindler fled Brünnlitz. It is identical to the April 18 list though quite messy, indicating that it was probably done in haste. The April 18 and May 8 women's lists are alphabetized while the male lists for these dates was not. Fortunately, the United States Holocaust Memorial Museum's (USHMM) archives has alphabetized the male and female lists of April 18, 1945, and blended them into one list. Aleksandra Kobielec of the Groß Rosen Museum did the same for the male and female lists, but did not combine them into one list.[57]

The USHMM list does enable us to look at one list and analyze its surname groupings. There were several large groupings on the list made up of families from prominent Jews, though they were more the exception than the rule. Most of the surname groupings on the list ranged from three to four individuals, and there is no way to know whether all the surname groupings were related. On the other hand, it is possible to determine from other sources which of these groupings were families and which were not. Regardless, it is interesting to note that of the 1,098 names on the April 18, 1945 lists, 545 were joined with those with identical surnames. We also know that the 98 new names added to the lists in 1945, as well as the 50 to 60 "Budzyners," were all males without relatives in Płaszów. This means that close to 60 percent of the individuals on "Schindler's List" were joined together with people, male and female, with identical surnames. Many of them were paired with someone with an identical surname, though there were also some very large surname groupings, many of them families. There were two groupings of eleven identical surnames, two with nine identical surnames, and quite a few with four, five, or six individuals with the same surnames. There were also linkages other than surnames. Stella Müller-Madej's extended family, for example, included the Grunbergs. So the prospect of even larger surname and/or family groupings on the list is probable. In the end, there is no doubt that there was a concentrated effort by Goldberg to save as many members of the same families as possible.[58]

The Schindler Men and Brünnlitz via Groß Rosen

Oskar Schindler's factory in Brünnlitz was formally known as *Arbeitslager Brünnlitz* and was a sub-camp of the Groß Rosen concentration camp. Groß Rosen (Polish, Rogoźnica) had been opened in 1940 as a small forced labor camp because a nearby quarry contained a blue-gray granite favored by Adolf Hitler and Albert Speer for some of the Führer's massive construction projects in Nuremberg and Berlin. In 1941, Groß

Rosen became an independent concentration camp and its prisoners were sent to work in the nearby quarries owned by the SS German Earth and Stone Works (DEST; *Deutsche Erd-und Steinwerke, GmbH*) or in the camp's brick works. Initially, Groß Rosen had a relatively small prisoner population, though by 1942 their numbers had begun to increase substantially. At first, the SS also used Groß Rosen as a training camp for prisoners willing to become stonemasons. Himmler falsely promised them better living conditions and even the hope of freedom. After they completed their training, they would then be sent to other camps to teach other prisoners their skills. Himmler, as usual, was thinking not only of wartime needs but also of SS postwar economic plans.[59]

Increased DEST demands for Groß Rosen's granite and bricks saw the camp population grow dramatically between 1940 and the end of the war. There were slightly fewer than 1,500 prisoners in Groß Rosen in 1941. By the time the camp was liquidated in February 1945, there were 97,414 prisoners in the main and satellite camps. Towards the end of the war, Groß Rosen became an important transit camp for prisoners being shipped westward from camps being liquidated in the face of Soviet moves. Estimates are that about 125,000 prisoners, almost half of them Jews, passed through Groß Rosen during the war. About 40,000 prisoners died in Groß Rosen's camps or in transports to or from them. Jews did not begin to arrive in Groß Rosen in significant numbers until 1943. Many of them would be forced to work not only in the main camp's quarries and brick works but in the various SS-run factories in Groß Rosen's hundred or so satellite camps in Poland, the Sudetenland, and Germany. Siemens Bauunion, for example, which had built a large factory building for Oskar Schindler at Emalia, ran a factory at Groß Rosen.[60]

When Oskar Schindler's seven hundred Jewish workers arrived for quarantine in Groß Rosen in mid-October 1944, the camp was under the command of *SS-Sturmbannführer* Johannes Hassebroek, a decorated Waffen SS officer who had once served with the SS Death's Head Division. Schindler said that Hassebroek and his staff soon became regular customers of his Schnaps-storage, and from the moment Schindler opened his factory camp at Brünnlitz, Hassebroek was in constant need of "fish, kilos of tea, Schnaps, valuable porcelain, etcetera." Groß Rosen's commandant frequently drove the two hundred or so miles from Groß Rosen to Brünnlitz to pick up Oskar's "donations and collections personally." He was always in a large car with a lot of storage space. Oskar said that because of these "donations," Hassebroek "became a benefactor of my camp, despite my Krakow reputation of friendliness towards Jews or even fraternity with Jews, the 'enemies of the state.'"[61]

But Hassebroek's later friendship with Schindler did little to help the seven hundred Schindler men when they arrived at Groß Rosen. The camp long had a reputation for brutality, and the death rate at its quarry was among the highest in DEST-run operations. But the SS at Groß Rosen did more than just work its prisoners to death. In early 1942, to reduce the camp's population, 127 inmates were sent to Aktion T4 (the Nazi code word for its "euthanasia" program for the handicapped) "euthanasia" center at Bernburg, where they were murdered by injection. This was part of "Special Treatment 14f13," the T4 program to murder concentration camp inmates.[62]

The trip for the Schindler men to Groß Rosen began at Płaszów at 5:00 A.M. on the morning of October 15, 1944, when all the remaining Jews at Płaszów were called to attention on the *Appellplatz*. After the names of the 1,000 Jews to be sent to Brünnlitz were read out, the women were separated from the men. About 4,000 Jewish males were then loaded onto train cars bound for the Groß Rosen concentration camp. The seven hundred male *Schindlerjuden* were put into the first seven cars; the eighth car carried Brünnlitz and non-Brünnlitz prisoners such as Dr. Aleksander Bieberstein. *SS-Hauptscharführer* Lorenz Landstorfer was in charge of the transport. The trip from Płaszów to Groß Rosen took about twenty hours.[63]

The prisoners got an inkling of what they were about to experience in Groß Rosen during the trip. The conditions in the cattle cars were so tense and overcrowded that Cantor Moshe Taubé's father, Emanuel, had a nervous breakdown. An SS guard sat in a corner of the car Emanuel was riding in. The guard drew an invisible circle around his chair and told the inmates that "whoever comes here to this chair where I sit will be shot." The prisoners dared not approach the guard; instead, they sat on top of each other. If they had to heed their bodily needs, they did so where they were sitting. Needless to say, the train car smelled of human excrement and body odor during the trip to Groß Rosen. But Taubé's father tried to reassure his son that wherever they were going, they would "be under the protection of Schindler."[64]

Groß Rosen terrified Leon Leyson, and Henry Wiener considered his time there "hell on earth." Leyson was so overwhelmed by his experience that he had no idea how long he was in the camp. On the other hand, Francisco Wichter told me that he was "treated generally well" while he was in Groß Rosen. But most Schindler Jews did not share his positive view of their time at Hassebroek's camp.[65] They arrived at Groß Rosen at about 3:00 P.M. on October 16. One inmate noted upon arrival that it was "a nice, large, graveled place and everywhere great barracks and green areas [met] the eye." The SS immediately began to unload the cars, putting the prisoners in columns of a hundred. The first seven columns were made up of the Brünnlitz men; the eighth column was mixed. Almost immediately, men in the eighth column tried to blend in with the Schindler columns in front of them. The SS immediately intervened and forced them back into the eighth column.[66]

As the new arrivals were being marched into the camp, Marcel Goldberg tried negotiating bribes with SS guards over the seven hundred places on the male "Schindler's List." According to Aleksander Bieberstein, Goldberg did this from memory because the written list had not arrived from Płaszów. Goldberg told the SS guards which men were supposed to be on the "list" and who was not on it. Goldberg was able verbally to remove about two dozen people from the male "list" made up in Płaszów, though it is unclear whether he was able to replace them with new men who had the resources to bribe him or their guards. And some of the bribes were significant. Sam Birenzweig, for example, remembered being approached by "a rich guy" who offered him "five thousand dollars American" for his place on the "list." Sam did not budge from his place in line, even after the inmate showed him the money in cash. Dr. Bieberstein was later put back on the list because of efforts by Mietek Pemper and Itzhak Stern. But most of the other men on the October 15 Płaszów to Groß Rosen transport were not as lucky. Mietek Pemper told me that most of the non-Schindler men on the transport would later die in forced death marches from other camps.[67]

Once in the camp, the SS marched the Brünnlitz men to the *Appellplatz* and ordered them to undress. They were also told to get rid of anything they had brought with them. These items, which included "a lot of valuables and currencies," were then taken to the camp's storehouse. The weather was freezing and the Schindler men had to stand naked for long periods for body searches, showers, disinfection, and clothing distribution. The individual body searches included a forced bowel movement to check for hidden valuables. Russian barbers then shaved each inmate's body hair, beginning with a "louse promenade" down the center of the head. The Schindler men were then forced to bathe in a sink, followed by a delousing with a caustic disinfectant. Still naked, they had to run to a distant storehouse, where they were given used shirts and pants, wooden or leather shoes, and a cap for the cold. They were also given a registration number on a wax disk that they had to wear around their necks.[68]

But the worst was yet to come. After spending hours in the cold, the Schindler men were then forced into rooms A and B of Block 9 (9/10). It was heated by one stove in the middle of the room. The windows were covered with tar paper and, when combined with natural body heat and the stove, made the room unbearable to live in. They were given fifty bowls to share at meal time. As they stood in line for food, the Schindler males had to pass the bowl from one man to another; if they did not do this quickly enough, the guards would knock the bowl from their hands and beat them. In fact, beatings by the *Stubendienst,* the German criminal prisoners assigned to guard the Schindler men, took place constantly. Few of the Schindler men escaped beatings by these sadists.[69]

For the next few days, the SS established a strict regimen of military-style calisthenics for the prisoners. After roll call at 8:00 A.M., they were taken to a ditch; here they had two minutes to relieve themselves, their only chance to do this. At other times, they had to soil their pants. After breakfast, they exercised until noon and then had an hour for lunch. They had calisthenics again in the afternoon and were then locked in their barracks for the night.[70] On October 20, the typewritten "Schindler's List" arrived from Płaszów, but was now out of date because Goldberg had verbally removed about twenty-four of the men from it. Most of them had been sent to some of Groß Rosen's sub-camps. The SS guards seemed unaware of this and began a frantic search of the camp for the missing men until they realized that most of them had already been sent elsewhere. To fill the void, Dr. Bieberstein and others were now added to the list to make up the full contingent of seven hundred. But Dr. Bieberstein is the only person we know of who was able to get on the list because of his personal ties to Stern and Pemper. A few of the men removed initially by Goldberg were put back on the list. Presumably, the other places were filled by inmates who bribed Goldberg or the SS guards.[71]

Thomas Keneally, who interviewed some of the Schindler men for his historical novel, said that the list never arrived from Płaszów. Consequently, Keneally wrote that, on October 20, the day before the Schindler men were to be shipped to Brünnlitz, the SS forced Goldberg to retype the original list from memory. It was supposedly at this point, says Keneally, that new alterations were made to the list. Dr. Bieberstein, though, says that Goldberg's original list arrived in Groß Rosen on October 20. But regardless of which of these stories is true, the first copy of the male "Schindler's List" we have is dated October 21, 1944. So whether the original list was lost or arrived late, the fact remains that Goldberg or someone else had to type a new list to take care of the new deletions and additions.[72]

This list, which is simply titled "*Konzentrationslager Groß-Rosen-Arbeitslager Brünnlitz*," contained the names of seven hundred men. Unlike the women's list, which is alphabetized, the male list is organized according to prisoner numbers. The men are listed last name first followed by their date of birth. Their individual wartime occupations are the last item listed by each man's name. There are some intriguing markings on the list. Someone, presumably Goldberg, went through and changed the occupations of twenty-seven of the men, mainly to *Bau* (construction). Ten more had their occupations typed on the list with a different typewriter, and the names of fifteen men were completely scratched out.[73] We know what happened to some of the males in this group. Soon after they arrived in Brünnlitz, it was discovered that four of them were children. Josef Leipold, Brünnlitz's commandant, ordered that the boys and their fathers be sent to Auschwitz. Those transferred were Dawid and Ryszard Horowitz, Abraham and Zugenusz Ginter, Leo and Zbigniew Groß, and Hermann and Aleksander Rosner. They were taken under SS guard to Auschwitz on a regular train and arrived in time for a few of the boys to see their mothers.[74]

The other seven names scratched out—Seriasz Fajszmann, Leon Ferber, Roman Ferber, Josef Isak Garde, Izak Gerstner, Wilhelm Schnitzer, and Zafel Naftali—never appeared on any of the later "Schindler's Lists," which means that they were never taken off the list, were removed from it soon after their arrival at Brünnlitz, or were no longer alive when it was created. Roman Ferber was one of the children hidden in Płaszów after the May 14, 1944, *Aktion*. So it is possible that he and his father, Leon, were also sent with the other group of fathers and sons to Auschwitz. Zafel Naftali was replaced by Szmul Cajg, and *"blieber"* (stay) was written beside Izak Gerstner's name. Wilhelm (Wilek) Schnitzer, a prominent OD man whom Amon Göth had killed months earlier as part of the Chilowicz murders, was also on the list. Why a dead man was on the list is a mystery, though it is possible that Goldberg created a few false places on the list for last-minute bribes. But regardless of what happened to those mentioned above on male list, it is apparent that the October 21, 1944, list was used as the official "Schindler's List" when the men got to Brünnlitz.[75]

On October 21, the prisoners were again deloused before boarding the trains for Brünnlitz. Igor Kling was uncertain of the destination until he "saw all the big shots from Płaszów." Just before the Schindler men boarded the train, they were given soup made of grass and water, which some of them refused, and a "sandwich wrapped in paper." The SS guards warned them, though, that they would be shot if they ate the sandwich before they got on the train. Once the car doors were locked, they all tore open the sandwich wrappings and discovered "two slices of bread with jam in the middle." At 3:00 P.M., the Brünnlitz transport left Groß Rosen for the twenty-one-hour trip to Schindler's factory camp in the Sudetenland.[76]

As the train left Groß Rosen, Igor Kling sensed that, other than the presence of the "big shots" on the transport, something was different. He saw a difference in the behavior of the SS guards. By this time, of course, the SS, like the rest of Germany's military and paramilitary forces, was suffering severe manpower shortages. The guards on the Brünnlitz transport were middle-aged "leftovers." Kling noted that the "viciousness from their faces had disappeared. The behavior we saw was completely different than in Płaszów."[77] Perhaps this easing of tension explains the almost anti-climatic arrival of the Schindler men at Brünnlitz at noon the next day. But more than likely, the men were simply too exhausted from their harsh treatment at Groß Rosen to appreciate fully their arrival at Schindler's sub-camp. Several of the Schindler men remembered Oskar waiting for them when they arrived; others also saw Emilie, and Commandant Josef Leipold, when the train pulled into the new camp. But they remembered little else.[78]

Steven Spielberg paints a far different picture of their journey and arrival in *Schindler's List*. He begins by showing the men riding in a frozen transport with icicles hanging from the windows, even though it is just late October. Outside, snow covers the ground. As the train pulled into Brünnlitz, a caption appears on the screen that reads, "Zwittau-Brinnlitz Schindler's Hometown." Zwittau, the German name for Oskar's birthplace, Svitavy, is about eight and a half miles north of Brněnec, or Brünnlitz, where Schindler's factory was located. Spielberg has the men dressed in normal street clothes, though in reality they wore shabby, used, ill-fitting clothing. When the SS guards have unloaded the seven hundred Schindler men from the transport, Oskar makes a short speech. "The train with the women has already left Płaszów, and will be arriving very shortly. I know you've had a long journey. But it is only a short walk to the factory where hot soup and bread is waiting for you. Welcome to Brinnlitz." If the men were arriving in "Zwittau-Brinnlitz," then it could not be a "short walk to the factory." Perhaps this confusion over geography comes from Keneally, who said that the men "dismounted" at the Zwittau depot and were then marched three or four miles to the industrial hamlet of Brinnlitz. While marching through Zwittau, Keneally wrote, the Schindler men saw graffiti on the walls that read, "KEEP THE JEWS OUT OF BRINNLITZ." Perhaps Keneally intended such graffiti to symbolize the general administrative opposition to the move of Jews into the Sudetenland. Such sentiments, though, were not reflective of the general population, which at the end of the war treated the Schindler Jews with great kindness.[79]

None of the Schindler men I interviewed ever talked about being marched eight miles or more from Svitavy (Zwittau) to Brněnec. In reality, it is hard to imagine such a march given the hilly terrain between the two towns. Moreover, there was an extensive network of rail lines running directly beside the factory's main gate. There was also a spur line that went into Schindler's sub-camp at one corner of this complex. So the idea that Oskar forced his new workers to march so many miles from Zwittau to Brünnlitz is illogical. Once they got to Schindler's sub-camp, what they found was an empty factory with no beds. Oskar had sent 250 wagonloads of goods from Emalia to Brünnlitz, and it was now the job of his new workers to construct a factory there. Oskar did not completely close Emalia. The enamelware portion of his factory in Kraków continued to operate with Polish workers until early 1945. But for the seven hundred Schindler men, there was a more serious problem than the reconstruction of Schindler's armaments factory: the whereabouts and safety of their wives, mothers, and daughters.[80]

The Schindler Women and Brünnlitz via Auschwitz

Aleksander Bieberstein states in his memoirs that a transport of 1,000 females, including the three hundred Schindler women, left Płaszów for Auschwitz on October 21, 1944. On the other hand, Auschwitz records state that more than 2,000 female Jews arrived from Płaszów on the evening of October 22. Because of space problems, they had to "spend the night in the so-called sauna." The "Sauna" was the nickname for the disinfection bath in Auschwitz II-Birkenau located near the "Kanada" warehouse for goods taken from the prisoners. Several of Birkenau's gas chambers were located nearby. But why were the women sent to Auschwitz instead of Groß Rosen? The myth is that they were sent to Auschwitz by mistake. But according to Mietek Pemper, this was not true. SS regulations required that the women, like the men, had to be quarantined, which involved intimate body searches, shaving, and delousing as part of their transfer to another camp. But as women had to do this to female prisoners, Groß Rosen simply did not have the personnel or facilities to handle the three hundred Schindler women.[81]

No one, of course, had informed the women that they would first be sent to Auschwitz, which was only thirty miles west of Płaszów on a direct rail link from Kraków. Helen Sternlicht Rosenzweig seemed to be the only one who knew precisely that they would go to Auschwitz before their final transfer to Brünnlitz. Before his arrest, Oskar Schindler had taken Helen aside in the commandant's villa in Płaszów and told her that he was opening a factory in Czechoslovakia. He said he had a list of names of people he wanted to take with him and that Helen would be on it. He asked whether she had family members. Helen told him she had two sisters, and Oskar wanted to know their names. He also asked whether she had personal items she wanted to take with her. Helen said she had a small suitcase and Oskar advised her to give it to him. He explained that his female workers would be sent to Auschwitz for a while before being sent to Brünnlitz and that the SS would take the suitcase from her when she arrived. Oskar then promised Helen that "she would be with him." When Helen got to Brünnlitz, she asked Oskar several times about her suitcase. He told her that it had been lost.[82]

Rena Finder told me that the Schindler women thought they were being sent to Brünnlitz, though Stella Müller-Madej remembered one woman in her train car telling her mother that Auschwitz was their real destination. But whether they knew about their temporary stopover in Auschwitz or not, the arrival of the Schindler women in Auschwitz on the evening of October 22, 1944, was terrifying. In fact, some of the Schindler women told me that the scene in *Schindler's List* about their arrival in Auschwitz II-Birkenau, the sprawling complex's killing center, was extremely realistic. Most of them also remembered the brutality and vulgarity of the female SS guards and *Kapos*. As they forced the women off of the train cars, they yelled *"Raus, raus, macht schnell"* (Get off quickly). The SS guards beat them with whips and rifle butts and "beautiful Alsatians" lunged at them. Rena also remembered the terrible stench of burning bodies and the ashes from the nearby crematory chimneys that fell on them like snow.

And several of the Schindler women remembered Josef Mengele, Auschwitz's "Angel of Death," whom some would meet again before they left the death camp.[83]

The women's facilities at Auschwitz had been opened in the main camp (later Auschwitz I) in 1942 to help meet its growing labor needs. The women's camp was later moved to Birkenau and expanded considerably. By the time the Schindler women arrived in Auschwitz's death camp, Birkenau (Auschwitz II-Birkenau), women lived in many of the barracks just inside the "gate of death," Birkenau's infamous arched entranceway. Upon their arrival, the Schindler women were given temporary registration numbers to sew on their clothing. They were initially housed in B-IIc, the Hungarian women's transit camp. When the Schindler women arrived at Auschwitz, it was under the command of *SS-Hauptsturmführer* Josef Kramer, who was soon transferred to Bergen-Belsen. Though Auschwitz records are a bit confusing on this next point, the women's camp at Auschwitz II-Birkenau was under the command of Austrian-born *SS-Lagerführerin* (camp supervisor) Maria Mandl (Mandel). She blended a passion for classical music with extreme cruelty towards her female prisoners. She was executed for war crimes in Kraków in 1947.[84]

When they arrived at Auschwitz in late October 1944, the Schindler women did not realize that it was normal to put newly arrived prisoners not designated for the nearby gas chambers in the "Sauna" for all aspects of the quarantine. After stripping, they were subjected to "gynecological examinations," the full shaving of all body hair with a dull razor and scissors, and a bath "under streams of boiling hot or freezing water." Occasionally, new inmates were subjected to a hot steam disinfection bath, though Stella Müller-Madej said that the delousing consisted of hitting each woman on her newly bald head with a "stinking rag that made every shaved place burn, whatever it was, carbolic acid or something."[85]

Stella remembered one of the *Aufseherinnen* (female SS guards) calling the Schindler women "whores" and "Płaszów scum." One shouted, "Why the hell do they order us to waste our time on this carrion?" And though only women could shave women, there were plenty of male *Kapos* working in the "Sauna." After the shaving and delousing, Stella's mother tried to reassure her daughter that if they intended to gas the Schindler women, they would not have shaved and deloused them. Next the *Aufseherin* forced the Schindler women into a large shower room.[86] Stella described the scene:

They started pushing us into that larger room without giving any soap-like mush. The iron doors opened. We stood waiting for the water to flow. Nothing. Women started going crazy and one shouted, "Do you smell the gas? I'm suffocating!"

Mummy hugged me so tight that I really couldn't breathe. I broke free. There was shouting all around. I felt a hand digging into my arm and couldn't shake it away. A woman fell, scratching my thigh.

"Mummy, Ilza [a friend]," I found my voice, "There's no gas." But I was choking. "The stink is coming from us." I wanted to say that it was coming from our heads, from that stuff on the rag [for disinfection], but I couldn't. Why don't they calm down before they kill each other?

"Hysteria! There's no gas! Calm down!" shouted a couple of strong voices.

A moment later, boiling water spurted onto us. We danced around and everyone tried to find shelter against the walls. The iron doors finally opened and they drove us outside naked. We immediately formed ranks, and many of us looked terrible, all scratched and bruised. It was drizzling. We shook, we shook from cold, hunger, and thirst.[87]

Each of the Schindler women I interviewed remembered this scene a little differently. Rena Finder, for example, told me that the water from the shower heads was cold. But everyone I talked to said the shower scene from Spielberg's *Schindler's List* was quite accurate. Helen Rosenzweig, though, told me that the scene in the film immediately afterwards was ridiculous. By 1942, Auschwitz authorities had begun to issue female prisoners used civilian clothing with red stripes painted on the back and crude wooden clogs. Stella, Rena, and Helen all remembered that the clothing was extremely mis-sized. But Halina Brunnengraber Silber remembered thinking there was "no room for miracles at Auschwitz." She believed there was no hope: "It is just a question of how or when it would be my turn [to die] in Auschwitz."[88]

The Schindler women were in Auschwitz from October 22 until either November 10 or November 12, 1944. Auschwitz records state that on November 10, a transport of three hundred women was sent from Auschwitz II-Birkenau to Groß Rosen's "Brünnlitz auxiliary camp in Czechoslovakia."[89] On the other hand, the official transport list for the women is dated November 12, 1944.[90] But whether they were in Nazi Germany's most horrific death camp for twenty-two or twenty-four days, it was far too long, even though they sensed they were only there temporarily. Word spread quickly that the Schindler group was bound for a favored labor camp and there were efforts by other inmates, particularly "Prominents," to somehow get on the Brünnlitz list. Mietek Pemper told me that only two women were taken off of the list in Auschwitz and replaced by others: his mother and Itzhak Stern's mother. Stern's mother contracted typhus and died; Mietek Pemper's mother, who survived Auschwitz and the war, was partially paralyzed. However, Aleksandra Kobeliec, who wrote a brief history of Brünnlitz for the Groß Rosen museum, said that five women were taken off the Brünnlitz list during selections at Auschwitz. On the other hand, Tushia Nusbaum Zilbering testified after the war that she and nine other Schindler women from Płaszów were removed from the list in Auschwitz and remained there until liberation.[91]

Stella Mülle-Madej became very ill at Auschwitz and was taken to the hospital. Like most of the Schindler girls and women, Stella's physical condition deteriorated rapidly at Auschwitz because of the harsh treatment and inadequate food. Genia Weinstein said their condition deteriorated further after the Germans insisted that each of the Schindler women donate half a liter of blood. The *Aufseherinnen* seemed to resent the Schindler women because they were to be transferred out, and did everything they could to make their lives miserable. They punished them if they violated one of the complex camp rules. If a Schindler woman had not properly sewn her number onto her ragged dress, an *Aufseherin* would dump crushed bricks on the floor and force the guilty prisoner to crawl over the bricks on her hands and knees. The *Aufseherinnen* would also withhold food for the slightest infraction and, one day, while Stella was standing in line for bread and marmalade, the *Blockälteste* (Senior prisoner block leader) threw Stella's portion of marmalade in her face and called her "an elegant whore" because she had absent-mindedly offered her bread for the marmalade instead of her hand.[92]

But the most frightening moments for a few of the Schindler women were their encounters with Josef Mengele. As chief physician at Birkenau, Mengele had been to Płaszów in the spring of 1944 to conduct a *Selektion* of male Jewish prisoners for shipment to Auschwitz. The day after the Schindler women arrived in Auschwitz, Mengele conducted a two-hour *Selektion* of the 2,000 or so women who had arrived on the Płaszów transport. He sent 1,765 women, including the *Schindlerjuden,* to Transit Camp B-IIc. The remaining women were sent to the gas chambers.[93] But this was not the last time the Schindler women encountered Mengele. Celina Karp Biniaz was part of a *Selektion* that involved everyone in her barracks. As the women walked past Mengele, he pushed those he chose to be gassed or shot to the left and those he wanted to live to the right. Celina was put into the left line. But for some reason, Mengele decided to go through the "death line" once more. As Celina walked past him, she blurted out, *"Lassen Sie mich gehen"* (Let me go). Mengele then pushed her into the right line.[94]

Margot Schlesinger had a similar experience during another selection. During the first *Selektion,* Celina's Biniaz's mother, Phyllis, had broken her promise to always stay with Celina when she volunteered to peel potatoes. Phyllis thought she could scrounge some extra food for both of them and left Celina in the barracks. While she was gone, a Mengele *Selektion* took place, and Phyllis almost lost her daughter. When yet another *Selektion* took place, Phyllis asked Margot to switch places so that she could be next to Celina. Mengele saw the women do this and put Margot in a group of four women about to be murdered. Margot, who spoke perfect German, then explained to Mengele that she was "young and frightened, and had made a mistake." Mengele let her live.[95]

The Schindler women also experienced other small miracles at Auschwitz. According to Elinor Brecher, Betty Bronia Groß Gunz was probably the only Schindler woman who looked forward to going to Auschwitz because she thought that her beloved husband, Roman, was there. Three months after their marriage in 1942, Roman had been taken in a roundup and sent to Auschwitz. Betty soon learned that she was pregnant and had an abortion because she knew that pregnancy was a "sure death sentence for mother and child."[96] One day while at Płaszów, a Jewish laborer who had spent a month at Auschwitz handed Betty a handkerchief with Roman's name on it. The worker told Betty that Roman wanted to let her know that he loved her. Later, some barrels were brought to Płaszów from Auschwitz. Written on the outside of one of them was "ROMAN GUNZ. I love you. I hope we will be together soon."[97] Betty reached Auschwitz full of hope and fear. "I was *dreaming* of it, if he aged, if he still loved me." But she soon learned that Roman had been sent to another part of the vast camp, and they did not reunite until they were in Kraków after the war.[98]

But Roman Gunz did play a important part in another small miracle at Auschwitz. He helped save the sons of the fathers who had been sent to Auschwitz from Brünnlitz soon after they had arrived in Schindler's subcamp. By this time, Roman was an Auschwitz "old timer." Consequently, he was one of the *Kapos* who met the male Brünnlitz group when they arrived in Birkenau in late October. But Roman also knew that children did not live long at Auschwitz; he told Henry Rosner: "Listen, if you want to live, try to save yourself, because about children, I don't know."[99] None of the fathers, though, was willing to sacrifice a son, so Roman put the children in "a bunker the Germans had prepared for themselves, and took care of them." Ryszard Horowitz said it was actually a barracks that had been set aside to quarantine typhus patients.[100]

But Ryszard was soon separated from his father, Dawid. After they arrived at Auschwitz, there was a small *Selektion* for the newly arrived Brünnlitz group. When they had lined up, one of the SS men ordered the sons to step back. But the officer winked at Henry Rosner, who took this to mean that he did not want his son, Alexander (Dolek), to step back. Just after the group had arrived at Auschwitz, one of the guards had given Dolek an accordion, which he played for the guards. All of Auschwitz's musicians were now dead, so Olek's musical skills probably saved his life. But Olek's cousin, Ryszard, was not as lucky. He was separated from his father, who was sent to Dachau along with Henry and Olek Rosner. After the selection, another miracle took place—some of the Brünnlitz boys were able to see their mothers briefly at Auschwitz just before they were shipped to Brünnlitz. On the day the Schindler women were being loaded onto the cattle cars for transport to Brünnlitz, Regina Horowitz, Manci Rosner's sister-in-law, looked through a peephole and saw her son, Ryszard, and Manci's son, Alex, with a group of other children. The guard who had escorted the Brünnlitz males to Auschwitz told Manci that they were in the camp. After Regina and Manci spotted their sons, they convinced the guard on their train car to pass a note to them. The guard then let Manci and Regina get out of the car to urinate beneath it. As they squatted down, they were "able to exchange a few words" with their sons, who lifted up their sleeves to show their mothers the new tattoos on their arms.[101]

The actual transfer of the Schindler women from Auschwitz to Brünnlitz is a story wrapped in mystery and myth. In Spielberg's *Schindler's List,* when Oskar Schindler learns to his surprise that the women are in Auschwitz, he dashes out of his office, telling his mistress and Stern as he goes, "They're in Auschwitz, the train was never routed here—a paperwork mistake." As Schindler's chauffered limousine races out of the factory grounds, Spielberg shifts back to the famous shower scene and an inspection by Josef Mengele at Auschwitz. Then we see Oskar Schindler in the office of Auschwitz's *Lagerkommandant,* at that time *SS-Sturmbannführer* Richard Baer. As Baer looks over a copy of the April 18, 1945, female list, he says,

You are not the only industrialist who needs labor, Herr Schindler. Earlier this year, I. G. Farben [I. G. Farben was the principal employer of forced and slave labor at its Auschwitz III-Monowitz complex, where it made artificial rubber and synthetic gasoline] ordered a train load of Hungarians for his chemical factory. The train came in through the archway, and the officer in charge of the selection went immediately to work and sent two thousand of them straight away to special treatment [Nazi euphemism for gassing]. It is not my responsibility to interfere with the processes that take place here. Why do you think I can help you if I can't help I. G. Farben?[102]

Oskar responds by slowly emptying a small pouch of six or seven large diamonds on Baer's desk. As he does this, he reassures Baer: "Allow me to express the reason. I'm not making any judgements about you. It's that I know in the coming months that we all are going to need portable wealth."[103] Baer responds by telling Oskar that he could have him arrested for this. Oskar explains that he is "protected by powerful friends," something he is sure the commandant knows.[104]

Baer now becomes less defensive and tells Oskar, "I do not say I'm accepting them. All I say is I am uncomfortable with them on the table." As Baer slides the precious gems into the top drawer of his desk, he offers Schindler a different group of Jewish women. "I have a shipment coming in tomorrow. I'll cut you three hundred units from it. New ones. These are fresh. The train comes, we turn it around. These are yours."[105] Needless to say, Oskar will have none of this. "Yes, yes, I understand. I want these."[106] Baer, who now begins to prepare himself a bicarbonate, tells Oskar that he "shouldn't get stuck on names."[107] Oskar, sitting stone-faced, says nothing. As Baer prepares to drink his bicarbonate, he explains to Schindler, "That's right, it creates a lot of paperwork."[108]

The scene then shifts to the rail lines just inside Birkenau's archway. The Schindler women are lined up for a final roll call just before they board the train for Brünnlitz. As they move towards the train cars, a male SS guard drags two of the young girls out of line. Suddenly, out of nowhere, Oskar Schindler appears. "Hey, hey, hey," he shouts, "What are you doing? These are mine. These are my workers. They should be on my train. They are skilled munitions workers. They're essential, essential girls. Their fingers polish the inside of shell metal casings. How else can I polish the inside of a 45 mm metal casing. You tell me?"[109] The dumbfounded guard now shouts, "Back on the train!"[110] In the next scene, the women are seen marching slowly into Brünnlitz as their husbands, fathers, and sons peer thankfully through the factory's windows. Leading them into the camp is their savior, Oskar Schindler.[111]

The myth of Schindler's personally saving the women in Auschwitz seems to have begun during the interviews that Oskar did with Martin Gosch and Howard Koch in 1964. According to the written summary of their discussions with Schindler, when Oskar learned that his three hundred women were in Auschwitz, he drove there and told the commandant, "Look, if you give me three hundred other women, I have to begin training them again, and this is pretty late to do this—the war effort needs the things that we are going to make, and you take away from me the women who are already skilled, the women I've already trained, and this is going to hurt our production there, so it doesn't make any sense." The commandant finally agreed to release the three hundred women to Schindler in return for a modest bribe.[112]

None of this took place. Oskar Schindler did not go to Auschwitz to save his female workers. He knew they were initially to be sent to Auschwitz before their ultimate transfer to Brünnlitz and did take action when they failed to show up soon after the arrival of his male workers. But what really happened was quite different from the Spielberg version of the story. So what was the basis for the dramatic scene surrounding Schindler's efforts to save his women in Auschwitz? The information certainly did not come from Schindler, who in his postwar accounts went into little detail about what happened. All he said about his women in Auschwitz in his 1945 report on his wartime activities was that the "men had been in the Groß-Rosen concentration camp for three days, while the women had been in Auschwitz for three weeks. Plundered, almost naked, they finally arrived, wearing old, striped uniforms; we had to adjust to 'Old Reich' methods."[113]

A decade later, he explained in a report to Yad Vashem that the biggest problem he faced when he tried to move his factory to the Sudetenland was local opposition. "The next great difficulty," he explained, "concerned my 1,100 Jewish inmates, who meanwhile had been assigned to the KZ *[Konzentrationslager]* camps Auschwitz and Groß Rosen, as to how to obtain them for my Brünnlitz plant. After several visits to Berlin, and with the support of Ob. Ing. Lange from the OKH military armament office Berlin, I succeeded in obtaining a telegraphed order from the superintendancy of the concentration camps Amtsgruppe D Oranienburg, the Reich leader SS, to take over my people by name from the KZ Groß-

Rosen and Auschwitz and to transport them to Brünnlitz."[114] At no point in either of these accounts does Oskar discuss anything similar to the accounts found in Spielberg's film.

So what was the basis of Spielberg's dramatic scenes involving the saving of the Schindler women? He drew it from Thomas Keneally, who admitted that it was part of the "Schindler mythology."[115] Keneally, who tried to be careful about the facts he used in his historical novel, made a few errors in this part of the book. He claimed, for example, that "according to the Schindler mythology," Oskar negotiated with Rudolf Höss, who "presided over the entire camp at the time the Schindler women occupied a barracks in Birkenau."[116] *SS-Obersturmbannführer* Rudolf Franz Ferdinand Höss was Auschwitz's first commandant. In the aftermath of Dr. Konrad Morgen's investigations into concentration camp corruption, the highly-decorated, well-thought-of Höss was transferred to WVHA's Office Group D1 office in Oranienburg, where he served as Deputy Inspector of Concentration Camps under Richard Glücks. He returned to Auschwitz for a few months in 1944 to oversee the murder of Hungarian Jews in operation *Aktion Höss* but returned to his post in Oranienburg in late summer. So, unless Oskar contacted Höss directly in Oranienburg, it was doubtful that he had any dealings with Auschwitz's former commandant about the release of three hundred women in the fall of 1944.[117]

Keneally, who interviewed *Schindlerjuden* for his historical novel, carefully discusses the various myths about Schindler and his female workers at Auschwitz. But he gives most credibility to a speech made by Itzhak Stern "years later."[118] Actually, Stern's remarks were part of a series of spontaneous testimonies given by Schindler Jews at a banquet to honor Oskar, who had recently been nominated as a Righteous Among the Nations by Yad Vashem in Tel Aviv on May 2, 1962. Dr. Moshe Bejski told me that the testimonies were not part of the evening's plans. But as various Schindler Jews stood up to praise Oskar, it occurred to Dr. Bejski that someone should take notes. He began furiously to write down everything that was being said on scraps of paper and napkins. He later organized his scribbled notes into a Hebrew transcript that he gave to Yad Vashem. He graciously shared an English translation with me.[119]

This is what Stern said:

After tremendous efforts he [Schindler] was able to transfer to Brinlitz only part of the prisoners, as potential workers. The men came to Brinlitz via Groß-Rosen, and the women through Auschwitz. We came to Brinlitz in October 1944. Days passed and the women did not arrive in spite of the confirmed list. I asked Schindler—under pressure of some of my comrades—to try to exert influence in this matter; just then his secretary [Hilde Albrecht] came in. Schindler looked at the pretty young woman, pointed to a big diamond ring on his finger and said, "Do you want this diamond?" The girl was very excited. Schindler told her: "Take the list of the Jewish women, put in your suitcase the best food and beverages, and go to Auschwitz. You know that the commander likes beautiful women. When you come back and the women arrive in camp, you will receive this diamond and more." The secretary went, and as she did not return within two days, Schindler took *Major* Polto (?) with him and they traveled to Auschwitz—and after a few days all the women arrived—only my mother (may she rest in peace) was missing. They were the wives, mothers and sisters of the men.[120]

This is a much more expansive account than the one Stern gave Dr. Ball-Kaduri in his interview with him in 1956.

After one week we realized that only the men had arrived, the women were missing. There was a great deal of anxiety, since many families had been separated. I consulted Schindler. The transport of the women had gone to Auschwitz. He showed a ring to his secretary and said: "This is my ring. Go to Auschwitz and get the women out of there and to Bruennlitz. Whatever it takes to do that, do it. If you are successful, you'll get this ring."

He accompanied her during that night. She traveled to Auschwitz in October 1944, and she made daily phone calls to Schindler. She was successful in getting the 300 women to Bruennlitz. Only two women were missing (among them my mother). When she came back, Schindler gave her the ring.[121]

Stern added that Schindler spoke to his secretary in even more drastic words: "Bring these women to Bruennlitz, use all possible means to do that, even if you have to sleep with the Nazi big shots."[122]

Stern then referred to a letter that Oskar had sent to Dr. Ball-Kaduri on September 9, 1956, to underscore his willingness to urge his secretary to use sex, if necessary, to help free the Schindler women in Auschwitz.[123] In the letter, Oskar said this:

Who can feel my inner conflict, which I encountered when I sacrificed a dozen women to the orgies of the *SS-Uebermenschen* (superior human beings), where alcohol and gifts had already lost attraction. Women, of which half of them must have known of the task awaiting them, if they were aware of only parts of my objective. This pain that I felt, was certainly not jealousy, but self-disgust of my actions. I was "throwing pearls to the swine." The saying that the end justifies the means was often only a shabby comfort.[124]

In reality, Oskar's statement of guilt about his misuse of women does little to back up Stern's account. But over time, Stern's explanation became an integral part of the Schindler mythology. Dr. Aleksander Bieberstein accepted it and added his own twist in his memoirs. According to his account, it took Schindler's secretary only two days to get the women out of Auschwitz and into Brünnlitz.[125]

Emilie Schindler had a different version of the story about the Auschwitz women. The problem with Emilie's story, though, is that she gets some of her basic facts wrong about events surrounding the Auschwitz controversy. She said that the Schindler women arrived in Brünnlitz in the spring of 1944 and that Oskar had "paid Goeth [Göth] a huge amount of money so he would let the thirteen hundred people named in the famous list leave without any problems."[126] The transfer of the Schindler Jews involved 1,000 workers and took place in the fall of 1944. Göth, of course, was in jail during this period, though it is possible that Oskar initially bribed him during the early negotiations for the transfer. Emilie went on to say that when Oskar learned "the transport with the women had been diverted to Auschwitz," he was "confused and nervous." Regardless, Emilie explained, "he decided not to be cowed and to try to do something, whatever that might be. As ever, I was ready to help him."[127]

Oskar and Emilie then went to the office, where Oskar telephoned Willi Schöneborn, the chief technical engineer at Brünnlitz, a position he had also held at Emalia. Oskar told Schöneborn to come to the office; he then took a "small bag out of his pocket, the contents of which were very familiar" and said,

I must entrust you with an important mission. Without the women we cannot go on with the factory. We need their labor, and besides, the men are getting very restless asking why their wives have not come yet. They fear something has gone seriously wrong. You are to go to Auschwitz immediately, speak to whomever you have to, pay whatever the price may be, but I want you to get those women here. I have full confidence in you; I know you are an honorable gentleman who can be trusted and will make good on your word.[128]

Schöneborn dutifully replied, "It will be done as you say, *Herr Direktor,*" and walked out of the office.[129]

It is unclear what happened next. Emilie says that though she was sure Schöneborn gave the SS the "precious stones," there was still no sign of the women. So a few days later, Oskar went to Zwittau (Svitavy), and asked an old friend, Hilde, to go to Auschwitz "and personally take care of the release of the women." Hilde, at least according to Emilie, "was strikingly beautiful, slender, and graceful." The daughter of a "wealthy German industrialist," her parents had been friends of Oskar's family before the war. During the war, Hilde worked for the Wehrmacht and had contacts with the "upper echelons of the Nazi bureaucracy." A few days after she left for Auschwitz, "the train with the three hundred female prisoners arrived at the esplanade." Emilie said that Hilde would never tell her what she did to free to the women, though Emilie suspected that "her great beauty played a decisive part."[130]

Mietek Pemper told me a different story. He said the idea that Oskar went personally to Auschwitz to save the women was simply not true. What really happened was much simpler. Oskar, of course, knew that the women had been sent to Auschwitz for quarantine. But when they did not show up, he called the Army Procurement Office (APO; *Heeresbeschaffungsamt*) in Berlin, which established production quotas and labor needs in Brünnlitz. The APO told Schindler to call Gerhard Maurer's Office Group D2 office in Oranienburg. Oskar did this and told them that the female workers in Auschwitz were essential to his armaments production. The women were soon on their way to Brünnlitz. Pemper's explanation fits closely with what Oskar said. He worked with his military contacts in Berlin to get Maurer's D2 office to issue the release for the women.[131]

So which account is true? In 1963, Oskar Schindler was interviewed by the West German criminal police who were investigating war crimes charges against Johannes Hassebroek. He was questioned about Hassebroek's corruption, random killings, and executions at Groß Rosen and Brünnlitz as well as Schindler's efforts to move his female prisoners out of Auschwitz. Oskar told the police that though he had never been to Groß Rosen, Hassebroek had visited Brünnlitz two or three times to collect various "gifts" that

were supposed to be used "for charitable purposes." During the early part of
the interview, Oskar told the investigators, who seemed to know about his
efforts to rescue his female workers in Auschwitz, the specifics of his efforts:

> It is true that I sent my secretary Hilde Albrecht (fate unknown) to
> Auschwitz with gifts (jewelry and alcohol) in order to obtain the release
> of my female workers from the responsible labor supervisor Schwarz [SS-
> Hauptsturmführer Heinrich]. Additionally, I asked Major Plate [Plathe] of
> the Abwehr office in Kattowitz and other people to push for a transfer of
> these women to Brünnlitz. I also approached the WVHA and the RSHA
> respectively to get them to send a telegram to Auschwitz, demanding the
> release of the workers (this telegram allegedly had been stored unopened
> in Schwarz's dispatch case for about a week).
>
> From these statements it becomes apparent that I consistently contacted
> the WVHA or the RSHA for the release of my workers after the evacua-
> tion of my Krakow factory. Whether the release of the workers would
> have been possible without contacting these Berlin institutions, therefore
> by just dealing with the camp commandants of Groß Rosen and
> Auschwitz, it is beyond my capacity to answer.[132]

It is hard to imagine that Schindler, who would testify or give evidence
in various West German war crimes investigations and trials from 1962 to
1972, would have exaggerated under oath to criminal police investigators.
At the same time, he made a point of underscoring his efforts to help save
his Jewish workers in Kraków and Brünnlitz. He did err, though, when he
told the investigators that he had 1,200 Jews working for him by the time
he relocated his armaments factory to the Sudetenland in the fall of 1944.
And unlike his 1955 report to Yad Vashem, in which he specifically mentioned the help of Erich Lange, this time Oskar mentioned the help of Lt.
Colonel Plathe. More than likely, Schindler used his important contacts in
the Wehrmacht to help free his female workers.[133]

The idea that Oskar sent Hilde Albrecht to see Heinrich Schwarz is not
that far-fetched, though by the fall of 1944, Schwarz was no longer head
(Arbeitseinsatzführer; employment supervisor) of Auschwitz's employment
section (Arbeitseinsatz-IIIa). A year earlier, he had been promoted to commandant of Auschwitz III-Monowitz, where he was responsible for all
Auschwitz's sub-camps except for those engaged in forestry and agriculture. Schwarz remained in this position until the liquidation of Auschwitz

in early 1945 and then became commandant of what remained of the Natzweiler-Struthof concentration camp satellite network near Strasbourg. As American forces advanced on these remnant camps in the spring of 1945, Schwarz was ordered to retreat with what remained of his prisoners to Dachau. He was tried and executed for war crimes in 1947.[134]

Schwarz was a very influential person at Auschwitz and had good contacts with Maurer's Office Group D2 in Oranienburg. According to Rudolph Höss, Schwarz had been Maurer's subordinate during the time he served as Auschwitz's employment supervisor. The only problem with these ties, though, was that Maurer did not seem to think very highly of Schwarz because "Maurer truly gave him a hard time." Höss, though, considered Schwarz "very conscientious and dependable." He wrote in his memoirs that "even during the extermination of the Jews, I could relax when Schwarz was on duty." But if Oskar Schindler did send Hilde Albrecht to Auschwitz III-Monowitz to try to convince Schwarz to release the three hundred Schindler women to Oskar's care in the Sudetenland, she probably had a hard time convincing Schwarz of the need for the transfer. Höss said that Schwarz's "particular frustration" was prisoners who were "transferred to other camps." From Schwarz's perspective, such transfers always caused headaches and incessant complaints from the receiving camps about the quality of the workers. These reports, which criticized Schwarz for being "undependable and incompetent," were then sent by Maurer to Schwarz "to liven up the Kommando leader."[135] The dedicated, serious-minded Schwarz was going to be suspicious of any request to send so many women out of Auschwitz to another camp not under his control. Why risk further criticism from Maurer? On the other hand, if he was pressured by Maurer's office to help with the transfer of the Schindler women, there was little he could do but obey.

So how did Oskar Schindler get the women out of Auschwitz? In reality, it probably took all these efforts to get them released. Oskar probably did first call the Army Procurement Office to prod them to contact Maurer's office because Schindler had a better relationship with the Wehrmacht than with the SS. It is evident from the information that Oskar earlier gave Jewish Agency representatives in Budapest that he was quite knowledgeable about SS operations in the concentration camps. Given all that he had gone through to win approval for his move to Sudetenland, he was well aware that Auschwitz was slowly closing down its operations and sending many inmates westward as slave laborers. The greatest danger to the Schindler women, who were housed first in a female transit camp at

Auschwitz II-Birkenau and later moved to its women's camp, came from the changes Goldberg had made to the ages of the younger and older women on the list to make them more acceptable to the SS as "essential workers." Several times the SS spotted such discrepancies, particularly those involving older Schindler women, and tried to send those women to their deaths. As gassing at Auschwitz had ended in early November, they would have been shot. Evidence shows that at least five Schindler women originally on the Płaszów-Auschwitz list were taken off while in Birkenau and replaced by other women.[136]

But for the most part, the SS accepted the Schindler women's transfer to the Sudetenland. The Auschwitz Labor Deployment List, for example, noted on November 3, 1944, that there were 1,156 "so-called transit Jews" in Auschwitz-Birkenau B-IIc, where the Schindler women were initially housed. Of this number, 320 were awaiting "transport to another camp," and another 696 remained in the camp "until further notice."[137] More than likely, most of the 320 women awaiting transport were part of the Schindler group. The following day, Birkenau B-IIc was liquidated and the women there were moved across the railroad tracks to Birkenau Ia, the Women's Camp.[138] Auschwitz records for this period show that far more prisoners were being sent westward as slave laborers than were being murdered. Between August 1944 and January 1945, the SS moved 65,000 prisoners westward to other slave labor camps and an additional 67,000 prisoners remained in Auschwitz until the final days of liquidation. The biggest problem for the SS, though, was transportation, which was increasingly tied up to meet military needs. The delay in shipping the Schindler women to Brünnlitz was probably more of a transportation issue than secret SS designs to murder them. But this in no way reduced the threat to them as long as they remained there, and Oskar Schindler knew this. They were at least fortunate that they got there by train when they did. Many Auschwitz prisoners were evacuated westward on deadly forced marches, and many others died on frozen transports during the winter of 1944–1945.[139]

Schindler must have known all this, which makes one wonder why he would have sent his chief engineer, Schöneborn, to Auschwitz at the very time he needed him at Brünnlitz to oversee the setting up of factory operations there. The idea that he sent a secretary or old girlfriend to get the women back with bribes and sex also seems a little farfetched, particularly in light of the dangers involved in such a venture. Allied air raids had intensified in the Auschwitz area and any such trip was going to be dangerous, particularly with Czech and Polish guerillas in the area and the Red Army only a hundred miles away.

On the other hand, given all the trouble that Oskar had gone through to set up the move to Brünnlitz, it seems unlikely that he would have simply sat around waiting for the women to arrive. If nothing else, Oskar Schindler was quite aggressive when it came to his factories and Jewish workers, which brings us back to Spielberg's version of the story. Oskar continued to operate Emalia until the Soviets occupied Kraków in early 1945, so it would have been easy for him to pay a visit to Auschwitz. According to Emilie, he spent a lot of time in Kraków before the Soviets occupied in January 1945. She said he "could not let go of the old enamelware factory."[140]

But Oskar probably wanted nothing to do with Kraków or the SS in the aftermath of his recent detention as part of the SS investigation of Amon Göth. After the Soviets took over Kraków, Oskar seemed seldom to stray too far from Brünnlitz. And even though he had acquired a comfortable villa just outside the factory grounds, he had an apartment built in the principal factory building where he lived with Emilie. Why? Oskar had already lost one factory to the Soviets and he wanted to protect his second one as much as possible. He was also afraid that if he was not around to protect his workers, they would fall victim to the whims of the SS. So it is highly unlikely that Oskar Schindler would have risked a trip to Auschwitz to save his women unless this was the only option left open to him. He well understood the dangers of such a trip for himself and his male workers, who were essential to the operation of his new factory in Brünnlitz.

10.

BRÜNNLITZ

SCHINDLERJUDE ROMAN FERBER ONCE REMARKED AFTER THE war that the arrival of the Schindler men at Brünnlitz was anticlimactic.[1] This was certainly not so with the Schindler women. Their weeks in Auschwitz had been terrifying and their mysterious trip to Brünnlitz was equally frightening. Stella Müller-Madej has written the most complete account of that journey in her memoirs, *A Girl from Schindler's List*. Stella had been put in Birkenau's *Krankenstube* (sick room) several days before the Brünnlitz transport left Auschwitz. Two friends, Bronia and Mira, managed to delude the SS into thinking that Stella was well and got her out of the sick room. All her clothes had been taken from her, so they carefully re-dressed her before they took her before the reporting officer *(Rapportführer)* to try to convince him to put Stella on the Brünnlitz transport. Their efforts were successful and Stella was ordered to join the other Schindler women.[2]

As the *Aufseherinnen* marched the Schindler women past the crematorium to the train, they decided to give them a "farewell flogging" with their whips. As soon as the cars were loaded, the train began to move. But uncertainty and fear continued to haunt the women as the train stopped and started time and again during what seemed an eternity. At one of the stops, the women called out to ask where they where. The response from outside was *"Československo."* The Schindler women then asked why the train was not moving. The voice outside responded that there was no locomotive to pull the cars. It had been taken by the Wehrmacht. Panic swept through the cars and many of the Schindler women were convinced they would be "taken out and finished off." Stella said that some women began to pray; others wailed "in a language I could not understand." She thought the wailing was going to drive her mad and pleaded with her mother and friends to make it stop.[3]

But soon another locomotive was found and the train again began its journey to Brünnlitz. Hunger and thirst now swept through the cars and some women feared they would starve to death. When the train stopped again, another voice from outside asked whether there was anyone in the cars. In unison, the women on Stella's car shouted, "We're here. Why have we stopped?" A person outside replied, "They want to take you back to Auschwitz." Stella said that everyone "went crazy. Anything except that. Let them kill us here."[4] After a while, the women heard more voices outside and asked for food and water. "I can't," was the reply. As the women debated about whether to use one corner of the car as a toilet, the train began moving. Were they returning to Auschwitz? No one knew. Even the stronger women now began to lose hope. Natka Feigenbaum tried to reassure everyone in Stella's car that "if Schindler doesn't save us, that means he's dead himself." Several women told her to "stop blabbering about your wonderful Schindler." Natka replied simply, "God will help. God will help."[5]

The train stopped again and Stella was convinced the SS was going to kill them all. For her, "to stand still and wait like this was horrible." The train stopped once more and everyone seemed certain this was the last stop. No one heard dogs barking and no guards were shouting from below. Someone did give instructions in German but spoke "calmly and without shouting." The women were filled with "a mixture of amazement and horror." No one beat them or hit them with rifle butts as they jumped out of the cars. Stella wondered how it was possible the Germans could have had "become so mild just before the end." As the women were being lined up, a car drove up and two tall Germans got out. One was dressed in an SS uniform; the other wore a "different uniform." The biggest of the two men, whom Stella described as "massive," was Oskar Schindler. Natka muttered, "on your knees, on your knees before him."[6]

Stella says the SS guards were offended by the women's smell, and one of them said, *"O, wie die Frauen stinken"* (Oh, how the women stink). Stella asked her mother whether she had noticed that the guards called them women and not swine as they did in Auschwitz and Płaszów. As Schindler walked along the rows and rows of dirty, lice-ridden, emaciated women, Stella wrote, he had a strange expression on his face, one of "horror, pity and benevolence."[7] Emilie Schindler, who saw the women a few minutes later, said that they were "in disastrous condition—fragile, emaciated, weak."[8]

As they marched the short distance to Schindler's factory, Stella began to wonder about the Schindler males. Were they in the factory? Once inside the two story main factory building, Stella and the other women saw the men in the distance on the other side of a screen on the ground floor. Men and women began to shout to each other or call out each other's name. An emotional tidal wave swept over the thousand women and men. In the midst of this tearful celebration, soup was brought in for the women. Afterwards, they were taken upstairs to the segregated living quarters. The bunks had not yet arrived and straw had been spread on the floor for sleeping.[9]

And then Oskar Schindler appeared in the doorway. He said in a powerful "but very gentle" voice:

> I know that you have been through hell on your way here. Your appearance says it all. Here also, for the time being, you will be forced to suffer many discomforts, but you are brave women. We did not have a great deal of hope that it would be possible to bring you here. That is in the past now. I am counting on your discipline and sense of order. I think that the worst has been overcome. The bunks should be here in a few days. Now you must put things in order yourselves. The [female] doctors should report to the head physician, and you should elect block supervisors. Doctor Hilfstein and [Mietek] Pemper will show you where you can wash. The sick and those who need bandaging should go with the doctors.[10]

But their fear and suffering was not over. Hunger and disease remained a serious problem, and Dr. Chaim Hilfstein, one of the Jewish physicians, told Stella and her parents that Brünnlitz's commandant, Josef Leipold, "was dangerous and had to be watched." Schindler was "doing everything he could to keep Leipold in line, but we should be careful."[11]

The small collection of factory buildings at one end of the sprawling Hoffmann factory complex in Brünnlitz (Czech, Brněnec) that Oskar Schindler took over for his Emalia operations in the Sudetenland could best be described as shabby and unused. The buildings were completely empty. Oskar would have to start from scratch and rebuild his factory from the ground up. He would use the machinery, tools, and raw materials sent from

Kraków to Brünnlitz in 250 train cars to do this. But in addition to transferring and rebuilding his small Kraków armaments operations, he also had
to construct a small concentration camp overseen by SS engineers from
Hans Kammler's WVHA construction Office Group C in Oranienburg. He
got no help from Reich authorities for this and had to pay the full construction costs from his own pocket. As Oskar explained after the war, the
"owner was free to decide on the equipment and design; he solely had to
comply with the safety and security standards of the SS" in the construction
of his factory camps. This involved the construction of "watch towers, barb
wire, high voltage lines, toilets, watch blocks, housing, separate quarters for
the sick, a camp kitchen."[12] After the war, Oskar estimated that he spent
RM 100,000 ($40,000) relocating his armaments factory to Brünnlitz and
another RM 200,000 ($80,000) building the new camp.[13]

To help run the camp, Oskar had a staff of twenty Germans and fifty
Polish volunteers who came with him from Kraków. The SS provided a
hundred SS guards under the command of *SS-Obersturmführer* Josef
Leipold. This figure was in line with SS statistics released in January 1945
that showed an average of seventy-four guards concentration camp-wide
for every 1,000 male prisoners. Over time, this contingent would probably have grown in size because Hassebroek prepared a memorandum in
November 1944 that discussed increasing the size of Brünnlitz's inmate
population to 1,400 women and eight hundred men. Needless to say, the
vicissitudes of war prevented the expansion from taking place. Schindler
never mentioned these plans after the war but it is hard to imagine, given
his relationship with Hassebroek, that he would not have been privy to
them. But this might explain why he was allowed to take in extra Jews
without question in 1945.[14]

Oskar was responsible for housing and feeding the SS contingent as his
sub-camp. He also had to pay the SS a daily fee for each of his Jewish
workers. In the General Government, Schindler had paid the SS via the
Armaments Inspectorate Zł 5 ($1.56) a day for his male Jewish workers
and Zł 4 ($1.25) a day for his female Jewish workers. Businesses there
were allowed to deduct up to Zł 1.60 a day for "maintenance." By the
time Schindler moved his armaments factory and its Jewish workers to the
Sudetenland Region *(Gauleitung Sudetenland),* which was an integral part
of the Greater German Reich, the fees he had to pay the SS to "rent" his
Jewish laborers had gone up. And because his Brünnlitz factory was in
Greater Germany, he would have to pay the SS in Reichsmarks. It now
cost Oskar RM 4 to RM 8 ($1.60 to $3.20) for skilled workers and RM

3 to RM 4 ($1.29 to $1.60) a day for unskilled workers. As each of his 1,000 Jewish workers had a specific trade listed by their names on the two "Schindler's Lists," we can presume that Oskar was paying the SS RM 4,000 ($1,600) to RM 6,000 ($2,400) a day to "rent" his workers. His costs would later increase after he added another ninety-eight names to his list of 1,000 Jewish laborers during the last four months that he operated his factory in Brünnlitz. After the war, Oskar noted that he always employed far more Jews than he needed in Kraków and Brünnlitz. In the latter camp, he had no work for the three hundred women, who spent most of their time knitting or sewing for their families. Yet he still had to pay the SS a daily fee for their skilled "services." After the war, he estimated that he paid the SS RM 250,000 ($59,524) during the "seven months" his three hundred female Jewish workers were in Brünnlitz. He added that he had had "no practical use" for these women but had to list them "as productive laborers" to insure their survival.[15]

When Oskar first prepared an estimated cost of what he had spent directly and indirectly to save his Jews in Kraków and Brünnlitz just after the end of the war, he said he had "invested" RM 1,935,000 ($774,000) in Poland and RM 705,000 ($282,000) for similar expenses in the Sudetenland. He added that he did not include in his estimates the "several hundred thousand Zl [złótys]" he paid to the SS "for small favors." In other words, Oskar claimed after the war that it cost him more than RM 2,640,000 ($1,056,000) to save his Jews. This included the fees he paid to the SS to "rent" his Jewish workers, the costs of constructing two small concentration camps at both factories, his expenses for black market food and feeding his SS contingents, and bribes to Reich officials and the SS. He admitted in his 1945 statement that these estimates were not meant to be "a balance sheet but instead it is intended to give an illustration of abstract and tangible values that were sacrificed."[16]

But beyond these figures were the greater costs of transferring a portion of his factory from Kraków to Brünnlitz and then building a new factory and camp in the Sudetenland. This was far more expensive than opening Emalia in Kraków. It should also be remembered that Schindler lost two factories at the end of the war. These losses traumatized him and he would devote half his postwar life to seeking compensation for them from the West German government. German authorities carefully but slowly investigated his claims and ultimately compensated Oskar for his losses. The detailed statistics compiled by Schindler after the war as part of his *Lastenausgleich* (equalization of burdens) compensation quest give us insight into the totality of his losses. He estimated, for example, that his Emalia losses in Kraków totaled DM 1,910,000 ($454,762) and those in Brünnlitz DM 4,246,400 ($1,011,047). Part of these losses were tied to helping his Jewish workers. He spent, for example, DM 270,000 ($64,285) for workers' quarters and facilities in Kraków. His losses for such facilities in Brünnlitz were even greater. He estimated that he had spent DM 293,700 ($69,928) to build an "installation" for his Jewish workers there and another 48,000 DM ($11,428) for similar facilities for his fifty Polish workers. He also had to spend another DM 39,950 ($9,512) in Brünnlitz on SS faciliites. Oskar also included in his Brünnlitz losses DM 320,000 ($76,190) for his "private quarters and fortune" and DM 300,000 ($71,428) in the Deutsche Bank in Zwittau.[17]

The difference between his Kraków losses and those in Brünnlitz was that Schindler was always able to counterbalance what he spent in Kraków on his Jewish workers with excess enamelware production that was then used to trade on the black market. During his years in Kraków, Oskar estimated that he produced about RM 15,000,000 ($6,000,000) in enamelware and RM 500,000 ($200,000) in armaments. His factory in Brünnlitz produced one wagon load of ammunition parts worth RM 35,000 ($14,000). In other words, Schindler had to dip into the profits he made from his Kraków operations to pay the expenses for his factory in Brünnlitz. Needless to say, whatever "fortune" he had made in Kraków was reduced significantly during his months in the Sudetenland at the end of the war.[18]

Bribery and black marketeering remained an integral part of Schindler's operations in Brünnlitz. The single greatest problem that Oskar faced was the shortage of food and medicines. But, as Oskar explained, there was a difference. In Poland, "one had to pay a lot of money but was able to get large amounts [of food]." There was simply little food available in the Sudetenland and "one sack of flour could potentially result in the death penalty." Yet Oskar needed "tens of thousands of kg [kilograms] of various food products every month in order to save many hundreds of people from dying of hunger and becoming skeletons." Oskar was determined that his "Schindler Jews would not become 'Muselmenen' [Muslims]," the term commonly used in the concentration camps to describe inmates on the verge of death from malnutrition, disease, or both. But Oskar also had to feed the one hundred SS men who served as guards at Brünnlitz. Oskar saw their well-being, at least when it came to keeping his SS contingent well supplied with alcohol, tobacco, and food, as essential to the health and well-being of his *Schindlerjuden*. In fact, soon after the opening of the

Brünnlitz factory camp, Oskar said, he "had the guards and supervisors under control, which primarily guaranteed humane treatment of my inmates, often against the will of the camp commandant."[19]

Oskar had to do more than keep his SS contingent well supplied with food, drink, and tobacco to insure the well-being of his Jewish workers. He also had to pay considerable bribes to SS and Reich officials in the Sudetenland to help him counter local opposition to his move there. After the war, he estimated that he had spent RM 75,000 ($17,857) to bribe SS and Reich officials during his eight months in the Sudetenland. Oskar wrote Fritz Lang in 1951 that local officials continued to protest his move to Brünnlitz even after he had already won final approval from Berlin. They were quite angry when his 250 train cars of factory goods tied up the town's small train station upon arrival. But local authorities were particularly afraid of disease when Schindler's 1,000 Jews arrived in Brünnlitz.[20] Johannes Hassebroek, Groß Rosen's commandant, was an occasional visitor to Brünnlitz and the recipient of regular bribes from Schindler. Another person who regularly took bribes from Schindler in return for his support of Oskar's operations in Kraków and Brünnlitz was Karl Heinz Bigell, a textile specialist who had once served as economic adviser to SS-Oberführer Julian Scherner, the HSSPF in Kraków from 1941 to 1944. Oskar said that Bigell as "an obscure figure, a drunkard," who was "always out of money." On the other hand, he had "very good connections to the highest SS circles in Krakow and Berlin." Oskar found Bigell useful when it came to questions about permits or items vital to Emalia's operations. In "exchange for small 'loans,' Bigell repeatedly took care of things like construction permits, wood-contingents, prison releases, wagons of SS cement, or 2–3 tons of Diesel oil or gasoline."[21]

Soon after he opened his new Brünnlitz factory, Oskar had occasion to call on Bigell after his problems with local Reich and SS officials "became unbearable." One day, Bigell showed up in Brünnlitz with SS-Standartenführer Ernst Hahn and an adjutant. Bigell evidently brought Hahn, who wore a "pompous uniform," not because he had anything to do with Jewish labor questions but because he simply worked for one of the most prominent men in Himmler's organization, SS-Obergruppenführer August Heissmeyer, who oversaw SS political education matters. Heissmeyer was also married to Reich's Women's Führerin (Reichsfrauenführerin), Gertrud Schlotz-Klink, who headed the National Socialist Women's Union (DFW; Nationalsozialistisches Frauenschaft) and the National Socialist Women's German Womens Organization (Deutsches Frauenwerk), making her one of the most powerful women in Nazi Germany. Hahn's visit seemed to impress everyone involved and Oskar reported afterwards that "the local administrators and also my camp commandant, *SS-Obersturmführer* Leipold, out of respect immediately stopped the intrigues against me; at least there were fewer denunciations against my firm due to my high-up connections."[22]

But this event did not end the need to bribe Reich officials. One of the principal recipients of Schindler's largess was *SS-Obersturmbannführer* Max Rausch, the HSSPF in Moravia and the former head of Kripo *(Kriminalpolizei)* in Kattowitz (Katowice) in East Upper Silesia. Schindler was introduced to Rausch by Josef Lasotta, whom Oskar described as a "Gestapo-Konfidentan" in Kattowitz who later then became director of security for Ferrum A. G. in Sossanowitz (Sosnowiec or Sosnowice). Oskar said that Rausch was "the highest SS official within 250 km (160 miles) of Brünnlitz" and was particularly helpful to Schindler during the latter days of the war in the face of "the renewed danger of liquidating Brünnlitz due to Russian advances." In return for Rausch's help in keeping Brünnlitz open and supplying Oskar with arms for the factory's defense, Oskar gave Rausch a diamond ring for his wife. Little did Rausch know, whose headquarters were in Brünn (Brno), that Oskar used the weapons to arm an illegal Jewish defense force.[23]

The factory itself was not particularly large or impressive. For all practical purposes, Oskar had one large factory building to house his armaments operation and his 1,000-plus Jews as well as several smaller buildings. He used the ground floor of the main factory building, which is still standing and is used today by the factory's current owner, Vitka Brněnec, as his armaments making facility. The second floor was divided into segregated living quarters for his male and female inmates. To call Brněnec (Brünnlitz) a factory town would be an understatement. Oskar Schindler leased about a quarter of the vast, sprawling factory complex that even today dominates the lush, heavily wooded valley basin of the Svitava River that flows beside the edge of the complex. Today, the center of the small village of Brněnec rests just across the railroad tracks that run beside Vitka's main gate. The rest of this sleepy hamlet covers the hills that overlook the town and the Vitka factory. It's small but attractive Catholic church is closed, and worshipers have to travel several miles into the hills to worship on Sundays. They also bury their dead in the Bela cemetery, also the resting place of the few Jews who died in Schindler's factory. The main road that runs between Svitavy, Schindler's hometown, and Brno to the south cuts through the middle of Brněnec. But it is doubtful whether the passing traveler would stop in village's few bars or restaurants unless she or he is familiar with the story of Oskar Schindler. But this very bucolic remoteness is one of the charms of Brněnec. And there is no doubt that Oskar Schindler was taken by its isolation, which at the end of the war offered some protection from snooping officials and Allied air raids.[24]

I was unable to find the official plans for Oskar Schindler's armaments factory in Brünnlitz during my research. There was a reference to such plans in his huge *Lastenausgleich* file in Bayreuth, but I was unable to find copies of his Brünnlitz factory plans there. The same is true for his *Koffer* (suitcase) files in the Bundesarchiv in Koblenz. I did locate what appeared to be a complete set of Brünnlitz plans in the archives of the United States Holocaust Memorial Museum (USHMM) in Washington, D.C. Museum archivists told me these were Schindler's factory plans, though I was confused by their title: *SS-Bekleidungslager* (Clothing Warehouse). Regardless, I decided that it was important to acquire a hard copy for my research, no easy task because they were on microfilm. I had to reproduce small parts of the plan and then carefully piece them together into several larger plans. Yet I remained uncertain that I had found the plans for Schindler's Brünnlitz factory.[25]

I did wonder whether the plans had somehow been mistitled because they had been drawn up in Kraków in September 1944, when Oskar was making final plans for his move to the Sudetenland. So I took copies to Augsburg, Germany, and asked Mietek Pemper to look at them. He told me they were not the plans for Oskar's factory but for the nearby SS uniform factory, which shared the Brünnlitz complex with Schindler. His analysis was, as usual, correct. As we were talking, I remembered a small plan of the Brünnlitz complex that Petr Henzl, the former deputy director of Vitka, gave me during my first visit to Brněnec during the summer of 1998. It was titled *Textilní továrna Arona-Jakub Löw Beera* (Textile Factory of Jakub and Aron Löw-Beer [the former Jewish owners of the factory]). The Henzl plan was a one-page, detailed plan of the factory complex during what it described as the "German occupation." When I returned home, I discovered that the detailed plans of the SS clothing factory I discovered in the USHMM archives fit perfectly over one side of the full complex plan given me by Mr. Henzl. The buildings, river, bridges, and other details on the SS master plan were a perfect match for that segment of the Henzl plan, which included details on Schindler's factory. After he had given me his plan, Mr. Henzl walked with me around the perimeter of the factory complex, showing me the location of the sub-camp's guard towers and other outlying buildings. He also pointed out which buildings had been built or replaced since the end of the war.[26]

Unfortunately, the Henzl plan does not give us any idea about the size of the buildings. Fortunately, Oskar Schindler supplied detailed information about the size and number of factory buildings, as well as the equipment and goods in each of them, in his initial *Lastenausgleich* application in the spring of 1957. He noted, for example, that he leased a 300 by 400 meters tract of land with buildings from the Hoffmann brothers. The Schindler factory camp rested at the north end of the Hoffmann complex. The three buildings already on the site were the main factory building (160 x 60 meters), a storehouse (80 x 15 meters), and an administrative building (40 x 40 meters). He also used one of these buildings to house his German staff. Schindler had six barracks built after he opened Brünnlitz to house his Polish workers and to use for further storage. Four of the barracks had been taken apart at Emalia and put back together in Brünnlitz; he filled these with machinery, raw materials, and others items shipped in from Kraków in 250 rail cars as well as food and black market trade goods. He prepared a detailed, eight-page list of everything he had shipped from Emalia to Brünnlitz or had acquired upon his arrival in the Sudetenland. Oskar also leased a beautiful villa near his factory that had once belonged to J. F. Daubek, the owner of a local grain mill. Schindler chose not to live in the villa. Instead, he kept the apartment, discussed earlier in this work, in the main factory building. Evidently, though, he intended to move into the villa after the war because Sol Urbach worked there to restore it to its former grandeur. The villa, which was torn down after the war, would have made Oskar and Emilie a fine home.[27]

For all practical purposes, the main factory building was the sub-camp. Oskar had concluded that if he built all the facilities for the prisoners here he would eliminate the necessity of building a camp outside the factory, which would require the inmates to be marched to work under SS guard. The living quarters for the workers were on the second floor of the main building. A screen ran through the middle of the large room separating the female living quarters from those of the Schindler men. A kitchen was built on the second floor where meals for both groups were prepared. The living, washing, and toilet facilities for the men and women were built at separate times because of the uncertainty about when the women would arrive. Soon after the men got to Brünnlitz, a latrine was built just outside the front entrance to the main factory building. Washing facilities remained a problem until proper bath facilities were constructed. By the time the women arrived, though, SS-approved washing, laundry, and disinfection facilities had been constructed by the men. Bunk beds also arrived during this period, and the inmates no longer had to sleep on straw thrown on the floor. Now they slept on traditional SS bunks equipped with straw mattresses. And though it was almost winter when the inmates arrived, the heat from the factory on the ground floor was enough to keep the living quarters warm.[28]

Beyond concern over adequate food, Schindler and the inmates had to worry about disease and illness. Wolfgang Sofsky said that "camp society was a society of the sick."[29] Leipold, like most SS commandants, was paranoid about the spread of infectious diseases; an outbreak of disease would not only cost him workers but also reflect negatively on his administrative skills. Consequently, Leipold set a strict limit of eighteen inmates who could be excused from work, though Stern said that many more were ill. When Leipold did complain to Schindler about the number of sick workers, Schindler reassured him: "I am also going to pay for the sick workers. I'll give you the money, don't worry about it."[30] Traditionally, illness in a concentration camp, particularly an infectious disease such as typhus, meant death. In larger camps, sick prisoners were put into quarantine barracks and those who were extremely ill were taken out and shot or gassed. It is obvious why inmates did everything they could to keep from being sent to a camp's infirmary or quarantine barracks. The SS was fearful of disease not only because of health reasons but also because it reflected badly on camp administration. Because most camps lacked adequate medical facilities and medicines, a variety of crude medicines and remedies were used by the inmate physicians and prisoners to keep serious ill-health at bay. Some prisoners would eat charcoal made from wood or dried bread crusts to fight diarrhea. Others used paper or linen suppositories to stop anal bleeding, or put urine or a cream made of lime and oil on scabies. Soap was a rare commodity in the camps and inmates often used herbs to clean their underwear.[31]

Most of the major concentration camps at one time or another were ravaged by typhoid fever, malaria, and other diseases. The first major wave of serious concentration camp epidemics took place in 1941–1942. As the SS gained better control over how to prevent and fight such outbreaks, the situation seemed to improve. However, the epidemics spread again in 1944 as the SS began to close camps and put inmates in the remaining overcrowded camps. One of the most feared epidemics was typhus, which was spread by the ever-present lice found in the prisoners' used and dirty clothing. If left unchecked, lice spread to bedding and even to food. Soon after Schindler's Jews arrived in Brünnlitz, a typhus epidemic swept through Dachau that killed thousands of prisoners.[32]

Though all the Schindler Jews had been disinfected in Groß Rosen and Auschwitz, they were covered with lice when they reached Brünnlitz; this infestation led to several cases of typhus. The only way to rid inmates of lice was through a "mass delousing," which involved all prisoners, their clothing, and their living quarters. This was a time-consuming process that meant disinfecting everything and then monitoring each prisoner for lice.[33] At Brünnlitz, a clinic and a sick room were set up on the first floor of the factory under Dr. Chaim Hilfstein, who oversaw the bathing and disinfection of the workers. Fortunately, Brünnlitz was blessed with excellent inmate physicians and they worked twenty-four hours a day to bathe and disinfect each of the Schindler Jews. Within three days, the inmates were "lice free." Dr. Aleksander Bieberstein reported only five cases of typhus at Brünnlitz during the time he was there.[34]

In addition to Dr. Hilfstein, there were six other physicians and one dentist at Brünnlitz, though it is uncertain how many of them worked in the camp clinic, which was under *SS-Obersturmführer* Streithof's control. Dr. Hilfstein, Dr. Aleksander Bieberstein, Dr. Juda Katz, Dr. Szaja Händler, and Dr. Matylda Löw were general practitioners; Dr. Ferdinand Lewkowicz was a surgeon. Dr. Aleksander Schubert was the camp's only dentist. There was another physician at Brünnlitz, Dr. Mirko Konowitsch, though it is a mystery when he arrived at the camp. Originally from Yugoslavia, Dr. Konowitsch was not on the October 21, 1944, Groß Rosen-Brünnlitz list; neither was he on the Golleschau, Landskron, or Geppersdorf lists. On the other hand, Dr. Konowitz is on the two final "Schindler's Lists" in April and May, 1945. Given the circumstances, Dr. Hilfstein and the other Jewish physicians played a key role in helping keep the Jewish prisoners alive. This was no easy task, given the serious lack of medical supplies. What little they had Oskar somehow acquired on the black market.[35]

Cantor Moshe Taubé remembered the infections covering his body from lack of nourishment while at Brünnlitz. When they filled with pus, Dr. Hilfstein's staff had to open them without anaesthesia and drain them. Few of the original Schindler Jews died in Brünnlitz. One who did was Janka (Janina) Feigenbaum, though there are questions about how she actually died. Janka, the sister of Lewis Fagen (Feigenbaum), had been ill for three years before she arrived at Brünnlitz. She had serious back problems, and by the time she got to Schindler's Sudeten sub-camp, she was completely bedridden. But Lewis Fagen and his parents, Jakub and Natalja, thought that if they could keep her alive until the end of the war, they would get her "the best medical care the West had to offer, and she'd live." Lew Fagen went to Emilie Schindler, who had begun to work with sick patients, and asked her to give Janka extra food. But two weeks before the end of the war, Dr. Hilfstein gave Janka a mysterious shot without consulting the family and she died soon afterwards. The family was devastated. Oskar Schindler gave them permission to bury Janka in an unmarked grave. Lew vividly remembered marking the exact site of her burial. After the war, her family exhumed Janka's body and reburied it in the New Jewish Cemetery in Prague.[36]

Oskar and Emilie played active roles in providing their Schindler Jews with the best medicines and medical care they could under the circumstances. And unlike Kraków, where Emilie was only a peripheral figure in Oskar's life, Emilie was constantly present and lived with her husband in their factory complex apartment. Occasionally, there were medical emergencies that only Oskar could resolve. On one occasion, he learned that one of the married Schindler women had become pregnant. This could mean a death sentence for the mother and child. A Hungarian Jew, Dr. Gisella Perl, ran a women's ward in Auschwitz and performed numerous illegal abortions to save the mothers' lives. An obstetrician and gynecologist by training, she was ethically repulsed by the need to do this, but knew that if she did not, "both mother and child would have been cruelly murdered."[37]

All prisoners knew that pregnancy was among the greatest crimes they could commit in the camps because it violated core Nazi ideals about Jewish "race" propagation and could result in transport to a death camp. Moreover, given the tenuousness of life, even in Brünnlitz, it was uncertain whether a pregnant woman could survive in the face of growing food shortages and the constant oversight of the SS. So Oskar arranged to have one of the Jewish camp physicians perform an abortion, which was also illegal. Because the physicians did not have the proper instruments, Oskar went to Kraków to buy them. Oskar later reported that the instruments cost him Zł 16,000 ($5,000) on the black market. Oskar willingly paid this price for the instruments because, if he had not, "the woman would have been murdered."[38] But lack of proper instruments was not the only problem they faced. They would have to hide the abortion from the ever present SS. Indeed, as the abortion was being performed, an *SS Lagerführer,* probably *SS-Obersturmführer* Streithof, walked into the factory's small sick room. Fortunately, Oskar had prepared for this eventuality and had posted someone to watch out for impromptu SS inspections. Consequently, the moment the *Lagerführer* walked into the sick room, the lights went out. Streithof left the factory building quite unaware that a successful abortion was taking place.[39]

The Golleschau and Landskron Transports

But the arrival of the Golleschau transport on January 29, 1945, and the Landskron transport on February 2, 1945, were the greatest of the medical challenges for Oskar, Emilie, and the camp's physicians. Thomas Keneally said that next to the "ransoming of the women in Auschwitz . . . the most astounding salvage of all was that of the Goleszów people."[40] He was right. Golleschau was an Auschwitz sub-camp located in the Polish village of Goleszów just across the border from Český Těšín in today's Czech Republic. In July 1942, an SS-owned company, the *Ostdeutsche Baustoffwerke GmbH* opened the *Golleschauer Portland-Zement AG* plant in Goleszów and began to use slave labor to operate it. In time, it became one of Auschwitz's most important factories.[41] About 70 percent of the workers at Goleszów, which was a sub-camp of Auschwitz III-Monowitz, were Jewish slave laborers. The camp opened with a Jewish labor force of about 350 workers. This number rose to 450 a year later and, by 1944, Golleschau employed about 1,000 Jewish workers. Sub-camps such as Golleschau were run by a *Kommandoführer* (labor supervisor) who had the unofficial title of *Lagerführer* (camp leader). Golleschau had three *Lagerführers* during its two-and-a-half-year history: *SS-Oberscharführer* Hans Picklapp, *SS-Oberscharführer* Hans Mirbeth, and *SS-Unterscharführer* Horst Czerwiřski.[42]

Prisoners at Golleschau worked in the cement factory or in the nearby quarries. They were involved in the actual production of cement as well as its packing and distribution. They also helped build the railroad tracks and cable car lines in the plant or helped make its wooden shipment cases. Conditions in Golleschau were "harsh," and prisoners who tried to escape were shot or hanged in public. We also know that when Hans Picklapp served as Golleschau's *Lagerführer,* he killed prisoners with a lethal injection of phenol, something favored in the Auschwitz main camp. Such injections were normally used for prisoners "exhausted to the point of physical collapse," and were part of the broader "euthanasia" experiment program at Auschwitz.[43]

As the Red Army moved deeper into Poland in early 1945, Golleschau was liquidated. Between January 18 and January 22, 1945, most of the sub-camp's remaining 900 to 1,008 prisoners were marched or shipped by rail to the Sachsenhausen and Flossenbürg concentration camps. Auschwitz records state that one of the last transports to leave Golleschau contained one train car "with ninety-six sick and exhausted prisoners and the corpses of four prisoners, who die[d] during the transport, [were] put in a sealed freight car and transferred to the Freudenthal A.C. (Auxiliary Camp] in Czechoslovakia."[44] Other than this note in the Auschwitz archives, the only documentation I could initially locate on this particular Golleschau trans-port was a two-page *Frachtbrief* (bill of lading) in the archives at Yad Vashem. During my research, I found the actual *Namenliste* (list of names or roll) of the eighty-one Jewish prisoners on the Golleschau transport that was created after they arrived in Brünnlitz on January 29, 1945. The bill of lading says that the Golleschau Jews were on car number 113264, which was originally built in France. We can trace the week-long odyssey of car number 113264 after it left Golleschau by looking at the station stamps on it. After it left Golleschau on January 22, it passed through Teschen, Oder-berg, and Schönnbrunn before it reached Freudenthal (Bruntál), the site of another Auschwitz sub-camp, three days later. However, because Freuden-thal was in the process of being liquidated, the Golleschau car was sent on to Zwittau (Svitavy), where it arrived on January 29.[45]

In a 1956 letter to Itzhak Stern, Oskar added more details about the transport's journey from Golleschau to Brünnlitz. He insisted that Stern share these details with Dr. Ball-Kaduri, who was investigating stories about Schindler's efforts to save Jews. First of all, Oskar told Stern, it was important to note that the Golleschau transport had taken ten days, not eight, to get to Brünnlitz. He said that the bill of lading was predated to January 22, but had a stamp on the back that showed that its first stop after it left Golleshau was in Teschen on January 21. He added that the bill of lading indicated that the Golleschau transport had been sent to Zwittau twice on January 29. It stood in the Zwittau station for eight hours before it was sent on to Brünnlitz. The transport spent another fourteen hours in Zwittau after Josef Leipold refused to accept it. The transport finally returned to Brünnlitz on the morning of January 30.[46]

In 1955, Oskar gave more details about events surrounding the Golleschau transport. According to Oskar, a friend of his with the *Reichs-bahn* (the German or Reich national railway), called him to tell him that "several wagons with Jewish inmates, some of which were already dead, stood at the Zwittau railway station." Oskar said that no one wanted these Jews and the two cars were "like a ship without a harbor." It was minus 16 degrees Celsius (c. 0° Fahrenheit) outside and Oskar called the station master in Zwittau and told him to send the wagons to Brünnlitz. Josef Leipold strongly objected to this action because the camp did not have a sanitarium to quarantine the Golleschau Jews. Oskar told Leipold that he would pay the SS the lost wages for the men on the transport, which Schindler explained was made up of men who had worked in Golleschau's stone quarries.[47]

The only problem with Oskar's accounts of what happened is that he was not there until the morning of the transport's arrival on January 29 or 30; indeed, Emilie Schindler and Itzhak Stern agree that Oskar was not at Brünnlitz when they first learned that the Golleschau car was sitting in the Zwittau train station. Stern said that Oskar was in Mauthausen trying to get extra workers for his factory. Emilie said that "he had not returned from one of his trips to Cracow," though this would have been unlikely because the Red Army had occupied the city ten days earlier.[48] Stern added that the transport had been made up not of Jewish prisoners from Golleschau but of inmates from a hospital in Buna (Auschwitz III-Buna at Monowitz) who had initially been left behind when Auschwitz was liquidated. At the last minute, though, they had been put on a transport before the Red Army occupied Auschwitz on January 27, 1945. Stern said that because *Reichsbahn* officials in Zwittau "believed that all Jewish transports were designated for Schindler," the station master in Zwittau called Brünnlitz to inform Oskar that there was a small transport awaiting him in the Zwittau station. As Schindler was away, Stern was asked about the transport; he said that it was "a transport Schindler had ordered." At this point, he said, the transport was accidentally sent back to Zwittau, though Oskar later told Stern it was ordered back to Zwittau by Leipold. Stern said that it was Emilie who ordered the transport back to Brünnlitz after she had learned of its return to Zwittau. By the time it finally arrived in Brünnlitz, Oskar had returned from his trip.[49]

Emilie tells a somewhat different story. One night, while a "terrible storm was raging outside," she heard "heavy pounding" on her door. She put on a robe and went downstairs to answer the door. When she asked who it was, she heard a male voice: "Please open up, Frau Schindler, I have to talk with you. It is important." She said it was the man in charge of the Golleschau transport. He asked her "to accept the two hundred and fifty Jews, crowded into four wagons." The man explained that the workers had been sent to a plant that had rejected them because Russian troops were nearby. Emilie said she knew that if she "rejected them, they were going to be shot." She then called Oskar and asked him whether it was all right to accept the transport. He agreed and Emilie then asked Brünnlitz's chief engineer, Willi Schöneborn, to help her unload the transport.[50]

So why such different stories? There is no question that Oskar probably investigated the matter of the Golleschau's transport's odyssey quite thoroughly when he returned to Brünnlitz. But why would he claim that he was there when he was not? He did not say much about the Golleschau transport in his immediate postwar account of his efforts to save Jews in Kraków and Brünnlitz. He said only that there were a hundred Jews on the transport and that seventeen were found dead when the train's doors were opened.[51] As this report was prepared just six months after the Golleschau Jews arrived in Brünnlitz, one would expect that someone actively involved in getting the transport to his own factory would have been more accurate about the number of people on the train. But in fairness to Oskar, the Golleschau transport was just one more dramatic episode in his daily Herculean efforts to keep his Brünnlitz Jews alive. But over time, at least among the *Schindlerjuden* closest to Oskar in Brünnlitz, the story of the Golleschau transport became a concrete example of the legendary deeds he performed there. And Oskar knew this. Yet it would have been far less heroic if Oskar had been absent when the transport was shuttling back and forth between Zwittau and Brünnlitz. In his own mind, Oskar probably thought that he had played an active role in efforts to bring the transport to Brünnlitz through his phone conversations with Emilie and others. And by the time he penned his more detailed accounts about the Golleschau transport a decade after the war, his efforts to save Jews had come to mean much, much more. By the mid-1950s, Oskar's efforts to start life anew in Argentina had failed, and he was thinking of returning to West Germany to push his claim for compensation for his lost factories. It was now extremely important, particularly in light of Yad Vashem's interest in his story, to make certain that he remained at the center of the growing Schindler legend. In some ways, the same thing can be said about Emilie. During the later years of her life, she desperately sought the recognition that Oskar had received decades earlier, particularly in the aftermath of the release of Steven Spielberg's *Schindler's List*. The Golleschau story became a centerpiece of her 1996 memoirs and was one way for her to underscore the important role she played in this period of Oskar's life. So in the end, as in most situations in which accounts vary, the truth lies somewhere in between.

Regardless of the different stories about the Golleschau transport's odyssey, we have fairly consistent information about what happened once it finally reached Brünnlitz. It was pulled onto the rail siding that ran directly into Schindler's sub-camp. It was dawn and snow was falling heavily. Voices were heard inside and efforts were made to open the frozen doors with long iron bars. When this did not work, some thought was given to opening them with a hand grenade. Victor Lewis said that straw-filled mattresses were burned underneath the car to try to melt the ice on the doors and locks.[52] A blow torch was then used to open the car's doors. Leipold, who stood watching everything with his two dogs, said to Emilie: "Stay away, Frau Schindler, it's a terrible sight. You'll never be able to erase it from your mind."[53] Itzhak Stern said that when he first looked into the car, he thought it must be a female transport because they all "looked so small and thin."[54] Dr. Aleksander Bieberstein, who helped open the frozen doors, described what he saw as "terrifying." Inside the car were "tens of human shadows in dirty clothes, lying cold in freezing urine and excrement." The car was filled with the stench of human excrement and dead bodies. Stella Müller-Madej said the bodies were frozen to the human waste inside. Murray Pantirer was assigned to help take the bodies out of the cars. He told me that their skin was frozen to the floor and when he tried to pick up a body, the skin came off. They then used hot water to thaw out the bodies before they removed them.[55] Victor Lewis said that one lone German guard was in the car with the prisoners. Later, he would be hanged by the Brünnlitz prisoners "on a pipe."[56]

Estimates vary about the number of inmates on the Golleschau transport and whether they were in one or two cars. Auschwitz records state that there were a hundred inmates on the car when it left Golleschau and that four died en route to Brünnlitz. Half the prisoners froze or starved to death; another twelve died within days of their arrival in Brünnlitz. Oskar also said that there were a hundred prisoners on the transport. But in one report he said that seventeen died in transit; in another, the number changed to sixteen. Emilie says the Golleschau transport had 250 prisoners on it. Mietek Pemper told me that there were eighty-six men on the transport when it arrived in Brünnlitz. Twelve were dead on arrival and another four died within a few days. He added that the Golleschau transport was made up of two train cars and that the men came from the Netherlands, Hungary, Belgium, France, and Germany. Dr. Aleksander Bieberstein said that there were eighty-six Jews on the Golleschau transport and that twelve of them were dead on arrival in Brünnlitz. Itzhak Stern never mentioned the number of Jews on the Golleschau transport, but did say that twelve or eighteen of the Jews on board were dead when it arrived in Brünnlitz.[57]

During my research, I discovered the *Namenliste des Häftlingszuganges vom Al Golleschau (KL Auschwitz) am 29. Januar 1945* (List of Names/Roll of the Prisoners from the Work Camp Golleschau [Concentration Lager Auschwitz] on 29 January 1945) with the names of eighty-one Jewish workers on it. Over time, ten of the names were scratched out after they had died, and the dates of their deaths were penciled in. As no one has ever before seen this list, I should like to list the names below in case there are families interested in the fate of their loved ones. I have listed their names exactly as they appeared on the January 29, 1945 list, which included their prisoner and camp registration numbers, their nationality, their full name, their date of birth, their date of death, and their occupation. They are buried in the cemetery at Bělá nad Svitavou, about two miles from Brněnec.

77101 15857 Hungarian **Aorias, Ladislaus** d. 12.III.45 Geb. 26.8.23. Schneider

77102 B11108 Hungarian **Friedman, Jenö** d. 9.II.45 Geb. 5.12.99. Chemiker

77130 B11185 Czech **Gellner, Artur** d. 1.III.45 Geb. 1.5.95 Kilfsarb.

77131 B11193 Czech **Hase, Josef** d. 18.II.45 Geb. 9.7.04 Schreibkraft

77139 B5771 Hungarian **Ilowicz, Moses** d. 8.II.45 Geb. 23.4.22. Weber.

77148 B5774 Hungarian **Kowatsch, Istewar** d. 4.II.45 Geb. 19.5.09 Sattler

77152 B11257 Czech **Löwy, Rudolf** d. 2.II.45 Geb. 13.12.21 Hilfsarb.

77169 B5638 Hungarian **Schwarz, Alexander** d. 4.II.45 Geb. 19.12.19 Hilfsarb.

77170 B15965 Hungarian **Schwarz, Bela** d. 7.II.45 Geb. 18.11.04 Bachhalter

77178 A16003 Hungarian **Török, Joseph** d. 6.III.45 Geb. 6.4.93 Bebenarb[58]

Five days after the arrival of the Golleschau transport, another train car was brought into the camp with six Jews on it from the small Landskron forced labor camp twenty-four miles northeast of Brünnlitz, and this could be the reason for the different figures given by various observers about how many prisoners were on the Golleschau transport and the number of cars they were in. Two of the six Jews on the Landskron transport died within a month after their arrival in Brünnlitz and were buried with full Jewish rituals in the Bělá cemetery. If you add up the figures from the Golleschau and Landskron transports drawn from their official *Namenliste,* it totals eighty-seven Jews with twelve dying within a month or so of their arrival. These figures are almost identical to those cited by Dr. Bieberstein and Mietek Pemper. Moreover, the fact that both lists indicate that the eighty-seven Jews on these transports came from Germany, France, Hungary, Poland, the Czech lands, Slovakia, and the Netherlands supports Mietek Pemper's comments about the Golleschau transport. It also means that he and Dr. Bieberstein were probably including the Golleschau and Landskron transports together in their general comments about the January 29, 1945, transport. As few people have ever seen the Landskron list and do not know about the burials at Bělá cemetery, I should like to list the names of the Landskron prisoners buried there:

  77185 13382 Polish **Schonfelt Alfred** 14.III.45 26.3.22 Tech.Zeicher
  77187 B53356 Polish **Willner Abraham** 1.III.45 5.6.11 Zimmermann[59]

One clue might help clarify the matter of how many Jews were on the Golleschau and Landskron transports, and it concerns the number of bodies in the burial plot that Oskar bought at the local cemetery in Bělá nad Svitavou in early February 1945. Oskar said little about this after the war, but he did comment that he was able to let Rabbi Jakob Levertov (Lewertow) bury the Golleschau dead in the cemetery with full Jewish rites. He thought this was the "only such case during the war in Germany."[60] But were the Golleschau and Landskron dead buried inside the grounds of the small cemetery or in a plot just beyond it?

What further complicates this issue is the confusing testimony that Rabbi Levertov gave to Howard Koch and Martin Gosch in New York in 1964 while they were collecting testimony for their proposed film on Schindler. After the arrival of the Golleschau transport, Schindler told Levertov, "Rabbi, we have these people from Golleschau. . . . Do everything your religion demands." Levertov told Oskar that he needed boards to put the bodies on, which was required by Jewish law. As Jewish law forbade breaking the bones of the dead, the bodies were placed on the boards in awkward positions. Levertov said that he and Schindler "looked over several places (within the factory grounds, not in a cemetery)" to bury the dead. After two days, they buried the first bodies from the Golleschau transport in graves lined with boards. Most important, the burials took place with a *Minyan,* a prayer quorum of at least ten males older than thirteen. Levertov conducted the service and led the burial *Kaddish.* The process took several days, during which Oskar kept Leipold and his officers drunk to keep them from finding out about the funerals.[61] What is confusing about Levertov's testimony is the time frame and the question of location. There was no place on Brünnlitz's grounds to bury bodies, so it had to be outside the camp. And though he states the burials took place over several days, Levertov said nothing about when they took place. We have to rely on others' testimony to supply us with information about the time and place for the Golleschau burials.

Peter Henzl took me to the small cemetery during my first visit to Brněnec and showed me two burial sites. The Schindler plot, he said, was originally outside the cemetery walls just beyond the mortuary. According to Thomas Keneally, one of the stories he heard about the Golleschau burials was that when Schindler tried to buy land within the cemetery, the priest instead offered him land just outside the cemetery walls usually reserved for suicides. Keneally said that Oskar told the priest that these were not suicides but "victims of a great murder." But they were also Jews and not Christians, and even given the wonderful stories of Czech kindness to the Brünnlitz prisoners, it is quite possible that the best Oskar could do was get land just outside the cemetery walls.[62]

Francisco Wichter worked on one of the details that buried the Jewish dead from the two transports. However, it was unlikely, because of the weather, that any of the dead on the two transports were buried soon after their arrival in Brünnlitz. The winter of 1944–1945 had been brutal and did not begin to moderate until mid-February. This meant that it would take some time for the ground to thaw before graves could be dug at Bělá cemetery. Though Jewish law stipulates that burial should take place as soon as possible after death, it also provides for extenuating circumstances. Francisco said the detail that he worked on, which was accompanied by an SS guard, took place at night without a rabbi or rituals. Keneally said that Oskar paid an *SS-Unterscharführer* to take care of the grave plot. During one of my visits with Francisco in Buenos Aires, I drew a diagram of the cemetery for him and described it in detail. I wanted to know whether he could remember where the bodies were originally buried. He said they were buried, without a tombstone, just in front of the mortuary.[63]

In 1946, a Czech commission under Dr. Josef Anděl and a physician, Dr. Eduard Knobloch, exhumed the bodies in two mass graves in Bělá cemetery. The two grave sites measured 9 x 5 x 0.6 meters and 2.5 x 4 x 1 meters. According to Jitka Gruntová, a Czech specialist who has published several books on Schindler, the smaller mass grave contained the bodies of sixteen Golleschau Jews and the other mass grave contained the bodies of twenty-six Jews who died elsewhere. This would tend to confirm estimates that sixteen Jews on both transports died while en route to Brünnlitz or sometime after they arrived. Gruntová and Radoslav Fikejz, a curator at the city museum in Svitavy who has also researched Schindler, told me that both grave sites rested outside the cemetery's walls; however, they disagreed on the location of these sites. After the Czech commission completed the autopsies of the bodies, they were respectfully re-buried within the cemetery's walls, though the graves remained unmarked. After he finished filming in Brněnec, Steven Spielberg had a small memorial plaque put on the wall overlooking the new burial site inside the cemetery's walls. He also had a large Star of David placed on the ground below the plaque. Bushes have been tastefully planted on either side of the memorial. The small plaque reads: *Památce idovskym Obětem 2 Světové Války* (In Memory of the Jewish Victims of the Second War).[64]

But even this does not fully clarify questions surrounding the number of Jews who died on the two transports because other Jews also died in Brünnlitz. In addition to Janka Feigenbaum, Keneally mentioned a Mrs. Hofstatter. Unfortunately, there is no Hofstatter on the two female lists from the fall of 1944. When the Polish historian Aleksandra Kobielec looked at the October 22, 1944, female list, she compared it to the April 18, 1945, list and noted that three women were missing from the latter list. Her conclusion was that the three Schindler women who died in Brünnlitz were Janina (Janka) Feigenbaum, Elisabeth Chotimer, and Anna Laufer. We do know that Elisabeth Chotimer and Anna Laufer died either in Brünnlitz or while in transit from Auschwitz because they are listed as *verstorben* (deceased) on the November 12, 1944, female list.[65] I have already mentioned the death of Janka Feigenbaum and her family's burial of her body. But we do not know what happened to the bodies of the other two women. Oskar did not acquire his burial plot until February 1945. Thomas Keneally said that Josef Leipold insisted initially that the bodies of the dead be cremated in the camp's furnace, so this is possible, though Keneally also makes the point that from the outset of the first deaths in Brünnlitz, Oskar insisted on ritual burials for his *Schindlerjuden*.[66]

Food and the Struggle for Survival

Oskar returned to Brünnlitz soon after the arrival of the Golleschau transport and ordered emergency hospital facilities to be set up in the factory to care for the Jews who were still alive. The dramatic efforts of Oskar, Emilie, and the camp's physicians to save the survivors of the Golleschau and Landskron transports is nothing short of miraculous. And though the Golleschau and Landskron Jews suffered from a variety of ailments, their greatest problem was malnutrition. Lack of food, unfortunately, was becoming a problem for the entire camp.

Emilie was in charge of caring for the transports' survivors and she did a remarkable job. A special clinic was set up in a large storage space on the main factory building's second floor. Dr. Chaim Hilfstein, Dr. Aleksander Bieberstein, and Dr. Szaja Händler were assigned to help Emilie care for the patients, each of whom required specialized care. The physicians needed certain medicines as well as frost cream and vitamins to restore them to good health. Brünnlitz had few medical supplies, so Oskar sent Emilie on a dangerous winter trip to Mährisch Ostrau (formerly Moravská Ostrava, Moravian Ostrava; today Ostrava) with suitcases full of vodka to trade for medical supplies. Emilie said that she obtained these goods from the Czechs, Poles, and Germans who arrived daily on the morning train in Mährisch Ostrau, "desperately trying to escape and not knowing where to go."[67] Emilie added that all the Golleschau and Landskron Jews "required extremely special attention and even had to be spoon-fed to prevent their choking to death. After not eating for so long, they had forgotten how." Emilie prepared them a special porridge and helped feed them this special diet until they were able to feed themselves. She used up the camp's reserves of grits, butter, milk, and other foodstuffs for this purpose.[68]

Emilie's need to use up the camp's small food surplus to feed the Golleschau and Landskron Jews underscored the serious problems that Oskar faced in obtaining food for his Jews, his staff, and the SS contingent. It was the biggest problem Schindler faced at Brünnlitz. Food had been readily available for the right price in Kraków, which was certainly not so in the Sudetenland. Johann Kompan, an old school friend of Oskar's in Zwittau and later a wholesale grocer there, wrote after the war that severe rationing and the attitude of local officials made it difficult for Schindler even to use the ration cards he had to obtain food for Brünnlitz.[69] Dr. Bieberstein said that when Brünnlitz first opened, Oskar was able to supply each worker with about 2,000 calories a day. Oskar had only brought a few wagon loads of food with him from Kraków, and this was not enough to feed his factory workers and staff for more than a week.[70]

In a much more personal way, Oskar Schindler's effort to keep his growing Jewish inmate population alive in Brünnlitz was as significant as the creation of the "list of life" that brought them to the Sudetenland. That was one miracle. Now he had to find a way to insure that they would survive until the end of the war. Oskar was well aware of the challenges he faced in finding food for the camp before he made the move to the Sudetenland. Once there, he did everything humanly possible to locate extra food for Brünnlitz. On November 1, 1944, for example, he rented a 3,000-square-meter tract of land from a family for RM 47 ($18.80) a year for "as long as the war lasted." The idea was to use the land to grow food for the factory.[71]

But the leasing of the farm plot was only one aspect of Oskar's efforts to supply his camp with food. More often than not, Oskar could be found traveling with illegal truckloads of goods that he traded for bread and other foodstuffs, tobacco, and other necessities. Tobacco was a highly prized trade commodity since cigarettes were simply unavailable in the Sudetenland. He estimated that he was able to obtain 12,000 tobacco packets for his workers, which they, in turn, could trade for food. By the end of the war, he estimated that he still had a month's supply of food as well as twenty animals for slaughter.[72]

But he did more than trade for food and other necessities. Sometimes he had to pay cash for it. Soon after the war ended, Oskar estimated that he had spent RM 80,000 ($32,000) on food and medicine for the camp. But sometimes he had to travel as far as 150 miles to find it. He often carried with him illegal papers with official-looking stamps made by Moshe Bejski, later a judge on the Israeli Supreme Court. The most useful stamp was the one that read *Der Höhere SS und Polizei Führer für Böhmen und Mähren* (Higher SS and Police Leader of Bohemia and Moravia), which permitted his trucks to pass through roadblocks without inspection. Dr. Bejski told me that he began his work as a forger during the war while still in Kraków, where he prepared illegal identity cards for Jewish girls who were to be sent to Germany. He began to make illegal documents for Oskar after Itzhak Stern told him that Schindler was going to Poland to buy food on the black market but needed forged documents to show that the food was bought legally from the Poles.[73]

If Oskar had a local benefactor, it was J. F. Daubek, the owner of the grain mill that was next to Oskar's factory. Oskar and Emilie quickly established good relations with Daubek and his wife. One afternoon, Emilie went to talk to the mill's manager to see if he could set up an interview with Frau Daubek. She soon received an invitation for tea, but she wondered how she could make a case for extra food for her workers given the serious food shortages in the region. In the end, she simply told Frau Daubek the truth. There was not enough food for Brünnlitz's Jewish workers and she "could not stand seeing our workers getting weaker by the day because of hunger." Emilie found Mrs. Daubek extremely warm and gracious. Over tea and a tray of delicacies, Emile told Mrs. Daubek that she urgently needed grain from her mill. Mrs. Daubek then asked her the reason for her request. Emilie replied, "I only want to help our Jews and the rest of the workers, so that they will not starve to death." Mrs. Daubek thought for a few moments and then said, "I understand your situation perfectly and realize we are going through unfortunate and difficult times. Anyway, I would like to help if I can. Please go to the mill and speak to the manager. Tell him from me that he is to give you whatever you need for your people." Later that afternoon, Emilie returned to the factory "with a veritable treasure in grains and semolina flour."[74]

There is no reason to doubt Emilie's story, though it is interesting that Oskar did not mention Daubek as a benefactor after the war. All he ever said about him was that he and Emilie had acquired the villa of this particular "local baron." The one specific thing we know about the relationship between Schindler and Daubek is that the mill owner allowed Schindler's Jews to steal grain quite freely from the mill. Sol Urbach and a friend, Max (Henryk) Blasenstein, worked as carpenters in the Daubek villa that Oskar was having renovated. Whenever he could, Sol would sneak into the Daubek mill and steal grain. He would fill his tool box and pockets with grain and then bring it back to the camp to share with others. Victor Lewis did the same thing. He worked as an electrician on the villa's renovations. "I was putting oatmeal in my toolbox and my tool belt, and bringing it [to the Brinnlitz camp]. My friends were cooking it. That is how Schindler saved my life."[75]

But Daubek must have done more than simply allow Brünnlitz's Jews to steal grain. After the war, many of them felt they owed Daubek a special thanks for the grain he had given them. About ten days after Oskar

and Emilie had fled the camp in 1945, Alfred Rozenfryd (Alfred Rosen-
fried) wrote J. F. Daubek a letter in the name of all of Brünnlitz's Jews
thanking him for providing them with flour, oatmeal, and semolina,
which he said often saved them from hunger. Aleksander Bieberstein was
equally complimentary of the mill owner, particularly his willingness to
allow Jews to steal grain from the mill.[76]

Oskar also had another benefactor in the area, Johann Kompan, a
wholesale grocer in Zwittau and a representative of the J. F. Daubek mill.
He had been a schoolfriend of Oskar's before the war and they renewed
their friendship after they met at the mill. According to Kompan, he did
everything that he could to supply Oskar with more food, particularly
bread, than Oskar's ration cards allowed. He said in a letter to the *"Religo" Comité pour la assistance la Populaston juife papée per la guerre*
(RELICO-Relief Committee for the War-Stricken Jewish Population) in
Geneva that Leib Salpeter, who was in charge of food storage in the
camp, and picked up the food from Kompan's warehouse, could attest to
this. Kompan estimated that he supplied Brünnlitz with extra weekly deliveries of 1,000 to 1,500 kilograms (2,200 to 3,300 pounds) of bread as
well as 500 kilograms (1,100 pounds) of grits, oats, and groats. He also
supplied extra rations of vegetables, carrots, flour, and cheese. He also
mentioned that he delivered 2,000 *Weizenmehlstriezel* wheat loaves for
Christmas 1944.[77]

His greatest effort, he told the Swiss committee, was to help Schindler's
Jews in the weeks after Oskar and Emilie had fled to the West. Some of
Brünnlitz's Jews remained in the camp and Kompan continued to supply
them with food. He said that he did this because no one seemed to care
for "these forced laborers" and "they had to eat." This all proved quite
costly to Mr. Kompan, particularly as Oskar did not pay him for the last
five weeks of food at the end of the war "because Schindler could not be
reached in the then upheaval." Stefan Pemper, Mietek Pemper's brother,
verified Kompan's account in the summer of 1945. In a statement prepared in Brněnec on July 14, he said that Kompan "supported us all during the entire time of our stay in Brněnec (Brünnlitz) by delivery of gro-
ceries in larger volume than our ration." He went on to explain how this
was done. Kompan established a separate warehouse in Zwittau for delivery of these goods for Brünnlitz. All the foodstuffs that Kompan supplied Schindler were paid for except the last deliveries, including one on
May 8, 1945, the last day of the camp's operation. The cost of the unpaid
goods was RM 12,800 ($5,120). Pemper explained that he was sent to

help pick up the food during this period, which included bread, flour, vegetables, asparagus, and carrots. His brother, Mietek, was then responsible for distributing the food. He concluded by stating that Johann Kompan "rendered us a great service and it is known to all of us that he put himself in great danger by making these deliveries."[78]

Kompan also had letters of support from other Schindler Jews. At the same time he prepared a thank-you letter for J. F. Daubek, Alfred Rosenfryd prepared a similar letter for Kompan that he later had translated into English and certified by a notary in Vienna. It stated that "H. Johann Kompan, resident of Zwickau, has given aid to the inmates of the concentration camp, Groß-Rosen, section Brünnlitz, materially by delivery of provisions outside the prescribed contingents."[79]

The following year, Kompan and his wife, Aloisia, who by this time were in Vienna, received two statements of support from another Schindler Jew, Alexander Goldwasser, and, in turn, the Jewish Committee *(Jüdisches Komitee)* in Vienna. Goldwasser befriended the Kompans after the war and was the one that suggested that they contact RELICO, an aid organization that had been created in the fall of 1939 by the World Jewish Congress to help Jews in Europe. Goldwasser assured the Kompans that once they identified themselves properly to the Geneva-based committee, they would receive the "most extensive support" because it was headed by Dr. Adolf Silberschein, a former member of the Polish Diet from Lemberg. Goldwasser wrote a statement in which he said that he saw with his "own eyes how Mr. Johann Kompan from Zwitau unselfishly and with the greatest danger to his life delivered to the KZ camp Brünnlitz in most ample measure amidst the greatest food difficulties, and we are therefore obliged to give him thanks for his efforts." The letter from the Jewish Committee in Vienna was addressed to the Jewish Committee in Innsbruck and was meant as part of the Kompans' request for food prompted by Mrs. Kompan's serious health problems. The letter said that the Kompans were to be regarded as "helpers of Jews."[80]

Oskar was equally grateful to Kompan for all he had done for the camp; before he left Brünnlitz, Kompan told Oskar that "the entire concentration camp feels obliged to thank me [Kompan] because of my steady, dangerous deliveries." Oskar added that when the war ended, Kompan's deeds would be "registered at the Jewish-American division of the International Red Cross [ICRC/IRC-International Committee for the Red Cross] in Geneva" under his full name. This would be done by "confidential Cracow people."

Kompan would also have a special number, KZ 24, and if he needed help, he should "introduce himself at this location of the I.R.T. [I.R.C.] with this stated number."[81] It is unclear whether Oskar meant American Red Cross representatives in Geneva or the Joint, the principal source of ICRC funding for efforts to aid Jews in Nazi-occupied Europe.[82]

While Oskar's instructions to Kompan sound a little far-fetched, it should be remembered that Oskar still had the mind of an Abwehr agent and, based on his immediate postwar efforts to seek aid from various Jewish groups, he probably thought that Kompan should do the same thing. And Oskar, who seemed to have planned his escape for some time, initially headed for Switzerland. So there was some logic, therefore, to his thoughts about registering Kompan with the ICRC there.

The foodstuffs and other goods that Oskar got from Daubek, Kompan, and others was meant for the camp's kitchen. Initially, the inmates were given three meals a day, though by the spring of 1945 they were reduced to two meals a day. The camp schedule was built around work and meals. Each prisoner received 25 dkg (1 dekagram = 0.353 ounces) of bread and coffee, and lunch consisted of a liter of "not very nourishing soup." For dinner, each inmate was given more bread and soup.[83] This was not sufficient for adults working nine-hour shifts and the workers were constantly scrounging for extra food. Cantor Moshe Taubé remembered thinking constantly about food. He and another bunk mate, Jerzy Sternberg, "dreamed about it: challah, cake, and fish, and pieces of wonderful meat, and roasted ducks, and goose livers! There was a sensual satisfaction just speaking about it."[84]

Oskar took particular pity on "Little" Leon Leyson and ordered extra rations for him. On another occasion, Oskar gave Leon a "hunk of bread," which Leyson described as "the most exciting thing" he had been given "in a long time." Leon immediately hid it and later shared it with his father and brother. The Budzyners controlled the inmate kitchen and they allowed Leon to take whatever scraps of food he could find after they had "swished water around" in the large soup kettles. He took the water that remained in the kettles, boiled it, and then ate what scraps were left after evaporation. When Oskar learned that several inmates had tuberculosis and that a few of the younger boys were losing weight, he ordered that they be given portions of Emilie's "magic" porridge.[85]

Stella Müller-Madej remembered Mietek Pemper sharing some baked beets with her family, "which were wonderful"; other men who worked outside the factory were occasionally able to find potatoes and extra grain in the Daubek mill. The inmates would grind the grain between two bricks and mix it with grain husks and water. This mixture was then baked into little cakes that "took a long time to chew and swallow. They looked like sawdust."[86] Polda Hirschfeld got a job in the kitchen that prepared food for the German staff. Whenever possible, she would take food scraps such as the heads of carp for her family. Igor Kling worked putting up the high SS-regulation fences around the perimeter of the camp. He and other Schindler Jews would steal potatoes from the fields surrounding the camp and bury them in a small hole under the fire they had built for their SS guards. They would cover the potatoes with a small sheet of tin and later enjoy a "feast" of baked potatoes.[87]

Iser Mintz was assigned to the Punishment Squad (Strafkommando) for four weeks, where he broke up rocks because he had stolen a turnip. And though the workers on the SS punishment squad were supposed to receive half rations only, Mintz ate well because he always managed to find potatoes hidden in the fields outside the camp. In time, Mintz learned to spot the ditches the Czech farmers had filled with potatoes and covered with straw. One day Iser decided to ask his SS guard, a sergeant, why they could not take some potatoes from the ditch. The sergeant said, "I can't. I'm afraid. It's against the order." But Iser sensed that the guard was a good man and in desperation decided to steal some of the potatoes. The next time they walked past the hidden potatoes, Iser told members of his squad to grab all they could while he held onto the guard with a big "bear hug." When the Strafkommando unit reached the hills overlooking Brünnlitz, they sat down and baked the potatoes. "This sergeant ate more than anyone, because he was hungry, too." And each day, Iser brought his brother, Jack Mintz, a baked potato.[88]

Such food shortages were not just a problem for Brünnlitz. One day Oskar was approached by Dr. Sternberg, a Jewish physician in a nearby camp, who had heard that there was food in Brünnlitz. Dr. Sternberg, who was allowed by his commandant, a Luftwaffe officer, to meet with Schindler, explained that the conditions in the Luftwaffe camp were "horrible," the work "very hard," and the food "very poor." Oskar immediately agreed to help supply the Luftwaffe camp with extra food and worked out a plan for Sternberg to get it from Brünnlitz's storehouses. Twice a week, Dr. Sternberg would come to Brünnlitz and, while Oskar looked the other way, he picked up extra supplies of "bread, cigarettes and other foodstuffs" for the nearby camp.[89]

Over time, food shortages became so serious that Oskar called a meeting of the entire camp in February 1945 to discuss the problem. He told everyone that they would have to limit their intake of food because he was having more and more difficulty finding provisions for the camp. The local landowners, he explained, had none to spare because they were "feeding the partisans." Some inmates began to contract scurvy and others lost their teeth. Leon Leyson told me that because of the food problems, the situation in Brünnlitz was much worse than it had been at Emalia. He said that if the war had lasted much longer, he was uncertain whether he would have survived. He recalled that he was "beginning to get double vision" and that his brother had "sores on his legs that weren't healing."[90] By late spring, rations were cut to two meals a day. The inmates were now given "a sort of paste made of flour," which was "good, hot and filling." They also got turnip soup, which "was doled out with a pharmacists's precision," though each bowl contained only few pieces of turnip. Stella Müller-Madej said that by this time she and her family had learned not to eat everything at once and they always tried to save some of their rations. But by early May, there was little food left. Stella remembered thinking that "if the liberators didn't come in a few days," they would all "die of hunger."[91]

The Challenges of Camp Work and Life in Brünnlitz

The chronic food problems in Brünnlitz were constant reminders that, despite the presence of Oskar Schindler, the Jews were still in a concentration camp. But what was different was the way that they were treated as prisoners and workers in the midst of an SS-regulated environment. Schindler's reputation was built less on how well he fed his workers than on how his prisoners were treated by the SS staff. Every Schindler Jew in Brünnlitz had suffered terribly from the random brutality and violence of the SS elsewhere. Most had spent some time in Płaszów under Amon Göth. Relatively speaking, Brünnlitz was a calm island in a sea of SS madness. And the person solely responsible for this was Oskar Schindler.

One of the few times this calm seemed to be really shaken was when Amon Göth showed up in the spring of 1945 to visit Oskar and check on the status of the sixty boxes of personal goods that Oskar had agreed to store for him at Brünnlitz. Göth had been released from prison in October 1944 on his own recognizance, though he remained under investigation by the SS. Ultimately, Oskar shipped Göth's war "booty" to his home in Vienna.[92] Stella Müller-Madej remembered the panic that swept through the women's quarters as news of Göth's visit spread among the inmates. Some of the prisoners were convinced that the former Płaszów commandant had come to liquidate Brünnlitz, and others talked of a mass escape.[93] But Rena Ferber Finder added that Göth did not look quite as threatening as he had in Płaszów because he was dressed in civilian clothes and was quite thin.[94] Victor Lewis said that several prisoners who saw him became angry and shouted, "What [do] you think, you are in Płaszów?" Göth, Lewis said, yelled back, "I'm gonna kill you guys!"[95] In reality, Göth did not stay very long in Brünnlitz because he was desperate to get back to Vienna. In addition to a brief meeting with Oskar, Göth also spent a few moments talking with Mietek Pemper. He wanted to know what the SS judges had asked Pemper when they interrogated him in 1944 and 1945. Dr. Aleksander Bieberstein also saw Göth in the camp's infirmary. Göth was suffering from heartburn and asked Dr. Bieberstein for some medicine which he gave him after examining the former Płaszów commandant.[96]

Göth's surprise visit to Brünnlitz was a reminder that Schindler still had to play the role of Nazi party loyalist and serious industrialist, whether it be with Göth or what seemed to be the incessant visits of SS and Wehrmacht teams to inspect his armament facilities. Several *Schindlerjuden* who came to adore Oskar after the war for what he did to save them admitted that even in Brünnlitz they were suspicious of him. Some found it hard to accept that this blond, tall German and Nazi Party member truly cared for them despite everything he did for them. Part of the problem centered around Oskar's ability to play the tough Nazi Party stalwart whenever one of the SS or Wehrmacht teams visited the factory. Perhaps one of the reasons for the frequent visits was Oskar's endless supply of alcohol. Every visit seemed to end in loud drinking parties in Oskar's factory apartment.[97] During one of these parties towards the end of the war, some of the inmates heard the following exchange:

"You know, Ossie, it's about time you scheduled the liquidation of your camp."

Schindler's reply was "No, let those Jewish swine work for the good of the Reich. I'll squeeze them till the pips squeak." At that, one of the big shots stood up and declared with a reverent look on his face that a patriot like Schindler should be an example to them all. He promised to try to get some sort of nomination or medal for such an outstanding citizen. Then there were drunken embraces and back-slapping. Schindler had tears in his eyes. The Germans thought he was so touched, but he was really just trying to keep from bursting out laughing.[98]

But perhaps they were tears of pain for having to say such awful things about people he cared for so much.

Oskar's ability to wine and dine SS and Wehrmacht big shots was not enough to convince Josef Leipold of his commitment to Nazi racial ideals or SS camp regulations. There was constant friction between both men over the treatment of prisoners. Though Leipold certainly could not be put in the same league as Amon Göth when it came to raw brutality, he still was a career SS man who had a certain mindset over how a camp should be run and how prisoners should be treated. Oskar bragged after the war that he "had the guards and supervisors under his control" at Brünnlitz, which assured that his Jews would be treated well. But, Schindler added, this was "often against the will" of Leipold.[99]

Like Schindler, SS-Obersturmführer Josef Leipold was a Sudeten German who was born in 1913 in Alt-Rohlau (Stará Role) in the western Sudetenland. A hairdresser by trade, he joined the Waffen-SS in 1938 and the Nazi Party the following year. He began his career in concentration camp administration in Mauthausen and also served in Lublin, Budzyń, Wieliczka, and Płaszów before he came to Brünnlitz. Leipold fled to Deggendorf, Germany, at the end of the war. In 1946, Henry Slamovich and several other Schindlerjuden living in Deggendorf's displaced persons (DP) camp, went to the Deggendorf Christmas fair, where they spotted Leipold. Slamovich and his friends surrounded Leipold while another told a nearby American MP that they had captured a former concentration camp commander. The MP asked Leipold for his identification, only to discover that he had changed his name. The MP told Slamovich and the others that there was nothing he could do. In the meantime, Slamovich noticed a Jewish officer in the U.S. Army's Counter Intelligence Corps (CIC) standing nearby who had attended religious services in the DP camp. Slamovich told him about Leipold and the CIC officer arrested the former Brünnlitz commandant. The CIC officer told Slamovich to find as many Brünnlitz Jews as possible and bring them to the DP camp to identify Leipold.[100]

Slamovich contacted various Schindler Jews in the area and told them that he needed them to help identify Leipold. One of those he got in touch with was Ryszard Lax, who, along with Oskar and Emilie, was living with Schindler Jews Gunther Singer and Hersch Licht in an apartment in Regensburg, which was only about thirty-five miles from Deggendorf. Oskar and about fifteen to twenty Schindler Jews showed up at the Deggendorf DP camp, where Leipold was being detained. During the line-up, Oskar went up to Leipold and said, "You are Leipold, and do not try to deny it. If you continue to deny it, downstairs there are three hundred Jews who will devour you." Leipold then admitted his true identity. Later, *Schindlerjude* Hersch Licht walked up to Leipold, who was now in a cell, and told him that he had "better not think" they wouldn't "prove all his deeds." Leipold was later deported to Poland, where he was tried for war crimes in Lublin and condemned to death on November 9, 1948.[101]

Itzhak Stern considered Leipold a "beast," and Dr. Chaim Hilfstein warned Stella Müller-Madej's family that the commandant "was dangerous and had to be watched."[102] Aleksander Bieberstein said that Leipold's goal was to destroy the camp and "kill the Jews." Yet somehow Oskar was able to maintain a good "diplomatic relationship with the commandant." Bieberstein wrote that "Schindler knew how to use the weak points and stupidity of Leipold, especially in moments of danger for the Jews. With bribes and parties he tempered his [Leipold's] determination."[103] Schindler often did this by intervening in situations that he thought would be harmful to the prisoners. One bitterly cold day in early January 1945, Leipold ordered everyone in the factory outside for roll call. Oskar stormed into the factory from his apartment and told Leipold that he needed healthy people to operate his machines, not "frozen dummies." This, Oskar told Leipold, "was what the Führer demanded of him." Needless to say, the roll call was held inside the factory.[104] Oskar again "outfoxed" Leipold when he convinced the Armaments Inspectorate that if they approved his use of the "highly skilled" Golleschau and Landskron workers, he could double his production output. Needless to say, Schindler was allowed to use these workers, even though some of them had limbs amputated because of frostbite.[105] There was no doubt that Leipold saw through this charade but seemed incapable of doing much about it.

Schindler had less trouble with the SS guards, most of whom, he said, had been released from the Waffen-SS "as unfit." Oskar attributed their fairly decent treatment of the prisoners to the ample supply of food, alcohol, and tobacco that he supplied his SS contingent. Emilie also played a role in helping temper the violence of the SS guards, particularly the *Auf-*

seherinnen or female guards. Whenever Oskar was away, Emilie would invite the female guards to tea in her apartment. Stella Müller-Madej said
this permitted the women to go to the toilet as they pleased. When the
Aufseherinnen were around, they strictly regulated trips to the bathroom.[106] But this did not mean that there were not problems, particularly
with some of the *Kapos*. The inmates nicknamed one *Kapo*, Müller,
"*Avanti*" because he constantly shouted "*Avanti*" with whip in hand to
get his workers to move faster. But the most feared *Kapo* was Willi, who
wandered into camp in March 1945 with a few other Jews. Though stories about Willi varied, they all agreed on two points—he was very brutal
and he quickly became Leipold's favorite *Kapo*. Willi had left with a hundred other prisoners from a nearby camp but by the time they reached
Brünnlitz, only a handful were alive. Rumor had it that Willi had taken a
steel club and beaten most of the Jews in his group to death before they
got to Brünnlitz.[107]

On his first day as a Brünnlitz *Kapo,* Willi viciously beat one of the
prisoners with his whip. He "cracked his head open with one blow, and
then made him do squats until he fainted." Oskar was away at the time
and Mietek Pemper reported the incident to Emilie. She told Pemper that
there was nothing she could do about it because she "wasn't allowed to
interfere" with the SS. Oskar returned to camp the next day and Mietek
Pemper overheard his conversation with Willi. Oskar told the *Kapo* that
he was now working in an armaments factory and that brave German soldiers depended on the work done at Brünnlitz. Consequently, it was important that everyone "be fit for work, not injured." He warned Willi that
if he ever struck a prisoner again, Oskar would have him arrested for
"sabotage and hampering the war effort."[108]

But during the eight months that he operated his factory sub camp,
Oskar had more to deal with than simply Leipold, the SS, and the wellbeing of his workers. He also had to maintain the façade of a viable armaments factory operation. Though there was no question that Oskar
had considerable contacts in the Armaments Inspectorate and the
Wehrmacht, he certainly would not have been permitted to keep his factory open if he had not shown evidence of considerable arms production.
Needless to say, it is absolutely remarkable that Schindler could produce
only one wagon-load of the 3.7 cm *Steilgranate* 41 *(Aufsteck Geschoß)*
shells for the *Panzerabwehrkanone 36* and continue to operate his factory,
particularly in the context of Germany's desperate need for armaments.
Oskar later explained that this wagonload of antitank shells was worth no

more than RM 35,000 ($14,000) and that even these shells had been half completed in Kraków before he moved his factory to Brünnlitz.[109]

How did he get away with it? Itzhak Stern said that they did it by "falsifying production charts," a skill that Mietek Pemper had mastered in Płaszów. Schindler's office staff made it appear that they were "working and producing but simply not making finished products."[110] When questioned about the lack of production, Schindler always fell back on the explanation that his factory was having "starting difficulties." But after a while, this excuse began to wear thin and Oskar feared for the safety of his workers, particularly in light of the increased demands from Albert Speer's Ministry for Armaments and Munitions.[111] This deception troubled some of Schindler's German staff. Stern recalled, for example, that Oskar had to get a fox fur coat in Poland as a Christmas present for the wife of one of the head German engineers "to ease his severe intentions."[112]

This also might explain why some of the German civilian staff were unkind to some of Schindler's Jews. One of the German engineers, for example, always refused to look or speak to his Jewish workers. But one day just before the war ended, the engineer tried to shake Dr. Ferdinand Lewkowicz's hand; but Dr. Lewkowicz said, "Yesterday you wouldn't shake hands with me; tonight I don't want to shake hands with you." The engineer "left with his head down." Victor Lewis remembered another incident in which a German foreman mistreated him after he had accidentally shorted out the lighting system in the factory while trying to hook up a welding machine. Though several electricians quickly fixed the problem, the German kicked Victor, called him a "son of a gun," and told him to go to his shop. Instead, Victor went to Oskar's office, where he ran into Emilie. He explained the situation to her and she told Oskar about the incident. Schindler told Victor to go back to the factory and wait for him. A few minutes later, Oskar went to see the German foreman and told him that he needed an electrician, specifically Victor Lewis. The foreman explained that Lewis was not an electrician. Oskar replied simply, "I want him." But there were other German staff members who were much kinder. Polda Hirschfeld remembers cleaning the office of a German engineer who would occasionally say, "Before you throw anything away from the wastebasket, you might want to look inside." When he said this, she always found several pieces of bread and jam in the wastebasket.[113] The lack of significant armaments production did not mean that the prisoners did not work hard. They did, though it was often at things made to look as if they were producing antitank shells. Some of the men worked setting up the large collection of machines that had been shipped from Emalia. In fact, Henry Weiner said, "We never finished. Schindler saw to it we never were." But no one worked as hard as they did at Emalia or Płaszów. In fact, Pola Gerner Yogev thought that comparatively speaking "we had easy jobs." Sam Birenzweig had similar memories. He described himself as "just a plain worker" who "didn't work too hard." His main job was to help make the cement that was used in the installation of the factory's machines.[114] Moshe Bejski said when they had free time, each of the men working on the factory floor made himself "a razor, spoons and other eating utensils, and even cigarette lighters."[115]

Camp life was built around a strict daily work schedule dictated by Leipold:

Wake up call—for the outside detachment 6:00
   for the inside detachment 7:30
   for the night shift 15:00
Beginning of work—for the outside detachment 7:15
   for the inside detachment 9:00
   for the night shift 20:30
End of work—for the outside detachment 16:30
   for the inside detachment 20:00
   for the night shift 7:00
Lunch break—for the inside shift 13:45–14:00
   for the outside shift 14:00–15:00
   for the night shift 1:00–1:30
Bedtime 22:00[116]

The women spent their free time knitting wool sweaters and underwear for the entire camp from wool that had been stolen from the Hoffmann mills next door. When Wilhelm Hoffmann, one of the owners, learned of the thefts, he threatened to call the Gestapo to investigate. Oskar stepped in and got Hoffmann to agree not to make an official complaint in return of a payment of RM 8,000 ($3,200) for the wool.[117] It was not particularly good wool. Stella Müller-Madej described it as "a strange kind of thick, springy wool" that was "so stiff that you could almost cut your fingers on it." Needless to say, the wool was also very scratchy and uncomfortable to wear. But it helped keep many of the workers warm in the chilly factory. More important, the knit goods "were life savers for those who left the camp to work in the open air."[118]

One of the most difficult aspects of Brünnlitz life was the living conditions. More than a thousand men and women were forced to live in extremely cramped conditions in the upper floor of the factory. Initially, the men had to sleep on straw until the standard three-tiered SS bunks arrived. Conditions were so tight for the women in the bunks that they had to turn over from one side to another in unison. And it was impossible to walk through the crowded living space. Stella Müller-Madej said that "there was bedlam when one woman got a stomach ache and couldn't make to it through the crowd in time." Some of the more ill-tempered women would scream out that she was a "pig." Very often such problems were caused by typhus.[119]

But some of the inmates tried to balance the harshness of camp life with adherence to traditional religious values and beliefs. Oskar acquired a *Teffilin* for Simon Jeret. The *Teffilin* are two small leather boxes worn by a male adult Jew on his head and forearm during morning prayer. Each leather box contains passages from the Jewish scriptures. Jeret kindly shared his *Teffilin* with anyone who wanted to use them. Each day, a line of men would gather near Jeret's bunk waiting to put on the *Teffilin* and then say the *Sh'ma*, the basic statement of Jewish faith from Deuteronomy 6:4:[120]

Hear, O Israel: The Lord our God is our Lord.[121]

As each man finished the *Sh'ma*, he would take off the *Teffilin* and Jeret would say, "Next one." Rabbi Moshe Taubé called it "a Sh'ma assembly line."[122]

During Passover, some of Brünnlitz's most observant Jews would literally "put their lives on the line" by not eating bread. Instead, "they ate the roots of the grass" because Jewish law prohibited eating leavened bread, or *hamets*, during Passover. Rabbi Moshe Taubé struggled with this question and finally decided to fast during the *Seder,* the special meal on the first night of Passover. As he explained, "We had to do everything possible in spite of ourselves to show that physical needs and deprivation would not annul the commitment to the Torah. When you are committed to your way of life and the past of your people and the continuance of your people your personal needs do not take precedence over the larger picture."[123]

Moses Goldberg remembered cooking rice for Abraham Bankier and Rabbi Jakob Lewertow during Passover because they also refused to eat *hamets*. He said the rice was not Kosher, meaning that it did not meet the standards of Jewish religious dietary laws, but it was better than eating *hamets*. Goldberg said that Schindler knew about the oven in the warehouse that he used to cook the rice for Passover; whenever Oskar smelled something cooking in the warehouse, he would ask, "What's cooking?"[124] Henry Slamovich was able to get potatoes for his friend, Josl (Josek) Ryba, who also did not want to eat *hamets* during Passover. But Henry chose not to observe his faith during his imprisonment. He said that he had seen too much violence and evil during the Holocaust and had lost his faith. He particularly remembered the taunts of German soldiers in Kraków, who would abuse and mock Orthodox Jews in their prayer shawls and beards and then ask, "Where is your God? Why doesn't he help you now?" After the war, Henry settled in San Francisco and became active in synagogue life there.[125]

Brünnlitz: The Final Weeks

By the middle of March 1945, Mährisch Ostrau, which was about 136 miles northeast of Brünnlitz, was the center of an assault led by the Soviet Fourth Ukrainian Front (Group) as part of its effort to break into the Sudetenland in its drive towards Dresden. By the end of March, German forces had momentarily halted the Soviet advance towards Mährisch Ostrau and Opava, both considered essential to Soviet efforts to enter the Sudetenland. The Germans put up staunch resistance and units of the Fourth Ukrainian Front did not reach the Brünnlitz area until May 8. Some *Schindlerjuden* reported hearing the fighting in the distance. What they did not know, of course, was that Czechoslovakia had become the last battleground of World War II. German forces under *Generalfeldmarschall* Ferdinand Schörner, a fanatical Nazi whom Hitler had designated his military heir, staged a last-stand defense with his Army Group Center about halfway between Prague and Brünnlitz. Though the German High Command surrendered on May 7, Schörner's forces continued to fight for four days. Needless to say, the situation in the Brünnlitz area was extremely unstable, particularly in light of a Czech uprising in Prague on May 5.[126]

Schindler's greatest concern as the front moved closer to Brünnlitz was the safety of his Jewish workers. He knew that Leipold would probably receive orders to liquidate the camp, but he was not certain whether this would simply mean moving the workers westward. There were instances where inmates were murdered as part of the liquidation process. His worries intensified after the arrival of thirty prisoners from Geppersdorf, another Groß Rosen sub-camp in southern Poland, on April 11, 1946. According to Henry Weiner, the prisoners from Geppersdorf were in "bad shape," though their condition was much better than that of the men on the Golleschau transport. It was at about this time that Schindler and Leipold had a big argument about how to deal with some of the prisoners who continued to arrive in Brünnlitz. Leipold wanted to take those in bad physical condition and shoot them in the nearby woods. Oskar told Leipold that if he did this he would have the SS men involved in the killings sent to the front as malingerers. Leipold said he would hold off on the executions because he needed the SS men.[127]

But this was not the end of Schindler's concerns over Leipold's eagerness to liquidate the camp. This is probably the reason for the April 18, 1945, list, which was drawn up to include all the Jews who were now in Brünnlitz. Groß Rosen had closed two months earlier, so any orders that Leipold received about an evacuation of the camp would come from WVHA D2 in Oranienburg. Oskar was also concerned about the presence in the area of units under *General* Andrei Vlasov, a Russian defector who had created, with the blessing of the Germans, two Russian Liberation Army divisions in the Wehrmacht. Only one became fully operational, and it was involved in the German defense of the Oder River line. Its most meaningful action was the aid it gave to Czech partisans in the Prague uprising on May 6, 1945. Actually, Schindler was wrong about the presence of Vlasov's units in the area. Though now theoretically under Field Marshal Schörner's command, Vlasov's units were trying to flee to the American lines and did not enter Czechoslovakia until late April. By then, they were well to the northwest of Brünnlitz.[128]

Stella Müller-Madej said that each day Leipold would take Oskar into the woods "to show off how carefully and precisely he had the ditches dug" that would hold the remains of the *Schindlerjuden*.[129] Betty (Bronia) Groß Gunz told a somewhat different story. She said that after Oskar received the order to close the factory and "execute all of us," he decided to dig graves to "deceive the Nazis." Bronia said that she helped dig the phony graves for two days until Oskar showed up with some documents with a red seal on them that he had gotten while on a trip to Germany. He walked into the factory and said, "Children, you are safe. You are going to make it. The war will not be forever."[130] On the other hand, another Schindler Jew, Ignacy (Israel) Falk, said that Leipold had "ordered Russian inmates of a neighboring camp to dig graves."[131] Thomas Keneally wrote that during the second half of April Leipold received a telegram from Hasse-broek, Groß Rosen's commandant, ordering him to prepare to march Brünnlitz's Jews to Mauthausen. But first he was to execute the elderly and the sick. But Leipold never saw the deadly telegram because Mietek Pemper, who worked in Leipold's office and served as liaison between Schindler and the commandant, intercepted it. He steamed it open and immediately told Oskar about its contents.[132]

According to Keneally, Schindler had already laid the groundwork for what would happen next. He lodged complaints with Richard Glücks, the head of WVHA Office Group D in Oranienburg about Leipold's treatment of the prisoners. He shared copies of these reports with Has-sebroek and Max Rausch, the regional HSSPF in Brno. Then, Keneally says, on April 27, the day before Schindler's birthday, Oskar put his scheme into motion. He invited Leipold to a party and got him very drunk. Around 11:00 P.M., Oskar brought Leipold onto the factory floor where the commandant raged against the camp's Jewish workers and cried out, "You fucking Jews. See that beam, see it! That's what I'll hang you from. Every one of you!" The next day, Oskar called Hassebroek "and others" to complain about Leipold's most recent outburst. His workers, Oskar proclaimed, were "not laborers!" They were "sophisti-cated technicians engaged in secret-weapons manufacture." Two days later, Keneally wrote, Leipold was transferred to a Waffen SS unit near Prague.[133]

Accounts by Stella Müller-Madej and Itzhak Stern tell a very different story. Moreover, there are some serious inconsistencies in Keneally's ver-sion of Leipold's departure. For one thing, Groß Rosen was closed in Feb-ruary 1945 and, though quite a bit has been written about Hassebroek, there is a mystery surrounding his last months in the SS. So it is doubtful that Oskar would or could have contacted the former Groß Rosen com-mandant. And there is no way he could have contacted Glück's office on April 28 in Oranienburg, on the outskirts of Berlin, because Soviet tanks had entered the suburb on April 24. So we have to look elsewhere to find out how Oskar Schindler managed to get rid of Josef Leipold and his SS contingent.[134]

Fortunately, Stella Müller-Madej and Itzhak Stern have given us more reliable testimony about how Oskar Schindler finally got rid of Leipold. Stella got her information from Mietek Pemper, who was close to her fam-ily in Brünnlitz. On April 27, Oskar invited Leipold to a party in his apartment, where he got the commandant drunk. Beforehand, Oskar had prepared forged documents that said Leipold and his SS men were requested "as great patriots who believe in the victory of the Third Reich and its great leader, to be transferred together to the front line." When Leipold was drunk, Oskar put the document in front of him and told him to sign it. It was, Oskar explained, the order "to liquidate the camp." Leipold, who had longed for this moment, signed willingly. Oskar then had someone in his office take the document to SS headquarters.[135]

Stern's account of how Oskar got rid of Leipold is much more complex. In mid-April, 1945, he and Mietek Pemper were working on the top floor in the Brünnlitz office building next to the factory. Only a glass partition separated their office from that of the German civilians who worked for Schindler. The Germans would listen three times a day to the radio, trying to find out the location of the front. As it moved closer and closer, the German staff became more nervous. One day, Stern was looking out the window and saw an *SS-Scharführer* walk over to Leipold's house. A few minutes later he came out with a letter in his hand. As he mounted his horse, he put the letter in his pocket. Stern asked Pemper, who served as "Leipold's unofficial secretary," how they could find out what was in the letter. Pemper said he had not written anything for Leipold that was important, so Stern concluded that there was something in the letter about the Jews because Pemper "would write all secret letters for Leipold." Stern and Pemper decided that it must have been written by Leipold's official secretary, a young SS officer.[136]

They agreed that they should talk to the young SS officer to see whether they could find out what was in the letter. But they needed an excuse to enter the SS offices on the floor below them. As they walked downstairs, they decided they would ask the officer's permission to see the sheets that were used to determine whether workers were to receive "so-called work bonuses." They explained that there were some errors on the sheets. The young officer became angry and began yelling at the two Jews. He said it was essential that these lists be correct. When he got up to check on the lists, Stern opened the notebook on his desk and found a copy of the letter Leipold had recently sent out with the SS courier. Stern took the letter out of the notebook and took it to Schindler. The letter "was a request by Leipold about what to do with the Jews."[137]

In the meantime, Leipold had received a response from the SS about the liquidation of the camp and called Schindler in to talk about it. His new orders were as follows:

All elements of disorder, young, old, and sick people to be deported, only 10% are allowed to stay. These absolutely essential workers are supposed to continue operating the factory or demolish it.[138]

Schindler quickly paid a visit to the regional Armaments Inspectorate office and then came back to talk with Leipold. He took the commandant to one of the storage rooms, where he noticed several large bottles on the shelves. Though Oskar knew what was in them, he asked Leib Salpeter, who was in charge of the storage room, what they contained. Salpeter said that they contained Slibowitz, a plum liqueur. Oskar told Leipold that they needed to find out what was in the bottles. Oskar gave Leipold glass after glass of Slibowitz and then walked him through the camp. While they were walking, Oskar put a velour cover on the commandant's head, which "made him look like a Chassidic Jew." Oskar then took Leipold into Emalia's office, where he introduced him to his staff. Afterwards, Oskar took Leipold on a drive to Brno, where he convinced Leipold to volunteer to join the fight at the nearby front.[139]

But Leipold changed his mind when he actually received his orders to report to the front. During their drive to Brno, Leipold told Oskar that he did not know how to use hand grenades and this was evidently the excuse he used to avoid joining the Waffen SS in the field. Schindler told him that he had a secret cache of hand grenades to protect the factory against the Russians and said he would teach Leipold how to use them. Emilie, Stern, and a few others criticized Oskar for telling Leipold about the secret weapons. But Oskar thought it was important for Leipold to know about them. One night, Oskar told Stern not to become concerned if he heard some explosions. He wanted the workers to go to their living quarters and remain quiet. He explained that he was going to show Leipold how to use hand grenades.[140]

Schindler later told Stern what happened next. The noise from the exploding hand grenades was extremely loud and, according to Oskar, they disturbed *Generalfeldmarschall* Ferdinand Schörner, the head of Army Group Central, whose headquarters were nearby. Schörner came to the factory and asked what was going on. Oskar told him that Leipold was "playing around with the grenades instead of going to the front." Schörner immediately ordered Leipold to report to his SS unit at the front. But Leipold still refused to go. So once again Oskar had to come up with a new scheme to force Leipold out of Brünnlitz.[141]

Several days later, Schindler had a party for some of the SS big shots from Brno. And as usual, everyone got drunk except Oskar. One of Schindler's secretaries, Ms. Hoffmann, then blurted out that Oskar had talked Leipold, "who had fought against the Jews, into going to the front." This, she said, was "a scandal." Someone else at the party suggested that it would "be a good idea to send the Jews to the Russians with white flags." When another SS officer began to criticize Schindler's actions, Oskar pushed him down a steep flight of stairs. As he was falling, the SS officer shouted, "Oskar shot me." One of the Jewish physicians was called in to tend to the fallen SS officer. Emilie, who was present at the party, was concerned about Oskar's behavior, though an officer from the Armaments Inspectorate pulled Oskar aside and told him that now that the war was, for all practical purposes, over, nothing must happen to him (Schindler) because he had "done so much for the Jews." At the end of the party, Oskar drove Leipold to the front. Stern concluded by saying that Leipold was replaced by a man of sixty-eight who was "a very calm and decent fellow." The rest of Leipold's SS contingent followed him to the front and was replaced with older SS men who were also "calm and decent."142

Stella Müller-Madej remembered the departure of Leipold and the SS men a bit differently. According to Stella, Oskar did drive Leipold to the front followed by the camp's SS contingent in a truck. Several hours later, Oskar returned to Brünnlitz with a new group of "older, jumpy" SS men who carried their "rifles under their arms like useless parcels." Oskar told two of them to guard the front gate and the rest were put up in Leipold's house. About an hour after he returned to Brünnlitz, Stella wrote, Schindler entered the factory wearing his Nazi Party uniform. He sat on a crate and slowly began to laugh like "a madman." He said to anyone who wanted to hear that "the man had not yet been born who could outfox Oskar." Schindler was finally in charge of the camp. The new SS contingent seemed bewildered by their fate, particularly after Oskar ordered them not to let any German vehicles into the camp because they could be partisans wearing German uniforms. And whenever he walked by, "they [the new SS men] stood at attention before him as if he were Hitler himself." Oskar also ordered the machinery shutdown. He told his *Schindlerjuden* to act as though the camp were empty.143

Yet how believable are these accounts? Though there will always be inconsistencies in any survivor's account, there is general agreement that

Oskar was desperate to rid himself of Leipold and the loyal SS unit that guarded Brünnlitz for fear of what they might do to the inmates if they were ordered to liquidate the camp. Itzhak Stern said that everyone in Brünnlitz was convinced that the "German leadership would attempt to liquidate them just before the end in some way or another."[144] Moreover, some of Schindler's Jews gave accounts of Schindler's role in the removal of Leipold that agree with the general thrust of the story provided by Stern and Müller-Madej. And as strange as it sounds, the story about *Generalfeldmarschall* Schörner is not that far-fetched. By the end of April or early May 1945, when Leipold and the original SS detachment finally left for the front, Brünnlitz sat at the edge of a German salient into the Russian lines that would have provided Schörner with a logical, protected place for his command headquarters. Though Soviet forces would ultimately force him westward to an enclave between Pardubice and Prague, it is quite possible that the ruthless and aggressive Schörner, worried and angered over explosions so near to his mobile command post, might very well have stormed into Schindler's factory to see what was going on. And what about Oskar's showing up on the factory floor in his Nazi Party uniform? Schindler occasionally wore the standard four-pocketed brown gabardine Nazi Party uniform to impress German military, SS, and government officials. If he put it on after he returned from delivering Leipold and his SS team to the nearby front, it was probably to give the new SS contingent, which was now under the command of a lowly *SS-Scharführer,* Motzek, a sense of Oskar's newfound authority.[145]

But getting rid of Leipold and Brünnlitz's original SS contingent was not the only thing that Oskar did to protect his Jews during the final weeks of the war. He also created and armed a secret Jewish underground force within the camp. Well before liberation, Schindler began to stockpile illegal arms. He got the weapons from HSSPF Max Rausch in return for a diamond for Rausch's wife. Schindler's arsenal consisted of rifles, machine guns, a few pistols, and some hand grenades. The idea was to build a secret camp defense force around workers and inmates who had military service. According to Itzhak Stern, Oskar created a committee that included Schindler, Stern, Hildegest, an Austrian who worked for Oskar and had once been in Dachau for his anti-Nazi writings, and a Polish engineer, Pawlink, to plan and lead the underground group. Uri (Urysz) Bejski, the younger brother of Moshe Bejski, was in charge of storing the arms. Stern said that the secret group planned a coup centered around dressing the underground members in SA uniforms. They would then

enter the village of Brünnlitz and cut off all communications with the factory. Their biggest problem, Stern said, was finding shoes to fit each underground team member.[146]

Victor Lewis, who was a member of Schindler's Brünnlitz defense force,
said the unit had contacts with the Czech underground, which also supplied the Jews with weapons. Lewis said the initial goal of this group was
to shoot Leipold when he tried to liquidate the camp. The Czechs said
they would try to help the Brünnlitz defense unit if the camp was attacked
but that for the most part the Schindler Jews would have to defend themselves.[147] Lewis said that the secret Brünnlitz defense squad consisted of
thirty men subdivided into units of five men each. As new men were
brought into the unit they were asked to recommend others. Lewis suggested Joe (Josef) Lipshutz and Joe (Josef) Jonas; Richard (Ryyszard)
Rechen, who would later help the Schindlers escape, recruited Lewis
Fagen into the Brünnlitz underground. Victor Lewis explained that
Schindler wanted people in the unit who were "mentally tough" to insure
that if they were caught, they would not reveal the names of the other
members of the group. Everything was kept very secret and few people
knew the names of the members of the six squads. In fact, Victor Lewis
said he did not know who was in charge of his particular squad until the
end of the war, when he learned it was Leopold "Poldek" Page. For the
most part, Lewis said, "I was with strangers." To insure the strength and
health of the unit, Oskar made sure that no one in the unit was malnour-
ished. When things became desperate, Schindler brought a horse into the
camp for the underground group to eat.[148]

Lewis Fagen was responsible for safeguarding some of the unit's
weapons, which were stored "under huge bales of wire in an electrical
transformer station." His job was to make sure the German staff did not
find the arms. And because one of the German supervisors lived in the
transformer station with his wife and child, Fagen's job was made doubly hard. Fagen said that every time the German supervisor got near the
bales of wire, his "heart stopped." As the war drew to a close, the
Czechs told the Brünnlitz squad to began their armed uprising. Once it
started, the Czechs promised, they would come in and help. Schindler,
who was coordinating these efforts, took out ten rifles and lined them
up against the wall for dispersal to the Brünnlitz underground.[149]
Leopold "Poldek" Page said that Oskar told the leaders of the unit,
"Look, when this moment comes, you have to stand up, maybe you will
get killed," but added that they could not execute everyone in the camp.

It would, he said, be "physically impossible" because when the SS began the executions, the Jewish prisoners would fight back. Some Jews would die in the fighting, but not everyone.[150] Fortunately, an uprising never took place because the SS guards left before the Russians took over the camp. When they had gone, the Brünnlitz underground took control of the camp and ordered everyone to stay inside because German units were still operating in the area. The underground group was now in charge of camp security.[151]

As part of his factory defense plan, Oskar also had radios put into the offices where his most prominent Jews worked. Stern said that this insured they were "always informed about the latest developments in the war." Elsewhere in the camp, Oskar arranged to have his car radios periodically repaired. This insured that the camp's two radio technicians, Zenon Senwic and Artur Rabner, could listen to one of the radios, particularly the illegal broadcasts of the BBC, and share what they heard with other prisoners. According to Dr. Moshe Bejski, each day Senwic would plug his earphone into Schindler's radio and listen to the 2:00 P.M. BBC broadcast. After a while, Senwic was worried that he had kept the radio too long and told Schindler it was repaired. Oskar replied, "Don't worry, I have another radio to repair."[152] A glass partition separated Stern's office from the German civilian staff's office. He and Pemper ran a wire from their office into the German office and hooked it up to the radio there. This enabled them to listen to German broadcasts. Stern also said in his 1956 report to Yad Vashem that the inmates began the construction of their own radio station in the final days of the war.[153] Sol Urbach remembered listening to the BBC while working on Schindler's villa. Occasionally, he explained, their SS guard would fall asleep. Sol and his coworker, Max Blasenstein, would then sneak behind the radio and "fiddle with it until [they] got the BBC."[154]

But Oskar did more than just worry about protecting the lives of his Schindlerjuden during the confusing final days of the war. He also concerned himself with their well-being once the war was over. In the final months of the war, he arranged, through a series of bribes, to purchase eighteen truckloads of various types of wool and other goods from a nearby Kriegsmarine (navy) depot. The shipment included navy-colored wool and khaki material as well as thread, shoes, leather, and other materials. Oskar's idea was to give each inmate enough material to make two suits, coats, underwear, and other clothing articles. The idea, he explained, was to have them "fitted out [properly] for their first steps as liberated people." Rena Finder told me that after Oskar left Brünnlitz on May 9, each inmate was given 3 meters of fabric, a pair of men's shoes, and a bottle of vodka. Each Schindler Jew found different uses for these goods. Victor Lewis added that the inmates were also given leather and scissors. It was apparent that Oskar wanted the prisoners not only to have new clothes but also items for trading and selling.[155]

As Oskar Schindler made final preparations for the defense of the camp, the Third Reich imploded from within. At about 3:30 P.M. on April 30, 1945, Adolf Hitler and his mistress, Eva Braun, committed suicide in the *Führerbunker* in Berlin as Soviet artillery bombarded Hitler's Reich Chancellery. The day before his suicide, Hitler appointed *Großadmiral* (Grand Admiral) Karl Dönitz to be his successor as head of state and the military with the title of Reich President. Dönitz, who was in Plön, near the Baltic Sea, did not learn of his appointment until early the next day. That evening, he broadcast the news of Hitler's "heroic death" fighting to defend the capital. The following day, German forces in Berlin surrendered to the Russians. Dönitz, now headquartered in Flensburg, near the Danish border, hoped in the final days of the war to do as Germany had done at the end of World War I—preserve the territorial integrity of the Third Reich and the Wehrmacht. But the Supreme Allied Commander, Dwight David Eisenhower, refused to consider anything but unconditional surrender. On May 6, Dönitz sent Chief of the Wehrmacht Command Staff (*Chef des Wehrmachtführungsstabs*) Alfred Jodl to Reims, France, to negotiate with the Allied powers. Soon after Jodl arrived, Eisenhower insisted on an immediate unconditional German surrender. Eisenhower told Jodl that if he did not accept these terms, the Allies would begin new air raids over Germany. At 2:41 A.M. on May 7, 1945, Jodl signed an agreement accepting Eisenhower's terms; a similar signing was held the next day for the Soviets in Berlin. Fighting was officially to cease at 12:01 P.M. on May 9. May 8 was declared V.E. (Victory in Europe) Day.[156]

When news of the end of the war in Europe slowly trickled through the camp, it seemed to have little impact on most of Schindler's Jews because they still worried about the heavy presence of Germans in the area. Stella Müller-Madej remembered the heavy rumble of German trucks and armor on the main road just outside the camp. Moreover, there was still heavy fighting nearby as Soviet forces pushed Schörner's army to the west. The camp's SS contingent became increasingly friendly with the prisoners and tried to explain to those who would listen that they had been drafted for guard service and had not harmed anyone. Thomas Keneally said that at noon on May 7, Schindler had Winston Churchill's V.E. day speech piped into the factory over its loud speakers. Churchill did not make any speeches on May 7, though he did make two on May 8, V.E. day. The first was to the gathered crowds in front of the Houses of Parliament, and the second, a longer version of the public speech, was given later that day to the House of Commons. Few of the Schindler Jews understood English, so the speech did not seem to mean much to many of them.[157]

But what did matter was the imminent departure of Oskar and Emilie Schindler. Mietek Pemper said that the Schindler Jews had to convince Oskar to leave and that he did not think the Soviets would hurt him. Oskar, though, told Fritz Lang that he was already familiar with "the methods of the Russians" because he had been one of the last people to leave Kraków amd Mährisch Ostrau before the Red Army took over. He explained that he was also "not keen on being pestered by that club [the Soviets]." But Oskar was also concerned about the Czechs. He said that he had already had a "small foretaste" of the "Czech way of doing things," a reference to his 1938 arrest and imprisonment by Czech authorities, and had no desire to receive "further demonstrations of their kindness."[158]

What happened next is the stuff of film legend. In Steven Spielberg's *Schindler's List,* Oskar walks into Josef Leipold's office as the commandant was listening to one of Winston Churchill's May 8 speeches. By that time, of course, Leipold had been at the front for a week. Regardless, Oskar then supposedly says, "I think it is time the guards came into the factory." From this moment on, just about everything in the film's final scenes is fictional. Once the inmates were gathered on the factory floor, Oskar delivered his farewell speech. This was not the first time they had come together to celebrate something important with Oskar. On New Year's day, the Schindler women had presented Oskar and Emilie with a hand-made steel bouquet and sung a Polish song, *"Sto Lat"* (A Hundred Years):

For a hundred years, for a hundred years,
May he/she live for us.
For a hundred years, for a hundred years,
May he/she live for us.
One more time, one more time, may he/she live
May he/she live (a hundred years).[159]

On April 28, 1945, the prisoners also had a birthday party for Oskar.[160] But the gathering on May 8 was a bittersweet victory celebration combined with a farewell to Oskar and Emilie.

Oskar's real speech, which he wrote beforehand, was transcribed by two stenographers, Mrs. M. Waldmann and Frau Berger. The speech that Oskar actually gave that night and the one in *Schindler's List* were as different as night and day. One of the few things they had in common was the opening line noting the unconditional surrender. In the real speech, Oskar emphasized the tone of humaneness and justice that Field Marshal Sir Bernard Montgomery, who had accepted the surrender of German forces in northern Europe four days earlier, asked to be observed towards the defeated Germans. If there was to be retribution, Oskar stated, it should be done "by those people who will be authorized to do so." In the short speech, Oskar tried to assure the gathered Jews that not all Germans were responsible for their fate. And though he mentioned that they were about to begin searching for their families, he would have been far too sensitive to state, as he did in *Schindler's List,* that in most cases [they would not] find them."[161]

Oskar spent much of the rest of the real speech reminding the Schindler Jews of all that he had done for them during the war. He also thanked Itzhak Stern, Mietek Pemper, J. F. Daubek, and "a few others, who, by fulfilling their task . . . looked death in the eye" and "thought and cared about all." At the end of his talk, Oskar reemphasized the importance of "vigilance and order" and reminded the *Schindlerjuden* again to make "humane and just decisions." He then thanked his German coworkers "for their restless sacrifice for [his] efforts" as well as the current SS contingent, who had been "ordered to serve [there]," for their "extraordinary humanness and correctness." The speech ended with a request for three minutes of silence for those "countless victims" who died during the war's "atrocious years."[162]

Oskar also mentioned in the speech that he would leave Brünnlitz at 12:05 A.M. on May 9. But before he left, the Brünnlitz Jews presented Oskar with a gold ring and a statement. The statement, signed by Itzhak Stern, Abraham Bankier, Leib Salpeter, Dr. Dawid Schlang, Natan Stern, and Dr. Chaim Hilfstein attested that from 1942 onwards, Oskar Schindler had done everything he could "to save the lives of the largest number of Jews possible." The statement added that Schindler "took care of our subsistence and during the entire time in the factory not one person died an unnatural death." It went into detail about the transfer of Oskar's factory to Brünnlitz and stated that because of this they owed their lives "exclusively to Dir. [Director] Schindler's efforts and humane treatment." Bankier, Stern, and the other authors considered the successful transfer from Kraków to Brünnlitz "a unique case in the entire territory of the Reich." The statement also explained in detail Schindler's efforts to save the Jews on the Golleschau transport. The camp's Jewish leaders ended their testimony by asking that those who read it "help Director Schindler in any way," and especially requested that he be allowed "to build up a new existence" because he had sacrificed his wealth to help his Jews in Kraków and Brünnlitz.[163]

The Schindler Jews also gave Oskar a going away present—a solid gold ring which, according to Keneally, was inscribed with the following phrase from the Talmud:

He who saves a single life saves the entire world.[164]

In *Schindler's List,* Itzhak Stern tells Oskar that the inscription, which was in Hebrew on the inside of the ring, read

Whoever saves one life saves the world entire.[165]

The gold for the ring came from Simon Jeret, whom Cantor Mose Taubé described as an "extremely religious and wealthy lumber dealer who sacrificed a gold tooth for Schindler's ring."[166] Keneally said the gold tooth was extracted by Hersch Licht, who had been a dentist in Kraków, though the only dentist in the camp was Dr. Aleksander Schubert. Dr. Moshe Bejski said that Jeret had an entire gold bridge taken out of his mouth for the ring, which Licht made. Dr. Bejski added that "during the hardships which Schindler encountered after the war he lost the ring." When the Israeli judge later asked Oskar what had happened to the ring, Schindler replied, "It went for schnaps." In 1962, Licht made a copy of the ring, which was then "symbolically offered again to Schindler."[167]

Few of the *Schindlerjuden* that I interviewed remembered anything about Oskar's departure. It was certainly nothing as dramatic as depicted in *Schindler's List.* The idea that Oskar collapsed sobbing into Itzhak Stern's arms and bemoaned his failure to save more Jews is preposterous. Oskar was proud of all he had done to save Brünnlitz's Jews and said so in his speech earlier that evening. In fact, given the increasing problems he had in finding food for his camp complex, it is amazing that he continued to take Jews into Brünnlitz when he knew that this would diminish Brünnlitz's tenuous food supply.[168]

Thomas Keneally said that before Oskar left Brünnlitz, two prisoners spent the afternoon taking out the upholstery in the ceiling and door panels of Oskar's Mercedes. When they had finished, they filled them with "small sacks of the *Herr Direktor's* diamonds." As midnight approached, Oskar gave Abraham Bankier the key to the storeroom containing the goods he wanted distributed to the workers. Then, Keneally wrote, Oskar and Emilie put on striped prisoners' uniforms and got in their Mercedes, which was driven by one of the eight Jews who had volunteered to accompany them to the American zone.[169]

If what Keneally wrote was true, it meant that by the end of the war, Oskar Schindler still had a great deal of money left, given the space in a Mercedes' door panels and ceiling. This completely contradicts what Oskar said about his final assets immediately after the war. He claimed that he had to bear all the costs of running Brünnlitz, RM 705,000 ($282,000), which emptied his bank account. Moreover, he listed personal losses of RM 620,000 ($248,000) in his detailed *Lastenausgleich* claim filed after the war. Given the thorough investigations that *Lastenausgleich* officials did of such claims, these figures are probably accurate. Of this amount, Oskar listed a loss of RM 60,000 ($24,000) for the Daubek villa and its belongings, including clothes, a RM 10,000 ($4,000) loss from the three-room apartment in Mährisch Ostrau, and a RM 250,000 ($100,000) loss from the "private capital of the proprietor and his wife, jewels, etc." In another part of his claim, he listed an additional loss of RM 300,000 ($120,000) from a "deposit in [his] favor" in the Deutsche Bank in Zwittau as a result of the blocking of this account on May 8, 1945. This means that counting the funds he spent to operate Brünnlitz from October 1944 until May 1945, Oskar Schindler lost or spent RM 1,325,000 ($530,000) during this period, a vast sum of money in those days. It is hard to imagine that he still had a collection of diamonds so large that it would fill the door and ceiling cavities of a Mercedes.[170]

Emilie totally discounted the idea that the two of them left Brünnlitz with a "fortune in diamonds," though she later admitted that Oskar did have a "huge diamond" hidden in the glove compartment of the Horch that they escaped in.[171] Yet it is still possible that Oskar did escape with some diamonds, though not the amount described by Keneally. Moreover, given the uncertainty of their journey, it is hard to imagine that Oskar would have hidden the last of his wealth in such an obvious place. In all likelihood, Oskar was driving what remained of his wartime valuables, not a Mercedes but his beloved blue Horch.

The Schindler party that left Brünnlitz soon after midnight on May 9, 1945, included a truck driven by *Schindlerjude* Ryszard Rechen. In the cab with Rechen was his future wife, Esther, and Schindler's mistress, Marta. Several other Schindler Jews, including Risha Grehen, Willim Schantz, Paul Degen and several German office workers, including Marta's brother, rode in the back of the truck along with the group's luggage and boxes full of cigarettes, vodka, and other trade goods. In fleeing from the Russians, the Schindler party faced a harrowing journey to the American zone. And if Oskar did leave Brünnlitz with any valuables, they were lost in the desperate effort to reach the American lines.[172]

11.

SCHINDLER IN GERMANY
(1945—1949)

As Steven Spielberg's film *SCHINDLER'S LIST* nears its climax, an impassive Itzhak Stern sits just in front of Brünnlitz's open gate; behind him the camp's Jews lie or sit slumped over like quiet sheep in a pasture. In the distance, Stern sees a soldier coming towards him on a mule. As he draws closer, we see that it is a Soviet army officer. The officer stops just in front of Stern and proclaims loudly, "You have been liberated by the Soviet Army!" At this point, the Schindler Jews sit up in unison, and some stand up. Stern asks the officer, "Have you been to Poland?" The officer responds, "I just came from Poland." Stern then asks, "Are there any Jews left?" And from the crowd, someone asks, "Where should we go?" The officer replies, "Don't go east, that's for sure, they hate you there!" He adds, "I wouldn't go west either if I were you." From the crowd another voice says, "We could use some food." The officer sits up on his mule and then points in the distance. "Isn't there a town over there?" This was Steven Spielberg's version of the liberation of Brünnlitz on May 9, 1945. This scene had little to do with reality.[1]

The Red Army did officially liberate Brünnlitz on May 9, 1945, as part of its occupation of that part of Czechoslovakia, but the first contact the *Schindlerjuden* had with the outside world was with the nearby villagers in the Czech village of Brněnec days earlier. Dr. Aleksander Bieberstein wrote in his memoirs that at 6:00 A.M. on the morning of May 7, five members of the town council in Brněnec approached him to ask whether there were any communicable diseases in the camp. The delegates had ventured into the camp when they realized that its gates were open. Dr. Bieberstein assured them that there were no contractible diseases in Brünnlitz. The delegation was glad to see the inmates were free and that afternoon returned with gifts of meat, milk, and other food. Over the next few weeks, this act of Czech kindness set the standard for relations between Brünnlitz's recently freed Jews and the Czechs living near the camp.[2]

The following day, a young female Czech partisan rode up to the front gate. She became for Henry Wiener the "harbinger of freedom." Formal liberation came the following day before noon, when a lone Soviet soldier rode up on his horse. Each of the Schindler Jews has a different memory of that important moment in the camp's history. Leon Leyson said that Spielberg "missed a bet" when he failed to depict the Russian soldier's first words to the gathered Jews once he realized who they were. He said that they were free and told them to rip the numbers from their prison uniforms. Cantor Moshe Taubé said that the Russian soldier was a Jew who spoke Yiddish. When the inmates learned he was Jewish, "he was mobbed. He was kissed from head to toe."[3]

The moment the inmates learned that the camp was officially liberated, some of them insisted that *Kapo* Willi, Leipold's favorite, be punished for his crimes. With the Soviet soldier presiding, Dawid Schlang, an attorney, helped draw up the charges against Willi. Bernard Goldberg said that some of the inmates wanted to hang Willi without a trial. But others insisted that he be given a trial. Later that day, he was hanged with thin wire from one of the factory's pipes. Needless to say, his death was ghastly. Later, when the prisoners told other Russians that they had executed a Nazi, the Russians asked, "Only one?"[4] But not all the Soviet troops who passed by Brünnlitz were as friendly. Soon after liberation, a gang of drunken Red soldiers entered the camp and began to rape some of the former female prisoners. Drunken rape became a hallmark of the Soviet conquest and occupation of German portions of the Third Reich. The soldiers often did not discriminate between Germans and non-Germans. Estimates are that as they occupied former German territory, the Russians raped 2 million German women. Some were raped many times. This happened to a friend of Bronia Gunz (Betty [Bronia] Groß Gunz), who was raped three times by Soviet soldiers in Brünnlitz. From the perspective of Soviet soldiers, this was their "casual right of conquest."[5]

Once the situation in the camp had stabilized, the Red Army set up a field kitchen to feed the former inmates and imposed a two-week quarantine of the camp. Bernard Goldberg remembered one Jewish officer in the Red army, Misha, who helped the inmates obtain clothes and food. Misha also helped organize a train for many of the inmates back to Kraków. After the war, Goldberg met Misha in Montreal, where the former Soviet officer had married and settled. The quarantine was not effective, and many of the inmates began gingerly to leave the camp to explore the village of Brněnec, which sat just across the main railroad tracks from the camp. Henry Blum (Hersch Blumenfrucht) and his nephew, Hersz Pomeranz, crept out of camp and went to Brněnec, where they met two German soldiers. The two Jews frightened both soldiers, who fled, leaving behind their backpacks. Harry and Hersz opened the packs and found honey inside. Harry told me they ate so much honey that day that they became sick. The only prisoner who immediately fled the camp was Marcel Goldberg, who escaped through a window and disappeared. It is not certain whether this was before or after the execution of *Kapo* Willi.[6]

The most distinctive thing that many Schindler Jews remembered after liberation was the kindness of the Czechs. Cantor Moshe Taubé called the Czechs "angels." He went on, "The goodness of their hearts is indescribable. They didn't have much, but they shared whatever they had with us: food, clothing. They are wonderful, warm people by nature. But the Slovaks were more like the Poles, the majority were hateful."[7] Several days after liberation, Margot Schlesinger ventured out of the camp and across the railroad tracks to the village of Brněnec, where she met a German woman. The woman, who seemed to like Margot, asked her to come live in her apartment. The woman was afraid that the Soviets would put people in her apartment. Margot explained that she had to ask her husband, Chaskel, if it would be all right to move in. She also told the woman that she had a brother-in-law. Margot, like the other Schindler Jews, had the fabric that Schindler had asked be distributed to all inmates after liberation. The German woman told Margot that she could use her sewing machine to make clothes. Margot made herself a skirt and blouse, and said she now felt "like a person again. Like a mensch." She was also surprised by the "wonderful food" that the woman had in her apartment. She excitedly baked a cake to share with her friends in the factory, only to discover that no one could eat it because it was too rich for their weakened digestive systems. But this newfound life ended after a week when Margot asked the woman about the photograph of a man in an SS uniform in her living room. The German housewife told Margot it was her husband. She explained that she had no idea where he was or whether he was ever coming back from the war. Needless to say, Margot quickly left the apartment, never to return.[8]

Each of the inmates reacted differently to news of liberation. Many were cautiously optimistic, but remembered the Soviet warning to be careful because German units were still operating in the area.[9] Most, though, were determined to return to Poland to try to find their families. But first they had to regain their strength and find transport. During this interval, Sol Urbach's close friend and fellow carpenter, Max Blasenstein, presented Sol with a handmade autograph book. The small book had a hand-carved wooden cover with Sol's initials and the date, May 7, 1945, carved on the front. On the back, Blasenstein had carved a picture of a Jewish inmate working in a carpentry shop. During the first days of liberation, Sol had some of his closest friends in Brünnlitz sign the book and write their comments about liberation.

> To remember!!!
> Everything passes, everything in the world.
> Sun ray fading, rivers flow
> Joy ends, and so does unhappiness—
> A moment of happiness will lighten your pain.
> Life goes by—and so ends suffering.
> The memories of good times remain.
> For a good friend.

> After a horrible, difficult German imprisonment.
> On the day we remove the ugly chains.
> I enter my name to a dear friend. 8.V.45

> It is not the one that lives in a palace
> or the one that is rich that is happy,
> but the one that is loved and loves in return.
> In remembrance of the happy moments in the evenings
> separated by a wall. Regina.

> If you forget about me I hope not.
> Because the common long imprisonment
> has bound us up in knots of a great friendship
> for life which you begin anew.

I wish you lots of luck and
above all you should find your close ones and
begin to live once again. Anita [Lampel]. 9.V.45

To remember the worst minutes of our lives and
in testimony of our heartfelt friendship.
Wishing happiness and rays of sunshine for the future. Yosel. 8.V.45

At cross roads when you are off into the world far away and
you will begin to live anew.
Remember dear Sol a friend from behind prison bars.
Wishing you lots of luck and
fulfillment of all your dreams. Rosia L. 10.V.45

If in the future you pick a splendid flower
then pleasantly remember a friend from
our younger years. From our time in
Koncentration Camp Brunlitz. Halina. 8.V.45

I am overjoyed on the day that World War II
came to an end. I can inscribe my name in the diary of my sincere friend
and coworker. Pinek Figowicz. 8.V.45

Life is difficult. Don't succumb.
New rays of sunshine are waking us to start anew. In remembrance of the
first postwar days. Tolek Schenierer. 8.V.45

Have heart and see heart.
As a reminder of our friendship in the concentration camp
I enter my name with love. Rena Ferber (Finder). 8.V.45

When you show this diary to your grandchildren's children,
I hope you will remember me as if in a dream.
To my generous friend from the concentration camp "Schindler Juden."
Olek Allerhand. 11.V.45

On the day that we awaited for a long time that brought such happiness.
Your friend wishes you fulfillment of your dreams.
Remember me sometimes. Genia Wohlfeiler. 9.V.45.[10]

Needless to say, one is struck by the tenderness and hopefulness of most of the farewells and remembrances in Sol Urbach's autograph book.

Most of the Schindler Jews were from the Kraków area and returned there in the months after liberation to try to find their families. Some, such as Abraham Bankier, Itzhak Stern and Mietek Pemper, tried to re-establish their lives there but ultimately fled abroad. Stella Müller-Madej and Niusia (Bronisława) Karakulska (Niusia Horowitz) were able to rebuild their lives in Kraków. What ultimately drove most Schindler Jews from Poland was the rising tide of post war anti-Semitism. Prewar Poland had a Jewish population of almost 3.3 million, of which almost 87 percent would die during the Holocaust. By the summer of 1946, there were 244,000 Jews in Poland. This figure included 86,000 Jews who had somehow managed to survive in Poland as well as 100,000 more who had been repatriated as a result of a Polish-Soviet repatriation agreement.[11]

What the Schindler and other Jews faced when they returned to or surfaced in Poland was a virulent outburst of nation-wide anti-Semitism that saw between 1,500 to 2,000 Jews murdered in Poland between 1944 and 1947. The worst of the violence took place in Kielce in the summer of 1946, when a mob attacked a home for Holocaust survivors. Forty-two Jews were murdered in the Kielce *pogrom* and more than a hundred were injured by the mob. It became apparent to many Holocaust survivors that Poland was no longer a place to try to re-establish a postwar home, particularly after the creation of Israel in 1948. By 1951, fewer than 80,000 Jews lived in Poland.[12] Many had emigrated to Israel, including almost three hundred *Schindlerjuden*.

Lewis Fagen was one of those who experienced Polish anti-Semitism firsthand. Several months after liberation, Lewis was walking towards his parents' apartment in Kraków. A woman stopped him on the street and asked him whether he was Jewish. When he said yes, she told him that "down the street they were beating up Jews." He could hear the mob as it shouted, "Kill the Jews!" A few minutes later, four policemen and a civilian appeared at his door and wanted to know who had been shooting a gun out of the apartment's window. Lewis told them that the family did not have a gun. The Feigenbaums (Fagens) were then taken into the street where they were surrounded by a screaming mob shouting, "Kill the Jews! Beat the Jews!" Lewis said that he was convinced the mob intended to lynch them. At that moment, he saw a militiaman and told him that he was the friend of an important militia official. The militia man told the police officers to protect the Feigenbaums. In the meantime, someone in the crowd shouted that they had "caught a Jew on the next block," and left. What Lewis Fagen witnessed was the beginning of the August 11, 1945, *pogrom* in Kraków that saw rioting anti-Semites initiate a mass assault on the city's Jews that resulted in many injuries and deaths as well as attacks against Jewish institutions and homes. The Polish army had to be called in to put down the anti-Jewish riots. The *pogroms* continued throughout Poland for several more years until the government stepped in and tried to end them.[13]

Stella Müller-Madej's family stayed in Kraków because of her father's deep love for Poland. Though they certainly experienced Poland's new wave of anti-Semitism firsthand, Stella also remembered the kindness of Poles after their return to Kraków. Stella, her brother, Adam, and their parents, Stella and Zygmunt, arrived in Kraków after a long journey in open coal trucks to Brno (Brün), where they boarded a train for Kraków. Each of the Müllers carried documents from the Brněnec city council that stated they had been political prisoners in the local Groß Rosen sub-camp and were "entitled to transportation from Brněnec to Kraków." The travel document asked that "all official bodies render any necessary help."[14]

Several days later, Stella and her family arrived at the Kraków-Płaszów train station, where they caught a tram to where they thought some of their family members might still be living. After they boarded the tram, the conductor wanted to know whether they had tickets. Stella's father, Zygmunt, explained that they were returning home from a concentration camp and had no money. The conductor responded, "No money for tickets, and as soon as they get off they buy a bottle of vodka." The Müllers were filthy and wearing ragged clothes. It was Pentecost, and the other passengers on the tram were dressed in their Sunday best. As a tear ran down Zygmunt's face, an elegantly dressed man stood up and told the conductor: "You animal. How dare you! Look at these people. Haven't you learned anything from the war?" He then turned to the Müllers: "With your permission, I will pay."[15]

The kind Polish gentleman then suggested that the family share a cab with him. He later told them that he had been in the Warsaw Uprising of 1944 and had lost his family in the war. As the cab neared the center of the city, he asked the driver to stop in front of a restaurant, where he bought the Müllers a meal. When they reached the house where Stella's family had once lived, they found it destroyed. Fortunately, neighbors had their new address and the Polish gentleman insisted on taking them there by cab. To everyone's delight, Stella's grandmother and other relatives were at their new home on Kolberg Street. After a wonderful doorstep reunion, Zygmunt went back to the cab to thank the Polish gentleman. But he had already left.[16]

Niusia (Bronisława) Horowitz Karakulska also returned to Kraków after the war and rebuilt her life there. Niusia was fortunate that there were eleven members of her family on "Schindler's List," though others died in the Holocaust. In addition, she was also closely related to the Rosner family. Niusia is best known as the young Jewish girl that Oskar Schindler kissed at his birthday party in the film *Schindler's List*. In reality, Niusia presented Oskar with a birthday cake at his party on April 28, 1945, but never kissed him. Steven Spielberg combined this occasion with another incident that took place earlier to create the birthday party scene for his film. Today, Niusia is a hairdresser at the Salon Kosmetyczny in the Hotel Forum in Kraków.[17]

One of the most mysterious figures to survive the war was Marcel Goldberg. It became apparent early in my research that Goldberg was an important figure in the Schindler story. And though I was in time able to clarify the important role he played in helping create the famous "Schindler's List," I could find no one who knew anything about what happened to him after the war. Dr. Moshe Bejski, certainly one of the most respected specialists on the Schindler story and a close friend of Oskar's after the war, told me that he had heard that Goldberg had fled to South America and had died soon thereafter. By the time that I left for Argentina in May 2001 to interview Emilie Schindler, I had pretty much concluded that the postwar fate of Marcel Goldberg would simply be one of the book's mysteries. Fortunately, Francisco Wichter was able to change all that. And with the story of Bronia Gunz's accidental sighting of Goldberg in Curaçao, I have been able to piece together a modest portrait of one of the most despised figures in the Schindler story.

When I first mentioned Goldberg to Francisco Wichter, he immediately knew who he was. But there was also someone else who knew more about him, though this source chose to remain anonymous. Francisco and I spent a lot of time together in Buenos Aires, and after each of our discussions he would call his friend for further information about Goldberg. After the war, Goldberg arrived in Argentina with his two sisters and his wartime gains. He settled about eighty miles outside Buenos Aires. He evidently kept his own name and became a builder. Later, he also owned a factory that employed about 120 people. His wife helped run the factory. According to Adolfo Smolarz, who helped Bronia Gunz track down Goldberg in Argentina, Goldberg was "loved" by his workers because he paid them a "very good salary."[18]

Bronia Gunz saw Goldberg and his wife in a linen shop one day in Curaçao, an island in the Netherlands Antilles. He was casually leaning on a counter while his wife looked at linens. Stunned, Betty did not know what to do. If she told her husband, Roman, she was certain he would kill him! Betty pulled Roman out of the shop as a friend, who was shopping with her, wondered what was going on. As she looked back into the shop, she saw that Goldberg's face had turned blood red. He must, she thought, "have been very grateful" that she had not confronted him. Betty realized almost immediately that she had made a mistake by not confronting Goldberg. For days she could not eat or sleep because of the guilt. Several months later, she went on a business trip with Roman to Argentina and stayed with the Smolarzs, the couple who had vacationed with them in Curaçao. After she told them about seeing Goldberg, Adolfo Smolarz told her she had been wrong not to confront Goldberg.[19]

But Adolfo decided he was going to do something. He informed Argentine Jewish organizations about Goldberg and reported his crimes to the Argentine authorities. He told Bronia to gather as many signatures as she could on a document that detailed Goldberg's crimes during the Holocaust. Adolfo took the document, which had the signatures of sixty-five Schindler Jews on it, to the authorities, who told him: "He is an Argentine citizen. He gives bread and butter to one hundred families. His behavior is excellent. We don't give up a person like that!" Later, Bronia heard that Goldberg had suffered a heart attack and died. From her perspective, they "should have cut him up in little pieces! Hung him! Most of the *Kapos* ran to Germany, and better stay there."[20]

But the story of Marcel Goldberg does not end there. Goldberg died in 1975 or 1976 and was buried in the vast Cemetario de Tablada run by the Asociación Mutual Israelita Argentina (AMIA; Israeli Mutual Association of Argentina) in the suburbs of Buenos Aires. After his death, Goldberg's family paid AMIA $100,000 Argentine to have him buried in one the cemetery's most prominent places near its Holocaust memorial. Francisco Wichter's anonymous friend was at the cemetery on the day Goldberg was buried and was struck by the presence of the many Argentine military officers at his graveside, the implication being that Goldberg had strong connections with Argentina's military dictatorship. According to Wichter's anonymous source, about a month later, an American Holocaust survivor, presumably a Schindler Jew, was walking through the cemetery and saw Goldberg's headstone. According to Francisco, this person complained so strongly about Goldberg's burial in such a prominent place in the cemetery that AMIA returned the $100,000 Argentine to Goldberg's family and reburied him in the section of the cemetery reserved for Jewish *"rufianes"*—pimps and prostitutes. More than likely, his disinterment and reburial was somehow linked to the efforts of Bronia Gunz and Adolfo Smolarz to bring charges against Goldberg.[21]

One afternoon, Adriana Brodsky, my research assistant, and I decided to try to find Goldberg's grave to see whether we could determine his exact date of death. The AMIA cemetery is huge, though with the help of several of the caretakers we were able to find the small, walled off *"rufianes"* section next to a public bathroom. Though some of the graves were unmarked, others had broken headstones. But we could not find the name of Marcel Goldberg on any of them. We then went to the cemetery office to ask whether they had a record of Goldberg or of a disinterment in 1975 or 1976. They said that disinterments were extremely rare because they violated Jewish law and they had no record of one during those two years. They added that though their records were quite complete, it was possible that a disinterment could have taken place and not been recorded. They also had no information about the burial of a Marcel Goldberg in the *"rufianes"* section of the cemetery. There are scores of Goldbergs in the Buenos Aires area, both in Jewish community records and in the local telephone book. Presumably some of them are related to Marcel Goldberg and know the whereabouts of his final resting place.

The Escape of Oskar and Emilie Schindler

More than likely, Oskar and Emilie Schindler never knew that Marcel Goldberg had settled near them in the suburbs of Buenos Aires. Francisco Wichter told me, for example, that he did not know that the Schindlers had lived there and did not meet Emilie until 1994. On the other hand, Francisco and the Schindlers both came to Argentina with the help of the Joint, Wichter in 1947 and the Schindlers two years later. But their paths never crossed; indeed, Oskar and Emilie would never have imagined four years earlier that they would wind up in Argentina. And one suspects that there were moments after they left Brünnlitz on May 9, 1945, when they doubted they would even survive their flight to the American zone.

Oskar discussed their harrowing journey in his 1951 letter to Fritz Lang, and Emilie spends quite a bit of time on it in her memoirs, *Where Light and Shadow Meet*. Unfortunately, parts of her account are at odds with her husband's recollections as well as Richard Rechen's. Esther Rechen, the wife of Richard (Ryszard) Rechen, the driver of the truck that accompanied the Schindler party, shared her memories with me. Kurt Klein, who would be responsible for insuring that the Schindler party reached the American zone safely, gave me a letter that Richard Rechen sent him in 1987 about the Schindlers' odyssey. Finally, Dr. Marjorie Zerin, a prominent journalist, sent me the notes of the interview she did with Emilie Schindler, Kurt Klein, and Marta (Eva "Marta" Kisza (Kisch) Scheuer) in 1994. These sources provide a confusing picture of what the Schindlers and others in their party went through before they reached the American lines.

According to Oskar, he and Emilie left with seven Jewish workers who wanted to find relatives in France or Switzerland. In addition, Marta, Schindler's mistress, and her brother, were with the rest of the Schindler party in the truck. Richard drove the truck and Esther and Marta rode with him in the cab. Oskar drove the two-seated Horch with Emilie by his side. Emilie said that ten German soldiers rode on the roof or the running boards of the Horch until the Soviets took it from them. As they moved westward, they were slowed down by "clogged roads" and the truck, which had trouble keeping up with the Horch. The Schindler convoy was stopped by Soviet troops once it reached the village of Havlíčův Brod (Deutsch Brod), which is about 180 miles west of Brněnec. This was about 50 miles south of Pardubice, where Field Marshal Ferdinand Schörner had commanded the last major pocket of German resistance to the Allies. Five days before Schindler's departure, General Dwight David Eisenhower had ordered that Allied forces halt at a line running between Karlovy Vary (Karlsbad), Plzeň (Pilsen), and Česky Budějovice (Budweis), which allowed the Soviets to take over most of Czechoslovakia. The region between the Eisenhower line in Czechoslovakia and Brünnlitz was extremely unstable and explains why the Schindler party had such difficulty reaching the American zone.[22]

Oskar was shocked that the Russians had already taken Havlíčův Brod. At the first checkpoint into the city, a Russian guard took their watches. When they reached the center of Havlíčův Brod, the Soviets took everything else from them, including the Horch. Inside was a large diamond that Emilie had discovered in the glove compartment soon after they left Brünnlitz and had then hidden under her seat. In the confusion, Oskar and Emilie lost contact with Richard Rechen and the other Jews in the truck. What followed on the night of May 9 was, according to Oskar "increasing sadism, rapes, and shootings" by the drunken Russian soldiers in the village. Emilie struggled to maintain her composure and Oskar seemed to be "in a trance."[23]

That night, Emilie wrote, she and Oskar met several people they had known before or during the war. The first person was "Annelie," who, Emilie said, had been Oskar's lover when he worked for Abwehr. This was probably Gritt Schwarzer, who played a key role in recruiting Oskar for Abwehr and carried on a three-year relationship with him.[24] Next to "Annelie" was another Sudeten German family with two children also named Schindler. Bewildered, Oskar and Emilie were not certain what to do in the midst of the growing chaos that night. Suddenly, Emilie heard someone call her name. It was a Russian cook who had once worked for her at Brünnlitz. The cook arranged for Oskar and Emilie to sleep in a truck that night. According to Emilie, Oskar befriended several Russian soldiers and drank with them through the night. This was Oskar's way of protecting Emilie from the Russians. But he was unable to protect one of the female Schindler Jews riding in the truck with Richard Rechen. Russian soldiers had taken her and evidently gang-raped her; when she showed up in Prague several months later, she was pregnant. The Russians had also tried to take Esther, but Marta was somehow able to hide her. Unknown to Oskar and Emilie, the Czech Red Cross had hidden the *Schindlerjuden* in the local jail for the night.[25]

The next morning, the Soviets began to separate the Germans into Sudeten, Austrian, and German groupings. Emilie said that Oskar knew that if he was put with the other Sudeten Germans, the two of them would spend months in a concentration camp. Consequently, they put on the concentration camp uniforms that Oskar had hidden in the truck and threw all their identification papers away. They got new travel documents from one of the Czech underground groups operating in the area. Oskar took these new documents to the Czech Red Cross in Havlíčův Brod, which issued the Schindlers new travel documents.[26] While they were in the Red Cross tent, a group of Czech soldiers began searching the contents of everyone's bags and found a German Luger in the handbag of one of the other Czech Germans in the tent, who was also named Schindler. Despite her husband's pleas, the Czech soldiers took the woman outside and shot her in the head.[27]

In the midst of the confusion, Oskar and Emilie worried about the rest of their party. Frantically, they began to search for them. Emilie said that at one point Oskar "almost went crazy, almost beserk" when he could not find them. Later, a Czech soldier approached them and inquired whether they were looking for the their companions. The Schindler Jews had told Czech authorities what the Schindlers had done for them during the war. But before they got very far, Emilie heard Oskar cry out, "They're going to shoot me, they're going to shoot me." After Emilie calmed Oskar down, he told her that he had overheard two Russian soldiers "say that they were looking for a certain Schindler of Mährisch Ostrau who had been with the Counterintelligence Service [Abwehr]." At this moment, a stranger walked up to Oskar and Emilie and told them that if they wanted to stay alive, they should not speak German in front of strangers.[28]

Oskar and Emilie soon found Richard Rechen, Marta, and the other Schindler Jews. The Red Cross put them up in a war-damaged hotel in Havlíčův Brod once used by traveling salesmen. Emilie, Gritt, Marta, and a new arrival, Emilie's niece, Traude, stayed in one wing of the hotel and the men stayed in the hotel's dining room. Emilie said that the party stayed in Havlíčův Brod for three days until the Czech Red Cross put them on a train bound for Plzeň (Pilsen), which would bring them to the edge of the American zone. The Red Cross advised Oskar not to venture outside of the hotel until the train left. By this time, the Schindlers had no goal in mind except to reach the American zone. However, as Richard Rechen had relatives in Switzerland, they decided to follow him there. Emilie's memoirs then state that they boarded a train for Plzeň on the night of May 11. After they got underway, Oskar had a nightmare and jumped up and pulled the the train's emergency cord. When the conductor chastised Oskar for his deed, Oskar explained that he had dreamed the train was hurtling down a steep grade and was about to crash. Emilie claimed that soon after this incident, the Schindler group had to change trains to go on to Plzeň. As they traveled westward, they were haunted by the presence of Russian soldiers in the area.[29]

Parts of Emilie's account of their escape, particularly the journey by train to Plzeň, are very different from the accounts by Oskar, Richard Rechen, and Kurt Klein. Oskar said nothing about a train trip but says that after the group left Havlíčův Brod they "moved along the road of the Bohemian Forest," where SS units were struggling "to beat their way to the Americans."[30] Richard Rechen never mentioned stopping in Havlíčův Brod but did say that they lost the truck somewhere near České Budějovice, where they later boarded a train. Kurt told me that he met the Schindler party just outside the village of Lenora, which is only about thirty miles from České Budějovice and more than seventy-five miles southeast of Plzeň. Emilie wrote her memoirs when she was in her mid-eighties, so it is easy to understand why she got some of the details wrong about their escape. The accounts by Oskar, Reichard Rechen, and Kurt Klein are more believable because an escape route through Céské Budějovice would have been much safer, particularly as Prague, a transit point for all trains traveling westward to Plzeň, had been under siege just days before.[31]

As the train neared the Czech-German border, it stopped and the conductor told everyone that it was too dangerous to go any further because SS

units were still operating in the area. At dawn on May 12, everyone was ordered out of the cars. Frustrated, the Schindler party began walking toward
what they hoped were the American lines. Richard Rechen said that the
group spent the next two hours "almost running" in their efforts to reach
the Americans. At one point they came across a soldier making eggs for
breakfast. They asked him to let them go through the checkpoint. He refused, but said they could go around to the next checkpoint. They managed
to get through this checkpoint and made their way to a small village, which
we now know was Lenora. The group, still dressed in their concentration
camp uniforms, was dirty and hungry. They tried to hitch a ride on a local
cart but did not have any money to pay the driver, so they continued walking. They were stopped again by American soldiers who then argued about
what to do with them. Richard Rechen said the Americans wanted to send
the Schindler group to a P.O.W. camp. At this point, an American lieutenant
arrived in a Jeep. He asked the sergeant, "What's wrong?" The sergeant
replied, "I don't know, they are some funny people refusing to go to the
camp." At this point, Richard Rechen spoke up and said, "Das wir sind
Juden aus einem K.Z." (We are Jews from a concentration camp). For a
moment, the lieutenant was speechless, but then said, "I have no right to let
you in but I'll go and try to settle this matter. Don't be afraid, I am a Jew
and my name is Kurt Klein." Unknown to the Schindlers, Klein was under
strict orders not to let any German soldiers, some of whom had put on
striped concentration camp uniforms to escape capture, into American-held
territory. Yet twenty minutes later, Lt. Kurt Klein, himself a German Jew
who had fled to the United States to escape Nazi persecution and had lost
his parents in the Holocaust, returned with a pass that allowed everyone in
the Oskar Schindler group to enter the American zone.[32]

I got to know Kurt Klein soon after I began my work on this book and
was struck by his kind, humble demeanor. Perhaps Sara J. Bloomfeld, the
director of the United States Holocaust Memorial Museum in Washington, D.C., best captured the special character of this man when she wrote,
after his death on April 19, 2002, that "Kurt Klein was a remarkable person of exceptional character. Beneath his warm and gentle demeanor was
a deeply humane man whose passion and compassion touched many
lives."[33] At the time he encountered the Schindler party, Kurt was part of
several two-man surrender specialist teams operating in western Czechoslovakia. These teams came from the Second Regiment of the Fifth U.S.
Infantry Division and were part of General George Patton's Third Army.
Kurt's sensitivity to the plight of the Jews in the Schindler group was not

isolated. Several days earlier he had begun to help the remnants of a group of female Jewish prisoners from Grünberg, a subcamp of Groß Rosen. Kurt and his team had been operating near Volary, a town seven miles from Lenora, when he came across the 120 Jewish women who had survived a forced march that began with 2,000. Over the next few months, Kurt became enamored with one of the survivors, whom he met in Volary, a young Jewish woman from Bielitz, Poland, Gerda Weissmann. A year later, they would marry in Paris.[34]

Kurt always downplayed the role he played in admitting the Schindler party into the American zone. Yet he told me that if he had not given the Schindlers and the others a pass to enter the zone, Oskar, Emilie, Traude, Marta, and her brother would have been separated from the Jews in the group and put in a special camp for Germans.[35] Kurt's job in the U.S. Army was "to interrogate and segregate Germans caught fleeing from the Russian and Czech guns."[36] If this had happened, it is uncertain what would have happened to Oskar and the Germans in his group. If the Soviets were looking for Oskar, and the Americans had turned him over to them, then he could have faced imprisonment or execution. When I interviewed Kurt, I asked him whether Oskar's height and striking looks had made him stand out from the other members of the group. Kurt replied that neither Oskar nor Emilie stood out, though several other members of the Schindler group did. He did, however, notice that all the members of the group were in much better shape than the Jewish women he had encountered several days earlier in Volary. After the war, Richard Rechen tried to find Kurt, and finally located him in Scottsdale, Arizona. They corresponded and the Rechens later visited the Kleins in the United States. After *Schindler's List* came out, Kurt met with Emilie and Marta in Los Angeles.[37]

After Kurt gave Oskar and the nine other members of his group their temporary travel permit, he took them to an empty house in Lenora. An American Jewish military chaplain came by to offer the group his help and over the next few days Jewish soldiers dropped in to talk to the Schindler party. They explained that they wanted to meet the first concentration camp survivors to enter the American zone. Most left with tears in their eyes after they learned what the *Schindlerjuden* had gone through during the war.[38] What Emilie remembered most was the "wonderful soup," the first thing they had eaten in three days.[39] But Oskar, Emilie, and the others were still not completely safe because the area they were in on the Czech-German border was about to be turned over to the Soviets. Consequently, the Jewish chaplain arranged to have a small bus and driver take Oskar and the others in his party to Passau, in the official American zone, where they were put in a displaced persons (DP) camp, which was only about sixty miles from Lenora. He also advised Oskar and Emilie to continue wearing their concentration camp uniforms.[40]

In Passau, another American Jewish officer, Colonel Cohen, helped them arrange train passage for Switzerland. When they reached Konstanz on the German-Swiss border, they ran into more difficulties trying to cross over to Kreuzlingen on the Swiss side. Frustrated by stubborn Swiss border guards, Oskar decided to slip through the "wire grill" that ran along the border; the next day he used wire cutters to cut his way into Switzerland when the guards changed at noon. In the meantime, two more people had joined the Schindler group. Oskar cut his way through the fence and then waited for everyone else in his group to come out of hiding and sneak through. One of the Jews who had joined the Schindlers before the "break-in" was a nephew of Helena Rubinstein, who insisted on shaving before he crossed the frontier "to please his aunt."[41]

Unfortunately, it took a half an hour for everyone to cross through the fence and by this time the new Swiss border guard contingent had taken up its posts and spotted the Schindler group trying to cross into Switzerland. About two thirds of a mile inside Switzerland, Oskar, Emilie, and seven other members of their party were stopped by Swiss customs officials and taken to the border customs house, where they were harassed by a Swiss official "who gesticulated wildly with his pistol." Five other members of the Schindler party had managed to escape after they crawled through the fence and were met by relatives and friends who took them away in cars. Oskar said the customs official was angry because the group had "disturbed his siesta" and was insulted by Oskar's loud, contagious laugh. Oskar said he was laughing at the official, a "Bourgeois figure" with a "face as red as a lobster." Oskar's outburst seemed to undermine the custom official's authority and he soon put his gun away. But he remained angry and snapped, "You bunch of Polish Jews, we have nothing to eat ourselves." He then turned all nine over to the French occupation forces operating just across the frontier in Germany.[42]

According to Oskar, the French detained those remaining in the Schindler party for two weeks in Konstanz. And when he had explained their situation to the French officials, he wrote Lang, they were put up in a local hotel and "given preferential treatment." In fact, he claimed, the day after they were turned over to the French by the Swiss, they were guests "at a feast of the local [French] commander for his officers."[43] In reality, the situation was much worse and Oskar remained in French custody for over three weeks. When the French realized that Schindler was a former Nazi Party member and factory owner they initiated an investigation into his background. What saved him were the detailed statements provided by three of the Schindler Jews still with him: Leopold Degen, Eduard Heuberger, and Adolf Grünhalt. Needless to say, their statements to the French police in Konstanz were detailed and profuse in their praise of Oskar and Emilie Schindler. At the end of his statement, Degen wrote: "[The] Brünnlitz camp was the one and only concentration camp in the entire Reich where not one case of unnatural death occurred. Today, men and women from Brünnlitz enjoy their new lives as free, proud Schindler-Juden.'"[44] These reports ultimately reached Captain Robert Monheit, a Jewish chaplain in the French army, who wrote in an August 27, 1945, memo that he had received "unanimous testimonies saying that Mr. Oskar SCHINDLER, director of a factory at KRAKOW, has rendered inestimable services to the allied cause." Captain Monheit went on to say that Schindler had protected and saved the lives of "1,200 persons during the war, in spite of great difficulties." His memo was meant as a notification "to Allied civilian and military authorities, that it may be examined with kindness." He finished by noting that Schindler was accompanied by his wife, Emilie, and "his relative, Miss Eva Kisza."[45]

During the summer of 1945, the five remaining *Schindlerjuden* with Oskar and Emilie obtained travel permits and left Germany; Oskar, Emilie, Traude, and Marta remained in Konstantz.[46] Oskar told Fritz Lang that he lived in "a state of apathy" that summer but finally decided to move to the American zone in Bavaria because conditions in the French sector "were rather bad." He also thought he would have better contacts abroad in Bavaria. But he did not completely waste his summer in the French zone. At the urging of a local rabbi, Oskar wrote the detailed financial report about his efforts to save Jews in Kraków and Brünnlitz. He was well aware of the denazification program underway in the American zone and the need to document his aid to Jews during the war.[47]

And though he never mentioned it, if he moved to Bavaria, he would be much closer to the Sudeten part of Czechoslovakia, where he hoped to rebuild his life as an industrialist making pots and pans for a war-torn Europe. But it did not take Emilie and Oskar long to realize that they could never return to Czechoslovakia.[48] In the midst of the collapse of Nazi power in the Protectorate of Bohemia and Moravia (Böhren und Mähren), Sudeten Germans fled en masse in the face of the Soviet onslaught. Czech troops occupied the former Sudetenland and inexperienced administrators tried to restore order in the former Nazi territory. Almost immediately, some Czechs decided to take revenge on the former Sudeten Germans who unwisely chose to remain behind in a restored Czechoslovakia. The new National Front government of Edvard Beneš issued harsh regulations in the summer of 1945 that declared all members of the Nazi party, the SS, Konrad Henlein's Sudeten German Party *(Sudetendeutsche Partei),* and its Voluntary Defense Service *(Freiwilliger Schutzdienst)* to be criminals. In addition, anyone who "had supported the Nazi regime, or consented to or defended the Nazi government, was to be prosecuted" by special Extraordinary People's Courts. Czech Germans who had acquired Reich German citizenship would automatically lose their Czechoslovak citizenship. The only Germans who could apply for the restoration of their Czechoslovak citizenship were those who could prove that they had "remained loyal to the Czechoslovak Republic," had "never committed any offense against the Czech or Slovak people," and had either "participated actively in the struggle against Nazism or suffered under Nazi terror."[49]

Needless to say, Oskar's work for Abwehr before World War II, and Emilie's support of his efforts, insured that they could never return to their former homeland or acquire Czechoslovak citizenship. More important, because of his Abwehr efforts to help destroy the Czechoslovak Republic between 1936 and 1938 and his membership in the Nazi Party, Oskar Schindler was now considered a war criminal in Czechoslovakia. And neither time nor Steven Spielberg's film have in any way reduced Czech antipathy towards Oskar Schindler. Czech historian Jitka Gruntová has written two scathing books on Schindler, *Oskar Schindler: Legenda a Fakta* and *Legendy a fakta o Oskar Schindlerovi,* that deal with his war criminality; and in 2002, the Regional Assembly of Eastern Pardubice, which includes Schindler's hometown of Svitavy, voted to exclude him from its list of outstanding personalities. The regional assembly's advisory council said that Schindler had been a member of the Nazi Party and was simply "too controversial" to be included on the list of famed Eastern Pardubicians. No doubt their decision was affected by Gruntová's works.[50]

And if they had any doubts about Czechoslovak intentions when they moved to Bavaria in the fall of 1945, they were dispelled over the next year as they watched a wave of German expulsions from Czechoslovakia. Between May and July 1945, for example, an estimated 800,000 Germans were forced from their homes by the Czech military or local revolutionary committees. These "wildcat expulsions" involved "mob action, lynchings, rapes" and large-scale "mistreatment." The most brutal of these expulsions took place in Brno (Brünn), where over 20,000 Germans were forced to try to walk to Vienna. When they were denied entry into Austria, they had to live in the open and many died of disease or malnutrition. To the north in Krásně Březno, between 1,000 to 2,700 Germans were murdered by a Czech mob. In the fall of 1945, the Allies approved the expulsion of 2,500,000 Germans from Czechoslovakia to Germany. Under this plan, the Czechoslovaks would be permitted to ship 1,750,000 Germans to the American zone and 750,000 to the Soviet zone. During the next eighteen months, the Czechoslovakian government would send 1,334,856 Germans to the American zone in Germany and 636,482 to the Soviet zone. Half the Czech Germans wound up in Bavaria; the other half were almost evenly distributed in the German states of Greater Hessen and Württemberg-Baden.[51]

But the expulsion of the Czech Germans not only meant that Oskar and Emilie could never return to Czechoslovakia. They would also find themselves increasingly resented and unwelcome in Bavaria, where many of the expelled Czech Germans were forced to settle. And if this was not bad enough, Oskar also had to face the possibility of denazification when he reached Bavaria. The denazification of Germany was an Allied policy aimed at bringing to justice all levels of the former Nazi leadership to insure that they played no significant role in its reconstruction. But as one U.S. Army intelligence officer noted just a month after the war ended, "The question who is a Nazi is often a dark riddle." But, he added, "The question what is a Nazi is also not easy to answer."[52] The question of who was a Nazi plagued denazification efforts in Germany during the three-year Allied effort to root out and punish the former Nazi leadership. Initially, the Allies agreed that anyone who had joined the Nazi Party after Hitler's accession to power and held some type of Party leadership role during the Hitler years was subject to denazification. The Allies were aided by the discovery of 12 million Party cards and photographs in Munich, which gave them some idea about the party's multilevel leadership. But the Allies had to differentiate between those Party members who actively embraced and engaged in Nazi Party activities and those who had joined, particularly after 1937, because of employment reasons. By the end of 1945, the Allies required any German who was employed or had business in occupied Germany to fill out a 131-question *Fragebogen* (questionnaire), which was used to determine the extent of one's relationship with the Nazi Party. What became most important in evaluating about 50 percent of the 1.4 million *Fragebogen* filled out by March 1946 was one's actions as a Party member, not mere membership itself. This was particularly true in the American zone.[53]

Almost immediately, Allied efforts to remove prominent Nazis from important positions in business and government began to cause problems. General George Patton, the Military Governor of Bavaria, was quite public in his criticisms of denazification. On August 11, 1945, he wrote General Dwight David Eisenhower, the Supreme Commander of Allied Forces in Europe, that "it is no more possible for a man to be a civil servant in Germany and not to have paid lip service to nazism than it is for a man to be a postmaster in America and not to have paid lip service to the Democratic Party or Republican Party when it is in power." Eisenhower reminded the controversial Patton that the "obliteration of nazism was a major U.S. war aim" and that the guidelines he was to follow were dictated by the Joint Chiefs of Staff.[54]

By the spring of 1946, the Allies had to shift responsibility for denazification to German authorities. Germany's new provincial assemblies *(Länderrat)* passed new Laws for Liberation that laid out five categories of Germans for denazification consideration: major offenders, offenders, lesser offenders, followers, and nonoffenders. All Nazi Party members were minimally considered followers. In time, 13 million Germans filled out the *Fragebogen* and 3 million were selected for appearances before denazification courts. How did these changing regulations affect Oskar Schindler? Oskar had applied for Nazi Party membership on November 1, 1938, about a month after the Sudetenland became a formal part of the Third Reich. And though his Nazi Party card is devoid of information about his Party activities, he was still hypothetically vulnerable to investigation and possible formal denazification proceedings because of his work for Abwehr and his role as an industrialist. But the key to determining one's potential criminality was Party leadership, and as there was nothing in his file to indicate significant leadership in the Nazi Party from 1938 to 1945, he probably had little to worry about. But at the time he was planning to move to Bavaria, the Americans were aggressively interning and interrogating tens of thousands of former Party members. Consequently, to deal with the possibility that he would be investigated as a former Nazi Party member, Oskar began to gather as many affidavits as he could from Schindler Jews to document what could be perceived as anti-Nazi activity. These documents would serve several purposes. They would underscore his impressive efforts to save more than a thousand of his Jewish workers and help open doors of opportunity for him because of this track record of anti-Nazi activity. Finally, Oskar would use these documents to try to recover professionally and economically.[55]

The first of these documents, of course, was the May 8, 1945, statement from Itzhak Stern, Abraham Bankier, and other prominent Schindler Jews attesting to his efforts to save his Jewish workers in Kraków and Brünnlitz. He also had a copy of the June 9, 1945, French interrogation reports of three of the Schindler Jews traveling with Oskar, as well as Captain Monheit's note to Allied authorities about these statements. Oskar prepared his detailed financial report in July 1945, and, on September 3, French authorities issued him a document based on Captain Monheit's recommendation that was addressed to the United Nations Relief and Rehabilitation Administration (UNRRA), which was responsible for aiding refugees and displaced persons. Later that month, *Schindlerjude* Leib Salpeter, now the head of the Zionist Democratic Union *(Zjednoczenie Sionistów-Demokratow)* in Kraków, sent a letter to "all Zionist Organizations and Societies" asking for "support to O. Schindler and his wife wherever they are in need." In the fall of 1946, Salpeter would send Oskar a more detailed account of his wartime efforts. This letter of support was signed by Salpeter and a representative of the Mizrachi Tora Waawoda in Kraków. On October 12, 1945, Oskar received another letter of support from twenty-four *Schindlerjuden* interned in a DP camp in Hert, Austria.[56]

There is no question that the letters helped keep Oskar from being forced to undergo one of the more serious denazification proceedings, and they also possibly led to an offer from the Bavarian government of a Privy Councillorship after he inquired about leasing a closed metal factory. Oskar told Fritz Lang that he turned down the government offer because it would condemn him to "a new idleness, even if it had a title."[57] The letters also helped him get a job in 1947 as an importer of metal ware and machines in the Munich office of the Jewish Agency for Palestine. However, in 1948, the Jewish Agency closed its office in Munich and Oskar was out of a job. Frustrated with what he later described as his idle, unproductive years in Germany, he began to consider emigration. Herbert Steinhouse, a Canadian journalist who befriended Schindler in the late 1940s before his emigration to Argentina, described Oskar as "stifled, bored, humiliated, desperate, worried—and obliged to live again as a virtual prisoner of Emilie, in too small and seedy a place. Oskar was too spoiled a high-flyer, and too intelligent and energetic a man to suffer poverty, but at the time had had little else but his charm to trade."[58]

Life in Regensburg, Germany: 1945–1949

But it was not just frustration over the lack of available employment that depressed Oskar and Emilie. After they arrived in Bavaria in the fall of 1945, Oskar and Emilie settled in Regensburg, a beautiful medieval Bavarian city on the Danube that was relatively untouched by the war. They ultimately moved into an apartment at 25 Nürnbergstraße, which remained their official residence until they left for Argentina in 1949. However, according to Herbert Steinhouse, sometime after they arrived in Regensburg, Oskar, Emilie, and many of their self-styled "Jewish bodyguards" moved into "bleak flats near the more interesting black markets of the Munich Zentrum," which is an hour south of Regensburg. They maintained their official addresses in Regensburg, Steinhouse explained, to get Joint and UNRRA rations from the nearby Regensburg DP camp.

But life in Regensburg was hard for the Schindlers. Emilie wrote in her memoirs that the Regensburgers went out of their way to let them know that they were unwelcome. She sensed that the people of Regensburg considered the Sudeten Germans "second-class Germans." She recalled one episode in which someone dumped a pail of "foul-smelling liquid" on her while she was walking down the street. She was rebuffed again and again when she tried to purchase or trade scarce goods in the city's shops and markets; in fact, the only shops willing to do business with her were those owned by Jews. Finally, Emilie decided to go to a vineyard in the countryside and buy grapes to sell on the black market. After a long, crowded train ride, she approached a vineyard owner and asked whether she could buy some grapes. He told her that his grapes left his vineyard only as wine. And from the window of his nearby home, his wife cried out, "Hans, they are not Germans, don't sell them wine either." Frustrated, that night, Emilie stole two bags of grapes from the irate farmer and his wife. But by the time she got back to Regensburg, most of the grapes had turned to raisins.[59]

On the other hand, Emilie said that for a while the romance had returned to their marriage. Oskar once again became the caring lover he had once been. But just as quickly as romance seemed to return to their marriage, it again disappeared. One evening at the movies, Emilie felt a terrible pain in the lower part of her stomach. Though she tried to put it out of her mind, the pains grew severe and Oskar had to rush her to the hospital. The next day, surgeons discovered a dead baby inside Emilie. This would be the last and worst of Emilie's four miscarriages, and she later blamed them on "the disappointments with Schindler."[60] But as she was coming out of the anaesthesia, she would suffer another loss that left her weeping inconsolably and deeply depressed. Above her, she saw Oskar's "smiling face." And just behind him stood his new lover, Gisa (Gisella Schein), who would later accompany Oskar, Emilie, and several others to Argentina. She now realized that Oskar would never change and remembered the rumors before the war about his two illegitimate children.[61]

In the meantime, Oskar began actively to seek the aid of various Jewish organizations because all they had to live on initially were monthly CARE packages. Emilie often traded the sugar, powdered eggs and milk, coffee, tea, and other items in the CARE packages on the black market for other goods. Oskar's first significant contact with a Jewish agency came in September 1945, when he sought help from James P. Rice, a representative of the Joint in Linz, Austria. Oskar was accompanied by some Schindler Jews who vouched for him and gave Rice a copy of the May 8, 1945, statement of support from the Jewish leaders at Brünnlitz. Two American Jewish soldiers, Corporal Jack Katzman and Lt. George Hillman, also verified Oskar's account of his wartime efforts to help Jews. Rice described Oskar as "quiet, modest, letting the survivors speak for him. He was, in fact, completely powerless," a person "completely dependent on others for his well-being and future." Rice wrote a letter of introduction for Oskar to Eli Rock at the Joint's office in Munich. He described Schindler as a man who had been of "great assistance to hundreds of Jews during the Nazi reign of terror." He knew that Rock, like other Jewish aid workers in Europe after the war, would be skeptical of such claims and made note of the various Jews who had verified these "incredible" claims. He asked Rock to do what he could to find Oskar work with the Joint in Bavaria or with UNRRA.[62]

Armed with this letter and the substantial affidavits that he had gathered from various *Schindlerjuden* and others, Oskar began to seek whatever support he could to rebuild his life in Bavaria. Initially, he seemed occupied with finding a job with German authorities, though he seemed unwilling to take just any job. In August 1946, Oskar read an account of the Amon Göth trial in Kraków in a local newspaper, which noted that Mietek Pemper was the main witness. Oskar sent a letter to the court in Kraków addressed simply to "Witness Pemper." He told Pemper that he and Emilie were in terrible shape in Regensburg and needed his help. Pemper went to see Lieb Salpeter in Kraków. On October 5, Salpeter sent a letter to Jewish organizations throughout West Germany asking them to do what they could to help Schindler. He went into detail about Oskar's wartime efforts to help and save Jews and noted his terrible plight in postwar Germany. During the war, Salpeter wrote, Schindler "did so much for us." Now it was time for the world's Jewish organizations to do what they could to help him.[63]

Several months later, Oskar wrote Dr. Reszőe Kasztner, whom he had met in Budapest in the fall of 1943, asking for his support in getting some type of compensation for his efforts to save Jews during the war. Dr. Kasztner, who coauthored a detailed report on his meeting with Schindler, *Die Bekenntnisse des Herrn X (The Confessions of Mr. X)* as well as a more comprehensive report on the activities of the Jewish Agency in Budapest during the war, *Der Bericht des jüdischen Rettungskomitees aus Budapest, 1942–1945 (A Report on the Jewish Rescue Committee in Budapest, 1942–1945)*, barely mentioned Schindler in his second report because he knew so little about Oskar's overall wartime activities. Consequently, though he expressed sincere gratitude for all Oskar had done to save Jews during the war, Dr. Kasztner asked Schindler to provide him with more details about when he began using Jewish workers in Kraków, his relationship with Dr. Rudi Sedlacek, the names of his Jewish workers, and what happened to the Jewish workers in nearby factories. In other words, could they have been rescued, and, if so, he wanted to know why they had not been. Kasztner assured Oskar that he wanted to do everything he could to help someone who had risked so much to help Jews during the war.[64]

These efforts finally began to pay off in 1947, though Emilie attributed the momentary improvement in their condition more to the announcement of the Marshall Plan, the four-year U.S. effort to invest heavily in the rebuilding of Europe, than to the job that Oskar got with the Jewish Agency in Munich.[65] Even with his job with the Jewish Agency, the Schindlers still seemed to struggle to make ends meet. In fact, Dr. Akiva Kohane wrote Samuel L. Haber, the director of the Joint's office in Munich, that during a visit to Kraków in May 1947, he attended a meeting of Zionist representatives during which the Schindler case was discussed. Attending the meeting were Leib Salpeter, Itzhak Stern, Jakob Sternberg, Hersch Licht, Markus Wulkan, and other *Schindlerjuden* then living in Kraków. Dr. Kohane, who had never heard of Oskar Schindler, was surprised by the stories of the gathered Schindler Jews. He was also taken aback by their "bitter resentment" over Oskar's postwar existence in Germany. They told Dr. Kohane that it angered them that while "many Nazis [were] living comfortable lives," Oskar was going hungry. They asked Dr. Kohane to inform Joint headquarters in Paris to see what they could do to help Oskar and Emilie.[66]

In the meantime, an article appeared in the *Jewish Chronicle* in London that described Schindler's wartime efforts to save his Jewish workers and the large sum he had spent to save them. The article also discussed his desperate plight in Germany. The British Jewish Refugee Association decided to contact the Jewish *Kultusgemeinde* (religious association) in Munich about Schindler because it was the largest Jewish community in the Regensburg area. The idea was to help him by sending him food parcels. In the meantime, Maria Rosner and Ludmilla Pfefferberg-Page, who were close to Oskar, gave Dr. I. Schwarzbart, a prominent Jewish leader in New York, a letter that Oskar had written in April 1947 asking for help. Dr. Schwarzbart had also heard stories about Oskar from another Schindler Jew, Mrs. Gerner-Schenk. Dr. Schwarzbart discussed Oskar's case with a prominent Joint leader in New York, who told him that the Joint was already considering Oskar's case "along with a number of similar claims in a special commission." Dr. Schwarzbart later wrote Oskar that though he was not in a position to help him financially, he wanted to thank him for what he had done during the war. He added, "Your deed shines like a star on the backdrop of the horizon of the horrible calamity which German men and women brought on the Jewish people."[67]

These developments ultimately led to Oskar's meeting with Ted Feder, the deputy director of Joint operations in Munich, to discuss his situation. The meeting, which took place in late 1947 or early 1948, marked the beginning of Schindler's long relationship with the Joint in Germany and Argentina. Over the next two years, Ted Feder would serve essentially as the Joint's "paymaster" for Oskar Schindler, distributing the various grants awarded to him. But it would take a while for the Joint to begin to help him because doubts about his story still lingered.[68]

In April 1948, Leib Salpeter sent Dr. Kohane a letter desperately asking him to do something for Schindler. Soon thereafter, Oskar visited Dr. Kohane in Munich, where he met Samuel Haber. Oskar showed both men the various affidavits, documents, and newspaper articles relating to his case. Oskar told them that he and his family were starving and that "he did not have a penny in his pocket. He could not afford a decent meal. Literally, he was hungry." Dr. Kohane immediately granted Oskar a substantial Joint monthly food allotment for himself, Emilie, Traude, and several others living with the Schindlers. Samuel Haber later noted that this allotment was more than sufficient to give him "a very decent living" in Germany at that time. Over the next few months, the Joint also gave Oskar $500 in Deutschmarks and found him a job in the Joint's nearby warehouse. As Haber noted, Oskar deserved "everything we can do for him."[69]

Once the Joint became Schindler's benefactor, he then decided to press his claims for full compensation for the funds he had spent saving his Jewish workers in Kraków and Brünnlitz. Oskar based his claim on the detailed financial report he had prepared in the summer of 1945, in which he estimated that he had spent RM 2,640,000 ($1,056,000) to save his Jewish workers. Oskar claimed that he had received instructions from Dr. Kasztner "to pay out any amount of money necessary to save Jewish lives."[70] Oskar also claimed that he always had the approval of Lieb Salpeter, Dr. Chaim Hilfstein, Natan Stern, or Itzhak Stern before he spent such funds. Unfortunately, he had no documentation to prove this. Moreover, though Oskar later claimed that Dr. Kasztner had sent him a list of prominent Jews, which, "upon the wish of Israeli organizations, should be looked for in the camps and brought to [his] factory and placed under [his] protection," there is nothing in the detailed report of the 1943 Budapest meeting prepared by Kasztner or Shmuel Springmann, who also attended the meeting with Schindler, or in Dr. Kasztner's postwar report, that would support Oskar's contention. And though Oskar did act as a conduit for funds from the Jewish Agency into Płaszów, there is nothing to indicate that he used any to compensate himself for his own expenses; and Dr. Hilstein wrote after the war that Oskar always promptly turned these funds over to Jewish representatives in Płaszów.[71]

Dr. Joseph J. Schwartz, the European director of the Joint in Paris, was not certain what to do about Schindler's claim, and decided to seek the legal advice of Dr. Kurt Wehle from the Joint's General Counsel Office in Paris. Dr. Wehle wrote a detailed memorandum on the entire Schindler claim based on some of the information gathered by the Joint in Paris and Munich. He also had the statement of Ignacy Schwebe (Izak Schweber) who enthusiastically confirmed the general details of the Schindler story, though Wehle admitted that he did not have the May 8, 1945, statement from the Jewish leaders in Brünnlitz. Dr. Wehle knew of Schindler's claim that he spent RM 2.6 million saving his Jewish workers but did not have a copy of Schindler's detailed 1945 financial report about his wartime expenses.[72]

Dr. Wehle analyzed the Schindler claim for compensation as an attorney and generally accepted the idea that he had done a great deal to help save the lives of between 1,100 to 1,500 Jews. He had the testimony from Schwebe and other survivors in Munich, though Dr. Wehle wondered whether some of the statements were based on hearsay evidence. The key question for Dr. Wehle was: whose money did Schindler spend in the process of saving his Jewish workers in Kraków and Brünnlitz? Schindler, he wrote, acquired his factories "through the arianization of Jewish factories." In addition, he made a great deal of money during the war in part because he paid little or nothing for the labor of his Jewish workers. Dr. Wehle assumed after reading Kasztner's postwar report on Jewish Agency operations in Budapest that Oskar was partially compensated for the money he spent to help his Jewish workers by the funds he was given by Dr. Sedlacek in Kraków, though we now know that this was not so. He estimated that Oskar probably received about RM 200,000 ($80,000) in compensation from Kasztner, though Oskar said in his 1945 financial report, which Wehle never saw, that Sedlacek brought him a little more than RM 125,000 ($50,000) during his three trips to Kraków, funds that were promptly turned over to Jewish leaders in Emalia and Płaszów. Wehle never saw Kasztner's more detailed report on his meeting with Schindler in Budapest and simply assumed that if money was sent by the Jewish Agency to help Jews in Kraków, then Schindler must have received some of it.[73]

Wehle's statement, based upon the documentation he had seen, read in part: "So far no proof has been given that Schindler's alleged expenses have been made out of his private means." The money Schindler made during the war either came from the property he had acquired through the Aryanization of Jewish property, from the labor of Jews, or from funds received from the Jewish Agency. Wehle, who had been in three concentration camps during the war, also thought that some of the stories about Schindler were exaggerated. He accepted that notion that Schindler had treated his Jews "very satisfactorily." However, he would need more evidence to accept fully "the intensity and extent of his action in favor of the Jewish prisoners."[74]

Dr. Wehle also wanted to know about Schindler's attitudes towards Nazism. He assumed he had been a member of the Nazi Party and was possibly a member of the SA, given his ties to the SS. Such allegiances were important in light of Schindler's claim that he had been forced to flee Czechoslovakia after the war because he was "threatened by the Czechs." If Schindler had indeed helped Jews during the war, then Wehle concluded that the Czechs should have treated him as an "antifascist." But Schindler's Nazi connections and activities were also important in determining the depth of his commitment to helping Jews. Wehle knew, for example, Germans who had helped "'their' Jews" but did "indescribable harm to other Jews." Finally, Oskar claimed after the war that he was penniless. Wehle wanted to know whether he had enjoyed "any means" before the war or whether he had acquired the wealth for which he now sought compensation during the war.[75]

Finally, Dr. Wehle evaluated the Joint's legal responsibilities to Schindler, who claimed that Dr. Kasztner gave him instructions to spend whatever he had to in order to save Jews in Brünnlitz and Płaszów. He questioned, of course, whether the Joint had indeed given Kasztner such authority; if it had, he argued, then the Joint might have some legal responsibilities towards Schindler. However, he concluded that there was no evidence to support Schindler's contention. He reminded Dr. Schwartz that the Joint was a "welfare organization whose duty was to help Jews and to lessen Jewish needs." It was not the Joint's responsibility "to reimburse individuals or organizations for their activities in the same field" regardless of the circumstances or reasons. If it did, then the Joint's welfare activities might become "ad absurdum." He added that the effort by Schindler and his friends to be reimbursed by the Joint was not the first request for such claims and certainly would not be the last. He added that the situation was complicated by Schindler's nationality. Was it, he asked, the Joint's moral responsibility "to indemnify a German who behaved decently with Jews?" Given what happened during the war, he thought not.[76]

The only recourse to this problem was a "revenge" for Schindler, which Wehle thought he certainly deserved. But who should be responsible for this? He thought it was the obligation of the Jews whom he saved to help him. He did not think the Joint should be directly involved in the "revenge," though it could help indirectly. He did not think the food and clothing the Joint had been supplying Schindler and his family for months should be included in this new indirect aid "revenge." He suggested that the Joint work through Dr. Chaim Hilfstein to aid Schindler to avoid any legal responsibility towards him.[77]

Given the times and the lack of information that Dr. Wehle and other Joint representatives had on Schindler, Dr. Wehle's points were reasonable. Oskar's contention that he had spent more than $1 million (RM 2,640,000) was incredible; even close friends such as Dr. Moshe Bejski, an attorney and Israeli Supreme Court Justice, told me the sum was probably exaggerated. Moreover, Oskar's claim that somehow Dr. Kasztner had authorized him to spend whatever necessary to save Jews with the promise of later Joint compensation is simply not true. There is nothing in Kasztner and Springmann's *Die Bekenntnisse des Herrn X*, the transcript of their 1943 meeting with Schindler in Budapest, to suggest this. Moreover, Schindler is barely mentioned in Kasztner's more detailed postwar report on the Jewish Rescue Committee or in Alex Weissberg's biography on Joel Brand, the head of the Rescue Committee *(Va'adah)* in Budapest. Kasztner has one paragraph in his detailed study on Schindler and describes briefly his meeting with Springmann and Kasztner in Budapest and his dealings with Sedlacek, who brought Oskar "several hundred thousand Reichsmarks" during his trips to Kraków. Weissberg verifies much of what Kasztner said and underscores Oskar's honesty.[78]

In his 1945 financial report, Oskar spent a lot of time on his work with Dr. Sedlacek, whom he claimed was working for the Joint. Though there is no doubt that some of the money Oskar received from Sedlacek came from the Joint, Sedlacek was working for the Jewish Agency, not the Joint. Oskar knew this, though immediately after the war he made a point of writing that Sedlacek was a Joint agent. This became the seed for his later claim. By the time he approached the Joint in Munich about compensation, he had convinced himself and others that he had been working directly for the Joint during the war and that it owed him more than $1 million. He was even able to convince Regensburg's small Jewish community to issue him a statement in the spring of 1948 certifying that during the war he had served as an "agent between Polish Jewry and the American Joint in Budapest."[79]

And there is no doubt that some of the Schindler Jews whom Oskar lived with or remained close to in Germany encouraged him to press his claim with the Joint. From their perspective, the Joint must have appeared to be a powerful, wealthy American Jewish organization with unlimited resources. It was certainly the most important Jewish welfare organization in Europe after the war, and its commitment to aid Holocaust survivors impressed other relief groups. Between 1946 and 1950, for example, the Joint spent $280 million to help Jewish survivors in Europe. It used its funds to deal with every aspect of rebuilding Jewish lives and later became involved in helping many of them emigrate to Palestine, later Israel, the United States, and other parts of the globe. The Joint remained active in Europe until 1957, when the last DP camp was closed. It was also involved in efforts to help survivors win reparations from West Germany. Given the extensive demands on the Joint's resources, Joint leaders were wise to be as careful as they could with their funds to insure that they could help as many survivors as possible. As Yehuda Bauer has noted, without the Joint, "the survivors' fate would have been much harder than it was."[80]

In light of all this, it is not surprising that Dr. Wehle took the position he did on Schindler's claim. The ultimate problem with it, of course, was that Schindler had absolutely no documentation to back up his demand for compensation; Dr. Wehle saw Schindler only as a German and Nazi Party member. This is in direct contrast with Schindler's later *Lastenausgleich* claim in West Germany, where, at the insistence of very particular German bureaucrats, Oskar was able to come up with an impressive collection of documents.

Schindler's claim for compensation centered around the bribes he had paid various officials, the daily fees he had paid the SS for his Jewish workers, extra food costs, and relocation expenses when he moved from Kraków to Brünnlitz. Bribery was so commonplace in the General Government that it was considered a normal part of doing business. Whether one did or did not use Jewish workers made no difference. It is a bit shocking to learn that Schindler insisted on including the fees he paid the SS for his "slave" laborers in his list of wartime costs. Schindler began to use Jewish workers early in the war because he needed the expertise of men such as Abraham Bankier or because they were cheaper than Polish workers. This was the standard practice followed by factory owners throughout the General Government, particularly later in the war when authorities encouraged this because of growing labor shortages. Many factories in Kraków used Jewish workers, and some of the factory owners treated them quite well. In other words, Schindler would have paid these fees to the SS whether he helped his workers or not. These fees went beyond normal labor expenses when he hired "useless" workers simply at their families' request.

The extra funds that Oskar spent for food for his Jewish and Polish workers was another matter, though, because he sacrificed a lot to insure that his workers were adequately fed. But his well-nourished workers were also more productive and the reason he made the kind of money he did during his years in Kraków. He also spent a lot of money relocating his factory to the Sudentenland, though part of the reason he did this was to insure himself a future in postwar Europe. He never dreamed that he would be driven out of Czechoslovakia, never to return. And though he did spend most of the money he made in Kraków keeping his Jewish workers alive in Brünnlitz, the fact remains that both the factories he acquired during the war had once been Jewish-owned. He came to Poland in 1939 essentially as a German carpetbagger, and took advantage, both there and in the Protectorate of Bohemia and Moravia, of Nazi Germany's Aryanization policies. Moreover, he used Jewish slave labor in each of them partially to keep production costs low and profits high. When he left

Brünnlitz, he still had some of the profits he had made during the war in his two factories, but they were lost within days after his flight began. Given all this, no reasonable Jewish organization involved deeply in the rebuilding of post-Holocaust Jewish lives could overlook Oskar Schindler's wartime membership in the German Nazi Party; neither could it ignore the vast amounts of money Schindler made by using Jewish slave laborers and the advantage Schindler took of German Aryanization policies to acquire property formerly owned by Jews.

Yet given all this and the questionable nature of some of Schindler's compensation claims, the Joint finally decided to award him a grant of $15,000, a substantial sum in postwar Germany. Dr. Schwartz suggested this amount to the Joint's Organization Committee in Paris in January 1949, and the grant was readily approved. Needless to say, Oskar was quite disappointed with the amount of the award. But once he learned of the grant, he quickly revealed plans to move to Argentina. He asked the Joint to give him $5,000 immediately and to pay him the rest when he reached Argentina.[81]

On January 29, 1949, Moses Beckelman, the vice chair of Joint operations in Paris, wrote a detailed letter of introduction for Schindler to Jacob Lightman, the head of the Joint office in Buenos Aires, the Argentine capital. Though Oskar would not arrive in Argentina until November 1949, the Joint offered to do everything it could to help the man who at "the constant risk of his own life and that of his wife . . . carried out his humanitarian work at considerable financial and material sacrifice." Beckelman went into details about Oskar's efforts to save Jews in Kraków and Brünnlitz and told Lightman, with whom he had once worked in South America, that now Schindler was about to begin life anew, they should help him, "as once he helped our brethren."[82]

But why Argentina? In a letter to Lightman a month later, Beckelman explained that once it had become known publicly that Schindler had helped Jews during the war, there was no chance for him to rebuild his life there. It was now unhealthy for him to remain in Germany. Beckelman wrote that the Joint would give him $5,000 in Germany to buy tools and machinery for an automobile radiator factory that Oskar planned to open in Argentina. The Joint would give him $10,000 more for upstart costs and other expenses when he got to South America.[83]

But there is nothing to indicate that he ever bought anything substantial with the $5,000 he received in Germany. Emilie was critical of how Oskar handled the Joint funds because, she said, he spent it "on small pleasures and on objects for which [the couple] had not the slightest need." In fact, she claimed, she never "received a penny of what he received." After he received the first Joint payment, he took his mistress, Gisa, who would also accompany him to Argentina, on a holiday in the Alps, while Emilie and her niece "had to perform miracles in order to obtain enough food on the black market." On the other hand, Emilie wrote, though Oskar continued "like a child, to follow his whims," he also clung to her, his "refuge in times of crisis," when "it came to important decisions."[84]

It soon became apparent to Joint officials in Europe that Oskar planned to take six other people with him to Argentina besides Emilie. In the spring of 1949, he told Moses Beckelman that he intended to divorce Emilie before he left Germany and marry Roma Horowitz. But he also wanted to arrange for Emilie's emigration to Argentina.[85] The question of divorce would come up again and again over the next two decades. Emilie said in her memoirs that she had often thought of leaving Oskar and beginning a new life in which she would be free of "his lies . . . his repeated deceits and constant insincere repenting." But her strong Catholic faith and her postwar impoverishment kept her with Oskar. She had briefly reunited with her brother, Franz, after the war, who disappeared again in 1946. So she decided to stay with Oskar in a loveless marriage. But she later told a German reporter after Steven Spielberg's film Schindler's List came out that her "wedding ring was good insurance against the claims of his many mistresses."[86] When Oskar returned to Germany in 1957, he talked occasionally of divorce, though finally decided it might complicate his Lastenausgleich claims and his new business dealings. Needless to say, he never married Roma Horowitz.[87]

What is peculiar about all of this is that, at least according to Emilie, Oskar's mistress during this period was not Roma Horowitz but Gisa Schein. All three women, Emilie, Roma, and Gisa, would accompany Oskar to Argentina. And it was Gisa, not Roma, who was Oskar's mistress during his years in Argentina. Oskar met Gisa in Munich while staying with some of the Schindlerjuden who lived there after the war. Their mutual friends gave them a room in their apartment for the liaison, and Oskar made frequent trips to Munich to see Gisa. Emilie was shocked to learn that Oskar intended to take Gisa with them to Argentina and said she "did not have the energy for futile reproaches anymore." She continued to hope that once they got to Argentina she would again be Oskar's "only woman." But Emilie went on to say that when they reached Argentina, the affair between Oskar and Gisa continued, even though the Schindlers lived in San Vicente, a small town more than an hour away from Buenos Aires. In fact, from what I could gather by talking to several Schindler neighbors in San Vicente, Oskar spent little time there, instead preferring life with Gisa in the Belgrano district of Buenos Aires. Emilie claimed that Gisa "used [her] husband for all he was worth" because he gave her jewelry and an otter-skin coat. Gisa felt abandoned when Oskar left for Germany in 1957 and wrote him some very critical letters, somehow hoping to persuade him to return. Oskar wrote Emilie and asked her to call Gisa and tell her that if she did not stop the insulting letters, he would "never come back to her."[88]

So why did Oskar tell Joint officials that he planned to marry Roma Horowitz? In two letters to Joint officials in early 1949, Herbert Steinhouse, a Canadian journalist who befriended Oskar at this time, wrote Joint officials in Paris about Edmund and Roma Horowitz, who hoped to accompany Oskar and Emilie to Argentina. Steinhouse had received several letters from Alex Madanes, the Paris correspondent for the *Jewish Chronicle* in London, who was a cousin of Roma and Edmund Horowitz. The Horowitzs, who lived in Munich, seemed desperate to join the Schindler party, but were uncertain of Joint support. Steinhouse told Dr. Joseph J. Schwartz that he had visited the Horowitzs in Munich and found them in a "fearful state of mind." Several weeks later, Oskar told Moses Beckelman that he intended to marry Roma Horowitz and divorce Emilie. Did Oskar tell Beckelman this to insure that Roma and Edmund would have a place on the new Argentine "Schindler's List," or was he also having an affair with Roma? We will never know. But what is interesting is that Moses Beckelman thought that Emilie was Jewish and that at least some of the people who traveled with her and Oskar to Argentina were members of her family.[89]

The Joint agreed to arrange Oskar's travel plans for the party of eight that planned to travel to Argentina with him and to deduct the costs of the trip from his $15,000 grant, though ultimately only Oskar and Emilie's fares and related expenses were paid from Joint funds. Once it was determined that everyone except the Schindlers were war refugees, the costs of the others were paid for by the United Nations International Refugee Organization. There seems to be some confusion about who actually joined Oskar and Emilie on the voyage. We know that the group initially consisted of Oskar, Emilie, Roma Horowitz and her brother, Edmund Horowitz, Gisa Schein, Jakob Goldfarb and his wife, Fanny Goldfarb, and Isaak Korczyn. At the last minute, Jakob Goldfarb became ill and could not make the trip. When the Schindler party arrived in Buenos

Aires, Joint officials informed its offices in New York that an additional person had traveled with the Schindlers, Alois Tutsch, a Sudeten German. Presumably he replaced Jakob Goldfarb. Later, though, Oskar told Joint officials in Buenos Aires that there had been more last-minute changes before his party left Genoa, and did not list Tutsch as one of the group. None of the Jews in Oskar's party was a Schindler Jew.[90]

If it is true that Oskar was partially driven to emigrate to Argentina because of his growing fame as a "savior" of Jews during the war, there is certainly evidence to support this. In early 1948, Oskar contacted Jacob Levy, a Jewish wine merchant in Manchester, England, about helping him out of his dire straits and advising on the possibility of emigrating to England. Levy sent Schindler a *Lebensmittelpackete* (food packet) and later offered to send Oskar £50 ($12.50) when he learned that he planned to emigrate to Argentina.[91]

What followed was a fascinating exchange of letters between Levy and Schindler that, at least on Oskar's part, were remarkable for their blunt, bitter tone. Oskar wrote the most interesting one to Levy on November 16, 1948. He thanked Levy for his "copious food package" of September 7. He told Levy that his letters were very important to him and had "strengthened [his] optimism and chased away [his] apocalyptic mood." In one of his letters, Levy had mentioned how difficult it must be for someone like Oskar to live in Germany. Schindler agreed, and decried the neo-Nazism developing in Germany that was taking the form of a "Nazi-Communism trickling through from the Eastern [Soviet] zone." In addition, Oskar wrote Levy, anti-Semitism was now stronger in Germany than during the war. He attributed this to the same "superman spirit" that was spreading quite openly in government circles and universities by unemployed war veterans and others. This spirit, Oskar argued, was leading to a sense of "collective innocence" among the German people."[92]

Oskar was particularly bitter over the fate of the millions of ethnic German refugees who were now forced to undergo denazification while more prominent Nazis "were hardly being reached by the law" or were only being modestly punished. When questions of "guilt, compensation, and penitence" arose, no one took responsibility. So where were the real Nazis, the real criminals? They were, Oskar told Levy, continuing to hold "influential positions" as they prepared Germany to "destroy Europe" in the next [international] dispute. And once again, the German people seemed ready to "run after the infallible supermen as cannon fodder." The current political strife between the East and the West helped protect the actual "guilty ones."[93]

Now, with a new threat of war hanging over Europe, Oskar thought it was important "to get out of Germany as quickly as possible." He would prefer going to Israel because he had so many friends there and thought that Israel would soon become a very prosperous country. But as Israel was "in the strategic line of attack of the Russians," he could not risk once again losing his "life's work and family assets to the red Czars." He ended his letter by asking Levy to help him with his compensation claim with the Joint. Once again, Oskar claimed that everything he spent during the war was approved by the Joint. Such a repayment would give him "an assured livelihood overseas." Finally, he thanked Levy for all his sacrifices as Oskar's advocate.[94]

A more significant relationship developed with Herbert Steinhouse, a Canadian journalist who became chief of the Paris bureau of the Canadian Broadcasting Corporation (CBC) in 1949. Before he assumed his post in Paris, Steinhouse met Itzhak Stern, who began to tell him about Schindler. Steinhouse, who had worked for UNRRA before he joined CBC, was initially skeptical of any stories about a "good German," but was intrigued by Stern's tales. After six sessions with Stern, he finally met Oskar and Emilie at their modest apartment in Regensburg in late 1948, though according to Tobe Steinhouse, Oskar had an apartment in Munich as well. Their wives "hit it off" and over several weeks, Steinhouse recorded Schindler's account of his wartime efforts to save "his" Jews. Tobe Steinhouse told me that she remembered Oskar as an extremely charming though manipulative person. On one occasion, he insisted on taking her to a local factory to buy her a special tea set, which she was hesitant to accept. Herbert Steinhouse returned to Paris and wrote an article about Oskar that he tried to get published. But his agent told him that magazines were no longer interested in stories about "good Germans" and that readers were tired of articles about the Holocaust. Steinhouse did not publish his account of his meetings with Schindler until 1994.[95]

After *Schindler's List* came out in 1993, Steinhouse wrote Steven Spielberg and Thomas Keneally a letter describing his relationship and views on Oskar Schindler in the late 1940s. Schindler's "Jewish bodyguard" deliberately tried to befriend Steinhouse because they thought he, as a journalist, could "help get Oskar and Emilie and perhaps themselves to Canada or the USA, where ex-Party member Oskar was automatically denied entry, by publicizing their story in America." Over the course of many months, Steinhouse and his wife Tobe became quite close to Oskar and Emilie and spent a great deal of time with them. In fact, it was Herbert Steinhouse who arranged a banquet in Paris for Oskar and a number of Schindler Jews in early 1949. Since Oskar could not legally enter France, Steinhouse smuggled him into Paris for the banquet. The banquet, which was attended by more than thirty-five Schindler Jews, was held in the Aux Armes de Colmar, an Alsatian restaurant in Paris. The *Jewish Chronicle* likened the gathering to that "of an English school speech day with Herr Schindler as the headmaster greeting former pupils." Schindler, the article continued, was quite interested in the "welfare of his protégés" even though they were now scattered around the globe. In turn, the *Schindlerjuden* "are deeply conscious that only his efforts saved them from the gas-chambers."[96]

The banquet was a very festive occasion. Steinhouse wrote that Oskar was toasted again and again for his efforts during the war. As they raised glasses of white wine, the gathered survivors sang *"Sto Lat"* (May you live a hundred years), a song that they had once sung for Oskar in Brünnlitz. The toasts and singing were followed by tributes to Schindler. One Schindler Jew proclaimed that "it was known throughout Poland that whoever went to Schindler's factory was safe." Another said they were sneered at as *Schindlerjuden* in Brünnlitz; but today, he boasted, they were "proud of that name." Oskar had tears in his eyes when it came time for him to speak. "Germans today seem to share a collective innocence," he said, "not the collective guilt they should." When he finished, Oskar went from table to table, hugging each of his beloved Schindler Jews.[97]

At the end of August 1949, Oskar, Emilie, and the six other members of their party left Munich for Genoa, where they made final preparations for their voyage to Argentina. On October 5, everyone except Edmund Horowitz, who had become ill, set sail on the SS *Genoa* for what became an "infernal" twenty-eight day voyage to Argentina. The ship docked in Buenos Aires on November 3, 1950. The trip across the Atlantic had been dreadful and everyone had suffered from sea-sickness. Though it was fall in Genoa, it was spring in Argentina. Hopefully Oskar and Emilie would now have a chance to begin life anew without the stigmas of the past haunting them. Perhaps they would be able to re-create the idyllic life that they had so hoped for in Germany.

12.

ARGENTINA, RETURN TO GERMANY, AND THE RIGHTEOUS GENTILE CONTROVERSY

DURING ONE OF THE EARLY INTERVIEWS I DID WITH SOL URBACH, he asked me why Oskar settled in Argentina. "Wasn't that," Sol wanted to know, "where many former Nazis settled after the war?" "Yes," I told him, "but so did many Jews." Argentina was and remains an historical enigma. More than 180,000 Jews fled Russia and Eastern Europe for Argentina from 1881 to 1930; by 1933, Argentina had the world's third largest Jewish population: 240,000. By the 1960s, 350,000 Jews lived in Argentina. Large numbers of Jews fled that country during the 1970s and early 1980s as military dictatorships and the resulting "Dirty [civil] War" devastated Argentina. More left after the bombings of the Israeli embassy in 1992 and the AMIA *(Kehilá Judia de Buenos Aires)* Jewish community center in Buenos Aires two years later. Many more fled the country during the financial crisis of the 1990s. Today, Argentina has 230,000 Jewish citizens, most of them living in Buenos Aires. Jewish religious and cultural institutions are now heavily guarded and I sensed a certain unspoken discomfort with life in Argentina among the Jews I interviewed there in 2001.[1]

But Argentina was also home to a large German population, and today 400,000 Argentines identify themselves as ethnic Germans by language.[2] Roberto Aleman, the co-editor of the German-language *Argentinisches*

Tageblatt, told me that during the war the German population was evenly split in terms of support or opposition to Hitler, a fact disputed by Uki Goñi in his *The Real Odessa: How Perón Brought the Nazi War Criminals to Argentina* (2002). What we do know is that Argentina's postwar dictator, Juan Perón, who ruled Argentina from 1946 to 1955 and again from 1973 to 1974, permitted hundreds of Nazi war criminals to enter Argentina at the same time he allowed Jews to enter the country.[3] Given Oskar Schindler's well-known reputation for helping Jews during the war, it is hard to imagine that he had anything to do with these former Nazis or, for that matter, the Nazi sympathizers among the large German population in Buenos Aires at the time, where he spent much of his time. Oskar had a Jewish girlfriend, Gisa Schein, during the years he lived in Argentina, and after 1953 it seems he lived with her in Buenos Aires. Yet, despite this, when he returned to Germany, Oskar showed a certain fondness for Sudeten German organizations, which surprised and confused his Jewish and German friends. But given the depth and nature of his ties to the Jewish community in Buenos Aires during his years there, it is hard to believe that he had much to do with anyone in the German community with links to Germany's Nazi past. But anything, of course, is possible.

What little we know about Oskar and Emilie's life in Argentina from late 1949 until 1957, when Oskar left for Germany, comes principally from Emilie's memoirs. Information about his life there also appears in scattered documents in the Schindler *Koffer* (suitcase) collection at the Bundesarchiv in Koblenz. Needless to say, Emilie was very critical of the film and of her husband in her memoirs and in the interviews she gave before her death in 2001. In a 1994 interview, she told a German journalist that Oskar was a "a womanizer, drinker, and good-for-nothing . . . an idiot" whom she had forgotten for thirty-seven years.[4] Oskar spoke or wrote little about his life in Argentina, perhaps because he was so embarrassed by his failures there.

But Emilie and Oskar were both full of hope when they arrived in Argentina in late 1949. In fact, in the summer of 1951, Oskar wrote Fritz Lang that he was now "free of complexes and depressions, and thank God once again full of vitality."[5] For the first time in many years he had an ample supply of money and unlimited prospects. The Joint had given him $5,000 before he left Germany to open an automobile radiator factory in Argentina. The Joint also paid the expenses for his trip to Argentina and loaned him Arg$5,000 (Argentine pesos) ($695) when he arrived in Buenos Aires to help with initial living expenses. The idea was that Oskar would repay the Joint for these expenses and for the loan, which totaled Arg$18,851 ($2,513), out of the final grant payment of $10,000, which he received soon after he arrived in Argentina. Unfortunately, Oskar repaid the Joint only Arg$10,000 ($1,180). After they made modest efforts to collect the rest of the money, Joint officials decided in 1952 to write off the debt. The Joint also put Oskar in contact with important Jewish businessmen in Buenos Aires who did what they could to help the storied German who had helped Jews during the Holocaust. One of them, Jacobo Murmis, had recently purchased a small farm in San Vicente, a village about forty miles from downtown Buenos Aires. He gave Oskar and Emilie jobs as caretakers at the farm.[6]

It is hard to imagine Oskar Schindler running a farm, but there is a picture of him on a tractor in the photographic archives at Yad Vashem. Emilie, coming as she did from a remote rural farm community in Czechoslovakia, took immediately to farm work. Their principal job was to raise chickens and egg-laying hens. Neither of them knew anything about this and they were hampered by their poor Spanish. But Emilie said that Oskar never really seemed interested in the chicken farm and was more intrigued by the "adventures the capital could provide," meaning Gisa Schein.[7] By the fall of 1950, Oskar had applied for a mortgage on a small ten-acre farm in San Vicente. At first, they continued to raise chickens and hens there, though in 1953, Oskar came up with the idea of raising fur-bearing otters. Emilie considered this a hare-brained, stupid idea: "just like marrying Oskar."[8]

On March 13, 1953, Oskar, Emilie, and Murmis established "Oskar Schindler and Company," which was to be a "hatchery of otters and wild animals in general" with a capital value of Arg$200,000 ($26,666). The new company was to be based on the new ten-acre farm in San Vicente. Oskar was the principal partner and owned shares worth Arg$80,000 ($10,507); Murmis's shares were worth Arg$70,000 ($9,333), and Emilie owned the rest of the shares (Arg$20,000; $2,667). The new firm was valued at Arg$200,000 ($26,667).[9] Problems started almost immediately, though Oskar assured Emilie that the otter-fur business was "the business of the century" and made her extravagant promises: "We're going to be millionaires," he said. "All the women wear fur coats."[10]

Neither of them knew anything about otters or furs and Emilie spent most of her free time before the animals arrived reading books on the subject. She quickly discovered that otters were not native to Latin America and that the animals Oskar had bought to start the farm were nutrias, not otters. When the nutrias arrived, Oskar disappeared, leaving Emilie to care for the farm and the nutrias by herself. In fact, she saw Oskar only on weekends, when he would bring Gisa or other friends to lunch. After a while, she became frustrated with his infrequent visits and often went horseback riding while he regaled his guests at the farmhouse.[11]

The 150-year-old-farm and the house on Viamonte 102–108 that Oskar and Emilie bought in 1953 are still there. Seven blocks away is Juan Perón's palatial country estate, which is now a museum. The family living in the former Schindler home was quite friendly when I visited them in the spring of 2001. They showed me through the home and even lent me a copy of a document signed by Oskar in 1957 transferring his property rights to Emilie. Though some renovations were made on the house after Emilie was forced to sell it, it still is very much as it was in the 1950s. It is a one-story hacienda-style home with a large front porch surrounded by large trees. The house is dark and damp inside. Much of the original land was sold off after Oskar left for Germany. In the early 1960s, Emilie moved to a house several blocks away on San Martin 353 built for her by B'nai Brith (Bene Berith). What particularly struck me about the house on Viamonte 102–108 was its rural setting vis-à-vis Emilie's more urban home near the center of San Vicente. Her new house was on a paved street just a block or so from San Vicente's quaint town square, but the house at Viamonte 102–108 still has a dirt road in front of it, as it did when Oskar lived there. While I was there, cattle wandered freely in front of the former Schindler home.

Within months after buying the new farm and setting up the nutria business, Oskar was already thinking about returning to Germany to pursue his reparations claims for his lost factories in Poland and Czechoslovakia. He contacted Beate Pollack, who worked for Joint offices in Buenos Aires, to help him find someone to file his claim in West Germany. On July 27, 1953, Pollack, who, along with her husband, Walter, would become two of Oskar's closest friends, wrote to Moses Beckelman, the head of Joint operations in Europe, to ask for help. This letter was prompted by Oskar's conversation a week or so earlier with Julius Lomnitz, the director of the Joint's Latin American operations in Buenos Aires. Oskar wanted Lomnitz to recommend "an influential person," such as Mr. Beckelman, "or another friendly institution" who could submit his application to the president of the Federal Compensation Office (Bundesausgleichsamt) in Bonn. Oskar told Lomnitz that he should immediately request DM 50,000 ($11,905) and possibly "an additional rebuilding credit" from this office in Bonn. Lomnitz suggested that the best person to do this would be Dr. E. G.

Lowenthal, the director of the Advisory Committee for the Claims Conference (Conference on Jewish Material Claims against Germany), which had been created by twenty-three major international Jewish organizations in New York in 1951 to negotiate with West Germany over Holocaust-related damages to Jewish individuals and the Jewish people. The Claims Conference would become the principal Jewish organization involved in negotiating compensation and indemnification programs for Holocaust victims, and in 1998 had paid out more than DM 118 billion ($66.6 billion) in indemnification payments to Holocaust victims.[12]

In her letter to Beckelman, Beate Pollack reminded him of Oskar's extraordinary assistance to Jews during the Holocaust and asked him to find him an attorney. After the discussion with Lomnitz, it was decided that Lowenthal would probably not be a good choice as Oskar's lawyer because he might not be able "to accept his power of attorney." Most important here, she reminded Beckelman, was the *"utmost urgency"* of Schindler's case because the deadline for filing claims was August 31, 1953. Oskar would have preferred that the Joint accept his power of attorney because it had awarded him the $15,000 grant earlier. She enclosed with her letter a second letter from Oskar to Beckelman that provided more details about the particulars of his claim. "It would be for us a real pleasure if we could be of real help to Mr. Schindler in this matter," she wrote, "because only a few of his kind deserve it so much." Pollack urged Beckelman to cable his response as quickly as possible.[13]

Oskar's letter to Beckelman, dated July 21, 1953, said that he still did not have an adequate income, "especially in light of the last economically difficult years." He explained that "high interest rates and high wages and new demands" made it imperative for him to press his claims against West Germany. He could not, he added, "allow the German government to keep [his] claim of over $30,000."[14] In fact, before he left Germany in 1949, he had already given Alfred Schindler, his former office manager in Kraków and Brünnlitz, his power of attorney to deal with claim opportunities and other matters relating to the two factories. He also wrote to the State Commissariat for Racial, Religious, and Political Persecutees in Munich, which opened a file on his claim in Regensburg, though this office told him in 1949 that they were uncertain when or whether such a compensation fund would be set up.[15]

The problem for Oskar, though, was that he did not know how to pursue his claim in light of the new 1952 *Lastenausgleich* law in West Germany. Consequently, he asked Beckelman for help in filing a *Lastenaus-*

gleich claim there. But Oskar also raised an issue that seemed to cast doubts on his prospect for *Lastenausgleich* compensation. From what he could determine, one had to have been living in Germany on December 31, 1950, to be eligible to file a claim. This date did not apply if the applicant had moved to another country as a public employee before that date. Oskar claimed that he made several trips abroad for the Joint in the summer of 1949 and considered his trip to Buenos Aires as foreign travel for the Joint. Consequently, he wanted Beckelman to certify that he was a Joint employee when he made these trips. He also asked for Beckelman's help in getting a position as an importer with the Israeli mission in Germany and mentioned the work he had done in a similar position for the Jewish Agency in Munich between 1947 and 1948. In return for the Joint's support, Oskar told Beckelman, he was willing to make the Joint his "legal heir," which would enable him to return to Argentina after a brief spell in Germany to file his claim.[16]

Beckelman immediately cabled Pollack after he received her letter and followed this up with a more detailed letter on August 4. But before he cabled her, he called Benjamin B. Ferencz, the director general of the Jewish Restitution Successor Organization (JRSO) office, which had been designated by the U.S. Military Government "to recover heirless property" in the Palace of Justice in Nürnberg, Germany.[17] Ferencz told Beckelman that neither JRSO nor the United Restitution Office (URO) could handle *Lastenausgleich* claims and later cabled him the name of Professor Dr. Robert Ellscheid in Cologne as the best person to handle Schindler's claim. He added that the deadline for filing such claims had been extended to March 1954.[18]

Beckelman immediately shared this information with Beate Pollack and told her that it was "out of the question" for the Joint or any other Jewish organization to handle *Lastenausgleich* matters because such actions were forbidden by the licensing arrangement the organizations had with the West German government. According to Beckelman, the logic of this was that "all the Jewish organizations [had] protested against the imposition of any Lastenausgleich obligations on Jewish survivors of Nazi persecutions," which made it "entirely inappropriate for any of these groups to concern themselves with such claims." He told her about Dr. Ellscheid and said he was "a reputable and reliable person." He also let her know about the new deadline for filing *Lastenausgleich* claims.[19]

But Beckelman was a little puzzled by the link between the $15,000 grant that the Joint had earlier awarded Schindler and his proposal to transfer his power of attorney to the Joint. This would be impossible for the Joint to do, though he added that it should not be taken as a sign of disinterest in Schindler's case. At this point, Beckelman was also uncertain about certifying Schindler's claim about travel for the Joint in 1949 and 1951 but wrote that he would look into the matter. He did not think, though, that travel for the Joint would fulfill the requirements of the *Lastenausgleich* law about such matters because the Joint was a "private philanthropic organization."[20]

Several days after Beckelman wrote Beate Pollack, he sent Benjamin Ferencz a letter and asked him whether he thought Oskar's claim of travel for the Joint in 1949 and 1951 "would reestablish his eligibility under the Lastenausgleich law." He included a copy of Oskar's July 21 letter. On the same day, August 8, Beckelman wrote Beate Pollack that he had looked into the possibility of Oskar's being employed by the Israel Purchasing Mission (IPM) in Germany. The director of the IPM told him that the nature of their ties to the German government specified that they could employ only people "directly connected with the Israel[i] Government."[21]

Ten days later, Beate Pollack clarified Oskar's request for a position with the IPM in a letter to Beckelman. One of the purposes of the *Lastenausgleich* law, she explained, was to help dispossessed ethnic Germans from Central and Eastern Europe reestablish themselves financially in West Germany. Oskar did not want a job with the IPM. Instead, he wanted to open an "intermediary agency" that would sell German goods to the IPM. What he needed now was a letter from the IPM stating that they would be interested in purchasing goods from him. This would, she went on to say, "serve him before the German authorities of the 'Lastenausgleich' as proof that he really had the intention to found such an agency" and really needed "the money he is asking for." She added that Oskar would then mortgage his *Lastenausgleich* claims to the Joint and use the attorney recommended by Beckelman and Ferencz. The Joint would become his creditor, which would enable Oskar to return to Argentina sooner because the Joint would be dealing directly with *Lastenausgleich* officials in Germany.[22] She went on to explain in another letter several weeks later that Oskar wanted to reimburse the Joint fully for the $15,000 it had given him earlier and thought that if the Joint was his *Lastenausgleich* beneficiary, the matter would be resolved much more quickly.[23]

In the meantime, Ferencz and another official at JRSO, Ernst Katzenstein, sought the advice of a German attorney, F. A. Stadler, about Oskar's *Lastenausgleich* questions and claim. According to Stadler and Katzenstein, the *Lastenausgleich* law stipulated that a person was eligible for such funds only if he had been a resident of the Federal Republic of Germany (West Germany) or West Berlin on December 31, 1950. The only exception to this was someone who, as a civil servant or a member of a "permanent trade commission," had been abroad on official business on or before this date. This meant that Schindler, who had emigrated for personal reasons, could not be included in this category. Stadler and Katzenstein added, though, that Schindler should pursue his claims as a Joint official traveling abroad in 1949 and 1951 because this was a gray area in the *Lastenausgleich* law. But more than likely, even employment by the Joint would probably not make him eligible for such claims because he was not *"Angehoeriger des oeffentlichen Dienstes"* (a member of the civil service).[24] When Ferencz sent Beckelman a copy of the Katzenstein-Stadler report, he added a note: "A good lawyer might persuade the competent German officials that the JDC is the same thing as an official German body. He would probably have to be a damn good lawyer. Nothing can be lost by trying."[25]

But this was not the end of the Joint's investigation into Oskar's questions about his *Lastenausgleich*. Beckelman also contacted the Joint's office in Munich about Schindler's claim that he had worked for the Joint between 1949 and 1951. On September 14, Samuel L. Haber, the director of the Joint's Munich operations, wrote to Charles Jordan, who worked for Beckelman in Paris and had formerly headed Joint operations in Cuba, that Schindler had never been employed by the Joint. A month later when Jordan shared this information with Beate Pollack, Oskar's effort to persuade the Joint to intercede for him in his *Lastenausgleich* claim seems to have ended.[26]

On the other hand, Oskar continued to look to the Joint as his benefactor and had no qualms about going back to the Joint again and again over the next four years for financial resources to live in Argentina and ultimately return to Germany to pursue his *Lastenausgleich* claims. Yet it is interesting that no one had any way of knowing who had originally owned the two factories Oskar had acquired during the war. If Joint officials had been aware that Oskar had taken over Aryanized Jewish property or that there would be charges of brutality leveled against him by Jewish Holocaust survivors, perhaps they would not have been as eager to help him. In fact, the principal accuser against Schindler, Nathan Wurzel, had first written to the Joint in Paris in the fall of 1951 under his new Israeli name, Antoni Korzeniowski, about Oskar's whereabouts. But instead of accusing Schindler of brutality, he said that he wanted to find him so that Oskar could help him locate his "lost relatives."[27]

It would be almost a year before Joint officials heard again from Oskar Schindler. On September 21, 1954, Oskar paid a visit to Joint offices in Buenos Aires, where he discussed with Moses Leavitt, the international head of the Joint, who was visiting the Argentine capital, the possibility of the Joint's granting him a two-year loan of $5,000 against a second mortgage on his property in San Vicente. Jacobo Murmis, who was still a partner in Oskar and Emilie's nutria farm, strongly backed the idea and said the loan would be "amply covered." Leavitt said he would agree to recommend the loan to the Joint's executive committee in New York only if Oskar took out a third mortgage on the property and agreed to pay it back in two years. With only one dissenting vote, the committee approved the loan because of Schindler's "assistance to so many of the people in whom [they] were interested." The only stipulation was that the third mortgage had to be in Murmis's name. On October 14, 1954, the Joint office in Buenos Aires gave Oskar Arg$130,000, the equivalent of $5,000. But when it came time to repay the loan two years later, Oskar was unable to do so because, Murmis explained, he had "economic difficulties" and had not yet received his "Widergutmachung [reparations] from Germany, which he [had] been awaiting for such a long time." Murmis advised the Joint to give Oskar a ten-month payment extension on the loan, which it did, though he also asked Joint officials in New York for an explanatory letter about the nature of the loan so that he would not to have to pay Argentine income taxes on the $5,000. Because Oskar never did repay the loan, he seriously damaged his relationship with Murmis; it seems that he even blamed Murmis for some of his financial difficulties.[28]

For all practical purposes, the scheme to farm and raise poultry and nutria had failed and the Schindlers were deeply in debt. At the end of 1955, Itzhak Stern, now acting as Oskar's "general attorney," received this letter from Schindler:

[My] farm has produced great debts, which I could balance out during normal times.

But agriculture is first of all a business with the good Lord, dependent on numerous factors, and second, there is only one harvest per year, which means that I have a very low capital flow. Necessary investments with extremely high interest rates were not successful. At least my wife enjoys animals, which makes the work a little more fun for her. Due to the enormously high social and food costs I gave up breeding poultry three years ago and have focused solely on the breeding of nutria. But even with nutria the relation between costs and sale prices is getting worse every year. Three months ago I began preliminary plans to sell half the farm as construction land to ease my debts. But the plans of the revolutionary [Argentine] government to devalue the peso will delay this sale of the property and the construction of apartments on it for several months. Right now everything seems paralyzed though my duties and obligations go on.[29]

Oskar frustratingly added that had he "been lazy over the past six years instead of working hard, [he] probably would not even have one third" of his current debts. Yet he also seemed willing to accept some of the blame for his financial problems. He explained that though he had no control over the Argentine economic crisis, which included the devaluation of the peso, he "should have long ago given up this occupation [farming], which kills your intelligence." He added, "I should have looked for a better way to earn a living."[30] In another letter to Stern the following spring, Oskar expressed frustration over his "isolation and mind-killing inactivity." But he hoped that his "good star" would soon be in the ascent. But what bothered him most was his "powerlessness" in confronting his most basic problems.[31]

But Oskar's failures in Argentina could not be solely blamed on the government or the economy. After Schindler died in Hildesheim in Germany in the fall of 1974, a memorial service was held for him in Frankfurt before his body was shipped to Israel for burial. When the service was over, Mietek Pemper approached one of the Argentine Schindler Jews and asked him how they could have let Oskar lose everything in Argentina. The Schindler Jew responded, "You cannot reprimand us for the fact that there were people in Buenos Aires who could play poker much better than Oskar Schindler."[32]

Oskar's financial situation continued to deteriorate during his last months in Argentina and, on November 20, 1956, he wrote another letter to Stern: "I am at the end and only a quick partial payment of my claim against the Federal Republic can save me."[33] Once again, his Schindler Jews came to his rescue. On January 23, 1957, Roma Horowitz and five Schindler Jews asked Sidney Nelson, now the head of Joint operations in Buenos Aires, to forward a letter they had written to Moses Leavitt in New York, further explaining Oskar's desperate financial situation and asking for more help. Schindler, they explained, had been living for the past few years "under really impossible and not–to–be borne circumstances." When he arrived in Argentina, he was "badly advised" on how best to invest the money he had received from the Joint and now stood "on the brink of a complete bankruptcy." Consequently, despite his willingness to work, Schindler was "totally unable to pay the enormous overheads and taxes from what he makes." His relationship with his former partner, Jacobo Murmis, was now over "since it [had] brought nothing but losses through the years." The only option open to Schindler at this point was to sell what remaining land he owned, which was impossible "due to the circumstances" current in Argentina. If Oskar could sell his land, the Schindler Jews wrote, then he could go to West Germany where he was supposed to receive "a great deal of money" from the *Lastenausgleich* fund. But he would need considerable travel and living funds and, consequently, the group asked the Joint to loan Oskar another $2,000 to help him make the trip. Oskar would repay this money as soon as he received his *Lastenausgleich* money. If they could, they explained, they would loan Oskar the money themselves but they simply did not have it. At the same time, they argued, $2,000 was "really a very small sum in comparison to what Mr. Schindler did to save so many of [them]." They went on to say that the "Jewry of the whole world and especially the thousand . . . whom he saved will undoubtedly be proud to know that it [the Joint] helped such a man and saved him from an extremely unpleasant fate."[34]

Several months later, Nelson informed New York of conversations he subsequently had with Murmis and several other Jews in Buenos Aires who knew Oskar well. They said that the Joint should not loan him any more because he might "use the money for some other purpose and fail to carry out his intended mission." They also told Nelson that Schindler had "a history of obvious financial irresponsibility." On the other hand, Murmis and others suggested that the Joint consider buying Schindler a round-trip airplane ticket to Germany and give him $200 to $300 for expenses. And even though they questioned Oskar's handling of money, they reminded Nelson of his "invaluable service" to fellow Jews during the Holocaust and of the "many friends who [had] been calling insistently on his behalf." As the Joint had gone this far with Schindler, they thought it should do everything reasonably possible to help him settle his claim.[35]

In late April 1957, Moses Leavitt told Nelson that he had talked to Mr. Mirelman, a prominent Jewish leader whom Oskar had also contacted about the loan. Oskar asked Mirelman, who was evidently quite fond of

Schindler, "to press the request upon [the Joint]" and also to let him visit the United States on his return trip from Germany. Oskar told Mirelman that he hoped to stop off in Venezuela on his way back from Germany to see whether he "could do something in that country." Leavitt added that Nelson should tell Mr. Schindler that the Joint could not keep making loans to him, though it was prepared to help him with his trip to Germany if he could provide the Joint with information regarding the status of his *Lastenausgleich* claim. But Leavitt also wanted to determine whether there was any need for Oskar to go to Germany. If so, he was ready to ask URO lawyers to look into Schindler's claim and determine whether they could help him win settlement sooner. But nothing more could be done until Oskar gave them an update on his *Lastenausgleich* application.[36]

Nelson informed Oskar of Leavitt's request and Schindler sent Leavitt a copy of the *Lastenausgleich* application that had been sent by several *Schindlerjuden* to Dr. Theodor Heuss, the president of the Society for Christian-Jewish Cooperation *(Gesellschaft Christlich-Jüdischer Zusammenarbeit)*, and the first president of the Federal Republic of Germany. Other than Konrad Adenauer, Heuss was West Germany's most prominent elder statesman. Oskar told Leavitt that he had also approached Dr. Nahum Goldmann, the president of the Claims Conference and the chairman of the World Jewish Congress, about the matter. When Schindler later met Goldmann in Buenos Aires, he gave Oskar a letter of introduction to present to Felix von Eckhardt, the chief of the press and information service of the West German government.[37] It stated that Schindler had become "an outright legendary figure among many Jewish refugees" because of his efforts to help them during the war. He mentioned Oskar's stalled claims efforts and asked Eckhardt to do everything he could to help him, particularly in regard to connections in Bonn. Separately, Goldmann told Schindler he would do whatever was necessary to help his case when the Jewish leader was in Germany that summer. Because of this, Oskar concluded that it was urgent for him to go to Germany as quickly as possible. In a May 11, 1957, letter to Moses Leavitt, Oskar said he needed a loan from the Joint to get there. He added that he now planned to stop in the United States on his way to Germany but assured Leavitt that it would not cost that much more to make this side trip.[38]

From what we can gather from Oskar's private papers, the United Restitution Office was now handling Oskar's application. On March 30, 1955, the Compensation Office *(Ausgleichsamt)* in Regensburg had written Dr. H. Wolf, of the URO's office in Munich, and reminded him that

Schindler had to be a resident of West Germany or West Berlin by December 31, 1950. In addition, Schindler was not registered at the local refugee office as an exiled person and had emigrated to Argentina on September 7, 1949. Consequently, he did not meet any of the residency criteria under the *Lastenausgleich* law for compensation. This, of course, did not prevent Oskar from continuing to press his case. In the fall of 1956, he forwarded a new set of application forms to Dr. Wolf in the URO office in Munich. When he heard nothing back, he again enlisted the help of *Schindlerjuden* in Argentina, which prompted the January 28, 1957, letter to Dr. Heuss in Bonn.[39]

This letter, which was signed by Roma and Edmund Horowitz as well as nine other Schindler Jews from Buenos Aires, went into detail about Oskar's aid to Jews during the war. The authors included a copy of the May 8, 1945, letter given to him by prominent Brünnlitz Jews and also mentioned Emilie's sacrifices and good deeds. What was so impressive about Schindler's efforts, the letter noted, was not the money he spent to save Jews or the danger to his own person. It was his consistent aid to Jews throughout the war. Oskar was, they explained, more determined to protect his Jews until liberation than to "bring his life and wealth to safety." For the past two years, the Schindler Jews wrote, he had lived without income and it was only through the efforts of the Joint that he was now able to return to Germany to press his *Lastenausgleich* claim. Unfortunately, despite the support of the Joint and the URO, his claim was tied up with "the usual bureaucratic rhythm" at the Regensburg refugee office. The Schindler Jews pleaded with Dr. Heuss to do everything he could to push Oskar's case to conclusion. They argued that it was essential to do whatever possible to help this "deserving man, who in the most dangerous time showed extraordinary heroism." It was important that he no longer be allowed "to vegetate in a catastrophic and shameful situation, without hope, in the shadow of [Germany's] economic miracle."[40]

In the meantime, the Joint continued to investigate the status of Oskar's claim through the URO in Munich. In June, the Joint bought him a round-trip airline ticket with a stopover in New York. In addition, the Joint also gave him about $750 in pocket money. Oskar flew to New York in mid-June, where he spent almost three weeks with Schindler Jews there, and arrived in Frankfurt in early July. Within a few weeks, he was out of money and called Dr. Katzenstein, who was now working with the Claims Conference in Frankfurt. He told Dr. Katzenstein that he had arrived in Germany with only $400 in his pocket and was now down to $100. Dr.

Katzenstein had helped Oskar quite a lot and had introduced him to Dr. Heuss and the Minister of Finance. He was also convinced that Oskar would soon receive his *Lastenausgleich* payment but needed some money to tide him over until he received it. Dr. Katzenstein called the Claims Conference about Schindler and they said that they could not help him. The Claims Conference suggested that Dr. Katzenstein contact the Joint, as it had already helped Oskar quite a bit. Officials at the Claims Conference also thought it might embarrass "Mr. Schindler if he were to be assisted by another organization."[41]

Oskar came to the Joint office in Frankfurt on August 6, 1957, and explained his predicament to officials there. He stated that he had left Argentina with $1,000 and arrived in Germany with only $400, meaning that he had spent $600 while in the United States. He added that he "had left his wife without money and he had to send her $100." What he wanted was a loan of DM 1,000 ($238), which he would repay when he received his *Lastenausgleich* payment, which he expected in a few months. He added that it had cost him about $400 to live during his first month in Germany and thought that DM 1,000 would get him through the next few months. Joint officials decided to grant Oskar the loan, which he agreed to pay back in three months.[42]

Needless to say, Schindler did not repay the loan because his *Lastenausgleich* payment was delayed. Furthermore, several months later he cashed in the return portion of his KLM ticket that the Joint had bought for him. And by January 1958, he was broke again and approached the Joint for another loan. But this time he at least had confirmation from his attorney, Dr. Alexander Besser, that he had been approved for a minimum *Lastenausgleich* payment of DM 50,000 ($11,905). Moreover, Dr. Katzenstein had now become Oskar's advocate and his story began to appear in publications such as *Reader's Digest* and the *Catholic Digest*. This was probably because of the publicity he got in the *New York Times*, *The Forward*, and other American publications while he was in New York in June. His trip to New York was also picked up by the Sudeten German *Der Sudetendeutsche* and other German publications. He stayed with Henry and Manci Rosner while in New York and held a press conference at Joint headquarters there. Slowly, Oskar Schindler was becoming famous. He was also becoming accustomed to the adoration of his Schindler Jews, who were vocal about his deeds and current plight.[43]

Consequently, after considerable discussion, the Joint approved a new loan of DM 1,200 DM ($286), which would be paid back in two installments with the proviso that this would be the last loan that it gave Oskar Schindler. But two months later, Dr. Katzenstein and Schindler's attorney, Dr. Besser, approached the Joint again about a new loan. Given the large amount of money that the Joint had loaned or given him over the years, it is not surprising that his request was turned down. Moreover, Oskar never repaid any of the loans that the Joint gave him between 1954 and 1958. In the end, the Joint simply had to absorb these losses. Yet it did not sever its ties with Schindler and still intervened on his behalf the following year when Jacobo Murmis tried to foreclose on the two mortgages he had on Schindler's property in Argentina.[44]

The Struggle to Succeed in Germany

The *Lastenausgleich* program was set up in West Germany to compensate Germans who had lost property during the war; ultimately, it paid out more than DM 140 billion ($93,000,000,000) in compensation, much of it in pensions. It was not designed to pay for full property loss and payments. Full restitution was available only for those with claims of DM 5,000 ($3,300); large claims such as Schindler's would receive only a small percentage of their actual property loss. Needless to say, West German *Lastenausgleich* officials reduced Oskar's initial claim of DM 5,256,400 ($1,251,524) substantially after he filed his claim. Between 1962 and 1968, the West German government gave him DM 177,651 ($42,298). According to Oskar, about two thirds of this money went to pay off his debts or his legal fees. What remained, about DM 50,000 ($11,905), was credited to him to help buy a new factory. His estate received another DM 10,886 ($4,252) after his death to cover various expenses, and Emilie received a final payment of DM 18,541.88 ($7,243) from the West German government two years after Oskar's death.[45]

Oskar was too young for a *Lastenausgleich* pension in 1957, so the only way he could be compensated for his losses was through the purchase of a bankrupt business with a loan guaranteed by the *Lastenausgleich* bank in Bad Godesberg.[46] Most of the deals fell through, and the one business he finally succeeded in acquiring in 1962 quickly failed. These failures compounded the tragedy of Oskar Schindler's postwar life and left him devastated.

Oskar settled in Frankfurt after he arrived in Germany and soon rented a small apartment at Arndtstraße 46. Soon after his return to Germany, Oskar contacted Mietek Pemper, who was now living in Augsburg, and

asked him to help him work his way through the *Lastenausgleich* bureaucratic maze. Pemper, an extremely gentle, kind man, reminded me several
times during my interviews with him that he was hesitant to say anything
critical of Schindler. He owed his life to Oskar and simply would not
make negative comments about him. I interviewed Mr. Pemper in Augsburg in May 1999 and in January 2000. During our last visit, I asked Mr.
Pemper for more details about his relationship with Oskar after the war.
Until this moment in our conversation, I had been writing down everything he said. He gently put his hand on mine, a sign that he would tell me
a few things but did not want me to take them down. To honor his request, I will not reveal these particular things about Oskar.[47]

But during our first visit, he told me several things about Oskar that he
later repeated in an interview with two journalists from the *Stuttgarter
Zeitung*, Claudia Keller and Stefan Braun. They later published their interview with Mr. Pemper in their *Schindlers Koffer: Berichte aus dem
Leben eines Lebensretters* (1999), a collection that included their series of
articles about the contents of the recently discovered Schindler *Koffer*,
which contained many of Oskar's private papers. Pemper helped Oskar
put together his list of claims and went with him in 1958 to Bad Godesberg to press his claim. It became apparent, at least to Pemper, that this
matter was not going to be settled quickly. Though there were many failed
businesses to take over, the "elderly gentlemen" in the claims office constantly "fixed new levies and always demanded new evidence and documents" from Oskar, delays that kept him from acquiring one of the bankrupt firms. On one occasion, as Schindler and Pemper left the claims
office, Oskar told Pemper: "You know, if I had murdered 1,200 Jews instead of rescuing them, I would have had no difficulty receiving my *Lastenausgleich* payment."[48]

But Pemper also admitted that you could not blame all the problems
Oskar had in getting his *Lastenausgleich* loan on officials in Bad Godesberg. Oskar, he said, "had absolutely no understanding about the whole
paper war." Oskar was not a good planner. This did not fit with his personality. Pemper stated that he always felt he had "two opponents" to
deal with as he helped Oskar try to settle his claim. The first was the bureaucracy and the second was Oskar himself. Schindler did not seem to
care about the financial state of any of the firms he looked at. All he
wanted to do was close the deal quickly, something that Pemper advised
him not to do. To some extent, Oskar's later failure was caused by this im-
patience and his seeming inability "to find his way again." Pemper said

that Oskar had never really gained entrepreneurial experience in Czechoslovakia, Kraków, and Brünnlitz. Emalia, for example, was run by Schindler's Jews. And Oskar did not invest all the money he received from the *Lastenausgleich* fund in the firm he finally acquired in 1962. Moreover, Oskar was simply not a desk person. It was one thing to run a large factory with thousands of employees as he did during the war, but Schindler was simply incapable of making the step "downwards."[49]

In his haste to find a business, any business, that he could quickly take over, Oskar first tried to buy into a firm owned by an Israeli, Benjamin Mayer, who owned a chemical and plastics company, "MAFIT." After this deal fell through, Oskar, working through his attorney, Dr. Alexander Besser, whom Mr. Pemper did not consider particularly helpful, then tried to purchase the Feinlederfabrik Albert Kastner, a fine-leather factory in Kemnath that made high-quality leather goods, in late 1958. Oskar and Dr. Besser spent months working out the deal to buy the leather factory, only to have it fall through because of problems with officials in Bad Godesberg. Oskar then unsuccessfully tried to buy a bankrupt box factory in Kemnath in early 1959.[50]

Next, Oskar tried to buy a cannery, the Konservenfabrik Remy & Kohlhaas in Erbach/Rheingau. After the cannery deal fell through, Oskar then briefly considered buying the Hotel Jung in Rüdesheim am Rhein.[51] But like the rest of his earlier deals, the venture fell through because of problems with *Lastenausgleich* funding. It was not until 1962, more than four years after Oskar arrived in West Germany, that he was finally able to purchase a business, the Kunststeinwerk Kurt Ganz in Hochstadt am Main, in early 1962, with the help of a DM 50,000 ($11,905) credit from his *Lastenausgleich* compensation. There is no doubt that the transfer of his claim from Bad Godesberg to Hessen state officials in Regensburg helped speed along a final decision on his case. He quickly renamed the company the Beton-und Kunststeinwerk Oskar Schindler (Concrete and Artificial Stone Work Oskar Schindler). The firm made window boards and stair cases made from stone and cement. But within a year, the factory went bankrupt, and, in the process of trying to run it, Oskar suffered a severe heart attack that almost killed him.[52]

Oskar later blamed the failure of his business in Hochstadt on the lack of adequate *Lastenausgleich* funds, a bad winter, and the high monthly rent for the factory. But he also had trouble with his thirty-five workers, particularly after he was nominated as a Righteous Among the Nations (Righteous Gentile) in Israel in the spring of 1962. According to Oskar, his workers physically attacked him and called him a *"Judenfreund"* (friend of the Jews).[53] This would not be the last time Oskar had trouble with accusations that he was sympathetic towards Jews. Richard Hackenburg, an old Sudeten German friend who lived in Frankfurt, said that on another occasion Oskar attacked a man who called him a *"Judenknecht"* (vassal or servant of the Jews). The accuser took Oskar to court over the matter and Schindler had to pay a fine for the incident.[54]

On January 24, 1963, Oskar sent a letter to Itzhak Stern, Jakob Sternberg, and Dr. Moshe Bejski in Israel:

> In the last two weeks I successfully delayed attempts to shut down my factory by promising improvements in the factory, at least in the short term. Unfortunately, we are experiencing a winter that I have not seen in Germany in many, many years. It even created problems for stable construction firms. I am very pessimistic about the upcoming weeks. We lack the most basic financial resources to last until we receive our next *Lastenausgleich* payment. Friendly talks at conference tables do not produce wages and without wages the workers are not motivated to work. The fact that I am physically and psychologically near the end is caused not only because of my coronary heart problems, which are continually being treated but have gotten much better since I lost 10 kg [22 lbs.] but also the ever tiring fight against hidden attacks.[55]

By the end of 1963, Oskar was forced to declare bankruptcy. He later stated that the "process of dissolving the business was paid for by me with a voluntary 20 percent settlement from delayed *Lastenausgleich* payments" received after the collapse of the concrete and stone business. Between 1962 and 1964, Oskar received over DM 45,000 ($10,714) from the *Lastenausgleich* fund to help settle his debts. In 1964, he had a massive heart attack and spent a month in a sanatorium. For the next ten years, Oskar struggled with growing health problems that would have crippled a weaker man.

Fame and the Righteous Gentile Controversy

From the late 1940s on, Schindler Jews in Europe and the United States had done everything they could to tell the world about Oskar Schindler's deeds during the war. Stories about Oskar's exploits appeared periodically in newspapers and magazines in Europe and the United States. But some Schindler Jews, such as Leopold "Poldek" Page and Itzhak Stern, were determined to tell Schindler's story to a broader audience. Their efforts resulted in his nomination as a Righteous Among the Nations (Righteous Gentile) by Yad Vashem in 1962, which became mired in controversy. In this particular instance, though, Oskar was able to mask his disappointment with the adoring tributes he received from the Schindler Jews who wined and dined him while he was in Israel to receive the award in 1962.

Leopold "Poldek" Page was one of the driving forces behind efforts to tell the world of Oskar's work to save more than a thousand Jews during the Holocaust. In the early 1950s he convinced the famed Austrian American film director Fritz Lang to consider doing a film on Schindler and in the 1960s was the driving force behind MGM's decision to make a film about Oskar on his wartime heroics. After Schindler's death, Page continued to promote Schindler's story and was the one who convinced Thomas Keneally to write *Schindler's Ark* (later *Schindler's List*). A decade or so later, Steven Spielberg, using Page as his film consultant, produced *Schindler's List* based on Keneally's historical novel.

After the war, Poldek Page and his wife, Ludmilla (Mila), fled to Bratislava, Slovakia, and then struggled to find a way to Palestine. Ludmilla Page shared this information with me when I interviewed her in November 2001. I was in Los Angeles to give The "1939" Club's Leopold Page Memorial Righteous Rescuers Lecture at Chapman University, which was sponsored by Steven Spielberg's Righteous Persons Foundation. Poldek had died earlier that year, which made my visit with Mrs. Page particularly special.

Ludmilla Page is a study in graciousness. Though she was never as well-known as her husband, she was an integral part of the Schindler story. She and Poldek married while they were still in the Kraków ghetto. Though she and Poldek knew Oskar throughout the war they did not begin working for him until they were put on the famous "Schindler's Lists" in the fall of 1944. When the war ended, Poldek and Ludmilla began a modest odyssey that took them to Bratislava, Budapest, and Prague before they wound up in Munich, where they reconnected with Oskar. They lived in Munich for two years and spent a great deal of time with Oskar, who traveled to Munich frequently to meet with the many Schindler Jews there. They would frequently meet him at the city's Deutsches Museum, which at the time served as a refugee center. Ludmilla particularly remembered Oskar's birthday party in Regensburg in 1946, which brought together Schindler Jews from throughout the area.[56]

After failing to find a way into Palestine, Poldek decided to try to get papers for the United States, which he received in the spring of 1947. But before he left Germany, Poldek promised Oskar that he would do everything he could "to make his name a household word."[57] The Pages lived in New York for three years. Though well-educated, Poldek had no trade or technical skills. He got a job in New York as a shipping clerk with a company that imported leather goods from Latin America. A friend, Arthur Rand, suggested that Page open a leather repair shop. Poldek then walked into a New York city bank and asked a banker for a $1,200 loan to start his new business. When the banker asked Page for collateral, he held up his hands and said, "These will pay back your loan." Page then persuaded the import company he was working for to let him repair their bags. When they had free time, Poldek and Mila (Ludmilla) would hand out leaflets advertising their repair service on Madison Avenue. Poldek repaired the bags and Mila, who also worked as a seamstress at Maximillan furs, delivered them to their customers. In 1950, Poldek and Mila followed Arthur Rand to California. Before they left New York, several of their friends suggested that they settle in the "triangle" area of Los Angeles, which included Beverly Hills. When they got to California, the Pages decided to open a small leather repair shop there. Throughout this period of transition, the Pages had maintained contact with Oskar. They were also friends with Roma and Edmund Horowitz, who traveled with the Schindlers to Argentina in 1949.[58]

Ludmilla described their first leather repair shop, which was on Linden Drive, as a "hole in the wall." However, it was significant enough to attract customers such as Lily Latté, who managed Fritz Lang's household and later became his wife. It was not until after the war that Schindler Jews such as Page came to appreciate the significance of what Oskar had done to save them. Page, though, was more than just appreciative. He would spend the rest of his life trying to tell the world of Oskar's exploits. And his small shop in Beverly Hills, the home of many Hollywood greats, would be his Schindler pulpit. Poldek and Ludmilla met Lang through Lily, who came into Poldek's shop to have a bag repaired. When the gregarious Poldek learned who she worked for, he told her Schindler's story. Latté, a statuesque native Berliner and a Jew, was a very influential figure in Lang's complex life, and he was quite dependent on her.[59]

Page's stories about Oskar evidently moved Ms. Latté and on April 27, 1951, she wrote Oskar expressing Lang's interest in his wartime efforts to save Jews. Oskar wrote back in June and said he knew that "a superb personality such as Mr. Fritz Lang could create a masterpiece of incalculable psychological value from this factual material." Oskar said that, in principle, he was agreeable to the filming of his experiences during the war as long as Lang based it on fact. "Pfefferberg [Page]" could provide Lang with the appropriate introductions to his story and even flesh out some of the important details. Oskar enclosed some important documents with his letter related to his story. He authorized Page, who had his "unconditional trust," to undertake the "required initial negotiations" for the film. On the other hand, he added, if these talks led to a movie deal, then Oskar wanted to be a direct part of the film project because he "had the chance during those sad years to experience the mentality of both fronts and to study them from both sides." He added: "I cannot imagine that a merely written transference of the material is possible, despite consideration of a sensitive movement, without distortion and shallowness being the consequence."[60]

A month later, Oskar sent Lang a letter that went into great detail about his life before and during the war. At some point in the talks about a film deal, Poldek and Mila invited Lang and Latté to their small apartment for dinner. Mila admitted that she was an inexperienced hostess, and was quite nervous, given Lang's fame as a film director. But the mercurial Lang, who could be quite harsh at times, was most complimentary of the meal. He was particularly taken by Mila's thoughtfulness in serving her guests chocolates afterwards. Lang told her that such niceties were "so refreshing. In the U.S., you finish dinner and that's it."[61]

It is difficult to say how serious Lang was about the Schindler story. He met the Pages at one of the lowest points in his career. His worst film, *American Guerilla*, had just been released and Lang was convinced that he was the subject of secret investigations by the House Committee on Un-American Activities. In some ways, he was a Hollywood "untouchable." Even so, his cinematic output during this low point in his career was still remarkable. He directed two films in 1952 and the same number a year later. So his interest in Oskar's story did not come from a directorial void in his life. It is possible, of course, that he was interested in Schindler's heroics during the war because they involved a fellow countryman who was that rare "good German." Yet Lang bore no love for Germany and in late 1944 he spoke out against Fred Zinnemann's *The Seventh Cross*, which told the story of escaped concentration camp inmates who were helped by the German resistance.[62] Lang thought it was "too soon to celebrate any good in the German character."[63] More than likely, though, Lang was interested in Schindler because he had saved

Jews. But Lang, who was half Jewish, always regarded himself as a Catholic and seldom talked about his Jewish background. On the other hand, most of the people he worked with in his company, Diana Productions, were Jewish, as was Lily, whom he married in a private Jewish ceremony.[64] He did this for Lily, who was "highly conscious of her Jewishness."[65] So in the end, it was probably Lily and the Jewish aspect of the Schindler legend that drew Lang to Poldek and Ludmilla.

Regardless, nothing ever came of the Lang film idea except for the seed that he planted in Oskar and Poldek's minds about a future movie deal. It is difficult to say why the film deal with Lang fell through, though Oskar provided a partial explanation in a letter he wrote to Page in early 1965 when they were working on another film idea about Schindler's wartime experiences. Oskar reminded Poldek how difficult it had been during his negotiations with Fritz Lang ten years previously "to find an idealist for a movie about concentration camps who was ready to sacrifice even one dollar."[66] According to Ned Comstock, the well-respected archivist who oversees the vast Fritz Lang collection in The Cinema-Television Library and Archives of the Performing Arts at the University of Southern California, Los Angeles, there is nothing in the collection on Schindler. The only written record we have of any contact between Oskar and Lang is the lengthy biographical letter that Oskar wrote Lang on July 20, 1951.[67]

But Page was not the only Schindler survivor who was trying to tell the world about Oskar. As early as June 1947, several Schindler women approached Kurt R. Grossman, a Jew who had fled Germany in 1933 and was at the time working for the World Jewish Congress (WJC), and asked him to send food packages to Oskar in Germany. After they explained why, Grossman, a prominent intellectual and scholar, became fascinated with Schindler's story and during the next decade discussed it frequently with his colleagues. In 1956, he asked Oskar to contribute an essay on his experiences to a collection of testimonies that Grossman was putting together on Gentiles who had helped Jews during the Holocaust. And prior to Oskar's return to Germany in 1957, Grossmann wrote letters of introduction for him to government officials and the editors of several newspapers such as the *Süddeutsche Zeitung* and the *Frankfurter Neue Presse*. Grossmann wanted them to know that the most prominent figure in his book, *Die unbesungenen Helden: Menschen in Deutschlands dunklen Tagen* (The Unsung Heroes: People in Germany's Dark Days), would be returning to Germany on the eve of its publication in Berlin.[68] By the time that Oskar left Argentina in 1957, he was gradually becoming famous in certain circles in the United States, Germany, and Israel. This was, of course, all due the efforts of his beloved Schindler Jews.

And Oskar had a no more devoted follower that Itzhak Stern, who had settled in Tel Aviv after the war and served as Oskar's legal adviser before his return to Germany. At the time, Stern was Oskar's closest confidant in Israel, though Oskar also had strong relationships with Simon Jeret, Dr. Moshe Bejski, and Jakob Sternberg, among others. But in the 1950s, it was Stern's advice that he most sought in Israel. Oskar sent Stern a rough draft of the article he planned to send Grossman for publication and asked his advice about it. At the time, in addition to offering Oskar legal advice about his *Lastenausgleich* efforts in Germany, Stern was also acting as Oskar's go-between with Dr. Kurt Jakob Ball-Kaduri, who was collecting testimony about Schindler's activities during the war for the newly established Holocaust memorial and archives in Jerusalem, Yad Vashem. Oskar sent Stern, whom he occasionally referred to as "Izu," various documents for Dr. Ball-Kaduri's investigation, including the April 18, 1945, Brünnlitz "Schindler's Lists." In December 1956, Stern gave the Yad Vashem archivist a detailed account of his own experiences with Schindler. The testimony and other documentation that Dr. Ball-Kaduri collected on Oskar would later help prod Yad Vashem to consider nominating Schindler as a Righteous Among the Nations in 1962. Schindler's nomination, though, was going to be clouded by a controversy over his actions during the war that begin in the 1950s and haunted him for years.[69]

One of the most interesting things about Oskar's correspondence with Stern at this time was his pro-Israeli attitudes. On October 29, 1956, a joint Anglo-French-Israeli alliance attacked Egypt. The British and the French wanted to end Egypt's nationalization of the Suez Canal and Israel was responding to a blockade of its shipping in the canal as well as to escalating Arab guerilla attacks and military threats from Egypt. Within a matter of days, Israel, as part of the Allied military effort, had captured the Gaza Strip and much of the Sinai desert. The crisis that led up to the invasion had been developing for more than a year. It almost exploded into war in April 1956, when Egypt mounted a series of deadly guerilla attacks against Israeli settlers in the Gaza Strip in response to Israeli mortar attacks in Gaza City.[70] Oskar wrote Stern on April 16 that he was "filled with unrest at having to experience [Israel's] difficult situation without being able to do anything to help [his] old friends." If he were in Israel, Oskar assured Stern, he would do something "to help ˉˉour good cause."[71]

And on November 20, 1956, Oskar congratulated Stern for Israel's recent military successes, particularly the capture of so many Arab weapons. He wrote Stern that he hoped that God would assure that "no serious complications occur" and regretted that Israel had not taken Jerusalem. But this could, he assured "Izu," come at a later time. Oskar added that he had "always advocated that one must defend Israel at the Suez and the Black Sea, the Bosporus, and not in Jerusalem." In fact, Oskar wrote Stern that he was willing to help Israel in any way, even if "it were only as a tank driver." All he needed was an airline ticket. Then he would "come immediately."[72]

Oskar's growing, deep love for Israel, unfortunately, did not protect him from scandal in that country, which could be traced back to the last months before World War II. It had its postwar incarnation in 1951 when Natan Wurzel, who by this time had changed his name to Antoni Korzeniowski, wrote the Tel Aviv office of the Joint requesting the whereabouts of Oskar Schindler. Wurzel explained that he was looking for certain family members that he had lost contact with during the war. Helen Fink, a Joint administrative assistant, told Wurzel that she thought that Schindler had moved to Argentina. Four years later, Wurzel, now working with a Schindler Jew, Julius Wiener, openly charged Schindler with theft and abuse. It is difficult to determine what prompted both men to choose this particular time to mount their attack against Schindler. In a letter to Wiener in the spring of 1955, Wurzel told Julius that he wanted Schindler, whom he thought "live[d] well, with wealth, without worries," partially to compensate him for his wartime losses.[73] Given Oskar's impoverished lifestyle at this time in Argentina, it is difficult to know where Wurzel got the idea that Oskar was well off. Regardless, this sense that Oskar was flourishing in Argentina was what drove both men to begin telling Jewish organizations in Israel that Schindler had mistreated them during the Holocaust.

What made all this so bad was that their stories about Schindler ran counter to the evolving Schindler legend. Yet their accusations also served to rally the leadership among the two hundred to three hundred or so Schindler Jews in Israel at that time to his side and strengthen the resolve of Itzhak Stern and others to begin to gather testimony about "Schindler's miracle" for Yad Vashem. In fact, when Oskar was corresponding with Stern and Dr. Ball-Kaduri about his efforts during the war, Natan Wurzel and Julius Wiener were supplying Yad Vashem with testimony about their mistreatment at the hands of Oskar Schindler. The charges came at a particularly low point in Oskar's life and his only defense was a detailed account that he wrote in April 1955 to prominent Schindler Jews in Israel that centered around an attack against Wurzel, whom he considered a thief and a collaborationist. He ended this lengthy defense statement with a list of twenty names of Jews, Poles and Germans in Israel, Poland, the United States, Germany, and Austria who could back up what he said in defense of himself. But despite his efforts, the Wurzel-Wiener controversy would be a cloud over Oskar's head for years.[74]

The charges themselves could be traced back to the summer of 1939, when Wurzel claimed that he had bought the machinery and dies from the Jewish-owned, recently bankrupt Kraków enamelware factory, Rekord, Ltd. The initial controversy that later led to charges against Schindler centered around whether Wurzel had the legal right to take possession of the machinery and dies, which the factory's owners, Michał Gutman and Wolf Luzer Glajtman, essentially "pawned" to him in return for a loan they hoped would help keep the factory running.[75]

By early August 1939, both sides had hired lawyers to resolve the matter, which then went before the regional trade court in Kraków. When Oskar decided to buy the factory in 1942, the court appointed a lawyer, Dr. Bolesław Zawisza, to determine who really owned the factory prior to its auction in late June 1939. He wrote Wurzel about the matter and also interviewed him in the Brzesko ghetto. Wurzel, perhaps frightened by the prospect of a conflict with a German, told contradictory stories about his claim of ownership of the machines and the factory's enamelware. In his final letter to Dr. Zawisza on August 3, 1942, Wurzel said that he had denounced his right to the machines in August 1939, which he said he had bought for the owners of the factory.[76]

By 1941, Wurzel, who worked for Schindler for a year and a half after the war began, had several unpleasant run-ins with Emalia's lessee. Schindler became particularly annoyed with him after the manipulative Wurzel tried to have Abraham Bankier removed from his managerial position at Emalia. Oskar warned Wurzel about his behavior but finally got rid of him after he discovered that Wurzel had stolen money paid to Emalia by a German customer. But even after his dismissal, Wurzel continued to drop by Emalia for handouts of food. The kindly Bankier could not say no to someone in need.[77] According to Schindler, during one of these visits in the summer of 1941, Wurzel said something that angered *SS-Hauptsturmführer* Rolf Czurda, the SD's liaison with the Armaments Inspectorate. Czurda slapped Wurzel twice in front of Oskar and his secretary. Wurzel would later claim that Oskar ordered Czurda to strike him.[78]

Julius Wiener later testified that he heard a different account of the beating from Wurzel's brother. According to this version, Oskar had asked Wurzel to come to the factory and, once there, demanded that he sign a false statement saying that Wurzel had earlier sold the factory to a Christian. When Wurzel refused, Oskar had two SS men beat him. Wurzel then signed the false statement. Oskar warned him that if he talked about the incident, he would be sent to Auschwitz. Oskar never denied that Czurda slapped Wurzel though he did disagree with the claim that he had ordered the SS man to do it. He added that Wurzel used the incident to establish "a quite profitable collaboration" between himself and the *SS-Hauptsturmführer*.[79] For the most part, Oskar's version of the story, particularly as it relates to the ownership transfer of Rekord, Ltd., is more in line with Polish trade court records that Wurzel's account. But the charges of abuse, both on the part of Wurzel and later his friend, Julius Wiener, are a different matter.

Oskar's staunch defense of himself and his countercharges against Wurzel never adequately dealt with the accusations of abuse, particularly against Julius Wiener and his father, Shlomo. Nor did Oskar say much about the charges that he brutally took over the Wieners' wholesale business, which he then turned over to his mistress, Marta, to manage. According to Wiener, about a month before Oskar leased Emalia in the fall of 1939, he came to the office of the profitable enamelware wholesale business owned by Wiener's father, Shlomo, and forced the Wieners to accept him as its trustee. In the process, Oskar, in league with Marta, who accompanied him, claimed the Wieners were thieves. Oskar verbally abused the elder Wiener, and, according to Julius, even made him kiss Hitler's portrait. After he acquired the Wiener business, Oskar briefly kept both men on the payroll though he refused to let Shlomo on the premises. After Oskar acquired Emalia, he accused Julius of theft and fired him. When Julius tried to discuss this matter with him, Schindler had him beaten by six SS or Gestapo men. Afterwards, they warned him that if he ever returned to Emalia, they would take him to "a place from where there is no return."[80]

Oddly enough, Wiener somehow made it on one of "Schindler's Lists" in the fall of 1944, though he wanted nothing to do with Schindler. He seldom saw Oskar during his eight months in Brünnlitz, and when he did, Oskar asked him whether he had enough to eat and the whereabouts of his father.[81] This was all that Oskar seemed to remember about the Wiener affair. In his lengthy April 1955 defense letter to Salpeter, Stern, and others, he mentioned the Wieners only once and then in a very positive way. He said that he "only decided to lease the bankrupt Record and take up enamelware production in Krakow after [he] held several day-long friendly negotiations with the Jewish enamelware wholesalers like the brothers Bossak, Samuel [Shlomo] Wiener and son [Julius], Kempler, among others." During the negotiations, Oskar continued, "these gentlemen guaranteed the sale of the total production [of Emalia products] and spurred [him] on toward taking over the business."[82] Needless to say, Oskar never really addressed the Wieners' charges other than to imply that they somehow approved his takeover of Emalia even though they knew that their property was on the verge of Nazi appropriation. The logic of his argument does not fit with the racial and political realities at the time.

The testimony that Natan Wurzel gave to Yad Vashem in late 1956 against Oskar seemed to be the last shot fired in this phase of the Wurzel-Wiener controversy until 1961, when it flared up again after Oskar began to be considered a nominee for one of the first Righteous Among the Nations awards. There are a few letters between Simon Jeret and Oskar at the end of 1956 that touch on the matter, though most Schindler Jews such as Jeret seemed to respond to the charges indirectly by simply accentuating the wonderful things that Oskar had done for them during the war. In fact, this was the line taken by a group that called itself "The Enterprising Committee of the Work Camp Survivors Oskar Schindler in Brünnlitz," when they wrote to Dr. Aryeh Kubovy, the head of Yad Vashem, which had been created in 1953 to commemorate the Holocaust. According to the Yad Vashem Law that created the Israeli Holocaust commemoration authority, one of its missions was to honor the *hasidei umot haolan* (Righteous Among the Nations or "Righteous Gentiles"), non-Jews who risked their lives to help Jews.[83]

By the time the "Enterprising Committee" wrote Dr. Kubovy, the Yad Vashem authority had created a Righteous Among the Nations committee headed by Dr. Moshe Landau to consider naming the first group of Righteous Gentiles. The Schindler committee's letter was prompted by news that Oskar was living in poverty. In early December 1962, an announcement appeared in the Polish-Israeli newspaper, *Nowiny I Kurier* asking "all former captives of concentration camp Brinnlitz who knew Oskar Schindler the German should contact the newspaper immediately." The newspaper editor, Edward Rosdal, strengthened the appeal when he wrote in an editorial that "the laws of God never forget that the just may forgive that there was goodness among oppression and friends among enemies." The newspaper was flooded with replies from Schindler Jews who wanted to help their savior.[84] Ultimately, the group collected $4,000 for Oskar and sent it to him in Germany. As the collection effort filtered through Israel's large *Schindlerjuden* community, Wurzel-Kozienowski and Wiener revived their charges against Oskar, who was now under consideration as a Righteous Among the Nations. The letter from the "Enterprising Committee," which was signed by fourteen Schindler Jews, among them Jakob Sternberg and Itzhak Stern, intended their letter to respond not only to the charges against him but also to document Schindler's actions as a "saving angel sent by Providence to Poland in 1939." From their perspective, it was imperative that Oskar "receive the recognition of the people and the State (of Israel)" for saving 1,200 Jews during the Shoah.[85]

In fact, the "Enterprising Committee" had conducted its own investigation into the charges and told Dr. Kubovy that there were so many "errors and contradictions" in Wurzel and Wiener's stories and charges that there was "doubt about the truth of their words." According to Moshe Bejski, he and the committee's leadership, Itzhak Stern, Jakob Sternberg, and Hersch Mandel met with Wiener in Stern's Tel Aviv apartment to discuss the charges against Schindler. Dr. Bejski asked Wiener whether the Germans had not taken his property outright in 1939. Wiener said no, the property was still under the control of the *Treuhänder* (trustee) system, which meant that his father still had indirect control over it. After Wiener repeated his accusations against Schindler to the group, Dr. Bejski asked Julius Wiener how he could make such charges. Wiener replied, "This was a testament to my late father." As he was dying in the Kraków ghetto, Shlomo Wiener told his son, "Do not forget what Schindler did to us."[86]

The committee, which had trouble accepting the charges even if they were true, was also upset because Oskar was not given an opportunity to respond to them. So because many of the committee members had known Wiener since he was a boy and were familiar with Wurzel's business dealings, they decided to testify for Oskar. And both men, the committee wrote, dealt more with "assumptions" than facts. The letter then went on to discuss the committee's major points of disagreement with Wiener and Wurzel. They were quite disturbed about Wiener's statement that Schindler saved Jews as an alibi to help save himself after the war. But, they asked, "an alibi for what?" For five and a half years "he was a man trusted by the Jews, he saved them; acted on their behalf; interfered in their favor every step of the way." The committee also pointed out that Wurzel and Wiener were the only Holocaust survivors who did not see Schindler "as a saving angel." They also disagreed with the charge that Oskar had fled Brünnlitz to escape punishment for his treatment of Jews. The committee reminded Dr. Kubovy of everything that Oskar had done to prepare them for his escape and the response of his survivors to his flight to the American zone.[87]

The letter went on to explain why they thought Julius Wiener had accused Oskar of stealing his father's business. It argued that the accusation "flowed from a personal hatred whose source [lay] in the fact that his late father, who died in the camp [Płaszów] from typhus (and was not murdered) said at the time of his death that Schindler took away his business." The letter added: "This is what Mr. Wiener holds as a testament against Schindler." The committee expressed sympathy for Shlomo Wiener's death, but stated: "Objectivity still compels us to view the matter correctly." In the end, the group explained, the source of Wiener and Wurzel's hatred of Schindler centered around an economic matter—"loss of property." Everyone on the committee had suffered financial and family losses. But in light of Wurzel's charges, one had to look "through the eyes of the situation of the Jews at that time," particularly "in light of the looting laws of the Nazis." Only then would "the actions of Mr. Schindler stand out."[88]

The committee then drew Dr. Kubovy's attention to a decree of September 6, 1939, and also cited an article that dealt with the creation of the trusteeship system, which either placed property in the hands of German *Treuhänder* or completely nationalized it. It is difficult to know what the committee meant by the decree of September 6. Was it a reference to several decisions made by Reinhard Heydrich at his Gestapo office in Berlin on September 7, 1939, regarding the forced expulsion and concentration of Jews in Poland and the expulsion and confiscation of the property of Polish Jews in Germany? Or could it be that the committee made an error on the date? Perhaps the letter was referring to the military order of September 29, 1939, which gave authorities the right to take over property owned by absentee owners or businesses that were not properly managed. This became the pretext for the seizure of Jewish property in Poland by trustees and others like Oskar Schindler. It might be, of course, that the committee was referring to Hermann Göring's decree of September 17, 1940, which ordered the immediate seizure of Jewish property in Poland with the exception of personal belongs.[89]

The committee went on to argue that Wurzel's charge that Schindler was dishonest was not valid because as late as 1942 he owned the machines in question and was working for Oskar. In fact, the Schindler committee noted, in light of German nationalization policies at the time, Wurzel's situation was unique because "he was still working in the business and did business as Schindler himself testifie[d]." And though the nationalization process was nothing more than "stealing Jewish property," Schindler thought that he was acting within German law when he acquired Emalia after it was nationalized. And, the committee told Dr. Kubovy, Wurzel benefitted from this situation until 1942. For a Jew to still own property this late in the war, the Schindler Jews wrote, was very unusual because by this time every Jew was willing to hand over everything he owned just to get a work permit.[90]

The committee argued that even if it accepted Wurzel's claim about the ownership of the machines as late as 1942, the fact remained that Jews were working in Emalia where the machines were located. Their work there allowed them to remain in the Kraków ghetto and avoid being expelled to a concentration camp. So if Wurzel was correct, and had refused to sign the papers transferring ownership of the machines to Schindler, his refusal "would have endangered the Jews that worked there under the protection of Mr. Schindler." And if you projected this situation forward to the last year of the war, when Oskar transferred "1,200" Jews to Brünnlitz and survival, then Wurzel's decision to transfer ownership of the machines kept these Jews "from the hell of Groß Rosen and Auschwitz." Moreover, what was the value of such property in light of ongoing Nazi Aryanization policies at the time? The "most valuable possession at that time was a work permit and bread and nothing more."[91]

The December 10 letter then asked about the nature of Wurzel and Schindler's relationship from 1939 to 1942. According to the committee's investigation, Wurzel claimed that his relations with Schindler were quite good until he left for Hungary in 1942. Certainly a Jew about to flee to Hungary would not have caused an uproar about property, particularly as Schindler knew all about his plans to flee. Moreover, was it possible for a man who was so kind and helpful to so many Jews during the war to be so "cruel and German like all Germans" towards only two Jews? To the "1,200" people he saved, the letter concluded, Oskar Schindler "was their rescuer from the moment that he happened on their path. . . . [It was] a singular and special occurrence and this [was] the attitude of all the survivors from all over the world." The committee had ample testimony to document Oskar's "deeds and actions" and thought it imperative that the people and the state of Israel honor this "man who gave his protection to the Jews in 1939, stayed with them for 5 1/2 years and risked his life for them; fed them; worried about them; and did for them more than any other man, and in the end saved them because of these actions."[92]

What is so interesting about this letter is that, unlike Schindler's April 1955 letter, it did not attack either Wiener or Wurzel and left open the possibility that some or all of their charges were true. There are really three issues here—whether Oskar Schindler stole Jewish property, abused Jews, and treated the bulk of the Jews he encountered with dignity for five and a half years and ultimately saved more than 1,000 of them from certain death. This was, of course, the crux of the whole Schindler controversy—the balance between Schindler's mistreatment of a few Jews and his kindness towards hundreds of others. From the perspective of the Schindler committee, it was hard to imagine a man who was so kind to his Jewish workers and risked life and limb for years to save them to have abused other Jews. Schindler was, of course, quite capable of abusing Jews and he even admitted this after the war. Moreover, he walked a fine line between the need to appear as a staunch Nazi in the eyes of Göth and the other Nazis he had to deal with every day and also be a good Samaritan to his Jewish workers. More than likely he did physically harm Julius and Shlomo Wiener and did take over their property as a trustee. Nazi law in this regard was simply a legalistic cover for theft and in that regard Oskar Schindler stole the Wieners' property. The question of Schindler's relationship and problems with Natan Wurzel is more complex and has been discussed in depth elsewhere in this study. Oskar's decision to acquire Emalia from the Polish trade court was really no different from what he did with the Wieners' property. It simply meant dealing with less German bureaucracy.

So the ultimate question unconsciously raised by some of Israel's most prominent Schindler Jews in their letter to Dr. Kubovy was whether Schindler's seizure of Jewish property and possible abuse of the Wieners and Natan Wurzel was morally counterbalanced by what he later did with the property to help a much larger group of Jews. Unfortunately, the Schindler committee seemed to discount the worst charges against their "savior" by arguing that the same person who was so kind to so many certainly could not have been so horrible to just three Jews. This argument is weak. The Oskar Schindler of 1939 or even 1942 was not the same man in the later months and years of the war. Oskar Schindler came to Poland on the coattails of the Wehrmacht in the fall of 1939 to avoid military service and make his fortune. If it meant humiliating and slapping a few Jews around while he took over their property, then it is quite possible he did this.

But why did he treat the Wieners so shabbily while being so kind at this time to Abraham Bankier and Itzhak Stern? Schindler was the ultimate opportunist who saw the Wieners as a nuisance standing in the way of his acquisition of their business. On the other hand, an opportunistic Schindler treated men such as Itzhak Stern, Abraham Bankier, and even Natan Wurzel with greater respect because he needed their advice or expertise to help run Emalia. In other words, his initial relationship with these Jews was simply business, though in time he developed a genuine affection for Bankier and Stern. On the other hand, he became quite uncomfortable with Wurzel's aggressive efforts to undercut Bankier, whom Oskar genuinely cared for and trusted. But the committee seriously erred when it claimed that Oskar and Wurzel had a rosy relationship until 1942. By this time, Wurzel was already living in a ghetto and efforts to make him sign away the machines, which he did in 1941, not 1942, to Oskar had more to deal with legal niceties than any legitimate claim that Wurzel might have had on the machines. In other words, in the context of German Aryanization policies at the time, Wurzel had no other choice but to sign them over, which makes one wonder whether he needed to be beaten to do this. On the other hand, Wurzel also seemed to be a bit of a manipulator and very feisty, so it is possible that he went too far in his aggressiveness towards Schindler and Czurda. And even after Czurda had him beaten, Wurzel somehow knew how to make political gain out of the beating. So although many of the most prominent Schindler Jews held out the prospect that Oskar Schindler might have abused two Jews and stolen their property, his deeds throughout the rest of the war to help more than "1,200" other Jews tended to diminish the significance of his earlier "sins."

Needless to say, the letter to Dr. Kubovy did little to still the controversy surrounding Oskar's possible nomination as a Righteous Gentile. At the time, there were no specific guidelines for nominating and choosing a Righteous Gentile. The refusal of two Israeli Holocaust survivors, one of them a Schindler Jew, to rescind their accusations of theft and abuse ran counter to the spirit of the Righteous Among the Nations award. Beyond this, Israel was in the throes of the Adolf Eichmann trial at the time and it was essential for the credibility of Yad Vashem and the Righteous Among the Nations awards that the first group of Gentiles selected for this award be of sterling character and reputation when it came to the matter of saving Jews during the Holocaust.[93]

The relationship of the Eichmann trial to the Schindler controversy was important. Eichmann, one of the architects of the Holocaust, had fled to Argentina after the war and had been kidnapped by Mossad, Israel's General Security Service, in May 1960 and brought to Israel, where he was put on trial the following spring for various crimes against the Jewish people. His capture and trial consumed Israel for the next two years. Dr. Landau was the presiding judge at the trial and Dr. Moshe Bejski testified against Eichmann. He was found guilty on December 15, 1961, and sentenced to death. Eichmann appealed the sentence, which the Israeli Supreme Court turned down on May 29, 1962. Two days later, he was hanged.[94]

The Eichmann trial prompted many Schindler Jews in Israel to make comparisons between Eichmann and Schindler. On December 11, 1961, an article appeared in the London *Daily Mail* that contrasted the actions of the two men during the Holocaust. Most of the article, which was based on interviews with Schindler Jews, concentrated on Schindler's story. It ended with a statement that several Schindler Jews had prepared as part of their efforts to convince Yad Vashem to recognize Oskar for his efforts to save Jews during the Holocaust:

> We cannot forget the sorrow of Egypt, we cannot forget Haman [ancient Persian official who plotted to kill Jews but was stopped by Esther and hanged], we cannot forget Hitler. But we also cannot forget the just among the unjust; remember Oskar Schindler.[95]

In light of such feelings, it is not surprising that some of the most prominent Schindler Jews in Israel continued to push for such recognition for Oskar. Compared to Adolf Eichmann, Schindler was a saint, an "angel of mercy." Dr. Mordecai Paldiel, the head of the Righteous Gentile Department at Yad Vashem, told me that many Schindler Jews were aware of Oskar's earlier wartime transgressions, but thought he had atoned for his earlier conduct when he saved more than a thousand Jews at the end of the war. But Oskar's nomination caused some problems within the twelve-member Yad Vashem Directorate. Dr. Bejski, who became head of the new Designation of the Righteous Commission in 1970, told me that Dr. Moshe Landau, the first head of the committee and the Israeli Supreme Court justice who presided at Eichmann's trial, opposed Schindler's selection, along with several other committee members. Dr. Landau thought that the committee should select only the most outstanding humanitarians for this first round of the award who would then become models for future nominees. On the other hand, Justice Landau did not accept Wurzel and Wiener's accusations against Schindler. The discussion surrounding Oskar's nomination was heated and contentious. According to Dr. Paldiel, there was some concern that one or two committee members might resign if Schindler was selected. Those who opposed his nomination argued that he was a German and a Nazi Party member who partied with and befriended other Nazis. His supporters pointed to the large body of testimony in support of his nomination and the fact that he had directly saved the lives of almost 1,100 Jews during the last year of the war. In the end, a majority of the Yad Vashem Directorate voted to allow Oskar Schindler to plant a tree along the Avenue of the Righteous along with others in the first group of Righteous Gentile recipients. Emilie Schindler was never seriously considered for the award at that time.[96] The controversy did not end here, though, but continued until the end of 1963.

In the meantime, the principal Schindler Jews in Israel informed Oskar of his selection and told him that the planting of his carob tree along the Avenue of the Righteous at Yad Vashem would take place on May 1, 1962. This date coincided with Yom ha-Sho'ah, Israel's Holocaust Remembrance Day. Oskar must have been thrilled when he learned that he had been named a Righteous Gentile, though it was difficult to get him to commit to specific arrival and departure times. Dr. Bejski wrote him in mid-April suggesting that he arrive on April 27 and depart on May 8. Itzhak Stern had kept Oskar abreast of the developments in Israel and in turn had told Dr. Bejski about Oskar's good fortune in acquiring the stone and cement factory in Hochstadt am Main. This was probably why Oskar delayed telling Bejski when he would arrive in Israel. Dr. Bejski informed Oskar that the World Jewish Congress would help coordinate his visit and that his participation in the tree planting ceremony was "already assured." But Dr. Bejski also pressed Oskar for his arrival and departure dates because the Schindler Jews in Israel wanted "to prepare the press" for his arrival and make final plans for a reception in his honor and a meeting with Israel's Schindler Jews.[97]

And prepare they did. Oskar's arrival at the Lydda Airport near Tel Aviv airport was tumultuous. Dr. Bejski told me that word of Oskar's arrival had spread like wildfire among Israel's Schindler Jewish community once the Israeli-Polish newspaper *Noviny I Kurier* had announced the date and time of his arrival. It was April 28, 1962, Oskar's birthday. Much to the surprise of the police, three hundred Schindler Jews and their families had gathered on the observation deck of the airport terminal to wait for Oskar's arrival. As Oskar came down the steps of the plane, the crowd began to shout "Oskar, Oskar!" Dr. Bejski, who as a judge had a special permit to go to the steps of the plane, then escorted Oskar into the terminal, where the crowd of Schindler Jews pushed forward to touch him and shake his hand. Tears were streaming down their faces. More than twenty reporters and TV crews from abroad were also there and news of his arrival quickly spread abroad. As Oskar moved towards the crowd, he exclaimed, "I recognize all of my Jews." The crowd now encircled him as many of his beloved Jews tried to hug him or touch him. He later told one reporter:

> I was born in Czechoslovakia and I had many Jewish friends. As the years were passing I realized that there were only two ways: either to-tally unite with the Jews and together with them risk your life or forget them and thus contribute to their extermination. Many opponents of the Nazi regime were not strong-willed and did not have the strength to maintain their opposition until the end and that is why so few Germans helped the Jews.[98]

Afterwards, a long caravan of cars and buses escorted Oskar to his hotel, the Spalier, in Tel Aviv.

The crowd followed Oskar into the hotel lobby, where many of his *Schindlerjuden* begged for a few minutes alone with the man who had "saved their lives." According to a *Deutsche Presse Agentur* (German Press Agency) account of the arrival, "an extensive visitor program awaited him over the next few days, including the tree planting on the Av-enue of the Righteous." But Oskar now decided that he wanted to forgo certain aspects of his official visit so that he could, as he told another re-porter, "be together" with his friends. He went on to say that "to do jus-tice to all of them," he would have to stay there "half a year instead of just two weeks." When he was finally able to break away from the ador-ing crowd in the lobby, he went up to his hotel room, which "looked like a flower shop." Oskar Schindler had come home. Or had he?[99]

Unfortunately, the joy of Oskar's arrival in Israel soon dissipated when the Yad Vashem Directorate decided not to let him plant his tree along with the eleven other new Righteous Gentiles. After Oskar's arrival, the

Yad Vashem Directorate learned that there was the possibility that Julius Wiener, angry about Schindler's selection, might either disrupt the tree planting ceremony or continue to make a public issue of it. So the committee decided it would be unwise to allow Oskar to take part in the ceremony. Instead, they decided to hold a separate tree planting ceremony for him on May 8. On May 2, the *Jerusalem Post* reported that Oskar "was taken ill" and did not take part in the tree planting ceremony at Yad Vashem with the other honorees. Perhaps it helped that another newly named Righteous Gentile, Jan Rijtsema, was also unable to attend this gathering.[100]

The decision infuriated many *Schindlerjuden.* Jakob Sternberg, one of Oskar's closest friends in Israel, wrote a letter to the editor of *Ha'aretz,* one of the country's leading newspapers, and said that the Israeli government had not treated Schindler fairly. Government officials had time to welcome Frank Sinatra, Sternberg noted, but not the man who had saved the Jews.[101] Oskar's quiet tree-planting ceremony took place on May 8 before a small gathering of friends and supporters. Perhaps the sting of Yad Vashem's decision not to include him in the official ceremony six days earlier was assuaged by a wonderful banquet held for him by his Schindler Jews in Tel Aviv on May 2. Three to four hundred Schindler Jews and their families attended. On the podium with Oskar were Dr. Bejski, Itzhak Stern, and three or four other prominent Schindler Jews. During the banquet, it was decided to let people in the audience stand up and say a few words to honor Oskar. According to Dr. Bejski, what followed "was something very great." As survivor after survivor stood up and began to give his testimony, Dr. Bejski realized it was important to take down what each one was saying because he had never heard many of these stories before. Using napkins and other scraps of paper, Dr. Bejski began to take down everything that was said that night. Afterwards, he went home and typed his notes. Two years later, when Leopold Page called him about the possibility of an MGM film on Schindler, Dr. Bejski told him about the banquet testimony and Page asked him to send the material to him. Dr. Bejski asked someone in the Israeli embassy in Washington to translate his notes into English, which were then sent to Page in California. This transcript provided Page with some of the survivor testimony he needed to help promote the film in its early planning stage.[102]

Dr. Bejski gave me a copy of the English translation of his forty-two-page transcript of the banquet testimonials. It began with a lengthy introduction by Jakob Sternberg, who asked the group to pay silent homage to the Jews who died in the Holocaust. He then went on to discuss the highlights of Schindler's efforts to save his Jews, and contrasted life under Amon Göth in Płaszów with that under Schindler in Brünnlitz. As most of the Jews at the banquet were only with Schindler in Brünnlitz, Sternberg talked about what happened there. He considered the "Herr Director's" efforts to save the Jews on the Golleschau transport to be "the peak of Schindler's humanitarian accomplishments." He went on to talk about Oskar's decision to permit Rabbi Levertov bury the Golleschau dead in a nearby cemetery and then told stories about Schindler's efforts to help individual prisoners maintain their human dignity. He ended by addressing Oskar: "Be thou blessed in thy arrival to and thy departure from Israel. We shall never forget you!"[103]

Dr. Leon Salpeter, a pharmacist in Tel Aviv, spoke next. He talked about the evolving Schindler legend in Płaszów and credited Abraham Bankier with putting him on "Schindler's List." According to Salpeter, when Oskar asked Bankier about him, Bankier told him that he was a "good accountant." Oskar responded: "Salpeter is more of a Zionist than an accountant, but enter his name on the list anyway." Salpeter was the first survivor at the banquet to bring up Emilie's name, who, he said, "was no less conscientious than her husband" in helping Jews. In fact, Dr. Salpeter told the group, the motto of both Schindlers in Brünnlitz was "Let not the Jews starve." From Salpeter's perspective, Oskar was a "messenger of God," particularly when it came to his efforts to save the Jews on the Golleschau transport. No ordinary man was capable of such deeds. Salpeter added, "Only a messenger of God takes upon himself such as mission of rescuing Jews in that time."[104]

Dr. Aleksander Bieberstein, a physician at Brünnlitz and the author of a valuable memoir on the history of the Kraków ghetto, *Zagłada Żydów w Krakowie,* was the next to speak. He talked about the grave health issues that everyone faced in the newly opened camp, particularly typhus. Soon after the men arrived at Brünnlitz, they discovered three cases of typhus, which could doom the camp if the SS found out. Oskar immediately ordered the opening of baths and a disinfection facility as well as a laundry and showers; in fact, whenever the medical staff asked for something, Oskar always managed to find it. Dr. Bieberstein also credited Emilie with helping to save lives. Dr. Bieberstein said that "she worked incessantly, caring for the sick. Not a day went by without her visiting at least twice, to inspect what had been done, and bring[ing] additional

food." Without her efforts, he added, no one on the Golleschau transport could have survived.[105]

Dr. Moshe Bejski then gave his testimonial, certainly one of the most thoughtful of the evening. He decided to speak in German so that Oskar could understand him. Dr. Bejski, an attorney and a judge, took a precise, judicial approach to the questions he raised at the beginning of his speech. Where, he asked, did Schindler find the "patience and perseverance to carry all [their] problems and solve them, when the solution of each single one involved risking his own life"? Moreover, why did Schindler do what he did? "As a German he would have fulfilled his humanitarian obligation by doing a small portion of what he achieved." In the end, he could only attribute this to "Schindler's personality." In fact, he told the audience, he had not understood the full truth about Schindler until Oskar arrived in Israel several days earlier. Since Oskar's arrival, Bejski explained, he had heard story after story about "the big feats" of Schindler, but also the "small, individual deeds." Oskar did not just care for "1,200 people collectively, but each one of them individually. Each of us was under the impression that he alone received that treatment."[106]

Dr. Bejski said that during the war Oskar was the only German he had not been afraid of: "On the contrary. And the same goes for every one of us!" Whenever a German walked into the factory in Brünnlitz, everyone scurried around, pretending to work. But when Oskar entered the factory, "nobody cared to even pretend, and the women went right on with their knitting of sweaters and underwear from wool they had pinched from the neighboring Hoffman factory." But not only were his workers not afraid of him, everyone expected Oskar "to stop by him" in hopes that he would leave a cigarette, or, if you had a problem, you could tell him about it. What Bejski had learned over the past four days was how Oskar "then knew, and still remember[ed], every small detail which occurred among [them]; whose child stayed with some gentile, and how the contact with the women was maintained. Everything!"[107]

Dr. Bejski went on to talk about how Oskar procured the instruments necessary for the camp's physicians to perform an abortion on one of the inmates because pregnancy "was the equivalent of a death sentence." On another occasion, Oskar told Bejski about his ongoing discussions with Itzhak Stern on the Talmud. Each one, Oskar told the future judge, always ended with "another request for an additional half loaf of bread for everybody." Bejski also told the story about Schindler's decision to allow the radio technician Zenon to continue to repair his personal radio so he could listen to the Voice of London each day, and then share the news with the rest of the camp. But along with many of the Schindler Jews that night, what Dr. Bejski remembered most were Oskar and Emilie's superhuman efforts to save the Jews on the Golleschau transport. Later, when the Golleschau survivors began to regain their strength, Oskar made sure they were given easy jobs so they could continue to recover. He also repeated the story about the burial of the Golleschau dead in a nearby cemetery.[108]

Dr. Bejski added that he knew that the other Schindler Jews in the audience had similar stories, though it was difficult for all of them to find the words to say what really needed to be said about Oskar. "But from all things," he added, "always the humanitarian in him stands out. He is to inherit Heaven not for a single rescue operation, but for his fatherly attitude and self-sacrifice, which are indescribable; he passed a test which has no equal." And he reminded them of the time when Oskar was arrested in Kraków in the fall of 1944 to be questioned about the Göth investigation. As long as Oskar was around, Bejski said, he was their "beam of hope." When word of his arrest spread among the remaining inmates in Płaszów, they all felt lost. When they learned that he had been released, "up surged . . . hope again" that they would survive. He reminded the group of Schindler's final departure on May 9 and the ring that they had given him. Oskar lost the ring after the war but Dr. Bejski told everyone that Hersch Licht, who had made the original ring, had made a new one, which they would present to Oskar at the end of the evening. In his closing remarks Bejski directly addressed Schindler: "Not a thing you and your wife have done for us have we forgotten, nor shall we ever forget as long as we live."[109]

Little was said by the other survivors who spoke about Yad Vashem's decision to delay the planting of Oskar's tree along the Avenue of the Righteous. Wilhelm-Zeev Nachhauser, though, mentioned recent statements by Dr. Kubovy and Dr. Nahum Goldmann, the head of the World Jewish Congress, recognizing that Schindler was "unique in the period of the Holocaust." Nachhauser added, "If Nansen [Nansen International Office for Refugees] received the Nobel prize for peace [in 1938]— Schindler ought to receive from the State of Israel a prize for the rescue of Jews in ways and numbers not to be compared anywhere. He did his deeds without any selfish interest, in times when nobody was willing to rebel and help. As a German, he found the courage to go against the general stream."[110]

Other Schindler Jews such as Maurice (Maurycy) Finder, Benno (Benzion) Florenz, Hersch Licht, Benjamin Wrozlavsky-Breslauer, Moshe Henigman, Meir (Marsk) Bossack, and Shmuel Springmann each stood and gave brief testimonials. Their words were often interspersed with comments from other survivors. Meir Bossak read a long poem, "Judgement of Jerusalem. To Oskar Schindler. The Lantern in the Darkness," which took a poetic overview of the Holocaust and the failure of "The Holy Father [Pope Pius XII]" to speak out.[111]

Finally, Oskar got up to speak. He thanked everyone for the reception and told them that for seventeen years he had lived in solitude. He went on: "The experiences of these last days have lifted my spirit very much, and I feel compensated. To see you all with your families and children, looking well, brings me happiness." He told everyone that he did what he had to do to save Jews and only wished that more Germans had done the same thing. If they had, "the situation would probably have been different." He reminded the audience that he had suffered a lot for his efforts to save them, and was used to such suffering. He went on: "[If] someone comes out now in Israel, complaining about me . . . the truth has already been told by you yourselves, and the things told here are truth itself—every part of it. As to myself, I do not attribute importance to the blame put on me, I am only sorry to have caused you to be chagrined." He then explained why he came to Poland in 1939 and what led him to begin to help his Jewish workers. He mentioned his work for the Jewish Agency and the numerous problems he had with the SS. He asked everyone to remember Abraham Bankier, Simon Jeret, and Uri Bejski. He ended by saying that though he had met with his Jews since the end of the war, he was most happy in Israel.[112]

The evening ended with speeches by Jakob Sternberg and Itzhak Stern. Sternberg said that everyone was deeply moved by what was said that evening by the survivors and the meeting with their "saviour Schindler." He added that the two happiest days of his life were his arrival in Israel twelve years earlier and April 28, 1962, when they welcomed their "saviour and friend Schindler." Sternberg then presented Oskar with the gold ring that Hersch Licht had made for him. It was engraved with the Hebrew saying "Whoever saves one life saves the world entire." Sternberg then addressed Oskar: "Be Blessed many fold, on your leaving Israel. May our blessings and wishes for all the very best, accompany you and your wife. May we meet again soon."[113]

Itzhak Stern was the last to speak and shared with the audience many of the stories he had told Dr. Ball-Kaduri at Yad Vashem seven years earlier. He talked about his first meeting with Schindler in 1939 and the contacts he had with him during his time in Płaszów. As the war went on and Schindler intensified his efforts to help Jews, Oskar "was already ready for anything." He never said no to any of Stern's requests about helping Jews. Stern went into great detail about the visit of the two Jewish Agency representatives to Płaszów in 1944 and Schindler's later arrest in the fall of 1944 as he was making plans for the move to Brünnlitz. According to Stern, the first thing he did after Emilie arranged his release was to come to Płaszów, "dirty and unshaven," to tell Stern and others that "he was with [them] again."[114]

He then mentioned Oskar's efforts to release the women from Auschwitz and the opening of "a symbolic Jewish cemetery" to bury the camp's Jewish dead. He also gave details about Schindler's decision to arm the inmates at the end of the war. He ended his remarks with a discussion of the Herculean efforts to save the Jews on the Golleschau transport. He was particularly complimentary of Emilie's work and Oskar's insistence that Rabbi Levertov perform a Jewish funeral for the dead at the new cemetery plot he had just acquired. "My brothers," Stern continued, "in the Hebrew language, there are three definitions of a human being: first he is born a man; secondly, he grows into a person; and third, he becomes like Adam, a full human being. Now, I think, there should be a last, and additional stage, and it should be called Oskar Schindler."[115]

The impact of the banquet on Oskar and the Schindler Jews in Israel is immeasurable. There would never be another gathering like this during Oskar's life. So many of the Jews he had saved during the Holocaust had the time to come together to celebrate the life of the man that they truly adored. The banquet also served to solidify the legend that was developing around Oskar. This would be the first of many trips that Oskar would make to Israel during the next twelve years. But none would mean as much to him as this one. Unfortunately, the words of adoration spoken at the Tel Aviv banquet had little impact on the Wurzel-Wiener controversy, which continued to haunt Oskar and Yad Vashem, particularly after their accusations appeared in the press.

On May 2, *Ha'aretz* published an interview with Julius Wiener, who worked as a customs officer in Jerusalem. He repeated his accusations against Schindler, whom he considered "a Nazi like all the other Nazis" who "began to save Jews only towards the end of the war in order to save his own skin." He admitted that Schindler had to be shown some gratitude for what he did to help Jews, but it must not be wrapped "in a halo of praise." *Ha'aretz* also interviewed Wurzel, who said he had once filed a law suit against Schindler but withdrew it when he learned of his rescue work later in the war. He did not think Schindler was "altogether innocent" but thought that his good deeds later in the war overshadowed his earlier mistreatment of Jews like himself. A *Ha'aretz* reporter also spoke to Dr. Bejski, who noted that he had only learned of the accusations on the eve of Schindler's arrival in Israel. He said that Schindler's friends in Israel talked to Mr. Wiener about his charges and then turned this information over to Dr. Kubovy. He in turn explained that Yad Vashem decided to do nothing about the accusations because Yad Vashem had not officially invited him to Israel. Instead, he, like the other Righteous Gentiles, had been invited by their survivors. Moreover, the only evidence that Yad Vashem had against Schindler were the charges of Julius Wiener. On the other hand, the Holocaust memorial institution had testimony from hundreds of Schindler Jews that told of his efforts to save them during the war. Later, the leadership among the Schindler Jews called a press conference to respond to Wiener's charges.[116]

In the meantime, the Schindler controversy prompted Yad Vashem to create a twelve-member Designation of the Righteous Commission headed by Justice Landau. One of the commission's first tasks was to develop a specific set of guidelines that it would use to select Righteous Among the Nations nominees. For one thing, the criteria for consideration for this award were precise when it came to a Gentile's treatment of Jews during the Shoah. According to Dr. Mordecai Paldiel, the specific requirements are:

1. The rescuer extended aid to a Jew or Jews in danger of being killed or sent to a concentration camp, thus ensuring their survival.
2. The rescuer was fully aware that by doing this he was risking his own life, freedom, and safety.
3. The rescuer did not exact any material reward or compensation at the time of the rescue, and did not require any promise of compensation, either oral or in writing, as a condition for the aid he was giving.
4. The rescuer's role was not passive but active; he acted on his own initiative, was directly involved and personally responsible, and in effect "caused" a rescue that would not otherwise have taken place.
5. The act of rescue or aid can be authenticated by evidence provided by the rescued persons or by other eyewitnesses and, whenever pos-

sible, by relevant bona fide documentation (e.g., German court records for those tried on the charge of harboring or extending aid to Jews).[117]

There were also other subcriteria that expanded on each of these points and looked into the extent to which the nominee fulfilled each of them.[118] In addition, Dr. Paldiel told me during one of our conversations about the Schindler controversy that the award was not to be given to anyone who "had caused pain or injury to Jews."[119] When the commission was formed in early 1963, it decided to use these new standards to reevaluate the twenty-five Gentiles who had been nominated as Righteous Among the Nations the year before. In August 1963, members of the Righteous Designation Commission interviewed Wiener, Esther Schwartz (Erna Lutinger), and Simah Hartmann (Gelcer) about the charges against Oskar Schindler. Jakob Sternberg, Itzhak Stern, and Dr. Moshe Bejski testified on Schindler's behalf at the four hour hearing. At one point, there was a confrontation with Wurzel over the charges that he and Wiener had leveled against Oskar. Several days later, Sternberg wrote Oskar that the Schindler Jews in Israel had sent Dr. Landau a number of documents that emphasized "the most important moments of your superhuman sacrifice for the rescued 1,100 inmates." In the meantime, Wurzel wrote Wiener that he had made some sort of "business agreement" with Schindler and suggested that Julius consider doing the same thing. By 1963, Oskar was in deep financial straits and did not have the resources to pay Wurzel off. More than likely, this was done by the Schindler Jews in Israel. Mrs. Schwartz's testimony supported Wiener's allegations, though the statement of another witness, Simah Hartmann (Gelcer), was inconclusive. Yad Vashem, of course, also had Wurzel and Wiener's testimony from late 1956.[120]

But what the Righteous Designation Commission heard in the summer of 1963 was not conclusive enough for them to launch a more detailed investigation into the charges. It decided formally not to name Schindler a Righteous Gentile and did not send him a certificate or a medal. Instead, on December 24, 1963, it sent Oskar two letters in German in two separate envelopes signed by Dr. Landau and Dr. Kubovy. The first explained that the commission was aware of the claims of Julius Wiener and Natan Wurzel that Schindler had stolen their property and physically abused them. However, it went on to say that "the commission [Designation of the Righteous Commission] [could not] come to a conclusion over these claims without a thorough investigation of these matters, that are disputed between Mr. Wiener and Mr. Wurzel on the one hand and Mr. Schindler on the other hand." Consequently, the commission did not feel that it could "undertake such an investigation."[121]

The second letter, which was titled "Official Citation to Oskar Schindler by the Government of Israel, December 24, 1963," dealt with the positive efforts of Oskar during the war:

> Based on the testimony of many witnesses, the "Righteous Gentile" commission of the national institution "Yad Vashem" has decided that Mr. Oskar Schindler has undertaken outstanding actions to rescue Jews during the Jewish catastrophe in Europe. Among other facts it should be emphasized that Mr. Schindler treated the Jews living in his factory in Zablocie humanely, that he transferred the Jews from the Płaszów camps into his factory to save their lives; that he transferred 700 Jewish men and 300 Jewish women from the Płaszów camp before its final liquidation; that he saved 300 Jewish women, who had already been transported to Auschwitz; that he got about 100 Jewish inmates from the Golszów [Golleschau] camp out of frozen train wagons and with the help of his wife saved them; that he constantly worried about the health of his Jewish workers and repeatedly supplied them with additional food and medicines; that he provided his Jewish workers with humane living conditions and medical treatment to ease their suffering; that he allowed the Jewish dead to have Jewish funerals.
>
> Mr. Schindler constantly endangered his life to do this.
>
> By doing this, Mr. Schindler has obtained the deepest gratitude of the hundreds of Jews that he saved and is worthy of recognition by the entire Jewish people.[122]

But Oskar Schindler was no longer officially considered a Righteous Gentile, even though no one gave any thought to removing his carob tree along the Avenue of the Righteous.[123] Regardless, Dr. Kubovy told Jakob Sternberg in 1965 that he considered Oskar "one of the great Righteous Ones." But how did Yad Vashem choose to deal with the fact that Schindler's tree remained on the Avenue of the Righteous?

I asked Dr. Paldiel, who shared all the Schindlers' files with me when I was working at Yad Vashem. One day, he called me to his office and said that because I was working on a scholarly biography of Schindler, he was going to tell me the real story about the Righteous Gentile controversy. We subsequently corresponded on this matter. He said that Oskar was given the certificate for the tree planting but was technically not considered a Righteous Gentile at the time. When Dr. Bejski became head of the Commission in 1970, some of the Schindler Jews asked him to rectify the Schindler matter and grant Oskar full recognition. Dr. Bejski refused to do so, saying that he did not want to use his position to overturn Judge Landau's earlier decision. Landau, who by this time was president of the Israeli Supreme Court, remained on the commission until the mid-1970s. Instead, Bejski arranged to send Oskar a certificate acknowledging that he had planted a tree along the Avenue of the Righteous.[124] Dr. Bejski told me that he regretted this decision. But, as a judge, he was familiar with controversy and was afraid that if he pushed too hard on the medal for Oskar, he would reignite the Wurzel-Wiener controversy.[125]

On the other hand, for the sake of the public, Yad Vashem diplomatically considered Oskar a Righteous Gentile because of the tree he had planted along the Avenue of the Righteous. In 1993, when the Designation of the Righteous Commission, which was now chaired by Dr. Bejski, learned that Emilie was coming to Israel to film the final scene in *Schindler's List*, Dr. Bejski decided it was time to clear up the matter. So on June 24, 1993, the Designation Commission declared Oskar and Emilie Schindler Righteous Gentiles and awarded them a single medal and certificate for both. She was later presented the medal and certificate in Buenos Aires by Israel's ambassador to Argentina. Emilie's name was then added to the plaque in front of Oskar's tree along the Avenue of the Righteous.[126]

But Dr. Paldiel also told me that if Emilie had not been in Israel for Spielberg's film, which prompted the Schindler Jews to ask Dr. Paldiel's help in getting Oskar declared a Righteous Gentile, he "would not have benefited from full recognition." From Dr. Paldiel's perspective, Schindler was "indeed a bona fide Righteous [Gentile]—though not a saint all his life." He later told me that Oskar "did save the lives of twelve hundred Jews; in fact, more than any other single rescuer during the Holocaust (Raoul Wallenberg had a trustworthy team at his side)."[127] Dr. Paldiel also told me that Oskar claimed that he did not care about the award but was pleased that a tree had been planted in his name. He said he did not need medals or awards. I doubt whether Oskar really felt this way. Though I can certainly see Oskar saying such a thing once he learned he would not get a medal, this was probably more of a rationalization than a statement of his true feelings. In fact, he wrote several of his friends in Israel after his return that his first trip to Israel and the recognition he received gave him the "strength in the future to find a way to want to live with people and to believe in people."[128] By the time that he received his letters from Yad Vashem in early 1964 he had suffered through a major heart attack and the collapse of his stone and cement business in Germany. All he had now in his life was the extraordinary love and dedication of his Schindler Jews and a growing reputation fueled by the stories of what he had done to save them during the war. Though he would suffer more disappointments, the support and adoration of his Jewish and German friends came to fill a big void in his life. Throughout the 1960s, the modest fame he would come to enjoy as well as the major disappointments he would suffer were inextricably linked with those of his Jewish friends and supporters. During this time, he lived in two worlds—one Jewish and one German. The same was true of Emilie, who struggled to rebuild her life in Argentina after Oskar left for Germany in 1957. Though they would never meet again, their lives remained intertwined throughout the last seventeen years of Oskar's life.

13.

THE EVENING OF
SCHINDLER'S LIFE

OSKAR SCHINDLER'S LIFE IN THE 1960S WAS FILLED WITH SERIOUS financial and health problems that were exacerbated by a humiliating failed movie deal with MGM (Metro-Goldwyn-Mayer) and an unscrupulous effort to use his name to raise funds for a phony Martin Buber prize in London. There were some momentary high points in his life during this period, though Oskar struggled with long bouts of depression. He came to depend more and more on his Schindler Jews in Israel and the United States for his emotional and financial well-being. The same was true of Emilie, who received similar support and friendship from the German Jewish community in Buenos Aires. This group was determined to care for what one Argentine German newspaper called "Mother Courage" for the rest of her life.[1]

Oskar left Emilie deeply in debt and emotionally devastated when he departed for Germany via New York in 1957. They said almost nothing to one another during the trip to the airport on that fateful day in June 1957. As Oskar boarded the plane, he said goodbye without looking directly into Emilie's eyes. And though she knew their marriage had ended long before and that Oskar was a complete stranger to her, she felt as though "a part of [herself] . . . was leaving." She felt "a tangible emptiness" when she returned to their farm in San Vicente. She was also broke and had no money to pay the workers who helped her with the small farm. Emilie estimated in her memoirs that she was a million pesos ($14,706) in debt and survived by selling milk from her cows.[2]

There is little evidence of much direct contact between Oskar and Emilie once he returned to Germany. He wrote her periodically, though Emilie said that his letters all "seemed copies of one another." From her perspective, they "amounted to a lot of excuses, delays, and confused stories, without the slightest reference to [her] repeated pleas for help and to the difficult situation" he had left her in. He sent her money only once, DM 200 ($47.62), along with a copy of the *Diary of Anne Frank*. At first, Emilie held out hope that Oskar planned to return to Argentina. After a while, she decided to ignore his letters.[3] On the other hand, Oskar still seemed to care for Emilie and expressed frustration over her failure to respond to his letters. Some of his concern, though, probably came more from their mutual financial interests in Argentina and the MGM film deal than any deep affection Oskar might have had for her.

Walter and Beate Pollack, two of Oskar's closest friends in Buenos Aires, were German Jews who had come to Argentina in the 1930s and met Oskar through their involvement with the Joint. The Pollacks adored Oskar and did everything they could to help Emilie after he left Argentina. In fact, most of what we know about Emilie's life after 1957 comes either from her memoirs or from Walter and Beate Pollack's correspondence with Oskar. Over time, Walter Pollack became the intermediary between Oskar and Emilie because of her refusal to have any contact with her husband.

As Emilie's financial plight worsened, she was forced to sell their *quinta* (house) and sold about half their farm in 1963 to cover back taxes and debt. She was fifty-six years old now and considered herself *"con mano atrás y otra delante"* (destitute: with nothing on and trying to cover oneself).[4] After she sold her beloved *quinta*, Emilie lived in an outhouse until a neighbor took pity on her and gave her a small shack to live in. One neighbor told me that she remembered Emilie picking and eating tangerines from neighbors' trees.[5] Another friend, Walter Pollack, wrote Leopold Page in 1965 that when he first got to know Emilie several years earlier she "almost literally" lay in the street. Her only steady companions seemed to be the growing menagerie of dogs and cats that she was so fond of, though she later had several boy friends and female live-in companions. She wrote that in the immediate years after Oskar's departure, her "loneliness was so absolute" that she hardly knew how to bear it.[6] Emilie, like Oskar, was deviled by long bouts of depression brought on by loneliness and financial desperation. But that would all change when Peter Gorlinsky, a writer for the *Argentinisches Tageblatt*, Buenos Aires' major German newspaper, wrote an article about Emilie's plight in January 1963, *Vater Courage bleibt unvergessen—aber wie steht es mit Mutter Courage* (Father Courage Has Not Been Forgotten—But How Does It Stand With Mother Courage?). Gorlinsky's article was stimulated by two things: news in the Argentine press of Oskar's Righteous Among the Nations nomination and efforts by Emilie's neighbors in San Vicente to contact B'nai B'rith about her plight.[7] Gorlinsky praised Oskar Schindler, whom he called the "'Scarlet Pimpernel' of the Second World War," and noted that he now lived modestly in Frankfurt. For the most part, he went on, the world seemed unmoved by Oskar's wartime deeds.[8]

But most of Gorlinsky's article dealt with Emilie, whom he argued deserved as much acclaim as her husband. Time and again, he noted, the Schindler Jews talked of her "kind smile" and her efforts to help save them. Yet few people knew of her efforts during the war and treated her as though she lived "on another planet." Argentinians, for example, would be surprised to know that she lived in Buenos Aires, "not as a legend, not as a modern fairytale, but as a human being made of flesh and blood." Yet, Gorlinsky continued, "Mother Courage" was struggling to survive and lived in far worse conditions than the survivors whom she helped save. All she had in life was a "small plot" of earth and it was possible that she would soon lose this; indeed, Emilie Schindler was "barely able to make a scant, humble living."[9]

This, Gorlinsky added, had to change. There had to be a way in the "evening of her life" to give some security to the woman who had helped so many others. There were pensions available for judges and civil servants (in Germany) who had once supported the Nazis but none for people like Emilie Schindler. So the only ones who could now help her were the people who had received [her] "good deeds." It was, Gorlinsky concluded, the responsibility of everyone to set right "a truly insufferable state of affairs."[10]

The impact of the article on Argentina's German Jewish community was electrifying. Its B'nai B'rith *(Bene Berith)* lodge, *Traducion* (Tradition), began to send her Arg$5,000 ($37.31) a month in March 1963 but soon increased this to Arg$9,000 ($67.16). That fall, the Joint decided to give her a additional monthly stipend of Arg$5,000 ($37.31). She would later receive stipends from the Argentine and German governments as well as some money from MGM after they began to consider making a

film about Oskar's wartime exploits. In addition, *Traducion,* which periodically held fund-raisers to help Emilie, created the Helen Strupp Foundation to build her a lovely home near the center of San Vicente. Walter
Pollack told Oskar in the summer of 1964 that the Buenos Aires German
Jewish community had "committed itself to care for [Emilie] for the rest
of her life." Emilie moved into the house at San Martin 353 in 1965 and
lived there until she was forced permanently to enter the *Hogar los Pinos*
(Home in the Pines), a German retirement home in the suburbs of Buenos
Aires, after she broke her hip in November 2000. But from the perspective of *Traducion,* which owned the deed to the house and land, it remained her home until her death in Germany in the fall of 2001.[11]

Oskar, Emilie, and MGM: "To the Last Hour"

Emilie's bitterness over Oskar's departure clouded her perspective when it
came to his explanations about why he was not able to help her anymore
than he did in the immediate years after his departure. She was very bitter,
for example, that he had "received a hundred thousand marks in compensation for the Brünnlitz factory" but that she "never saw a penny of it." It
was evidently never explained to her that this money was not paid directly
to Oskar but was used to help him purchase a bankrupt business in West
Germany. Though she never mentions it in her memoirs, she must have
known about his failed stone-and-concrete business because Oskar had
told the Pollacks, who were very close to Emilie. But by the time that
Oskar began to involve her in the contractual issues surrounding the planning for the film deal with MGM, Emilie refused to have direct contact
with her husband and worked with him through Walter and Beate Pollack.

By the early 1960s, Oskar had become something of a media figure in
Europe. In the fall of 1960, *Bayerischer Rundfunk* did a radio play, "Licht
in der Finsternis" (Light in the Darkness), that included a section on
Oskar's wartime efforts to save Jews. In 1962, he was approached by
MCA (Germany) about signing a multi-media contract. He ultimately
signed a contract with George Marton with the idea of developing a film
script with Austrian writer Jochen Huth. When filming began, Oskar was
to receive $10,000. Oskar was also working with Walt Disney Produc-
tions in Vienna, which prepared an eleven-page synopsis for a film project
that was essentially based on the article he had done years earlier for Kurt
Grossmann. It is difficult to determine whether this was linked to the
movie envisioned by George Marton. Regardless, nothing ever came of ei-

ther of these projects, though they no doubt did help generate some interest in Europe and the United States in Oskar's story.[12]

This new interest in Oskar's efforts to save his Jewish workers during the war came from widespread news reports about his Righteous Among the Nations nomination in Israel. But it would be another year and a half before any serious effort to make a film about his life bore fruit. And that would come not in Europe but in the United States. Leopold Paul ("Poldek") Page was the person responsible for what would become the most serious effort to memorialize Oskar Schindler's wartime exploits in film prior to Steven Spielberg's *Schindler's List*. From 1964 on, Page would be the driving force behind Hollywood's interest in telling the story of his beloved Oskar Schindler.

Page stubbornly talked to anyone who would listen to his stories about Oskar. In the summer of 1963, he met a *Los Angeles Times* reporter, Anton Calleia, and told him about Schindler. Calleia decided to interview Page as well as many other Schindler Jews in the Los Angeles area and finally contacted Oskar in Frankfurt as part of his research. Calleia told Schindler that although he was impressed by his heroism during the war, what touched him the most was "the deep love and reverence" that these people had for him: "You are their angel." He wanted to share these thoughts and sentiments with Oskar so that they might comfort him in his "moments of loneliness, discouragement or sadness."[13] Several months later, an article appeared in the *New York Herald Tribune* on Oskar. This time, it was not Leopold Page but his close friend, the violinist Henry Rosner, who provided the author, Robert Parrella, with information about Oskar's wartime exploits and his current problems in Germany. Rosner noted, for example, that earlier in the year Schindler had been stoned in Frankfurt for helping Jews during the war. But, Parrella added, Schindler Jews in Israel and the United States were doing everything they could to help their "old friend." The Schindler Jews in Los Angeles, for example, were "contributing one day's pay per year to assist the Schindler cement plant" in Germany.[14]

Three months later, Lucille "Chip" Gosch, the wife of Hollywood film director and writer Martin Gosch, had walked into Leopold Page's luggage shop in Beverly Hills to have a bag repaired. Poldek immediately recognized her and said: "I have an interesting story for your husband. I am one of thirteen hundred Jews saved by Oskar Schindler." Gosch, who had been blacklisted in the 1950s and had recently returned to Hollywood from Spain to rebuild his career, was fascinated by what his wife told him about Oskar Schindler. He went to Page's shop and asked him to repeat the story.

Gosch later told a reporter with the *Los Angeles Times* that he was astounded. "How could such a story be kept out of the public limelight for so long?" Gosch asked. But he also found Page's tale about Schindler hard to believe. He had the Schindler story checked out by the State Department and other sources abroad and found Page's account "to be true and incredibly exciting." He did more research on the subject and in May 1964, prepared a thirty-six-page preliminary analysis titled "The Oskar Schindler Story." Gosch showed his analysis to Delbert Mann, who had received an Academy Award in 1956 for his film *Marty*. According to Gosch, Mann "jumped" at the chance to film the story of Oskar Schindler.[15]

Once Mann agreed to direct the film, contractual preparations for the film moved along very quickly. On May 1, 1964, Page sent Gosch a preliminary contract for the film with Poldek acting as Oskar Schindler's "Attorney in Fact." On January 24, 1964, Oskar had agreed to give Page his power of attorney. The draft contract gave Gosch "exclusive rights" for a period of nine months commencing on February 28, 1965, to develop a film script of the Oskar Schindler story. Gosch would pay Schindler through Page $50,000 for the story rights. Oskar would receive a $25,000 advance for these rights during the option period and another $25,000 on the first day of filming. Once the film was completed, Gosch, who would now own the rights to the Schindler story "in perpetuity," would give Schindler through Page 5 percent of the producer's profits, which in this case amounted to 50 percent of the film's net profits. Other clauses required additional payments of 50 percent or $10,000, whichever was greater, if Gosch sold the Schindler story rights for purposes other than a film. Page was to receive 2.5 percent of the producer's profits and 10 percent of the profits from any sale of the Schindler story to other media outlets once Oskar had received his payments for the non-film story rights. If for some reason Gosch was not successful in commercially exploiting the Schindler story, then the contract with Schindler and Page would become "null and void."[16]

The preliminary contract also stipulated that if Gosch and his associates did complete the film script, Schindler and Page would serve as paid film consultants. Prior to filming, Oskar and Poldek would offer their expertise without compensation. However, once filming began, then they would be paid consultants for a minimum of ten weeks with a fee of $300 a week apiece. In addition, Gosch would fly each of them as well as Emilie first class to any film site not in "the environs of Frankfurt, Germany." He would also pay for their daily living expenses during the filming.[17]

A month later, Irving Glovin, an attorney in Beverly Hills, wrote Oskar that he had been hired by Leopold Page to represent the two of them "with reference to [their] war experiences." Glovin told Oskar that he, Gosch and Page were working "with people and companies whom [they] consider of sufficiently high caliber and standing to be capable and worthy of doing a story such as this." Operating under Page's power of attorney, they expected soon to enter into a commitment to develop the film. At this time, Page would sign a new contract for Schindler after which he would "be advised of its complete provisions." Glovin added that Page's "personal co-operation will be necessary" and that everyone involved in the film development process thought that this would be a "very successful and profitable venture." He hoped that they would have the opportunity to meet soon. In the meantime, Glovin asked Oskar not to discuss these exclusive arrangements with anyone. "The arrangements we are making are intended to be world wide in scope and the parties with whom we are dealing undertake all of the necessary publicity at that time." He concluded by asking Oskar to acknowledge the receipt of his letter and his "understanding of its contents." He added: "This could be persuasive with the parties with whom we are negotiating that you do understand and approve our proceeding."[18]

Several days later, Page wrote Oskar about the film and other matters. He told him that their lawyer [Glovin] was working on a contract with a movie producer and that the terms of this contract "will be good" for him. Page said that the producer thought the "film must be monumental" and wanted Gregory Peck to play the role of Oskar.[19] It is difficult to tell from the extensive correspondence between Page and Schindler in the summer of 1964 how much Oskar knew about the details of the film deal. He told Dr. Moshe Bejski about the project and Bejski suggested that he use the testimony he had compiled during the May 2, 1962, banquet in Tel Aviv to help with the script development. Bejski thought that the testimony of the individual Schindler Jews at the banquet was "good material." He added that he would write Page separately about the film contract.[20]

But Oskar had a lot more on his mind at this time than just the film. He was still having to deal with the bankruptcy court over his failed stone-and-cement business and was also working with the Schindler Jews in Israel who were trying to convince the West German government to grant Oskar an honorary pension. Oskar was in bad shape financially and unable to work because of his heart problems. In fact, in August, he checked himself into a sanatorium in Bad Wildungen to recover from his heart attack. He had planned to stay ten days but instead was there for a month. He hoped to use his time in the sanatorium to work on the synopsis for the film.[21]

Several weeks after Oskar got out of the sanatorium, Gosch flew him to London, where they spent time with Irving Glovin discussing the film. Oskar later wrote Page that he believed he had found a new friend in Gosch. Schindler was particularly pleased to discover that Gosch spoke fluent Spanish, which meant the two of them could converse without a translator.

He also liked Glovin, whom he considered an "iron-hard, clever attorney." Oskar was a bit overwhelmed with the amount of money they thought he might make on the film. And though Oskar was personally interested in the financial aspects of the film, he told Gosch that he should make arrangements to cover Page's business losses while he was away from his leather shop in Beverly Hills. It was not that he did not trust Gosch, Oskar wrote Page, but "the burnt child shies away from fire," a reference to his own recent financial and business difficulties. This was, he explained, perhaps his "last chance to prepare for the evening of [his] life." The only thing he asked of Page, who was Oskar's sole representative in the film negotiations in California, was that he be honest and open with him throughout the project's development.[22]

When Gosch met with Oskar in London, he told him that he had close ties with Cardinal Joseph Francis Spellman of New York and to Democrats close to U.S. President Lyndon Johnson. This impressed Oskar, who thought such contacts would help when it came time to promote the film. Such recognition, Schindler wrote Page, whether it be "from the government of Israel, the Pope in Rome, or the President in Washington, is a slap in the face for the highest local authorities [in West Germany], who for years took notice of articles [about Schindler] in the press, but have not officially offered . . . a solid piece of dry bread until today."[23]

In a different letter on the same day, Oskar asked Page to arrange for a power of attorney document in Page or Glovin's name for Emilie. Once he received this document, which was to be in English, Schindler would send it to Stern in Israel, who in turn would send it to Walter Pollack for Emilie to sign in Buenos Aires. He went on to explain that he had told Gosch that he should consider paying Emilie $10,000 for her film rights, although this amount could be less depending on what Gosch had to pay Schindler Jews for the rights to their stories. Oskar added that Gosch had promised to "transfer a considerable sum as advance for expenses . . . within the next few days" to cover his costs for doing preliminary research, travel, and interviews for the film.[24]

As plans for the film matured, Oskar became more excited about the project. In light of his financial difficulties, he wrote Walter Pollack that he saw it as an opportunity to achieve "a higher standard of living" both for himself and for Emilie. But Oskar was also concerned about Emilie's ability to handle money, whether it be from the film or other sources. He had learned, for example, that Emilie had a boyfriend, Cascho Bosetti, who was thirty years her junior. Oskar, in a surprising bit of jealousy, described Bosetti as her "one-time peon and horse lackey." Schindler was concerned that if Emilie received a large fee for her film rights, that would give the ten-member "family Bosetti illusions of grandeur." Oskar added that he could have flown Emilie to London to meet Gosch. However, this would have cost $1,000 and that sum could be used to insure a "secure life for 1-2 years" for her as well as a vacation in the Mar de Plata, a seaside resort south of Buenos Aires. Oskar ended his letter to Pollack by asking him to serve as his trustee for Emilie over the next few months. Oskar would voice these concerns over and over again in letters to Pollack during the next few years. The odd thing about all this is that Oskar had just as much trouble handling money as his wife.[25]

According to Pollack, Oskar's concerns about Emilie's ability to handle money were well placed. He told him in a letter on October 19, 1964, that she had lost the Arg$4,000 ($27.78) that *Traducion* had recently given her as a Yom Kippur gift. Earlier that year, Pollack continued, she spent another Arg$100,000 ($694) that *Traducion* friends had given her to fence in her five acres of land. In a letter to Page in early 1965, Pollack explained that the land she had just fenced in did not even belong to her. What frustrated Pollack was that she promised to use the money only for emergencies. Moreover, Emilie had told him earlier that the land was already fenced. Pollack advised Oskar that the best thing to do with Emilie when it came to money was to give it to her in small portions. Otherwise, she would spend it all at once.[26]

On the same day that Pollack wrote Schindler in Frankfurt, Oskar sent Gosch and Page a telegram asking for more details about the film project. Page responded hurtfully the same day and asked him whether he was "serious" about the concerns he had raised in his telegram. Page, who almost always wrote Oskar in Polish, told him that he had spent fourteen years trying to get the film made and had knocked on "thousands of doors" to persuade someone to make a movie about Oskar. He considered Oskar his "best friend" and intended to do as much for him as Schindler had done for Page. People, he added, laughed at him because of his efforts to tell Schindler's story. And when they did, he always told them that as long as he was alive he would "always try to do something for Oskar." Page then told him that he was setting up an Oskar Schindler Fund that would last forever. He advised Oskar not to interfere in the film project because the professionals involved in developing it were preoccupied with the movie and "don't like to be disturbed." He advised Oskar to leave everything to Martin Gosch and promised to explain everything to him when they met in Paris in a few weeks. He also told Schindler to take care of himself: "Don't drink and don't smoke too much." Page, who had been sending Oskar money almost every month, ended his letter by asking whether he needed money for underwear or clothes.[27]

Page included in his letter another letter of the same date from Irving Glovin, who told Oskar that work on the film project was "serious" but warned him to be patient because "nothing is certain until it is completed." He said that a "fine writer" had been hired to write the screen play and that the writer would go with Gosch and Page when they traveled to Europe in November and December to do further research and look at possible film sites. Glovin said that he greatly admired what Oskar had done during the war, though he thought that Schindler's story was more than simply a "war story" and that it "had the quality of greatness." He also had the "deepest admiration and respect for the man who was responsible for preserving the life of . . . Paul [Page]," and the many others with him who were "now useful and productive human beings the world over." Glovin said his firm would charge Schindler a small contingency fee of 10 percent but he would not make any money unless Oskar did. He reiterated that it was important for Oskar to "be patient" and keep his "own confidences." He added that "big plans" were being made in his honor but warned Oskar that his interference in the film's development could "complicate and perhaps destroy the project completely." Glovin asked Schindler "to avoid further communication with Mr. Gosch" and not to talk with anyone about the film. He ended by advising Oskar to please be patient and "don't complicate matters."[28]

A week later, Martin Gosch wrote Schindler on an MGM letterhead to tell him of their planned research trip to Europe and plans to meet him in Paris from November 17–20. This would give Oskar a chance to meet Howard Koch, who would write the film script. Koch was considered one of Hollywood's finest screenwriters and had coauthored scripts for *Sergeant York* (1941) and *Casablanca* (1942). He had also adapted H. G. Welles's *War of the Worlds* for radio, which became the basis of Orson Welles's terrifying national radio broadcast in October 1938. Koch's 1943 script for *Mission to Moscow* got him into trouble with the House Un-American Activities Committee in 1950 and he was blacklisted. He lived in Europe for several years and returned to the United States in 1956, hoping to revive his writing career. Koch was to be paid $55,000 for the script for *To the Last Hour*, and its success would hopefully play a role in reviving his career.[29]

It is uncertain at this point, though, whether Oskar knew much about Koch. Before he departed for Europe, Gosch wrote Oskar and asked him to give him the names of Schindler Jews in Paris whom he could talk to while he was there. But Gosch said he wanted to spend most of his time in Paris tape recording his wartime memories. He added: "[I am] making some very important plans for you to receive world recognition for your efforts, in addition to the other compensations." Page would tell him about other developments that should make life "much easier and more pleasant" for Oskar. Gosch ended by asking Oskar to control his "very excited and nervous enthusiasm," and added, "We want you to be well and healthy and to enjoy a good life."[30]

As Oskar began to plan for his meeting in Paris with Gosch, Page, and Koch, he wrote Moshe Bejski to ask him whether he could meet with the group in the French capital. Oskar had come to trust Dr. Bejski implicitly and, with the exception of Walter Pollack, wrote to him more frequently than to anyone else. Oskar respected Bejski's judicious approach to his concerns and wanted him to be with him in Paris during the final negotiations on the film. He sent Bejski all the letters he had received from Gosch and Glovin and told him that Stern had advised him in a telegram that it was important "to hold out stubbornly" when it came to the contract discussions. Over the next few years, Oskar would become increasingly frustrated with the pace of the movie's evolution and came to rely heavily on the advice of Dr. Bejski and the other prominent Schindler Jews in Israel for advice and direction regarding his role in its development.[31]

Unknown to Oskar, Gosch had contacted Bejski and Stern about a trip to Israel in late November to interview the Schindler Jews there. Dr. Bejski immediately wrote Oskar about these developments and told him that Stern had recently sent Page a telegram telling him that the Schindler Jews in Israel would need a copy of Emilie's power of attorney before they would consider giving their testimony to Gosch. Bejski was a little surprised that Oskar was not coming with them to Israel and said that Page had written him earlier to warn him to deal "very carefully with MGM— in order not to ruin the whole thing." Dr. Bejski evidently did not appreciate Page's advice and instead warned Schindler to be careful with Gosch and MGM, particularly when it came to the type of film they might produce. Bejski said it was important that they "try to influence" the film by insuring that it was based on fact.[32] It is uncertain whether Oskar received Dr. Bejski's letter before he left for Paris.

In the meantime, Gosch was hard at work on the film. About two weeks before he left on his trip to meet with Oskar in Paris, he sent a memo to MGM's Maurice Silverstein and Delbert Mann about selecting a film title. Gosch preferred *The Third Face of War*, which would highlight war's third element such as Schindler's efforts to save his Jews. He also was considering *No Sound of Trumpets*, *The Man Who Dared*, *The Final Chapter*, *The Last Index*, *They Live Again*, *My Brother's Keeper*, and the one ultimately chosen, *To the Last Hour*.[33]

Gosch was also desperately trying to get Gregory Peck to play the role of Oskar Schindler in the film. In a November 9 letter to the character actor Syl Lamont, who was close to Peck and had worked with him in several films, Gosch discussed the importance of the film, and called the role of Oskar Schindler "a great tour de force." He discussed the honors he planned for Schindler, including a special Humanities Medal to be awarded by Congress and President Johnson. He noted that *Readers Digest* and *Life Magazine* intended to publish extended articles on Schindler. Gosch, possibly in an effort to draw Lamont more deeply into the project and entice him to influence Peck, said there would be seven or eight important costarring roles in the movie. Normally, Gosch told Lamont, actors of Peck's stature wanted to read a script before they committed to a film. But given its special nature, Gosch hoped that Peck would consider the thirty-six-page preliminary analysis of the film, "The Oskar Schindler Story," sufficient to make a decision. He added that he had met with Schindler in London in September, and that Oskar was "enormously impressed with the shadings of the character which Greg brought to 'Mockingbird [*To Kill a Mockingbird*].'" Schindler thought that Peck, of all that period's film actors, best resembled the way he was "as a human being inside." Gosch added that 92 percent of the Schindler Jews he had interviewed agreed with the choice of Peck for the role of Oskar Schindler. From Gosch's perspective, Gregory Peck had "the same warm regard for the humanities of life which are so clearly evidenced by the things that Schindler did at great danger and sacrifice to himself."[34]

Gosch, Koch, and Page's research trip abroad took place from November 11 to December 8. Gosch and Koch followed this up with a trip to

Poland to explore film sites. They began their interviews in New York on November 14, where they spoke with Rabbi Menashe Levertov (Lewertow), Edith Wertheim, Pauline Boyman, Ryszard Horowitz, Alex Rosner, Frances Spira, Lewis Fagin, and Roman Ginter. They flew to Paris where they met Oskar on November 18 and did an extensive series of interviews with him. This was followed by a trip to Vienna, where they interviewed Raimund Titsch, the manager of Julius Madritsch's sewing factories in the Kraków ghetto and Płaszów, and Regina Bankier, the wife of Abraham Bankier. From there they flew to Tel Aviv, where they interviewed Itzhak Stern, Josef and Rebeka Bau, Helen Hirsch Horowitz, one of Göth's two Jewish maids, Dr. Moshe Bejski, Mr. and Mrs. Yanuk Sternberg, Israeli Supreme Court Justice Moshe Landau, and Dr. Steinberg, a physician at one of the factories next to Emalia in Kraków. Afterwards, Jakob Sternberg wrote Oskar and told him that Gosch only talked in "vague contours" about the film. Like Dr. Bejski, Sternberg was worried about the film's accuracy. Using background documents and notes supplied to them by Oskar, Page, Dr. Bejski, and others, Gosch, Koch, and Page gathered the most complete body of testimony about Schindler up to that time. The transcript of these interviews, as well as Gosch and Koch's post interview notes, which are in the Delbert Mann Papers at Vanderbilt University, provided Thomas Keneally and Steven Spielberg with some of their most poignant stories.

Oskar never said much about the meetings with Gosch, Page, and Koch, but did express some frustration over the new contract he signed with MGM while he was in Paris. Before he left for Paris, Oskar asked Schindler Jew Henry Orbach for advice on the proposed contract, which Gosch had recently sent him. Orbach suggested that they go to see Robert J. Fiore, an American lawyer in Frankfurt. Orbach, a prominent diamond trader to whom Ian Fleming devoted a full chapter in his only non-fiction work, *The Diamond Smugglers*, had used Fiore to do some work for him in New York. Oskar wanted Fiore's advice on "the form and enforceability" of his contract with Gosch. Since Oskar knew little English, Orbach served as translator during the discussion.[35] Fiore, who received Germany's highest civilian award, the Order of Merit, in 2003, told Oskar "that the contract would be a binding legal document and he could look forward to receiving at least $50,000." Orbach explained that Schindler was having some financial problems and was concerned that his creditors in Germany would get his film advance if it was transferred to a German bank. Fiore suggested that Oskar have the money deposited in a US dollar account at the Chase Manhattan Bank where the US military deposited its funds. German officials, Fiore went on, "rarely scrutinized" accounts at Chase Manhattan.[36] Mr. Fiore met Oskar only once more, when he dropped by to give him photos of Amon Göth during his trial in Kraków in 1946. At the time, Fiore knew little about Oskar Schindler. Orbach later told him that Oskar was a hero, but "not here in Germany, Mr. Fiore, they don't want to know about him." After Emilie's death in 2001, her heir, Erika Rosenberg, approached Fiore about filing a lawsuit against Steven Spielberg for 5 percent of the profits of *Schindler's List*. Mr. Fiore respectfully declined the offer.[37]

The new agreement, which was dated November 13, was similar to the one that Page had originally drawn up with a few exceptions. Emilie had evidently signed over her power of attorney to Page and the contract was now in the names of Oskar and Emilie Schindler. It stated that they would receive $25,000 once Gosch decided to exercise his option to make the movie and another $25,000 on February 28, 1966, or on the date when filming began, whichever was earliest. The option date for Gosch had now been moved ahead by one year. Oskar would receive 80 percent of the advance and Emilie would receive 20 percent, but only after legal fees and other expenses were deducted from Oskar and Emilie's advances. Oskar was still to receive 5 percent of the "Producer's Profits," though neither he nor Page were to be paid as consultants for the movie once filming began. On the other hand, Page would receive 2.5 percent of the "net profits" of the film and no less than 1.25 percent of the "Producer's Profits."[38]

Oskar returned from Paris revitalized and generally enthusiastic about the film despite some small frustrations over certain aspects of the contract. He thought these could be changed later but was annoyed because Page had taken Emilie's contract from him "under false pretenses." He considered Martin Gosch a real friend and, in a letter a few days after Christmas, he wrote him: "You have given me the nicest Christmas I can think of." He had heard good reports from his Schindler Jews in Israel about Gosch's trip there in November. He noted that Gosch's personality and "unheard-of-initiative" deeply impressed them. Yet even in the midst of Oskar's joy over the pace of the film's development, he still wanted more specific details about Gosch's trip to Israel and the movie itself, particularly as reports about the film had appeared in the press throughout the world.[39]

Oskar wrote Walter Pollack on December 30 that the film would be made by MGM with Martin Gosch as producer. It would be titled *To the Last Hour*. He expected filming to begin in London at the end of January;

the following month the production company would move to Madrid, where they would film the outside shots. It would cost $9 million to make. He told Pollack: "I am happy, after vegetating the last years, to have reached my goal with perseverance." Their mutual friends in Israel were equally pleased because the film would create "a historical monument for the Polish Jewish victims" of the Shoah.[40]

Oskar expected to be on hand for the filming in London and Madrid, yet still felt uneasy about the contracts he had signed for himself and Emilie and questions of historical accuracy. He wrote Dr. Bejski that though he had no reason to distrust Gosch, he had to remind himself that the film's producer was "merely a free coworker of the president of MGM." But, Oskar told Bejski, the only way the film could be a success was if they did not allow themselves to be "pushed aside altogether and, at least in the historical part" they should "develop a united obstinacy." He assured the Israeli judge that he would pay attention to the question of historical accuracy "like a pointer (dog)" and would regularly keep him abreast of developments once filming began.[41] Oskar and Bejski sensed almost from the beginning of the planning for the film that something was not quite right. Little did they know at the time that the film would never be made and that Gosch was not quite the honest, creative force that he seemed to be.

News of the film, *To the Last Hour,* began to appear in the press about a week before Oskar signed the contract in Paris. The *New York Times* did a small article on the film on November 8, 1964, though it said the film would be shot in Portugal, not Spain, and at MGM's Elstree studio in Boreham Wood north of London. News of the film appeared in the Israeli press about a week later and, just before Christmas 1964, a lengthy article on it appeared in the *Los Angeles Times*. It reported that MGM had offered Richard Burton $750,000 to play the role of Oskar Schindler. *Ma'ariv,* Israel's most prominent daily newspaper, also noted Gosch's plans to have Burton play Schindler in the film. Oskar Schindler, the article went on, was a "hero in life, a hero in reality," but Burton was a stage hero, a hero with makeup. But the article also noted that while Schindler received no reward for his heroism, Burton was to be paid $750,000 for his stage "heroism." Several weeks later, *Variety Weekly* reported that Gosch and Koch, who would jointly write the film script, had just returned from a research trip to Poland where officials had tried to convince them to make the film using original locations. Several months earlier, Oskar had advised against this and told Page that there were plenty of factories in Germany that produced the same goods and had scenery similar to that in Brünnlitz.

There were also plenty of concentration camps in Bavaria, such as Dachau and Flossenbürg, that could duplicate the camps in Poland.[42]

Gosch wrote Oskar about his trip to Poland and Israel a month or so after he returned to California. However, he provided Oskar with far less information about his trip than he gave to the Israeli press and *Variety Weekly*. He also told reporters about the new Oskar Schindler Foundation and why he and Koch rejected the idea of shooting the film in Poland. Gosch told the Israeli-Polish newspaper, *Nowiny i Kurier*, that Oskar did not save just 1,300 people but at least 28,000. As he explained: "There are thousands of other Jews saved by him, who are now in other countries and owe their lives to the courage and sacrifice of this man." Gregory Peck would play Oskar and Danny Kaye would play an Auschwitz prisoner. Both actors "declared that they would give their salaries for this movie to the 'Schindler Foundation.'" The Schindler Foundation, Gosch went on, would be used to give out awards for "outstanding humanitarian acts," and its funding would come from "ticket sales." Profits from the film would also be given to the Schindler Foundation annually to insure that $20,000 would be "devoted to this noble purpose." The Schindler Foundation prize would be "some kind of Nobel Prize from the movie industry." Gosch hoped that the U.S. and Israeli governments would support the foundation, which would insure that history would remember and honor the great work of Oskar Schindler.[43]

But all Gosch told Oskar in a letter in mid-January 1965 about shooting in Poland was that there would simply be too many political and bureaucratic problems filming there. Instead, he thought MGM's new studio in Madrid would be a perfect site for the outdoor shots, and most of the interior shots could be done in London (Boreham Wood). On the other hand, Gosch told *Variety Weekly* that Polish officials had made a "big pitch" for the film, which he had rejected because of the weather and because there were "few signs of the purported abatement of government controls." Gosch felt that Poland was still a pretty closed society when compared to Yugoslavia and Czechoslovakia and he did not want his movie to be the "guinea pig" to see how open Poland had become. Gosch and Koch found a visit to the site of Schindler's former factory in Kraków particularly troubling. When they asked whether they might film the interior and exterior of the factory, their guide told them that this would be prohibited. Gosch said, "This seemed pretty silly . . . if it's an example of the problems we would face." The *Variety Weekly* article ended by saying that James Garner would be one of the stars in the film.[44]

Gosch followed up his January 15, 1965, letter to Oskar with another one ten days later that told him about his efforts to pressure the West German government to acknowledge Schindler's wartime heroics by honoring him through a pension or a substantial contribution to the Oskar Schindler Humanities Foundation. He told Oskar that he had just had lunch at MGM with Dr. Irene Weinrowsky, the press and cultural attaché of the West German Legation in Los Angeles. Gosch said he understood that Schindler was not entitled to a pension until he was sixty-five. However, he warned Dr. Weinrowsky that the West German government might find itself embarrassed if other governments were the first to recognize Oskar for his accomplishments. He explained "that the only way . . . Bonn could preserve its dignified face in the international spectrum would be to act *before* other nations, and not afterwards." If West German authorities wished to make a one time gift to the Schindler Foundation, then the foundation could use the funds to hire Oskar in some capacity. As usual, Gosch reminded Oskar to keep this information confidential.[45]

Gosch wrote Schindler again two weeks later in response to a letter Oskar had written him on February 1. Schindler had included several newspaper clippings about the film in the German press. One discussed several programs that the state-run television station Westdeutscher Rundfunk (WDR) was going to do on Schindler in March. Gosch told Oskar that such programs would violate his film contract. Television, Gosch went on, "should only be used to *assist* the film industry when it can do the most good." He again reminded Schindler that media contacts should be directed to his office at MGM. Gosch immediately cabled the program director of Westdeutscher Rundfunk, Dr. Hans Joachim Lange, and told him that he, MGM, and Delbert Mann owned the exclusive rights to the life of Oskar Schindler.[46]

After chastising Schindler once more, Gosch went on to tell him that he had been in contact with Gunther von Hase, the Minister of Information in West Germany, who oversaw Westdeutscher Rundfunk. He hoped to use the conflict over WDR's programs to pressure the West German government to do more to help Oskar: "I cannot permit them to make you into a national hero while still owing you a great deal of money." He added that Howard Koch was hard at work on the film script and should complete a preliminary script or "treatment" by the end of February.[47]

In the meantime, Gosch was trying to drum up publicity for the film in the United States. His biggest coup came on the floor of the United States House of Representatives on February 24, 1965, when Congressman

James C. Corman of California gave a short speech about Oskar Schindler and *To the Last Hour*. Corman, whose congressional district included Hollywood and Beverly Hills, began his brief comments by noting that the American film industry was often criticized because of its "almost unlimited freedom" to express itself. But occasionally, he added, a motion picture comes forward that "is very nearly above criticism." This was true of MGM's upcoming film, *To the Last Hour*. It was about Oskar Schindler, a man recently honored by the State of Israel for saving 1,300 Jews during the war. The theme of the film, "that man's humanity to man must always prevail," certainly was the case with Schindler, a German and a Catholic. The fact, Corman went on, that Schindler, in the "face of incredible dangers and adversities" was still willing to "become his brother's keeper" was certainly a "sign of hope that one day a true peace [would] be built from friendship and understanding." Congressman Corman concluded by saying that he knew of no recent film "that convey[ed] so great a message or that ha[d] the potential to weave all peoples into the common thread of individual brotherhood."[48]

Corman's remarks thrilled Gosch, who sent a copy by special delivery to Dan Terrell with MGM's publicity office in New York. Gosch wrote Terrell that he had spent the past two months with the leading Hollywood artists' representatives "using every persuasive means . . . to mind-condition . . . difficult and temperamental people to one inalienable fact: that for an important star to appear in their forthcoming film vehicle [would] be tantamount to a status symbol within the industry." Gosch then went to the heart of the matter about the progress of the film: finding a top notch star to play the role of Oskar Schindler. He thought that Corman's remarks were "the final seal of approval . . . to break down the one rule-of-thumb of [their] business—no star wants to commit to a picture without seeing the screenplay." He and Delbert Mann felt that if proper use were made of these remarks in the *Congressional Record* they would "fire the strongest opening gun that a picture has ever had in the difficult area of top casting." He assured Terrell that he would have a script treatment ready in a few weeks that would then be used to cast the leading actors. The final script would be ready in May. He hoped to begin production in December though it would take several months to build a set near MGM's studio in Madrid. Gosch said that he had some top rate actors interested in the film. He added: "Agents for Burt Lancaster, Paul Newman and a number of other players of similar category are giving the Oskar Schindler role so much consideration that, literally, they are holding open any likelihood of conflict with a possible December starting date until they have had an opportunity to read and discuss the treatment of our picture."⁴⁹

In the meantime, Gosch sent Delbert Mann a list of the main characters for the film. Howard Koch would use the real names of Oskar and Emilie only; all other characters would be given new names. Leopold Page was now "Poldi" Resnick and Amon Göth would become Karl Gunter. Itzhak Stern was the character Solomon Kravitz and Herman Rosner became the model for Herman Spivak. Helen Hirsch Horowitz was now Rebecca Bartok and Rabbi Menashe Levertov was the character Rabbi Julius Levy. All the major and minor characters in the film were many of the same people interviewed by Gosch and Koch in late 1964. Steven Spielberg chose to feature many of the same people in his 1993 motion picture, though he used their real names. What is also different about this earlier film proposal is the expansion of the story to include Schindler's Abwehr contacts and Righteous Gentiles such as Raimund Titsch.⁵⁰

The Film Treatment for To The Last Hour

Koch finished a 130-page screenplay treatment, or preliminary script, on March 15. The "Producer's Statement" at the beginning declared: "The amount of fictionalization content is *minimal*" though, in reality, there is a great deal of fiction in this early draft. Emilie, for example, plays a major role in the March 15 treatment. But as no one ever interviewed her for the film, much of what she did in this treatment was fictional. The same is true of Helen Hirsch, who figured prominently in the 1964 MGM treatment and Spielberg's 1993 film. In Koch's preliminary screenplay, for example, there is a preposterous scene in which Karl Gunter (Göth) forces Rebeka Bartok (Helen Hirsch) slowly to strip in front of Schindler. In another scene, Koch's tale of Oskar's first trip to Budapest to meet Jewish Agency representatives in 1943 is much more exciting than his real trip there using a German travel visa. Koch has Oskar flown to Hungary by Rudi Froelich, an Abwehr agent enamored with Emilie, where Oskar parachutes into the countryside and is met by armed men who lead him to Jewish Agency representatives in Budapest.⁵¹

Other than the shocking moment where Koch has Rebeka Bartok strip for Schindler, one of the most outrageous scenes is where Oskar plays poker with Gunter (Göth) to make up the list of Jews that he wants to take with him to Brünnlitz. There is no hint of the sacred "Schindler's

List" made up by Stern and Schindler in Spielberg's film. Instead, every time Oskar wins a hand in Koch's 1965 film treatment, and he seems to win handily that particularly day, he adds a new name to his list. This is how, supposedly, Schindler is able to put Poldi Resnick (Leopold Page) and Rebeka Bartok (Helen Hirsch) on his list. When the lengthy game ends, Gunter flies into a rage, calling Schindler a "Jew-lover." Oskar in turn calls Gunter "an inhuman bastard." As Gunter pulls out his pistol, Schindler warns him that he has a letter in his safe detailing Gunter's corruption. His secretary had orders to send it to *General* Otto Wechsler (*General* Maximilian Schindler of the Armaments Inspectorate) if Oskar never returned from Gunter's villa.[52]

Wechsler also plays a fictional role in granting Schindler Armaments Inspectorate permission to make the move to Brünnlitz. In real life, *General* Schindler (Wechsler) did everything he could to help his Sudeten German namesake save Jews. But in the Koch treatment, Wechsler tells Oskar after he grants him permission for the move that "he would be accountable for every one of them [Jewish inmates] and for their eventual liquidation." But before the move can take place, there is one last hurdle: SS approval. To get this, Emilie, against Oskar's wishes, volunteers to go to SS headquarters in Prague, where she beguiles the commanding general, Schemerhorn, with her beauty. To avoid Schemerhorn's efforts to seduce her, Emilie gets him drunk, but not before he gives his permission for the move. Oskar's wife did all this "without either surrendering herself to the obnoxious General or incurring his enmity."[53]

The trip to Brünnlitz for the men is also fictionalized. They make the long trip mostly on foot, though Oskar did manage to "get together an assortment of vehicles ranging from lorries to bicycles and horse-drawn wagons" for some of them. The account of Oskar's efforts to save the women in Auschwitz is a mixture of fiction and fact. After Oskar goes to Auschwitz and fails to convince the commandant to release his three hundred women, Oskar's secretary, Ilse Schoen, volunteers to go to Auschwitz to try to free the Schindler females. Early one morning, Ilse suddenly appears at the front gate of Brünnlitz, leading the women. A surprised Oskar rushes out of his office to greet the group, but Ilse pleads: "Please don't ask me anything." She then falls weeping into Emilie's arms. Though about a fifth of the script deals with Brünnlitz, there is no mention of the Golleschau transport and the remarkable efforts to save the Jews on it. For many Schindler survivors, this was the most memorable event in the Schindler story other than those surrounding liberation.[54]

Koch became really creative when it came to the days leading up to the liberation of the camp. Oskar, presumably away trying to find a way to prevent the murder of his Jews, leaves Emilie, who has emerged as the script's principal heroine, in charge. As Jewish workers dig a death pit with a large bulldozer, a member of the Czech underground infiltrates the camp dressed as an SS officer and convinces Emilie to come with him in a truck to get hidden arms. When Oskar returns, he organizes a Jewish commando unit under Poldi Reznick (Leopold Page). As the armed Jewish group begins to take over the camp, Oskar confronts the commandant, Bischel (Josef Leipold) and tells him that he is taking over Brünnlitz. A fight ensues and Bischel tries to shoot Oskar with his Luger. As the struggle continues, Oskar knocks the Luger out of Bischel's hand. A few moments later, Oskar hits Bischel with "a hard blow on the side of his head. Bischel falls back, trips, and plunges through the open window, landing on the cement pavement below."[55]

Now that the Jewish commandos have control of the camp, Oskar tells them to put signs "warning of typhus" outside the gates to prevent Germans from entering the lager. Now the scene shifts to a gathering of all the inmates inside. Oskar, with Emilie and Ilse by his side, tells his Jewish workers that Hitler is dead and that the war is over. He warns them of the danger of German units still operating in the area but assures them that he will remain with them to protect them *"to the last hour."* He also asks them to keep order and discipline and not to harm their guards. There had already been enough killing and enough inhumanity: "Let us behave like human beings." In the final scene, Oskar, "standing at the head of the Jewish throng," greets the Soviet officer, Colonel Rakov, who heads the Russian squad about to liberate the camp. When Rakov learns that Schindler is a German, he puts his hand on his pistol. Quickly, Poldi (Page) and the other Jewish commandos surround Oskar as Emilie and Ilse protect him with their bodies. Poldi then steps forward and tells Rakov, "We are Schindler Jews." In a flash, first Francischa Resnick, Poldi's mother, and then others behind Schindler rush forward to embrace the Russians. "This spontaneous emotional gesture," the film's treatment reads, "breaks the ice and now the repressed joy and relief surge over the group in a wave of wild celebration." The Russians reciprocate this loving outpouring while Oskar stands proudly with his arm around Emilie. They watch the celebration knowing that they have saved 1,300 souls "who will live to testify to one man's humanity to his fellow beings."[56]

The sad thing about this early script treatment is that it contained the very inaccuracies and fictionalization that so concerned Schindler and Bejski. It also explains why Gosch refused to give Oskar a copy. He knew that both men would have been outraged at the liberties taken with the Schindler story. Oskar seemed to sense all along that something was amiss with the film's progress and accuracy, which in turn fed his uncertainties. This explains, for example, his comments to Walter Pollack in mid-February when he told him that because of his "precarious [financial] situation [he] had no chance of placing demands [during the contract negotiations] and had to accept and sign the completed outcome." In this particular situation, he added, he had to "eat bird or die." But on reflection, he was determined "to achieve an increase of . . . material fees from the collaboration and successes."[57] He hoped to do this with meetings with Gosch in Germany in March. Leopold Page expressed the same frustrations in a letter to Oskar several weeks later. He had lost his consultancy position in the final contract, though Gosch promised to hire him and Mila during the actual filming. He only hoped that Gosch would keep his promise. Page had spent a great deal of time away from his business dealing with film matters, and he was not doing too well at the time. So, like Oskar's, Gosch's plans were very important not only to tell the world about Schindler's dramatic efforts during the war but also to help ease serious financial difficulties for both men. The same could be said for Emilie.[58]

Despite this, Oskar and Page remained deeply trustful of Martin Gosch, whom Oskar still considered his friend. Yet finances remained at the forefront of his concerns. His attorney, Dr. Alexander Besser, had recently reached a settlement in Schindler's bankruptcy case, though Oskar still owed his creditors some money. He hoped to use money from his advance to pay them off. According to the contract, Oskar was to receive 80 percent of the first half of the advance minus $6,250 in expenses and legal fees for a total payment of $13,750; Emilie was to receive 20 percent or $5,000 minus expenses and legal fees, or $4,375. In some ways, it proved more difficult getting the money to Emilie than to Oskar. In addition to exchange rate problems with the weak Argentine peso, there were questions about whether it would be wise to send Emilie a lump sum or to give her a monthly stipend. In fairness to Gosch, Page, and Glovin, their only concern through all this was the welfare of Oskar and Emilie. They knew that each of them had financial problems, though Oskar's were worse because he did not have someone caring for him as Emilie did in Buenos

Aires. The modest problems that arose about the distribution of these particular advances were perceptual and arose more out of their concern to be certain that both Schindlers got the most for their money in terms of exchange rates and bank interest. In late February, for example, Oskar, desperate for money, asked Page to wire him $7,500 immediately. Page advised holding the money in a California account to gain more interest, but Oskar insisted on being paid immediately.[59]

Oskar's financial problems intensified his frustrations with Gosch, particularly when Gosch told him that he did not want Oskar to take part in Brünnlitz liberation ceremonies in Israel in May. Initially, Oskar told Dr. Bejski that if necessary he would sneak into Israel to see his friends despite the restraints from MGM. Gosch wanted to coordinate the celebration with Oskar and the Schindler Jews with the film and asked the organizers in Israel to delay it because he wanted the celebration to be a part of "the planned propaganda for the film."[60] On March 8, Schindler wrote Irving Glovin and expressed his frustration with the amount of his advance and with the problems of getting Emilie's money to her. Glovin reminded Oskar of the difficulties of getting that kind of advance, particularly as it was based only on an idea for a film when the contract was signed. Oskar, of course, was thinking of his payments in light of the projected costs of the film, $9 million. Glovin told him that these were merely cost projections and had nothing to do with the value of the story. He simply felt it was unrealistic for Oskar to expect any more money from the project than laid out in the contract. In fact, he wrote, Schindler's receiving cash in advance at all was remarkable; and to have "gained a participating interest in the production [was] extraordinary." He went on to explain the delays in getting the advance to Emilie. The check for the full amount had been written early and sent to Argentina. But concern over the distribution of the money there delayed the payment.[61]

Glovin's letter did little to still Oskar's frustration over what he perceived to be the failure to send Emilie her advance. To his credit, Oskar remained protective of Emilie's interests throughout the film's development and seemed to care about her well-being, though this was partially driven by their contractual arrangement on the film. In the fall of 1964, Emilie applied for a certificate of citizenship at the German consulate in Buenos Aires so that she could obtain a German passport. She had lost her birth and marriage certificates; all she had for identification was an invalid Allied zone pass from occupied Germany. Oskar was called to Regensburg to verify their marriage. The official questioning him asked why they were not divorced after living apart for so long. Several years before, Oskar had asked Walter Pollack to find out whether Emilie was willing to grant him a divorce. She told him that she had no reason to divorce her husband. The citizenship matter and the question of divorce upset Oskar, who misunderstood the reasons for Emilie's request for a certificate of citizenship. He wrote Pollack that he was quite willing to grant Emilie a divorce, but was afraid that he would lose title to what remained of their property in Argentina as well as his claim to their "bungalow" in San Vicente.[62]

Pollack gave Oskar frequent updates about money, which he claimed Emilie often mishandled, and expressed concern about her relationship with Cascho Bosetti, whom Oskar thought was simply a gold digger. On December 20, 1965, Schindler wrote Pollack again about his concerns for Emilie's welfare and the question of divorce. Several people told him he was a fool not to divorce his wife, which, Oskar explained, would give him the right to free himself "from a burden which has as the only positive result the tie to a person who is to be described as outside any social order even in the generous Argentinian society and was laughed at." In another letter, Oskar told Pollack that the question of a divorce was really not important to him because it would not change Emilie. He had to, "for better or worse, leave her [Emilie] at liberty to be a fool." Regardless, Oskar still wished the best for Emilie though she was also the reason he did not return to Argentina for a visit. If he did, he explained to Pollack, he would sneak into the country to avoid her "with one crying and one laughing eye." He added: "I do not know how I myself could stomach such situations incognito."[63] In part, Oskar was probably reacting to Emilie's decision to have nothing to do with him. On one occasion, when Walter Pollack begged her to write Oskar, she responded, "Oh, leave me in peace. I have no time."[64]

Yet despite his mixed feelings towards his wife, Oskar was still angered by what he perceived to be the unwarranted delays in getting her the film advance. Oskar wrote Walter Pollack at the end of March that Glovin's letter was simply "beating around the bush" when it came to Emilie's money. When angry, Oskar was at his verbal best. He added that "for Borscht one needs no teeth, after all, nor any 15 minute conversations in the Plaza Hotel." He then laid out the terms of a letter that Emilie should write to Glovin to insure that he sent her the film money promptly. A quick payment, he noted, will "eliminate all doubts about cheating my wife." Oskar followed up this letter with one to Glovin in which he reemphasized the need to send Emilie her money as soon as possible. But he took a much less angry and more conciliatory tone than the one he displayed in the letter to Pollack of the same day. He was not, as Glovin's earlier letter implied, dissatisfied with the pace of the film's development. On the other hand, he reserved the right as Glovin's client "to express . . . [his] part of the problems." Finally, he wanted to know what fees Glovin planned to charge him in the future.[65]

In reality, Emilie was doing fine. One of the things that had angered Oskar, Pollack, and Emilie's other *Traducion* friends was a report to Gosch and Glovin by an MGM representative who happened to be in Buenos Aires, that Emilie was in bad financial shape and "without shoes and accommodation, first aid, etc. She was just living in a terrible condition."[66] Oskar wrote to Page that this was ridiculous. The MGM representative, Mr. Silvestre, Oskar noted, had seen Emilie for only fifteen minutes. *Traducion* had just built a lovely furnished home for her and she was doing "as well as [Page's] dear children." In fact, *Traducion* had done so much for Emilie that she had asked the head of the B'nai B'rith lodge, Helmuth Heinemann, who was also serving as her trustee, not to give her any more furniture once she had received her film money. When she got her advance from Page in April, she explained, she wanted to buy more furniture with her own funds. Emilie finally decided, in consultation with Heinemann and Pollack, to ask Page to put her money, $4,375 (Arg$30,000) in the Gibraltar Savings Bank and Loan Association in California. Page would then send her $100 a month stipend with the proviso that she could ask for additional funds as needed.[67]

War Crimes Investigations, Continued Financial Problems, and the Film's Failure

For the next few months there was no news on the film, though Oskar probably had his hands full dealing with a drunken driver charge. He lost his driver's license for six months and, as a result, the police impounded his car. He was also "sentenced to a jail term of three weeks for violating German driving laws."[68] When he got out of jail, Oskar's attentions turned to the West German war crimes investigations against former *SS-Hauptscharführer* Wilhelm Kunde, *SS-Hauptscharführer* Franz Müller, and SS-man Herman Heinrich, who had all served in Kraków and Płaszów. Between 1962 and 1972, Oskar would testify in five war crimes investigations against former SS men and Nazis in West Germany (Federal Republic of Germany). However, according to Professor C. F. Ruter of the Institute for Criminal Law of the University of Amsterdam, with one exception, Schindler's testimony was not relevant to the German courts' findings because most of those investigated were not brought to trial or had died before they could be prosecuted. And when Oskar's testimony did appear in the court transcript, it had little impact on the outcome of the case.[69]

This was so in the trial of *SS-Hauptsturmführer* Walter Fellenz, the deputy HSSPF in the Kraków district. After the war, Fellenz returned to Germany, where he became a prominent leader of the small but politically important Free Democratic Party *(Freie Demokratische Partei)*. Fellenz was arrested and charged with war crimes in the summer of 1960. He was accused of responsibility for the murder of 40,000 Jews in Poland. His six-week trial began in Flensburg in November 1962. Oskar was required to testify in the case against Fellenz after he received a subpoena from the chief of police in Frankfurt. His testimony, which was taken on June 6, 1962, meant little in terms of the specific charges against Fellenz, whom Oskar admitted he knew well by name but did not know personally. His five pages of testimony, though, did help re-create the environment in which Fellenz operated during his time in Kraków. At the end of the trial, Fellenz was convicted and sentenced to seven years at hard labor, though the prosecutor had asked for life imprisonment. The Federal Supreme Court *(Bundesgerichtshof)* later overturned the verdict and Fellenz was re-tried and convicted of war crimes in 1965. On January 27, 1966, he was sentenced to a seven-year prison term but was freed on the same day for time served.[70]

About ten months after he had provided investigators with information about Fellenz, Oskar gave the criminal police in Frankfurt testimony in the case against *SS-Sturmbannführer* Johannes Hassebroek. After the war, the British arrested the former Groß Rosen commandant and placed him on trial for war crimes. In 1948, a British court sentenced him to death but later commuted the sentence to fifteen years imprisonment. In 1954, Hassebroek was released from prison. In the early 1960s, West German authorities investigated him and in 1967 arrested him for war crimes. Hassebroek was put on trial in the District Court in Braunschweig for the murder of nine Jews and three non-Jews during his time as Groß Rosen's commandant, but was acquitted. State prosecutors appealed the acquittal to the Federal Supreme Court, which upheld the lower court's ruling. This did not end the West German investigation against Hassebroek, which continued until his death in 1977. In his 1963 testimony, Schindler explained his relationship with Hassebroek, who periodically inspected Brünnlitz because it was a sub-camp of Groß Rosen. Oskar told investigators that he had interacted with Hassebroek during his eight months at Brünnlitz. He mentioned the considerable bribes he gave Hassebroek, but added that "no arbitrary killings occurred at Brünnlitz."[71]

Schindler's testimony in the investigations against Fellenz and Hassebroek set the stage for testimony against Kunde, Müller, and Heinrich at the end of 1965. Seven months earlier, Oskar had written Dr. Bejski and suggested that he, Stern, and Page should consider giving testimony against the three former SS men. When Martin Gosch learned of Oskar's proposal, he tried to use this potential gathering of Schindler Jewish witnesses in Kiel to help publicize the film. What drove him to this were the movie's dwindling prospects.[72]

The first serious hint of problems with *To the Last Hour* came in the fall of 1965, when Gosch wrote Oskar to tell him that MGM liked the script prepared by Howard Koch but wanted to replace Delbert Mann as director. He asked Oskar not to be impatient and again explained that it took a long time to put the details of a film project together. Oskar responded on November 28 in poor English and seemed pleased that the script was finally ready. He requested a confidential copy of the script in English because his memories could add "valuable colouring" to the script. Schindler wrote, "I want to prevent any mistake in bringing forth the facts," which would be a great disappointment not only to him, but also for his "freinds [sic], who trusted [him] during all those years of the awful war." He invited Gosch to visit him whenever he could because he felt isolated in Germany. It was contact with his American and Israeli friends that gave him "the feeling of worth living," particularly in light of his upcoming testimony against Kunde, Heinrich, and Müller. Such testimony, he explained, "before courts against Nazi people can only deprimate [*deprimiert*; depressed]" him.[73]

Despite the friendly tone of his letter to Gosch, Oskar was quite upset over the delay in shooting. He wrote Walter Pollack that he was nervous and depressed about the delay: "It would be easier to sell a film in which sex and large breasts dominate, but my stuff is just not so popular."[74] What is interesting about this letter is that he does not mention that he had just been awarded the Cross of Merit, First Class, of the Order of Merit of the Federal Republic of Germany. Gosch, to his credit, had been the driving force behind the medal. After she lunched with Gosch in January, Dr. Weinrowsky of the German Legation in Los Angeles sent a detailed report about Schindler and the film's development to the Foreign Office *(Auswärtiges Amt)* in Bonn, which recommended that the Federal president, Dr. Heinrich Lübke, award the Cross of Merit to Schindler. Dr. Lübke approved the award on November 5, 1965, and Oskar received it on January 12, 1966.[75]

Though Oskar certainly appreciated the medal, his greater concern was money, and that was one of the principal reasons for his nervousness about the film's progress. Dr. Bejski wrote Gosch just before Christmas 1965 about this very issue. He told Gosch that the past year had been a good one for Oskar. "After many years," he explained, "Mr. Schindler had regained his composure." He now looked much different than in years past and was "well and calm." But his many friends in Israel continued to worry about him and wanted him to emigrate there because Oskar seemed so isolated in Frankfurt. However, Schindler hesitated because he hoped to be busy with the film and "eagerly" awaited news about its progress. Oskar underscored these concerns to Gosch in a January 19, 1966, letter in which he said that he was "a little afraid for the future, without any hope of economic security." His financial situation seemed precarious and he asked for an early payment of the second portion of his advance. He evidently was still hounded by creditors from his failed stone-and-cement business, and a former Brünnlitz employee who had filed charges against Oskar for back wages. He was quite discouraged by these problems and frustrated because Gosch had still not sent him a script. He begged him for a copy of the script, which he needed for "a moral push" for himself.[76]

For some strange reason, Schindler's letter reached Gosch overnight and on January 20 he responded to Oskar's letter of the day before. He explained that he had not sent Schindler a copy of the script because it was obvious from the poorly translated letters he had sent Gosch that Oskar would have trouble understanding the script. Moreover, it would cost Gosch $2,500 to translate into German what had become a very long script. Gosch wrote that he knew of film deals that were ruined by mistranslated scripts. He again asked Oskar to be patient with the film's progress and pointed to MGM's recently released *Dr. Zhivago,* which had cost $11 million to make and four years to develop. *To the Last Hour* was going through the same "growing pains," Gosch pointed out. They now had a rough draft of a script that would take up four hours of film time. Moreover, Gosch was still unsure whether just covering Oskar's life from 1938 to 1945 would be adequate. Perhaps it was important to expand the story line to include more of his life. And it might be, Gosch noted, better "to publish a book version of the story" as a way of "pre-exploiting the film, and to condition the world audience to the name and deeds of Oskar Schindler." Finally, Oskar had to remember that MGM had the "right to refuse" any film proposal. This was a "large and expensive film" and "it might start out with Paramount and finish up at MGM. Or vice versa." Once again, Gosch told Oskar that "PATIENCE" was needed as plans for the film moved forward. Gosch went on to say that it greatly annoyed him that the German government did not coordinate Oskar's receipt of the Cross of Merit with him. He had anticipated building a "SCHINDLER CAMPAIGN" around the ceremony. Gosch added, "Bonn hopes to escape their righteous economic obligations to you by giving you a medal." He intended to make a stink about this matter with the German ambassador to the United States and threatened negative publicity if Bonn refused to grant Oskar a pension.[77]

Oskar sent Dr. Bejski a copy of Gosch's letter, which the Israeli judge analyzed and, with great hesitancy, concluded, in a letter to Oskar, that the film deal with MGM seemed to have fallen through. Dr. Bejski also told Oskar that he was also troubled by "Poldek's silence."[78] Page soon confirmed Bejski's suspicions. In fact, he explained, MGM had rejected the film deal in October 1965 and initially was not going to pay Oskar his advance until Page and Gosch threatened to sue them. Page went on to say that the reason for his silence centered around the fact that he had lost his business in Beverly Hills and was consumed with his own financial difficulties. This news greatly depressed Oskar, who was about to leave on a trip to the United States to discuss the future of the film with Gosch. Page told Bejski later that summer that MGM was still interested in *To the Last Hour* but would not make a decision about it until the spring of 1967.[79]

Oskar now gave some thought to finding a job. Several of his friends recommended him for a position with Hoechst Aktiengesellschaft, a giant chemical company based in Frankfurt. Since 1925, Hoechst had been part of the chemical conglomerate I. G. Farbenindustrie, but had been broken up into subsidiaries in 1950 after its most prominent leaders had been tried in Nuremberg in 1947 and 1948 for crimes against peace and humanity and for being part of a criminal organization. Hoechst, Bayer, and BASF were some of the more prominent firms to emerge from the breakup. Nothing ever came of this job prospect as Oskar was interested in working for Hoechst only if it made him its Israeli representative.[80]

Camille Honig, the Martin Buber Prize Fiasco, and Conflicts with Martin Gosch

By early 1967, things seemed to improve for Schindler. The German government provided him with an interim honorary pension and he was nominated for the Martin Buber Peace Prize in London, which involved the promise of several financial awards. The press reported that Oskar was to receive £20,000 ($48,192) from the prize while Oskar told Leopold Page in March 1967 that Dino de Laurentis was going to give him £10,000 ($24,096). In addition, Martin Gosch had gained full control of the rights for *To the Last Hour* and wanted to revitalize the project, using the upcoming war crimes investigative trial against Kunde, Müller, and Heinrich to publicize the wartime deeds of Oskar Schindler. But the Buber Prize proved to be a scam and the film project was for all practical purposes dead. Moreover, Schindler's involvement with Camille Honig, the head of the Martin Buber Society, brought him into serious conflict with Martin Gosch and almost destroyed their relationship.[81]

The most important developments over the next few years were the decisions of the Hessian and Federal governments to grant Oskar several pensions. In 1967, the governor of the State of Hesse granted Schindler a monthly temporary honorary pension of DM 500 ($125) that later became permanent. To a great extent, the Hessian pension could be attributed to Martin Gosch and Oskar's supporters in Israel, who had put pressure on West German officials. Gosch had chosen to threaten the Germans into action, whereas the Schindler Jews in Israel chose a diplomatic course, which meant gaining the support of the West German ambassador to Israel, Dr. Rolf Pauls, and other prominent Germans, such as Earl Graf Yorck von Wartenberg, who would play an important role in helping Oskar get the Hessian pension. Unfortunately, this first pension was barely enough for Oskar to pay for his small apartment at Am Hauptbahnhof 4, across the street from Frankfurt's main train station, and his basic living expenses. However, when Oskar turned sixty in 1968, his financial situation began to improve. The Federal government in Bonn awarded him an additional monthly pension of DM 200 ($50). He also began to receive a monthly stipend of DM $405 ($101.25) from the local reparations office as well as a monthly compensation pension of DM 118.80 ($29.70).[82]

It is fortunate that German authorities finally came through for Oskar because nothing ever came of *To the Last Hour* and the Martin Buber Prize. As news of the film became more discouraging, Oskar briefly thought he might realize some sort of financial windfall when Camille Honig, the head of the Martin Buber Society in London, contacted Oskar in the fall of 1966 with news that he had been nominated for the first Martin Buber Peace Prize, which Oskar was to receive in early 1967. We now know that Honig was a con artist who simply tried to use Oskar's growing fame to raise money from his many supporters in Europe, Israel, and the United States. Honig, in fact, was so slick that he conned everyone close to Schindler, even his friends in Israel, who sent Honig several glowing letters of support for Oskar's nomination in the fall and winter of 1966.[83]

Once Honig got a list of Schindler's supporters, he then asked them to apply for membership in the International Martin Buber Society & Institute, which would include a subscription to the society's journal, *I and Thou*, a play on one of Buber's most important philosophical works. Honig not only used Buber's name illicitly, he also adorned his publications with the names of some of the world's most prominent intellectuals and artists without their consent. Albert Schweitzer, for example, was listed as the Late President and Dag Hammarskjold, the second Secretary-General of the United Nations, as the Late First Sponsor. Igor Stravinsky served as the Life President and Yehudi Menuhin the Vice President for the British Commonwealth. Max Brod, Marc Chagall, Andre Maurois, and Reinhold Neibuhr were listed as Sponsors; the Advisory Committee included Saul Bellow, Arthur Miller, and Sir Alec Guinness. Needless to say, this list was impressive and Honig's publications were slick. It was hard for anyone to imagine that all this was just a façade to hide the scam.

Honig invited Oskar to London in January 1967 to discuss details of the award and help him plan the invitation list for the awards ceremony. Oskar told Martin Gosch that it would take place at the Hilton Hotel in London before two to three hundred selected guests. Even the wise Moshe Bejski was taken in by Honig's offer and told Oskar that he could use the award to pressure the government in Bonn to award him a permanent Federal pension.[84] Martin Gosch was upset when he learned about plans for the Martin Buber prize. Oskar wrote him on March 6, 1967, about his meeting with Honig in London and sent him materials about the Martin Buber Society. He added that though he thought that ties to Honig, with his "superb connections in London," might help with the film's publicity, he would do nothing to harm their "film affair" and would discuss anything of importance with Gosch relating to the matter.[85]

Gosch, though, was deeply suspicious of Honig and went to London soon after he received Oskar's letter and looked into Schindler's ties with the head of the Buber Society. When he had completed his investigation, Gosch asked the Criminal Investigative Division of Scotland Yard to look into Honig's "efforts in connection with Oskar Schindler." Gosch claimed that he and MGM had full legal rights to Schindler's story and was troubled because Honig was attempting to raise money for Schindler with the claim that Oskar was "both poverty-stricken and destitute." Gosch also claimed that Honig had entered into negotiations with the BBC and other media outlets as Schindler's representative. Gosch evidently spoke with Honig while he was in London and wrote him on March 27 and ordered him to "cease and desist" in all his activities involving Oskar Schindler, both then and in the future.[86]

Gosch was particularly angry about the Honig affair because he was trying to convince West German officials to turn the investigative trial of Wilhelm Kunde into a "show trial" that would center around the testimony of Oskar and prominent Schindler Jews such as Leopold Page and Dr. Moshe Bejski. Gosch also claimed that he was continuing to "negotiate" with German officials about a permanent pension for Oskar and the creation of an Oskar Schindler International Humanities Foundation. He was also talking with officials in the Vatican about "some fitting tribute" to Schindler. All this, of course, centered around efforts to publicize the war time heroics of Schindler and in turn create new interest for *To the Last Hour.*[87]

Honig was shocked by Gosch's letter and wrote Bejski and Sternberg asking them whether the Hollywood producer had "the rights over Mr. Schindler" and over them. He also wondered whether he had to obtain Gosch's permission to give Oskar the Martin Buber Prize.[88] In the meantime, Oskar met with Gosch in Frankfurt and came away from the meeting quite disturbed about the entire Martin Buber Prize affair. He learned that the promise of £20,000 from the Buber prize and £10,000 from Dino de Laurentis was, like the Buber Society, "a paper-puff." The whole idea of Honig's using his name to raise money fictitiously depressed Oskar, who later told Dr. Bejski: "I have not experienced such a spiritual low since the collapse of my factory three years ago." His only hope was that there was enough time left in his life to "survive this hit." Oskar was also discouraged when Gosch's efforts to use the Kunde investigative trial as a "propaganda" launching pad for the Schindler film were not successful even though Oskar and several Schindler Jews gave West German investigators their testimony in Kiel. Kunde was supposed to be tried for crimes centering around deportations to Bełżec and Auschwitz but died in Bremen in 1969 before he could be brought to justice.[89]

But Oskar was soon to suffer further indignities at the hands of Camille Honig and Martin Gosch. On April 19, Honig wrote Schindler in Israel telling him that the plans for the Martin Buber Prize ceremony on May 21 in London had fallen apart because of Gosch. Honig explained that Gosch's efforts to discredit him in London had destroyed six months of work on the prize for Schindler and "the bottom fell out" of his world. Yet he begged Schindler to contact him so that they could discuss future plans for the Martin Buber Prize.[90] On the same day, Martin Gosch wrote to Oskar in Israel in care of Dr. Bejski. Gosch was furious with Schindler for writing Honig letters filled with "threats of scandal." Gosch claimed he preferred a more subtle approach and chastised Oskar for his methods: "If they continue you will lose my personal interests and help." Oskar had evidently signed a conditional letter with Honig in London earlier in the year that had led to negotiations between Honig and various media outlets such as the BBC interested in the Schindler story. To a point, Gosch added, he was willing not to say anything about Schindler's relationship with Honig because he hoped Oskar might gain something financially out of it. "You cannot," Gosch went on, "ride with both the hares and the hounds and expect to come away unmarked." He was deeply hurt by Oskar's behavior and personally disillusioned "regarding the true greatness of Oskar Schindler." He ended by telling Oskar that if he did not give him "unreserved authority to continue in regard to London and Bonn," he preferred that Oskar handle his own affairs.[91]

Oskar never said much about Gosch's letter and continued to maintain ties with Honig even though he was deeply suspicious of him. But Dr. Bejski did say something about Gosch's letter to Oskar and a separate letter that Gosch had written Bejski that he included with the April 19 letter to Schindler, which Gosch asked Dr. Bejski to translate. What most disturbed Dr. Bejski was the threatening nature of this separate letter, which Gosch asked him to share with the Schindler committee in Israel. From Bejski's perspective, Gosch had attempted to blackmail the Schindler Jews when he told him that "if he [Gosch] doesn't get $50,000 at once" he would use the same threats that he had used against the German government when he tried to get them to award Schindler a pension. If the Schindler Jews were not forthcoming financially, then Gosch threatened to write the real Oskar Schindler story, naming names, dates, and places: "I will publicize the worthy and castigate the unworthy in the gaze of public light." Bejski's worry now was that Gosch would do something to hurt Oskar. At the same time, Bejski wrote Leopold Page that he [Bejski] "won't be the object of threats and blackmail."[92]

It is difficult to know the exact purpose of Gosch's letter because we do not have anything other than Dr. Bejski's references to it. It was probably motivated, at least according to Gosch, by the fact that he had spent $250,000 on pre-production costs for *To the Last Hour* and was somehow trying to recoup his losses. But why he threatened the Schindler Jews in Israel is a mystery. They had done nothing but support the film project and each of them who were interviewed by Gosch had turned over their individual $500 honorariums to him to help support the Oskar Schindler Humanities Foundation. And though the money from this fund was meant partially to help Oskar, Gosch always rebuffed efforts to give the money to him, which, depending on whose figures you believed, amounted to anywhere between $2,000 and $10,000. Towards the end of Schindler's life, Leopold Page told Dr. Bejski what had happened to the money. Gosch, who died in 1972, had taken all the money that the survivors had given him for the Oskar Schindler International Humanities Foundation, though he claimed that it had been stolen. Some thought was given to suing Gosch's estate, but the idea was dropped when Gosch's wife promised to pay back the stolen funds. However, Dr. Bejski doubted that Oskar would ever see any of this money because Gosch had left his wife destitute.[93]

Yet even though Gosch and Honig had defrauded Schindler and his friends, Oskar continued to maintain relationships with both men, in part because he could not pull away from their continuing promises of fame and fortune. After many stops and starts, Honig finally gave the promised banquet for Oskar on December 4, 1967, and the evening's other honoree, Dr. Gerhard Wolf, the former German consul in Florence who also helped save Jews during the war. Oskar later told Dr. Bejski that he had decided to take part in the ceremony because he did not want to be the "victim of public disgrace" at an event attended by so many prominent people. He felt that he had to put on "a good face to the evil game, so as to at least save face to the outside [world]." Honig, who had published a special edition of *I and Thou* beforehand to highlight the exploits of Schindler and Dr. Wolf, somehow managed to convince the renowned British author J. B. Priestley to give the keynote address, and two well-known artists and Holocaust survivors, Natalia Karp and Zwi Kanar, provided the entertainment. Many of the prominent guests were there to support Oskar, and were well aware of the humiliation he had already suffered at the hands of Honig. The banquet began with a speech by Priestley, though Oskar arrived at the end of it because Honig had picked him up late from his hotel. Priestley gave another impromptu speech welcoming Oskar. Reginald, Lord Sorensen (the Rev. R. W. Sorensen), a prominent member of the House of Lords and vice president of the Buber Society, and Rabbi Leslie Hardman, an important British Jewish leader and activist, followed with short speeches applauding Oskar's wartime exploits. Both men, like Oskar, were conned by Honig's missteps regarding the peace prize and promised to look into the prospect of creating a new Oskar Schindler Committee independent of Honig. The evening finished with a short speech by Oskar. When the Honig scandal finally hit the press in 1968 after Honig failed to pay the bills for the Schindler-Wolf banquet (which Wolf did not attend), Lord Sorensen explained that he had tried time and again to have his name removed from letters sent out by Honig. He told the *Jewish Chronicle* that he had no ties with the Martin Buber Society.[94]

Oddly enough, Oskar partially blamed Martin Gosch for his failure to follow through on his promise publicly to expose Honig. In some ways, this was more of an expression of Oskar's frustration over the failure of the movie deal. By early 1968, he was again having heart problems and suffered from renewed bouts of depression. He continued to have money problems and told Walter Pollack that he had lost more than DM 8,000 ($2,000) in the Honig affair. He asked Page to help him obtain funds from the Oskar Schindler International Humanities Foundation and wrote Gosch on April 8, 1968, urging send him to send some portion of the funds in the foundation's account. He needed the money to live on and to help pay for the medical tests he desperately needed. Though Gosch expressed sympathy for Schindler's current economic problems, he argued that it would violate the trust of those who had contributed money to create the Oskar Schindler International Humanities Foundation. Instead, Gosch proposed that Dr. Bejski and others create an Oskar Schindler Survivors Fund that would provide Oskar with an income. Oskar later told Page that if Gosch had sent the money as requested instead of offering him "pedagogical suggestions," he could have undergone a test that showed he had severe diabetes. Instead, he had to wait until he got to Israel later that spring to find this out. His health had deteriorated to the point that several Israeli physicians suggested that he have heart surgery later that year to correct problems he had with angina pectoris. He planned to return to Israel later that summer for further medical checkups.[95]

Revival and Hope

Oskar later admitted that if it had not been for the help of his Israeli friends that spring and summer, his health might have deteriorated further. Instead, he began to feel better and by November was able to travel to Israel. He was the guest of Lufthansa, West Germany's national airline, on its inaugural flight to Israel. In fact, his second trip to Israel in 1968 seemed to represent a major turning point in Oskar's life. In late October, Pope Paul VI made him a Knight of the Order of Saint Sylvester, though Oskar was annoyed because the Vatican's bureaucracy had prevented him from receiving it earlier on his birthday. This event was followed by a wonderful trip to Israel in December, where he was fêted at a banquet held in his honor by the Kraków Society at the Hilton Hotel in Tel Aviv.[96]

This was followed by a trip to the United States, where Oskar was honored at Temple Beth Am in Los Angeles on January 5, 1969, for his efforts to save Jews during the war. Leopold Page and the other organizers of the tribute used the occasion to announce the creation of the Oskar Schindler Survivor's Fund. The ceremony began at exactly 2:00 P.M. Page explained that this was the exact time on April 28, 1945, Schindler's birthday, that he told his gathered workers in Brünnlitz that the war was almost over. Page added: "And he told us not to worry." Page went on to say that Oskar had promised he would stay with them "until the Last Hour." He then asked: "Can we do less for him?" Rabbi Jacob Pressman opened the commemoration service by reciting an ancient Jewish prayer of deliverance that was repeated simultaneously by Schindler Jews in cities throughout the world. Leopold Page then spoke about Schindler, whom he called "a living God to us," and announced the creation of the Survivor's Fund, which was meant to insure that Oskar would never "have to worry for the rest of his life." Martin Gosch, who helped organize the gathering, then spoke and said he had grave doubts whether the Schindler story would "ever be seen on the screen." Several months earlier, an article had appeared in the California Jewish newspaper, *Heritage*, that laid the failure of the film on the shoulders of the head of MGM, Robert O'Brien.[97]

Regardless, he remained dedicated "to the proposition that in the consideration of man being, in truth, his brother's keeper, the name of Oskar Schindler must be preeminent." Gosch concluded his remarks by announcing the creation of an Oskar Schindler Humanities Foundation that he hoped would begin to award an annual prize in 1971 to honor "those individuals in the world who best symbolize the true meaning of Man's Humanity to Man." Oskar then gave a brief address in which he thanked everyone, particularly his Schindler Jews, for the creation of the Survivor's Fund. He mentioned something newly dear to his heart, an exchange program of young people between Germany and Israel. For Oskar, children, whether they be those of his beloved Schindler Jews or anyone, were "mankind's best, and last hope." He went on: "Like the young of all creatures, they want to like, they want to *love*, and they will *love*, unless deliberately and carefully taught otherwise. For this is the *true* education—*of the heart.*"98

The idea of an exchange program of German and Israeli youth had become something very dear to Oskar's heart by this time. Several years earlier, he had been contacted by Dr. Dieter Trautwein, the city youth minister *(Stadtjugendpfarrer)* in Frankfurt who was involved in planning a workbook for young people in conjunction with the 450th anniversary of Martin Luther's 95 Theses (1517). Dr. Trautwein's committee wanted to know whether there were any contemporary German reformers they could put in the workbook. One of the documents they looked at was an article on Oskar Schindler that was based on a radio play by Maria Lahusen, the widow of a Berlin pastor. She had gotten her idea for the radio script from Kurt Grossman's *Die unbesungenen Helden: Menschen in Deutschlands dunklen Tagen* (The Unsung Heroes: People in Germany's Dark Days). Trautwein was intrigued by Schindler's story but also suspicious of it because he knew little about him even though he had seen Schindler's tree at Yad Vashem. When he learned that Oskar lived in Frankfurt, Trautwein decided to pay him a visit. He showed Schindler the article on the radio play and asked him whether it was accurate. Oskar responded: "More or less." Once he heard the full account of Schindler's wartime exploits, Trautwein decided that it was important for him to speak at the Frankfurt Church Youth Day on May 25, 1967. Oskar, along with Leopold Page, who was in Germany to testify in the Kunde hearing, spoke before a gathering of approximately 450 young people. Page's presence was particularly important because he, as a Schindler Jew, was able to back up what Schindler said. Oskar considered the meeting "a great success" and noted that the discussions with the young people at the meeting "took an hour longer than anticipated."99

His connections with Trautwein, who was becoming not only one of the German Lutheran (Evangelical) church's most important youth leaders but also one of its most creative composers, helped lead to new ties with the West German Catholic Church. In the summer of 1968, Oskar took part in several Lutheran and Catholic discussion forums that dealt with a new Christian-Jewish dialogue. His participation in the Catholic symposium, "Tempted and Engaged Faith" at the Hedwig-Dansfeld House in Bendorf am Rhein, was promoted by Dr. Lotte Schiffler, a former Frankfurt city councilwoman who became very close to Oskar during this period. There is no doubt that Oskar was sincerely interested in becoming more involved in youth work, but he was also driven by hopes that Dr. Trautwein and other church leaders would help him obtain his pension from the West German government in Bonn. Yet what heartened Oskar most in all these discussions that summer was that no one, either Catholic or Lutheran, had "tired of taking an unequivocal position" for his Israeli friends "and their splendid country."[100]

Dr. Trautwein told me that Oskar spoke frequently about the importance of bridge building among German youth through the *Aktion Sühnezeichen* (sign of atonement) movement, which sent German young people to countries that Germany had invaded during World War II. Oskar was particularly proud of the role he played in helping organize one of the first Israeli-West German youth exchange programs in 1969. He played an important role in helping raise the funds to send thirty "Schindler-Sabres" [Sabras, native-born Israelis] to West Germany in July 1969 to spend a month in Frankfurt, the Catholic home in Bendorf, and Munich.[101]

This newfound interest in Israel among Oskar's Catholic and Lutheran acquaintances meant a great deal to him and helped build an important psychological bridge for Schindler between Israel and West Germany that helped erase his confusing ties to both countries. He was particularly heartened by the positive reception to his work among Lutheran and Catholic youth groups and now considered himself "their partner in faith." As a result, Oskar Schindler had, at least according to Dr. Trautwein, "returned in a certain way to his church, with which he had not had any ties for thirty years." These ties, first to Israel and then to West Germany's Lutheran and Catholic communities, would play important roles in finally giving Oskar Schindler a sense of self-worth and mission in the final years of his life. This, combined with his growing involvement with Hebrew University in the early 1970s and the appearance of the final love of his life, Ami (Annemarie) Staehr, would seem to point finally to a stable, happy time in his life. Unfortunately, that was never to be because of mounting health problems that left him weak and depressed.[102]

14.

LOVE, BITTERNESS, AND DEATH

It WAS A TYPICAL, HOT, LATE JULY DAY IN TEL AVIV IN 1970.
Ami (Annemarie) Staehr had just arrived in Israel's beautiful coastal city
with her husband, Dr. Heinrich Staehr, who was working with West Germany's reparations *(Wiedergutmachungen)* program for Israel's Holocaust survivors. Dr. Staehr was there medically to investigate and help determine the amount each survivor was to receive, which was to be based on
the trauma he or she had suffered during the war. Ami Staehr was sitting
alone on the beach when she noticed someone standing near her. The soles
of the man's bare feet were covered in blood. Standing before her was
Oskar Schindler, so drunk that he did not know he had blistered his feet
on the hot sand.[1] A month earlier, Oskar had done the same thing at the
Dead Sea.[2] Entranced by this tall, handsome German, Ami bandaged his
feet. Several days later, she wrote her daughter-in-law, Tina Staehr, that
she had met "a real hero, a hero named Oskar Schindler."[3] Thus began
the last, and perhaps most important romance in Oskar Schindler's life.
After Oskar died in Hildesheim in 1974, Ami gathered many of his private papers from his apartment in Frankfurt and took them back to her
home in Hildesheim, which is about two hundred miles northeast of
Frankfurt. These famed *Koffer* (suitcase) files were later discovered by her
son, Chris, after the death of his father, Heinrich, in 1997. In the midst of
two pending lawsuits by Emilie Schindler, who still lived in Argentina,
Chris Staehr managed to spirit this vast collection of Oskar Schindler's
private papers out of Germany to Yad Vashem in Israel.

Oskar Schindler had many girlfriends throughout his life. But apart from his marriage to Emilie and his relationships with his wartime mistress, Eva "Marta" Kisza (Kisch) Scheuer, Gisa Schein, and Ami Staehr, none of his other romances seemed very important, with the exception of his staid affair with Herta Kluge, who was Oskar's girlfriend and secretary in the 1960s. As he grew older, Oskar, unlike many men his age, sought ties with attractive mature women. Oskar had a magnetic personality and remained handsome even as he aged. He never had trouble attracting women; his only problem was keeping them. I asked several of the Schindler women who had worked for Oskar at Emalia or Brünnlitz whom they found most attractive, Oskar or Liam Neeson, the actor who played Oskar in Steven Spielberg's film, *Schindler's List*. Each time, and without hesitation, they answered with a sigh, "Oskar!"

Dr. Dieter Trautwein said that the main reason Oskar had trouble keeping girlfriends was his drinking. Oskar knew he drank too much and that his heavy drinking was partly responsible for his poor health. In fact, his heavy drinking was one of the few criticisms I ever heard about him from his Schindler Jews. Oskar tried time and again to stop drinking, but always slipped back.[4] His close friend Lotte Schiffler wrote him an "SOS" letter in 1970 in which she, along with his physician in Frankfurt, Dr. Horst Metz, gave Oskar a blunt warning: "You are completely ruining yourself with alcohol." Lotte Schiffler told him that he had many friends who wanted to "spend a decade of friendship" with him. But they wanted him this time to be "rosy red and not blue [drunk]."[5] Unfortunately, about the best Oskar could do about his drinking problem was try to limit the amount he drank each day. An autopsy report, two days after his death in Hildesheim on October 9, 1974, noted that Oskar drank from two to four cognacs a day and smoked twenty cigarettes (down from forty).[6]

By the time Oskar met Ami Staehr on the beach in Tel Aviv, he had already suffered one heart attack and had serious kidney problems and diabetes. Ami fell madly in love with Oskar, though in a mature, distant way. She remained true to her marriage and husband, Heinrich, who had previously indulged in numerous affairs, and Oskar was drawn into their family circle as a friend.

Consequently, though Oskar had a special relationship with Ami, he also seemed close to Heinrich, at least from the perspective of some of Oskar's Israeli friends. Klara Sternberg, for example, wrote Ami in early 1973 that Oskar's "greatest fortune" was Ami and her husband; she added: "We cannot imagine what would happen to him [Oskar] without your selfless and loving help." Klara's only concern was that Ami might sacrifice her life "as his caretaker."[7]

Oskar occasionally traveled with Ami and Heinrich and became close friends with their son and daughter-in-law, Chris and Tina, who approved of Ami's relationship with Oskar. Chris and Tina had always fretted over Heinrich's affairs with other women and knew that they depressed Ami. They were overjoyed that her relationship with Oskar made Ami happy. Oskar's death devastated Ami but also led to the revitalization of her marriage to Heinrich. Dr. Staehr, who became one of Oskar's physicians, was well aware of their relationship and a bit jealous of Oskar. Fortunately, he and Ami became closer after Oskar's death in 1974 and had a happy marriage in the years before Ami's death in 1988.[8]

What we know about Ami's relationship with Oskar comes from her modest diary, the comments from Oskar's friends, Dieter Trautwein and Dr. Lotte (Charlotte) Schiffler, and the extensive conversations I had with Chris and Tina Staehr in Stuttgart, Germany, in 2000 and 2003. His chance meeting with Ami Staehr came at a particularly meaningful time for Oskar, who had broken up with Herta Kluge the year before. Though Oskar never said much about it, his friends sensed his pain over the breakup. For years, Herta had accompanied Oskar on his visits to Israel and the United States. Jakob Sternberg blamed the breakup on Herta's daughter. Lotte Schiffler, who seemed infatuated with Oskar even though she was married, also sensed his loneliness and told Oskar that he needed "the sympathy of a woman," one "who is quite free of other baggage, who has no grandchildren on her lap"; in other words, a woman who would "make herself beautiful" for him alone. Ami Staehr, though she had a grandchild, was able to give herself totally to Oskar within the context of her married life in Hildesheim. She became his intimate friend, confidant, and nurse, and the times they spent together, particularly in Israel, were some of the happiest in Oskar's life. Oskar called Ami "a piece of gold" for all she did for him when he was sick in the summer of 1973, and Lottie Schiffler added that Ami was even better than gold for Oskar.[9]

The day after Ami met Oskar on the beach, she sent an elegant, handmade get-well card to his room, No. 74, at the Hotel Narciss. It is difficult to describe the care and love that went into making this card, but it let Oskar know that it was sent by someone who had more than just a passing interest in this "real hero." Later that year, they vacationed together in Dubrovnik, Yugoslavia, and the following spring spent some time together in Israel. Some of the most memorable photographs taken of Oskar during the last years of his life show him with Ami in Israel. They depict a happy, content couple and a surprisingly tanned, healthy-looking Oskar. When they were not together abroad, Oskar would go to Hildesheim for Christmas and other family gatherings. It was no secret, of course, that their relationship was more than platonic. Chris Staehr told me that his father was well aware of this, though there was little he could do about it, considering his own track record with other women. Beyond this, Dr. Staehr considered Oskar his friend and patient and evidently never let Oskar's relationship with Ami affect his professional and personal ties to Schindler.[10]

It is said that pictures are worth a thousand words, though I suspect that those of Oskar and Ami in Israel in 1973 do not reveal the delicate state of Oskar's health. In their 1974 autopsy report on Oskar, Dr. H. Kleinsorg and Dr. Rosemeyer indicated that he was "always healthy until December 1973," when he had a stroke. In reality, he was a very sick man and in a lot of pain well before this date.[11] As early as 1972, Oskar talked about problems with "circulatory collapse" and "severely high blood pressure." In a detailed letter to Leopold "Poldek" Page on October 30, 1972, he said that he had been "seriously ill with a variety of ailments for three months." These problems included a defect of the lower spine that was "similar to arthritis" and was so painful that it kept him from sleeping. In addition, Oskar talked about a "strophantinkur for the heart" and constant "kidney-basin suppuration." He also had nerve pain in the foot and had an "oscillograph" treatment for his legs. He also wrote Page that he had received "radioactive isotopes" for his kidneys as well as a hundred injections. He became quite ill in Israel during a visit with the Staehrs in June 1973, and, though Oskar returned to Germany, Dr. Moshe Bejski told him that he needed "constant medical supervision."[12]

I asked Dr. James C. Osborne, a prominent internist in Greensboro, North Carolina, to look over Schindler's medical files and evaluate them for me. Dr. Osborne told me that it is important to remember that, until recently, European, and particularly German, medical traditions were different in that the Germans used a "whole pharmacopia" of herbal medications that were not used in the United States. The long list of drugs that Oskar took indicated serious problems with high blood pressure, diabetes, and heart failure. But Oskar also had other issues that affected his health. The "circulatory collapse" he referred to in several of his letters meant that he simply passed out, possibly due to congestive heart failure. Dr. Osborne told me that the pain in his lower spine was probably caused by some degenerative disc disease. The "strophantinkur" for the heart was a reference to tincture of stophan, an herbal medication to help with congestive heart failure. The problems with "kidney-basin suppuration" meant simply an infection. Other medical reports indicate that Oskar suffered from frequent kidney infections during the last years of his life. The "nerve pain in the foot," Dr. Osborne explained, was neuropathy, something common in people with diabetes. Neuropathy causes pain and numbness in the feet and is worse at night or when someone is resting. This, of course, would be another reason for Oskar's problems with insomnia. The "oscillograph" he mentioned to Page was a painful procedure that looked for nerve activity in his legs. The "radioactive isotope of the kidneys" was probably another test, this time to gauge the function of his kidneys.[13]

These problems paled compared to the stroke Oskar suffered in December 1973, which left him paralyzed on his right side. However, according to his autopsy report, Oskar did not lose the ability to speak, which Dr. Osborne found surprising because the left side of the brain, which includes the speech center, is affected by a right-sided stroke. This meant that Oskar might have been one of those rare people whose speech center was either missed by the stroke or whose speech center was on the right side of his brain, occasionally found among people who are left-handed, as Oskar was. These problems left Schindler bedridden for months and under the care of Ami Staehr. Ami Staehr's sole entry in her diary, dated December 8, 1973, evidently the date of Oskar's stroke, and January 14, 1974, mentioned that there were discussions about Oskar's weak heart caused by arteriosclerosis (hardening of the arteries).[14]

Until his stroke, Oskar lived a reasonably normal life, though he must have been in constant pain. In 1972, he testified in a preliminary war crimes investigative against a former guard in Płaszów, Laaf, and told the investigating judge in the district court in Bochem that he was the volunteer director of the German Association for the Society of Friends of the Hebrew University in Germany *(Geschäftsführer des Bundesverbandes der Gesellschaften der Freunde der hebräischen Universität Jerusalem in Deutschland).*[15] His involvement with Hebrew University in Jerusalem was very important to Oskar, particularly the development of the Truman Center and the creation of the Oskar Schindler scholarship. His involvement with the German Friends of Hebrew University began in 1968 and continued until the end of his life. Oskar deeply loved Israel, which Lotte Schiffler called the true love of his life, and his work for Hebrew University was simply an extension of the affection he had for that country. Oskar's work for Israel was such that Walter Hesselbach, the chairman of the board of the Bank für Gemeinwirtschaft (BfG) in Frankfurt and the chairman of the German Friends of Hebrew University, paid Oskar a modest salary for his work as honorary chair of the German Friends organization.[16]

Oskar's work with the Friends of Hebrew University in Germany centered mainly around fund-raising efforts. Hebrew University, which is Israel's most prominent institution of higher learning, was opened in 1925 on Mount Scopus in Jerusalem. During the 1948 War of Independence, Mount Scopus was cut off from the Jewish sections of the ancient Israeli capital. A new campus was built in Givat Ram in western Jerusalem. After Israel's victory in the Six Day War in 1967, a new Hebrew University campus was begun on Mount Scopus, which was completed in 1981. In 1972, Oskar became actively involved in trying to help raise money for a scholarship in his name at Hebrew University. In January of that year, he went to New York, where he was honored by Schindler Jews at the headquarters of the American Friends of Hebrew University in Manhattan. The group, led by three prominent Schindler Jews, Isaac Levenstein, Murray Pantirer, and Abraham Zuckerman, announced that they had raised $125,000 for an Oskar Schindler scholarship at Hebrew University. They also wanted to honor Schindler and the Jews he saved with a plaque somewhere on the university's Mount Scopus campus. Oskar was deeply moved by this news, and explained to his gathered friends, first in German, then in Yiddish, and finally in halting English, why he did what he did during the Holocaust: "What is there to say? They are my friends. I would do it again, over and over—for I hate cruelty and intolerance."[17] After his death, a special corner was devoted to Oskar at the Truman Institute for International Peace at Hebrew University. It includes a plaque honoring Schindler as well as a statue and a bust of him. The latter was donated to the Truman Institute in 1999 by Pantirer and Zuckermann. They also donated copies of this beautiful and striking bust to Steven Spielberg and Kean College, and keep the original in their Oskar Schindler office complex in Union, New Jersey.[18]

The first recipient of the Oskar Schindler Scholarship was Yossi Windzberg, a graduate student in Hebrew University's Institute of Communications. The university informed Oskar about the award to Windzberg in the spring of 1974. Eliyahu Honig, the director of Hebrew University's Department of Information and Public Affairs office, told Oskar that Windzberg was a young army veteran who had earlier served as an artillery officer in the Israeli Defense Forces. He noted that students who had recently served in the military, a reference to the recent 1973 Yom Kippur

War, faced special problems. Scholarships such as this one enabled students such as Windzberg, who came from a family with little money, to complete their education.[19] It would have pleased Oskar to know that this scholarship continues to be awarded by Hebrew University to this day. The fact that the first scholarship was given to an army veteran in the aftermath of the outbreak of the Yom Kippur War also had special meaning for Oskar.

The war began on October 6, 1973, which was also Yom Kippur (Day of Atonement), the holiest and most solemn day in the Jewish religious calendar. At 2:00 P.M., Syrian and Egyptian forces began simultaneous attacks along the Golan Heights and the Suez Canal. Soon other Arab countries, as well as a large contingent of men and tanks from Iraq, joined Syria and Egypt, and the war for the survival of Israel raged over the next two and a half weeks.[20] Stunned by the early successes of the Arabs, Prime Minister Golda Meier of Israel went on television four days later and promised that Israel would not let itself be destroyed. Her government, she reassured her audience, had done everything possible to prevent the invasion, which she called "an act of madness."[21] She asked Israeli citizens not to allow themselves the "'luxury' of despair" and added: "I have one prayer in my heart, that this will be the last war."[22]

But Israelis did worry about the fate of their country, as evidenced by a letter that Yad Vashem sent to Oskar Schindler and other Righteous Gentiles throughout the world. Signed by Gideon Hausner, the prosecutor at Adolf Eichmann's trial, a member of Israel's parliament, the Knesset, and later chairman of the World Council of Yad Vashem, and Dr. Chaim Pazner, the deputy chairman of Yad Vashem's executive council, the letter told Schindler and the other Righteous Gentiles that the purpose of the current "criminal attack" was the destruction of Israel and the extermination of its people. They reminded them that the Yom Kippur assault was similar to a tactic used by the Nazis, who liked to begin their "actions" against Jews when they were most unsuspecting and vulnerable. At this tragic moment, the letter went on, Yad Vashem "thankfully remember you, following the natural human feeling, who risked your lives in the horror of the Nazi regime to save persecuted and endangered Jews. The efforts of the Righteous Gentiles encouraged Israelis to fight once again for their survival. We are convinced that just as back then, you are with us today. Raise your voice during this fateful hour for the state of Israel and declare your solidarity with us in any way you can."[23]

Dr. Dieter Trautwein said that Oskar was deeply upset by the Yom Kippur War. Throughout the years, Oskar had gotten into a lot of arguments with people who called him the "servant of the Jews." This did not dissuade Schindler from voicing support for Israel, which occasionally offended people with more pro-Arab sensibilities. After Oskar got the letter from Yad Vashem, he went to Dr. Trautwein's house in a "furious mood." He insisted on repeating his well-known opinions on Israel and the Arabs, which to a great extent were driven by his worries about the lives and well-being of his friends in Israel. And he had every right to be worried. Few Israeli households were untouched by the deaths of more than 2,600 Israelis in the conflict. On November 21, for example, Dr. Moshe Bejski wrote Oskar that he was "almost paralyzed" by the death of his nephew, Haim. The following day, Dr. Bejski wrote Ami Staehr that the situation in Israel was far worse than she could imagine and that he wondered whether the family would ever recover. Golda Meir spoke of those times as ones of national "trauma."[24]

Oskar's special fondness for Israel and his decision to live permanently in Germany confounded his Israeli and German friends. Several Schindler Jews ask me why Oskar chose to live in Germany, particularly as he loved Israel so much and would later be buried there. From their perspective, Oskar had suffered nothing but hardship and pain in Germany. Dieter Trautwein was extremely sensitive about this issue and a bit defensive when it came to the question of Oskar's life and friendships in Germany. He was particularly troubled by the idea among some Schindler Jews, particularly in Israel, that Oskar died poor and alone in Frankfurt. Trautwein, who became the *Propst* (conference minister) in Frankfurt, was a devout friend of Israel and an important figure, along with Dr. Lotte Schiffler, in developing a mature German-Jewish dialogue in West Germany. He thought that this perspective on Schindler's life in Germany was too simplistic. Though Trautwein agreed that Oskar was, to a point, poor and alone in Frankfurt, he pointed out that Schindler had a special relationship with Ami Staehr, who lived in Hildesheim, and Dr. Lotte Schiffler. Unfortunately, Oskar and Dr. Schiffler's relationship was contentious, because, at least from Schindler's perspective, she was trying to control his life. Dr. Schiffler was an extremely kind, ecumenical person who hated any form of racism and helped raise children of different ethnic and racial backgrounds. But she and Oskar had numerous fights and, after his stroke, he banned Lotte from his apartment. Oskar was also befriended by Walther Kampe, a Suffragan Catholic bishop, who offered Oskar his private apartment in Frankfurt after Oskar's stroke. In fact, Oskar had already made arrangements to move into a retirement home, the Haus Leonhard, in Frankfurt after his pacemaker operation in 1974.[25]

On the other hand, Dr. Trautwein agreed that the West German government in Bonn did not do enough for Schindler. He thought this might have been deliberate because the "politics of that era" dictated that "certain issues be suppressed." West German officials, Dr. Trautwein told me, were particularly leery of Schindler because he "brought Auschwitz with him." Yet discussions were underway in West Germany at the time of Oskar's death to upgrade the level of his Federal Cross of Merit in order to increase the amount of his honorary pension given by the president of West Germany. Several years earlier, there had also been efforts to nominate Oskar for the Heinrich Stahl Prize, which was given out annually by the Jewish community of Berlin. There is nothing to indicate whether either of these efforts bore fruit.[26]

One of the things that Dr. Trautwein had difficulty understanding was Oskar's relationship with Frankfurt's Sudeten German community and his friendships in the bars around the train station near his apartment. Dr. Trautwein said that Oskar would occasionally take him "bar hopping" to meet his many local friends. Oskar evidently saw himself as "the agency of the church [Catholic] in the train station area." He once told Dr. Trautwein that he had taken a young couple aside when he discovered that they had a child but were not married: "What, you're not yet married?" he lectured. "Now that you have a child, you can't just stay unmarried. Go and see the city deacon, you have to resolve this now!"[27]

In some ways, these relationships defined Oskar in a very different way than his friendships with prominent churchmen such as Dr. Trautwein and Bishop Kampe, or his ties with Israel and his Schindler Jews. It is doubtful that Oskar would ever have been comfortable living permanently in Israel. Though he was always happy there, it was an artificial existence, dependent on the adoring presence of his Schindler Jews. And there was some tension in Israel over Oskar. The Schindler Committee in Israel tried to do what it could to help Oskar financially and usually covered his expenses when he was there. Some Schindler Jews, though, resented the fund-raising efforts of the Schindler Committee because they said the money would just go for "vodka" for Oskar. Other Schindler Jews were still struggling to make ends meet in Israel and simply did not have the money to donate to the Schindler Committee. Oskar could go through large sums of money in two or three days and had no qualms about calling Dr. Bejski and asking for more.[28]

Oskar's life in Frankfurt was quite different and centered around his modest, smoky apartment (No. 63) on Hauptbahnhof 4. But what Dr.

Trautwein and others in West Germany failed to see was Oskar's more pedestrian side. He enjoyed living next to the central train station with its interesting people and bars. Moreover, Oskar was by heritage and birth a Sudeten German and he never forgot it. His ties and friendships in the Sudeten German exile community in Frankfurt and its *Zwittau Heimatrunde* (Svitavy Home Circle) helped him maintain his links to this past; and his friendships in the pubs around the train station allowed him to "let loose" and simply be Oskar Schindler—a hard-drinking man-of-the-world. Many of Oskar's Israeli and German friends suggested time and again that he consider living all or part of the year in Israel. Dr. Moshe Bejski asked him to move to Israel on several occasions, and Lotte Schiffler suggested that he take a small apartment in Israel and keep a "tent" in Frankfurt.[29] To some extent, Oskar remained in West Germany because of the various stipends he received there. If he had moved to Israel, it is doubtful that he would have continued to receive all of them. Oskar was also a proud man, and though he had no trouble taking money from his friends, he knew that if he moved to Israel he would probably become almost totally dependent on his Schindler Jews, many of whom still struggled to build a comfortable life. But the main reason that Oskar chose to remain in Frankfurt, despite the fact that Jakob Sternberg considered him a "Jewicized Christian," was because he was ethnically, culturally, and socially a German. Simply stated, he felt more comfortable being a German in West Germany than a "Jewicized Christian" in Israel.[30]

The Death of Oskar Schindler: Tribute and Mourning

For the most part, Oskar never fully recovered from his stroke, though Lotte Schiffler told him when she saw him in April 1974 that he seemed "fresh and rested." Yet a month earlier Oskar would not permit her in his apartment to help him with small things such as "clipping the nails and other things." Oskar was still having trouble with the paralysis on the right side of his body, and Lotte suggested that he receive a salt water treatment to help "revive the right side again." She also wondered whether the expensive injections he was receiving were helping his paralysis.[31] Oskar was able to travel and went to Hildesheim for four days for Ami Staehr's birthday in early March. After the stroke, the Staehrs made up a small room for Oskar in their apartment in Hildesheim, which in a way became his second home. He returned for a visit to Hildesheim in late May and stayed with the Staehrs for about ten days.[32]

Oskar returned to Hildesheim on August 8, and, except for a brief trip back to Frankfurt approved by his physician, Dr. Kleinsorg, he would spend the remaining weeks of his life in Hildesheim with the Staehrs. Oskar's health was deteriorating and Ami Staehr called Dieter Trautwein in late August to let him know of Oskar's continuing heart problems. Dr. Trautwein then called Lotte Schiffler, who wrote to Ami Staehr and asked her about the prospect of a heart operation for Oskar. Dr. James Osborne told me that heart surgery was still in its infancy at the time, so he was uncertain what Schiffler meant by this. Instead, the decision was made to give Schindler a pacemaker to help stabilize his heart rhythms.[33]

It is possible to piece together what happened next from the autopsy report prepared two days after Oskar died, a letter that Ami wrote to Dr. Bejski and Itzhak Stern's wife for all Oskar's Israeli friends just before he died on October 9, and one that she sent to Oskar's niece, Traude Ferrari, in December 1974. The autopsy report noted that a week before he was admitted to the hospital (September 24), Schindler was suffering from "swollen feet as well as severe breathing problems, lack of appetite, and sleep." The decision was then made to give him a pacemaker at the St. Bernward Krankenhaus, a Roman Catholic hospital, in Hildesheim. During the operation Oskar slipped into a coma and never regained consciousness. He was placed in the intensive care unit of St. Bernward's. Ami described what happened next in her letter to Dr. Bejski and Mrs. Stern. She wrote it on October 7, and described Oskar's condition after he slipped into the coma. For the most part, she told them, he was "dozing along in constant unconsciousness though he was periodically responsive to those around him. When his name was mentioned, he would open his eyes and sometimes say 'Yes.'" But for the most part, Ami explained, he had no idea where he was or what was happening to him. Because Oskar was in intensive care, Ami was not able to be with him all the time, though she frequently called the hospital to find out how he was doing. And she was always told the same thing: "No change, but Mr. Schindler is still alive." She reassured Bejski and Stern that everything was being done medically and personally to care for him. On the day she wrote the letter, it was decided to put Oskar on "liquids and astronaut food" to help flush his kidneys. Oskar was now nothing more than "skin and bones." She was glad that Dr. Bejski and Mrs. Stern did not have to see Oskar like this. She ended by writing that she felt it was "a greeting from God" that Oskar was oblivious to what was happening to him "since the unconsciousness also spare[d] him the pains, the tortures."[34] Two days later, October 9, 1974, Oskar Schindler passed away. During this period, the pacemaker worked very well. His body, damaged by his diabetes as well as his kidney, heart, and other problems, simply gave out.[35] From Ami Staehr's perspective, his slow death "was more an extinguishing of his spirit, a diminishing of all energies, a break down of all functions." Oskar Schindler was sixty-five years old.[36]

Oskar's death devastated Ami Staehr. She wrote Dr. Bejski a month after his death that, for her, "time now stood still":

> I have been frozen in grief over my dead Oskar. I am still waiting for him. I would sit for hours before Oskar's bed, holding a conversation with him, yes, conversation. I hear him, know what he wants to say to me, would say—I hear him. Without Oskar I am nothing, don't exist anymore. I draw some comfort knowing what I meant to Oskar, that is, after all, worth much, much more, nothing is equal to it. My life is empty, painfully empty without Oskar. No one could tear my Oskar out of my heart; he will live on in me until I am again with him."[37]

Ami was particularly troubled when, despite specific instructions from Oskar, Dr. Schiffler entered his apartment after he died and took keepsakes that meant so much to Ami. Somehow, Dr. Schiffler had been given Oskar's power of attorney and had taken away many of his private belongings. Ami later wrote Oskar's niece, Traude, that she considered Schiffler's efforts a *"Blitzaktion"* (lightning operation). Dr. Schiffler gave many of Oskar's private possessions away and, at least according to Ami, even paid people to take them. Schiffler completely cleaned out his apartment. Fortunately, before this happened, Ami, who had a key to Oskar's apartment, had the foresight to go with her son, Chris, to gather up as many of Oskar's private papers as she could find. But, according to Ami's letter to Traude, for some reason the papers she took out that day wound up in the hands of Stefan Pemper, the brother of Mietek Pemper. Her efforts to get him to return them to her, at least by the end of December 1974, were unsuccessful. Fortunately, some time earlier, Oskar had shipped a very heavy, hard-sided Samsonite suitcase filled with some of his most important personal papers to the Staehrs in Hildesheim. This was the storied suitcase, which Chris and Tina Staehr later found after Heinrich Staehr's death in 1997, that became the basis of the world-wide stories about the discovery of the original "Schindler's List."[38]

Ami and Chris knew Oskar's apartment well, and he kept papers scattered everywhere. However, one of his favorite places to store his papers was a sideboard in the kitchen. Ami and Chris had a soft-sided suitcase with them and filled it with about a third of the papers in Oskar's apartment at the time. When they came back the next day, they discovered that Dr. Schiffler had taken the rest. Within three days, the apartment was completely empty. Chris and Tina Staehr both think that Ami and Dr. Schiffler were looking for their love letters to Oskar. Ami had hidden the letters that Oskar had sent to her in her apartment in Hildesheim. After Heinrich Staehr's death in 1997, the apartment was sold and the people who bought it found the papers and threw them away. Chris Staehr later asked them whether they knew how important the letters were historically. They said they had no idea they were from Oskar Schindler's estate.[39]

What troubled Ami most about Dr. Schiffler's *"Blitzaktion"* was the fact that Oskar told her where to find handwritten instructions in the apartment detailing exactly what he wanted done should he not survive the pacemaker operation. Oskar did not expect to die during surgery and talked with Ami about future plans. But he also had enough foresight to realize that the operation might not go as planned. It was possible, Ami later wrote, that Oskar, who was "already quite forgetful and so weakened by illness," might have forgotten where he had put the instructions. Ami looked where Oskar told her he had put them but could not find them. It was possible, of course, that Dr. Schiffler had taken Oskar's statement of his last wishes along with everything else she took out of the apartment. Ami later wrote Traude that being prevented from carrying out this wish left her "no rest."[40]

As a result, Ami had to make plans for Oskar without knowing his exact wishes. She worked night and day over the next three weeks making arrangements for his memorial service and Requiem Mass in Frankfurt and burial in Israel. But were these Oskar's wishes? Dr. Moshe Bejski told me that Oskar never said anything to him about wanting to be buried in Israel. On the other hand, Dr. Dieter Trautwein told me that Oskar said he wanted to be cremated and have his ashes scattered around his tree along the Avenue of the Righteous at Yad Vashem. Instead, he was buried at the Latin Cemetery on Mount Zion just outside Jerusalem's Old City.[41]

Ami called Dr. Bejski in Tel Aviv on October 9 and told him that Oskar wanted to buried in Israel. Dr. Bejski set to work with several other members of the Schindler Committee planning for Oskar's funeral; at the same time, Ami and Dr. Trautwein made plans for his memorial service in the Trauerhalle of the Hauptfriedhof in Frankfurt on October 16 and his Requiem Mass several days later. Five dignitaries spoke at Oskar's October 16 memorial service, which began at 2:00 P.M.—Dr. Moshe Bejski, Dr. Dieter Trautwein, Stadtdekan Msgr. Walter Adloch, Dr. Walter Hesselbach, and Dr. Heinrich Staehr. Msgr. Adloch, the rector for Frankfurt's St. Bartholomew's Cathedral, began the service and provided the religious intercessions. Dr. Trautwein preached the memorial sermon, and Shlomo Raiß, the Senior Cantor for Frankfurt's Jewish community, sang Psalm 16 in Hebrew. Songs written to honor Schindler's life and works were also performed during the service. Richard Hackenberg, a leader in Frankfurt's Sudeten German community and a friend of Oskar's from the Svitavy region, also spoke at the memorial service.[42]

Dr. Trautwein began his sermon with two biblical verses from the Torah that he thought would be most fitting on Oskar's tomb, "Love your Lord" and "Love your neighbor as yourself." Or, he added, you could use Martin Buber's words, "Love your neighbor, because he is like you." He told those in the congregation that they knew whom to thank for this commandment—Israel and its God. When Oskar Schindler arrived in Kraków, Trautwein continued, such commandments were "despised and ridiculed . . . everything stopped: love, humanity, the simplest decency was gone." But not for two people, Oskar and Emilie Schindler. Their accomplishments during the war could not be expressed in words. Today, there were 3,000 to 4,000 people, the Schindler Jews and their descendants, who "entered the arch built by Schindler and thereby entered a new world." Dr. Trautwein recalled the old Talmudic saying: "Whoever has saved one single life has saved the entire world! The Schindlers and their helpers have saved more than a thousand worlds." [43]

Dr. Trautwein reminded everyone that Oskar never took sole credit for what he did during the war. He could not, Dr. Trautwein explained, have saved as many lives as he did without the help of "many supporters, even supporters on the side of the enemy." But the question was, why? It began with his friendships with Jews when he was a young man in Svitavy. And when he saw what was happening to Jewish children in Kraków, Buber's commandment of life, "Love your neighbor, because he is like you," came to life. Later, a Schindler Jew addressed Oskar: "That wasn't you, someone else saved you through the thousand worlds." Oskar's achievements during the war, what Dr. Trautwein called Schindler's "high hour of confirmation, had been so unique and extraordinary," that Oskar, this "generous, goal-oriented person," could never top his wartime deeds. "And that's why," Dr. Trautwein thought, "a lot of things that came after this depressed him, whether they were his own fault or the misfortune of the moment."[44]

Despite these problems, Oskar remained "an agent of peace" in this city [Frankfurt] through his bridge building between Germany and Israel. "Who among our people, which has shown so little mourning and gratitude, knows what he has done to improve the German reputation throughout the world?" But we should not be sad, he told the congregation. "We need to be very thankful," he went on, "thankful that God has given him a palette of generous engagement for other people!" Schindler had many friends, including his Schindler Jews, his acquaintances among the German Friends of Hebrew University and, most important, Ami and Heinrich Staehr. They were with him to the end, "when his suffering became worse and worse, when surgery became unavoidable, when only imploring and praying with him and for him were possible."[45]

Dr. Trautwein ended his sermon by reminding the congregation of the words, "Nothing is bad except if we lose our love." Even in mourning, the "love that God let shine through this Oskar Schindler ha[d] not perished." Such love can flourish through those present while Oskar's tree at Yad Vashem would remind everyone of love. "Our hope is that we will be together with this beloved deceased in the 'bundle of life,' and that the enigmas and sorrows of his life, and the bitter questions of the many, too many, who were not saved, will find answers." Most important, he told everyone, "the commandment, which has become the offer of life for Jews and Christians and all people, should not and must not be ridiculed and despised; love your Lord—and love your neighbor as yourself!"[46]

Richard Hackenburg, Oskar's Sudeten German friend, also spoke and talked about Oskar's deep love for his home town, Svitavy, and his Sudeten German homeland. He found a piece of the Sudetenland in Frankfurt, Hackenburg noted, among his Sudeten German friends there. Hackenburg concluded his brief remarks: "We thank God he was one of us." Hackenberg also spoke at a Requiem Mass for Oskar three days later at Frankfurt's St. Bartholomew's Cathedral. A number of prominent German officials spoke at the Mass as well as Richard Rechen, who drove the truck that accompanied Oskar and Emilie during their escape from Brünnlitz at the end of the war. Rechen noted that the Chief Rabbi of Tel Aviv had recently said that "Oskar Schindler was an ambassador of the Almighty." Oskar's greatness, Rechen thought, rested on the fact that even during the time of greatest Nazi victories, he [Schindler], as a young man, "simply did not participate." He saw Schindler as a great humanist:

> Alone, and often at the risk of his life, he swam against the superior forces of the torrent of hatred and cruelty. He not only saved our bodies but our souls as well. If we did not lose our faith in humanity, it was only thanks to his assistance. He showed that there were and are Christians who in the spirit of Good Samaritans will pour oil and wine into the wounds of those who have fallen among thugs.

> Oskar, you were a Good Samaritan. It was your wish that your place of last repose should be in the sacred city of Jerusalem. We promise to do our utmost to honor that wish.[47]

And Rechen, Dr. Bejski, Jakob Sternberg, and other members of the Schindler Committee in Israel were able to fulfill that promise. On October 24, his body was flown to Israel where, four days later, he was buried in the Latin cemetery in Jerusalem. The State of Hesse, BfG, and the Lutheran and Catholic churches of West Germany paid the costs of his transport to Israel.[48]

Ami Staehr was in charge of the preparations for shipping Oskar's body to Israel. This involved extensive paperwork and phone calls, overseeing the embalming of the body, and shipment preparation that required three caskets. Working with Dr. Bejski and other members of the Schindler Committee in Israel, Ami also arranged for Oskar's burial in a Christian cemetery in Jerusalem. Ami later admitted that she was so busy making these arrangements that she did not have time to grieve for Oskar. She was so exhausted from making his funeral arrangements that, though she went to the airport to see his body off, she did not accompany the body to Israel, nor did she attend the funeral there. She would later visit his grave with Dr. Trautwein and Dr. Bejski in the summer of 1975.[49]

A Requiem Mass was held for Oskar at St. Saviour's Roman Catholic Church in Jerusalem's Old City near the New Gate on October 28, 1974. The church was filled with four hundred Schindler Jews and their families as well as prominent figures such as Jesco von Puttkamer, West Germany's ambassador to Israel, Yitzhak Arad, the head of Yad Vashem, and representatives from Hebrew University. Dr. Bejski said that he was surprised to see a group of Orthodox Schindler Jews at the service in the church.

One, Mordechai Broder, told Bejski that for Oskar, he "would even go to Hell."[50] Another devout Schindler Jew told a reporter: "For him it is not only permissible to carry his Christian coffin on our shoulders, but it is a *mitzvah* [religious commandment or duty] to accompany him on his last journey even inside the church. He was a saint in his lifetime."[51]

When the Requiem Mass was over, six Schindler Jews gently placed Oskar's coffin on their shoulders and, led by three Franciscan monks, began the long procession through Jerusalem's Old City to the Franciscan Latin Cemetery on Mount Zion just outside the Zion Gate. A group of Schindler Jews walked in front of the coffin carrying wreaths in honor of Oskar. Yad Vashem asked Dr. Moshe Bejski to deliver the graveside eulogy. Each Righteous Gentile, Dr. Bejski noted, deserved "the full measure of recognition and gratitude" for their rescue actions. But Oskar Schindler's deeds, he added, were "without precedent" as evidenced by the three hundred women he saved in Auschwitz. The fact that he "snatched" 1,200 Jews "from the jaws of death, place[d] Schindler in the first rank of Righteous Among the Nations."[52]

But, Dr. Bejski went on, Oskar was more than a rescuer: "He became a legend in his lifetime among the survivors because of his humanity, his personal care of his protégés, his willingness to listen and find solutions to countless personal, everyday problems." There were many examples of this during the war though the one that stood out most for Dr. Bejski was Oskar's efforts to save the Jews on the Golleschau transport in early 1945: "Oskar Schindler revealed himself as a humanist, a person with a sensitive heart, who was deeply moved by the suffering of his fellow men, a person who spared no effort to ease our suffering and protect us to the limit of what was possible under the circumstances. No matter how extensive is the chronicle of his acts of kindness, it still cannot relay the full measure of his benevolence."[53]

After the war, Dr. Bejski continued, Oskar "remained bound with the strongest ties to his survivors and the State of Israel, in which he rebuilt part of his life." He "continued to experience the trauma of the Jewish people" and worried a great deal about the threats against Israel. He was extremely devoted to Hebrew University and to a "rapprochement between Jews and Christians." This was a Christian burial service, Dr. Bejski acknowledged, though he told everyone that he would like to add one Jewish element to it. After the mourner's *Kaddish* (Sanctification) is said at the grave site of a Jewish funeral, it is normal to ask forgiveness of the deceased for "any harm done to him by persons close to him." Dr. Bejski continued:

I consider it my duty to ask forgiveness from Oskar Schindler on behalf of all the survivors in Israel and in the Diaspora, not only for the injuries we had caused him, whether intentionally or unintentionally, but also for not having done enough for him as we were duty bound to do for the rescuer and benefactor that he was. We could have done much more.

Blessed be his memory.[54]

In her letter to Traude two months after Oskar's death, Ami wrote that "if only in his lifetime so many had thought of him, helped him, supported him, not left him alone so much." She went on: "Sometimes I think that much was done from a bad conscience." As a result, she added, "Oskar was very disappointed in everyone and refused everything from the past."[55]

Today Oskar's grave is among the most frequently visited in Jerusalem. The inscription on his tomb, in German and in Hebrew, simply reads: "Oskar Schindler, 28.4.1908–9.10.1974. 'Der unvergessliche Lebensretter 1200 verfolgter Juden. [The Unforgettable Savior of 1200 Persecuted Jews].'" It somehow seems fitting that the man who saved the lives of almost 1,100 Jews during the Holocaust and spent much of his time after the war trying to build bridges between Israel and West Germany should be buried in this beautiful, quiet setting among Arab Christians overlooking the rolling hills beyond Mount Zion.[56]

Life in Death

It is not certain when Emilie learned of Oskar's death. However, in early 1976, she gave Dr. Lotte Schiffler her power of attorney to settle Oskar's will and to enter into negotiations with the *Lastenausgleich* authorities over any balance owed Oskar after his death. On June 20, 1976, the main *Lastenausgleich* office sent Emilie a check for DM 18,541.88 ($7,856.73), the final balance on Oskar's account.[57] In the meantime, Oskar's friends in West Germany became involved in the production of a forty-five-minute television documentary film on Oskar's life, *Die Juden nennen Ihn, 'Vater Courage'* (The Jews Call Him 'Father Courage'). Produced by Reinhard Albrecht, *Vater Courage* was the first detailed television documentary on Oskar's life. It first aired on November 28, 1975, on Südwestfunk 3, and copies were sent to Israeli television, which helped produce it, the BBC, and NBC. The program centered around a series of interviews that Hessische Rundfunk did with Oskar in 1965 in Frankfurt in the midst of the final trials of twenty Germans who had served in Auschwitz as well as interviews with Emilie Schindler, Walter Pollack, Mietek Pemper, Dr. Dieter Trautwein, Dr. Lotte Schiffler, and Ami Staehr. Albrecht also spent a week in Israel interviewing Schindler Jews such as Dr. Moshe Bejski, who, as always, insisted upon "seriousness, tact, and responsibility," Jakob Sternberg, and others. Ami Staehr and Lotte Schiffler served as the documentary's historical consultants and Ami provided Albrecht with photographs of Oskar in Israel and some of his private papers. Albrecht also used Oskar's own account of his wartime activities from Kurt Grossmann's *Die unbesungenen Helden: Menschen in Deutschlands dunklen Tagen* (1957).[58]

Lotte Schiffler, who was one of the driving forces behind the documentary, wrote Ami Staehr in March 1975 that the Schindler project was not a "blauer Dunst [blue mist]" production "like all of the USA promises," but one fully approved by Südwestfunk. Schiffler hoped that the film would create new sympathy for Israel and that "Schindler's life should be a last call to activate everything 'for his land.'" She also hoped to obtain an honorarium for their work on the documentary to help pay for a tombstone at Oskar's grave in Jerusalem.[59]

From Albrecht's perspective, the program was aimed at German youth, and, using the famed "list" with its bare listing of names, concentration camp numbers, nationality, race, and occupation, was the documentary's "red thread" by which Albrecht tried to bring each of the Jewish survivors and their testimonies to life. Albrecht saw Oskar Schindler as an "anti-hero," a "Father Courage," a "Schweijk"-like figure, a daredevil, and a humanitarian who was willing to take responsibility for the fate of his Jewish workers and do whatever was necessary, even if it meant sacrificing his own life, to save them. Albrecht thought that Oskar Schindler was a man "who was touched by God's finger, human like you and I, with all the human weaknesses and strengths of a person of stature."[60]

The program began with a brief overview of the Holocaust and the statement that only 330,000 of the 2 million Polish Jews in the General Government survived, 60,000 of them in labor and death camps. Out of this latter number, 1,200 were saved by one man, "a German, a man, a mixture of Schweijk and the devil's general, an anti-hero, who succeeded in outplaying the Nazis. His name: Oskar Schindler."[61] According to Schiffler, Oskar went with Admiral Canaris to Dachau in 1939, a trip which "opened his eyes so much that he decided to find ways to prevent the same fate from happening to his Jewish friends." Though there is no evidence to document this experience or that Oskar ever met Canaris, it had entered the Schindler mythology by this time. The rest of the program was based on statements from Oskar's friends and numerous Schindler Jews such as Dr. Moshe Bejski and Dr. Aleksander Bieberstein as well as lesser known *Schindlerjuden* such as Mordechai Bruder (Markus Broder), Dolek Gruenhaut (Adolf Grünhalt) and Moritz Reichgoot (Mortiz Reichgod), who survived the Golleschau transport.[62]

At some point in his interview with Hessiche Rundfunk, Oskar was asked about his relationship with Emilie and their work together during the war. He said that they did have problems which were exacerbated by their childless marriage. Regardless, Oskar stated, Emilie "always proved to be a loyal and good comrade. She played a particularly important role in Brünnlitz and oversaw feeding the workers in the camp." This was, Oskar explained, "a gigantic task," since she was also responsible for the camp's hospital. He told Hessiche Rundfunk that it was important to understand that "whenever necessary, [Emilie] fearlessly protected and stood up for the endangered Jewish workers." The German television crew also interviewed Emilie, who, it noted, lived in poverty in a suburb of Buenos Aires in a house built for her by "Schindler Jews." It added that the West German government never granted her a pension. Emilie was asked to explain Oskar's failures after the war. They were caused, she noted, by the fact that "Herr Schindler was thrown out of the ordered paths," and that all the changes after the war "really affected him . . . and he didn't get back on track. He didn't have the people, the personnel, he didn't understand it [new postwar life], that was missing, that's why it [his recovery] failed."[63]

The last part of the documentary explored Oskar's last years in Germany. This was a time, Lotte Schiffler stated, when Oskar was "very broken, quiet, sick." Jehuda Kahrwisch, the press coordinator for Hebrew University, said that once Oskar's Israeli friends realized how sick he was, they decided to speed up contributions to an Oskar Schindler scholarship so that it could be awarded before Oskar died. Oskar, Kahrwisch told Albrecht, was not interested in having buildings or monuments named after him. Instead, he wanted his name to be used "to help actually living young people." The program ended with a statement by Mordechai Bruder, one of the pallbearers at Oskar's funeral in Jerusalem. Broder told Albrecht that someone later asked him how he could carry a coffin with a cross on it. He responded that it was not the coffin of an ordinary man: "It is the coffin of a man who saved me and many other Jews; there are not many people like him, and this is my obligation. I was happy to do this, and I believe that it is a command from God that it be done."[64]

The interviews done for *Vater Courage* were important in keeping Oskar Schindler's story alive in the minds of the people who so cared for him. This was particularly true in the case of the Schindler Jews in Israel, who would become the principal source of information for the next major look at Oskar's life—Thomas Keneally's novelized biography, *Schindler's Ark*. The person initially behind Keneally's work was the irrepressible Leopold Page, who continued to pester anyone who came into his leather goods shop about Oskar's story. In 1980, the Australian novelist was in Italy to attend a film festival. While there, his publisher called him to ask whether he would be interested in going to the United States for a book tour for his recently published novel, *Confederates* (1979).[65]

One day as he was strolling in downtown Beverly Hills, Keneally stopped in front of a luggage store. It was 105 degrees outside, and the owner asked Keneally to come in and get out of the heat. After looking around, Keneally decided to buy a new briefcase. While he was waiting for the processing of his credit card, Page asked Keneally what he did for a living. Keneally told him, "I am a writer." Page responded excitedly, "If you are a writer, I have a story for you." He then told the Australian novelist about Oskar Schindler and took him to the back of the store to show him the documents he had on Schindler.[66] Keneally, though fascinated by Page's story and documents, told the Schindler Jew that he was not the person to write the story because he was only three when the war broke out and, as a Catholic, knew little about the Holocaust and the fate of the Jews. Page said those were the very reasons Keneally should write the book. Page, who became Keneally's consultant on the novel, took him on a detailed research trip to Europe and Israel very similar to the one he had taken with Martin Gosch and Howard Koch in 1964. Ultimately, Keneally, who had access to the script for *To the Last Hour*, would interview fifty Schindler Jews for his book. Their testimony became the basis of his historical novel, which was first published as *Schindler's Ark* in Great Britain in 1982. When it came out in the United States, it was re-titled *Schindler's List*. In 1982, *Schindler's Ark* won Great Britain's most prestigious literary award, the Booker Prize for Fiction (today the Mann Booker Prize for Fiction). Once Page convinced Keneally to write his book on Schindler, he sold the film rights to Irving Glovin, who in turn sold them to Sid Sheinberg, the head of Universal Studios, who was interested in having one of his younger, most brilliant directors, Steven Spielberg, make

a film based on Keneally's novel. It would be a decade, though, before
Spielberg was ready to make his film about Oskar Schindler.[67]

Keneally's novel, though, did more than just spur interest in a film account of Oskar Schindler's life. Its publication in Germany *(Schindlers
Liste)* in 1983 prompted further efforts by Oskar's friends to memorialize
his wartime heroics. On October 14, 1984, the Ackermann Gemeinde
Hessen (Ackermann Congregation of Hesse), a community of Sudeten
German Catholics in the state of Hesse, organized a large memorial service for Oskar on the tenth anniversary of his death in Frankfurt celebrating his life and his saving of almost 1,100 Jews during the Holocaust.
The speakers at the service represented a broad range of important German religious and political leaders as well as letters of support from
prominent Jews such as Jerusalem's mayor, Teddy Kollek and Dr. Moshe
Bejski, who was now a member of Israel's Supreme Court. The Ackermann Congregation published a full account of the memorial service in
1985, which included excerpts from press reports about the service, reviews and portions of Keneally's novel, and selections from an article in a
Polish journal on Schindler, "Eine Krakauer Stimme zu Oskar Schindler"
(A Kraków Voice on Oskar Schindler) by Maciej Kozlowski. [68]

Suffragan Bishop Walther Kampe, a close friend of Schindler's, wondered how God could "just silently watch" the mass murder of the Jews
during the Holocaust. Edward Knechtel, the chairman of the Ackermann
Congregation, while noting the presence of many distinguished guests and
letters of support from others, said that if it had not been for Thomas Keneally's novel, Oskar would hardly have been noticed in Germany. It was
important to learn from Schindler's example, a proud son of Moravia, to
insure that brutal expulsions, whether it be "in Moravia, Uganda, or Bi-
afra," did not happen again. The Ackermann Community felt it was particularly important to remember Schindler because it thought it was "an
essential part of its agenda to fight for humanity and the right to live and
for practical Christian charity." If Schindler provided the world with an
example, it was "that the human being remains the measure of things, but
also, as a continuous model, to remember the words of Tobias: 'Compassion covers sin.'"[69]

Dr. Dieter Trautwein expressed sympathy for the fate of the expelled
Sudeten Germans and thanked the congregation for permitting one of
them to "become one of us." Dr. Trautwein then talked about his seven-
year relationship with Schindler and his correspondence with Thomas Keneally. Though he was generally pleased by Keneally's novel, he was disap-

pointed that there was so little in it about Oskar's Frankfurt years. He was particularly troubled that Keneally seemed to know nothing about Schindler's close friendship with Ami and Heinrich Staehr, who were in the audience and had done so much for Oskar during the last years of his life. Regardless, Trautwein went on, Keneally's novel finally brought to life the story of a light [Schindler] that "professes that our world still has hope and mercy." He then mentioned the struggles that Steven Spielberg was having with producing a movie about Oskar Schindler. Any film about Schindler, Dr. Trautwein thought, had to express what he [Dr. Trautwein] stated in the last verse of a song that he had written for Oskar in 1968:

A tree grows in Israel
telling what courage can achieve.
A tree grows in Yad Vashem
deeply ashamed of indolence.
A tree grows in Israel
asking, who is helping today.[70]

Michael Friedman, a member of the board of the Jewish Congregation in Frankfurt and the son of Schindler Jews, described Oskar as an "opalescent personality, an epicurean" but "mainly a human being [a Mensch]," a man "who took the Ten Commandments seriously," a man "who fulfilled the demand 'Love thy neighbor as you love yourself.'" Dr. Lotte Schiffler continued with this theme by talking about Schindler's respect for Judaism and Jews. She described Oskar's childhood friendships with Jews and his determination not to allow any of his Jewish school friends to be bullied by others. Oskar agreed with the idea that "we had to understand Judaism as God's first love" and supported ongoing efforts to "renew the friendship between Jews and Christians." Richard Hackenburg, a friend of Oskar's and a prominent Sudeten German leader, ended the service by praising Oskar's "courage and humanitarian undertakings." He "should remain our continuous admonition for active solidarity with persecuted and suppressed people all over the world."[71]

But Thomas Keneally's novel and the 1984 memorial service in Frankfurt also prompted renewed interest on the part of Emilie, her friends, and family about Oskar and his story. In early 1983, Mila Pfefferberg-Page wrote Emilie to see how she was doing. Mila mentioned that though she had written Emilie a few years earlier she had never received a response. She told Emilie that the Schindler Jews in their mutual circle of friends thought of her "often and with love." She then went on to tell Emilie about Thomas Keneally's new book, which was mostly about her, about Oskar, and about Płaszów and Brünnlitz.[72] In the meantime, Bernard Scheuer, a close friend of Emilie's and the husband of Oskar's wartime mistress, Marta (Eva Kisch Scheuer), decided to look into the question of Emilie's legal rights via-à-vis Keneally's novel and the film rights to the Schindler story. Scheuer wrote Irving Glovin about this, who told Scheuer that he and Poldek Pfefferberg (Leopold Page) had purchased "all of the rights from M.G.M. and commissioned Mr. Keneally to write the book." Glovin added that he had sold these rights to Universal Pictures. Glovin explained that once Oskar sold his film rights to MGM, he "no longer had a claim." Glovin also sent Scheuer an excerpt from the original 1964 contract underscoring these points. Scheuer wrote Emilie to explain the terms of the excerpt of the contract but admitted that this was a matter for an attorney. Consequently, he hired a lawyer for $1,000 to look into the book and film rights for Emilie. He added that he presumed Glovin would want to settle the matter out of court to avoid "a legal scandal."[73]

Scheuer continued to pester Glovin and Page about this matter, though he had no legal basis to challenge their claim to ownership of the Schindler story.[74] Erika Rosenberg, Emilie Schindler's legal heir, claimed in 2002 that she had received a letter from Glovin dated July 13, 1984, promising Emilie 5 percent of the net from any film on Oskar Schindler.[75] The original 1964 contract, which was signed by Schindler, Page, and Martin A. Gosch, stated that if the film was never made, ownership would revert back to Schindler and Page. Emilie signed away her rights to her husband's story in return for the $5,000 advance she received in 1965. When Oskar died in 1974, Leopold Page became the sole proprietor of the Oskar Schindler story. Consequently, he had full legal rights to commission Thomas Keneally's novel and to sell these rights to Irving Glovin. The ownership issue is very important, not only because of the success of Keneally's novel and Spielberg's film, but also later charges by Emilie and lawsuits by her heir, Erika Rosenberg, that claim that Keneally, Steven Spielberg, and even Universal Pictures owed Emilie and/or her estate considerable profits from the book and motion picture. There is nothing in Oskar Schindler's extensive documentary collection scattered in archival and private collections in Israel, Germany, and the United States to support this. Moreover, it must be remembered that Irving Glovin was a top-notch, well-respected Hollywood attorney who knew his way around the film business. He had been deeply involved in the initial legal stages of the contracts with Oskar Schindler and was knowledgeable on who owned the rights to the Schindler story.

But this question continued to crop up. In 1985, Traude Ferrari, Oskar's niece, called and wrote Ami Staehr about certain letters and other documents relating to this matter in her uncle's papers in Hildesheim. Traude was particularly interested in anything between Oskar, Leopold "Poldi" Pfefferberg [Page], and Martin Gosch. Ami sent Traude two letters as well as Oskar's empty check register, but added in a letter on May 30, 1985, that "nothing remain[ed]." She explained that her husband, Heinrich, told Ami that the Polish letters in the suitcase, which he could not read, would probably not interest anyone. The letters, of course, were from Leopold Page, who wrote to Oskar almost exclusively in Polish. Ami added that she knew nothing of the "Martin" in one of the letters and expressed worry that the letters she sent Traude might fall into the wrong hands.[76]

Traude responded to Ami's letter a month later and explained why this matter was so important to her. She was looking for correspondence between her uncle and "Poldi Pfefferberg and otherwise with 'America' which could give information about possible monetary gifts." Traude explained that the letters and other documents that Ami had earlier sent her were of no value. She was evidently looking for evidence of hidden funds in the United States, not for herself, but for Emilie. Her aunt, she noted, had "worked hard for thirty years to pay off the debts left by [her] uncle of a million [pesos] so as not to defile the name of 'Schindler.'" In fact, Traude explained, though her uncle had always claimed that Emilie did not want to go with him to Germany, the truth was that she could not leave Argentina because of their debts. All Traude now wanted to do was "help a woman who sacrificed thirty years of her life" for Schindler's debt and to make her "last remaining years as comfortable as possible." She appealed to Ami to help her find "a few useful letters in the suitcase full of documents" in her attic to help her with Emilie's cause. Traude assured Ami that these documents would not fall into the "wrong hands" and reminded her that she "loved [Oskar] above everything, like a daughter." She ended by expressing bitterness that Ami had failed to inform her of Oskar's death in 1974.[77]

Ami did not send Traude any more documents from her uncle's suitcase and Traude remains bitter about it to this day. In an interview with *Der Spiegel*'s Jürgen Dahlkamp in 1999, Traude was harsh in her criticism of Ami Staehr. She complained that she learned of her uncle's death from a newspaper and that all Ami sent her afterwards were five photographs and an un-mailed postcard written by Oskar addressed to "Dear Traude." Oskar's niece also told Dahlkamp that she was shocked to learn that there had been a suitcase full of his documents in his Frankfurt apartment, and that she felt "deceived" by the whole matter. When she asked Ami for some of the letters from the suitcase in 1985, she claimed that Ami "curtly refused" to send her anything.[78] The reality of the situation, though, is quite different. What Traude did not realize was how difficult it was for Ami, both emotionally and physically, to dig around in the mass of papers in the suitcase in the attic. From what Chris and Tina Staehr told me, once the suitcase and the papers from the suitcase had been stored in a large wooden crate in the attic, they were left mostly untouched because Ami did not have the physical or emotional strength to go through them and that to do so would possibly put a strain on a marriage that had been reborn and was in good health. Ami had not been in good health for some time and would pass away in 1988. It is hard to imagine that the kind-hearted, gentle Ami Staehr could be "curt" with anyone. Ami seemed to know little about Oskar's business dealings with Leopold Page and Martin Gosch and could not be expected to dig through thousands of pages of letters and other files to try to find the few vague documents that Traude wished to locate. She did mention the Polish letters from Page to Oskar, though Traude never responded to this point. After Ami died in 1988, Heinrich Staehr told his family not to go through the suitcase and other Schindler documents until after his death. His family respected his wishes.[79]

Steven Spielberg, Schindler's List, and Emilie

Questions about the contents and ownership of the collection of Oskar Schindler papers in the attic of the Staehr apartment in Hildesheim would not come up again until the late 1990s, when they were rediscovered by Chris and Tina Staehr after the death of Dr. Heinrich Staehr in 1997. By this time, Steven Spielberg's blockbuster film, Schindler's List, had made Oskar Schindler's name a household word throughout much of the world. But the film and its success, financial and otherwise, brought increasing criticism from Emilie Schindler, who felt not only left out of the story of her husband's incredible exploits during the Holocaust but also from the film's financial success. Emilie and her legal partner and heir, Erika Rosenberg, traveled widely criticizing Spielberg and his film. They also filed several law suits in Germany to gain control of the Schindler collection found in Hildesheim two years earlier and to seek damages from the newspaper that published a series of articles on the collection's contents.

The story of Steven Spielberg's decision ultimately to make *Schindler's List* has been amply told elsewhere. Initially, Spielberg tried to turn the project over to other directors such as Billy Wilder, Roman Polanski, Sidney Pollack, and Martin Scorcese. Despite Spielberg's entreaties, Polanski, who as a child lived in the Kraków ghetto and whose mother was murdered at Auschwitz, felt the story was too close to home. Pestered by Leopold Page, who called him every week from 1983 onwards about the film, Spielberg had various scripts drafted by Thomas Keneally and Kurt Luedtke, who wrote the script for *Out of Africa*. None of these scripts satisfied Spielberg, so he approached Martin Scorcese in 1988 with an offer to produce *Schindler's List* if Scorcese would direct it. Scorcese asked Steven Zaillian to prepare a new script. However, after he saw Zaillian's script, Spielberg had a change of heart. He convinced Scorcese, who thought only a Jewish director could adequately film the story of Oskar Schindler, to trade him *Schindler's List* for another film on Spielberg's production list, *Cape Fear*.[80]

Spielberg's decision finally to make a film of Keneally's book was based on emotional growth and a need to come to grips with his own Jewishness after the birth of his first child. The results astounded everyone, including Spielberg, who was uncertain that the three-and-a-half hour film would break even financially. And, he wondered, how receptive was the world to a film as graphic as this one on the Holocaust? *Schindler's List,* which opened in December 1993, received eleven Academy Award nominations and won seven for Best Film, Best Director [Steven Spielberg], Art Direction, Editing, Original Score, Cinematography, and Screenplay. During the next ten years, *Schindler's List* grossed $321 million worldwide. Spielberg made $65 million on the film.[81]

To Spielberg's credit, he donated his profits to the Righteous Person Foundation, "which was set up to encourage the flourishing of Jewish Life in the United States," and the Survivors of the Shoah Visual History Foundation, which was to create an archive made up of the testimony of 50,000 Holocaust survivors throughout the world. In early 2004, the Shoah Foundation had recorded the testimony of 52,000 Holocaust survivors. When the project is completed, these testimonies will be placed in prominent archives and museums throughout the world for public use. The Shoah Foundation is also involved in other educational projects for young people on the Holocaust and genocide.[82]

But Spielberg's post-*Schindler's List* humanitarian efforts meant little to Emilie Schindler, who achieved newfound fame as a result of the film. On June 24, 1993, she, along with Oskar, was declared a Righteous Among the Nations by Yad Vashem. She received the Righteous Gentile medal in both names in a special ceremony in Buenos Aires, and the sign in front of Oskar's carob tree along the Avenue of the Righteous was changed to read "Oskar and Emilie Schindler." Such recognition, though, only fueled Emilie's criticism of her husband. Her first broadside came in a lengthy interview for the British tabloid, the *Daily Mail* (London) at the end of 1993, which was quickly republished in *Ma'ariv*, one of Israel's most important daily newspapers. Emilie began the interview by discussing her disastrous marriage to Oskar, which she claimed began with his arrest on the day of her wedding because of trumped-up charges by a former lover. She spent her wedding night alone and considered her husband's actions "beyond forgiveness." She added: "My marriage was finished." Expressing frustration over his fame, awards, and legend, Emilie considered "him simply as 'the asshole.'" From her perspective, at the end of his life he was "a broken-down alcoholic, unable to come to terms with his diminishing sexual powers," though it is hard to determine how she knew this because she had absolutely no contact with him during the latter part of his life.[83]

The *Daily Mail* article by Corinna Honan depicted Emilie as an impoverished widow living "her last years at a subsistence in a shantytown outside the southernmost suburbs of Buenos Aires, Argentina." She lived in a small house provided her by a local Jewish organization and her income was $300 a month. Emilie expressed particular contempt for Thomas Keneally and "roll[ed] her eyes at some of Spielberg's more romantic fictions." Yet she was more fair-minded when it came to the reasons for her husband's actions during the Holocaust and the role she played in helping save Jews. Oskar, she explained, was motivated partly by humanitarian reasons because he had befriended some of the Jews that he saved. But, she added, "he was also looking after himself." With the Russians moving closer and closer, Oskar, whom she considered a coward, "used the Jews as support" to avoid being sent to the front to fight the Russians. Emilie explained that her husband also regarded his Jewish workers as a "cushion." She went on: "He felt more secure taking them with him. They seemed to give him courage." She was equally forthright when it came to her involvement in helping saving Jews, which began when they all moved to Brünnlitz in the fall of 1944.[84]

Emilie also told Honan, who spent quite a bit of time with her in San Vicente, that she did not enjoy the trip to Israel to film the final scene for Spielberg's film. She expressed annoyance with the hundreds of Schindler Jews who tried to thank her for saving them and said she felt nothing at Oskar's grave. She considered the Latin Cemetery where he was buried "a dump." As she told the reporter: "My dogs have better graves. Ugly is not the word; it is worse." She also felt nothing when she learned of her husband's death. "I can only feel pity for myself, not for him." She was equally distraught over her trip to Washington to see the premiere of Spielberg's film. There, she saw the film twice. First with President Bill Clinton, when she fell asleep, and later in New York. "It was terrible, too much. First the museum [the United States Holocaust Memorial Museum, which had just opened], the film; I felt ill. The film looked just like it was then, and it took me back in time. It upset me very much. I lost my peace of mind."[85]

A flood of reporters made their way to Emilie's home in San Vicente after the release of the film at the end of 1993. For the most part, the reclusive Emilie seemed to enjoy the fame and the opportunity to continue to criticize her husband, Thomas Keneally, and Steven Spielberg. To Katherine Ellison of Knight-Ridder Newspapers in early 1994, she insisted that Oskar was "stupid. Useless. Half crazy." She added: "To hell with him." She remained extremely critical of Thomas Keneally because she saw him as the source of the distorted view of her husband. Keneally, she claimed, relied too much upon Oskar's memoirs and interviews with the Schindler Jews. She claimed that Keneally had never interviewed her and therefore downplayed her role in the "Schindler story." But Keneally said that he tried to contact Mrs. Schindler through her attorney but was told at the time that she was too sick to do an interview. Instead, he sent her a list of questions to which she responded by mail. From Emilie's perspective, her husband did little to save his beloved Jews: "It wasn't Schindler, it was me. Schindler didn't do anything. He was pitiful."[86] This consistent and false complaint, particularly when coupled with Emilie's harsh criticism of her husband, annoyed a lot of people who otherwise were ready to acknowledge all the wonderful things that she did for the Jews in Brünnlitz. This was particularly true of many of the Schindler Jews I interviewed. Though they were certainly sympathetic to Emilie's sad, difficult life and her unfortunate marriage to Oskar, they had trouble embracing someone who was so openly critical of their beloved savior.

Emilie continued to criticize not only her husband but the Schindler Jews in a detailed interview she did with the German magazine *Bunte* in

1994, though she at least gave Oskar credit for coming up with the idea of saving his Jewish workers. But it was she, and not her husband, she claimed, who really did the hard work of saving the Schindler Jews. Yet she did agree that "Schindler [she refused to call him Oskar] really did worry greatly about [their] Jewish friends and workers." But he had no idea about how to run a factory and how to protect people: "Thus I had to pull all of the strings together and regulate everything." Emilie attributed his drinking, which became a particular problem for Oskar after the war, to the constant demands of partying with the SS.[87] She was also less than gracious when it came to the Schindler Jews, who, she claimed, never even thanked her for saving them.[88] This, of course, was simply not true. All the Schindler Jews I spoke to were extremely grateful for all that Emilie and Oskar had done for them. Moreover, people such as Itzhak Stern and Dr. Moshe Bejski had repeatedly tried to persuade Emilie to move to Israel in the 1960s and had been the ones who insisted that she be included in the financial aspects of the MGM film deal. Emilie, unfortunately, chose to cut herself off from the Schindler Jews, at least until after Spielberg's film came out in the 1990s. This was her way, I suspect, of dealing with the pain of Oskar's return to Germany in 1957.

Emilie's tone was somewhat different in the memoirs she prepared with the help of Erika Rosenberg in 1996. Published first in Spanish as *Memorias,* they came out in the United States the same year as *Where Light and Shadow Meet,* and in Germany a year later as *In Schindlers Schatten* (In Schindler's Shadow). Perhaps Emilie became more temperate because of her growing fame and the presence of Rosenberg, who increasingly saw herself as Emilie's closest confidant and biographer. Emilie presented a much softer and more revealing side of herself in her memoirs, particularly as it related to her relationship and feelings towards her famous husband. It is apparent now from reading the interviews she gave soon after Spielberg's film came out that she was initially shocked out of the protective psychological cocoon that she had built around herself in the years after Oskar's return to Germany. The bitterness that she had held in check for so long exploded in the midst of her husband's newfound fame.[89]

She stated in her memoirs that she was particularly moved and troubled by her trip to Jerusalem in 1993 for the filming of the final scene in Steven Spielberg's film. She remained bitter, though, towards "others in Los Angeles, whose names [she] would rather forget, who were very much aware of [her] existence and had made a lot of money selling the rights to the movie without any consideration for [her] whatsoever."[90] Her trip to

Jerusalem really made her come to grips with her repressed feelings towards her husband. Though she admitted that she knew little about his death, she claimed that he planned to return to Argentina a month before he died, a trip thwarted by "his latest lover." She was uncertain whether she would have "taken him back" if he had returned to San Vicente. She then drifted into thoughtless accusations against Dr. Heinrich Staehr, who was, according to Emilie, "in charge of the operation" and the "husband of one of [Oskar's] lovers." Emilie said in her memoirs that she decided not to press charges against Dr. Staehr, but considered the nature of her husband's death peculiar: "A defenseless man places his life in the hands of a potential enemy . . . perhaps in some way, it was Oskar's last flirtation with danger." These are strange comments and charges for a person who claimed she had no feelings for her husband.[91]

But perhaps more revealing was her new account of her visit to his grave in the Latin Cemetery in Jerusalem. She now admitted that she had placed a ritual stone on his grave and "silently said to him"

Well, Oskar, at last we meet again, but this is not the time for reproaches and complaints. It would not be fair to you or to me. Now you are in another world, in eternity, and I can no longer ask you all those questions to which in life you would have given evasive replies . . . and death is the best evasion of all. I have received no answer, my dear, I do not know why you abandoned me. . . . But what not even your death or my old age can change is that we are still married, this is how we are before God. I have forgiven you everything, everything . . .

Emilie left Oskar's grave knowing somehow that "the power of [her] thoughts had reached him, and felt, after all those years, a strange inner peace filling [her] spirit."[92] She went on to explain later in her memoirs her feelings about forgiveness, which she considered "magnificent," particularly as it related to the Holocaust. "It requires us," she explained, "at once to understand and to not forget, to value life and at the same time to not abandon the memory of those who died or the passion for justice."[93]

To say that Emilie's world was forever changed by Spielberg's film would be an understatement. In addition to meeting President Bill Clinton, she would also be received by numerous other dignitaries, such as President Roman Herzog of Germany, who earlier had given her Germany's Federal Cross of Merit, and Pope John Paul II. She was particularly excited by her visit with the Holy Father in Rome in the spring of 1995. Though not a devout Roman Catholic, Emilie held closely to her beliefs and occasionally went to mass in the beautiful Catholic church just a block from her home in San Vicente. As she prepared to leave for her trip to Europe, she admitted her frustration: "I couldn't tell then what it was I hated more: Oskar, or myself for being unable to expel him from my mind." Her audience with the Holy Father in the Vatican reminded Emilie of her special ties to Oskar. The Pope, who spoke to her in "perfect German," told her that as a Pole, he was "very grateful" for what she had done. Many Polish Jews, particularly in the Kraków area, had thanked Emilie and Oskar for saving their lives. John Paul II then added: "Your example of solidarity also saved Polish Catholics." After her meeting with the Holy Father, Emile met the Chief Rabbi of Rome, Elio Toaff, who held a wonderful reception for her and presented her with two books on the history of Italian Jewry.[94]

But perhaps the most moving part of her trip to Europe that spring was her return to Germany for the first time in forty-six years. While in Bonn waiting to be received by President Herzog, she had a reunion with her beloved niece, Traude Ferrari. Emilie had helped raise Traude, and called her "my little girl." Traude brought with her a photo album of family pictures that Emilie had given her in Brünnlitz. Emilie had few family pictures with her in San Vicente and only two of Oskar. This album was Emilie's "only existing testimony" of her family, her childhood, her "years with Oskar." Traude, who was, along with her mother and younger brothers, at Brünnlitz at the end of the war, had torn the photos out of the album and stuffed them under her blouse as Russian soldiers marched into the camp. The photographs, which Emilie included in her memoirs, gave Emilie "back an important part of her life."[95]

Emilie would not return to Europe for four years, when she made a trip back to visit Germany and her hometown, Maletín, in the Czech Republic. But she could not escape the shadow of her husband, who continued to be honored in both countries. In the summer of 1993, the Ackermann Congregation in Frankfurt and the Jewish congregations in the Czech Republic erected a memorial plaque in honor of Oskar outside the house where he had been raised in Svitavy. In 1994, ZDF (Zweites Deutsches Fernsehen), Germany's public television station, produced a documentary about Oskar, *Oskar Schindler: Retter and Lebemann* (Oskar Schindler: Rescuer and Man of the World). The film, which was stimulated by *Schindler's List* and included an interview with Spielberg, also had comments from Schindler Jews such as Dr. Moshe Bejski, Michael Garde, Ester Rechen, Joseph Bau, and Zeev Nahir. ZDF also interviewed Robin

O'Neil, a retired British police inspector and scholar who had conducted considerable research on Schindler, and Dr. Dieter Trautwein.[96]

The Koffer (Suitcase) Controversy

A few years before Emilie's return to Germany in 1999, a discovery took place that had the potential to change dramatically the Oskar Schindler story as constructed by Thomas Keneally and Steven Spielberg. Once Emilie learned of it, she initiated two lawsuits in Germany, first to gain possession of her husband's private papers, and then to win damages from the newspaper that published a series of articles on the famed collection. The discovery, of course, was Oskar Schindler's forgotten suitcase *(Koffer)* containing many of his personal papers in the attic of the apartment of Ami and Heinrich Staehr in Hildesheim, Germany. Oskar had sent the first part of this collection in his grey, hard-sided Samsonite suitcase to the Staehrs sometime before his death. A few days after he died, Ami and her son Chris were able to retrieve more of his papers from his apartment in Frankfurt. Ami evidently loaned them briefly to Stefan Pemper, who later returned them. She then put the entire collection in Oskar's Samsonite suitcase and stored them in a large wooden crate in the attic of her Hildesheim apartment. For the most part, at Heinrich's insistence, the files were left untouched except for the times when Traude Ferrari asked for documents from the collection. After Ami died in 1988, Heinrich asked that the Schindler papers be left untouched by the family until after his death. After *Schindlers Liste* came out, he also refused to allow plaques to be erected to Oskar outside their home, fearing that neo-Nazis might use the site as a shrine. He asked his daughter-in-law, Tina, to handle all questions from the press about his relationship with Oskar Schindler. In time, the family completely forgot about the Schindler papers in the attic.[97]

Dr. Heinrich Staehr died on June 3, 1997. A few days after his death, Chris, his brother Konrad, and Tina were cleaning out the apartment and collecting Dr. Staehr's medical records and other private papers. Towards the end of the day, they decided to check the attic to see whether there was anything there. All they saw was a large wooden crate. As Chris looked inside, he saw a large stack of bundled papers. When he lifted the papers from the box, he saw a large, grey Samsonite suitcase at the bottom of the crate. He turned the suitcase's luggage tag over, which read "O. Schindler." Though Chris had helped his mother take papers out of Oskar's Frankfurt apartment in 1974, he knew little about the suitcase full of documents that Oskar had sent earlier to Hildesheim. He also did not know that his mother had stored most of Schindler's private papers in the Samsonite suitcase. Because his father had insisted that the family not touch or discuss the Schindler papers in the attic, Chris and the rest of the family presumed that Ami had earlier sent most of Oskar's papers to Yad Vashem.[98]

As Konrad seemed to have no interest in the suitcase, Chris and Tina decided to bring it home with them to Stuttgart, where they stored it in their basement. Though they were fully aware of the importance of its contents, they were not sure what to do with it, though their first instinct was that it should go to Yad Vashem. Several months later, Chris called Dr. Moshe Bejski in Israel and asked him about the prospect of donating the suitcase and Schindler's private papers to Yad Vashem. Dr. Bejski told Chris that there was no hurry giving the papers to Israel's national Holocaust memorial and archives. But questions about what to do with the suitcase collection were put on hold after it was discovered that Tina had breast cancer. Chris initially gave some thought to taking the suitcase to Yad Vashem himself but gave up that idea because of Tina's illness. It would be another year before the Staehrs revisited the question about what to do with the suitcase. By Christmas 1998, Tina had fully recovered from her cancer and decided to organize the contents of the suitcase. When she had completed her work, Chris thought of writing an article about Oskar based on his own memories and the documents in the suitcase to commemorate Oskar's birthday on April 28, 1999. But after a while, Chris decided that the topic was too personal for him. Consequently, he contacted a friend, Dr. Wolfgang Borgmann, who was the science editor at the *Stuttgarter Zeitung,* and asked whether he had any suggestions about what to do with the suitcase.[99]

Dr. Borgmann suggested that Chris and Tina let one of his younger colleagues, Stefan Braun, who had just returned from Israel, look over the Schindler papers. Braun spent two days going through the suitcase files at the Staehr's home in Stuttgart. Braun quickly concluded that the files were extremely important. Chris and Tina told him to take them back to his apartment where he could carefully go over them with another reporter from the *Stuttgarter Zeitung,* Claudia Keller. Claudia, a freelance reporter, spent the summer of 1999 going through the Schindler papers and decided to write a series of articles summarizing the most important documents in the suitcase. She was not certain, though, whether the *Stuttgarter Zeitung's* editor, Dr. Uwe Vorkötter, would be interested in such a series because the articles were quite long. She thought she might have a better chance of publishing the articles in another German newspaper, *Die Zeit,* or in the German magazine *Der Spiegel.* However, once Stefan told Dr. Vorkötter about Claudia's series, which Stefan coauthored, the editor insisted that they publish them in the *Stuttgarter Zeitung.* Claudia wrote most of the articles, which Stefan and Dr. Vorkötter edited before publication.[100]

But before he decided to publish the series, Dr. Vorkötter invited Chris and Tina to his offices to make sure they were comfortable with its publication. He also wanted confirmation that the collection was genuine. He was a bit suspicious because of the 1983 scandal involving another German publication, *Stern,* and the fake Hitler diaries. On the eve of the publication of what became one of the longest series to run in a German newspaper, Stefan Braun brought the suitcase to the offices of the *Stuttgarter Zeitung* because, Dr. Vorkötter assured him, the newspaper had insurance to protect its contents. The series, which began in the *Stuttgarter Zeitung* on October 16, 1999, became an international sensation, mainly because it was thought that the Schindler collection contained the long lost original "Schindler's List." We now know, of course, that it did not. The excellent, well-written seven-part series, which appeared from October 16 through 26, was interspersed with articles about Emilie and comments from the international press on the discovery of the suitcase files. The *Stuttgarter Zeitung* later published the entire collection of articles, along with a lengthy interview with Mietek Pemper, as *Schindlers Koffer: Berichte aus dem Leben eines Lebensretters* (Schindler's Suitcase: Report on the Life of a Rescuer).[101]

I first learned of the series while watching the late-night news in Washington, D.C. As a picture of Oskar Schindler was flashed on the screen, the reporter announced that the original "Schindler's List" and Oskar's other private papers had, according to the *Stuttgarter Zeitung,* been discovered in Germany. When I returned home several days later, I went to the *Stuttgarter Zeitung*'s Web site and downloaded the articles that had already been published. I knew immediately from reading the articles that the collection was genuine and that it would be invaluable to my research. I had long suspected that Schindler's private papers were somewhere in Germany, though I thought the family of Dr. Lotte Schiffler probably had them. I decided to send an e-mail to Dr. Vorkötter and ask whether he could tell me more about the collection. He responded immediately and told me that the Schindler papers, along with the suitcase, had been sent to the Bundesarchiv in Koblenz. He suggested that I contact Dr. Wolf Buchmann, the head of the Bundesarchiv there, about access to the collection. What I did not know at the time was that Emilie Schindler was preparing to file a lawsuit in Stuttgart to gain control of her husband's private papers. I sent an e-mail to Dr. Buchmann, who told me that I was welcome to come to Germany and review the collection, though he could not guarantee access to it when I got there because of the impending lawsuit. I decided to take a chance, and spent much of January 2000 working in the Schindler collection in Koblenz.

It is difficult to know how Emilie and Erika Rosenberg first learned of the discovery of the suitcase. Erika worked at the Goethe Institute in Buenos Aires and was known to be very close to Emilie, so she probably learned about it as soon as the *Stuttgarter Zeitung* articles began to appear. Regardless, several days later, one of Germany's most prominent magazines, *Der Spiegel,* called Emilie and asked her opinion about the recent discovery. Another magazine, *Stern,* also contacted Emilie in an effort to determine whether the suitcase files were genuine. Emilie said she could not tell until she saw them. She added, "I will fly to Germany within the next few days . . . to take the suitcase with me."[102]

But Emilie, who was about to turn ninety-two, was not physically able to make the trip. Instead, she sent Erika Rosenberg to Germany to retrieve the suitcase. Erika immediately flew to Stuttgart, thinking that the suitcase and the Schindler collection was still in the Staehr's apartment. On the evening of October 21, Chris heard the bell ring at the gate outside their home. Tina, oddly enough, was talking on the telephone with Oskar's daughter, Edith Schagl. Chris opened the outer gate leading to their home. A few seconds later, Erika Rosenberg knocked on their front door. She introduced herself and explained that she was a friend of Emilie's who worked at the Goethe Institute in Buenos Aires. "Emilie," Erika went on, "sent me to fetch the suitcase." Chris remembers that Erika was extremely nervous and was trembling. Chris asked Erika to come inside and offered her a glass of wine. Chris told Erika that though he believed the suitcase belonged to Emilie, he no longer had it.[103]

When she had finished her white wine, Erika told Chris and Tina that she had to go. Chris, ever gracious, offered to call a taxi for Erika. She declined, saying that someone was waiting outside for her. Chris walked Erika to the front gate and noticed a TV crew from ZDF across the street. When the crew spotted Chris and Erika, they rushed over, and a ZDF journalist asked Chris about the location of the suitcase. Chris, who dislikes interviews and photographs, declined to be interviewed. Early the next morning, Erika called Tina and suggested that they meet at the Hotel Gloria at 9:00 A.M. Tina agreed, with one proviso—they be alone. When Tina drove up to the hotel, she saw the ZDF crew with Erika. She turned around and went home. Later, Erika called Tina to ask whether they could meet alone. Tina told her that she was too busy. With the exception of another telephone call from Erika four or five months later asking for another meeting, this was the last contact the Staehrs had with her. In light of Emilie's lawsuit, Tina again declined to meet with Erika.[104]

What Erika did not know when she first showed up at the Staehr's home was that the suitcase and its files were being prepared for shipment to Yad Vashem via the Bundesarchiv in Koblenz. Chris Staehr wanted the Bundesarchiv to make two copies of the files before they were sent to Israel—one on microfilm for researchers to use in Koblenz and a hardbound copy for Emilie. I was able to work in the Koblenz collection during much of January 2000. Each day, Dr. Buchmann would come by to see how I was doing. One evening, he invited me up to his office for coffee. As we were talking, he pointed to a library cart that was filled with grey bound volumes. This was the carefully reproduced, bound set of every letter and document in the Schindler suitcase that was to be sent to Emilie in Buenos Aires. Erika Rosenberg used this bound collection to produce her two edited, documentary collections on the Schindlers, *Ich, Oskar Schindler: Die persönlichen Aufzeichnungen, Briefe und Dokumente* (I, Oskar Schindler: The Personal Notes, Letters, and Documents) and *Ich, Emilie Schindler: Erinnerungen einer Unbeugsamen* (I, Emilie Schindler: Memories of an Inflexible One).

The transfer of the suitcase with all its valuable papers from the Bundesarchiv in Koblenz to Yad Vashem in Israel took place in early December 1999. It was initially sent in a diplomatic pouch from Frankfurt to David Ben Gurion Airport in Tel Aviv via Lufthansa, the German national airline. For some strange reason, it was mysteriously sent back to Frankfurt. It was then re-shipped to Israel in two separate packages—one containing the suitcase and another with the actual Schindler files—and arrived at Ben Gurion on December 4, 1999. As it was *Shabbat,* no one could pick it up from Yad Vashem and it remained there until the next day, when it was transferred to Yad Vashem. About ten days later, Chris and Tina arrived in Israel to check the status of the suitcase files. They were given a tour of Yad Vashem and spent about two hours meeting with Dr. Mordecai Paldiel, the head of the Righteous Gentile Department, who told them it would be about two years before scholars could have access to the collection. They also spent several days with Dr. Bejski in Tel Aviv.[105]

But before all this took place, Emilie's attorneys had contacted the police about the suitcase. About a week before it was sent to Israel, the police came to the offices of the *Stuttgarter Zeitung* looking for it. By this time, of course, the collection was at the Bundesarchiv in Koblenz. The police search was part of the first lawsuit that Emilie filed against the *Stuttgarter Zeitung* and Chris Staehr in November 1999 in an effort to gain control of Oskar's suitcase and its contents. By the time the matter was brought before the court in Stuttgart on January 20, 2000, the suitcase and its contents were already in Israel, though Yad Vashem agreed to return everything if Chris Staehr and the *Stuttgarter Zeitung* lost the lawsuit. The court in Stuttgart quickly dismissed Emilie's suit and held her responsible for the costs of her failed legal action.[106]

The matter did not end there. Emilie and Erika decided to file a second lawsuit against the *Stuttgarter Zeitung* that asked for damages of DM 100,000 ($58,823). According to Emilie's new lawsuit, the publication of the series by Claudia Keller and Stefan Braun in the *Stuttgarter Zeitung* in October 1999 had "infringed upon the ownership and author-rights to the papers in the suitcase." According to Emilie's attorney, had the suitcase and its contents been sold to a publication such as *Der Spiegel,* DM 100,000 was the estimated amount they would have fetched. But from Emilie and Erika's perspective, there was more at stake here than just the assessed value of the suitcase and its contents. Before the trial, Rosenberg also asserted that the publication of the Schindler series in the Stuttgart newspaper had prevented her edited collection of documents, *Ich, Oskar Schindler,* from becoming a "bestseller." The trial, which began on April 26, 2001, lasted only two days. Attorneys for the *Stuttgarter Zeitung* argued that the suitcase and its valuable papers had been a gift from Oskar Schindler to Ami Staehr and belonged to her estate and heirs. The court agreed and on April 27 Judge Werner Müller ruled that the *Stuttgarter Zeitung* had not acted "culpably" in printing the series eighteen months earlier. But though the court supported the position of the Stuttgart newspaper, Judge Müller suggested that it consider making, "as a charitable gesture and without recognition of a legal obligation," a gift of DM 20,000 to DM 25,000 ($11,695 to $14,620) to Emilie. The judge said he doubted that Emilie could ever win a long legal battle in German courts over the matter, which meant that she would probably not live long enough to see the outcome.[107]

I had been in contact with Dr. Vorkötter during this period and told him that I was going to Argentina in May to interview Emilie. Initially, he had been hesitant to agree to the humanitarian gift to Emilie because it might be seen as an admission that the *Stuttgarter Zeitung* had done something wrong in publishing the series on Oskar's suitcase files. However, after some reflection, Dr. Vorkötter realized it was the right thing to do. But he was concerned that the money would go to Erika Rosenberg and not Emilie. Consequently, he asked whether I could contact someone with B'nai B'rith or another prominent Jewish organization in Buenos Aires who would be willing to accept the contribution from the *Stuttgarter Zeitung* and use it to create a trust fund to help Emilie. Fortunately, my research assistant in Buenos Aires, Adriana Brodsky, was a member of a very prominent Jewish family in the Argentine capital, and she was able to put me in contact with Elias Zviklich, the international senior vice president of B'nai B'rith International. I met with Mr. Zviklich, and he expressed interest in helping Emilie by creating a trust fund for her. I shared this information with Dr. Vorkötter when I returned to the United States several weeks later, though nothing ever came of these plans. In late June, the *Stuttgarter Zeitung* decided to give Emilie a "gift" of DM 25,000, which presumably went directly to Erika Rosenberg.[108]

But my meeting with Mr. Zviklich was not the most important reason for my trip to Argentina. I went there to interview Emilie and to see what I could find out about her life and that of her husband while they lived in Argentina. Working with Adriana Brodsky, I was able to meet some of Emilie's closest friends there, including Francisco Wichter, the last Schindler Jew in Argentina, and Ilse Chwat, Monika Caro, and Ilse Wartenleben. Each was a long time member of *Traducion* and had known Emilie for decades. They considered Emilie a friend and had played important roles in helping and befriending her. Ilse, Monika, and Ilse agreed to take me to see Emilie and to do anything they could to help me with my research. Their only stipulation was that they would not be in the same room with Erika Rosenberg. They said this without malice or anger. They just did not like her or trust her.[109]

Francisco, Ilse Chwat, and Ilse Wartenleben took me to see Emilie on May 22 at Hogar los Pinos (Home in the Pines), the German rest home where she was living in the suburbs of Buenos Aires. Emilie had been there since November 2000 after she fell and broke her hip while trying to move a wheelbarrow full of bricks. She lay alone in her yard for five hours before someone found her. Rosenberg, who visited Emilie only on weekends, was in Germany at the time promoting her book on Oskar Schindler, though she had people checking on Emilie twice a day. Before we went to visit Emile, I asked Francisco and Ilse Chwat whether I should bring anything for Emilie. They told me she had a sweet tooth and liked flowers. Adriana, who accompanied us on the visit, took me to a wonderful *confiteria* in Buenos Aires, R. Mossuti, where we picked up a pound of delicious handmade chocolates for Emilie. Francisco also had his wife make her a wonderful apple strudel, a Sudeten speciality. Ilse Chwat brought her flowers.

Needless to say, everyone was a little nervous about the visit because they were concerned that Erika would find out about it and try to intervene. There were a few tense moments when we arrived at the front gate. The staff was protective of Emilie's privacy but, with the exception of Adriana and myself, knew everyone in our party because they visited Emilie frequently. Everyone warned me beforehand that Emilie had good days and bad days and they were not certain how receptive she would be. She evidently was quite bitter and depressed about being in the rest home and constantly talked about wanting to go home while we were together. Personally, I had less interest in an actual interview with Emilie than simply being in the presence of someone for whom I had high regard.

It was a cool, crisp fall day at los Pinos and Emilie met us outside. She was in a wheelchair and her nurse had settled her in a small pavilion. Fortunately, this was one of Emilie's good days and she was quite talkative. I brought some photographs I had taken of her hometown, Maletín, and when she saw them she kept saying "Alte, alte." It was fairly obvious that she was suffering from some form of dementia, common for someone of her age. Yet she was also full of life, particularly when we took her inside for strudel. I had taken some photos of her outside and she really warmed up to the camera when we went inside. Even at her age, Emilie had a radiant smile. You could also tell that she was accustomed to being in front of cameras. It took little prompting to get her to pose for a photograph. Periodically, she would look back at me and smile. Ilse Chwat said Emilie was very proud to know that an American had come so far to see her. Though she spoke heavily accented Spanish in San Vicente, she had reverted to German during our visit, though she would periodically mumble "Santa Maria y Jesus."[110]

I left los Pinos late that afternoon with some wonderful memories of Emilie Schindler. I also hoped that my modest efforts to help set up a trust fund for her with B'nai B'rith would benefit her. Yet I was also worried about her well-being and health. Her wheelchair was rather shabby and I told one of the nurses that I would be more than happy to buy her a new one. But I was also concerned about her health. Her nurses told me that she was extremely depressed and slept most of the time because of the medication she was taking. This was why visitors were so important to her—at least they got her out of bed. But she was so frail and mentally sluggish that I asked Monika Caro, another close friend of Emilie's, whether it was possible to talk with her physician to discuss her condition. Several days later, Dr. Alfredo May called me at my hotel. He confirmed that Emilie suffered from dementia and would never be able to leave the rest home. She was simply too ill.[111]

I returned to the United States a week later thinking that Emilie would spend the last days of her life in Hogar los Pinos aided by the gift from the *Stuttgarter Zeitung.* Needless to say, I was stunned to learn five weeks later that Erika Rosenberg had checked Emilie out of los Pinos and taken her to Germany. The reason I was so upset was that I instinctively knew that the trip would kill Emilie. And I was not the only one concerned about Emilie's well-being. Linda Diebel, a reporter with the *Toronto Star,* and Cristine Hurtado, an Argentine journalist who had spent a great deal of time with Emilie over the years, interviewed Rosenberg and visited Emilie just before Erika took her to Germany. Diebel, the *Star*'s Latin American correspondent who published a featured article on the interview and visit just after Emilie arrived in Germany, was extremely critical of Rosenberg's treatment of Emilie, who, she claimed, now "languishes in a German hospital, drugged, and appearing to be under the complete control of one Erika Rosenberg." Moreover, Deibel went on, Rosenberg checked Emilie out of los Pinos against the advice of her doctors and flew her to Germany, a trip that coincided "with the imminent German publication of Rosenberg's fourth Schindler book."[112]

Yet who was this person who seemed to wield such power over Emilie Schindler's life? Erika Rosenberg, the child of German Jews who fled to Argentina in 1936, got to know Emilie in the early 1990s as part of a research project she was doing on German Jewish immigrants to Argentina. Peter Gorlinsky, the editor of Argentina's principal German newspaper, the *Argentinisches Tageblatt,* told Rosenberg about Emilie and asked her whether she knew of "Mother Courage." Rosenberg, intrigued, contacted Emilie in San Vicente and slowly established a very close relationship with her. After she gained Emilie's confidence, she asked to record their conversations, which centered around the story of Emilie's life. Over time, Erika put their talks on four hundred tapes, which became the basis of

Emilie's published memoirs. Over time, Rosenberg came to consider herself Emilie's "voice" and "mouthpiece."[113]

Linda Diebel considered Rosenberg's relationship with Emilie pure opportunism. Moreover, Diebel and Hurtado blamed Rosenberg for Emilie's criticism of Steven Spielberg and the suggestion that she did more to help Jews during the Holocaust than her husband, Oskar Schindler. Hurtado, who had interviewed Emilie many times between 1993 and 2001, said that "Emilie never, ever talked about money, or claimed that she was greater than Oskar." Hurtado went on, "She never tried to take attention for her self. She would always say, 'I don't understand the fuss. It was not heroism. If you had been there, you would have done the same thing.'" Emilie also revealed her true feelings for Oskar. "I still love Oskar, I married him for life, until death." Hurtado once asked Emilie whether she believed in heaven. "Who knows. But if there is, and I see Oskar, I will ask him: Why did you leave me alone?"[114]

Though Cristine Hurtado had established her own, special relationship with Emilie, she and Linda Diebel found it difficult to see Emilie in the summer of 2001. Diebel wrote that the only way Rosenberg would allow the two reporters to see her was if they paid for the interview. But the *Toronto Star,* Diebel explained, "doesn't pay for interviews." Finally, after a great deal of effort on Hurtado's part, Rosenberg agreed to let them spend some time with Emilie in los Pinos. It was not a pleasant visit. They found her "lying in her bed, uncovered and exposed." They were upset to find that Emilie's wheelchair had no footrest and that "her feet drag[ged] along the ground." Rosenberg was unresponsive when Hurtado mentioned this to her. Later, she was equally silent when both reporters complained about leaving Emilie outside in the cold. When Hurtado finally insisted on moving her back into her room, "Rosenberg complied." Once inside, Rosenberg kept asking Emilie, "Isn't Spielberg a pig?" Emilie did not respond and stared out the window.[115]

From Diebel's perspective, Rosenberg's relationship with Emilie "seem[ed] to be pretty much about money."[116] This, in part, also seemed to have been Emilie's take on her friend. While I was in Argentina, several of the *Traducion* women I spoke to told me that during a Christmas party for Emilie the previous year, someone had asked her about Erika Rosenberg. Emilie responded that all Rosenberg wanted was "money, money, money."[117] The idea that Emilie was living in poverty was absurd. This idea is insulting not only to her neighbors in San Vicente but to her *Traducion* friends who cared for her over the years. Her home in San Vicente, though modest, was quite lovely and in a very desirable section of the town. If her house was a mess, it was, in part, because she allowed her many pets to roam freely through the house. Who would want or have nice furniture that twenty cats and multiple dogs would destroy? If Emilie had financial problems, some of it was because she had never handled money particularly well. This was a trait she shared with her husband, Oskar. In her article, Linda Diebel correctly noted that Emilie received various Argentine, German, and Jewish pensions, had received a $50,000 gift from Steven Spielberg, and royalties from the books that Rosenberg published under her name. Moreover, groups were constantly trying to find other ways to help her. Rosenberg, though, refused to discuss her financial relationship with Emilie. On the other hand, she claimed that Emilie needed a lot of money because her various pensions did not cover her medical expenses. Rosenberg claimed, for example, that she owed los Pinos thousands of dollars for Emilie's care; but the director, Arno Hinckedeyn, said the German charity hospital required patients to pay only what they could afford. Moreover, B'nai B'rith had earlier offered to put Emilie in a German-speaking Jewish rest home free of charge, but Rosenberg rejected the offer.[118]

But all was moot once Rosenberg decided to take Emilie to Germany. According to Rosenberg, Emilie signed a notarized statement in 1997 stipulating that, upon her death, she be cremated and her ashes scattered along the La Plata River in Buenos Aires. But she also claimed that Emilie wanted to return to Germany. So, even though Emilie was too weak to get out of bed by herself, Rosenberg was determined to take her to Germany. Diebel, who interviewed Rosenberg just before she took Emilie to Germany on July 6, 2001, questioned the wisdom of taking this frail, ninety-three-year-old woman to Germany. After they left, Diebel asked Arno Hinckedeyn about this. He told her that the rest home's physicians had advised against it. But Rosenberg somehow managed to find a physician in the German embassy to sign her out. Rosenberg, though, promised the los Pinos staff that she would return Emilie to Buenos Aires on July 21. But Diebel wondered how a person "so frail it is a huge deal to get her to the bathroom" could cope "with such a long flight [thirteen hours] to Germany." Rosenberg told her that "Emilie would be medicated." But this did not reduce the stress of the flight. Once in Germany, they had to wait for four hours in the Frankfurt airport for their flight to Bonn. When Emilie failed to wake up after the landing in Bonn, an emergency medical crew was brought on board and she was admitted to the Porzer Hospital for observation.[119]

But did Rosenberg really intend to return Emilie to Argentina as she had promised? Just before Rosenberg left with Emilie for Germany, Linda Diebel interviewed Erika in her apartment in Buenos Aires. Erika had now completed her last book on the Schindlers, *Ich, Emilie Schindler,* and she told Diebel: "It is enough. I am finished. I can only be responsible for myself." As she looked around Rosenberg's apartment, Diebel noticed several brochures on nursing homes in Germany on a nearby table, an indication that Rosenberg was at least looking into the prospect of leaving Emilie in Germany. Rosenberg explained that she might do this is "if that is what she [Emilie] wants."[120]

Rosenberg had planned for Emilie to be with her at their first news conference in Bonn on July 9 at the House of History (Haus der Geschichte) to announce the presentation of several items to the museum and the opening of a permanent exhibit on the Schindlers. Emilie, who was still in the hospital, was unable to meet Chancellor Gerhard Schröder of Germany, who also attended the ceremony. But the next morning, Rosenberg checked Emilie out of the Porzer Hospital and took her by car to Berlin—a four-hundred-mile trip. The following day, Emilie and Erika went on a tour of the Berlin's New Synagogue-Centrum Judaicum and held a short press conference. Afterwards, they attended a lunch sponsored by the Oskar Schindler School (Oskar-Schindler-Oberschule) where, according to Rosenberg, "Emilie spoke with everyone at the table and even made a few jokes." This was followed by a reception at the Bundestag, the lower house of the German parliament. It was apparent that Emilie was confused by everything going on around her because she frequently asked, "Where are we?" Rosenberg always explained that they were in Germany.[121]

The following day, they attended a special ceremony at the Oskar Schindler School, where Emilie signed autographs for an hour. Over the next few days, Emilie and Rosenberg visited the Rosa-Luxemburg Foundation, a local Protestant church, and the Berlin Zoo. Emilie, Rosenberg explained, "accepted everything naturally . . . and seemed to enjoy the attention she received." Two days later, Rosenberg took Emilie to the Katharinenhof in nearby Fredersdorf, where she could rest before her final journey to Bavaria. On July 16, the State of Bavaria offered to find and pay for a suitable rest home for Emilie should she wish to settle in the southern German state. Rosenberg quickly accepted the Bavarian offer and arrangements were made to send Emilie to the Adalbert-Stifter Nursing Home, a Sudeten German rest home in Waldkreiburg. According to

Rosenberg, this was where she wanted "to spend the evening of her life in the circle of her fellow Sudeten German friends." But on July 21, the day before they were to leave for Waldkreiburg, Emilie had a stroke and was sent to the Märkisch-Oberland Hospital in Strasbourg, outside Berlin. Emilie's physicians told Rosenberg that their patient could no longer speak and was physically too weak to travel to Bavaria. They also advised her to expect the worst. Emilie seemed to recover and regain some of her speech just as Rosenberg prepared to leave for Argentina, where she had pressing obligations. Soon after she returned to Buenos Aires, Rosenberg completed her final editing for her book on the Schindlers, *Ich, Emilie Schindler.* Her final statement in this work, dated August 2, 2001, was "All the best and love, Emilie!"[122]

Rosenberg might have also gone back to Argentina to escape growing press criticism of her treatment of Emilie in Germany. Though she claims in *Ich, Emilie Schindler* that Emilie enjoyed the visits and the press conferences, the truth is somewhat different. Reporters were particularly critical of the 80 Euro ($97) fee that Rosenberg demanded for each interview, regardless of whether Emilie took part or not, and what seemed to be Rosenberg's insensitivity to Emilie's deteriorating health. When someone asked Rosenberg about the fees, she responded: "Journalists earn money from the interviews we give them, so why shouldn't we, Mrs. Schindler, have the right to earn money to live from?" Derek Scully of the *Irish Times,* though, was more concerned about Emilie's physical condition than the fees. The same was true of Kate Connolly at the *Observer* (London). Scully noted, for example, that during a press conference in the German parliament, Emilie sat with her "eyes shut, looking exhausted." During her visit to the Oskar Schindler School, students rushed her wheelchair, pushing books in her lap to sign and "asking one question after another about her husband." The visit, Scully observed, "overwhelmed and exhausted" Emilie. Rosenberg had to cancel several television interviews with the BBC and other networks because of Emilie's growing exhaustion. Scully said that "the rapid deterioration of Emilie's health is no surprise to those who watched her as she was dragged along from one reception to another for a week, accompanied always by Rosenberg." During one of the few interview sessions that Emilie was able to attend, she was "so mentally unaware that it had to be abandoned." Needless to say, the interview was never aired. When Kate Connolly asked Rosenberg whether she had brought Emilie to Germany to help promote her new book, Rosenberg denied it. But Erika told Derek Scully of the *Irish Times* that she hoped Emilie would "recover for the October launch of *Ich, Emilie Schindler,* which . . . would tell the full story of the woman behind Oskar Schindler."[123]

Emilie seemed to recover a bit after Erika left and by mid-August was able to sit up in bed and smile. But during the next seven weeks, her condition deteriorated and on Friday, October 6, 2001, she died of a stroke, just sixteen days short of her ninety-fourth birthday. But it would be another week before a cemetery could be found to bury her. With the help of Dr. Herbert Flessner, a prominent Sudeten German who owned Langen Müller Herbig, the publishing house that did Erika Rosenberg's books on the Schindlers, it was decided to inter her in the cemetery in Waldkreiburg, which is about an hour's drive east of Munich. I visited Emilie's grave in Waldkreiburg in the fall of 2003, and I have to say that it is exquisitely beautiful. In fact, once I got beyond the confines of Munich and into the rolling hills of southeastern Bavaria, I felt that I was once again back in the Sudetenland. It was most appropriate that Emilie be buried here. According to Dr. Eva Habel of the Sudetendeutsche Landsmannschaft in Munich, Waldkreiburg was founded after World War II by Sudeten Germans forced out of Czechoslovakia. Though the village's population is now only about half Sudeten German, the cemetery is a quiet tribute to its Sudeten German heritage.[124] Emilie's white tombstone is simple but beautiful. It has a cross carved on the left with two inscriptions to the right—"Emilie Schindler: Alt Moletein/Sudeten 1907-Strausberg/Brandenburg 2001" and "Wer einen Menschen Rettet, Rettet die Ganze Welt [Whoever saves one life saves the whole world]." Just to the right of the tombstone is a crucifix. As I placed a stone on her headstone and a candle just in front, I thought of Francisco Wichter's final tribute to Emilie. I had written Franciso in the summer of 2001 after I learned that Emilie had been taken to Germany. I wanted to know when he had learned of Emilie's departure. He told me that he did not know about it until after Emilie left for Germany but had suspected something as we were leaving los Pinos on the day of our visit. Emilie, he said, bid us goodbye in a very "maternal way," something she had never done before. Needless to say, he and Emilie's other *Traducion* friends, who had loved and cared for her for many years, were upset because they never had a chance to say goodbye. These are the last words in his mournful letter: "Emilie, may your soul rest in peace and wholeness. She was a great fighter in the good and bad times."[125]

15.

AFTERTHOUGHTS

WHEN I BEGAN WORKING ON THIS BOOK MORE THAN SEVEN
years ago, I knew little about Oskar Schindler other than what I had read
in Thomas Keneally's historical novel and in the few scattered works written about him after Steven Spielberg's film, *Schindler's List,* came out in
1993. Though I had a copy of Elinor Brecher's wonderful collection of
Schindler survivor testimonies, *Schindler's Legacy* (1994), I had not come
to understand its richness and diversity. As I began my research, I struggled with the images in Spielberg's film. This was particularly the case during my first trip to Kraków. Though I had been to this beautiful medieval
Polish city before, this time was different. I wanted to explore first-hand
each of the sites discussed by Keneally and depicted in the Spielberg film.
What I slowly discovered over the course of my research travels, which
brought me back to Kraków and Brünnlitz several times, was that I could
escape Keneally and Spielberg's literary and cinematographic images of
Oskar Schindler only by creating new ones based solely on my own exacting scholarly research.

Over time, I became very comfortable with my own, separate image of
Oskar Schindler, whom I found to be a far more complex, and, at times,
sad figure, than the person captured in the pages of Keneally's historical
novel or in Spielberg's film. Moreover, I found my own views constantly
changing towards a person who was one of the most remarkable figures
to come out of the Holocaust. In the early part of the book, I was disgusted by Oskar Schindler's continual affairs and his decision to spy for

Nazi Germany. One of the first people I interviewed in the Czech Republic was Dr. Jitka Gruntová, a Czech historian who has written quite a bit about Schindler. She was extremely critical of Schindler's work for Abwehr and his efforts to help destroy Czechoslovakia in the immediate years before World War II. Needless to say, I did not have a high opinion of Schindler at this point in my research, and this did not change as I explored his move to Kraków in the early days of the war. At this point, I saw Oskar Schindler as nothing more than a greedy ethnic German "carpetbagger" who sought to take advantage of Poland's despair to enrich himself and escape further service in the military.

But then something changed, both on the part of Oskar Schindler and within myself. I have to admit that up until this point in my research and writing, I had begun to doubt the merits of Schindler's postwar acclaim. But as I went through the vast body of personal testimonies and other material I had gathered, my opinion of him slowly became more positive. Oskar was in Kraków to do one thing—make money. But in the process of trying to set up a factory that he did not seem to know how to run, Schindler befriended a handful of Jews who became not only the key to his success during his five years in Kraków but also close, trusted associates. Though much has been made of Oskar's supposed signs of pro-Jewish sentiments well before the war began, there is little concrete evidence to support this. It was the war and the growing horror of the Shoah that forced Oskar Schindler to reevaluate his relationship with the Nazi regime and his Jewish workers.

So when did Oskar Schindler change from being a greedy factory owner into one of the most remarkable Righteous Gentiles in the Holocaust? I think his transformation took place slowly over a long period. Oskar did not begin to use a significant number of Jewish workers until several years after he arrived in Kraków. Jewish workers were much cheaper than Poles and in many ways more dependable. I concluded early in my research that I would have to separate my own image of Schindler as a heavy drinker and womanizer, which I drew partially from Keneally and Spielberg, from the almost god-like figure adored by most Schindler Jews. It became obvious to me as I began to interview Schindler Jews that few of them knew much about Oskar during the war. At the time, most accepted him, at a distance, as a kind, caring man, though it was not until after the war, when they began to compare notes with other Holocaust survivors, that they came to understand everything Oskar Schindler had done and sacrificed to save them. I also decided that I would have to separate the stories of the Schindler Jews who had worked for Oskar in Emalia from those who only knew him during the last eight months of the war in Brünnlitz. Life in this latter factory sub-camp was quite different from the one that Schindler ran in Kraków.

In the end, there was no one, dramatic, transforming moment when Oskar Schindler decided to do everything he could to save his Jewish workers. I think that Keneally and Spielberg found such a moment very useful. I also think they were wrong. One of the most frightening things about the Holocaust is the "ordinariness" of most of the Germans and others in the supporting network of businesses and factories that fed off the SS slave labor pool in the ghettos and concentration camps. In some ways, at least in the Kraków area, Oskar Schindler was not particularly unique in his initial treatment of his Jewish workers. Giving your Jewish workers adequate food and modest protection from SS mistreatment was simply good business and something other factory owners and managers such as Julius Madritsch and Raimund Titsch also did in Kraków.

But Oskar took his care and concern for the well-being of his Jewish workers a step further than Madritsch, Titsch, and others. But the question remains—why? I think that Oskar Schindler was, at heart, a fairly decent human being despite his womanizing and heavy drinking. Over time, I think the growing violence and death that enveloped Kraków's Jews disgusted him and prompted him to do whatever he could to protect his Jewish workers from the SS. This development probably started as good business but evolved into something more humane as the Holocaust became more deadly. I am fairly certain, based on the information Oskar provided Shmuel Springmann and Reszőe Kasztner in Budapest in November 1943, that Schindler was quite knowledgeable about the most deadly aspects of the Final Solution.

In part, the key to understanding Oskar's transformation can be found in his Abwehr contacts. Oskar was a part of many German and Nazi circles in Kraków, and I think he was probably most comfortable with his old friends in Abwehr and the Wehrmacht. I also feel that his continual run-ins with the Gestapo and the SS helped form his own attitudes towards Jews. In other words, helping his Jews became one of the ways Oskar acted out his own disillusionment with the Nazi system.

Dr. Moshe Bejski, a Schindler Jew and one of Oskar's closest postwar friends, has a pragmatic and unromantic view of Schindler. He told me that, for him, the defining measure of Schindler's commitment to doing everything possible to save his Jewish workers came in the fall of 1944, when Oskar chose to risk everything to move his armaments factory to Brünnlitz. Oskar could easily have closed his Kraków operations and retreated westward with the profits he had already made. Instead, he chose to risk his life and his money to save as many Jews as he could. Though there is no doubt in my mind that Oskar had vague dreams of transforming his Brünnlitz factory into a postwar economic powerhouse, I do not see that as the prime motive for his move. At this point in the war and in his life, I think Oskar Schindler was absolutely determined to do everything he could to save as many Jews as he could regardless of the cost, either personal or financial. During the last two years of the war, he had undergone a dramatic moral transformation, and, in many ways, he came more and more to associate himself with his Jews than with other Germans.

It could be argued here, and Emilie at one point says this, that Oskar's growing closeness with his Jews was a self-protective measure adopted to insure his post-war safety. Oskar was well aware that the Allies could possibly prosecute him as a Nazi Party member who used Jewish slave labor during the war. Yet there was something beyond just mere self-protection that motivated Oskar to go to such extremes to save his growing number of Jewish workers. I am hesitant to get into the dangerous realm of pop psychology, but I think that as the war went on, and the Nazi system, wrapped as it was in its self-serving, irrational propaganda and racial ideology, he found moral comfort in his association with his Jewish workers, who clung to their ancient faith and cultural traditions in the midst of absolute horror.

By the end of the war, Oskar became so close to his Jewish workers that it became difficult for outsiders, particularly in Germany, to separate Oskar from his Schindler Jews. In some ways, his efforts to help Jews during the war created a unique symbiosis between himself and his Jewish workers, and in many ways they became one. The only difference is that after the war, the Schindler Jews traded places with Oskar, now himself part of a dispossessed ethnic minority, and collectively became his protector and benefactor. I am not certain, though, that Oskar fully appreciated the richness of these relationships, because he was constantly using his Jewish friends to try to regain his professional footing. I have to admit that I have been dismayed by Schindler's sense of opportunism, particularly when it came to his efforts to gain economic benefit from his friendships with his Jewish friends after the war. But it should be remembered that whenever he did this, it was with the active encouragement of his numerous Jewish acquaintances, whether they be Schindler Jews or not, remained in awe of what he had done for Jews during the Holocaust. Moreover, I think that had Oskar been able successfully to rebuild his life after the war, he would have developed a more mature, less opportunistic relationship with his Schindler Jews. I think we see a hint of the true Oskar Schindler in the final years of his life, when, with a steady income and more stable life, he was able to give himself fully to something that he came to love most deeply—Israel. His love of Israel was a mere reflection of the close relationship that he had developed after the war with his many Jewish friends throughout the world. These friendships were buffered by equally close ties with many Germans who shared Oskar's passion for Israel and a closer German-Jewish relationship.

So how should history judge Oskar Schindler? From my own perspective, I look to the Schindler Jews for guidance, who knew and observed Oskar Schindler with all his virtues, strengths, and flaws. As I researched and wrote this book, I had the opportunity to interview and correspond with many Schindler Jews. With one or two exceptions, their feelings towards Oskar are pragmatically romantic. To a person, they will tell you that if it had not been for Oskar Schindler, they and their families would not be here today. Most of them were well aware of Oskar's human flaws but put these moral qualms aside when it came to judging him. They felt he deserved all the accolades that the modern world has to offer. The only negative in all this was the guilt that most of them expressed about not having done more to help their beloved Oskar after the war. I have seen many Schindler Jews weep when it came to this issue.

Finally, I go back to a conversation that I had with Dr. Mordecai Paldiel, the head of the Righteous Among the Nations Department at Yad Vashem. Other than Dr. Moshe Bejski, there has been no other person in Israel more intimately involved in investigating the thousands of nominations for Righteous Gentile status over the past few decades. From Dr. Paldiel's perspective, there was no person more deserving of Righteous Gentile status than Oskar Schindler, including Raoul Wallenberg. I agree. I think that Oskar Schindler's heroism is unique because of the fact that what he did, both in Kraków and Brünnlitz, took place in the midst of the most horrible killing center in modern history. Moreover, while his most dramatic efforts took place during the last year of the war, Oskar Schindler's efforts to help and later save Jews was a stance that evolved over three or four years.

Yes, Oskar Schindler was a flawed human being. But he also personally risked his fortune and his life to save almost 1,100 people. Beyond this, he provided hundreds of other Jews who worked for him at Emalia with a quality of life that better enabled many of them to survive the Holocaust. Finally, Oskar Schindler should also be remembered for his willingness to supply Jewish aid organizations with information about the Final Solution and life in the General Government and his efforts to help these organizations bring money, food, and medicine into Kraków to help sustain Jewish life in the Płaszów concentration camp. Such unique acts of humanity were rare during the Holocaust.

SS Ranks *(Based on US Army Equivalents)*

Reichsführer-SS	General of the Army
SS-Oberstgruppenführer	General
SS-Obergruppenführer	Lt. General
SS-Gruppenführer	Major General
SS-Brigadeführer	Brigadier General
SS-Oberführer	Senior Colonel
SS-Standartenführer	Colonel
SS-Obersturmbannführer	Lt. Colonel
SS-Sturmbannführer	Major
SS-Hauptsturmführer	Captain
SS-Obersturmführer	First Lieutenant
SS-Untersturmführer	Second Lieutenant
SS-Sturmscharführer	Sergeant Major
SS-Hauptscharführer	Master Sergeant
SS-Oberscharführer	Technical Sergeant
SS-Scharführer	Staff Sergeant
SS-Unterscharführer	Sergeant
SS-Rottenführer	Corporal
SS-Sturmmann	Corporal
SS-Oberschütze	Private First Class
SS-Schütze	Private

SOURCE: Heinz Höhne, *The Order of the Death's Head: The Story of Hitler's SS* (New York: Ballantine Books, 1971, 744.

German Army Ranks *(Based on U.S. Army Equivalents)*

Generalfeldmarschall	General of the Army
Generaloberst	General
General	Lt. General
Generalleutnant	Major General
Generalmajor	Brigadier General
Oberst	Colonel
Oberstleutnant	Lt. Colonel
Major	Major
Hauptmann	Captain
Oberleutnant	First Lieutenant
Leutnant	Second Lieutenant
Stabsfeldwebel	Master Sergeant
Oberfeldwebel	Technical Sergeant
Feldwebel	Staff Sergeant
Unterfeldwebel	Sergeant
Unteroffizier	Corporal
Gefreiter	Private First Class
Obersoldat	No U.S. Army equivalent
Soldat	Private

SOURCE: U.S. War Department, *Handbook on German Military Forces* (Baton Rouge: Louisiana State University press, 1990), 6–7.

NOTES

Chapter 1

1. Theodore D. (Ted) Feder, interview by the author, New York, April 24, 1997.

2. Österreichisches Patentamt Büro, Vienna, "Report on Oskar Schindler," December 12, 1991, Yad Vashem, Department of the Righteous, M 31/20, 1–2; Sčítání lidu 1930 Volkszählung 1930 (1930 Census), Zwittau, Odbočka zpravodajské ústředny při policejním ředitelství Praha (Branch Office of the Intelligence Headquarters of the Police Directorate in Prague), S 54/1, 202-48-159, Státní Ústřední Archiv v Praze, 1–2 (hereafter referred to as OZU).

3. Letter from Radoslav Fikejz to David Crowe, March 27, 2000. In the midst of the park is a building that now houses the office of the mayor. It was built by a German industrialist, Robert Langer, in 1892. Emilie Schindler, with Erika Rosenberg, *Where Light and Shadow Meet*, trans. Dolores M. Koch (New York: W. W. Norton & Company, 1997), 26.

4. "Oskar Schindler, Retter und Lebemann." ZDF Film (1994); Ackermann Gemeinde Hessen, *Zur Erinnerung an Oskar Schindler dem unvergeßlichen Lebensretter 1200 verfolgter Juden: Dokumentation der Gedenkstunde zum 10. Todestag am 14. Oktober 1984 in Frankfurt am Main* (Frankfurt am Main: Ackermann-Gemeinde, 1985), 18; Thomas Keneally, *Schindler's List* (New York: Touchstone Books, 1992), 32–33.

5. Radoslav Fikejz, *Oskar Schindler (1908–1974)* (Svitavy: Městské muzeum a galerie Svitavy, 1998), 18; Jana Šmídová, "Oskar Schindler—anděl nebo gauner? (Oskar Schindler: Angel or Crook?), *Lidové noviny,* February 8, 1994, 9; Oskar Schindler, *Daten meines Lebensweges,* July 13, 1966, 1, Bundesarchiv (Koblenz), Nachlaß Oskar Schindler, 1908–1974, Bestand N 1493, No. 1, Band 1 (hereafter referred to as Oskar Schindler, BA(K)).

6. Schindler, *Light and Shadow,* 129.

7. Ibid., 7, 10–11; Fikejz, *Oskar Schindler,* 19.

8. Schindler, *Light and Shadow,* 3–7.

9. Ibid., 8–9.

10. Ibid., 9.

11. Ibid.

12. Ibid., 23–26; Christoph Stopka, "Ich bin Frau Schindler," *Bunte* (1994):24.

13. Schindler, *Light and Shadow,* 26–27; Stopka, "Frau Schindler," 24.

14. Ernst Tragatsch, "Eine Erinnerung: Oskar Schindler," *Motorrad*, no. 12 (1964):1; Fikejz, *Oskar Schindler*, 19.

15. Tragatsch, "Eine Erinnerung," 1.

16. "Schindler Protokol," 23 July, 1938, Zpravodajská ústředna při policejním ředitelství Praha, 200-299-50, Státní Ústřední Archiv v Praze, 1 (hereafter referred to as "Schindler Protokol," ZUP 200). This thirteen-page document is Oskar Schindler's official interrogation statement (in German and Czech) to the Czech secret police about his life and Abwehr activities. The page numbers cited are those used in this archival collection, which also includes the secret police report on Leo Pruscha and Dr. Sobotka's report on Schindler and Pruscha. I have chosen to use these handwritten archival numbers so that future researchers can easily locate them. Each report also contains separate typed numbers that are referenced only to the individual reports. "Dr. Sobotka Report: Schindler Oskar and Pruscha Leo—Suspected Crime Against Paragraph 6, No. 2, of the Law for the Protection of the Republic," ZUP 200, Policajní ředitelství v Brně (Police Directorate in Brno), No. 3382/2/38, 28 July, 1938, Státní Ústřední Archiv v Praze, 40–41 (hereafter referred to as "Sobotka Report," ZUP 200). The handwritten numbers of pages 29–41 correspond to the typed page numbers of 1 through 13; "Oskar Schindler to Fritz Lang," July 20, 1951, BA (K), N 1493, 5/28, 4 (hereafter referred to as "Schindler to Lang," July 20, 1952, BA(K)).

17. "Schindler Protokol," ZUP 200, 1; Schindler, *Light and Shadow*, 27; in the notes of their interview with Schindler in Paris in 1964, Martin Gosch and Howard Koch stated that Schindler told them that he received a DM 100,000 dowry from Emilie's father. Given that they were still living in Czechoslovakia at the time, it was probably 100,000 Czech crowns, as Emilie stated in her memoirs. Martin A. Gosch and Howard Koch, "Interview with Oskar Schindler," November 18, 1964, Paris, France, in the Delbert Mann Papers, Special Collections Library, Vanderbilt University, 7-A, 11.

18. "Schindler to Lang," July 20, 1951, BA(K), 3.

19. MVP, Č, 193/66-K, March 9, 1966, 1; Dr. Mečislav Borak, "Zatykac na Oskara Schindlera," Česka televize Ostrava, 1999; Fikejz, *Oskar Schindler*, 20, 27.

20. Jitka Gruntová, *Oskar Schindler: Legenda a Fakta* (Brno: Barrister & Principle, 1997), 14 n. 13.

21. "Schindler Protokol," ZUP 200, 1.

22. Schindler, *Light and Shadow*, 27–28.

23. "Edith Schlegl to David M. Crowe," November 17, 1999; "Edith Schlegl to David M. Crowe," September 26, 2000. See the Czech secret police comments on Oskar's affair and its impact on his relationship with Emilie in "Sobotka Report," ZUP 200, 34; Matthias Kessler, *Ich muß doch meinen Vater lieben, oder?: Die Lebensgeschichte von Monika Göth, Tochter des KZ-Kommandanten aus 'Schindlers Liste'* (Frankfurt am Main: Eichborn, 2002), 224.

24. "Tina Staehr to David Crowe (report of a conversation with Edith Schlegl)," October 23, 2000; Gerhard Rempel, *Hitler's Children: The Hitler Youth and the SS* (Chapel Hill: University of North Carolina Press, 1989), 233, 248–250.

25. "Schlegl to Crowe," November 17, 1999; Chris Staehr and Tina Staehr, interview by the author, Stuttgart, Germany, October 31, 2003.

26. Schindler, *Light and Shadow*, 115.

27. Keneally, *Schindler's List*, 37.

28. *Vollmacht* (Power of Attorney), *Lastenausgleichsarchiv* (Lastenausgleich Archive), Bayreuth, 306 2230 D (Oskar Schindler). Oskar Schindler's extensive *Lastenausgleich* files are hereafter referred to as LAG (OS). This file states that soon after Fanny's death, Elfriede, by then Elfriede Tutsch, died at University Hospital in Munich. Given that she later bore three children, this account is inaccurate.

29. "Martin Gosch interview with Oskar Schindler," November 18, 1964, Paris, France, Delbert Mann Papers, Special Collection Library at Vanderbilt University, 2 (hereafter re-

---

ferred to as "Gosch-Schindler Interview," November 18, 1964, Delbert Mann Papers, Vanderbilt University).

30. "Gosch-Schindler Interview," November 18, 1964, Delbert Mann Papers, Vanderbilt University, 3–4.

31. Fikejz, *Oskar Schindler,* 21–22.

32. "Schindler to Lang," 1; Dieter Trautwein and Ursula Trautwein, interviews by the author, Frankfurt, Germany, May 25, 1999, and January 18, 2000.

33. Joseph Rothschild, *East Central Europe Between the Two World Wars,* vol. IX, *A History of East Central Europe* (Washington: University of Washington Press, 1990), 76–78; Victor S. Mamatey, "The Establishment of the Republic," in Victor S. Mamatey and Radomír Luža, eds., *A History of the Czechoslovak Republic, 1918–1948* (Princeton: Princeton University Press, 1973), 24–27.

34. Václav L. Beneš, "Czechoslovakia Democracy and Its Problems, 1918–1920," in Mamatey and Luža, *History,* 39; Herman Kopecek, *"Zusammenarbeit* and *Spoluprace:* Sudeten German–Czech Cooperation in Interwar Czechoslovakia," in Nancy M. Wingfield, ed., *Czech-Sudeten German Relations,* Special Topic Issue, *Nationalities Papers* 24, no. 1 (March 1996):63; J. W. Brügel, "Die Aussiedlung der Deutschen aus der Tschechoslowakei," *Vierteljahrshefte für Zeitgeschichte* 8 (April 1960):134–135; Radomír Luža, *The Transfer of the Sudeten Germans: A Study of Czech-German Relations, 1933–1962* (New York: New York University Press, 1964), 1, 2 n. 6, 3 n. 9, 30.

35. Kopecek, *"Zusammenarbeit* and *Spoluprace,"* 63–65.

36. Ibid., 66, 70; J. W. Bruegel, "The Germans in Pre-War Czechoslovakia," in Mamatey and Luža, *History,* 184; Rothschild, *East Central Europe,* 110–111, 116–117.

37. Kopecek, *"Zusammenarbeit* and *Spoluprace,"* 63–64, 70–72; Bruegel, "Germans in Pre-War Czechoslovakia," 173–175; Luža, *Transfer,* 30.

38. Rothschild, *East Central Europe,* 123–124.

39. Ibid., 110, 116.

40. Ibid.; Bruegel, "Germans in Pre-War Czechoslovakia," 182; Kopecek, *"Zusammenarbeit* and *Spoluprace,"* 72–73.

41. Ronald M. Smelser, *The Sudeten Problem, 1933–1938: Volksturmpolitik and the Formation of Nazi Foreign Policy* (Middletown, Conn.: Wesleyan University Press, 1975), 50, 52–53, 270 n. 25; Malbone W. Graham, *New Governments of Central Europe* (New York: Henry Holt and Company, 1926), 61 n. 30, 329; Victor S. Mamatey, "The Development of Czechoslovak Democracy, 1920–1938," in Mamatey and Luža, *History,* 113; Volker Zimmermann, *Die Sudetendeutschen im NS-Staat: Politik und Stimmung der Bevölkerung im Reichsgau Sudetenland (1938–1945)* (Essen: Klartext Verlag, 1999), 39.

42. Luža, *Transfer,* 68 n. 25, 69–71; Kopecek, *"Zusammenarbeit* and *Spoluprace,"* 72; on January 1, 1933, the German Nazi Party said that it had only fifty German party members in Czechoslovakia; Donald M. McKale, *The Swastika Outside of Germany* (Kent, Ohio: Kent State University Press, 1977), 41; Mamatey, "Czechoslovak Democracy," 148.

43. McKale, *Swastika,* 41, 45, 55–56. The VDA had been established in 1881 to further German culture and education among ethnic Germans living outside Germany. In 1933, it supported 9,200 German schools abroad. Luža, *Transfer,* 26 n. 8; Smelser, *The Sudeten Problem,* 71–72; Zimmermann, *Die Sudetendeutschen im NS-Staat,* 49; Dr. Reinhard Barth, "Volk League for Germandom Abroad," in Christian Zentner and Friedemann Bedürftig, eds., *The Encyclopedia of the Third Reich* (New York: Da Capo Press, 1997), 1003; Gerhard L. Weinberg, *The Foreign Policy of Hitler's Germany: Diplomatic Revolution in Europe, 1933–1936* (Chicago: University of Chicago press, 1970), 109.

44. Smelser, *The Sudeten Problem,* 105–112; Luža, *Transfer,* 71–75; Rothschild, *East Central Europe,* 127–128; Weinberg, *Foreign Policy, 1933–1936,* 110, 225; McKale, *Swastika Outside Germany,* 56.

45. Smelser, *The Sudeten Problem*, 101–102; Luža, *Transfer*, 76; Elizabeth Wiskemann, *Czechs and Germans: A Study of the Struggle in the Historic Provinces of Bohemia and Moravia* (London: Oxford University Press, 1938), 205–206.

46. Wiskemann, *Czechs and Germans*, 204–205, 227; Luža, *Transfer*, 76.

47. Luža, *Transfer*, 77.

48. Ibid., 77–79; Rothschild, *East Central Europe*, 128.

49. Mamatey, "Czechoslovak Democracy," 153–154; Rothschild, *East Central Europe*, 96, 128; James Ramon Felak, *At the Price of the Republic: Hlinka's Slovak People's Party, 1929–1938* (Pittsburgh: University of Pittsburgh Press, 1994), 134–135, 139–140, 209–210; David Kelly, *The Czech Fascist Movement, 1922–1942* (Boulder/New York: East European Monographs and Columbia University Press, 1995), 120, 123.

50. Luža, *Transfer*, 79–80; Rothschild, *East Central Europe*, 116, 126–128; Kopecek, *"Zusammenarbeit* and *Spoluprace,"* 72–73.

51. Mamatey, "Czechoslovak Democracy," 154–156; Rothschild, *East Central Europe*, 130–131.

52. Weinberg, *Foreign Policy*, 225, 312.

53. Canaris became a rear admiral in 1935 and a full admiral in early 1940. Zimmermann, *Die Sudetendeutschen im NS-Staat*, 50 n. 82; Smelser, *Sudeten Problem*, 184–185.

54. Smelser, *Sudeten Problem*, 168–169; Heinz Höhne, *Canaris*, trans. J. Maxwell Brownjohn (New York: Doubleday, 1979), 163.

55. Smelser, *The Sudeten Problem*, 169–172.

56. Wiskemann, *Czechs and Germans*, "Distribution of Sudeten German Population in Bohemia and Moravia-Silesia," map at end of book; Fikejz, *Oskar Schindler*, 22; Gruntová, *Oskar Schindler*, 9; "Dr. Gerlach to the District Court of the NSDAP," Zwittau, June 26, 1939, in NSDAP-spojovací ústedna pŕi úřadu řiššého protektora, 123-592-2 (fólie 24), Státni Ústřední archiv v Praze, 1 page.

57. Schindler, *Light and Shadow*, 30; Fikezj, *Oskar Schindler*, 25; Schindler to Lang, 4; "Schindler Protokol," ZUP 200, 2.

58. "Schindler Protokol," ZUP 200, 2; "Report on Ilse Pelikánová," July 28, 1938, Státni zastupitelstvíbv Olomouc, Tkxvi 1733/38, Zemský archiv Opava pobočka Olomouc, 1 page; Dr. Jitka Gruntová, "Schindlerův Seznam Tentokrát Jinak (Schindler's List This Time in a Different Light)," *Rovnost*, March 8, 1995, 9.

59. Oskar Schindler, *"Daten meines Lebensweges,"* July 13, 1966, OS Bundesarchiv, N 1493, No. 1/ Band 1, 1; Höhne, *Canaris*, 287–288.

60. Patrick McGilligan, *Fritz Lang: The Nature of the Beast* (New York: St. Martin's Press, 1997), 170, 174–177. Lang fled Germany in the spring of 1933 after a meeting with Hitler's Reich Minister for Volk Enlightenment and Propaganda, Joseph Goebbels. The Reich Minister, who had just banned Lang's *Das Testament des Dr. Mabuse*, apologized for this and told Lang that Hitler was one of his greatest admirers. He then offered Lang, who was regarded as Germany's best film maker, a job as head of an agency that would oversee film production in the Third Reich. The Führer, Goebbels assured Lang, felt he would make great films for the Reich. Goebbels dismissed Lang's confession that he had Jewish ancestors and told him that he could become an "Honorary Aryan." It was the Nazis, Goebbels explained, who decided who was a Jew. Within hours after his meeting with Goebbels, Lang left Germany for Paris, never to return. "Schindler to Lang," July 20, 1951, BA(K), 3–4.

61. "Schindler to Lang," July 20, 1951, BA(K), 4; "Schindler Protokol," ZUP 200, 2; Keneally, *Schindler's List*, 39.

62. "Sobotka Report," ZUP 200, 34–35, 39. The statement in Czech about Schindler's spying was "nutno označiti Schindlera za vyzvěda če velkého formátu a typu zvláště nebezpečného"; "Alois Polanski Protokol," November 2, 1945. Ředitelství Národní bezpečnosti v Mor. Ostravě. Státně bezpečnostní oddělení. Kčj.: II/I 6314/1945, Státni Ústřední Archiv v Praze, 4 (hereafter referred to as "Polanski Protokol," MV MO).

63. "Schindler to Lang," July 20, 1951, BA(K), 4; "Sobotka Report," ZUP 200, 34–35. Dr. Sobotka's statement about Schindler in Czech was "je člověk krajně lehkomyslný a nevalného charakteru, jehož jedinou snahou je lehce a bez práce získati hodně penez."

64. Robin O'Neil, "The Man from Svitavy: The Enigma of Oskar Schindler" (unpublished manuscript, 1994), 45; Schindler, *Light and Shadow,* 30–31; Höhne, *Canaris,* 295.

65. Zimmermann, *Die Sudetendeutschen im NS-Staat,* 50–51; Höhne, *Canaris,* 291; Smelser, *The Sudeten Problem,* 184–185.

66. Smelser, *The Sudeten Problem,* 185; Höhne, *Canaris,* 289.

67. According to Heinz Höhne, Groscurth was a deeply religious Christian who hated Nazism. Höhne, *Canaris,* 189–190.

68. *"Bericht Eugen Sliva,"* Geheime Staatspolizei, Staatspolizeistelle Bruenn, Maerisch Ostrau, May 8, 1940, Moravský zemsky archiv Brno, sign, 100-162-20, III 85/40g-Eugen Sliwa, 1.

69. Dr. Mečislav Borak, "Zatykac na Oskara Schindlera," Česka televize Ostrava, 1999; "Schindler Protokol," ZUP 200, 4. Kreuziger's warning to Schindler in German was "ausserdem sehr ans Herz jedes Angebot zur Mitarbeit von Seiten der Abteilung A II, die sich mit rein politischen Sachen, so wie Propaganda Flugblätter usw. beschäftigt, abzulehnen um mich nicht zu zersplittern"; "Sobotka Report," ZUP 200, 30; in 1939, Abwehr became Amt Ausland/A, or the Abwehr Foreign Office. Höhne, *Canaris,* 287–288.

70. Weinberg, *Foreign Policy,* 312–320; Gerhard L. Weinberg, *The Foreign Policy of Hitler's Germany: Starting World War II, 1937–1939* (Chicago: University of Chicago Press, 1980), 316–317.

71. Smelser, *The Sudeten Problem,* 196–206.

72. Weinberg, *Foreign Policy,* 318–319; Weinberg, *Foreign Policy, 1937–1939,* 373; Smelser, *The Sudeten Problem,* 201–207.

73. Smelser, *The Sudeten Problem,* 205–207, 217; Weinberg, *Foreign Policy, 1937–1939,* 334; Unsigned Report with Enclosures: "Preliminary Report on My Conversations with Konrad Henlein, the Leader of the Sudeten German Party, and Karl Hermann Frank," March 28, 1938, No. 107, *Documents on German Foreign Policy, 1918–1945,* Series D (1937–1945), vol. 2, *Germany and Czechoslovakia, 1937–1938* (Washington, D.C.: United States Government Printing Office, 1949), 197–198. Though this memorandum is unsigned, it bears the initials of Hans Georg von Mackensen, a state secretary in the German Foreign Office (hereafter referred to DGFP, D, II).

74. "Memorandum of the Eight Demands Made by Konrad Henlein at the Sudeten German Party Congress at Karlsbad," April 24, 1938, No. 135, DGFP, D, II, 242; Weinberg, *Foreign Policy, 1937–1939,* 337–339.

75. Weinberg, *Foreign Policy, 1937–1939,* 357, 363, 370–371. The complete draft of the May 20 directive and Keitel's cover letter can be found as No. 175, in DGFP, D, II, 299–303.

76. Weinberg, *Foreign Policy, 1933–1936,* 224, 370; Weinberg, *Foreign Policy, 1937–1939,* 32–33; "Directive for Operation 'Green' from the Führer to the Commanders in Chief, with Covering Letter from the Chief of Supreme Headquarters, the Wehrmacht (Keitel)." May 30, 1938, No. 221, DGFP, D, II, 358.

77. Höhne, *Canaris,* 293–294.

78. Ibid., 294–295.

79. "Pruscha Protocol," ZUP 200, 17.

80. Ibid.; "Sobotka Report," ZUP 200, 39–40; "Ladislav Novak Protokol," July 27, 1938, ZUP 200, Státní Ústřední Archiv v Praze, 1 (hereafter referred to as "Novak Protokol," ZUP 200).

81. "Schindler Protokol," ZUP 200, 4–5, 8.

82. "Sobotka Report," ZUP 200, 30.

83. "Schindler Protokol," ZUP 200, 4–6; "Sobotka Report," ZUP 200, 30–31: Höhne, *Canaris,* 295.

84. Felak, *At the Price of the Republic,* 184, 194–195, 204; Smelser, *The Sudeten Problem,* 188–189.

85. "Schindler Protokol," ZUP 200, 6–7; "Sobotka Report," ZUP 200, 30–31.

86. "Schindler Protokol," ZUP 200, 7.

87. Ibid., 7–8.

88. Ibid., 8; "Pruscha Protokol," ZUP 200, 18.

89. "Schindler Protokol," ZUP 200, 8; "Pruscha Protokol," ZUP 200, 18.

90. "Pruscha Protokol," ZUP 200, 18–19; "Schindler Protokol," ZUP 200, 8–9.

91. "Pruscha Protokol," ZUP 200, 19; "Schindler and Pruscha Report," ZUP 200, 91.

92. "Pruscha Protokol," ZUP 200, 19–20; "Schindler Protokol," ZUP 200, 9.

93. "Schindler Protokol," ZUP 200, 9; "Pruscha Protokol," ZUP 200, 20.

94. "Schindler Protokol," ZUP 200, 9; "Pruscha Protokol," ZUP 200, 20–21; No. 221, DGFP, D, II, 360.

95. "Pruscha Protokol," ZUP 200, 21; Höhne, *Canaris,* 293.

96. "Pruscha Protokol," ZUP 200, 21.

97. Ibid., 21; "Directive for Operation 'Green' from the Führer to the Commander in Chief, with Covering Letter from the Chief of the Supreme Headquarters, the Wehrmacht (Keitel)," No. 221 (Operation Green), Berlin, May 30, 1938, DGFP, D, II, 359–360.

98. Matthew Cooper, *The German Army, 1933–1945* (Lanham, Md: Scaborough House Publishers, 1990), 102; Luža, *Transfer of the Sudeten Germans,* 147–148; J. E. Kaufmann and Robert M. Jurga, *Fortress Europe: European Fortifications of World War II,* translations by H. W. Kaufmann (Conshohocken, Pa.: Combined Publishing, 1999), 240, 242–245, 252; Höhne, *Canaris,* 311.

99. Luža, *Transfer of the Sudeten Germans,* 149; Weinberg, *Foreign Policy, 1937–1939,* 362–363, 368 n. 213, 370; Kaufmann and Jurga, *Fortress Europe,* 252.

100. "Pruscha Protokol," ZUP 200, 21–22.

101. Ibid., 22; Weinberg, *Foreign Policy, 1937–1939,* 370, n. 220; No. 221 (Operation Green), DGFP, D, II, 360–361.

102. "Schindler Protokol," ZUP 200, 10; "Pruscha Protokol," ZUP 200, 22.

103. "Pruscha Protokol," ZUP 200, 22–23.

104. Ibid., 11; "Pruscha Protokol," ZUP 200, 23.

105. "Schindler Protokol," ZUP 200, 11; "Pruscha Protokol," ZUP 200, 23.

106. "Schindler Protokol," ZUP 200, 11; "Pruscha Protokol," 23–24.

107. "Schindler Protokol," ZUP 200, 11–12.

108. "Pruscha Protokol," ZUP 200, 24.

109. "Ladislav Novak Protokol," July 27, 1938, ZUP 200, 1 page; "Pruscha Protokol," ZUP 200, 24–26; "Schindler and Pruscha Report," ZUP 200, 38.

110. "Schindler Protocol," ZUP 200, 12; "Pruscha Protokol," ZUP 200, 25.

111. "Pruscha Protokol," ZUP 200, 25–26; "Schindler Protokol," ZUP 200, 12–13.

112. "Pruscha Protokol," ZUP 200, 26; "Schindler Protokol," 13.

113. "Schindler Protokol," ZUP 200, 14.

114. "Schindler and Pruscha Report," ZUP 200, 90; Robin O'Neil, "An Analysis of the Actions of Oskar Schindler Within the Context of the Holocaust in German Occupied Poland and Czechoslovakia" (master's thesis, University College, London, 1996), 19.

115. "Schindler, Oskar," April 13, 1966, Archiv Ministerstva vnitra (Prague), Krajská Správa Ministerstva vnitra, Č.j. Sv-90/01-66, 2 (hereafter referred to as Archiv MV); "Oskar Schindler," March 9, 1966, Archiv MV, Ministervo Spravedlinosti v Praze, Č. 193/66-K, 1–2).

116. Fikejz, *Oskar Schindler,* 29; "Agreement Reached on September 29, 1938, between Germany, the United Kingdom, France, and Italy," September 29, 1938, No. 675, DGFP, D, II, 1015.

117. Trautwein and Trautwein, interview, Frankfurt, Germany, May 25, 1999.

118. Schindler, *Light and Shadow,* 33; Stanislav Motl, "Schindlerův Rok, *Reflex* 12 (1994):13; O'Neil, "An Analysis of the Actions of Oskar Schindler," 19.

119. Cooper, *The German Army,* 95–99; Weinberg, *Foreign Policy, 1937–1945,* 384–386.

120. Keith Eubank, "Munich," in Mamatey and Luža, *History,* 243–244; Weinberg, *Foreign Policy, 1937–1939,* 374–377, 390–391; Smelser, *The Sudeten Problem,* 234–238; Zimmermann, *Die Sudetendeutschen im NS-Staat,* 62.

121. Smelser, *The Sudeten Problem,* 237–240; "Memorandum by an Official of Political Division IV (Altenburg)," September 13, 1938, DGFP, D, II, 751 n. 95.

122. "Unsigned Foreign Ministry Minute," September 13, 1938, No. 469, DGFP, D, II, 754; "Letter from the Leader of the Sudeten German Party (Henlein) to the Führer," September 15, 1938, No. 489, DGFP, D, II, 801; "Text of the Joint Communication by the British and French Governments to the President of Czechoslovakia," September 19, 1938, No. 523, DGFP, D, II, 831–832.

123. Weinberg, *Foreign Policy, 1937–1939,* 433–434; Peter Hoffmann, *The History of the German Resistance, 1933–1945,* 3d ed., trans. Richard Barry (Montreal: McGill-Queen's University Press, 1996), 69–96; Cooper, *The German Army,* 95–103.

124. Klemens von Klemperer, *German Resistance Against Hitler: The Search for Allies Abroad, 1938–1945* (Oxford: Clarendon Press, 1994), 23–25; Höhne, *Canaris,* 258–260, 275–276, 303–311; for more on Oster's 1938 plot to kill Hitler, see Terry Parssinen, *The Oster Conspiracy of 1938: The Unknown Story of the Military Plot to Kill Hitler and Avert World War II* (New York: HarperCollins, 2003).

125. Luža, *Transfer of the Sudeten Germans,* 142–144; Weinberg, *Foreign Policy of Hitler's Germany,* 434, 446–453.

126. Eubank, "Munich," 248–250; "Agreement Signed at Munich Between Germany, the United Kingdom, France, and Italy," September 29, 1938, No. 675, DGFP, D, II, 1014–1015.

Chapter 2

1. Alois Polanski Protokol, November 2, 1945, V Mor. Ostravé.-Stáněbezpečnostní oddělení-Kčj.: II/1/1945, Archiv Ministerstva Vnitra (Prague), 8 (hereafter referred to as Polansky Protokol, MV); "Report on Oskar Schindler," April 13, 1966, Krajská Správa Ministerstva Vnitra, Č.j. Sc-90/01-66, 1. This report was prepared by Major Karel Stedry for the Deputy Minister of the Interior, Comrade Colonel Klima; Thomas Keneally, *Schindler's List* (New York: Simon & Schuster, 1992), 13; E.W.W. Fowler, *Nazi Regalia* (Secaucus, N.J.: Chartwell Books, 1992), 46–48; Jay W. Baird, *To Die for Germany: Heroes in the Nazi Pantheon* (Bloomington: Indiana University Press, 1990), 49–50, 65; "Testimony of Julius Wiener before Messrs. Shatkai and Laudau, in the Presence of Mr. Alkalai," Jerusalem, August 6, 1953 (in Hebrew). Yad Vashem Archives, M 31/30, RGD, 423; John Weitz, *Hitler's Banker: Hjalmar Horace Greeley Schacht* (Boston: Little, Brown and Company, 1997), 214.

2. "Golden Party Badge," http://www.geocities.com/goldpartypin/ahaward.html., 1–2.

3. "Oskar Schindler to Fritz Lang," July 20, 1951, 4, Bundesarchiv (Koblenz), Nachlaß Oskar Schindler, 1908–1974, Bestand N 1493, Band 23; Dietrich Orlow, *The History of the Nazi Party, 1933–1945* (Pittsburgh: University of Pittsburgh Press, 1973), 205; "Oskar Schindler's Nazi Party Application," NSDAP-Mitgliederkartei, Berlin Documentation Center, Bundesarchiv (Berlin), 1–2.

4. "Dr. Gerlich an das Kreisgericht der NSDAP," June 26, 1939, Reg. 4746/39 (Oskar Schindler), NSDAP-spojovací ústředna při úřadu říšského protektora, 123-592-2 (fólie 24), 1 page.

5. "Agreement Reached on September 29, 1938, Between Germany, the United Kingdom, France, and Italy," No. 675, *Documents on German Foreign Policy, 1918–1945*, Series D (1937–1945), vol. 2, *Germany and Czechoslovakia, 1937–1938* (Washington: United States Government Printing Office, 1949), 1014-1015; Theodor Prochazka, "The Second Republic, 1938–1939," in Victor S. Mamatey and Radomír Luža, eds. *A History of the Czechoslovak Republic, 1918–1948* (Princeton: Princeton University Press, 1973), 256.

6. Volker Zimmermann, *Die Sudetendeutschen im NS-Staat: Politik und Stimmung der Bevölkerung im Reichsgau Sudetenland (1938–1945)* (Essen: Klartext, 1999), 82–87, 102–108, 119–125; Radomír Luža, *The Transfer of the Sudeten Germans: A Study of Czech-German Relations, 1933–1962* (New York: New York University Press, 1964), 157–159; Prochazka, "The Second Republic, 1938–1939," 261; Franz Neumann, *Behemoth: The Structure and Practice of National Socialism, 1933–1944* (New York: Harper and Row, 1944), 561–562.

7. Ralf Gebel, *'Heim ins Reich!': Konrad Henlein und der Reichsgau Sudetenland (1938–1945)* (Munich: R. Oldenbourg, 2000), 118; Zimmermann, *Die Sudetendeutschen im NS-Staat*, 210–211; letter from Ronald Smelser to David M. Crowe, July 7, 2000, 1 page; Ronald M. Smelser, "The Expulsion of the Sudeten Germans, 1945–1952," *Czech-Sudeten German Relations*, Special Topic Issue, *Nationalities Papers* 24, no. 1 (March 1996):83.

8. Dr. Mečislav Borak, "Zatykac na Oskara Schindlera," Ceska televize Ostrava (1999).

9. Gerhard L. Weinberg, *The Foreign Policy of Hitler's Germany: Starting World War II, 1937–1939* (Chicago: The University of Chicago Press, 1980), 467; Prochazka, "The Second Republic," 265; Hans Höhne, *Canaris*, trans. J. Maxwell Brownjohn (New York: Doubleday & Company, 1979), 323–324.

10. Prochazka, "The Second Republic," 256–258.

11. Ibid., 263, 266; Weinberg, *Foreign Policy, 1937–1939*, 468.

12. Jörg K. Hoensch, "The Slovak Republic, 1939–1945," in Mamatey and Luža, *History*, 271–272; James Ramon Felak, *"At the Price of the Republic": Hlinka's Slovak People's Party, 1929–1938* (Pittsburgh: University of Pittsburgh Press, 1994), 202–208.

13. Hoensch, "The Slovak Republic," 272.

14. Ibid., 273–274; Luža, *Transfer*, 173–174.

15. Hoensch, "The Slovak Republic," 274–275; Luža, *Transfer*, 174.

16. Luža, *Transfer*, 176–177; Hoensch, "The Slovak Republic," 275.

17. Hoensch, "The Slovak Republic," 274–276, 278, 290.

18. Weinberg, *Foreign Policy, 1937–1939*, 419, 479, 498.

19. Dr. Mečislav Borak, interview by the author, Ostrava, Czech Republic, 22 September, 2000; "Zatykac na Oskera Schindlera"; Emilie says that the address was 24 Sadova; Emilie Schindler, with Erika Rosenberg, *Where Light and Shadow Meet*, trans. Dolores M. Koch (New York: W. W. Norton & Company, 1997), 31. I have chosen to use Dr. Borak's address because he lives in Ostrava and has done extensive research on Schindler's life in the city; there are conflicting accounts about where Emilie lived when war broke out in 1939. According to Robin O'Neil, she said in an interview with him that she returned to Svitavy in the fall of 1939, though in her memoirs Emilie says she remained in the apartment in Mährisch Ostrau until 1941, when she joined Oskar in Kraków. O'Neil, "An Analysis of the Actions of Oskar Schindler Within the Context of the Holocaust in German Occupied Poland and Czechoslovakia" (master's thesis, University College, London, 1996), 27 n. 20; Schindler, *Light and Shadow*, 43, 46–48.

20. Policejní ředitelství v hor. Ostrae, č.j. D-100/40, March 29, 1940, 1 page; Policejni ředitelství Praha, 1931–1940, S. 2370/82; Elizabeth Wiskemann, *Czechs and Germans: A*

Study of the Struggle in the Historic Provinces of Bohemia and Moravia (London: Oxford University Press, 1938), 83, 134, 113–114.

21. "Oskar Schindler to Fritz Lang," July 20, 1951, OS Bundesarchiv, N 1493, 5, No. 28, 4. "*kaiserliche und königliche*" is a reference to the dual powers held by the Austrian emperor after the *Ausgleich* (Compromise) of 1867. The Austrian empire now became the Austrian-Hungarian empire. The Habsburg ruler became the emperor of the Austrian lands and king of Hungary. *Kaiserliche* refers to his imperial powers in the Austrian portions of his kingdom; *Königliche* to his royal powers in Hungary.

22. Alois Polanski Protokol, 3; Frantisek Moravec, *Master of Spies: The Memoirs of General Frantisek Moravec* (Garden City, N.Y.: Doubleday & Company, 1975), 128.

23. Schindler, *Light and Shadow,* 30–31; "Ilona Klimova to David Crowe, 23 September 2000"; Borak, interview, 22 September, 2000; "*Bericht Eugen Sliva,*" Geheime Staatspolizei, Staatspolizeistelle Bruenn, Maerisch Ostrau, May 8, 1940, Moravský zemský archiv Brno, sign., 100-162-20, III 85/40g-Eugen Sliwa, 1.

24. Schindler, *Light and Shadow,* 30–31; O'Neil, "An Analysis of the Actions of Oskar Schindler," 25.

25. Schindler, *Light and Shadow,* 49.

26. Höhne, *Canaris,* 334–336; Borak, "Zatykac na Oskara Schindlera."

27. Borak, "Zatykac na Oskara Schindlera." In the post-war Czechoslovak investigations, an agent mentioned with some frequency was Waltraud Vorster. It is possible that Forster and Vorster were one and the same; see Polansky Protokol, MV, 4–7; Martin A. Gosch and Howard Koch, "Interview with Oskar Schindler," November 18, 1964, Paris, France, in Delbert Mann Papers, Special Collections Library, Vanderbilt University, 7-A, 6.

28. Weinberg, *Foreign Policy, 1937–1939,* 537–538, 553–555, 559–560.

29. "Directive for the Armed Forces 1939/40, April 3, 1939, WFA Nr. 37/39 Top Secret Officer Only L Ia, and "Annex II to OKW No. 37/39, Top Secret L 1, C-120," *Nazi Conspiracy and Aggression,* vol. 4 (Washington, D.C.: United States Government Printing Office, 1946), 916–925 (hereafter referred to as NCA); these directives are summarized in Telford Taylor, *Sword and Swastika: Generals and Nazis in the Third Reich* (New York: Barnes & Noble Books, 1952), 256–260; Höhne, *Canaris,* 331.

30. Höhne, *Canaris,* 335–336.

31. Ibid., 336.

32. Ibid., 336–367, 350; "*Bericht Eugen Sliva,*" May 8, 1940, Moravský zemský archiv Brno," 1.

33. Höhne, *Canaris,* 337–339.

34. Ibid., 339.

35. "Affidavit of Alfred Helmut Naujocks," 20 November 1945, Document 2751-PS, NCA, vol. 5, 390–391; Walter Schellenberg, *The Labyrinth: Memoirs of Walter Schellenberg, Hitler's Chief of Counterintelligence,* trans. Louis Hagen (New York: Da Capo Press, 2000), 48–50; Donald Cameron Watt, *How War Came: The Immediate Origins of the Second World War: 1938–1939* (New York: Pantheon Books, 1989), 485–486.

36. Schindler, *Light and Shadow,* 32.

37. Dr. Mečislav Borak, "Zatykac na Oskara Schindlera." Dr. Jaroslav Valenta of the Czech Academy of Sciences also says that the large body of historical literature on the Gliwice operation suggests that Schindler had nothing to do with it. Edouard Calic, *Reinhard Heydrich* (New York: Military Heritage Press, 1982), 194–195; "Ilona Kilmova to David Crowe, September 23, 2000"; Borak, interview, September 22, 2000.

38. Geheime Staatspolizei, Staatspolizei Brünn, Grenzpolizeikommissariat Mähr.-Ostaru, Abt. III, B. Nr. 770/39g, July 23, 1939, Betriff: Polnisches Konsulat Mähr.-Ostrau und *Protokoll* Eugen Slíva; Moravský zemský archiv Brno, sign. 100-162-20, III 85/40 g. Eugen Sliwa, 1–5; Geheime Staatspolizei, Staatspolizei Brünn, "Eugen Sliwa," May 8, 1940, Moravský zemský archiv Brno. 100-162-20, III 85/40 g.-Eugen Sliwa, 2–3 (hereafter re-

ferred to as Geheime Staatspolizei, Brünn, "Eugen Sliwa," May 8, 1940, Moravský zemský archiv Brno, "Eugen Sliwa").

39. Geheime Staatspolizei, Brünn, "Eugen Sliwa," May 8, 1940, Moravský zemský archiv Brno, "Eugen Sliwa," 4–5.

40. Geheime Staatspolizei, Brünn, May 8, 1940, Moravský zemský archiv Brno, "Eugen Sliwa," 5–6.

41. Geheime Staatspolizei, Mährisch Ostrau, III L-85/40g, June 17, 1940, Moravský zemský archiv Brno, "Eugen Sliwa," 1 page.

42. Deutsche Kriminalpolizei, Mährisch Ostrau, June 14, 1940, Moravský zemský archiv Brno, "Eugen Sliwa," 1 page; Das Deutsche Amtsgericht, 3 Gs 119/40, "Strafsache gegen Eugen Sliva wegen schweren Diebstahls," June 15, 1940, Moravský zemský archiv Brno, "Eugen Sliwa," 1–3.

43. "Der Oberrechtsanwalt beim Volksgericht, Berlin to Geheime Staatspolizei, Mährisch Ostrau," 11 J 263/40g, July 23, 1940, Moravský zemský archiv Brno, "Eugen Sliwa," 1 page.

44. "Kanzlei von dem Oberrechtsanwalt beim Volksgerichtshof," 11 J 263/40g, August 10, 1940, Moravský zemský archiv Brno, "Eugen Sliwa," 3 pages.

45. "Geheime Staatspolizei, Staatspolizeistelle Brünn to Geheime Staatspolizeileitstelle Mährisch Ostrau," III L-85/40g, 1 page. Moravský zemský archiv Brno, "Eugen Sliwa," 1 page.

46. "Schlussbericht III-85/40g, Mähr. Ostrau, September 27, 1940, Moravský zemský archiv Brno, "Eugen Sliwa," 1 page; "Kanzlei an die Staatspolizei, Brünn, III-L-85/40g, September 1940, Moravský zemský archiv Brno, "Eugen Sliwa," 3 pages.

47. "Kreisgericht in Mähr. Ostrau an die Geheime Staatspolizei, III 85/40g, November 2, 1940, Moravský zemský archiv Brno, "Eugen Sliwa," 1 page; "Kreisgericht in Mähr. Ostrau, "Eugen Sliva," November 26, 1941, Moravský zemský archiv Brno, "Eugen Sliwa," 1 page; "Nachrichten-übermittlung, Stapoleit Bruen, an Adst. Maehr. Ostrau," November 13, 1940, Moravský zemský archiv Brno, "Eugen Sliwa," 1 page.

48. Schindler, Light and Shadow, 32.

49. "Abwehrstelle-zpráva," May 12, 1947, Čis.bZ/z-1157/3–47, Appendix 1, Ministerstvu vnitra, odbor VII v Praze, 2 (hereafter referred to as "Abwehrstelle-zpráva," MV Archiv); "Alois Polansky Protokol," MV Archiv, 1, 3.

50. "Alois Polansky Protokol," MV Archiv, 3; "Abwehr-zpráva," April 8, 1947 Č. VIII-4669/taj-47-A-11, Ministeratvu národní obrany-hlavní štáb 5. oddělení-V Praze, Archiv Ministerstvo Vnitra (Prague), 2, 8 (hereafter referred to as "Abwehr-zpráva" MV). According to postwar Czechoslovak investigations, Moschkorsch was a Gestapo operative in Mährisch Ostrau who was later killed by Czech partisans on March 20, 1945, for his collaboration. Though the Czechs investigated Fischer's activities, they were never able to find him and concluded that he had probably disappeared into the Wehrmacht. "Abwehrstelle-zpráva," MV Archiv, 2.

51. "Alois Polansky Prokotol," MV Archiv, 3–5, 7, 9. Unger's wife was also at the meeting. As of 1947, all three had escaped the Czech dragnet and were never brought to justice for their espionage activities.

52. "Abwehrstelle-zpráva." MV Archiv, 2, 6–7; Dr. Mečislav Borak, "Zatykac na Oskara Schindlera;" Polansky Protokol, MV, 12; "Abwehr zpráva" MV Archiv, 4, 6–7; Jitka Gruntová, Oskar Schindler: Legenda a Fakta (Brno: Barrister & Principal, 1997), 19.

53. "Josef Aue Protokol," August 6, 1946, Č.j. II/1.-7219/46, Oblastní státní bezpečnosti v Mor. Ostravě, Ministerstvu vnitra Archiv (Prague), 1. The 12-page Aue Protokol is actually four investigative reports dated Ausgust 6, 1946, August 9, 1946, October 17, 1946, and October 23, 1946 (hereafter referred to as Josef Aue Protokol MV Archiv with specific date of interrogation); Sepp Aue to Itzhak Stern, December 7, 1948, Yad Vashem

Archives, 0/1/64, 1–2 (hereafter referred to as Aue to Stern, YVA); Gruntová, *Oskar Schindler*, 19.

54. Josef Aue Protokol, MV Archiv, August 6, 1946, 1–2; Josef Aue Protokol, October 17, 1946, MV Archiv, 1–2; Weinberg, *Foreign Policy of Nazi Germany, 1937–1939*, 479; O'Neil, "An Analysis of the Actions of Oskar Schindler," 27, n. 20.; Aue to Stern, YVA, 1.

55. Aue Protokol, October 23, 1946, MV Archiv, 1–3; O'Neil, "An Analysis of the Actions of Oskar Schindler," 25–26; Aue to Stern, YVA, 1.

56. Aue Protokol, August 6, 1946, MV Archiv, 2; "Abwehr-zpráva," MV Archiv, 6. Gassner escaped the Czech dragnet after the war, at least as of 1947. The secret police suspected he was in the Salzberg area where his wife had undergone a "healing cure."

57. O'Neil, "An Analysis of the Actions of Oskar Schindler," 21; "Abwehr zpráva" MV Archiv, 5.

58. Schindler to Lang, 3; "Schindler Financial Report, 1945," Yad Vashem Archives, 01/164, 15 (hereafter referred to as "Schindler Financial Report, 1945").

59. Zprava V Mor. Ostravě, November 7, 1945, Ministerstvo vnitra Archiv (Prague), 2, 5 (hereafter referred to as Zprava V Mor. Ostravě, MV Archiv); Schindler, *Light and Shadow*, 30; Schindler to Lang, 3; O'Neil, "An Analysis of the Actions of Oskar Schindler," 38; "Schindler Financial Report, 1945" 15.

60. We have little information on *Hauptmann* Kristiany. At one point, he was in command of Abwehr operations in Brno. *Leutnant* Decker was injured in an automobile accident during the war and disappeared. Polanski Protokol, MV Archiv, 4–6; Zprava V Mor. Ostravě, 2.

61. *Schindler*. A film written, directed, and produced by Jon Blair, Thames Television Production, 1981; Schindler, *Light and Shadow*, 100.

62. Polanski Protokol, MV Archiv, 8; Schindler to Lang, 2.

63. Dr. Mečislav Borak and Dr. Jaroslav Valenta, "Zatykac na Oskara Schindlera."

64. Borak, interview, September 22, 2000.

65. David M. Crowe, *The Baltic States and the Great Powers: Foreign Relations, 1918–1940* (Boulder: Westview Press, 1993), 68–81.

66. Höhne, *Canaris*, 346–347; Taylor, *Sword and Swastika*, 286–291.

67. Höhne, *Canaris*, 348–350; Weinberg, *Foreign Policy, 1937–1939*, 635–637.

68. Höhne, *Canaris*, 350–352; Taylor, *Sword and Swastika*, 304–308.

69. Weinberg, *Foreign Policy, 1937–1939*, 636–638.

70. Höhne, *Canaris*, 351–353.

71. Taylor, *Sword and Swastika*, 315; Höhne, *Canaris*, 352–353.

72. Weinberg, *Foreign Policy of Hitler's Germany, 1937–1939*, 646–652; Pat McTaggart, "Poland '39," in *Hitler's Army: The Evolution and Structure of German Forces* (Conshohocken, Pa.: Combined Publishing, 1995), 220.

73. Schindler, *Light and Shadow*, 50; *Hitler's Army*, 199, 211–212; Richard M. Watt, *Bitter Glory: Poland and Its Fate, 1918–1939* (New York: Simon and Schuster, 1979), 422.

74. Schindler, *Light and Shadow*, 43; O'Neil, "An Analysis of the Actions of Oskar Schindler," 29–30; Höhne, *Canaris*, 357–358.

75. Höhne, *Canaris*, 315–322; John A. Armstrong, *Ukrainian Nationalism*, 2d ed. (New York: Columbia University Press, 1963), 33–35.

76. Armstrong, *Ukrainian Nationalism*, 42–44; Ukrainian scholars are justifiably sensitive about the entire question of collaboration with the Germans before and during World War II. According to Bohdan Krawchenko, this relationship was an opportunistic one for the Ukrainians, caught as they were between two dictatorial powers. Given Stalin's policies in the Soviet portions of Ukraine, Germany seemed to offer the best hope for Ukranian national aspirations. See his *Social Change and National Consciousness in Twentieth-Century*

Ukraine (New York: St. Martin's Press, 1985), 156; Robert M. Slusser and Jan F. Triska, eds., *A Calendar of Soviet Treaties, 1917–1957* (Stanford: Stanford University Press, 1959), 127–128; Albert Seaton, *Stalin as Military Commander* (New York: Praeger Publishers, 1975), 89; Leonid N. Kutakov, *Japanese Foreign Policy on the Eve of the Pacific War: A Soviet View*, ed. George Alexander Lensen (Tallahassee: Diplomatic Press, 1972), 152–153; David J. Dallin, *Soviet Russia's Foreign Policy, 1939–1942*, trans. Leon Dennen (New Haven: Yale University Press, 1942), 70–71; Jane Degras, ed., *Soviet Documents on Foreign Policy*, vol. 3, *1933–1941* (New York: Octagon Books, 1978), 374–376; Pavel Zhilin et al., *Recalling the Past for the Sake of the Future: The Causes, Results and Lessons of World War Two* (Moscow: Novosti Press Agency, 1985), 23.

77. The Ukrainians in Poland in 1931 made up almost 14 percent of the population. Paul Robert Magocsi, *Historical Atlas of East Central Europe* (Seattle: University of Washington Press, 1998), 131; Orest Subtelny, *Ukraine: A History*, 2d ed. (Toronto: University of Toronto Press, 1994), 457; Höhne, *Canaris*, 357–359.

78. Ian Kershaw, *Hitler, 1936–1945: Nemesis* (New York: W. W. Norton, 2000), 234–235, 244; Louis L. Snyder, ed., *Hitler's Third Reich: A Documentary History* (Chicago: Nelson-Hall, 1981), 329; Hans Umbreit, "Stages in the Territorial 'New Order' in Europe," in Bernhard R. Kroener, Rolf-Dieter Müller, and Hans Umbreit, eds., *Germany and the Second World War*, vol. 5, *Organization and Mobilization of the German Sphere of Power*, part 1, *Wartime Administration, Economy, and Manpower Resources, 1939–1941*, trans. John Brownjohn, Patricia Crampton, Ewald Osers, and Louise Willmot (Oxford: Clarendon Press, 2000), 41.

79. Umbreit, "Stages," 44; Kershaw, *Hitler, 1936–1945, Nemesis* (New York: W. W. Norton, 2000), 235–236, 244; Raul Hilberg, *The Destruction of the European Jews*, vol. 1 (New York: Holmes & Meier, 1985), 188–189; Richard C. Lukas, *Forgotten Holocaust: The Poles under German Occupation, 1939–1944* (New York: Hippocrene Books, 1990), 3–5.

80. Kershaw, *Hitler, 1936–1945*, 240–241.

81. According to *The Black Book of Polish Jewry*, the population swelled to 72,000 because of an influx of Jewish refugees from Germany, the former Czechoslovakia, and the war. Jacob Apenszlak, Jacob Kenner, Dr. Isaac Lewin, and Dr. Moses Polakiewicz, *The Black Book of Polish Jewry: An Account of the Martyrdom of Polish Jews Under the Nazi Occupation* (New York: The American Federation for Polish Jews, 1943), 77; Umbreit, "Stages in the Territorial 'New Order' in Europe," 42 n. 68, 43–44; Omar Bartov, "Preface," Hamburg Institute for Social Research, ed., *The German Army and Genocide: Crimes Against War Prisoners, Jews, and Other Civilians, 1939–1945* (New York: The New Press, 1999), 12–13. This volume was prepared to accompany the controversial exhibit by the same title. Because of errors found in some of the photographs in the German exhibit, it has yet to appear in the United States. It should also be noted that the English language exhibit book is very different from that of the German edition, Hamburger Institut für Sozialforschung (Hg.), ed., *Vernichtungskrieg. Verbrechen der Wehrmacht 1941 bis 1944* (Hamburg: Hamburger Edition, 1996). The German edition does not cover the years from 1939–1940 and does not contain the lengthy opening comments by Michael Geyer and Omar Bartov; Kershaw, *Hitler, 1936–1945*, 236; Kershaw's figures differ considerably from those of Richard Lukas, who stated that the Poles lost 200,000 men and had 420,000 captured. The Germans, he claimed, lost 45,000 men. See his *Forgotten Holocaust*, 2.

82. Höhne, *Canaris*, 364–365; Kershaw, *Hitler, 1936–1945*, 243; Woyrsch's group was composed of regular policemen. Umbreit, "Stages," 44.

83. Kershaw, *Hitler, 1936–1945*, 245–246.

84. Ibid., 238; see, for example, Britain's warning and ultimatum messages to the Germans in the early days of the war, "Viscount Halifax to Sir. N. [eville] Henderson (Berlin)," Foreign Office, September 1, 1939, No. 109, "Viscount Halifax to Sir N. Henderson

(Berlin)," Foreign Office, September 1, 1939, No. 110, "Viscount Halifax to Sir. N. Henderson (Berlin)," Foreign Office, September 3, 1939, No. 118, "Memorandum Handed to Sir N. Henderson at 11:20 a.m. on September 3, 1939, by Herr von Ribbentrop," No. 119, in *Documents Concerning German-Polish Relations and the Outbreak of Hostilities between Great Britain and Germany on September 3, 1939* (London: His Majesty's Stationery Office, 1939), 168, 175–178; Donald Cameron Watt provides an excellent, detailed overview of these developments in the early days of the war in chapters 28, 30, and 31 in his *How War Came,* 530–550, 568–604; Geoffrey Roberts, *The Unholy Alliance: Stalin's Pact with Hitler* (Bloomington: Indiana University Press, 1989), 156–159.

    85. Umbreit, "Stages," 45–47.

    86. Ibid., 50; Christopher Ailsby, *SS: Roll of Infamy* (Osceola, Wisc.: Motorbooks International, 1997), 47–48, 57, 157–158. Forster had SS number 158, indicating his high rank among the "Old Fighters." Forster, a protegé of virulent Nazi anti-Semite Julius Streicher, had served as a Nazi Party member in the Reichstag and as *Gauleiter* (area commander) of the Free City of Danzig. He later become Reich governor *(Reichsstatthalter)* of the Danzig *Gau.* A bitter enemy of Forster, Greiser would soon become the Reich governor of a new Wartheland *Gau,* which would consist of the Posen, Łódź, and Hohensalza districts. Greiser's SS number was 10,795. Kershaw, *Hitler, 1936–1945,* 69–72, 74–79, 250–252.

    87. Umbreit, "Stages," 20.

    88. Ibid., 52–53; Kershaw, *Hitler, 1936–1945,* 246–247.

    89. Richard Giziowski, *The Enigma of General Blaskowitz* (New York: Hippocrene Books, 1997), 179–180, 203–207.

    90. Michael Burleigh, *The Third Reich: A New History* (New York: Hill and Wang, 2000), 438–440; Kershaw, *Hitler, 1936–1945,* 247–248; Jeremy Noakes and Geoffrey Pridham, eds. *Nazism, 1919–1945: A History in Documents and Eyewitness Accounts,* vol. 2, *Foreign Policy, War and Racial Extermination* (New York: Schocken Books, 1988), 938–941.

    91. United States Holocaust Memorial Museum, *Historical Atlas of the Holocaust* (New York: Macmillan Publishing, 1996), 34; Umbreit, "Stages," 53–55; Hilberg, *Destruction,* 193–196. Lower Silesia was governed by *Oberpräsident* and *Gauleiter* Karl Hanke and Upper Silesia by *Oberpräsident* and *Gauleiter* Fritz Bracht.

    92. Stanisław Piotrowski, *Dziennik Hansa Frank* (Warszawa: Wydawnictwo Prawnicze, 1956), 11–13. An English edition of this work is available but it is not as extensive as the Polish edition. See Stanisław Piotrowski, *Hans Frank's Diary* (Warszawa: Państwowe Wydawnictwo Naukowe, 1961); Christoph Klessmann, "Hans Frank: Party Jurist and Governor-General in Poland," in Ronald Smelser and Rainer Zitelmann, *The Nazi Elite* (New York: New York University Press, 1993), 39–40; Ian Kershaw, *Hitler, 1889–1936: Hubris* (New York: W. W. Norton, 1999), 333, 337, 338.

    93. Smelser and Zitelmann, *The Nazi Elite,* 40, 47. It is important not to confuse Hans Frank's wartime diary with his postwar prison memoirs, *Im Angesicht des Galgens: Deutung Hitlers und seiner Zeit aufgrund eigener Erlebnisse und Erkenntnisse,* ed. O. Schloffer (Munich: Neuhaus, 1953).

    94. Umbreit, "Stages," 49, 53, 56, 58, 60; Piotrowski, *Dziennik Hansa Frank,* 29.

    95. Jan Tomasz Gross, *Polish Society Under German Occupation: The Generalgouvernment, 1939–1944* (Princeton: Princeton University Press, 1979), 51; Joachim C. Fest, *The Face of the Third Reich: Portraits of the Nazi Leadership,* trans. Michael Bullock (New York: Ace Books, 1970), 315; Niklas Frank, *In the Shadow of the Third Reich,* trans. Arthur S. Wensinger, with Carole Clew-Hoey (New York: Alfred A. Knopf), 109; Piotrowski, *Dziennik Hansa Franka,* 21–22.

    96. Office of United States Chief of Counsel for Prosecution of Axis Criminality, *Nazi Conspiracy and Aggression,* Volume II (Washington, D.C.: United States Government Printing office, 1946), 956–957; on October 18, 1945, the International Military Tribunal at

Nuremberg indicted Seyß Inquart on all four counts and convicted him of crimes against peace, war crimes, and crimes against humanity. Frank was charged with three of four counts and convicted of war crimes, and crimes against humanity. Office of United States Chief of Counsel for Prosecution of Axis Criminality, *Nazi Conspiracy and Aggression: Opinion and Judgement* (Washington, D,C.: United States Government Printing Office, 1947), 123–126, 153–156.

97. Piotrowski, *Dziennik Hansa Frank,* 52, 134, 239; Gross, *Polish Society under German Occupation,* 51–52.

98. Gross, *Polish Society,* 51–52; Hilberg, *Destruction of the European Jews,* 1:197–198; Dr. Max Freiherr du Prel, *Das General Gouvernement* (Würzburg: Konrad Triltsch Verlag, 1942), 375, 380–382.

99. Umbreit, "Stages," 60.

100. Gross, *Polish Society,* 51; Hilberg, *Destruction of the European Jews,* 1:203–204.

101. Umbreit, "Stages," 60.

102. Hilberg, *Destruction of the European Jews,* 1:199; Umbreit, "Stages," 60.

103. Omar Bartov, *Hitler's Army: Soldiers, Nazis, and War in the Third Reich* (New York: Oxford University Press, 1991), 61–68; Umbreit, "Stages," 60.

104. Schindler to Lang, 4; "Schindler Financial Report, 1945," 15; "Oskar Schindler *Bericht*," October 30, 1955, Bundesarchiv (Koblenz), Nachlaß Oskar Schindler, 1908–1974, Bestand N 1493, No. 1/15, 3, 4 (hereafter referred to as "Oskar Schindler *Bericht* (1955).")

105. Schindler to Lang, 3; "Schindler Financial Report, 1945," 15; Military Intelligence Service, *German Army Order of Battle: October 1942* (Mt. Ida, Ark.: Lancer Militaria, n.d), 172; Georg Thomas, *Geschichte der deutschen Wehr-und Rüstungswirtschaft (1918-1943/45),* ed. Wolfgang Birkenfeld (Boppard am Rhein: Harald Boldt Verlag, 1966), 293, n. 78. This volume is part of the Bundesarchiv series, *Schriften des Bundesarchiv.*

106. "Oskar Schindler *Bericht* (1955)," 4; Schindler to Lang, 3.

107. "Schindler Financial Report, 1945," 15; "Oskar Schindler *Bericht* (1955)," 4; Schindler, *Light and Shadow,* 83–84.

108. Thomas, *Geschichte der deutschen Wehr-und Rüstungwirtschaft,* 1 2; R.J. Overy, *War and Economy in the Third Reich* (Oxford: Oxford University Press, 1994), 178, 203, 242; Rolf-Dieter Müller, "The Mobilization of the German Economy for Hitler's War Aims," in Kroener, Müller, and Umbreit, *Germany and the Second World War,* vol. 1, *Wartime Administration, Economy, and Manpower Resources, 1939–1941,* 415–421; Höhne, *Canaris,* 344.

109. Initially, the economics minister held the title as General Plenipotentiary for the War Economy (GBK; *Generalbevollmächtiger für die Kriegswirtschaft*). He became the GBW in 1938. Müller, "Mobilization," 410, 413; Overy, *War and Economy in the Third Reich,* 183–187, 203. The influential Thomas had once headed the army's Defense Economy and Weapons Bureau; Hans-Erich Volkmann, "The War Economy under the Four Year Plan, in Wilhelm Diest, Manfred Messerschmidt, Hans-Erich Volkmann, and Wolfram Wette, eds., *Germany and the Second World War,* vol. I: *The Buildup of German Aggression,* trans. P. S. Falla, Dean S. McMurry, and Ewald Osers (Oxford: Clarendon Press, 2000), 281–285.

110. Müller, "Mobilization," 420–421.

111. Thomas, *Geschichte der deutschen Wehr-und Rüstungswirtschaft,* 10–11; Norman Rich, *Hitler's War Aims: Ideology, the Nazi State, and the Course of Expansion* (New York: W. W. Norton, 1973), 69–71; Alfred C. Mierzejewski, *The Collapse of the German War Economy, 1944–1945: Allied Air Power and the German National Railway* (Chapel Hill: University of North Carolina Press, 1988), 9–11; Müller, "Mobilization," 777–779.

112. Burleigh, *The Third Reich*, 679–683; Kershaw, *Hitler, 1936–1945*, 52–60; Höhne, *Canaris*, 254–258, 263–264, 270–271, 276; Klemens von Klemperer, *German Resistance Against Hitler: The Search for Allies Abroad, 1938–1945* (Oxford: Clarendon Press, 1994), 86.

113. Thomas, *Geschichte der deutschen Wehr-und Rüstungswirtschaft*, 11–15; Klemperer, *German Resistance*, 172–173; Peter Hoffmann, *The History of the German Resistance, 1933–1945*, trans. Richard Barry, 3d ed. (Montreal: McGill-Queens University Press, 1996), 158–160.

114. Thomas, *Geschichte der deutschen Wehr-und Rüstungswirtschaft*, 15–17; Ulrich von Hassell, *The Von Hassell Diaries, 1938–1944* (New York: Doubleday, 1947), 116–118, 125–128, 130–132; Hoffmann, *History*, 161–168; Klemperer, *German Resistance*, 172–178.

115. Höhne, *Canaris*, 449–450; Müller, "Mobilization of the German War Economy for Hitler's War Aims," 608, 610–615, 629–630, 648–649; Danuta Czech, "Origins of the Camp, Its Construction and Expansion," in Franciszek Piper and Teresa Świebocka, eds., *Auschwitz: Nazi Death Camp* (Oświęcim: The Auschwitz-Birkenau State Museum, 1996), 26–27, 29–30.

116. Thomas raised these points in a talk before the Military Policy and Military Sciences Association *(Gesellschaft für Wehrpolitik und Wehrwissenschaften)* on November 29, 1940. Müller, "Mobilization," 618–619, 652, 659; Kershaw, *Hitler: 1936–1945*, 344–346; *The Memoirs of Field-Marshal Wilhelm Keitel*, ed. Walter Gorlitz (New York: Cooper Square Press, 2000), 183.

117. Von Hassell, *Diaries*, 218; Höhne, *Canaris*, 463–464; Hoffmann, *History*, 270.

118. Hoffmann, *History*, 270; Hamburg Institute, *German Army and Genocide*, 132.

119. Hoffmann, *History*, 269–270; Thomas, *Geschichte der deutschen Wehr- und Rüstungswirtschaft*, 19; Müller, "Mobilization," 664, 666.

120. Höhne, *Canaris*, 507, 515–518; Hoffmann, *History*, 293–294, 529–530. On the day the military arrested Dohnányi, the Gestapo arrested his wife and her brother, Dietrich Bonhoeffer, and Dr. Josef Müller; Thomas, *Geschichte der deutschen Wehr-und Rüstungswirtschaft*, 5.

121. Schindler, *Light and Shadow*, 55–56, 83–84.

Chapter 3

1. Emilie Schindler, *Where Light and Shadow Meet: A Memoir* (New York: W. W. Norton, 1997), 43; Thomas Keneally, *Schindler's List* (New York: Touchstone Books, 1992), 41–42; Robin O'Neil, "The Man from Svitavy: The Enigma of Oskar Schindler" (unpublished manuscript, 1994), 51; *Bericht*, Eugen Sliwa, May 11, 1940, Mährisch Ostrau, III-85/40g, May 11, 1940, Moravský zemský archiv Brno, 100-162-20 (hereafter referred to as Eugen Sliwa *Bericht*, MzaB, 1).

2. O'Neil, "The Man from Svitavy," 51; Robin O'Neil, "An Analysis of the Actions of Oskar Schindler Within the Context of the Holocaust in German Occupied Poland and Czechoslovakia" (Master's Thesis, University College, London, September 1996), 34.

3. O'Neil, "The Man from Svitavy," 51; O'Neil, "An Analysis of the Actions of Oskar Schindler," 29–30, 34; "Leasehold Agreement between Dr. Romuald Goryyczko and Oskar Schindler," January 15, 1940, Akta Rejestru Handlowego przy Sądzie Okręgowym w Krakowie (akta dotyczące firmy: Pierwsza Małopolska Fabryka Naczyń Emailowanych i Wyrobów Blaszanych "Rekord", Spółka z o ow. Krakowie), Archiwum Państwowe w Krakowkie Oddział III, 2022, III U 5/39, 288. This set of court records, 2022, and 2023 will hereafter be referred to as SOKC 2022 or 2023, III U 5/39. Though this document is dated January 15, 1940, it deals with Schindler's leasing of the factory in the fall of 1939; *Verhandelt*, Oskar Schindler, August 22, 1940, Krakau, III C 1, Moravský zemský archiv

Brno, sign. 100-162-20, 1 page (hereafter referred to as *Verhandelt,* Oskar Schindler, MzaB); the Germans renamed most of the major streets in Kraków, which they spelled Krakau. Strszewskiego became simply the Westring and Fenna Serena Gasse was changed to Schillinggasse. Krasiński became the Außenring. Dr. Max Freiherr du Prel, ed., *Das General Gouvernement* (Würzburg: Konrad Triltsch Verlag, 1942), 264–266; Karl Baedeker, *Das Generalgouvernement: Reisehandbuch von Karl Baedeker* (Leipzig: Karl Baedeker, 1943), 33, map 2.

4. Leopold Page Testimony, March 11, 1992, United States Holocaust Memorial Museum Archives, RG-50.042*0022, 1 (hereafter referred to as Leopold Page Archives, USHMM); Douglas Martin, "Leopold Page, Who Promoted Story of Schindler, Dies at 87," *New York Times,* March 15, 2001, A21; "Leopold Page: Businessman, Community Leader & the Singular Catalyst for the *Schindler's List* Story," in Nick del Calzo, with Renee Rockford, Drew Myron, and Linda J. Raper, *The Triumphant Spirit: Portraits & Stories of Holocaust Survivors—Their Messages of Hope & Compassion* (Denver: Triumphant Spirit Publishing, 1997), 119; Celia S. Heller, *On the Edge of Destruction: Jews of Poland between the Two World Wars* (New York: Columbia University Press, 1977), 119–124; Ezra Mendelsohn, *The Jews of East Central Europe Between the World Wars* (Bloomington: Indiana University Press, 1983), 83; Keneally, *Schindler's List,* 49.

5. Leopold Page, interviews by the author, Beverly Hills, California, April 3, 2000, and September 13, 2000; Martin, "Leopold Page," A21; del Calzo, "Leopold Page," 119; Keneally, *Schindler's List,* 49; Pat McTaggart, "Poland '39," in *Editors of Command Magazine, Hitler's Army: The Evolution and Structure of German Forces* (Conshohocken, Pa.: Combined Publishing, 2000), 215–216.

6. Keneally, *Schindler's List,* 49–50.

7. Bob Keeler, "Schindler's Survivors: Five People Whose Experiences Contributed to 'Schindler's List' Came Together to Talk About Their Lives and the Movie and About Horror and Survival," *New York Newsday,* March 23, 1994, B49; Keneally, *Schindler's List,* 50–51.

8. Isaiah Trunk, *Judenrat: The Jewish Councils in Eastern Europe Under Nazi Occupation* (New York: Stein & Day, 1977), 196–197; Lucjan Dobroszycki, *Reptile Journalism: The Official Polish-Language Press Under the Nazis, 1939–1945* (New Haven: Yale University Press, 1994), 108–109; Richard C. Lukas, *Forgotten Holocaust: The Poles under German Occupation, 1939–1944* (New York: Hippocrene Books, 1990), 10.

9. Keneally, *Schindler's List,* 51–52; Jacques Delarue, *The Gestapo: A History of Horror* (New York: Paragon House, 1987), 187–189; Lukas, *Forgotten Holocaust,* 28–29.

10. Leopold Page Testimony, USHMM Archives, 1; Keneally, *Schindler's List,* 51–52.

11. Leopold Page Testimony, USHMM Archives, 1; Keneally, *Schindler's List,* 53–54.

12. R. J. Overy, *War and Economy in the Third Reich* (Oxford: Clarendon Press, 1994), 281–286; Trunk, *Judenrat,* 99.

13. Jan Tomasz Gross, *Polish Society Under German Occupation: The Generalgouvernement, 1939–1944* (Princeton: Princeton University Press, 1979), 99–102; Trunk, *Judenrat,* 99–100; Eugeniusz Duranczyński, *Wojna i Okupacja: Wrzesień 1939–Kwiecień 1943* (Warsaw: wieza Powszechna, 1974), 69; Lukas, *Forgotten Holocaust,* 30; Jacob Apsenszlak, Jacob Kenner, Isaac Lewin, and Moses Polakiewicz, eds., *The Black Book of Polish Jewry: An Account of the Martyrdom of Polish Jewry Under the Nazi Occupation* (New York: The American Federation for Polish Jews, 1943), 37; according to Clive Cookson, "modern nutritionists regard 3,000–3,500 calories as a healthy minimum consumption." "Hunger, Horror and Heroism," *Financial Times,* July 28/29, 2001, Weekend II. These figures were probably a bit less more than a half century ago.

14. Trunk, *Judenrat,* 99–103.

15. In 1939, the official exchange rate was 5.30 złotys to the U.S. dollar and RM 2.49 to the U.S. dollar. The Germans would later inflate the value of the Reichsmark to the złoty by

---

about 33 percent so that $1 was now equal to about 3.2 złotys. R. L. Bidwell, *Currency Conversion Tables: A Hundred Years of Change* (London: Rex Collins, 1970), 23, 37; Gross, *Polish Society,* 97; Keneally, *Schindler's List,* 54–55.

16. Eugeniusz Duda, *The Jews of Cracow,* trans. Ewa Basiura (Kraków: Wydawnictwo 'Hagada' and Argona-Jarden Jewish Bookshop, 2000), 60.

17. Duda, *Jews of Cracow,* 60–61.

18. Ibid., 61–62; "Dr. Roland Groyczko to Handlowego przy Sądzie Okręgowym w Krakowie," September 11, 1941, SOKC 2023: III U 5/39, 2.

19. Czesław Madajczyk, *Polityka III Rzeszy w Okupowanej Polsce,* vol. 1 (Warszawa: Państwowe Wydawnictwo Naukowe, 1970), 516; Gross, *Polish Society,* 93–94; Trunk, *Judenrat,* 63–64.

20. Trunk, *Judenrat,* 62.

21. Madajczyk, *Polityka III Rzeszy w Okupowanej Polsce,* vol. 1, 516–519; Trunk, *Judenrat,* 63–64; Gross, *Polish Society,* 94–96.

22. Trunk, *Judenrat,* 65.

23. Ibid., 64–65; Gross, *Polish Society,* 94, 100–101; Czesław Madajczyk, *Polityka III Rzeszy w Okupowanej Polsce,* vol.2 (Warszawa: Państwowe Wydawnictwo Naukowe, 1970), 66–67.

24. Trunk, *Judenrat,* 65–66; Stella Müller-Madej, interview by the author, Kraków, Poland, August 9, 2000; Stella Müller-Madej, *A Girl from Schindler's List* (London: Polish Cultural Foundation, 1997), 7, 10–11.

25. *Schindler's List,* Steven Spielberg, Director, Universal/MCA and Amblin Entertainment (1993) (hereafter referred to as Spielberg, *Schindler's List*).

26. "Josef Aue Protokol," August 6, 1946, Č.j. II/1.-7219/46, Oblastní státní bezpečnosti v Mor. Ostravě, Ministerstvu vnitra Archiv (Prague), 3–5 (hereafter referred to as Josef Aue Protokol, August 6, 1946, MVA (Prague)); Hans Höhne, *Canaris* (New York: Doubleday & Company, 1979), 365–366; 508–511; O'Neil, "An Analysis of the Actions of Oskar Schindler," 35–36.

27. Josef Aue Protokol, August 6, 1946, MVA (Prague), 4.

28. Ibid.; O'Neil, "An Analysis of the Actions of Oskar Schindler," 35–36; Gruntová, *Oskar Schindler,* 19–20.

29. Keneally, *Schindler's List,* 41–48.

30. "The Trial of Adolf Eichmann," Session 37, Part 2 of 5, The Nizkor Project, 5; an example of Dr. Ball-Kaduri's scholarly interests can be seen in his "Illegale Judenauswanderung aus Deutschland nach Palästina, 1939–1940: Planung, Durchführung und internationale Zusammenhänge," in *Jahrbuch des Instituts für deutsche Geschichte* 4 (1975).

31. "Martin Gosch Interview with Itzhak Stern," November 24, 1964, Tel Aviv, Israel, Delbert Mann Papers, Special Collections Library, Vanderbilt University, 3–4 (hereafter referred to as "Gosch-Stern Interview," Delbert Mann Papers, Vanderbilt University).

32. Ibid., 6–7.

33. "Stern Report 1956," Yad Vashem Archives, 01/164; Dr. Moshe Bejski, "Notes on the Banquet in Honor of Oskar Schindler, May 2, 1962, Tel Aviv, Israel," 31–32. Dr. Bejski's transcript of the banquet testimonies is also available in Hebrew at Yad Vashem's Archives, M 21/20.

34. Douglas Brode, *The Films of Steven Spielberg,* (New York: Citadel Press, 2000), 233; John Baxter, *Steven Spielberg: The Unauthorized Biography* (London: HarperCollins, 1996), 382; Mietek Pemper, interview by the author, Augsburg, Germany, January 17, 2000; Franciszek Palowski, *The Making of Schindler's List: Behind the Scenes of an Epic Film,* trans. Anna and Robert G. Ware (Secaucus, N.J.: Birch Lane Press, 1998), 133.

35. "Oskar Schindler to Dr. K. J. Ball-Kaduri," September 9, 1956," Yad Vashem Archives, 01/164.

36. "Stern Report 1956," YVA, 8–9, 24; Yehuda Bauer, *American Jewry and the Holocaust: The American Jewish Joint Distribution Committee, 1939–1945* (Detroit: Wayne State University Press, 1981), 103.

37. Keneally, *Schindler's List,* 43; "Stern Report 1956," YVA, 1, 23.

38. Palowski, *Making of Schindler's List,* 38–39; Sol Urbach, interview by the author, Flemington, New Jersey, April 13, 1999.

39. O'Neil, "An Analysis of the Actions of Oskar Schindler," 68 n. 3; "Schindler Survivor Remained Aloof from Postwar Hype (Obituary), *The Australian,* May 26, 2000, 15.

40. Ralf Eibl and Norbert Jessen, "Im Schatten Schindlers," *Die Welt* (February 22, 2000):10.

41. Ibid.

42. "The Confessions of Mr. X," Budapest, November 1943, Bundesarchiv (Koblenz), Nachlaß Oskar Schindler, 1908–1974, Bestand N 1493, No. 1, Band 18, 4 (hereafter referred to as "The Confessions of Mr. X," BA(K)).

43. "Oskar Schindler to Salpeter, Isac Stern, Rabiner Levetov, Dr. N. Stern, Edel Elsner Henek Licht, and Others," April 1955, Bundesarchiv (Koblenz), Nachlaß Oskar Schindler, 1908–1974, Bestand, N 1493, No. 1, Band 23, 4 (hereafter referred to as "Oskar Schindler to Salpeter et al.," BA(K)).

44. "Oskar Schindler to Itzhak Stern," October 22, 1956, Bundesarchiv (Koblenz), Nachlaß Oskar Schindler, 1908–1974, Bestand 1493, No. 1, Band 23, 1.

45. Małopolska, or Little Poland, is a reference to a specific region in Poland that has Kraków as its capital.

46. "Wypis Pierwszy. Akt Notarialny, Numer Repertorium 228/37, March 17, 1937 (Krakow), Akta Rejestru Handlowego przy Sądzie Okręgowym w Krakowie, Oddział II (akta dotyczęce firmy: Pierwsza Małopolska Fabryka Naczyń Emaliowanychg i Wyrobów Balszanych "Rekord", Spółka z o. o w Krakowie), RH 401-RHB XII 35, 1–2, 6 (hereafter referred to as SOK, RH 401-RHB XII 35); "Oświadczenie," March 17, 1937, SOK, RH 401-RHB XII 35, "Rekord," 1; there were 5.28 złotys to the U.S. dollar in 1937, Bidwell, *Currency Conversion,* 37.

47. "Wypis Pierwszy. Akt Noytarialny," Numer Repertorium 977/37, October 27, 1937, SOK RH 401-RHB XII 35, 1, 3–4, 6–7; "Numer Repertorium 613, September 12, 1938, SOK RH 401-RHB XII 35, 1–2, 8; the exchange rate for the złoty to the U.S. dollar was 5.28 in 1937 and 5.30 in 1938. Bidwell, *Currency Conversion,* 37.

48. Mendelsohn, *The Jews of East Central Europe,* 69–70; Joseph Rothschild, *East Central Europe Between the Two World Wars* (Seattle: University of Washington Press, 1974), 40–41, 68–69; Norman Davies, *God's Playground: A History of Poland,* vol. 2, *1795 to the Present* (New York: Columbia University Press, 1982), 415–418.

49. The official date of the bankruptcy declaration was June 23, 1939; "Stanislaw Frühling to Sad Okręgówy w Krakowie," September 1, 1939, SOKC 2022: III U 5/39, 244–245; "Michał Gutman and Wolf Luzer Galjtman to Dr. Zbigniew Reczyński," July 10, 1939, SOKC 2022: III U 5/39, 235–236.

50. "Wypis Pierwszy. Akt Norarialny," Numer Repertorium: 371/39, March 17, 1939, SOK, RH 401-RHB XII 35, "Rekord," 5.

51. "Gutman and Glajtman to Reczyński," July 10, 1939, SOKC 2022: III U 5/39, 235–236; "Natan Wurzel to Dr. Zbigniew Reczyński," July 30, 1939, SOKC 2022: III U 5/39, 1 page; "Natan Wurzel to Dr. Zbigniew Reczyński," August 8, 1939, SOKC 2022: III U 5/39, 1 page; "Natan Wurzel to Wolf Gleitman i Michał Gutman," August 9, 1939, SOKC 2022: III U 5/39, 1 page.

52. Frühling to Sad Okręgówy w Krakowie, September 1, 1939, SOKC 2022: III U 5/39, 244–245.

53. "Dr. Bolesław Zawisza to Sad Okręgowy w Krakowy," August 4, 1942, SOKC 2023: III U 5/39, 1–2 plus "Odpis," July 24, 1942 and "Odpis" August 3, 1942. These lat-

ter documents are summaries of the meeting with Natan Wurzel and his last two letters to Dr. Zawisza.

54. Brzesko's Jewish cemetery was opened in 1846; the last of its three cemeteries was completed in 1904. The synagogue on ul. Puszkina was turned into a public library after the war. Martin Gilbert, *Holocaust Journey: Traveling in Search of the Past* (New York: Columbia University Press, 1997), 196; Joram Kagan, *Poland's Jewish Heritage* (New York: Hippocrene Books, 1992), 56–57.

55. "Dr. Roland Goryczko to Sąd Okręgowy w Krakowie," January 15, 1940, SOKC 2022: III U 5/39, 1–4; "Treuhänder für Werke und Gewerbe to Oskar Schindler," November 13, 1939, SOKC 2022: III U/59, 1–2; "Protokol," November 14, 1939, SOKC 2022: III U/59, 1–2.

56. Goryczko to SOK, January 15, 1940, SOKC 2022: III U 5/39, 1–4; Sad Grodzki w Krakowie, November 13, 1940, SOKC 2022: III U 5/39, 1 page.

57. "Dr. Roland Goryczko to Sąd Okręgowy w Krakowie," November 23, 1939, SOKC 2022: III U 5/39, 1–4.

58. Palowski, *Making of Schindler's List*, 111.

59. "Natan Wurzel to Julius Wiener" (in Hebrew), May 21, 1955, Yad Vashem Archives, M31/30, 1.

60. "Antoni Korzeniowski to American Jewish Joint Distribution Committee, Tel Aviv," October 10, 1951, American Jewish Joint Distribution Committee Archives, Jerusalem (File: Oskar Schindler), 1 page (hereafter referred to as AJJDC Archives, Jerusalem (O. Schindler); "Helen Fink to Antoni Korzeniowski," November 8, 1951, AJJDC Archives, Jerusalem (O. Schindler), 1 page.

61. "Wurzel to Wiener," May 21, 1955, YVA, M31/30, 2.

62. "Oskar Schindler to Salpeter et al.," BA(K), Oskar Schindler, N 1493, 1/23, 6–7; Oskar Schindler *Bericht*, October 30, 1955, Bundesarchiv (Koblenz), Nachlaß Oskar Schindler, 1908–1974, Bestand, N 1493, No. 1, Band 15, 15 (hereafter referred to as Oskar Schindler *Bericht*, BA(K); "Wurzel to Wiener," May 21, 1955, YVA, M31/30, 1.

63. "Oskar Schindler to Salpeter et al.", April 1955, BA, Oskar Schindler, N 1493, 1/23, 1–2.

64. Ibid.

65. Oskar Schindler *Bericht*, BA(K), 1; "Oskar Schindler to Salpeter et al.," BA(K), 2.

66. "Oskar Schindler to Salpeter et al.," BA(K), 2.

67. Ibid., 3; Gross, *Polish Society*, 80, 107.

68. "Oskar Schindler to Salpeter et al.," BA(K), 3.

69. Ibid.

70. Ibid.

71. "Oskar Schindler to Salpeter et al.," BA(K), 4; "Testimony of Julius Wiener before Messrs. Shatkai and Landau, in the Presence of Mr. Alkalai (in Hebrew) Jerusalem, 6 August 1963, Yad Vashem Archives, M 31/30 (RGD), 1 (hereafter referred to as "Testimony of Julius Wiener," August 6, 1963, YVA, M31/30); "Testimony of Esther Schwartz in the Matter of Oskar Schindler" (in Hebrew), 1963, Yad Vashem Archives, M 31/30 (RGD), 2–3 (hereafter referred to as "Testimony of Esther Schwartz, 1963," YVA, M 31/30).

72. "Testimony of Julius Wiener" (in Polish), October 10, 1956, Yad Vashem Archives, 01/164, 4 (hereafter referred to as "Testimony of Julius Wiener," 10 October 1956, YVA, 01/164).

73. Ibid., 4–5.

74. Ibid., 5. *Lapuvka* is from the Polish word *łapówka* (bribe). According to Yudit Natkin, my Hebrew translator, and her network of Yiddish specialists, there is also a word in Yiddish, *Lapuvka,* that means a small shovel or shoulder blade. In this context, *Lapuvka* could mean a pat on the back, or, more literally, a bribe. Schindler often used Yiddish and Hebrew words in letters to his Jewish friends.

75. "Oskar Schindler to Salpeter et al.," BA(K), 5.

76. Ibid.; Bauer, *American Jewry*, 320.

77. Tadeusz Pankiewicz, *Apteka w Getcie Krakowskim* (Kraków: Wydawnictwo Literackie, 1995), 65–66; Malvina Graf, *The Kraków Ghetto and the Płaszów Camp Remembered* (Tallahassee: University of Florida Press, 1989), 40.

78. Pankiewicz, *Apteka w Getcie Krakowskim*, 66–67; Graf, *The Kraków Ghetto*, 40–41.

79. Graf, *The Kraków Ghetto*, 41.

80. Pankiewicz, *Apteka w Getcie Krakowskim*, 67–68.

81. Ibid., 68–69.

82. "Oskar Schindler to Salpeter et al.," BA(K), 5–6; Palowski, *Making of Schindler's List*, 37–38.

83. Ibid., 5; Palowski, *Making of Schindler's List*, 35–36.

84. Palowski, *Making of Schindler's List*, 37–38.

85. Ibid., 39–42.

86. "Oskar Schindler to Salpeter et al.," BA(K), 6.

87. Ibid., 7.

88. "Testimony of Julius Wiener," October 10, 1956, YVA. 01/164, 1. "Testimony of Julius Wiener" (in Hebrew), August 6, 1963, Yad Vashem Archives, M 31/30, 1 (hereafter referred to as "Testimony of Julius Wiener," August 6, 1963, YVA, M 31/30, 1); "Testimony of Esther Schwartz," 1963, YVA, M 31/30, 1.

89. "Testimony of Esther Schwartz," 1963, YVA, M 31/30, 1; "Testimony of Julius Wiener, August 6, 1963, YVA, MVA 31/30, 1.

90. "Testimony of Julius Wiener," October 10, 1956, YVA, 01/164, 1–2.

91. Ibid.; "Testimony of Natan Wurzel" (in Hebrew), November 26, 1956, Yad Vashem Archives, M 31/30 (RGD), 1.

92. "Testimony of Esther Schwartz," 1963, YVA, M 31/30, 1; "Testimony of Julius Wiener," October 10, 1956, YVA, 01/164, 1–2; "Testimony of Julius Wiener," August 3, 1963, YVA, M 31/30, 1.

93. "Testimony of Julius Wiener," October 10, 1956, YVA, 01/164, 2; "Testimony of Julius Wiener," August 6, 1963, YVA, M 31/30, 1; "Testimony of Esther Schwartz, 1963, YVA, M 31/30, 1; "Testimony of Natan Wurzel," November 26, 1956, YVA, M 31/30, 1.

94. "Testimony of Esther Schwartz," 1963, YVA, M 31/30, 2; "Testimony of Julius Wiener," August 3, 1963, YVA, M 31/32, 1.

95. "Testimony of Julius Wiener," October 10, 1956, YVA, 01/164, 3; "Testimony of Natan Wurzel," November 26, 1956, YVA, M31/30, 1.

96. "Testimony of Esther Schwartz," 1963, YVA, M 31/30, 2.

97. "Testimony of Julius Wiener," August 6, 1963, YVA, M 31/30, 1–2.

98. "Moshe Landau and A. L. Kubovy to Oskar Schindler" (in German), December 24, 1963, Yad Vashem Archives, M-31/20-1, 1 page; "Testimony of Mrs. Simah Hartmann (Gelcer) before Shatkai and Landau, in the Presence of Alkalai and Wiener" (in Hebrew), August 28, 1963, Yad Vashem Archives, M 31/30 (RGD), 1.

99. "The Enterprising Committee of the Work Camp Survivors: Oskar Schindler in Brinnlitz, to Mr. Aryeh Leon Kovivi" (in Hebrew), December 10, 1961, Yad Vashem Archives, Oskar and Emilie Schindler Collection, Department of the Righteous, 2–4 (hereafter referred to as "The Enterprising Committee of the Work Camp Survivors," December 10, 1961, YVA, Schindler Collection).

100. "Schindler to Salpeter et al.," BA(K), 7–8; "The Enterprising Committee of the Work Camp Survivors," December 10, 1961, YVA, Schindler Collection, 1–4.

101. "Simon Jeret to Oskar Schindler" (in German), December 17, 1956, Bundesarchiv (Koblenz), Nachlaß Oskar Schindler, 1908–1974, Bestand 1493, No. 1, Band 23, 1.

102. Urbach, interviews by the author, April 13, 1999, and February 15, 2000.

103. Ibid.

104. Ibid.

105. Ibid.

106. Ibid.

107. "Schindler Financial Report 1945," Yad Vashem Archives, 01/164, 1.

108. Urbach, interview, March 19, 2000; Urbach, interviews, April 13, 1999, February 15, 2000, and March 19, 2000.

109. "Testimony of Julius Wiener," August 6, 1963, YVA, 2.

110. "Oskar Schindler to Dr. K. J. Ball-Kaduri" (in German), September 9, 1956, Bundesarchiv (Koblenz), Nachlaß Oskar Schindler, 1908–1974, Bestand 1493, No. 1, Band 25, 2; "Oskar Schindler to Simon Jeret" (in German), November 25, 1956, Bundesarchiv (Koblenz), Nachlaß Oskar Schindler, 1908–1974, Bestand 1493, No. 1, Band 25, 3.

111. "Notes of Dr. Moshe Bejski on the Banquet in Honor of Oskar Schindler," May 2, 1962, Tel Aviv, Israel (in Hebrew), 29. Dr. Bejski kindly gave me a copy of his typed transcript of the evening's testimonials and speeches when I interviewed him in Tel Aviv on May 17, 1999.

Chapter 4

1. *Krakauer Zeitung,* May 30, 1943, 15.

2. Karl Baedeker, *Das Generalgouvernement: Reisehandbuch von Karl Baedeker* (Leipzig: Karl Baedeker, 1943), iv.

3. Ibid., 10, 102, 137.

4. Ibid., 32–34, 142.

5. Dr. Max Freiherr du Prel, ed., *Das General Gouvernement* (Würzburg: Konrad Triltsch Verlag, 1942), v, viii-xii, 375–391.

6. Ibid., 147.

7. "Die Juden schwingen sich in den Sattel," *Krakauer Zeitung,* September 18, 1943, 3; "Jüdisches Parasitentum ohne Maske," *Krakauer Zeitung,* September 28, 1943, 5; Hanns Stock, "Fünf Jahre befreites Sudetenland," *Krakauer Zeitung,* September 28, 1943, 3.

8. Hans Frank, *Dziennik Hansa Franka,* vol. 1 (Warsaw: Wydawnictwo Prawnicze, 1956), 35, 71.

9. Ulrich Herbert, *Hitler's Foreign Workers: Enforced Foreign Labor in Germany under the Third Reich,* trans. William Templer (Cambridge: Cambridge University Press, 1997), 62, 70, 198, 462.

10. Herbert, *Hitler's Foreign Workers,* 79–84; Jan Tomasz Gross, *Polish Society under German Occupation: The Generalgouvernement, 1939–1944* (Princeton: Princeton University Press, 1979), 79–80.

11. Oskar Schindler *Bericht,* October 30, 1955, Bundesarchiv (Koblenz), Nachlaß Oskar Schindler, 1908–1974, Bestand N 1493, No. 1, Band 15, 1; Oskar Schindler *Lebenslauf,* October 26, 1966, Bundesarchiv (Koblenz), Nachlaß Oskar Schindler, 1908–1974, Bestand N 1493, No. 1, Band 1, 1–2; the General Government took over the Polish State Monopolies for Tobacco, Spirits, Salt, Matches, and the Lottery on November 1, 1939. Du Prel, *Das General-Gouvernement,* 104–105, 377.

12. Oskar Schindler *Bericht,* BA(K), 1.

13. Sol Urbach, interview by the author, Delray Beach, Florida, February 15, 2000.

14. "Testimony of Edith Wertheim," June 20, 1994, T-2956, Fortunoff Archives, Yale University.

15. "Schindler Financial Report 1945," Yad Vashem Archives, 01/164, 1 (hereafter referred to as Schindler Financial Report 1945, YVA).

16. "Testimony of Edith Wertheim," November 13, 1964, Martin A. Gosch and Howard Koch, "The Oskar Schindler Story," Delbert Mann Papers, Special Collections Library, Vanderbilt University, 1B, 9–10.

17. "Testimony of Menachim Stern," July 15, 1979, T-152, Fortunoff Archives, Yale University.

18. Gross, *Polish Society under German Occupation*, 109–110; Czesław Madajczyk, *Polityka III Rzeszy w Okupowanej Polsce*, vol. 2 (Warszawa: Państwowe Wydawnictwo Naukowe, 1970), 67–68.

19. Gross, *Polish Society*, 110.

20. Ibid., 110–111.

21. Isaiah Trunk, *Judenrat: The Jewish Councils in Eastern Europe Under Nazi Occupation* (New York: Stein & Day, 1977), 64–65; Gross, *Polish Society*, 94, 100–101; Madajczyk, *Polityka III Rzeszy w Okupowanej Polsce*, II, 66–67.

22. Eugeniusz Duda, *The Jews of Cracow*, trans. Ewa Basiura (Kraków: Wydawnictwo 'Hagada' and Argona-Jarden Bookshop, 2000), 60–62; Czesław Madajczyk, *Polityka III Rzesy w Okupowanej Polsce*, vol. 1 (Warszawa: Państwowe Wydawnictwo Naukowe, 1970), 516–519; Gross, *Polish Society*, 93–96; Trunk, *Judenrat*, 63–64; Piotrowski, *Dziennik Hansa Frank*, I, 265–266; the Polish edition of Hans Frank's diary is more complete than the English version, Stanisław Piotrowski's *Hans Frank's Diary* (Warszawa: Państwowe Wydanictwo Naukowe, 1961), 217–218.

23. Jeremy Noakes and Geoffrey Pridham, eds., *Nazism: A History in Documents and Eyewitness Accounts, 1919–1945*, vol. 2, *Foreign Policy, War and Racial Extermination* (New York: Schocken Books, 1988), 1051.

24. Noakes and Pridham, *Nazism*, 1052–1053; Raul Hilberg, *The Destruction of the European Jews*, vol. 1 (New York: Holmes & Meier, 1985), 191.

25. Haim Hillel Ben-Sasson, "The Middle Ages," in Haim Hillel Ben-Sasson, ed. *A History of the Jewish People* (Cambridge, Mass.: Harvard University Press, 1994), 639; Shmuel Ettinger, "The Modern Period," in Ben-Sasson, *A History of the Jewish People* (Cambridge, Mass.: Harvard University Press, 1994), 762, 807, 811–812.

26. Hilberg, *Destruction of the European Jews*, 1:205–206; efforts were also made in the immediate months after the outbreak of the war to set up ghettos in Piotrków just southwest of Łódź and in Warsaw. Plans for the Warsaw ghetto collapsed after *Judenrat* leaders appealed to Warsaw's military commandant, *General* Karl von Neumann-Neurode.

27. Duda, *The Jews of Cracow*, 62.

28. Piotrowski, *Dziennik Hansa Frank*, 266; Aleksander Bieberstein, *Zagłada Żydów w Krakowie* (Kraków: Wydawnictwo Literackie, 1985), 32; Duda, *Jews of Cracow*, 62. The *Gazeta Żadowska*, which was edited by a German Jew, Fritz Seifert, was published from July 23, 1940 until August 30, 1942.

29. Duda, *Jews of Cracow*, 62.

30. Ibid.

31. Arieh L. Bauminger, *The Fighters of the Cracow Ghetto* (Jerusalem: Keter Press Enterprises, 1986), 30–31.

32. Hilberg, *Destruction of the European Jews*, 2:668–669, 3:1108; Shmuel Krakowski, "The Fate of Jewish Prisoners of War in the September 1939 Campaign," *Yad Vashem Studies*, vol. 12 (1977), 316–317. Wächter's dutiful enforcement of these regulations served him well. He became Governor of Galicia when it was integrated into the General Government after the invasion of the Soviet Union in 1941. Two years later, Wächter, now an *SS-Gruppenführer*, became the Chief of Military Administration of German occupied Italy after the collapse of Mussolini's first regime. Wächter remained in Italy after the war ended and died in Rome in 1949 under the protection of Bishop Alois Hudal, the rector of Santa Maria del Anima and confessor to the German Catholic community in Rome. A year ear-

lier, the controversial Bishop had helped Franz Stangl, the commandant of the Treblinka death camp, escape to Syria. Duda, *Jews of Cracow,* 62–63; Frank, *Dziennik Hansa Franka,* 52. Frank cites November 10 as Independence Day in the Polish edition. The editors of the English edition corrected the date. Piotrowski, *Hans Frank's Diary,* 49; *Trial of War Criminals before the Nuernberg Military Tribunals under Control Council Law No. 10 (Nuernberg October 1946-April 1949),* vol. 12 (Washington, D.C.: United States Government Printing Office, 1951), 107; Gitta Sereny, *Into That Darkness: An Examination of Conscience* (New York: Vintage Books, 1983), 275, 289–290.

33. Duda, *Jews of Cracow,* 63.

34. Tadeusz Pankiewicz, *Apteka w Getcie Krakowskim* (Kraków: Wydawnictwo Literackie, 1995), 12–13; Malvina Graf, *The Kraków Ghetto and the Płaszów Camp* (Tallahassee: Florida State University Press, 1989), 35–36.

35. Duda, *Jews of Cracow,* 63; Emilie Schindler, *Where Light and Shadow Meet,* trans. Dolores M. Koch (New York: W. W. Norton & Company 1997), 50–51; Robin O'Neil, "An Analysis of the Actions of Oskar Schindler Within the Context of the Holocaust in German Occupied Poland and Czechoslovakia" (Master's Thesis, University College, London, September 30 1996), 34. According to Emilie and O'Neil, Thomas Keneally called Amelia "Ingrid" in his novel. See Thomas Keneally, *Schindler's List* (New York: Touchstone Books, 1992), 25, 78, 127–128.

36. Pankiewicz, *Apteka w Getcie Krakowskim,* 13–14.

37. Anna Pióro and Wiesława Kralińska, *Krakowskie Getto* (Kraków: Muzeum Pamięci Narodowej "Apteka pod Orłem, 1995), 37–38; Stella Müller-Madej, interview by the author, Kraków, Poland, August 9, 2000.

38. Stella Müller-Madej, *A Girl from Schindler's List,* trans. William R. Brand (London: Polish Cultural Foundation, 1997), 12.

39. Ibid., 12–13.

40. Duda, *Jews of Cracow,* 66; Pióro, *Krakowskie Getto,* 36; Pankiewicz, *Apteka w Getcie Krakowskim,* 19–20.

41. Müller-Madej, *A Girl from Schindler's List,* 13.

42. "Zbioru fotohgrafii z 'akcji zydowskiej' w Krakowie/eksmisje, wysiedlenia, rejestracje, getto." Starosty Miasta Krakowa/Der Stadthauptmann der Stadt Krakau/ z lat 1939–1945, SMKr 211, Archiwum Państwowe w Krakowie.

43. Pankiewicz, *Apteka w Getcie Krakowskim,* 16, 19–23, 33.

44. Trunk, *Judenrat,* 485–487; Pankiewicz, *Apteka w Getcie Krakowskim,* 16, 19–23; Pióro, *Krakowskie Getto,* 58–59.

45. Pankiewicz, *Apteka w Getcie Krakowskim,* 25; Graf, *The Kraków Ghetto and the Płaszow Camp Remembered,* 39.

46. Pankiewicz, *Apteka w Getcie Krakowskim,* 25; Trunk, *Judenrat,* 475, 489.

47. Graf, *Kraków Ghetto,* 39; Trunk, *Judenrat,* 478, 499–500.

48. Yehuda Bauer, *American Jewry and the Holocaust: The American Jewish Joint Distribution Committee, 1939–1945* (Detroit: Wayne State University Press, 1981), 85–86; du Prel, *Das General Gouvernement,* 311; Weichert's appointment as chair of the JSS in Kraków and his relationship with Czerniakow and the Warsaw *Judenrat* is discussed in some depth in *The Warsaw Diary of Adam Czerniakow: Prelude to Doom,* ed. Raul Hilberg, Stanislaw Staron, and Josef Kermisz, trans. Stanislaw Staron and the staff of Yad Vashem (New York: Stein and Day, 1979), 33, 161, 164–165, 168–169, 174.

49. Bieberstein, *Zagłada Żydów w Krakowie,* 31, 96, 129, 132, 135, 159–163; Bauer, *American Jewry and the Holocaust,* 90–92, 318–322; Bauminger, *Fighters,* 33; Jean-Claude Favez, *The Red Cross and the Holocaust,* ed. and trans. John and Beryl Fletcher (Cambridge: Cambridge University Press, 1999), 143–144.

50. Pankiewicz, *Apteka w Getcie Krakowskim,* 74–75.

51. Pióro, *Krakowskie Getto,* 4043; Pankiewicz, *Apteka w Getcie Krakowskim,* 26; Bieberstein, *Zagłada Żydów w Krakowie,* 73; Sol Urbach, interview by the author, Flemington, New Jersey, July 15, 2002.

52. Bieberstein, *Zagłada Żydów w Krakowie,* 223; Pankiewicz, *Apteka w Getcie Krakowskim,* 25–26.

53. Pankiewicz, *Apteka w getcie Krakowskim,* 26–27; Duda, *Jews of Cracow,* 28.

54. Müller-Madej, *A Girl from Schindler's List,* 13–17.

55. Ibid., 22, 27–29; Gross, *Polish Society,* 108–109.

56. Müller-Madej, *A Girl from Schindler's List,* 13–14, 40.

57. Pankiewicz, 33, 65–66; Manci Rosner, interview by the author, Hallandale, Florida, March 21, 2000.

58. Christopher R. Browning, *Nazi Policy, Jewish Workers, German Killers* (Cambridge: Cambridge University Press, 2000), 61–62; du Prel, *Das General Gouvernement,* 379; according to Frauendorfer, in the spring of 1940, his office planned to send a half million Poles to work in the Greater Reich. There were already 160,000 Poles being used there as agricultural workers and another 50,000 Poles working in German factories. By the end of 1941, Frauendorfer said that Poles made up 47 percent of the foreign labor force in the Greater Reich. In 1943, Frank proudly noted that the General Government had sent two million workers to the Greater Reich. Piotrowski, *Dziennik Hansa Frank,* 72–74.

59. Gross, *Polish Society,* 111; Browning, *Nazi Policy,* 25, 62–63, 71–73.

60. Pióro, *Krakowskie Ghetto,* 42.

61. Julius Madritsch, *Menschen in Not! Meine Erlebnisse in den Jahren 1940 bis 1944 als Unternehmer im damaligen Generalgouvernement* (Vienna: V. Roth, 1962), 6–8; Mila Levinson-Page, interview by the author, Beverly Hills, California, December 2, 2001; Helen Sternlicht Rosenzweig, interview by the author, Boca Raton, Florida, March 20, 2000.

62. Mietek Pemper, interview by the author, Augsburg, Germany, January 17, 2000; "Oskar Schindler to Dr. Ball-Kaduri," 21 October 1956, 01/165, Yad Vashem Archives, 1–2.

63. Keneally, *Schindler's List,* 230–231.

64. Madritsch, *Menschen,* 27.

65. Ibid., 6.

66. Ibid., 7–8.

67. Ibid., 9–10.

68. Ibid., 9.

69. Ibid., 9–12.

70. Browning, *Nazi Policy,* 71–73.

71. *Das Protokoll der Wannsee-Konferenz, January 20, 1942* (Berlin: Haus der Wannsee-Konferenz, 2002), 15.

72. Ibid., 15.

73. Browning, *Nazi Policies,* 75.

74. Hilberg, *Destruction of the European Jews,* 2:524, n. 137, 525–526; Albert Speer, *The Slave State: Heinrich Himmler's Masterplan for SS Supremacy,* trans. Joachim Neugroschel (London: Weidenfeld and Nicolson, 1981), 257; Browning, *Nazi Policy,* 73–74; General Georg Thomas, the head of the Armaments Inspectorate in Berlin, who was in a power struggle with Albert Speer, the new Armaments Minister, briefly alludes to the new problems with the SS over labor in his *Geschichte der deutschen Wehr-und Rüstungswirtschaft (1918–1943/45),* ed. Wolfgang Birkenfeld (Boppard am Rhein: Harald Boldt Verlag, 1966), 357–358.

75. Speer, *The Slave State,* 257; Browning, *Nazi Policy,* 76–77; Hilberg, *The Destruction of the European Jews,* 2:526.

76. Richard Breitman, *The Architect of Genocide: Himmler and the Final Solution* (New York: Alfred A Knopf, 1991), 235; Gross, *Polish Society Under German Occupation*, 66–67, n. 22; Browning, *Nazi Policies*, 77.

77. Browning, *Nazi Policies*, 77; Hilberg, *Destruction of the European Jews*, 2:526.

78. Speer, *The Slave State*, 260; Browning's translation of the phrase "would retain Jews until the end of the war" is different from Speer's but is probably more accurate. Browning, *Nazi Policies*, 77–78.

79. Speer, *The Slave State*, 260–261.

80. Ibid., 261.

81. Ibid., 262–263.

82. Ibid., 263.

83. Hilberg, *Destruction of the European Jews*, 2:527.

84. Ibid., 2:527–528.

85. Ibid., 2:528; Wolfgang Sofsky, *The Order of Terror: The Concentration Camp*, trans. William Templer (Princeton: Princeton University Press, 1997), 175; "Schindler Financial Report, 1945," YVA, 3.

86. Hilberg, *Destruction of the European Jews*, 2:529.

87. Yitzhak Arad, Shmuel Krakowski, and Shmuel Spector, eds. *The Einsatzgruppen Reports* (New York: The Holocaust Library, 1989), v-vi; Hilberg, *Destruction of the European Jews*, 2:341.

88. Breitman, *Architect of Genocide*, 192–193.

89. Henry Friedlander, *Origins of Nazi Genocide: From Euthanasia to the Final Solution* (Chapel Hill: University of North Carolina Press, 1995), 68, 108–109, 111, 237, 243–245, 296–300; Yitzhak Arad, *Belzec, Sobibór, Treblinka: The Operation Reinhard Death Camps* (Bloomington: Indiana University Press, 1987), 17–18.

90. Hilberg, *Destruction* of the European Jews, 3:893, 1219; Daniel Niewyk and Francis Nicosia, *The Columbia Guide to the Holocaust* (New York: Columbia University Press, 2000), 198; Judith Tydor Baumel, "Extermination Camps," in Walter Laquer and Judith Tydor Baumel, eds. *The Holocaust Encyclopedia* (New Haven: Yale University Press, 2001), 178; Shmuel Krakowski, "Chełmno," in Israel Gutman, ed., *Encyclopedia of the Holocaust*, vol. 1 (New York: Macmillan Publishing Company, 1990), 283.

91. Yisrael Gutman, "Auschwitz–An Overview," in Yisrael Gutman and Michael Berenbaum, eds., *Anatomy of the Auschwitz Death Camp* (Bloomington: Indiana University Press in Association with the United States Holocaust Memorial Museum, 1994), 28–30; Raul Hilberg, "Auschwitz and the 'Final Solution,'" in Gutman and Berenbaum, eds., *Anatomy of the Auschwitz Death Camp*, 84–85; Franciszek Piper, "Gas Chambers and Crematoria," in Gutman and Berenbaum, eds., *Anatomy of the Auschwitz Death Camp*, 157–158; Franciszek Piper, *How Many Perished: Jews, Poles, Gypsies . . .* (Kraków: Poligrafia, 1991), 52.

92. Arad, *Belzec, Sobibór, Treblinka*, 14–15, 370.

93. Ibid., 14–16, 23–26, 126–127.

94. Ibid., 30–34, 333, 341.

95. Ibid., 297–298.

96. Józef Marszałek, *Majdanek: The Concentration Camp in Lublin* (Warsaw: Interpress, 1986), 18, 23; the name Majdanek was never used officially. It was taken from the Polish district it bordered, Majdan Tatarski, and was known in official German documents as *Kriegsgefangenenlager der Waffen SS in Lublin* (KGL Lublin) until 1943 and then as *Konzentrationslager der Waffen SS Lublin* (KL Lublin).

97. Marszałek, *Majdanek*, 69, 142. Of those who died at Majdanek from various causes, 100,000 were Poles, 80,000 were Jews, and 50,000 were Soviet citizens. Edward Gryń and

Zofia Murawska-Gryń, *Majdanek* (Lublin: Państwowe Muzeum na Majdanku, 1984), 93–95, 98–99. About a half million prisoners passed through Majdanek.

98. Madritsch, *Menschen*, 5, 9, 14. Madritsch only mentions the last name of his Polish "collaborators." The list consists of "Felix Holeczek and [his] brother, the Soltys brothers, the Pajong brothers, Paczesnika, Kleinmann, Gonczarcik, Zbroja, and many others." In the extensive list of Polish publications on wartime resistance among Poles, only a few of these names crop up, and even then it is not certain if they refer to some of the Poles on Madritsch's list. See, for example, Tadeusz Wroński's *Kronika Okupowanego Krakowa* (Kraków: Wydawnicto Literackie, 1974), 289, 331 and Aleksander Bieberstein's *Zagłada Żydów w Krakowie*, 113.

99. Madritsch, *Menschen*, 14.

100. Ibid., Madritsch said that 60 percent of his Jewish workers knew nothing about sewing since most of them had been "physicians, lawyers, engineers, and merchants" before the war.

101. Madritsch, *Menschen*, 9–10.

102. Ibid., 24; "Schindler Financial Report 1945," YVA, 3.

103. Madritsch, *Menschen*, 2; Harry M. Rabinowitz, *Hasidism: The Movement and Its Masters* (Northvale, N.J.: Jason Aronson, 1988), 318–319; Leo Rosten, *The Joys of Yiddish* (New York: Pocket Books, 1970), 418–419.

Chapter 5

1. Oskar estimated that he spent a great deal more than the estimated 2.64 million RM to help his Jews, though this excess varied by no more than 10 percent of his actual expenses for his *Schindlerjuden*. "Schindler Financial Report 1945," July 1945, Yad Vashem Archives, 01/164, 12–13.

2. "Emalia Bilanz für 31 Dezember 1943," Kraków, May 15, 1944, *Lastenausgleicharchiv* (Bayreuth), 306 2230a (Oskar Schindler), 1–4 (hereafter referred to as LAG (OS) 306 2230a).

3. "Oskar Schindler *Antrag*," March 16, 1954, Bundesarchiv (Koblenz), Nachlaß Oskar Schindler, 1908–1974, Bestand N 1493, No. 1, Band 3, 2.

4. "Oskar Schindler *Bericht*," October 30, 1955, Bundesarchiv (Koblenz), Nachlaß Oskar Schindler, 1908–1974, Bestand N 1493, No. 1, Band 15, 1; "Oskar Schindler *Lebenslauf*," 26 October 1966, Bundesarchiv (Koblenz), Nachlaß Oskar Schindler, 1908–1974, Bestand N 1493, No. 1, Band 1, 1–2; "Schindler Financial Report 1945," YVA, 1; Jan Tomasz Gross, *Polish Society under German Occupation: The Generalgouvernement, 1939–1944* (Princeton: Princeton University Press, 1979), 109–110; Czesław Madajczyk, *Polityka III Rzeszy w Okupowanej Polsce*, vol. 2 (Warszawa: Państwowe Wydawnictwo Naukowe, 1970), 67–68.

5. "Oskar Schindler to Fritz Lang," July 20, 1951, Bundesarchiv (Koblenz), Nachlaß Oskar Schindler, 1908–1974, Bestand N 1493, Band 23, 5 (hereafter referred to as "Schindler to Lang," BA(K)); in 1942, the HSSPF in the General Government became the HSSPF Ost. Włodzimierz Borodziej, *Terror und Politik: Die Deutsche Polizei und die Polnische Widerstandsbewegung im Generalgouvernement, 1939–1944* (Mainz: Verlag Philipp von Zabern, 1999), 33.

6. "Schindler to Lang," BA(K), 5.

7. Ibid., 3; "Schindler Financial Report 1945," YVA, 3–4; Roman Kiełkowski, *Zlikwidować na Miejscu! Z dziejów hitlerowskiej w Krakowie* (Kraków: Wydawnictwo Literackie, 1981), 104–105.

8. "Schindler Financial Report 1945," YVA, 4.

9. "*Aufstellung der in Krakau und Brünnlitz verbliebenen Fabrikgebäude, Maschinen, und Einrichtungen einschl. der Forderungen an das Reich*," May 6, 1945, Bundesarchiv

(Koblenz), Nachlaß Oskar Schindler, 1908–1974, Bestand 1493, No. 1, Band 14, 2 (hereafter referred to as *"Aufstellung der in Krakau,"* May 6, 1945, BA(K)); *"Situations-Skizze, mit angrenzenden Industrien für Deutsche Emaliwarenfabrik-Oskar Schindler,"* n.d., Bundesarchiv (Koblenz), Nachlaß Oskar Schindler, 1908–1974, Bestand N 1493, No. 1, Band 3, 1 page (hereafter referred to as *"Situations-Skizze"* Emalia, BA(K)); "Oskar Schindler *Teilbescheid unter Vorbehalt,"* Der Magistrat Sozialverwaltung-Ausgleichsamt, Stadt Frankfurt am Main, March 5, 1959, 8, Bundesarchiv (Koblenz), Nachlaß Oskar Schindler, 1908–1974, Bestand N 1493, No. 1, Band 3 (hereafter referred to as "Oskar Schindler *Teilbescheid,* March 5, 1959," BA(K)); "Oskar Schindler *Fragebogen,"* Regensburg Stadt *Ausgleichsamt,* April 18, 1957, V 15 591, Bundesarchiv (Koblenz), Nachlaß Oskar Schindler, 1908–1974, Bestand N 1493, No. 1, Band 3, 1–3 (hereafter referred to as "Oskar Schindler *Fragebogen,* BA(K)).

10. "Kurt Müller to Oskar Schindler," October 30, 1957, Bundesarchiv (Koblenz), Nachlaß Oskar Schindler, 1908–1974, Bestand 1493, No. 1, Band 3, 1–3. Müller was a representative of Siemens-Bauunion Gmbh responding to Schindler's request for information about the construction of the Siemens built facility at Emalia; "Oskar Schindler, *Anlage zu Az.* V 15-591," April 18, 1957, Archives of the American Jewish Joint Distribution Committee (New York), 1 page.

11. *"Aufstellung der in Krakau,"* May 6, 1945, BA(K), 2; "Oskar Schindler Notarized Compensation Statement," Regensburg, August 27, 1949, LAG (OS) 306 2230a, 45.

12. *"Feuerversicherung, Versicherungsschein* Nr. 109 128," July 10, 1943, Bundesarchiv (Koblenz), Nachlaß Oskar Schindler, Bestand 1493, No. 1, Band 3, 1–2 and *"Abschrift,"* February 11, 1944, 1; *"Feuerversicherung Versicherungsschein* Nr. 109 129," July 10, 1943, Bundesarchiv (Koblenz), Nachlaß Oskar Schindler, Bestand 1493, No. 1, Band 3, 1–3, and *"Abschrift"* February 11, 1944," 1–2.

13. "Dr. Roland Goryczko to Sad Okręgowy w Krakowie," January 15, 1940, Akta Rejestru Handlowego przy Sądzie Okregowym w krakowie (akta dotyczące firmy: Pierwzsa Małopolska Fabryka Naczyń Emailowanych i Wyrobów Blaszanych "Rekord", Społka z o o. Krakowie), Archiwum Państwowe w Krakowie Oddział III, 2022, III U 5/39, 1–4. This set of court records, 2022 and 2023 will hereafter be referred to as SOKC 2022 or 2023; "Treuhänder für Werke und Gewerbe to Oskar Schindler," November 13, 1939, SOKC 2022: III U/59, 1–2; "Protokol," November 14, 1939, SOKC 2022: III U/59, 1–2.

14. Dr. Goryczko hints of this in his September 11, 1941, report to the Polish Trade Court. "Report of Dr. Roland Goryczko," September 11, 1941, SOKC 2023: III U 5/39, 1–4.

15. "Report of Dr. Roland Goryczko," September 11, 1941, SOKC 2023: III U 5/39, 1–4; "Dr. Zawisza's General Report to the Polish Trade Court," April 18, 1942, SOKC 2023: III U 5/39, 1–4; Dr. Zawisza's Report to the Polish Trade Court," August 4, 1942, SOKC 2023: III U5/39, 1–4; "Statement of Judge Dr. Stanisław Zmudny," September 16, 1942, SOKC 2023: III U 5/39, 1 page; "Dr. Zawisza to the Polish Trade Court," May 7, 1946, SOKC 2023: III U 5/39, 1–3; "Dr. Zawisza to the Polish Trade Court," May 31, 1946, SOKC 2023: III U 5/39, 1–2; by 1946, there were 100 złotys to $1. R.L. Bidwell, *Currency Conversion Tables; A Hundred Years of Change* (London: Rex Collins, 1970), 37.

16. Mietek Pemper, interview by the author, Augsburg, Germany, May 26, 1999.

17. "Schindler Financial Report 1945," YVA, 1; Sol Urbach, interviews by the author, Delray Beach, Florida, April 13, 1999 and February 15, 2000, and Flemington, N.J., July 15, 2002; "Testimony of Edith Wertheim," November 13, 1964, Martin A. Gosch and Howard Koch, "The Schindler Story," Delbert Mann Papers, Special Collections Library, Vanderbilt University, 1B, 9–10.

18. Urbach, interview, July 15, 2002; Pankiewicz, *Apteka w Getcie Krakowskim,* 205–206; Aleksander Bieberstein, *Zagłada Żydów w Krakowie* (Kraków: Wydawnicto Literackie, 1985), 78–79.

19. Urbach, interview, July 15, 2002.

20. "Schindler to Lang," July 20, 1951, 3; Franciszek Palowski, *The Making of Schindler's List: Behind the Scenes of an Epic Film,* trans. Anna and Robert G. Ware (Secaucus, N.J.: Birch Lane Press, 1998), 40; Tadeus Wroński, *Kaźń Polaków przy Ulica Pomorskiej 2 w Krakpowie w Latach 1939–1945* (Kraków; Wydawnictwo "Sport i Turystyka," 1985), 53–54, 70–71.

21. "Schindler to Lang," July 20, 1951, 3; Palowski, *The Making of Schindler's List,* 40; Thomas Keneally gives a more lively account of Schindler's arrest and interrogation. However, this was an historical novel and he chose not to include footnotes; consequently, it is difficult to verify his account. My sources, including those by Oskar, Emilie, and Itzhak Stern, do not mention such details. Thomas Keneally, *Schindler's List* (New York: Simon & Schuster, 1992), 103–104.

22. "Summary of Interview with Oskar Schindler and Notes re Ahmon Goeth," November 18, 1964, in Howard Koch and Martin A. Gosch, "The Oskar Schindler Story," Delbert Mann Papers, Special Collections Library, Vanderbilt University, 7-A, 6–7, 9–10 (hereafter referred to as "Interview with Oskar Schindler," November 18, 1964, Delbert Mann Papers, Vanderbilt University).

23. "Interview with Oskar Schindler," November 18, 1964, Delbert Mann Papers, Vanderbilt University, 7–9.

24. Ibid., 7–10.

25. Ibid., 9.

26. Pankiewicz, *Apteka w Getcie Krakowskim,* 97–99; Malvina Graf, *The Kraków Ghetto and the Płaszów Camp Remembered* (Tallahassee: Florida State University, 1989), 43; Bieberstein, *Zagłada Żydów w Krakowie,* 57–58.

27. Pankiewicz, *Apteka w Getcie Krakowskim,* 99–103.

28. Ibid.,103–104.

29. Ibid., 108–109.

30. Ibid., 115.

31. Ibid., 116–119; Bieberstein, *Zagłada Żydów w Krakowie,* 60–63.

32. Pankiewicz, *Apteka w Getcie Krakowskim,* 99–108; Bieberstein, *Zagłada Żydów w Krakowie,* 63.

33. Pankiewicz, *Apteka w Getcie Krakowskim,* 128–129; Bieberstein, *Zagłda Żydówska w Krakowie,* 63–64.

34. Pankiewicz, *Apteka w Getcie Krakowskim,* 130–131; Bieberstein, *Zagłada Żydóska w Krakowie,* 64–65.

35. Pankiewicz, *Apteka w Getcie Krakowskim,* 100–107; Yitzhak Arad, *Belzec, Sobibór, Treblinka: The Operation Reinhard Death Camps* (Bloomington: Indiana University Press, 1987), 72–73, 126–127, 387–389. Arad says that the Germans deported only 5,000 Kraków Jews in June 1942. However, he erroneously lists their deportation dates as June 1–6.

36. Keneally, *Schindler's List,* 117–125.

37. "Oskar Schindler *Bericht,*" BA(K), 2; There were two Lesers and five Reichs listed on the fall 1944 and spring 1945 "Schindler's Lists." Jakob Leser was a thirty-one-year-old engine fitter and the twenty-eight-year-old Szulim Leser was listed as a mechanic's apprentice. There were two Kalman Reichs on the lists (ages thirty-three and thirty), one a metal worker, and the other a mechanic. Jerzy Reich was an eighteen-year-old machine mechanic; the fifty-year-old Emil Reich was listed as a metal press operator. The thirty-one-year-old Mendel Reich was listed initially as a mechanic's apprentice, but this was

scratched out and changed to building contractor on the 1944 list. "Konzentrationslager Groß-Rosen-Arbeitslager Brünnlitz: *Namenliste der männlichen Häftlinge*," October 21, 1944, Państwowe Muzeum Auschwitz-Birkenau w Oświęcimiu, KL Gross-Rosen Zugangs a. Häftlingslisten, ss. 80–92, Sygn., D-Gr-3/1, Nr. 150003, 80–92; "KL Groß-Rosen-AL Brünnlitz/Häftl.-Liste (Männer)," April 18, 1945. Bundesarchiv (Koblenz), Nachlaß Oskar Schindler, 1908–1974, Bestand 1493, No. 1, Band 12, 1–14.

38. Leon Leyson, interview by the author, Anaheim, California, March 29, 2000.

39. Pankiewicz, *Apteka w Getcie Krakowskim*, 135.

40. Ibid., 199–200.

41. Ibid., 139.

42. Yehuda Bauer and Robert Rozett, "Estimated Jewish Losses in the Holocaust," *Encyclopedia of the Holocaust*, Israel Gutman, ed. vol. 4 (New York: Macmillan Publishing Company, 1990), 1799. The authors estimate that there were 3.3 million Jews in Poland on the eve of World War II and 3.02 million in the Soviet Union. They add that there were almost 9.8 million Jews in Europe at the time, with 5,860,000 murdered in the Holocaust; Arad, *Belzec, Sobibór, Treblinka*, 165; Raul Hilberg, *The Destruction of the European Jews* vol. 3 (New York: Holmes & Meier), 1985, 1219. Hilberg says that 5.1 million Jews died in the Holocaust, up to 2.7 million killed in the six death camps.

43. Pankiewicz, *Apteka w Getcie Krakowskim*, 155–159; Bieberstein, *Zagłada Żydów w Krakowie*, 71–72.

44. Pankiewicz, *Apteka w Getcie Krakowskim*, 159–160; Albert Speer, *The Slave State: Heinrich Himmler's Masterplan for SS Supremacy*, trans. Joachim Neugroschel (London: Weidenfeld and Nicolson, 1981), 262–263; Hilberg, *Destruction of the European Jews*, 2, 527–528.

45. "Oskar Schindler *Bericht*," BA(K), 1; Julius Madritsch, *Menschen in Not! Meine Erlebnisse in den Jahren 1940 bis 1944 als Unternehmer im damaligen Generalgouvernement* (Vienna: V. Roth, 1962), 13.

46. Madritsch, *Menschen*, 13.

47. Pankiewicz, *Apteka w Getcie Krakowskim*, 162.

48. Ibid., 154.

49. Ibid., 164–171.

50. Pankiewicz, *Apteka w Getcie Krakowskim*, 173–179; Bieberstein, *Zagłada Żydów w Krakowie*, 73–76; Eugeniusz Duda, *The Jews of Cracow*, trans. Ewa Basiura (Kraków: Wydawnictwo "Hagada" and Argona-Jarden Jewish Bookshop, 2000), 66–67; Arad, *Belzec, Sobibor, Treblinka*, 387.

51. Pankiewicz, *Apteka w Getcie Krakowskim*, 186, 188, 190–19. Pankiewicz erroenously lists Bełżec as one of the five remaining ghettos; Bieberstein, *Zagłada Żydów w Krakowie*, 78–79.

52. Pankiewicz, *Apteka w Getcie Krakowskim*, 200–206.

53. Arieh L. Bauminger, *The Fighters of the Cracow Ghetto* (Jerusalem: Keter Press Enterprises, 1986), 37–43, 49–68; Richard C Lukas, *Forgotten Holocaust: The Poles under German Occupation, 1939–1944* (New York: Hippocrene Books, 1990), 76–77. The Soviet-sponsored Polish Workers Party was formed on January 5, 1942, by Polish communists. Two months later, they formed the People's Guard (later the *Armia Ludowa*) as the vanguard of their partisan efforts.

54. Bauminger, *Fighters*, 72.

55. Ibid., 69–72.

56. Ibid., 69–77; Wroński, *Kronika Okupowanego Krakowa*, 240. There is some disagreement on the date of the attack, which some Polish sources put on December 24, 1942.

57. Kiełkowski, *Zlikwidować na Miejscu*, 68.

58. Bauminger, *Fighters*, 73.

59. A third source claims the attack took place on December 23. Kielkowski, *Zlikwidować na Miejscu*, 68; Wroński, *Kronika Okupowanego Krakowa*, 240; Duda, *The Jews of Cracow*, 67; Pankiewicz, *Apteka w Getcie Krakowskim*, 183–184.

60. *"Situations-Skizze"* Emalia, BA(K), 1 page; "Verzeichnis jüdischer Arbeiter welche am 25.5.1943 an N.K.F., Deutsche Emaliwarenfabrik, Kistenfabrik und Chmielewski in Krakau überstellt wurden," Zydowski Instytut Historyczny, Instytut Naukowo-Badawezy, Warsaw, 7–10.

61. Hilberg, *Destruction of the European Jews*, 2:526.

62. "Interview with Oskar Schindler," November 18, 1964, Delbert Mann Papers, Vanderbilt University, 7-A, 9.

63. Robin O'Neil, "An Analysis of the Actions of Oskar Schindler Within the Context of the Holocaust in German Occupied Poland and Czechoslovakia" (Master's Thesis, University College, London, 1996), 64.

64. Keneally, *Schindler's List*, 190.

65. Pankiewicz, *Apteka w Getcie Krakowskim*, 139; Keneally, *Schindler's List*, 190; Urbach, interview, July 15, 2002.

66. Pankiewicz, *Apteka w Getcie Krakowskim*, 218.

67. Ibid., 219–223; Bieberstein, *Zagłada Żydów w Krakowie*, 82–83.

68. Pankiewicz, *Apteka w Getcie Krakowskim*, 223–224; *Proces Ludobójcy Amona Leopolda Goeth przed Najwyższym Trybunałem Narodowym*, No. 35 (Kraków: Centralna Żydowska Komisja Historyczna przy Centralnym Komitecie Żydów w Polsce, 1947), 25. This is the official transcript of the trial of Amon Göth in Kraków.

69. Pankiewicz, *Apteka w Getcie Krakowskim*, 224–230.

70. Ibid., 235–241; Elinor Brecher, *Schindler's Legacy: True Stories of the List Survivors* (New York: Plume, 1994), 306.

71. Pankiewicz, *Apteka w Getcie Krakowskim*, 242–243.

72. Ibid., 244–245; O'Neil, "An Analysis of the Actions of Oskar Schindler," 97–98; Murray Pantirer, interview by the author, Union, New Jersey, August 3, 1999; Urbach, interview, April 13, 1999.

73. Pankiewicz, *Apteka w Getcie Krakowskim*, 246–248; Urbach, interview, April 13, 1999; Pantirer, interview, August 3, 1999.

74. Pankiewicz, *Apteka w Getcie Krakowskim*, 123–125; Heinz Höhne, *The Order of the Death's Head: The Story of Hitler's SS*, trans. Richard Barry (New York: Ballantine Books), 1971, 302–303.

75. Pankiewicz, *Apteka w Getcie Krakowskim*, 125–126; *The SS* (New York: Time-Life Books, 1989), 95; Bieberstein, *Zagłada Żydów w Krakowie*, 173–174; Madritsch, *Menschen*, 5. Madritsch said that Bousko was a sergeant major, not a lieutenant. Letter from Bozenna Rotman to David Crowe, August 18, 2002, 1 page; Keneally, *Schindler's List*, 97, 117, 138–139; Mordecai Paldiel, *The Path of the Righteous: Gentile Rescuers of Jews during the Holocaust* (Hoboken, N.J.: KTAV Publishing House, and The Jewish Foundation for Christian Rescuers/ADL, 1993), 5.

76. Madritsch, *Menschen*, 3, 13, 16–18. Madritsch's memoir was used by Yad Vashem to investigate Bousko's efforts saving Jews during the Holocaust.

77. Pankiewicz, *Apteka w Getcie Krakowskim*, 126–127.

78. Danuta Czech, *Auschwitz Chronicle, 1939–1945: From the Archives of the Auschwitz Memorial and the German Federal Archives* (New York: Henry Holt and Company, 1990), 352, 354; Duda, *The Jews of Cracow*, 68.

79. French L. MacLean, *The Field Men: The SS Officers Who Led the Einsatzkommandos—the Nazi Mobile Killings Squads* (Atglen, Pa.: Schiffer Military History, 1999), 20, 42; Richard Rhodes, *Masters of Death: The Einsatzgruppen and the Invention of the Holocaust* (New York: Alfred A. Knopf, 2002), 258–262; *Concentration Camp in Plaszow*, 2.

This publication was printed in Kraków though it has no listed author, date of publication, or publisher; Shmuel Spector, "Aktion 1005," in Israel Gutman, *Encyclopedia of the Holocaust*, vol. 1 (New York: Macmillan Publishing Company, 1990), 11–14; Hilberg, *Destruction*, 976–979; Leni Yahil, *The Holocaust: The Fate of European Jewry* (New York: Oxford University Press, 1990), 449–450.

80. Douglas Brode, *The Films of Steven Spielberg* (New York: Kensington Publishing, 2000), 230–231.

81. Schindler, *Light and Shadow*, 50–51; Erika Rosenberg, ed., *Ich, Emilie Schindler: Errinerungen einer Unbeugsamen* (München: F.A. Herbig Verlagsbuchhandlung GmbH, 2001), 56; Keneally, *Schindler's List*, 62–63; Palowski, *The Making of Schindler's List*, 37–42, 101.

82. Keneally, *Schindler's List*, 126–130.

83. Ibid., 107–108; Palowski, *The Making of Schindler's List*, 101.

84. Roma Logocka, *The Girl in the Red Coat*, trans. Margot Bettauer Dembo (New York: St. Martin's Press, 2002), 1–292.

85. Keneally, *Schindler's List*, 130–133; "Schindler's Survivors," *New York Newsday*, March 24, 1994, B49.

86. Keneally, *Schindler's List*, 126–130.

87. Ibid., 130.

88. Dr. Moshe Bejski, "Notes on the Banquet in Honor of Oskar Schindler," May 2, 1962, Tel Aviv, Israel, 27.

89. Kurt Grossmann, *Die unbesungenen Helden: Menschen in Deutschlands dunklen Tagen* (Frankfurt: Verlag Ullstein GmbH, 1961), 160.

90. Schindler, *Light and Shadow*, 15–16.

91. Keneally, *Schindler's List*, 33.

92. "Georg Pták to Radio Jerusalem," July 5, 1990, Yad Vashem Archives, M31/20, 152 (hereafter referred to as "Pták to Radio Jerusalem," YVA M31/20); Keneally, *Schindler's List*, 33.

93. Schindler, *Light and Shadow*, 15–16; Herbert Steinhouse, "The Real Oskar Schindler," *Saturday Night*, April 1994, 43–44; Thomas Fensch, *Oskar Schindler and His List: The Man, the Book, the Film, the Holocaust and Its Survivors* (Forest Dale, Vt.: Paul S. Eriksson, Publisher, 1995), 13; "Pták to Radio Jerusalem," YVA M31/20; "Svitavy," in Shmuel Spector and Geoffrey Wigoder, eds., *The Encyclopedia of Jewish Life Before and During the Holocaust*, vol. 3 (New York: New York University Press, 2001), 1270.

94. Ian Kershaw, *Hitler: 1936–1945* (New York: W. W. Norton, 2000), 562.

Chapter 6

1. "Monika Knauss geb. Göth to *Der Spiegel*," *Der Spiegel*, no. 11 (March 14, 1983):12; Matthias Kessler, *Ich muß doch meinen Vater lieben, oder? Die Lebensgeschichte von Monika Göth, Tochter des KZ-Kommandanten aus "Schindlers Liste"* (Frankfurt am Main: Eichborn AG, 2002), 251–252.

2. *Frankfurter Allgemeine Zeitung*, August 5, 2002, 35.

3. Kessler, *Ich muß doch meiner Vater lieben, oder?*, 35–39; Kathryn Knight, "My Father Was the Nazi Officer Who Shot Jews for Fun," *London Daily Mail on Sunday*, April 21, 2002, 30.

4. Kessler, *Ich muß doch meiner Vater lieben, oder?*, 35, 41–42; Louise Potterton, "Daughter to the Devil," *Jerusalem Report*, September 9, 2002, 44.

5. Kessler, *Ich muß doch meiner Vater lieben, oder?*, 103; Knight, "My Father," 30.

6. Potterton, "Daughter to the Devil," 44; Knight, "My Father," 30; Kessler, *Ich muß doch meiner Vater lieben, oder?*, 35.

7. Potterton, "Daughter to the Devil," 44.

8. Kessler, *Ich muß doch meiner Vater lieben, oder?*, 142–144.

9. Ibid., 144–145; Potterton, "Daughter to the Devil," 44.

10. Kessler, *Ich muß doch meiner Vater lieben, oder?*, 101–102; Potterton, "Daughter to the Devil," 44.

11. Knight, "My Father," 30.

12. Ibid.

13. Kessler, *Ich muß doch meiner Vater lieven, oder?*, 165–168.

14. Potterton, "Daughter to the Devil," 44.

15. Kessler, *Ich muß doch meiner Vater lieber, oder?*, 147–149; Potterton, "Daughter to the Devil," 44.

16. Jon Blair, interview, *Sony Pictures Classics*, February 8, 1996, http://www.sonypictures.com/classics/annefrank/misc/interview.html, 1.

17. Ruth Kalder, interview by Jon Blair, *Schindler*, Thames Television Production, 1983; Ruth Rosensweig, interview by the author, Boca Raton, Florida, March 20, 2000.

18. Ibid.

19. Kessler, *Ich muß doch meiner Vater lieben, oder?*, 200–206.

20. Ibid., 22–24, 29–30; Potterton, "Daughter to the Devil," 44.

21. Kessler, *Ich muß doch meiner Vater lieben, oder?*, 10, 244–245; Potterton, "Daughter to the Devil," 44.

22. Emilie Schindler, *Where Light and Shadow Meet: A Memoir* (New York: W.W. Norton, 1996), 59.

23. Tom Segev, *Soldiers of Evil: The Commandants of the Nazi Concentration Camps*, trans. Haim Watzman (New York: McGraw Hill, 1987), 151.

24. Heinz Höhne, *The Order of the Death's Head: The Story of Hitler's SS*, trans. Richard Barry (New York: Ballantine Books, 1971), 150–154.

25. "*Lebenslauf* of Amon Leopold Göth," Personal-Akte, PA Nr. G 886, Göth, Amon-Leopold, SS-Nr. 43 673, Der Reichsführer-SS, SS-Personalhauptamt, BDC (Berlin Documentation Center) SS-Offiziere, Bundesarchiv (Berlin), 1 (hereafter referred to as "*Lebenslauf* of Amon Leopold Göth," BA(B)). Future documents from Göth's SS "Personal Akte" will be cited as "Personal-Akte," PA Nr G 886, Göth, Amon Leopold, BA(B), preceded by the individual document title and page reference; Elinor J. Brecher, *Schindler's Legacy: True Stories of the List Survivors* (New York: Plume/Penguin Books, 1994), 164.

26. Segev, *Soldiers of Evil*, 151.

27. Ibid.

28. Ibid.

29. Ibid., 151–152; Bruce F. Pauley, *Hitler and the Forgotten Nazis: A History of Austrian National Socialism* (Chapel Hill: The University of North Carolina Press, 1981), 36, 38–41.

30. Pauley, *Hitler and the Forgotten Nazis*, 24–25, 28–29, 32–33.

31. Segev, *Soldiers of Evil*, 151–152; "*Lebenslauf* of Amon Göth," BA(B), 1.

32. "*Lebenslauf* of Amon Göth," BA(B), 1; Pauley, *Hitler and the Forgotten Nazis*, 76.

33. "*Lebenslauf* of Amon Göth," BA(B), 1; Pauley, *Hitler and the Forgotten Nazis*, 64–66, 74–75; Nazi Party Card, Bundesarchiv Zehlendorf, Personal-Akte, PA Nr. G 886, Göth, Amon-Leopold, BA(B), 1 page. Göth's Party card lists his birth date as December 14, 1905. All other Nazi Party and SS files on Göth, though, list the correct date of his birth, December 11, 1908; Michael H. Kater, *The Nazi Party: A Social Profile of Members and Leaders, 1919–1945* (Cambridge: Harvard University Press, 1983), 193, 262. The Nazi Party had almost 130,000 members in 1930 and close to 850,000 three years later. There were an estimated 8 million Party members at the end of World War II.

34. "*Lebenslauf* of Amon Göth," BA(B), 1.

35. Segev, *Soldiers of Evil*, 152.

36. Höhne, *Order of the Death's Head*, 27–28, 86, 161–162, 166–168, 171; Thomas H. Flaherty, *The SS* (Alexandria, Va.: Time Life Books, 1989), 29.

37. Höhne, *Order of the Death's Head*, 66. Höhne says that an SS-*Sturmführer* was a captain, but technically an SS-*Hauptsturmführer* was a captain. See Christopher Ailsby's *SS: Roll of Infamy* (Osceola, Wisc.: Motorbooks, 1997), 187, for a complete list of SS ranks and the British and American equivalents.

38. "*Lebenslauf* of Amon Göth," BA(B), 1; "*Personal-Bericht* of Amon Leopold Göth," January 30, 1941, Personal-Akte, PA Nr. G 886, Göth, Amon Leopold, BA(B), 1–2; "*Dienstleistungszeugnis* for *Oberscharführer* Göth, Amon Leopold," July 14, 1941, Personal Akte, PA Nr. G 886, Göth, Amon Leopold, BA(B), 1 page.

39. Segev, *Soldiers of Evil*, 152.

40. Gottfried-Karl Kindermann, *Hitler's Defeat in Austria, 1933-1934: Europe's First Containment of Nazi Expansionism*, trans. Sonia Brough and David Taylor (Boulder: Westview Press, 1988), 10.

41. Pauley, *Hitler and the Forgotten Nazis*, 105–108.

42. Ibid., 109.

43. "*Lebenslauf* of Amon Göth," BA(B) 2; Pauley, *Hitler and the Forgotten Nazis*, 109, 114.

44. Segev, *Soldiers of Evil*, 152.

45. Pauley, *Hitler and the Forgotten Nazis*, 131–138, 142, 146; Kindermann, *Hitler's Defeat in Austria*, 99–110; Ian Kershaw, *Hitler, 1889–1936 Hubris* (New York: W. W. Norton, 1999), 522–523; "*Lebenslauf* of Amon Göth," BA(B), 2.

46. "*Personal Bericht* of Amon Göth," BA(B), 1–2; Pauley, *Hitler and the Forgotten Nazis*, 141–142, 144, 146.

47. "Amon Göth to the N.S.D.A.P. Refugee Relief Organization, Berlin," July 16, 1937, Personal-Akte, PA Nr. G 886, Göth, Amon-Leopold, BA(B), 1–2.

48. Pauley, *Hitler and the Forgotten Nazis*, 139–140; Segev, *Soldiers of Evil*, 152.

49. Segev, *Soldiers of Evil*, 152.

50. Ibid.; Höhne, *Order of the Death's Head*, 176–177.

51. Segev, *Soldiers of Evil*, 152; "*Personal Bericht* of Amon Göth," BA(B), 1; "*Personalangaben* of Göth, Amon Leopold," 26 July 1941, Personal-Akte, PA Nr. G 886, Göth, Amon-Leopold, BA(B), 1; "*Ernennungsvorschlag* für SS-*Untersturmführer* Amon Leopold Göth zum SS-*Hauptsturmführer*, Höhrer SS-u.Polizeiführer Ost, Krakau to SS-Personalhauptamt, Berlin," July 23, 1943, 1. It is impossible to pinpoint exactly the date of birth of Göth's daughter from his SS files, which list the month his sons were born and places only an asterik in the spot where a daughter's date of birth would be listed; one source, Michael Miller, Jeff Chrisman, et al., *Axis Biographical Research: An Apolitical Military History Site*, http://www.geocities.com/~orion47/, states that Anny Göth gave birth to a daughter in July 1939, who died seven months later. It adds that she later bore two more children. Göth's SS files state that he had only two sons, born in July 1939 and February 1940. This would mean possibly that Anny gave birth to twins in the summer of 1939.

52. "*Personal Bericht* of Amon Göth," BA(B), 2.

53. Alfred C. Mierzejewski, *The Collapse of the German War Economy, 1944-1945: Allied Air Power and the German National Railway* (Chapel Hill: University of North Carolina Press, 1988), 25, 33; Sybille Steinbacher, "In the Shadow of Auschwitz: The Murder of the Jews of Upper East Silesia," in Ulrich Herbert, ed., *National Socialist Extermination Policies: Contemporary German Perspectives and Controversies* (New York: Berghan Books, 2000), 300 n. 31.

54. "SS-*Sturmbannführer* Otto Winter SS-*Personalhauptamt*," October 10, 1941, SS-File of Amon Leopold Göth," 2, Records of the Reich Leader of the SS and Chief of the

German Police, RG 242 (National Archives Collection of Foreign Records Seized, 1941-), National Archives of the United States II, College Park, Maryland; all records from this file will hereafter be referred to as "SS-File of Amon Leopold Göth," Reich Leader SS Collection, RG 242, NA-US II.

55. *"Dienstleistungszeugnis* for Göth, Amon Leopold," BA(B), 1 page; Steinbacher, "Shadow of Auschwitz," 278–280.

56. *Dienststelle der Schutzstaffel der NSDAP (SS-Obergruppenführer-SS-Standartenführer), Stand vom 30, Januar 1942, Herausgegeben vom SS-Personalhauptamt* (SS Officers List as of January 30, 1942, SS-Standartenführer to SS-Oberstgruppenführer—Assignments and Decorations of the Senior SS Officer Corps) (Atglen, Pa.: Schiffer Military History, 2000), 10; Robert L. Koehl, *RKFDV: German Resettlement and Population Policy, 1939–1945* (Cambridge, Mass.: Harvard University Press, 1957), 56–58; Höhne, *Order of the Death's Head,* 351–352.

57. Steinbacher, "In the Shadow of Auschwitz," 284–286.

58. "Der Höhere SS- und Polizeiführer Ost (Krakau) an den Chef des SS-Personalhauptamtes, Berlin," June 12, 1942, 1 page. "SS File of Amon Leopold Göth," Reich Leader SS Collection," RG 242, NA-US II; "Der Reichsführer-SS, SS-Hauptamt-Amt II, Berlin," 10 August 1942, "Personal-Akte, PA Nr. G 886, Göth, Amon Leopold," BA(B), 1 page.

59. Siegfrid J. Pucher, *". . . in der Bewegung führend tätig:"* Odilo Globočnik-Kämpfer *für den 'Anschluß,' Vollstrecker des Holocaust* (Klagenfurt/Celovac: Drava Verlag, 1997), 38–41, 54–56, 62, 68, 74, 76–77, 79–82, 85; Ailsby, *SS: Roll of Infamy,* 54; Globočnik held the Nazi Party's highest award, the *Goldenes Ehrenzeichen der NSDAP,* which Hitler gave to only about 650 "stars" in the Nazi firmament. *Dienststelle der Schutzstaffel der NSDAP,* 13; "Golden Party Badge," http://www.geocities.com/goldpartypin/ahaward.html, 1.

60. Pucher, *". . . in der Bewegung führend tätig,"* 56–66, 69, 82–89, 104, 109–110; Yitzhak Arad, *Belzec, Sobibór, Treblinka: The Operation Reinhard Death Camps* (Bloomington: Indiana University Press, 1987), 14–15; Włodzimierz Borodziej, *Terror und Politik: Die Deutsche Polizei und die Polnische Widerstandsbewegung im Generalgouvernement, 1939–1944* (Mainz: Verlag Philipp von Zabern, 1999), 50 n. 112; Richard Rhodes, *Masters of Death: The SS-Einsatzgruppen and the Invention of the Holocaust* (New York: Alfred A. Knopf, 2002), 106–109.

61. Pucher, *". . . in der Bewegung führend tätig,"* 10–11; "SS-*Untersturmführer* [signature illegible] to Der *Reichsführer*-SS, SS-Hauptamt-Ergänzungsamt der Waffen-SS, Berlin," August 12, 1942, Personal-Akte, PA Nr G 886, Göth, Amon Leopold, BA(B), 1 page; *Proces Ludobójcy Amona Leopolda Goetha przed Najwyższym Trybunałem Narodowym* (Kraków: Centralna Żydowska Komisja Historyczna w Polsce, 1947), 25–26, 29; Arad, *Belzec, Sobibór, Treblinka,* 15–19.

62. Mietek Pemper, interview by the author, Augsburg, Germany, May 26, 1999.

63. Raimund Titsch, interview, Vienna, Austria, November 25, 1964, in Martin A. Gosch and Howard Koch, "The Oskar Schindler Story," Delbert Mann Papers, Special Collections Library, Vanderbilt University, 8A, 7 (hereafter referred to as Raimund Titsch, interview, November 25, 1964, Delbert Mann Papers, Vanderbilt University).

64. Pucher, *". . . in der Bewegung führend tätig,"* 113–116; Arad, *Belzec, Sobibór, Treblinka,* 44–45, 54, 119–130; "*Dienstlaufbahn des* Göth, Amon-Leopold," Personal-Akte, Nr. 10 022, Göth, Amon Leopold, BA(B), 1 page.

65. Mietek Pemper, interview by Dr. Reich, Augsburg, Germany, October 26, 1996 (hereafter referred to as Pemper-Reich interview, October 26, 1996); *Proces Ludobójcy Amona Leopolda Goetha,* 77, 84.

66. "*Dienstleistungszeugnis* of *Oberscharführer* Göth, Amon Leopold, 1/11," July 14, 1941, "Personal-Akte, PA Nr. G 886, Göth, Amon Leopold," BA(B), 1 page; "*Personal-Bericht* des Göth Amon Leopold, 1/11," October 10, 1941, "Personal-Akte, PA Nr. G 886, Göth, Amon Leopold, BA(B), 1–2.

67. "*Personal Bericht* des Göth, Amon Leopold, 1/11," October 10, 1941, "Personal-Akte, PA Nr. H 886, Göth, Amon Leopold," BA(B), 1–2.

68. *Proces Ludobójcy Amona Leopolda Goetha*, 29–36.

69. "Tarnów," in Shmuel Spector and Geoffrey Wigoder, eds., *The Encyclopedia of Jewish Life Before and After the Holocaust*, vol. 3 (New York: New York University Press, 2001), 1293–1295; Aharon Weiss, "Tarnów," in Israel Gutman, ed., *Encyclopedia of the Holocaust*, vol. 4 (New York: Macmillan Publishing Company, 1990), 1451–1452.

70. *Proces Ludobójcy Amona Leopolda Goetha*, 164; Weiss, "Tarnów," 1295; "The Tarnów Jewish Trail," *Tarnów City Guide*, http://www.tarnow.pl/tarnow/ang/historia/index-szalki.php, 1.

71. Julius Madritsch, *Menschen in Not! Meine Erlebnisse in den Jahren 1940 bis 1944 als Unternehmer im damaligen Generalgouvernement* (Vienna: V. Roth, 1962), 13.

72. Madritsch, *Menschen*, 13.

73. "Jakob Sternberg to Yad Vashem, June 11, 1963," Yad Vashem Archives, Department of the Righteous, File on Julius Madritsch, Raimund Titsch, and Oswald Bosko, 31/21-22-23 (RGD), 1–4 (hereafter referred to as "Sternberg to Yad Vashem" June 11, 1963, YVA).

74. "Sternberg to Yad Vashem, June 11, 1963," YVA, 3.

75. Photos of Bochnia Ghetto, Nos. 02347, 02348, and 74708, Photographic Archives, United States Holocaust Memorial Museum., Washington, D.C.

76. Madritsch, *Menschen*, 13, 16.

77. Ibid., 16.

78. *Proces Ludobójcy Amona Leopolda Goetha*, 161–163, 258.

79. Madritsch, *Menschen*, 16; *Proces Ludobójcy Amona Leopolda Goetha*, 34–35, 165–166, 226–230, 257; Danuta Czech, *Auschwitz Chronicle, 1939–1945* (New York: Henry Holt and Company, 1990), 475, 477–478. The Germans killed immediately 1,845 Jews on the first transport from Bochnia and used the others as slave laborers. "Bochnia," in *Encyclopedia of Jewish Life*, 1:160; Joram Kagan, *Poland's Jewish Heritage* (New York: Hippocrene Books, 1992), 56; though very little has been written about the Bochnia ghetto, a gruesome collection of photographs that documents German atrocities is housed in the archives of Beit Lohamei Haghetaot (Ghetto Fighters' House) in Israel; see particularly photo numbers 6726, 6954, 6955, 6956, 6957, 6958, 6960, and 22093.

80. Pemper-Reich interview, October 26, 1996.

81. "*Ernennungsvorschlag* für SS-*Untersturmführer* Amon Leopold Göth," July 23, 1943, 2; "SS-File of Amon Leopold Göth," Reich Leader SS Collection, RG 242, NA-US II.

82. "*Ernennungskunde* SS-*Untersturmführer* Amon Leopold Göth," July 23, 1943, 1 page, "SS-File of Amon Leopold Göth," Reich Leader SS Collection, RG 242, NA-US II. Though this document was originally dated July 23, 1943, his promotion and appointment to the Waffen-SS Fachgruppe did not go into effect until August 1. It took about a week after the document was initially prepared for it to go up the chain of command for full approval by the SS Personnel office in Berlin.

83. Raul Hilberg, *The Destruction of the European Jews*, vol. 3 (New York: Holmes & Meier, 1985), 1201–1202, 1219–1220. Hilberg estimates that 5.1 million Jews died in the Holocaust but admits that it is impossible to estimate accurately the actual number of Jewish deaths, which some put as high as 6 million. Using this conservative estimate, he calculated that over 800,000 Jews died of "ghettoization and general deprivation," 1.3 million

in "open air shootings," and up to 3 million in death and other types of camps. Martin Gilbert estimates that 5.7 million Jews died in the Holocaust in his *Macmillan Atlas of the Holocaust* (New York: The Macmillan Publishing Co., 1982), 245, and the United States Holocaust Memorial Museum's *Historical Atlas of the Holocaust* (New York: Macmillan Publishing USA, 1996), 221, estimates that 6 million Jews died in the Shoah; Arad, *Belzec, Sobibór, Treblinka*, 44–45.

84. Supreme Headquarters Allied Expeditionary Force (SHAEF), Evaluation and Dissemination Section, G-2, *Basic Handbook: KL's (Konzentrationslager) Axis Concentration Camps and Detention Centers Reported As Such in Europe* (Middlesex: World War II Investigator Limited, n.d.), 1–3, A1.

85. SHAEF, *Basic Handbook: KL's*, 104.

86. Iwo Cyprian Pogonowski, *Jews in Poland: A Documentary History* (New York: Hippocrene Books, 1993), 127.

87. John Roth, Marilyn Harran, et al., *The Holocaust Chronicle* (Lincolnwood, Ill.: Publications International Ltd., 2000), 480.

88. Ibid., 496; Danuta Czech, Stanisław Kłodziński, Aleksander Lasik, Andrzej Strzelecki, *Auschwitz, 1940–1940: Central Issues in the History of the Camp*, vol. 5 (Oświęcim: Auschwitz-Birkenau State Museum, 2000), 188–189; Czech, *Auschwitz Chronicle*, 520).

89. *Proces Ludobójcy Amona Leopolda Goetha*, 35.

90. Ibid., 249, 252–254.

91. Ibid., 271.

92. Ibid., 271–272.

93. Ibid., 35.

94. Jaroslav Zotciak, interview by the author, Kraków, Poland, August 7, 2000; *Proces Ludobócjy Amona Leopolda Goetha*, 81; Eugeniusz Duda, *The Jews of Cracow*, trans. Ewa Basiura (Kraków: Wydawnictwo "Hagada" and Argona-Jarden Jewish Bookshop, 2000), 71; *Concentration Camp in Plaszow*, n.p., n.d., 2, 6.

95. Zotciak, interview, August 7, 2000; Duda, *Jews of Krakow*, 71.

96. Wolfgang Sofsky, *The Order of Terror: The Concentration Camp*, trans. William Templer (Princeton: Princeton University Press, 1997), 59–61; the most complete set of photographs of Płaszów can be found in the photographic archives of the Beit Lohamei Haghetaot (Ghetto Fighters' House) Archive in Nahariya, Israel. There is also an excellent collection in the photo archives section of the United States Holocaust Museum in Washington, D.C.

97. Elinor J. Brecher, *Schindler's Legacy: True Stories of the List Survivors* (New York: Plume/Penguin Books), 398, 409–410; Aleksander Bieberstein, *Zagłada Żydów w Krakowie* (Kraków: Wydawnictwo Literackie, 1985), 101–102.

98. "Schindler Financial Report, 1945," YVA, 15; "Oskar Schindler *Bericht*" (1955), Bundesarchiv (Koblenz), Nachlaß Oskar Schindler, 1908–1974, Bestand 1493, No. 1, Band 15, 4; Mietek Pemper, interview by the author, Augsburg, Germany, January 17, 2000. Mietek Pemper said that Schindler went first to someone in the *Heeresbeschaffungsamt* (Army Procurement Office), who in turn negotiated with Maurer. Michael Thad Allen, *The Business of Genocide: The SS, Slave Labor, and the Concentration Camps* (Chapel Hill: University of North Carolina Press, 2002), 139, 154–155, 157, 182–183; Sofsky, *Order of Terror*, 40–41.

99. Allen, *The Business of Genocide*, 138, 179–190, 201.

100. The entire edition of The Main Commission's journal, *Pamięć i Sprawiedliwość*, vol. XXXVIII (1995), was dedicated to the fiftieth anniversary of this organization, one of the principal depositories in Poland for war crimes during World War II. In 1991, this organization was reconstituted and now looks at crimes during the Soviet area as well as war crimes during World War II. Joseph Bau, *Dear God, Have You Ever Gone Hungry?* trans. Shlomo "Sam" Yurman (New York: Arcade Publishing, 1990), 116–117.

101. *Proces Ludobójcy Amona Leopolda Goetha,* 61–62, 75–77; Pemper, interviews, May 26, 1999, and January 17, 2000.

102. French L. Maclean, *The Camp Men: The SS Officers Who Ran the Nazi Concentration Camp System* (Atglen, Pa.: Schiffer Military History, 1999), 17; "Jan Sehn to Mieczysław Pemper," July 8, 1946, List of SS Officers in Kraków-Płaszów," Bundesarchiv (Berlin) 2M 1402 A.12, 1–2. This list is incomplete, given the constant changeover in concentration camp staff during the latter phases of the war. See, for example, the two investigative "Protokolls" prepared by the Polska Misja Wojskowa Badania Zbrodni Wojennych (Polish War Crimes Mission) for the prosecution of the Płaszów SS men, Anton Schulz and Wilhelm Matle, both of whom are not listed on the Pemper-Sehn list. Bundesarchiv (Berlin), 2M 1402 A. 12.

103. Pemper-Reich interview, October 26, 1996; Bieberstein, *Zagłada Żydów w Krakowie,* 109.

104. Brecher, *Schindler's Legacy,* 410.

105. Ibid., 411.

106. Höhne, *Order of the Death's Head,* 493; Sofsky, *Order of Terror,* 100, 102, 109–110; *The Buchenwald Report,* trans. and ed. David A. Hackett (Boulder: Westview Press, 1995), 36, 176; SHAEF, *Axis Concentration Camps and Detention Centers,* 11.

107. Pemper-Reich interview, October 26, 1996; Allen, *The Business of Genocide,* 251; Sofsky, *Order of Terror,* 48–52; the observations about the physical structure of the camp are based on the detailed map of the camp given to me by Jaroslav Zotciak. There is also a detailed written description of the camp's structure in Bieberstein's *Zagłada Żydów w Krakowie,* 103–113, which substantiates the accuracy of the Zotciak map and, one suspects, was used in creating it.

108. Sofsky, *Order of Terror,* 50, 130–131, 145.

109. Ibid., 49.

110. Ibid.

111. Bieberstein, *Zagłada Żydów w Krakowie,* 108; Zotciak map.

112. Zotciak map; Brecher, *Schindler's Legacy,* 398.

113. Pemper-Reich interview, October 26, 1996; Allen, *The Business of Genocide,* 178, 205; MacLean, *The Camp Men,* 202.

114. Dr. Moshe Bejski, interview by the author, Tel Aviv, Israel, May 17, 1999; Pemper-Reich interview, October 26, 1996; Pemper, interviews, May 26, 1999, and January 17, 2000.

115. Pemper, interview, May 26, 1999.

116. Ibid., May 26, 1999 and January 17, 2000.

117. Pemper-Reich interview, October 26, 1996.

118. Pemper, interview, May 26, 1999. Mietek Pemper also served as a translator for the Auschwitz war crimes trials in 1947 and the trial of Dr. Josef Bühler, the state secretary of the General Government and its representative at the Wannsee Conference, the following year; Pemper-Reich interview, October 26, 1996.

119. Pemper-Reich interview, October 26, 1996.

120. Ibid.

121. Ibid.

122. Pemper, interview, January 17, 2000.

123. Pemper-Reich interview, October 26, 1996; Pemper, interview, January 17, 2000; Sofsky, *Order of Terror,* 102.

124. Pemper-Reich Interview, October 26, 1996.

125. "Mietek Pemper to Oskar Schindler," July 27, 1969, 1–2. BA 1/24.

126. Allen, *The Business of Genocide,* 95.

127. Ibid., 140.

128. "Stern Report 1956," Yad Vashem Archives, 01/164 ; Allen, *Business of Genocide,* 157, 242, n. 7.

129. "Stern Report 1956," YVA, 26–27; Hilberg, *Destruction of the European Jews,* 3:81; United States Holocaust Memorial Museum, *Historical Atlas of the Holocaust* (New York: Macmillan Publishing, 1996), 63. Four towns in Poland are named Janów. The one mentioned by the Ukrainian guard was possibly the one near Lemberg, which had a ghetto where some armaments work was done before the SS ordered the entire ghetto burned to the ground in late 1942. It is also possible that the guard was talking about the DAW Janówska forced labor camp in the suburbs of Lemberg.

130. "Stern Report 1956," YVA, 27.

131. Ibid., 27.

132. Pemper-Reich interview, October 26, 1996.

133. Ibid.

134. Ibid.

135. "Stern Report 1956," YVA, 27–28.

136. Ibid., 28.

137. Ibid.; Pemper-Reich interview, October 26, 1996.

138. "Selbst Schindler's List konnte nicht das Schlimmste zeigen," *Süddeutsche Zeitung,* January 27, 1997, 3; *Proces Ludobójcy Amona Leopolda Goetha,* 75.

139. *Proces Ludobójcy Amona Leopolda Goetha,* 53, 38–39; Claudia Keller and Stefan Braun, *"Ohne Führung fressen sich die Menschen gegenseitig auf: Mietek Pemper im Gespräch mit Claudia Keller und Stefan Braun,"* in *Schindlers Koffer: Berichte aus dem Leben eines Lebensretters* (Stuttgart: *Stuttgarter Zeitung,* 1999), 37–38; Helen Sternlicht Rosenzweig, interview by the author, Boca Raton, Florida, March 20, 2000; Brecher, *Schindler's Legacy,* 162, 377; Stella Müller-Madej, interview by the author, Kraków, Poland, August 9, 2000.

140. Raimund Titsch, interview, November 25, 1964, Delbert Mann Papers, Vanderbilt University.

141. Brecher, *Schindler's Legacy,* 350.

142. For Henry Slamovich's brief statement about Göth during his trial, see *Proces Ludobójcy Amona Leopolda Goetha,* 370.

143. Sofsky, *Order of Terror,* 105.

144. Brecher, *Schindler's Legacy,* 185.

145. *Proces Ludobójcy Amona Leopolda Goetha,* 60; Brecher, *Schindler's Legacy,* 75, 87–88.

146. Brecher, *Schindler's Legacy,* 101–102.

147. Ibid., 102.

148. Ibid., 186, 360.

149. Ibid.; "Stern Report 1956," YVA, 20.

150. Helen [Hirsch] Horowitz, interview, Tel Aviv, Israel, December 3, 1964, in Martin A. Gosch and Howard Koch, "The Oskar Schindler Story," Delbert Mann Papers, Special Collections Library, Vanderbilt University, 10-B, 2 (hereafter referred to as Interview with Helen [Hirsch] Horowitz, December 3, 1964, Delbert Mann Papers, Vanderbilt University).

151. Ibid., 3–4.

152. Ibid., 3.

153. Ibid., 5.

154. Ibid., 8–9.

155. Ibid., 9–10.

156. Izak (Itzhak) Stern, interview, Tel Aviv, Israel, November 29, 1954, in Martin A. Gosch and Howard Koch, "The Oskar Schindler Story," Delbert Mann Papers, Special Collections Library, Vanderbilt University, 11A, 10–11.

157. Rosenzweig, interview, March 20, 2000.

158. Ibid.

159. Pemper, interviews, May 26, 1999, and May 26, 2000.

160. Rosenzweig, interview, March 20, 2000.

161. Ibid.

162. Brecher, *Schindler's Legacy*, 59.

163. Rosenzweig, interview, March 20, 2000.

164. Ibid.

165. *Proces Ludobójcy Amona Leopolda Goetha*, 62.

166. Ibid., 57, 69, 91.

167. Ibid., Brecher, *Schindler's Legacy*, 87.

168. Ibid., 60.

169. Ibid.

170. *Proces Ludobójcy Amona Leopolda Goetha*, 78.

171. Ibid., 78–79; Franciszek Piper, "Gas Chambers and Crematoria," in Yisrael Gutman and Michael Berenbaum, eds., *Anatomy of the Auschwitz Death Camp* (Bloomington: Indiana University Press, 1994), 164.

172. Biberstein, *Zagłada Żydów w Krakowie*, 140; at his 1947 *Einsatzgruppen* trial, Paul Blobel, who commanded *Sonderkommando* 4a and later *Sonderkommando* 1005 units, stated that he preferred not to use *Genickschußspezialisten*. Instead, he used large execution squads where each man was relieved after an hour of killing. "Affadavit of Paul Blobel," June 6, 1947, Office of Chief of Counsel for War Crimes, U.S. Army, No. 3824, International Military Tribunal at Nuernberg in John Mendelsohn and Donald S. Detwiler, eds. *The Holocaust*, vol. 10, *The Einsatzgruppen or Murder Commandos* (New York: Garland Publishing, 1982), 128.

173. Brecher, *Schindler's Legacy*, 398.

174. Piper, "Gas Chambers and Crematoria," 163.

175. Breitman, *Architect of Genocide*, 211.

176. Arad, *Belzec, Sobibór, Treblinka*, 170–171; Piper, "Gas Chambers and Crematoria," 163; Rhodes, *Masters of Death*, 258–260.

177. Michael A. Musmanno, *Justice: The Eichmann Kommandos* (London: Peter Davies, 1961), 145–155; MacLean, *The Field Men*, 42; Shmuel Spector, "Paul Blobel," in *Encyclopedia of the Holocaust*, 1:220.

178. Shmuel Spector, "Aktion 1005," *Encyclopedia of the Holocaust*, 1:14; Francisco Wichter, interview by the author, Buenos Aires, Argentina, May 17, 2001.

179. Brecher, *Schindler's Legacy*, 320–321.

180. Ibid., 410–411.

Chapter 7

1. Claudia Keller and Stefan Braun, "*Ohne Führung fressen sich die Menschen gegenseitig auf; Mietek Pemper im Gespräch mit Claudia Keller und Stefan Braun,*" in *Schindlers Koffer: Berichte aus dem Leben eines Lebensretters* (Stuttgart: *Stuttgarter Zeitung*, 1999), 39.

2. Ibid., 39.

3. Ibid., 38–39.

4. Peter Steiner, *The Deserts of Bohemia: Czech Fiction and Its Social Context* (Ithaca: Cornell University Press, 2000), 27.

5. Steiner, *Deserts*, 44.

6. Ibid., 44.

7. Ibid., 67–68.

8. Helen Sternlicht Rosenzweig, interview by the author, Boca Raton, Florida, March 20, 2000.

9. Oskar Schindler, interview by Martin Gosch, November 18, 1974, Paris, France, Delbert Mann Papers, Special Collections Library, Vanderbilt University, 7-B, 6.

10. Sternlicht Rosenzweig, interview, March 20, 2000.

11. Michael Thad Allen, *The Business of Genocide: The SS, Slave Labor, and the Concentration Camps* (Chapel Hill: University of North Carolina Press, 2002), 95, 140.

12. Allen, *The Business of Genocide*, 173, 175; after the war, Speer claimed that Schieber was "Himmler's confidential agent in my ministry." Albert Speer, *The Slave State: Heinrich Himmler's Masterplan for SS Supremacy*, trans. Joachim Neugroschel (London: Weidenfeld, 1981), 16. Yet it should be remembered that many educated Germans had honorary SS ranks. Moreover, according to Michael Thad Allen, Schieber was extremely loyal to Speer and there is nothing to indicate that he was an SS spy. Allen, *The Business of Genocide*, 174.

13. Allen, *The Business of Genocide*, 176.

14. Ibid., 189.

15. Wolfgang Sofsky, *The Order of Terror: The Concentration Camp*, trans. William Templer (Princeton: Princeton University Press, 1997), 40–41; Allen, *The Business of Genocide*, 139, 154–155, 157, 182–183.

16. Allen, *The Business of Genocide*, 182–188.

17. Ibid., 199.

18. Ibid., 198–199.

19. Sofsky, *Order of Terror*, 178; Allen, *The Business of Genocide*, 156–157. Speer considered Kammler "a relentless but capable robot." Speer, *Slave State*, 236.

20. Allen, *The Business of Genocide*, 202–203, 206; Bieberstein, *Zagłada Żydów w Krakowie*, 109; Elinor J. Brecher, *Schindler's Legacy: True Stories of the List Survivors* (New York: Plume/Penguin Books), 199, 185.

21. Raul Hilberg, *The Destruction of the European Jews*, vol. 2 (New York: Holmes & Meier, 1985), 528.

22. Speer, *Slave State*, 257, 261, 265–267, 269, 273, 275–280; "Stern Report 1956," Yad Vashem Archives, 01/164, 56; Mietek Pemper, interview by Dr. Reich, Augsburg, Germany, October 26, 1996 (hereafter referred to as Pemper-Reich interview, October 26, 1996).

23. Sofsky, *Order of Terror*, 181.

24. Allen, *The Business of Genocide*, 241–242.

25. "Oskar Schindler Financial Report 1945," July 1945, Yad Vashem Archives, 01/164, 3–4.

26. Pemper-Reich interview, October 26, 1996.

27. Julius Madritsch, *Menschen in Not! Meine Erlebnisse in den Jahren 1940 bis 1944 als Unternehmer im damaligen Generalgouvernement* (Vienna: V. Roth, 1962), 20.

28. Ibid., 20–21.

29. Ibid., 25.

30. Ibid., 22.

31. "Schindler Financial Report 1945," YVA, 3–4; Madritsch, *Menschen*, 24.

32. Madritsch, *Menschen*, 24.

33. From March 1943 until October 1944 Madritsch paid the SS Zł 10 million ($3,187,500) for food and subsistence. Schindler claimed he spent over Zł 4 million ($1.25 million) on similar costs between 1942 and 1944 in Kraków and RM 750,000 ($282,000) in Brünnlitz. Madritsch, *Menschen*, 24, and "Schindler Financial Report 1945," YVA, 4, 9–12.

34. Raimund Titsch, interview by Martin Gosch, November 25, 1964, Vienna, Austria, Delbert Mann Papers, Special Collections Library, Vanderbilt University, 8-A, 6.

---

35. "Schindler Financial Report 1945," YVA, 1–2.

36. "Stern Report 1956," Yad Vashem Archives, 01/164, 24 (hereafter referred to as "Stern Report 1956," YVA); Keller and Braun, *Ohne Führung fressen sich die Menschen gegenseitig auf,* 39.

37. *Die Bekenntnisse des Herrn X,* Budapest, November 1943, Bundesarchiv (Koblenz), Nachlaß Oskar Schindler, 1908–1974, Bestand N 1493, No. 1, Band 18, 3–4 (hereafter referred to as *Die Bekenntnisse des Herrn X,* BA(K)).

38. *"Situation's-Skizze mit angrenzenden Industrieen für Deutsche Emailwarenfabrik-Oskar Schindler,"* n.d., Bundesarchiv (Koblenz), Nachlaß Oskar Schindler, 1908–1974, Bestand 1493, No. 1, Band 3, 1 page. Another neighboring factory that housed Jews in Schindler's sub-camp was the *Krakauer Drahtgitter Fabrik* (Kraków Wire Gauze Factory); "Verzeichnis jüdischer Arbeiter welche am 25.5.1943 an N.K.F., Deutsche Emailwarenfabrik, Kistenfabrik und Chmielewski in Krakau überstellt wurden," Zydowski Instytut Historyczny, Instytut Naukowo-Badawezy, Warsaw, 7–10. The Schindler Jews on this list are Hirsch Danzig, Wigdor Dortheimer, Motie Geller, Bernhard Goldstein, Wolf Horowitz, Jerzy Scheck, and Dawid Urbach.

39. Sol Urbach, interview by the author, Flemington, New Jersey, February 15, 2000.

40. "Schindler Financial Report 1945," YVA, 2.

41. *"Aufstellung Krakau und Brünnlitz,"* May 6, 1944, Bundesarchiv (Koblenz), Nachlaß Oskar Schindler, 1908–1974, Bestand N 1493, No. 1, Band 14, 3–4; "Müller (Siemens) to Oskar Schindler," October 10, 1957, Bundesarchiv (Koblenz), Nachlaß Oskar Schindler, 1908–1974, Bestand 1493, No. 1, Band 3, 1 page; Urbach, interview, March 21, 2003.

42. Karl Friedrich von Siemens, the head of Siemens at this time, joined with thirty-seven other German industrial leaders to voice support for the Nazis after their setback in the November 1932 Reichstag elections. Joseph Borkin, *The Crime and Punishment of I.G. Farben* (New York: Pocket Books, 1978), 70–71; Siemens, for example, had representatives on Heinrich Himmler's special business support group, "Friends of the Reichsführer SS." Membership in this group, which involved significant contributions to the SS, insured one, hopefully, of protection "from SS encroachment" and special considerations when it came to SS contracts. Heinz Höhne, *The Order of the Death's Head: The Story of Hitler's SS,* trans. Richard Barry (New York: Ballantine Books, 1971), 158–159; Allen, *The Business of Genocide,* 72; "Dr. Frank Wittendorfer, Head of the Siemens Archives, Munich, Germany, to David Crowe," March 21, 2003; in a letter to me on March 31, 2003, Alexander Görbing of Walter Bau-AG, informed me that they were unable to find any documents on Oskar Schindler's dealings with Siemens-AG in the files of Dyckerhoff & Widman; Benjamin B. Ferencz, *Less than Slaves: Jewish Forced Labor and the Quest for Compensation* (Bloomington: Indiana University Press in association with the United States Holocaust Memorial Museum, Washington, D.C., 2002), 28, 117, 119, 125; Aleksander Bieberstein, *Zagłada Żydów w Krakowie* (Kraków: Wydawnicto Literackie, 1985), 111.

43. Ferencz, *Less than Slaves,* 127; Stuart Eizenstat, *Imperfect Justice: Looted Assets, Slave Labor, and the Unfinished Business of World War II* (New York: Public Affairs, 2003), 209–210; John Authers and Richard Wolfee, *The Victim's Fortune: Inside the Epic Battle over the Debts of the Holocaust* (New York: HarperCollins, 2002), 189–191, 194–195, 218; "Germany Unveils Holocaust Fund," *BBC News Online,* February 16, 1999, 1; Tony Cuczka, "German Firms Announce Fund for Holocaust Claims," Associated Press, February 16, 1999, 1–2, *LexisNexis;* "German Firms Agree to Fund Holocaust-era Victims," February 16, 1999, Jewish Telegraph Agency, *Jewish Bulletin of Northern California Online,* 1–2, *LexisNexis;* Roger Boyes, "Bonn Tackled on Hitler Slaves Cash," *Times* (London), March 10, 1999; 1 page, *LexisNexis;* "Australians File US Suit on Nazi-

era Forced Labor," Agence France Presse, April 14, 1999, 1 page, *LexisNexis;* David E. Sanger, "German Companies Offer $3.3 Billion in Slave-Labor Suit," *New York Times,* October 8, 1999, 1 page, *LexisNexis;* despite its role in supporting the Nazi dictatorship, Siemens has suffered little in postwar Germany and plays the same dominant role in the German electrical engineering field as it did before World War II. Neil Gregor, *Daimler-Benz in the Third Reich* (New Haven: Yale Univesity Press, 1998), 3; the use of slave labor by Siemens during the war, particularly the question of reparations, is glossed over in its "official" company history, Wilfried Feldenkirchen, *Siemens, 1918–1945* (Columbus: Ohio State University Press, 1999), 237–240.

44. "Julius Lomnitz to the United Restitution Office, London," October 29, 1953, Archives of the American Jewish Joint Distribution Committee, New York, Oskar Schindler Collection, 1 page; Urbach, interview, March 21, 2003; *Die Bekenntnisse des Herrn X,* YVA, 4.

45. "Schindler Financial Report 1945," YVA, 2.

46. Bieberstein, *Zagłada Żydów w Krakowie,* 104–105; Robert-Jan Van Pelt, "A Site in Search of a Mission," in Yisrael Gutman and Michael Berenbaum, eds., *Anatomy of the Auschwitz Death Camp* (Bloomington, Ind.: Indiana University Press in association with the United States Holocaust Memorial Museum, 1994), 119, 126–127.

47. *Proces Ludobójcy Amona Leopolda Goetha, przed Najwyższym Trybunałem Narodowym* (Kraków: Centralna Żydowska Komisja Historyczna w Polsce, 1947), 63–64.

48. Urbach, interview, March 21, 2003.

49. Madritsch, *Menschen,* 23; "Testimony of Rabbi Menashe Levertov," in Martin Gosch and Howard Koch, "The Oskar Schindler Story," Delbert Mann Papers, Special Collections Library, Vanderbilt University, 1-A, 12.

50. "Schindler Financial Report 1945," YVA, 2–3.

51. *Proces Ludobójcy Amona Leopolda Goetha,* 273–274; Brecher, *Schindler's Legacy,* 351.

52. *Proces Ludobójcy Amona Leopolda Goetha,* 278–279.

53. Brecher, *Schindler's Legacy,* 305; "Stern Report 1956," YVA, 24.

54. Brecher, *Schindler's Legacy,* 387.

55. Ibid., 261, 429.

56. Urbach, interview, February 15, 2000.

57. Brecher, *Schindler's Legacy,* 350–351.

58. Ibid., 429; "Testimony of Edith Wertheim," in Martin A. Gosch and Howard Koch, "The Oskar Schindler Story," Delbert Mann Papers, Special Collections Library, Vanderbilt University, 2-A, 2.

59. "Oskar Schindler *Bericht,*" October 30, 1955, Bundesarchiv (Koblenz), Nachlaß Oskar Schindler, 1908–1974, Bestand N 1493, No. 1, Band 15, 2; Thomas Keneally, *Schindler's List* (New York: Touchstone Books, 1992), 213–214.

60. "Oskar Schindler *Bericht* 1955," BA(K), 2.

61. Brecher, *Schindler's Legacy,* 225.

62. "Oskar Schindler *Bericht,* 1955," BA(K), 2–3.

63. Brecher, *Schindler's Legacy,* 102.

64. Ibid.

65. Ibid.

66. Ibid.

67. Ibid., 294–295.

68. Ibid., 294–295, 297–299.

69. Ibid., 305.

70. Ibid.

71. Ibid., 200.

72. Emilie Schindler, *Where Light and Shadow Meet: A Memoir,* trans. Dolores M. Koch (New York: W. W. Norton, 1996), 59–60.

73. Franciszek Palowski, *The Making of Schindler's List: Behind the Scenes of an Epic Film,* trans. Anna and Robert G. Ware (Secaucus, N.J.: Birch Lane Press Books, 1998), 40.

74. "Oskar Schindler to Fritz Lang," July 20, 1951, Bundesarchiv (Koblenz), Nachlaß Oskar Schindler, 1908–1974, Bestand N 1493, Band 23, 2; "Josef Aue Protokol," August 6, 1946, and October 17, 1946, Č.j. II/1.-7219/46, Oblastní státní bezpečnosti v Mor. Ostravě, Ministerstvu vnitra Archiv (Prague), 2, 6–7.

75. "Schindler to Lang," July 20, 1951, BA(K) 2.

76. David Kahn, *Hitler's Spies: German Military Intelligence in World War II* (New York: Macmillan, 1978), 240, 242.

77. Ibid., 100; Donald M. McKale, *The Swastika Outside Germany* (Kent: Kent State University Press, 1977), 45–46, 116, 177–180.

78. Franz von Papen, *Memoirs,* trans. Brian Connell (New York: E. Dutton & Company, 1953), 489; McKale, *Swastika Outside Germany,* 108, 115–116, 172; Heinz Höhne, *Canaris,* trans. J. Maxwell Brownjohn (New York: Doubleday & Company, 1979), 489.

79. Kahn, *Hitler's Spies,* 60–61.

80. Walter Schellenberg, *The Labyrinth: Memoirs of Walter Schellenberg: Hitler's Chief of Counterintelligence,* trans. Louis Hagen (New York: Da Capo Press, 2000), 140–143.

81. Gerhard L. Weinberg, *The Foreign Policy of Hitler's Germany: Starting World War II, 1937–1939* (Chicago: University of Chicago Press, 1980), 591.

82. Von Papen, *Memoirs,* 481.

83. McKale, *Swastika Outside Germany,* 172–173.

84. "Schindler to Lang," July 20, 1951, BA(K) 3.

85. Kahn, *Hitler's Spies,* 243, 248.

86. "Schindler to Lang," July 20, 1951, BA(K) 3.

87. Ibid., 3–4.

88. Schindler, *Light and Shadow,* 30, 55–56, 83–84.

89. "Schindler Financial Report 1945," YVA, 6.

90. Alex Weissberg, *Desperate Mission: Joel Brand's Story as Told by Alex Weissberg,* trans. Constantine FitzGibbon and Andrew Foster-Melliar (New York: Criterion Books, 1958), 36.

91. "Oskar Schindler *Bericht,* 1955," BA(K), 3; Weissberg, *Desperate Mission,* 16–18, 20.

92. Weissberg, *Desperate Mission,* 30, 33–34; Andrew J. Janos, *The Politics of Backwardness in Hungary, 1825–1945* (Princeton: Princeton University Press, 1982), 302–307; Randolph L. Braham, "The Holocaust in Hungary: A Retrospective Analysis," in Michael Berenbaum and Abraham J. Peck, eds., *The Holocaust and History: The Known, the Unknown, the Disputed, and the Reexamined* (Bloomington: Indiana University Press in association with the Untied States Holocaust Memorial Museum, 1998), 432.

93. Yehuda Bauer, *American Jewry and the Holocaust: The American Jewish Joint Distribution Committee, 1939–1945* (Detroit: Wayne State University Press, 1981), 385–386.

94. Weissberg, *Desperate Mission,* 33.

95. Stanford J. Shaw, *Turkey and the Holocaust: Turkey's Role in Rescuing Turkish and European Jewry from Nazi Persecution, 1933–1945* (New York: New York University Press, 1993), 256.

96. Ibid., 257, 270, 271, 275.

97. Ibid., 272–273.

98. Ibid., 273–276.

99. Ibid., 275–276.

100. "Interview with Hansi Brand," Martin A. Gosch and Howard Koch, "The Story of Oskar Schindler," 12-A, 12, 12-B, 1, Delbert Mann Papers, Special Collections Library, Vanderbilt University.

101. Reszőe Kasztner, *Der Bericht des Jüdischen Rettungskomitees aus Budapest* (Self-published by the author, 1946), 14.

102. "Schindler Financial Report 1945," YVA, 7; Weissberg, *Desperate Mission,* 37; Bieberstein, *Zagłada Żydów w Krakowie,* 16, 149; Dr. Kasztner says in his *Der Bericht des jüdischen Rettungskomitees aus Budapest: 1942–1945* (Budapest: Private manuscript published by the author, 1946), 14, that Sedlacek made only three trips to Kraków.

103. Keneally, *Schindler's List,* 153.

104. Weissberg, *Desperate Mission,* 37; "Schindler Financial Report 1945," YVA, 6.

105. *Die Bekenntnisse des Herrn X,* BA(K), 1, 7.

106. Ibid., 1; "Schindler Financial Report 1945," YVA, 7.

107. *Die Bekenntnisse des Herrn X* BA(K), 1.

108. Ibid.

109. Ibid.

110. Ibid.

111. Ibid.

112. Ibid.

113. Ibid.

114. Christopher R. Browning, *Nazi Policy, Jewish Workers, German Killers* (Cambridge: Cambridge University Press, 2000), 86–87.

115. *Die Bekenntnisse des Herrn X,* BA(K), 2.

116. Ibid.; Jeremy Noakes and Geoffrey Pridham, *Nazism: A History in Documents and Eyewitness Accounts, 1919–1945,* vol. 2 (New York: Schocken Books, 1988), 1087 n. 1; Omer Bartov, *Hitler's Army: Soldiers, Nazis, and War in the Third Reich* (New York: Oxford University Press, 1991), 84–88. Though the Commissar Order *(Kommissarbefehl)* did not contain specific instructions to murder Jews, each unit commander was allowed freely to interpret whom his troops could murder under this order, resulting in the deaths of many Jewish POWs and others.

117. Hamburg Institute for Social Research, *The German Army and Genocide: Crimes Against War Prisoners, Jews, and Other Civilians, 1939–1944* (New York: The New Press, 1999), 7. This is the English edition guidebook for the Hamburg Institute's controversial exhibit that was supposed to appear in the United States. However, the controversy over it in Germany, combined with the discovery that some of the photos were inaccurately described, resulted in the cancellation of the exhibit in New York and, ultimately, the United States. The German edition of the guidebook, *Vernichtungskrieg. Verbrechen der Wehrmacht 1941 bis 1944* (Hamburg: Hamburger Edition, 1996), is less descriptive than the English edition and covers only the period from 1941 to 1944.

118. *Die Bekenntnisse des Herrn X,* BA(K), 3.

119. Ibid.

120. Ibid., 3–4.

121. Ibid., 4.

122. Ibid.

123. Ibid.

124. Ibid.

125. Ibid.

126. Ibid.

127. Bauer, *American Jewry and the Holocaust,* 85–86, 90–92, 318–322; Bieberstein, *Zagłada Żydów w Krakowie,* 31, 96, 129, 132, 135, 159–163.

128. *Die Bekenntnisse des Herrn X,* BA(K), 4.

129. Ibid., 4–5.

130. Ibid., 5.

131. Ibid.

132. Ibid.

133. Ibid.

134. "Schindler Financial Report 1945," YVA, 3.

135. Ibid.

136. *Die Bekenntnisse des Herrn X*, BA(K), 5; Danuta Czech, *Auschwitz Chronicle, 1939–1945* (New York: Henry Holt and Company, 1990), 556–557; the most thorough investigation of the Katyń massacres in English is Allen Paul's *Katyń: The Untold Story of Stalin's Polish Massacre* (New York: Charles Scribner's Sons, 1991), 114.

137. *Die Bekenntnisse des Herrn X*, BA(K), 5–6.

138. Ibid., 6.

139. Ibid.

140. Abraham J. Edelheit & Hershel Edelheit, *History of the Holocaust: A Handbook and Dictionary* (Boulder: Westview Press, 1994), 295.

141. *Die Bekenntnisse des Herrn X*, BA(K), 6.

142. Ibid.

143. Ibid.

144. "Oskar Schindler *Bericht*, 1955," BA(K), 3.

145. *Die Bekenntnisse des Herrn X*, BA(K), 6.

146. Ibid.

147. Ibid., 6–7; Paul, *Katyń*, 270–274.

148. Israel Gutman, *Resistance: The Warsaw Ghetto Uprising* (Boston: Houghton Mifflin, 1994), 254; Ruta Sakowska, "The Warsaw Ghetto," in *The Warsaw Ghetto: The 45th Anniversary of the Uprising* (Warsaw: Interpress, 1988), 10; "Stroop to Krueger," Warsaw, 24 May 1943, in *The Stroop Report*, trans. Sybil Milton (New York: Pantheon Books, 1979), 2 pages.

149. "Schindler Financial Report 1945," YVA, 7.

150. Ibid.; Breitman, *Official Secrets*, 200–201; Shaw, *Turkey and the Holocaust*, 291; Bauer, *American Jewry and the Holocaust*, 406.

151. Richard Breitman, *Official Secrets: What the Nazis Planned, What the British and Americans Knew* (New York: Hill & Wang, 1998), 137–154.

152. "Stern Report 1956," YVA, 25; Weissberg, *Dangerous Mission*, 36–37; Kasztner, *Der Bericht des jüdischen Rettungskomitees aus Budapest: 1942–1945*, 14.

153. Weissberg, *Desperate Mission*, 33–34.

154. Ibid., 30.

155. "Schindler Financial Report 1945," YVA, 7; Weissberg, *Desperate Mission*, 36.

156. "Schindler Financial Report 1945," YVA, 7.

157. Ibid.

158. "Stern Report 1956," YVA, 25.

159. Keneally, *Schindler's List*, 220–224.

160. "Stern Report 1956," YVA, 25.

161. Ibid.

162. Ibid.

163. Weissberg, *Desperate Mission*, 96–97.

164. Breitman, *Official Secrets*, 204–205.

Chapter 8

1. *Schindler's List*, Steven Spielberg, Director, Universal/MCA and Amblin Entertainment (1993) (hereafter referred to as *Schindler's List* (1993)).

2. Ibid.

3. Thomas Keneally, *Schindler's List* (New York: Simon & Schuster, 1992), 278–279.

4. *Schindler's List* (1993).

5. *Proces Ludobójcy Amona Leopolda Goetha przed Najwyżym Trybunałem Naro-dowym* (Kraków: Centralna Żydowska Komisja Historyczna w Polsce, 1947), 62–63.

6. Ibid., 282–283.

7. Heinz Höhne, *The Order of the Death's Head: The Story of Hitler's SS* (New York: Ballantine Books, 1977), 433.

8. Ibid.

9. Ibid.; for a more in-depth look at the career of Franke-Gricksch, particularly his interests in ideological issues and as they related to the Holocaust, see Charles W. Sydnor, Jr., *Soldiers of Destruction: The SS Death's Head Division, 1933–1945* (Princeton: Princeton University Press, 1990), 85 n. 28, 315–316, 337–338.

10. Höhne, *Order of the Death's Head*, 433; Wolfgang Sofsky, *The Order of Terror: The Concentration Camp*, trans. William Templer (Princeton: Princeton University Press, 1997), 105, 112.

11. Sofsky, *Order of Terror*, 113.

12. Höhne, *Order of the Death's Head*, 433.

13. Sofsky, *Order of Terror*, 40–41; Michael Thad Allen, *The Business of Genocide: The SS, Slave Labor, and the Concentration Camps* (Chapel Hill: University of North Carolina Press, 2002), 139, 154–155, 157, 182–183.

14. *Proces Ludobójcy Amona Leopolda Goetha*, 63–64.

15. Ibid., 64–65.

16. Randolph L. Braham, "The Holocaust in Hungary: A Retrospective Analysis," in Michael Berenbaum and Abraham J. Peck, eds., *The Holocaust and History: The Known, the Unknown, the Disputed, and the Reexamined* (Bloomington: Indiana University Press in association with the United States Holocaust Memorial Museum, 1998), 434–436. Braham correctly concludes that Eichmann's commandos alone could not have implemented the Final Solution of Hungarian Jewry with such quick efficiency. It succeeded because of considerable support from Hungarian fascists and the failure of the Horthy regime to do more to save the country's Jews; Randolph L. Braham, "Hungarian Jews," in Yisrael Gutman and Michael Berenbaum, eds., *Anatomy of the Auschwitz Death Camp* (Bloomington: Indiana University Press in association with the United States Holocaust Memorial Museum, 1994), 462–465; Randolph L. Braham is the foremost scholar on the Holocaust in Hungary. His classic work is *The Politics of Genocide: The Holocaust in Hungary*, 2 vols. (New York: Columbia University Press, 1981).

17. Braham, "Hungarian Jews," 466; *Proces Ludobójcy Amona Leopolda Goetha*, 45.

18. Ana Novac, *The Beautiful Days of My Youth: My Six Months in Auschwitz and Plaszow*, trans. George L. Newman (New York: Henry Holt and Company, 1997), 52–53.

19. Ibid., 56.

20. Ibid., 84–85, 88–89, 98–101.

21. Keneally, *Schindler's List*, 259–260.

22. Aleksander Bieberstein, *Zagłada Żydów w Krakowie* (Kraków: Wydawnictwo Literackie, 1985), 138–139; Murray Pantirer, interview by the author, Union, New Jersey, August 3, 1999; Elinor Brecher, *Schindler's Legacy: True Stories of the List Survivors* (New York: Plume Books, 1994), 186.

23. Bieberstein, *Zagłada Żydów w Krakowie*, 138–139; *Proces Ludobójcy Amona Leopolda Goetha*, 65–66.

24. Bieberstein, *Zagłada Żydów w Krakowie*, 139. The children saved were Romek Ferber, the brother of a Jewish clerk; Wilek Schnitzer, the son of a supervisor in Madritsch's sewing factory; Zbyszek Gross, the son of one of the camp's Jewish physicians, Dr. Leon Gross; Genek Gunter, the child of a camp *Kapo;* Rysiek Horowitz, the son of another *Kapo;*

Marysia Finkelstein, the stepdaughter of a *Kapo;* Ewa Ratz, the child of a camp servant; and Marcel Gruner, the son of a *Kapo.* Although it is difficult to determine the nature of the influence that each of these Jewish leaders had on Chilowicz, many of the few children saved on May 14 were part of larger family groupings that appeared on the two "Schindler's Lists." This included the Ferber, Gross, Gruner, Horowitz, and Ratz families.

25. Stella Müller-Madej, *A Girl from Schindler's List* (London: Polish Cultural Foundation, 1997), 123–124.

26. Müller-Madej, *A Girl from Schindler's List,* 124.

27. Ibid., 124–125.

28. Joseph Bau, *Dear God, Have You Ever Gone Hungry? Memoirs by Joseph Bau,* trans. Shlomo "Sam" Yurman (New York: Arcade Publishing, 1996), 114.

29. Müller-Madej, *A Girl from Schindler's List,* 125–126.

30. Brecher, *Schindler's Legacy,* 163.

31. Müller-Madej, *A Girl from Schindler's List,* 132.

32. Bieberstein, *Zagłada Żydów w Krakowie,* 139; *Proces Ludobójcy Amona Leopolda Goetha,* 66–67, 92; Danuta Czech, *Auschwitz Chronicle, 1939–1945* (New York: Henry Holt and Company, 1990), 625.

33. Julius Madritsch, *Menschen in Not! Meine Erlebnisse in den Jahren 1940 bis 1944 als Unternehmer im damaligen Generalgouvernement* (Vienna: V. Roth, 1962), 25.

34. Alfred C. Mierzejewski, *The Collapse of the German War Economy, 1944–1945: Allied Power and the German National Railway* (Chapel Hill: University of North Carolina Press, 1988), 17–20; R. J. Overy, *War and Economy and the Third Reich* (Oxford: Clarendon Press, 1994), 113, 117; Christopher R. Browning, *Nazi Policy, Jewish Workers, German Killers* (Cambridge: Cambridge University Press, 2000), 85–86; Albert Speer, *The Slave State: Heinrich Himmler's Masterplan for SS Supremacy,* trans. Joachim Neugroschel (London: Weidenfeld and Nicolson, 1981), 276–277.

35. Ulrich Herbert, *Hitler's Foreign Workers: Enforced Foreign Labor in Germany Under the Third Reich,* trans. William Templer (Cambridge: Cambridge University Press, 1997), 278–279, 281–282, 298. By the summer of 1944, there were more than 2.7 million Soviets working as forced laborers in the Reich and almost 1.7 million Poles.

36. Speer, *The Slave State,* 278, 280–281.

37. Sol Urbach, interview by the author, Delray Beach, Florida, February 15, 2000.

38. "Oskar Schindler Financial Report 1945," July 1945, Yad Vashem Archives, 01/164, 9.

39. Urbach, interview, February 15, 2000; Keneally, *Schindler's List,* 288.

40. Urbach, interview, February 15, 2000; Harald Hutterberger (*Republik Österreich, Bundesministerium für Inneres*) to David M. Crowe, 20 October 2000, 1 page; "10. August 1944 vom KL. Plaszow," *Archiv der KZ-Gedenkstätte Mauthausen, Abschrift Häftlingszugangsbuch* (E/13/1), 42-121; Konnilyn G. Feig, *Hitler's Death Camps: The Sanity of Madness* (New York: Holmes & Meier, 1979), 124.

41. Brecher, *Schindler's Legacy,* 187, 437.

42. "Oskar Schindler *Bericht,*" October 30, 1955, Bundesarchiv (Koblenz), Nachlaß Oskar Schindler, 1908–1974, Bestand N 1493, No. 1, Band 15, 3; Abraham Zuckerman, *A Voice in the Chorus: Memories of a Teenager Saved by Schindler* (Stamford, Conn.: Longmeadow Press, 1991), 86–87.

43. Abraham Zuckerman and Murray Pantirer, interview by the author, Union, New Jersey, August 3, 1999; Abraham Zuckerman also discusses the train incident in his memoirs, *A Voice in the Chorus,* 85–87.

44. Murray Finder, interview by the author, Delray Beach, Florida, March 19, 2000.

45. Zuckerman and Pantirer, interview, August 3, 1999; Brecher, *Schindler's Legacy,* 186–187; "Testimony of Al Bukiet," March 29, 1995, Fortunoff Archives, T-2831, Yale University.

46. "Stern Report 1956," Yad Vashem Archives, 01/164, 30.

47. Mietek Pemper, interview by the author, Augsburg, Germany, May 26, 1999.

48. Schindler, *Light and Shadow,* 62–63.

49. "Schindler Financial Report 1945," YVA, 12–13.

50. Keneally, *Schindler's List,* 341.

51. Francisco Wichter, interview by the author, Buenos Aires, Argentina, May 17, 2001; Jitka Gruntová, *Legendy a fakta o Oskaru Schindlerovi* (Praha: Vydalo nokladatelstvín Naše vojsko, 2002), 144–145; Ian V. Hogs, *German Artillery of World War Two* (London: Greenhill Books, 2002), 189–192.

52. Schindler, *Light and Shadow,* 62–63.

53. Pemper, interview, May 26, 1999.

54. "Oskar Schindler *Bericht* 1955," BA(K), 24; Volker Zimmermann, *Die Sudetendeutschen im NS-Staat: Politik und Stimmung der Bevölkerung im Reichsgau Sudetenland (1938–1945)* (Essen: Klartext Verlag, 1999), 141, 460.

55. "Oskar Schindler *Bericht* 1955," BA(K), 3; Zimmermann, *Die Sudetendeutschen im NS Staat,* 387–395; Rudolph Höss, *Death Dealer: The Memoirs of the SS Kommandant at Auschwitz,* ed. Steven Paskuly, trans. Andrew Pollinger (New York: Da Capo Press, 1996), 229–230; Andrew Konieczny, "Organisation Schmelt," in Israel Gutman, ed., *Encyclopedia of the Holocaust,* vol. 3 (New York: Macmillan Publishing Company, 1990), 1093–1095.

56. Jan Kopecký, *Historie textilního závodu v Brněnci* (Svitavy: Grafickou úpravu a obálku navrhl Lad. Vejda, 1965), 22–24. This is an excellent history of textile manufacture in Brněnec and particularly of the Löw-Beer family; Jitka Gruntová, *Oskar Schindler: Ledgenda a Fakta* (Brno: Barrister & Principal, 1997), 43–44; "Schindler Financial Report 1945," YVA, 8.

57. "Schindler Financial Report 1945," YVA, 8.

58. Schindler, *Light and Shadow,* 83–84; "Oskar Schindler *Bericht* 1955," BA(K), 4.

59. "Oskar Schindler *Bericht* 1955," BA(K), 4; "Oskar Schindler to Fritz Lang," July 20, 1951, Bundesarchiv (Koblenz), Nachlaß Oskar Schindler, 1908–1974, Bestand N 1493, No. 1, Band 23, 3; "Schindler Financial Report 1945," YVA, 15; Sofsky, *Order of Terror,* 181.

60. "Oskar Schindler *Bericht* 1955," BA(K), 4.

61. Ibid.; Danuta Czech, *Auschwitz Chronicle, 1939–1945* (New York: Henry Holt and Company, 1990), 728, 731, 733, 738–739, 744–745; the three hundred women in the Freudenthal sub-camp worked for the Emmerich Machold company that made "vitaminized juices." The three Auschwitz sub-camps in the Protectorate of Bohemia and Moravia—Freudenthal, Světlá, and Brno—were the most distant in the Auschwitz network. Tadeusz Iwaszko, Helena Kubica, Franciszek Piper, Irena Strzelecka, and Andrzej Strzelecki, *Auschwitz 1940–1945,* vol. 2, *The Prisoners: Their Life and Work* (Oświęcim: Auschwitz-Birkenau State Museum, 2000), 117, 120.

62. "Schindler Financial Report 1945," YVA, 9–10.

63. Primo Levi, *The Drowned and the Saved,* trans. Raymond Rosenthal (New York: Summit Books, 1988), 41–42; Browning, *Nazi Policy, Jewish Workers, German Killers,* 102.

64. Primo Levi, *Survival in Auschwitz: The Nazi Assault on Humanity,* translated by Stuart Woolf (New York: Collier Books, 1961), 82–83; Browning, *Nazi Policy, Jewish Workers, German Killers,* 102.

65. Sofsky, *Order of Terror,* 145–149; Levi, *Survival in Auschwitz,* 83.

66. *Proces Ludubócjy Amona Leopolda Goetha,* 71–72.

67. Levi, *The Drowned and the Saved,* 40.

68. Isaiah Trunk, *Judenrat: The Jewish Councils in Eastern Europe under Nazi Occupation* (New York: Stein and Day, 1977), 573.

69. Levi, *Survival in Auschwitz,* 83.

70. Malvina Graf, *The Kraków Ghetto and the Płaszów Camp Remembered* (Tallahassee: Florida State University Press, 1989), 115, 117, 121.

71. Ibid., 121.

72. Ibid., 115.

73. Bieberstein, *Zagłada Żydów w Krakowie*, 139.

74. Spielberg, *Schindler's List* (1993).

75. Sofsky, *Order of Terror*, 145.

76. Brecher, *Schindler's Legacy*, 161–162.

77. Ibid., 429.

78. Zuckerman, *A Voice in the Chorus*, 66–67.

79. Müller-Madej, *A Girl from Schindler's List*, 89.

80. Ibid.

81. Bieberstein, *Zagłada Żydów w Krakowie*, 142.

82. Brecher, *Schindler's Legacy*, 236.

83. Ibid., 332–333.

84. Müller-Madej, *A Girl from Schindler's List*, 89.

85. Bieberstein, *Zagłada Żydów w Krakowie*, 142.

86. Müller-Madej, *A Girl from Schindler's List*, 89.

87. Bieberstein, *Zagłada Żydów w Krakowie*, 142.

88. Müller-Madej, *A Girl from Schindler's List*, 89–90.

89. Mietek Pemper, interview by Dr. Reich, Augsburg, Germany, October 26, 1996; *Proces Ludobójcy Amona Leopolda Goetha*, 60.

90. Madritsch, *Menschen*, 24.

91. Bieberstein, *Zagłada Żydów w Krakowie*, 142.

92. *Proces Ludobójcy Amona Leopolda Goetha*, 62.

93. Ibid., 76–77.

94. Ibid., 77, 93; Bieberstein, *Zagłada Żydów w Krakowie*, 142.

95. Keneally, *Schindler's List*, 271–272; *Proces Ludubójcy Amona Leopolda Goetha*, 92.

96. Brecher, *Schindler's Legacy*, 168.

97. Ibid., 132.

98. Ibid., 132–133.

99. Ibid., 114; *Proces Ludobójcy Amona Leopolda Goetha*, 142.

100. Müller-Madej, *A Girl from Schindler's List*, 140.

101. *Proces Ludobójcy Amona Leopolda Goetha*, 92.

102. Brecher, *Schindler's Legacy*, 133.

103. Müller-Madej, *A Girl from Schindler's List*, 140.

104. Ibid., 141.

105. Israel Gutman, *Resistance: The Warsaw Ghetto Uprising* (New York: Houghton Mifflin Company in association with the United States Holocaust Memorial Museum, 1994), 152–153.

106. Stella Müller-Madej, interview by the author, Kraków, Poland, August 9, 2000; Bieberstein, *Zagłada Żydów w Krakowie*, 139–140; Müller-Madej, *A Girl from Schindler's List*, 141.

107. Müller-Madej, *A Girl from Schindler's List*, 141.

108. Ibid.

109. Bieberstein, *Zagłada Żydów w Krakowie*, 140.

110. Ibid., 142.

111. *Proces Ludobójcy Amona Leopolda Goetha*, 71.

112. Brecher, *Schindler's Legacy*, 133, 161; Müller-Madej, *A Girl from Schindler's List*, 141.

113. Brecher, *Schindler's Legacy*, 411.

114. Höhne, *Order of the Death's Head,* 261; Raul Hilberg, *The Destruction of the European Jews* (New York: Holmes & Meier, 1985), 2:528.

115. Speer, *The Slave State,* 39.

116. Richard Breitman, *The Architect of Genocide: Himmler and the Final Solution* (New York: Alfred A. Knopf, 1991), 34; Peter Padfield, *Himmler: Reichsführer-SS* (New York: Henry Holt and Company, 1990), 100–105.

117. "Testimony of Guenther Reinecke," August 8, 1946, International Military Tribunal in Session at Nuremberg, Germany, *The Trial of German Major War Criminals: Proceedings of the International Military Tribunal Sitting at Nuremberg Germany,* part 20, *29 July, 1946 to 8 August, 1946* (London: H.M. Attorney General by His Majesty's Stationery Office, 1949), 340 (hereafter referred to as *Trial of Major War Criminals,* part 20); see Hannsjoachim W. Koch's *In the Name of the Volk: Political Justice in Hitler's Germany* (New York: Barnes & Noble, 1997), 53, 86–125, for a discussion of what he calls a "complete capitulation of the judiciary in general and the VGH [*Volksgerichtshof;* Volk Court] in particular Himmler's SS state," particularly as it related to Nazi Germany's broadly defined *Kriegsstrafrecht* dealing with espionage and partisans. Though this statement is in reference to questions of espionage and other broadly defined anti-German acts, it does capture the spirit of the growing power of the SS autonomous legal authority, particularly in the occupied territories.

118. Höhne, *Order of the Death's Head,* 14, 169, 242–243, 362; Hans Frank, *Dziennik Hansa Frank,* ed. and trans. Stanislaw Piotrowska (Warszawa: Wydawnictwo Prawnicze, 1956), 21–22; *Trial of the Major War Criminals,* part 20, 334.

119. Höhne, *Order of the Death's Head,* 434.

120. Ibid.

121. Włodziemierz Borodziej, *Terror und Politik: Die deutsche Polizei und die polnische Widerstandsbewegung im Generalgouvernement, 1939–1944* (Mainz: Verlag Philipp von Zabern, 1999), 175; Gerald Reitlinger, *The SS: Alibi of a Nation, 1922–1945* (New York: Da Capo Press, 1981), 170–174, 375–377; Padfield, *Himmler,* 442, 524–525, 527, 538; Hilberg, *Destruction of the European Jews,* 3:966.

122. Reitlinger, *Alibi of a Nation,* 173–174; Höhne, *Order of the Death's Head,* 434; Hilberg, *Destruction of the European Jews,* 3:1093; Christian Zentner and Friedemann Bedürftig, eds., *The Encyclopedia of the Third Reich,* trans. Amy Hackett (New York: Da Capo Press, 1997), 200.

123. Höhne, *Order of the Death's Head,* 435.

124. "Testimony of Georg Konrad Morgen," August 7–8, 1946, *Trial of the Major War Criminals,* part 20, 380, 393, 395; Höhne, *Order of the Death's Head,* 435–436.

125. Tom Segev, *Soldiers of Evil: The Commandants of the Nazi Concentration Camps,* trans. Haim Watzman (New York: McGraw-Hill Book Company, 1987), 144–145. The first escape, in March, involved two hundred Soviet POWs; the second, in April, involved fewer prisoners but resulted in the death of four guards. Józef Marszałek, *Majdanek: The Concentration Camp in Lublin* (Warsaw: Interpress, 1986), 39, 170–171.

126. David A. Hackett, ed. and trans., *The Buchenwald Report* (Boulder: Westview Press, 1995), 335–341; "Testimony of Georg Konrad Morgen," August 7, 1946, *Trial of the Major War Criminals,* part 20, 381; Höhne, *Order of the Death's Head,* 436–438; Segev, *Soldiers of Evil,* 154; Drexel A. Sprechter, *Inside the Nuremberg Trial: A Prosecutor's Comprehensive Account,* vol. 2 (Lanham, Md.: University Press of America, 1999), 1188–1190.

127. Hackett, *The Buchenwald Report,* 126, 341. Another prisoner, Jan Robert, echoed Heymann's statement about how SS officers feared Morgen.

128. Drexel A. Sprecher, *Inside the Nuremberg Trial: A Prosecutor's Comprehensive Account,* vol. 1 (Lanham, Md.: University Press of America, 1999), 99–100. Only three of the six accused organizations were declared criminal at the end of the trial: the Nazi Leadership

Corps, the SD and the Gestapo, and the SS. The SA, the Reich Cabinet, the General Staff, and the High Command were declared not to be criminal organizations. Telford Taylor, *The Anatomy of the Nuremberg Trials: A Personal Memoir* (Boston: Little, Brown and Company, 1992), 583–587; Christopher Ailsby, *SS: Roll of Infamy* (London: Motorbooks International, 1997), 121.

129. "Schindler Financial Report 1945," YVA, 4; Tadeusz Pankiewicz, *Apteka w Getcie Krakowskim* (Kraków: Wydawnictwo Literackie, 1995), 278–279; Tadeusz Wroński, *Kronika Okupowanego Krakowa* (Kraków: Wydawnicto Literackie, 1974), 220.

130. Pankiewicz, *Apteka w Getcie Krakowskim*, 280.

131. "Schindler Financial Report 1945," YVA, 5.

132. Ibid.

133. *SS-Wirtschafts-Verwaltungshauptamt*, A V/2/5/Ni./Schf. Memo on Amon Göth to SS-Personalhauptamt, II 8, Berlin-Charlottenburg 4, April 14, 1944, Personal-Akte, PA Nr. G 886, Göth, Amon Leopold, SS-Nr 43 673, Der Reichsführer-SS, SS-Personalhauptamt, BDC (Berlin Documentation Center), Bundesarchiv (Berlin), 1 page; future documents from Göth's SS "Personal Akte" will be cited as "Personal-Akte," PA Nr G 886, Göth, Amon Leopold, BA(B), preceded by the individual document title and page reference.

134. Dr. Adolf Katz to WVHA," April 26, 1944, Personal-Akte, PA Nr G 886, Göth, Amon Leopold, SS-Offiziere, BA(B), 1 page.

135. Sydnor, *Soldiers of Destruction*, 324–326.

136. SS-Personalhauptamt II/8 En./We., June 9, 1944, Personal-Akte, PA Nr 886, Göth, Amon Leopold, BA(B), 1 page; Göth's Certificate of Discharge from the HSSPF Ost was issued on 23 June 1944. "Dr. Katz Memorandum," June 23, 1944, Personal-Akte, PA Nr 886, Göth, Amon Leopold, BA(B), 1 page; one document in Göth's SS file shows that the date of his transfer became effective on April 20, 1944. *Personalverfügung* Hauptsturmführer Amon Leopold Göth, Der Reichsführer SS-Personalhauptamt, Amt II a 1 a Za/Sch., September 26, 1944, SS-Files of Amon Leopold Göth, 1 page; records of the Reich Leader of the SS and Chief of the German Police, RG 242 (National Archives Collection of Foreign Records Seized, 1941-), National Archives of the United States II, College Park, Maryland.

137. "Aktennotiz," I2a, K/Mü., August 31, 1944, Personal-Akte, PA Nr 886, Göth, Amon Leopold, BA(B), 1 page.

138. "Hans Stauber to Heinrich Himmler," August 18, 1944, in Personal-Akte, PA Nr 886, Göth, Amon Leopold, BA(B), 1–2.

139. *Proces Ludobójcy Amona Leopolda Goetha*, 70.

140. Howard Koch and Martin A. Gosch, "Summary of Interview with Oskar Schindler and Notes re Ahmon Goeth," in "The Oskar Schindler Story," 6-B, 3-4 in Delbert Mann Papers, Special Collections Library, Vanderbilt University (hereafter referred to as Koch and Gosch, "Summary of Interview with Oskar Schindler," Delbert Mann Papers, Vanderbilt University).

141. "HSSPF Koppe to SS-Standartenfuehrer Brandt," September 6, 1944, Personal-Akte, PA Nr 886, Göth, Amon Leopold, BA(B), 1 page.

142. *Proces Ludobócja Amona Leopolda Goetha*, 69–70; Pemper, interview, May 26, 1999.

143. Brecher, *Schindler's Legacy*, 68.

144. Ibid.

145. Höhne, *Order of the Death's Head*, 435.

146. Pemper, interview, May 26, 1999.

147. Ibid.; Bieberstein, *Zagłada Żydów w Krakowie*, 149;

148. Joseph Bau, *Dear God, Have You Ever Gone Hungry? Memoirs by Joseph Bau*, trans. Shlomo "Sam" Yurman (New York: Arcade Publishing, 1998), 118.

149. Müller-Madej, interview, August 9, 2000; Müller-Madej, *A Girl from Schindler's List*, 63, 110. There is no one by the name of Huth on the list of Płaszów officers that

Mietek Pemper prepared for the Polish court in the summer of 1946; there is, however, an *SS-Unterscharführer* Rolf Lüth on the list. See "Jan Sehn to Mieczysław Pemper, July 8, 1946, 'List of SS Officers in Kraków-Płaszów,'" Bundesarchiv (Berlin) 2M 1402 A.12, 1.

150. Bieberstein, *Zagłada Żydów w Krakowie*, 102, 104, 111, 116; Pemper, interview, May 26, 1999.

151. Bau, *Dear God*, 121.

152. Pemper, interview, May 26, 1999; *Proces Ludobójcy Amona Leopolda Goetha*, 71.

153. *Proces Ludobójcy Amona Leopolda Goetha*, 70.

154. Bieberstein, *Zagłada Żydów w Krakowie*, 141.

155. Höhe, *Order of the Death's Head*, 433.

156. *Proces Ludobójcy Amona Leopolda Goetha*, 71.

157. Ibid.

158. Koch and Gosch, "Summary of Interview with Oskar Schindler," Delbert Mann Papers, Vanderbilt University, 6-B, 4–5.

159. Ibid., 4–6.

160. Ibid., 6–7.

161. Ibid., 7–9.

162. Ibid.

163. Ibid., 9–10.

164. Ibid., 10–11.

165. Ibid., 7-A, 1–2.

166. Ibid., 2–3.

167. "Oskar Schindler *Bericht*," October 30, 1955, Bundesarchiv (Koblenz), Nachlaß Oskar Schindler, 1908–1974, Bestand 1493, No. 1, Band 15, 4; Dr. Moshe Bejski, interview by the author, Tel Aviv, Israel, May 17, 1999; Dr. Moshe Bejski, "Notes on the Banquet in Honor of Oskar Schindler," May 2, 1962, Tel Aviv, Israel, 37–38; "Stern Report 1956," Yad Vashem Archives, 01/164, 30–31; Pemper, interview, May 26, 1999; "Kriminalpolizei *Bericht*-Oskar Schindler Ge. 28.4. 1908 in Zwittau/Sudetenland, Frankfurt/M, Am Hauptbahnhof 4/63," March 18, 1963, Frankfurt/Main, West Germany, Zentrale Stelle der Landesjustizverwaltung (ZSL), Ludwigsburg, Germany, 1–3.

168. "Oskar Schindler *Bericht*, 1955," BA(K), 4.

169. Ibid.; Bejski, "Notes on the Oskar Schindler Banquet," May 2, 1962, 37.

170. Höhne, *Order of the Death's Head*, 436–438.

171. Pemper, interview, May 26, 1999.

172. Koch and Gosch, "Summary of Interview with Oskar Schindler," Papers of Delbert Mann, Vanderbilt University, 6-B, 1.

173. *Proces Ludobójcy Amona Leopolda Goetha*, 286–287.

Chapter 9

1. Thomas Keneally, *Schindler's List* (New York: Touchstone Books, 1992), 292.

2. Ibid., 290.

3. Elinor J. Brecher, *Schindler's Legacy: True Stories of the List Survivors* (New York: Penguin Books, 1994), 430.

4. Keneally, *Schindler's List*, 291–292.

5. Dr. Moshe Bejski, interview by the author, Tel Aviv, Israel, May 17, 1999.

6. Mietek Pemper, interview by the author, Augsburg, Germany, May 26, 1999.

7. Dr. Aleksander Bieberstein, *Zagłada Żydów w Krakowie* (Kraków: Wydawnictwo Literackie, 1985), 145.

8. Rena Ferber Finder, interview by the author, Boca Raton, Florida, March 19, 2000. The first transport from Kraków to Auschwitz in 1943 was on January 19. Auschwitz

records indicate that all the Jews on that transport were murdered soon after their arrival. It is possible that Moses Ferber was on that transport. Danuta Czech, *Auschwitz Chronicle, 1939–1945* (New York: Henry Holt and Company, 1990), 308.

9. Finder, interview, March 19, 2000.

10. Sol Urbach, interview by the author, Delray Beach, Florida, April 13, 1999.

11. Brecher, *Schindler's Legacy*, 166.

12. Ibid., 133, 282.

13. Ibid., 166, 306, 340.

14. Ibid., 166.

15. Ibid., 423.

16. "Hans Stauber to Heinrich Himmler," August 18, 1944, in Personal-Akte, Nr 886, Göth, Amon Leopold, SS-Nr 43 673, Der Reichsführer-SS, SS Personalhauptamt, BDC (Berlin Documentation Center) Bundesarchiv (Berlin), 2.

17. Pemper, interview, May 26, 1999.

18. "Oskar Schindler Financial Report 1945," July 1945, Yad Vashem Archives, 01/164, 8.

19. "Oskar Schindler to Dr. K. J. Ball-Kaduri," September 9, 1956, Yad Vashem Archives, 01/164, 5; Oskar Schindler to Dr. K. J. Ball-Kaduri, October 21, 1956, Yad Vashem Archives, Department of the Righteous, 1.

20. "Schindler to Dr. Ball-Kaduri," October 21, 1956, YVA (DR), 1; Martin A. Gosch and Howard Koch, interview with Raimund Titsch, November 25, 1964, Vienna, Austria, 8-A, 9, Delbert Mann Papers, Special Collections Library, Vanderbilt University (hereafter referred to as "Interview with Riamund Titsch," November 25, 1964, Delbert Mann Papers, Vanderbilt University).

21. "Schindler to Dr. Ball-Kaduri," October 21, 1956, YVA (DR), 1–2.

22. "Interview with Raimund Titsch," November 25, 1964, Delbert Mann Papers, Vanderbilt University, 3.

23. "Schindler to Dr. Ball-Kaduri," October 21, 1956, YVA (DR), 1-2; "Interview with Raimund Titsch," November 25, 1964, Delbert Mann Papers, Vanderbilt University, 9–10.

24. "Raimund Titsch to Marcel Goldberg: Madritsch List," October 1944, Bundesarchiv (Koblenz), Nachlaß Oskar Schindler, 1908–1974, Bestand N 1493, Miscellaneous Files, 1 page (hereafter referred to as "Madritsch List," BA(K); "Interview with Raimund Titsch," November 25, 1964, Delbert Mann Papers, Vanderbilt University, 1).

25. Tadeusz Wroński, *Kronika Okupowanego Krakowa* (Kraków: Wydawnictwo Literackie, 1974), 356–363; Czech, *Auschwitz Chronicle*, 680, 684; Julius Madritsch, *Menschen in Not! Meine Erlebnisse in den Jahren 1940 bis 1944 als Unternehmer im damaligen Generalgouvernement* (Vienna: V. Roth, 1962), 39.

26. Wroński, *Kronika*, 372; Bieberstein, *Zagłada Żydów w Krakowie*, 145. Bieberstein says there were 550 men and 156 women remaining in the camp after the major October transports.

27. Mietek Pemper, interview by the author, Augsburg, Germany, January 17, 2000.

28. Madritsch, *Menschen*, 26.

29. Ibid., 25.

30. Pemper, interview, January 17, 2000.

31. Madritsch, *Menschen*, 22, 25–27.

32. Ibid., 28.

33. Brecher, *Schindler's Legacy*, 111–114, 264.

34. Pemper, interview, May 26, 1999; Helen Sternlicht Rosenzweig, interview by the author, Boca Raton, Florida, March 20, 2000.

35. The closest Oskar Schindler ever came to publishing an account of his wartime experiences was the testimony he provided Kurt R. Grossmann in *Die unbesungenen Helden: Menschen in Deutschlands dunklen Tagen* (Frankfurt/Berlin/Wien: Verlag Ullstein GmbH,

1957), 147–161. This essentially the same account found in his 1945 "Financial Report" and in his 1956 story for Yad Vashem.

36. Brecher, *Schindler's Legacy*, 133.

37. "Interview with Raimund Titsch," November 25, 1964, Delbert Mann Papers, Vanderbilt University, 1–2.

38. Pemper, interview, January 17, 2000; Francisco Wichter, interview by the author, Buenos Aires, Argentina, May 17, 2001.

39. Michael Thad Allen, *The Business of Genocide: The SS, Slave Labor, and the Concentration Camps* (Chapel Hill: University of North Carolina Press, 2002), 167, 170, 213, 255; Wolfgang Sofsky, *The Order of Terror: The Concentration Camp*, trans. William Templer (Princeton: Princeton University Press, 1997), 183, 323–324 n. 10; Shmuel Spector, "Budzyń," in Israel Gutman, ed., *Encyclopedia of the Holocaust*, vol. 1 (New York: Macmillan Publishing Company, 1990), 259–260; Jósef Abzug, "Budzyń: Sadyzm. Tortury skazańców. 'Czarni," in Michał M. Borwicz, Nella Rost, and Józef Wulf, eds., *Dokumenty Zbrodni i Męczeństwa* (Kraków: Wojewódzkiej Żydowskiej Komisji Historycznej w Krakowie, 1945), 72–75.

40. Francisco Wichter, *Undécimo Mandamiento: Testimonio del sobreviviente argentino de la lista de Schindler* (Buenos Aires: Grupo Editorial Agora, 1998), 88–90; Brecher, *Schindler's Legacy*, 422.

41. Allen, *The Business of Genocide*, 232–233; Albert Speer, *The Slave State: Heinrich Himmler's Masterplan for SS Supremacy*, trans. Joachim Neugroschel (London: Weidenfeld and Nicolson, 1981), 235–237.

42. Pemper, interview, January 17, 2000; Czesław Madajczyk, *Polityka III Rzeszy w Okupowanej Polsce*, vol. 1 (Warszawa: Państwowe Wydawnictwo Naukowe, 1970), 579; Małgorzata Międzobrodzka, "Jews in Wieliczka during the Nazi Occupation," Muzeum Up Krakowskich Wieliczka (Cracow Salt-Works Museum), http://www.muzeum.wieliczka.pl/en/Zydzi.html, 2 pages; David Donald, ed., *Warplanes of the Luftwaffe: Combat Aircraft of Hitler's Luftwaffe, 1939–1945* (New York: Barnes and Noble, 2000), 128–134; Rondall R. Rice, "Bombing Auschwitz: U.S. Fifteenth Air Force and the Military Aspects of a Possible Attack," in Michael J. Neufeld and Michael Berenbaum, eds., *The Bombing of Auschwitz: Should the Allies Have Attempted It?* (New York: St. Martin's Press in Association with the United States Holocaust Memorial Museum, 2000), 167–168; Wichter, interview, May 17, 2001; Brecher, *Schindler's Legacy*, 422.

43. Wichter, interview, May 17, 2001.

44. Spector, "Budzyń," 260.

45. Brecher, *Schindler's Legacy*, 422.

46. "Madritsch List," BA(K), 1 page; *"Namenliste der männlichen Häftlinge,"* Konzentrationslager Groß-Rosen-Arbeitslager Brünnlitz, October 21, 1944, Państwowe Muzeum Auschwitz-Birkenau w Oświęcimiu, 13 pages (hereafter referred to as *"Namenliste der männlichen Häftlinge,"* October 21, 1944, Muzeum Auschwitz-Birkenau); *"Namenliste der weiblichen Häftlinge,"* Konzentrationslager Groß-Rosen-Arbeitslager Brünnlitz, October 22, 1944, Muzeum Auschwitz-Birkenau, (hereafter referred to as *"Namenliste der weiblichen Häftlinge,"* October 22, 1944, Muzeum Auschwitz-Birkenau); *"KL Groß Rosen-AL Brünnlitz (Frauenlager)-Namenliste,"* November 12, 1944, Państwowe Muzeum Auschwitz-Birkenau w Oświęcimiu, 4 pages (hereafter referred to as *"KL Groß Rosen-AL Brünnlist (Frauenlager)-Namenliste,"* November 12, 1944, Muzeum Auschwitz-Birkenau); "Interview with Raimund Titsch," Delbert Mann Papers, Vanderbilt University, 5–6.

47. Bejski, interview, May 17, 1999.

48. Brecher, *Schindler's Legacy*, 40.

49. Bieberstein, *Zagłada Żydów w Krakowie*, 145, 150.

50. Joseph Bau, *Dear God, Have You Ever Gone Hungry?* trans. Shlomo "Sam" Yurman (New York: Arcade Publishing, 1998), 158.

51. Hadasah Bau, interview by the author, Winnipeg, Canada, November 15, 2000; Bau, *Dear God*, 223.

52. Bieberstein, *Zagłada Żydów w Krakowie*, 149.

53. Ibid.

54. Brecher, *Schindler's Legacy*, 351, 437.

55. Ibid., 412–413.

56. Magdalena Kunicka-Wrzykowska, *Indeks imienny Więźniów obozu w Płaszowie*, Ministerstwo Sprawiećliwości, Archiwum Głównej Komisji Badania Zbrodni Hiterlowskich w Polsce, Okręgowa Komisja Badania Zbrodni Przeciwko Narodowi Polskiemu-Instytut Pamięci Narodowej w Krakowie, Kraków, Poland.

57. *"Namenliste der weiblichen Häftlinge,"* October 22, 1944, Muzeum Auschwitz-Birkenau; *"Namenliste des Häftlingszuganges vom AL Golleschau (KL Auschwitz am 29. Januar 1945,"* Muzeum Auschwitz-Birkenau (hereafter referred to as *"Namenliste des Häftlingszuganges vom AL Golleschau,"* January 29, 1945, Muzeum Auschwitz-Birkenau); *"Namenliste der am 2.2.1945 vom Amtsgerichtsgefängnis Landskron zum Arbeitslager Brünnlitz überstellten Häftlinge,"* February 2, 1945, Muzeum Auschwitz-Birkenau (hereafter referred to as *"Namenliste Landskron-Brünnlitz,"* February 2, 1945, Muzeum Auschwitz-Birkenau); *"Namenliste des Häftlingszuganges am 11.4.45 vom AL Geppersdorf (KL Gr. Ro.),"* Muzeum Auschwitz-Birkenau (hereafter referred to as *"Namenliste Geppersdorf-Brünnlitz,"* April 11, 1945, Muzeum Auschwitz-Birkenau; Aleksandra Kobielec, *Filia Obozu Koncentracyjnego Groß-Rosen Arbeitslager Brünnlitz* (Wałbrzych: Państwowe Muzeum Groß-Rosen, 1991), 14–44. There is also a German translation of this work, Aleksandra Kobielec, *Außenlager des Konzentrationslagers Groß-Rosen Arbeitslager Brünnlitz* (Wałbrzych: Państwowe Muzeum Groß-Rosen, 1991); "Schindler's List: Name Index with Line and List Number," United States Holocaust Memorial Museum Archives, RG-20.003*01, USHMM Registry GR0306, 8 pages (hereafter referred to as "Schindler's List: Name Index," USHMM Archives, RG-20.003*01/GR0306); "Notes of Dr. Moshe Bejski on the Banquet in Honor of Oskar Schindler, May 2, 1962," 21; "Stern Report 1956," Yad Vashem Archives 01/164, 35.

58. "Schindler's List: Name Index," USHMM Archives, RG-20.003*01/GR0306, 8 pages.

59. Paul B. Jaskot, *The Architecture of Oppression: The SS, Forced Labor and the Nazi Monumental Building Economy* (London: Routledge, 2000), 70, 74–75.

60. Aahron Weiss, "Categories of Camps: Their Character and Role in the Execution of the 'Final Solution of the Jewish Question,'" in Yisrael Gutman and Avital Saf, eds., *The Nazi Concentration Camps* (Jerusalem: Yad Vashem, 1984), 132; Shmuel Krakowski, "Death Marches in the Period of the Evacuation of the Camps," in Gutman and Saf, *Nazi Concentration Camps*, 479, 482; Alfred Konieczny, "Groß-Rosen," in Gutman, *Encyclopedia of the Holocaust*, vol. 2, 623–626; Wilfried Feldenkirchen, *Siemens, 1918–1945* (Columbus: Ohio State University Press, 1999), 168, 364.

61. French L. Maclean, *The Camp Men: The SS Officers Who Ran the Nazi Concentration Camp System* (Atglen, Pa.: Schiffer Military History, 1999), 100; "Schindler Financial Report 1945," YVA, 10; Karin Orth, "Ich habe mich nie getarnt: Brücke und Kontinuitäten in der Lebensgeschichte des KZ-Kommandanten Johannes Hassebroek," *Sozialwissenschaftliche Informationen* 24, no. 2 (April-June 1995), 145–150.

62. Allen, *The Business of Genocide*, 8–10, 125–126, 185; Henry Friedlander, *The Origins of Nazi Genocide: From Euthanasia to the Final Solution* (Chapel Hill: University of North Carolina Press, 1995), 68, 142, 149. The name T4 came from the address in Berlin where the "euthanasia" program was headquartered, Tiergarten Straße 4; *The State Museum of Groß Rosen*, 1–7.

63. Bieberstein, *Zagłada Żydów w Krakowie*, 149–150; Kobielec, *Filia Obozu Koncentracyjnego Groß-Rosen Arbeitslager Brünnlitz*, 3.

----

64. Brecher, *Schindler's Legacy*, 210–211, 237.

65. Leon Leyson, interview by the author, Anaheim, California, March 29, 2000; Brecher, *Schindler's Legacy*, 90, 401; Wichter, interview, May 17, 2001.

66. Bieberstein, *Zagłada Żydów w Krakowie*, 149–150; Wichter, interview, May 17, 2001; Kobielec, *Filia Obozu Koncentracyjnego Groß-Rosen Arbeitslager Brünnlitz*, 3.

67. Bieberstein, *Zagłada Żydów w Krakowie*, 150; Brecher, *Schindler's Legacy*, 423; Pemper, interview, May 26, 1999.

68. Bieberstein, *Zagłada Żydów w Krakowie*, 150; Brecher, *Schindler's Legacy*, 237, 413; Kobielec, *Filia Obozu Koncentracyjnego Groß-Rosen Arbeitslager Brünnlitz*, 3.

69. Bieberstein, *Zagłada Żydów w Krakowie*, 150; Brecher, *Schindler's Legacy*, 133–134; Konieczny, *Filia Obozu Koncentracyjnego Groß-Rosen Arbeitslager Brünnlitz*, 623. Sadistic German criminal prisoners ran Block 4 of the camp and were now prominent in the new "Auschwitz" camp; *The State Museum of Groß-Rosen* (Rogoznica: The Groß-Rosen Muzeum in Rogoznica, n.d.), 8; Kobielec, *Filia Obozu Koncentracyjnego Groß-Rosen Arbeitslager Brünnlitz*, 4.

70. Wichter, interview, May 17, 2001; Bieberstein, *Zagłada Żydów w Krakowie*, 150.

71. Bieberstein, *Zagłada Żydów w Krakowie*, 150; Kobielec, *Filia Obozu Koncentracyjnego Groß-Rosen Arbeitslager Brünnlitz*, 4.

72. Keneally, *Schindler's List*, 301; Bieberstein, *Zagłada Żydów w Krakowie*, 150.

73. *"Namenliste der männlichen Häftlinge,"* October 21, 1944, Muzeum Auschwitz-Birkenau, 2–13.

74. Keneally, *Schindler's List*, 322–323; Pemper, interview, May 26, 1999.

75. *"Namenliste der männlichen Häftlinge,"* October 21, 1944, Muzeum Auschwitz-Birkenau, 3, 6, 7, 9.

76. Brecher, *Schindler's Legacy*, 134, 238; Wichter, interview, May 17, 2001.

77. Brecher, *Schindler's Legacy*, 238.

78. Ibid., 170, 250; Wichter, interview, May 17, 2001.

79. *Schindler's List*, Steven Spielberg, director, Universal/MCA and Amblin Entertainment (1993) (hereafter referred to as *Schindler's List* (1993)); Keneally, *Schindler's List*, 301–302.

80. "Oskar Schindler *Lebenslauf*," 26 October 1966, Bundesarchiv (Koblenz), Nachlaß Oskar Schindler, 1908–1974, Bestand N 1493, No. 1, Band 1, 2; "Schindler Financial Report 1945," YVA, 9; Kobielec, *Filia Obozu Koncentracyjnego Groß-Rosen Arbeitslager Brünnlitz*, 5.

81. Bieberstein, *Zagłada Żydów w Krakowie*, 144; Czech, *Auschwitz Chronicle*, 737; Irena Strzelecka, "Women," in Yisrael Gutman and Michael Berenbaum, eds. *Anatomy of the Auschwitz Death Camp* (Bloomington: Indiana University Press in association with the United States Holocaust Memorial Museum, 1994), 399; Pemper, interview, May 26, 1999.

82. Sternlicht Rosenzweig, interview, March 20, 2000.

83. Finder, interview, March 19, 2000; Stella Müller-Madej, interview by the author, Kraków, Poland, August 9, 2000; Stella Müller-Madej, *A Girl from Schindler's List*, trans. William R. Brand (London: Polish Cultural Foundation, 1997), 163, 165.

84. Czech, *Auschwitz Chronicle*, 737, 816, 818; Irena Strzelecka and Piotr Setkiewicz, "The Construction, Expansion and Development of the Camp and Its Branches," in Aleksander Lasik, Franciszek Piper, Piotr Setkiewicz, and Irena Strzelecka, eds., *Auschwitz, 1940–1945: Central Issues in the History of the Camp*, vol. 1, *The Establishment and Organization of the Camp*, trans. William Brand (Oświęcim: Auschwitz-Birkenau State Museum, 2000), 88; Aleksander Lasik, "The Auschwitz SS Garrison," in Lasik et al., *Auschwitz, 1940–1945*, 1:284–285; Irena Strzelecka, "Women in the Auschwitz Concentration Camp," in Tadeusz Iwaszko et al., eds., *Auschwitz 1940–1945: Central Issues in the History of the Camp*, vol. 2, *The Prisoners: Their Life and Work*, trans. William Brand (Oświęcim: Auschwitz-Birkenau State Museum, 2000), 175–176; Aleksander Lasik, "Structure and Char-

acter of the Camp SS Administration," in Franciszek Piper and Teresa Świebocka, eds., *Auschwitz: Nazi Death Camp* (Oświęcim: The Auschwitz-Birkenau Museum, 1996), 49; The Auschwitz-Birkenau State Museum, *KL Auschwitz Seen by the SS: Rudolf, Pery Broad, Johann Paul Kremer,* trans. Constantine Fitzgibbon, Krystyna Michalik, and Zbigniew Bezwiński (Oświęcim: The Auschwitz-Birkenau State Museum, 1997), 244.

85. Strzelecka, "Women," 399–400; Müller-Madej, *A Girl from Schindler's List,* 167.

86. Müller-Madej, *A Girl from Schindler's List,* 167–168.

87. Ibid., 168.

88. Finder, interview, March 19, 2000; Sternlicht Rosenzweig, interview, March 20, 2000; Müller-Madej, interview, August 9, 2000; Strzelecka, "Women," 400; "Testimony of Halina Silber," June 26, 1994, Fortunoff Archives, Yale University, HVT 2747.

89. Czech, *Auschwitz Chronicle,* 747.

90. *"KL Groß Rosen-AL (Frauenlager)-Namenliste,"* November 12, 1944, Muzeum Auschwitz-Birkenau.

91. Müller-Madej, interview, August 9, 2000; Pemper, interview, May 26, 1999; Kobielec, *Filia Obozu Koncentracyjnego Groß-Rosen Arbeitslager Brünnlitz,* 5; "Testimony of Tushia Zilbering," n.d., Fortunoff Archives, Yale University, T-3175.

92. Müller-Madej, interview, August 9, 2000; Müller-Madej, *A Girl from Schindler's List,* 171–172; Manci Rosner, interview by the author, Hallandale, Florida, March 21, 2000; Brecher, *Schindler's Legacy,* 14–15; "Testimony of Genia Weinstein," January 20, 1994, Fortunoff Archives, Yale University, T-2259.

93. Czech, *Auschwitz Chronicle,* 738.

94. Brecher, *Schindler's Legacy,* 115, 132; Irena Strzelecka, "Experiments," in Piper and Świebocka, *Auschwitz: Nazi Death Camp,* 94–95.

95. Brecher, *Schindler's Legacy,* 115, 134.

96. Ibid., 359.

97. Ibid., 361–362.

98. Ibid., 362, 364.

99. Ibid., 362.

100. Ibid.

101. Ibid., 13–14, 14–15; Rosner, interview, March 21, 2000.

102. *Schindler's List* (1993).

103. Ibid.

104. Ibid.

105. Ibid.

106. Ibid.

107. Ibid.

108. Ibid.

109. Ibid.

110. Ibid.

111. Ibid.

112. Howard Koch and Martin A. Gosch, "Summary of Interview with Oskar Schindler and Notes re Ahmon [Amon] Goeth," 7-A, 2–3, Delbert Mann Papers, Special Collections Library, Vanderbilt University.

113. "Schindler Financial Report 1945," YVA, 9.

114. "Oskar Schindler *Bericht,*" October 30, 1955, Bundesarchiv (Koblenz), Nachlaß Oskar Schindler, 1908–1974, Bestand N 1493, No. 1, Band 15, 4 (hereafter referred to as "Oskar Schindler *Bericht,*" October 30, 1955, BA(K)).

115. Keneally, *Schindler's List,* 318.

116. Ibid., 318.

117. Aleksander Lasik, "Rudolf Höss: Manager of Crime," in Gutman and Berenbaum, *Anatomy of the Auschwitz Death Camp,* 294–295.

118. Keneally, *Schindler's List*, 318.
119. Bejski, interview, May 17, 1999.
120. Dr. Moshe Bejske, "Notes on the Oskar Schindler Banquet, May 2, 1962, Tel Aviv, Israel," 37–38.
121. "Stern Report 1956," YVA, 30–31.
122. Ibid., 31.
123. Ibid.
124. "Oskar Schindler to Dr. K. J. Ball-Kaduri, September 9, 1956," Yad Vashem Archives, 01/164, 5.
125. Bieberstein, *Zagłada Żydów w Krakowie*, 152.
126. Emilie Schindler, *Where Light and Shadow Meet: A Memoir*, trans. Doris M. Koch (New York: W. W. Norton, 1996), 65.
127. Ibid., 65–66.
128. Ibid., 66.
129. Ibid.
130. Ibid., 66, 68–69.
131. Pemper, interview, May 26, 1999.
132. "Kriminalpolizei Bericht-Oskar Schindler ge. 28.4.1908 in Zwittau/Sudetenland, Frankfurt/M., Am Hauptbahnhof 4/63," March 18, 1963, Frankfurt/Main, West Germany, Zentrale Stelle der Landesjustizverwaltung (ZSL), Ludwigsburg, Germany, 2–3; for more on these investigations into war crimes charges after World War II, see Orth, "Ich habe mich nie getarnt," 145–150, and Tom Segev, *Soldiers of Evil: The Commandants of the Nazi Concentration Camps,* trans. Haim Watzman (New York: McGraw-Hill), 1987, 181–182.
133. "Kriminalpolizei Bericht-Oskar Schindler," March 18, 1963, ZSL, Ludwigsburg, 1; "Oskar Schindler Bericht," October 30, 1955, BA(K), 4.
134. Aleksander Lasik, "Structure and Character of the Camp SS Administration," in Piper and Świebocka, *Auschwitz: Nazi Death Camp,* 46, 109; *KL Auschwitz Seen by the SS,* 250–251; Aleksander Lasik, "The Apprehension and Punishment of the Auschwitz Camp Staff," in Danuta Czech, Stanisław Kłodziłski, Aleksander Lasik, and Andrzej Strzelecki, eds., *Auschwitz 1940–1945: Central Issues in the History of the Camp,* vol. 5, *Epilogue* (Oświęcim: Auschwitz-Birkenau State Museum, 2000), 115; Rudolph Höss, *Death Dealer: The Memoirs of the SS Kommandant at Auschwitz,* ed. Steven Paskuly, trans. Andrew Pollinger (New York: Da Capo Press, 1996), 320.
135. Höss, *Death Dealer,* 318–319.
136. Pemper, interview, May 26, 1999; Czech, *Auschwitz Chronicle,* 743–744; Brecher, *Schindler's Legacy,* 90–91, 438–439.
137. Czech, *Auschwitz Chronicle,* 744.
138. Ibid.
139. Andrzej Strzelecki, "Evacuation, Liquidation and Liberation of the Camp," in Piper and Świebocka, *Auschwitz: Nazi Death Camp,* 269–270.
140. Emilie Schindler, *Light and Shadow,* 92.

Chapter 10

1. Elinor Brecher, *Schindler's Legacy: True Stories of the List Survivors* (New York: Penguin Books, 1994), 170.
2. Stella Müller-Madej, *A Girl from Schindler's List,* trans. William R. Brand (London: Polish Cultural Foundation, 1997), 185, 194–199.
3. Müller-Madej, *A Girl from Schindler's List,* 204.
4. Ibid., 204–205.

5. Ibid., 205–206.

6. Ibid., 206–207.

7. Ibid., 208.

8. Emilie Schindler, *Where Light and Shadow Meet: A Memoir,* trans. Dolores M. Koch (New York: W. W. Norton, 1996), 69.

9. Müller-Madej, *A Girl from Schindler's List,* 208–209.

10. Ibid., 209–210.

11. Ibid., 213.

12. "Oskar Schindler Financial Report 1945," July 1945, Yad Vashem Archives, 01/164, 2, 10 (hereafter referred as "Schindler Financial Report 1945," YVA).

13. Ibid., 10.

14. "Oskar Schindler *Lebenslauf,*" October 26, 1966, Bundesarchiv (Koblenz), Nachlaß Oskar Schindler, 1908–1974, Bestand N 1493, No. 1, Band 1, 1; Aleksandra Kobielec said that Brünnlitz's SS contingent consisted of "40 SS guards and 4 female attendants." See her *Filia Obozu Koncentracyjnego Groß-Rosen Arbeitslager Brünnlitz* (Wałbrzych: Państwowe Muzeum Groß-Rosen, 1991), 6, 8.

15. Scholars differ on the amounts German businesses had to pay the SS for slave laborers. Raul Hilberg, *The Destruction of the European Jews,* vol. 2 (New York: Holmes & Meier, 1985), 528; Wolfgang Sofsky, *The Order of Terror: The Concentration Camp,* trans. William Templer (Princeton: Princeton University Press, 1997), 175; Albert Speer, *The Slave State: Heinrich Himmler's Masterplan for SS Supremacy,* trans. Joachim Neugroschel (London: Weidenfeld and Nicolson, 1981), 36 and 36 n. 50; Eugen Kogon, *The Theory and Practice of Hell: The German Concentration Camps and the System Behind Them,* trans. Heinz Norden (New York: Berkley Publishing Corporation, 1975), 93; "Schindler Financial Report 1945," YVA, 2, 11–12; "Oskar Schindler *Bericht,*" October 30, 1955, Bundesarchiv (Koblenz), Nachlaß Oskar Schindler, 1908–1974, Bestand N 1493, No. 1, Band 15, 2 (hereafter referred to as "Oskar Schindler *Bericht,*" October 30, 1955, BA(K)).

16. "Schindler Financial Report 1945," YVA, 1, 4, 12.

17. "*Aufstellung der in Brünnlitz verbliebenen Maschinen und Einrichtungen einschl. der Forderungen an das Reich,*" *Räumung* auf Grund des *Befehls* der *Rüstungs-Inspektion, Troppau (Zwittau)* vom 6. Mai 1945, Lastenausgleicharchiv (Bayreuth), 1/306 2230a (Oskar Schindler), 1–8 (hereafter referred to as "*Aufstellung* der in Brünnlitz," LAG (B), 1/306 2230a (OS)). Though this document was dated May 6, 1945, it was actually prepared later by Schindler while he lived in Regensburg, Germany.

18. "Schindler Financial Report 1945," YVA, 13.

19. Ibid., 11.

20. "Oskar Schindler to Fritz Lang," July 20, 1951, Bundesarchiv (Koblenz), Nachlaß Oskar Schindler, 1908–1974, Bestand N 1493, No. 1, Band 28, 5 (hereafter referred to as "Schindler to Lang," July 20, 1951, BA(K)); "Schindler Financial Report 1945," YVA, 11.

21. "Schindler Financial Report 1945," YVA, 10.

22. Ibid., 10–11.

23. Ibid., 11; "Oskar Schindler *Bericht,*" October 30, 1955, 5; Jitka Gruntová, *Legendy a fakta o oskaru Schindlerovi* (Praha: Vydalo nakladatelstvín Naše vojsko, 2002), 133, 136–137.

24. *Vitka Brněnec,* brochure prepared by Vitka Brněnec, 4 pages.

25. "*SS-Bekleidungslager Brünnlitz: Krakau im September 1944,*" in Records of Nazi Concentration Camps, 1939–1945, RG-04.006M, Reel 8: Dachau-Flossenbürg-Groß-Rosen, No. 12, "Request for information by Judge Stanisław Zmuda about Jewish labor in camps and transport of Jewish prisoners to Czechoslovakia and response with plan of Brunnlitz camp November 1947." Judge Zmuda's request was part of the Polish government's ongoing war crimes investigation and prosecution efforts after World War II.

26. Petr Henzl, interview by the author, Břenenec, Czech Republic, June 29, 1998; Petr Henzl gave me a copy of this unpublished plan during our visit on June 29, 1998; *"Textilní Továrna Arona-Jakuba Löw Beera"*; Mietek Pemper, interview by the author, Augsburg, Germany, January 17, 2000.

27. *"Aufstellung* der in Brünnlitz von 6 Mai 1945," LAG (B), 1/306 2230a (OS), 4, 8; Sol Urbach, interview by the author, Flemington, New Jersey, April 13, 1999.

28. Kobielec, *Filia Obozu Koncentracyjnego Groß-Rosen Arbeitslager Brünnlitz,* 5–6, 8; Aleksander Bieberstein, *Zagłada Żydów w Krakowie* (Kraków: Wydawnictwo Literackie, 1985), 151.

29. Sofsky, *Order of Terror,* 206.

30. "Stern Report 1956," Yad Vashem Archives, 01/164, 32 (hereafter referred to as "Stern Report 1956," YVA).

31. Sofsky, *Order of Terror,* 208–210.

32. Ibid., 206; Paul Berben, *Dachau, 1933–1945: The Official History* (London: Comité International de Dachau, 1975), 107–108.

33. Jacob Sternberg said that the prisoners were "tormented by lice" when they got to Brünnlitz. "Notes of Dr. Moshe Bejski on the Banquet in Honor of Oskar Schindler," May 2, 1962, Tel Aviv, Israel, 4, 7–8; Kobielec, *Filia Obozu Koncentracyjnego Groß-Rosen Arbeitslager Brünnlitz,* 6; Sofsky, *Order of Terror,* 211.

34. Bieberstein, *Zagłada Żydów w Krakowie,* 152; Itzhak Stern said that Brünnlitz had "six doctors for 1000 Jews in the camp, some young physicians, and 6–8 nurses," "Stern Report 1956," YVA, 32.

35. Kobielec, *Filia Obozu Koncentracyjnego Groß-Rosen Arbeitslager Brünnlitz,* 10; Bieberstein, *Zagłada Żydów w Krakowie,* 152.

36. Brecher, *Schindler's Legacy,* 211, 267–268.

37. Gisella Perl, "A Doctor in Auschwitz," in Carol Rittner and John K. Roth, eds., *Different Voices: Women and the Holocaust* (New York; Paragon House, 1993), 104, 114.

38. "Oskar Schindler Financial Report 1945," YVA, 5.

39. "Stern Report 1956," YVA, 32.

40. Thomas Keneally, *Schindler's List* (New York: Simon and Schuster, 1992), 353–354.

41. Shmuel Krakowski, "The Satellite Camps," in Yisrael Gutman and Michael Berenbaum, eds., *Anatomy of the Auschwitz Death Camp* (Bloomington: Indiana University Press in association with the United States Holocaust Memorial Museum, 1994), 42–43, 53.

42. Irena Strzelecka and Piotr Setkiewicz, "The Construction, Expansion and Development of the Camp and Its Branches," in Aleksander Lasik et al., eds., *Auschwitz 1940–1945: Central Issues in the History of the Camp,* vol. 1, *The Establishment and Organization of the Camp* (Oświęcim: Auschwitz-Birkenau State Museum, 2000), 118; Franciszek Piper, "The Exploitation of Prisoner Labor," in Tadeusz Iwaszko et al., eds., *Auschwitz 1940–1945: Central Issues in the History of the Camp,* vol. 2, *The Prisoners: Their Life and Work* (Oświęcim: Auschwitz-Birkenau State Museum, 2000), 102; Franciszek Piper, "Exploitation of Prisoner Labor," in Franciszek Piper and Teresa Świebocka, eds., *Auschwitz: Nazi Death Camp* (Oświęcim: The Auschwitz-Birkenau State Museum, 1996), 116; Krakowski, "The Satellite Camps," 53.

43. Piper, "Exploitation of Prisoner Labor," 102; Irena Strzelecka, "Hospitals at Auschwitz Concentration Camp," in Tadeusz Iwaszko et al., eds., *Auschwitz 1940–1945: Central Issues in the History of the Camp,* vol. 2, *The Prisoners: Their Life and Work* (Oświęcim: Auschwitz-Birkenau State Museum, 2000), 325.

44. Danuta Czech, ed., *Auschwitz Chronicle, 1939–1945* (New York: Henry Holt and Company, 1990), 796.

45. "Golleschauer *Frachtbrief,"* January 22, 1945, Yad Vashem Archives, 01/164, 2 pages; Andrzy Strzelecki, "The Liquidation of the Camp," in Danuta Czech, et al,

Auschwitz 1940–1945: Central Issues in the History of the Camp, vol. 5 (Oświęcim: Auschwitz-Birkenau State Museum, 2000), 31; Piper, "Exploitation of Prisoner Labor," 117, 120. The three hundred women in the Freudenthal sub-camp worked at the Emmerich Machold plant making "vitaminized juices."

46. "Stern Report 1956," YVA, 35.

47. "Oskar Schindler *Bericht*, " October 30, 1955, BA(K), 4.

48. "Stern Report 1956," YVA, 34; Schindler, *Light and Shadow*, 89–90.

49. "Stern Report 1956," YVA, 34–35.

50. Schindler, *Light and Shadow*, 89–90.

51. "Schindler Financial Report 1945," YVA, 13–14.

52. Pemper, interview, January 17, 2000; Brecher, *Schindler's Legacy*, 224.

53. Schindler, *Light and Shadow*, 90.

54. "Stern Report 1956," YVA, 34.

55. Bieberstein, *Zagłada Żydów w Krakowie*, 153; Müller-Madej, *A Girl from Schindler's List*, 228; Murray Pantirer, interview by the author, Union, New Jersey, August 3, 1999.

56. Brecher, *Schindler's Legacy*, 224.

57. Czech, *Auschwitz Chronicle*, 796–797; "Schindler Financial Report 1945," YVA, 13–14; "Oskar Schindler *Bericht*," October 30, 1955, BA(K), 4; Schindler, *Light and Shadow*, 90; Pemper, interview, January 17, 2000; Bieberstein, *Zagłada Żydów w Krakowie*, 153.

58. *"Namenliste des Häftlingszuganges vom AL Golleschau (KL Auschwitz) am 29. Januar 1945,"* Państwowe Muzeum Auschwitz-Birkenau w Oświęcimiu, 2 pages.

59. *"Namenliste der am 2.2.45 vom Amtsgerichtsgefängnis Landskron zum Arbeitslager Brünnlitz überstellten Häftlinge."* Państwowe Muzeum Auschwitz w Oświęcimiu, 1 page.

60. "Schindler Financial Report 1945," YVA, 14.

61. Howard Koch and Martin A. Gosch, "The Testimony of Rabbi Menashe Levertov," November 13, 1965, New York, Delbert Mann Papers, Special Collections Library, Vanderbilt University, 1-B, 4–6. Rabbi Levertov said that Oskar rescued him from the Mauthausen transport in August 1944 by telling the SS guards that Levertov was "one of his best workers."

62. Henzl, interview, June 29, 1998; Keneally, *Schindler's List*, 357.

63. Francisco Wichter, interview by the author, Buenos Aires, Argentina, May 17, 2001; Keneally, *Schindler's List*, 357–358.

64. Jitka Gruntová, interview by the author, Březova nad Svitavou, Czech Republic, June 27, 1998; Radoslav Fikejz, interview by the author, Svitavy, Czech Republic, June 27, 1998; Gruntová, *Legendy a fakta o Oskaru Schindlerovi*, 152.

65. Keneally, *Schindler's List*, 357; Kobielec, *Filia Obozu Koncentracyjnego Groß-Rosen Arbeitslager Brünnlitz*, 11. To further complicate matters, Bogdan Cybulski interviewed Czech researchers who claimed that fifty-eight people died in Brünnlitz during the last months of the war; *"KL Groß Rosen-AL Brünnlitz (Frauenlager)-Namenliste,"* November 12, 1944, Państwowe Muzeum Auschwitz-Birekenau w Oświęcimiu, 1–2.

66. Keneally, *Schindler's List*, 356–357.

67. "Oskar Schindler *Bericht*," October 30, 1955, BA(K), 4; Kurt R. Grossmann, *Die unbesungenen Helden: Menschen in Deutschlands dunklen Tagen* (Frankfurt/M: Zeitgeschichte, 1961), 156; Schindler, *Light and Shadow*, 92.

68. Schindler, *Light and Shadow*, 91; "Oskar Schindler *Bericht*," October 30, 1955, BA(K), 4.

69. "Schindler Financial Report 1945," YVA, 11; "Oskar Schindler *Bericht*," October 30, 1955, BA(K), 4; *"Johann Kompan to "'Religo' Comité pour l'assistance la Populaston*

juife papée per la guerre," n.d., 1, private papers of Margarete Kompan-Bazzanella, Trazegnies, Belgium (hereafter referred to as "Kompan to *Comité*").

70. Bieberstein, *Zagłada Żydów w Krakowie,* 152.

71. Robin O'Neil, "An Analysis of the Actions of Oskar Schindler Within the Context of the Holocaust in German Occupied Poland and Czechoslovakia" (Master's Thesis, University College, London, September 30, 1996), 159.

72. "Schindler Financial Report 1945," YVA, 12.

73. Ibid.; Dr. Moshe Bejski, interview by the author, Tel Aviv, Israel, May 17, 1999.

74. Schindler, *Light and Shadow,* 86–87.

75. Sol Urbach, interview by the author, Delray Beach, Florida, July 4, 2003; Brecher, *Schindler's Legacy,* 223.

76. "Alfred Rozenfryd to J. F. Daubek," May 18, 1945, Brněnec, Czechoslovakia, 1 page, private collection of David M. Crowe; Bieberstein, *Zagłada Żydów w Krakowie,* 152; Urbach, interview, July 4, 2003.

77. "Kompan to *Comité,"* 1.

78. "Stefan Pemper *Bestätigung,"* July 14, 1945, Brněnec, Czechoslovakia, 1 page, private papers of Margarete Kompan-Bazzanella, Trazgnies, Belgium.

79. "Certified Translation from the Polish," Brünnlitz, May 18, 1945, 2 pages; this document also includes the original Polish statement in support of Johann Kompan, private papers of Margarete Kompan-Bazzanella, Trazegnies, Belgium.

80. "Statement of Alexander Goldwasser for the Jewish Committee of Vienna," July 23, 1946, 1 page, private papers of Margarete Kompan-Bazzanella; "Goldwasser to Johann and Aloisa Kompan," December 13, 1949, 1 page, private papers of Margarete Kompan-Bazzanella; "Michael Kohn for the Jewish Committee of Vienna to the Jewish Committee of Innsbruck," July 23, 1946, 1 page, private papers of Margarete Kompan-Bazzanella; Yehuda Bauer, *American Jewry and the Holocaust: The American Jewish Joint Distribution Committee, 1939–1945* (Detroit: Wayne State University Press, 1982), 97, 221, 283.

81. "Kompan to *Comité,"* 2.

82. Jean-Claude Favez, *The Red Cross and the Holocaust,* ed. and trans. John and Beryl Fletcher (Cambridge: Cambridge University Press, 1999), 103–104.

83. Kobielec, *Filia obozu koncentracyjnego Groß-Rosen Arbeitslager Brünnlitz,* 9–10.

84. Brecher, *Schindler's Legacy,* 211.

85. Ibid., 91–92; Bejski, "Notes on the Oskar Schindler Banquet," 14.

86. Müller-Madej, *A Girl from Schindler's List,* 218, 220, 222.

87. Brecher, *Schindler's Legacy,* 238, 296–297.

88. Ibid., 414.

89. Bejski, "Notes on the Oskar Schindler Banquet," 26.

90. Leon Leyson, interview by the author, Anaheim, California, March 29, 2000; Brecher, *Schindler's Legacy,* 92.

91. Müller-Madej, *A Girl from Schindler's List,* 229, 242, 245.

92. Heinz Höhne, *The Order of the Death's Head: The Story of Hitler's SS* (New York: Ballantine Books, 1977), 436–438; Pemper, interview, May 26, 1999; *Proces Ludobójcy Amona Leopolda Goetha* (Kraków: Centralna Żydowska Komisja Historyczna w Polsce, 1947), 286–287.

93. Müller-Madej, *A Girl from Schindler's List,* 227.

94. Rena Ferber Finder, interview by the author, Boca Raton, Florida, March 19, 2000.

95. Brecher, *Schindler's Legacy,* 224.

96. Pemper, interview, May 26, 1999; Bieberstein, *Proces Ludobójcy Amona Leopolda Goetha,* 287.

97. Müller-Madej, *A Girl from Schindler's List,* 220.

98. Ibid., 223.

99. "Schindler Financial Report 1945," YVA, 11.

100. Brecher, *Schindler's Legacy*, 353; Kobielec, *Filia Obozu Koncentracyjnego Groß-Rosen Arbeitslager Brünnlitz*, 6 n. 11.

101. Bejski, "Notes on the Oskar Schindler Banquet," 20; Kobielec *Filia Obozu Koncentracyjnego Groß-Rosen Arbeitslager Brünnlitz*, 6 n. 11.

102. "Stern Report 1956," YVA, 33; Müller-Madej, *A Girl from Schindler's List*, 213.

103. Bieberstein, *Zagłada Żydów w Krakowie*, 153.

104. Müller-Madej, *A Girl from Schindler's List*, 226–227.

105. Ibid., 229.

106. "Schindler Financial Report 1945," YVA, 10–11; Müller-Madej, *A Girl from Schindler's List*, 223, 227.

107. Bieberstein, *Zagłada Żydów w Krakowie*, 153–154; Müller-Madej, *A Girl from Schindler's List*, 219–220, 240.

108. Müller-Madej, *A Girl from Schindler's List*, 240–241.

109. "Schindler Financial Report 1945," YVA, 13.

110. "Stern Report 1956," YVA, 31.

111. "Schindler Financial Report 1945," YVA, 13.

112. "Stern Report 1956," YVA, 32.

113. Brecher, *Schindler's Legacy*, 135, 223, 297.

114. Ibid., 283, 401, 423–424.

115. Bejski, "Notes on the Oskar Schindler Banquet," 13.

116. Kobielec, *Filia Obozu Koncentracyjnego Groß-Rosen Arbeitslager Brünnlitz*, 9.

117. Bejski, "Notes on the Oskar Schindler Banquet," 12.

118. Müller-Madej, *A Girl from Schindler's List*, 219.

119. Ibid., 219.

120. Brecher, *Schindler's Legacy*, 212.

121. *The Fifth Book of Moses Called Deuteronomy* (London: F. Kiernan, 1902), 22.

122. Brecher, *Schindler's Legacy*, 212.

123. Ibid.

124. Ibid., 341.

125. Ibid., 351, 355.

126. Earl F. Ziemke, *Stalingrad to Berlin: The German Defeat in the East* (Washington, D.C.: Office of the Chief of Military History, 1968), 463, 465–466; Radomír Luža, *The Transfer of the Sudeten Germans; A Study of Czech-German Relations, 1933–1962* (New York: New York University Press, 1964), 258–260; John Keegan, ed., *HarperCollins Atlas of the Second World War* (London; HarperCollins, 1997), 186–187.

127. "*Namenliste des Häftlingszuganges am 11.4.45 vom AL Geppersdorf (KL Gr.Ro.),*" Muzeum Auschwitz-Birkenau, 2 pages. There is little information available on Geppersdorf; it is mentioned briefly in Martin Weinmann's *Das nationalsozialistische Lagersystem* (Frankfurt am Main: Zweitausendeins, 1990), 643, and states that Geppersdorf, which was opened in the fall of 1940, used from three hundred to five hundred Jewish workers to work for firms building the *Reichs-Autobahn*, the vast German interstate highway system. This account, which is based upon information provided by the International Tracing Service, today a part of the International Committee for the Red Cross, states that Geppersdorf was closed in the spring of 1942 and its prisoners were shipped to other camps; Brecher, *Schindler's Legacy*, 401; Müller-Madej, *A Girl from Schindler's List*, 240.

128. "Schindler *Bericht*," October 30, 1955, 5; Sven Steenberg, *Vlasov* (New York; Alfred A. Knopf, 1970), 180–181, 187, 193–194, 195–202.

129. Müller-Madej, *A Girl from Schindler's List*, 243.

694

NOTES

130. Brecher, *Schindler's Legacy*, 363.
131. Kobeliec, *Filia Obozu Koncentracyjnego Groß-Rosen Arbeitslager Brünnlitz*, 12.
132. Keneally, *Schindler's List*, 362; Pemper, interview, January 17, 2000.
133. Keneally, *Schindler's List*, 362–363.
134. Karin Orth, "'Ich habe mich nie getarnt: Brüche und Kontinuitäten in der Lebensgeschichte des KZ-Kommandanten Johannes Hassebroek," *Sozialwissenschaftliche Informationen*, vol. 24, no. 2 (April-June 1995), 149; Isabell Sprenger, "Das KZ-Groß-Rosen in der letzten Kriegsphase," in Ulrich Herbert, Karin Orth, und Christoph Dieckmann, editors, *Die nationalsozialistischen Konzentrationslager*, Band II: *Entwicklung und Struktur* (Frankfurt am Main: Fischer Taschenbuch Verlag, 2002), 1123–1124; Anthony Bevor, *The Fall of Berlin 1945* (New York: Viking, 2002), 291–292.
135. Müller-Madej, *A Girl from Schindler's List*, 244.
136. "Stern Report 1956," YVA, 37.
137. Ibid.
138. Ibid.
139. Ibid., 38.
140. Ibid.
141. Ibid., 38–39.
142. Ibid., 39–40.
143. Müller-Madej, *A Girl from Schindler's List*, 244.
144. "Stern Report 1956," YVA, 36.
145. Bieberstein, *Zagłada Żydów w Krakowie*, 154; Kobielec, *Filia obozu koncentracyjnego Groß-Rosen Arbeitslager Brünnlitz*, 12; Christopher Chant, ed., *Hitler's Generals* (London: Salamander Books, 1998), 192–195.
146. "Stern Report, 1956," YVA, 36; Bejski, interview, May 17, 1999.
147. "Schindler *Bericht*," October 30, 1955, BA(K), 5; Brecher, *Schindler's Legacy*, 224; Kobielec, *Filia obozu koncentracyjnego Groß-Rosen Arbeitslager Brünnlitz*, 12, said that the secret Schindler defense group went under the name "Zakonspirowane Piątki (Secret Friday).
148. Brecher, *Schindler's Legacy*, 224–225, 268; Howard Koch and Martin A. Gosch, "Testimony of Lewis Fagin," November 14, 1964, New York, Delbert Mann Papers, Special Collections Library, Vanderbilt University, 4-A, 10.
149. Brecher, *Schindler's Legacy*, 225, 268.
150. "Testimony of Leopold Page, 1992," United States Holocaust Memorial Museum Archives, RG-50.042*0022, 15.
151. Brecher, *Schindler's Legacy*, 225.
152. Bejski, "Notes on the Oskar Schindler Banquet," 14.
153. "Stern Report 1956," YVA, 37.
154. Brecher, *Schindler's Legacy*, 251.
155. "Schindler Financial Report 1945," YVA, 14; "Oskar Schindler *Bericht*," October 30, 1955, YVA, 5; Pemper, interview, January 17, 2003; Finder, interview, March 19, 2000; Brecher, *Schindler's Legacy*, 225.
156. Ian Kershaw, *Hitler*, vol. 2, *1936–1945 Nemesis* (New York: W. W. Norton, 2000), 826, 827–828, 831–832.
157. Müller-Madej, *A Girl from Schindler's List*, 245.
158. Pemper, interview, May 26, 1999; "Oskar Schindler to Fritz Lang," July 20, 1951, BA(K).
159. "Sto Lat," The University of Texas, College of Liberal Arts, http://www.utexas.edu/courses/sla323/stolat.htm.
160. Keneally, *Schindler's List*, 364.

161. "Schindler Speech in Brünnlitz on May 8, 1945," Yad Vashem Archives, 01/164 (hereafter referred to as "Schindler Speech in Brünnlitz on May 8, 1945," YVA); *Schindler's List*, Steven Spielberg, Director, Universal/MCA and Amblin Entertainment (1993) (hereafter referred to as *Schindler's List* (1993)).

162. "Schindler Speech in Brünnlitz on May 8, 1945," YVA.

163. Ibid.; "Brothers! Letter of Schindler Jews," Brünnlitz, Protectorate of Bohemia and Moravia, May 8, 1945, Yad Vashem Archives, 01/1643 (150015). Kurt Klein also provided me with his own translation of Schindler's May 8, 1945, speech.

164. Keneally, *Schindler's List,* 368.

165. *Schindler's List* (1993).

166. Brecher, *Schindler's Legacy,* 212.

167. Bejski, "Notes on the Oskar Schindler Banquet," 16–17.

168. *Schindler's List* (1993); Bejski, interview, May 17, 1999.

169. Keneally, *Schindler's List,* 368, 374, 375.

170. "Schindler Financial Report 1945," YVA, 13; *"Aufstellung der in Brünnlitz,"* LAG(B), 1/306 2230a (OS), 8.

171. Schindler, *Light and Shadow,* 100–101.

172. "Testimony of Lewis Fagin," November 14, 1964, Delbert Mann Papers, Vanderbilt University, 4-A, 11.

Chapter 11

1. *Schindler's List*, Steven Spielberg director, Universal/MCA and Amblin Entertainment (1993) (hereafter referred to as *Schindler's List* (1993)).

2. Aleksander Bieberstein, *Zagłada Żydów w Krakowie* (Kraków: Wydawnictwo Literackie, 1985), 155.

3. Elinor Brecher, *Schindler's Legacy: True Stories of the List Survivors* (New York: Plume Books, 1994), 92, 213, 401.

4. "Testimony of Bernard Goldberg," December 7, 1989," Fortunoff Archives, T-3084, Yale University.

5. Stella Müller-Madej, *A Girl from Schindler's List* (London: Polish Cultural Foundation, 1997), 248–250; Anthony Bevor, *The Fall of Berlin 1945* (New York: Viking, 2002), 28–32, 409–410; Brecher, *Schindler's Legacy,* 363.

6. Müller-Madej, *A Girl from Schindler's List,* 247; "Testimony of Bernard Goldberg," Fortunoff Archives, T-3084; Harry Blum, interview by the author, Miami Beach, Florida, April 27, 2001; Brecher, *Schindler's Legacy,* 225.

7. Brecher, *Schindler's Legacy,* 213.

8. Ibid., 136.

9. Müller-Madej, *A Girl from Schindler's List,* 251.

10. "Autograph Book of Sol Urbach," May 7, 1945, private collection of Sol Urbach.

11. Raul Hilberg, *The Destruction of the European Jews,* Rev. ed., vol. 3 (New York: Holmes & Meier, 1985), 1212; Michael C. Steinlauf, "Poland," in David S. Wyman, ed., and Charles H. Rosenzveig, project director, *The World Reacts to the Holocaust* (Baltimore: Johns Hopkins University Press, 1996), 109.

12. Steinlauf, "Poland," 112–113.

13. Brecher, *Schindler's Legacy,* 269–270; Yisrael Gutman and Shmuel Krakowski, *Unequal Victims: Poles and Jews During World War II* (New York: Holocaust Library, 1986), 370–372; Bernard D. Weinryb, "Poland," in Peter Meyer et al., eds., *The Jews in the Soviet Satellites* (Syracuse: Syracuse University Press, 1953), 252–253.

14. Müller-Madej, *A Girl from Schindler's List,* 261–263.

15. Ibid., 265–266.

16. Ibid., 266–270.

17. Niusia Bronisława Karakulska, interview by the author, Kraków, Poland, August 8, 2000; Franciszek Palowski, *The Making of Schindler's List: Behind the Scenes of an Epic Film*, trans. Anna and Robert G. Ware (Secaucus, N.J.: Birch Lane Press, 1998), 55, 63, 94, 113–122, 154, 157.

18. Francisco Wichter, interview by the author, Buenos Aires, Argentina, May 17, 2001, and May 22, 2001; Brecher, *Schindler's Legacy*, 364.

19. Brecher, *Schindler's Legacy*, 363–364.

20. Ibid., 364.

21. Wichter, interview, May 17, 2001, and May 22, 2001.

22. "Oskar Schindler to Fritz Lang," July 20, 1951, Bundesarchiv (Koblenz), Nachlaß Oskar Schindler, 1908–1974, Bestand N 1493, No. 1, Band 23, 6; Emilie Schindler, *Where Light and Shadow Meet: A Memoir*, trans. Dolores M. Koch (New York: W.W. Norton, 1996), 100; Christopher Duffy, *Red Storm on the Reich: The Soviet March on Germany, 1945* (Edison, N.J.: Castle Books, 2002), 294–297.

23. "Schindler to Lang," July 20, 1951, 6; Schindler, *Light and Shadow*, 103.

24. Schindler, *Light and Shadow*, 103; "Schindler to Lang," BA(K), 4; "Schindler Protokol," July 23, 1938, Zapravodajská úředna při policejním ředitelství Praha, 200–299–50, 1; Keneally, *Schindler's List*, 39.

25. Schindler, *Light and Shadow*, 103–104; Dr. Marjory Zerin, "Notes on Klein/Emilie Schindler Reunion," May 12, 1994, 4, private collection of Dr. Marjory Zerin.

26. "Schindler to Lang," BA(K), 6.

27. Schindler, *Light and Shadow*, 104.

28. Ibid., 105–106; Zerin, "Notes on Klein/Emilie Schindler Reunion," 4.

29. Schindler, *Light and Shadow*, 108; Zerin, "Notes on Klein/Emilie Schindler Reunion," 4.

30. "Schindler to Lang," BA(K), 6.

31. Kurt Klein, interview by the author, Greensboro, North Carolina, January 11, 1998; "Schindler to Lang," BA(K), 6; "Richard Rechen to Kurt Klein," April 21, 1987, 1 page, private collection of Esther Rechen.

32. "Rechen to Klein," April 21, 1987; Duffy, *Red Storm on the Reich*, 294–295.

33. "In Memoriam, Kurt Klein, 1920–2002," *United States Holocaust Memorial Museum* 1, no. 1 (Summer 2002): 8.

34. Gerda Klein Weissmann and Kurt Klein, *The Hours After: Letters of Love and Longing in War's Aftermath* (New York: St. Martin's Press, 2000), 4–7; Gerda Weissmann Klein, *All But My Life: A Memoir* (New York: Hill and Wang, 1995), 4, 166, 182, 214–221; Martin Weinmann, Anne Kaiser, and Ursula Krause-Schmitt, eds., *Das nationalsozialistische Lagersystem (CCP)* (Frankfurt am Main: Zweitausendeins, 1990), 277, 579.

35. Klein, interview, January 11, 1998.

36. Marjory Zerin, "The Jew Who Saved Schindler," *Jerusalem Report* (June 2, 1994): 36.

37. Klein, interview, January 11, 1998; Zerin, "The Jew Who Saved Schindler," 35–36.

38. "Schindler to Lang," BA(K), 6; "Rechen to Klein," April 21, 1987.

39. Schindler, *Light and Shadow*, 110–111.

40. "Rechen to Klein;" April 27, 1987; Zerin, "The Jew Who Saved Schindler," 36; "Schindler to Lang," BA(K), 6.

41. "Schindler to Lang," BA(K), 6.

42. Ibid. For more on the changing French occupation zone in Germany at that time see Earl F. Ziemke, *The U.S. Army in the Occupation of Germany, 1944–1946* (Washington,

D.C.: Center of Military History, United States Army, 1975), 307–308; Dennis L. Bark and
David R. Gress, *A History of West Germany,* vol. 1, *From Shadow to Substance,*
1945–1963 (Oxford: Basil Blackwell, 1989), 60.
43. "Schindler to Lang," BA(K), 6.
44. French Interrogation Report: Leopold Degen," June 9, 1945, Konstanz, Germany,
Yad Vashem Archives, 01/164, 4 pages; "French Interrogation Report: Eduard Heuberger,"
June 9, 1945, Konstanz, Germany, Yad Vashem Archives, 01/164, 5 pages.
45. "Memorandum of Captaine Robert Monheit, Aumonier Militaire Israélite," August
27, 1945, Strasbourg, Bundesarchiv (Koblenz), Nachlaß Oskar Schindler, 1908–1974, Bestand N 1493, No. 1, Band 26, 1 page.
46. Schindler, *Light and Shadow,* 111–112.
47. Schindler to Lang, BA(K), 6; "Oskar Schindler Financial Report, 1945," July 1945,
Yad Vashem Archives, 01/164, 1.
48. "Schindler to Lang," BA(K), 6; Schindler, *Light and Shadowe,* 111.
49. Radomír Luža, *The Transfer of the Sudeten Germans: A Study of Czech-German Relations, 1933–1962* (New York: New York University Press, 1964), 126, 270–271; about
300,000 Czechs had acquired Reich citizenship during the war. Chad Bryant, "Either German or Czech: Fixing Nationality in Bohemia and Moravia, 1939–1946, *Slavic Review* 61,
no. 4 (Winter 2002): 699.
50. *Oskar Schindler: Legenda a Fakta* (Brno: Barrister & Principle, 1997), 159, and
Jitka Gruntová, *Legenda a fakta o Oskar Schindlerovi* (Prague: Naše vojsko, 2002), 247;
"No Place for Schindler on Czech List," *RFE/RL Newsline* 6, no. 31, pt. 2 (February 15,
2002): 1 page.
51. Ronald M. Smelser, "The Expulsion of the Sudeten Germans, 1945–1952," *Nationalities Papers* 24, no. 1, (1996): 86–89.
52. Ziemke, *Occupation of Germany, 1944–1946,* 380.
53. Bark and Gress, *A History of West Germany,* 1:74–75; Ziemke, *Occupation of Germany, 1944–1946,* 381–382.
54. Ziemke, *Occupation of Germany, 1944–1946,* 384.
55. Bark and Gress, *A History of West Germany,* 1:75–76; "Oskar Schindler's Nazi
Party Application," NSDAP-Mitgliedkartei, Berlin Documentation Center, Bundesarchiv
(Berlin), 1–2.
56. "Brothers! Letter of Schindler Jews," Brünnlitz, Protectorate of Bohemia and
Moravia, May 8, 1945, Yad Vashem Archives, 01/1643 (150015), 2 pages; FIR, Leopold
Degen, June 9, 1945, YVA, 4 pages; FIR Eduard Heuberger, June 9, 1945, YVA, 5 pages;
"Monheit Memorandum, August 24, 12945, BA(K), 1 page; "Schindler Financial Report
1945," YVA, 15 pages; "Memorandum to UNNRA," September 3, 1945, Yad Vashem
Archives, 01/164, 1 page; "Leib Salpeter to Zionist Organizations and Societies," Septem-
ber 30, 1945, Bundesarchiv (Koblenz), Nachlaß Oskar Schindler, 1908–1974, Bestand N
1493, Band 1, No. 1, 1 page; "*Schindlerjuden* Statement," October 12, 1945, Lager 67,
Hert, Austria, Yad Vashem Archives, 01/164, 1 page.
57. "Schindler to Lang," July 20, 1951, BA(K), 7.
58. "Oskar Schindler to M.W. Beckelman," July 21, 1953, Buenos Aires, Argentina,
Oskar Schindler Collection, Archives of the American Jewish Joint Distribution Committee,
(Jerusalem), 3; "Schindler to Lang," July 20, 1951, BA(K), 6; Herbert Steinhouse to
Thomas Keneally and Steven Spielberg, March 1994, Herbert and Tobe Steinhouse Collection, Montreal, Canada, 2.
59. Steinhouse to Keneally and Spielberg, March 1994, 2; Schindler, *Light and Shadow,*
112–114.
60. Ibid., 114–115; Christoph Stopka, "Ich bin Frau Schindler," *Bunte* (1994), 25.

61. Schindler, *Light and Shadow,* 114–115; Stopka, "Ich bin Frau Schindler," 25.

62. James Rice, "The Breakers: Oskar Schindler and the Holocaust," unpublished manuscript (April 28, 1994), 2, James Rice Collection, San Francisco and Washington, D.C.; "James Rice to Eli Rock," AJJDC, Munich, September 25, 1945, James Rice Collection, San Francisco and Washington, D.C.

63. Mietek Pemper, interview by the author, Augsburg, Germany, January 17, 2000; "Salpeter and Markus Memorandum: Oskar Schindler," October 5, 1946, Yad Vashem Archives, 01/164, 3 pages.

64. "Dr. Rsezőe Kasztner to Oskar Schindler," January 17, 1947, Bundesarchiv (Koblenz), Nachlaß Oskar Schindler, 1908–1974, Bestand 1493, No. 1, Band 23, 1–2.

65. Schindler, *Light and Shadow,* 117.

66. "Dr. Akiba Kohane to Samuel L. Haber," July 9, 1948, Munich, Germany, American Jewish Joint Distribution Committee Archives (Jerusalem), 1 page.

67. "Dr. I. Schwarzbart to Dir. Oskar Schindler," August 29, 1947, Bundesarchiv (Koblenz), Nachlaß Oskar Schindler, 1908–1974, Bestand 1493, No. 1, Band 24, 1 page.

68. "Rosalie Westreich to A.J.D.C. Paris," December 28, 1947, American Jewish Joint Distribution Committee Archives (Jerusalem), 1 page; "Dr. George Weis to H. [Herbert] Katzki," January 9, 1948, American Jewish Joint Distribution Committee Archives (Jerusalem), 1 page; Ted Feder, interview by the author, New York, New York, April 24, 1997.

69. "Kohane to Haber," July 9, 1948, AJJDC Archives (J), 2; "Samuel L. Haber to M. [Moses] Beckelman," November 4, 1948, Munich, Germany, American Joint Distribution Committee Archives (Jerusalem), 1 page.

70. "Schindler Financial Report," July 1945, 12; "Kohane to Haber," July 9, 1948, AJJDC Archives (J), 3.

71. Kohane to Haber, July 9, 1948, AJJDC Archives (J), 3; "Oskar Schindler *Bericht,*" October 30, 1955, Bundesarchiv (Koblenz), Nachlaß Oskar Schindler, 1908–1974, Bestand N 1493, No. 1, Band 15, 3; *Die Bekenntnisse des Herrn X,* Budapest, November 1943, Bundesarchiv (Koblenz), Nachlaß Oskar Schindler, 1908–1974, Bestand N 1493, No. 1, Band 18, 1–6; Dr. Reszőe Kasztner, *Der Bericht des jüdischen Rettungskomitees aus Budapest: 1942–1945* (Budapest: Private manuscript published by the author, 1946), 14; Alex Weissberg, *Desperate Mission: Joel Brand's Story As Told by Alex Weissberg,* trans. Constantine FitzGibbon and Andrew Foster-Melliar (New York: Criterion Books, 1958), 37.

72. Dr. Kurt Wehle to Dr. Joseph J. Schwartz," December 22, 1948, Paris, France, American Jewish Joint Distribution Committee Archives (Jerusalem), 1.

73. "Wehle to Schwartz," December 22, 1948, AJJDC Archives (J), 1–2; "Schindler Financial Report 1945," YVA, 7; Weissberg, *Desperate Mission,* 37; "Schindler Financial Report 1945," YVA, 7; Kastzner, *Der Bericht des jüdischen Rettungskomitees aus Budapest,* 14.

74. "Wehle to Schwartz," December 22, 1948, AJJDC Archives (J), 2.

75. Ibid.

76. Ibid., 3.

77. Ibid., 3–4.

78. Dr. Moshe Bejski, interview by the author, Tel Aviv, Israel, May 17, 1999; *Die Bekenntnisse des Herrn X* (Budapest, November 1943), 7 pages, Bundesarchiv (Koblenz), Nachlaß Oskar Schindler, 1908–1974, Bestand N 1493, Band 1, No. 18; Kasztner, *Der Bericht des jüdischen Rettungskomitees aus Budapest,* 14; Weissberg, *Desperate Mission,* 36–37.

79. "*Bescheinigung.*" Jewish Community-*Jüdische Gemeinde,* Regensburg, Germany, May 5, 1948, Yad Vashem Archives, 01/164, 1 page.

80. Mark Wyman, *DPs: Europe's Displaced Persons, 1945–1951* (Ithaca: Cornell University Press, 1998), 129; Yehuda Bauer, "Joint Distribution Committee," in *Encyclopedia*

of the Holocaust, ed. Israel Gutman, vol. 2 (New York: Macmillan Publishing Company, 1990), 755.

81. "Evelyn M. Morrissey to Accounting Department," February 1, 1949, American Jewish Joint Distribution Committee Archives (New York), 1 page; "Joint Cable to Joseph J. Schwartz," January 17, 1949, American Jewish Joint Distribution Committee Archives (New York), 1 page.

82. "M. W. Beckelman to J. B. Lightman, January 29, 1949, American Jewish Joint Distribution Archives (Jerusalem), 1–2.

83. "Lightman to Jacob [Jack] Lightman," February 22, 1949, American Jewish Joint Distribution Archives (Jerusalem), 1.

84. Schindler, *Light and Shadow,* 117; M. W. Beckelman to Amy Zahl, April 29, 1949, 1, American Jewish Joint Distribution Committee Archives (Jerusalem).

85. "Beckelman to Zahl," April 29, 1949, AJJDC Archives (J), 1.

86. Schindler, *Light and Shadow,* 117; Stopka, "Ich bin Frau Schindler," 24.

87. "Oskar Schindler to Walter Pollack," December 10, 1964, Bundesarchiv (Koblenz), Nachlaß Oskar Schindler, 1908–1974, Bestand N 1493, Band 1, No. 24, 1 page.

88. Schindler, *Light and Shadow,* 131; Graciela La Rocca, interview by the author, San Vicente, Argentina, May 24, 2001.

89. "J. B. Lightman to M. W. Beckelman," March 17, 1949, American Jewish Joint Distribution Committee Archives (Jerusalem), 1; "Herbert Steinhouse to Dr. Joseph J. Schwartz," April 6, 1949, American Jewish Joint Distribution Committee Archives (Jerusalem), 1 page; "Beckelman to Zahl," April 29, 1949, AJJDC Archives (J), 1; "M. W. Beckelman to C. Jordan," July 12, 1950, American Jewish Joint Distribution Archives (Jerusalem), 1 page.

90. "Hyman Gottlieb to Evelyn M. Morrissey," November 30, 1949, American Jewish Joint Distribution Archives (New York), 2; "Morrissey to Hyman Gottlieb," January 20, 1950, American Jewish Joint Distribution Committee Archives (New York), 1 page; "Hyman Gottlieb to JDC New York," March 13, 1950, American Jewish Joint Distribution Committee Archives (New York), 1.

91. "Jacob Levy to Oskar Schindler," February 25, 1948, Bundesarchiv (Koblenz), Nachlaß Oskar Schindler, 1908–1974, Bestand N 1493, Band 1, No. 23, 1 page; "Jacob Levy to J. Schwartz," January 13, 1949, American Jewish Joint Distribution Committee Archives (Jerusalem), 1 page; "Jacob Levy to M. W. Beckelmann," February 3, 1949, American Jewish Joint Distribution Committee Archives (Jerusalem), 1 page.

92. "Oskar Schindler to A.J. Levy," November 16, 1948, Bundesarchiv (Koblenz), Nachlaß Oskar Schindler, 1908–1974, Bestand 1493, No. 1, Band 23, 1.

93. "Schindler to Levy," November 16, 1948, BA(K), 1–2.

94. Ibid., 1–3.

95. Herbert Steinhouse, "The Real Oskar Schindler," *Saturday Night* 109, no. 3 (April 1994): 43–44; Tobe Steinhouse, interview by the author, Montreal, Canada, February 12, 2004.

96. Dr. Bejski became a member of the Righteous Gentile committee in 1966. "Unique Reception in Paris," *Jewish Chronicle* (1949), Yad Vashem Archives, 01/164; Steinhouse, "The Real Oskar Schindler," 49; Steinhouse, interview, February 12, 2004.

97. Steinhouse, "The Real Oskar Schindler," 49.

Chapter 12

1. Paul Mendes-Flohr and Jehuda Reinharz, eds. *The Jew in the Modern World: A Documentary History,* 2d ed. (Oxford: Oxford University Press, 1995), 705, 707, 716; Calvin Sims, "Jewish Graves in Argentina Are Smashed; 3rd Time in '96," *New York Times* (Oc-

tober 22, 1996), A4; Anthony Faiola, "Exiting Argentina by Bloodline," *Washington Post* (January 13, 2002), A17, A20; Miriam Jordan, "As Prospects Dim in Argentina, Its Jews Hear the Call of Israel," *Wall Street Journal* (January 31, 2002), A1, A8; Larry Rohter, "Iran Blew Up Jewish Center in Argentina, Defector Says," *New York Times* (July 22, 2002), A1, A6; Elio Kapszuk and Damián Lejzorowicz, eds., *Shalom Buenos Aires* (Buenos Aires: Gobierno de la Ciudad de Buenos Aires, 2001), 287.

2. "Languages of Argentina" (September 16, 2003), Ethnologue.com, 1.

3. Roberto Aleman, interview by the author, Buenos Aires, Argentina, May 21, 2001; Uki Goñi, *The Real Odessa: How Péron Brought the Nazi War Criminals to Argentina* (London: Granata Books, 2002), 63; James Woodall, "J'accuse: The Other Dirty War," *Financial Times* (January 26/January 27, 2002), Weekend, 4; Nathaniel C. Nash, "Argentina Files Show Huge Effort to Harbor Nazis," *New York Times* (December 14, 1993), A4.

4. Christoph Stoph, "Ich bin Frau Schindler," *Bunte* (1994): 24.

5. "Oskar Schindler to Fritz Lang," July 20, 1951, Bundesarchiv (Koblenz), Nachlaß Oskar Schindler, 1908–1974, Bestand N 1493, No. 23, Band 1, 7.

6. "Hyman Gottlieb to JDC New York," January 12, 1950, American Jewish Joint Distribution Committee Archives (New York), 1 page; "Account Oskar Schindler," June 19, 1950, American Jewish Joint Distribution Archives (New York), 1–2; "Summary File on Oskar Schindler," October 1, 1954, American Jewish Joint Distribution Archives (New York), 1 page.

7. Emilie Schindler, *Where Light and Shadow Meet: A Memoir,* trans. Dolores M. Koch (New York: W. W. Norton, 1997), 127.

8. "Hyman Gottlieb to JDC New York," September 28, 1950, American Jewish Joint Distribution Committee Archives (New York), 1 page; "Hyman Gottlieb to JDC New York," December 27, 1950, American Jewish Joint Distribution Archives (New York), 1 page; Juan Alonso, "Una lista de reclamos," *Noticias* (June 12, 1999), 101.

9. "Document of Incorporation: Oscar Schindler y Compania, Sociedad de Responsabilidad Limitada," March 16, 1953. Bundesarchiv (Koblenz), Nachlaß Oskar Schindler, 1908–1974, N 1493, No.1, Band 1, 5.

10. Schindler, *Light and Shadow,* 127.

11. Paul Armony, "Entrevista con la Sra. Emilie Schindler," *Toldot,* No. 12 (Aogost 2000), 15.

12. The Conference on Jewish Material Claims against Germany, *Claims Conference: 1998 Annual Report with 1999 Highlights* (New York: The Conference on Jewish Material Claims against Germany, 1998), 1, 7.

13. "B. F. Pollack to Moses W. Beckelman," July 27, 1953, American Jewish Joint Distribution Committee Archives (Jerusalem), 1–2.

14. "Oskar Schindler to M. W. Beckelman," July 21, 1953, American Jewish Joint Distribution Committee Archives (Jerusalem), 3.

15. "*Beglaubigte Abschrift* von Oskar Schindler," October 3, 1949, Bundesarchiv (Koblenz), Nachlaß Oskar Schindler, 1908–1974, Bestand N 1493, No. 1, Band 1, 1–2; "Staatskommissariat to Oskar Schindler," February 2, 1948, Bundesarchiv (Koblenz), Nachlaß Oskar Schindler, 1908–1974, Bestand N 1493, No. 1, Band 1, 1 page; "Karl Gnath to Oskar Schindler," September 9, 1949, Bundesarchiv (Koblenz), Nachlaß Oskar Schindler, 1908–1974, Bestand N 1493, No. 1, Band 1, 1 page.

16. "Schindler to Beckelman," July 21, 1953, AJJDC Archives (J), 2.

17. "Benjamin B. Ferencz to M. Beckelman," American Jewish Joint Distribution Committee Archives (Jerusalem), 1 page; Benjamin B. Ferencz, *Less Than Slaves; Jewish Forced Labor and the Question for Compensation* (Bloomington: Indiana University Press in association with the United States Holocaust Memorial Museum, 2002), 37; for more on U.S.

Military Government laws in occupied Germany, see Earl F. Ziemke, *The U.S. Army in the Occupation of Germany* (Washington, D.C.: Center of Military History, 1975).

18. "Ferencz to Beckelman," August 4, 1953, AJJDC Archives (J), 1 page.

19. "Beckelman Cable to Joint Fund (Argentine)," July 31, 1953, American Jewish Joint Distribution Committee Archives (Jerusalem), 1 page; "M. W. Beckelman to B. F. Pollack," August 4, 1953, American Jewish Joint Distribution Archives (Jerusalem), 1.

20. "Beckelman to Pollack," August 4, 1953, AJJDC Archives (J), 1–2.

21. Ibid., August 8, 1.

22. Ibid., August 18, 1953, 1–2.

23. Ibid., September 4, 1953, 1.

24. Ferencz, *Less than Slaves*, 46–47; "*Bericht* of Dr. Katzenstein from F. A. Stadler," August 12, 1953, American Jewish Joint Distribution Committee Archives (Jerusalem), 1–2.

25. "Benjamin B. Ferencz to Moses W. Beckelman," August 25, 1953, American Jewish Joint Distribution Committee Archives (Jerusalem), 1 page.

26. Yehuda Bauer, *American Jewry and the Holocaust: The American Jewish Joint Distribution Committee, 1939–1945* (Detroit: Wayne State University Press, 1981), 180, 202; "Charles H. Jordan to Samuel L. Haber," September 9, 1953, American Jewish Joint Distribution Committee Archives (Jerusalem), 1 page; "Samuel L. Haber to C. Jordan," September 14, 1953," American Jewish Joint Distribution Committee Archives (Jerusalem), 1 page; "Charles H. Jordan to B. F. Pollack," October 14, 1953, American Jewish Joint Distribution Committee Archives (Jerusalem), 1 page.

27. "Antoni Korzeniowski to American Jewish Joint Distribution Committee, Paris," October 30, 1951, American Jewish Joint Distribution Committee Archives (Jerusalem), 1 page.

28. "Oskar Schindler to Moses A. Leavitt," September 21, 1954, American Jewish Joint Distribution Committee Archives (New York), 1 page; "Moses A. Leavitt to Morris Laub," September 23, 1954, American Jewish Joint Distribution Committee Archives (New York), 1 page; "Morris Laub *File Memorandum: Oskar Schindler,* October 14, 1954, American Jewish Joint Distribution Committee Archives (New York), 1 page; "Felix Tronik, *Accounting Letter No. 267/54: Loan to Mr. Oskar Schindler,*" American Jewish Joint Distribution Committee Archives (Jerusalem), 1 page; "Felix Tronik, *Accounting Letter No. 332/55: Loan to Mr. Oskar Schindler,*" March 14, 1955, American Jewish Joint Distribution Committee Archives (New York), 1 page. This letter also contains the formal six page mortgage agreement signed and notarized on November 24, 1954; "Felix Tronik *Accounting Letter No. 722; Loan to Mr. Oskar Schindler, Buenos Aires,*" October 11, 1956, American Jewish Joint Distribution Archives (New York), 1 page.

29. Claudia Keller and Stefan Braun, "Schindlers Koffer (3): Als Unternehmer nach dem Krieg gescheitert," *Stuttgarter Zeitung* (October 22, 1999), 6.

30. Keller and Braun, "Schindlers Koffer (3)," 6.

31. "Oskar Schindler to Itzhak Stern," April 16, 1956, Bundesarchiv (Koblenz), Nachlaß Oskar Schindler, 1908–1974, N 1493, No.1, Band 25, 3.

32. Claudia Keller and Stefan Braun, *Schindlers Koffer: Berichte aus dem Leben eines Lebensretters* (Stuttgart: Stuttgarter Zeitung, 1999), 41.

33. "Oskar Schindler to Itzhak Stern," November 20, 1956, Bundesarchiv (Koblenz), Nachlaß Oskar Schindler, 1908–1974, N 1493, No.1, Band 25, 1 page.

34. "*Schindlerjuden* to Herrn Director Nelson and Herrn Moses A. Leavitt," January 23, 1957, Bundesarchiv (Koblenz), Nachlaß Oskar Schindler, 1908–1974, Bestand 1493, No. 1, Band 17, 2 pages. This letter was then translated into English and re-dated January 28, 1957. See "*Schindlerjuden* to Mr. Nelson and Moses A. Leavitt," January 28, 1957, American Jewish Joint Distribution Committee Archives (New York), 1–2.

35. "Sidney Nelson to Dorothy Speiser," March 28, 1957, American Jewish Joint Distribution Committee Archives (New York), 1–2.
36. "Moses A. Leavitt to Sidney Nelson," April 26, 1957, American Jewish Joint Distribution Committee Archives (New York), 1 page; "Beate Pollock to Oskar Schindler," July 22, 1957, Bundesarchiv (Koblenz), Nachlaß Oskar Schindler, 1908–1974, Bestand N 1493, No.1, Band 4, 1–2.
37. "Oskar Schindler to Moses A. Leavitt," May 11, 1957, American Jewish Joint Distribution Committee Archives (New York), 1 page.
38. "Dr. Nahum Goldmann to Felix von Eckhardt," May 9, 1957, American Jewish Joint Distribution Committee Archives (New York), 1 page; "Schindler to Leavitt," May 11, 1957, AJJDC Archives (NY), 1 page; for more on Heuss and his career, see Charles Williams, *Adenauer: The Father of the New Germany* (New York: John Wiley & Sons, 2000), 335, 345–348, 366, 395–396, 399–400, 452–453, 464.
39. "Stadtoberinspektor Heller to Dr. H. Wolf, United Restitution Office, München," March 30, 1955, Bundesarchiv (Koblenz), Nachlaß Oskar Schindler, 1908–1974, Bestand 1493, No.1, Band 3, 1 page; "Oskar Schindler to Dr. H. Wolf, United Restitution Office, München," April 28, 1957, Bundesarchiv (Koblenz), Nachlaß Oskar Schindler, 1908–1974, Bestand 1483, No.1, Band 3, 1 page.
40. "Dr. Maximo Biedermann, et al., to Dr. Theodor Heuss," May 3, 1957, American Jewish Joint Distribution Committee Archives (New York), 1–3.
41. "Oskar Schindler File, No. 4167," October 3, 1957, American Jewish Joint Distribution Committee Archives (New York), 1 page; Friedl Reifer to Mr. Charles H. Jordan," August 13, 1957, American Jewish Joint Distribution Committee Archives (Jerusalem), 1.
42. "Reifer to Jordan," August 13, 1957, JDC Archives (J), 2; "Charles H. Jordan to Mr. Saul Kagan," August 14, 1957, American Jewish Joint Distribution Committee Archives (Jerusalem), 1 page.
43. "Unsigned Letter to the American Jewish Joint Distribution Committee, Buenos Aires," December 13, 1957, American Jewish Joint Distribution Committee Archives (New York), 1–2; "Sidney Nelson to Dorothy Speiser," December 24, 1957, American Jewish Joint Distribution Archives (New York), 1 page; Emanuel Perlmutter, "Jews Here Honor Hitler Arms Aide," *New York Times* (June 26, 1957), 4. Copies of all of these articles can be found scattered throughout the Oskar Schindler collection at the Bundesarchiv in Koblenz. Unfortunately, many of them are undated and without page numbers.
44. "Fred Ziegellaub to Charles H. Jordan," January 14, 1958, American Jewish Joint Distribution Committee Archives (Jerusalem), 1 page; "Charles H. Jordan to Fred Ziegellaub," January 21, 1958, American Jewish Joint Distribution Archives (Jerusalem), 1 page; "Friedl Reifer to Dr. E. Katzenstein," March 7, 1958, American Jewish Joint Distribution Committee Archives (Jerusalem), 1 page; "Saul Kagan to Dr. Ernst Katzenstein," March 13, 1958, American Jewish Joint Distribution Committee Archives (Jerusalem), 1 page; "Fred Ziegellaub to Charles H. Jordan," March 28, 1958, American Jewish Joint Distribution Committee Archives (Jerusalem), 1 page; "Charles H. Jordan to Fred Ziegellaub," April 2, 1958, American Jewish Joint Distribution Archives (Jerusalem), 1 page.
45. This is the sum that Oskar initially claimed and presented to Joint officials in Buenos Aires in 1953. His detailed breakdown of wartime losses was then forwarded by Julius Lomnitz, the director of Joint Operations in Latin America, to URO officials in London. "Julius Lomnitz to United Restitution Office, London," October 29, 1953, American Jewish Joint Distribution Committee Archives (New York), 3 pages and Emalia factory plans. Similar documents can be found in Bundesarchiv (Koblenz), Nachlaß Oskar Schindler, 1908–1974, Bestand 1493, No. 1/ Band 3; "Der Lastenausgleich—was er war und was er heute noch ist." *Frankfurter Allgemeine Zeitung*, February 24, 1996, n.p.; "*Aufstellung* der

in Brünnlitz verliebenen Maschinen und Einrichtungen einschl. der Forderungen an das Reich, *Räumung* auf Grund des *Befehls* der *Rüstungs-Inspektion, Troppau (Zwittau) vom 6. Mai 1945,"* Lastenausgleicharchiv (Bayreuth), 306 2230a (Oskar Schindler), 8; "Ausgleichsamt 55.31: *Erfüllungsübersicht,* Oskar Schindler 40333," June 21, 1976, Lastenausgleicharchiv (Bayreuth), 306 2230a (Oskar Schindler), 1 page; Oskar Schindler's *Lebenslauf,* October 10, 1966, Bundesarchiv (Koblenz), Nachlaß Oskar Schindler, 1908-1974, Bestand N 1493, No. 1, Band 1, 2.

46. Mietek Pemper, interview by the author, Augsburg, Germany, January 17, 2000.

47. Pemper, interviews, May 26, 1999, and January 17, 2000.

48. Ibid., interview, May 26, 1999; Keller and Braun, *Schindlers Koffer,* 41.

49. Pemper, interviews, May 26, 1999, and January 17, 2000; Keller and Braun, *Schindlers Koffer,* 42.

50. "Dr. Alexander Besser to Oskar Schindler," January 31, 1958, Bundesarchiv (Koblenz), Nachlaß Oskar Schindler, 1908–1974, Bestand N 1493, No.1, Band 1, 1–3; Pemper, interview, May 26, 1999; "Dr. Alexander Besser to Benjamin Mayer," January 31, 1958, Bundesarchiv (Koblenz), Nachlaß Oskar Schindler, 1908–1974, Bestand N 1493, No. 1, Band 1, 1–2; "Oskar Schindler to Benjamin Mayer," February 9, 1958, Bundesarchiv (Koblenz), Nachlaß Oskar Schindler, 1908–1974, Bestand 1493, No. 1, Band 23, 2 pages; "Dr. Hans Pietsch, *Aktenverwerk,"* September 20, 1958, Bundesarchiv (Koblenz), Nachlaß Oskar Schindler, 1908–1974, Bestand 1493, No. 1, Band 2, 1–6; "Dr. Hans Pietsch, *Aktennotiz: Exposée betreffend Fa. Schindler in Kemanth [sic],"* November 16, 1958, Bundesarchiv (Koblenz), Nachlaß Oskar Schindler, 1908–1974, Bestand 1493, No.1, Band 2, 1–8; "Dr. Alexander Besser to Oskar Schindler," November 26, 1958, Bundesarchiv (Koblenz), Nachlaß Oskar Schindler, 1908–1974, Bestand 1493, No. 1, Band 2, 1 page; "Dr. Hans Petsch to Oskar Schindler," December 10, 1958, Bundesarchiv (Koblenz), Nachlaß Oskar Schindler, 1908–1974, Bestand 1493, No. 1, Band 2, 1 page; "Dr. Hans Pietsch, *Aktennotiz,"* January 30, 1959, Bundesarchiv (Koblenz), Nachlaß Oskar Schindler, 1908–1974, Bestand 1493, No. 1, Band 2, 1–4; "Dr. Hans Petsch, *Aktennotiz: Betr.: Vorhaben Oskar Schindler, Kemnath-Stadt,"* February 18, 1959, Bundesarchiv (Koblenz), Nachlaß Oskar Schindler, 1908–1974, Bestand 1493, No. 1, Band 2, 1–5; "Dr. Hans Pietsch to Oskar Schindler," February 27, 1959, Bundesarchiv (Koblenz), Nachlaß Oskar Schindler, 1908–1974, Bestand 1493, No. 1, Band 2, 1 page; "Oskar Schindler, *Aktennotiz. Betr.: Errichtung einer Kartonagenfabrik von Oskar Schindler in Kemnath/Opf.,"* March 20, 1959, Bundesarchiv (Koblenz), Nachlaß Oskar Schindler, 1908–1974, Bestand 1493, No. 1, Band 2, 1–3.

51. "*Aktennotiz* zur Besprechung beim hessischen Innenministerium, Wiesbaden Luisenstraße-Referant Herr Gilfert, Erdgeschoß, Zimmer 29 in Sachen Lastenausgleichsanspruch Oskar Schindler, Frank/Main, Arndtstraße 46," August 24, 1959, Bundesarchiv (Koblenz), Nachlaß Oskar Schindler, 1908–1974, Bestand 1493, Band 1, No. 1, 1–4; Pemper, interview, January 17, 2000; *"Abschrift Nr./59 Urkundenrolle,"* n.d., Bundesarchiv (Koblenz), Nachlaß Oskar Schindler, 1908–1974, Bestand 1493, Band 1, No. 1, 1–4.

52. "*Verpfändungserklärung,"* November 6, 1961, Lastenausgleicharchiv (Bayreuth), 30 62230b (Oskar Schindler), 1 page; "*Auszugsweise beglaubigte Abschrift:* Hans Kuhn and Oskar Schindler," January 10, 1962, Lastenausgleicharchiv (Bayreuth), 30 62230b (Oskar Schindler), 1–3; Pemper, interview, May 26, 1999.

53. Keller and Braun, "Schindlers Koffer (3)," 6.

54. "Erhard Knechtel to David M. Crowe," May 13, 2000, 2.

55. Keller and Braun, "Schindler's Koffer (3)," 6.

56. Ludmilla Page, interview by the author, Beverly Hills, California, November 28, 2001.

57. "Schindler's Survivors," *New York Newsday,* March 23, 1994, B29.

58. Page, interview, November 28, 2001; "Leopold Page-Shopkeeper-Philosopher," *Beverly Hills City Directory: Golden Anniversary* (Beverly Hills: City of Beverly Hills, n.d.), 64.

59. Page, interview, November 28, 2001; Patrick McGilligan, *Fritz Lang: The Nature of the Beast* (New York: St. Martin's Press, 1997), 159, 178, 198–199, 473.

60. "Oskar Schindler to Lily Latté," June 1951, Bundesarchiv (Koblenz), Nachlaß Oskar Schindler, 1908–1974, Bestand 1493, No. 1, Band 28, 1 page.

61. Page, interview, November 28, 2001; McGilligan, *Fritz Lang,* 159, 178, 198–199, 473.

62. McGilligan, *Fritz Lang,* 373, 377, 498–499.

63. Ibid., 327–328.

64. Ibid., 11, 158, 169–172, 176–177, 179–180, 288, 350, 475.

65. Ibid., 178.

66. "Oskar Schindler to Leopold Page," February 14, 1965, Bundesarchiv (Koblenz), Nachlaß Oskar Schindler, 1908–1974, Bestand 1493, No. 1, Band 21, 1.

67. Ned Comstock, interview by the author, Los Angeles, California, March 14, 2000; McGilligan, *Fritz Lang,* 509; "Oskar Schindler to Fritz Lang," July 20, 1951, Bundesarchiv (Koblenz), Nachlaß Oskar Schindler, 1908–1974, Bestand 1493, Band 1, No. 28, 8 pages.

68. "Kurt Grossmann to Oskar Schindler," July 18, 1956, Bundesarchiv (Koblenz), Nachlaß Oskar Schindler, 1908–1974, Bestand 1493, No. 1, Band 23, 1 page; "Kurt Grossmann to Oskar Schindler," September 4, 1956, Bundesarchiv (Koblenz), Nachlaß Oskar Schindler, 1908–1974, Bestand 1493, No. 1, Band 23, 2 pages; "Oskar Schindler to Kurt Grossmann," April 6, 1957, Bundesarchiv (Koblenz), Nachlaß Oskar Schindler, 1908–1974, Bestand 1493, No. 1, Band 23, 1 page; "Kurt Grossmann to Oskar Schindler, Bundesarchiv (Koblenz), Nachlaß Oskar Schindler, 1908–1974, Bestand 1493, No. 1, Band 23, 1 page; "Kurt R. Grossmann to Herrn Rechtsanwalt Dr. Georg Krauss," June 26, 1957, Bundesarchiv (Koblenz), Nachlaß Oskar Schindler, 1908–1974, Bestand 1493, No. 1, Band 23, 1 page; "Kurt R. Grossmann to Herrn Hermann Proebst," June 26, 1957, Bundesarchiv (Koblenz), Nachlaß Oskar Schindler, 1908–1974, Bestand 1493, No. 1, Band 26, 1 page; "Kurt R. Grossmann to Herrn Richard Kirn," June 26, 1957, Bundesarchiv (Koblenz), Nachlaß Oskar Schindler, 1908–1974, Bestand 1493, No. 1, Band 26, 1 page. What is interesting about these last two letters, which were to the editors of the *Süddeutsche Zeitung* and the *Frankfurter Neue Presse,* is that they were written on The Jewish Agency for Palestine letterhead. Grossmann normally used his own personal stationery for such letters; Kurt Grossman, *Die unbesungenen Helden: Menschen in Deutschlands dunklen Tagen* (Berlin: Ullstein, 1957), 147. The first edition of this book was published by Arani-Verlags in Berlin in 1957; the Kurt Richard Grossman Papers, 1913–1973, are located at the Hoover Institution Archives at Stanford University. The entire finding aid for this large collection is available online.

69. "Oskar Schindler to Itzhak Stern," August 6, 1956, Bundesarchiv (Koblenz), Nachlaß Oskar Schindler, 1908–1974, Bestand 1493, Band 1, No. 25, 1 page; "Itzhak Stern to Oskar Schindler," August 25, 1956, Bundesarchiv (Koblenz), Nachlaß Oskar Schindler, 1908–1974, Bestand 1493, Band 1, No. 25, 1–2; "Dr. Ball-Kaduri to Oskar Schindler," October 1, 1956, Bundesarchiv (Koblenz), Nachlaß Oskar Schindler, 1908–1974, Bestand 1493, Band 1, No. 25, 1 page; "Oskar Schindler to Itzhak Stern," October 22, 1956, Bundesarchiv (Koblenz), Nachlaß Oskar Schindler, 1908–1974, Band 1, No. 25, 1 page; "Itzhak Stern to Oskar Schindler," October 25, 1956, Bundesarchiv (Koblenz), Nachlaß Oskar Schindler, 1908–1974, Bestand 1493, Band 1, No. 25, 1–2; "Oskar Schindler to

Itzhak Stern," November 20, 1956, Bundesarchiv (Koblenz), Nachlaß Oskar Schindler, 1908–1974, Bestand 1493, Band 1, No. 20, 1 page; "Stern Report 1956," December 1956, Yad Vashem Archives, 01/164, 40 pages.

70. Benny Morris, *Righteous Victims: A History of the Zionist-Arab Conflict, 1881–2001* (New York: Vintage Books, 2001), 282–296.

71. "Oskar Schindler to Itzhak Stern," April 16, 1956, Bundesarchiv (Koblenz), Nachlaß Oskar Schindler, 1908–1974, Bestand 1493, Band 1, No. 25, 3.

72. "Oskar Schindler to Itzhak Stern," November 20, 1956, Bundesarchiv (Koblenz), Nachlaß Oskar Schindler, 1908–1974, Bestand 1493, Band 1, No. 25, 1 page.

73. "Natan Wurzel to Julius Wiener (in Hebrew)," May 21, 1955, Yad Vashem Archives, M 31/30, 1.

74. "Oskar Schindler to Leib Salpeter, Itzhak Stern, Rabiner Levertov, Dr. N. Stern, Edel Elsner Henek Licht, and Others," April 1955, Bundesarchiv (Koblenz), Nachlaß Oskar Schindler, 1908–1974, Bestand 1493, No. 1, Band 23, 1–8.

75. "Wypis Pierwszy. Akt Norarialny," Numer Repertorium: 371/39, March 17, 1939, SOK, RH 401-RHB XII 35, "Rekord," 5; "Gutman and Glajtman to Reczyński," July 10, 1939, SOKC 2022: III U 5/39, 235–236; "Natan Wurzel to Dr. Zbigniew Reczyński," July 30, 1939, SOKC 2022; U 5/39, 1 page; "Natan Wurzel to Dr. Zbigniew Reczyński," August 8, 1939, SOKC 2022: III U 5/39, 1 page; "Natan Wurzel to Wolf Gleitman, I Michałman," August 9, 1939, SOKC 2022: III U 5/39, 1 page.

76. "Stanislaw Frühling to Sad Okręgowy w Krakowy," September 1, 1939, SOKC 2022: III U 5/39, 244–245; "Dr. Bolesław Zawisza to Sad Okręgowy w Krakowy," August 4, 1942, SOKC 2023: III U 5/39, 1–2 and "Odpis," July 24, 1942, 1 page, and "Odpis," August 3, 1942, 1 page.

77. "Schindler to Salpeter et al.," April 1955, BA(K), 2–3.

78. Ibid., 4; "Testimony of Julius Wiener Before Messrs. Shatkai and Landau, in the Presence of Mr. Alkalai (in Hebrew)," August 6, 1963, Jerusalem, Yad Vashem Archives, M 31/30 (RGD), 1–3; "Testimony of Esther Schwartz in the Matter of Oskar Schindler (in Hebrew)," 1963, Yad Vashem Archives, M 31/30 (RGD), 2–3.

79. "Testimony of Julius Weiner," October 10, 1956, Yad Vashem Archives, 01/164, 4–5.

80. "Testimony of Julius Wiener (in Hebrew)," October 10, 1956, Yad Vashem Archives, 01/164, 1–2; "Testimony of Esther Schwartz," 1963, YVA, 1; "Testimony of Julius Wiener," August 6, 1963, YVA, 1; "Testimony of Natan Wurzel (in Hebrew)," November 26, 1956, Yad Vashem Archives, M 31/30 (RGD), 1.

81. "Testimony of Julius Wiener," October 10, 1956, YVA, 1; "Testimony of Julius Wiener," August 6, 1963, YVA, 1; "Testimony of Esther Schwartz," YVA, 1.

82. "Oskar Schindler to Salpeter et al.," April 1955, BA(K), 2.

83. Martin Gilbert, *The Righteous: The Unsung Heroes of the Holocaust* (New York: Henry Holt and Company, 2003), xv; Mordecai Paldiel, *The Path of the Righteous: Gentile Rescuers of Jews during the Holocaust* (Hoboken, N.J.: KTAV Publishing House in conjunction with The Jewish Foundation for Christian Rescuers/ADL, 1993), 4–5.

84. James Cameron, "The Good German Schindler," *Daily Mail*, December 11, 1961, 8.

85. Dr. Moshe Bejski, interview by the author, Tel Aviv, Israel, May 17, 1999; "The Enterprising Committee of the Work Camp Survivors: Oskar Schindler in Brünnlitz to Mr. Aryeh Leon Kubovy (in Hebrew)," December 10, 1961, Yad Vashem Archives, 4 pages.

86. "The Enterprising Committee to Mr. Kubovy," December 10, 1961, YVA, 1; Bejski, interview, May 17, 1999.

87. "The Enterprising Committee to Mr. Kubovy," December 10, 1961, YVA, 2.

88. Ibid., 2.

89. Alexander B. Rossino, *Hitler Strikes Poland: Blitzkrieg, Ideology, and Atrocity* (Lawrence: University Press of Kansas, 2003), 92; Isaiah Trunk, *Judenrat: The Jewish Councils in Eastern Europe Under Nazi Occupation* (New York: Stein and Day, 1977), 62–64.

90. "The Enterprising Committee to Mr. Kubovy," December 10, 1961, YVA, 2–3.

91. Ibid., 3.

92. Ibid., 4.

93. Dr. Mordecai Paldiel, interview by the author, Yad Vashem, Jerusalem, Israel, May 12, 1999.

94. Gideon Hausner, *Justice in Jerusalem* (New York: Holocaust Library, 1968), 305–446. Hausner was the Attorney General of Israel at the time of the Eichmann trial and prosecuted the State of Israel's case against Eichmann; State of Israel, Ministry of Justice, *The Trial of Adolf Eichmann: Record of Proceedings in the District Court of Jerusalem,* vol. 1 (Jerusalem: Israel State Archives and Yad Vashem, 1992), 343–355.

95. "The Good German Schindler," *Daily Mail* (London), December 11, 1961, 8.

96. Paldiel, interview, May 12, 1999; Bejski, interview, May 17, 1999; "Dr. Mordecai Paldiel to David M. Crowe," January 19, 2004, 1 page.

97. "Dr. Moshe Bejski to Oskar Schindler," April 11, 1962, Bundesarchiv (Koblenz), Nachlaß Oskar Schindler, 1908–1974, Bestand 1493, No. 1, Band 23, 1 page.

98. "Oskar Schindler-wybawca 1100 Żydów entuzjastrycznie powitany w Lud," *Izraelskie Nowiny I Kurier,* April 29, 1962, 1.

99. "Bewegender Empfang für Herrn Schindler in Israel," Deutsche Presse Agentur, May 1, 1962.

100. Paldiel, interview, May 12, 1999; "National Remembers Six Million: Eleven 'Righteous Gentiles,' *Jerusalem Post,* May 2, 1962, 3.

101. "Jakob Sternberg to *Ha'aretz,*" May 13, 1962, n.p.

102. Bejski, interview, May 17, 1999.

103. Dr. Moshe Bejski, "Notes on the Banquet in Honor of Oskar Schindler," May 2, 1962, Tel Aviv, Israel, 1–5.

104. Ibid., 5–7.

105. Ibid., 7–9.

106. Ibid., 9–12; excerpts of this transcript, including Dr. Bejski's remarks, can be found in an article he published, "Oskar Schindler and *Schindler's List,*" edited by Aharon Weiss, *Yad Vashem Studies,* vol. 24 (Jerusalem 1994), 317–348. This article also includes a copy of the eulogy that Dr. Bejski delivered at Oskar's funeral in Jerusalem on October 28, 1974.

107. Bejski, "Notes on the Oskar Schindler Banquet," 12–13.

108. Ibid., 12–16.

109. Ibid., 16–17.

110. Ibid., 18–19.

111. Ibid., 19–26.

112. Ibid., 27–29.

113. Ibid., 30–31.

114. Ibid., 31–37.

115. Ibid., 37–42. Itzhak Stern made a point of correcting Dr. Bejski's original quote, "There are three definitions in three stages: a man, a person, a human being. I think there should be an additional one, Schindler," when he met Martin Gosch and Howard Koch in Tel Aviv in 1964. Martin A. Gosch and Howard Koch, "Interview with Itzhak Stern," November 29, 1964, Tel Aviv, Israel, Delbert Mann Papers, Special Collections Library, Vanderbilt University, 10-A, 10. Leo Rosten explains this folk saying more clearly in his *The Joys of Yiddish* (New York: Simon & Schuster, 1970), 237. "Mensh, Mensch: 1. A human

being. 2. An upright, honorable, decent person. 3. Someone of consequence; someone to admire and emulate; someone of noble character."

116. "Strong Accusations against Oskar Schindler (in Hebrew)," *Ha'aretz*, May 2, 1962, n.p. There was also an article, "Schwere Anklagen gegen Oscar Schindler," in German on the controversy surrounding Schindler that was based on the *Ha'aretz* article in Yad Vashem's collection on Schindler. However, as it is only a clipping, it is difficult to determine its origin. See Yad Vashem Archives (RGD), M 31/30, 519 and Bundesarchivs (Koblenz), Nachlaß Oskar Schindler, 1908–1974, Bestand 1493, No. 1, Band 33, 1 page; Bejski, interview, May 17, 1999.

117. Paldiel, *Path of the Righteous,* 5–6.

118. Ibid.

119. Paldiel, interview, May 12, 1999.

120. "Testimony of Julius Wiener," August 6, 1963, YVA, 1–2; "Testimony of Esther Schwartz," 1963, YVA, 1–3; "Testimony of Mrs. Simah Hertmann (Gelcer) before Shatkai and Landau, in the Presence of Alkalai and Wiener (in Hebrew)," August 28, 1963, Yad Vashem Archives, M 31/30, 1–2; Jakob Sternberg to Oskar Schindler, February 25, 1964, Bundesarchiv (Koblenz), Nachlaß Oskar Schindler, 1908-1974, Bestand N 1493, No. 1, Band 1, 1 page); "Dr. Mordecai Paldiel to David M. Crowe," January 19, 2004.

121. "Statement of Moshe Landau and A.L. Kubovy to Oskar Schindler, December 24, 1963," Bundesarchiv (Koblenz), Nachlaß Oskar Schindler, 1908–1974, Bestand 1493, No. 1, Band 21, 1 page.

122. "Official Citation Given to Oskar Schindler by the Government of Israel," December 24, 1963, Bundesarchiv (Koblenz), Nachlaß Oskar Schindler, 1908–1974, Bestand 1493, No. 1, Band 17, 1 page.

123. "Dr. Mordecai Paldiel to David M. Crowe," January 20, 2004, and January 21, 2004.

124. Jakob Sternberg to Oskar Schindler, November 1, 1965, Bundesarchiv (Koblenz), Nachlaß Oskar Schindler, 1908-1974, Bestand N 1493, No. 1, Band 25, 1 page; "Dr. Mordecai Paldiel to David M. Crowe," Jan. 20, 2004.

125. Bejski, interview, May 17, 1999.

126. Paldiel, interview, May 12, 1962, and May 13, 1999; "Dr. Mordecai Paldiel to David M. Crowe," January 20, 2004.

127. Dr. Mordecai Paldiel to David M. Crowe," January 21, 2004.

128. "Oskar Schindler to My Very Honored and Dear Friends," June 22, 1962, Bundesarchiv (Koblenz), Nachlaß Oskar Schindler, 1908-1974, Bestand N 1493, No. 1, Band 28, 2.

Chapter 13

1. Peter Gorlinsky, "'Vater Courage' bliebt unvergessen—aber wie steht es mit 'Mutter Courage,'" *Argentinisches Tageblatt,* January 30, 1963, 2.

2. Emilie Schindler, *Where Light and Shadow Meet: Memoirs,* trans. Dolores M. Koch (New York: W.W. Norton, 1997), 135–136.

3. Ibid., 135.

4. Ibid., 138.

5. Graciela La Rocca, interview by the author, San Vicente, Argentina, May 24, 2001; in her memoirs, *Light and Shadow,* 134, Emilie mentioned that her meals consisted of "tangerines [she] picked in the orchard, some bread, and lots of coffee."

6. Walter Pollack to Leopold Page, February 20, 1965, Bundesarchiv (Koblenz), Nachlaß Oskar Schindler, 1908-1974, Bestand N 1493, No. 1, Band 26, 1 page; Schindler, *Light and Shadow,* 134.

7. "Walter Pollack to Oskar Schindler," July 9, 1962, Bundesarchiv (Koblenz), Nachlaß Oskar Schindler, 1908–1974, Bestand 1493, No. 1, Band 24, 1; Rocca, interview, May 24, 2001.

8. Peter Gorkinsky, "Vater Courage bleibt unvergessen—aber wie steht es Mutter Courage," *Argentinisches Tageblatt,* January 30, 1963, 2.

9. Ibid., 2.

10. Ibid.

11. Juan C. Caro to the Editor, *The Jerusalem Post,* December 21, 1982, n.p.; "Walter Pollack to Oskar Schindler," July 7, 1964, Bundesarchiv (Koblenz), Nachlaß Oskar Schindler, 1908–1974, Bestand 1493, No. 1, Band 24, 1; Monica Caro, Ilse Chwat, and Ilse Wartensleben, interviews by the author, Buenos Aires, Argentina, May 18, 2001; Erika Rosenberg, ed., *Ich, Emilie Schindler: Erinnerungen einer Unbeugsamen* (Munich: Herbig, 2001), 218.

12. Joseph Wulf, "Licht in der Finsternis," Bayerischer Rundfunk Production, September 9 and 12, 1960, 13–16. Bundesarchiv (Koblenz), Nachlaß Oskar Schindler, 1908–1974, Bestand 1493, No. 1, Band 18, 22 pages; "Annie Capell to Oskar Schindler," July 18, 1962, August 13, 1962, and September 22, 1962, Bundesarchiv (Koblenz), Nachlaß Oskar Schindler, 1908–1974, Bestand 1493, No. 1, Band 28, 1 page; "Contract between Oskar Schindler and George Marton," November 3, 1962, Nachlaß Oskar Schindler, 1908–1974, Bestand 1493, No. 1, Band 28, 2 pages; "Oskar Schindler to Annie Capell," November 3, 1962, Bundesarchiv (Koblenz), Nachlaß Oskar Schindler, 1908–1974, Bestand 1493, No. 1, Band 28, 1 page; "Peter V. Herald to Oskar Schindler," October 16, 1962, Bundesarchiv (Koblernz), Nachlaß Oskar Schindler, 1908–1974, Bestand 1493, No. 1, Band 18, 1 page. Included with the letter were two copies, in English, of an 11-page synopsis that Herald had written on Schindler's actions during the war.

13. "Anton Calleia to Oskar Schindler," August 20, 1963, Bundesarchiv (Koblenz), Nachlaß Oskar Schindler, 1908–1974, Bestand 1493, No. 1, Band 22, 1 page.

14. Robert Parrella, "Jews Move to Help German Who Saved 1,200," *New York Herald Tribune,* November 23, 1963, 1.

15. A. H. Weiler, "Biography," *New York Times,* November 8, 1964, n.p.; Natan Gurdus, "Gregory Peck Odtworzy Postać Oskara Schindlera," n.d., *Nowiny I Kurier,* n.p. This is a clipping from Bundesarchiv (Koblenz), Nachlaß Oskar Schindler, 1908–1974, Bestand 1493, No. 1, Band 30, 1 page; Philip K. Scheuer, "Burton Possibility for Schindler Epic," *Los Angeles Times,* December 22, 1964, n.p. This article is part of a collection of articles on Oskar Schindler, Martin Gosch, and the film, *To the Last Hour,* that I discovered in the archives of the Academy of Motion Pictures, Arts and Sciences in Beverly Hills, California. All subsequent articles from this archive will be cited as Archives of the Academy of Motion Pictures, Arts and Sciences.

16. "Leopold Page to Martin Gosch," May 1, 1964, Bundesarchiv (Koblenz), Nachlaß Oskar Schindler, 1908–1974, Bestand 1493, No. 1, Band 28, 1–3.

17. Ibid., 3–5.

18. "Irving Glovin to Oskar Schindler," June 1, 1964, Bundesarchiv (Koblenz), Nachlaß Oskar Schindler, 1908–1974, Bestand 1493, No. 1, Band 23, 2 pages.

19. "Leopold Page to Oskar Schindler," June 3, 1964, Bundesarchiv (Koblenz), Nachlaß Oskar Schindler, 1908–1974, Bestand 1493, No. 1, Band 24, 4 pages.

20. "Moshe Bejski to Oskar Schindler," July 16, 1964, Bundesarchiv (Koblenz), Nachlaß Oskar Schindler, 1908–1974, Bestand 1493, No. 1, Band 22, 3.

21. "Mietek Pemper to Oskar Schindler," August 4, 1964, Bundesarchiv (Koblenz), Nachlaß Oskar Schindler, 1908–1974, Bestand 1493, No. 1, Band 24, 2 pages; "Oskar Schindler to Moshe Bejski," August 19, 1964, Bundesarchiv (Koblenz), Nachlaß Oskar

Schindler, 1908–1974, Bestand 1493, No. 1, Band 22, 1 page; "Oskar Schindler to Walter Pollack," October 9, 1964, Bundesarchiv (Koblenz), Nachlaß Oskar Schindler, 1908–1974, Bestand 1493, No. 1, Band 24, 1.

22. "Oskar Schindler to Leopold Page," October 5, 1964, Bundesarchiv (Koblenz), Nachlaß Oskar Schindler, 1908–1974, Bestand 1493, No. 1, Band 24, 1 page.

23. Ibid., 2.

24. Ibid., 1–2.

25. "Oskar Schindler to Walter Pollack," October 9, 1964, Bundesarchiv (Koblenz), Nachlaß Oskar Schindler, 1908–1974, Bestand 1493, No. 1, Band 24, 2 pages.

26. "Walter Pollack to Leopold Page," February 2, 1965, Bundesarchiv (Koblenz), Nachlaß Oskar Schindler, 1908–1974, Bestand N 1493, No. 1, Band 26, 1 page; "Walter Pollack to Oskar Schindler," October 19, 1964, Bundesarchiv (Koblenz), Nachlaß Oskar Schindler, 1908–1974, Bestand 1493, No. 1, Band 24, 2 pages.

27. "Leopold Page to Oskar Schindler," October 19, 1964, Bundesarchiv (Koblenz), Nachlaß Oskar Schindler, 1908–1974, Bestand 1493, No. 1, Band 24, 2 pages.

28. "Irving Glovin to Oskar Schindler," October 19, 1964, Bundesarchiv (Koblenz), Nachlaß Oskar Schindler, 1908–1974, Bestand 1493, No. 1, Band 28, 2 pages.

29. Howard Koch, *As Time Goes By: Memoirs of a Writer* (New York: Harcourt Brace Jovanovich, 1979), 1–9, 71–84, 96–108, 163–170, 178–192, 210–220; "Arthur I. Weinberg to Benjamin Melniker, MGM," October 9, 1964, 3 pages, Delbert Mann Papers, Special Collections Library, Vanderbilt University.

30. "Martin Gosch to Oskar Schindler," October 26, 1964, Bundesarchiv (Koblenz), Nachlaß Oskar Schindler, 1908–1974, Bestand 1493, No. 1, Band 28, 2 pages.

31. "Oskar Schindler to Moshe Bejski," October 30, 1964, Bundesarchiv (Koblenz), Nachlaß Oskar Schindler, 1908–1974, Bestand 1493, No. 1, Band 22, 1 page.

32. "Moshe Bejski to Oskar Schindler," November 5, 1964, Bundesarchiv (Koblenz), Nachlaß Oskar Schindler, 1908–1974, Bestand 1493, No. 1, Band 22, 1.

33. "Martin A. Gosch to Maurice Silverstein and Delbert Mann," October 28, 1964, 1 page, Delbert Mann Papers, Special Collection Library, Vanderbilt University.

34. "Martin A. Gosch to Syl Lamont," November 9, 1964, 1 page, Delbert Mann Papers, Special Collections Library, Vanderbilt University.

35. Robert A. Fiore to David M. Crowe, March 7, 2000; Ian Fleming, *The Diamond Smugglers* (New York: Dell, 1957), 84–97.

36. Robert J. Fiore to David M. Crowe, March 7, 2000; Robert J. Fiore to David M. Crowe, February 10, 2004; "Würdigung Fiore Verdienste um die deutsch-amerikanische Freundschaft," *Kronberger Bote,* January 22, 2004, n.p.

37. Fiore to Crowe, March 7, 2000; Robert J. Fiore to David M. Crowe, August 13, 2003.

38. "Oskar Schindler to Martin Gosch," November 13, 1964, Nachlaß Oskar Schindler, 1908–1974, Bestand 1493, No. 1, Band 28, 3 pages; "Jakob Sternberg to Oskar Schindler," December 15, 1964, Bundesarchiv (Koblenz), Nachlaß Oskar Schindler, 1908–1974, Bestand N 1493, No. 1, Band 1, 1 page; "Leopold Page to Martin Gosch," November 13, 1964, Bundesarchiv (Koblenz), Nachlaß Oskar Schindler, 1908–1974, Bestand 1493, No. 1, Band 28, 5 pages.

39. "Oskar Schindler to Moshe Bejski," December 24, 1964, Bundesarchiv (Koblenz), Nachlaß Oskar Schindler, 1908–1974, Bestand 1493, No. 1, Band 22, 1 page; "Oskar Schindler to Leopold Page," December 24, 1964, Bundesarchiv (Koblenz), Bestand 1493, No. 1, Band 24, 1 page; "Oskar Schindler to Martin Gosch," December 28, 1964, Ami Staehr Collection, Stuttgart, Germany, 1 page.

40. "Oskar Schindler to Walter Pollack," December 30, 1964, Bundesarchiv (Koblenz), Nachlaß Oskar Schindler, 1908–1974, Bestand 1493, No. 1, Band 24, 1 page.

41. "Oskar Schindler to Moshe Bejski," December 30, 1964, Bundesarchiv (Koblenz), Nachlaß Oskar Schindler, 1908–1974, Bestand 1493, No. 1, Band 22, 1 page.

42. Uri Kaisari, "Real Heroes and Heroes with Makeup," *Ma'ariv*, January 7, 1965, n.p.; "Gosch Evades Poland's Fog and Bureaucrats," *Variety Weekly*, January 20, 1965, n.p. Archives of the Academy of Motion Pictures, Arts, and Sciences; "Schindler to Page," October 5, BA(K), 2.

43. Gurdus, "Gregory Peck Odtworzy Postać Oskara Schindlera," n.p.

44. "Martin Gosch to Oskar Schindler," January 15, 1965, Bundesarchiv (Koblenz), Nachlaß Oskar Schindler, 1908–1974, Bestand 1493, No. 1, Band 28, 1; "Gosch Evades Poland's Fog and Bureaucrats," January 20, 1965, n.p.

45. "Martin Gosch to Oskar Schindler," January 25, 1965, Bundesarchiv (Koblenz), Nachlaß Oskar Schindler, 1908–1974, Bestand 1493, No. 1, Band 2, 2 pages.

46. "Martin A. Gosch to Oskar Schindler," February 9, 1965, Bundesarchiv (Koblenz), Nachlaß Oskar Schindler, 1908–1974, Bestand 1493, No. 1, Band 28, 1; "Martin A. Gosch to Dr. Hans Joachim Lange," February 9, 1965, 1 page, Delbert Mann Papers, Special Collections Library, Vanderbilt University.

47. "Gosch to Schindler," February 9, 1965, BA(K), 1.

48. "*To the Last Hour*, Factual Story of a Living Man: Extension of Remarks of Hon. James C. Corman," *Congressional Record-Appendix* (February 24, 1965), A796.

49. "Martin A. Gosch to Dan Terrell," February 26, 1965, Delbert Mann Papers, Special Collections Library, Vanderbilt University, 1–2.

50. "Martin A. Gosch to Delbert Mann," January 14, 1965, 8 pages, Delbert Mann Papers, Special Collections Library, Vanderbilt University.

51. Howard Koch, "Script for *To the Last Hour*," Delbert Mann Papers, Special Collections Library, Vanderbilt University, 1–86.

52. Koch, "Script for *To the Last Hour*," Delbert Mann Papers, Vanderbilt University, 87–89.

53. Ibid., 101–104.

54. Ibid., 104, 115–120.

55. Ibid., 120–125.

56. Ibid., 126–130.

57. "Oskar Schindler to Walter Pollack," February 14, 1965, Bundesarchiv (Koblenz), Nachlaß Oskar Schindler, 1908–1974, Bestand 1493, No. 1, Band 21, 2 pages.

58. "Oskar Schindler to Leopold Page," February 14, 1965, Bundesarchiv (Koblenz), Nachlaß Oskar Schindler, 1908–1974, Bestand 1493, No. 1, Band 21, 1; "Leopold Page to Oskar Schindler," February 28, 1965, Bundesarchiv (Koblenz), Nachlaß Oskar Schindler, 1908–1974, Bestand 1493, No. 1, Band 24, 2 pages; Ludmilla Page, interview by the author, Beverly Hills, California, November 28, 2001.

59. "Oskar Schindler to Dr. Moshe Bejski," March 31, 1965, Bundesarchiv (Koblenz), Nachlaß Oskar Schindler, 1908–1974, Bestand 1493, No.1, Band 22, 2; "Leopold Page to Oskar Schindler," February 28, 1965, Bundesarchiv (Koblenz), Nachlaß Oskar Schindler, 1908–1974, Bestand 1493, No. 1, Band 24, 2 pages.

60. "Oskar Schindler to Dr. Moshe Bejski," March 31, 1965, Bundesarchiv (Koblenz), Nachlaß Oskar Schindler, 1908–1974, Bestand 1493, No. 1, Band 22, 1; "Dr. Moshe Bejski to Oskar Schindler," March 27, 1965, Bundesarchiv (Koblenz), Nachlaß Oskar Schindler, 1908–1974, Bestand 1493, No. 1, Band 22, 1 page.

61. "Irving Glovin to Oskar Schindler," March 17, 1965, Bundesarchiv (Koblenz), Nachlaß Oskar Schindler, 1908–1974, Bestand 1493, No. 1, Band 23, 3 pages.

62. "Oskar Schindler to Walter Pollack," December 10, 1964, Bundesarchiv (Koblenz), Nachlaß Oskar Schindler, 1908–1974, Bestand 1493, No. 1, Band 24, 1 page; "Walter Pol-

lack to Oskar Schindler," January 10, 1965, Bundesarchiv (Koblenz), Nachlaß Oskar Schindler, 1908–1974, Bestand 1493, No. 1, Band 24, 1 page.

63. "Oskar Schindler to Walter Pollack," December 20, 1965, Bundesarchiv (Koblenz), Nachlaß Oskar Schindler, 1908–1974, Bestand 1493, No. 1, Band 24, 1–2; "Walter Pollack to Oskar Schindler," December 30, 1965, Bundesarchiv (Kolbenz), Nachlaß Oskar Schindler, 1908–1974, Bestand 1493, No. 1, Band 24, 2; "Oskar Schindler to Walter Pollack," January 27, 1966, Bundesarchiv (Koblenz), Nachlaß Oskar Schindler, 1908–1974, Bestand 1493, No. 1, Band 24, 1 page.

64. "Walter Pollack to Oskar Schindler," April 5, 1965, Bundesarchiv Koblenz, Nachlaß Oskar Schindler, 1908–1974, Bestand 1493, No. 1, Band 24, 1.

65. "Oskar Schindler to Walter Pollack," March 31, 1965, Bundesarchiv (Koblenz), Nachlaß Oskar Schindler, 1908–1974, Bestand 1493, No. 1, Band 24, 2 pages; "Oskar Schindler to Irving Glovin," March 31, 1965, Bundesarchiv (Koblenz), Nachlaß Oskar Schindler, 1908–1974, Bestand 1493, No. 1, Band 23, 2 pages; Oskar Schindler to Leopold Page, March 10, 1965, Bundesarchiv (Koblenz), Nachlaß Oskar Schindler, 1908–1974, Bestand 1493, No. 1, Band 24, 1 page.

66. "Leopold Page to Oskar Schindler," February 28, 1965, Bundesarchiv (Koblenz), Nachlaß Oskar Schindler, 1908–1974, Bestand 1493, No. 1, Band 24, 1.

67. "Oskar Schindler to Leopold Page," March 10, 1965, Bundesarchiv (Koblenz), Nachlaß Oskar Schindler, 1908–1974, Bestand 1493, No. 1, Band 24, 1 page; "Walter Pollack to Oskar Schindler," April 5, 1965, Nachlaß Oskar Schindler, 1908–1974, Bestand 1493, No. 1, Band 24, 1; "Beate Pollack to Oskar Schindler," April 5, 1965, Bundesarchiv (Koblenz), Nachlaß Oskar Schindler, 1908–1974, Bestand 1493, No. 1, Band 24, 1 page; "Emilie Schindler to Irving Glovin," April 5, 1965, Bundesarchiv (Koblenz), Nachlaß Oskar Schindler, 1908–1974, Bestand 1493, No. 1, Band 26, 1 page; "Emilie Schindler to Leopold Page," April 5, 1965, Bundesarchiv (Koblenz), Nachlaß Oskar Schindler, 1908–1974, Bestand 1493, No. 1, Band 26, 1 page; "Irving Glovin to Walter Pollack," January 25, 1965, Bundesarchiv (Koblenz), Nachlaß Oskar Schindler, 1908–1975, Bestand N 1493, No. 1, Band 26, 1 page; "Walter Pollack to Leopold Page," March 15, 1965, Bundesarchiv (Koblenz), Nachlaß Oskar Schindler, 1908–1974, Bestand N 1493, No. 1, Band 26, 1 page.

68. Helmut Schmitz, "Wie ein großzügiger Habenichts zur Ehrenrente kam: Ein Blick in die Akte Oskar Schindler der hessischen Staatskanzlei deckt die Wege deutscher Bürokratie auf," *Frankfurter Allgemeine Zeitung,* March 1, 1994, n.p.

69. "Professor C. Ruter to David M. Crowe," December 22, 2003, 1 page; "Professor C. F. Ruter to David M. Crowe," January 26, 2004, 1 page.

70. "Oskar Schindler in dem Ermittlungsverfahren gegen Martin Fellenz," June 16, 1962, BKB-Stelle Flensburg, 2 Js 117/63, aus Zst 206 AR 225/63, Zentrale Stelle der Landesjustizverwaltungen, Ludwigsburg, 5 pages; Hannah Arendt, *Eichmann in Jerusalem: A Report on the Banality of Evil* (New York: Penguin Books, 1977), 16; Albert Speer, *The Slave State: Heinrich Himmler's Masterplan for SS Supremacy,* translated by Joachim Neugroschel (London: Weidenfeld and Nicolson, 1981), 258.

71. Karen Orth, *Die Konzentrationslager-SS: Sozialstrukturelle Analysen und biographische Studien* (Göttingen: Wallstein Verlag, 2000), 290–291; Tom Segev, *Soldiers of Evil: The Commandants of the Nazi Concentration Camps,* trans. Haim Watzman (New York: McGraw Hill, 1987), 181–182; "Kriminalpolizei und Oskar Schindler," March 13, 1963, aus FSK 405 AR 3681/65, Zentrale Stelle der Landesjustizverwaltungen, Ludwigsburg, 3 pages.

72. "Oskar Schindler to Dr. Moshe Bejski," May 2, 1965, Bundesarchiv (Koblenz), Nachlaß Oskar Schindler, 1908–1974, Bestand 1493, No. 1, Band 22, 1 page.

73. "Martin A. Gosch to Oskar Schindler," October 13, 1965, Bundesarchiv (Koblenz), Nachlaß Oskar Schindler, 1908–1974, Bestand 1493, No. 1, Band 28, 2 pages; "Oskar Schindler to Martin Gosch," November 28, 1965, Bundesarchiv (Koblenz), Nachlaß Oskar Schindler, 1908–1974, Bestand 1493, No. 1, Band 28, 2 pages.

74. "Oskar Schindler to Walter Pollack," December 20, 1965, Bundesarchiv (Koblenz), Nachlaß Oskar Schindler, 1908–1974, Bestand 1493, No. 1, Band 24, 1.

75. "Der Staatssekretär des Auswärtigen Amts to President Dr. Heinrich Lübke," February 17, 1965, in "Vorschlagsliste Nr. 115/65 für die Verleihung des Verdienstordens der Bundesrepublik Deutschland," October 26, 1965, Bundesarchiv (Koblenz), 3–4; "Stadtrat Dr. Wilhelm Fay to Oskar Schindler," December 31, 1965, Bundesarchiv (Koblenz), Nachlaß Oskar Schindler, 1908–1974, Bestand 1493, No. 1, Band 19, 1 page; "Martin A. Gosch to Oskar Schindler," January 20, 1966, Bundesarchiv (Koblenz), Nachlaß Oskar Schindler, 1908–1974, Bestand 1493, 3.

76. "Dr. Moshe Bejski to Martin A. Gosch," December 22, 1965, Bundesarchiv (Koblenz), Nachlaß Oskar Schindler, 1908–1974, Bestand 1493, No. 1, Band 28, 2 pages; "Oskar Schindler to Martin A. Gosch," January 19, 1966, Bundesarchiv (Koblenz), Nachlaß Oskar Schindler, 1908–1974, Bestand 1493, No. 1, Band 29, 2 pages; for more on Schindler's continued financial problems at this time, see "Joachim Kügler to Dr. Otto Toepper," December 19, 1966, Bundesarchiv (Koblenz), Nachlaß Oskar Schindler, 1908–1974, Bestand 1493, No. 1, Band 1, 3 pages; "Landkreis Düsseldorf-Mettmann to Oskar Schindler," September 19, 1968, Bundesarchiv (Koblenz), Nachlaß Oskar Schindler, 1908–1974, Bestand 1493, No. 1, Band 1, 2 pages.

77. "Martin A. Gosch to Oskar Schindler," January 20, 1966, Bundesarchiv (Koblenz), Nachlaß Oskar Schindler, 1908–1974, Bestand 1493, No. 1, Band 28, 3 pages.

78. "Dr. Moshe Bejski to Oskar Schindler," February 19, 1966, Bundesarchiv (Koblenz), Nachlaß Oskar Schindler, 1908–1974, Bestand 1493, No. 1, Band 22, 2 pages.

79. "Leopold Page to Oskar Schindler," March 30, 1966, Bundesarchiv (Koblenz), Nachlaß Oskar Schindler, 1908–1974, Bestand 1493, No. 1, Band 24, 4 pages; "Dr. Moshe Bejski to Oskar Schindler," April 22, 1966, Bundesarchiv (Koblenz), Nachlaß Oskar Schindler, 1908–1974, Bestand 1493, No. 1, Band 22, 1 page; "Dr. Moshe A. Bejski to Oskar Schindler," August 29, 1966, Bundesarchiv (Koblenz), Nachlaß Oskar Schindler, 1908–1974, Bestand 1493, No. 1, Band 22, No. 1, 2.

80. "Mietek Pemper to Oskar Schindler," October 10, 1966, Bundesarchiv (Koblenz), Nachlaß Oskar Schindler, 1908–1974, Bestand 1493, No. 1, Band 24, 1; "Oskar Schindler to Dr. Moshe Bejski," January 12, 1967, Bundesarchiv (Koblenz), Nachlaß Oskar Schindler 1908–1974, Bestand 1493, No. 1, Band 22, 1 page; Joseph Borkin, The Crime and Punishment of I. G. Farben (New York: Simon and Schuster, 1979), 54–55, 172–198, 202–203.

81. "Oskar Schindler to Leopold Page," April 14, 1967, Bundesarchiv (Koblenz), Nachlaß Oskar Schindler, 1908–1974, Bestand 1493, No. 1, Band 24, 1 page; "Martin A. Gosch to The Right Honorable Earl of Harewood," April 18, 1967, Bundesarchiv (Koblenz), Nachlaß Oskar Schindler, 1908–1974, Bestand 1493, No. 1, Band 28, 2 pages.

82. "Oskar Schindler to Martin A. Gosch," January 30, 1967, Bundesarchiv (Koblenz), Nachlaß Oskar Schindler, 1908–1974, Bestand 1493, No. 1, Band 23, 1; Schmitz, "Wie ein großzügiger Habenichts zur Ehrenrente kam," n.p.; "Graf Yorck von Wartenburg to Oskar Schindler," July 3, 1966, Bundesarchiv (Koblenz), Nachlaß Oskar Schindler, 1908–1974, Bestand 1493, No. 1, Band 24, 1 page; "Der Bundesminister der Finanzen to Oskar Schindler," II a/1-AF 2262-60/68, September 11, 1968, Bundesarchiv (Koblenz), Nachlaß Oskar Schindler, 1908–1974, Bestand 1493, No. 1, Band 22, 1 page.

83. "Izak Stern to Herrn Ge. Sekretär Honig," September 30, 1966," Bundesarchiv (Koblenz), Nachlaß Oskar Schindler, 1908–1974, Bestand 1493, No. 1, Band 21, 2 pages;

"Camille R. Honig to Oskar Schindler," October 10, 1966, Bundesarchiv (Koblenz), Nachlaß Oskar Schindler, 1908–1974, Bestand 1493, No. 1, Band 21, 2 pages.

84. Jewish Chronicle Reporter, "Martin Buber's Name 'Exploited,'" *Jewish Chronicle,* August 23, 1968, 18; "Oskar Schindler to Martin A. Gosch," January 30, 1967, Bundesarchiv (Koblenz), Nachlaß Oskar Schindler, 1908–1974, Bestand 1493, No. 1, Band 23, 1; "Moshe Bejski to Oskar Schindler," February 9, 1967, Bundesarchiv (Koblenz), Nachlaß Oskar Schindler, 1908–1974, Bestand 1493, No. 1, Band 22, 1.

85. "Oskar Schindler to Martin Gosch," March 6, 1967, Bundesarchiv (Koblenz), Nachlaß Oskar Schindler, 1908–1974, Bestand 1493, No. 1, Band 23, 1 page.

86. "Martin A. Gosch to Sir Keith Joseph," March 27, 1967, Bundesarchiv (Koblenz), Nachlaß Oskar Schindler, 1908–1974, Bestand 1493, No. 1, Band 21, 1 page; "Martin A. Gosch to Axel Springer," March 28, 1967, Bundesarchiv (Koblenz), Nachlaß Oskar Schindler, 1908–1974, Bestand 1493, No. 1, Band 21, 2 pages; "Martin A. Gosch to the Earl of Harewood," March 28, 1967, Bundesarchiv (Koblenz), Nachlaß Oskar Schindler, 1908–1974, Bestand 1493, No. 1, Band 21, 2 pages; "Martin A. Gosch to Camille Honig," March 27, 1967, Bundesarchiv (Koblenz), Nachlaß Oskar Schindler, 1908–1974, Bestand 1493, No. 1, Band 21, 1 page.

87. "Martin A. Gosch to Axel Springer," March 28, 1967, Bundesarchiv (Koblenz), Nachlaß Oskar Schindler, 1908–1974, Bestand 1493, No. 1, Band 21, 1; "Martin A. Gosch to The Very Reverend Stefan Schmidt, S.J.," March 28, 1967, Bundesarchiv (Koblenz), Nachlaß Oskar Schindler, 1908–1974, Bestand 1493, No. 1, Band 21, 2 pages.

88. "Camille Honig to Dr. Moshe Bejski and Jakob Sternberg," March 27, 1966, Bundesarchiv (Koblenz), Nachlaß Oskar Schindler, 1908–1974, Bestand 1493, No. 1, Band 21, 1 page.

89. "Oskar Schindler to Dr. Moshe Bejski," April 14, 1967, Bundesarchiv (Koblenz), Nachlaß Oskar Schindler, 1908–1974, Bestand 1493, No. 1, Band 22, 1 page; "Oskar Schindler to Leopold Page," April 14, 1967, Bundesarchiv (Koblenz), Nachlaß Oskar Schindler, 1908–1974, Bestand 1493, No. 1, Band 24, 1 page; "J. Ruter to David M. Crowe," December 22, 2003, 1 page; "Martin A. Gosch to The Right Honorable Earl of Harewood," April 18, 1967, Bundesarchiv (Koblenz), Nachlaß Oskar Schindler, 1908–1974, Bestand 1493, No. 1, Band 28, 2 pages.

90. "Camille Honig to Oskar Schindler," April 19, 1967, Bundesarchiv (Koblenz), Nachlaß Oskar Schindler, 1908–1974, Bestand 1493, No. 1, Band 21, 8 pages.

91. "Martin A. Gosch to Oskar Schindler," April 19, 1967, Bundesarchiv (Koblenz), Nachlaß Oskar Schindler, 1908–1974, Bestand 1493, No. 1, Band 21, 2 pages.

92. "Dr. Moshe A. Bejski to Leopold Page," November 29, 1967, Bundesarchiv (Koblenz), Nachlaß Oskar Schindler, 1908–1974, Bestand 1493, No. 1, Band 22, 5 pages.

93. "Martin A. Gosch to Dr. Irene Weinrowsky," January 19, 1967, Bundesarchiv (Koblenz), Nachlaß Oskar Schindler, 1908–1974, Bestand 1493, No. 1, Band 28, 1; "Oskar Schindler to Dr. Moshe Bejski," March 3, 1968, Bundesarchiv (Koblenz), Nachlaß Oskar Schindler, 1908–1974, Bestand 1493, No. 1, Band 22, 1 page; "Martin A. Gosch to Oskar Schindler," March 3, 1968, Nachlaß Oskar Schindler, 1908–1974, Bestand 1493, No. 1, Band 30, 1; "Moshe A. Bejski to Oskar Schindler," January 17, 1974, Bundesarchiv (Koblenz), Nachlaß Oskar Schindler, 1908–1974, Bestand 1493, Band 1, No. 22, 1.

94. "Oskar Schindler to Dr. Moshe Bejski," December 10, 1967, Bundesarchiv (Koblenz), Nachlaß Oskar Schindler, 1908–1974, Bestand 1493, No. 1, Band 22, 1–2; Jewish Chronicle Reporter, "Martin Buber's Name 'Exploited,'" *Jewish Chronicle,* August 23, 1968, 18.

95. "Oskar Schindler to Dr. Moshe Bejski," February 16, 1968, Bundesarchiv (Koblenz), Nachlaß Oskar Schindler, 1908–1974, Bestand 1493, No. 1, Band 22, 1 page; "Oskar Schindler to Leopold Page," February 24, 1968, Bundesarchiv (Koblenz), Nach-

laß Oskar Schindler, 1908–1974, Bestand 1493, No. 1, Band 24, 2 pages; "Oskar Schindler to Walter Pollack," April 6, 1968, Bundesarchiv (Koblenz), Nachlaß Oskar Schindler, 1908–1974, Bestand 1493, No.1, Band 24, 1; "Oskar Schindler to Martin Gosch," April 8, 1968, Bundesarchiv (Koblenz), Nachlaß Oskar Schindler, 1908–1974, Bestand 1493, No. 1, Band 23, 1 page; "Martin A. Gosch to Oskar Schindler," April 18, 1968, Bundesarchiv (Koblenz), Nachlaß Oskar Schindler, 1908–1974, Bestand 1493, No. 1, Band 23, 1; "Leopold Page to Oskar Schindler," April 20, 1968, Bundesarchiv (Koblenz), Nachlaß Oskar Schindler, 1908–1974, Bestand 1493, No. 1, Band 4, 2 pages; "Oskar Schindler to Leopold Page," June 10, 1968, Bundesarchiv (Koblenz), Nachlaß Oskar Schindler, 1908–1974, Bestand 1493, No. 1, Band 24, 1; "Oskar Schindler to Dr. Moshe Bejski," June 10, 1968, Bundesarchiv (Koblenz), Nachlaß Oskar Schindler, 1908–1974, Bestand 1493, No. 1, Band 22, 1; "Dr. Moshe Bejski to Oskar Schindler," July 4, 1968, Bundesarchiv (Koblenz), Nachlaß Oskar Schindler, 1908–1974, Bestand 1493, No. 1, Band 22, 2 pages.

96. "Päpstlicher Orden für Rettung von Juden," *Frankfurter Allgemeine Zeitung,* October 25, 1968, 5; "Oskar Schindler to Walter Pollack," January 23, 1969, Bundesarchiv (Koblenz), Nachlaß Oskar Schindler, 1908–1974, Bestand 1493, No. 1, Band 24, 2 pages; "Oskar Schindler to Dr. Moshe Bejski," June 10, 1968, Bundesarchiv (Koblenz), Nachlaß Oskar Schindler, 1908–1974, Bestand 1493, No. 1, Band 22, 2.

97. Press Release, Oskar Schindler Survivors Fund, January 5, 1969, Bundesarchiv (Koblenz), Nachlaß Oskar Schindler, 1908–1974, Bestand 1493, No. 1, Band 4, 1–3; *"Leopold Page Address,"* January 5, 1969, Temple Beth Am, Los Angeles, California, Bundesarchiv (Koblenz), Nachlaß Oskar Schindler, 1908–1974, Bestand 1493, No. 1, Band 4, 2 pages; "Schindler Jews Remember Savior," January 6, 1969, *Los Angeles Herald Examiner,* A-3; Tom Tugend, "Holocaust Survivors Thank German Savior," *Jewish Heritage,* January 9, 1969, 1, 6.

98. Press Release, Oskar Schindler's Survivors Fund, January 5, 1969, 3–4; *"Mr. Oskar Schindler's Address,"* January 5, 1969, Temple Beth Am, Los Angeles, California, Bundesarchiv (Koblenz), Nachlaß Oskar Schindler, 1908–1974, Bestand 1493, No. 1, Band 30, 2 pages; "Schindler Jews Remember Savior," A-3; Tugend, "Holocaust Survivors Thank German Savior," 1, 6.

99. Dr. Dieter Trautwein," interview by the author, Frankfurt, Germany, December 17, 1998; Dieter Trautwein, *Oskar Schindler, . . . immer neue Geschichten: Begegnungen mit dem Retter von mehr als 1200 Juden* (Frankfurt: Societäts-Verlag, 2000), 16–28; "Oskar Schindler to Dr. Moshe Bejski," June 4, 1967, Bundesarchiv (Koblenz), Nachlaß Oskar Schindler, 1908–1974, Bestand 1493, No. 1, Band, 22, 1.

100. "Schindler to Bejski," June 10, 1968, BA(K), 1.

101. Trautwein, interview, May 25, 1999; "Oskar Schindler to Leopold Page," March 1, 1969, Bundesarchiv (Koblenz), Nachlaß Oskar Schindler, 1908–1974, Bestand 1493, No. 1, Band 2, 1, 2.

102. "Oskar Schindler to Dr. Mose Bejski," June 10, 1968, Bundesarchiv (Koblenz), Nachlaß Oskar Schindler, 1908–1974, Bestand 1493, No. 1, Band 22, 1.

Chapter 14

1. Chris Staehr and Tina Staehr, interview by the author, Stuttgart, Germany, October 22, 2000, and October 31–November 1, 2003.

2. "Dr. Lotte Schiffler to Oskar Schindler," June 22, 1970, Private Collection of Ami Staehr, Stuttgart, Germany.

3. Staehr and Staehr, interview, October 22, 2000.

4. Dieter Trautwein, interview by the author, Frankfurt, Germany, December 17, 1998.

----

5. "Lotte Schiffler to Oskar Schindler," August 4, 1970, Bundesarchiv (Koblenz), Nachlaß Oskar Schindler, 1908–1974, Bestand 1493, No. 1, Band 27, 1 page.

6. "Prof. Drs. Kleinsorg and Risemeyer to Dr. Heinrich Staehr," October 11, 1974, Bundesarchiv (Koblenz), Nachlaß Oskar Schindler, 1908–1974, Bestand 1493, No. 1, Band 8, 1; Oskar's favorite drink was "Doornkaat" schnaps. Staehr and Staehr, interview, October 22, 2000.

7. "Klara Sternberg to Ami Staehr," February 3, 1973, Bundesarchiv (Koblenz), Nachlaß Oskar Schindler, 1908–1974, Bestand 1493, No. 1, Band 27, 1–2.

8. Staehr and Staehr, interviews, October 22, 2000, and October 31–November 1, 2003.

9. "Janek (Jakob) Sternberg to Oskar Schindler," October 11, 1969, Bundesarchiv (Koblenz), Nachlaß Oskar Schiindler, 1908–1974, Bestand 1493, No. 1, Band 25, 1 page; "Lotte Schiffler to Oskar Schindler," April 23, 1970, Bundesarchiv (Koblenz), Nachlaß Oskar Schindler, 1908–1974, Bestand 1493, No. 1, Band 24, 1 page; "Lottie Schiffler to Oskar Schindler," August 17, 1973, Nachlaß Oskar Schindler, 1908–1974, Bestand 1493, No. 1, Band 22, 1 page.

10. Diary of Ami Staehr, Ami Staehr Collection, Stuttgart. The pages of Ami's diary are unnumbered; Staehr and Staehr, interviews, October 2, 2000, and October 31-November 1, 2003.

11. "Oskar Schindler Autopsy Report: Drs. H. Kleinsorg and Rosemeyer," Innere Abteilung St.-Bernard-Krankenhaus, Hildesheim, Germany," October 11, 1974, Bundesarchiv (Koblenz), Nachlaß Oskar Schindler, 1980–1974, Bestand 1493, No. 1, Band 8, 1.

12. "Oskar Schindler to Walter Pollack," June 22, 1970, Bundesarchiv (Koblenz), Nachlaß Oskar Schindler, 1908–1974, Bestand 1493, No. 1, Band 24, 1; "Oskar Schindler to Murray Pantirer," June 4, 1972, Bundesarchiv (Koblenz), Nachlaß Oskar Schindler, 1908–1974, Bestand 1493, No. 1, Band 24, 1 page; "Oskar Schindler to Leopold Page," June 4, 1972, Nachlaß Oskar Schindler, 1908–1974, Bestand 1493, No. 1, Band 24, 1 page; "Oskar Schindler to Leopold Page," October 30, 1972, Nachlaß Oskar Schindler, 1908–1974, Bestand 1493, No. 1, Band 24, 1 page; "Dr. Moshe Bejski to Oskar Schindler," August 27, 1973, Bundesarchiv (Koblenz), Nachlaß Oskar Schindler, 1908–1974, Bestand 1493, No. 1, Band 22, 1; Staehr and Staehr, interview, October 22, 2000.

13. "Dr. James C. Osborne, MD, FACP, to David M. Crowe," February 19, 2004.

14. "Oskar Schindler Autopsy Report," October 11, 1974, BA(K), 1; "Dr. James Osborne to David M. Crowe," February 19, 2004; Diary of Ami Staehr, December 8, 1973–January 14, 1974.

15. "Testimony of Oskar Schindler," Der Untersuchungsrichter bei dem Landgericht, 10 Vus 6/65, July 26, 1972, aus 206AR 2622/65 Z st, Zentrale Stelle der Landesjustizverwaltung, Ludwigsburg, 1.

16. "Lotte Schiffler to Oskar Schindler," October 31, 1971, Ami Staehr Collection, Stuttgart, Germany, 1 page; Claudia Keller and Stefan Braun, "Schindler's Koffer (5): Späte Orden und Ehren für den notleidenden Retter," Stuttgarter Zeitung, October 25, 1999, 5.

17. Irving Spiegel, "Jews Here Honor West German Who Rescued 1,400 in Nazi Era," New York Times, January 9, 1972, 24.

18. Murray Pantirer and Abraham Zuckerman, interview by the author, Union, New Jersey, August 3, 1999; "Felicia Kobylanski to Abraham Zuckerman and Murray Pantirer," July 26, 1999, 2 pages, private papers of Abraham Zuckerman; "Professor Menahen Ben-Sasson to Abraham Zuckerman," April 22, 1999, 2 pages, private papers of Abraham Zuckerman.

19. "Eliyahu Honig to Oskar Schindler," April 18, 1974, Bundesarchiv (Koblenz), Nachlaß Oskar Schindler, 1908–1974, Bestand 1493, No. 1, Band 23, 1 page.

20. Howard M. Sachar, *A History of Israel from the Rise of Zionism to Our Time*, 2d ed. (New York: Alfred A. Knopf, 1996), 755–756.

21. Golda Meir, *My Life* (New York: G. Putnam's Sons, 1975), 429.

22. Martin Gilbert, *Israel: A History* (New York: William Morrow and Company, 1998), 440–441.

23. "Gideon Hausner and Dr. Chaim Pazner, Yad Vashem, to Oskar Schindler," October 12, 1973, M 31/20, Yad Vashem Archives, 2 pages.

24. Trautwein, interview, December 17, 1998; "Dr. Moshe Bejski to Oskar Schindler," November 21, 1973, Bundesarchiv (Koblenz), Nachlaß Oskar Schindler, 1908–1974, Bestand 1493, No. 1, Band 22, 1; "Dr. Moshe Bejski to Annemarie Staehr," November 22, 1973, Bundesarchiv (Koblenz), Nachlaß Oskar Schindler, 1908–1974, Bestand 1493, No. 1, Band 22, 1; Meir, *My Life*, 453.

25. Trautwein, interviews, December 17, 1998, and May 25, 1999; "Dr. Lotte Schiffer to Oskar Schindler," March 20, 1970, Ami Staehr Collection, Stuttgart, Germany, 1; "Dr. Lotte Schiffler to Oskar Schindler," April 10, 1974, Ami Staehr Collection, Stuttgart, Germany, 1; "Bishop Walther Kampe to Oskar Schindler," August 1, 1974, Bundesarchiv (Koblenz), Nachlaß Oskar Schindler, 1908–1974, Bestand 1493, No. 1, Band 23, 1 page; Dieter Kittlauß, "Dr. Charlotte Schiffler (1909–1992): Stadtälteste von Frankfurt und Großmutter des Hedwig-Dransfeld-Hauses in Bendorf," http://www.wkutsche.de, 11 pages.

26. Trautwein, interview, December 17, 1998; "Klara Sternberg to Oskar Schindler," August 22, 1970, Ami Staehr Collection, 1 page; "Jakob Sternberg to Dr. Lotte Schiffler," September 29, 1972, Bundesarchiv (Koblenz), Nachlaß Oskar Schindler, 1908–1974, Bestand 1493, No. 1, Band 26, 2 pages.

27. Trautwein, interviews, December 17, 1998, and May 25, 1999.

28. Dr. Moshe Bejski, interview by the author, Tel Aviv, Israel, May 17, 1999.

29. Bejski, interview, May 17, 1999; "Dr. Lotte Schiffler to Oskar Schindler," December 22, 1970, Ami Staehr Collection, Stuttgart, Germany; "Erhard Knechtel to David M. Crowe," Wiesbaden, Germany, May 13, 2000, 3 pages.

30. "Jakob Sternberg to Oskar Schindler," December 19, 1972, Bundesarchiv (Koblenz), Nachlaß Oskar Schindler, 1908–1974, Bestand 1493, No. 1, Band 23, 1 page.

31. "Lotte Schiffler to Oskar Schindler," May 17, 1974, Ami Staehr Collection, 1 page; "Lotte Schiffler to Oskar Schindler," April 10, 1974, Ami Staehr Collection, 1.

32. "Diary of Ami Staehr," Ami Staehr Collection; Staehr and Staehr, interview, October 22, 2000.

33. "Diary of Ami Staehr," Ami Staehr Collection; "Dr. Lotte Schiffler to Ami Staehr," August 24, 1974, Bundesarchiv (Koblenz), Nachlaß Oskar Schindler, 1908–1974, Bestand 1493, No. 1, Band 26, 1 page; "Dr. James C. Osborne to David M. Crowe," February 19, 2004, 2.

34. Ami Staehr to Dr. Moshe Bejski and Mrs. Dr. Stern," October 7, 1974, Bundesarchiv (Koblenz), Nachlaß Oskar Schindler, 1908–1874, Bestand 1493, No. 1, Band 28, 2 pages.

35. "Prof. Drs. Kleinsorg and Risemeyer to Dr. Heinrich Staehr," October 11, 1974, Bundesarchiv (Koblenz), Nachlaß Oskar Schindler, 1908–1974, Bestand 1493, No. 1, Band 8, 2 pages.

36. "Diary of Ami Staehr," Ami Staehr Collection; "Ami Staehr to Traude Ferrari," December 12, 1974, Ami Staehr Collection, 1.

37. "Ami Staehr to Dr. Moshe Bejski," November 9, 1974, Bundesarchiv (Koblenz), Nachlaß Oskar Schindler, 1908–1974, Bestand 1493, No. 1, Band 22, 1–2.

38. "Ami Staehr to Traude Ferrari," December 12, 1974, 1–2; Staehr and Staehr, interviews, October 22, 2000, and October 31-November 1, 2003.

39. Staehr and Staehr, interviews, October 22, 2000, and October 31-November 1, 2003.

40. "Ami Staehr to Traude Ferrari," December 12, 1974, 2.

41. Bejski, interview, May 17, 1999; Trautwein, interview, May 25, 1999.

42. Bejski, interview, May 17, 1999; Ernie Meyer, "Saving Jewish Lives Was 'a Moral Obligation,'" *Jerusalem Post,* October 29, 1974, n.p.; Dieter Trautwein, *Oskar Schindler . . . immer neue Geschichten: Begegnungen mit dem Retter von mehr als 1200 Juden* (Frankfurt: Societäts Verlag, 2000), 86–88.

43. "Sermon of Dr. Dieter Trautwein," October 16, 1974, 1. Private papers of Dr. Dieter Trautwein. There is also a copy of his sermon in his *Oskar Schindler,* 88–90.

44. "Sermon of Dr. Dieter Trautwein," October 16, 1974.

45. Ibid.

46. Ibid.

47. "Speech by Richard Rechen for Oskar's Schindler Requiem Mass," October 19, 1974, Frankfurt Germany, Private Papers of Kurt Klein. It can also be found in Dr. Dieter Trautwein's *Oskar Schindler . . . immer neue Geschichten,* 91.

48. "Diary of Ami Staehr"; Ami Staehr said that it cost over DM 20,000 ($8,333) to ship his body to Israel, but Helmut Schmitz said that the cost was DM 10,000 ($4,166). The difference might have involved the costs of the caskets, embalming, and other funeral costs. The State of Hesse paid for its portion of the costs out of lottery proceeds. "Ami Staehr to Traude Ferrari," December 12, 1974, BA(K), 1; Helmut Schmitz, "Wie ein großzügiger Habenichts zur Ehrenrente kam," *Süddeutsche Zeitung,* March 1, 1994, 3.

49. "Ami Staehr to Traude Ferrari," December 12, 1974, BA(K), 1; Bejski, interview, May 17, 1999; Trautwein, *Oskar Schindler,* 109.

50. Bejski, interview, May 17, 1999.

51. Joseph Waksman, "It is a Mitzvah (Commandment) to Accompany Him on His Last Journey—Even in a Church," *Ha'aretz,* October 29, 1974, n.p.

52. Moshe Bejski, "Oskar Schindler and *Schindler's List,*" *Yad Vashem Studies,* vol. 24, ed. Aharon Weiss (Jerusalem: Yad Vashem, 1994), 345–346.

53. Bejski, "Oskar Schindler and *Schindler's List,*" 346–347.

54. Ibid., 347–348.

55. "Ami Staehr to Traude Ferrari," December 12, 1974, 1–2.

56. The original inscription on the gravestone was done in copper which was stolen by thieves, which had nothing to do with Schindler. This was later replaced with a new tombstone top with black lettering. Dr. Mordecai Paldiel, interview by the author, Yad Vashem, Jerusalem, Israel, May 12, 1999.

57. *"Vollmacht Emilie Schindler,"* January 22, 1976, Lastenausgleicharchiv (Bayreuth), 306 2230 D (OS), 1 page; Ausgleichsamt 55.31: *Erfüllungsübersicht*: Oskar Schindler, June 21, 1976, Lastenausgleicharchiv (Bayreuth), 403333, 1 page.

58. "Reinhard Albrecht to Dr. Moshe Bejski," July 21, 1975, Bundesarchiv (Koblenz), Nachlaß Oskar Schindler, 1908–1975, Bestand 1493, No. 1, Band 18, 1–5; *"Die Juden nennen Ihn 'Vater Courage,'* Private Papers of Dr. Dieter Trautwein, Frankfurt, Germany, 12 pages, hereafter referred to as "Script for *Vater Courage,* Trautwein Papers"; Dr. Trautwein also discusses the production of the documentary in some depth in his *Oskar Schindler,* 111–121.

59. "Dr. Lotte Schiffler to Ami Staehr," March 14, 1975, Bundesarchiv (Koblenz), Nachlaß Oskar Schindler, 1908–1974, Bestand 1493, No. 1, Band 18, 1 page.

60. "Albrecht to Bejski," July 21, 1975, BA(K), 3–5.

61. Trautwein, *Oskar Schindler,* 111–113; script for *Vater Courage,* Trautwein Papers.

62. Script for *Vater Courage,* Trautwein Papers, 1–8.

63. Ibid., 8–9.

64. Ibid., 10–12.

65. "Poldek Pfefferberg," *Lest We Forget,* http://www.oskarschindler.com/19.htm, 2; Ian Freer, *The Complete Spielberg* (London: Virgin Publishing Ltd., 2001), 223.

66. "Noah's Ark of Oskar Schindler," *Ma'arev* (Israel), November 5, 1982, 21.

67. Joseph McBride, *Steven Spielberg: A Biography* (New York: Simon & Schuster, 1997), 424–425; "Thomas Keneally to David M. Crowe," February 2, 2004; "Poldek Pfefferberg, *Lest We Forget,* 2; Freer, *Spielberg,* 223–224.

68. Ackermann Gemeinde Hessen, *Zur Erinnerung an Oskar Schindler dem unvergeßlichen Lebensretter 1200 verfolgter Juden: Dokumentation der Gedenkstunden zum 10.Todestag am 14. Oktober 1984 in Frankfurt am Main* (Frankfurt: Geschäftsstelle der Ackermann-Gemeinde Diözese Limburg, 1985), 1–52.

69. Ackermann Gemeinde Hessen, *Zur Erinnerung an Oskar Schindler,* 4–9.

70. Ibid., 11–18.

71. Ibid., 20–23.

72. Erika Rosenberg, ed. *Ich, Emilie Schindler: Erinnerungen einer Unbeugsamen* (Munich; F. A. Herbig, 2001), 162.

73. "Bernard Scheuer to Emilie Schindler," June 12, 1983, in Rosenberg, *Ich, Emilie Schindler,* 163–165.

74. Ibid., September 16, 1983, 166.

75. Christoph Elflein, "Schindlers Last: Die Witwe des Judenretters ging beim Kinoerfolg leer aus. Ihre Erbin will nun Millionen von Universal," *Focus,* No. 23, 2002, 58.

76. "Ami Staehr to Traude Ferrari," May 30, 1985, Ami Staehr Collection, Stuttgart, Germany, 1 page.

77. "Traude Ferrari to Ami Staehr," June 30, 1985, Ami Staehr Collection, Stuttgart, Germany, 1 page.

78. Jürgen Dahlkamp, "Die letzte Gefährtin," *Der Spiegel,* No. 43, 1999, 116.

79. Staehr and Staehr, interviews, October 20, 2000, and October 31-November 1, 2003.

80. Terrence Rafferty, "Polanski and the Landscape of Aloneness," *New York Times,* January 26, 2003, Section 2, 1; McBride, *Steven Spielberg,* 426–427; Freer, *Spielberg,* 223–224.

81. John Baxter, *Steven Spielberg: The Unauthorized Biography* (London: HarperCollins, 1996), 392–393; Bernard Weinraub, "For Spielberg, an Anniversary Full of Urgency," *New York Times,* March 9, 2004, B1, B4.

82. Weinraub, "For Spielberg," B1, B4; Daisy Miller, interview by the author, Survivors of the Shoah Visual History Foundation, Universal Studios, Los Angeles, California, March 28, 2000; Stryk Thomas, interview by the author, Survivors of the Shoah Visual History Foundation, Universal Studios, Los Angeles, California, March 28, 2000; Peter Gumbel, "Making History: Steven Spielberg's Oral History of the Holocaust Survivors Has Videotaped 50,000 Interviews. Now Comes the Hard Part," *Wall Street Journal,* March 22, 1999, R9; Ralph Blumenthal, "To Point, Click and Never Forget," *New York Times,* January 13, 2001, A17, A22.

83. Corinna Honan, "Interview with Emilie Schindler," *Daily Mail* (London), December 24, 1993, 22–23; Yoav Limor, "Schindler's List: The Version that Spielberg Did Not Know," *Ma'ariv,* December 28, 1993, 4–5.

84. Honan, "Emilie Schindler," 22–23.

85. Ibid., 25; Christoph Stopka, "Ich bin Frau Schindler," *Bunte* (1994), 23.

86. Katherine Ellison, *Times-Picayune* (New Orleans), February 6, 1994, A16.

87. Stopka, "Ich bin Frau Schindler," 24.

88. Ibid., 23–24.

89. Emilie Schindler, *Where Light and Shadow Meet,* trans. Dolores M. Koch (New York: W. W. Norton, 1997), 143.

90. Ibid., 142.

91. Ibid., 144–145.

92. Ibid., 144.

93. Ibid., 146–147.

94. Ibid., 147–151.

95. Ibid., 155–158.

96. "Memorial Service to Oskar Schindler," August 3, 1993, Yad Vashem Archives, 2 pages. Later, a much more elegant monument was erected to Oskar in a park just across the street from his boyhood home; *Oskar Schindler: Retter und Lebemann,* ZDF Mainz, 1994.

97. Staehr and Staehr, interviews, October 22, 2000, and October 31-November 1, 2003.

98. Ibid.

99. Ibid.

100. Claudia Keller and Stefan Braun, interview by the author, Berlin, Germany, January 13, 2000, and November 1, 2003; Staehr and Staehr, interviews, October 22, 1999, and October 31-November 1, 2003.

101. Staehr and Staehr, interviews, October 22, 2000, and October 31-November 1, 2003; Claudia Keller and Stefan Braun, *Schindlers Koffer: Berichte aus dem Leben eines Lebensretters* (Stuttgart: Stuttgarter Zeitung, 1999), 1–77.

102. Ingrid Eißele, "Schindlers Liste gehört mir," *Stern* 43 (1999): 19; Jürgen Dahlkamp, *Der Spiegel* 43 (1999): 116–117; Staehr and Staehr, interviews, October 22, 2000, and October 31-November 1, 2003.

103. Staehr and Staehr, interviews, October 22, 1999, and October 31-November 1, 2003.

104. Ibid.

105. Ibid.; Keller and Braun, interview, November 1, 2003.

106. Landgericht Stuttgart *Beschluß,* "In dem Verfahren, Emilie Schindler gegen Christian Staehr und Fa. Stuttgarter Verlagsgesellschaft Eberle GmbH & Co.," November 11, 1999, 3 pages, Ami Staehr Collection, Stuttgart, Germany; "Dr. Jur. Tilo. Bodendorf to Christian Staehr," December 21, 1999, 2 pages, Ami Staehr Collection; "Witwe von Oskar Schindler klagt zum zweiten Mai-Streit um Ansprüche aus Urheberrecht," April 25, 2001, *Stuttgarter Zeitung,* http://www.stuttgarter-zeitung.de, 1 page.

107. "Witwe von Oskar Schindler klagt zum zweiten Mai-Streit um Ansprüche aus Urheberrecht," 1–2; "Witwe hat wenig Aussicht auf Schadenersatz-Richter: Zeitung hat nicht schuldhaft gehandelt," April 27, 2004, 1–2, http://www.stuttgarter-zeitung.de; "Streit und Schindlers Koffer beigelegt: Witwe soll 25,000 Mark erhalten," *Frankfurter Allgemeine Zeitung,* June 27, 2001, 9; Wulf Reimer, "Vergleich für Schindlers Koffer," *Süddeutsche Zeitung,* April 28, 2001, 12.

108. "David M. Crowe to Dr. Uwe Vorkötter," May 7, 2001; "Dr. Uwe Vorkötter to David M. Crowe," May 8, 1002; "Witwe hat wenig Aussicht auf Schadenersatz," *Sttutgarter Zeitung,* April 27, 2001, 2; Elias Zviklich, interview by the author, Buenos Aires, Argentina, May 21, 2001; "Streit um Schindlers Koffer beigelegt," 9; "Einigung über Nachlaß-Dokumente," *Süddeutsche Zeitung,* June 20, 2001, 20; "Streit um Schindlers Koffer beigelegt," *Frankfurter Allgemeine Zeitung,* June 27, 2001, 9.

109. Monika Caro, Ilse Chwat, and Ilse Wartensleben, interview by the author, Buenos Aires, Argentina, May 18, 2001.

110. Emilie Schindler, interview by the author, Buenos Aires, Argentina, May 22, 2001.

111. Dr. Alfredo May, interview by the author, Buenos Aires, Argentina, May 24, 2001.

112. Linda Diebel, "A Tale of Intrigue, Feuds, Hollywood Tycoons, Widow's Book Accuses Oskar Schindler of Being a 'Coward.' 'It Pains Me to See Emilie So Alone But That Is How Life Goes': The Complex Friendship of an Author and Schindler's Widow," *Toronto Star,* July 8, 2001, NEO1.

113. Uta Rasche, "Schindlers lange Schatten: Das Leben seiner Frau blieb im Dunkeln," *Frankfurter Allgemeine Zeitung,* October 28, 1999, 67; "Die Frau in Schindlers Schatten," *Welt am Sonntag,* October 15, 2000, 36; "Die Stimme Emilie Schindlers," November 13, 2003, *Frankfurter Allgemeine Zeitung,* 59.

114. Diebel, "A Tale of Intrigue, Feuds, Hollywood Tycoons," NEO1.

115. Ibid.

116. Ibid.

117. Caro, Chwat, and Wartensleben, interview, May 18, 2001.

118. Diebel, "A Tale of Intrigue, Feuds, Hollywood Tycoons," NEO1; Caro, Chwat, and Wartensleben, interview, May 18, 2001.

119. Diebel, "A Tale of Intrigue, Feuds, Hollywood Tycoons," NEO1; Rosenberg, *Ich, Emilie Schindler,* 217–218.

120. Diebel, "A Tale of Intrigue, Feuds, Hollywood Tycoons," NEO1.

121. Rosenberg, *Ich, Oskar Schindler,* 221–222; Gernot Wolfram, "Reise zum späten Ruhm," *Frankfurter Allgemeine Zeitung,* July 13, 2001, 11.

122. Rosenberg, *Ich, Emilie Schindler,* 222–226; "Bavaria Offers Retirement Home to Schindler's Widow, Who Says She Wants to Return to Germany," July 16, 2001, Associated Press, Lexus Nexus, 1 page.

123. Derek Scully, "The Forgotten Schindler," *Irish Times,* July 28, 2001, 61; Kate Connolly, "Schindler's Widow Left to Die in Bitterness and Poverty," *Observer* (London), July 29, 2001, 3.

124. Dr. Eva Habel, interview by the author, Munich, Germany, October 27, 2003.

125. "Francisco Wichter to David M. Crowe," Buenos Aires, Argentina, July 27, 2001, 7 pages.

BIBLIOGRAPHY

Archives and Private Collections

AUSTRIA

Archiv der KZ-Gedenkstätte Mauthausen.

BELGIUM

Private papers of Margarete Kompan-Bazzanella, Trazegnies, Belgium.

CANADA

Herbert and Tobe Steinhouse Collection, Montreal.

CZECH REPUBLIC

Archiv Ministerstvo Vnitra (Prague).
Moravský zemský archiv Brno.
Státní Ústřední Archiv v Praze.
Zemský archiv Opava pobočka Olomouc.

GERMANY

Ami Staehr Collection, Stuttgart, Germany.
Berlin Documentation Center. Bundesarchiv (Berlin).
Bundesarchiv (Koblenz). Nachlaß Oskar Schindler, 1908–1974, Bestand N 1493.
Lastenausgleicharchiv (Bayreuth).
Private Papers of Dr. Dieter Trautwein, Frankfurt, Germany.
Zentrale Stelle der Landesjustizverwaltung (ZSL), Ludwigsburg, Germany.

ISRAEL

American Jewish Joint Distribution Committee Archives, Jerusalem.
Beit Lohamei Haghetaot (Ghetto Fighters' House), D. N. Western Galilee, Israel.
Private Collection of Dr. Moshe Bejski, Tel Aviv, Israel.
Private Collection of Esther Rechen, Haifa, Israel.
Yad Vashem, Jerusalem.

POLAND

Archiwum Głównej Komisji Badania Zbrodni Hitlerowskich w Polsce.
Archiwum Państwowe w Krakowkie, Kraków.

Muzeum Up Krakowskich Wieliczka.
Państwowe Muzeum Auschwitz-Birkenau w Oświęcimiu.
Państwowe Muzeum Gross-Rosen.

UNITED STATES
American Jewish Joint Distribution Committee. New York.
Archives of the Academy of Motion Pictures, Arts and Sciences, Beverly Hills, California.
Fortunoff Archives, Yale University, New Haven, Connecticut.
National Archives of the United States II. College Park, Maryland.
Private Collection of David M. Crowe, Greensboro, North Carolina.
Private Collection of Sol Urbach, Delray Beach, Florida.
Private Collection of Dr. Majorie Zerin, Westlake, California.
Private Papers of Kurt Klein, Scottsdale, Arizona.
Private Papers of Abraham Zuckerman, Union, New Jersey.
James P. Rice Collection, San Francisco and Washington, D.C.
United States Holocaust Memorial Museum, Washington, D.C.
The Papers of Delbert Mann, Special Collections Library, Vanderbilt University, Nashville,
    Tennessee.

Interviews

Aleman, Roberto. Buenos Aires, Argentina, May 21, 2001.
Bau, Hadasah. Winnipeg, Canada, November 15, 2000.
Bejski, Dr. Moshe. Tel Aviv, Israel, May 17, 2000.
Blum, Harry. Miami Beach, Florida, April 27, 2001.
Borak, Dr. Mečislav. Ostrava, Czech Republic, September 22, 2000.
Caro, Monika. Buenos Aires, Argentina, May 18, 21, 2001.
Chwat, Ilse. Buenos Aires, Argentina, May 18, 22, 2001.
Feder, Theodore D. (Ted). New York, New York, April 24, 1997.
Finder, Murray. Delray Beach, Florida, March 19, 2000.
Finder, Rena Ferber. Boca Raton, Florida, March 19, 2000.
Fikejz, Radoslav. Svitavy, Czech Republic, June 27, 1998.
Gruntová, Jitka. Březova nad Svitavou, Czech Republic, June 27, 1998.
Habel, Dr. Eva. Munich, Germany, October 27, 2003.
Keller, Claudia, and Stefan Braun. Berlin, Germany, January 13, 2000, and November 1,
    2003.
Petr Henzl, Brněnec, Czech Republic, June 29, 1998.
Karakulska, Niusia Bronisłwa. Kraków, Poland, August 8, 2000.
Klein, Kurt. Greensboro, North Carolina, January 11, 1998.
La Rocca, Graciela. San Vicente, Argentina, May 24, 2001.
Levinson-Page, Mila. Beverly Hills, California, December 2, 2001.
Leyson, Leon. Anaheim, California, March 29, 2000.
May, Dr. Alfredo. Buenos Aires, Argentina, May 24, 2001.
Miller, Daisy. Los Angeles, California, March 28, 2000.
Müller-Madej, Stella. Kraków, Poland, August 9–10, 2000.
Page, Leopold. Beverly Hills, California, April 3, 2000, and September 13, 2000.
Page, Ludmilla. Beverly Hills, California, November 28, 2001.
Paldiel, Dr. Mordecai. Yad Vashem, Jerusalem, Israel, May 12, 1999.
Pantirer, Murray. Union, New Jersey, August 3, 1999.
Pemper, Mietek. By Dr. Reich. Augsburg, Germany, October 26, 1996.
Pemper, Mietek. Augsburg, Germany, May 26, 1999, and January 17, 2000.
Rosner, Manci. Hallandale, Florida, March 21, 2000.

Schindler, Emilie. Buenos Aires, Argentina, May 22, 2001.
Staehr, Chris, and Tina Staehr. Stuttgart, Germany, October 22, 2000, and October 31-November 1, 2003.
Sternlicht Rosenzweig, Helen. Boca Raton, Florida, March 20, 2000.
Steinhouse, Tobe. Montreal, Canada, February 12, 2004.
Thomas, Stryk. Los Angeles, California, March 28, 2000.
Trautwein, Dieter, and Ursula Trautwein. Frankfurt, Germany, May 25, 1999, and January 18, 2000.
Urbach, Sol. Flemington, New Jersey, March 19, 2000, and July 15, 2002.
Urbach, Sol. Delray Beach, Florida, April 13, 1999, February 15, 2000, and March 21, 2003.
Wartensleben, Ilse. Buenos Aires, Argentina, May 18, 22, 2001.
Wichter, Francisco. Buenos Aires, Argentina, May 17, 22, 2001.
Zotciak, Jaroslav. Kraków, Poland, August 7, 2000.
Zuckerman, Abraham. Union, New Jersey, August 3, 1999.
Zviklich, Elias. Buenos Aires, Argentina, May 21, 2001.

Correspondence

"David M. Crowe to Dr. Uwe Vorkötter." May 7, 2001.
"Radoslav Fikejz to David Crowe." March 27, 2000.
"Robert J. Fiore to David M. Crowe." March 7, 2000.
"Robert J. Fiore to David M. Crowe." August 13, 2003.
"Robert J. Fiore to David M. Crowe." February 10, 2004.
"Alexander Görbing, Walter Bau-AG," to David M. Crowe." March 31, 2003.
"Harald Hutterberger *(Republik Österreich, Bundesministerium für Inneres)* to David M. Crowe." October 20, 2000.
"Ilona Klimova to David M. Crowe." September 23, 2000.
"Erhard Knechtel to David M. Crowe." May 13, 2000.
"Dr. James C. Osborne, MD, FACP, to David M. Crowe." February 19, 2004.
"Dr. Mordecai Paldiel to David M. Crowe." January 19, 20, 21, 2004.
"Bozenna Rotman to David Crowe." August 18, 2002.
"Edith Schlegl to David M. Crowe." November 17, 1999.
"Edith Schlegl to David M. Crowe." September 26, 2000.
"Ronald Smelser to David M. Crowe." July 7, 2000.
"Tina Staehr to David Crowe" (report of a conversation with Edith Schegl). October 23, 2000.
"Dr. Uwe Vorkötter to David M. Crowe." May 8, 2002.
"Francisco Wichter to David M. Crowe." July 27, 2001.
"Dr. Frank Wittendorfer, Head of the Siemens Archives, Munich, Germany, to David Crowe," March 21, 2003.

Diaries and Memoirs

Arendt, Hannah. *Eichmann in Jerusalem: A Report on the Banality of Evil.* New York: Penguin Books, 1977.
Bau, Joseph. *Dear God, Have You Ever Gone Hungry?* Translated by Shlomo "Sam" Yurman. New York: Arcade Publishing, 1998.
Bejski, Dr. Moshe. "Notes on the Banquet in Honor of Oskar Schindler." May 2, 1962, Tel Aviv, Israel (in Hebrew and English).
Bieberstein, Aleksander. *Zagłada Żydów w Krakowie.* Kraków: Wydawnictwo Literackie, 1985.

"The Confessions of Mr. X." Budapest, November 1943, Bundesarchiv (Koblenz), Nachlaß Oskar Schindler, 1908–1974.

Hans Frank's Diary. Edited by Stanisław Piotrowski. Warszawa: Państwowe Wydanictwo Naukowe, 1961.

Frank, Hans. *Dziennik Hansa Franka.* 2 Volumes. Warsaw: Wydawnictwo Prawnicze, 1956.

Frank, Hans. *Im Angesicht des Galgens. Deutung Hitlers und seiner Zeit aufgrund eigener Erlebnisse und Erkenntnisse.* Edited by O. Schloffer. Munich: Neuhaus, 1953.

Frank, Niklas. *In the Shadow of the Third Reich.* Translated by Arthur S. Wensinger, with Carole Clew-Hoey. New York: Alfred A. Knopf, 1991.

Graf, Malvina. *The Kraków Ghetto and the Płaszów Camp Remembered.* Tallahassee: University of Florida Press, 1989.

Hausner, Gideon. *Justice in Jerusalem.* New York: Holocaust Library, 1968.

Höss, Rudolph. *Death Dealer: The Memoirs of the SS Kommandant at Auschwitz.* Edited by Steven Paskuly and translated by Andrew Pollinger. New York: Da Capo Press, 1996.

Kasztner, Dr. Reszőe. *Der Bericht des jüdischen Rettungskomitees aus Budapest: 1942–1945.* Budapest: Private manuscript published by the author, 1946.

Kessler, Matthias. *Ich muß doch meinen Vater lieben, oder? Die Lebensgeschichte von Monika Göth, Tochter des KZ-Kommandanten aus "Schindlers Liste."* Frankfurt am Main: Eichborn, 2002.

Klein, Gerda Weissmann. *All But My Life: A Memoir.* New York: Hill and Wang, 1995.

Klein, Gerda Weissmann, and Kurt Klein. *The Hours After: Letters of Love and Longing in War's Aftermath.* New York: St. Martin's Press, 2000.

Koch, Howard. *As Time Goes By: Memoirs of a Writer.* New York: Harcourt Brace Jovanovich, 1979.

The Labyrinth: Memoirs of Walter Schellenberg, Hitler's Chief of Counterintelligence. Translated by Louis Hagen. New York: Da Capo Press, 2000.

Levi, Primo. *The Drowned and the Saved.* Translated by Raymond Rosenthal. New York: Summit Books, 1988.

_____. *Survival in Auschwitz: The Nazi Assault on Humanity.* Translated by Stuart Woolf. New York: Collier Books, 1961.

Logocka, Roma. *The Girl in the Red Coat.* Translated by Margot Bettauer Dembo. New York: St. Martin's Press, 2002.

Madritsch, Julius. *Menschen in Not! Meine Erlebnisse in den Jahren 1940 bis 1944 als Unternehmer im damaligen Generalgouvernement.* Vienna: V. Roth, 1962.

Meir, Golda. *My Life.* New York: G. P. Putnam's Sons, 1975.

The Memoirs of Field-Marshal Wilhelm Keitel. Edited by Walter Gorlitz. New York: Cooper Square Press, 2000.

Moravec, Frantisek. *Master of Spies: The Memoirs of General Frantisek Moravec.* Garden City, N.Y.: Doubleday & Company, 1975.

Müller-Madej, Stella. *A Girl from Schindler's List.* London: Polish Cultural Foundation, 1997.

Novac, Ana. *The Beautiful Days of My Youth: My Six Months in Auschwitz and Plaszow.* Translated by George L. Newman. New York: Henry Holt and Company, 1997.

"Oskar Schindler Financial Report 1945" (in German). July 1945, Yad Vashem Archives, 01/164.

Palowski, Franciszek. *The Making of Schindler's List: Behind the Scenes of an Epic Film.* Translated by Anna and Robert G. Ware. Secaucus, N.J.: Birch Lane Press, 1998.

Pankiewicz, Tadeusz. *Apteka w Getcie Krakowskim.* Kraków: Wydawnictwo Literackie, 1995.

Piotrowski, Stanisław, ed. *Dziennik Hansa Frank.* Warszawa: Wydawnictwo Prawnicze, 1956.

_____. *Hans Frank's Diary.* Warszawa: Państwowe Wydawnictwo Naukowe, 1961.

Rosenberg, Erika, ed. *Ich, Emilie Schindler: Errinerungen einer Unbeugsamen.* München: F.A. Herbig Verlagsbuchhandlung GmbH, 2001.

Schindler, Emilie with Erika Rosenberg. *Where Light and Shadow Meet.* Translated by Dolores M. Koch. New York: W. W. Norton & Company, 1997.

Speer, Albert. *The Slave State: Heinrich Himmler's Masterplan for SS Supremacy.* Translated by Joachim Neugroschel. London: Weidenfeld and Nicolson, 1981.

Sprecher, Drexel A. *Inside the Nuremberg Trial: A Prosecutor's Comprehensive Account.* 2 Volumes. Lanham, Md.: University Press of America, 1999.

Taylor, Telford. *The Anatomy of the Nuremberg Trials: A Personal Memoir.* Boston: Little, Brown and Company, 1992.

Thomas, Georg. *Geschichte der deutschen Wehr-und Rüstungswirtschaft (1918–1943/45).* Edited by Wolfgang Birkenfeld. Boppard am Rhein: Harald Boldt Verlag, 1966.

Trautwein, Dieter. *Oskar Schindler, . . . immer neue Geschichten: Begegnungen mit dem Retter von mehr als 1200 Juden.* Frankfurt: Societäts-Verlag, 2000.

Von Hassell, Ulrich. *The Von Hassell Diaries, 1938–1944.* New York: Doubleday, 1947.

Von Papen, Franz. *Memoirs.* Translated by Brian Connell. New York: E. P. Dutton & Company, 1953.

The Warsaw Diary of Adam Czerniakow: Prelude to Doom. Edited by Raul Hilberg, Stanislaw Staron, and Josef Kermisz. Translated by Stanislaw Staron and the staff of Yad Vashem. New York: Stein and Day, 1979.

Weissberg, Alex. *Desperate Mission: Joel Brand's Story as Told by Alex Weissberg.* Translated by Constantine FitzGibbon and Andrew Foster-Melliar. New York: Criterion Books, 1958.

Wichter, Francisco. *Undécimo Mandamiento: Testimonio del sobreviviente argentino de la lista de Schindler.* Buenos Aires: Grupo Editorial Agora, 1998.

Zuckerman, Abraham. *A Voice in the Chorus: Memories of a Teenager Saved by Schindler.* Stamford, Conn.: Longmeadow Press, 1991.

Documentary Collections

Ackermann Gemeinde Hessen. *Zur Erinnerung an Oskar Schindler dem unvergeßlichen Lebensretter 1200 verfolgter Juden: Dokumentation der Gedenkstunde zum 10. Todestag am 14. Oktober 1984 in Frankfurt am Main.* Frankfurt am Main: Ackermann-Gemeinde Hessen, 1985.

Apenszlak, Jacob, Jacob Kenner, Dr. Isaac Lewin, and Dr. Moses Polakiewicz, eds. *The Black Book of Polish Jewry: An Account of the Martyrdom of Polish Jews Under the Nazi Occupation.* New York: The American Federation for Polish Jews, 1943.

Arad, Yitzhak, Shmuel Krakowski, and Shmuel Spector, eds. *The Einsatzgruppen Reports.* New York: The Holocaust Library, 1989.

The Auschwitz-Birkenau State Museum. *KL Auschwitz Seen by the SS: Rudolf Höss, Pery Broad, Johann Paul Kremer.* Translated by Constantine Fitzgibbon, Krystyna Michalik, and Zbigniew Bezwiński. Oświęcim: The Auschwitz-Birkenau State Museum, 1997.

Borwicz, Michał M., Nella Rost, and Józef Wulf, eds. *Dokumenty Zbrodni i Męczeństwa.* Kraków: Wojewódzkiej Żdowskiej Komisji Historycznej w Krakowie, 1945.

The Buchenwald Report. Translated and edited by David A. Hackett. Boulder: Westview Press, 1995.

Czech, Danuta. *Auschwitz Chronicle, 1939–1945: From the Archives of the Auschwitz Memorial and the German Federal Archives.* New York: Henry Holt and Company, 1990.

Das Protokoll der Wannsee-Konferenz, January 20, 1942. Berlin: Haus der Wannsee-Konferenz, 2002.

Degras, Jane, ed. *Soviet Documents on Foreign Policy.* Vol. 3, *1933–1941.* New York: Octagon Books, 1978.

*Dienststelle der Schutzstaffel der NSDAP (SS-Obergruppenführer-SS Standartenführer).
Stand vom 30. Januar 1942. Herausgegeben von SS-Personalhauptamt* (SS Officers List
as of January 30 1942-SS Standartenführer to SS-Oberstgruppenführer: Assignments and
Decorations of the Senior SS Officer Corps). Atglen, Pa.: Schiffer Military History, 2000.

*Documents Concerning German-Polish Relations and the Outbreak of Hostilities between
Great Britain and Germany on September 3, 1939.* London: His Majesty's Stationery
Office, 1939.

Du Prel, Dr. Max Freiherr. *Das General Gouvernement.* Würzburg: Konrad Triltsch Verlag,
1942.

Kunicka-Wrzykowska, Magdalena. *Indeks imienny Więźniów obozu w Płaszowie.* Ministerstwo Sprawiećliowości, Archiwum Głównej Komisji Badania Zbrodni Hiterlowskich
w Polsce, Okręgowa Komisja Badania Zbrodni Przeciwko Narodowi Polskiemu-Instytut
Pamięci Narodowej w Krakowie. Kraków, Poland, n.d.

Mendelsohn, John and Donald S. Detwiler, eds. *The Holocaust.* Vol. 10, *The Einsatzgruppen or Murder Commandos.* New York: Garland Publishing, 1982.

Mendes-Flohr, Paul and Jehuda Reinharz, eds. *The Jew in the Modern World: A Documentary History.* 2d ed. Oxford: Oxford University Press, 1995.

Military Intelligence Service. *German Army Order of Battle: October 1942.* Mt. Ida, Ark.:
Lancer Militaria, n.d.

Noakes, Jeremy and Geoffrey Pridham, eds. *Nazism, 1919–1945: A History in Documents
and Eyewitness Accounts.* Vol. 2, *Foreign Policy, War and Racial Extermination.* New
York: Schocken Books, 1988.

Office of United States Chief of Counsel For Prosecution of Axis Criminality. *Nazi Conspiracy and Aggression,* Vols. 2, 4. Washington: United States Government Printing Office, 1946.

Office of United States Chief of Counsel for Prosecution of Axis Criminality, *Nazi Conspiracy and Aggression: Opinion and Judgement.* Washington: United States Government Printing Office, 1947.

Pogonowski, Iwo Cyprian. *Jews in Poland: A Documentary History.* New York: Hippocrene Books, 1993.

Proces Ludobójcy Amona Leopolda Goetha przed Najwyższym Trybunałem Narodowym.
Kraków: Centralna Żydowska Komisja Historyczna w Polsce, 1947.

Rosenberg, Erika, ed. *Ich, Oskar Schindler: Die persönlichen Aufzeichnungen, Briefe und
Dokumente.* Munchen: F.A. Herbig Verlagsbuchhandlung GmbH, 2000.

Slusser, Robert M. and Jan F. Triska, eds. *A Calendar of Soviet Treaties, 1917–1957.* Stanford: Stanford University Press, 1959.

Snyder, Louis L., ed. *Hitler's Third Reich: A Documentary History.* Chicago: Nelson-Hall,
1981.

State of Israel. Ministry of Justice. *The Trial of Adolf Eichmann: Record of Proceedings in the
District Court of Jerusalem.* Vol. 1. Jerusalem: Israel State Archives and Yad Vashem, 1992.

"Stern Report 1956." Yad Vashem Archives, 01/164.

The Stroop Report. Translated and annotated by Sybil Milton. New York: Pantheon Books,
1979.

Supreme Headquarters Allied Expeditionary Force, Evaluation and Dissemination Section, G-
2. *Basic Handbook: KL's (Konzentrationslager) Axis Concentration Camps and Detention
Centers Reported as Such in Europe.* Middlesex: World War II Investigator Limited, n.d.

*The Trial of German Major War Criminals: Proceedings of the International Military Tri-
bunal Sitting at Nuremberg Germany,* Part 20: *29 July, 1946 to 8 August, 1946.* London:
H.M. Attorney General by His Majesty's Stationery Office, 1949.

*Trial of War Criminals before the Nuernberg Military Tribunals under Control Council
Law No. 10 (Nuernberg October 1946-April 1949).* Vol. 12. Washington, D.C.: United
States Government Printing Office, 1951.

United States Department of State. *Documents on German Foreign Policy, 1918–1945*, Series D (1937–1945). Vol. 2, *Germany and Czechoslovakia, 1937–1938*. Washington, D.C.: United States Government Printing Office, 1949.

Articles

Armony, Paul. "Entrevista con la Sra. Emilie Schindler." *Toldot*, no. 12 (Aogost 2000): 15.

"Australians File US Suit on Nazi-era Forced Labor." Agence France Presse (April 14, 1999): 1.

Ball-Kaduri, Dr. Kurt Jakob. "Illegale Judenauswanderung aus Deutschland nach Palästina, 1939–1940. Plannung, Durchführung und internationale Zusammenhänge." In *Jahrbuch des Instituts für deutsche Geschichte* 4 (1975): n.p.

Barth, Dr. Reinhard Barth. "Volk League for Germandom Abroad." In Christian Zentner and Friedemann Bedürftig, eds., *The Encyclopedia of the Third Reich* (New York: Da Capo Press, 1997): 1003.

"Bavaria Offers Retirement Home to Schindler's Widow, Who Says She Wants to Return to Germany" (The Associated Press, July 16, 2001): 1.

Bejski, Moshe. "Oskar Schindler and *Schindler's List*." *Yad Vashem Studies*. Vol. 24. Edited by Aharon Weiss (1994): 317–348.

"Biographische Freakshow." *Frankfurter Allgemeine Zeitung* (August 5, 2002): 35.

Blumenthal, Ralph. "To Point, Click and Never Forget." *New York Times* (January 13, 2001): A17, A22.

Boyes, Roger. "Bonn Tackled on Hitler Slaves Cash." *The Times* (London, March 10, 1999): 1.

Brügel, J. W. "Die Aussiedlung der Deutschen aus der Tschechoslowakei." *Vierteljahreshefte für Zeitgeschichte* 8 (April 1960): 134–135.

Bryant, Chad. "Either German or Czech: Fixing Nationality in Bohemia and Moravia, 1939–1946. *Slavic Review* 61, no. 4 (Winter 2002): 683–706.

Cameron, James. "The Good German Schindler." *Daily Mail* (December 11, 1961): 8.

Caro, Juan C. Letter to the Editor. *The Jerusalem Post* (December 21, 1982): n.p.

Connolly, Kate. "Schindler's Widow Left to Die in Bitterness and Poverty." *Observer* (London, July 29, 2001): 3.

Cookson, Clive. "Hunger, Horror and Heroism." *Financial Times* (July 28/29, 2001), Weekend II.

Cuczka, Tony. "German Firms Announce Fund for Holocaust Claims." The Associated Press, (February 16, 1999): 1–2.

Dahlkamp, Jürgen. "Die letzte Gefährtin." *Der Spiegel* 43 (1999): 116–117.

Diebel, Linda. "A Tale of Intrigue, Feuds, Hollywood Tycoons, Widow's Book Accuses Oskar Schindler of Being a 'Coward.' 'It Pains Me to See Emilie So Alone But That Is How Life Goes'; The Complex Friendship of an Author and Schindler's Widow." (*Toronto Star*, July 8, 2001): NEO1.

Eibl, Ralf and Norbert Jessen. "Im Schatten Schindlers," *Die Welt* (February 22, 2000): 10.

"Einigung über Nachlaß-Dokumente." *Süddeutsche Zeitung* (June 20, 2001): 20.

Eißele, Ingrid. "Schindlers List gehört mir." *Stern* 43 (1999): 19.

Elflein, Christoph. "Schindlers Last: Die Witwe des Judenretters ging beim Kinoerfolg leer aus. Ihre Erbin will nun Millionen von Universal." *Focus*, no. 23 (2002): 58.

Ellison, Katherine. *Times-Picayune* (February 6, 1994): A16.

Faiola, Anthony. "Exiting Argentina by Bloodline." *Washington Post* (January 13, 2002): A17, A 20.

"Die Frau in Schindlers Schatten." *Welt am Sonntag* (October 15, 2000): 36.

"German Firms Agree to Fund Holocaust-era Victims." Jewish Telegraph Agency. *Jewish Bulletin of Northern California Online* (February 16, 1999): 1–2.

"Germany Unveils Holocaust Fund." *BBC News Online* (February 16, 1999): 1.

Glowa Komisja Badana Zbrodni Przecwko Narodowi Polskiemu Instytut Pamieci Narodowej Okregowa Komizja. *Pamięć i Sprawiedliwość* 38 (1995).

"Golden Party Badge." http://www.geocities.com/goldpartypin/ahaward.html: 1–2.

"The Good German Schindler." *Daily Mail* (London, December 11, 1961): 8.

Gorlinsky, Peter. "'Vater Courage' bliebt unvergessen-aber wie steht es mit 'Mutter Courage.'" *Argentinisches Tageblatt* (January 30, 1963): 2.

"Gosch Evades Poland's Fog and Bureaucrats." *Variety Weekly* (January 20, 1965): n.p.

Gruntová, Dr. Jitka. "Schindlerův Seznam Tentokrát Jinak. *Rovnost* (March 8, 1995): 9.

Gumbel, Peter. "Making History: Steven Spielberg's Oral History of the Holocaust survivors has videotaped 50,000 interviews. Now comes the hard part." *Wall Street Journal* (March 22, 1999): R9.

Gurdus, Natan. "Gregory Peck Odtworzy Postać Oskara Schindlera." *Nowiny I Kurier* (n.d.): n.p.

"In Memoriam, Kurt Klein, 1920–2002." *United States Holocaust Memorial Museum* 1, no. 1 (Summer 2002): 8.

Honan, Corinna. "Interview with Emilie Schindler." *Daily Mail* (London, December 24, 1993), 22–23.

"An Interview with Jon Blair." February 8, 1996. *Sony Pictures Classics*. http://www.sonypictures.com/classics/annefrank/misc/interview.html: 1.

"Jakob Sternberg to *Ha'aretz*." *Ha'aretz* (May 13, 1962): n.p.

Jewish Chronicle Reporter. "Martin Buber's Name 'Exploited.'" *Jewish Chronicle* (August 23, 1968): 18.

Jordan, Miriam. "As Prospects Dim in Argentina, Its Jews Hear the Call of Israel." *Wall Street Journal* (January 31, 2002): A1, A8.

"Die Juden schwingen sich in den Sattel." *Krakauer Zeitung* (September 18, 1943): 6.

"Jüdisches Parasitentum ohne Maske." *Krakauer Zeitung* (September 28, 1943): 5.

Kasari, Uri. "Real Heroes and Heroes with Makeup." *Ma'ariv* (January 7, 1965): n.p.

Keeler, Bob. "Schindler's Survivors: Five People Whose Experiences Contributed to 'Schindler's List' Came Together to Talk About their Lives and the Movie and About Horror and Survival." *New York Newsday* (March 23, 1994): B49.

Keller, Claudia, and Stefan Braun. "Schindler's Koffer (5): Späte Orden und Ehren für den Notleidenden Retter." *Stuttgarter Zeitung* (October 25, 1999): 5.

Kittlauß, Dieter. "Dr. Charlotte Schiffler (1909–1992): Stadtälteste von Frankfurt und Großmutter des Hedwig-Dransfeld-Hauses in Bendorf." http://www.wkutsche.de: 1–11.

Knight, Kathryn. "My Father Was the Nazi Officer Who Shot Jews for Fun." *Daily Mail on Sunday* (April 21, 2002): 30.

Kobielec, Aleksandra. *Außenlager des Konzentrationslagers Gross-Rosen Arbeitslager Brünnlitz*. Wałbrzych: Państwowe Muzeum Gross-Rosen, 1991.

———. *Filia Obozu Koncentracyjnego Gross-Rosen Arbeitslager Brünnlitz*. Wałbrzych: Państwowe Muzeum Gross-Rosen, 1991.

Kopecek, Herman. *"Zusammenarbeit and Spoluprace: Sudeten German-Czech Cooperation in Interwar Czechoslovakia."* In Nancy M. Wingfield, ed., *Czech-Sudeten German Relations*. Special Topic Issue. *Nationalities Papers* 24, no. 1 (March 1996): 63–78.

Krakowski, Shmuel. "The Fate of Jewish Prisoners of War in the September 1939 Campaign. *Yad Vashem Studies,* 12 (1977): 297–333.

"Languages of Argentina." Ethnologue.com (September 16, 2003): 1.

Limor, Yoav. "Schindler's List—the Version that Spielberg Did Not Know." *Ma'ariv* (December 28, 1993): 4–5.

"Der Lastenausgleich—was er war und was er heute noch ist." *Frankfurter Allgemeine Zeitung* (February 24, 1996): n.p.

Martin, Douglas. "Leopold Page, Who Promoted Story of Schindler, Dies at 87." *New York Times* (March 15, 2001): 21.

Meyer, Ernie. "Saving Jewish Lives Was 'a Moral Obligation.'" *Jerusalem Post* (October 29, 1974): n.p.

"Monika Knauss geb. Göth to *Der Spiegel.*" *Der Spiegel,* no. 11 (14 March 1983): 12.

Motl, Stanislav. "Schindlerův Rok." *Reflex* 12 (1994): 13.

Nash, Nathaniel C. "Argentina Files Show Huge Effort to Harbor Nazis." *New York Times* (December 14, 1993): A4.

"Nation Remembers Six Million: Eleven 'Righteous Gentiles.'" *Jerusalem Post* (May 2, 1962): 3.

"No Place for Schindler on Czech List." *RFE/RL Newsline* 6, no. 31, pt. 2 (February 15, 2002): 1.

"Noah's Ark of Oskar Schindler." *Ma'arev* (November 5, 1982): 21.

Orth, Karin. "Ich habe mich nie getarnt: Brücke und Kontinuitäten in der Lebensgeschichte des KZ-Kommandanten Johannes Hassebroek." *Sozialwissenschaftliche Informationen* 24, no. 2 (April-June 1995): 145–150.

"Oskar Schindler and *Schindler's List.*" Edited by Aharon Weiss. *Yad Vashem Studies.* Vol. 24 (Jerusalem 1994): 317–348.

"Oskar Schindler-wybawca 1100 Żydów entuzjastrycznie powitany w Lud." *Izraelskie Nowiny I Kurier* (April 29, 1962): 1.

"Leopold Page-Shopkeeper-Philosopher." *Beverly Hills City Directory: Golden Anniversary* (Beverly Hills: City of Beverly Hills, n.d.): 64.

"Päpstlicher Orden für Rettung von Juden." *Frankfurter Allgemeine Zeitung* (October 25, 1968): 5.

Parrella, Robert. "Jews Move to Help German Who Saved 1,200." *New York Herald Tribune* (November 23, 1963): 1.

Perlmutter, Emanuel. "Jews Here Honor Hitler Arms Aide." *New York Times* (June 26, 1957): 4.

"Poldek Pfefferberg." *Lest We Forget.* http://www.oskarschindler.com/19.htm: 2.

Potterton, Louise. "Daughter to the Devil." *Jerusalem Report* (September 9, 2002): 44.

"Press Release, Oskar Schindler's Survivor Fund." (January 5, 1969): 1.

Rafferty, Terrence. "Polanski and the Landscape of Aloneness." *New York Times* (January 26, 2003): 2, 1.

Rasche, Uta. "Schindlers langer Schatten: Das Leben seiner Frau blieb im Dunkeln." *Frankfurter Allgemeine Zeitung* (October 28, 1999): 67.

Reimer, Wulf. "Vergleich für Schindlers Koffer." *Süddeutsche Zeitung* (April 28, 2001): 12.

Rohter, Larry. "Iran Blew Up Jewish Center in Argentina, Defector Says." *New York Times* (July 22, 2002): A1, A6.

Sanger, David E. "German Companies Offer $3.3 Billion in Slave-Labor Suit." *New York Times* (October 8, 1999): 1 page.

Scheuer, Philip K. "Burton Possibility for Schindler Epic," *Los Angeles Times* (December 22, 1964): n.p.

"Schindler Jews Remember Savior." *Los Angeles Herald Examiner* (January 6, 1969): A-3.

"Schindler Survivor Remained Aloof from Postwar Hype" (Obituary). *The Australian* (May 26, 2000): 15.

"Schindler's Survivors." *New York Newsday* (March 24, 1994): B27-B29, B47-B50.

Schmitz, Helmut. "Wie ein großzügiger Habenichts zur Ehrenrente kam." *Süddeutsche Zeitung,* (March 1, 1994): 3.

Schmitz, Helmut. "Wie ein großzügiger Habenichts zur Ehrenrente kam: Ein Blick in die Akte Oskar Schindler der hessischen Staatskanzlei deckt die Wege deutscher Bürokratie auf," *Frankfurter Allgemeine Zeitung* (March 1, 1994): n.p.

Scully, Derek. "The Forgotten Schindler." *Irish Times* (July 28, 2001): 61.

"Selbst Schindler's List konnte nicht das Schlimmste zeigen." *Süddeutsche Zeitung* (January 27, 1997): 3.

Sims, Calvin. "Jewish Graves in Argentina are Smashed; 3rd Time in '96." *New York Times* (October 22, 1996), A4.

Smelser, Ronald M. "The Expulsion of the Sudeten Germans, 1945–1952." In *Czech-Sudeten German Relations*. Special Topic Issue. *Nationalities Papers* 24, no. 1 (March 1996): 73–92.

Šmídová, Jana. "Oskar Schindler-anděl nebo gauner?" *Lidové noviny* (February 8, 1994): 9.

Spiegel, Irving. "Jews Here Honor West German Who Rescued 1,400 in Nazi Era." *New York Times* (January 9, 1972), 24.

Steinhouse, Herbert. "The Real Oskar Schindler." *Saturday Night* (April 1994): 40–49.

"Die Stimme Emilie Schindlers." *Frankfurter Allgemeine Zeitung* (November 13, 2003): 59.

Stock, Hanns. "Fünf Jahre befreites Sudetenland." *Krakauer Zeitung* (September 28, 1943): 3.

"Sto Lat." The University of Texas, College of Liberal Arts, http://www.utexas.edu/courses/sla323/stolat.htm:1.

Stopka, Christoph. "Ich bin Frau Schindler," *Bunte* (1994): 24–25.

"Streit und Schindlers Koffer beigelegt: Witwe soll 25,000 Mark erhalten." *Frankfurter Allgemeine Zeitung* (June 27, 2001): 9.

"Strong Accusations against Oskar Schindler (in Hebrew)." *Ha'aretz* (May 2, 1962): n.p.

"The Tarnów Jewish Trail." *Tarnów City Guide,* http://www.tarnow.pl/tarnow/ang/historia/index-szalki.php: 1.

"*To the Last Hour* Factual Story of a Living Man: Extension of Remarks of Hon. James C. Corman." *Congressional Record, Appendix* (February 24, 1965): A796.

Tragatsch, Ernst. "Eine Erinnerung: Oskar Schindler." *Motorrad,* no. 12 (1964): 1.

"The Trial of Adolf Eichmann." Session 37, Part 2 of 5, The Nizkor Project: 5.

Tugend, Tom. "Holocaust Survivors Thank German Savior." *Jewish Heritage* (January 9, 1969): 1, 6.

"Unique Reception in Paris." *Jewish Chronicle* (1949): 1.

Waksman, Joseph. "It is a Mitzvah (Commandment) to Accompany Him on His last Journey—Even in a Church." *Ha'aretz* (October 29, 1974): n.p.

Weiler, A.H. "Biography." *New York Times* (November 8, 1964), n.p.

Weinraub, Bernard. "For Spielberg, an Anniversary Full of Urgency." *New York Times* (March 9, 2004): B1, B4.

"Witwe von Oskar Schindler klagt zum zweiten Mai-Streit um Ansprüche aus Urheberrecht." *Stuttgarter Zeitung* (April 25, 2001): 1.

"Witwe hat wenig Aussicht auf Schadenersatz." *Stuttgarter Zeitung* (April 27, 2001): 2.

Wolfram, Gernot. "Reise zum späten Ruhm." *Frankfurter Allgemeine Zeitung* (July 13, 2001): 11.

Woodall, James. "J'accuse—the Other Dirty War." *Financial Times* (January 26/January 27, 2002): IV Weekend.

"Würdigung Fiores Verdienste um die deutsch-amerikanische Freundschaft." *Kronberger Bote* (January 22, 2004): n.p.

Zerin, Marjory. "The Jew Who Saved Schindler." *Jerusalem Report* (June 2, 1994): 36.

Books

Ailsby, Christopher, *SS: Roll of Infamy*. Osceola, Wisc.: Motorbooks International, 1997.

Allen, Michael Thad. *The Business of Genocide: The SS, Slave Labor, and the Concentration Camps*. Chapel Hill: University of North Carolina Press, 2002.

Arad, Yitzhak. *Belzec, Sobibór, Treblinka: The Operation Reinhard Death Camps.* Bloomington: Indiana University Press, 1987.

Armstrong, John A. *Ukrainian Nationalism.* 2d ed. New York: Columbia University Press, 1963.

Authers, John, and Richard Wolfee. *The Victim's Fortune: Inside the Epic Battle over the Debts of the Holocaust.* New York: HarperCollins, 2002.

Baedeker, Karl. *Das Generalgouvernement: Reisehandbuch von Karl Baedeker.* Leipzig: Karl Baedeker, 1943.

Baird, Jay W. *To Die for Germany: Heroes in the Nazi Pantheon.* Bloomington: Indiana University Press, 1990.

Bark, Dennis L. and David R. Gress. *A History of West Germany.* Vol.1, *From Shadow to Substance, 1945–1963.* Oxford: Basil Blackwell, 1989.

Bartov, Omar. *Hitler's Army: Soldiers, Nazis, and War in the Third Reich.* New York: Oxford University Press, 1991.

Bauminger, Arieh L. *The Fighters of the Cracow Ghetto.* Jerusalem: Keter Press Enterprises, 1986.

Bauer, Yehuda. *American Jewry and the Holocaust: The American Jewish Joint Distribution Committee, 1939–1945.* Detroit: Wayne State University Press, 1981.

Baxter, John. *Steven Spielberg: The Unauthorized Biography.* London: HarperCollins, 1996.

Ben-Sasson, Haim Hillel, ed. *A History of the Jewish People.* Cambridge: Harvard University Press, 1994.

Berben, Paul. *Dachau, 1933–1945: The Official History.* London: Comité International de Dachau, 1975.

Berenbaum, Michael, and Abraham J. Peck, eds. *The Holocaust and History: The Known, the Unknown, the Disputed, and the Reexamined.* Bloomington: Indiana University Press in association with the United States Holocaust Memorial Museum, 1998.

Bevor, Anthony. *The Fall of Berlin 1945.* New York: Viking, 2002.

Bidwell, R. L. *Currency Conversion Tables: A Hundred Years of Change.* London: Rex Collins, 1970.

Borkin, Joseph. *The Crime and Punishment of I.G. Farben.* New York: Pocket Books, 1978.

Borodziej, Włodzimierz. *Terror und Politik: Die Deutsche Polizei und die Polnische Widerstandsbewegung im Generalgouvernement, 1939–1944.* Mainz: Verlag Philipp von Zabern, 1999.

Braham, Randolph L. *The Politics of Genocide: The Holocaust in Hungary.* 2 vols. New York: Columbia University Press, 1981.

Brecher, Elinor J. *Schindler's Legacy: True Stories of the List Survivors.* New York: Plume/Penguin Books, 1994.

Breitman, Richard. *Official Secrets: What the Nazis Planned, What the British and the Americans Knew.* New York: Hill & Wang, 1998.

_____. *The Architect of Genocide: Himmler and the Final Solution.* New York: Alfred A. Knopf, 1991.

Brode, Douglas. *The Films of Steven Spielberg.* New York: Citadel Press, 2000.

Browning, Christopher R. *Nazi Policy, Jewish Workers, German Killers.* Cambridge: Cambridge University Press, 2000.

Burleigh, Michael. *The Third Reich: A New History.* New York: Hill and Wang, 2000.

Chant, Christopher, ed. *Hitler's Generals.* London: Salamander Books, 1998.

Concentration Camp in Plaszow. N.p., n.d.

The Conference on Jewish Material Claims against Germany. *Claims Conference: 1998 Annual Report with 1999 Highlights.* New York: The Conference on Jewish Material Claims against Germany, 1998.

Cooper, Matthew. *The German Army, 1933–1945*. Lanham, Md.: Scaborough House Publishers, 1990.

Crowe, David M. *The Baltic States and the Great Powers: Foreign Relations, 1918–1940*. Boulder: Westview Press, 1993.

Czech, Danuta, Stanisław Kłodziński, Aleksander Lasik, Andrzej Strzelecki. *Auschwitz, 1940–1945: Central Issues in the History of the Camp*. Vol. 5. Oświęcim: Auschwitz-Birkenau State Museum, 2000.

Dallin, David J. *Soviet Russia's Foreign Policy, 1939–1942*. Translated by Leon Dennen. New Haven: Yale University Press, 1942.

Davies, Norman. *God's Playground: A History of Poland*. Vol. 2, *1795 to the Present*. New York: Columbia University Press, 1982.

Delarue, Jacques. *The Gestapo: A History of Horror*. New York: Paragon House, 1987.

Del Calzo, Nick, with Renee Rockford, Drew Myron, and Linda J. Raper. *The Triumphant Spirit: Portraits & Stories of Holocaust Survivors . . . Their Messages of Hope and Compassion*. Denver: Triumphant Spirit Publishing, 1997.

Diest, Wilhelm, Manfred Messerschmidt, Hans-Erich Volkmann, and Wolfram Wette, eds. *Germany and the Second World War*. Vol. 1, *The Buildup of German Aggression*. Translated by P. S. Falla, Dean S. McMurry, and Ewald Osers. Oxford: Clarendon Press, 2000.

Dobroszycki, Lucjan. *Reptile Journalism: The Official Polish-Language Press under the Nazis, 1939–1945*. New Haven: Yale University Press, 1994.

Donald, David, ed. *Warplanes of the Luftwaffe: Combat Aircraft of Hitler's Luftwaffe, 1939–1945*. New York: Barnes and Noble, 2000.

Duda, Eugeniusz. *The Jews of Cracow*. Translated by Ewa Basiura. Kraków: Wydawnictwo 'Hagada' and Argona-Jarden Jewish Bookshop, 2000.

Duffy, Christopher. *Red Storm on the Reich: The Soviet March on Germany, 1945*. Edison, N.J.: Castle Books, 2002.

Duranczyński, Eugeniusz. *Wojna i Okupacja: Wrzesień 1939-Kwiecień 1943*. Warszawa: Wieza Powszechna, 1974.

Eizenstat, Stuart. *Imperfect Justice: Looted Assets, Slave Labor, and the Unfinished Business of World War II*. New York: Public Affairs, 2003.

Favez, Jean-Claude. *The Red Cross and the Holocaust*. Edited and translated by John and Beryl Fletcher. Cambridge: Cambridge University Press, 1999.

Feig, Konnilyn G. *Hitler's Death Camps: The Sanity of Madness*. New York: Holmes & Meier, 1979.

Felak, James Ramon. *At the Price of the Republic: Hlinka's Slovak People's Party, 1929–1938*. Pittsburgh: University of Pittsburgh Press, 1994.

Feldenkirchen, Wildfried. *Siemens, 1918–1945*. Columbus: Ohio State University Press, 1999.

Fensch, Thomas. *Oskar Schindler and His List: The Man, the Book, the Film, the Holocaust and Its Survivors*. Forest Dale, Vt.: Paul S. Eriksson, Publisher, 1995.

Ferencz, Benjamin B. *Less than Slaves: Jewish Forced Labor and the Quest for Compensation*. Bloomington: Indiana University Press in association with the United States Holocaust Memorial Museum, Washington, D.C., 2002.

Fest, Joachim C. *The Face of the Third Reich: Portraits of the Nazi Leadership*. Translated by Michael Bullock. New York: Ace Books, 1970.

The Fifth Book of Moses Called Deuteronomy. London: F. Kiernan, 5583 (1902).

Fikejz, Radoslav. *Oskar Schindler (1908–1974)*. Svitavy: Městské muzeum a galerie Svitavy, 1998.

Flaherty, Thomas H. *The SS*. Alexandria, Va.: Time Life Books, 1989.

Fleming, Ian. *The Diamond Smugglers*. New York: Dell, 1957.

Fowler, E.W.W. *Nazi Regalia*. Secaucus, N.J.: Chartwell Books, 1992.

Freer, Ian. *The Complete Spielberg*. London: Virgin Publishing Ltd., 2001.

Friedlander, Henry. *The Origins of Nazi Genocide: From Euthanasia to the Final Solution.* Chapel Hill: University of North Carolina Press, 1995.

Gebel, Ralf. *'Heim ins Reich!' Konrad Henlein und der Reichsgau Sudetenland (1938–1945).* Munich: R. Oldenbourg, 2000.

Gilbert, Martin. *Holocaust Journey: Traveling in Search of the Past.* New York: Columbia University Press, 1997.

_____. *Israel: A History.* New York: William Morrow and Company, 1998.

_____. *The Righteous: The Unsung Heroes of the Holocaust.* New York: Henry Holt and Company, 2003.

Giziowski, Richard. *The Enigma of General Blaskowitz.* New York: Hippocrene Books, 1997.

Goñi, Uki. *The Real Odessa: How Péron Brought the Nazi War Criminals to Argentina.* London: Granata Books, 2002.

Graham, Malbone W. *New Governments of Central Europe.* New York: Henry Holt and Company, 1926.

Gregor, Neil. *Daimler-Benz in the Third Reich.* New Haven: Yale University Press, 1998.

Gross, Jan Tomasz. *Polish Society Under German Occupation: The Generalgouvernment, 1939-1944.* Princeton: Princeton University Press, 1979.

Grossmann, Kurt. *Die unbesungenen Helden: Menschen in Deutschlands dunklen Tagen.* Frankfurt: Verlag Ullstein GmbH, 1961.

Gruntová, Jitka. *Legendy a fakta o oskaru Schindlerovi.* Praha: Vydalo nakladatelstvín Naše vojsko, 2002.

_____. *Oskar Schindler: Legenda a Fakta.* Brno: Barrister & Principle, 1997.

Gryń, Edward, and Zofia Murawska-Gryń, *Majdanek.* Lublin: Państwowe Muzeum na Majdanku, 1984.

Gutman, Israel. *Resistance: The Warsaw Ghetto Uprising.* Boston: Houghton Mifflin, 1994.

Gutman, Yisrael, and Avital Saf, eds. *The Nazi Concentration Camps.* Jerusalem: Yad Vashem, 1984.

Gutman, Yisrael, and Shmuel Krakowski. *Unequal Victims: Poles and Jews during World War II.* New York: Holocaust Library, 1986.

Gutman, Yisrael, and Michael Berenbaum, eds. *Anatomy of the Auschwitz Death Camp.* Bloomington: Indiana University Press in Association with the United States Holocaust Memorial Museum, 1994.

Hamburg Institute for Social Research, ed. *The German Army and Genocide: Crimes Against War Prisoners, Jews, and Other Civilians, 1939–1945.* New York: The New Press, 1999.

Hamburger Institut für Sozialforschung (Hg.), ed. *Vernichtungskrieg. Verbrechen der Wehrmacht 1941 bis 1944.* Hamburg: Hamburger Edition, 1996.

Heller, Celia S. *On the Edge of Destruction: Jews of Poland Between the Two World Wars.* New York: Columbia University Press, 1977.

Herbert, Ulrich. *Hitler's Foreign Workers: Enforced Foreign Labor in Germany under the Third Reich.* Translated by William Templer. Cambridge: Cambridge University Press, 1997.

_____, ed. *National Socialist Extermination Policies: Contemporary German Perspectives and Controversies.* New York: Berghan Books, 2000.

Herbert, Ulrich, Karin Orth, und Christoph Dieckmann, eds. *Die nationalsozialistischen Konzentrationslager,* Band II: *Entwicklung und Struktur.* Frankfurt am Main: Fischer Taschenbuch Verlag, 2002.

Hilberg, Raul. *The Destruction of the European Jews.* Rev. and def. ed. 3 vols. New York: Holmes & Meier, 1985.

Hitler's Army: The Evolution and Structure of German Forces. Ed. by *Command* Magazine eds. Conshohocken, Pa.: Combined Publishing, 1995.

Hoffmann, Peter. *The History of the German Resistance, 1933–1945*. Translated by Richard Barry. 3d ed. Montreal: McGill-Queen's University Press, 1996.

Hogs, Ian V. *German Artillery of World War Two*. London: Greenhill Books, 2002.

Höhne, Heinz. *Canaris*. Translated from the German by J. Maxwell Brownjohn. New York: Doubleday & Company, 1979.

———. *The Order of the Death's Head: The Story of Hitler's SS*. Translated by Richard Barry. New York: Ballantine Books, 1971.

Iwaszko, Tadeusz, Helena Kubica, Franciszek Piper, Irena Strzelecka, and Andrzej Strzelecki. *Auschwitz 1940–1945*, Volume 2: *The Prisoners: Their Life and Work*. Oswięcim: Auschwitz-Birkenau State Museum, 2000.

Janos, Andrew J. *The Politics of Backwardness in Hungary, 1825–1945*. Princeton: Princeton University Press, 1982.

Jaskot, Paul B. *The Architecture of Oppression: The SS, Forced Labor and the Nazi Monumental Building Economy*. London: Routledge, 2000.

Kagan, Joram. *Poland's Jewish Heritage*. New York: Hippocrene Books, 1992.

Kahn, David. *Hitler's Spies: German Military Intelligence in World War II*. New York: Macmillan, 1978.

Kapszuk, Elio, and Damián Lejzorowicz, eds. *Shalom Buenos Aires*. Buenos Aires: Gobierno de la Ciudad de Buenos Aires, 2001.

Kater, Michael H. *The Nazi Party: A Social Profile of Members and Leaders, 1919–1945*. Cambridge, Mass.: Harvard University Press, 1983.

Kaufman, J. E., and Robert M. Jurga. *Fortress Europe: European Fortifications of World War II*. Translations by H. W. Kaufmann. Conshohocken, Pa.: Combined Publishing, 1999.

Keller, Claudia, and Stefan Braun. *Schindlers Koffer: Berichte aus dem Leben eines Lebensretters*. Stuttgart: *Stuttgarter Zeitung*, 1999.

Kelly, David. *The Czech Fascist Movement, 1922–1942*. Boulder/New York: East European Monographs and Columbia University Press, 1995.

Keneally, Thomas. *Schindler's List*. New York: Touchstone Books, 1992.

Kershaw, Ian. *Hitler, 1936–1945: Nemesis*. New York: W. W. Norton, 2000.

———. *Hitler, 1889–1936: Hubris*. New York: W. W. Norton, 1999.

Kiełkowski, Roman. *Zlikwidować na Miejscu: Z dziejów okupacji hitlerowskiej w Krakowie*. Kraków: Wydawnictwo Literackie, 1981.

Kindermann, Gottfried-Karl. *Hitler's Defeat in Austria, 1933-1934: Europe's First Containment of Nazi Expansionism*. Translated by Sonia Brough and David Taylor. Boulder: Westview Press, 1988.

Klemperer, Klemens von. *German Resistance against Hitler: The Search for Allies Abroad, 1938–1945*. Oxford: Clarendon Press, 1994.

Kobielec, Aleksandra. *Filia Obozu Koncentracyjnego Gross-Rosen Arbeitslager Brünnlitz*. Wałbrzych: Państwowe Muzeum Gross-Rosen, 1991.

Koch, Hannsjoachim W. *In the Name of the Volk: Political Justice in Hitler's Germany*. New York: Barnes & Noble, 1997.

Koehl, Robert L. *RKFDV: German Resettlement and Population Policy, 1939–1945*. Cambridge, Mass.: Harvard University Press, 1957.

Kogon, Eugen. *The Theory and Practice of Hell: The German Concentration Camps and the System Behind Them*. Translated by Heinz Norden. New York: Berkley Publishing Corporation, 1975.

Kopecký, Jan. *Historie textilního závodu v Brněnci*. Svitavy: Grafickou úpravu a obálku navrhl Lad. Vejda, 1965.

Krawchenko, Bohdan. *Social Change and National Consciousness in Twentieth-Century Ukraine*. New York: St. Martin's Press, 1985.

Kroener, Bernhard R., Rolf-Dieter Müller, and Hans Umbreit, eds. *Germany and the Second World War.* Vol. 5, *Organization and Mobilization of the German Sphere of Power,* part 1, *Wartime Administration, Economy, and Manpower Resources, 1939–1941.* Translated by John Brownjohn, Patricia Crampton, Ewald Osers, and Louise Willmot. Oxford: Clarendon Press, 2000.

Kutakov, Leonid N. *Japanese Foreign Policy on the Eve of the Pacific War: A Soviet View.* Edited by George Alexander Lensen. Tallahassee, Fla.: Diplomatic Press, 1972.

Lasik, Aleksander, Franciszek Piper, Piotr Setkiewicz, and Irena Strzelecka, eds. *Auschwitz, 1940–1945: Central Issues in the History of the Camp.* Vol. 1, *The Establishment and Organization of the Camp.* Translated by William Brand. Oświęcim: Auschwitz-Birkenau State Museum, 2000.

Liste der NS-Konzentrationslager. http://www2.3dresearch.com/~june/Vincent/Camps/ListeEng.html, and http://www.uni-duisburg.de/dings/Holocaust/KZ-Liste.html.

Richard C. Lukas. *Forgotten Holocaust: The Poles Under German Occupation, 1939–1944.* New York: Hippocrene Books, 1990.

Luža, Radomír. *The Transfer of the Sudeten Germans: A Study of Czech-German Relations, 1933–1962.* New York: New York University Press, 1964).

Maclean, French L. *The Camp Men: The SS Officers Who Ran the Nazi Concentration Camp System.* Atglen, Pa.: Schiffer Military History, 1999.

———. *The Field Men: The SS Officers Who Led the Einsatzkommandos—the Nazi Mobile Killings Squads.* Atglen, Pa.: Schiffer Military History, 1999.

Madajczyk, Czesław. *Polityka III Rzeszy w Okupowanej Polsce.* 2 vols. Warszawa: Państwowe Wydawnictwo Naukowe, 1970.

Magocsi, Paul Robert. *Historical Atlas of East Central Europe.* Seattle: University of Washington Press, 1998.

Mamatey, Victor S., and Radomír Luža, eds. *A History of the Czechoslovak Republic, 1918–1948.* Princeton: Princeton University Press, 1973.

Marszałek, Józef. *Majdanek: The Concentration Camp in Lublin.* Warsaw: Interpress, 1986.

McBride, Joseph. *Steven Spielberg: A Biography.* New York: Simon & Schuster, 1997.

McGilligan, Patrick. *Fritz Lang: The Nature of the Beast.* New York: St. Martin's Press, 1997.

McKale, Donald M. *The Swastika Outside of Germany.* Kent, Ohio: Kent State University Press, 1977.

Mendelsohn, Ezra. *The Jews of East Central Europe Between the World Wars.* Bloomington: Indiana University Press, 1983.

Meyer, Peter, Bernard D. Weinryb, Eugene Dushinsky, and Nicolas Sylvain, eds. *The Jews in the Soviet Satellites.* Syracuse: Syracuse University Press, 1953.

Mierzekewski, Alfred C. *The Collapse of the German War Economy, 1944–1945: Allied Air Power and the German National Railway.* Chapel Hill: University of North Carolina Press, 1988.

Miller, Michael, et al. *Axis Biographical Research: An Apolitical Military History Site.* http://www.geocities.com/~orion47/.

Morris, Benny. *Righteous Victims: A History of the Zionist-Arab Conflict, 1881–2001.* New York: Vintage Books, 2001.

Musmanno, Michael A. *Justice: The Eichmann Kommandos.* London: Peter Davies, 1961.

Neufeld, Michael J., and Michael Berenbaum, eds. *The Bombing of Auschwitz: Should the Allies Have Attempted It?* New York: St. Martin's Press in Association with the United States Holocaust Memorial Museum, 2000.

Neumann, Franz. *Behemoth: The Structure and Practice of National Socialism, 1933–1944.* New York: Harper and Row, 1944.

Orth, Karen. *Die Konzentrationslager-SS: sozialstrukturelle Analysen und biographische Studien.* Göttingen: Wallstein Verlag, 2000.

Orlow, Dietrich. *The History of the Nazi Party, 1933–1945.* Pittsburgh: University of Pittsburgh Press, 1973.

Overy, R.J. *War and Economy in the Third Reich.* Oxford: Oxford University Press, 1994.

Padfield, Peter. *Himmler: Reichsführer-SS.* New York: Henry Holt and Company, 1990.

Paldiel, Mordecai. *The Path of the Righteous: Gentile Rescuers of Jews During the Holocaust.* Hoboken, N.J.: KTAV Publishing House, and The Jewish Foundation for Christian Rescuers/ADL, 1993.

Parssinen, Terry. *The Oster Conspiracy of 1938: The Unknown Story of the Military Plot to Kill Hitler and Avert World War II.* New York: HarperCollins, 2003.

Paul, Allen. *Katyń: The Untold Story of Stalin's Polish Massacre.* New York: Charles Scribner's Sons, 1991.

Pauley, Bruce F. *Hitler and the Forgotten Nazis: A History of Austrian National Socialism.* Chapel Hill: University of North Carolina Press, 1981.

Pióro, Anna and Wiesława Kralińska. *Krakowskie Getto.* Kraków: Muzeum Pamięci Narodowej Apteka pod Oręem, 1995.

Piper, Franciszek. *How Many Perished: Jews, Poles, Gypsies.* Kraków: Poligrafia, 1991.

Piper, Franciszek, and Teresa Świebocka. *Auschwitz: Nazi Death Camp.* Oświęcim: The Auschwitz-Birkenau State Museum in Oświęcim, 1996.

Pucher, Siegfrid J. *". . . in der Bewegung führend tätig:" Odilo Globočnik-Kämpfer für den 'Anschluß,' Vollstrecker des Holocaust.* Klagenfurt/Celovac: Drava Verlag, 1997.

Rabinowitz, Harry M. *Hasidism: The Movement and Its Masters.* Northvale, N.J.: Jason Aronson, 1988.

Reitlinger, Gerald. *The SS: Alibi of a Nation, 1922–1945.* New York: Da Capo Press, 1981.

Rempel, Gerhard. *Hitler's Children: The Hitler Youth and the SS.* Chapel Hill: University of North Carolina Press, 1989.

Rhodes, Richard. *Masters of Death: The Einsatzgruppen and the Invention of the Holocaust.* New York: Alfred A. Knopf, 2002.

Rich, Norman. *Hitler's War Aims: Ideology, the Nazi State, and the Course of Expansion.* New York: W. W. Norton, 1973.

Rittner, Carol and John K. Roth, eds. *Different Voices: Women and the Holocaust.* New York; Paragon House, 1993.

Roberts, Geoffrey. *The Unholy Alliance: Stalin's Pact with Hitler.* Bloomington: Indiana University Press, 1989.

Rossino, Alexander B. *Hitler Strikes Poland: Blitzkrieg, Ideology, and Atrocity.* Lawrence, Kans.: University Press of Kansas, 2003.

Rosten, Leo. *The Joys of Yiddish.* New York: Pocket Books, 1970.

Roth, John, et al. *The Holocaust Chronicle.* Lincolnwood, Ill.: Publications International Ltd., 2000.

Rothschild, Joseph. *East Central Europe Between the Two World Wars.* Vol. 9, *A History of East Central Europe.* Seattle: University of Washington Press, 1990.

Sachar, Howard M. *A History of Israel from the Rise of Zionism to Our Time.* 2d ed. New York: Alfred A. Knopf, 1996.

Seaton, Albert. *Stalin As Military Commander.* New York: Praeger Publishers, 1975.

Segev, Tom. *Soldiers of Evil: The Commandants of the Nazi Concentration Camps.* Translated by Haim Watzman. New York: McGraw Hill, 1987.

Sereny, Gitta. *Into That Darkness: An Examination of Conscience* (New York: Vintage Books, 1983).

Shaw, Stanford J. *Turkey and the Holocaust: Turkey's Role in Rescuing Turkish and European Jewry from Nazi Persecution, 1933–1945.* New York: New York University Press, 1993.

Smelser, Ronald, and Rainer Zitelmann. *The Nazi Elite*. New York: New York University Press, 1993.

Smelser, Ronald M., *The Sudeten Problem, 1933–1938: Volkstumpolitik and the Formation of Nazi Foreign Policy*. Middletown, Conn.: Wesleyan University Press, 1975.

Sofsky, Wolfgang. *The Order of Terror: The Concentration Camp*. Translated by William Templer. Princeton: Princeton University Press, 1997.

The State Museum of Gross Rosen. Rogoznica: The Gross-Rosen Muzeum in Rogoznica, n.d.

Steiner, Peter. *The Deserts of Bohemia: Czech Fiction and Its Social Context*. Ithaca: Cornell University Press, 2000.

Subtelny, Orest. *Ukraine: A History*. 2d ed. Toronto: University of Toronto Press, 1994.

Sydnor, Charles W., Jr. *Soldiers of Destruction: The SS Death's Head Division, 1933–1945*. Princeton: Princeton University Press, 1990.

Textilní Továrna Arona-Jakuba Löw Beera. Brněnec, n.p., nd.

Taylor, Telford. *Sword and Swastika: Generals and Nazis in the Third Reich*. New York: Barnes & Noble Books, 1952.

Trunk, Isaiah. *Judenrat: The Jewish Councils in Eastern Europe under Nazi Occupation*. New York: Stein & Day, 1977.

Vitka Brněnec. Brochure prepared by Vitka Brněnec. n.d.

United States Holocaust Memorial Museum. *Historical Atlas of the Holocaust*. New York: Macmillan Publishing, 1996.

The Warsaw Ghetto: The 45th Anniversary of the Uprising. Warsaw: Interpress, 1988.

Watt, Donald Cameron. *How War Came: The Immediate Origins of the Second World War: 1938–1939*. New York: Pantheon Books, 1989.

Watt, Richard M. *Bitter Glory: Poland and Its Fate, 1918–1939*. New York: Simon and Schuster, 1979.

Weinberg, Gerhard L. *The Foreign Policy of Hitler's Germany: Diplomatic Revolution in Europe, 1933–1936*. Chicago: University of Chicago Press, 1970.

_____. *The Foreign Policy of Hitler's Germany: Starting World War II, 1937-1939*. Chicago: The University of Chicago Press, 1980.

Weinmann, Martin, Anne Kaiser, and Ursula Krause-Schmitt, eds. *Das nationalsozialistische Lagersystem*. Frankfurt am Main: Zweitausendeins, 1990.

Weitz, John. *Hitler's Banker: Hjalmar Horace Greeley Schacht*. Boston: Little, Brown and Company, 1997.

Williams, Charles. *Adenauer: The Father of the New Germany*. New York: John Wiley & Sons, 2000.

Wiskemann, Elizabeth. *Czechs and Germans: A Study of the Struggle in the Historic Provinces of Bohemia and Moravia*. London: Oxford University Press, 1938.

Wroński, Tadeusz. *Kaźń Polaków przy Ulica Pomorskiej 2 w Krakpowie w Latach 1939–1945*. Kraków: Wydawnictwo "Sport i Turystyka," 1985.

_____. *Kronika Okupowanego Krakowa*. Kraków: Wydawnicto Literackie, 1974.

Wyman, David S, ed., and Charles H. Rosenzveig, project director. *The World Reacts to the Holocaust*. Baltimore: The Johns Hopkins University Press, 1996.

Wyman, Mark. *DPs: Europe's Displaced Persons, 1945–1951*. Ithaca: Cornell University Press, 1998.

Yahil, Leni. *The Holocaust: The Fate of European Jewry*. New York: Oxford University Press, 1990.

Zhilin, Pavel, et al. *Recalling the Past for the Sake of the Future: The Causes, Results and Lessons of World War Two*. Moscow: Novosti Press Agency, 1985.

Ziemke, Earl F. *Stalingrad to Berlin: The German Defeat in the East*. Washington, D.C.: Office of the Chief of Military History, 1968.

_____ *The U.S. Army in the Occupation of Germany, 1944–1946.* Washington, D.C.: Center of Military History, United States Army, 1975.

Zimmermann, Volker. *Die Sudetendeutschen im NS-Staat: Politik und Stimmung der Bevölkerung im Reichsgau Sudetenland (1938–1945).* Essen: Klartext Verlag, 1999.

Unpublished Manuscripts

O'Neil, Robin. "An Analysis of the Action of Oskar Schindler Within the Context of the Holocaust in German Occupied Poland and Czechoslovakia." Master's thesis, University College, London, 1996.

_____. "The Man from Svitavy: The Enigma of Oskar Schindler." 1994.

Rice, James P. "The Breakers: Oskar Schindler and the Holocaust." April 28, 1994.

Atlases and Encyclopedias

Edelheit, Abraham J. & Hershel Edelheit, eds. *History of the Holocaust: A Handbook and Dictionary.* Boulder: Westview Press, 1994.

Gilbert, Martin. *The Macmillan Atlas of the Holocaust.* New York: The Macmillan Publishing Co., 1982.

Gutman, Israel, ed. *Encyclopedia of the Holocaust.* 4 vols. New York: Macmillan Publishing Company, 1990.

Keegan, John, ed. *HarperCollins Atlas of the Second World War.* London: HarperCollins, 1997.

Laquer, Walter and Judith Tydor Baumel, eds. *The Holocaust Encyclopedia.* New Haven: Yale University Press, 2001.

Niewyk, Daniel and Francis Nicosia. *The Columbia Guide to the Holocaust.* New York: Columbia University Press, 2000.

Spector, Shmuel, and Geoffrey Wigoder, eds. *The Encyclopedia of Jewish Life Before and During the Holocaust.* 3 vols. New York: New York University Press, 2001.

United States Holocaust Memorial Museum. *Historical Atlas of the Holocaust.* New York: Macmillan Publishing USA, 1996.

Zentner, Christian and Friedemann Bedürftig, eds. *The Encyclopedia of the Third Reich.* Translated by Amy Hackett. New York: Da Capo Press, 1997.

Films

"Die Juden nennen Ihn Vater Courage." Südwestfunk 3, West Germany. 1975.

"Oskar Schindler, Retter und Lebemann." ZDF. Mainz. 1994.

Schindler. A film written, directed, and produced by Jon Blair. Thames Television Production. 1981.

Schindler's List. Steven Spielberg, Director. Universal/MCA and Amblin Entertainment. 1993.

"Zatykac na Oskara Schindlera." Česka televize Ostrava. 1999.

INDEX

Silber, Ernestine, 211
Silber, Halina Brunnengraber, 391
Silberschein, Dr. Adolf, 431
Silesia (Śląsk), 11, 33, 52, 121, 332
    East Upper Silesia, 75, 224–25, 412
    Upper Silesia, 75, 224
Silver, Henry (Hersch Silberschlag), 257
Silverstein, Maurice, 550
Sinatra, Frank, 528
Singer, Gunther, 437
Sinnemann, Fred, 513
Składkowski, Felicjan Sławoj, 108
Slamovisch, Henry (Chaim Wolf
    Szlamowicz), 257, 259, 287–88, 436,
    442
Sliwa, Eugen, 58–61
Slovakia
    Abwehr and, 26–27, 32
    Czechoslovakia, invasion of, and, 49
    Slovak People's Party, 26–27, 50
Slovak People's Party, 26–27, 50
Smolarz, Adolfo, 464, 465
Sobibór death camp, 164, 166–67, 188,
    267
Sobotka, Dr., 19, 21, 22
Society for Christian-Jewish Cooperation
    (Gesellschaft Christlich-Jüduscher),
    504
Society for the Protection of Health (TOZ;
    Towarzystwo Ochrony Zdrowi), 103
Sofsky, Wolfgang, 240, 244, 317–18, 335,
    338, 415
Soldinger, Sam, 288
Sommer, Herr, 118
Sonnenschein, 258
Sorensen, Lord Reginald, 573
Southern California, University of, Los
    Angeles, 514
Soviet Union (USSR; Union of Soviet
    Socialist Republics)
    Czechoslovakia and, 22
    German invasion of Poland and, 66–67,
        69, 70
    Red Army, 140, 175, 202, 243, 301,
        324, 404, 420, 457
    Russian Liberation Army, 443
    Soviet Fourth Ukrainian Front (Group)
Sowinski, SS-Oberwachmann Josef, 340
Speer, Albert, 80, 83, 86, 272, 275–76,
    277, 325, 375, 439
Spellman, Joseph Francis, 546

Spielberg, Steven, 45–46, 97, 102, 105,
    106, 113, 184–85, 187, 193, 194,
    202, 204, 213, 256, 259–60, 267,
    358, 362–63, 387, 421, 452, 464,
    488, 578, 597–98, 602–8
    Academy Awards, 603
Spira, Francis, 551
Spira, Jerzy, 323
Spira, Symche, 119, 149, 182–83, 184,
    188, 190, 196
Spitz, Mr., 105
Springmann, Shmuel, 280, 284, 296,
    298–311, 532
SS (Schutzstaffeln; Nazi Party defense and
    protection squads), 22
    Abwehr and, 98
    concentration camp regulations and,
        257–58
    corruption and, 342–49
    Ethnic German Central Office (VoMi;
        Volksdeutsche Mittelstelle), 23
    General Government and, 73–74,
        76–78
    Higher SS and Police Leader (HSSPF,
        Der Höhere SS-und Polizeiführer),
        78, 115
    HSSPF General Government, 78
    Jewish labor controversy and, 159
    Sudeten German affairs and, 15–16
SS and Police Courts
    Chief Judge of the Supreme SS and
        Police Court, 345
    Legal Department (Hauptamt SS-
        Greicht), 345
    SS and Police Court VI, 345
SS-Waffen (Armed), 98
Stadkomissar (city commissioner), 92
Stadler, F. A., 499–500
Staehr, Ami (Annemarie), 576, 577–81,
    584, 586–90
Staehr, Chris, 368, 577, 580, 587–89,
    609–14
Staehr, Dr. Heinrich, 577–81, 578–80, 587,
    590
    Wiedergutmachungen work in Israel,
        577
Staehr, Konrad, 609–10
Staehr, Tina, 577, 588–89, 609–14
Stalin, Joseph, 67, 70, 120, 140, 313
Stalingrad, Battle of, 241, 250, 313, 325
Staré Maletín (Alt Moletein), Moravia, 4, 6